YIANNOPOULOS' CIVIL LAW PROPERTY COURSEBOOK

TENTH EDITION
2014

By
Dian Tooley-Knoblett
Jones Walker Distinguished Professor of Law
Loyola University College of Law
Lead Editor

Jeanne Louise Carriere
John Minor Wisdom Professor of Civil Law
And Director, Civil Law Program
Tulane University School of Law
Co-editor

John Randall Trahan
Louis B. Porterie Professor of Law
Paul M. Hebert Law Center
Louisiana State University
Co-editor

Published and for sale by
CLAITOR'S PUBLISHING DIVISION
3165 S. Acadian at I-10, P.O. Box 261333
Baton Rouge, LA 70826-1333
Tel: 800-274-1403 (In LA 225-344-0476)
Fax: 225-344-0480
Internet address:
e-mail: claitors@claitors.com
http://www.claitors.com

Acknowledgments

Appreciation is expressed to Shaneil Strava, who assisted in the typing and layout of the book and to Christopher Arruebarrena (St. Louis University Class of 2015) and Alexander Arruebarrena (Loyola University Class of 2015) who assisted in the table of contents and table of cases.

Excerpts from Louisiana Civil Law Treatise vols. 2, 3, and 4, from Civil Law Translations, from the Louisiana Revised Statutes, and decisions from the Southern Reporter Series have been reproduced with permission of Thomson Reuters/West, copyright holder, with reservation of all its rights. Excerpts from legal periodicals have been reproduced with the permission of the Louisiana and Tulane Law Reviews, copyright holders, and with reservation of their rights. The authors wish to express their thanks for the permission to use these copyright materials.

Published and for sale by
CLAITOR'S PUBLISHING DIVISION
3165 S. Acadian at I-10, P.O. Box 261333
Baton Rouge, LA 70826-1333
Tel: 800-274-1403 (In LA 225-344-0476)
Fax: 225-344-0480
Internet address:
e-mail: claitors@claitors.com
http://www.claitors.com

INTRODUCTION

"The civil law is beautiful."
–A.N. Yiannopoulos

Over ten years ago, the three editors of this book were selected by Professor A.N. Yiannopoulos to take over his Civil Law Property Coursebook, beginning with the ninth edition that was published in 2009, the year marking Professor A.N. Yiannopoulos' 50th anniversary teaching law in Louisiana. Although he officially retired in May 2008, after 20 years of law teaching at LSU and 29 years at Tulane, he continues to teach at Tulane as an emeritus law faculty member. Moreover, he still edits the annual edition of Louisiana's Civil Code, he continues to serve the Louisiana State Law Institute as a member of the council and as a reporter, and he annually updates the volumes he has contributed to the Louisiana Civil Law Treatise series.

Professor Yiannopoulos' mind remains razor sharp, his heart is still a mile wide and his spirit has not diminished one iota. Professor Yiannopoulos continues to envision and to produce works that benefit greatly not only Louisiana's law students, practitioners, and judges, but all who are interested in the civil law tradition in the 21st century. He is the embodiment and inspiration for one of my favorite sayings: "The best is yet to come." Professor Yiannopoulos may not have yet penned his magnum opus, and I wait in anticipation for his next masterpiece.

Given Professor Yiannopoulos' amazing energy, enthusiasm and vitality, it is almost curious that he relinquished control over the Civil Law Property Coursebook. Of course, it is not surprising that it has taken three veteran law professors[1] to replace him, though the truth is that Professor Yiannopoulos is irreplaceable. As stated in a tribute celebrating Professor Yiannopoulos' 40th anniversary of teaching law in Louisiana: "Professor Yiannopoulos can claim the rare honor of having changed the legal landscape of American civil law. He helped usher in the legal renaissance that began in Louisiana in the 1970s leading to the first systematic revision of the Louisiana Civil Code in a century."[2]

Dian Tooley-Knoblett, lead editor
November 11, 2014

---

[1] Professor Tooley-Knoblett is so "veteran" that she can boast having studied property under the first edition of the Civil Law Property Coursebook.
[2] Sherman, "Introduction: A Tribute to Professor Athanassios Yiannopoulos," 73 Tul. L. Rev. 1017, 1017 (1999).

TABLE OF CONTENTS

PART I: THINGS, POSSESSION, AND OWNERSHIP

INTRODUCTION: THE DOMAIN OF CIVIL LAW PROPERTY

A.N. YIANNOPOULOS, CIVIL LAW PROPERTY
§§ 1-8 (4th ed. 2001)
(footnotes omitted)

§ 1. Property

Property is a word with high emotional overtones and so many meanings that it has defied attempts at accurate all-inclusive definition. The English word *property* derives from the Latin *proprietas,* a noun form of *proprius,* which means one's own. In the United States, the word *property* is frequently used to denote indiscriminately either the *objects* of rights that have a pecuniary content or the *rights* that persons have with respect to things. Thus, lands, automobiles, and jewels are said to be property and rights, such as ownership, servitudes, and leases, are likewise said to be property. This latent confusion between rights and their objects has its roots in texts of Roman law and is also encountered in other legal systems of the western world. Accurate analysis should reserve the use of the word property for the designation of rights that persons have with respect to things.

Property may be defined as an exclusive right to control an economic good, corporeal or incorporeal; it is the name of a concept that refers to the rights, obligations, privileges and restrictions that govern the relations of man with respect to things of value. People everywhere and at all times desire the possession of things that are necessary for survival or valuable by cultural definition and that, as a result of the demand placed upon them, become scarce. Laws enforced by organized society control the competition for, and guarantee the enjoyment of, these desired things. What is guaranteed to be one's own is property.

§ 2. Objects of Property Rights

Not all things are objects of property rights, and not all rights that persons have with respect to things are governed by the law of property. Legislation, doctrine, or jurisprudence in various legal systems determines which things may become objects of property rights. In most legal systems, including common law jurisdictions, Louisiana, and legal systems of the French family, the word things applies to both physical objects and incorporeals. In legal systems following the model of the German Civil Code, however, the word things applies only to corporeal objects that are susceptible of appropriation. In these systems, incorporeals, such as rights and obligations, are neither things nor objects of property rights.

Accurate definition of the word things is indispensable in view of the fact that only things in the legal sense may be objects of property rights. Entities that are not things in the legal sense may, however, be objects of a variety of other rights. For example, according to modern conceptions, living human bodies and members or parts thereof are not things; they are objects of a comprehensive right of personality. Nevertheless, blood plasma, hair, and organs separated from a human body are things and objects of property rights. Dead bodies, though ordinarily destined to be disposed of by burial or cremation, are likewise regarded as things.

With respect to things, persons may have a variety of rights, of which some confer a direct and immediate authority while others confer the possibility of enjoyment through the intervention of another person. For example, according to appearances, a lessee and an owner have the use and enjoyment of a house in much the same way. The owner, however, has a direct and immediate authority over the house; the lessee has a right against the lessor to let him enjoy the house. All rights that are susceptible of pecuniary evaluation are property in the sense that they are guaranteed by the legal order and form part of a person's patrimony. But only rights that confer a direct and immediate authority over a thing, that is, real rights, are governed by the civil law of property.

§ 3. Technical Terms: Property, Ownership, Patrimony and Real Rights

In the Louisiana Civil Code, the word property is at times a translation of the French *propriete* and at times a translation of *biens.* In context, it may mean things, ownership, or patrimony. In the new legislation, the word property is used consistently to mean things. In Louisiana jurisprudence, the word property is used broadly to denote rights forming part of a person's patrimony and narrowly to denote rights conferring on a person a direct and immediate authority for the use and enjoyment of a thing that is susceptible of appropriation. Thus, leases, contractual or delictual causes of action, interests in pension plans, the rights to pursue employment and to conduct a business, and uncopyrighted designs are property in the broad sense. Property in the narrow sense refers exclusively to real rights. All real rights, such as ownership, personal servitudes, predial servitudes, and mineral servitudes, are property in the narrow sense. Since, according to accurate civilian usage, objects of ownership and of other real rights may only be corporeal things that are susceptible of appropriation, the word property in the narrow sense does not apply to personal rights. Though having a value and forming part of a person's patrimony, these rights bear on an incorporeal, such as a credit or an obligation.***

§ 4. Civil Law Property

According to civilian classification, the law of property is a branch of private law, particularly of the civil law.***

In civil law jurisdictions, the law of property deals with the principal real rights that a person may have in things. This definition of the domain of property law distinguishes it the from other main branches of the civil law, namely, the law of persons, the law of obligations, the law of family, and the law of successions.

The law of persons deals with the incidents of natural and juridical personality; the law of obligations is preoccupied with relations whereby a person called creditor is entitled to demand a performance from another person called debtor; the law of family regulates legal relations arising out of blood relationship or marriage; and the law of successions deals with the devolution of property upon death. These branches deal with relations that may, and frequently do, give rise to property rights. Due to their origin and purpose, however, these property rights are often subject to special rules rather than the general law of property which may apply to them only subsidiarily and in the absence of specific regulation. These classifications are not rigorously logical abstractions but merely working generalizations devised for the purpose of convenience of understanding and regulation.***

§ 6. Louisiana Property Law: Civil Codes of 1808, 1825 and 1870

Book II of the Louisiana Civil Code of 1870, titled "Things, and of the Different Modifications of Ownership," included the fundamental precepts of the Louisiana property law and regulated selectively a number of institutions.

Following closely the conceptual framework of the French Civil Code and borrowing freely rules from a number of civilian sources, the redactors of the Louisiana Civil Codes of 1808, 1825, and 1870 produced a text that proved both functional and durable. However, it was correctly pointed out that the Louisiana Civil Code, promulgated in the first quarter of the nineteenth century, expressed and inculcated to a large extent the social, political and economic philosophy of the seventeenth and eighteenth centuries. Thus, while as a product of its era the Louisiana Civil Code has been justly considered to be an achievement of juridical craftsmanship, in the light of subsequent experience and doctrinal developments the Code proved in some respects deficient from the viewpoints of both form and substance.

The deficiencies of the Code in the field of property law related mostly to its formal characteristics and conceptual technique rather than substantive regulation. With respect to formal aspects, Book II of the Louisiana Civil Code did not exhaust the regulation of property institutions. This Book dealt with the law of things, ownership, usufruct, habitation, rights of use, and predial servitudes. Possession, which according to modern conceptions is a *sui generis* patrimonial right, was relegated to Title XXIII of Book III along with acquisitive prescription and prescription of nonuse which are, respectively, methods of acquisition and loss of real rights. Likewise, rents of lands, and rights of real security, in spite of their unambiguous characterization as real rights, are dealt with in Titles X, XX, and XXII of Book III.

The substantive deficiencies of the Code in the field of property were almost entirely the result of omission rather than commission; and, in fairness to the memory of its redactors, it must be added that deficiencies became apparent mostly in the light of new social, economic, and political demands. For example, the Code was mostly occupied with immovable property which, at the time of its promulgation, was clearly the foundation of wealth. Movables were dealt with scantily and new sources of riches, like intellectual property, were not regulated at all. A creative jurisprudence and an active Louisiana legislature joined efforts to keep the property law up to date. New legislation was either incorporated into the Civil Code by amendment of original articles or was digested in Title 9 of the Louisiana Revised Statutes as ancillary to the Civil Code. With the exception of trusts legislation and commercial laws, neither the gloss of jurisprudence nor statutes have deeply altered the conceptual framework of the Code and its fundamental precepts in the field of property law.

The question whether Louisiana has a civil law system at all has been hotly debated in the past. The answer to this question depends entirely on the criteria adopted for the distinction between civil law and common law. If emphasis were to be placed on the nature of the judicial process, one might be inclined to classify the legal system of Louisiana within the orbit of the common law. Yet, this generalization would be contrary to fact since, depending on the subject matter of litigation and predilections of judges, decisions are frequently rendered that do justice to the civilian tradition at its best. If, however, emphasis were placed on the origin and content of the substantive regulation of private law relations, one would be entirely justified to affirm that Louisiana has a civil law system of its own. This is particularly so in the domain of property law.

Due to the essentially local and conservative nature of property institutions, attendant constitutional guarantees, the different structure of common law institutions which excludes interstitial seepage, and finally the logic, simplicity, and adequacy of the Civil Code, the civilian tradition in the field of property law has not only been maintained but has flourished. It is in this field that a creative jurisprudence has developed on the basis of the Code a new body of law for the regulation of building restrictions and mineral rights.

§ 7. Historical Sources of Louisiana Property Law

Professor Batiza of the Tulane Law Faculty has undertaken the task of ascertaining in detail the historical sources of each article in Book II of the Louisiana Civil Code. There is no *projet* for the 1808 or 1870 Codes. In the *projet* of the 1825 Code, published by the Louisiana State Law Institute, the sources of particular provisions are not always identified. Comments and citation of sources occur ordinarily in connection with proposed amendments.

The redactors of the Louisiana Civil Code of 1808 had at their disposal the *Projet du Gouvernement* as well as the finished version of the Napoleonic Code. Book II of the Louisiana Civil Code of 1808 differs in many respects from the Napoleonic Code, and it may be a safe assumption that the redactors of the Louisiana Code derived their text not only from French sources but also from Spanish and Roman materials.

In the 1825 revision, as indicated by the large number of amendments proposed and the heavy reliance on the treatises of Pothier, Domat, Toullier, and other French commentators, the redactors sought to follow more closely the French model. Yet, in the field of property, the sources of a number of newly proposed articles are identified as the Digest, the Siete Partidas, Febrero, and other Spanish materials.

For the most part, the Codes of 1825 and 1870 contain provisions that have an exact equivalent in the French Civil Code. Deviation from that model occurred most frequently with respect to definitions and didactic materials in general which were kept to a minimum in France. While according to the better view these materials have no place in a legal text, their inclusion in the Louisiana Civil Code was, perhaps, a practical necessity due to the scarcity of doctrinal works in English.

§ 8. Revision of the Louisiana Civil Code: the New Law of Property

The need for revision of the Louisiana Civil Code of 1870 was felt since the turn of the century. In many respects the Louisiana Civil Code of 1870 represented a "law in the books" as contrasted to "living law." It was stated several decades ago that "the entire foundation of the Code is swept from beneath it, leaving the superstructure of its articles suspended *in vacuo* and in contact but remotely and tenuously with the life, the *moeurs* and the demands of the civilization." While this may be an exaggeration, revision *is* desirable. Respect for the law and for our Civil Code demands an effort at establishing a clear correspondence between legal precepts and rules in the Code and in actual practice.

Sensitive to the need for change, the Louisiana legislature in 1948 passed an act by which the Louisiana State Law Institute was specifically directed to prepare a *projet* for the revision of the Louisiana Civil Code. The legislative mandate was implemented by the Institute in 1961 with the organization of a Civil Law Section consisting of sixty persons elected for a period of over three years. They are Louisiana lawyers, judges, and faculty members who are particularly learned in the civil law and who desire to engage actively in the work of the Civil Law Section. The objectives that this section aspires to fulfill may be summarized in two propositions: the development of civil law studies in Louisiana and the accomplishment of a revision of the Civil Code.

The work of revision began with Book II of the Louisiana Civil Code and this project was completed in 1979. The new law of property, adopted title by title, reflects the work of a committee of experts over more than ten years. It conforms with the Louisiana civilian tradition in both substance and form and with solutions suggested by doctrine, jurisprudence, and legislation in developed civil law countries, such as France, Germany, and Greece. It also contains significant innovations made in the light of local and contemporary conditions.

The redactors worked within the confines of Book II of the Civil Code, which they did not feel free to alter significantly as to coverage. They mostly re-drafted provisions, repealed obsolete rules, and added texts when this was desirable or necessary. As a whole, the new Louisiana law of property is the result of evolution. It rests on tested values, and has retained the accumulated wisdom of the past within the scheme of a modern, comprehensive, and comprehensible organization of the subject matter. It has been drafted, and is expected to function, in the light of Louisiana civilian doctrine. Indeed, a proper interpretation and application of the revised texts presupposes the development of studies, monographs and treatises, furnishing a sound doctrinal foundation. It is hoped that this treatise will contribute to this objective as a useful expose of the new law of property and that it will assist the Louisiana legal profession in the fulfillment of its solemn responsibility.

CHAPTER I. COMMON, PUBLIC, AND PRIVATE THINGS
La. Civil Code arts. 448-460

A. N. YIANNOPOULOS, CIVIL LAW PROPERTY
§ 45 (4th ed. 2001)
(footnotes omitted)

§ 45. Basis of the Division

Under the Louisiana Civil Code, the first division of things is into common things, public things, and private things. This division derives from the Romanist tradition and corresponds with divisions in other civil codes.

In Louisiana, the division of things into common, public, and private rests on the idea that things may fall into three broad categories. The first category consists of common things, such as the air and the high seas, that are *insusceptible of ownership.* Neither public bodies nor private persons may own these things. The second category consists of public things, such as state highways and municipal roads dedicated to public use, that are susceptible only of public ownership. These things are *insusceptible of private ownership* and may only be owned by the state and its political subdivisions in their capacity as public persons. The third category consists of private things, namely things that are *susceptible of private ownership;* these may be owned by private persons or by the state and its political subdivisions in their capacity as private persons.

The division of things according to their susceptibility or insusceptibility of private ownership has been abandoned in modern civil codes in favor of the analytically preferable division of things as being "in commerce" or "out of commerce." However, the traditional division has been maintained in the revision of the Louisiana Civil Code for both historical and practical reasons. Thus, common things are insusceptible of any ownership, public things are insusceptible of private ownership, and private things are the only ones susceptible of private ownership. The parallel division of things "in commerce" and "out of commerce," however, remains implicit in the Civil Code, in special legislation, and in the jurisprudence.

1. COMMON THINGS

LOUISIANA CONSTITUTION (1974)

Article 9, § 1. The natural resources of the state, including air and water, and the healthful, scenic, historic, and esthetic quality of the environment shall be protected, conserved, and replenished insofar as possible and consistent with the health, safety, and welfare of the people. The legislature shall enact laws to implement this policy.

A. N. YIANNOPOULOS, CIVIL LAW PROPERTY
§§ 46-48 (4th ed. 2001)
(footnotes omitted)

§ 46. Common Things; Definition

Article 449 of the Louisiana Civil Code declares: "Common things may not be owned by anyone. They are such as the air and high seas that may be freely used by everyone conformably with the use for which nature has intended them." The corresponding provision of the 1870 Code reproduced a passage of the Institutes of Justinian, based on the questionable assumption that common things are insusceptible of ownership by their nature. This idea has been abandoned in modern civil codes as it became clear that insusceptibility of ownership is a matter of legal prohibition rather than an inherent characteristic of common things. Thus, in the German Civil Code there is no reference to common things; in the French Civil Code there is merely an allusion to such things; and in the Greek Civil Code, in which the traditional classification has been retained, the category of common things has merely academic significance.

In Louisiana, in accordance with the desire of the state to secure administrative and financial advantages, statutes have been enacted since the last quarter of the nineteenth century asserting state ownership over certain things that were classified in the Civil Code as common things. This legislation resulted in near elimination of the category of common things and in substantial augmentation of the category of public things, but the reclassification brought into line Louisiana law and modern continental doctrine and legislation. The revision, following this trend, has limited the category of common things to air and the high seas.

§ 47. Air

According to Article 449 of the Louisiana Civil Code "air," that is, the atmospheric air in its entirety, is not susceptible of ownership. It may not belong to anyone, whether a private or public person. Everyone, however, may reduce finite quantities of air into possession and ownership.

Article 449 refers to air as a mixture of chemical compounds rather than as the airspace. According to Article 490 of the Louisiana Civil Code, airspace is a private thing; it belongs to the owner of the ground. Though a private thing, airspace may be used for aerial traffic above certain altitudes. Congress has recognized the need for modification of the notion of private ownership of airspace, and has declared that the airspace above a minimum altitude for safe flight is navigable airspace subject to the public right for free transit.

§ 48. High Seas

According to Romanist tradition, the sea is a common thing. Deviating from this tradition, Article 449 of the Louisiana Civil Code, as revised in 1978, includes only the "high seas" in the category of common things. This was necessary in the light of legislation asserting the state's "full and complete ownership" of the waters and bottoms of the Gulf of Mexico and of adjacent bodies of water within Louisiana territorial limits.

The words "high seas" in Article 449 of the Louisiana Civil Code have the same meaning as in Article 1 of the Convention of the High Seas of April 29, 1958: they refer to the column of water, the surface, and airspace beyond the territorial sea. The continental shelf beneath the water is subject to the paramount rights of the United States. Further, the United States claims "sovereign rights and exclusive fishery management authority" over the "exclusive economic zone," that is, a zone stretching two hundred nautical miles from the outer limits of the territorial sea.

2. PUBLIC THINGS

A. N. YIANNOPOULOS, CIVIL LAW PROPERTY
§§ 49, 52 (4th ed. 2001)
(footnotes omitted)

§ 49. Public Things; Definition

Public property, that is, property of the state and its political subdivisions, is comprised of two classes of things; public things and private things. The first class consists of things that the state or its political subdivisions own in their capacity as *public persons* and the second of things that the state or its political subdivisions own in their capacity as *private persons*.

Public things that belong to the state are such as running waters, the waters and bottoms of natural navigable water bodies, the territorial sea, and the seashore. Public things that belong to the political subdivisions of the state are such as streets and public squares. The enumeration is merely indicative. In contrast with common things that may not be owned by anyone, public things are susceptible of ownership, though not of private ownership. They are owned by the state or its political subdivisions; but this ownership is of a public law nature for the benefit of all persons, citizens and non-citizens.

§ 52. The Public Domain and the Private Domain — The 1978 Revision of the Louisiana Civil Code

Public property is no longer divided in Louisiana into property of the public domain and property of the private domain. Things which under the prior law were considered to be part of the public domain are now "public things," and things which were considered to be a part of the private domain are "private things." The criterion for the distinction between the two classes of public property is the capacity in which a public body owns a particular thing. Things that the state or its political subdivisions own in their capacity as public persons are public things, and things that the state or its political subdivisions own in their capacity as private persons are private things.

Determination of the question whether the state or a political subdivision of the state owns a particular thing in its capacity as a public person or private person depends on inherent characteristics of particular things and pertinent provisions of law. For example, the state owns naturally navigable water bodies in its capacity as a public person; if the water body ceases to be navigable, the state owns the same water body in its capacity as a private person. Further, a political subdivision owns a street or a square that is subject to public use in its capacity as a public person; if the public use terminates, in the absence of other provisions of law, it owns the same street or square in its capacity as a private person.

The essential characteristic of public things is that they are insusceptible of private ownership. Things are not insusceptible of private ownership because they are owned by the state or its political subdivisions in their capacity as public persons. The contrary is true: things are owned by the state or its political subdivisions in their capacity as public persons because they are insusceptible of private ownership. Insusceptibility of private ownership is not a natural quality of things but a legal determination. Certain things that are subject to, or needed for, public use are for that reason designated by the law as insusceptible of private ownership. Insusceptibility of private ownership is a guarantee for continuous enjoyment of certain things by all persons, citizens or non-citizens. Public things are subject to public use by express legislative text, but not all things subject to public use are public things. For example, the banks of navigable rivers are private things subject to public use, even if they are owned by the state or its political subdivisions.

It would have been analytically preferable to adopt in the 1978 revision the distinction between things "in commerce" and "out of commerce" and to dispense with the distinction of things according to their susceptibility of private ownership. All things subject to public use could be designated as "out of commerce," that is, as insusceptible of private relations incompatible with public use. Such things could be owned by the state, by its political subdivisions, or by private persons. This scheme would have been in accord with both early civilian sources and modern continental doctrine. However, it would have been contrary to established patterns of thought in contemporary Louisiana practice.

LOUISIANA CONSTITUTION (1974)

Article 9, §§ 3, 4. The Legislature shall neither alienate nor authorize the alienation of the bed of a navigable water body, except for purposes of reclamation by the riparian owner to recover land lost through erosion. This Section shall not prevent the leasing of state lands or water bottoms for mineral or other purposes. Except as provided in this Section, the bed of a navigable water body may be reclaimed only for public use.

(A) Reservation of Mineral Rights. The mineral rights on property sold by the state shall be reserved, except when the owner or person having the right to redeem buys or redeems property sold or adjudicated to the state for taxes.

(B) Prescription. Lands and mineral interests of the state, of a school board, or of a levee district shall not be lost by prescription.

Article 12, § 10. (A) No Immunity in Contract and Tort. Neither the state, a state agency, nor a political subdivision shall be immune from suit and liability in contract or for injury to person or property.

(B) Waiver in Other Suits. The legislature may authorize other suits against the state, a state agency, or a political subdivision. A measure authorizing suit shall waive immunity from suit and liability.

(C) Procedure; Judgments. The legislature shall provide a procedure for suits against the state, a state agency, or a political subdivision. It shall provide for the effect of a judgment, but no public property or public funds shall be subject to seizure. No judgment against the state, a state agency, or a political subdivision shall be exigible, payable, or paid except from funds appropriated therefore by the legislature or by the political subdivision against which judgment is rendered.

3. PRIVATE THINGS

a. The Nature of Private Things

A. N. YIANNOPOULOS, CIVIL LAW PROPERTY
§§ 59-61 (4th ed. 2001)
(footnotes omitted)

§ 59. Private things; Definition

Private things are the only things that are susceptible of private ownership, that is, they are capable of becoming objects of property rights held by private persons. Article 453 of the Louisiana Civil Code declares: "Private things are owned by individuals, other private persons, and by the state or its political subdivisions in their capacity as private persons." This provision is a necessary counterpart of Article 449, dealing with common things, which cannot be owned by anyone, and of Article 450, dealing with public things, are not susceptible of private ownership.

Private things are not necessarily owned at all times; they are things that the law permits persons to own. Thus, res nullius and abandoned movables are private things though they are not owned by anyone in particular.

Private things are, in principle, alienable, prescriptible, and subject to seizure. Certain exceptions to the principle, however, may be established by law or by juridical act.

§ 60. Things of Private Persons

Private things are divided into two classes. One class consists of things belonging to individuals or other private persons, such as partnerships and corporations, and the other of things belonging to the state or its political subdivisions in their capacity as private persons.

The division is important because different rules of law apply to each class of things. In principle, private persons may freely dispose of private things under modifications established by law, whereas private things belonging to the state, its agencies, and its political subdivisions may only be disposed of in accordance with applicable laws and regulations.

§ 61. Things of the State and Its Political Subdivisions

Things owned by the state or its political subdivisions in their capacities as private persons are private things. These, like similar things belonging to private persons, are alienable, unless the law provides otherwise. Private things of political subdivisions are, in principle, prescriptible but exempt from seizure. Private things of the state, for reasons of policy, are both imprescriptible and exempt from seizure.***

The category of private things of the state and its political subdivisions includes things which, though serving a public purpose, are not subject to, or needed for, public use. Thus, money in the state treasury or in the treasury of a political subdivision, rentals accruing from leases of public property, revenues from public enterprise, and movables or immovables of a nature that private persons may own, are private things.

b. Protection of Private Ownership

The following provisions of constitutional law restrict the ability of the State to interfere with the rights of property owners through the State's private or public law.

THE CONSTITUTION OF THE UNITED STATES OF AMERICA

Amendment V. No person ... shall be compelled in any criminal case to be a witness against himself, nor be deprived of life, liberty, or property, without due process of law; nor shall private property be taken for public use without just compensation.

LOUISIANA CONSTITUTION (1974)

Article. 1, § 4. Every person has the right to acquire, own, control, use, enjoy, protect, and dispose of private property. This right is subject to reasonable statutory restrictions and the reasonable exercise of the police power.

Property shall not be taken or damaged by the state or its political subdivisions except for public purposes and with just compensation paid to the owner or into court for his benefit. Property shall not be taken or damaged by any private entity authorized by law to expropriate, except for a public and necessary purpose and with just compensation paid to the owner; in such proceedings, whether the purpose is public and necessary shall be a judicial question. In every expropriation, a party has the right to trial by jury to determine compensation, and the owner shall be compensated to the full extent of his loss. No business enterprise or any of its assets shall be taken for the purpose of operating that enterprise or halting competition with a government enterprise. However, a municipality may expropriate a utility within its jurisdiction. Personal effects, other than contraband, shall never be taken.

This Section shall not apply to appropriation of property necessary for levee and levee drainage purposes.

CHAPTER II. WATER BODIES AND RELATED LANDS

See A. N. YIANNOPOULOS, CIVIL LAW PROPERTY
§ 62 (4th ed. 2001)

1. STATE OWNERSHIP OF WATER BODIES
La. Civil Code arts. 450–452

a. Running Waters
La. Civil Code art. 450

A. N. YIANNOPOULOS, CIVIL LAW PROPERTY
§ 57 (4th ed. 2001)
(footnotes omitted)

§ 57. Running Waters

According to Article 450 of the Louisiana Civil Code, running water is a public thing. As such, it is owned by the state in its capacity as a public person and it is subject to public use.

Under the Civil Code, running water is distinguishable from the space it occupies and from the bed that contains it. Thus, the bed of a non-navigable river is a private thing, whereas the water is a public thing subject to public use. Further, the bed of a navigable river or stream is a public thing, as is the water. However, the water is subject to public use but the bed is not.

The riparian owner may use running water for his purposes, but he may not interfere with or exclude the public use. Legislation and jurisprudence stress the public interest and require that the user of running water should consider the rights of other persons and refrain from pollution.

According to continental doctrine, running water is conceptually inseparable from its bed. Thus, running water belongs to the owner of the bed, whether he is a public or a private person. However, regardless of ownership, running water under modern civil codes is a thing subject to public use.

NOTES AND QUESTIONS

1. Article 450 of the Louisiana Civil Code classifies running water as a public thing; it is owned by the State in its public capacity. Thus running water is subject to public use under art. 452. However, that use must be, as the article declares, "in accordance with applicable laws and regulations." A statutory provision expands the public's right to use the state's waters; see La. R. S. 9:1101 *infra*. Besides "running waters," what waters qualify as "waters of the state," subject to public use?

2. Who owns waters that are not "waters of the state," and who may use them? See La. Civ. Code art. 490 and *Adams v. Grigsby*, 152 So. 2d 619 (La. App. 2d Cir. 1963).

3. Until Act 258 of 1910, running water was classified as a common thing; see La. Civil Code art. 449 for the current rule on common things. The 1910 act reclassified running water as public. Upon the revision of Book II of the Civil Code, the new status for running water was incorporated into art. 450. See A.N. YIANNOPOULOS, PROPERTY, 2 La. Civil Law Treatise 4th ed., § 57 (2001). What is achieved by reclassifying running water as a public thing of the State rather than as a common thing?

4. Does the fact that running water is a public thing require that the private riparian landowner permit public access to that water? In *Buckskin Hunting Club v. Bayard*, 868 So. 2d 266 (La. App. 3d Cir. 2004), seven Louisiana hunters argued that the privately owned land leased by the plaintiff was subject to public use by virtue of its waterway. In its multitude of reasons for upholding the issuance of a permanent injunction against the seven defendants, the Louisiana Third Circuit Court of Appeal included the following:

> The obligations arising from water being a public thing require the owner through whose estate running waters pass to allow water to leave his estate through its natural channel and not to unduly diminish its flow; however, this does not mandate that landowner allow public access to [the] waterway. LSA - C.C. arts. 450, 452, 658. *People For Open Waters. Inc. v. Estate of Gray*, 643 So. 2d 415 (La.App. 3d Cir. 1994). Landowners and members of [the] general public have [the] right to use running water for their needs, if they have access to it, but neither landowners nor members of general public have the right to cross private lands in order to avail themselves of running water, and such right may only be established by agreement, destination of owner, or prescription. No public right to use of a canal located on private property arises from the fact that water flows through channel. Cf. *People For Open Waters, Inc., supra.*

Id. at 274.

The federal Fifth Circuit Court of Appeals more recently re-iterated this as the Louisiana rule on public use of running water; see *Parm v. Shumate, infra* and at 513 F. 3d 135 (5th Cir. 2007).

The *Buckskin* case is one of many in which Louisiana hunters or fishermen claim the existence of a right in the general public either of access from or of use of a privately owned thing owing to its proximity to a public thing. The scenario has been repeated frequently despite consistency in the results.

5. Individual use of running waters may be regulated by the state to insure that it does not interfere with the rights of others. This regulation includes prohibitions on diverting or obstructing the flow of the waters, La. Civ. Code arts. 655-658; criminal penalties for contaminating the water supply and irrigation waters, e.g., La. R.S. 14:58 and 38:216; and the establishment of district authorities to control water usage within their areas, e.g., La. R.S. 38: 2101, 2321, and 2551.

b. Natural Navigable Water Bodies

Under Louisiana Civil Code article 450, the State of Louisiana owns running waters, the waters and bottoms of natural navigable water bodies, and the territorial sea as public things; they are thus subject to public use under article 452. Given that the area comprising most of the present State of Louisiana was purchased from France by the United States of America in 1803, why does the State, rather than the United States, own these waters? The answer lies in two Constitutional doctrines established by the U.S. Supreme Court.

COYLE v. SMITH
221 U.S. 559 (1911)

MR. JUSTICE LURTON delivered the opinion of the court. ***The power of Congress in respect to the admission of new States is found in the third section of the fourth Article of the Constitution. That provision is that, "new States may be admitted by the Congress into this Union." ...

But what is this power? It is not to admit political organizations which are less or greater, or different in dignity or power, from those political entities which constitute the Union. It is, as strongly put by counsel, a "power to admit States."

The definition of "a State" is found in the powers possessed by the original States which adopted the Constitution, a definition emphasized by the terms employed in all subsequent acts of Congress admitting new States into the Union. The first two States admitted into the Union were the States of Vermont and Kentucky, one as of March 4, 1791, and the other as of June 1, 1792. No terms or conditions were exacted from either. Each act declares that the State is admitted "as a new and entire member of the United States of America." 1 Stat. 89, 191. Emphatic and significant as is the phrase admitted as "an entire member," even stronger was the declaration upon the admission in 1796 of Tennessee, as the third new State, it being declared to be "one of the United States of America," "on an equal footing with the original States in all respects whatsoever," phraseology which has ever since been substantially followed in admission acts....The power is to admit "new States into this Union."

"This Union" was and is a union of States, equal in power, dignity and authority, each competent to exert that residuum of sovereignty not delegated to the United States by the Constitution itself. ...

hence States own water b/c not delegated to U.S.

POLLARD v. HAGAN
44 U.S. 212, 3 How. 212, 230 (1845)

McKINLEY, J. ***[W]e have arrived at these general conclusions: First, [t]he shores of navigable waters, and the soils under them, were not granted by the Constitution to the United States, but were reserved to the states respectively. Secondly, [t]he new states have the same rights, sovereignty, and jurisdiction over this subject as the original states....

NOTES

1. Under the Equal Footing Doctrine summarized in *Coyle v. Smith*, every new state granted admission to the Union enters with the same dignity and powers held by the original States that adopted the U.S. Constitution. *Pollard v. Hagan* earlier had recognized that ownership of navigable waters and their bottoms was reserved to the original States rather than transferred to the U.S. under its Constitution. Thus, new states have ownership of these water bodies upon admission to statehood, even if, as is the case with regard to Louisiana, they did not have this incident of sovereignty prior to statehood.

2. Louisiana was admitted to statehood in 1812. As the cases in this chapter will indicate, establishing navigability *vel non* as of this date becomes a crucial issue in disputes over the ownership of water bodies, and the nature of that ownership.

c. The Territorial Sea and the Seashore
La. Civil Code arts. 450-451

See A. N. YIANNOPOULOS, CIVIL LAW PROPERTY
§§ 69-72 (4th ed. 2001)

LOUISIANA REVISED STATUTES

R.S. 49:3. Ownership of waters within boundaries

The State of Louisiana owns in full and complete ownership the waters of the Gulf of Mexico and of the arms of the Gulf and the beds and shores of the Gulf and the arms of the Gulf, including all lands that are covered by the waters of the Gulf and its arms either at low tide or high tide, within the boundaries of Louisiana.

MILNE v. GIRODEAU
12 La. 324 (1838)

CARLETON, J., delivered the opinion of the court. This being a petitory action brought for the recovery of a lot of ground in the town of Milneburg, at the end of the rail road, on Lake Pontchartrain, composed, according to the plan of that town, of a part of lots 1 and 2, in square No. 1, being sixty feet front on Champs Elysées street, and extend-ing in depth one hundred and twenty feet, and fronting on the American wharf.

The defendant, who is in possession of the lot, avers, in his answer, that it makes a part of the sea shore, is common property, and that plaintiff cannot have the ownership thereof. There was judgment for the defendant, and plaintiff appealed.

It appears to us that the testimony shows fully, the ground in question, lies much below high water mark, and forms part of the bed of the lake, and is not, therefore, susceptible of private ownership. Louisiana Code, Articles 440, 1, 2, 3, and 4 (1825) [Revised C.C. arts. 449, 450]...It is, therefore, ordered, adjudged and decreed, that the judgment of the District Court be affirmed, with costs.

NOTES

1. *Procedural terminology:* A *petitory action* is an action to establish ownership; see Chapter X, *infra.*

2. *Milne v. Girodeau* is the jurisprudential ancestor of the notion that Lake Pontchartrain is an "arm of the sea," thus belonging to the State in its public capacity under article 450; and that its shores are therefore a public thing as well, the seashore, under article 451. For the proposition that additions to the shores of Lake Pontchartrain and of all navigable "lakes, bays, arms of the sea, or other large bodies of water" other than rivers belong to the state, see Zeller v. Southern Yacht Club, 34 La. Ann. 837 (1882); Brunning v. City of New Orleans, 165 La. 511, 115 So. 733 (1928).

In *Zeller v. Southern Yacht Club*, the plaintiff, "having title by purchase to a lot situated on Lake Pontchartrain," sought to be declared owner "of the batture, accession or accretion, formed and to be formed between the former frontage of the lot and the waters of the lake, and to recover of the defendant two thousand dollars for trespassing thereon." The defendant filed an exception of no cause of action and argued that "the plaintiff seeks to recover an accession or accretion on the shore of Lake Pontchartrain, and the right of property does not exist in such accession or accretion on said lake, the same being an arm of the sea." The court sustained the exception; plaintiff appealed. The court of appeal affirmed, stating: "The plaintiff...denies that Lake Pontchartrain is either the sea or an arm of the sea, and, therefore, contends that this question of accretions or alluvion on the sea shores has no applicability to this case ...[W]e consider this question virtually disposed of in the case of Milne vs. Girodeau, 12 La. 324."

BURAS v. SALINOVICH
154 La. 594, 97 So. 748 (1923)

O'NIELL, C.J. The question in this case is whether the conservation laws of the state give, to the holder of a license to hunt and trap wild game and fur bearing animals, the right to hunt and trap on any and all marsh land, even against the protest of the owner of such land, if the land be subject to tidal overflow, unfenced, not in cultivation or used as a pasture, and not set apart as a game preserve.

Plaintiff here owns a tract of marsh land, exceeding 5,000 acres in area, fronting nearly 4 miles on the east bank of the Mississippi river, about 85 miles below New Orleans. The land is not fenced, or cultivated, or used for a pasture; and, excepting the ridge that extends back only a few acres from the river, and the ridges forming the banks of several bayous in the land, it is subject to tidal overflow, and not fit for cultivation.

Each of the six defendants holds a state license, declaring that he "has paid the license fee required by law, and is entitled to hunt such game birds and game animals, and to catch or trap such animals as are defined under the laws of the state of Louisiana, during the open season, and in such manner and at such times and places as permitted by law." The defendants, pursuing a custom which had prevailed among the local hunters and trappers from time immemorial, went upon plaintiff's land, without his consent and, for their own profit, engaged in hunting the wild game and in trapping the fur-bearing animals on the land.

The plaintiff had posted notices, printed in bold letters, on boards measuring 18 inches square, along the boundaries of the land and along the banks of the bayous running through the land, forbidding trespassing within the line of stakes, under penalty of the law. The notices and intervening stakes were placed close enough together to serve their purpose. Similar notices, describing the land, were published in the two newspapers published in the parish where the land is situated.

Plaintiff also had a man employed patrolling the land, making the rounds regularly through the bayous, warning hunters and trappers against trespassing upon the land. He delivered to each of the defendants personally a written demand that they should quit hunting and trapping on the land. The defendants refused to quit. Thereupon plaintiff brought this suit, alleging the facts which we have stated, and praying for a preliminary injunction, to be eventually made perpetual, forbidding the defendants to go upon the land for the purpose of hunting or trapping. The district judge issued a rule, ordering the defendants to show cause why the preliminary injunction should not issue.

Answering the petition, and the rule to show cause, the defendants denied that plaintiff was entitled to any relief, on the facts stated, and they set up a reconventional demand for a judgment in their favor, declaring that they had the right to go upon any part of the land described in plaintiff's petition "for the purpose of trapping, taking, capturing, killing, or removing from the land, any animal, fowl, bird, or quadruped, without the consent or permission of the plaintiff or of any other person, and further condemning the said Manuel Oscar Buras to pay to respondents, as plaintiffs in reconvention, the sum of $3,250, as damages, with legal interest," etc. The damages claimed were said to be $2,500 for the alleged or approximated value of the fur-bearing animals which, defendants alleged, this suit had prevented their trapping, and $750 for attorneys' fees alleged to have been incurred in defending the suit.

Having heard argument on the rule, the district judge refused to issue a temporary injunction. The case was then heard on its merits, resulting in a judgment for the defendants, rejecting the plaintiff's demand for an injunction "and recognizing the defendants' right to enter upon the premises described in the petition herein, for the purpose of trapping and removing therefrom such wild life and fur-bearing animals as are permitted by state license." The plaintiff has appealed.

The Civil Code, in Article 3415 [Revised C.C. art. 3413], after declaring that the wild beasts and birds have no owner while they are at large, and that when captured they become immediately the property of their captor, whether he takes them from his own land or from the land of another, says: "But the proprietor of a tract of land may forbid any person from entering it for the purpose of hunting thereon."

The argument of the defendants is twofold. It is contended, first, that this provision of the Code, recognizing the right of any and every landowner to forbid hunting on his land, was repealed by implication, or superseded, by Section 20 of the Conservation Law (Act 204 of 1912), as to marsh land, subject to tidal overflow, and not fenced, or in cultivation, or used as a pasture, or set apart as a game preserve. In the alternative, the defendants contend that plaintiff's land, being subject to overflow regularly from the gulf tides, is "seashore," according to the definition in the Civil Code, and is therefore not subject to private ownership....

The district judge, in his written opinion, maintained the defendants' contention that the provision in Article 3415 [Revised C.C. art. 3413] of the Civil Code, recognizing the right of every landowner to forbid hunting on his land, was repealed by implication, or superseded, by section 20 of Act 204 of 1912, in so far as it had applied to marsh land, subject to tidal overflow, and unfenced, and not cultivated or used for a pasture, or set apart as a game preserve. The judge did not maintain that the land was "seashore," not subject to private ownership. He must have concluded or assumed that the land was not "seashore"; otherwise there would have been no occasion for pronouncing judgment upon the repealing effect of section 20 of Act 204 of 1912, as to marsh land that is subject to private ownership.

We concur in the opinion that plaintiff's land should not be classed as "seashore," or public property. The fact that it is subject to tidal overflow does not characterize the land as "seashore," under the provisions of the Code. The statutes providing for disposing of such lands, either by the state or by the federal government, describe them as being subject to tidal overflow. It has never heretofore been supposed that the definition in

Article 451 of the Civil Code was intended to include in the term "that space of land over which the waters of the sea spread in the highest water during the winter season," any and all land that is subject to tidal overflow, however remote from the "seashore" as it is generally understood. The waters of the Gulf of Mexico, or the bays or coves behind plaintiff's land, do not "spread" upon it, during the ordinary high tides, or in the highwater seasons. The tide waters back up into the coves behind the land, and cause the bayous in the land to rise and spread over most of the areas. These expressions in the Code "the sea and its shores," and "seashore," have reference to the gulf coast, and to the lakes, bays and sounds along the coast. The nearest body of water that could reasonably be characterized as a part of the sea, or as having a seashore, in this case, is a small bay nearly a mile away from plaintiff's land.

In the case of Morgan v. Negodish, 40 La. Ann. 246, 3 South. 636, the question presented was whether the plaintiff's marsh land was "seashore, under the definition in Article 451 of the Civil Code." The land was situated very much like that of the plaintiff in this case, with relation to the gulf, a small bay, and a bayou penetrating the land, which was subject to tidal overflow. The court's ruling in the case is accurately expressed in the head notes, thus: "If the salt water ascertained to be in a bayou, lake, cove, or inlet adjacent to, or connected with, an arm of the Gulf of Mexico, does not result from an overflow that is occasioned by high tides flooding its banks, out, in the first instance, enters an arm of the gulf, and thence passes into said bayou, lake, etc., and is there combined with fresh water derived from other sources, same cannot be considered as an arm of the sea, nor its banks the seashore."***

The fundamental doctrine that the wild beasts and birds belong to the state in her sovereign capacity, and for the benefit of all of her citizens, is not at all contrary to the right of every landowner to forbid other persons to hunt or trap wild beasts or birds on his land. Although a landowner does not, literally, own the wild beasts and birds on his land, he controls the right to enter upon his land for the purpose of hunting or trapping the wild beasts or birds. That right, on the part of the landowner, is, of course, subject to the conservation laws of the state enacted in the exercise of her police power. But the state does not undertake to deprive a landowner, for the benefit or profit of other individuals, of his exclusive right of possession of his land.

Counsel for appellant have argued, very forcibly, that, if the Act 204 of 1912 should be construed as depriving him of his right to forbid others to hunt on his land, the law would be unconstitutional, in that it would deny him the equal protection of the laws, and deprive him of his property without due process of law, and without compensation. Having concluded that the statute does not purport to deprive any landowner of his right to forbid hunting or trapping on his land, we have no occasion for saying whether the law would be unconstitutional if it did purport to have that effect. The judgment appealed from is annulled.

NOTE AND QUESTION

1. *Procedural terminology:* A *rule* is a motion, and a *rule to show cause*, as the procedural history of this case indicates, requires the defendant to show a cause why some action requested by a plaintiff—in this case, issuance of the preliminary injunction—should not be granted. The defendants in this case not only responded with arguments against issuance, but also made a *reconventional demand*, i.e., made their own claim for damages against Mr. Buras; thus the defendants in Buras' case are *plaintiffs in reconvention* against him.

2. Generally stated, what factors did the Louisiana Supreme Court consider to be significant in determining whether land subject to overflow is to be classified as "seashore" or not?

d. The "Oyster Statutes"

LOUISIANA ACTS. NO. 106, § 1 (1886)

Be it enacted by the General Assembly of the State of Louisiana, that all the beds of the rivers, bayous, creeks, lakes, coves, inlets and sea marshes bordering on the Gulf of Mexico, and all that part of the Gulf of Mexico within the jurisdiction of this State, and not heretofore sold or conveyed by special grants, or by sale by this State, or by the United States to any private party or parties, shall continue and remain the property of the State of Louisiana, and may be used in common by all the people of the State for the purposes of fishing and of taking and catching oysters and other shell fish, subject to the reservations and restrictions hereinafter imposed, and no grant or sale, or conveyance shall hereafter be made by the Register of the State Land office to any estate, or interest of the State in any natural oyster bed or shoal, whether the said bed or shoal shall ebb bare or not.

LOUISIANA ACTS NO. 258 (1910)

Be it enacted by the General Assembly of the State of Louisiana, That the waters of and in all bayous, lagoons, lakes and bays and the beds thereof, within the borders of the State not at present under the direct ownership of any person, firm, or corporation are hereby declared to be the property of the State. There shall never be any charge assessed against any person, firm or corporation for the use of the waters of the State for municipal, agricultural or domestic purposes.

LOUISIANA REVISED STATUTES

R.S. 9:1101. Ownership of waters and beds of bayous, rivers, streams, lagoons, lakes and bays

The waters of and in all bayous, rivers, streams, lagoons, lakes and bays, and the beds thereof, not under the direct ownership of any person on August 12, 1910, are declared to be the property of the state. There shall never be any charge assessed against any person for the use of the waters of the state for municipal, industrial, agricultural or domestic purposes.

A. N. YIANNOPOULOS, CIVIL LAW PROPERTY
§ 61 (4th ed. 2001)
(footnotes omitted)

§ 61. Things of the State and its Political Subdivisions

Things owned by the state or its political subdivisions in their capacity as private persons are private things. These, like similar things belonging to private persons, are alienable, unless the law provides otherwise. Private things of political subdivisions are, in principle, prescriptible but exempt from seizure. Private things of the state, for reasons of policy, are both imprescriptible and exempt from seizure.

Under the regime of the Louisiana Civil Code of 1870, private things of the state and its political subdivisions were designated as things of the private domain in contradistinction with public things, which formed part of the public domain. The notions of the public and private domain were avoided in the 1978 revision of the Louisiana Civil Code; accordingly, private things of the state and its political subdivisions are merely contrasted with public things.

The category of private things of the state and its political subdivisions includes things which, though serving a public purpose, are not subject to, or needed for, public use. Thus, money in the state treasury or in the treasury of a political subdivision, rentals accruing from leases of public property, revenues from public enterprises, and movables or immovables of a nature that private persons may own, are private things. In addition, in Landry v. Council of East Baton Rouge Parish, the court concluded after careful analysis of all pertinent authorities that a municipal airport is a private thing.

Swamp lands acquired by Louisiana from the United States and state owned bottoms of inland non-navigable water bodies are also private things. The state acquired the ownership of the beds or bottoms of all inland navigable waters upon its admission into the Union in 1812. Such water bodies that continue to be navigable are public things; however, if they cease to be navigable, they become private things of the state. Thus, it may be important to determine whether a body of water was navigable in 1812 and whether or not it continues to be navigable. Navigability is ordinarily a question of fact; if a body of water is navigable in fact, it is navigable in law. In order to be navigable, bodies of water must be used, or be susceptible of being used, "in their ordinary condition, as highways of commerce, over which trade and travel are or may be conducted in the customary modes of trade and travel on water."

By Act 258 of 1910, the state asserted its ownership of the waters and beds of all "bayous, lagoons, lakes, and bays ... not under the direct ownership of any person, firm, or corporation." This act has been largely ignored by Louisiana courts. Despite its broad language, the act is inapplicable to running waters and to the beds or bottoms of natural navigable water bodies because these are public things owned by the state in its capacity as a public person. Moreover, the act may not be constitutionally applied to waters already owned on its effective date. It is true that the statute exempts from its application only water bodies "directly" owned, but there is no such notion as direct or indirect ownership under Louisiana law. A person either owns or does not own a thing.

Perhaps the words "directly owned" were inserted into the statute to exclude claims by riparian owners under the law of accession, that is, claims to beds or bottoms of water bodies and to accretions by virtue of the ownership of the banks or shores. Ownership by right of accession might be described as indirect ownership. Even if this interpretation were acceptable, the act would be without purpose today. The beds of non-navigable rivers belong by accession to the riparian owners along a line drawn in the middle of the bed; the state may not divest a riparian of his ownership of the bed of a non-navigable river, even if such ownership were to be termed "indirect." For different reasons, the act is equally without purpose as to claims to bottoms and accretions formed at the shores of non-navigable lakes: such lakes are treated as dry lands. The riparian owners do not own the bottoms of non-navigable lakes by accession and have no claim to alluvion or derelictions formed at their shores.

R.S. 9:1115.2. Ownership of inland non-navigable water bottoms

A. Inland non-navigable water bodies are those which are not navigable in fact and are not sea, arms of the sea, or seashore.

B. Inland non-navigable water beds or bottoms are private things and may be owned by private persons or by the state and its political subdivisions in their capacity as private persons.

NOTE AND QUESTION

1. La. R.S. 9:1115.2 differs from the rest of the statutes above in declaring possible ownership by private individuals of some water bodies. The Louisiana Legislature passed it to clarify Louisiana's position under the U.S. Supreme Court's decision in *Phillips Petroleum v. Mississippi*, 484 U.S. 469 (1988). In that case, the U.S. Supreme Court concluded that

ownership of non-navigable inland water bodies subject to the ebb and flow of tidal waters was an aspect of State sovereignty, though a State could choose to divest itself of such ownership.

2. What are the likely purpose(s) of the "Oyster Statutes" of 1886 and 1910? Why are they, as Professor Yiannopoulos points out, of limited significance?

2. NAVIGABILITY
La. Civil Code arts. 450-453

A. N. YIANNOPOULOS, CIVIL LAW PROPERTY
§ 64 (4th ed. 2001)
(footnotes omitted)

§ 64. Navigability

The question of whether a body of water is or has been navigable is important in a variety of contexts. From the viewpoint of Louisiana property law, navigability is ordinarily determinative of the classification of a natural body of water as a public thing and of the question of whether its water and banks or shores are subject to public use.

In determining whether a body of water is or has been navigable, Louisiana courts have in the main followed the test developed by the United States Supreme Court for the delimitation of federal admiralty jurisdiction. In general, a body of water is navigable if it is susceptible of being used, in its ordinary condition, as a highway of commerce "over which trade and travel are or may be conducted in the customary modes of trade and travel on water." Navigability must thus be proven unless the court is prepared to take judicial notice that a body of water is navigable in fact.

STATE v. TWO O'CLOCK BAYOU LAND CO.
365 So. 2d 1174 (La. App. 3d Cir. 1978)

WATSON, J. Plaintiffs, the State of Louisiana and the Police Jury of the Parish of St. Landry, asked that defendants, Two O'Clock Bayou Land Company, Inc., and its lessee,

Creighton James Nail,[1] be enjoined from maintaining a cable across Two O'Clock Bayou.[1] Plaintiffs also sought a declaration that the stream is navigable and subject to public use. The trial court declared the stream navigable and granted the permanent injunction. Defendants have appealed.

The question presented is whether the bayou is navigable, entitling the Parish and the State to enjoin its obstruction by privately owned barriers. C.C. art. 453; R.S. 14:96, 97....

Two O'Clock Bayou[1] runs roughly north and south through St. Landry Parish in the Atchafalaya Basin Swamp area, crossing sections 14 and 13, T-6-S, R-6-E, and sections 11 and 12, T-6- 5, R-7-E. The bayou, at one time, connected with Darbonne Bay on the north and Craft Lake on the south, but dams have now closed off boat access to these areas. Two O'Clock Bayou crosses Cowan Bay and Close Lake. A recent dam was built by a pipeline company roughly half-way between Close Lake and Craft Lake.

In 1808, the bayou appeared on the Darby survey as an unnamed tributary feeding into Bayou De Grasse. Two O'Clock Bayou's northern portion, above Cowan Bay, has apparently moved half a mile to the west. Although it was not meandered by Darby, defendants' expert forester, Lewis C. Peters, admitted that the bayou could in fact have been navigable in 1808. Darby also failed to meander Bayou Courtableau, a primary navigable stream in the area. At times, in the intervening years, the bed of Two O'Clock has been dry enough to allow germination of cypress trees. The younger trees are approximately 100 years old, showing that the bed was dry 100 years ago. The stumps of the older cypress trees were about four hundred years old when cut in the early nineteen hundreds. Photographs in evidence show large trees and stumps in the bayou, but there is a passage space 10 to 12 feet wide between the old cypress stumps. The water level at the time the photos were taken was admittedly low.

Creighton James Nall, the lessee, testified in deposition that there are pilings and a trestle at Cowan Bay which he believed to be the remnants of a dummy railroad line used for timbering operations. Nail testified on oral examination that he placed the cable at the northern end of the bayou just south of the old Missouri Pacific right of way to control access by the public. A dam had been built just north of the cable's location some ten years before by Walter Buchanan. Nall said the shallowest portion of the bayou is from 3½ to 7 feet deep. At the narrowest part of the bayou, where there are old pilings at the abandoned railroad right of way, there is an opening 8 to 10 feet wide.

Preston Scruggins testified in deposition that he helped build the railroad trestle at Cowan Bay around 1935, when there was only a foot of water in the bayou. According to Scruggins, Two O'Clock was only suitable for pirogue use at that time.

Joe Elder testified in deposition that he is a lumber man and had a mill at Bayou Close near Lottie in 1931. His company harvested timber around Two O'Clock Bayou, snaked the logs to the bayou and floated them out behind small motor boats. The logs were tied together in rafts or cribs about four feet wide.

---

[1] Title to the bed of the bayou is not at issue. Obstruction of the bayou can be enjoined if it is navigable, D'Albora v. Garcia, 144 So. 2d 911 (La. App. 4th Cir. 1962) writ denied; Discon v. Saray, Inc., 262 La. 997, 265 So. 2d 765 (1972). Here, in contrast to Vermillion Corp. v. Vaughn, 356 So. 2d 551 (La. App. 3d Cir. 1978) writ denied 357 So. 2d 558 and National Audubon Society v. White, 302 So. 2d 660 (La. App. 3d Cir. 1974), writ denied 305 So. 2d 542 (La. 1975); the bayou is not artificial and its bed does not lie wholly within the confines of defendants' land. See 33 La. Law Review 172.

Fifteen people attested to their use of Two O'Clock Bayou for fishing over various periods of time, commencing as early as 1930. Emile Miller testified that he had used the bayou for fishing for 26 or 27 years. Ernie Kovack did sport fishing in the bayou, going as far south as Craft Lake in a boat with a two foot draft. A. K. Miller said he had fished the bayou since around 1936 and had seen many commercial fishing boats there.

W. A. Welch has utilized the bayou for fishing since the mid-fifties and has traversed the bayou its entire length beginning at Craft Lake on the south. Welch witnessed use of the bayou by a motion picture company filming "Nevada Smith." The company operated barges on the bayou measuring about 12 feet wide and twenty feet long. Their draft was estimated by Welch at about three feet. According to Welch, the bayou is about three feet deep in the shallowest part of the main channel at low water.

Arthur Roy Shay said he had used the bayou for fishing since 1948, using motors up to 50 horsepower in size. A dam at the northern crossing of old highway 190 and the Missouri Pacific Railroad now obstructs passage into Darbonne Bay on the north. Shay measured a spot 37 feet deep in the bayou where it empties into Close Lake on the south. Another spot at the northern edge of Cowan Bay is twenty feet deep. Shay estimated the average depth of the bayou at nine feet. In his opinion, based on frequent use of a depth finder, the bayou's depth fluctuates three or four feet during periods of high water.

Sherby J. Skrantz testified that he had been familiar with Two O'Clock Bayou since 1949 when he assisted his father in commercial fishing operations there, using a "Joe-boat" four feet wide and fourteen feet long. They caught two to three hundred pounds of fish a night, fishing as far south as Craft Lake. He knew of four other commercial fishermen who used the bayou. Some garfish from Craft Lake weighed in at up to 110 pounds.

In evidence are 1860 patents to sections 14 and 11 and part of section 13 issued by the Louisiana Land Office. Tax receipts were introduced in evidence to prove that Two O'Clock Bayou Land Company had paid taxes on all of sections 13 and A, T-6-S, R-6-E, without any deduction for a navigable waterway. The land company also paid taxes on the part of section 11, T-6-S, R-7-E, crossed by the bayou, but the tax receipt notes that this W ½ of the W½ of section 11 "Includes 13 acres used by the U.S. Government for levee and high level crossing rights-of-way." Payment of taxes on section 12, T-6-S, R-7-E, where the southern part of the bayou empties into Craft Lake, is not claimed by the land company.

Savano Bernard Langlois, an expert surveyor, testified that Two O'Clock Bayou appears in its present location south of Cowan Bay on Darby's 1808 survey notes and the U.S. geodetical map (Exhibit 8) but not north of Cowan Bay. The northern portion of Two O'Clock Bayou is a new stream a half mile to the west. In Langlois' opinion, the 1829 and 1842 maps and surveys indicate that Two O'Clock Bayou was not considered navigable when they were made.

The trial court concluded that the bayou has an average depth of nine feet, and averages 18 to 30 feet in width. The trial court made a factual finding that the bayou is capable of sustaining commerce despite occasional obstructions in its flow.

Navigability is not presumed; the burden of proof rests with the party seeking to establish it. Johnson v. State Farm Fire and Casualty Company, 303 So. 2d 779 (La. App. 3d Cir. 1974); Burns v. Crescent Gun & Rod Club, 116 La. 1038, 41 So. 249 (1906). The trial court concluded that plaintiffs had sustained the burden of proving Two O'Clock Bayou to be a navigable stream.

A body of water is navigable in law when it is navigable in fact. State v. Jefferson Island Salt Mining Co., 183 La. 304, 163 So. 145 (1935), cert. den. 56 S.Ct. 591, 297 U.S. 716, 80 L.Ed. 1001, rehearing denied 56 S.Ct. 667, 297 U.S. 729, 80 L.Ed. 1011. The factual question turns on whether the evidence shows a body of water to be suitable by its depth, width and location for commerce. However, lack of commercial traffic does not preclude a finding of navigability. State v. Capdeville, 146 La. 94, 83 So. 421 (1919), cert. den. 40 S.Ct. 346, 252 U.S. 581, 64 L.Ed. 727. A stream, to be navigable, must be usable for commerce in its natural state or ordinary condition. Madole v. Johnson, 241 F.Supp. 379 (1965); The Daniel Ball, 10 Wall. 557, 19 L.Ed. 999 (1870); Delta Duck Club v. Barrios, 135 La. 357, 65 So. 489 (1914). Construction of a dam across a bayou does not change its status as a navigable stream. Beavers v. Butler, 188 So. 2d 725 (La. App. 2d Cir. 1966), writ refused 249 La. 739, 190 So. 2d 242. A body of water can be navigable despite natural or man-made obstructions. Terrebonne Parish School Board v. Texaco, Inc., 178 So. 2d 428 (La. App. 1st Cir. 1965), writ refused, 248 La. 465, 179 So. 2d 640; U.S. cert. den., 348 U.S. 950.

In the instant case it is difficult to determine whether Two O'Clock Bayou was navigable in its ordinary condition because the bayou is not presently in a natural state, having been dammed, bridged and otherwise interfered with over a period of time.

The question of navigability of Two O'Clock Bayou in 1812 is only pertinent to the question of ownership of the bed of the bayou. It has no relevance to the question of whether or not passage on the stream can be obstructed by defendants. Begnaud v. Grubb & Hawkins, 209 La. 826, 25 So. 24 606 (1946); Discon v. Saray, Inc., supra. Therefore, the evidence that parts of the bayou bed were dry as recently as 100 years ago does not affect the State's right to enjoin its obstruction if it is in fact a navigable waterway. Here, unlike the situation in National Audubon Society v. White, 302 So. 2d 660 (La. App. 3d Cir. 1974), writ denied, 305 So. 2d 542 (La. 1975) and Vermilion Corp. v. Vaughn, 356 So. 2d 551 (La. App. 3d Cir. 1978), writ den., 357 So. 2d 558, the waterway is not privately constructed and does not lie wholly within the confines of the property owned by the defendant land company.

The evidence allows a reasonable inference that Two O'Clock Bayou is navigable in fact, except for various man-made obstructions. It has in the past sustained commercial fishing and logging, which are types of commerce. There is no prescription right to obstruct navigation on a navigable stream. Ingram v. Police Jury of Parish of St. Tammany, 20 La.Ann. 226 (1868). The bayou, in its natural state, afforded a channel for navigation although there are now certain difficulties in the form of natural and man-made barriers. The fact that bridges have been built, with or without legal authority, and there is a resulting accumulation of timber, which, to some extent, obstructs and impedes navigation, does not preclude a finding that a stream is navigable. Goodwill v. Police Jury, 38 La.Ann. 752 (1886). See the discussion of navigability in fact and law in D'Albora v. Garcia, 144 So. 2d 911 (La. App. 4th Cir. 1962), cert. den.

The trial court's conclusion that Two O'Clock Bayou is navigable is not manifestly erroneous and therefore must be affirmed. For the foregoing reasons, the judgment of the trial court herein is affirmed at the cost of defendants-appellants.

NOTES AND QUESTIONS

1. The types of evidence considered in this case, such as eyewitness testimony, surveys, maps, and photographs, underscore Professor Yiannopoulos' observations that navigability is a question of fact, and that navigability is not usually presumed, but must be proven.

2. The Court of Appeal concludes that Two O'Clock Bayou is navigable despite the existence of obstructions to navigation. How is this result reconcilable with the factual nature of the determination? Would the result be the same if the obstruction was a sandbar that had developed in the middle of the bayou?

3. The Court observes that the navigability of the bayou in 1812 is only relevant to ownership of its bed, not to the question of whether navigation on it can be obstructed by the defendants. If the statement in *Buckskin Hunting Club v. Bayard*, et al. cited above in section 1, N&Q 4 reflects the law on this issue, should this be the case?

3. NAVIGABLE RIVERS

See R.S. 9:1102; A. N. YIANNOPOULOS, CIVIL LAW PROPERTY
§ 74 (4th ed. 2001)

a. Ownership of the Beds and of the Banks of Rivers and Streams
La. Civil Code arts. 450, 456, 506

WEMPLE v. EASTHAM
150 La. 247, 90 So. 637 (1922)

O'NIELL, J. Pursuant to Act 30 of 1915, authorizing the leasing of state lands, including river and lake beds and bottoms, for the production of oil, gas, and other minerals, the Governor leased to Mally Eastham, on the 4th of November, 1918, all of the land that the state then owned "within the meandering lines of Bayou Pierre river and Dolet Bayou, in sections 14, 15, 22, 23 25, 26, 27, 35 and 36 in T. 12N., R. 11 W., La. Mer."***

Plaintiff owns lands bordering on one side of Bayou Pierre and lands through which Bayou Dolet runs, in sections 14, 15, 22, 23. Defendants commenced operations for the drilling of a well on the bank of Bayou Pierre, that is, between the ordinary high-water mark and the ordinary low-water mark, and between the upper and lower boundary lines of plaintiff's land. Thereupon plaintiff, averring that the recording of the contract of lease was a slander of his title to the lands forming the banks and beds of the two bayous within his property lines, brought this suit to cancel the lease and to enjoin defendants from drilling wells on the land. Plaintiff contends that the two bayous are not and never have been navigable streams, and that therefore he owns the bed or bottom of the bayou that crosses his land and owns to the thread or middle of the bayou on which his land borders. In any event — that is, even if either bayou should be held to be a navigable stream — he claims the bayou banks, or land between the ordinary high-water mark and the ordinary low-water mark.

Defendants admit that Dolet Bayou is not, and never has been, a navigable stream, and that the state therefore had no right to lease the bed or bottom of that bayou within the boundary lines of plaintiff's land. Defendants contend that Bayou Pierre was once a navigable stream, and has ceased to be such, and that therefore the state had authority to lease the bed or bottom of that stream, and the banks or land between what was once the ordinary high-water mark and what was once the ordinary low-water mark. Defendants asserted a reconventional demand for damages alleged to have been caused by plaintiff's interference with their alleged right of possession of the land once forming the bed of Bayou Pierre, and a demand for a right of passage over plaintiff's adjacent land to the public road.

There was judgment in favor of plaintiff, recognizing his title to the bed and banks of Dolet Bayou within the boundaries of his adjacent land, and recognizing his title to the bank of Bayou Pierre, being the land between the ordinary high-water mark and the ordinary low-water mark, between the upper and lower boundary lines of plaintiff's land. Defendants were therefore [enjoined not to] go upon the lands thus recognized as plaintiff's property. The lease to the defendants was recognized as affecting the bed of Bayou Pierre, being the land covered by the waters of the bayou at its ordinary low stage....

Defendants have appealed from the judgment, and plaintiff, answering the appeal, prays that the judgment be amended so as to declare him the owner of the bed of Bayou Pierre to the middle or thread of the stream....

Appellant assigns as error that the district court erred in holding that the bed of Bayou Pierre was the land covered by water at its ordinary low stage, instead of holding that the bed of the bayou was the land between the banks covered by water at its ordinary high stage, and that the court therefore erred in holding that the well which defendants had commenced drilling was on the land of plaintiff. On the original hearing of the appeal, a majority of the members of the court, taking that view of the case, rejected plaintiff's demand, except as to the bed of Dolet Bayou.... A rehearing was granted on the application of plaintiff appellee.

The evidence sustains the conclusion of the district judge that Bayou Pierre was once a navigable stream, and that for many years it has not been navigable. When the bayou had ceased to be navigable, the state, having been theretofore the owner of the bed of the bayou, subject to the right of the public to navigate the bayou and to use the banks, which belonged to the owners of the adjacent lands, had the right to lease the bed of the bayou. Board of Commissioners v. Glassel, 120 La. 400, 45 South. 370; State v. Bayou Johnson Oyster Co., 139 La. 604, 58 South. 105; Perry v. Board of Commissioners, 132 La. 415, 61 South. 511; State ex rel. Board of Commissioners v. Capdeville, Auditor, 146 La. 94, 83 South. 421.

The bed of a navigable river — that is, the land which the state holds in her sovereign capacity — is only the land that is covered by the water at its ordinary low state. The land lying between the edge of the water at its ordinary low stage and the line which the edge of the water reaches at its ordinary high stage — that is, the highest stage that it usually reaches at any season of the year — is called the bank of the stream and belongs to the owner of the adjacent land, subject to the right of the public to use the bank, to land and unload boats, to dry nets, etc. Rev. Civ. Code, arts. 455 and 457 [Revised C.C. art. 456]; Morgan v. Livingston, 6 Mart. (0.5.) 19; De Ben. Gerard, 4 La. Ann. 30 [additional citations omitted].***

The land on which defendants had commenced or prepared to drill a well, being the bank of Bayou Pierre — that is, the land between the ordinary high-water mark and the ordinary low-water mark — belongs to plaintiff. The judgment appealed from in that respect is correct.

Of course, there is no dispute that the judgment is correct in so far as it recognizes plaintiff's ownership of the bed of Dolet Bayou, which, it is admitted, is and always has been nonnavigable. The beds of streams that are not and never were navigable belong to the riparian owners, to the thread or middle of the stream. The judgment appealed from is affirmed at the cost of defendants, appellants.

Holding

Disposition

NOTES AND QUESTIONS

1. In *Smith v. Dixie Oil Co.*, 156 La. 691, 101 So. 24 (1924), a river that was navigable in 1812 was not navigable at the time of litigation. The court held that "all of its bed below its ordinary low-water mark" belongs to the state.

2. In *Begnaud v. Grubb & Hawkins*, 209 La. 826, 25 So.2d 606 (1946), plaintiff owned lands along the bank of Bayou Sale; his title described the property as "fronting" on the river. He claimed that since Bayou Sale was non-navigable in 1812 and also non-navigable at the time of litigation, his ownership extended to the thread of the bayou. Defendants, the state and its lessees, claimed the plaintiff's ownership extended merely to the water's edge. *Held*, one acquiring lands fronting on a stream that was nonnavigable in 1812 acquires ownership to the thread. The court relied on Spanish sources, and on articles 513, 514, and 515 of the Louisiana Civil Code of 1870. If your client wishes to transfer land along a non-navigable river, but not the bed of the river, to another, what must he do to avoid transferring the bed? What general principle of private law governs the situation?

3. How is the ordinary low water mark established? In *Seibert v. Conservation Commission*, 181 La. 237, 159 So. 375 (1935), plaintiff sued the state and its lessee for the wrongful taking of sand from batture in front of his property on the Mississippi River. The state claimed that the sand was taken from the bed of the river, that is, below the ordinary low water mark. Plaintiff sought to establish the low mark by the method of the Mississippi River Commission: he computed the low water mark by taking the lowest depth to which the water receded in each year over a period of 43 years and then adopted the average over that period of time. The state sought to establish the low ordinary water mark by the method of the State Board of Engineers: taking the daily average of the low water mark stage of the river during each year and computing the average low water mark therefrom; then taking the averaged low water mark of each and averaging it over a period of 43 years. The court rejected both of these "scientific" methods; it gave weight instead to eyewitness reports that the batture in question had been exposed during the low stages of the river in recent years, and held for the plaintiff.

4. Compare: *DeSambourg v. Board of Commissioners*, 621 So.2d 602 (La. 1993). Plaintiffs, riparian landowners, filed suit against the Plaquemines Parish claiming compensation for lands appropriated for levee construction. The Louisiana Supreme Court denied the claim on the ground that the property taken was "batture" for which no compensation is due under the Louisiana Constitution. The court defined *batture* as "*alluvial accretions annually covered by ordinary high water, the highest stage the river can be expected to reach annually in season of high water,*" and determined the ordinary high water mark in light of expert testimony.

definition of "batture"

5. Does the court's definition of batture accord with the definition of the banks of a navigable river in Article 456 of the Civil Code? For discussion, see Comment, Batture, Ordinary High Water, and the Louisiana Levee Servitude, 69 Tul. L. Rev. 561 (1994).

b. Alluvion and Dereliction
La. Civil Code arts. 482, 499-501

Alluvion and dereliction are ownership rights that arise through the principle of accession. Accession is a default rule that, in the absence of other rights, what is produced by or joined to a thing belongs to the owner of the thing. Alluvion and dereliction, defined in art. 499, are two processes by which additional dry land becomes joined to the bank of a river, and is owned by the owner of the bank. Art. 500 expressly excludes the right of accession by alluvion or dereliction on the shores of the sea or of lakes. Art. 501 provides guidance on the division of alluvion that forms in front of the property of several owners; the factual scenario that gave rise to it is reported in *Jones v. Hogue*, 241 La. 407, 129 So. 2d 194 (1960).

c. Avulsion; Opening of New Channel
La. Civil Code arts. 502-505

NOTE
Sudden Action of Waters

In contrast with alluvion and dereliction, which are changes occurring "successively and imperceptibly" on riverbanks, the changes dealt with in Louisiana Civil Code articles 502–504 occur suddenly. Article 502 allows a riparian owner to retain ownership of an identifiable part of his land that has been carried away by the sudden action of a river or stream and united to riparian land belonging to another. This event, called *avulsion* in Roman law,[2] has never been the subject of analysis in a reported Louisiana case.

Sudden changes in a river's channel, such as opening a new channel or even abandoning its bed for a new one, regularly appear in Louisiana's jurisprudence. Articles 503 and 504 deal with the ownership of land affected by the change—formerly riparian land cut off from its bank to become an island, formerly private land now the bed of a navigable river, a navigable river's former bed that has been abandoned. While the ownership of the new island does not change, in the latter two cases, the State takes the new riverbed, and the private owner who has lost it takes the State's former riverbed.

Relying on nature to indemnify those who have lost their land because of the natural

---

[2]A.N. YIANNOPOULOS, PROPERTY—THINGS, REAL RIGHTS, REAL ACTIONS, Louisiana Civil Law Treatise Series vol. 2, § 76 (4th ed. 2001). Note 1 in this section points out that meaning of *avulsion* in common law jurisdictions is not applicable in Louisiana.

actions of a navigable river does not result in an orderly exchange, however. As a result, in *State v. Bourdon*, 535 So. 2d 1091 (La. App. 2d Cir. 1988), *writ denied*, 536 So. 2d 1223 (1989), the Louisiana Second Circuit Court of Appeal faced an interpretive conflict between two Code articles. A portion of the Red River had jumped its banks, creating a new and shorter channel far away from its former bed. While most of the bed it left behind was dry land, a portion of it still contained water, a large (123 acre) navigable lake. Under Code article 450, the waters and bottoms of natural navigable water bodies are public things of the State; under article 504, the abandoned bed belonged to the private owners of the land on which the new bed was located. The court rejected the State's contention that article 504 was not intended to include abandoned beds that contained navigable waters, seeing the language of that article as unambiguous. The conflict was resolved by invoking the interpretive principle that the specific provisions with respect to abandoned riverbeds displace the general provisions concerning navigable waterways' bottoms in article 450.

Not all the discrepancies inherent in article 504 can be as easily resolved. The *Bourdon* court resolved another issue by ruling that the new owner of the old bed does not have to be a riparian owner along the old river bed; he takes the abandoned bed no matter how far it is from the land that he lost. In some cases, such a trade could have little to offer by way of indemnification. And in a case like *Bourdon*, in which the abandoned bed is much larger than land lost to the new bed, what quantity of it does the former owner of the new bed take?

d. Public Use of Privately Owned Riverbanks

1) The Uses Permitted to the Public
La. Civil Code arts. 455, 456

WARNER v. CLARKE
232 So. 2d 99 (La. App. 2d Cir. 1970)

DIXON, J. This is a suit to enjoin the district attorney and the sheriff of East Carroll Parish from prosecuting the plaintiffs for trespass under R.S. 14:63. The lands involved lie adjacent to the Mississippi River south of the Arkansas line and include the levee and land between the levee and the river. There are various bodies of water located on this land which are, or have been, navigable.

The petition alleges that considerable quantities of fish and game abound in the area involved, and that petitioners hold hunting and fishing licenses, and desire to hunt and fish on the lands involved. Their arrest, and threatened prosecution by the district attorney, they allege, will result in irreparable harm by loss of their alleged right to use the lands involved, or by wrongful prosecution ....

It was stipulated that the lands are owned by private individuals or corporations, and that the vast majority of the owners or lessees of the land have posted it in accordance with the requirements of R.S. 14:63. There are roads on the levee, constructed with public funds, but not open to the public.

The appellants claim that their rights to the land come from provisions of the Civil Code. Article 455 of the Civil Code [Revised C.C. art. 456] declares that the use of the banks of navigable rivers is public. Article 453 [Revised C.C. arts. 450, 452] states that public things are those, the property of which is vested in a whole nation, and the use of which is allowed to all the members of the nation. Article 457 [Revised C.C. art. 456] says that the levees form the banks on the borders of the Mississippi River. Plaintiffs claim that although the land between the levee and the river is subject to private ownership, that ownership is imperfect, according to Article 490 [Revised C.C. art. 478]. The statutory basis for the plaintiffs' claimed right to hunt and fish on the levee and the land between the levee and the river is Article 455 [Revised C.C. art. 456] of the Civil Code. The prayer of the petition is for judgment "decreeing that the lands are subject to a servitude in favor of the public or, that is, subject to public use" and for an injunction against the arrest and prosecution of the plaintiffs when hunting, fishing or walking on the lands described.

At the outset, it must be noted that we cannot render a declaratory judgment in this case, principally because of the absence of indispensable parties. No owner of land involved is a party to this litigation, yet we are asked to hold that private lands are subject to a servitude in favor of these plaintiffs and the public generally....

...[I]t seems clear that the plaintiffs here have no right to an injunction because they do not possess a property right threatened with invasion.

Whatever Article 455 [Revised C.C. art. 456] once meant about the use of banks of navigable rivers, subsequent legislation has made it apparent that the legislature did not intend to maintain a right in these plaintiffs or in the general public to hunt and fish upon the levees and the land that lies between the levees and the Mississippi River. R.S. 14:63 defines "criminal trespass" as follows:

(2) The unauthorized and intentional entry upon any:
(a) Plot of immovable property in excess of one acre which is posted but not enclosed, unless said property is situated in an open range area; or
(b) Plot of immovable property which is posted and enclosed, including property situated in open range areas; or
(c) posted lands belonging to public institutions; or * * *
(d) where an entry is made from a waterway for emergency purposes the party in distress may use the banks of said waterway without violating the provisions of paragraph 2.

B. Definitions
(1) 'Posted' property means any immovable property which is designated as such by the owner, lessee or other person lawfully authorized to take such action, provided the following requirements are satisfied:* * *

(2) 'Enclosed' property means any immovable property which is surrounded or encompassed by natural and/or artificial barriers. Natural barriers include:

(a) The Gulf of Mexico,

(b) Lakes or ponds or other bodies of water which hold water during twelve months of the year,

(c) Any river, stream, bayou or canal in which water is held or runs during twelve months of the year,

(d) Other similar natural barriers * * *

...Our courts have repeatedly held that the riparian servitudes are not subject to a broad and liberal construction, as contended by the plaintiffs, but exist "only for that which is incident to the nature and the navigable character of the stream washing the land of such proprietor." Hebert v. T. L. James & Company, Inc. et al., 224 La. 498, 70 So. 2d 102, 106 (1953), quoting from Carollton R. Company v. Winthrop, 5 La.Ann. 36 (1850); Lake Providence Port Commission v. Bunge Corporation, La. App., 193 So. 2d 363.

It does not seem that a fair interpretation of [1870] Revised C.C. 455 [Revised C.C. art. 456], which gives everyone the right to land his vessel and tie up to trees on the banks, and there "to dry his nets, and the like" could construe that article to grant to the public the right to hunt and fish upon the lands and waters between the river and the levee. The right to hunt and fish on these lands seems unrelated to the nature and the navigable character of the Mississippi River.***

Since we find no property right in these plaintiffs which enables them to hunt and fish between the river and the levee, they are not entitled to an injunction. Consequently, the judgment of the district court is affirmed, at the cost of the appellants.

NOTES AND QUESTIONS

1. Do members of the public have the right to cross private lands in order to gain access to the bank of a navigable river? See *Pizanie v. Gauthreaux*, 173 La. 737, 138 So. 650 (1931).

2. The Second Circuit Court of Appeal somewhat wearily observes, "Our courts have repeatedly held that the riparian servitudes are not subject to a broad and liberal construction, as contended by the plaintiffs, but exist 'only for that which is incident to the nature and the navigable character of the stream washing the land of such proprietor.'" The end to assertions of the Divine Right of Louisiana Fishers and Hunters to use private lands belonging to another is still not in sight; see our next case, *Parm v. Shumate*, and the notes that follow.

3. Is picketing on the levee a "public use" within the meaning of Article 455 of the Civil Code? See *Tenneco, Inc. v. Oil, Chemical, Atomic Workers Union*, 234 So.2d 246 (La. App. 4th Cir. 1970).

PARM v. SHUMATE
513 F.3d 135 (5th Cir. 2007)

KING, Circuit Judge. Plaintiffs-appellants Normal Parm, Jr., Harold Eugene Watts, Roy Michael Gammill, William T. Rogers, and Robert Allen Balch ("Plaintiffs"), recreational fishermen, appeal the district court's denial of their summary judgment motion and the grant of the cross-motion for summary judgment by defendant-appellee East Carroll Parish Sheriff Mark Shumate ("Sheriff Shumate"). Plaintiffs brought their claims against Sheriff Shumate under 42 U.S.C. § 1983, alleging that they were falsely arrested for trespass when they refused to cease fishing on waters covering ordinarily dry, private property (the "Property") owned by Walker Cottonwood Farms, L.L.C., successor-in-title to Walker Lands, Inc. (collectively "Walker"). Plaintiffs argue that Sheriff Shumate lacked probable cause to arrest them for fishing on the Property because the public has a federal and state right to fish on the Property when it is submerged under the Mississippi River. Because we disagree, we AFFIRM the district court's judgment.

I. FACTUAL AND PROCEDURAL BACKGROUND

The underlying dispute in this case began over a decade ago, and the facts have been considered in various forms by multiple courts, including this one. Plaintiffs are lifelong boaters, hunters, and fisherman who fish on the Mississippi River in East Carroll Parish and other river parishes in northeast Louisiana. The water levels of the Mississippi River fluctuate seasonally. In East Carroll Parish, the normal low water mark is seventy-seven feet above mean sea level. Yet during the spring season the river floods well beyond its normal channel—as a result of increased rainfall and snow melt in the North—and the river regularly rises to as high as one hundred and twelve feet above mean sea level. It is normal for the river to remain at this level for at least two months.

The Property is located in East Carroll Parish. On its eastern side, the Property is bound by the Mississippi River, and on its western side, it is bound by the Mississippi River's levees. Buildings, crop lands and forests, with trees as tall as one hundred and forty feet, are located on the Property. In addition, waterways known as Gassoway Lake, Little Gassoway Lake, and other bodies of water are contained within its boundaries. Gassoway Lake, which Plaintiffs consider the most ideal venue for fishing on the Property, is located on the Property's western side, nearly three-and-a-half miles from the ordinary low water mark of the Mississippi River and its channel. Gassoway Lake is connected by a man-made drainage ditch to Bunch's Cutoff, which, in turn, flows into the Mississippi River. When the river floods in the spring, Gassoway Lake, along with the rest of the Property, is submerged under its waters.

Plaintiffs have fished the waters of Gassoway Lake when it was flooded by the Mississippi River, even though they knew that Walker objected to their presence. In 1996, Walker began filing complaints with Sheriff Shumate against boaters fishing on Gassoway Lake. Sheriff Shumate responded by arresting Plaintiffs, and others found on the Property, for trespass. While admitting that they did not have Walker's permission, Plaintiffs claimed that they were entitled to fish on the Property when it was flooded because Gassoway Lake was either: (1) owned by the State of Louisiana on behalf of the public; or (2) subject to state and federal servitudes.

The Attorney General for the State of Louisiana agreed with Plaintiffs' position and issued Louisiana Attorney General Opinion No. 96-206, concluding that channels of the Mississippi River traversed the Property and were "river bed" owned by the State. His opinion stated that "Lake Gassoway is a naturally navigable body of water under both State and Federal law and actually supports navigation for such purposes as hunting, fishing, [and] trapping...." He also determined that the Property was subject to a public servitude....

On June 10, 1996, Walker filed suit in Louisiana state court...seeking a declaration that it owned the Property and an injunction prohibiting members of the public from entering without permission....On March 16, 1998, the court granted Walker's motion for summary judgment and issued a permanent injunction. The State appealed to the Second Circuit Court of Appeal of Louisiana, which reversed, holding that the issues could not be resolved on summary judgment. *Walker Lands, Inc. v. East Carroll Parish Police Jury*, 738 So. 2d 205 (La. Ct. App., March 5, 1999).

On December 17, 2001, with the state trial court yet to issue a final decision, Plaintiffs filed this case in federal district court. Plaintiffs alleged that Sheriff Shumate lacked probable cause to arrest them in light of the opinion of the State Attorney General and the decision of the Second Circuit Court of Appeal....Plaintiffs sought damages for false arrest under 42 U.S.C. § 1983 and an injunction prohibiting further arrests for fishing on the Property until a "final judgment is rendered by a court of competent jurisdiction, specifying the ownership and navigational rights of the State of Louisiana and [Walker] relative to the [Property]...during normal water heights...." [The Federal court stayed the plaintiff's case until the state proceedings were concluded.]

.... On May 1, 2003, the state trial court ruled that Walker owned the Property and had the right to exclude the public from it. *Walker Lands, Inc. v. East Carroll Parish Police Jury*, 871 So. 2d 1258, 1261 (La. Ct. App. 2004). The court first noted that it was undisputed that the Property was either woodland or farmland in 1812, the year that Louisiana was admitted to the Union as a State. It found that during the 1860s and 1870s, the Mississippi River slowly but gradually shifted westward and submerged the Property. When the river subsequently shifted back eastward, it left behind a swale—a shallow depression in the land—which became Gassoway Lake through alluvion or accretion. Gassoway Lake and the other natural bodies of water on the Property were formed before 1910, when private landowners purchased it. Moreover, the court determined that none of the waters on the Property were navigable. But for the man-made drainage ditch connected to Bunch's Cutoff and other structures, the court held, Gassoway Lake itself would be non-existent during the summer months. Since the waters lying on the Property were not navigable in fact, the trial court entered a permanent injunction prohibiting the public-at-large from going on Gassoway Lake, or on the land between Gassoway Lake and the Mississippi River.

The State appealed the trial court's decision to the Second Circuit Court of Appeal, which affirmed in part and reversed in part. The appellate court accepted the trial court's findings of fact and held that the Property was privately owned. The court rejected the State's argument that the Property was the bed of the Mississippi River— and therefore owned by the State—because a river's bed consists only of the land lying below the river's ordinary low water mark. It did not matter that the Mississippi River sometimes flooded the Property.

> Privately owned land does not become part of a navigable body of water when a nearby navigable body of water overflows its normal bed and temporarily covers the property. Gassoway Lake is landlocked and does not now lie in the bed of the Mississippi river, which is some three and one-half miles to the east; likewise, it is not a channel of the river, since it is cut off from it.

In addition, the court held that Gassoway Lake was not a navigable body of water owned by the State because it was not a navigable body of water in fact.

Nevertheless, the Second Circuit Court of Appeal lifted the state trial court's injunction because Walker lacked standing to seek relief against a hypothetical public-at-large. The court stated that while "[o]wners of private property may forbid entry to anyone for purposes of hunting or fishing and the like[,]" Walker could only ask for relief against a specific individual after that person had invaded the Property. The court declined to resolve whether there was a public servitude on the Property during the Mississippi River's peak stage. It observed that under Louisiana law, the bank of the Mississippi River consists of all the land lying between its ordinary low and high water marks, which includes all of the Property, and noted that a public servitude preserves a river's bank for the public's navigational use. And while it stated that "[f]ishing and hunting on flooded lands do not meet the definition of using the bank of a river at its high water mark for a navigational purpose[,]" it "pretermit[ted] discussion" of the issue because the State had not properly raised it.

On June 3, 2005, the Second Circuit Court of Appeal's decision became final when the Louisiana Supreme Court denied the State's application for a writ of certiorari. In light of the conclusion of the state court proceedings, on August 16, 2005, the district court lifted the stay in this case....Sheriff Shumate filed briefs arguing that...there is no federal or state right to fish on private property above the Mississippi River's ordinary low mark....Plaintiffs, on the other hand, argued that they were entitled to summary judgment because there is both a state and federal right to fish on the Property when it is submerged under the Mississippi River....

[The plaintiffs' federal claims were based on the federal navigational servitude and on federal common law. The district court rejected both.]

[A]lthough the district court found that the Property is a bank of the Mississippi River under Louisiana law and subject to a state servitude, the servitude "is limited to activities that are incidental to the navigable character of the Mississippi River and its enjoyment as an avenue of commerce....[F]ishing and hunting are not included in these rights." Accordingly, the district court found that Sheriff Shumate had probable cause to arrest Plaintiffs for trespass and entered summary judgment on Sheriff Shumate's behalf. This timely appeal followed.

II. DISCUSSION

...The key issue...is whether Plaintiffs have either a federal or state right to fish on the Property in the spring during the Mississippi River's normal flood stage. If they do not, Sheriff Shumate had probable cause to arrest them for trespass and was entitled to prevail on summary judgment.

A. Federal Rights

[The Fifth Circuit upheld the District Court's determination that neither the federal navigation servitude nor federal common law provide a right to fish on private property when overflowed by waters from a navigable river.]

B. State Navigational Servitude

Plaintiffs argue that a state servitude burdens the Property and grants them the right to fish upon it when it is flooded....They...find support in the Louisiana Civil Code, which provides that everyone has the right to fish in the State's rivers. See LA. CIV. CODE ANN. art. 452. Finally, they contend that the Property is burdened by the State for the public's use because Louisiana owns all of the running waters in the State. See id. art. 456. In response, Sheriff Shumate argues that the right to fish in Louisiana is explicitly limited to public lands and does not extend to private riparian property. Moreover, he argues that the Second Circuit Court of Appeal, while failing to hold that the Property is free of a state servitude because the issue was not properly raised, left a "guide post" for this court by noting in passing that the public does not have a right to fish on private lands. We agree with Sheriff Shumate....

[T]he Louisiana Civil Code does not create a right to fish upon the Property, even if we assume that the Property in its entirety is a bank of the Mississippi River. Under Louisiana law, the "banks of navigable rivers are private things that are subject to public use." LA. CIV. CODE ANN. art. 452;....The public use, however, is limited to use for navigational purposes. As stated in the comments to article 456, "[a]ccording to well-settled Louisiana jurisprudence, which continues to be relevant, the servitude of public use under this provision is not 'for the use of the public at large for all purposes' but merely for purposes that are 'incidental' to the navigable character of the stream and its enjoyment as an avenue of commerce." LA. CIV. CODE ANN. art. [456] cmt. b (citations omitted). The Second Circuit Court of Appeal noted, in the parallel state proceeding, that fishing on the banks of the Mississippi River does not meet the definition of a navigational use. We agree. *See, e.g.*, *State v. Barras*, 602 So. 2d 301, 305 (La. Ct. App. 1992) (holding that fishing was not incidental to navigation); *Edmiston v. Wood*, 566 So. 2d 673, 675-76 (La. Ct. App. 1990) (same).

Finally, we reject Plaintiffs' argument that they have the right to fish on the Property when it is submerged under the Mississippi River because "running waters" are public things owned by the State. "Under Louisiana law, "public things" belong to the State, and "public things" include "running waters." LA. CIV. CODE ANN. art. 456. Plaintiffs argue that the public has a right to fish on the running waters of the State based on *Chaney v. State Mineral Bd.*, 444 So. 2d 105 (La. 1983). In that case, the Louisiana Supreme Court stated that the running waters over non-navigable streams are preserved for the general public. *Id.* at 109. This court has since determined that claims to the use of waterways based on *Chaney* have "failed to carry the day in Louisiana courts." *Dardar*, 385 F.2d at 834 (citation omitted). We have no reason to deviate from that holding. To the contrary, the Third Circuit Court of Appeal of Louisiana recently stated that although an owner must permit running waters to pass through his estate, Louisiana law "does not mandate that the landowner allow public access to the waterway." *Buckskin Hunting Club*, 868 So. 2d at 274.

NOTES AND QUESTIONS

1. *Federal Common Law:* The magistrate judge who handled this case prior to its advancing to the District Court found that federal common law created a right of the public to fish in the waters of a navigable river, and that this public right burdens private property when it is submerged by waters of a navigable river. The District Court and the Court of Appeals rejected this conclusion, holding that "Plaintiffs' argument to the contrary based on purported federal common law is unavailing. Plaintiffs point us to state court decisions that provide citizens with a state right to fish on navigable waters. But those cases merely prove that states generally regulate the use of public trust lands."

2. In the Louisiana Court of Appeal cases *Warner v. Clarke*, supra, and in *Edmiston v. Wood* and *State v. Barras*, cited by the federal Fifth Circuit in support of its rejection of recreational fishing as a public use under the 456 servitude, the hunters and fishermen were not using a navigable river's bed or bank to hunt or fish in the navigable river's waters. In *Warner*, the defendants were hunting and fishing on land between the river and the levee. In *State v. Barras*, the Barras brothers were arrested for crawfishing on privately owned overflowed acreage in the Atchafalaya Basin, four miles from the Atchafalaya River itself. They accessed the land using a system of private man-made canals. They appealed to the Louisiana Supreme Court after their convictions, but did not succeed in getting these overturned. In a majority opinion, Justice Watson stated:

"The beds of navigable waters are insusceptible of private ownership. R.S. 9:1107; Gulf Oil Corporation is. State Mineral Board, 317 So. 2d 576 (La. 1975).

Professor Yiannopoulos points out in his Louisiana Civil Law Treatise on Property that the banks of a navigable river are private things subject to public use, while swamp lands subject to overflow are private things. The crawfish bottoms, which are covered with water only part of the year and vary in depth from six inches to six feet, do not qualify as navigable waters....

"The trial court recognized that this property lies within the levees of the Atchafalaya River but concluded that it was not part of the Atchafalaya River's banks. The court of appeal decided that the area comprised part of the Atchafalaya River's flood plain. The record supports these conclusions.

"The Barras brothers were crawfishing on flooded swampland, not on the submerged banks of a navigable stream or in navigable waters. The evidence establishes with the requisite certainty, R.S. 15:271 (the state must prove each element of a crime beyond a reasonable doubt), that they were on privately owned property and not on private property subject to public use or public navigable waters. For the foregoing reasons, the trial court judgment convicting defendants is affirmed."

See also *Buckskin Hunting Club v. Bayard*, 868 So. 2d 266 (La. App. 3d Cir. 2004), in which the defendants, who were not members of the plaintiff hunting club, were hunting within the boundaries of the plaintiff's land using the plaintiff's private artificial canal system.

3. In *Edmiston v. Wood*, the plaintiffs were hunting from a boat in waters covering land that occasionally flooded. The *Edmiston* plaintiffs contended that when the land flooded to a depth that allowed navigation, it became a part of a navigable water body. Because the land was not normally flooded, the court found that it was situated above the ordinary high stage of water, and thus did not constitute the bank of a navigable river. It was therefore not subject to the public use servitude. Is the case of *Parm v. Shumate* distinguishable on its facts, and if so, how?

4. One difficulty facing the Fifth Circuit in the principal case was the inconsistency in the Louisiana jurisprudence on the methods of establishing the ordinary high and the ordinary low of the water that distinguish the bank and the bed of a navigable river. See notes 3 and 4 following *Wemple v. Eastham, supra*.

5. What name does the Fifth Circuit give to the State servitude created by article 456 in *Parm*? Is that name contained in the Code article itself? Is it synonymous with "incidental to the navigable character of the stream and its enjoyment as an avenue of commerce"?

6. If the plaintiffs in *Parm* had been commercial fishermen, would the Fifth Circuit find on the reasoning employed in it that their activities were not covered by the 456 servitude?

7. What reason does the Fifth Circuit give for rejecting the plaintiffs' argument, based on art. 452, that they were in fact fishing in a State-owned navigable water body, the Mississippi River? Does use of the public servitude on a *public* thing require that the use be incidental to the stream's navigability and to commerce?

A. N. YIANNOPOULOS, CIVIL LAW PROPERTY
§§ 82-86 (4th ed. 2001)
(footnotes omitted)

§ 82. Nature of the Public Use of River Banks

Public use is generally regarded in Louisiana as a charge in the interest of the public akin to a servitude. It is neither a predial nor a personal servitude, but a *sui generis* burden, which confers on administrative authorities and courts broad powers for the regulation and protection of the rights of the public. This conception is also applicable to the public use of the banks of navigable rivers; and, in the interest of simplification of terminology, the expression "servitude of public use" will be utilized in the following discussion.

The servitude of public use that burdens the banks of navigable rivers has been recognized by the Supreme Court of the United States, and has been held to be consistent with the Fourteenth Amendment of the United States Constitution. Louisiana courts have likened this servitude to a usufruct, the public being "a great usufructuary," with the right to all the profit, utility, and advantages that the property may produce, and the public authorities being the "administrator." According to well-settled Louisiana jurisprudence, the servitude of public use burdening the banks of navigable rivers under Article 456 of the Civil Code is distinguishable from other servitudes burdening riparian lands and especially from the road or levee servitude of Article 665 of the Civil Code. This last servitude is "a very much [more] onerous one, extending much farther inland."

§ 83. Prerequisites of Public Use

The servitude of public use under Article 456 of the Louisiana Civil Code burdens the privately owned banks of *navigable rivers.* The banks or shores of non-navigable inland waters are private things that are not subject to public use. The seashore and the shores of navigable lakes are public things that are subject to public use under Articles 450 and 452 of the Civil Code. It is thus important to determine in each case whether the prerequisites for public use under Article 456 of the Civil Code are met, namely, whether a body of water is a river and whether it is *navigable....*

The servitude of public use clearly burdens the banks of rivers that were navigable in 1812, the year Louisiana was admitted into the Union, and continue to be navigable. Question may arise, however, whether the servitude exists on the banks of rivers that have ceased to be navigable or that have become navigable since 1812. A literal interpretation of Article 456 of the Civil Code leads to the conclusion that the banks of a river that is no longer navigable are freed of the servitude of public use. This conclusion is bolstered by the consideration that a non-navigable river is no longer an avenue of commerce and the servitude for the public use of its banks has no reason to exist. Analogous application of Article 751 of the Civil Code, establishing the general rule for the termination of predial servitudes would lead to the same result.

A literal interpretation of Article 456 of the Civil Code also leads to the conclusion that the banks of a river that was non-navigable in 1812 but is navigable today are burdened with the servitude of public use. This interpretation, however, may give rise to a question of constitutionality under the Fifth and Fourteenth Amendments of the United States Constitution. Strong argument may be made that the imposition of a servitude of public use on the banks of formerly non-navigable rivers is a taking of property without compensation. The original acquirer of the land that is now traversed by a navigable river did not acquire his property *sub modo,* as did an acquirer of land fronting a navigable river. But, on the other hand, argument may also be made that any acquisition of property in Louisiana is subject to the terms of Article 456 of the Civil Code, namely, should the property ever front a navigable river, it would be burdened with a servitude of public use. Perhaps the best solution is to exclude public use of the banks of rivers that were non-navigable in 1812, in accordance with the modern tendency to limit the scope and burden of riparian servitudes.

Non-navigable rivers may become navigable either as a result of natural forces or as a result of artificial works, such as drainage, irrigation, or dredging. Further, formerly dry lands may become banks of a man-made navigation canal. Although a man-made waterway is not a river within the meaning of Article 456 of the Civil Code, questions may arise as to the ownership of water bottoms, freedom of navigation, and public use of its banks. A navigation canal constructed by public authorities on public lands is a public thing under Article 450 of the Civil Code and a navigation canal constructed by public authorities on a right of way servitude is a private thing subject to public use. In either case, the canal is a public waterway. If the banks of such a canal are within the right of way acquired by the public authorities, they are ordinarily subject to public use. If, however, the banks of the canal belong to private persons, public use should be excluded. Even if private ownership of lands eroded by man-made navigable waters is extinguished, it does not follow that the banks of such waters are subject to public use. The two questions are distinct and distinguishable.

§ 84. Area Subject to Public Use: Banks

A river consists of three things "the water, the bed, and the banks." The water and bed of a navigable river are public things, whereas the banks are private things subject to public use. Determination of the area that is subject to public use under Article 456 of the Civil Code necessitates accurate definition of the bed and banks....

§ 85. Rights of the General Public

According to well-settled Louisiana jurisprudence, the servitude of public use burdening the banks of navigable rivers is not for the use of the public at large for all purposes. The language of Article 452 is indicative of possible uses but any use of the banks must be incidental to the navigable character of the river and its enjoyment as an avenue of commerce. Thus, the use must not only be a public one, but it must be of the particular public use specified in the reservation.

Members of the general public do not have the right to hunt on the banks of navigable rivers nor the right to trap fur bearing animals without permission from the riparian owner. Moreover, when there are levees, hunting or trapping may be excluded by the rules and regulations of the levee board, which has authority to post levees against such uses. The public has the right to fish from the banks of a navigable river, but has no right to fish in ponds or pit bars between the levee and the water. Further, the public does not have the right to cross privately owned lands in order to go to the banks of navigable rivers. The list of rights that members of the general public do not have is, indeed, a long one. Louisiana decisions indicate that the public does not have the right to camp on the banks, to keep vessels or dry docks tied to the bank indefinitely, to use without compensation wharves or other facilities at the bank, to drive piles into the bank for the mooring of vessels, to use the bank as a coal or wood yard, or to erect permanent structures thereon without the consent of the riparian owner or without license from the authorities. Persons acting without authority may be prosecuted as trespassers, and structures erected by them may be removed or demolished on an action brought by the riparian owner or by the public authorities upon proof that these structures obstruct the public use. These persons are squatters on public or on private property, as the case may be.

The long list of negatives limits substantially the scope of public use of the banks of navigable rivers. Changed circumstances, special legislation and possibly *contra legem* customs have derogated from a broader conception of public use. Louisiana courts held in the past that the rights of landing or launching boats, receiving or shipping freight … may be exercised by every individual, whenever his interests require, and that vessels may be temporarily moored at the banks of navigable rivers. There is strong doubt, however, whether these rights may be exercised freely. Public authorities are entitled to charge fees for the use of port facilities, and there is indication that custom permits riparians to charge fees for the use of the banks in rural areas. The rights to unload vessels and to deposit goods may be exercised in public landings or other facilities, but it is at best questionable whether these rights may be exercised on all banks. One can hardly imagine a modern tanker depositing a cargo of oil on the banks of navigable rivers that are not designed for such a use.

The Louisiana Civil Code may be taken to mean that the general public has a right of free passage over the banks of navigable rivers in their natural state. This does not mean, however, that a member of the public may construct a roadway on the banks or use a private road that may be located there. If there is a public road on the banks, established by virtue of the road servitude under Article 665 of the Civil Code or in any other way in which public roads may be established, the general public has the right to use this road.

§ 86. Powers of Public Authorities

The real significance of the servitude of public use burdening the banks of navigable rivers in Louisiana does not lie in the rather limited rights of use accorded to members of the general public. It lies instead in the powers that it confers upon the state and its political subdivisions to regulate the public use of the banks and to appropriate the banks for the construction of works serving the general interest. Along with inherent police powers and several other articles of the Louisiana Civil Code, the servitude of public use under Article 456 invests public authorities with broad powers of regulation and administration....

The power of the state to control the public use of the banks of navigable rivers, and to grant exclusive rights of use to private persons, individuals or corporations, was early recognized. Further, it was early established that the state may delegate its powers to the governing bodies of its political subdivisions which may develop the banks or grant, within certain limits, exclusive rights of use to private individuals and corporations. Political subdivisions may thus lease the riverfront for limited periods of time and for such public purposes as the establishment of a ferry landing or the construction of a coal yard and coaling station. A municipality, however, may not give to private persons "a right to erect permanent structures upon the batture which will obstruct or embarrass the free use of a public servitude, and to maintain the same in perpetuity." The discretion of political subdivisions to regulate commerce and traffic on the banks of navigable rivers is not to be disturbed by the courts lightly; but when this discretion is abused, courts may intervene. Further, when administrative action violates the equity of all persons under the law with respect to the use of the banks of navigable rivers, both state and federal courts may intervene for the protection of individual rights.

The broad powers of the political subdivisions of the state that are charged with the administration of the public use of the banks of navigable rivers are specified in comprehensive special statutes.

2) The Rights of the Private Owner of the Riverbank
La. Civil Code arts. 458-460

A. N. YIANNOPOULOS, CIVIL LAW PROPERTY
§ 87 (4th ed. 2001)
(footnotes omitted)

§ 87. Prerogatives of Bank Ownership

The banks of navigable rivers in Louisiana are private things burdened with a servitude of public use; the ownership of the ground, down to the ordinary low water mark, remains vested in the riparian proprietors. The private ownership of the banks may be severely impaired by the exigencies of public use, but, on principle, the riparian owner retains all prerogatives of ownership that are not incompatible with public use. In effect, the rights of the private owner of the banks of navigable rivers are residual; the content of these rights is determined in the light of the superior claims of the general public or of the public authorities that are charged with the control and administration of the servitude of public use.

The riparian owner cannot himself enjoy the bank in such a way as to prevent its common enjoyment by all, nor is he entitled to be preferred over others in the use of the banks as a landing place, but he may use the bank, provided he does not prevent the use of it by others, as regulated by the Code and in conformity to the police regulations. As a general rule, the riparian owner in rural areas enjoys more prerogatives of ownership over the banks than the riparian owner within ports or within the limits of municipalities. Thus, the rural riparian owner may be entitled to fish and to hunt or trap fur-bearing animals on the banks; he may also undertake mineral operations for the discovery and production of oil and gas. Further, in all areas, the owner may lease whatever rights he has on the banks, and in rural areas he may exact fees from the public for the permanent mooring of vessels or for camping on the banks. When the owner uses or leases his rights, his ownership of the banks may be assessed and taxed.

The riparian proprietor owns the batture, and he may also own trees, buildings, and other constructions located thereon. He may enjoin members of the general public from crossing his land to go to the banks and from using his facilities without his consent. Structures erected by third persons on the banks may be removed or demolished on an action by the owner unless these structures were erected under license from the public authorities. When the banks are appropriated by political subdivisions of the state according to law, the owner may still claim from the public authorities part of the batture that is not needed for public use. No one, not even public authorities, may take gravel and sand from the batture without the consent of the owner in rural areas, unless the taking is for levee purposes.

One of the most important prerogatives of riparian ownership is the qualified right of the owner to build on the banks structures for the accommodation of the public or for his private use and enjoyment....

The Louisiana Supreme Court has allowed a warehouse, erected by the owner on the bank of a navigable river, to remain on the ground that it merely encroached upon but did not "absolutely" prevent the use of the bank by the public. This formula, and especially the use of the word "absolutely," has been criticized as out of line with prior jurisprudence and as an unwarranted distortion of the text of the Civil Code. Louisiana decisions indicate that constructions erected on public property must be removed on proof that they obstruct the public use although they may not absolutely prevent it. In an early case, which has been followed broadly, a house built on the bank of the Red River was ordered to be removed merely on proof that it was placed on the bank of a navigable river, and that it interrupts the use of it, which is common to all.

The question whether a building obstructs the public use is not to be decided as a matter of law, unless it is obvious that the obnoxious structure absolutely prevents the public use. This interpretation does justice to the text of Article 459 as well as to that of Article 456, which does not contemplate an absolute prohibition to the rural riparian owner to build between the waterline and the levee.

LAKE PROVIDENCE PORT COMM'N v. BUNGE CORP.
193 So. 2d 363 (La. App. 2d Cir. 1966)

BOLIN, J. Lake Providence Port Commission, created as an executive department of the State of Louisiana by Louisiana Revised Statutes 34:1501 and Article 6, Sec. 33 of the Louisiana Constitution, is vested with authority over all the river front land in East Carroll Parish for the development of port facilities on the Mississippi River. Pursuant to this authority the Port Commission acquired 284 acres of land and developed a portion thereof as a port.

Bunge Corporation, desiring to use a portion of the improved land owned by the port commission, submitted a sealed bid for such a site in order to construct a grain facility for the loading and unloading of grain. These efforts were fruitless. Subsequently, Bunge bought 24 acres of land several miles from the property owned by the port commission and began construction of its grain facility on the banks of the Mississippi between the levee and the waterfront. This construction precipitated the present action which was instituted by the port commission to enjoin Bunge from building an elevator on the banks of the river. Plaintiff also seeks judgment declaring its rights under the statutes and constitutional provisions creating it. Judgment was rendered recognizing the port commission as an executive department of the state with exclusive authority to reasonably regulate navigable river commerce and traffic in the port area of East Carroll Parish, Louisiana . . . .

The position of the port commission is:

(1) The riparian servitude established by the Louisiana Civil Code prohibits the erection of any permanent improvement or structure on the bank, batture, accretion and alluvion of the Mississippi River in East Carroll Parish, Louisiana.

(2) The port commission alone is exempt from this prohibition by reason of the Constitution and legislation which created it.

The record establishes Bunge Corporation is engaged in extensive grain and soybean business and in furtherance of such operation had located numerous elevators on navigable inland waterways. It also owns and operates a fleet of barges for river transportation of grain. Defendant had lengthy negotiations with the plaintiff in an effort to obtain an elevator site but, being unsuccessful, it sought permission of the U.S. Corps of Engineers to construct its grain facilities on its own land on the banks of the Mississippi River in East Carroll parish approximately nine miles south of the port commission facilities.

Pursuant to the rules of its department the U.S. District Engineer gave public notice of the application and in due time advised defendant the structure was unobjectionable from the standpoint of navigation but the consent of the United States would be withheld due to the opposition filed by the port commission.

By virtue of Article 6, Sec. 33 and Article 14, Sec. 30 of the Louisiana Constitution (1921). Louisiana Revised Statutes 34:1501 et seq. and Louisiana Civil Code Articles 455, 457, 665, 861 [Revised C.C. arts. 456, 665], plaintiff contends it has absolute and complete authority over the use of the entire river bank throughout the parish of East Carroll and defendant cannot place any permanent structure thereon without its consent.

Defendant corporation admits the port commission is legally created with power to reasonably regulate commerce and traffic on the Mississippi within the entire parish of East Carroll, but contends it, as a rural riparian owner, may not be prohibited by the commission from placing improvements upon its property so long as the structures do not seriously obstruct or prevent the public use of the navigable stream or banks thereof.

Plaintiff's principal argument is that the site for defendant's proposed facility is located on the bank of the Mississippi and that as such it is subject to a servitude of use in favor of the public which forbids the erection of a permanent structure even on "one inch" of the bank and cites as authority Article 453 [Revised C.C. arts. 450, 452], Louisiana Civil Code....Plaintiff admits that the case of Town of Madisonville v. Dendinger (Sup.Ct., 1949) 214 La. 593, 38 So. 2d 252 is favorable to defendant but contends the facts are inapposite to the instant case and further that the case is a "maverick" in our jurisprudence.

We direct our attention now to the proper interpretation of the cited code articles. Article 455 [Revised C.C. art. 456] is the basic article establishing a servitude of use in the public in and to the banks of navigable rivers or streams of Louisiana. It is to be noted, however, that this article also provides the ownership of the bank of the river is vested in the owner of the adjacent land. It seems reasonable that the owners outside of municipalities can use and develop these river banks so long as the use by the public is not obstructed. The character of the use reserved to the public must be considered as well as the nature of the land so burdened.

Article 457 [Revised C.C. art. 456] designates the levees as the banks of the Mississippi and as related to the property herein the levee is more than one-quarter of a mile from the ordinary high water line. In the instant case, the land in the vicinity is classified as rural and the expanse of land between the levee and the high water mark is relatively wide, compared to that in cities, and the waterborne traffic is not congested. For these reasons the restrictions on development of land by riparian owners or their representatives need not be as extensive as in cities.

The instant case is therefore distinguishable from the cases cited, *supra*, by plaintiff, all of which dealt with the banks of streams within corporate limits. However, in the Dendinger case, cited *supra*, the Supreme Court denied the municipality the right to remove or destroy a warehouse owned by the landowner under the provisions of Article 861 [Revised C.C. art. 458] of the Louisiana Civil Code holding the warehouse merely encroached upon the bank and did not prevent its use within the contemplation of the code article.

There is no evidence in the present case to establish that defendant's elevator would obstruct or prevent the public use of the banks of the river. Plaintiff admits its opposition to defendant's construction is stimulated by its duty to protect and increase the commission's income and in return relieve the burden of the taxpayers, all of which is admirable and noble, but is incompatible with the type of use reserved for the public by Louisiana Civil Code Article 455 [Revised C.C. art. 456]....

In conclusion, it is our holding that although the land owned by defendant in the instant case is between a levee and a navigable river and is burdened with a servitude of public use, [the defendant], as a riparian owner, may construct any manner of works on its land provided it does not obstruct the public use. If and when a structure on a riverbank interferes with the servitude of public use, the owner, by appropriate legal procedure, may be required to remove it. We do not agree with plaintiff's position that the proposed construction is prohibited per se as a matter of law. We find that the constitutional and legislative acts creating the port commission conferred upon it the right to acquire land, construct wharves, etc., and to regulate river navigation in East Carroll Parish but did not confer the right to prohibit reasonable use of property owned by others adjacent to the banks of navigable waters in the parish.

There is no dispute over the lower court's declaratory judgment. Accordingly, the judgment appealed from is affirmed at Appellant's cost.

NOTE AND QUESTION

May a municipality exclude the public use of the bank of a navigable river within its limits by zoning the batture as "R-1, single family, residential?" See *Parish of Jefferson v. Universal Fleeting Co.*, 234 So. 2d 88 (La. App. 4th Cir. 1970). In this case, the court held that Jefferson Parish could not supersede the provisions of the Civil Code.

4. LAKES

See A. N. YIANNOPOULOS, CIVIL LAW PROPERTY
§ 80 (4th ed. 2001)

a. Identifying a Lake

STATE v. PLACID OIL COMPANY
300 So. 2d 154 (La. 1973)

ON REHEARING

SANDERS, C.J. We granted a rehearing in this case because of the importance of the legal issues to the people of the State of Louisiana. Although the bare controversy between the State and defendants is the ownership of a tract of land located below the high-water mark of Grand Lake-Six Mile Lake in St. Mary Parish, the decision has far reaching consequences, affecting that State's natural resources, ecology, and the public fisc.

For the purposes of rehearing, the facts set forth in the original opinion may be summarized. The State of Louisiana, joined by Gulf Oil Corporation, its lessee, seeks to be declared the owner of an area of land, on which several oil wells are located, lying below the high-water mark of a large body of water known as Grand Lake-Six Mile Lake in St. Mary Parish, adjacent to Sections 49, 50, and 88, Township 15 South, Range 11 East. In 1812, when Louisiana was admitted into the Union, Grand Lake-Six Mile Lake was navigable. The areas in dispute are referred to as the Woodland Tract, Barnetts Cove, and The Island area. As found on original hearing, the Woodland tract is part of the bank of the water body. The record discloses that the remaining area was as late as 1935 a part of the bottom of Grand Lake. During the ensuing years, however, sedimentary deposits caused a buildup, transforming the area into alluvion lying below the ordinary high-water mark. A fair inference, we think, is that the sedimentary deposits were accelerated by the channeling and dredging performed by governmental agencies as part of an extensive water-resource program.

Although State-Gulf makes a most persuasive argument that the land formation in the Barnett and Island areas is not alluvion, we accept the findings of the lower courts that it is alluvion, that is, accretions formed successively and imperceptibly on the shore.

As correctly noted in our original opinion, the State of Louisiana upon its admission to the Union acquired title to all lands within its boundaries below the ordinary high-water mark of navigable bodies of water, with the power to determine the rights of riparian owners. Shively v. Bowlby, 152 U.S. 1, 14 S.Ct. 548, 38 L.Ed. 331 (1894); State v. Richardson, 140 La. 329, 72 So. 984 (1916).

Through statutory provisions, the State of Louisiana has defined the rights of riparian owners.

As to navigable rivers and streams, the State holds in its sovereign capacity all the land that is covered by water at its ordinary low state. The bank belongs to the owner of the adjacent land, subject to public use. C.C. Arts. 455, 457 [Revised C.C. art. 456]. As to lakes, the State has never ceded, and still holds, the land below the ordinary high-water mark. See [1870] Revised C.C. art. 455 [Revised C.C. art. 456]; State v. Aucoin, 206 La. 786, 20 So. 2d 136 (1944); State v. Bozeman, 156 La. 635, 101 So. 4 (1924); State v. Capdeville, 146 La. 94, 83 So. 421 (1919); Mime v. Girodeau, 12 La. 324 (1838).

Article 509 [Revised C.C. art. 499] of the Louisiana Civil Code, regulating the ownership of alluvion, provides:

> "The accretions, which are formed successively and imperceptibly to any soil situated on the shore of a river or other stream, are called alluvion.

> "The alluvion belongs to the owner of the soil situated on the edge of the water, whether it be a river or stream, and whether the same be navigable or not, who is bound to leave public that portion of the bank which is required by law for the public use."

By its terms, the foregoing article applies only to rivers and other streams. Thus, alluvion formed on the shores of rivers or streams belongs to the adjacent landowners. The principle of accretion, however, is inapplicable to lakes. As to lakes, the adjacent landowners have no alluvial rights. Esso Standard Oil Company v. Jones, 233 La. 915, 98 So. 2d 238 (1957); Amerada Petroleum Corporation v. Case, 210 La. 630, 27 So. 2d 431 (1946); Zeller v. Southern Yacht Club, 34 La. Ann. 837 (1882).

The crucial determination is whether at the time of Louisiana's admission to the Union, Grand Lake-Six Mile Lake was a stream or lake. If it was a stream, the banks belong to the riparian owners, and the law of accretion applies. Thus, the disputed land would belong to the adjacent landowners. If, on the other hand, it was a lake, the banks are state-owned and accretion is inapplicable. Thus, the disputed land would belong to the State in its sovereign capacity.

On original hearing, in holding that Grand Lake-Six Mile Lake was a stream, as distinguished from a lake, we stated: "[A] body of water through which a current flows or runs with such capacity and velocity and power as to form accretions is characterized as a river or stream, depending upon all attending circumstances, for the purpose of applying the rules of accretion and dereliction set forth in Articles 509 and 510 [Revised C.C. arts. 499, 500] of the Civil Code." We now think we erred in holding the body of water to be a stream, primarily because of two basic errors:

(1) In holding that Amerada Petroleum Corporation v. State Mineral Board, 203 La. 473, 14 So. 2d 61 (1943) overruled State v. Erwin, 173 La. 507, 138 So. 84 (1931).

(2) In giving undue weight to the existence of water current capable of forming accretions as a basis of classification.

In State v. Erwin, *supra*, this Court was concerned with the classification of Calcasieu Lake in Cameron Parish as a lake, river, or stream. That body of water was 18 miles long and varied in width from 4 ½ to 14 miles. The Calcasieu River traversed the water body from north to south, then continued its flow toward the Gulf of Mexico. At times, there were perceptible currents in the water, and it was affected by tides.

In holding that the water body was a lake rather than a stream on original hearing, this Court stated: "In our opinion, however, the better view — with reference to the laws, governing alluvion and dereliction — is to regard such a vast expanse of water as Calcasieu Lake as being in fact a lake, although a river empties into the sea through it." (138 So. at 86).

On rehearing, the Court adhered to the holding that the body of water was a lake.

In Miami Corporation v. State, 186 La. 784, 173 So. 315 (1937), this Court dealt with the stream-lake classification of Grand Lake in Cameron Parish. The Court described it as a "navigable body of running water." It was about ten miles long and from three to nine miles wide. The Mermentau River flowed into and out of the lake. There was sufficient current to carry sediment. The Court overruled State v. Erwin, *supra*, as to a point not pertinent here. In holding the body of water to be a lake, however, it reaffirmed the Erwin lake classification, stating: "Grand Lake, like Calcasieu Lake, was a navigable lake. when Louisiana was admitted to the Union in 1812." (173 So. at 319).***

First Amerada makes only one reference to State v. Erwin, *supra*. That reference is not to overrule, but to distinguish.*** We conclude, contrary to our first impression, that the holding of State v. Erwin as to the classification of lakes has not been overruled.

It is true that sectors of the Court's language in several of the above cases focus strongly upon the existence of accretion-forming current in the water body. When these decisions are read as a whole, however, it is evident that the Court considered, not one, but several characteristics of the water body in making its classification. Our synthesis of these cases yields a conclusion that the existence of accretion-forming current is not, by itself, decisive of a stream's classification. As noted in the dissenting opinion on original hearing, a holding that accretion-forming current alone is determinative that the water body is a stream would mean that all alluvion on all water bodies accrues to the riparian owners, contrary to the intent of Article 509 [Revised C.C. art. 499], the formal expression of legislative will.

In our opinion, the jurisprudence, as well as the expert testimony, supports a multiple-factor test for classifying a water body as a lake or a stream. A judgment must be based upon a consideration of pertinent characteristics. Among these are the size, especially its width as compared to the streams that enter it; its depth; its banks; its channel; its current, especially as compared to that of streams that enter it; and its historical designation in official documents, especially on official maps....

Considering these factors in the present case, we find that Grand Lake-Six Mile Lake is one of the five largest water bodies in Louisiana. From earliest times, it has been designated on official maps as a lake. In 1812, at the time Louisiana was admitted to the federal union, the body was also known as Lake Chetimaches or Lake Sale (Salt Lake). It was about 30 miles long by 3 to 10 miles wide. It had a "Thalweg depth of only 8 feet."

The water body was subject to the ebb and flow of the tide. Because of the tidal action, the water was brackish and populated by salt water fish. The record reflects that Grand Lake is about 20 times wider than the Atchafalaya River, which enters it; that currents are reduced substantially in the lake; that 75% of the sedimentation is deposited in the lake, and only 25% is carried out.

In summary, Grand Lake-Six Mile Lake is a wide, irregularly shaped body of water of great size, relatively shallow in depth, with a current substantially slower than that of the inflowing river. In its main characteristics, it is similar to Lake Pontchartrain and Lake Calcasieu. Historically, it has always been designated as a lake.

We hold that it was a lake in 1812, when Louisiana was admitted to the Union. Accordingly, it must now be classified as such. It follows under the principles already announced that the State owns its banks and that the accretion rule of Louisiana Civil Code Article 509 [Revised C.C. art. 499] is inapplicable to it.

Consistent with the views expressed, we hold that the State of Louisiana owns the disputed areas, located below the ordinary high-water mark of Grand Lake-Six Mile Lake, subject to the rights of its mineral lessee, Gulf Oil Corporation.

For the reasons assigned, the judgment of the Court of Appeal, insofar as it decreed the defendants to be the owners of the area hereinafter described, is reversed. Judgment is rendered in favor of plaintiffs, State of Louisiana and Gulf Oil Corporation, against Placid Oil Company, J. Ray McDermott & Co., Inc., and all other defendants decreeing the State of Louisiana to be the owner of the property covered by State Lease 2963, dated April 18, 1956, to Gulf Oil Corporation....

SUMMERS, J. (dissenting). In classifying Six Mile Lake as a lake the Court disregards the most important characteristic of a water body for the purpose of classification under Civil Code Article 509 [Revised C.C. art. 499], that is, a moving or running body of water principally endowed with the capacity for change. Instead the Court has emphasized other physical features which are either not supported by the record or which have pertinence only in the limited fields of geology or cartography. And this notwithstanding the fact that the State expressly admitted in its application for writs that the issue before the Court was the classification of the water body under our laws relating to accretion and dereliction.

This reasoning of the Court is based upon the erroneous premise that if the capacity to form accretions is the test for classification, a minimal amount of accretion in any type of water body would satisfy the requirements of Article 509 [Revised C.C. art. 499] of the Civil Code because the presence of accretions proves up the capacity to form them. This overly simplistic approach is irrelevant to the facts of this case. It disregards the admitted fact that Six Mile Lake is a dynamic body of water carrying a substantial portion of the waters of the Atchafalaya Basin to the Gulf. This approach requires classification of Six Mile Lake as a placid or immobile body of water having no real capacity for undergoing physical change. Nothing could be further from the facts. The characteristics of Six Mile Lake are otherwise.

b. Legal Effect of Erosion of Lake Shore

MIAMI CORPORATION v. STATE
186 La. 784, 173 So. 315 (1936)

HIGGINS, J. This is an action of boundary by a riparian or littoral owner…seeking to be decreed the owner of an eroded area which now forms a part of the bed of Grand Lake in Cameron Parish, La. The defenses are that the State owns the disputed inundated area under either one or both of two distinct rules or principles of law:

    1. That the property forms a part of the bottom or bed of a navigable lake, which was such when Louisiana was admitted into the Union in 1812, and therefore owned by the State by virtue of its inherent rights of sovereignty, and thus insusceptible of private ownership under Articles 450 and 453 [Revised C.C. art. 452] of the Civil Code found in Book 2, Title 1, "Of Things, and of the Different Modifications of Ownership."

    2. That the State acquired title to the disputed area under the law of accretion, dereliction, and reliction, as set forth in Articles 509 and 510 [Revised C.C. arts. 499, 500] of the Civil Code, found in Book 2, Title 2 Chapter 3, dealing with "the right of accession to what unites or incorporates itself to the thing," because Grand Lake is a navigable body of running water and was such in 1812, when Louisiana was admitted to statehood.

There was judgment in favor of the State, and plaintiff has appealed. The district judge has so clearly stated the issues, the facts, and the law pertinent thereto, we quote approvingly, in part, from his written opinion:

"Plaintiff further alleges that the shore line has receded eastward until at present a large part of several of the original sections of land is inundated and permanently covered by the waters of the lake.

"Relying on the rule established in the case of State v. Erwin, 173 La. 507, 138 So. 84, plaintiff prays that the boundary of its property in Sections 3, 4, and 9 of Township 14 South, Range 3 West, be established along the shoreline as it was on May 24, 1883, and that plaintiff be decreed the owner of all the area east of the said line, whether inundated or not, and the State be decreed the owner of all the area west of said line whether inundated or not.

"From the record the Court finds the following facts: Grand Lake and the Mermentau River are navigable, and were navigable in 1812. Grand Lake is a body of water in Cameron Parish, Louisiana, approximately ten miles long from North to South, and from three to nine miles wide from east to west. The Mermentau River, flowing generally in a north to south direction, flows into the north end of the lake and out of the south end. The south end of the lake, by river, is 27 miles from the Gulf of Mexico. The waters of the Lake are fresh to brackish, and are affected to some extent by the tides. The Mermentau River meanders through and across alternate areas and being confined within a comparatively narrow channel through the higher, harder areas. Where the river widens in the marshy areas, it is in each instance locally called a lake, and the river is made up of a chain of lakes, connected by a narrow channel.

"The name 'Lake' is applied to various wide places in the river, some of which are widened to so little extent that the widening is scarcely perceptible. Such wide places in the river are: Lake Arthur, considerably below Grand Lake, both of which are shown in scale on the plats introduced in evidence. Grand Lake is the largest of these so-called lakes in the entire chain.

"The evidence further conclusively shows that there is a current running through Grand Lake with sufficient force to carry the sediment brought into the north end of the lake by the river out the south end, and it is also of sufficient force to remove the earth as it is eroded from the banks, so that the depth of the lake is practically the same near the receding shore as it is in the middle of the lake.

"The recession of the shore is caused by a combination of natural forces and conditions. The area involved in this suit is the southeast side of the lake, at a point where the force of the waves, due to the prevailing winds, is probably the greatest. The current or currents in the lake must also be a considerable factor, as there are no flats or shoals formed in front of the receding area. All material eroded is carried out of the Lake, through the river and into the Gulf of Mexico. Another natural force which has to do with the recession of the banks is subsidence. The entire area of Cameron Parish is subsiding. The percentage of erosion or recession due to the waves, current, or subsidence is not and cannot be determined by the court[;] they work jointly to accomplish the result.

"Of the three natural forces which cause the encroachment in this case, it is agreed by the parties that the waves and currents are factors. There is a contest on the question of subsidence.

"Plaintiffs expert plausibly contends that the entire area is being gradually built up, while defendant's experts, representing the opposite school of geological thought, just as plausibly maintain that there is a constant subsidence of the entire area.

"After a study of the reports and the testimony of the experts, which contain their theories, findings of fact and conclusions, this Court is of the opinion that subsidence of the area is irrefutably established...

"*The law.* Counsel on both sides have materially assisted the court by reviewing the case in oral argument and by filing able and exhaustive briefs.

"Article 509 of the Civil Code [Revised C.C. art. 499] treats of alluvion along navigable streams or rivers, and defines alluvion as 'accretions, which are formed successively and imperceptibly.' Article 510 of the Civil Code [Revised C.C. arts. 499, 500] treats alluvion and dereliction and provides that the owner of the shore which is encroached upon by running water cannot claim the land he has lost. This article uses the term 'running water' instead of river or streams.

"Article 453 [Revised C.C. arts. 450, 452] of the Civil Code lists as public things the beds of navigable rivers, as long as they are covered by water. Article 457 [Revised C.C. art. 456] of the Civil Code defines the banks of a river or stream as that which contains it in its ordinary stage of high-water, temporary overflow not changing it.

"From the facts, and the above articles of the Civil Code, if the bank encroached upon in this case were located on the Mermentau River instead of the Lake, all parties agree the articles of the Code would clearly apply.

"The articles quoted in reality make the riparian owner a party to an aleatory contract, in which the State as the owner of the bed of the stream is the other party, and which contract provides that in the event one party loses by the encroachment of the stream and the other gains, the loss is offset by the possibility of a reversal of the condition. Delachaise v. Maginnis, 44 La. Ann. 1043, 1048, 11 So. 715.***

"Counsel for plaintiff contends that because the land encroached upon in this case is located not upon the bank of the Mermentau River but upon the bank of the body of water called Grand Lake, through which the Mermentau River flows, the articles of the Civil Code above quoted do not apply, and the riparian owner on the lake is not a party to an aleatory contract such as we have described above....

"The Louisiana courts have repeatedly interpreted Article 453 [Revised C.C. art. 450, 452] of the Civil Code, and the Articles immediately preceding and following it, exactly as have the French courts interpreted the similar Articles of their Code. In other words, although Article 453 [Revised C.C. art. 450, 452] and the other Articles cited do not specially mention navigable lakes among public things, the courts have included such lakes among public things, and have repeatedly held that if a lake is navigable in fact, and was navigable in fact as of date 1812, the bed of the lake is a public thing, and title is vested in the State.***

"To apply the rule established in the Erwin Case, would be impracticable. A study of the plat attached to plaintiff's petition clearly shows that there is no discernable point where the Mermentau River ceases to be a river and becomes a lake. A property owner whose property extended two miles up the river, and two miles along the lake — we use this merely as an illustration — would be subject to two rules of property. On the river he would be entitled to alluvion and on the lake he would not. In the event alluvion was formed on both the river shore and the lakeshore, at some point the owner's land would extend from where it is today, and beyond that point it would remain fixed. In the case of encroachment of both, which is the case here, up to a certain point the owner would lose the land covered by the water, and beyond that point he would retain it, and neither the owner nor any court could definitely fix the point of offset. From a practical standpoint, also, since both the lake and the river are navigable, the rule established by the Erwin Case, since Grand Lake is expanding in all directions, would eventually result in a public thing partially owned by the State and partially owned by private individuals. If individuals owned the lake bottom around the edge of Grand Lake, such individuals could prevent trespass. Beyond the point where the shore was in 1812, one using the lake, although navigable, would be a trespasser on private property, and the trespasser would have no right to use the bank which was not inundated, since it would not be the bank of a navigable public water."***

Grand Lake, like Calcasieu Lake, was a navigable lake when Louisiana was admitted to the Union in 1812. It was shown that Calcasieu Lake is situated about 7 or 8 miles from the Gulf of Mexico, while Grand Lake is about 27 miles from the Gulf. The Mermentau River enters Grand Lake on the north and flows out at the south end to the Gulf, just as the Calcasieu River enters Calcasieu Lake on the north and flows out of the south end to the Gulf. The district judge found that conditions surrounding Grand Lake and Calcasieu Lake "are similar, though not identical."

Counsel for the State argue that the rule announced in State v. Erwin, *supra*, is not binding on this court under the common-law doctrine of stare decisis or its rigorous application as establishing a rule of property, because this doctrine is, at most, accepted in Louisiana only in a modified form; that the decision in State v. Erwin became final on November 30, 1931; that it was rendered by a divided court; that it has not been followed to date in a single instance; and that it not only stands alone in the jurisprudence of Louisiana, but that it is contrary to a series of decisions which have formed a part of the jurisprudence of this state for nearly one hundred years.***

Learned counsel for both parties litigant stated that the main point in the case is the correctness or incorrectness of the decision in State v. Erwin, *supra*, and whether or not it should be followed or overruled. They also agree that the facts in this case are so substantially similar to those in the Erwin Case that this case must be decided under the rule declared therein, in the event we reach the conclusion that the case of State v. Erwin is correct.

There the State instituted an action to try title to certain lands which were submerged by the waters of Lake Calcasieu, an inland, navigable body of water. The Calcasieu River flowed through the lake and from it to the Gulf of Mexico or sea, through a channel 6 miles in length. The shores of the lake had been eroded to a considerable extent by the forces of nature — wind and wave. The State claimed the bed of the lake up to its then present shore line as belonging to it as a sovereign State, because the lake was a navigable body of water in 1812. The defendants asserted ownership of the land in question under patents which conveyed title up to the shore line of the lake, as it was in 1812, when Louisiana was admitted to the Union. This court held that Calcasieu Lake is a true lake, and that Articles 509 and 510 [Revised C.C. art. 499] of the [1870] Revised Civil Code, covering alluvion, dereliction, and reliction had no application to the case, and that the submerged lands belonged to the riparian owners. On rehearing, the court held that the lake was not an arm of the sea and reiterated its previous views.***

Three of the justices dissented on the ground that Calcasieu Lake, even though it was an inland fresh water lake, was nevertheless a navigable lake, and therefore title to the bed thereof vested in the State under its inherent sovereign rights, and that it was against public policy for such lands to be privately owned, being a public thing....

Since it is conceded that Grand Lake is a navigable body of water, and the law is settled that the title to the bed of such a body of water is vested in the State, the question arises whether the eroded or disputed area, which has been added to the bed of the lake by the combined forces of nature — subsidence and erosion — has so become a part of the bed of the lake, that it is now the property of the State, and the riparian proprietors have lost their title. It appears to be the rule that where the forces of nature — subsidence and erosion — have operated on the banks of a navigable body of water, regardless of whether it be a body of fresh water or the sea, or an arm of the sea, the submerged area becomes a portion of the bed and is insusceptible of private ownership. This is of necessity the law, because, to hold otherwise would be contrary to sound principles and public policy upon which the rule is predicated. It is the rule of property and of title in this State, and also a rule of public policy that the State, as sovereignty, holds title to the beds of navigable bodies of water.***

The mere fact that a portion of the bed of a navigable body of water may have been formed by the action of natural forces does not change the situation, for the rule is, that when submersion occurs, the submerged portion becomes a part of the bed or bottom of the navigable body of water in fact, and therefore the property of the State, by virtue of its inherent sovereignty, as a matter of law. If this were not so, there could be a complete rim of privately owned submerged lands around the entire circumference of a navigable lake. This is wholly undesirable and destructive of progress, because it would practically deprive the public of the use of the lake under State laws. To say that the federal government could regulate the use, by the public, of such navigable bodies of water under the commerce clause and its admiralty jurisdiction, is not a satisfactory reply.

In the Tulane Law Review, Vol. VII, No. 3, p. 438, dated April, 1933, the author of a well-written article on this subject, after discussing the authorities of both the common and civil law, including our own decisions, concluded by saying: "The instant case (State v. Erwin) sets a dangerous precedent, contrary to the whole spirit of the Code, which forbids private ownership of the beds of navigable waters." Citing Articles 450, 453, 455, 512, and 518 [Revised C.C. arts. 449, 450, 452, 456, 504, 505] of the Louisiana Civil Code, "***The Calcasieu Lake case or State v. Erwin seems therefore, to be entirely out of line with the rest of Louisiana jurisprudence on the subject of lakes, and since it is clearly bad policy to allow private ownership of the beds of navigable waters of any kind, it is submitted that the conclusion of that case will produce undesirable results."***

The author of the majority opinion in State v. Erwin was apparently endeavoring to give application to the maxim of Roman Law "*Qui sentit onus, sentire debet et commodum*" ["he who bears the burden ought to receive the benefit"], the equitable principle underlying the rule of title to alluvion and dereliction in the Civil Law system....He must have discerned by reading the decisions of this court that where a riparian owner was claiming alluvion and dereliction which took place along the shores of a navigable lake, he was denied title to this land; whereas, when the State claimed an eroded area along the shore of a navigable lake, the court recognized the State's title to the property, a public thing, as a result of its inherent sovereignty. This must have impressed the court as being inequitable and therefore the reason for overruling the case, i.e., New Orleans Land Co. v. Board of Commissioners, etc., *supra*, which recognized the State's title to the eroded area. It appears that the purpose was to make the law equitable — neither the State nor the riparian owner gaining or losing when the water line of the lake expanded or contracted. The majority opinion accomplished this result by stating Articles 509 and 510 [Revised C.C. arts. 499, 500] of the Civil Code with reference to alluvion and dereliction did not apply to fresh water, navigable lakes. But, in order to reach this conclusion, the court had to go counter to the long-established sound principles of public policy in our jurisprudence — that the title to the bottoms of navigable bodies of water belong to the State as a result of its inherent sovereignty and are insusceptible of private ownership.

Consequently, the effect of the decision was more harmful and destructive of the rule of property and public welfare than the correction of an alleged inequitable situation in the jurisprudence or law.

The majority view on rehearing in the State v. Erwin Case sought to explain the authorities cited in support of the dissenting opinion, simply on the ground that they had no application, because Lake Pontchartrain was an arm of the sea, and therefore within the exception provided for in Article 510....

It is to be noted that, in the decisions of this court dealing with Lake Pontchartrain, there is no description of the Lake and no definition of the phrase "arm of the sea." In State v. Erwin, it is said that Lake Pontchartrain has been held to be "an arm of the sea." In the same opinion, the court also states that Lake Calcasieu is not "an arm of the sea." However, both lakes empty into the Gulf of Mexico and Lake Calcasieu is closer and more directly connected with the Gulf than Lake Pontchartrain, as clearly appears from the map filed in evidence herein. No explanation is made why one lake is held to be "an arm of the sea" and the other lake held not to be "an arm of the sea." Certainly this phrase should have some definite meaning and its explanation should not be left to the discretion of the court in a particular case, in order that the jurisprudence and the law may be uniform and effective.***

Finally, there is no explanation — not even a word in the opinion in support of the expression that it is a "better view" to hold that the lake bottom or bed is susceptible of private ownership, than to hold, as was stated in New Orleans Land Co. v. Board of Levee Commissioners, 171 La. 718, 722, 723, 132 So. 121, 123, that:

> "In determining the issues involved in this case, it is of no practical value to ascertain whether Lake Pontchartrain should be classed as a salt-water tidal lake or a fresh-water inland navigable lake. The legal situation with which we are concerned here is the same in either case. The water bottoms of both classes of lakes are owned by the state to the high-water mark. McGilbra v. Ross, 215, U.S. (70) 77, 30 S. Ct. 27, 54 L. Ed. 95; Barney v. Keokuk, 94 U.S. 324, 24 L. Ed. 224; Civ. Code, art. 451; Milne v. Girodeau, 12 La. 324; State v. Bozeman, 156 La. 635, 101 So. 4; Bruning v. City of New Orleans, 165 La. 511, 115 So. 733."

We believe that reasons of public policy readily suggest themselves why the above-quoted expression of the law is correct. It is our opinion that...the case of State v. Erwin, *supra*, is erroneous and is hereby overruled. We are further of the opinion that the bed or bottom of Grand Lake, a navigable body of water, including the area in controversy, which has been submerged since 1883, belongs to the State of Louisiana, by virtue of its sovereignty, it being a public thing and insusceptible of private ownership under the provisions of Articles 450 and 453 [450] of the Revised Civil Code. Having reached the above conclusion, it is unnecessary to consider the applicability of Articles 509 and 510 [Revised C.C. arts. 499, 500] of the [1870] Revised Civil Code to this case....For the reasons assigned, the judgment appealed from is affirmed, at appellant's costs.

O'NIELL, C.J. (dissenting). It is suggested in the prevailing opinion in this case that the Erwin Case set a dangerous precedent, and might produce undesirable results. No danger is pointed out; no undesirable results are specified; nor has any broad principle of public policy ever entered into this case. The State officials do not intend to dedicate the land in contest to a work of public improvement, as in the case of the public-improvement project on Lake Pontchartrain. The intention is for the State to lease the land in contest for the production of oil, gas, or other minerals, and to receive the bonuses and royalties thereon, as the State leased the land under the edge of Calcasieu Lake, without avail, to the Louisiana Land & Exploration Company, co-plaintiff in the Erwin Case. What is it that constitutes the "dangerous precedent" in the Erwin case? The oil companies that lease these lake bottoms from the State are obliged to obtain permission from the War Department — in the same way that an oil company leasing from the [private] land owner has to obtain such permission — to construct derricks or other obstructions on the lake. The oil derricks erected by the oil companies holding leases from the State are not any less objectionable to navigation on the lakes than the derricks erected by the oil companies holding leases from the owners of the submerged lands.

It is true, of course, that the state treasury will profit to the extent of the bonuses and royalties if the State is permitted to take these submerged lands from the owners, and lease them to operating companies for the production of oil, gas, and other minerals; but the taking of these lands by the State, for any such purpose, after the State has sold the lands and collected the price, and has collected taxes on them for many years, would not be sanctioned by any consideration of public policy, not any more than it is sanctioned by express law....

LOUISIANA REVISED STATUTES

R.S. 9:1151. Change in ownership of land or water bottoms as a result of action of navigable stream, bay or lake; mineral leases

In all cases where a change occurs in the ownership of land or water bottoms as a result of the action of a navigable stream, bay, lake, sea, or arm of the sea, in the change of its course, bed, or bottom, or as a result of accretion, dereliction, erosion, subsidence or other condition resulting from the action of a navigable stream, bay, lake, sea or arm of the sea, the new owner of such lands or water bottoms, including the state of Louisiana, shall take the same subject to and encumbered with any oil, gas, or mineral lease covering and affecting such lands or water bottoms, and subject to the mineral and royalty rights of the lessors in such a lease...; the right of the lessee or owners of such lease and the right of the mineral and royalty owners thereunder shall be in no manner abrogated or affected by such change in ownership.

NOTE

Since 1952, this "freeze statute" has insured that changes in ownership resulting from actions of navigable waters do not affect outstanding mineral rights. The Court of Appeal for the Second Circuit has held that the mere existence of a lease triggers the statute; actual mineral production is not required. See *Cities Service Oil and Gas Corp. v. State*, 574 So. 2d 455 (La. App. 2d Cir. 1991).

5. CANALS

See A. N. YIANNOPOULOS, CIVIL LAW PROPERTY
§ 79 (4th ed. 2001)

VERMILION CORPORATION v. VAUGHN
356 So. 2d 551 (La. App. 3d Cir. 1978)

DOMENGEAUX, J. This suit involves the right of the public to use man-made navigable canals on private property constructed and maintained with private funds.

Vermilion Corporation, plaintiff-appellee, leases 125,000 acres of land in Vermilion Parish owned by the Exxon Company. The land is traversed by a system of man-made canals. The canals are approximately 60 feet wide and 8 feet deep, are subject to tidal fluctuations, and are navigable in fact. They were constructed with private funds and have been under the continuous control, possession, and supervision of Vermilion Corporation, Exxon Company, and all prior owners since the 1900s.

The canal system enters other naturally navigable waterways and lies between the Intercoastal Canal on the north, the Gulf of Mexico on the south, West Cheniere Au Tigre Canal on the east, and Rollover Bayou on the west. The canals are used to facilitate hunting, trapping, and fishing activities, and are also used by the Exxon Company for hydrocarbon exploration and development activities. Vermilion Corporation subleases portions of the land to hunters, trappers, and fishers. The right to use the canals is part of the lease arrangement.

In order to control access to the land and canals, over 400 "No Trespassing" signs are posted in various locations. In addition persons have been continuously employed to supervise activities in the canal and on the land. On numerous occasions Vermilion Corporation has prohibited persons from entering and using the property.

The present controversy arose when the defendant appellants, Norman Vaughn, Freddie Broussard, and Larry J. Broussard, continued to enter the property and travel the canals in order to engage in commercial fishing and shrimping activities without obtaining plaintiff's permission. These individuals disregarded several written warnings issued by plaintiff. Consequently, these suits were filed seeking permanent injunctions enjoining the three defendants from trespassing on the property and in the canals. In the present case the parties are in agreement on all relevant facts that are genuinely material to this case and upon which a judgment can be rendered. There is no question that the canals are navigable and were built and maintained with private funds on private property. It is not contested that defendants did engage in fishing and shrimping activities in the canals without permission.

Defendants contend, however, that there is a fact in dispute which is genuinely material to this litigation and that summary judgment was improper. They claim that plaintiff's system of artificial waterways destroyed the navigability of surrounding natural waterways. They argue that this is material because, if true, the court could conclude that the system of artificial waterways was substituted for the pre-existing natural system of navigable waterways. If such a conclusion were reached, the canals would not be private and could not be privately controlled under state and federal law.

We do not agree. A similar argument was raised in McIlhenny v. Broussard, 172 La. 895, 135 So. 669 (1931), the facts of which are almost the same as in the present case. The plaintiff in that case, E. A. McIlhenny, constructed a private canal on his property. The defendant, Broussard, continued to use this canal without McIlhenny's permission. McIlhenny sought to enjoin Broussard from using his private waterway. The contention was made that the waters from a natural canal were diverted by the man-made waterway and that therefore the man-made waterway was substituted for the natural waterway. The Louisiana Supreme Court rejected the argument stating that the diversion of water from a natural channel by a private man-made waterway does not give rise to a right of the public to use the man-made waterway.

Defendants contend that the injunctions should not have been granted as a matter of state and federal law. They argue that under La. R.S. 14:97 and under 33 U.S.C.A. Sec. 403 (§ 10 of the Rivers and Harbors Act) a private individual may not exert dominion over a navigable waterway.

With regard to state law, this court discussed the application of La. R.S. 14:97 to a private canal in National Audubon Society v. White, 302 So. 2d 660 (La. App. 3d Cir.1974), writ denied 305 So. 2d 542 (La. 1975), a case which defendants contend was erroneous and should be overruled.

The facts of *Audubon* mirror those in the present controversy. In that case a private canal was constructed in 1912 by E. A. McIlhenny on his property in Vermilion Parish. The canal, which was the same canal involved in McIlhenny v. Broussard, *supra*, was navigable and connected with Vermilion Bay. In 1924 a portion of the land, including a part of the canal, was donated to the National Audubon Society. That organization used the property to operate the Paul J. Rainey Wildlife Sanctuary. The Audubon Society maintained their portion of the McIlhenny canal with its own funds. Access to the canal was restricted by the Audubon Society as it was restricted prior to the donation. The defendant in that case, Joseph White, used the canal without permission for fifty years to haul cattle, cotton, vegetables, and fruit to the market. In 1971 and 1972 he was notified by the Audubon Society that he could no longer use the canal. These notices were disregarded and suit for a permanent injunction to enjoin him from using the canal followed.

This court granted the injunction and held that a canal built entirely on private property with private funds for private purposes is a private thing. White contended that a landowner was prohibited from obstructing any navigable waterway, regardless of whether it was constructed with private funds, by virtue of La. R.S. 14:97, as applied by the Supreme Court in Discon v. Saray, Inc., 262 La. 997, 265 So. 2d 765 (1972), and the Fourth Circuit in D'Albora v. Garcia, 144 So. 2d 911 (La. App. 4th Cir. 1962).

In *Discon*, landowners whose property bordered on a navigable canal dedicated for the use of the property owners sought to enjoin another landowner from obstructing a portion of the canal. The Supreme Court concluded that plaintiffs were entitled to injunctive relief under La. R.S. 14:97. In D'Albora an injunction was sought to enjoin the owner of land from restricting passage on a navigable canal running through his property. The canal was dug by the State of Louisiana to obtain dirt for the construction of a highway. The Fourth Circuit affirmed the action of the trial court in granting the injunction on the basis of La. R.S. 14:97.

We distinguished *Discon* and *D'Albora* in *Audubon* on the basis that the canals in those cases were either built with public funds or involved a dedicated right of way. We held that La. R.S. 14:97 was inapplicable to a private canal which was not part of the public domain or was not dedicated to the public use, stating the following:

We distinguish the *D'Albora* and *Discon* cases from the instant suit, because in each of those cases the canal was either a part of the public domain or it had been dedicated for use by the owners of property in the subdivision in which the canal was located.

We have concluded that R.S. 14:97 does not apply to a privately owned canal, even though it may be navigable. We agree with the views expressed by Professor A. N. Yiannopoulos, in discussing the case of Discon v. Saray, Inc., *supra*, where he stated:

> The majority opinion necessarily rests on the assumption that the canal in question was burdened with a servitude of public use. Indeed, it would be inconceivable to apply Article 97 of the Criminal Code to a strictly private waterway. The majority proceeded on the idea that this article was applicable because the canal was navigable, and, therefore, was burdened with a servitude of public use; in the alternative, that the canal was burdened with a servitude of public use by virtue of dedication. No one, however, should be prepared to accept the proposition that all navigable waterways in Louisiana are subject to public use merely by virtue of the fact they are navigable. A privately owned canal, though navigable in fact, may not be subject to public use, for the same reasons that a private road, though used by commercial traffic, may not be subject to public use. Thus, the disposition of the case would be correct only if the canal in question had been dedicated to public use. 302 So. 2d 660, 667-668.

We are convinced that the decision of National Audubon Society v. White was correct and apply it to this case. We hold that a canal on private property constructed and maintained with private funds and used for private purposes is a private canal subject to private control.

With regard to federal law, defendants have cited several federal cases for the proposition that under 33 U.S.C.A. Section 403, private individuals cannot control navigable waterways.

In any event, we fail to see how 33 U.S.C.A. Section 403 would forbid a landowner from prohibiting the general public from using his private canal. The statute grants authority to the Chief of Engineers and the Secretary of the Army to control waterways, but it does not grant individuals the unrestricted right to use a privately owned navigable canal.

If the public has no right of use on a natural waterway made navigable by private funds under federal law, then *a fortiori* it has no right of use on an artificial navigable waterway constructed with private funds.

Thus, under state and federal law a canal on private property constructed and maintained with private funds for private purposes is a private canal, the use of which can be restricted by the landowner or his assigns. The injunctions in these cases in favor of the landowner's lessee [were] proper.

For the above reasons we affirm the judgment of the District Court. All costs are to be assessed against the defendant-appellant.

NOTES AND QUESTION

1. In *Kaiser-Aetna v. United States*, 444 U.S. 164 (1979), the United States Supreme Court held that a navigable water body made by a private person on his land and with his own funds, either by excavation of fast lands or by dredging of non-navigable waters, is not subject to a federal navigation servitude. Having granted writs in the case of *Vermilion Corp. v. Vaughn, supra,* the United States Supreme Court held in this companion case that a navigable water body made by a private person on his land and with his own funds by the improvement or alteration of previously natural navigable waters is subject to a federal navigation servitude. Accordingly, the matter was remanded to the Louisiana court from which it originated for determination of the question whether Vermilion Corporation has improved or altered previously navigable waters. *Vermilion Corp. v. Vaughn*, 444 U.S. 206 (1979). On remand, the court of appeal for the third circuit affirmed its previous judgment on the ground that the alleged trespassers did not timely raise the defense that artificial canals diverted the waters or destroyed the navigability of surrounding naturally navigable public waterways. *Vermilion Corp. v. Vaughn*, 387 So. 2d 698 (La. App. 3d Cir. 1980).

2. In *Buckskin Hunting Club v. Bayard*, 868 So. 2d 266 (La. App. 3d Cir. 2004), the defendants argued for a servitude of public use on a man-made, privately owned canal system. They claimed that the plaintiff had destroyed the navigability of the natural waterways surrounding its system. Without finding that the plaintiff had done so, the court held that despite the importance of maintaining the navigability of natural waterways, their destruction by the private canal system would not create a right in the public to use privately owned canals at will for hunting. Can this decision be reconciled with the U.S. Supreme Court's instructions on remand in *Vermilion*?

3. Can the public acquire by acquisitive prescription a navigational servitude over a private canal? Now we may find out. In *People for Open Waters, Inc. v. Estate of Gray*, 643 So. 2d 415 (La. App. 3d Cir. 1994), the court held that plaintiffs did not acquire a servitude of passage by the acquisitive prescription of thirty years because such a servitude could not be acquired by prescription prior to the 1977 revision of Title IV, Book II of the Louisiana Civil Code, and thirty years had not elapsed since the revision.

6. PATENTS CONVEYING NAVIGABLE WATER BOTTOMS

A. N. YIANNOPOULOS, CIVIL LAW PROPERTY
§§ 66-67 (4th ed. 2001)
(footnotes omitted)

§ 66. Principle of Inalienability

It has been a well-established general proposition of Louisiana property law that the beds or bottoms of navigable water bodies are public things, inalienable by the state and insusceptible of private ownership. Functionally, the state ownership of public things corresponds clearly with the common law notion of a public trust for the benefit of future generations. Yet, in Louisiana's past, an involved legislative action and judicial interpretation resulted in the recognition of private ownership over certain navigable water bottoms and parts of the sea and its shores despite the provisions of the Civil Code that have always designated such things as insusceptible of private ownership.

Originally, the prohibition against the alienation by the state of its navigable water bottoms was grounded on the interpretation of Articles 449, 450, and 453 of the Louisiana Civil Code of 1870. The first direct legislative prohibition of alienation of state-owned water bottoms is found in Act No. 106 of 1886 which declared that the state owned all waters adjoining the Gulf of Mexico and that the public ownership of these waters should be continued and maintained. Subsequently, the prohibition against alienation was fortified by the judicial doctrine of "inherent sovereignty" and by the adoption of a constitutional provision in 1921 which prohibited alienation of the "bed of any navigable stream, lake or other body of water, except for purposes of reclamation."

In the meanwhile, however, the United States had conveyed to Louisiana by the Swamp Land Acts of 1849 and 1850 "swamp lands subject to overflow" that were unfit for cultivation. In contrast with navigable water bottoms and the sea and its shores, these lands were susceptible of private ownership and could be conveyed to private persons. By a series of legislative acts, commencing with Act No. 247 of 1855, the Louisiana legislature authorized the alienation of shallow non-navigable lakes and swamp lands that the state had acquired from the United States under the Swamp Land Grant Acts. Further, Act No. 124 of 1862 assimilated dried up navigable lakes to swamp lands and removed the prohibition against the alienation of such lands. Congress made no reference in either the Act of 1849 or in the Act of 1850 to "tidal" overflow. Yet, by Act No. 75 of 1880, the Louisiana legislature authorized the sale by the state of "sea marsh or prairie, subject to tidal overflow." This Act was destined to create confusion as it seemed to obliterate the difference between lands "subject to the ebb and flow of the tide" that Louisiana acquired from the United States under the equal footing doctrine, and "swamp lands subject to overflow" that Louisiana acquired from the United States under the Swamp Land Grant Acts.

Under the authority of these statutes, the state issued patents purporting to convey to private persons and to public bodies, such as levee boards, large areas that occasionally included navigable water bottoms or lands subject to the ebb and flow of the tide. The patents did not reserve to the state the ownership of such water bottoms and, consequently, a question arose as to their validity.

§ 67. The Repose Statute: Act 62 of 1912

In order to promote security of title, the Louisiana legislature passed Act 62 of 1912, a repose statute. This Act declared: "All suits or proceedings of the State of Louisiana, private corporations, partnerships or persons to vacate and annul any patent issued by the State of Louisiana, duly signed by Governor of the State and the Register of the State Land Office, and of record in the State Land Office on any transfer of property by any subdivision of the state, shall be brought within six years from the passage of this act." The same act was reenacted in the Louisiana Revised Statutes of 1950 to read: "Actions, including those by the State of Louisiana, to annul any patent issued by the state, duly signed by the governor and the register of the state land office, and of record in the state land office, are prescribed by six years, reckoning from the day of the issuance of the patent."

On the basis of Act 62 of 1912, Louisiana courts held that patents which included beds of navigable waters without reserving title to them in the state were valid and no longer assailable. It is in this way that Louisiana arrived at private ownership of the bottoms of navigable waters.

At the time Act 62 of 1912 was enacted, Louisiana legislation prohibited alienation of navigable water bottoms to private interests. Question, therefore, arose whether the 1912 statute was intended to apply to all patents indiscriminately or only to patents that did not include the beds of navigable waters. Since it is clear that the Louisiana legislature could, due to the absence of constitutional prohibition at that time, authorize the sale of navigable waters, it is merely a problem of statutory interpretation whether Act 62 of 1912 intended to cure patents conveying only non-navigable water or both navigable and non-navigable waters. The majority view in the celebrated case of California Co. v. Price was that "the Legislature intended that the Act was to be all-inclusive, in conformity with the language used therein." A vigorous dissent indicated that "a reasonable construction of the statute would be that it only applies to property susceptible of ownership...." The reasoning of the majority opinion in the Price decision has been subjected to criticism on a variety of grounds. It is indeed a strained interpretation of a repose statute to maintain that it repealed by implication all prior legislation expressly prohibiting alienation of navigable waters and that it rendered valid patents that were absolute nullities at the time they were issued. As a prescriptive statute, Act 62 of 1912 is *stricti juris* and must be narrowly construed.

This view was adopted in Gulf Oil Corporation v. State Mineral Board, a landmark decision that overruled Price. The law is now clear: state patents conveying navigable water bottoms to private persons are absolute nullities, and, to that extent, they may not be cured by the repose statute of 1912.

In order to resolve authoritatively the question of the effect of patents conveying to private persons the beds of navigable water bodies, the Louisiana legislature enacted Act 727 of 1954. This act declares that the intent of the legislature at the time of enactment of Act 62 of 1912 was "to ratify and confirm only those patents which conveyed or purported to convey public land susceptible of private ownership," the alienation of which was authorized by law, but not patents which purported to "convey or transfer navigable waters and the beds of same." Any doubt as to the constitutionality of this act has been removed by the overruling of the Price decision.

NOTE

For the ownership of inland non-navigable water bottoms, see La. R.S. 9:1115.2, *supra.*

CHAPTER III. MOVABLES AND IMMOVABLES; CORPOREALS AND INCORPOREALS
Civil Code arts. 462-475

1. IMMOVABLES

a. Tracts of Land and Their Component Parts
Civil Code arts. 462-469, 472

A. N. YIANNOPOULOS, CIVIL LAW PROPERTY
§§ 114-115 (4th ed. 2001)
(Footnotes omitted)

§ 114. Tracts of Lands

Tracts of land, namely, portions of the surface of the earth individualized by boundaries, are immovables par excellence....

§ 115. Component Parts of Tracts of Land

Tracts of land are not empty space; they contain organic as well as inorganic substances, such as soil, minerals, vegetation, and buildings or other constructions permanently attached to the ground. In systems of the French family, such things are considered to be parts of an immovable by nature, unless owned by a person other than the owner of the ground. In central European systems, and in Louisiana, civil code provisions deal specifically with component parts of tracts of land. In common law jurisdictions, fixtures and vegeta[tion] are treated either as chattels or as part of realty.

According to Article 463 of the Louisiana Civil Code, buildings, other constructions permanently attached to the ground, standing timber, and unharvested crops or ungathered fruits of trees are component parts of a tract of land when they belong to the owner of the ground. Buildings and standing timber are *separate immovables* when they belong to a person other than the owner of the ground; in contrast, other constructions and crops are *movables* when they belong to a person other than the landowner.

Articles 465 through 467 of the Louisiana Civil Code deal with the status of things incorporated in, or attached to, another thing. Article 465 declares that things incorporated into a tract of land, a building, or other construction "so as to become an integral part of it, such as building materials, are its component parts." Thus, anything that has merged with a tract of land, or with a building or other construction belonging to the owner of the ground, is a component part of the tract of land. Article 466 declares that things permanently attached to a building or other construction, such as plumbing, heating, cooling, electrical or other installations, are its component parts. This provision seems to deal specifically with component parts of buildings or other constructions; however, such component parts are also component parts of a tract of land when a building or other construction belongs to the owner of the ground.

NOTE

The Louisiana legislature made extensive changes to Article 466 during the 2008 regular session. See the notes in subsection iii, *infra*.

LANDRY v. LeBLANC
416 So. 2d 247 (La. App. 3d Cir. 1982)

DOUCET, J. Plaintiff-lessor brought suit to recover damages allegedly occasioned by defendant-lessee's removal of topsoil from the leased premises. Defendant asserted plaintiff's agent had authorized him to remove and haul away the soil, and presented parol evidence in support thereof, over plaintiff's objection, which was admitted. The trial judge held that lessor had not sustained her burden of proof and dismissed plaintiff's demands. Plaintiff appeals. We reverse.

The parties entered into a verbal farm lease for 8 1/2 acres in 1976. The lessee, Adley LeBlanc, maintained the farm lease for the first year and the lease was thereafter verbally renewed for 1977 and 1978. Immediately after the third renewal period commenced, on or about April 1, 1978, lessee made arrangements with R.J. Thibodeaux Shell Yard, Inc. to remove the headland comprising the southeast portion of the property allegedly without lessor's permission. Thereafter, the lessor, Adelaide L. Landry, notified the lessee that the lease would not be renewed. Lessor additionally requested that the land be returned to its original condition by replacing the soil which had been removed earlier that year. Suit followed wherein the lessor claimed lessee's failure to return the property to its original condition resulted in damage to the property consisting of [the] cost of returning the property to its original condition. The lessee filed an exception of prescription which was overruled. At trial on the merits, the lessee claimed that he received permission to remove the soil from one Lucien Landry, brother of plaintiff and lessor's alleged agent. Tommy Thibodeaux, whose father owned property adjacent to plaintiff's, testified that he excavated the unplowed land at the end of the plowed furrow on the leased premises at defendant's request and that the removal thereof improved the drainage of both fields. Plaintiff denied any authorization to alter the property.

The trial judge was of the opinion that the lessor failed in her burden of proof and rendered judgment in favor of lessee. Plaintiff-lessor appeals alleging ... that the trial judge erred in admitting parol evidence relative to the alleged agent's authorization for defendant to remove the soil.

Defendant assert[ed] the affirmative defense of mandate, alleging plaintiff's brother, Lucien Landry, as agent of lessor, had granted authority for removal of the topsoil. ... The only matter seriously disputed is whether lessee's removal of the soil was authorized. Thus resolution of the dispute turns on whether defendant established the affirmative defense of mandate.

Topsoil is immovable as tracts of land with their component parts are immovables. C.C. art. 462. Comment (c) to art. 462 provides: "Lands may be defined as portions of the surface of the earth. The ownership of land carries, by accession, the ownership of 'all that is directly above and under it.' C.C. art. 505 (1870)." Related thereto is the Louisiana Mineral Code Section listing substances to which the code applies: "The provisions of this Code are applicable to... rights to explore for or mine or remove from the land the soil itself...." R.S. 31:4. The right to minerals is an incorporeal immovable. R.S. 31:18. Thus, whether Civil Code or Mineral Code articles are applied, the result remains the same in that the interest asserted herein is to an immovable, *Cf.* R.S. 31:2. Plaintiff-owner's topsoil did not become movable by its placement in trucks to be hauled away.

As the property involved was immovable, any transfer of ownership thereto was required to be in writing. C.C. art. 2275 [Revised C.C. arts. 1839, 1832]. Indeed any dealing with realty, onerous or gratuitous, must be in writing unless the adverse party admits under oath that he made a contract affecting realty.... As there was no such admission under oath, the verbal sale of immovable property was null. That the parties admittedly had a preexisting lease agreement is of no consequence as the oral lease did not effect an ownership transfer of the immovable topsoil. In this regard it should be noted that we are not concerned with defendant's use of the immovable property per se, to which the parol evidence prohibition would not apply, but rather the transfer thereof. It is the rights to immovables acquired under a lease which cannot be established by parol evidence. [Citations omitted.]

Likewise, parol evidence could not be received to prove an agency to buy or sell immovable property. McKenzie v. Bacon, 40 La. Ann. 157, 4 So. 65 (1888). A contract to sell affecting title to immovable property is required to be in writing and any mandate authorizing Lucien Landry to dispose of such property must have been express, special, and also in writing. C.C. art. 2997 [Revised C.C. art. 2993] [Citation omitted]. None of the above formalities were followed. In fact, Lucien Landry testified at trial that he did not authorize lessee LeBlanc to remove the soil. The trial judge erred in admitting parol evidence concerning Landry's alleged mandate.

H1d18

Considering all admissible evidence we conclude that the trial judge was clearly wrong in finding plaintiff had failed to establish her claim by a preponderance of evidence. Accordingly we turn to the issue of damages. Clarence Thibodeaux, a civil engineer accepted as an expert in said field, estimated that 287 cubic yards of soil had been removed from the headland. According to Miller Lewis, Jr., who was accepted as a "dirt hauling" expert, the cost of a seven yard load, or truck full, of dirt was $59.20, and testified that forty (40) loads would be required to fill the excavation in question. Clarence Begnaud, a motor grader operator expert, testified that the cost to level the dirt is $100.00. Defendant offered no testimony to controvert these figures. Therefore we find that the sum required to return the property to its original condition [is] Two Thousand, Four Hundred Sixty-Eight ($2,468.00) dollars and hereby award plaintiff this sum as damages with legal interest from the date of judicial demand. Furthermore, we hereby assess expert witness fees as follows: Two Hundred ($200.00) Dollars to Clarence Thibodeaux, and One Hundred ($100.00) Dollars each to Messrs. Lewis and Begnaud. All costs, both at the trial level and on appeal, are taxed to Defendant-appellee.

NOTES AND QUESTION

1. For the meaning of *mandate*, the basis of Landry's defense, see La. Civ. Code art. 2989; see art. 1839 for the writing requirement for transfers of immovable property. Louisiana Civil Code art. 2993 provides that when the law prescribes a certain form for an act, a mandate authorizing the act must be in that form. Present Louisiana Civ. Code art. 1832 contains the rule prohibiting proof of a contract that is required by law to be in writing by means of testimony (parol evidence) or of presumption, except in a case in which the writing has been destroyed, lost, or stolen.

2. If the topsoil had been removed by someone authorized to do so, would it constitute a movable or an immovable? See La. Civ. Code art. 468 on de-immobilization and *Sales Tax Collector v. Westside Sand Co.*, 534 So. 2d 454 (La. App. 5th Cir. 1988), *writ denied*, Jan. 20, 1989 (sand pumped from the Mississippi River and sold became a corporeal movable on detachment and was therefore subject to the State and Parish sales taxes on movables).

i. Buildings
La. Civ. Code arts. 463-464

See A. N. YIANNOPOULOS, CIVIL LAW PROPERTY §§ 137-142 (4th ed. 2001)

P.H.A.C. SERVICES v. SEAWAYS INTERNATIONAL, INC.
403 So. 2d 1199 (La. 1981)

DIXON, C. J. This is a suit instituted by two unpaid subcontractors who supplied labor and materials for the construction of an offshore drilling platform living quarters unit; defendants are the general contractor and the owner. The primary issue is what, if any,

Issue What, if any, privileges are available to these plaintiffs. The unit involved in this litigation is a three story steel structure which was built on blocks at a construction site in St. Mary Parish. It was then transported by the owner, Pennzoil Company and Pennzoil Producing Company, and attached to an offshore drilling platform located in the Gulf of Mexico off the coast of Texas.

Pennzoil contracted with Seaways International, Inc. for construction of the unit. This contract was not recorded and no bond was required of Seaways as contractor. Seaways contracted with P.H.A.C. Services, Inc. for installation of plumbing, heating and air conditioning in the unit, and with Acoustical Spray Insulators, Inc. for labor and acoustical materials for the unit.

It is uncontested that P.H.A.C. and Acoustical performed their work in accordance with their subcontracts with Seaways, and that they have not been paid. They have timely filed lien affidavits, and have instituted suit to enforce their privileges.***

The Private Works Act, R.S. 9:4801 et seq., confers a privilege to certain persons who supply labor or materials "for the erection, construction, repair, or improvement of immovable property." R.S. 9:4801(A). The parties agree that the act applies if the living quarters unit is an immovable.

The Civil Code articles on the classification of things were recently amended. 1978 La. Acts, No. 728, amending the Civil Code of 1870 Articles 448-87. Because the revision became effective in 1979, and the operative facts leading to this litigation occurred in 1978, the rights of the parties are governed by the articles as they existed prior to the revision. Nonetheless, examination of the revision provides guidance and insight into a proper interpretation of the pre-amendment articles.

3 categories of immovables] The Civil Code of 1870 divided immovables into three categories: immovables by nature, immovables by destination and immovables by the object to which they are applied. C.C. of 1870 art. 463. The Code attempted to define immovables by nature as things which "can not move themselves or be removed from one place to another." C.C. of 1870 art. 462. This definition was followed by a listing of those things considered to be immovables by nature.

This definition was deleted from the Code by the 1978 revision, because, as explained by the revision's redactors:

> "This analytical scheme — definition and illustrations — contradicts reality. Contemporary mechanical means make possible the relocation of immense quantities of earth, timber, buildings, and various kinds of constructions. It appears, therefore, that immovability by nature under present Louisiana law is a legal fiction based partly on practical considerations and partly on inherent characteristics of things. In the light of contemporary conceptions the only immovables by nature are tracts of land, i.e., portions of the surface of the earth individualized by boundaries."

Exposé des Motifs of Act 728, 1978 La. Acts, Vol. 11, p. 1908.

Immovability is a legal concept and not merely an inherent quality of a thing. Whether a thing is classified as an immovable depends upon whether the legislature has accorded to that thing the preferred status of immovability. Immovability "in fact" is not itself a prerequisite to immovability "in law," and things regarded as immovables by the law might be moved through the application of extraordinary mechanical means. To determine whether this living quarters unit is an immovable by nature, the Code articles listing the things which are immovables by nature should be considered.

The 1870 Code classified as immovables by nature buildings and other constructions. Although the Code did not define these terms, it did provide that buildings and other constructions are immovables regardless of "whether they have their foundations in the soil." C.C. of 1870 art. 464. Integration with the soil was not a prerequisite to immovability under former Article 464, and the courts have properly classified as immovables things whose foundations rested upon blocks or posts. [Citations omitted.]

Nor did former Article 464 require unity of ownership as a prerequisite to immovability. Buildings and other constructions erected by persons other than the owner of the land are nonetheless immovables by nature under the 1870 Code. [Citations omitted.]

The 1978 revision effects several changes. Constructions other than buildings are now classified as movables unless they are component parts of a tract of land. To be a component part of a tract of land, a construction must meet two requirements: it must be permanently attached to the ground, and it must belong to the owner of the ground. C.C. 463, as amended by 1978 La. Acts, No. 728.

The 1978 legislation made no changes in the classification of buildings. Under the revision, buildings which belong to the owner of the ground are considered component parts of a tract of land, C.C. 463, as amended by 1978 La. Acts, No. 728, and, when there is no unity of ownership, the building is considered a separate immovable. C.C. 464, as amended by 1978 La. Acts, No. 728. Thus, under the revision, as under the 1870 Code, buildings are always classified as immovables.

The trial court concluded that the living quarters unit was not a building because it "was not being used as a building; rather it was set upon wooden blocks while it was under construction." The Court of Appeal reversed, correctly noting that there is no code requirement that a building have its foundation in the soil. Additionally, the trial court's reasoning would frustrate the purpose of the Private Works Act, which is to protect the claims of laborers and workmen. Many lien claimants perform work for the erection of new structures which naturally are not placed into use until completion. If classification must await actual use, then these lien claimants would find themselves unprotected by the act.

We agree with the conclusion of the Court of Appeal that this living quarters unit is a building. As the picture of the unit demonstrates, the facts speak eloquently for themselves. This is a three story high permanent steel structure with a helicopter landing pad constructed above it, built at a cost of over $400,000. It is designed to house offshore workers. Under prevailing notions, such a structure is a building and is therefore classified as an immovable.

Pennzoil maintains that the unit should not be classified as an immovable because the unit was intended to be moved offshore. The fact that the unit is capable of being moved by a powerful crane does not defeat classification of that thing as an immovable, for, as mentioned earlier, immovability is a legal concept and not an inherent quality of a thing.

Implicit in Pennzoil's position is the concept that classification of a thing as an immovable by nature is somehow contingent upon the owner's intentions. We do not believe the Code granted the owner such flexibility, nor do we believe that immovability by nature should hinge upon such a subjective factor as the owner's intentions. Such a contention may have been meritorious in connection with the 1870 Code's category of immovables by destination, but is not applicable to immovables by nature. As this court has previously explained:

> "There is a vast distinction between immovables by destination and immovables by nature. The status of an immovable by destination can be changed by an act of the landowner, but there is no provision of law that we are aware of, and none has been cited to that effect, that the act of the landowner, or any other person, can change the status of an immovable by nature....The status of an immovable by nature is never changed by any act of the owner, while the status of an immovable by destination changes according to its use by the owner....In the instant case, the status of the property could not be changed by the intention or act of the landowner because its status is fixed by law and does not depend upon its use."
> Buchler v. Fourroux, 193 La. at 477-78, 190 So. at 650-51.

The legislature has determined that a building is an immovable regardless of whether its foundation is integrated with the soil. This three story high permanent steel structure qualifies as a building and therefore is an immovable, and subject to the laws governing immovables. Consequently, the Private Works Act (including R.S. 9:4812) applies to this case. For the foregoing reasons, the judgment of the Court of Appeal is affirmed, at the cost of defendants.

ii. Other Constructions
La. Civ. Code arts. 463, 475

BAYOU FLEET PARTNERSHIP v. DRAVO BASIC MATERIALS CO.
106 F.3d 691 (5th Cir. 1997)

POLITZ, C.J. Bayou Fleet Partnership, plaintiff, and Dravo Basic Materials Company, Inc. and Dravo Corporation, defendants, both appeal a judgment against Dravo Basic for $25,000 in damages caused by Dravo's unauthorized removal of limestone working bases from Bayou Fleet's property. We conclude that under controlling provisions of the Louisiana Civil Code the limestone working bases were a component part of the immovable property belonging to Bayou Fleet. For the reasons assigned, we reverse and render judgment in favor of Bayou Fleet.

BACKGROUND

From 1989 to 1993, pursuant to an oral lease, Dravo operated an aggregate yard in Hahnville, Louisiana on a tract of Mississippi River batture property owned by Neal Clulee. Dravo established the aggregate yard to store, stockpile, and sell limestone extracted from quarries in Illinois and Kentucky and transported down the Mississippi River to the yard.

Dravo established three stockpiles of limestone on the Clulee property, each of which was placed on a foundation made from hardened limestone commonly called a "working base." The working bases were formed by putting a fabric liner on the batture and placing large quantities of loose, saleable limestone thereon until the weight compressed the batture and the limestone became compacted. Once formed, tons of loose limestone could be stored on the working bases.

On August 13, 1992, the Sheriff of St. Charles Parish seized the Clulee property and on January 27, 1993 sold it at a sheriff's sale. [Originally, the tract of land was sold to Louisiana Materials, Inc., but that company promptly sold it to the plaintiff.] Bayou Fleet acquired ownership and intended to continue to lease to Dravo or some other aggregate yard operator. Bayou Fleet and Dravo could not reach a lease agreement and Dravo determined to vacate the premises but did not do so until the weekend of March 6-8, 1993.

On March 6, 1993 Dravo began to remove the limestone from the property, utilizing a Cat 225 Excavator, a backhoe, a bulldozer, front-end loaders, and dump trucks. Over the weekend Dravo removed all of the loose stockpiles of limestone as well as the three working bases. In all, Dravo removed approximately 26,000 tons of limestone. On March 9, 1993 Bayou Fleet learned that Dravo had removed the stockpiles and the working bases.

Dravo filed a declaratory judgment action in state court seeking to be declared the owner of the limestone removed from the property. Bayou Fleet then filed this action for damages and removed Dravo's state court action to federal court. The two actions were consolidated and tried to the bench. The district court found that Dravo was entitled to remove a majority of the limestone in the working bases. Dravo was held liable, however, for the excavation of the portion of the working bases that had become a component part of the property. The court stated that Dravo's surreptitious removal of the limestone was "unusual and unbusinesslike," and it held Dravo liable for $25,000 in damages caused by its trespass on Bayou Fleet's property. Both Bayou Fleet and Dravo timely appealed.

ANALYSIS

The sole issue presented by this appeal is whether Dravo had the right to remove the limestone working bases and the loose stockpiles of limestone from Bayou Fleet's property. The resolution of this issue turns on the classification of the limestone as either movable or immovable under Louisiana property law. Findings of fact are upheld unless clearly erroneous. The classification of the limestone is a matter of law which we review *de novo*.

The Civil Code classifies things as either movable or immovable. An immovable is defined as a tract of land with its component parts. Article 463 of the Civil Code provides that component parts of a tract of land include, among other things, other constructions that are permanently attached to the ground. The Civil Code does not, however, specifically define what qualifies as an "other construction" under Article 463; that determination is left to the judiciary giving due consideration to prevailing societal notions.[1] Louisiana courts have found "other constructions" to include a cistern, corn mill, gas tank, barbed wire fence, outdoor advertising sign, and a railroad track. [Citations omitted.] We now conclude that the limestone working bases at issue herein can and properly should be classified under Article 463 as other constructions permanently attached to the ground.

In determining whether an object is an "other construction" within the meaning of Article 463, Louisiana courts generally rely on three criteria: the size of the structure, the degree of its integration or attachment to the soil, and its permanency. If there is a failure of any of these criteria, an object will not be deemed to be an immovable.[2]

The limestone working bases were massive in size. The volume of the limestone excavated by Dravo was 26,628.98 cubic yards and approximately 46,721.5 cubic yards of dirt would be required for fill to restore the land to its prior condition. The working

---

[1] *Bailey v. Kruithoff,* 280 So. 2d 262 (La. App. 1973); *Benoit v. Acadia Fuel & Oil Distributors, Inc.,* 315 So. 2d 842 (La. App.), *writ refused,* 320 So. 2d 550 (1975).

[2] *Bailey; Benoit; Telerent Leasing Corp. v. R & P Motels, Inc.,* 343 So. 2d 267 (La. App. 1977). Although these cases were decided prior to the 1978 revision of the Louisiana Civil Code, they remain relevant to the determination of what qualifies as an other construction under Article 463, a matter not addressed by the revision. A.N. Yiannopoulous, Property, Louisiana Civil Law Treatise, § 141, p. 311 (1991) [2001 ed. p. 318].

bases were capable of supporting the weight of tons of loose limestone, dump trucks, tractor-trailers, and other heavy equipment used in the operation of the aggregate yard.

The limestone working bases were attached firmly to the property. The weight of the limestone working bases compressed the batture property and, having done so, actually formed the surface level of the property. To remove the working bases Dravo had to dig them out of the ground, using heavy equipment, including a Cat 225 Excavator, to break loose the compacted limestone.

Finally, the limestone working bases achieved the necessary degree of permanency, having been placed on the Clulee property in 1989 and continuing thereon undisturbed until Dravo's action. In its regular course of business Dravo did not remove any of the limestone from the working bases; only loose limestone from the stockpiles on top of the working bases was sold to customers.

We conclude that the size, degree of attachment, and permanence of the limestone working bases, all combine to establish beyond peradventure that the limestone working bases of the aggregate yard were other constructions permanently attached to the ground within the intendment of Article 463. The loose stockpiles of limestone were not; nor do they qualify as an immovable under any other applicable provision of the Civil Code. Although the stockpiles were massive in size, they were neither attached to the ground nor permanent.

The classification of the working bases as other constructions does not, however, end our inquiry. The ownership of the working bases must be determined by reference to Civil Code articles concerning accession in relation to immovables.[3] Other constructions, such as the limestone working bases, may belong to a person other than the owner of the ground to which they are attached. They are presumed, however, to belong to the owner of the ground unless separate ownership is evidenced properly by a recorded document. Absent such a public recordation, another construction is considered to be a component part of the land and is transferred with it.[4]

Dravo was the original owner of the materials composing the working bases, but it recorded no evidence of its ownership. It could have protected its interest in the limestone working bases by recording its lease with Clulee. This was not done and Bayou Fleet acquired the immovable property free and clear of any claim Dravo may have had to the land or any constructions thereon.

Ownership of the working bases transferred to the purchaser at the sheriff's sale. Dravo had no right to remove the working bases and is thus liable for their reasonable replacement cost. Uncontroverted expert testimony in the record establishes that it would cost $263,222.22 to restore the property to its former condition. We therefore reverse the judgment of the district court and render judgment in favor of

---

[3] La. Civ. Code arts. 490-506.
[4] *See* La. Civ. Code art 491; Yiannopoulos, Property, § 141, p. 312 [2001 ed. p. 320].

Bayou Fleet and against Dravo Basic Materials Company, Inc. and Dravo Corporation in that amount. We defer to the district court on the matter of interest and return this matter for entry of an appropriate judgment.

NOTES AND QUESTIONS

1. After concluding that the limestone working bases were other constructions permanently attached to the ground, the court turned to the principles of *accession* to determine their ownership. Accession is the concept that, in the absence of other law, "the ownership of a tract of land carries with it the ownership of everything that is directly above or underneath it." See La. Civ. Code art. 490.

2. The presumption that appears in La. Civ. Code art. 491 is interpreted by the *Bayou Fleet* court as rebuttable only by a recordation of separate ownership of the items in controversy prior to sale to a third party of the immovable to which they are attached. The jurisprudence has consistently interpreted article 491 in this way, despite the fact that the wording of the article does not explicitly state that the presumption can *only* be overcome by such recordation; see the footnotes in Yiannopoulos' commentary cited by the court in footnote 14. Whose interests would be negatively affected if the courts permitted introduction of other evidence of separate ownership, and whose would be favored? What policies underlie limiting the rebuttal of the presumption to this one method?

iii. Component Parts of Buildings and Other Constructions
La. Civ. Code arts. 465-467

NOTE
Millenial Fever: Recent Changes in the Law
of Component Parts of Immovables

From 1999 through July, 2008, the Louisiana property law community witnessed an unprecedented furor over the proper interpretation of Civil Code article 466. This article, innocuously titled "Component parts of a building or other construction," inspired literary analysis by the federal bench,[5] an oblique response and explanatory footnote from the Louisiana Supreme Court,[6] a flurry of law review commentaries,[7] a Louisiana Supreme Court decision overruling its earlier explanation,[8] three dissents to that aspect of the decision,[9] two

---

[5] See Prytania Park Hotel v. General Star Indemnity, 179 F.3d 169, 180-183 (5th Cir. 1999).
[6] See Showboat Star Partnership v. Slaughter, 789 So. 2d 554, 558n.4 (La. 2001).
[7] See, e.g., A.N. Yiannopoulos, *Of Immovables, Component Parts, Societal Expectations, and the Forehead of Zeus*, 60 LA. L. REV. 1379 (2000); John A. Lovett, *Another Great Debate? The Ambiguous Relationship between the Revised Civil Code and Pre-revision Jurisprudence as Seen through the Prytania Park Controversy*, 48 LOY. L. REV. 615 (2002).
[8] Willis-Knighton Medical Center v. Caddo-Shreveport Sales and Use Tax Commission, 903 So. 2d 1071, 1092 (La. 2005).

revisions of the article within two years,[10] a further flurry of law review commentaries,[11] followed by a further revision made by the Legislature during the 2008 regular session.[12] The eye of the storm was the "societal expectations test" of a component part, formerly codified as "prevailing notions in society."

Historical context of the debate: Three articles in the present-day Code describe the circumstances under which a movable becomes subject to the laws governing immovables by becoming a component part of an immovable. Article 465 gives component part status to a thing that is so completely incorporated into an immovable that it becomes an "integral part of it." Our present concern, article 466, identifies things permanently attached to a building or to an immovable other construction as component parts of the immovable. Article 467 makes component parts of things that fulfill certain characteristics of place, ownership, and use, and that are declared in the public records to be component parts of an immovable by its owner.

In the Civil Code of 1870, the situations corresponding to those in present article 466 had appeared in articles 467 through 469. Article 467 and 468 employed the French Code's terminology of "immovables by nature" and "immovables by destination," describing attachment of listed items "for the use or convenience of the building" (nature) or "attached permanently" by the owner (destination). Article 469 employed a test of injury to the immovable or to the attached former movable. Jurisprudence under the 1870 Code's version of article 466 dealt with such important interpretive issues as whether the list of specific immovables by nature in article 467 was illustrative, and whether the method of "attachment" described in article 469 was exclusive, or was supplemented by article 468.

The list in article 467 was found to be illustrative in a number of cases in the early twentieth century; ultimately, the societal expectations test was introduced to provide an objective standard where the thing attached was non-enumerated, and the parties' intentions not specified. The cases on the exclusivity of the method of attachment in article 469 were inconsistent, but some cases held that in the absence of that method (which was the injury test described above), article 468 justified a finding of permanent attachment using evidence of owner intent and of ease of removal.

The 1978 revision of Book II, "Things," resulted in the combination of the 1870 Code's arts. 467 – 469 into a single article on immobilization by attachment, article 466, which then read:

> Things permanently attached to a building or other construction, such as plumbing, heating, cooling, electrical or other installations, are its component parts.

> Things are considered permanently attached if they cannot be removed without substantial damage to themselves or to the immovable to which they are attached.

---

[9] See id. at pp. 1097 (Kimball, J., concurring and dissenting); 1101 (Johnson, J., concurring and dissenting); 1102 (Knoll, J., concurring only in the result). All three justices dissented from the rejection of the societal expectations test

[10] See Acts 2005, No. 301, sec. 1 (eff. June 29, 2005); Acts 2006, No. 765, sec. 1.

[11] See, e.g., Elizabeth Ruth Carter, *Comment: Ghosts of the Past and Hopes for the Future: Article 466 and Societal Expectations*, 81 TUL. L. REV. 1665 (2007); Katie Drell Grissel, *Comment: The Legal Fiction of the "Clear Text" in Willis-Knighton v. Caddo-Shreveport Sales and Use Tax Comm'n.*, 67 LA. L. REV. 523 (2007).

[12] See Act 632 *supra.*

While the revision sought to abrogate articles 467 and 468 of 1870, with their French categories, the Comments make clear the intent to reproduce the substance of article 469, thus preserving the relevance of interpretive jurisprudence.[13]

Jurisprudence after the revision, like jurisprudence before it, recognized the possibility that the classification of a thing as a component part by virtue of attachment to a building might require examination of conceptions prevailing in society to determine its status. The most influential case in the post-revision jurisprudence was *Equibank v. I.R.S.*, 749 F.2d 1176 (5th Cir. 1985), which follows.

EQUIBANK v. UNITED STATES INTERNAL REVENUE SERVICE
749 F. 2d 1176 (5th Cir. 1985)

POLITZ, C.J. Equibank appeals the denial of a petition for injunction against the Internal Revenue Service, which removed certain chandeliers from a house subject to an Equibank mortgage. Concluding that under controlling provisions of the Louisiana Civil Code the chandeliers are component parts of the house and, as such, are subject to the priming mortgage of Equibank, we reverse.

FACTS

Norman L. Johnson and Gayfred Dorothea McNabb Johnson owned a fine home, appropriately called a mansion, on St. Charles Avenue in New Orleans, Louisiana. Equibank held a mortgage in favor of Hibernia National Bank. The Johnsons defaulted on the mortgages and failed to pay their income taxes. The IRS made jeopardy assessments, secured a lien and served notices of levy and seizure of the residence. Hibernia brought a foreclosure action and Equibank intervened. The Louisiana state court ordered the foreclosure of both mortgages and the sale of the property to satisfy the mortgage indebtednesses. The mortgages primed the IRS lien.

Prior to the auction sale ordered by the court, with the consent of the Johnsons the IRS took physical possession of the residence. The house was valued at $3,000,000 and the contents had an approximate value of $1,500,000 at the time of the seizure. The interior house lighting included several valuable antique crystal chandeliers.

---

[13] Changes in the law in the 1978 revision of Art. 466 include: Suppression of the French terminology in favor of "component parts of an immovable"; ratcheting up the attachment required for immobilization to *permanent* attachment; suppression of old article 467's "use and convenience of the immovable" requirement; suppression of the old article 468's requirement of the unity of ownership for immovable and movable; replacement of the detailed illustrative list of old article 467 with a shorter illustrative list of categories of things that qualify as component parts of the immovable as a matter of law; replacement of the test of injury on removal that appeared in old article 468 with a broader "substantial damage" test.

The IRS removed and stored the contents of the house, including the furniture, fixtures, appliances and decorations. The IRS took the chandeliers, some valued as high as $75,000, and other light fixtures. In order to remove these electrical units, it was necessary to disconnect the internal house wiring from the wiring of the chandeliers and other fixtures. This disconnect took place in electrical workboxes located inside the ceiling and within the walls. In addition, the bolts and other fasteners securing the chandeliers and fixtures were taken off and the units were lowered to the floor. Upon completion of the removal, the workboxes containing the internal house wiring were exposed along with the holes made by the securing connectors. Persons effecting the safe removal had to have sufficient knowledge of electricity and electrical wiring to separate the internal wires from the unit wires without risking harm to the worker, or damage to the house and fixtures by the touching of exposed wires or the "shorting-out" of the circuitry. This type of removal is not comparable to the simple and ordinary unplugging of a lamp or other electrical appliance from a wall socket. The latter requires little knowledge of the mysteries and vagaries of electricity, and involves minimal risk absent abuse.

Equibank filed a state court injunctive action seeking the return of the chandeliers. The IRS removed the suit to federal court. After hearing the district court denied the injunction requested, based on a finding that the chandeliers were not component parts of the residence and were thus not covered by Equibank's mortgage.

ANALYSIS

Whether the chandeliers were component parts of the Johnson residence or separate movables depends upon the interpretation of articles in the 1978 revision of Book 2 of the Louisiana Civil Code. As is usually the case in civilian interpretative methodology, several articles are to be considered *in pari materia* but the critical code provision is Article 466. . . .

Professor A. N. Yiannopoulos, the official reporter for the Louisiana State Law Institute's revision of Book 2 of the Civil Code, called as an expert witness by the IRS, gave testimony about the history of the revision of those articles and of his opinion as to their meaning, with particular emphasis on Article 466. The professor was of the opinion that under Article 466 items are component parts of a building or other construction: (1) if they fit within one of the categories listed in the first paragraph of the article, in which event they are considered permanently attached as a matter of law, or (2) if they are actually permanently attached as described in the second paragraph. He stated:

> The first paragraph considers, or meant to consider these things as component parts as a matter of law as to which the test of permanent attachment would be immaterial. *** I would consider these things as a matter of law being component parts...you do not need to worry about the test of damage to themselves or to the building as to things covered by 466, first paragraph. These are component parts even if their removal

would not cause damage to the building or to themselves.

To complete the discussion, the professor testified that the second paragraph of Article 466 covered items other than those listed in the first paragraph. A second paragraph item was to be considered a component part only if its removal occasioned substantial damage to itself or the immovable to which it was attached. Professor Yiannopoulos concluded by expressing his opinion that the chandeliers were not component parts of the Johnson residence, although he was of the view that an electrical hot water heater would be so classified. He explained the difference by referring to societal expectation:

> We are talking about [what] an ordinary man who purchases a house with ordinary prudence ought to know and ought to expect. We are talking about what ideas prevail in society today with respect to an ordinary buyer of ordinary prudence. Or an ordinary mortgagor or an ordinary mortgagee of ordinary prudence. It is an objective test rather than a subjective test.

The Louisiana Legislature did not define or otherwise describe an electrical installation when it enacted Article 466 in 1978. We find no post-1978 jurisprudence addressing the issue. The Exposé des Motifs and history of the predecessor articles, however, lend some guidance to today's interpretative task.

Prior to the 1978 revisions to Book 2, Articles 467 and 469 governed the inquiry whether a particular item was a component part of a building. Former Article 467 declared that wire screens, water pipes, gas pipes, sewerage pipes, heating pipes, radiators, electric wires, electric and gas lighting fixtures, bathtubs, lavatories, closets, sinks, gasplants, meters and electric light plants, heating plants and furnaces were immovables when actually connected or attached to the building. Albert Tate, Jr., a civilian scholar, then an intermediate appellate court judge, later a justice of the Louisiana Supreme Court and now a member of this court, expressed the view that the 1912 Legislature amended Article 467, vastly expanding the items specifically covered, to overrule decisions of the Louisiana courts classifying items such as chandeliers as movable despite the fact that society considered such items integral parts of buildings. LaFleur v. Foret, 213 So. 2d 141 (La. App. 1968). The Exposé des Motifs notes the position of societal views in the determination of items which compose component parts of a building, observing that

> Lines of demarcation [between movables and immovables] are ordinarily drawn in accordance with prevailing ideas in society....In contemporary civil law, the distinction rests, in principle, on physical notions of mobility and on "inherent" characteristics of things.

Thus, the views of the public on which items are ordinarily regarded as part of a building must be considered in defining those items which the legislature meant to include within the term electrical installation. See also Yiannopoulos, Property, 2

Louisiana Civil Law Treatise § 22 (1980).

In this technological age many electrical units are designed for connection to the electrical power source by persons with little or no knowledge of electricity. This is accomplished by the simple expedient of inserting a male plug into a female socket. The electrical unit can be disconnected just as readily by simply pulling the plug out of the socket. Such items are legion: table and floor lamps, toasters, can openers, blenders, drills, soldering irons, mixers, knife sharpeners, radios, television sets, record players, stereo units, and on, and on *ad infinitum.* We are persuaded that these units, in the eyes of society, are movable; they are not electrical installations. They are not fixed in place. No special knowledge or expertise is needed to engage or disengage the electrical power source. They do not constitute component parts of the building or other construction in which they are found.

Other electrical units do not access the electric energy source through the plug arrangement but are "permanently" connected to the interior wiring of the building or other construction. The connection and disconnection from the power source poses a danger to the untutored or unskilled and requires knowledge of electricity and of electrical wiring. Such items include built-in stoves or ovens, wall and ceiling electric heaters, central heating and air conditioning, heat pumps, electrical hot water heaters, built-in public address and alarm systems, overhead fans, interior lighting, automatic garage door controls, and like electrical equipment. We are persuaded that these electrical units, from the societal viewpoint, are not movable; they are electrical installations which become a component part of the building or construction to which they are attached.

From the foregoing we conclude that a lamp which is simply plugged into a socket is a movable and may be removed from a residence without violating the mortgage, but an installed light fixture, be it an expensive, antique chandelier or a garden-variety fixture, becomes a component part of the building.

The ordinary view of society being a relevant consideration, we conclude our consideration by asking the near-rhetorical question, Does the average, ordinary, prudent person buying a home expect the light futures to be there when he or she arrives to take possession? Does that person expect the room to become illuminated when the light switch is thrown or should that person reasonably expect no response to the switch and, upon looking up, reasonably expect to see only a hole in the ceiling with the interior house wiring sticking out of the electrical workbox? In our view, the societal expectation is to have the lights go on. We therefore conclude that the Louisiana Legislature intended that the physically attached light fixtures were electrical installations and, as such, were component parts of the residence, thus respecting what "everybody knows" about which items "go with the house." See Simonett, "The Common Law of Morrison County," 49 ABAJ 203 (March 1963).

The chandeliers are electrical installations. They are component parts of the Johnson residence despite the fact that they could be removed without damage to the chandeliers or the residence. They are subject to Equibank's mortgage.

The judgment of the district court is reversed and the matter is remanded for entry of a judgment consistent herewith.

NOTE

In *Equibank*, the federal Fifth Circuit Court of Appeal, first, treated the two paragraphs of art. 466 as disjunctive, providing two mechanisms by which a thing might become a component part by virtue of attachment; and used "societal expectations" as a test of whether the legislature intended things—in this case, antique chandeliers—to be considered "electrical installations," and thus covered by the illustrative list of component parts. This interpretation of article 466 was consistently relied upon in subsequent decisions in Louisiana courts, such as the case below.

AMERICAN BANK & TRUST COMPANY v. SHEL-BOZE, INC.
527 So. 2d 1052 (La. App. 1st Cir. 1988)

COVINGTON, C.J. This is a devolutive appeal by plaintiff, American Bank & Trust Company, from a judgment in favor of defendants, Jenkins Tile Company, Inc., Shel-Boze, Inc., William J. Jenkins and Hugh A. Shelton, dismissing plaintiff's action at its costs.

Appellant, American Bank & Trust Company, (hereinafter referred to as "AmBank") is the holder of a number of promissory notes executed by A & M Builders, Inc. (A & M) and secured by collateral mortgages affecting two residential lots in Riverbend Subdivision, Fourth Filing, East Baton Rouge Parish, Louisiana. Financing was provided to A & M by AmBank for the construction of a single-family dwelling on each of the lots. In the course of the construction of these residences, A & M contracted with appellees, Shel-Boze, Inc. (Shel-Boze) and Jenkins Tile Company, Inc. (Jenkins Tile) respectively, for the purchase of and installation of light fixtures and related electrical paraphernalia, and carpeting. All of these items were installed in the residences constructed by A & M.

On November 10, 1985, after each of the residences had been substantially completed, A & M surrendered physical possession of the two residences in question to AmBank, because A & M was unable to meet its financial obligation to AmBank. A letter of surrender from the principal of A & M is in evidence. After the residences were substantially completed and ready for occupancy, and after AmBank had advanced funds to the owner to pay for the materials purchased from the defendants, representatives of Shel-Boze and Jenkins Tile went to the two residences and removed all of the items which had been sold and/or installed by them with the permission of A & M. Neither Shel-Boze nor Jenkins Tile received payment from A & M for the materials they supplied. Additionally, Jenkins Tile was not paid its installation charges.

A petition for foreclosure was filed by AmBank on November 22, 1985, in the 19th Judicial District Court. The record of that proceeding was introduced at trial as evidence. Pursuant to orders of the court, the subject lots and residences were seized and sold at sheriff's sale. By sheriff's deed recorded on July 22, 1986, the subject residences were purchased by AmBank. As shown at trial by the testimony of representatives of Stuart Distributors and Lacour's Carpet World, AmBank purchased light fixtures and related electrical paraphernalia and carpeting for the subject residences to replace those previously removed by Shel-Boze and Jenkins Tile. The cost of purchasing and installing these replacement items was introduced at trial.

AmBank filed suit against the corporate defendants, Shel-Boze and Jenkins Tile, and the individual defendants, Hugh Shelton and William Jenkins, asserting that the light fixtures and related electrical paraphernalia and the carpet all had become component parts of each of the respective residences upon installation, and each of these items thus became encumbered with the mortgages in favor of AmBank. The acts of defendants in removing the items from the residences allegedly caused substantial damage to the immovables at that time possessed by AmBank, and subject to their mortgages. (Originally, Dayton Heating and Air Conditioning, Inc. and Donald Levatino were also joined as party defendants, but AmBank settled its claims against them prior to trial).

AmBank claims that defendants are liable for the value of the various items removed by them from the two residences, together with the costs of reinstallation of said items.

The case was tried by bench trial on February 9, 1987. After trial, judgment was rendered in favor of the defendants, with the trial judge assigning oral reasons for judgment. It is that judgment by the trial court signed February 12, 1987, dismissing AmBank's demands against Shel-Boze, Jenkins Tile, Shelton and Jenkins which AmBank appeals. The case presents questions of law, rather than questions of fact. No conflicting testimony was presented at trial on the merits for the trial judge to resolve. We find that the trial judge erred in his conclusion that the light fixtures and other electrical paraphernalia removed by Shel-Boze, and the carpeting removed by Jenkins Tile had not become component parts of the residences. Applicable law can be found in Louisiana Civil Code Article 466... An analysis of the application of this code article is found in the case of Equibank v. United States, Internal Revenue Service, 749 F.2d 1176 (5th Cir. 1985).***

As to the liability of Shel-Boze, in the instant matter, we find that the *Equibank* is directly on point. The testimony of Hugh Shelton, President of Shel-Boze, establishes the fact that all fixtures removed by him were wired-in as opposed to things one plugs in, such as a floor lamp, or other movable electrical appliances.

The *Equibank* case may also be applied by analogy, to include the carpeting which was installed, and then subsequently removed by Jenkins Tile. Undoubtedly, a reasonable person buying a residence expects finished flooring to be there when he or she takes possession. The societal expectation is to have finished flooring, such as carpeting.

The testimony of William J. Jenkins, President of Jenkins Tile Company, Inc., shows that the carpet was completely installed in the residences, and as far as the carpet installation was concerned, the houses were ready for occupancy.

A review of the evidence leads us to the conclusion that the light fixtures, other electrical paraphernalia and carpeting had become component parts of the two residences in question prior to their removal by Shel-Boze and Jenkins Tile, respectively. We further find that the trial judge erred in his conclusion that the mortgages in favor of AmBank did not perfect, from the date of recordation of the mortgages, a security interest in the component parts of the two residences.

Applicable to the issue at hand are Louisiana Civil Code Articles 462, 463, 469 and La.R.S. 9:2721, which provide as follows:

> Article 462: Tracts of land, with their component parts, are immovables.

> Article 463: Buildings, other constructions permanently attached to the ground, standing timber, and unharvested crops or ungathered fruits of trees, are component parts of a tract of land when they belong to the owner of the ground.

> Article 469: The transfer or encumbrance of an immovable includes its component parts.

> La.R.S. 9:2721: No sale, contract, counter letter, lien, mortgage, judgment, surface lease, oil, gas or mineral lease or other instrument or writing relating to or affecting immovable property shall be binding on or affect third persons or third parties unless and until filed for registry in the office of the parish recorder of the parish where the land or immovable is situated; and neither secret claims or equities nor other matters outside the public records shall be binding on or affect such third parties.

By reading Articles 462, 463 and 469 *in pari materia*, it is clear that residences, such as the ones at issue, built on concrete slabs, are classified as immovables. Moreover, according to Article 469, an encumbrance of an immovable, such as a mortgage on a building, includes the encumbrance of its component parts.

In order to finance the construction of the property in question, the owner-contractor entered into two separate collateral mortgage agreements with AmBank. The mortgages provided for a security interest in the two lots, together with all the buildings and improvements thereon. All of the necessary exhibits to establish the indebtedness of the owner of the property to AmBank were introduced at trial, as well as all exhibits and testimony necessary to perfect AmBank's mortgage. In applying Civil Code Article 469 to these facts, we conclude that the mortgages also encumbered the component parts of the two residences. Additionally, according to La.R.S. 9:2721, the security interest in the component parts of the two residences, perfected by the mortgage agreements entered into between the owner and AmBank, became effective as to third parties from the time the mortgages were filed for recordation in the office of the recorder of mortgages in East Baton Rouge Parish. Certified copies of the mortgages were introduced into evidence. These documents establish that the date of recordation was May 7, 1985, which is a date before construction began.

We find that the trial judge was in error in holding that November 22, 1985, the date the foreclosure proceeding was filed by AmBank, was the operative date when AmBank acquired a security interest in the property, including the electrical fixtures and carpet. This ruling fails to consider Articles 462, 463, 469 and La.R.S. 9:2721, and must be reversed. Mortgages rank from the date of their filing for recordation, not the date when a foreclosure is filed.

We further find that the trial judge erred in his failure to award a money judgment against the defendants for the cost of replacing the items which were removed from the residences by the defendants.

Just as the plaintiff in Equibank v. United States, *supra*, AmBank sued initially for injunctive relief herein. Later, believing that most, if not all, of the items removed from the property had been disposed of by the defendants, AmBank amended its petition to seek a money judgment against the defendants for the value of the fixtures removed, plus the cost of reinstallation.

The evidence presented at trial clearly establishes the measure of Am-Bank's damage. With respect to the carpet, W.E. Williams, Jr., an officer of AmBank, who for five years managed and dealt with all real estate owned by AmBank, testified that the removed carpet was replaced with carpet of a similar grade and in keeping with the general style and value of homes in the neighborhood. His testimony was supported by the testimony of Verien Flaherty of Lacour's Carpet World, who supplied and installed the replacement carpet. The new carpet cost AmBank $4,275.40.

With regard to the light and other electrical fixtures, Williams testified that the fixtures removed and the replacement fixtures were of similar quality and in keeping with the style and quality one would expect in a home in Riverbend Subdivision. This was corroborated by the testimony of John Stuart of Stuart Distributors, who supplied the replacement fixtures at a cost of $2,330.57. Included in these replacement fixtures were ceiling fans which were not in the houses previously. These ceiling fans cost approximately $500.00. Hence, the net cost of the replacement fixtures amounted to $1,830.57.

Williams hired Cal Hamilton to install the fixtures. He was paid $810.00 by AmBank to install the fixtures, including the ceiling fans. Hamilton testified that he would have charged $90.00 for installing the fans alone. Therefore, the net cost of installation was $720.00.

In summary, the damage claim proven by AmBank is as follows:

Carpet and installation	$4,275.40
Electric fixture	1,830.57
Electrical installation	720.00
Total	$6,825.97

For the foregoing reasons, we reverse the judgment appealed in part and affirm in part, and render judgment in favor of American Bank & Trust Company, as follows: 1. Judgment against Shel-Boze, Inc. in the full sum of $2,550.57; 2. Judgment against Jenkins Tile Company Inc. in the full sum of $4,275.40.

We affirm the judgments of dismissal against Hugh Shelton and William Jenkins. Costs of the trial are to be paid one-third each by AmBank, Shel-Boze and Jenkins Tile. Costs of this appeal are to be borne one-half by AmBank, one-fourth by Shel-Boze and one-fourth by Jenkins Tile.

NOTE

The appropriate tests to be applied in determining whether an attachment to an immovable qualified as a component part remained settled for more than a decade. However, in a 1999 case arising in Louisiana, the Federal Fifth Circuit offered its own interpretation of article 466, with results described by Professor Yiannopoulos in the following commentary from 2006.

A.N. Yiannopoulos, "On the Wake of *Prytania Park*"

In *Prytania Park Hotel, Ltd. v. Gen. Star Indemnity. Co.*, 179 F.3d 169 (5th Cir. 1999), the federal court questioned the reasoning of the *Equibank* decision. The question before the court was whether custom-made furniture attached to the walls of a hotel were component parts of the building or simply movable property. In applying article 466, the court questioned the appropriateness of using the societal expectations test in determining whether something is immovable under that article. However, it did not overrule *Equibank* and finally concluded that the furniture involved did not satisfy either the societal expectations test or the substantial damage standard of article 466. This decision spawned critical commentary and progeny. See Yiannopoulos, Of Immovables, Component Parts, Societal Expectations and the Forehead of Zeus, 60 La. L. Rev. 1379; Note 74, Tul. L. Rev. 1543 (2000); Note, 60 La. L. Rev. 947 (2000). For a lone defender of *Prytania Park*, see Lovett, Another Great Debate? The Ambiguous Relationship Between the Revised Civil Code and the Pre-Revision Jurisprudence as Seen Through the Prytania Park Controversy, 48 Loy. L. Rev. 615 (2002).

Neither federal nor Louisiana courts adopted the *Prytania Park* interpretation. In the case of *In Re Exxon v. Coker Fire*, 108 F.Supp. 628 (M.D. La. 2 d 2000), Chief

Judge Polozola adopted the disjunctive approach of *Equibank* instead of the conjunctive mandate of *Prytania Park*, and held that an elbow portion of a pipe spool in a Coker facility was a component part of an immovable. In a sensitive, sensible and scholarly opinion, the court reasoned:

It is clear the Court may find that the elbow falls within the first paragraph of article 466 even if it does not precisely fit within the plumbing category in article 466. It is also well established that the list in article 466 is merely illustrative of those things that may be component parts. Although the plumbing label may not apply under the facts of this case, the Court finds the "other installations" category is sufficiently broad to include the piping elbow involved in this case. ... Because the elbow qualifies as an "other installation," the Court now considers the requirements of the second paragraph of article 466. Under the second paragraph, things are considered permanently attached if "they cannot be removed without substantial damage to themselves or to the immovable to which they are attached." The question of whether removal damage is substantial is a fact-intensive determination which must be decided in the context of the case. Based on the facts of this case, including the numerous exhibits presented by the parties, the Court finds that substantial damage would occur to both the elbow and the East Coker device if the elbow were removed (footnotes omitted).

Subsequently, in *Showboat Star Partnership v. Slaughter,* 789 So. 2d at 558 (2001), the Louisiana Supreme Court stated: "[t]he judicial interpretations of Article 466 have not been consistent, but the courts generally have applied a societal expectations analysis." Recognizing the discrepancy in federal jurisprudence created by Prytania Park, the court in Showboat nevertheless validated the reasoning of Lafleur and Equibank regarding the relevance of societal expectations and the disjunctive nature of the two paragraphs of article 466.

Later, in the case of *In Re Exxon Corporation v. Foster Wheeler Corporation,* 805 So. 2d 432 (La. App. 1st Cir. 2002), under the same facts as in *Coker Fire, supra,* the court held in accord with the federal court that the elbow portion of the pipe spool in the coker facility was component part of an immovable. Relying on *Equibank v. United States, Internal Revenue Service,* 749 F.2d 1176 (5th Cir. 1985) and *Showboat Star Partnership v. Slaughter,* 789 So. 2d 554 (La. 2001), the court declared:

The reasoning in Lafleur and Equibank, regarding the relevance of societal expectations and the disjunctive nature of the two paragraphs of article 466, has been adopted in Louisiana state courts. See, e.g., Hyman v. Ross, 26,096 (La. App. 2d Cir. 9/21/94), 643 So. 2d 256; In re Chase Manhattan Leasing Corp., 626 So. 2d 433 (La.App. 4 Cir.1993), writ denied, 93-2943 (La.1/28/94), 630 So.2d 797; American Bank & Trust Co. v. Shel-Boze, Inc., 527 So.2d 1052 (La. App. 1st Cir. 1988), writ denied, 532 So. 2d 155 (La. 1988). Also, in Coulter v. Texaco, Inc., 117 F.3d 909 (5th Cir. 1997), the Fifth Circuit applied the Equibank test in determining whether a drilling rig was a component part of a drilling platform and, therefore, immovable property....

In the ill starred *Willis-Knighton Medical Center v. Caddo Shreveport Sales and Use Tax Comm'n.*, 903 So. 2d 1071 (La. 2005), a plurality of a deeply divided Louisiana Supreme Court overruled well-settled *jurisprudence constante* and opted for a novel interpretation of Article 466 of the Civil Code. The Louisiana Legislature acted swiftly and by Acts 2005, No. 301, effective June 29, 2005, amended article 466 and reinstated the interpretation of that article that Louisiana courts have been following for decades. Under pressure from the circumstances, the Louisiana Supreme Court declared in a *per curiam* opinion on rehearing that *Willis-Knighton* has prospective application only.

Art. 466. Component parts of a building or other construction

Things permanently attached to a building or other construction are its component parts.

Things such as plumbing, heating, cooling, electrical, or other installations are component parts of a building or other construction as a matter of law.

Other things are considered to be permanently attached to a building or other construction if they cannot be removed without substantial damage to themselves or to the building or other construction or if, according to prevailing notions in society, they are considered to be its component parts.

Acts 1978, No. 728, § 1, eff. Jan. 1, 1979. Amended by Acts 2005, No. 301, § 1, eff. June 29, 2005; Acts 2006, No. 765, § 1.

This is the...text of much maligned Article 466 of the Louisiana Civil Code, as amended by Acts 2006, No. 765. Contrary to the 2005 amendment that applies to *an immovable*, the 2006 amendment limits the application of Article 466 to a *building or other construction*.

Acts 2005, No. 765, acquired the force of law on August 15, 2006. However, Section 2 of Acts 2006, No. 765 declares: "The provisions of this Act shall have retroactive application to June 29, 2005." The constitutionality of this section is highly questionable. Indeed, application of the current text to transactions and facts involving immovable property that arose prior to August 15, 2006, is unconstitutional to the extent that it impairs the obligation of contracts or divests vested rights. Article I, § 23, of the Louisiana Constitution declares: "No bill of attainder, ex post facto law, or law impairing the obligation of contracts shall be enacted." Further, according to firm and well-settled Louisiana jurisprudence, laws impairing the obligation of contracts or divesting vested rights are unconstitutional. For discussion and citation of authorities, see Yiannopoulos, Civil Law System §§ 110 to 112 (2d ed. 1999; *id.*, Civil Law Property § 10 (2001)).

Article 466, as amended by Acts 2005, No. 301, § 1, effective June 29, 2005, provided:

Art. 466. Component parts of an immovable

Things permanently attached to an immovable are its component parts.

Things, such as plumbing, heating, cooling, electrical or other installations, are component parts of an immovable as a matter of law.

Other things are considered to be permanently attached to an immovable if they cannot be removed without substantial damage to themselves or to the immovable or if, according to prevailing notions in society, they are considered to be component parts of an immovable.

The 2005 amendment was a sequel to Willis-Knighton Medical Center v. Caddo Shreveport Sales and Use Tax Comm'n., 903 So. 2d 1071 (La. 2005). To ensure constitutionality, Section 2 of Acts 2005, No. 301 declares that "This Act shall apply to existing immovables and shall be used in any determination of whether a thing is a component part, *but no provision may be applied to divest already vested rights or to impair obligations of contracts*" (emphasis added).

Section 3 of Acts 2005, No. 301 declares that "Article 466 of the Louisiana Civil Code that governs the component parts of buildings and other constructions was enacted in 1978. It was drafted by the Property Committee of the Louisiana State Law Institute, was discussed and adopted by the Council of the Institute and was enacted into law as submitted to the Louisiana Legislature. The Reporter of the Institute's Committee (A.N. Yiannopoulos) has explained the scope, purpose, and function of the Article. See Yiannopoulos, Civil Law Property § 116.142 (4th ed. 2001). The two Paragraphs of Article 466 of the Louisiana Civil Code were presented to the Council of the Louisiana State Law Institute as two independent Articles and were so adopted. However, the provisions of Title I, Book II of the Louisiana Civil Code—Things, of which Article 466 is a part, were renumbered when submitted to the legislature and the two independent Articles governing component parts of buildings or other constructions become the two Paragraphs of Article 466.

According to legislative intent, the two Paragraphs of Article 466 contemplate distinct tests for the classification of things as component parts of building or other constructions. The things that are indicatively enumerated in the first Paragraph of Article 466 are component parts as a matter of law. All other things are considered to be permanently attached and, therefore, component parts of a building or other construction under the second Paragraph of Article 466 if they cannot be removed without substantial damage to themselves or to the immovable. Further, Louisiana courts have correctly superimposed on the two Paragraphs of Article 466 the realistic test of "societal expectations." Things attached to an immovable may be component parts of the immovable or may remain movables depending on societal expectations, namely, prevailing notions in society and economy concerning the status of those things.

Section 4 of Acts 2005, No. 301 declares that "This Act is intended to clarify and re-confirm interpretation of Louisiana Civil Code Article 466, including the "societal expectations" analysis, that prevailed prior to the decision in Willis-Knighton Medical Center v. Caddo Shreveport Sales, 903 So. 2d 1071, 2005 WL 737481 (La.) 2004-0473 (La. 4/1/05)."

Section 5 of Acts 2005, No. 301 declares that "[a]s provided by R.S. 24:175, the provisions of this Act are severable. If any Provision, Item or Section of this Act, or the application thereof, is held invalid, such invalidity shall not affect other Provisions, Items, Sections, or applications of this Act or applications of this Act which can be given effect without the invalid provision, Item, Section, or application."

NOTE

Millenial fever hadn't broken, however. On May 18, 2007, the Council of the Louisiana State Law Institute adopted two proposals, to be recommended to the Louisiana legislature in its 2008 session. In most respects, they are identical to the versions of article 466 and of article 508 contained in Act 632 of 2008, *supra*.

Why, despite the uncertainty created by another change in article 466 in the daily business of Louisiana banks and realtors, as well as in the affairs of ordinary home sellers and homebuyers, did the Law Institute propose yet another revision? While the Institute's motivation has never been fully explained—the Revision Comments reference a "fresh start" without explaining why such a start is necessary, or even desirable—a couple of possibilities suggest themselves. The societal expectations test incorporated into the 2006 version of article 466 in the term "prevailing notions" provided flexibility to the article. It avoided restricting courts to the absurdly narrow category of immovables through permanent attachment that resulted from the *Willis-Knighton* reading. However, without specific methods by which prevailing notions were to be gauged, the door was opened to inconsistency affecting a large number of property transactions. In addition, the proposal reflected an approach taken from the state Supreme Court's decision in *Showboat Star*: That the societal expectations test should be applied at a level of generality that ignores the particular use of the immovable. This argument had succeeded for the plaintiff in *Willis-Knighton* in the Louisiana Court of Appeal for the Second Circuit.[14] The first paragraph of the proposal, with its reference things that "serve to complete a building of the same general type, without regard to its specific use," echoed this argument.

The changes in language in the new version of Art. 466 are likely to increase the uncertainty in the law of component parts. A much broader array of movables have the potential to be categorized as component parts of an immovable because things merely "attached," rather than "permanently attached," to a building or to another immovable construction are candidates. The new language used to constrain the category is too vague and to furnish much guidance to attorneys and courts. For example, such new tests as whether the part "serves to complete a building," is "of the same general type, without regard to specific use," or "serves [the

---

[14] The state Supreme Court, while reaching the same result, rejected that argument.

building's] primary use" will require jurisprudential interpretation before those who find themselves relying on article 466 in litigation arising out of their transactions can feel confident that they understand their position. Mistaken expectations in both personal and commercial dealings are likely as the meanings are fleshed out over time. Meanwhile, time-honored certainties have vanished. For example, the classification of such things as electrical systems, historically regarded as component parts of buildings and other constructions, is now an ad hoc decision because the illustrative list, a feature of this area of the law since the 1870 Code, is expressed in non-mandatory terms: "Component parts of this kind *may* include...."

It is true that one rule cannot cover every contingency. However, the legislature ignored the sensible alternative of providing a default rule in the Civil Code for the ordinary and usual case; specific statutes could then be passed to deal with specialized situations. These wholesale changes in the law necessitate increased reliance on the judiciary, working on a case-by-case basis, with little doctrine to guide it. Unfortunately, unpredictability is the inevitable result. Even more unfortunately, this unpredictability will affect the interests of substantial numbers of Louisiana citizens—purchasers and sellers of immovable buildings (including residential real estate), banks and mortgage companies, which utilize immovables in secured transactions; and insurers of immovable property.

DELAGE LANDEN FINANCIAL SERVICES v. PERKINS ROWE ASSOC.
2011 WL 1337381 (U.S. Dist. Ct. M.D. La. 4/7/2011)

BRADY, J. This matter is before the Court on cross motions for summary judgment [by Plaintiff De Lage Landen Financial Services ("DeLage") and by Intervenors KeyBank National Association ("Keybank") and Jones Lang LaSalle Americas, Inc. ("JLLA").] This court's jurisdiction exists pursuant to 28 U.S.C. § 1332.

I. FACTS

This case arises out of the alleged failure of Defendants to pay Plaintiff DeLage for the construction an integrated security and informational System ("the System") for the Perkins Rowe Development ("the Development"), a mixed residential, retail and entertainment complex....The following facts are undisputed. On July 21, 2006, Defendants Perkins Rowe and Perkins Rowe Associates II, LLC, executed a mortgage ("the Mortgage") with KeyBank. Under the terms of the Mortgage, Keybank retained a security interest in "[a]ll buildings, structures, component parts, other constructions and improvements now located on or later to be constructed on the premises" *(Id.)*. The Mortgage was recorded with the Clerk of Court and Recorder of Mortgages of East Baton Rouge Parish on July 21, 2006.

On October 3, 2007, Perkins Rowe executed a master lease agreement ("the Lease") with Cisco Systems Capital Corporation ("Cisco") for the System. On November 20, 2007, a UCC–1 Financing Statement was filed and recorded covering the collateral described in the Lease, including the System's equipment. On or about December 11, 2007, Cisco assigned its rights under the Lease to DeLage, at which point DeLage began acquiring equipment, software and services necessary to complete and operate the System.

The System was to be installed for the purpose of controlling the Development's security, fire safety, lighting, music, etc., from a central location. The System is comprised of individual units which are bolted to large black racks which are themselves bolted to the floors of various buildings in the Development. The units' wires run throughout the walls and ceilings of the Development's buildings and through underground conduits in between buildings. Removing the system would require unbolting the units from the racks and pulling the wires from the holes through which they were connected to the individual units. If the System were to be removed, the security, fire safety, lighting, music, etc., would continue to function, but could not be centrally controlled. In addition, questions remain as to how much damage would result from removing the system.[1]

II. PROCEDURAL HISTORY

On November 19, 2009, DeLage filed suit against Defendants to recover the almost $1.5 million due under the October–2007 Lease. In its complaint, DeLage seeks to enforce its alleged security interest in the System under the Lease. On April 20, 2010, Keybank and JLLA intervened to protect their alleged security interest in the Development under the Mortgage. KeyBank asserts that the System is a component part of the Development, subject to the July–2006 Mortgage, and that its security interest is superior to DeLage's security interest under the Lease, which was perfected no earlier than October 2007.

On January 20, 2011, DeLage filed its Motion for Summary Judgment. DeLage asserts that its security interest under the Lease is superior to Intervenors' security interest under the Mortgage because the System is not a component part of the Development, and is therefore not covered by the Mortgage.

On January 20, 2011, Intervenors filed their Motion for Summary Judgment. Intervenors assert that (1) DLL's lease is not valid; (2) DLL's security interest under the lease is invalid because DLL failed to file a fixture filing; and (3) even if DeLage's lease is valid and its security interest is perfected, Intervenors' security interest is superior because the Mortgage encumbering the Development was filed before the Lease, and the System is a component part of the Development.

---

[1] Plaintiffs claim that removing the System would result in no "damage" other than exposing the holes where the units were bolted to the racks or the racks to the floor and exposing the holes where the wires connected to the individual units. Intervenors claim that (1) it is impossible to tell what wires are related to the System—and could be removed—and which are not; and (2) removing the System may also damage these other wires. However, because there are no "as built" drawings of the Development, Intervenors are not certain whether these "other" wires even exist and state that an electrician will need to be hired to determine their presence and/or location.

STANDARD OF REVIEW

A motion for summary judgment should be granted when the pleadings, depositions, answers to interrogatories, and admissions on file, together with the affidavits, show that there is no genuine issue as to any material fact and that the moving party is entitled to a judgment as a matter of law. Fed.R.Civ.P. 56(c)....

DISCUSSION

....Under Louisiana Law, an encumbrance on an immovable, such as a mortgage, includes the immovable's component parts. La. Civ.Code art. 469.... There are two tests for determining whether a particular thing is a component part [under] La. Civ.Code. art. 466. Under first test, "[t]hings that are attached to a building and that, according to prevailing usages, serve to complete a building of the same general type, without regard to its specific use, are its component parts." La. Civ.Code. art. 466. Under the second test, things are component parts if "they are attached to such a degree that they cannot be removed without substantial damage to themselves or to the building or other construction." La. Civ.Code. art. 466. The United States Court of Appeals for the Fifth Circuit has stated that items such as "central heating and air conditioning, ... built-in public address and alarm systems, ... interior, physically attached light fixtures, exterior lighting, ... and like electrical equipment" are component parts under Louisiana Law. *Equibank v. U.S. I.R.S.,* 749 F.2d 1176, 1179 (5th Cir.1985).

The Court finds that there are genuine issues of material fact. KeyBank's Mortgage granted a security interest in the debtor's "Property" which was defined as including the buildings comprising the Development and their component parts. The processes that the System centrally controlled can still be controlled without the System in place,[sic] however, Keybank has introduced evidence suggesting that doing so would be inappropriate and likely impracticable, especially with regards to lighting and fire safety. That is, the evidence suggests that such a System "completes" a large mixed-use complex "under prevailing usages." The Court finds that this testimony creates genuine issues of material fact as to whether the System is a component part under Louisiana Civil Code article 466.

The Court also finds that there are genuine issues of material fact as to whether removing the System would cause substantial damage to the System itself or the Development. Plaintiff states that removing the system would require nothing more than unbolting the individual units and pulling the wires from the ceilings, walls and conduits through which they run. According to Plaintiffs, the only "damage" that will occur is that the holes into which the units were bolted and through which the wires ran will be exposed. Intervenors claim that (1) it is impossible to tell what wires are related to the System—and could be removed—and which are not; and (2) removing the System may also damage these other wires. Because there are no "as built" drawings of where the various wires are located, Intervenors are not certain whether these "other" wires even exist and state that an electrician will need to be hired to determine their presence and/or location.

Because resolution of both parties' motions requires the Court to determine whether the System is a component part of the Development, the Court will DENY both Motions for Summary Judgment.

Disp Needs to lessens as Dis of Cat valves version

NOTE

Service One Cable TV v. Scottsdale Ins. Co., 2012 Westlaw 602209, is another post-revision case invoking art. 466. In it, the Louisiana 1st Circuit court of appeal applied art. 466 to a request by the plaintiff cable television company for summary judgment against the defendant, its commercial property insurer. Defendant insurer had denied coverage of damage by 2008's Hurricane Gustav to the 49-mile-long coaxial cable via which the cable company disseminated its programming to customers. The plaintiff claimed that the cable fell under the contract term designating "fixtures, including outdoor fixtures" of the insured building as a covered loss. The court looked to pre-revision jurisprudence to identify "fixture" in an insurance contract with an art. 466 "component part." Noting that "Courts applying Louisiana law have equated the term "fixture" with "component part," as used in the Louisiana Civil Code," the first circuit found that Service One had failed to show that it could meet its burden of proving that the coaxial cable was a component part, and thus a fixture. The plaintiff, the court said, offered no evidence that the cable was "permanently installed," (which would not necessarily make it a component part under the language of revised art. 466 in any event). The plaintiff also failed to offer evidence that removal of the coaxial cable line from the building would cause "substantial damage" to either the building or to the cable. The court did not consider paragraph 1 of art. 466, and given the restrictions in the first sentence of that paragraph, may have considered it unnecessary.

iv. Standing Timber and Crops
Civil Code arts. 463-464, 474, R.S. 9:3204

A. N. YIANNOPOULOS, CIVIL LAW PROPERTY
§ 133 (4th ed. 2001)
(footnotes omitted)

§ 133. Classification: Component Part or Separate Immovable

Under Article 465(1) of the Louisiana Civil Code of 1870, trees were immovables by nature as a part of the land to which they were attached. The provision was interpreted by Louisiana courts in the light of its source, and with reference to French doctrine and jurisprudence, to mean that standing timber was an inseparable component part of the ground. As in France, the landowner could sell standing timber as a movable by anticipation. The purchaser acquired the ownership of a movable, and his right was governed by the rules applicable to movable property.

The legal status of standing timber was altered in 1904. Act 188 of that year declared that "standing timber shall remain an immovable, and be subject to all the laws relating to immovables, even when separated in ownership from the land on which it stands." There has been some speculation as to the reasons that prompted this sweeping enactment. The most plausible explanation is that the Louisiana legislature, impressed with the value of standing timber which may by far exceed the value of land stripped of timber, sought to secure maximum protection for interests in this valuable natural resource. Application of the laws governing immovable property would enhance security of transaction and acquisition. Transfers would be subject to the requirements of written act and recordation, and real actions would become available for the protection of the ownership of standing timber. As a side effect, lumber companies would be encouraged to buy, and landowners to sell, standing timber alone rather than both the timber and the ground.

The 1978 revision of the Louisiana Civil Code has systematized the prior law. Standing timber is a component part of a tract of land when it belongs to the owner of the ground and a separate immovable when it belongs to another person. Fallen timber is movable property, whether it belongs to the owner of the ground or to another person.

Article 464 of the Louisiana Civil Code, as revised in 1978, permits horizontal division of timberlands into two separate immovables, the standing timber and the ground. When this happens, the timber ceases to be a component part of the ground and a sale or encumbrance of the land does not include standing timber, unless, of course, the owner of the timber fails to file for registry an instrument evidencing his ownership. Despite the segregation of standing timber from the ownership of the ground, a vendor of timberlands is liable for breach of warranty when he commits himself to convey both the ground and the standing timber.

The owner of segregated timber is owner of corporeal immovable property governed by the laws applicable to such property. Thus, separate ownership of standing timber may be asserted toward third persons only if it is evidenced by an instrument filed for registry in the appropriate public records; the owner of standing timber may convey his interest in accordance with the rules of form and substance governing immovable property; and he may protect his ownership by all sorts of personal and real actions. A sale of standing timber may be rescinded for lesion, and the purchaser may also claim redhibition or diminution of the price.

Standing timber may be segregated from the ground by an act translative of ownership, such as sale, donation, or exchange. A landowner may sell the standing timber or sell the land and reserve the timber.***

A. N. YIANNOPOULOS, CIVIL LAW PROPERTY
§§ 128-132 (4th ed. 2001)
(footnotes omitted)

§ 128. Classification: Component Parts or Movables by Anticipation

In Louisiana, growing crops are component parts of lands when they belong to the owner of the ground and movables by anticipation when they belong to another person. When encumbered with security rights of third persons, crops are movables by anticipation insofar as the creditor is concerned. Thus, standing crops are not necessarily a part of a tract of land.

Separate ownership of standing crops may derive from a variety of contractual relationships, such as lease of land, emphyteusis, or sale of standing crops. It may also derive from real rights on the land of another, such as usufruct or antichresis or even from the possession of land in good faith. The owner of the crops may always assert his rights against the owner of the land, but he may assert his ownership against third persons only if his interest is recorded. It is only in this way that purchasers of standing crops as well as lessees and their creditors are amply protected in case of transfer, mortgage, or seizure of the land.

§ 129. Transfer, Mortgage or Seizure of Land

The question of the status of crops as component parts of the ground arises typically in cases involving transfer, mortgage, or seizure of lands. In the absence of express contractual provisions concerning rights to crops, interested parties claim standing or even gathered crops as included in or excluded from, the transfer, mortgage, or seizure. As to gathered crops, however, the rule is clear: they are movables rather than a part of the ground; and, accordingly, they are not included by implication in either transfer or mortgage.

In cases involving transfer of lands, as by purchase at private or public sale, Louisiana courts have held that standing crops and ungathered fruits of trees are part of the ground and follow it, unless, of course, they belong to third persons as movables by anticipation. This is an application of the principal that no one can transfer a greater right than he himself has as well as of the rule that the transfer of immovable property does not include movables located thereon. Thus, when the ungathered crops and fruits of trees do not belong to the owner of the ground, a transfer of the land does not include these crops and fruits.

Like a sale or any other disposition of immovable property, the establishment of a real mortgage extends to standing crops and ungathered fruits or trees, unless they belong to a person other than the mortgage debtor. This is an application of the principle that no one can transfer a greater right then he himself has as well as of the rule that standing crops belonging to a person other than the landowner are movables by anticipation. Whether the standing crops belong to the landowner or to other persons is determined by application of the rules governing acquisition of ownership.

In the case of a seizure of lands by general creditors or by mortgage creditors of the landowner, standing crops and ungathered fruits of trees are included in the seizure as a part of the immovable only to the extent that they belong to the debtor.

§ 130. Transfer, Pledge, and Seizure of Growing Crops

The owner of growing crops, be he the landowner or another person, may sell, pledge, or otherwise dispose of his interest. Creditors of the owner of the growing crops may seize them separately from the land to which they are attached. Legislation applicable to crop pledges declares that a pledge must be recorded in order to be effective against third persons. In the absence of similar legislation applicable to transfers of growing crops, however, question may arise as to the requirement of recordation. A proper application of the doctrine of mobilization by anticipation ought to lead to the conclusion that recordation is not required. The Louisiana Supreme Court has declared, however, that a sale of growing crops by the landowner is the sale of immovable property; therefore, it is effective against third persons from the date of recordation. This rule should not apply to sales of growing crops made by persons other than the landowner, because the interest of these persons is an interest in movable property.

§ 131. Lessee's Crops

Question has arisen, in a variety of contexts, as to whether crops raised by a predial lessee belong to him or to the landowner. There has never been doubt that the lessee owns the crops that he has harvested in accordance with the terms of the lease. It was contended last century that standing crops were part of the immovable property and necessarily belonged to the lessor. This contention was considered in a number of cases, but it was definitely rejected by Louisiana courts. Today, standing crops are susceptible of separate ownership, namely, they may belong to a person other than the owner of the ground; and it is settled that a predial lessee owns growing crops as movables by anticipation.

The contract of lease gives rise to purely personal obligations. The lessor is bound by a personal obligation to deliver to the lessee the thing leased, and the lessee is likewise bound by a personal obligation to pay the rent to the lessor. This is clearly the case under the Civil Code, whether the price of the lease is fixed in a certain amount of money, in a certain amount of commodities, or in a portion of the fruits yielded by the leased property. The landowner does not own the growing crops, which are the fruits of the industry of the lessee, but he has a privilege for the payment of the rent.

The rules of the Civil Code, however, have been affected by special legislation. Act 211 of 1908, now R.S. 9:3204, declares: "In a lease of land for part of the crop, that part which the lessor is to receive is considered at all times the property of the lessor." Whereas under the Civil Code the lessee is owner of all crops and he is merely bound by a personal obligation to deliver to the landowner the rent in money, in a determinate amount of crops, or in a proportion of the crops, under R. S. 9:3204, the lessor is owner of his part of the crops at all times. This means that the lessor, as owner, has direct and immediate authority over his portion of the crops without the need of any delivery or payment by the lessee. Further, under the statute, the lessor is owner of his portion of the crops at all times, that is, when they are growing as well as after harvest. Argument might be made that the statute refers to the undivided part of the crops, but the avowed purpose of the act is to protect the lessor and its strong language attributes ownership to the lessor of a divided part of corporeal things, the crops themselves.

It is a critical question whether the lessee may assert his ownership of standing crops against the creditors of the landowner or against third acquirers of the land. In this respect, Louisiana courts have held that the separate ownership of standing crops may be asserted against creditors and transferees of the landowner only if the lease is recorded. The Louisiana Supreme Court has held that "an unrecorded lease of real estate has no effect as to third persons and seizing creditors." In this case the lessee lost his standing crops to a purchaser of the property because his lease was unrecorded. When the lease is recorded, however, the lessee is allowed to assert his ownership of the crops against both creditors of the landowner and purchasers of the land. In these circumstances, courts declare that standing crops are not a part of the land or that they are movables by anticipation.

§ 132. Crops of Other Persons

Not only lessees may own standing crops on the land of another; good faith possessors, purchasers of standing crops, and persons having a contractual or real right may also own crops on the land of another. When the separate ownership of these persons derives from a juridical act made by the owner, the act must be recorded in order to affect third persons. If, however, separate ownership of growing crops arises from acts of possession, recordation is not required. In all cases, the interests of these persons ought to be classified as an interest in movable property by application of the doctrine of mobilization by anticipation.

PORCHE v. BODIN
28 La. Ann. 761 (1876)

WYLY, J. Plaintiff leased in March, 1873, by act under private signature and duly recorded, sixty arpents of land, being part of the plantation purchased by Mrs. Emma Bodin from F. S. Goode, in June, 1868. Pending the lease, to wit: in August, 1873, the plantation was seized under foreclosure of the mortgage given to secure the purchase price, and it was sold in September following to the defendants, Bonvillain and Burguieres.

The purchasers claimed the corn crop standing the field leased to plaintiff, on the ground that the mortgage under which they purchased the property containing a non-alienation clause, the sale dissolved the lease, and the standing crop, being a part of the plantation, passed to them by the sale.

By the terms of the lease plaintiff was to give one fourth of the corn produced in payment of the rent. The contract of lease was mentioned in the mortgage certificate incorporated in the deed to the purchasers. Plaintiff sues to be decreed the owner of three fourths of the corn, and he enjoins the defendants from gathering and appropriating the corn.

Defendants, Bonvillain and Burguieres, caused the injunction to be released on bond for one thousand dollars. The court below gave judgment on the verdict of a jury, rejecting plaintiff's demand and dismissing his suit. Plaintiff appeals.

We think the court erred. If the sale under the foreclosure of the mortgage containing the non-alienation clause dissolved the lease, still this did not transfer to the purchasers the crop of corn, which was fully matured and ready to be gathered, and which did not belong to the mortgagor debtor. Indeed, the mortgage certificate read at the sale and copied in the deed to the purchasers shows that the corn belonged to plaintiff. The crop was made before there was a seizure. It was the property of plaintiff, less one fourth due for rent, and his title could not be divested in a proceeding to which he was not a party. By the sale the purchasers acquired the property of the mortgage debtor, and the lessee had the right to remove his property, whether in the field or in the houses, from the leased premises.

It is true, Article 465 of the Civil Code [Revised C.C. art. 463] says that standing crops are considered as immovable and as part of the land to which they are attached, and Article 466 [Repealed] declares that the fruits of an immovable gathered or produced whiie it is under seizure are considered as making part thereof, and inure to the benefit of the person making the seizure. But the evident meaning of these articles is, where the crops belong to the owner of the plantation, they form part of the immovable, and where it is seized, the fruits gathered or produced inure to the benefit of the seizing creditor.

A crop raised on leased premises in no sense forms part of the immovable. It belongs to the lessee, and may be sold by him, whether it be gathered or not, and it may be sold by his judgment creditors. If it necessarily forms part of the leased premises the result would be that it could not be sold under execution separate and apart from the land. If the lessee obtains supplies to make his crop, the factor's lien would not attach to the crop as a separate thing belonging to his debtor, but the land belonging to the lessor would be affected with the recorded privilege. The law cannot be construed so as to result in such absurd consequences.

Besides, the law, if literally construed, would only give the benefit of fruits gathered or produced during seizure to the seizing creditor. Here it is the purchasers who claim the benefit. The seizing creditor did not set up such a claim, either in the proceedings to foreclose the mortgage, or in the advertisement and sale. He took no proceeding contradictorily with plaintiff looking to the sale of the property of the latter. On the contrary, the evidence shows that the crop was not sold. Defendants should be satisfied to get what they purchased. They will not be permitted to despoil the plaintiff of the fruits of his industry or labor. No one should be permitted to enrich himself at the expense of another.

As the evidence fails to disclose the value of the corn belonging to plaintiff which has been taken and appropriated by defendants, the case must be remanded.

MORGAN, J., dissenting. On the twelfth of June, 1868, F. S. Goode sold a certain tract of land, cultivated as a plantation, to Mrs. Emma Bodin. The sale was made by public act, and was duly recorded. The terms of sale were notes, to secure which, special mortgage and vendor's privilege was reserved. The act of sale contained the pact *de non alienando*.

The act of sale was notice to all persons having dealings with regard to the property conveyed by it, who were charged with notice of the terms upon which it was sold and the encumbrances which existed upon it. When, therefore, the plaintiff leased a portion of the land, he knew what responsibilities he was incurring and what risk he ran. I consider him to be in the same position that his lessor was. The lease was, in my opinion, a violation of the pact, and could not, therefore, affect the conditions of the sale or the condition of the property, and when the defendants purchased it they did so without any regard to the lease or the rights of the lessee as between the lessor and the lessee. When they acquired the land they became the owners of everything which was growing thereon.

b. Immovables by Their Object

See A. N. YIANNOPOULOS, CIVIL LAW PROPERTY
§§ 145-147 (3d ed. 2001)

A. N. YIANNOPOULOS, CIVIL LAW PROPERTY
§ 236 (4th ed. 2001)
(footnotes omitted)

The right of ownership confers on a person direct, immediate, and exclusive authority over a thing. The owner may use, enjoy, manage and dispose of the thing he owns within the limits and under the conditions established by law. However, not all persons are capable or willing to manage their property, and the law permits management to be detached from ownership. This may be accomplished by the use of the corporate device, namely, the transfer of property to a juridical person, such as a corporation, a partnership, or a foundation. It may also be accomplished without the interposition of an artificial person between a human being and his property, as in cases of administration of the property of a minor or an incompetent.

In common law jurisdictions, detachment of management from ownership is frequently accomplished by means of a trust. A trust is a legal relationship by which a *trustee* undertakes the obligation to deal with property over which he has control, that is, the *property in trust,* for the benefit of a *beneficiary* or *beneficiaries,* of whom he may himself be one. All sorts of things, movable or immovables, and corporeals or incorporeals, may be held in trust, but the things most frequently so held are lands, stocks and bonds.

Separation of the management from the beneficial enjoyment of property is always allowed in common law jurisdictions. In civil law jurisdictions, as a rule, separation of management from the enjoyment of property without the interposition of an artificial person is allowed only when a person is incompetent to manage his own affairs on account of absence, minority, or unsound mind. Competent persons are forced, in effect, to manage their own property or at least undertake the risk of mismanagement by other persons. In common law jurisdictions, however, the use of the trust device enables competent as well as incompetent persons to have their property managed by others without much risk of mismanagement.

When management and beneficial enjoyment are separated question arises as to the nature of the interests of the manager and of the person having the beneficial enjoyment. It might be possible to say that the manager owns the property but he is under duty to manage it for the benefit of another who has nothing more than a correlative personal right against the manager. It might also be possible to say that the beneficiary owns the property but the manager has power of administration without owning the property. This second possibility has materialized in civil law jurisdictions: the property administered by the tutor of a minor or by the curator of a person of unsound mind belongs to the incompetent. Neither possibility has materialized in common law jurisdictions. In these jurisdictions, both the trustee and the beneficiary own the property but in different ways. Neither owns the property in the sense of the Roman *dominium,* but each owns an interest in it, called respectively, the legal estate and the equitable interest.

Thus, in the framework of the institution of trust, there is no single object of ownership. The property in trust is fragmented into two separate abstract objects, the legal estate that the trustee owns for the purpose of managing the property and the equitable interest that the beneficiary owns for the purpose of enjoyment. The legal estate is a way of explaining that the trustee may act as owner of the property, enjoying wide powers of administration and disposition. The equitable estate means that the beneficiary has during the term of the trust advantages of the use and enjoyment of the property. In the light of the historical development of the law of trusts, it would be misleading to ask the question who owns the property subject to a life estate, that is, the tenant or the remainderman. Each of these persons owns an abstract thing, an estate, rather than the property.

Property may be given to a trustee for the benefit of a person or for the accomplishment of certain purposes, usually charitable. In either case, a trustee may not take any benefit in his capacity as such, unless he is entitled to charge for his services under the instrument creating the trust. He must obey the terms of the trust and is personally responsible toward the beneficiary for the proper management of the property. Correlatively, the beneficiary has a personal right against the trustee. If the trustee fails in his duties toward the beneficiary, the beneficiary may bring an action against the trustee to have the provisions of the trust enforced.

Question has arisen in common law jurisdictions whether the beneficiary of a trust has only a personal right against the trustee, a right *in personam,* or also a proprietary interest in the trust property, a right *in rem.* The better view is that the beneficiary as well as the trustee has a proprietary interest. Thus, the beneficiary may follow the trust property that has been disposed of in breach of the trust in the hands of any person other than a purchaser in good faith for value without notice of the breach of the trust or one who acquires the property from or through such a purchaser, even with notice of a previous breach of the trust.

The fragmentation of ownership into a legal estate and an equitable interest is an original common law institution that serves a variety of functions. There is no equivalent institution in civil law jurisdictions unless one may regard as equivalent a substitution or a fideicommissum, whereby an instituted heir or legatee is bound to restore the succession to another person. But analogy fails because the instituted heir, though a temporary owner of the property, has both management and beneficiary enjoyment as long as his right lasts.

As a single device to accomplish a variety of purposes, the trust has no equal but nearly everything that the trust can accomplish may actually be achieved within the framework of civil law institutions, the policies of the law permitting. When something achievable with the trust is not achievable in civil law jurisdictions, it is usually because the result is forbidden for reasons of social policy. Nevertheless, rather than restructure civilian institutions in the light of new policy objectives, certain civil law jurisdictions having close ties with the United States or with countries of the British Commonwealth, such as Mexico and Liechtenstein, have adopted legislation governing trusts. The same technique has long been followed in mixed jurisdictions, such as Quebec and Louisiana.

Louisiana enacted legislation governing charitable trusts in 1882. Certain private trusts of limited duration were first allowed in 1920 until 1935. In 1938, the legislature adopted the Trust Estates Law which again permitted the creation of certain private trusts of limited scope and duration. Mostly due to economic pressures, and, especially, for tax savings, Louisiana enacted in 1964 the Trust Code which allows much flexibility in the use of the trust device.

An overall effort has been made by the legislature, jurisprudence, and doctrine to fit the Louisiana trust into the framework of the prevailing civil law. According to Article 1781 of the Trust Code, the "title of the trust property" is transferred to the trustee, and this seems to imply that he is owner of the property. However, according to doctrine and jurisprudence, the "title" of the trustee is merely a power of administration and disposition rather than ownership. Despite the broad legislative formulation, the ownership of the trust property is vested in the principal beneficiary. In Louisiana, there is neither need nor room for a fragmentation of ownership into the components of legal title and equitable interest. The trustee has a real right that permits him to manage and dispose of the trust property. The beneficiary has likewise a real right, which is ownership subject to trust, that is, ownership without power of administration and disposition. Thus, functionally, the trust device has been accommodated in Louisiana without the implications of a split ownership that is unknown to civil law.

The trust device has proven its usefulness in Louisiana. It may fulfill various legitimate purposes in a most flexible manner in connection with onerous transactions as well as donations inter vivos and mortis causa. In principle anything that may be accomplished out of trust may be accomplished in trust, and vice versa. There is no reason why dispositions not permitted out of trust should be permitted in trust. Nevertheless, the Louisiana legislature, bowing to special interests, has expressly permitted certain dispositions in trust that may not be made out of trust, such as certain narrowly defined substitutions and class gifts. For the rest, dispositions in trust must conform with the principles of the Civil Code under penalty of nullity.

ST. CHARLES LAND TRUST v. ST. AMANT
253 La. 243, 217 So. 2d 385 (1968)

SANDERS, J. The trustees of the St. Charles Land Trust, holders of mineral interests in St. Charles Parish, applied to the Court for instructions pursuant to R.S. 9:2233. They seek authority to transfer a deceased beneficiary's interest in the trust under the order of a court of California, where the beneficiary was domiciled, without ancillary succession proceedings or the payment of inheritance taxes in Louisiana.

The district court instructed the trustees that the decedent's beneficial interest was incorporeal, immovable property, subject to Louisiana inheritance taxes and transferable only pursuant to ancillary succession proceedings in this state.

The Court of Appeal reversed and instructed the trustees that the decedent's beneficial interest was incorporeal, movable property, exempt from Louisiana inheritance taxes and transferable upon the order of the California Court. Judge Chasez dissented from these instructions. La. App., 206 So. 2d 128.***

The St. Charles Land Company, a Maryland corporation, owned mineral leases and servitudes on lands located in St. Charles Parish, Louisiana. An amendment to its Articles of Incorporation adopted by its shareholders provided that in the event of liquidation the directors could transfer the corporate property to a trust for the benefit of the shareholders. Acting under this authority, the liquidator transferred the mineral leases and servitudes to the trustees of the St. Charles Land Trust for the benefit of the former shareholders. The transfer in trust was made by an authentic act entitled "Transfer and Trust Instrument" dated April 2, 1962. The instrument designated the shareholders as beneficiaries for both principal and income in the same proportion as their former stock ownership.

Under. the terms of the trust instrument, the sole purpose of the trust is to conserve the trust estate and distribute the income to the beneficiaries after the payment of expenses. The trustees are prohibited from engaging in the development of mineral property or other business activities.....

The instrument further provides: "The interests of the beneficiaries are classified as movable property, notwithstanding that the trust estate consists in whole or in part of immovable property; provided that the trustees shall have the right, but shall not be bound, to require, as a condition precedent to recognition of the validity or effectiveness of any transfer of the interest of a beneficiary, compliance in respect thereof with the formalities attendant on like transfers of immovable property."

Mrs. Ella E. Watkins, a beneficiary, died in California where she was domiciled on October 28, 1965. She left no forced heirs. In due course, a California court granted an order as to the Louisiana trust interest.

Louisiana levies a tax on inheritances. As to the scope of the tax, R.S. 47:2404 provides:

> "Except to the extent of the exemptions provided in R.S. 47:2402 the tax shall be imposed with respect to all property of every nature and kind included or embraced in any inheritance legacy or donation or gift made in contemplation of death, including all immovable property and tangible movable property physically in the State of Louisiana, whether owned or inherited by, or bequeathed, given, or donated to a resident or non-resident, and whether inherited, bequeathed, given or donated under the laws of this state or of any other state or country. The tax shall also be imposed with respect to all movable property, tangible or intangible, owned by residents of the State of Louisiana, wherever situated; provided that the tax shall not be imposed upon any transfer of intangible movable property owned by a person not domiciled in this state at the time of his death."

Under the above provision, the inheritance of a nonresident's immovable property, tangible or intangible, situated in this state is taxable. The inheritance of intangible movable property owned by a nonresident is immune from the tax.

The trustees assert that the beneficiary's interest in the trust, like that of a corporate stockholder, is an incorporeal movable, both under the terms of the trust instrument and Louisiana law. Hence, they reason, the interest is free from Louisiana inheritance taxes.

The opponents first assert the instrument relied on created no trust, but rather a partnership or agency. Alternatively, they contend the beneficiary's interest in the trust is an immovable under Louisiana law. Hence, they submit, the Louisiana inheritance tax law applies.

A trust is a relationship resulting from the transfer of title to property to a person to be administered by him as a fiduciary for the benefit of another....

No particular language is required to create a trust. Former R.S. 9:1815. It suffices if the instrument as a whole reflects the intent to establish a trust relationship. When it can reasonably do so, the Court will construe the trust instrument to sustain the validity of the trust.

Our examination of the instrument in contest here discloses that it transfers legal title of the property to the trustees, defines their duties and powers as fiduciaries, designates the shareholders as income and principal beneficiaries, and fixes the term of the trust as the maximum period permitted by law. The trustees appeared in the instrument to accept the trust.

The relationship has all the features of a trust and lacks certain essential features of both partnership and agency. A partnership is created by contract among the partners. C.C. art. 2801. The beneficiaries were not parties to the trust instrument. Clearly, therefore, there can be no contract of partnership among them.

The contention that the relationship is a mandate, or agency, rather than a trust, is equally weak. Without attempting to enumerate all the distinctions between a trust and agency, we note that the trust instrument vests title to the property in the trustees in a relationship that is neither terminable at the will of the beneficiaries nor upon the death of any of them. In an agency, on the other hand, title to the property normally remains in the principal and the mandatory has the power to bind the principal by contract. C.C.art. 3021. An agency terminates upon the death or at the will of the principal. C.C.art. 3027.

We conclude, as did the Court of Appeal, that the instrument creates a trust.

The classification of the beneficiary's interest in the trust in terms of recognized property concepts raises difficult questions. This classification has been the subject of much controversy in the common law. See 1A Bogert, Trusts and Trustees, § 183, pp. 174-179 (1951) and 2 Scott on Trusts, § 130, pp. 1050-1062 (1967). To remove uncertainty, a number of states have enacted statutory provisions classifying the interest. See 1A Bogert, *supra*, § 184, pp.179-182.

Louisiana trust laws contain no provision classifying the principal beneficiary's interest as movable or immovable. It is quite clear, however, that the trustees hold title to the property for the benefit of the income and principal beneficiaries. Furthermore, upon the death of a principal beneficiary, his interest vests in his heirs, subject to the trust. Former R.S. 9:1921. Hence, it may be said that the principal beneficiary's interest is an incorporeal right enforceable at law. But fixing title in the trustees does not resolve the question of whether the beneficiary's incorporeal right is movable or immovable. Since the trust laws are silent, a resolution of the question depends upon basic property concepts of the Louisiana Civil Code and related statutes. Article 470 of the Louisiana Civil Code (1870) provides:

"Incorporeal things, consisting only in a right, are not of themselves strictly susceptible of the quality of movables or immovables; nevertheless they are placed in one or the other of these classes, according to the object to which they apply and the rules hereinafter established."

Under Louisiana law, the mineral leases and servitudes held by the trustees are immovable property. C.C. art. 471 [Revised C.C. art. 470]; R.S. 9:1105; Succession of Simms, 250 La. 177, 195 So. 2d 114. Since the trust is upon such property, the object to which the beneficial interest applies is immovable property. Hence, under the above code article, the right itself is immovable, unless the right is excepted from this classification by other code articles. C.C. art. 470; Yiannopoulos, Civil Law of Property, §§ 60, 61, pp. 178-182 (1966); 2 Aubry & Rau, Property, § 165 (20), p. 35 (English translation by the Louisiana State Law Institute).

Louisiana Civil Code Article 471 [Revised C.C. art. 470] provides that a usufruct of immovable things, a servitude on an immovable estate, and an action for the recovery of an immovable estate or an entire succession "are considered as immovable from the object to which they apply." The language of this article and its history leave no doubt that the immovable rights mentioned are illustrative and not exclusive. See Yiannopoulos, *supra*, § 61, pp. 180-181 and the authorities cited. For this reason, other rights may be classified as immovable when they apply to an object that is immovable.

The trustees contend, however, that the trust interest is classified as a movable by Article 474 of the Louisiana Civil Code [Revised C.C. art. 473]. That article declares movable "shares or interests in banks or companies of commerce, or industry or other speculations, although such companies be possessed of immovables."

The provision creates a special exception to the general rule of Article 470. The exception originated in Article 529 of the Code Napoléon. The code language refers to shares or interests in business organizations, such as corporations or partnerships. Yiannopoulos, *supra*, § 66, pp. 194-195; 2 Aubry & Rau, *supra*, § 165 (31), pp. 39-40; 1 Planiol, Traité Élémentaire De Droit Civil No. 2260, pp. 335-336 (English Translation by the Louisiana State Law Institute). The trust is a unique institution of Anglo-American origin. It has a wide variety of uses in making dispositions of property, especially in estate planning. It may contain any conditions not forbidden by law or public policy. See, generally, Rubin and Rubin, Louisiana Trust Handbook (1968) and 1 Scott, *supra*, § 1, pp. 3-5. Based upon any type of property susceptible of private ownership, a trust can be created either by testament or inter vivos transfer. Although we respect analogy in code application, we are of the opinion the beneficial interest in the trust does not fall within the exception of Article 474 [Revised C.C. art. 473].

Finally, the trustees rely on the clause of the trust instrument itself which classifies the beneficiary's interest as movable. It is true, as contended by the trustees, that such clauses are recognized and enforced in some common law jurisdictions. In essence, these clauses are applications of the doctrine of equitable conversion. See 1A Bogert, *supra*, § 185, pp. 182-184. We find no sound basis in Louisiana law for enforcing such a clause against the State of Louisiana. To give it effect here, moreover, would permit the parties to a trust instrument to upset long-established, legislative property classifications to the prejudice of state tax agencies, though the State is a stranger to the instrument.

We hold that the principal beneficiary's interest in the trust is an incorporeal immovable for Louisiana inheritance tax purposes. Recognizing its interest in protecting the rights of local creditors and in assuring proper administration of its tax laws, Louisiana has for many years required ancillary probate proceedings when a non-resident dies leaving property situated in the state. See C.C.P. Book VI, Title IV [citations omitted]. Since we have determined that the decedent owns immovable property situated in Louisiana, it follows that the code provisions relating to ancillary probate procedure apply. C.C.P. Arts. 2811, 3401.

For the reasons assigned, the judgment of the Court of Appeal is reversed, and the judgment of the district court is reinstated and made the judgment of this Court.

BARHAM, J. (dissenting). The majority properly concludes that the instrument under consideration created a valid trust. The question for resolution is the nature of the principal beneficiary's interest in that trust. For more precise resolution is the query: Is the quality of the beneficiary's interest in the trust governed by the nature of the property owned by the trust?

Civil Code Articles 470, 471, 474, and 475 [Revised C.C. arts. 470, 471, 473, 475] determine the quality of the beneficiary's interest. Article 470 provides that incorporeal things take on the quality of movables or immovables "***according to the object to which they apply and the rules hereinafter established." The majority correctly finds that Article 471 [Revised C.C. art. 470] is merely illustrative and not exclusive in enumerating certain incorporeal immovables. However, the majority contends that Article 474 [Revised C.C. art. 473], which says that "Things movable by the disposition of the law, *are such as***", is a special exception to Article 470. This is error, for Article 474 [Revised C.C. art. 473] by its very language is merely illustrative of incorporeal movables and not exclusive, just as Article 471 [Revised C.C.

art. 470] is illustrative but not exclusive of incorporeal immovables. Yiannopoulos, 1 Louisiana Practice (Civil Law of Property), § 66, p. 193.

The majority has failed to apply what I believe to be a most important code provision in determining the qualities of movables and immovables — i.e., Article 475, which states: "All things corporeal or incorporeal, which have not the character of immovables by their nature or by the disposition of the law, according to the rules laid down in this title, are considered as movables." It is to be seen, then, that under Article 475 all incorporeal things are movables which are not specifically identifiable as immovables from the nature of the object to which they apply or not designated by law as immovables. In short, under our law movables form the residual category. Yiannopoulos, op. cit. *supra*, § 64, p. 189.

The incorporeal interest of the beneficiary is not one of those immovables enumerated in Article 471 [Revised C.C. art. 470] (usufruct and use of an immovable, servitude on an immovable, action to recover an immovable or the entirety of a succession), nor is it analogous to those others not named but included by implication (ownership, habitation, etc.,) of an immovable. If the beneficiary's interest is not an immovable according to the object to which it applies, as indicated by Article 47 [Revised C.C. art. 470], and if special disposition or fiction of law has not classified it immovable, this court is obligated to conclude under Article 475 that it is an incorporeal movable.

The majority has erred by disregarding the legal personality of the trust and by treating the mineral leases owned by the trust as the "object" of the beneficiary's interest. The majority has destroyed the entity of the trust, which is the only and real "object" of the beneficiary's interest, and has incorrectly treated the mineral leases owned by the trust as the "object" of the beneficiary's interest. It is true that the ownership of the mineral leases which is the right vested in the trust is an incorporeal immovable right, but this is not the right vested in the beneficiary. The majority has found her right to be "*** an incorporeal right enforceable at law." The beneficiary does not own the mineral leases, nor does she possess any other immovable right in them while the trust exists.

I believe this reasoning alone adequately fixes her interest as an incorporeal movable, but this conclusion is buttressed by the use of analogy in the application of Article 474 [Revised C.C. art. 473]. That article, being merely illustrative of incorporeal movables, necessarily includes the beneficiary's interest in a trust, which is analogous to "*** shares or interests in banks or companies of commerce, or industry or other speculations, although such companies be possessed of immovables depending upon such enterprises."

Yiannopoulos says: "*** Although shares or interests in various associations could be regarded as either movable or immovable property depending on the type of property owned by the association, Article 474 [Revised C.C. art. 473] indicates that these shares or interests are movable 'although such companies be possessed of immovables.' ***" Yiannopoulos, op. cit. *supra*, § 66, p. 194. He further points out that in Louisiana all associations are to be considered as included within Article 474

[Revised C.C. art. 473]. In the absence of recognition of trusts in our civil law sources as well as in our own law at the time of the adoption of this article, obviously trusts could not have been included by name, but just as obviously trusts are meant to be included by analogy.

I conclude that the interest of the beneficiary in the trust is an incorporeal movable right, and that the character of the property owned by the trust does not affect the nature of that interest. I respectfully dissent.

c. Non-immobilization

LOUISIANA REVISED STATUTES

R.S. 9:1106, Storage tanks placed on land by one not owner of land as movable property

Tanks placed on land whether urban or rural by other than the owner of the land for the storage or use of butane, propane or other liquefied gases, or for the storage or use of anhydrous ammonia or other liquid fertilizer, be and they are declared to be and shall remain movable property, and the ownership of such tank or tanks shall not be affected by the sale, either private or judicial, of the land on which they are placed.

IN RE RECEIVERSHIP OF AUGUSTA SUGAR CO.
134 La. 971, 64 So. 870 (1914)

PROVOSTY, J. The Augusta Sugar Company, being insolvent and in the hands of a receiver, Payne & Joubert intervened in the receivership proceedings, asking that their vendor's privilege upon a vacuum pan, a vacuum pump, a water pump, a tower tank, an oil storing tank, and three Magma tanks, sold by them to the now insolvent company, and erected by them on its plantation, and never paid for, be recognized, and that the receiver be ordered to sell said machinery at once to satisfy their said claim.

The learned counsel for the receiver have argued this case as if the question presented were as to whether these objects had become immovables by destination by having been permanently attached to the plantation of the company for its exploitation; but that is not the question at all. No one can contend for a single moment that these objects were not attached permanently, and did not become immovables by destination. But hardly anything is better settled in our jurisprudence than that the vendor's privilege upon movables is not lost by their becoming immovables by destination.

In all cases like the present the question is, not as to whether or not the movables have become immobilized by destination, under Articles 468 and 469, C.C. [Revised C.C. arts. 466, 467] for they unquestionably have, but it is whether they have become so incorporated into, or merged in, the immovable property, as to have become part and parcel of it, and thereby ceased to be movables; with the consequence that the vendor's privilege upon them, qua movables, has ceased to exist. Swoop v. St. Martin, 110 La. 237, 84 South. 426.***

The question of when or under what circumstances this merger will be held to have taken place is one to be determined from the particular facts of each case.

Where the things sold are mere materials for the construction or repair of a building, or of machinery, these materials when put into the building constructed or repaired or into the repaired machinery lose their identity and become merely a part of the building or repaired machinery. In such case the vendor's privilege is lost; but out of its ashes springs another privilege, that of the furnisher of materials, which rests upon the structure as a whole, and upon one acre of the ground upon which the structure stands. Swoop v. St. Martin, 110 La. 237, 84 South. 426.

Much testimony was taken on the point of what damage would have to be done to the company's sugarhouse for removing this machinery. This evidence showed no damage at all would have to be done except for the vacuum pan. For removing it an opening would have to be made in the corrugated iron wall of the structure enclosing it, and a wooden platform built around it for the sugar maker to stand on would have to be removed in part. But the evidence shows that this could be done and the premises restored to their present condition at a comparatively trifling expense. We do not think that machinery like this vacuum pan, costing thousands of dollars, loses its identity and becomes merged in the building within which it is placed (becomes mere building material, as it were) simply because for removing it an opening easily repaired would have to be made in the side of the building, or a wooden platform built around it would have to be taken down in part or in whole—all at a small expense.

The vacuum pan does not lose its identity as a piece of machinery complete in itself and retaining its individuality after removal, simply because this corrugated iron building is constructed around and above it to protect it from the weather, or because this inexpensive wooden platform is constructed around it.

The learned counsel for the receiver argue also that the sugarhouse will be disabled by the removal of this machinery. No doubt of that; but that result is merely the legal consequence of the machinery not having been paid for. In all the cases cited above and in all others where the vendor was allowed to assert his privilege or other rights upon machinery forming part of an operating plant, the effect was to disable the plant; but it never occurred to any one that this result was an obstacle to the enforcement of the vendor's legal rights. Judgment affirmed.

MONROE, J. I dissent in so far as the judgment recognizes a vendor's privilege on the machinery which can be removed only by taking down the side of the factory in which it is contained.

LOUISIANA CODE OF CIVIL PROCEDURE

Art. 1092. Third person asserting ownership of, or mortgage or privilege on, seized property

A third person claiming ownership of, or a mortgage or privilege on, property seized may assert his claim by intervention. If the third person asserts ownership of the seized property, the intervention may be filed at any time prior to the judicial sale of the seized property, and the court may grant him injunctive relief to prevent such sale before an adjudication of his claim of ownership.

If the third person claims a mortgage or privilege on the entire property seized, whether superior or inferior to that of the seizing creditor, the intervention may be filed at any time prior to the distribution by the sheriff of the proceeds of the sale of the seized property, and the court shall order the sheriff to hold such proceeds subject to its further orders. When the intervenor claims such a mortgage or privilege only on part of the property seized, and the intervention is filed prior to the judicial sale, the court may order the separate sale of the property on which the intervener claims a mortgage or privilege; or if a separate sale thereof is not feasible or necessary, or the intervenor has no right thereto, the court may order the separate appraisement of the entire property seized and of the part thereof on which the intervenor claims a mortgage or privilege.

An intervenor claiming the proceeds of a judicial sale does not thereby admit judicially the validity, nor is he estopped from asserting the invalidity, of the claim of the seizing creditor.

NOTE
"Fixture Filings" and UCC-9

The topic of "non-immoblization" is a legal fiction that is concerned with protecting a creditor who has acquired a right in a movable thing. Although such a creditor may need protection for a number of reasons, non-immobilization is concerned with the legal effects upon such a creditor's rights when that movable becomes a component part of an immovable. Since immobilization has the legal effect of converting the movable into an immovable with no distinct legal identity apart from the immovable into which it has been incorporated, the term "non-immobilization" refers to the continued recognition of the rights of a creditor, obtained when the thing was still movable, after that thing has been immobilized.

In *Augusta Sugar*, the creditor asserted that he was a vendor who extended credit to his buyer, thereby entitling him to a vendor's privilege. Thus, the creditor in that case sought protection as a preferred creditor. Privilege is one of the bases of preference for a creditor; a preferred creditor stands ahead of the debtor's general unsecured creditors. La. Civ. Code art. 3184. Although privileges are created by law, La. Civ. Code art. 3186, Louisiana's other causes of preference typically are created by contract, *e.g.*, a conventional mortgage, in which the debtor confers upon a creditor the right to cause the mortgaged property to be seized and sold if the principal obligation is not performed. La. Civ. Code art. 3278. In Louisiana, mortgage was initially limited to immovable property, but in the early twentieth century this security device was extended to movables through enactment of legislation creating the chattel mortgage.

Chattel mortgages were eliminated effective January 1, 1990, the date on which Louisiana became the last state to adopt article 9 of the Uniform Commercial Code, "Secured Transactions." Called the most innovative of the original UCC articles, article 9's "grand innovation was the introduction of a 'unitary' security device," designated as a security interest. Located in Chapter 9 of Title 10 of the Revised Statutes, Louisiana's version of article 9 was renamed "Chapter 9."

As of January 1, 1990, the date on which Louisiana's version of UCC-9 took effect, the only consensual security right in movables that Louisiana recognizes is a security interest. A security interest, as defined in Louisiana's UCC chapter 1, entitled "General Provisions," is "an interest in personal property or fixtures, created by contract, which secures payment or performance of an obligation." Although Louisiana continues to recognize privileges on movables (as well as on immovables), a security interest pursuant to UCC-9 (including an attached but unperfected security interest) will have priority over conflicting privileges in most instances. La. R.S. 10:9-322(h). Today, a creditor in the shoes of the seller in the *Augusta Sugar* could protect himself more effectively by obtaining a security interest and complying with the requirements for a "fixture filing." What is a fixture, you are probably wondering. That term is defined in Louisiana's UCC chapter 9:

> "Fixtures means goods, other than consumer goods and manufactured homes, that after placement on or incorporation in an immovable have become a component part of such immovable as provided in Civil Code Articles 463, 465, and 466, or that have been declared to be a component part of an immovable under Civil Code Article 467."

La. R.S. 10:9-102(a) (41).

A fixture filing serves an analogous role in protecting creditors' rights to movables as registry serves in protecting third persons' rights to immovables. UCC-9 is studied either in a Louisiana Security Devices course, or in the more specialized course on Secured Transactions. The purpose of introducing you to the concept of a security interest and to the notion of a "fixture filing" is to provide you some understanding of how the law protects creditors of movables in the specific situation described in this note. Hopefully, this will help you to conceptualize the outcome that non-immobilization is striving to attain as well as the reason for its existence.

d. De-immobilization; Separate Immovables
Civil Code arts. 464, 468

FOLSE v. TRICHE
113 La. 915, 37 So. 875 (1904)

LAND, J. There seems to be no dispute about the facts, and the question of law is whether the machinery and appliances of the sugar house destroyed by fire, ("all in a demolished and ruined condition, but containing much valuable metal,") are movables or immovables.

The district judge held that said machinery and appliances had not lost their character as immovables by the conflagration which destroyed the house in which they were located. He therefore rendered judgment in favor of the plaintiff, who, as a creditor of her husband, claiming a legal mortgage, had enjoined the sale of said machinery, etc., separately from the mortgaged premises. Defendant, an ordinary judgment creditor, who had caused the said property to be seized under a writ of fieri facias, appealed to the Court of Appeal.

It is conceded that before the destruction of the sugar house, the machinery and appliances contained therein were immovable by destination. This accords with the textual provisions of Article 468 of the Civil Code [Revised C.C. art. 467].

Our learned Brother of the district court ruled that immovables by destination can be mobilized only by the act of the owner in removing or disposing of them in good faith. Movables are converted into immovables by destination when placed by the owner of a tract of land upon it "for its service and improvement." Civ. Code, art. 468 [Revised C.C. art. 467]. Movables which do not perform this function do not fall within the terms of the definition. Hence it would seem that when, from any cause, a movable ceases to be of service to a tract of land, or is detached from a building or tenement of which it formed a part as an accessory, there is no longer ground for the claim that such movable appertains to the realty.

The text of the Civil Code teaches us that the materials arising from the demolition of a building are movables until they have been made use of in raising a new building. Civ. Code, art. 476 [Revised C.C. art. 472]. It matters not whether the building be demolished by the act of the owner or by natural causes. The French courts hold that, where a house has been burned, a mortgage thereon cannot be enforced against the materials which escaped the flames. Dalloz, Code Civil, vol. 2, pt. 1070, 1483. This results from the doctrine of the civil law that mortgages can exist only on immovables and their accessories considered likewise as immovables. Civ. Code, art. 3289.

In Bank v. Knapp, 22 La. Ann. 117, our Supreme Court held that machinery, when detached from a sugar house, and removed from the plantation by the purchaser, became again movables, not subject to the mortgage resting on the land.... This doctrine was reaffirmed in Weil v. Lapeyre, 38 La. Ann. 303, after a review of the French jurisprudence on the subject.

In both of the cases cited, the Supreme Court held that the machinery again became movable by sale made in good faith and removal from the premises.

It does not follow that a sale and delivery is the only mode by which machinery in a sugar house or other factory can regain its true nature as a movable. If so attached as to become a part of the building, the demolition or destruction of the building leaves the machinery, or what is left of it, in the condition of a movable not attached to the realty. In such case no distinction can be drawn between such machinery and materials arising from the demolition of the building. Both become movables under Civ. Code, art. 476 [Revised C.C. art. 472]. Laurent says:

> "Quand des choses immeubles par incorporation sont détachées du sole ou du batiment, elles reprennent, de fait comme de droit, leur nature mobilière." Droit Civil Français, Tome 5, p. 534.

If such machinery be not incorporated with the building, but placed therein for the service and improvement of the land, it becomes immovable by destination, not because the owner so wills or intends, but by reason of such service and improvement. *Id.* pp. 537, 564. While immovables by destination remain on the land in a condition fit for service, it may be that the will of the owner or his action is necessary to change their status; but when, as in the case at bar, they become unfit for service as the result of accident, there is no reason for the continuation of the legal fiction made in the interests of agriculture and industry. The immobilization and hypothecation of movables by destination cease when the movable objects are detached from the immovable, or cease to be applied to the cultivation or service of the tract of land to which they were attached as accessories. Paul Pont, 1, No. 376, p. 374. The case is stronger where such movables are rendered by accident incapable of further service.

We cannot consider the demolished and ruined machinery valuable only as scrap metal as in the category of "machinery made use of in carrying on plantation works." Civ. Code, art. 468 [Revised C.C. art. 466, 467]. In the Succession of Allen, 48 La. Ann. 1047, 1048, 20 South, 193, 55 Am. St. Rep. 295, this court held that a lot of "old iron" was not an immovable by destination, because it was not essential for the use of the plantation, and not employed in the cultivation of the same. Doubtless such "old iron" was the remnant of implements or machinery which had been used on the plantation, because otherwise there could have been no question of its immobilization.

Holding that plaintiff cannot have a legal mortgage on the remnants of machinery in question, her injunction must be dissolved, and her suit dismissed, with costs. There is no evidence in the record on the reconventional demand for damages, and therefore the rights of defendants will be reserved.

NICHOLLS, J., dissents, holding that the rights of the mortgage creditor being vested upon each and every part of the building is not lost by the fortuitous burning of the building when any part of the building still remains upon the mortgaged property. He reserves the right to amplify this proposition.

ON REHEARING (Jan. 30, 1905.)

PROVOSTY, J. The court adheres to the views expressed in the opinion heretofore handed down in so far as the law is concerned, but does not find itself sufficiently informed of the facts to come to a final conclusion. The decision handed down is therefore reinstated, in so far as it sets aside the judgment below, and the case is remanded to the district court for further trial, with instructions that if, as a result of the fire, the property seized has ceased to be a sugar mill and machinery such as need only to be repaired and properly sheltered for continuing in the service of the plantation, and has become merely a lot of material, more or less susceptible of being utilized in the reconstruction of the destroyed sugar house, it shall be held to have lost its character of immobility; otherwise not. All costs to abide final result.

See P.H.A.C. Services v. Seaways International, Inc., *supra*

See A.N. Yiannopoulos, Civil Law Property § 133 (4th ed. 2001), *supra*

BROWN v. HODGE-HUNT LUMBER CO.
162 La. 635, 110 So. 886 (1926)

THOMPSON, J. This suit is for the value of timber cut and removed from a certain tract of land claimed by the plaintiff and fully described in the petition. The plaintiff's title to the land has its origin in a deed from the defendant company to G. A. Woods, of date December 4, 1906. The ownership of the timber is claimed by virtue of a tax sale in the name of the estate of said Woods for the taxes of 1918.***

The land, with the timber thereon, was originally owned by the Huie-Hodge Lumber Company. By an amendment to the charter the name of the company was changed to that given in the title of the case. On December 4, 1906, the then owner (Huie-Hodge Lumber Company) sold the land to A. Woods, reserving unto said company all of the merchantable timber on the land, together with right of way for railroad, wagons, etc., for the removal of the timber. There was no time limit fixed in the deed for the removal of the timber, and no application was ever made to the court to have the timber cut and removed within a fixed and definite period.

The reservation of the timber in the sale of the land was clearly a segregation of ownership of the timber from the land and created two separate and distinct estates one to the land in Woods, and the other to the timber in the lumber company. This is so well settled since Act No. 188 of 1904 as to need no citation of authorities. It is equally well settled that the failure to fix a time limit in the deed for the removal of the timber does not affect the validity of the transfer of the timber; since the omission may be supplied by application to the courts, and until such a period is fixed the right to remove the timber remains in the grantee (in this case the owner of the timber) indefinitely. Kavanaugh v. Frost-Johnson Lbr. Co., 149 La. 972, 90 So. 275.

Some time after his purchase of the land, Woods died, and in 1919 the land was sold for the taxes of 1918, under an assessment in the name of the estate of G. A. Woods. At this sale, Dr. W. S. Jones bought the land, and a year thereafter sold the same to the present plaintiff... It does not appear that the timber was included in the assessment and valuation of the land as a basis for the tax sale. The timber is not specially mentioned, either in the assessment or the tax deed. The value placed on the land for taxing purposes would seem to indicate that it was not intended to include the timber.

From the allegations of plaintiffs petition and the proof in the record, the timber on the land was worth more than eight times the value of the land without the timber.

The same may be said in reference to all of the deeds to the land subsequent to the tax deed. In none of these deeds was any reference made to the timber on the land, and price stated in the deeds indicates very clearly, we think, that the sale was not to include the timber.

The plaintiff concedes, and very properly so, that since Act No. 188 of 1904, where timber has been segregated in ownership from the land, there should be separate assessments; that the land should be assessed to its owner, and the timber to its owner...

The only authority relied on in support of the contention that the timber was a part of the land is Article 465 [Revised C.C. art. 463] of the Civil Code, which provides, among other things, that trees before they are cut down are immovable, and are considered as a part of the land to which they are attached.

This article has no application to the question here presented since the passage of the act of 1904, which retained the immovable character of standing timber, but classified it as a separate and distinct estate from that of the land, when segregated in ownership from the land by the act of the owner, who held the title to the combined estate of timber and land.

Our conclusion is that the timber in question was reserved to the defendant in the original sale of the land to Woods; that the title to the timber never vested in Woods, was not covered by the assessment of the land to the estate of Woods, and did not pass under the tax sale, nor any of the subsequent sales of the land. Our further conclusion is that the failure of the lumber company to assess the timber did not have the effect of a forfeiture of the title to the timber.

The judgment appealed from is reversed and set aside, and plaintiff's demand is rejected, with costs.

WILLETTS WOOD PRODUCTS CO. v. CONCORDIA LAND & TIMBER CO.
169 La. 240, 124 So. 841 (1929)

THOMPSON, J. This is a suit to have the court fix a term within which the timber on certain described lands situated in Concordia Parish should be removed and in default of such removal to have plaintiff, owner of the land, decreed to be the owner of the timber.

After certain exceptions were filed and overruled, the case was put at issue and tried, resulting in a judgment in favor of plaintiff fixing a term of four years to run from the date of the judgment, and providing that all timber not removed within the time fixed shall revert to the plaintiff.

There is no dispute as to the facts except on the question as to what is a reasonable time in which to remove the timber. The legal controversy results from the interpretation sought to be given by counsel for defendant to the many decisions of this court in which the precise question here involved was at issue. The defendant was at one time the owner of both the land and timber, and some time during 1917 or 1918 granted a mortgage in favor of the Continental & Commercial Trust & Savings Bank and Frank H. Jones, trustees. The mortgage debt not having been paid, foreclosure proceedings were brought in the federal court, as a result of which the land was sold to Roy H. Goddard. From Goddard the land passed to the Black River Lumber Company, and from the latter to the present plaintiff. In each and every one of the sales mentioned the timber on the land described in paragraph 2 of plaintiffs petition was expressly excepted, and hence remained the property of the defendant.

One of the contentions of defendant is that there was no contractual relation between the defendant and the plaintiff and its authors in title with reference to the removal of the timber, and for that reason the court was without authority to order the removal within any fixed time.

But the defendant gave a mortgage on the land and consented that the land be sold in default of the payment of the debt. The defendant remained silent, permitted the land to be sold separately from the timber, and acquiesced therein, and now claims to own the timber while admitting that the land belongs to the plaintiff. The defendant by its conduct placed it in the power of, and made it possible for, the mortgagee to sell the land separately from the timber and thereby to bring about the creation of two separate estates. Hence there were created two separate estates as perfectly and completely as if the defendant had made a conventional sale of the land and reserved to itself the timber. The plaintiff therefore occupies the same position towards the defendant with respect to the timber as it would have occupied if it has purchased the land from the defendant. Whatever contractual relations existed between the defendant and its mortgagee with regard to the timber passed to the present plaintiff, owner of the land.

Person The further contention is made that, when separated in ownership from the land on which it stands, the timber becomes an immovable possessing equal rank and dignity with the land, and that the owner of the land has no more inherent right to compel the owner of the timber to sell his timber than the owner of the timber has to compel the owner of the land to sell the land. The contention amounts to a legal heresy, and is contrary to numerous decisions of this court. It is true there may be created court under the statute two separate estates, and the title to the land rested in one person and that of the timber in another, but it was never intended and will not do to say that the respective titles are of equal rank and dignity, in the sense that the owner of the timber can require that the timber be permitted to remain on the land in perpetuity without any right in the owner of the land to cause the timber to be removed. No such impossible situation was ever intended or contemplated. Statutes must be construed, if possible, so as to make them practicable, and to hold that the owner of the land must subordinate the use of the land to the will and pleasure of the owner of the timber would effectually put the land out of commence. It is further contended that this court has never fixed a time limit for the removal of timber in a case where the contract between the parties is silent on the subject, and that any expressions that the court might in some cases fix such a limit, are purely obiter. The very cases which counsel cite in support of this contention hold to the contrary.

We will say, however, as said in one of the very latest cases, Ward v. Hayes-Ewell Co., 155 La. 18, 98 So. 740, 741, "that this court has always held,***that standing timber was property subject to be acquired separately from the land on which it grows; but that when sold it must be cut and removed within the period agreed upon by the parties or fixed by the court in default of agreement; otherwise said timber reverts to the owner of the land."

The only remaining question is as to the time allowed for the removal of the timber. The evidence is somewhat conflicting, but we think that the great preponderance of the evidence supports the finding of the trial judge. Indeed his ruling could not be said to be manifestly wrong if he had fixed a shorter period than four years.

The judgment appealed from is amended by making the term for the removal of the timber to commence from the date this judgment becomes final. In all other respects the judgment is affirmed, at the cost of defendant in both courts.

2. MOVABLES

See A. N. YIANNOPOULOS, CIVIL LAW PROPERTY
§§ 148-152 (4th ed. 2001)

STEINAU v. PYBURN
229 So. 2d 153 (La. App. 2d Cir. 1969)

DIXON, J. Plaintiffs seek a judgment recognizing them as owners of one-third of $8000.00 deposited in the registry of the court in another suit. They appealed from an adverse judgment. Appellee is Lawrence T. Beck, widower of Sybil Loewenberg.

When the Murphy Oil Corporation deposited the $8000.00 in the registry of the court in 1954 it sought a judgment for specific performance against Lawrence T. Beck and Sybil Loewenberg Beck, owners of a certain tract of land in Caddo Parish, basing its suit on an alleged contract to enter into an oil and gas lease. The funds deposited represented lease bonus money at $50.00 per acre for 160 acres. This suit was dismissed with prejudice on June 7, 1954, but the funds were never withdrawn.

Sybil Loewenberg Beck died July 7, 1954. Her husband, Lawrence T. Beck, was named in her New York will as principal legatee. Mrs. Beck's mother (Minnie S. Loewenberg) survived her, and was subsequently recognized as owner of one-third of the Caddo Parish real property. Plaintiffs here are the heirs of Minnie S. Loewenberg.

Plaintiffs claim ownership of the funds deposited, contending that the fund is an interest arising out of an oil and gas lease and therefore an incorporeal immovable. What plaintiffs claim here is not an interest in a lease, nor even an interest in a lawsuit. What they claim is ownership of one-third of $8000.00 which has been deposited in the registry of the court. The suit in which the $8000.00 was deposited had been dismissed with prejudice one month prior to the death of Mrs. Beck. The Murphy Oil Corporation has filed a disclaimer to the funds which it deposited for the benefit of Lawrence T. Beck and Sybil L. Beck. In order for the plaintiffs to prevail, it is necessary for the court to hold that the fund of money is immovable and subject to the succession laws of Louisiana. The authorities relied on by plaintiffs do not support this contention.

Plaintiffs rely on R.S. 9:1105, Code of Civil Procedure Article 3664, and the Succession of Simms, La. App., 175 So. 2d 113, affirmed in 250 La. 177, 195 So. 2d 114 (1965). R.S. 9:1105 provides in part:

"Oil, gas, and other mineral leases, and contracts applying to and affecting these leases or the right to reduce oil, gas, or other minerals to possession, together with the rights, privileges, and obligations resulting therefrom, are classified as real rights and incorporeal immovable property."

Article 3664 of the Code of Civil Procedure provides in part:

> "A mineral lessee or sublessee, owner of a mineral interest in immovable property, owner of a mineral royalty, or of any right under or obligation resulting from a contract to reduce oil, gas, and other minerals to possession, is the owner of a real right."

It is to be noted that, although these statutory provisions provide that rights resulting from mineral contracts are immovable, they do not provide that money resulting from mineral contracts is an immovable.

In the case before us, it is money which the plaintiffs claim to own. The judgment they seek is a judgment ordering the clerk to pay them money. Money is not an immovable. It is movable (Civil Code Articles 473 and 475 [Revised C.C. art. 471]) and therefore subject to the dispositions contained in the New York will of Mrs. Beck. The judgment of the district court is affirmed, at the cost of appellants.

BEARD v. DURALDE
23 La. Ann. 284 (1871)

TALIAFERRO, J. Archinard, administrator of the succession of Giquel, having obtained a judgment against Mrs. Beard, issued an execution and seized a lot of lumber and bricks on her plantation. She enjoined the sale on the ground that the articles were being put to the use for which they were intended, that is the erection of a framed sugarhouse, at the time they were seized by the sheriff, and were immovables by destination, and could not be seized separately from the land on which the building was in progress of construction.

This ground was considered by the judge a quo as sufficient to warrant the plaintiff in staying the execution by injunction, and rendered judgment perpetuating it. The defendant appealed.

Article 468 of the Civil Code [Revised C.C. art. 472] is relied upon to support the position assumed by the plaintiff. That article reads thus:

> "Materials arising from the demolition of a building, those which are collected for the purpose of raising a new building are movables until they have been made use of in raising a new building.

> "But if the materials have been separated from the house or other edifice only for the purpose of having it repaired or added to, and with the intention of replacing them, they preserve the nature of immovables and are considered as such."

The evidence is that a portion of the bricks had been used in building the foundation of the sugarhouse; that about half the foundation had been laid; that the workmen were putting up the building at the time the bricks and lumber were seized. But, as appears from the evidence, the sheriff seized only the bricks and lumber that were lying around convenient to be used as the work progressed, and not any of the material which was already worked into or attached to the new structure. A part of the lumber seized was still lying at the landing where it had been delivered, having been brought there by water, as had also the bricks.

We do not see the parity of reasoning by which it is maintained on the part of the plaintiff that building material intended to be used in the construction of an edifice, although never having been so used, becomes immovable by its distinctive quality like materials are which, having formed part of a house, have been separated from it only for the purpose of having it repaired or added to, and with the intention of replacing the materials. In the latter case, the materials had acquired their character of immovables by having been previously constituted part of the fabric, and they retain that character where the intention exists of replacing them in repairing or enlarging the edifice. In the former case, the materials have not that character because they have never constituted a part of any structure or work of any kind to give them that character.

We think the court below erred in the conclusions it aimed at in supposing the facts of this case analogous to one in which materials are detached from a building with the intention of using them in repairing or enlarging that building. The first paragraph of Article 468 [Revised C.C. art. 472], already quoted, seems explicit on the subject. Two classes of materials are enumerated in that paragraph, and both classes are declared to be movables: First, materials arising from the demolition of a building. This is where the building or work is destroyed. Its component parts are permanently separated, and they lose their character of immovables because the destination which was imparted to them and which gave them the character of immovables is at an end. Second, materials which are collected for the purpose of raising a new building are movables until they have been used in raising a new building-the very case presented here. We see from the second paragraph that it treats of materials having a different condition from that of those spoken of in the first paragraph. The materials in this category are not those of a demolished building, nor such as are collected for the purpose of raising a new building. They are such as have been separated from a building temporarily, and to be again attached to it, in the operation of repairing or enlarging it. The cases in (Nimmo v. Allen) 2 An. 451, (Woodruff v. Roberts) 4 An. 127, and (Key v. Woolfolk) 6 Rob. 424, harmonize with the views here taken.

It is therefore ordered, adjudged and decreed that the judgment of the district court be annulled, avoided and reversed. It is further ordered that the injunction be dissolved, and that the defendant in injunction recover of the plaintiffs and their sureties, in solido, eight per cent interest per annum on the amount of the judgment enjoined, ten percent thereon general damages, and seventy-five dollars as special damages, and all costs of suit.

3. CORPOREALS AND INCORPOREALS
La. Civ. Code arts. 461, 470-471, 473, 475

SOUTH CENTRAL BELL TELEPHONE CO. v. BARTHELEMY
643 So. 2d 1240 (La. 1994)

HALL, J. ***During the pertinent taxing periods, January 1, 1986 through April 30, 1990, Bell operated a telephone system in Orleans Parish. As part of its system, Bell set up in the parish sixteen telephone central offices. Each telephone central office is a system, in and of itself, as well as part of the larger telephone system. Simply put, each central office is a place where the caller's telephone line is connected to the line of the person being called, if that person is served by the same central office, or, if not, to a line connected to another telephone central office. Depending upon the location of the person being called, a given call may pass through multiple central offices.

Each central office consists of, among other things, switching equipment. Switching equipment includes computer processors that are directed and operated by computer software programs. Each central office is unique; consequently, each central office requires specifically tailored software designed to meet that office's operations.

During the pertinent taxing periods, Bell licensed specific switching system software programs for use in specific central offices pursuant to license agreements confected out of state with three vendors, AT&T Technologies, Inc., Northern Telecomm and Erickson.

The vendors delivered the switching system software programs to Bell via magnetic tapes. Once received, the software programs were loaded onto Bell's switching system processors, and the magnetic tapes were either used or discarded.

The second type of software at issue in this case is data processing software. This software guides the functions of the computers located in Bell's data processing center in Orleans Parish. Bell's data processing center handles basic accounting functions, including processing customer billings and payments, storing and managing customer data and maintaining a voucher and disbursement system. Bell acquired the right to use the data processing software through its affiliate, BellSouth Services, Inc. (BellSouth). BellSouth entered into a master license agreement regarding the software out of state. BellSouth also tested, evaluated and adapted the software out of state. BellSouth then transmitted the software electronically via telephone lines to Bell's modem in Orleans Parish.

The taxes at issue in this case are use taxes levied by the City on Bell's use of the two types of software programs under § 56-21 of the City Code, and sales taxes levied by the City on Bell's payment for the related maintenance service under §§56-21 and 56-15(7) of the City Code.

In October 1990, following an audit, the City notified Bell of a proposed tax deficiency assessment for, among other things, Bell's use of the two types of computer software and Bell's payment for maintenance services for such software during the pertinent taxable period. Bell paid the full amount of the proposed tax deficiency under protest. Thereafter, in November 1990, Bell commenced the instant action, seeking to recover the taxes paid under protest and contending that the items at issue were not taxable under the pertinent provisions of the City Code.

Each party filed cross-motions for summary judgment. After a hearing on the motions, the trial court denied the City's motion and granted Bell's motion in part, finding "that the sale/use tax of the City of New Orleans is not applicable to the licensing of the data processing software or to the switching software." . . . [T]he district court found "that the sale/use tax of the City of New Orleans is not applicable to the maintenance of software," and granted judgment in favor of Bell for the sum of taxes paid under protest.

Affirming, the court of appeal reasoned that computer software does not fall within the definition of "tangible personal property"; rather, it, falls within the definition of incorporeal property as it constitutes "intellectual property." In support of the latter conclusion, the court cited jurisprudence from other jurisdictions holding that computer software is intangible because the essence of the transaction is the acquisition of intangible information or knowledge. South Cent. Bell Tel. Co. v. Barthelemy, 93-1072, p. 5 (La. App. 4th Cir. 1/27/94), 631 So. 2d 1340, 1343. Likewise, the court found that since the maintenance services related to such intangible property and did not constitute "repairs," such services were not subject to the City's sales tax. Id. at 8-9, 631 So. 2d at 1344-45. On the City's writ application, we granted certiorari to consider the correctness of that decision.

II

The city use tax is imposed by § 56-21 of the Code of the City of New Orleans:

> There is hereby levied, for general municipal purposes, a tax upon the sale at retail, the use, the consumption, the distribution and the storage for use or consumption in the city of each item or article of tangible personal property, upon the lease or rental of such property and upon sale of services within the city.

"Tangible personal property" is defined in § 56-18 of the City Code as follows:

> [P]ersonal property which may be seen, weighed, measured, felt or touched, or is in any other manner perceptible to the senses. The term "tangible personal property" shall not include stocks, bonds, notes or other obligations or securities.

Construing this provision, we held in City of New Orleans v. Baumer Foods, Inc., 532 So. 2d 1381 (La. 1988), that "the term 'tangible personal property' in the City Code's use *"tangible personal prop." = "corporeal movable prop."*

tax is synonymous with corporeal movable property as used in the Louisiana Civil Code." 532 So. 2d at 1383. The reasoning behind applying property concepts in such a tax context is that the use of the common law term "tangible personal property" by the legislature, or by the various political subdivisions, was not intended to import the common law into Louisiana for purposes of sales and use tax law, nor to require the development of an entirely new body of property law for sales and use tax purposes only, but rather, the term was intended to be interpreted consistently with our civilian property concepts embodied in the Civil Code. The pertinent Civil Code provisions are Louisiana Civil Code Articles 461, 471 and 473.

As a noted property law scholar has observed, under Roman law, "Material objects that could be felt or touched were given as illustrations of corporeal things. Incorporeal things were abstract conceptions, objects having no physical existence but having a pecuniary value. The illustrations given were rights of various kinds...." A. N. Yiannopoulos, Louisiana Civil Law Treatise, Property § 25 (3d ed. 1991) (hereinafter Yiannopoulos). The Louisiana Civil Code departed from the narrow Roman law conception that only "tangible objects" were corporeal; instead, "the Louisiana Civil Code of 1870 declared that perceptibility by any of the senses sufficed for the classification of a material thing as corporeal." Yiannopoulos, § 26. While the 1978 revision to the property articles used slightly different language, the official comments indicate that it was not intended to change the law. La. Civ. Code art. 461, 1978 Official Revision Comment (a). "The word 'felt' in [Article 461] refers to perceptibility by any of the senses." Yiannopoulos, § 26.

Planiol points out that corporeals are "things" and that incorporeals are "rights." 1 M. Planiol, Treatise on the Civil Law, No. 2174 (12th ed. La. State Law Inst. Trans. 1939) (hereinafter Planiol). Planiol goes on to state that corporeal movables comprise "all things (physical objects) which are not immovables" and that incorporeal movables are "rights." 1 Planiol, Nos. 2238 and 2244. As illustrative of incorporeal movables, Planiol cites literary, artistic and industrial ownership, stating that "[t]he temporary monopoly of exploitation which the law grants to authors and inventors is also tantamount to a right of ownership." 1 Planiol, No. 2248. Hence, the civilian concept of corporeal movable encompasses all things that make up the physical world; conversely, incorporeals, i.e., intangibles, encompass the non-physical world of legal rights.

The term "tangible personal property" set forth in the City Code, and its synonymous Civil Code concept "corporeal movable," must be given their properly intended meaning. Physical recordings of computer software are not incorporeal rights to be comprehended by the understanding. Rather, they are part of the physical world. For the reason set out below, we hold the computer software at issue in this case constitutes corporeal property under our civilian concept of that term, and thus, is tangible personal property, taxable under § 56-21 of the City Code.***

IV

To correctly categorize software, it is necessary to first understand its basic characteristics. In its broadest scope, software encompasses all parts of the computer system other than the hardware, i.e., the machine; and the primary non-hardware component of a computer system is the program.

When stored on magnetic tape, disc, or computer chip, this software, or set of instructions, is physically manifested in machine readable form by arranging electrons, by use of an electric current, to create either a magnetized or unmagnetized space. The computer reads the pattern of magnetized and unmagnetized spaces with a read/write head as "on" and "off", or to put it another way, "0" and "1". This machine readable language or code is the physical manifestation of the information in binary form. [Citations omitted.]

Ordinarily, at least three program copies exist in a software transaction: (i) an original, (ii) a duplicate, and (iii) the buyer's final copy on a memory device....

South Central Bell argues that the software is merely "knowledge" or "intelligence," and as such is not corporeal and thus not taxable. We disagree with South Central Bell's characterization. The software at issue is not merely knowledge, but rather is knowledge recorded in a physical form which has physical existence, takes up space on the tape, disc, or hard drive, makes physical things happen, and can be perceived by the senses. As the dissenting judge at the court of appeal pointed out, "In defining tangible, 'seen' is not limited to the unaided eye, 'weighed' is not limited to the butcher or bathroom scale, and 'measured' is not limited to a yardstick." 93-1072, at p. 8-9, 631 So. 2d at 1348 (dissenting opinion). That we use a read/write head to read the magnetic or unmagnetic spaces is no different than any other machine that humans use to perceive those corporeal things which our naked senses cannot perceive. [Citations omitted.]

The software itself, *i.e.*, the physical copy, is not merely a right or an idea to be comprehended by the understanding. The purchaser of computer software neither desires nor receives mere knowledge, but rather receives a certain arrangement of matter that will make his or her computer perform a desired function. This arrangement of matter, physically recorded on some tangible medium, constitutes a corporeal body.

We agree with Bell and the court of appeal that the form of the delivery of the software—magnetic tape or electronic transfer via a modem — is of no relevance. However, we disagree with Bell and the court of appeal that the essence or real object of the transaction was intangible property. That the software can be transferred to various media, i.e., from tape to disk, or tape to hard drive, or even that it can be transferred over the telephone lines, does not take away from the fact that the software was ultimately recorded and stored in physical form upon a physical object. [Citations omitted.] As the court of appeal explained, and as Bell readily admits, the programs cannot be utilized by Bell until they have been recorded into the memory of the electronic telephone switch. 93-1072, at p. 6, 631 So. 2d at 1343. The essence of the transaction was not merely to obtain the intangible "knowledge" or "information", but rather, was to obtain recorded knowledge stored in some sort of physical form that Bell's computers could use. Recorded as such, the software is not merely an incorporeal idea to be comprehended, and would be of no use if it were. Rather, the software is given physical existence to make certain desired physical things happen.

One cannot escape the fact that software, recorded in physical form, becomes inextricably intertwined with, or part and parcel of the corporeal object upon which it is recorded, be that a disk, tape, hard drive, or other device. [Citations omitted.] That the information can be transferred and then physically recorded on another medium is of no moment, and does not make computer software any different than any other type of recorded information that can be transferred to another medium such as film, video tape, audio tape, or books....

Once the software is reduced to physical form and has come to rest in the City of New Orleans, be it on tape, disk, hard drive, or other device the use tax attaches.

The court of appeal found that computer software constitutes "intellectual property" and thus classified such software as an incorporeal under Louisiana Civil Code Article 461. In so doing, the court of appeal relied on a line of out of state jurisprudence holding that intangible information stored on magnetic tapes or punch cards is not taxable. That line of jurisprudence is premised on the notion that a computer software program constitutes intangible knowledge or information.

We find this line of reasoning flawed and inconsistent with our civilian property concepts outlined above. As the dissenting court of appeal judge in this case perceptively pointed out, this reasoning confuses the corporeal computer software copy itself with the incorporeal right to the software. Explaining this often confused distinction, the dissenting judge noted that the incorporeal right to software is the copyright, which in this case, as is typical in such license agreements, was reserved to the vendors. 93-1072, at p. 2, 631 So. 2d at 1345 (dissenting opinion). What Bell acquired, and what the City was attempting to tax, was not the copyright to the software, but the copy of the software itself. It was not the copyright that operated the telephone central office switching equipment, but rather the physical copy of the software.

We likewise decline to adopt the canned versus custom distinction invoked by a few state legislatures, commentators and courts. "Canned" software is software which has been pre-written to be used by more than one customer, or mass marketed; "custom" software is specially designed for exclusive use by one particular customer. Under the canned versus custom distinction, canned programs are classified as taxable on the theory that the buyer acquires an end product; whereas, custom programs are classified as non-taxable services on the theory that the buyer acquires professional services. [Citations omitted.]

In sum, once the "information" or "knowledge" is transformed into physical existence and recorded in physical form, it is corporeal property. The physical recordation of this software is not an incorporeal right to be comprehended. Therefore we hold that the switching system software and the data processing software involved here is tangible personal property and thus is taxable by the City of New Orleans. Affirmed in part, reversed in part, and remanded. *Holds*

SUCCESSION OF MILLER
405 So. 2d 812 (La. 1981)

On Rehearing

CALOGERO, J. Rehearing was granted in this case to reconsider our determination that Ms. Miller gave Mrs. Meyer the funds from the savings account and the bearer bonds and that each such gift constituted a valid inter vivos donation.

The facts surrounding the transfer of these items, in chronological order, are essentially as follows. About August 21, 1974, decedent and Mrs. Meyer went to the office of Schwegmann Brothers Giant Super Market and purchased the bearer bonds involved in this case. Decedent had previously consulted Mrs. Meyer's husband, *Facts* a ranking employee in the management of Schwegmann's, and had told him of her intentions to buy the bonds and give them to Mrs. Meyer. After the bonds were issued, decedent gave the bonds to Mrs. Meyer, according to Mr. and Mrs. Meyer's testimony. Mrs. Meyer testified that she understood that the bonds were hers, but that she would have returned them to the decedent if she had been asked to. She also testified that she gave the decedent the interest coupons from the bonds until her death.

On January 30, 1976, after having discussed her plans with Mr. and Mrs. Meyer, and accompanied by Mrs. Meyer, the decedent closed out a savings account in her name and transferred the funds to an account styled "Mildred M. Miller or Mrs. Albertha S. Meyer (payable to either or survivor)." Mrs. Meyer testified that at the time of the transfer, decedent told her, "Albertha, I want you to have that." Nothing more was said about this money until shortly before decedent's death.

On May 19, 1976, Ms. Miller was brought to the hospital in an ambulance, suffering from a stroke. Mrs. Meyer accompanied Ms. Miller to the hospital. Both Mr. and Mrs. Meyer testified that Ms. Miller had told them that she was about to die and instructed Mrs. Meyer to go to the savings and loan association and withdraw the funds from the joint account. Mrs. Meyer testified that she first protested, but later complied with the decedent's instructions. The withdrawal was made on May 24, 1976.

During Ms. Miller's six day stay in the hospital prior to her death, the hospital records indicate that the decedent was comatose and could not speak upon entering the hospital on May 19, was drowsy but cooperative on May 20, was semicomatose on May 21, continuing to mumble, and again reverted back to the comatose condition on May 22, with no improvement noted on the charts until her death on May 25, 1976. Mrs. Meyer testified that she and the decedent did talk to each other during this period, and they could both understand each other. No other witnesses were called by either party.

Ms Miller had never married, and was survived only by cousins, one of whom was Mrs. Albertha Meyer. Ms. Miller had lived alone but saw Mrs. Meyer daily, and had a room in Mrs. Meyer's house which was treated as Ms. Miller's room. Although Ms. Miller had written a will, it was invalid for want of form. The succession proceedings followed those for an intestate succession, and a succession inventory was filed by the administratrix. In the inventory of Ms. Miller's property, the administratrix had listed, among other things, the money from the joint savings account which had been withdrawn by Mrs. Meyer from the account prior to decedent's death and also the bearer bonds issued by Schwegmann's.

Mrs. Meyer filed a motion to traverse the inventory contending that the funds from the joint savings account and the bearer bonds were erroneously listed in the succession inventory, and that she was the owner of that property by virtue of an inter vivos manual donation from Ms. Miller. After a hearing on Mrs. Meyer's motion the trial court held that the bonds and cash were properly included in the succession inventory and the Court of Appeal affirmed. 378 So. 2d 543.

This Court granted Mrs. Meyer's application to review the lower court rulings and in our original opinion reversed the rulings, finding that a valid inter vivos donation by manual gift had been made of both the funds from the savings account and the bearer bonds, and that the items belonged to Mrs. Meyer. After granting a rehearing in this case, we now affirm our original opinion insofar as it relates to the funds from the savings account, but find that there was no valid inter vivos donation of the bearer bonds.

Mrs. Meyer contends that Ms. Miller gratuitously gave her both the funds from the savings account and the bearer bonds and that those items thus belong to her. The administratrix of Ms. Miller's estate included both items in the succession inventory contending that a valid inter vivos donation had not been made of the property.

It is well settled that property can neither be acquired nor disposed of gratuitously except by donations inter vivos or mortis causa. La. Revised C.C. art. 1467. Since Ms. Miller's will has already been held invalid (that is not contested here), for Mrs. Meyer to prevail in this case, it must be shown that a valid inter vivos donation of the property was made.

A donation inter vivos (between living persons) is an act by which the donor divests himself, at present and irrevocably, of the thing given, in favor of the donee who accepts it. La. C.C. art. 1468. The Code requires that such donations meet strict form requirements. La. C.C. art. 1467. It is provided that donations of immovables and movables, whether corporeal or incorporeal, be made by "an act passed before a notary public and two witnesses." La. C.C. art. 1536; La. C.C. art. 1538. The only Code exception to this form requirement is found in Article 1539 which provides:

> The manual gift, that is, the giving of corporeal movable effects, accompanied by a real delivery, is not subject to any formality.

Since no authentic act was executed for either the donation of the funds in the savings account or the bearer bonds, the validity of these donations hinges on whether they were "manual gifts" under La. C.C. art. 1539, that is, whether they were *corporeal* movables actually delivered.

Corporeals and incorporeals are defined in the Civil Code in Article 461 which provides:

> Corporeals are things that have a body, whether animate or inanimate, and can be felt or touched.

> Incorporeals are things that have no body, but are comprehended by the understanding, such as the rights of inheritance, servitudes, obligations, and right of intellectual property.

Corporeal movables are things that normally move or can be moved from one place to another. La. C.C. art. 471. Incorporeal movables are the rights, obligations and actions that apply to a movable thing, such as *bonds*, annuities, and interests or shares in entities possessing juridical personality. La. C.C. art. 473.

As concerns the funds in the savings account, while it is true that the savings account, or the right to the funds therein, is an incorporeal movable, and thus as such not subject to manual gift, the cash, withdrawn from the savings account, is a corporeal movable and subject to manual gift provided there was actual delivery of the funds.

Mrs. Meyer contends that there was actual delivery of the funds even though it was she who withdrew the funds from the account. She contends that Ms. Miller did not have to actually hand her the cash, but that it was sufficient that she withdrew and possessed the funds at Ms. Miller's request.

As noted in our original opinion, the donor expressed her unqualified intent, on several occasions, that Mrs. Meyer have the money, the last such expression being just prior to her death, while she was in the hospital. In fact, it was this final insistence which prompted Mrs. Meyer to go and withdraw the funds before Ms. Miller's death. Therefore, although Ms. Miller did not actually hand the funds to Mrs. Meyer, there was nevertheless a valid inter vivos donation by manual gift of the funds from the savings account.

As for the bearer bonds, we now conclude that the bonds are incorporeal movables and simply, by statute, not susceptible of manual gift...

The Legislature has provided that incorporeal movables are not subject to manual gift and cannot be donated inter vivos except by an act passed before a notary and two witnesses. La. C.C. art. 1536; La. C.C. art. 1539. La. C.C. art. 473 specifically provides that the rights and obligations that apply to bonds are incorporeal movables. Because of this, and because there was no such notarial act passed in this case, we conclude that the bonds, even if delivered, were not validly donated. Thus, the bonds remained the property of the deceased and were properly included in the succession inventory.

WATSON, J., concurs as to the bonds but dissents as to the savings account.

DIXON, C. J. (dissenting). I respectfully dissent. It is not necessary for us to thwart the will of the decedent and hold that bearer bonds cannot be the subject of a manual gift....

A quick reading of the Louisiana Civil Code would easily lead to the conclusion that bonds of business concerns, transferable by delivery, are not subject to manual donation. Donations of movables, immovables and "incorporeal things, such as rents, credits, rights or actions" are invalid unless an act of donation is passed before a notary and two witnesses. C.C. 1536, 1538; only the "manual gift, that is, the giving of corporeal movable effects, accompanied by a real delivery, is not subject to any formality." C.C. 1539. Bonds (since Act 728 of 1978) are specifically mentioned in the definition of incorporeal movables:

> "Rights, obligations, and actions that apply to a movable thing are incorporeal movables. Movables of this kind are such as bonds, annuities, and interests or shares in entities possessing juridical personality. . . ." C.C. 473

Rights, obligations and actions that apply to bonds, therefore, are incorporeal movables. Rights, obligations and actions that apply to a cow are also incorporeal movables. Cows are movable, but corporeal. Bearer bonds are movable, but are they incorporeal, like the actions which apply to them? C.C. 461 defines:

> "Corporeals and things that have a body, whether animate or inanimate and can be felt or touched.

> "Incorporeals are things that have no body, but are comprehended by the understanding, such as the rights of inheritance, servitudes, obligations, and right of intellectual property."

....C.C. 1536 should not be extended to instruments the transfer of which is governed by the commercial law. No reason has been advanced for requiring an act of donation before a notary and two witnesses to validate the gift of an instrument which can be transferred by mere delivery. Negotiable instruments are what they seem to be — movables which can be felt and touched. They are themselves proof of the obligations expressed within them, and are therefore something in addition to those obligations.

French doctrine permits the manual donation of such instruments, as does most of the Louisiana jurisprudence since the earliest years of the state.

NOTES AND QUESTIONS

1. Ms. Miller's bearer bonds were a type of negotiable instrument. A bearer instrument can be negotiated—that is, is capable of valid transfer—by endorsement or delivery. Thus the physical paper itself, rather than merely representing an underlying debt obligation on the part of the issuer, has intrinsic value; the owner of a lost or stolen bearer bond would face the same difficulty in recovering it as the owner of lost or stolen cash. A negotiable instrument to the bearer is now negotiated by delivery under Uniform Commercial Code Article 3, adopted in Louisiana as La. R.S. 10:3-202(1). That legislation did not exist at the time that *Miller* was decided. However, as Justice Dixon points out in dissent, such an instrument was treated under past jurisprudence as a corporeal movable, rather than as an incorporeal, because its nature is more like that of a cow than like that of a right.

2. In *Succession of Walker*, 533 So. 2d 70 (La. App. 4th Cir. 1990), the court held that a certified cashier's check, though an incorporeal movable under the Civil Code, is a negotiable instrument that may be donated in accordance with the Louisiana Commercial Paper Law, R.S. 10:3-201(4). See also La. Civ. Code art. 1550, *as amended by* 2008 La. Acts, No. 204, § 1, effective Jan. 1, 2009.

3. It has been held that R.S. 10:3-201(4) has superseded the Civil Code as to matters of form only. The underlying validity of a donation is still subject to the substantive requirements of the Civil Code. *Fogg v. Fogg*, 571 So. 2d 838 (La. App. 3d Cir. 1990).

4. What was Ms. Miller likely trying to accomplish through the bearer bonds and the joint savings account with Ms. Meyer, and why?

INNOVATIVE HOSPITALITY SYSTEMS v. ABRAHAM
61 So. 3d 740 (La. App. 3d Cir.), *cert. denied* 63 So. 3d 2011)

EZELL, J. Innovative Hospitality Systems, LLC, alleged in its petition that in March 2007, at least 108 of its checks were fraudulently presented for cashing at Abe's Grocery in Lake Charles, Louisiana. The applicant, First Specialty Insurance Corporation, provided a commercial general liability policy for Abe's. First Specialty filed a motion for summary judgment asserting that the cashing of these fraudulent checks was not covered by its policy. The trial court denied First Specialty's motion. First Specialty sought supervisory writs from the judgment denying the motion for summary judgment. This court denied writs. First Specialty then sought relief from the Louisiana Supreme Court, which remanded the case for briefing, argument, and a full opinion. Innovative Hospitality Systems, LLC v. Abraham, 10-1285 (La. 11/5/10), 51 So. 3d 1. For the reasons that follow, we deny the writ.

ANALYSIS

The original petition in this suit avers that Abe's Grocery, in addition to functioning as a grocery store, also cashed checks and that numerous fraudulent checks had been negotiated on Innovative Hospitality's bank account by the various check-cashing businesses-defendants, including Abe's. In addition to naming the businesses, Innovative Hospitality eventually joined the businesses' insurers, including First Specialty[,] who provided a commercial general liability (CGL) policy to Abe's. The suit also was brought against the banks in which the checks had been deposited by the various check-cashing businesses; therefore, these banks filed cross-claims against these businesses and their insurers, including First Specialty.

First Specialty filed a motion for summary judgment claiming that its policy did not provide coverage for the losses at issue because the losses did not constitute either "bodily injury" or "property damage" as defined by the policy. In support of its motion, First Specialty attached a certified copy of the policy it issued to Abe's. Abe's opposed the motion, not on the basis that any genuine issue of material fact existed, but rather on the basis that the language of the First Specialty policy afforded coverage for its loss.

Louisiana Code of Civil Procedure Article 966(B) provides that summary judgment shall be granted where the pleadings, depositions, answers to interrogatories, admissions on file and affidavits show that there is no genuine issue of material fact and that the mover is entitled to judgment as a matter of law. The Louisiana Supreme Court discussed the standard applicable to appellate review of summary judgments involving insurance contracts in Robinson v. Heard, 01-1697, pp. 3-4 (La. 2/26/02), 809 So.2d 943, 945:

> ***Summary judgment declaring a lack of coverage under an insurance policy may not be rendered unless there is no reasonable interpretation of the policy, when applied to the undisputed material facts shown by the evidence supporting the motion, under which coverage could be afforded." Reynolds v. Select Props., Ltd., 93-1480, p. 2 (La. 4/11/94), 634 So.2d 1180, 1183.

An insurance policy is a contract between the parties and should be construed employing the general rules of interpretation of contracts set forth in the Louisiana Civil Code. The parties' intent, as reflected by the words of the policy, determine[s] the extent of coverage. La. Civ. Code art. 2045. Words and phrases used in a policy are to be construed using their plain, ordinary and generally prevailing meaning, unless the words have acquired a technical meaning. La. Civ. Code art. 2047. An insurance policy should not be interpreted in an unreasonable or a strained manner so as to enlarge or to restrict its provisions beyond what is reasonably contemplated by its terms or so as to achieve an absurd conclusion. Where the language in the policy is clear, unambiguous, and expressive of the intent of the parties, the agreement must be enforced as written. However, if after applying the other rules of construction an ambiguity remains, the ambiguous provision is to be construed against the drafter and in favor of the insured.

The purpose of liability insurance is to afford the insured protection from damage claims. Policies therefore should be construed to effect, and not to deny, coverage. Thus, a provision which seeks to narrow the insurer's obligation is strictly construed against the insurer, and, if the language of the exclusion is subject to two or more reasonable interpretations, the interpretation which favors coverage must be applied.

It is equally well settled, however, that subject to the above rules of interpretation, insurance companies have the right to limit coverage in any manner they desire, so long as the limitations do not conflict with statutory provisions or public policy.

Id. (case citations omitted).

The policy provides, "We will pay those sums that the insured becomes legally obligated to pay as damages because of 'bodily injury' or 'property damage' to which this insurance applies." The policy defines "property damage" as:

Property damage" means:

a.   Physical injury to tangible property, including all resulting loss of use of that property. All such loss of use shall be deemed to occur at the time of the physical injury that caused it; or

b.   Loss of use of tangible property that is not physically injured. All such loss of use shall be deemed to occur at the time of the "occurrence" that caused it.

For the purposes of this insurance, electronic data is not tangible property.

As used in this definition, electronic data means information, facts or programs stored as or on, created or used on, or transmitted to or from computer software, including systems and applications software, hard or floppy disks, CD-ROMS, tapes, drives, cells, data processing devices or any other media which are used with electronically controlled equipment.

First Specialty contends that because Innovative Hospitality and the cross-claim plaintiffs are seeking to recoup funds withdrawn from Innovative Hospitality's bank account, such transactions do not involve physical items; thus, the object of this suit is to recoup intangible things. Therefore, First Specialty asserts that its policy provides no coverage under the policy's express definition of "property damage" as being limited to tangible things.

The trial court found that since Abe's paid out cash on the fraudulent checks, this cash was in fact tangible. Therefore, the trial court held that First Specialty was not entitled to summary judgment dismissing it from this action because it had failed to show that the policy did not provide coverage.

The term "tangible property" in such policies carries the same meaning as the civilian term "corporeal property." (Ctations omitted.)

In South Central Bell Telephone Co. v. Barthelemy, 94-499 (La. 10/17/94), 643 So. 2d 1240, the supreme court discussed the meaning of "tangible personal property" utilizing the civilian property concepts embodied in the Louisiana Civil Code. The supreme court observed that the Civil Code differentiates between corporeals and incorporeals in La. Civ. Code art. 461 as follows: "Corporeals are things that have a body, whether animate or inanimate, and can be felt or touched. Incorporeals are things that have no body, but are comprehended by understanding, such as the rights of inheritance, servitudes, obligations, and right of intellectual property."

The supreme court, citing La. Civ. Code art. 471, also noted that corporeal movables are " 'things, whether animate or inanimate, that normally move or can be moved from one place to another.' " Id. at 1244. The supreme court also recognized La.Civ.Code art. 473 as defining incorporeal movables as " 'rights, obligations, and actions that apply to a movable thing....Movables of this kind are such as bonds, annuities, and interests or shares in entities possessing juridical personality.' " Id.

The supreme court then held that "the civilian concept of corporeal movable encompasses all things that make up the physical world; conversely, incorporeals, i.e., intangibles, encompass the non-physical world of legal rights." Id.

First Specialty argues that Innovative Hospitality and the co-defendant banks are seeking to recover incorporeals; that is, amounts withdrawn from Innovative Hospitality's bank account. First Specialty asserts that Innovative Hospitality does not have actual dollar bills sitting in a bank; rather, Innovative Hospitality has a right to go to the bank where it holds an account and ask to withdraw in dollars an amount equal to its account balance. In countering the trial court's reasoning that Innovative Hospitality and the co-defendant banks are seeking reimbursement for the physical dollars that First Specialty's insured, Abe's, paid out on the fraudulent checks, First Specialty suggests that those dollars were not damaged or destroyed in any fashion so as to bring the dollar bills within the coverage of its insurance policy. Furthermore, First Specialty points out that Innovative Hospitality never had ownership of the actual dollar bills paid out by Abe's on the fraudulent checks. Instead, the dollars were simply handed over by Abe's to those cashing the fraudulent checks. Accordingly, First Specialty contends that the trial court's reasoning for finding coverage was incorrect.

Innovative Hospitality, on the other hand, contends that its injury occurred when the fraudulent check and cash were exchanged at Abe's. In Innovative Hospitality's words, "The operative reality of negotiable instruments is that while Abe's employee was reaching into its cash drawer...that employee was effectively reaching into Plaintiff's bank account."

At issue in this case is the specific language in the policy: "Loss of use of tangible property that is not physically injured." Specifically, damage to the property is not required. What is required is a "loss of use" of "tangible property".

In Succession of Franklin, 42,496 (La. App. 2d Cir. 10/17/07), 968 So.2d 811, the court held that an "uncashed check" was an incorporeal movable. The court reasoned that the check represented the bank's obligation to pay the funds, but was not the funds themselves. Obviously, the funds themselves are corporeal movables or tangible property.

Once Abe's Grocery presented cash in exchange for the check, the check was converted into actual funds which were corporeal movables. It was at this point that any responsibility Abe's Grocery may have attached. This action resulted in a loss of use of funds to Innovative Hospitality. It is ridiculous to argue that Innovative Hospitality has not lost actual cash as a result of the cashing of fraudulent checks. The funds in its bank account are actual funds deposited at the bank by Innovative Hospitality. As a result of Abe's Grocery cashing the checks, Innovative Hospitality Systems suffered a "loss of use" of its cash money, a corporeal movable and therefore, tangible property. See Succession of Miller, 405 So. 2d 812; 405 So. 2d 812 (La. 1981); Succession of Walker, 533 So.2d 70 (La. App. 3d Cir. 1988), writ denied, 536 So. 2d 1254 (La. 1989). If Abe's Grocery is held responsible for this loss, it will be for the loss of cash money it handed over in cashing the fraudulent checks.

We find that the CGL policy of insurance issued by First Speciality to Abe's Grocery provides coverage for the type of claims asserted in this case. Therefore, we find no error in the trial court's ruling denying First Specialty's motion for summary judgment. Writ denied.

GREMILLION, J., dissenting....Until Abe's bank presented the fraudulent check to Innovative Hospitality's bank, and that bank then honored the check and debited Innovative Hospitality's account, Innovative Hospitality still had the use of those funds. Innovative Hospitality did not lose cash, but the right to use its funds.

Innovative Hospitality makes the valid point that a check is also considered a corporeal. However, it is not making a claim for the damage to the check. It is making a claim for funds that were fraudulently withdrawn from its checking account.

It has been further suggested that because the policy states that First Specialty insures against "[l]oss of use of tangible property that is not physically injured," the loss experienced by Innovative Hospitality is covered. I believe the "loss of use" coverage does not apply. Our colleagues on the first circuit held that "loss of use" coverage did not extend to compensate a business for its employee's embezzlement of funds. Jim Carey Dist. Co., Inc. v. Zinna, 589 So.2d 526 (La. App. 1st Cir. 1991). I agree with that analysis.

CONCLUSION

The miscreants who stole and forged checks drawn on Innovative Hospitality's account withdrew cash. The cash, however, was not what Innovative Hospitality lost. It lost the right to use its funds on deposit with its bank. The loss did not consist of tangible property. As such, First Specialty, as the insurer of Abe's Grocery, does not afford Abe's coverage for that loss. I would grant First Specialty's application for writs and make that grant peremptory.

CHAPTER IV. POSSESSION
Civil Code arts. 3421-3444, 3476-3479, 481

1. DEFINITION, NATURE, AND EFFECTS OF POSSESSION
Civil Code arts. 3421-3423, 3446

1(2) PLANIOL, TRAITÉ ÉLÉMENTAIRE DE DROIT CIVIL 340-346
(an English translation by the Louisiana State Law Institute 1959)

Definition. Possession is a state of fact which consists in holding a thing in an exclusive manner and in carrying out on it the same material acts of use and of enjoyment as if its possessor were its owner.

Thus defined, possession is taken in its narrow and original sense. It recalls the idea of both the material thing and the idea of ownership.

Progressive Extension of the Idea of Possession. Roman jurisconsults at first knew of possession and understood it solely in its most perfect application. They envisaged the case where a person holds a thing, may make use of it, and if need be destroy it or consume it. Thus conceived, possession appears as being a physical power, something material. And thus was it held that possession was possible only as regards material things. But, with the passage of time, these jurisconsults recognized, in addition to this possession of corporeal things or *possessio rei,* another kind of possession. It consisted in the factual exercise upon a thing of a mere right of servitude. It was called the *possessio jurist* or *quasi-possessio.* Not only have we preserved this extension of the concept of possession but in our modern law the concept of possession has even been removed from the domain of real rights and has been extended to other rights.

Elements That Constitute Possession. According to an old doctrinal tradition of Roman origin, possession is made up of two elements. One is physical, and is called the *corpus.* The other is a matter of intent, and is known as *animus.*

The *corpus* consists of facts that constitute the possession. They are the physical acts of detention, use, enjoyment and transformation carried out upon the thing. Juridical acts, such as a lease or sale do not suffice to form the corporeal element of possession (Cass., Nov. 14, 1910, D. 1912. 1.483). These acts may be performed by persons who are not in possession. It is not necessary to possess a thing in order to grant a lease upon it, or to sell it. The contract is valid; it is merely its execution that becomes impossible. Such contracts rest on the right of ownership, not upon the thing.

According to the current opinion in France, "*animus*" on the incorporeal element, is the possessor's intent to act on his own behalf. Thus it is called "*animus domini*" or "*animus rem sibi habendi.*" These expressions, which were invented to express the Roman concept of possession, are all Roman. They are not found in any law. They are moreover rejected by Ihering and many of his school, who reduce the element of intent to the mere will to exercise upon the thing that physical power known as possession.

Animus is taken for granted. When a man holds a thing physically he is not called upon to prove that he is acting on his own behalf and that he is really its possessor. It devolves upon his adversary to prove that he merely holds the thing, and is in possession of it for the account of a third party.

Moreover the law does not require that there be a deliberate and special act of will at each entry into possession. In most cases, a general act of will suffices, when conditions are such that they are consistent with a new possession. This is what takes place when postmen deposit letters in the boxes found near the door of private residences. The person to whom the letters are addressed becomes their possessor before he knows that the letter has been deposited in his box.

PELOQUIN v. CALCASIEU PARISH POLICE JURY
367 So. 2d 1246 (La. App. 3d Cir. 1979)

FORET, J. Plaintiff, Robert Peloquin, filed suit on behalf of himself, his wife and their two minor children against Mr. and Mrs. Joseph A. Linscomb and the Calcasieu Parish Police Jury for damages for conversion of their pet cat, "George," for the value of the cat, and for mental anguish, inconvenience, and humiliation suffered due to the alleged actions of the defendants.

Mrs. Linscomb, a neighbor of the plaintiffs, borrowed an animal trap from the Calcasieu Parish Animal Control Center, an agency of the Calcasieu Parish Police Jury, placed it in her yard, and eventually succeeded in trapping a cat, allegedly "George." After trapping the cat, Mr. and Mrs. Linscomb returned the trap with the enclosed cat to the Calcasieu Parish Animal Control Center where it was destroyed. The defendants deny that the cat disposed of was in fact, the plaintiffs' cat.

Prior to trial on the merits, defendants filed exceptions of no right of action and no cause of action on the grounds that as the plaintiffs had no ownership interest in George they had no legal grounds to sue for damages for mental anguish, etc. occasioned by his alleged conversion at the hands of defendants. These exceptions were maintained by the trial court, leaving plaintiffs the right to sue for only the worth of the cat, which the court determined was less than the statutorily required amount necessary for a jury trial and thus also denied plaintiffs' request for same. Plaintiffs have appealed dismissal of this part of their claim.***

The plaintiffs allege their ownership of George and their subsequent dispossession of him by acts of the defendants. This in itself is sufficient to state a cause of action.

It is stipulated by the parties that:

(1) appellants did not purchase the cat nor did they receive it as a gift;

(2) the Peloquins had possessed the cat for more than seven years since Mrs. Peloquin found it as a kitten in or near her yard;

(3) the Peloquins did not advertise the finding of the kitten in the newspaper or make other attempts to locate the owner except to ask their neighbors.

The trial court, citing Civil Code Article 3422 [Revised C.C. art. 3419], held that the Peloquins were not the owners of the cat and as mere possessors, did not have the right to sue for mental anguish, etc. suffered as a result of George's alleged demise at the hands of the defendants but could sue only for any actual damages (the worth of the cat).

Article 3422 is contained in the chapter of the Louisiana Civil Code of 1870 entitled "Occupancy," which is defined in Article 3412 (1870):

Article 3412. Occupancy is a mode of acquiring property by which a thing which belongs to nobody, becomes the property of the person who took possession of it, with the intention of acquiring a right of ownership upon it.

Further examination of this chapter reveals that property, subject to occupancy, may be acquired by possession of it for different periods of time, depending on the prior ownership status of the property. Article 3421 [Revised C.C. art. 3418] allows a person who acquires a movable that has been abandoned to immediately become its "master." Article 3415 [Revised C.C. art. 3413] allows the captor who reduces to possession a wild animal to immediately become the owner of the captured creature.

Mrs. Peloquin stated that approximately seven years prior to the disappearance of George, she had found him as a kitten while putting her children on a school bus. After first asking her neighbors if they had lost a kitten, the Peloquins raised George as a family pet. In applying Article 3422 [Revised C.C. art. 3419], the trial court must have determined that George was "lost" when taken in by the Peloquins; however, from the record this appears to be a factual determination that the jury should have had a chance to consider. It is at least as likely that George was either abandoned by his prior owner or perhaps never had an owner (a wild beast or animal). Cursory observation of the streets of our cities reveals many "alley cats" which exist by their wiles without being owned by any person.***

However, we do not decide this appeal on these grounds as we are persuaded by plaintiffs' further alternative argument that they should be allowed to sue for all claimed damages because of their status as George's possessor...

In French law, Aubry & Rau Property state:

> "The possession of corporeal things creates in favor of the possessor a presumption that he has legal title which the possession manifests. More precisely it has the following effects:
>
> A simple possessor or even a precarious holder of a movable of whose possession he is deprived can recover it against a third party simple possessor in all cases in which the owner of the thing could do so."

Holding

We conclude that a possessor has the same rights as an owner of a movable to sue for damages for conversion thereof by the defendant, and those damages may include awards for mental anguish, humiliation, etc. as well as special and/or actual damages.... If plaintiffs can prove possession, and that they suffered provable and compensable damages as a result of the conversion of the cat involved, we are of the opinion that they are entitled to recover for these damages.*** Accordingly, we reverse the judgment of the trial court, and overrule the exceptions of no right of action and no cause of action, and remand the case for further proceedings.

LOUISIANA CIVIL CODE, BOOK III, TITLE XXIII
Exposé des Motifs

Chapter 2. Possession

According to civilian conceptions, *possession* is the physical control over a corporeal thing with the intent to have it as one's own. The physical control over a thing, in the absence of intent to have it as one's own, is called detention. Thus, a lessor has possession, whereas the lessee has *detention*. A precarious possessor is not a possessor; he merely has physical control over a thing and thus has detention of it.

In Louisiana, the distinction between possession and detention has not been drawn neatly in legislation or jurisprudence. On the contrary, possession was defined broadly in the 1870 Code to include detention. Article 3421(1) follows the Louisiana legal tradition; possession is defined broadly as the detention or enjoyment of a corporeal thing, movable or immovable, that one holds or exercises by himself or through another who keeps it or exercises it in the possessor's name. Thus, under the revision, a precarious possessor may be called a possessor even though he does not intend to possess as owner.

Possession, as defined, properly applies to corporeal things only. The exercise of a right, such as a servitude, with the intent to have it as one's own is quasi-possession. This distinction between possession and quasi-possession has been made for systematic reasons. Practically speaking there is no difference between possession and quasi-possession because the rules governing possession apply by analogy to the quasi-possession of incorporeals. Article 3421(2).

Possession is a matter of fact; however, one who has possessed a thing for over a year acquires the right to possess it. Article 3422. This distinction between possession and right to possess has been established by Louisiana jurisprudence on the basis of the provisions of the Civil Code.

Although possession is a matter of fact, it gives rise to certain rights. For example, a possessor may be entitled to reimbursement for certain expenses. Articles 486, 488, 527 and 529. Moreover, a possessor is considered provisionally to be the owner of the thing he possesses until the right of the true owner is established. Article 3423. Under this provision, a possessor is vested with the prerogatives of ownership as long as there is no other owner.

OLIVER WENDELL HOLMES
THE COMMON LAW 213-215 (1881)

I think we are now in a position to begin the analysis of possession. It will be instructive to say a word in the first place upon a preliminary question which has been debated with much zeal in Germany. Is possession a fact or a right? This question must be taken to mean, by possession and right, what the law means by those words, and not something else which philosophers or moralists may mean by them; for as lawyers we have nothing to do with either, except in a legal sense. If this had always been borne steadily in mind, the question would hardly have been asked.

A legal right is nothing but a permission to exercise certain natural powers, and upon certain conditions to obtain protection, restitution, or compensation by the aid of the public force. Just so far as the aid of the public force is given a man, he has a legal right, and this right is the same whether his claim is founded in righteousness or iniquity. Just so far as possession is protected, it is as much a source of legal rights as ownership is when it secures the same protection.

Every right is a consequence attached by the law to one or more facts which the law defines, and wherever the law gives anyone special rights not shared by the body of the people, it does so on the ground that certain special facts, not true of the rest of the world, are true of him. When a group of facts thus singled out by the law exists in the case of a given person, he is said to be entitled to the corresponding rights; meaning, thereby, that the law helps him to constrain his neighbors, or some of them, in a way in which it would not, if all the facts in question were not true of him. Hence, any word which denotes such a group of facts connotes the rights attached to it by way of legal consequences, and any word which denotes the rights attached to a group of facts connotes the group of facts in like manner.

The word "possession" denotes such a group of facts. Hence, when we say of a man that he has possession, we affirm directly that all the facts of a certain group are true of him, and we convey indirectly or by implication that the law will give him the advantage of the situation. Contract, or property, or any other substantive notion of the law, may be analyzed in the same way, and should be treated in the same order. The only difference is, that while possession denotes the facts and connotes the consequence, property always, and contract with more uncertainty and oscillation, denotes the consequence and connotes the facts. When we say that a man owns a thing, we affirm directly that he has the benefit of the consequences attached to a certain group of facts, and, by implication, that the facts are true of him. The important thing to grasp is, that each of these legal compounds, possession, property, and contract, is to be analyzed into fact and right, antecedent and consequent, in like manner as every other. It is wholly immaterial that one element is accented by one word, and the other by the other two. We are not studying etymology, but law. There are always two things to be asked: First, what are the facts which make up the group in question; and then, what are the consequences attached by law to that group. The former generally offers the only difficulties.

Hence, it is almost tautologous to say that the protection which the law attaches by way of consequence to possession, is as truly a right in a legal sense as those consequences which are attached to adverse holding for the period of prescription, or to a promise for value or under seal. If the statement is aided by dramatic reinforcement, I may add that possessory rights pass by descent or devise, as well as by conveyance, and that they are taxed as property in some of the States.

1(2) PLANIOL, TRAITÉ ÉLÉMENTAIRE DE DROIT CIVIL 351-357
(an English translation by the Louisiana State Law Institute 1959)

Effects of Possession. Possession, taken in itself, is a pure fact. A person enjoys a thing. A person claims to be the owner of it or to have a right of servitude or a usufruct upon it and acts as if he has this right. In all this, there is but a fact and nothing juridical. But the fact of possession, alone or joined to other circumstances, produces various juridical consequences.

First of all it is protected for its own sake:

(1) by means of a presumption of ownership, which safeguards it against attacks of a juridical nature directed against it in the form of suits and

(2) by means of special units called possessory actions, which defend it against physical violence.

And, in the next place, it leads to the acquisition of ownership:
(1) as regards the fruits, which the possessor of a fruit-bearing thing gains, that is to say is permitted to keep indefinitely, when he possesses it under certain conditions; and

(2) as regards the thing itself and this either in an immediate manner, through the occupation of things without an owner or at the end of a certain delay (ordinarily one of 30 years in the case of immovables) through *"usucapion,"* or acquisitive prescription of immovable real rights.

Presumption of Ownership Based on Possession. All possessors are presumed to be owners, because this factual state of affairs is generally conformable to the legal state of affairs (Cass., April 15, 1863, D. 63. 1. 396).

In matters affecting immovable property, the sole effect of this presumption of ownership is that the possessor becomes defendant in suits known as actions of revendication. This affords him a distinct advantage. The requirement that the plaintiff must establish his right of ownership often places him in a difficult position. If the plaintiff be unable to adduce this proof, the defendant will remain in possession, not because the latter is recognized as owner, but because his adversary has not demonstrated that he is. The state of affairs which existed before the suit will continue because there is no reason why it should be changed. This is the natural effect of the rules of proof.

Reference. Most of the effects of possession will find their appropriate place later on, either in studying actions in revendication or the different modes of acquiring ownership. All that is necessary to bring out for the moment is (1) the acquisition of fruits by the possessor in good faith and (2) possessory actions.

2. CORPOREAL, CIVIL, AND CONSTRUCTIVE POSSESSION
Civil Code arts. 3425, 3426, 3431

See A. N. YIANNOPOULOS, CIVIL LAW PROPERTY §§ 301-305 (4th ed. 2001)

NOTE
Introduction to *Ellis v. Prevost*

Most students find the opinion that follows (*Ellis*) difficult to understand, partly because the case is so old, and partly because it is the second in what was a series of three inter-related Louisiana Supreme Court opinions. The courts struggled with this case for years. Ellis originally filed suit against Madame Prevost in February, 1837, and trial was held in March, 1838. The Louisiana Supreme Court rendered its first opinion in April 1839, remanded for a new trial, and rendered its second opinion July 1841. But wait, there's more. Madame Prevost thereafter sued Ellis, resulting in a third trial and yet a third supreme court opinion rendered in May, 1845. So, if you have struggled with the case (and you should be struggling with the case), be comforted. The Louisiana Supreme Court reversed the trial court all three times!

To understand the opinion, you must first recognize the nature of the litigation between Ellis and Madame Prevost. Information on this topic appears in the middle of the third paragraph of this (the second) opinion, in which the court references its first opinion:

> Under the legal principles established in the former decision of this case, which however we are not ready to adopt to the same extent, it is clear, that the plaintiff had a right to institute an action of possession against the defendants by virtue of his civil possession, based on the previous actual and corporeal possession of his vendor. This doctrine, so far as it regards the civil possession to be preceded by an actual and corporeal detention of the thing, and as it allows to the plaintiff the benefit of the previous corporeal possession of his author, appears to be correct, and we are not disposed to controvert it; but we cannot accede to the proposition, that our laws recognize but one kind of possession, and that a civil possession will suffice in all cases.

As you can see from this excerpt, the lawsuit filed by Ellis against Prevost was an "action of possession," more commonly called a "possessory action."

Though you'll study the possessory action in greater detail later in this chapter, you need to know at least something about the action now if you're going to be able to understand the opinion. The legislation that governs the action today – a series of articles in the Code of Civil Procedure – is reproduced on pages 170-173. You should give them a quick read now. When *Ellis* was decided, this legislation did not yet exist. There was, however, comparable legislation, legislation that, as it came to be interpreted in *Ellis* and other cases, was later codified in these very articles of the Code of Civil Procedure. That legislation was part of the so-called "Code of Practice", which was the predecessor to the Code of Civil Procedure. Of particular interest to the *Ellis* court was Article 49 of the Code of Practice, which the court quoted in the ninth paragraph of the opinion. You should take a look at it now. The substance of that article, together with its jurisprudential interpretation, is today reproduced in several articles of the Code of Civil Procedure. Of particular significance for our present purposes are Article 3655 of the Code of Civil Procedure, which defines the possessory action, and Article 3658, which sets forth the requirements imposed upon a plaintiff in a possessory action:

Article 3655. Possessory action

The possessory action is one brought by the possessor of immovable property or of a real right therein to be maintained in his possession of the property or enjoyment of the right when he has been disturbed, or to be restored to the possession or enjoyment thereof when he has been evicted.

Art. 3658. Same; requisites

To maintain the possessory action the possessor must allege and prove that:

1. He had possession of the immovable property or real right therein at the time the disturbance occurred;

2. He and his ancestors in title had such possession quietly and without interruption for more than a year immediately prior to the disturbance, unless evicted by force or fraud;

3. The disturbance was one in fact or in law, as defined in Article 3659; and

4. The possessory action was instituted within a year of the disturbance.

As you can see from Article 3655, a plaintiff in a possessory action is seeking legal protection of his possession. According to Article 3658, the plaintiff can get such legal protection only if he can show, among other things, that he acquired and maintained possession for at least one year prior to the defendant's disturbance. If he meets these criteria, the plaintiff gets legal protection of his possession – a "legal right to possess" – which is a "property" right. La. Civ. Code arts. 3422, 3444.

What that all means for our case is this: Ellis is claiming that his possession of the disputed property has resulted in the attainment of a property right that the court should recognize – a right to possess – and, further, that the court should protect that right by ordering Madame Prevost to stop disturbing his possession. The critical issue before the court was whether Ellis had ever acquired such a property right.

When you look at the dates on which the various events occurred, you can easily see the difficulty Ellis might have had in meeting the requisites for a possessory action. Ellis bought the property on June 28, 1936, and he never resided there, yet he sued in February 1837 for the disturbance by Madame Prevost. Ellis did not even own the property for a year, let alone reside there for a year at the time he instituted the suit. Moreover, Madame Prevost and her ancestors had been living on the west side of the bayou "for a long time" and Champagne and Daspit had begun to reside on the east side around September of 1836, only three months after Ellis bought the land. If Madame Prevost and the defendants were on the west side long before Ellis bought the property, how could he claim that they were disturbing his possession? How does the court unravel this mystery?

For purposes of the present discussion, we can streamline the court's focus. First, we'll learn later on in the course that Ellis is entitled to rely upon the physical acts of possession (i.e., corporeal detention) that were exercised by his ancestors. La. Civ. Code arts. 3441, 3442. So whatever acts were performed by John Hutchings, you can pretend these acts were performed by Ellis. Second, we'll learn later on in the chapter that physical acts of possession performed with another's permission are treated as though they were performed by the one who gave the permission. Take, for example, the overseer and seven hands who were on the east side with Hutchings' permission – it is as though Hutchings himself cultivated the east side for 22 months, built some cabins, girdled the trees, and raised the crops. The same is true of Champagne and Daspit's activities on the east side with Madame Prevost's permission – it is as though she had performed thacts. La. Civ. Code art. 3437.

Let's now sum up what we've discovered. We can pretend that Ellis bought the property from P.S. Cocke in 1829 or 1830 and that for 22 months thereafter Ellis performed the listed acts on the east side. Ellis performed no acts on the west side at any time. Ellis then physically left the property, performing no more physical acts but filing this suit in February of 1837. Ellis claims that he has the legal right to possess the property – both the east and west sides. He brings a possessory action, which is the type of action brought by one with the right to possess whose possession has been disturbed. Under article 49 of the Code of Practice, he must show he "had the real and actual possession of the property, at the instant when the legal disturbance occurred." Did Ellis fulfill this requirement? What does the court say about this? Read on.

ELLIS v. PREVOST
19 La. 251 (1841)

SIMON. J. delivered the opinion of the court. The record shows, that on the 28th of June, 1836, plaintiff purchased from one John Hutchings, by a notarial act, a tract of land, containing thirty-six arpents in front, by forty in depth, on the east side of bayou Grant Caillou, and eleven arpents and one-third in front, by forty in depth on the west side of the said bayou; and that Hutchings had acquired the same from P.S. Cocke, by an act of sale executed on the 6th of February, 1829. That in the years 1829 or 1830, Hutchings took possession of the tract as owner, and put an overseer and seven hands upon it, who lived on and cultivated the place for about twenty-two months, built some cabins, girdled the trees on about one hundred and fifty arpents on the east side, raised a crop on said land, nearly opposite where Madame Prevost then and now lives, and that two individuals also cultivated the said land at different times by the permission of Hutchings.

The plaintiff never resided there, and after his purchase, he abandoned the improvements made by his vendor. It is also established, that the defendants and their ancestors resided for a long time on the west side of the bayou, and that they occupied and cultivated at different periods an inconsiderable part of the land in controversy on both sides; it is not shown however, that the portions thus cultivated and which were unenclosed, were ever possessed by metes and bounds, but there is proof resulting from the testimony of the witnesses and from the plat returned by the surveyor, and that their enclosures around the house on the west side have existed for a long time, and contain a small tract of four arpents in front, by two arpents and a half in depth, which is the spot which the defendants and their father have actually occupied for a certain number of years before the institution of this suit.

The evidence further shows, that about eighteen months previous to the first trial of this suit (in March, 1838; the suit was brought in February, 1837), two persons named Champagne and Daspit, came to reside on the land on the east side, with Madame Prevost's permission; the spot by them occupied is shown on the plat to be five arpents in front, by two and half in depth. Under the legal principles established in the former decision of this cause, which however we are not ready to adopt to the same extent, it is clear, that the plaintiff had a right to institute an action of possession against the defendants by virtue of his civil possession, based on the previous actual and corporeal possession of his vendor. This doctrine, so far as it regards the civil possession to be preceded by an actual and corporeal detention of the thing, and as it allows to the plaintiff the benefit of the previous corporeal possession of his author, appears to us to be correct, and we are not disposed to controvert it; but we cannot accede to the proposition, that our laws recognize but one kind of possession, and that a civil possession will suffice in all cases.

We are aware, that the distinction between natural and civil possession is peculiar to the Roman law, and among the French commentators of the highest authority on the Napoléon Code, there are several who consider it as having no sense or direct meaning. But we are not able to say, that with us it is a distinction without a difference: it is evident from the different provisions contained in our system of legislation, that our laws on this subject, too clear and too explicit to be disregarded, recognize two species of possession, natural possession, which may be called possession, in fact, is, when a man detains a thing corporeally, as by occupying a house, cultivating a field; and civil possession, or possession in right, is, when a person ceases to reside in the house or on the land which he occupied, but without intending to abandon the possession. La. Code, Articles 3390 [Revised C.C. art. 3427], 3391 [Revised C.C. art. 3428], 3392 [Revised C.C. art. 3429] (1825). Another difference is established by Pothier, on possession, No. 55, which, it seems to us, explains clearly the object and meaning of the distinction made under our laws between natural and civil possession; it is this:

> Pour acquérir la possession d'une chose, la seule volonté ne suffit pas; il faut une préhension corporelle de la chose, ou par nous-mêmes, ou par quelqu'un qui l'appréhende pour nous et en notre nom. Au contraire, lorsque nous avons acquis la possession d'une chose, la seule volonté que nous avons de la posséder suffit pour nous en faire conserver la possession, quoique nous ne détenions pas cette chose corporellement, ni par nous-mêmes, ni par d'autres.[12]

This distinction, therefore, is very obvious: possession is acquired by the actual and corporeal detention of the property; this is the natural possession or possession in fact; and it is preserved and maintained by the mere will or intention to possess; and this is the civil possession or possession in right. Now, in order to acquire prescription by the possession of ten years, founded on a just title, it is necessary, among requisites, that the possessor should have held the thing in fact and in right as owner, (ait possédé la chose naturellement et civilement[13],) and yet, to complete a possession already begun, the civil possession shall suffice, provided it has been preceded by the corporeal detention of the thing. La. Code, art. 3453 (1825). So it is with regard to the right of possession:

> "When a person has once acquired possession of a thing, by the corporeal detention of it, the intention which he has of possessing, suffices to preserve the possession in him, although he may have ceased to have the thing in actual custody, either himself or by others." La. Code. Articles 3405, 3406 and 3407 (1825).

Thus, if after having abandoned the corporeal possession of my house, or the cultivation of my field, I continue to possess it civilly; the intention which I have of

---

[12] *Ed.'s note.* English translation: "In order to acquire the possession of a thing, the will [to possess it] alone does not suffice; it is necessary that there [also] be a corporeal taking hold of the thing, be it by ourselves or by someone who apprehends it for us and in our name. It is different when we have [already] acquired the possession of a thing: even if we do not [any longer] detain the thing corporeally, neither by ourselves nor by others, the will that we have to possess it alone suffices for us to retain the possession."

[13] *Ed.'s note.* English translation: "have possessed the thing naturally and civilly".

possessing, will preserve the possession in me, during the time required by law, or I have failed to exercise an actual possession for ten years; and if in the mean time, I am disturbed in my possession, I have the right before the expiration of one year, and by virtue of my civil possession, founded on my previous and anterior corporeal and actual possession of the property, to institute a possessory action to recover it.

This is undoubtedly tne meaning of the art. 49 of the Code of Practice (1825), which must be construed in relation to the articles of the Louisiana Code on the subject of possession; this article says:

"In order that the possessor may be entitled to bring a possessory action, it is required: 1st that he should have had the real and actual possession of the property, at the instant when the disturbance occurred: a mere civil or legal possession is not sufficient."

Now, we understand the expressions, real and actual possession, contained in this law, as used in contradistinction with the possession which is purely civil and legal, that is to say: with the possession, which is entirely devoid of the quality of having its source in or being derived from a previous actual and corporeal one; such possession is not sufficient; but when it has been preceded by the corporeal enjoyment of the thing, and the possessor has not ceased to exercise such enjoyment for ten years, the actual possession previously acquired is preserved and maintained, and it continues in the same manner and with the same effect, as if the thing has always been actually and corporeally possessed....

It is clear, therefore, that if the Article 49 of the Code of Practice was to be construed strictly and according to its literal meaning, there would follow the absurdity, that if a person was to absent himself temporarily, and leave his house unoccupied for a certain lapse of time, he could not on his return bring a possessory action against an intruder, who would have taken possession of it during his absence, and would be obliged to resort to the petitory action; his adversary would always successfully oppose to him the plea in the words of the Code of Practice: that he was not in the real and actual possession of the house, at the instant when the disturbance occurred. This cannot have been the intention of the law giver; and such an interpretation is too absurd, to be for a moment countenanced at our hands. We must consequently conclude, that the possession acquired by the plaintiff's vendor, which possession is shown to have existed really and actually for more than one year, according to the extent and under the limits exhibited by the acts of sale, ought to inure to the benefit of said plaintiff; and that having not failed to exercise the said natural possession for ten years, the same was preserved in his favor by the civil possession, and was sufficient to entitle him to bring and maintain the present action.

With this view of the question, the plaintiff, under the evidence, would have a right to recover the whole tract, unless he is shown to have suffered a year to elapse after the disturbance, without bringing his possessory action, and unless the defendants have succeeded in establishing an adverse possession to it or to any part thereof during the period prescribed by law. C. of Pr., art. 59 (1825); La. Code, art. 3419 (1825). It is true that the defendants have, at various times, occupied and cultivated, for a certain number of years, different inconsiderable parts of the land in dispute; but they have shown no possession according to metes and bounds of the land which was unenclosed, and the testimony is so vague and uncertain as to the extent of the several spots, which they have successively occupied, and of the limits of the fields which they may have cultivated, that it would be impossible to ascertain and indicate the fractions of the plaintiffs land, upon which they may have exercised their alleged acts of possession.....

In the case of Prevost's Heirs v. Johnson 9 M.R., 123, this court held, that when a person claims by possession alone, without showing any title, he must show an adverse possession by enclosures, and his claim will not extend beyond such enclosures. In the case of Bernard vs. Shaw, 1 Martin, N.W., 480, the facts proved established the plaintiffs right of possession, (as in this case,) to the whole body of land sued for; the defendant, however, gave in evidence his possession and cultivation of a field of fifteen arpents, but neither the pleadings, nor the evidence ascertained the particular spot where this possession was exercised; and the defendant's pretensions were disregarded. In the case of McDonough vs. Childress et al., 15 La. Rep., 560, we said that it was necessary, in an action of possession, not only to show acts of limited and restricted possession, but also to establish by legal evidence the extent and full limits of the property so possessed. These principles are clearly applicable to the present case; and as the defendants have not shown their adverse possession to extend, by metes and bounds, with any degree of certainty, four arpents in front, by two arpents and a half in depth, and as the evidence fully establishes their actual and continued possession for a number of years to the quantity of arpents of land comprised within their said enclosures, we are of opinion, that the said defendants should be maintained in their said possession of the said tract of four arpents in front, by two and a half in depth, on the west side of bayou Grand Caillou; and that the plaintiff should recover the possession of the balance of the whole trace to the extent and limits described in his petition.

With regard to the parcel of land possessed by Champagne and Daspit, with the permission of the defendants, on the east side of the bayou; it is clear from the evidence, that they had not been in possession of it for one year, at the time of the institution of this suit, and that consequently, the defendants cannot derive any benefit from their said possession.

It is therefore ordered, adjudged and decreed, that the judgment of the district court be annulled, avoided and reversed, and proceedings to give such judgment, as, in our opinion, ought to have been rendered in the lower court; it is ordered, adjudged and decreed, that the plaintiff and appellant do recover and be maintained in the possession of the tract of land described in his petition; except, however, of that portion of the said tract on the west side of the bayou Grand Caillou, shown in the surveyor's map to contain four arpents in front, by two arpents and a half in depth; and that the defendants and appellees be maintained in their possession of the said small tract according to the metes and bounds designated in the said surveyor's map; the costs in both courts to be borne by the said defendants.

NOTE
Constructive Possession

An instructive case of "constructive" possession is *Whitley v. Texaco, Inc.*, 434 So. 2d 96 (La. App. 5th Cir. 1983).

Back before 1930, two persons, Louisiana Land & Exploration Company (LLEC) and Cole, unknowingly held title to overlapping estates, that is, the area described in LLEC's title overlapped with the area described in Cole's title. The area of overlap consisted of undeveloped woodland. Before or during 1930, LLEC leased its tract to Price, who raised vegetables for market there. For this purpose, he used the cleared part of the tract, but not the wooded part (i.e., the part that included the overlap). At some point during that year, while Price was still on the tract, Sunset Realty & Planting Company (Sunset) acquired title to the tract through a tax sale. Hibernia Bank later acquired title to the tract from Sunset, and Texaco later acquired it from Hibernia Bank. Each of these title holders, including Texaco, leased the tract out on a more or less continuous basis. The lessees limited their activities to the cleared part of the tract. Precisely what, if anything, the Coles did on, to, or with their tract before or during 1930 was unclear. According to some witnesses, the Coles had lived on and had farmed the cleared part of their tract for a brief period prior to that time. But that evidence was shaky. All that was known for certain was that the Coles sold their tract to Nave, who later sold it to Whitley. Both Nave and Whitley, at different times, but well after 1930, lived on and farmed the tract themselves or leased the tract out. But except for sporadic forays into the woods (including the overlap) to hunt, pick berries, or chop wood, the title holders and the lessees limited their activities to the cleared part of the tract.

Not long after the Whitleys and Texaco discovered that their titles overlapped, Whitley brought a petitory action against Texaco to settle the dispute. Both parties relied on theories of acquisitive prescription. The trial court, for reasons that remain obscure, ruled for the Whitleys. The court of appeal reversed that judgment. The court's rationale can be summarized as follows. A possessor does not lose possession against his consent unless he is evicted, that is, he is forcibly expelled or the disturber usurps his possession. This generalization holds true not only for corporeal and civil possession, but also for constructive possession. Here, the evidence, properly evaluated, shows that the first person to establish possession (albeit it merely constructive possession) of the disputed area was LLEC, Texaco's ancestor-in-title. Thereafter neither the Coles nor Nave nor Whitley ever evicted LLEC or Sunset or Texaco from that area. Consequently, LLEC's constructive possession of the area, which now redounds to the benefit of its successor-in-title, Texaco, still continues in full force.

MANSON REALTY CO. v. PLAISANCE
196 So. 2d 555 (La. App. 4th Cir. 1967)

JANVIER, J. Plaintiff brought this action to enjoin Defendant from trespassing on land claimed by it in Elmwood Subdivision, Jefferson Parish, and to remove certain shacks and fences Defendant had allegedly erected on the property.***

Defendant answered alleging he had been in possession of the tract in question for one year prior to the filing of the suit. The district judge concluded, as do we, that Defendant had not been in possession of the property for a year preceding the institution of this suit...

However, the district judge found that Plaintiff itself had not been in actual possession for more than a year prior to the filing of the action, and therefore was barred from bringing it. We do not agree that Plaintiff was not in possession. The record discloses plaintiff performed the following acts with respect to the property: granted a pipeline servitude to United Gas Pipeline Company, which pipeline was actually laid in 1950, and has been in continuous operation since then, with the company clearing the right-of-way approximately two or three times a year; that Plaintiff has paid state and parish ad valorem taxes; has granted mineral leases, although no actual drilling operations have been conducted and that intermittently Plaintiff had conducted inspections of the property.

Admittedly the laying of the pipeline and the use and maintenance thereof are the only acts of corporeal possession; the others evidencing only civil possession.

As Plaintiff is the record owner of the property, possession of part of the tract through the pipeline would constitute possession of the whole. Vidrine v. Vidrine, 14 La. App. 484, 130 So. 244; Haas v. Currie, 169 La. 1041, 126 So. 547; Jones v. Goss, 115 La. 926, 40 So. 357.***

When one claiming possession has title, the requirements for establishing possession are simpler than those which are required of a mere trespasser. In Lecomte v. Smart, 19 La. 484, the Supreme Court, in a possessory action, said:

"If the defendant had have taken possession of the land under an apparent title, we should regard *slight acts* as evidence of an intention to take possession, but when a man without any pretense of title goes upon land which he is informed is claimed by another, he must show unequivocal and continued acts of possession for more than a year, to maintain a plea of prescription. (Emphasis added.) (The Code of Practice of 1825, Article 49 also provided that a possessory action must be brought by one who had been in possession for more than a year previous to the disturbance thereof.)

The following appears in a Tulane Law Review article thoroughly discussing the possessory action:

"It is difficult to set forth definite rules which will determine whether there is actual and real possession in any given case. Where the possessor has a title and is in good faith, the requirements for showing possession should be fewer than where the possessor has no title, and therefore is a usurper or trespasser who is obviously in bad faith." 20 Tul.L.Rev. 524, 530.

Here, considering that Plaintiff was the record owner and that the land was undeveloped, we feel that the continuous operation of a pipeline and the continuous maintenance thereof was sufficient evidence of corporeal possession...

However, assuming arguendo that the laying of the pipeline in 1950 was the only act of actual possession on the part of the Plaintiff, we conclude that its acts of civil possession subsequent to the commencement of the acts which evidenced corporeal possession were sufficient to enable it to bring this action .***

We conclude, therefore, that Plaintiff was disturbed in the possession which it had for more than a year prior to such disturbance; that it brought this action within a year of such disturbance and is thus entitled to relief under C.C.P. art. 3663.

3. ACQUISITION, EXERCISE, RETENTION, AND LOSS OF POSSESSION
Civil Code arts. 3424-3434, 3465

LOUISIANA CIVIL CODE, BOOK III, TITLE XXIII
Exposé des Motifs

Acquisition, exercise, retention and loss of possession. To acquire possession, one must intend to possess as owner and must take corporeal possession of the thing. Article 3424. However, one is presumed to have the intent to possess as owner unless he began to possess precariously, that is, in the name of another. Article 3427.

Possession may be corporeal, civil, or constructive. Corporeal possession is the exercise of physical acts of use, detention, or enjoyment over a thing. Article 3425. Civil possession is the retention of an acquired possession solely by virtue of an intent to possess as owner. Thus, one may have civil possession even though he has ceased to possess corporeally. Article 3431. The intent to possess as owner is presumed to exist, but the presumption may be rebutted by clear proof of an intent to abandon possession. Article 3432. Constructive possession is a substitute for corporeal or civil possession. One who possesses a part of an immovable by virtue of a title is deemed to have constructive possession within the limits of his title. Article 3426. In the absence of title, one has corporeal or civil possession only of the area that he actually possesses.

Possession may be acquired through another person who takes it for the possessor and in the name of the possessor. Article 3428. It may be exercised by the possessor or by another who holds for and in the name of the possessor. Article 3429. A juridical person necessarily acquires and holds possession through its representatives. Article 3430. A natural person who labors under some incapacity may acquire possession through his tutor or curator.

Possession is lost when the possessor manifests an intention to abandon it or when he is evicted by force or usurpation. Article 3433. The right to possess is lost upon the abandonment of possession, though not upon eviction. In case of eviction, the right to possess is lost if the possessor does not recover possession within a year of the eviction. Article 3434. Naturally, if the evicted possessor institutes a possessory action within a year and later obtains a judgment in his favor, he is considered to have recovered possession within one year from the eviction even if the judgment is rendered after the lapse of one year from the date of the eviction. Article 3465.

1(2) PLANIOL, TRAITÉ ÉLÉMENTAIRE DE DROIT CIVIL 340-346
(an English translation by the Louisiana State Law Institute 1959)

A. Acquisition of Possession

Acquisition by a Third Party. Is it necessary that the two elements of possession be united in the very person who is become the possessor? A distinction must be drawn between the element of intent and the physical element.

(1)   The element of intent, the intention of becoming a possessor, is in principle, necessary in the very person who is to possess. The will of a third person cannot make a man a possessor without his knowing it. Nevertheless, in the case of persons who are incapable of having an *animus* of their own, such as insane persons and children, it had to be held that possession could take place in their favor through the *animus* of another. They borrow, as it were, the *animus* of their representatives.

(2)   The physical element is governed by a contrary principle. It is never necessary that the acts of enjoyment, which make up the possession, be carried out by the possessor in person. It has always been recognized, and this was admitted by the Romans, that possession may be taken of a thing *"corpore alieno,"* that is to say through the intervention of any representative, a mandatary, an agent, etc. Whenever this person takes possession of the thing in the name of another intending to make this other person acquire it, possession is acquired by the latter, if the latter so desires.

B. Loss of Possession

Simultaneous Loss of the Two Elements of Possession. Possession is lost first of all, when the two elements which form the possession, disappear at the same time. This first manner is the normal case. Ordinarily, he who loses the possession of a thing loses at the same time the *corpus* and the *animus*. This takes place in two series of different cases: (1) Where there is alienation. The old possessor of the thing transmits it to the acquirer who immediately possesses it in his place. (2) Where there is an abandonment. The possessor throws the thing away, with intent to give it up. It becomes *"res derelicta."*

Loss Of The Corporeal Element. The second manner of losing possession consists in losing the *corpus* while preserving the *animus*. This also takes place in two series of cases: (1) where a third party takes possession in fact of the thing; (2) where without any intent on the part of the person, the thing gets away physically from him. For example, if the thing in question is an inanimate object, it is misplaced; if it is an animal held in captivity, it escapes. In all these cases, the possessor not being able to carry out the physical acts which form possession, remains animated by the desire to possess the thing. He has lost possession and his intent does not suffice to preserve it.

Loss Of The Element of Intent. The third manner of losing possession is the loss of the *animus* alone. This is more difficult to comprehend. It is difficult to imagine that a person who had ceased to have the intent to possess a thing should still continue to carry out the physical acts of possession. But it may well be supposed that the possessor, in selling the thing, agrees to preserve it for the account of the purchase, although he had previously held it for his own account. This is what the old writers called the *constitut possessoire* (Pothier *Propriété* no. 108). The seller made of himself the possessor for account of another. Thenceforth the true possession belongs to the purchaser and the vendor, who has preserved the *corpus*, loses possession when he loses the *animus*.

Preservation of Possession Through Another. Possession may be preserved, just as it can be acquired through the intermediary of a third person. Thus, he who gives a lease upon his field or his house, ceases to be in physical possession of the thing. But as the tenant holds it for him, he does not thereby cease to retain possession with all the advantages thereto appertaining. The owner confines himself to performing juridical acts that are not creative of possession. He draws up leases. He gives receipts for rent that is paid. But the physical acts that make of him the possessor of the thing are performed by a third party. He therefore possesses *"corpore alieno."*

Preservation of Immovable Possession Merely By Intent. He who, after having had the possession of an estate, ceases to perform the acts that make up the corporeal element of possession remains nonetheless the possessor of the estate through the mere fact that he preserves the intent of possessing it. It is said that in such cases possession is preserved *solo animo*. This rule comes from the Roman law (Digest, Book XLI, Title 2, Fr. 2 § 1). And it is true solely for that species of property known as immovables. (Civ., March 27, 1929, D. H. 1929. 250.)

But in order that mere *animus* preserve possession, it is necessary that the thing remain physically at the disposal of the possessor. If a new fact arises which interferes with a continuance of the acts of possession, possession is lost, notwithstanding the preservation of the *animus*. This happens if another person takes possession of the estate, and enjoys it peaceably during a year. This possession of one year assures the new possessor success in a possessory suit (citations omitted).

HARPER v. WILLIS
383 So. 2d 1299 (La. App. 3d Cir. 1980)

STOKER, J. This is a possessory action. It was dismissed in the trial court on a motion for summary judgment brought by the defendant-appellee, Ray Preston Willis. Plaintiff, Leroy Harper, seeks to be maintained in the possession of immovable property consisting of a rectangular tract of open land measuring 323.6 feet by 435.6 feet. The plaintiff asserts he "possessed" the land by grazing his cattle on it and doing certain other acts upon the land. Plaintiff alleges be has been disturbed in his possession by the recordation of a document which purports to convey the property to defendant Willis. The motion for summary judgment, and the judgment granting it, are based solely on a deposition given by plaintiff.

In our opinion the sole issue in this matter is whether plaintiff ever had the intent to acquire possession as required by Article 3436 [Revised C.C. art. 3424] of the Louisiana Civil Code. That article reads:

Art. 3436 [Revised C.C. art. 3424]. To be able to acquire possession of property, two distinct things are requisite:

1. The intention of possessing as owner.

2. The corporeal possession of the thing.

For the purpose of determining whether the trial court was justified in dismissing the possessory action, we may assume that plaintiff could establish the corporeal possession of the land in question requisite number two of C.C. art. 3436 [Revised C.C. art. 3424] quoted above. We may so assume because, even if plaintiff can establish that required element of the article, he gave testimony in his deposition in which he specifically negatived any "intention of possessing as owner". The concept of "possessing as owner" is the crux of this case and will be discussed later in this opinion.

In order to better follow the principles to be discussed it is appropriate here to set forth briefly certain facts related by plaintiff-appellant, Leroy Harper, in his deposition. It appears that the property in question is part of what was created several decades ago as the Old Pecan Orchard Subdivision. The whole property consisted of two sections of land one mile by two miles. Apparently the subdivision venture encountered difficulty of some nature, and in the early 30's some of the lots began to be sold for taxes. In the beginning a caretaker, a Mr. Crowe, looked after the property. By 1946 or 1947 the caretaker gave up this job, and the property was left untended. None of the lot purchasers ever occupied or used the lots acquired by them, and Mr. Crowe did not look after these lots. Plaintiff-appellant had begun to run cattle on the whole two-section tract in about 1939 and continued thereafter to do so. At some time, perhaps about 1947, plaintiff-appellant began to acquire lots through tax redemptions, or he acquired an interest with others. At some time before Mr. Crowe abandoned his caretaker responsibilities, he gave plaintiff-appellant permission to run his cattle on the land without payment of rent by Harper if Harper would look after the property, keep the fire out and the brush down. Harper testified he took over the property in 1947. By 1952, plaintiff-appellant had acquired sufficient interest in lots in the subdivision that whatever he did for the whole property he considered to be for his own interests. From 1952, some clearing took place year by year. In 1952, this property was overgrown in thickets. Through purchases at tax sales and from individuals, plaintiff-appellant continued to acquire lots in the subdivision. At some time not clear, plaintiff-appellant became interested in the property subject of this law suit. He was interested in purchasing it, but it was sold to defendant-appellee, Willis. The property apparently consists of three lots. Plaintiff-appellant testified there has never been a fence around the three lots in question, but there was a fence around the entire two sections of land.

The facts set forth above are taken entirely from the deposition given by plaintiff-appellant on which the motion for summary judgment of defendant-appellee is founded. Mr. Harper never testified that he acquired the property subject of this possessory action by any species of title. The action is strictly a possessory action based upon his alleged possession quietly and without interruption for more than a year prior to the recordation of the conveyance to Willis.

The critical testimony given by Leroy Harper himself which establishes the actual subjective intention of plaintiff-appellant regarding the tract purchased by Willis, beginning on transcript page 33, is as follows:

> Q. So, the possession that you have had of this property that Mr. Willis has the deed to now, you never have possessed that property as the owner of that property, have you the lots Mr. Willis has the deed to?
>
> A. No.
>
> Q. Alright. You knew all along you didn't own that lot.
>
> A. Yeah.

***The foregoing excerpts from plaintiff's deposition show that plaintiff, testifying very candidly, has completely destroyed the foundation for his possessory action. As stated above we have assumed, for the purposes of this appeal, that plaintiff can establish the necessary corporeal possession. We focus on his intent. We find that plaintiff did not have the requisite intent to maintain this possessory action. We affirm the trial court action.

INTENT AS REQUIRED BY CIVIL CODE ARTICLE 3436

We will discuss in some detail the requirement of C.C. art. 3436 [Revised C.C. art. 3424] that to "acquire possession of property" one of the "two distinct things [which] are requisite" is "(1) The intention of possessing as owner." We are prompted to do so by the suggestion that a possessory action may be maintained without the necessity of possessing as owner....

No matter in what quality a person professes to be a possessor, whether in good faith or otherwise, it is clear that the person who asserts that he is a possessor must have had the intention of possessing as owner. The matter is aptly stated in the case of Buckley v. Dumond, 156 So. 784 (La. App. 1st Cir. 1934). A possessory action was brought by Buckley. Plaintiff had title to the area in dispute, but the defendant, Dumond, had none. Plaintiff prevailed in the possessory action and the Court of Appeal reasoned as follows:

> We find that Dumond's claim to have had possession, as owner, of any part of the land, called for in plaintiff's title, is not well founded, because in the beginning and all along since then, in entering on the land, he did not have "the intention of possessing as owner," but hunting and looking after his cattle and hogs ranging thereon was his only purpose in view. Dumond is not to be regarded as an occupant of the land, but as indicating the importance of intent in a matter of taking possession, we refer to the Civil Code, arts. 3412 and 3413 [Revised C.C. art. 3412]. Under these articles, occupancy is not a mode of acquiring the possession, except when it is retained by the acquirer with the intention of keeping it as his own property. And on the subject of possession, the Code, art. 3436 [Revised art. 3424], provides that: "To be able to acquire possession of property, two distinct things are requisite: 1. The intention of possessing as owner. 2. The corporeal possession of the thing." There must be a positive intention to take and commence a possession, as owner, in order that possession, as owner, may be created and commenced.

In typical litigation in which possession is the issue, whether it be a possessory action, a petitory action, or whether it concerns some other question resting on possession, the usual inquiry involves a determination of the subjective intent of the party who claims to be a possessor by reference to objective facts. In Humble v. Dewey, 215 So. 2d 378 (La. App. 3d Cir. 1968), this court stated the proposition as follows in a petitory action:

> In some cases, we think the intention to possess as owner may be inferred from the surrounding facts and circumstances. We believe, however, that ordinarily the intent to possess as owner should not be inferred unless the actions of the possessor or the surrounding facts and circumstances are sufficient to reasonably apprise the public, and the record title owner of the property, of the fact that the possessor has the positive intent to possess as owner.

The concept stated in Humble v. Dewey, *supra*, was recently reiterated in Wm. T. Burton Industries, Inc. v. McDonald, 346 So. 2d 1333 (La. App. 3d Cir. 1977). However, the need to infer intent from facts, and circumstances is not present in the case before us. The plaintiff, out of his own mouth, has denied any intent to possess as owner. In his deposition he stated, without any equivocation, that he did not possess as owner.***

From the foregoing it is clear that if someone, without legal claim or intention to possess as owner, uses the property in any manner, it is without legal significance or detriment to the true owner..***

Buckley v. Dumond, *supra*, stated: "There must be a positive intention to take and commence a possession, as owner, in order that possession, as owner, may be created and commenced." C.C. 3436 [Revised C.C. art. 3424] requires two distinct elements for a person to acquire possession: (1) the intention of possessing as owner and (2) the corporeal possession of the thing. Our jurisprudence usually states that the term "corporeal possession means the actual, physical, open, public, unequivocal, continuous, and uninterrupted possession of property with the intent of possessing it as owner. Gerrold v. Barnhart, 128 La. 1099, 55 So. 688 (1911); Wm. T. Burton Industries, Inc., v. McDonald, *supra*, Succession of Kemp v. Robertson, 316 So. 2d 919 (La. App. 1st Cir. 1975), writ denied, 320 So. 2d 906.***

It is clear that the intent to possess as owner has to do with the subjective intent of one who professes to possess and does not mean that the possessor must pretend to have valid title rights. The possessor may actually have title, but in the possessory action that factor is significant only in determining intent. The intent may exist without title to the knowledge of the possessor, for as shown above, even our codes permit a person in bad faith or a usurper to maintain the possessory action. C.C. arts. 3450, 3452, and 3454 [Revised C.C. art. 3481] and C.C.P. art. 3660. Inasmuch as the corporeal possession required as a predicate to a possessory action is the same as that required for acquisitive prescription of 30 years, the corporeal possession must be open and notorious and adverse or hostile to the true owner and everyone else.

In the case before us Mr. Leroy Harper has affirmed in every way possible that he intended no adverse claim to the property in question. While we have assumed that Mr. Harper could prove corporeal possession (although he may very well not be able to), none of those acts show in themselves a claim of rights to the land hostile to the true owners. Harper makes no pretense of title. He has acknowledged that he does not own the property. He has also acknowledged that his corporeal possession (if such it be) was not with the intention of possessing it as owner.***

This case is before us on appeal from the action of the trial court which dismissed plaintiff-appellant's possessory action on a motion for summary judgment. Among his reasons for judgment the trial court observed: "From a reading of [plaintiff's] deposition it appears that plaintiff's case must fail because he does not contend that he possessed as owner...". We agree with that holding and affirm the judgment of dismissal.

SOUTHER v. DOMINGUE
238 So. 2d 264 (La. App. 3d Cir. 1970)

FRUGÉ, J. This is a possessory action. La. C.C.P. arts. 3655-3664. Defendants appeal from an adverse judgment on the merits. Walter A. Souther, plaintiff herein, acquired a tract of land by notarial act of sale in 1953. As shown by the plat paraphed for identification with that sale (though not filed until eleven years later), that tract was bounded on the north, west, and south by the property of defendants, the Prejeans, and on the east by the Vermilion River, and included the property over which this controversy has arisen. The eastern and western portions of the tract are highland; the center is swamp. Plaintiff has bridged the Vermilion to make the eastern end of the property accessible, has cleared and built a barn upon that eastern end, fenced it, and grazed cattle and grown crops there. The western end of the property, however, was practically inaccessible to Souther because of the swamp, and he at no time prior to the institution of this suit attempted to make any actual use of that portion of the property. The area in dispute is approximately 9.7 acres in the southwest corner of this tract.

Louis Charles Prejean, Oran Vincent Prejean, and Lucille Ann Prejean, who with their tenant Louis A. Domingue are made defendants, acquired the property surrounding that claimed by Souther (including, they allege, the property in dispute) from the succession of Dr. Louis A. Prejean. The Prejeans and their tenants, who live nearby, have for at least thirty years used the disputed property as a pasture for their cattle. Prior to December 4, 1961, no fences were erected by the Prejeans or their tenants to the east of the disputed tract or to its north, where it admittedly abuts land owned by Souther, because the heavy woods to the north and the heavy woods and swamp to the east served as a natural barrier to cattle. It does not appear that fences were erected to the south and west, but land admittedly belonging to the Prejeans abuts the disputed area on those sides. The north and east boundary claimed by plaintiff was clearly marked, however. Markers which several tenants of the Prejeans testified represented the boundary between the Prejeans and Souther for at least thirty years were located by a 1953 survey in precisely the locations shown by a 1921 plat showing the property lines in the area. These markers were still visible in 1961. Only cattle belonging to the Prejeans or to their tenants grazed on the land in dispute. The tenants regularly cleared the pasture of underbrush to allow their cattle to graze.

For about two years prior to the activities out of which this dispute arises, no cattle were maintained by the Prejeans or their tenants on the property. Then, the Prejeans leased to defendant Domingue, who again had the area cleared, this time by using a bulldozer. On October 17, 1961, one year and one month before this action was filed, Mr. C.J. Langlinais, a surveyor hired by Souther to reestablish his northern boundary against some timber operations off his property, noticed that the disputed 9.7 acres were "being cleared off by a bulldozer. There was no trees, hardly any trees standing there." Souther knew prior to November 23, 1961, when he admits he first became aware that there was a question as to the disputed area, that a bulldozer had cleared the land. On the last mentioned date, Souther joined Prejean on the property to discuss boundaries, and learned that there was a difference of opinion, and that defendants claimed to possess the area in dispute, and intended to resume grazing cattle on it. Souther stated that he believed he owned the property, and when on December 4, 1961, Domingue erected a fence around the disputed property, Souther claims in his petition filed November 27, 1962, that the defendants thereby took possession of his property.

The Prejeans appealed suspensively from the trial court's judgment ordering them to restore to Souther possession of the disputed area. They contend that Souther has failed to prove that he ever possessed the land, La. C.C.P. art. 3660; La. C.C. arts. 3426-3456 [Revised C.C. arts. 3421-3423], and therefore was not entitled to bring the action, La. C.C.P. art. 3658. Alternatively, they contend that Souther's possessory action has prescribed because it was not brought within one year of the disturbance, citing La. C.C.P. art. 3658. We believe that both of these contentions are well founded.

Souther relies on the principle of law that where a contiguous body of land is conveyed by a single deed, possession exercised on any part of that tract (in this case, the eastern portion) extends constructively to the limits of the land as called for in the deed itself. La. C.C. arts. 3437, 3498; Lewis v. Standard Oil Co., 154 La. 1048, 98 So. 662 (1923).

The Prejeans, however, have proved actual corporeal possession of the disputed area followed by civil possession. Souther has done nothing, other than bringing this action, to interfere with their possession. Our jurisprudence has established that the maintenance of cattle or a pasture on an enclosed tract of land constitutes corporeal possession. Kilchrist v. Conrad, 191 So. 2d 705 (La. App. 3d Cir. 1966). "Enclosed" does not necessarily mean fenced in, but requires "that the land actually, physically, and corporeally possessed by one as owner must be established with certainty, where by natural or by artificial marks; that is, that they must be sufficient to give definite notice to the public and all the world of the character and extent of the possession, to identify fully the property possessed, and to fix with certainty the boundaries or limits thereof." Hill v. Richey, 221 La. 402, 59 So. 2d 434, 440 (1952). We believe that the boundaries of the area possessed by the Prejeans were sufficiently marked, both naturally, by the heavy wood lines and the swamp, and artificially, by the stakes and tree blazes, to be considered "enclosed."

The Prejeans had physically and corporeally possessed the land in dispute. Their possession was neither abandoned, Culpepper v. Weaver Bros. Lbr. Corp., 194 La. 897, 195 So. 349 (1940), nor physically usurped by another. Souther's mere constructive possession was therefore insufficient to oust their corporeal possession, or at least uninterrupted civil possession commencing with actual possession (citations omitted). ***For the foregoing reasons, the judgment appealed from is reversed, and plaintiff-appellee's suit is dismissed at his cost. All costs of this appeal are assessed against the plaintiff-appellee.

LINER v. LOUISIANA LAND & EXPLORATION CO.
319 So. 2d 766 (La. 1975)

DIXON, J. This possessory action was brought by Oliver Liner against Louisiana Land and Exploration Company as a result of conflicting claims to marshlands in Terrebonne Parish. Liner's land, he claims, lies in Sections 30, 31 and 32 of Township 20 South, Range 16 East, and in Sections 25 and 36 of Township 20 South, Range 15 East, all in Terrebonne Parish. The portion in dispute is the western end, west of the range line which separates Range 15 from Range 16. Liner's title, in the record before us, includes only land in Range 16. Louisiana Land and Exploration Company's record title covers all that portion of Liner's claim lying in Range 15.

All the land involved is marshland. It forms, roughly, a parallelogram 2909 feet on the easterly side, 6823 feet on the northerly side and 7036 feet along the southerly side. Liner claims that the westerly boundary of his property is the easterly bank of Bayou Dufrene (also known as Ash Point Bayou). Defendant claims Liner's westerly boundary is the line dividing Ranges 15 and 16.

The portion in dispute, which Liner claims that he and his family have possessed as owner for over one hundred years, is bounded on the west side by the east bank of Bayou Dufrene, and is adjacent to Liner's land in Range 16 East....

The trial court gave judgment in favor of the plaintiff, finding that the evidence strongly supported his claim of possession. The Court of Appeal reversed (303 So. 2d 866 (1974)), holding that the construction in the year 1956 and the continued operation of the Tennessee Gas Transmission Company's 24 inch gas pipeline disturbed Liner's possession, and the disturbance was continuing and uninterrupted, a "usurpation" permitted by Liner for a period in excess of one year.

We granted writs in this case because it appeared that the construction of the pipeline across Liner's claim was with his permission, and not such a usurpation. (C.C. 3449) [Revised C.C. art. 3433] as would result in the loss of possession by Liner. See also C.C. 3490 [Revised C.C. art. 3477].

Oliver Liner's contention is that he and his family have possessed the land involved since the acquisition of a tract of land by Jacob Liner, Oliver's grandfather, in 1869.***

In spite of having no record title to land in Range 15, the Liner family, from earliest times, occupied and used all the land which lay between Bayou Dufrene and Bayou DuLarge, treating Bayou Dufrene as the western boundary of the Liner tract. . . .

Oliver Liner was seventy-seven years old at the time of the trial in 1973. For fifty-six years, he testified, he had occupied this land, trapping, raising cattle, and raising his family. For three or four months of each year, during the trapping season, the family would occupy a "camp" constructed on the bank of Bayou DuLarge.

Before 1909, his grandfather and an aunt lived in houses constructed on the bank of Bayou DuLarge. That part of the property used as a farm lay on the westerly side of Bayou DuLarge, and was fenced on the north and south sides between Bayou DuLarge and Bayou Dufrene. These houses and the fence were destroyed by a devastating storm in 1909. Oliver Liner and his family were also living on his grandfather's place in 1909.

Oliver's grandfather planted cotton, pecan trees and orange trees on the farm, and raised cattle. Liner testified that he helped his father replace the fences on the upper end after the storm of 1909, and some fence remained along the northern boundary until about twenty years before the trial. The southerly boundary was marked with stakes after the fence was destroyed, and the stakes along the property line were continually maintained by Liner and his family. One engineer who surveyed the property found evidence of old stakes and markers beneath the water line at almost every place where one of Liner's markers was located.

Each year Oliver Liner followed a practice of burning the marsh — the beneficial nature of which practice is not explained by the record. (There was some testimony that this practice made the disputed tract "too poor to trap."). Although the burning sometimes destroyed some of the property stakes, they were replaced, indicating continuing activity on the part of the Liners in inspecting and replacing the boundary stakes.

The quality of the marshland deteriorated after the 1909 storm. Liner, however, continued to make his living on the land, using it all for the purposes of trapping and for raising cattle. The Liner boundaries, as staked by Jacob Liner, were recognized by other trappers in the area, even those employed by agents of Louisiana Land and Exploration Company. Oliver Liner and his family occupied the camp on the property every trapping season, for the purpose of tending the traps. Oliver Liner himself only missed the season preceding the trial of this case, having suffered a stroke; and during that season his unmarried son, Randolph, who lived with Oliver Liner, trapped the land involved in this litigation.***

The only source of income for Oliver Liner disclosed by the record during his entire life is the land which he thought he owned. There is no evidence in this record of any occurrence which might have cast any doubt upon the extent of Liner's ownership until a survey of Louisiana Land and Exploration Company properties in 1952. As a result of that survey, Louisiana Land and Exploration Company set two concrete markers and two iron pipes with Louisiana Land and Exploration Company signs along the 3000 feet of the range line which Louisiana Land and Exploration Company claims is the boundary between its land and Oliver Liner's. The concrete markers were located at a section corner and a quarter section corner along the range line.

In February of 1956 Oliver Liner granted Tennessee Gas Transmission Company a pipeline right-of-way.***

The record leaves no doubt but that Oliver Liner intended to grant a pipeline right-of-way across all the land he owned. Contrary to the finding of the Court of Appeal, there was no loss of possession "against his consent." The pipeline canal and the pipeline which crossed Liner's land were constructed with his knowledge and consent.

In 1958 Louisiana Land and Exploration Company undertook to mark the boundaries of its holdings in this area with a ditch, monuments and signs. The ditch was originally 6 feet wide and 4 feet deep, but had been somewhat widened by subsequent maintenance operations.

Oliver Liner testified that when he found the ditch on his land he did not know who had dug it, and saw no other activity. Therefore, he appropriated the ditch to himself, constructing bulkheads with planks at tow points in the ditch. The purpose of the bulkheads was to minimize the intrusion of salt water with the tidal flow, and to maintain a source of fresh water for his cattle. These bulkheads remained in place until removed by Louisiana Land and Exploration Company in 1971. When removed, they were replaced by the Liners.

Several seismograph crews crossed the disputed area from 1958 to 1965, with permission from Louisiana Land and Exploration Company, only.

Louisiana Land and Exploration Company retraced its survey lines in 1965, following Hurricane Hilda, and undertook to clean out the boundary ditch. There was testimony by an engineer for Louisiana Land and Exploration Company that some of the Liner stakes were pulled up during this process.

In 1971 when Louisiana Land and Exploration Company again undertook to clean its boundary ditch with an amphibious dragline, Liner's stakes were noticed by Louisiana Land and Exploration Company employees. On August 2, 1971 the boundary stakes were removed by the amphibious dragline. By August 17 it was reported that stakes were again in place along the Liner claim. On September 24 Louisiana Land and Exploration Company employees again removed the boundary stakes. On September 30 they returned and removed the remaining stakes. There was a confrontation with one of the Liners. On October 25 Louisiana Land and Exploration Company employees again removed the obstructions from the ditch and the Liner boundary markers.

On August 20, 1971 and on October 1, 1971 Oliver Liner's attorneys notified Louisiana Land and Exploration Company that their employees had reportedly removed Liner's boundary stakes. Louisiana Land and Exploration Company was requested to assist in the termination of such activities, in order to avoid legal proceedings. The defendant did not answer the letters, and no further action came to Liner's attention until February of 1972. On that occasion a Louisiana Land and Exploration Company crew, with deputies for protection, again removed Liner's boundary markers. Suit followed on February 9 — a possessory action alleging the February 3, 1972 incident as the disturbance of plaintiff's possession.***

Oliver Liner's possession of the disputed property satisfies all requirements for bringing the possessory action. The nature of the possession changed as the character of the marsh changed. From 1909, when the land was fenced and subject to some cultivation, the land deteriorated until the north boundary fence was abandoned after 1920. But the fence lines were continually marked. The camp was occupied each year. Trapping continued over the entire claim. Other trappers recognized Liner's boundaries. Hunters and fishermen used Liner's property only with his permission. He burned the prairie marsh every year. He ran his herd of cattle on the land.

Liner's claim continued to have visible boundaries until Louisiana Land and Exploration Company destroyed them. His possession had been preserved by "external and public signs" . . . .

Nor did Louisiana Land and Exploration Company's "acts of possession" dispossess Liner. The 1952 survey did not. The boundary ditch was appropriated by him to his own use. The water control structure on Bayou Dufrene extended only to the east bank of that stream, which Liner claimed as his westerly boundary. The seismic explorations, although an act of possession, did not serve to end the possession of Liner nor to evict him. The Tennessee Gas Transmission Company's pipeline ditch was dug with Liner's consent — not against it.***

The evidence in this case leaves no doubt but that Oliver Liner had the corporeal possession of the property here in dispute for many years. The quality of his possession was that of owner. It extended to visible boundaries. It was neither precarious, clandestine, violent nor ambiguous. Aubry & Rau, Civil Law Translations, Vol. 2, § 100 (1966). One having acquired the corporeal possession of an immovable does not thereafter lose it against his consent except in the manner prescribed by law. "Possession," say Aubry & Rau, *supra*, § 179, "is not necessarily lost just because a third person has occupied the immovable. It is lost only if he remained occupied for a year (art. 2243). If the former possessor lets this period elapse without any act of enjoyment or any claim for return of possession, he is considered as having lost it, whether he did or did not know of the adverse occupancy "

Our Civil Code provisions make it clear that one who has acquired corporeal possession continues in possession until he transfers it or abandons it, or until another expels him from it, or until he permits the estate to be usurped and held for a year without doing any act of possession or without interfering with the usurper's possession.***

A disturbance might interrupt possession. It might bring a corporeal possession to an end. (If, however, the disturbance results in an eviction by force or fraud, the one year possession requirement is eliminated). A disturbance may be an eviction, but it might also be "any other physical act which prevents the possessor of immovable property or of a real right from enjoying his possession quietly, or which throws any obstacle in the way of that enjoyment." C.C.P. art. 3659.

The acts of Louisiana Land and Exploration Company for the year preceding February 3, 1972 did constitute a disturbance of Liner's possession. However, he was not evicted. He and his son continued to trap on the disputed property. He continued to replace the boundary stakes removed by Louisiana Land and Exploration Company. Liner protested the August and September "invasions" by Louisiana Land and Exploration Company employees. Liner was not expelled, nor did he acquiesce in a usurpation. C.C. 3449 [Revised C.C. arts. 3433, 3434].***

Oliver Liner has proven each of the requisite elements of the possessory action set out in C.C.P. art. 3658. He is entitled to a judgment of possession.

ON APPLICATION FOR REHEARING

Under the Civil Code, possession is not interrupted when it is merely disturbed. A possessor does not lose possession against his consent unless he is forcibly expelled or unless the disturber usurps possession and holds it for more than a year.***

We therefore conclude that one may possess quietly and without interruption for more than a year so as to be entitled to bring a possessory action, La. C.Civ.P. art. 3658(2), even though during that year disturbances in fact or law have occurred, La. C.Civ.P. art. 3659. The application for a rehearing is denied.

TATE, J. (concurring in denial). The writer subscribes to the majority opinion and to the denial of rehearing. The additional sources and analysis are set forth below for what aid they may be in study for future applications of the article.

The Louisiana Civil Code and the Louisiana Code of Civil Procedure draw a distinction between a disturbance in fact that results in eviction and such a disturbance that falls short of eviction. In the first case, the possessor is evicted, and the person who caused the disturbance may commence to possess for himself. In the second case, the disturbance merely questions or places an obstacle to the enjoyment of quiet possession. Civil Code Article 3454(2) [no corresponding article after Revision]; La. C.Civ.P. arts. 3655, 3658 (4), 3659.

Under the facts before us, as the majority states, Louisiana Land's act clearly amounted to no more than a disturbance. They did not amount to an eviction. Nevertheless, whether an eviction or a disturbance, the possessor must within a year bring the possessory action. La. C.Civ.P. art. 3658(4).***

RICHARD v. COMEAUX
260 So. 2d 350 (La. App. 1st Cir. 1972)

COLE, J. We have before us an appeal from a judgment of the 17th Judicial District Court, parish of Terrebonne, in which a rule for a preliminary injunction incidental to a possessory action was made absolute in favor of the plaintiffs. This action was initiated by the seven heirs of Alice Trahan Bonvillain and Joseph Bonvillain and is in response to attempts by the defendant herein to possess certain real property allegedly left those heirs by their parents.***

Comeaux owns the tract immediately adjoining and paralleling their property to the west. Both estates front to the south on a Terrebonne Parish public road bordering Bayou Black and appear to run to the north between generally parallel lines. In March of 1970, the defendant began the construction of a fence dividing his estate from that of the Bonvillain heirs along a line which he believed to be his easternmost boundary. On March 24, 1970, the plaintiffs herein demanded by letter that Comeaux cease and desist his activities concerning the fence and that all construction be immediately removed. This action failing to gain the desired results, the present litigation was instituted on April 23, 1970. The matter came on for hearing on July 23, 1970, and on October 7, 1970; and, in a subsequent judgment, the action was decided favorably to the plaintiffs; therein, the defendant was enjoined from further action along the line which he claimed to be his easternmost boundary and was directed to remove all construction which he had placed thereon.

As noted in the thorough and exhaustive written reasons for judgment rendered by the trial judge, the record reflects that the plaintiffs' mother acquired the Bonvillain tract as her separate and paraphernal property on January 30, 1916. The testimony of her children at the trial indicates that she lived upon this property until approximately a year and a half prior to her death in 1966. For that period of time and for possibly a year after her death, no one lived on the property. However, Edward J. Giroir continued to grow sugar cane under a lease for that purpose on all of the property except the home site and the grounds and gardens immediately surrounding it. He and the plaintiffs testified that during this period of time they maintained the property in the way and to the extent that it had always been cared for through the years. During the year 1967, the southernmost part of the tract, including the family house, was leased to Donald Joseph Giroir who positively stated that he continued to maintain the property on its western boundary to the limits exercised by its previous occupants.

It seems that in the weeks prior to March of 1970, Comeaux ordered a survey of his eastern boundary which indicated to him that he owned along a line some five to ten feet to the east of the Bonvillain's old fence line. Although we note that the results of that survey were not testified to at the trial, they apparently satisfied Comeaux to such an extent that he commenced the construction of his fence immediately thereafter, this structure being a wooden fence for the first thirty or forty feet running south to north, and from that point, northerly, barbed wire.

The Bonvillain heirs claim continued and uninterrupted possession to a point along the disputed boundary represented by the middle of what was once a drainage ditch or canal running in a north-south direction along the western edge of their property. The record indicates that the ditch was once a viable drainage canal which has, in time, become filled by the cutting of debris, gradual filling, and the development by the adjoining landowners of their lawns. The remains of the ditch, although readily visible, are now a part of those lawns and amounts to nothing more than an indentation on the landscape.

In addition to the natural boundary created by the ditch, it seems that Mr. Bonvillain, prior to his death in 1949, constructed a barbed wire fence on the east bank of the canal as a cattle enclosure, the remains of which were still evident at the time of trial. The fence was well remembered by several of the plaintiffs' witnesses and, indeed, seems to be partially visible on photographs entered as P-20 and P-21, which were taken in 1957.

The Bonvillain heirs contend that possession sufficient to maintain the possessory action has been established to the middle of the drainage canal and certainly to the remains of the fence constructed on its east bank.

At the hearing, numerous witnesses testified concerning the events which have transpired between these estates since Comeaux's acquisition of his tract in 1963. Although much contradiction exists which is incapable of reconciliation, certain consistencies are evident in the testimony. It seems that at the time of his purchase, a heavy undergrowth existed along and around the ditch which Comeaux set out to clean up and beautify, even to the extent of bringing a bulldozer in to remove stumps. These commendable efforts on his part apparently caused no friction at the outset; however, as time passed, Mr. Comeaux began to include in the mowing of his lawn certain of the property east of the ditch and east of the remains of the fence, which was in disrepair by this time.

Mr. Comeaux, and other defense witnesses, testified that he continued to mow the grass several feet beyond and east of the ditch through the years preceding and subsequent to Mrs. Bonvillain's death. By his own admission, however, he stated that, at no time prior to the construction of his fence, did he place any structure or edifice of any kind at any point beyond the drainage ditch which would indicate adverse possession to the adjoining landowner.

In supporting the plaintiffs' demand, the trial judge relied upon our Supreme Court's decision in the case of Hill v. Richey, 221 La. 402, 59 So. 2d 434 (1952). He found the case at bar to be within the ambit of pronouncements therein which preserve to the landowner the possessory action where he civilly possesses only, and such civil possession has followed corporeal possession. In so concluding, he found that the possessory action would lie here due to the Bonvillain's and their heirs' and assigns' continued and undisturbed possession of the disputed area to the drainage ditch and old fence line. We are in accord with that judgment and find that the evidence fully supports such a conclusion.***

Plaintiffs have adequately proven possession sufficient to sustain the possessory action. Mr. Stanley Marchand, an employee of T. Baker Smith & Son, Inc., Civil and Consulting Engineers, testified that they were hired by the plaintiffs to inspect the disputed area to determine what vestiges of the old fence remained or to discover any other indications of possession that might be present. He testified that he and a crew checked the line from south to north for the entire depth of the property and that, though neglected, numerous remains of the Bonvillain fence still existed. Indeed, the photographs taken by Marchand and his group, and filed into evidence as plaintiffs' exhibits, plainly show wire still imbedded in trees and old fence posts with wire still attached down along the line described by plaintiffs.

Furthermore, the plaintiffs have testified that their possession to the ditch and old fence line has remained undisturbed for some fifty-four years. Even after the drainage ditch filled and the surrounding underbrush was removed, they and their lessees maintained the property to the center of the ditch and remained cognizant of the presence of the old fence line erected by their father.

Of paramount importance also is the defendant's inability to demonstrate that he established possession of that property claimed by the Bonvillain heirs in a way sufficient to oust the plaintiffs from their occupancy, other than the construction of the fence which immediately precipitated the filing of this suit. Clearly, such inoffensive acts as the mowing of grass on the Bonvillain side of the ditch could not be considered to constitute a usurpation of plaintiffs' dominion over the disputed area and obviously, the Bonvillains, if they knew that such was going on, did not consider it to be so. See Hebert v. Chargois, 106 So. 2d 15 (La. App. 3d Cir. 1958), and authorities cited therein. Had the defendant been able to offer evidence that the plaintiffs had not enjoyed quiet and uninterrupted possession for more than a year prior to the disturbance created by the construction of his fence, it is conceivable that, under the terms of C.C.P. art. 3658 (2), *supra*, the possessory action might have been defeated. The occasional encroachment by a lawnmower, however, is not sufficient indication that one's possession is endangered.

We find that each of the requisites of C.C.P. Article 3658 has been satisfied and that the plaintiffs are entitled to have their right to possession of the contested property recognized and are further entitled to be maintained in possession thereof ***Judgment reversed in part, affirmed in part as amended, and recast.

NOTE
Is Mowing Grass Sufficient to Establish Corporeal Possesion?

When, if ever, will "mowing grass" on a certain stretch of land be considered sufficient to establish "corporeal possession" of that land? This question has been addressed in at least two reported opinions: *Richard v. Comeaux*, 260 So. 2d 350 (La. App. 1st Cir. 1972) and *Wagley v. Cross*, 347 So. 2d 859 (La. App. 3d Cir. 1977). There are some who have argued that these authorities are in conflict. See what you think.

1. *Richard v. Comeaux.*

Back in the early 20th century, the Bonvillains, owners of a certain tract of rural land, assumed control of a strip of land that lay between the western boundary of their tract and a north-south drainage canal that was located some distance into the tract to their west. This strip of land, like their own, they devoted to farming and cattle ranching.

Years later, Comeaux acquired title to the tract of land on the west (including the strip that had been used by the Bonvillains). Comeaux, finding the drainage ditch overgrown with weeds, immediately "set out to clean and beautify [it], even to the extent of bringing a bulldozer in to remove stumps." He later expanded his "beautification" efforts, which consisted primarily of mowing, to the land that lay just to the east of the canal, that is, the strip of land that had theretofore been used by the Bonvillains. He thereafter continued to mow that land on a fairly regular basis.

The Bonvillain heirs (including Richard) eventually filed a possessory action against Comeaux. Though Comeaux did not dispute that the Bonvillains had established possession of the disputed area once upon a time, he contended that, by virtue of his acts within that area, namely, his "beautification" efforts, he had effectively evicted the Bonvillain heirs, thereby bringing their possession to an end. Neither the trial court nor the court of appeal found the argument persuasive:

> Of paramount importance...is the defendant's [Comeaux's] inability to demonstrate that he established possession of that property claimed by the Bonvillain heirs in a way sufficient to oust the plaintiffs [the Bonvillain heirs] from their occupancy.... Clearly, such inoffensive acts as the mowing of grass on the Bonvillain side of the ditch could not be considered to constitute a usurpation of plaintiffs' [the Bonvillain heirs'] dominion over the disputed area.... The occasional encroachment by a lawnmower...is not sufficient indication that one's possession is endangered.

Id. at 353-354.

2. *Wagley v. Cross.*

After Cross's father died, Cross moved into his father's place, located on a lot in a residential subdivision. The first time Cross went out to mow the grass, he mowed not only that which lay on his own lot, but also a wide strip of that which lay on the lot immediately to the west. (That neighboring lot was then undeveloped.) This practice Cross continued, at two-week intervals, for the next 12 years.

At some point Wagley, the record title holder of the lot to Cross's west (including the strip that had been mowed by Cross), had his lot surveyed. Cross, insisting that at least part of that lot was "his", ordered the surveyor to leave.

Wagley and Cross then filed possessory actions against each other. In support of his claim that he had established corporeal possession of the disputed area, Cross was able to point to only one act: grass mowing. Though the court of appeal rejected the notion that "mere mowing grass over a long period of time will, in of itself, enable a person" to establish possession (the court insisted that "[m]ore must be shown"), the court nevertheless noted that "every case must be judged on its own facts." *Id.* at 864. Further, the court, looking at the peculiar "facts" before it, concluded that Cross had, indeed, managed to show the required more-than-mere-mowing. How so? By proving (1) that he had acted "as owner" while "claiming ownership", *id.*, and (2) that at no time during the many years through which he had mowed the area had anyone, least of all Wagley, ever done anything that would have constituted a "disturbance" of possession, *id.* at 865.

EVANS v. DUNN
458 So. 2d 650 (La. App. 3d Cir. 1984)

CUTRER, J. This is a possessory action affecting a strip of land 36 feet wide and 210 feet long located along the common boundary of properties owned by plaintiff, G.B. Evans, and defendant, J. E. Dunn. The strip of land is located along plaintiff's northern border which is contiguous to land owned by defendant.

Plaintiff alleged that his possession of the strip of land had been wrongfully disturbed by the defendant who erected a fence across the *northern* portion of it in July 1982. The erection of the fence terminated plaintiff's access to the strip.

Plaintiff alleges that the defendant destroyed numerous flowers, shrubs and plants that were on the strip in dispute. Finally, plaintiff claims that less than one year had elapsed since the disturbance and he desires to be maintained and restored to peaceful possession of the property.

The defendant filed a reconventional demand for damages in the amount of $600.00 for the loss of the use and enjoyment of the land in question.

After trial on the merits, judgment was rendered in favor of the defendant, dismissing plaintiff's possessory action. The trial court held that the plaintiff had failed to meet the requirements of C.C.P. art. 3658(2) which require that the possessor must allege and prove that he and his ancestors-in-title had possession quietly and without interruption for more than a year immediately prior to the disturbance. Plaintiff appeals from this ruling. We affirm.

FACTS

The plaintiff and the defendant own contiguous property. The plaintiff acquired his one acre tract of land by deed on November 2, 1951. He testified that, at the time of purchase, there was a wire fence which was located 36 feet past what the deed called for on the northern side of the property. The plaintiff testified that he had possessed the disputed area for several years by mowing it and by tending to a flower garden that he and his wife planted there.

At the time the defendant acquired his property in 1978, there was no visible boundary line between the two properties. The plaintiff testified that the wire fence, that was present at the time of the sale in 1951, was eventually torn down about a year before the defendant acquired the adjacent property in 1978. In May 1981, the defendant had his land surveyed and, pursuant to this survey, built a chain link fence across his southern boundary. The fence erected by defendant encompassed the thirty-six foot strip of land which the plaintiff claimed to have possessed. After the defendant's chain link fence was built, many of the plaintiff's plants were isolated at various distances up to 40 feet north of the chain link fence on property that the defendant was signifying by the presence of the fence that he intended to possess.

The plaintiff's plants north of the chain link fence continued to grow until July 1982, when the defendant replaced the chain link fence with a barbed wire fence. The plaintiff admitted in his testimony that this second barbed wire fence was placed on the same spot as the chain link fence had occupied.

Soon after this fencing change, the defendant destroyed the plaintiff's remaining plants north of the fence. This possessory action was filed on September 28, 1982.

Both the plaintiff and his wife testified at trial that, after the chain link fence was built, they never went on the disputed strip of land again. They also testified that they did not tend or care for the plants north of the chain link fence except to occasionally water the plants that could be reached with a hose being sprayed from their side of the fence.

The defendant testified that, after the chain link fence was built, he kept the property north of the fence mowed and that, after the fence was changed to barbed wire, he allowed his cattle to grace that area.

The principal issue presented on appeal is whether the plaintiff has met all of the requirements for maintaining the possessory action listed in C.C.P. art. 3658.

In Louisiana, the possessory action is governed primarily by C.C.P. art. 3658. The law of this subject matter is interpreted in Pitre v. Tenneco Oil Co., 385 So. 2d 840 (La. App. 1st Cir. 1980), as follows:

"HOW THE RIGHT IS ACQUIRED

"A person acquires the right to possess immovable property by possessing the property quietly and without interruption for more than a year. La. C.C.P. art. 3658(2); La. C.C. art. 3454(2) [no corresponding article after Revision]; see also La. C.C. arts. 3449(2) and 3487 [Revised C.C. arts. 3434-3437]. The species of possession required to acquire the right to possess is either corporeal possession or civil possession preceded by the corporeal possession of the plaintiff or his ancestors in title. La. C.C.P. art. 3660. In all cases, a person must possess as owner and for himself. Thus, to acquire the right to possess, 'one must combine the intention of possessing as owner with the corporeal detention' of the thing. Norton v. Addie, 337 So. 2d 432, 436 (La. 1976).

"Once a person shows he has possessed the property as required by law quietly and without interruption for more than a year, he has proven his right to possess. There is no need to show he acquired this right in the year immediately preceding suit, but only that he obtained the right at one time and that he has not lost it prior to the disturbance. Liner v. Louisiana Land and Exploration Company, 319 So. 2d 766 (La. 1975).

"HOW THE RIGHT IS LOST"

"A person loses the right to possess immovable property either voluntarily, by transferring or abandoning the property; or involuntarily, by being evicted or expelled for more than a year or by acquiescing a third party's usurpation of the property for more than a year. La. C.C. arts. 3447, 3448, 3449 [Revised C.C. arts. 3433-3434]. A question often arises as to what type of activity by an adverse party will sufficiently interrupt a person's right to possess so as to usurp his possession and strip him of his right upon passage of more than a year's time. Not every disturbance is strong or long enough to interrupt another's right to possess. Disturbances which do not interrupt another person's right to possess may be challenged in court and the disturber cast for appropriate damages and other appropriate relief. But such minor disturbances will be insufficient, even if unchallenged within a year's time, to strip the right to possess from the person who presently has that right. See *Liner, supra*, particularly the per curiam opinion on rehearing, 319 So. 2d 778; Plaisance v. Collins, *supra*; Richard v. Comeaux, 260 So. 2d 350 (La. App. 1st Cir. 1972); Yiannopoulos, *supra*, § 217 page 582, and Work of the Appellate Courts — 1974-1975, Property, 36 L.L.Rev. 354 (1976).

"Louisiana courts have indicated that for a disturbance to be sufficient to interrupt another's right to possess, the disturbance must bring home to the actual possessor the realization that his dominion is being seriously challenged. Pittman v. Bourg, 179 La. 66, 153 So. 22 (1934); Southern v. Domingue, 238 So. 2d 264 (La. App. 3rd Cir. 1970), writ refused, 256 La. 891, 239 So. 2d 544 (1970); Hebert v. Chargois, 106 So. 2d 15 (La. App. 1st Cir. 1958). In addition, the person with the right to possess must acquiesce in the interruption for more than a year without conducting any act of possession or without interfering with the usurper's possession. La. C.C. art. 3449(2)."

As we apply the principles to the facts at hand, we find that the trial court correctly held that plaintiff failed to meet the requirements of C.C. art. 3658 as interpreted by Pitre v. Tenneco Oil Co., *supra*.

A person loses the right to possess immovable property either voluntarily, by transferring or abandoning the property, or involuntarily, by being evicted or expelled for more than a year or by acquiescing in a third-party's usurpation for more than a year. C.C. arts. 3447, 3448, 3449, now C.C. art. 3433. See also, Pitre v. Tenneco Oil Co., *supra*.

In this case, we agree with the trial judge that:

"In May 1982, one year after the chain-link fence was built, the property north of that fence had thus been usurped and held for a year without the plaintiff acting to possess the property or interfere with the defendant's possession of it. Therefore in May, 1982 the plaintiff lost his right to possess the property north of the chain-link fence."

The act of building a fence around the land (which the plaintiff claimed to possess) was a disturbance that was sufficient to interrupt his right to possess and to bring home to him the realization that his dominion was being seriously challenged. This action was not a mere disturbance of the possession of the plaintiff, but an actual interruption of the plaintiff's right to possess. Since this interruption to his possession began in May 1981, the plaintiff lost his right to possess the property in May 1982. Plaintiff did not show that he had possessed the property one year before the alleged disturbance in July 1982. The trial court correctly dismissed the plaintiff's suit.

For these reasons, the judgment of the trial court is affirmed. Plaintiff-appellant is to pay all costs of this appeal.

NOTE
Acquisition of Possession

An interesting recent case regarding the acquisition of possession is *Page v. Wise*, 10-1273 (La. App. 3 Cir. 3/9/11), 58 So.3d 1062.

In 2009 the Pages filed a possessory action against Wise, seeking recognition of their supposed right to possess certain property and to be maintained in possession thereof. At dispute were 20 acres of immovable property that the Pages purchased in 2001 and that Wise had purchased in 1983. The Pages, contending that had been in possession of the property since 2001, claimed that their possession had been established by the following acts: having the property surveyed, painting lines on the boundaries, raising pine trees, and paying taxes on the property. Wise, in addition to denying the Pages' assertions, testified that *he* had had possession of the property since 1983: not only had he lived on the property, but he had, he claimed, maintained wood roads, mowed, hunted, and installed deer stands on the land and, further, had ridden on the land periodically with a four wheeler.

The trial court found that the Pages failed to meet their burden of proof to establish their possession. According to the trial court, the Pages had not performed any "acts of possession" on the property. The mere surveying of the property, the trial court reasoned, is not an act of possession. Further, the court noted that paying taxes on the property does not entail the kind of "physical" interaction with a thing that is required for possession. Finally, the court found, as a matter of fact, that the Pages had not actually planted, cultivated, or cut any of the timber on the land, but, at most, had allowed timber to grow up there through purely natural processes.

The court of appeal, in answer to the Pages' appeal, affirmed the trial court's judgment. In the view of the court of appeal, the Pages failed to "clearly and overtly" establish possession. As the court pointed out, the Pages, by their own admission, had not set foot on the property since they had purchased it, an admission that precluded the possibility of either corporeal or constructive possession. Further, having the land surveyed without Wise's knowledge was insufficient to establish either corporeal or constructive possession, the court ruled. For these reasons, the court concluded, the Pages' actions "did not demonstrate an intent to possess to Wise or anyone else."

Though the court of appeal's conclusion – that the Pages failed to prove "possession" – is correct, its reasoning may nevertheless be questioned. If one can take seriously the language of the court's opinion, then it would seem that, in the court's judgment, the Pages' case had failed for want of proof of "intent to possess as owner", in other words, *animus domini*. But how can that be so? Did the Pages even have the burden of proof on this issue? See C.C. art. 342 7. Isn't the problem with the Pages' case something else aside from *animus domini*? If so, what is it? *Hint:* see C.C. art. 3425.

4. TRANSFER OF POSSESSION; TACKING
Civil Code arts. 936, 3441-3444, 3506(28)

2 AUBRY ET RAU, DROIT CIVIL FRANÇAIS 100-105
(an English translation by the Louisiana State Law Institute 1966)

Transfer and Continuation of Possession

When Tacking of Possession Takes Place. Possession considered in itself and as a state of fact cannot pass from one person to another; but the benefits of possession, especially actions for restitution of or maintenance in possession, can. These benefits and actions pass *ipso facto* to the universal or particular successors of the possessor together with the presumed title of which the possession was the exercise or manifestation.

It follows that universal or particular successors as such and independently of any personal entry into possession can exercise possessory actions which their grantor had, provided of course that they prove his possession.

On the other hand, it follows that in cases where the possession must continue over a certain period of time in order to have a given legal effect, these successors are authorized to cumulate the period of possession of their grantor and the period during which they have held (art. 2235). Without this accumulation, their benefit of possession would often be lost.

The transfer and cumulation (tacking) of possession operate not only in favor of successors in the proper sense, but also in favor of all those to whom the possessor is under obligation to return or abandon the possession, either on grounds of a duty to deliver, or of the dissolution, annulment or rescission of his title.

The Conditions of Tacking of Possession. The Effect of Defects of Possession. Tacking can operate only with regard to two possessions which follow each other without an interruption, that means a separation by an interim possession by a third party lasting at least one year. The fact that the possession remained simply not exercised is not an obstacle to tacking.

On the other hand, it is necessary that both the possession which the new possessor wants to accumulate, and his own possession, be free from any defect. It follows, among others, that the buyer of an immovable from a person who holds precariously cannot cumulate the possession of the seller with his own possession (*Cf.* art. 2239).

5. VICES OF POSSESSION; PRECARIOUS POSSESSION
Civil Code arts. 3435-3440

1(2) PLANIOL, TRAITÉ ÉLÉMENTAIRE DE DROIT CIVIL 346-351
(an English translation by the Louisiana State Law Institute 1959)

Definition and Enumeration. Possession exists just as soon as its two essential elements, the *corpus* and the *animus* are united. It, however, can be affected by certain vices that make it useless, principally for the bringing of possessory actions and for the acquisition of ownership by prescription. These two effects, which are the principal advantages of possession, are attached solely to a possession free of vices (or defects). A vice of possession is therefore a certain state of affairs which, without destroying possession, makes it judicially valueless. There are four of these vices. They are: discontinuity, violence, secrecy and uncertainty.

Criticism of the Law. The Code speaks of vices of possession in art. 2229, in connection with prescription. Certain remarks are called for by this article. Instead of envisaging the vice itself which makes possession sterile, the law gives, in a positive form, the converse attribute that flows from the absence of this vice. Thus the law requires that possession be peaceable (free of violence), public (not concealed) and continuous (free of discontinuity). It would have been better to have dealt with the vice, which is an accidental condition of possession, rather than with the corresponding attribute, which is its normal condition. In this way it is easy to note than an error has been made by the law in its enumeration. Instead of limiting itself to the four vices enumerated above, which are the only ones that exist, the law seems to assume that there are six, in as much as it sets forth six attributes instead of four. The two supplementary qualities are the following: the possession must be uninterrupted and must be enjoyed under the title of owner. It is however easy to see that these latter two attributes have been borrowed from another chain of thought and that they really have no corresponding vice. When they do not exist there is an absence of possession. There is not vitiated possession.

The interruption concerns the theory of prescription not that of possession. It is moreover not a mere vice of possession. When prescription is interrupted, it is because possession is lost.

The same thing may be said of the third attribute enumerated by the law. The possession must be enjoyed "under the title of owner." What the law means by this is that the possession must not be precarious. "Under the title of owner" signifies "under a non-precarious title," as says art. 23 of the Code of Civil Procedure. Precariousness is not a mere vice of possession. It is something far graver. It is the absence of possession. Precarious possession is in reality the mere holding of a thing, that is to say, a juridical state of affairs entirely different from possession. It follows that in requiring that the possessor act as owner, the law is not dealing with a vice or an attribute. It is the *"animus domini"* which it exacts of him, that is to say one of the essential elements of possession. It is accordingly but proper to insist that vices of possession be reduced to four.

1. Vice of Discontinuity

Definition. The possession must be continuous. Continuity consists in the regular succession of acts of possession at sufficiently short intervals not to form lacunae. The constant handling or use of the thing is not required, every moment and with no interval. This would be impossible and absurd. Continuity flows from a series of acts performed at normal intervals, such as a careful owner would perform them who desired to get the best returns out of his property. A possession which is not carried on in a regular manner does not sufficiently indicate the reality of the right to be protected.

The question of deciding whether the intervals that have factually separated the acts of possession, are sufficiently prolonged to constitute lacunae and to make the possession discontinuous, is one of fact. Its solution depends upon the nature of the thing possessed. Thus, in the upper valleys of mountainous regions where sheep are sent only during the summer, and in poor lands which are allowed to lie fallow for a year or two in order to rest the soil, acts of possession at intervals of six months, a year or more, may suffice to make the possession continuous. As a case put it, possession is continuous "when use is made of it on all occasions and at all times, when it should be," (Cass., June 5, 1939, S. 39. 1. 621. Comp. Cass., March 19, 1884, D. 85. 1. 212).

2. VICE OF VIOLENCE

Difference Between Old Law and the New. The vice of violence is not now understood as it was formerly. Formerly, cognizance was taken solely of the violence that had accompanied the taking of possession. A possession that had been peaceable at its inception did not become violent merely because a third party had disturbed the possessor's enjoyment and he had to use force to maintain his possession. It was deemed to be proper to repress force by force (Ulpian in the *Digest*, Book XLIII, Title 16, Fr. 1, § 18. Compare Pothier, *De la possession,* no. 26).

Art. 2233 seems to be conceived in the same sense. "Acts of violence cannot be the basis of a possession engendering prescription." This is manifestly a case of the initial violence alone. Modern authors and the jurisprudence nevertheless require that the possession be peaceable even during its duration (Garsonnet, Vol. 1, no. 136, page 584). They bring out that the law, in art. 2229, requires a peaceable possession and that there would be no sense attached to the term "peaceable," if it applied to some one who could retain his possession only by resorting to violence. art. 113 of the Customs of Paris already carried out this idea. It assumed that the possessor had enjoyed the thing "frankly and without disturbance."

The new principle is nevertheless subject to two restrictions:

(1) Acts of violence committed after the taking of possession have no effect when they form what is known as passive violence, that is to say when the possessor suffers violence but does not commit any himself. It is inadmissible, so it is held, that a third person should be able to affect adversely the possessor's tenure by committing acts of violence against him.

(2) The acts of violence, even when committed by the possessor himself in order to maintain himself in possession, have no effect when committed at long intervals (Cass., March 24, 1868, D. 69. 1. 83).

Was not this double attenuation a condemnation of the modern system? There should be no defective possession other than that which was acquired through violence.

How Effect of Act of Violence Is Wiped Out. The vice due to violence is temporary. As soon as the violence ceases, the effective possession commences (art. 2233). This rule creates a differentiation between French Law and Roman Law. According to the latter, possession acquired through violence, remained defective after the cessation of the violence. In order to cure the defect, it was necessary that the thing return to the custody of the legitimate possessor.

Relative Nature of Violence. Violence is but a relative vice. The present possessor has expelled a person who claimed to be owner. There has been a violent taking of possession as regards this alleged owner. But if the true owner be a third person, untouched by these acts of violence, the possession will be free from violence as far as he is concerned and will give rise to possessor actions against him and to prescription.

3. VICE OF BEING CLANDESTINE

Definition. To be useful, possession must be public. The possessor must act without hiding himself, as generally do those who make use of a right. His possession will be clandestine, when he attempts to hide his acts from those who are interested in knowing of them.

Relative and Temporary Nature of Clandestine Possession. The vice of being clandestine is relative as is that of violence. The possession may be clandestine for some persons and not for others, if the possessor lets some know what he hides from others. It is also temporary. As soon as the concealment ceases, effective possession commences and prescription begins to run.

Its Rarity. Concealed possession is readily understandable as regards movables. But instances of concealment applicable to immovables are very few in number. Practically no examples are found in adjudged cases because it is extremely difficult to hide the fact that one occupies a house or cultivates a field. Those cited in text books are purely hypothetical. It is assumed that an owner digs a pit that extends beneath the home of his neighbor. If there be no exterior sign, such as an opening that reveals the encroachment, the possession will be clandestine.

4. VICE OF BEING EQUIVOCAL

Proof of Its Existence. It is often contended that equivocal character cannot form a special vice of possession, distinct from other vices which may affect it. Possession will be uncertain when one of its attributes, such as continuity or public character is doubtful. This interpretation of the word "not unequivocal," appearing in art. 2229, reduces the matter to a question of proof. To state that the attributes of the possession must be certain, is the equivalent to saying that they must be proved. If the fact of possession is established, the possessor has proved his case. It then devolves upon his adversary to establish the special circumstances of violence, concealment or discontinuity from which he seeks to profit. And if these circumstances are not proved, the existing possession will not be held to be defective.

It is nevertheless quite clear that being equivocal is a special vice, that sometimes makes an existing possession ineffective. But in such a case it must be assumed that the doubt or equivocal character does not concern one of the secondary attributes of possession but one of its constituent elements, the intent to hold for one's own account.

Examples: Possession is equivocal when the acts of enjoyment can be explained in two ways. Most practical examples of equivocal possession come up in cases dealing with property in a state of indivision. Each of the co-owners has a right to perform acts of possession upon the totality of the thing. Such acts are ambiguous because they could be performed in virtue of the owner's partial ownership, as well as in virtue of exclusive ownership. As long as this ambiguity lasts his possession remains ineffective as against his co-owners. In order to dissipate this uncertainty it is necessary that he exclude his co-owners in some manifest manner. (Cass., Dec. 16, 1873, S. 75. 1. 203; Cass., May 13, 1889, D. 90. 1. 273).

LOUISIANA CIVIL CODE, BOOK III, TITLE XXIII
Exposé des Motifs

Vices of possession. Possession has no legal effect if it is tainted with vice. Possession is tainted with vice when the possession is violent, clandestine, discontinuous, or equivocal. Article 3435. Each of these vices is defined in Article 3436.

Thus, if possession is tainted with vice, the possessor is not entitled to possessory protection, and the plea of acquisitive prescription is not available to him.

Precarious possession. The exercise of possession over a thing with the permission of or on behalf of the owner is precarious possession. Article 3437. Strictly speaking, a precarious possessor is not a possessor at all; he is a person who merely has physical control over a thing, which amounts to detention rather than possession. A precarious possessor is presumed to possess for another even though he may intend to possess for himself. Article 3438.

The presumption of precariousness is rebuttable because precarious possession may terminate in accordance with the terms of Article 3439. For example, a co-owner may commence to possess for himself when he demonstrates this intent by overt and unambiguous acts sufficient to give notice to his co-owner. From that time he ceases to possess precariously for his co-owner. However, any other precarious possessor commences to possess for himself when he gives *actual* notice of this intent to the person on whose behalf he is possessing. These rules were inherent in the Louisiana Civil Code of 1870.

In the past, the possessory action was not available to a precarious possessor. However, in the light of contemporary conditions, it seems desirable to accord him possessory protection against anyone except the person for whom he possesses. Article 3440 makes this significant change in the law.

Comment, Possession — The 1982 Revision Of The Louisiana Civil Code, 58 Tul. L. Rev. 573-592 (1983)

Precarious Possession

As previously mentioned, Louisiana legal texts sometimes use the word "possession" to mean the physical detention of the thing without the intent to own. In order to be analytically correct, this situation should be termed "precarious possession," or merely "detention." Only the element of physical detention is supplied by the precarious possessor, while the second element of proper possession — the intent to possess as owner — is satisfied by the owner or actual possessor.

Once a person enters into a relationship with another that places him in the category of precarious possessor, the Code presumes that such condition continues throughout the duration of his detention of the thing. The policy behind this presumption (and, indeed, behind the entirety of Chapter 2, Title XXIII, Book III dealing with possession) is that the Owner or possessor must be given an adequate opportunity to ascertain the fact that another party is adversely possessing his property so that he may institute a possessory action. To allow a precarious possessor to change his mind covertly and begin to possess in his own name clearly would circumvent this policy. As with all of the presumptions imposed by the Code articles dealing with possession, the presumption of precariousness imposed by this article is rebuttable.

The converse of the prohibition against a covert conversion from precarious to adverse possession would be a rule that an outwardly manifested change in intention should allow a mere detainer to become a true possessor. This is indeed the policy of the Code. Revised Article 3439 provides that a co-owner can change his relationship as precarious possessor vis-à-vis his other co-owners through overt and unambiguous acts which are sufficient, to give notice to his co-owners that he intends to possess for himself. Precarious possessors other than co-owners, however, must give actual notice of such intent to the person on whose behalf they are possessing.

It appears at first glance that this article imposes a heavier burden of notice on a lessee or depositary than upon a co-owner. Upon closer examination, however, it can be seen that the opposite is true. Because each co-owner may exercise all of the attributes of ownership, overt acts which would be sufficient to demonstrate the intent of a co-owner to possess on his own behalf would have to be of an extraordinary nature. Such acts would include forcibly preventing a co-owner from exercising any of the attributes of ownership over the thing. An example of actual notice by a precarious possessor other than a co-owner would be the sale of the leased premises by the lessee to a third party.

In addition to specifically delineating the methods by which a precarious possessor may change the nature of his possession, the new revision also provides him with a procedural route to follow to protect his precarious possession. The introduction of Article 3440, which allows a precarious possessor to file a possessory action, constitutes a change in the law of Louisiana. Under the old law, only the one for whom the precarious possessor was possessing was entitled to bring the possessory action. The precarious possessor only had an action against the person for whom he was possessing for breach of his obligation to deliver quiet possession of the property. Some courts circumvented this harsh rule by holding that a precarious possessor could obtain an injunction against trespassers pursuant to Article 3663(2) of the Code of Civil Procedure, which allows injunctive relief for a disturbance of enjoyment as well as possession. The introduction of Article 3440 renders this strained interpretation of Code of Civil Procedure Article 3663 unnecessary, and places the precarious possessor in a position analogous to that of co-owners, who are considered precarious possessors vis-à-vis other co-owners, but who have all of the rights of full owners as to the rest of the world.

FALGOUST v. INNESS
163 So. 429 (La. App. Orl. Cir. 1935)

WESTERFIELD, J. Plaintiff is the owner of a tract of land in the Vacherie Settlement, St. James Parish, La. On September 1, 1932, she gave John William Inness, who was married to her adopted daughter, permission to erect a building for the purpose of operating a garage and filling station on a part of her land adjacent to the public road. Inness constructed a garage and operated it until the 12th day of June, 1933, when she caused written notice to vacate to be served upon him through her attorney. Inness refused to comply with her demand, and this suit was instituted on September 2, 1933, for the purpose of compelling him to vacate the property and remove all buildings which he had erected thereon, and for the sum of $10 per month as rental beginning June 12, 1933, the date on which the notice to vacate was served and continuing as long as plaintiff occupies the property and fails to remove the buildings.

After interposing exceptions of vagueness and of no right or cause of action, which were overruled, the defendant answered admitting practically all the allegations of the plaintiff's petition and averring that he had been given a verbal permission to occupy the land for a period of five years. He reconvened and claimed the sum of $1,823.58 as the cost of the building which he had constructed, the stock which he had on hand, the profits which he expected to earn, and the enhanced value of the plaintiff's land resulting from the improvements which he had erected thereon.

There was judgment below in favor of plaintiff on the main demand ordering the defendant to vacate the property within forty days, and, in the event of his default or neglect to do so, the sheriff for the parish of St. James was ordered to demolish the buildings erected by defendant. Plaintiff's claim for rent was rejected as was defendant's reconventional demand. From this judgment, defendant has appealed.

It is suggested in brief and in argument that plaintiff's reason for her desire to evict the defendant grows out of the fact that the marital relations between defendant and plaintiff's foster daughter were unpleasant, and it has been proven that two days before the institution of this suit his wife, plaintiff's adopted daughter, instituted proceedings against him for separation from bed and board. The explanation of the reason for the litigation seems to us plausible, but immaterial, the important consideration being her legal right to dispossess defendant.

In so far as the main demand is concerned, the only disputed question of fact relates to the character of the oral permission given by plaintiff to defendant to erect a building on plaintiff's property — plaintiff claiming that it was indefinite, and defendant that it was for a definite period of five years, and on this point plaintiff must prevail because of the defendant's failure to establish his claim concerning the five-year term.***

Article 3436 of the Civil Code [Revised C.C. art. 3424] reads:

"To be able to acquire possession of property, two distinct things are requisite:

"1. The intention of possessing as owner.
"2. The corporeal possession of the thing."

It is apparent from a consideration of the articles we have quoted, that the defendant is not a possessor in good faith, and, in fact, not a possessor at all, in the sense of the articles of the Code, because he does not possess as owner, and whatever may be the status of his claim, it involves the recognition of the ownership and legal possession of the plaintiff through whom he holds.

The best that can be said for the defendant is that he had been given the right to erect his garage building on the plaintiff's property and to keep it there for a reasonable period of time. Before this judgment can become final he will have been in possession for more than three years, a period which we consider reasonable.

The claim for rent was properly rejected below. The reconventional demand will be dismissed. Affirmed.

6. PROTECTION OF POSSESSION: THE POSSESSORY ACTION
Civil Code arts. 3440, 3444

LOUISIANA CODE OF CIVIL PROCEDURE

Art. 3655. Possessory action

The possessory action is one brought by the possessor of immovable property or of a real right therein to be maintained in his possession of the property or enjoyment of the right when he has been disturbed, or to be restored to the possession or enjoyment thereof when he has been evicted.

Art. 3656. Same; parties; venue

A plaintiff in a possessory action shall be one who possesses for himself. A person entitled to the use or usufruct of immovable property, and one who owns a real right therein, possesses for himself. A predial lessee possesses for and in the name of his lessor, and not for himself.

The possessory action shall be brought against the person who caused the disturbance, and in the venue provided by Article 80(1), even when the plaintiff prays for a judgment for the fruits and revenues of the property, or for damages.

Art. 3657. Same; cumulation with petitory action prohibited; conversion into or separate petitory action by defendant

The plaintiff may not cumulate the petitory and the possessory actions in the same suit or plead them in the alternative, and when he does so he waives the possessory action. If the plaintiff brings the possessory action, and without dismissing it and prior to judgment therein institutes the petitory action, the possessory action is abated.

When, except as provided in Article 3661(1)-(3), the defendant in a possessory action asserts title in himself, in the alternative or otherwise, he thereby converts the suit into a petitory action, and judicially confesses the possession of the plaintiff in the possessory action.

If, before executory judgment in a possessory action, the defendant therein institutes a petitory action in a separate suit against the plaintiff in the possessory action, the plaintiff in the petitory action judicially confesses the possession of the defendant therein.

Art. 3658. Same; requisites

To maintain the possessory action the possessor must allege and prove that:

(1) He had possession of the immovable property or real right therein at the time the disturbance occurred;

(2) He and his ancestors in title had such possession quietly and without interruption for more than a year immediately prior to the disturbance, unless evicted by force or fraud;

(3) The disturbance was one in fact or in law, as defined in Article 3659; and

(4) The possessory action was instituted within a year of the disturbance.

Art. 3659. Same; disturbance in fact and in law defined

Disturbances of possession which give rise to the possessory action are of two kinds: disturbance in fact and disturbance in law.

A disturbance in fact is an eviction, or any other physical act which prevents the possessor of immovable property or of a real right therein from enjoying his possession quietly, or which throws any obstacle in the way of that enjoyment.

A disturbance in law is the execution, recordation, registry, or continuing existence of record of any instrument which asserts or implies a right of ownership or to the possession of immovable property or of a real right therein, or any claim or pretension of ownership or right to the possession thereof except in an action or proceeding, adversely to the possessor of such property or right.

Art. 3660. Same; possession

A person is in possession of immovable property or of a real right therein, within the intendment of the articles of this Chapter, when he has the corporeal possession thereof, or civil possession thereof preceded by corporeal possession by him or his ancestors in title, and possesses for himself, whether in good or bad faith, or even as a usurper.

Subject to the provisions of Articles 3656 and 3664, a person who claims the ownership of immovable property or of a real right therein possesses through his lessee, through another who occupies the property or enjoys the right under an agreement with him or his lessee, or through a person who has the use or usufruct thereof to which his right of ownership is subject.

Art. 3661. Same; title not at issue; limited admissibility of evidence of title

In the possessory action, the ownership or title of the parties to the immovable property or real right therein is not at issue.

No evidence of ownership or title to the immovable property or real right therein shall be admitted except to prove:

(1) The possession thereof by a party as owner;

(2) The extent of the possession thereof by a party; or

(3) The length of time in which a party and his ancestors in title have had possession thereof.

Art. 3662. Same; relief which may be granted successful plaintiff in judgment; appeal

A judgment rendered for the plaintiff in a possessory action shall:

(1) Recognize his right to the possession of the immovable property or real right therein, and restore him to possession thereof if he has been evicted, or maintain him in possession thereof if the disturbance has not been an eviction;

(2) Order the defendant to assert his adverse claim of ownership of the immovable property or real right therein in a petitory action to be filed within a day to be fixed by the court not to exceed sixty days after the date the judgment becomes executory, or be precluded thereafter from asserting the ownership thereof, if the plaintiff has prayed for such relief; and

(3) Award him the damages to which he is entitled and which he has prayed for.

A suspensive appeal from the judgment rendered in a possessory action may be taken within the delay provided in Article 2123, and a devolutive appeal may be taken from such judgment only within thirty days of the applicable date provided in Article 2087(1)-(3).

Art. 3663. Sequestration; injunctive relief

Sequestration of immovable property or of a real right therein involved in a possessory or petitory action during the pendency thereof is available under the applicable provisions of Chapter 1 of Title I of Book VII.

Injunctive relief, under the applicable provisions of Chapter 2 of Title I of Book VII, to protect or restore possession of immovable property or of a real right therein, is available to:

(1) A plaintiff in a possessory action, during the pendency thereof; and

(2) A person who is disturbed in the possession which he and his ancestors in title have had for more than year of immovable property or of a real right therein of which he claims the ownership, the possession, or the enjoyment.

OLIVER WENDELL HOLMES
THE COMMON LAW 206-213 (1881)

POSSESSION is a conception which is only less important than contract.***

Why is possession protected by the law, when the possessor is not also an owner? That is the general problem which has much exercised the German mind. Kant, it is well known, was deeply influenced in his opinions upon ethics and law by the speculations of Rousseau. Kant, Rousseau, and the Massachusetts Bill of Rights agree that all men are born *free* and *equal*, and one or the other branch of that declaration has afforded the answer to the question why possession should be protected from that day to this. Kant and Hegel start from freedom. The freedom of the will, Kant said, is the essence of man. It is an end in itself; it is that which needs no further explanation, which is absolutely to be respected, and which it is the very end and object of all government to realize and affirm. Possession is to be protected because a man by taking possession of an object has brought it within the sphere of his will. He has extended his personality into or over that object. As Hegel would have said, possession is the objective realization of free will. And by Kant's postulate, the will of any individual thus manifested is entitled to absolute respect from every other individual, and can only be overcome or set aside by the universal will, that is, by the state, acting through its organs, the courts.

Savigny did not follow Kant on this point. He said that every act of violence is unlawful, and seemed to consider protection of possession a branch of protection to the person. But to this it was answered that possession was protected against disturbance by fraud as well as by force, and his view is discredited. Those who have been contended with humble grounds of expediency seem to have been few in number, and have recanted or are out of favor.***

It follows from the Kantian doctrine, that a man in possession is to be confirmed and maintained in it until he is put out by an action brought for the purpose. Perhaps another fact besides those which have been mentioned has influenced his reasoning, and that is the accurate division between possessory and petitory actions or defenses in Continental procedure. When a defendant in a possessory action is not allowed to set up title in himself, a theorist readily finds a mystical importance in possession.

But when does a man become entitled to this absolute protection? On the principle of Kant, it is not enough that he has the custody of a thing. A protection based on the sacredness of man's personality requires that the object should have been brought within the sphere of that personality, that the free will should have unrestrainedly set itself into that object. There must be then an intent to appropriate it, that is, to make it part of one's self, or one's own.

Philosophy by denying possession to bailees in general cunningly adjusted itself to the Roman law, and thus put itself in a position to claim the authority of that law for the theory of which the mode of dealing with bailees was merely a corollary. Hence I say that it is important to show that a far more developed, more rational, and mightier body of law than the Roman, gives no sanction to either premise or conclusion as held by Kant and his successors.

In the first place, the English law has always had the good sense to allow title to be set up in defense to a possessory action.... The rule that you cannot go into title in a possessory action presupposes great difficulty in the proof, the *probatio diabolica* of the Canon law, delays in the process, and importance of possession *ad interim*, — all of which mark a stage of society which has long been passed. In ninety-nine cases out of a hundred, it is about as easy and cheap to prove at least a *prima facie* title as it is to prove possession.

In the next place, and this was the importance of the last Lecture to this subject, the common law has always given the possessory remedies to all bailees without exception. The right to these remedies extends not only to pledgees, lessees, and those having a lien, who exclude their bailor, but to simple bailees, as they have been called, who have no interest in the chattels, no right of detention as against the owner, and neither give nor receive a reward.

Modern German statutes have followed in the same path so far as to give the possessory remedies to tenants and some others. Bruns says, as the spirit of the Kantian theory required him to say, that this is a sacrifice of principle to convenience. But I cannot see what is left of a principle which avows itself inconsistent with convenience and the actual course of legislation. The first call of a theory of law is that it should fit the facts. It must explain the observed course of legislation. And as it is pretty certain that men will make laws which seem to them convenient without troubling themselves very much what principles are encountered by their legislation, a principle which defies convenience is likely to wait some time before it finds itself permanently realized.

It remains, then, to seek for some ground for the protection of possession outside the Bill of Rights or the Declaration of Independence, which shall be consistent with the larger scope given to the conception in modern law.

The courts have said but little on the subject. It was laid down in one case that it was an extension of the protection which the law throws around the person.

Those who see in the history of law the formal expression of development of society will be apt to think that the proximate ground of law must be empirical, even when that ground is the fact that a certain ideal or theory of government is generally entertained. Law, being a practical thing, must found itself on actual forces. It is quite enough, therefore, for the law, that man, by an instinct which he shares with the domestic dog, and of which the seal gives a most striking example, will not allow himself to be dispossessed, either by force or fraud, of what he holds, without trying to get it back again. Philosophy may find a hundred reasons to justify the instinct, but it would be totally immaterial if it should condemn it and bid us surrender without a murmur. As long as the instinct remains, it will be more comfortable for the law to satisfy it in an orderly manner than to leave people to themselves. If it should do otherwise, it would become a matter for pedagogues, wholly devoid of reality.

a. Possession at the time of disturbance
C.C.P. art. 3658(1)

NOTE

In *Antulovich v. Whitley*, 289 So. 2d 164 (La. App. 1st Cir. 1973), a "possessory action" case, the court was called upon to determine whether Antulovich, the plaintiff, had been "in possession" of the disputed land "at the time of the disturbance" by Whitley, the defendant. The disputed land, which was covered by timber, lay within the confines of the tract of land to which Whitley held title. Whitley's land lay immediately to the south of that to which Antulovich held title. At the trial, it was established that Antulovich had once caused a survey of his tract to be conducted; that the surveyor, apparently in error, had located the southern boundary 100 feet south of where it actually lay (that is, 100 feet "into" Whitley's tract); that the surveyor had "blazed" this supposed boundary on the trees; that Antulovich had periodically thereafter re-marked the line by applying paint to the trees; that Antulovich, on three occasions, had sold the timber on the disputed land and that, on each of these occasions, the timber had been cut down to the blazed-painted line. As for Whitley, he did nothing that even arguably could have amounted to a disturbance until years later, when he finally sent his own surveyor out onto the disputed land. Under these circumstances, the court of appeal concluded, Antulovich had met his burden of proof, namely, that of showing that he had possessed the disputed land within a veritable "enclosure" up until the time of the disturbance:

> . . . The property in question is rural, wooded land, and plaintiffs exercised possession over that tract in an appropriate manner, by cutting timber...and maintaining the southern boundary line throughout their ownership.... We think that the fact that the...line was surveyed and blazed, and that plaintiffs marked the line with paint periodically thereafter, brings it within the legal definition of enclosure....
> Id. at 176.

b. Possession for one year "quietly and without interruption"
C.C.P. art. 3658(2)

LINER v. LOUISIANA LAND & EXPLORATION CO.
319 So. 2d 766 (La. 1975)

DIXON, J. Defendant advances two main reasons for affirming the Court of Appeal. The first is that plaintiff has failed to prove possession within enclosures; the second reason is that the extensive activities of Louisiana Land and Exploration Company on the disputed property during the year preceding February of 1972 prevented a finding that plaintiff was in peaceful possession for the time required to maintain the possessory action.***

C.C.P. art. 3658 requires the possessor to prove that he had possession at the time of the disturbance; that his quiet, uninterrupted possession shall have existed more than a year prior to the disturbance; that suit was instituted within a year of the disturbance.***

Defendant's second argument is based on subparagraph (2) of C.C.P. art. 3658 which requires the possessor to allege and prove that he "had such possession quietly and without interruption for more than a year immediately prior to the disturbance, unless evicted by force or fraud." Defendant would interpret the article literally, and maintains its actions for the year before February 3, 1972 prevent any conclusion that Oliver Liner had the quiet uninterrupted possession. The activities relied on by Louisiana Land and Exploration Company are: the August 2, 1971 cleaning of the property line ditch; the August 4, 1971 pulling of Liner's stakes and the continued cleaning of the ditch; the use of an air horn to communicate between the dragline and the marsh buggy while cleaning the ditch; the presence of no trespassing signs along the ditch; the August 17, 1971 removal of the stakes Liner had used to replace those previously removed by Louisiana Land and Exploration Company; the awareness by Liner of the August 17 operation; the September 24 and September 30, 1971 removal of Liner's property line stakes, and Liner's awareness shown by his attorney's letter to the defendant; the October 25, 1971 removal of stakes and obstructions in the property line ditch; and, finally, the February 3, 1972 operation which precipitated the suit.

We must conclude then that the words "quietly and without interruption" do not mean that a possessor who suffers a "disturbance" on several occasions in the year preceding the suit has lost his right to bring the possessory action. The possessor may suffer disturbances throughout the year preceding the filing of the possessory action, and unless his possession comes to an end in such a way that he cannot show that he was in possession for more than a year prior to the disturbance complained of, he has the right to bring the action within a year of the disturbance.

C.C.P. art. 3658 (2) cannot, without adding a new requirement to the possessory action, be read literally. It cannot mean that there must be no adverse claim for a year before the disturbance. "Quietly" appears in C.P. 49 and may be compared to "peaceably" in C.C. 3454, subd. 2 (1870) [no corresponding article after Revision; *Cf.* Revised C.C. art. 3444], and in contrast to the violence referred to in C.C. 3491 (1870) [Revised C.C. art. 3436]:

> "A possession by violence, not being legal, does not confer the right of prescribing. That right only commences when the violence has ceased."

As stated in Aubry & Rau, *supra*, § 180:

> "Possession is marred by violence, that means it is not peaceful, if it was acquired and continued by acts accompanied by physical or psychological violence."

Consequently, we interpret the requirement of C.C.P. art. 3658(2) to mean that there must have been no interruption of the possession for one year, prior to the disturbance which caused the suit.

Oliver Liner has proven each of the requisite elements of the possessory action set out in C.C.P. art. 3658. He is entitled to a judgment of possession.

On Application for Rehearing

PER CURIAM. Our original opinion has adequately disposed of the contentions advanced by the application for rehearing. However, a strong argument has been made that we have misapplied La.C.Civ.P. art. 3658(2).

The applicant points out that in our opinion we pointed out several acts by which the defendant Louisiana Land disturbed the plaintiff Liner's "quiet" possession during the year prior to the February 3, 1972 disturbance alleged as the basis for this suit.

The defendant correctly points out that each of these acts was a disturbance of possession which would entitle Liner to bring this possessory action, just as did the February 3, 1972 disturbance. Thus, Louisiana Land contends, due to these late 1971 disturbances, plainly Liner did not possess "quietly and without interruption" during the year preceding the February 3, 1972 disturbance upon which this suit is based.

This contention overlooks that the term to possess "quietly and without interruption," as used in the Louisiana Code of Civil Procedure (and by Article 49(2) of the Louisiana Codes of Practice of 1825 and 1870 preceding it), is equated with its traditional meaning in the Louisiana Civil Code. There, as a substantive right of possession, the Code recognizes the right of a possessor for a year or more who has possessed "peaceably and without interruption" to bring a possessory action against one who disturbs his possession. Louisiana Civil Code of 1808, art. 23, p. 478; Louisiana Civil Code of 1825, art. 3417(2) [Revised C.C. art. 3423]; Louisiana Civil Code of 1870, art. 3454(2). See art. 3454, La.C.C. Comp. ed. in West's C.C., pp. 656-57 (1972).***

We therefore conclude that one may possess quietly and without interruption for more than a year so as to be entitled to bring a possessory action, La.C.Civ.P. art. 3658(2), even though during that year disturbances in fact or law have occurred, La.C.Civ.P. art. 3659. The application for a rehearing is denied.

TATE, J. (concurring in denial). ***According to Article 3658(2) of the Louisiana Code of Civil Procedure, the plaintiff in a possessory action must allege and prove that he and his ancestors in title had possession of the immovable property or real right *"quietly and without interruption* for more than a year immediately prior to the disturbance, unless evicted by force or fraud." (Italics mine.) This provision was derived from Article 49(2) of the Codes of Practice of 1825 and 1870. This prescribed that the plaintiff in the possessory action ought to have possession *"quietly and without interruption . . .* for more than a year previous to his being disturbed," unless he had been evicted by force or fraud (Italics mine). An official comment under Article 3658 of the Louisiana Code of Civil Procedure indicates that "this article makes no change in the law."***

We may now return to the interpretation of Article 3658(2) of the Louisiana Code of Civil Procedure.

Does this provision contemplate interruption of possession by an eviction of any duration or only by an eviction that has lasted for more than a year?

In other words, does this provision contemplate interruption of possession by the loss of physical control (Civil Code Article 3449(1)) [Revised C.C. art. 3486], or only interruption of possession by the loss of the right to possess? (Civil Code Article 3449 (2) [Revised C.C. art. 3486]. In the final analysis, the question is open to either interpretation and must be resolved in the light of policy consideration.

If possession is interrupted within the meaning of Article 3658(2) of the Louisiana Code of Civil Procedure by the mere loss of physical control at sometime during the period of one year immediately preceding the disturbance, consider the following illustration. A is disturbed in his possession by eviction or otherwise on January 4, 1974. He must bring the possessory action within one year and he must allege and prove that he was in possession on January 4, 1974, and that he was *not evicted at all* during the period between January 4, 1973, and January 4, 1974.

If possession is interrupted within the meaning of Article 3658(2) of the Louisiana Code of Civil Procedure by the loss of the right to possess during the period of one year immediately preceding the disturbance, consider the following illustration. A is disturbed in his possession, by eviction or otherwise, on January 4, 1974. He brings a possessory action on January 3, 1975, meeting the requirement of C.C.P. art. 3658(4). He must also allege and prove that he was in possession on January 4, 1974, and that he *did not lose the right to possess* during the period between January 4, 1973 and January 4, 1974. If he was evicted, at any time, for less than a year and recovered possession prior to January 4, 1974, he may still bring the possessory action. If he was evicted for more than a year but recovered possession prior to January 4, 1973, again he may still bring the possessory action. The possessory action is barred to him only if he recovered possession during the period from January 4, 1973 to January 4, 1974, after having been out of possession for more than a year, namely, if he was evicted prior to January 4, 1972, and his eviction lasted for more than a year.

The second interpretation is preferable. Under this interpretation, an interruption of possession for purposes of the possessory action coincides with an interruption of acquisitive prescription under Article 3517 of the Civil Code [Revised C.C. arts. 3434, 3465]. Moreover, under this interpretation, the loss of the right to possess under Article 3449(2) of the Civil Code [Revised C.C. art. 3486] coincides in time with the acquisition of the right to possess by another under Articles 3454(2) and 3456 of the Civil Code [no corresponding articles after Revision].

This preferred interpretation accords with the apparent intent of the redactors of the Code of Practice and of the Code of Civil Procedure. The redactors intended to accord possessory protection to a person who acquired the right to possess, under Civil Code Articles 3449(2), 3454(2), and 3487.

Thus, the legislative intent of the provisions of Article 49(2) of the Code of Practice and 3658(2) of the Code of Civil Procedure seems to be that possessory protection is available to anyone who has previously acquired the right to possess and did not lose it in the year immediately preceding the disturbance.

MIRE v. CROWE
439 So. 2d 517 (La. App. 1ˢᵗ Cir. 1983)

CARTER, J. This is a possessory action involving a triangular piece of property located in St. Tammany Parish.

Karl Mire instituted this possessory action on December 10, 1981, against Levi L. Crowe, Jr. claiming that the defendant had disturbed his possession by advising plaintiff's lessee that Crowe claimed ownership of a portion of the property. After trial on the merits, judgment was rendered in favor of plaintiff and defendant perfected this appeal.

On March 16, 1968, Karl Mire bought from Levi L. Crowe, Jr. property located in Slidell, Louisiana described as follows:

"A certain tract or parcel of land, together with all the buildings and improvements thereon, and all rights, ways, advantages, and appurtenances thereunto belonging or in anywise appertaining situated in St. Tammany Parish, Louisiana, and more particularly described as Lot Six (6) of Section Eighteen (18) in Township 8 South, Range 15 East, of the St. Helena Meridian Louisiana, containing two (2) acres and sixteen hundredths of an acre, according to the official plat of survey of the said lands, in file in the General Land Office."

Prior to passage of this act of sale, Mire and Levi Crowe, Jr. walked the boundaries of the property to be conveyed. The area pointed out to Mire by Crowe included an area in Lot 7, which could be generally described as lying east of Lot 6 and bounded on the north and south by an extension of the north and south lines of Lot 6 and on the east by Langston's Bayou.

Crowe does not question Mire's possession of Lot 6. Crowe claims, however, that Mire's title is limited to Lot 6 and does not cover any property in Lot 7. Both parties assert ownership of the disputed land, although the only issue on this appeal is whether Mire is entitled to be maintained in possession of the property. Crowe did not reconvene for possession of the property, but simply denied plaintiff's possession.

MIRE'S ACTS OF POSSESSION

Upon acquisition of Lot 6 in 1968, Mire immediately took possession of the disputed property. Mire employed a surveyor and had the property surveyed. Mire and his nephews then walked the property and placed stakes for construction of a fence. A new fence was built along the northern boundary of the property to Langston Bayou and along the southern boundary to a point referred to as the "gully". No fence was erected through the "gully" because the area was under water during parts of the year. Mire also maintained and repaired the fences.

Hunting and fishing activities were also conducted on the disputed area. Family members and friends of Karl Mire often used a portion of the disputed property known as the 'hill" to conduct these activities, with Mire's permission.

Several of Mire's nephews (with Mire's consent) raised hogs in the area west of the gully and allowed cattle to graze over the entirety of the area, including the "hill".

Mire erected a barn on the disputed area west of the gully and maintained a garden for several years in the general vicinity of the barn. Grass was clipped and maintained by Mire on the disputed tract.

In July, 1981, Mire leased the property to John Buttrey for the purpose of housing and maintaining horses on the premises.

CROWE'S ACTS OF POSSESSION

Crowe lived on the property in dispute as a child and conducted various activities on the property prior to the sale to Mire in 1968. Crowe now owns a campsite south of and adjacent to the Mire property. The Crowe camp is bounded on the north by the disputed "hill", on the east by Langston Bayou, and on the west by other Mire property. Crowe and his friends have used the disputed tract on several occasions to get to his camp.

THE TRIAL COURT'S JUDGMENT

The trial court found that Mire was entitled to be maintained in possession of the disputed area and stated: "... since acquisition of the property, Mr. Mire has been in actual, physical, open, public, unequivocal continuous, and uninterrupted possession of the property with the intent to possess as owner. The Court is also convinced by the evidence that upon execution of the act of sale on March 16, 1968, Mr. Crowe terminated his prior possession of the disputed area. Mire was in possession at the time of Crowe's disturbance and had been so without interruption for more than a year prior to the disturbance. Crowe's disturbance was a disturbance in fact, and the possessory action was instituted by Mire well within a year of the disturbance. The few trespasses upon the property by Crowe and his friends, without knowledge of Mire, are of no significance. These trespasses are inadequate to establish possession by Crowe or his usurpation of the property in dispute. These disturbances--unknown to Mire--are not strong enough to interrupt Mire's right to possess. These activities would in no way bring home to Mire the realization that his possession and control of the property is being challenged by Crowe...."

Defendant has appealed the trial court judgment, contending that the trial judge erred in finding that the plaintiff maintained the necessary possession of the area in dispute.

THE LAW

This action is governed primarily by LSA-C.C.P. art. 3658.***Although Article 3658 lists four requirements for bringing the possessory action, the battle lines are often drawn over the question posed by paragraph (2): Who has the *right to possess?* This question, in turn, is often decided by a determination of whether any acts of the defendant have sufficiently interrupted the plaintiff's possession so as to strip the plaintiff of his right to possess.

HOW THE RIGHT IS ACQUIRED

A person acquires the right to possess immovable property by possessing the property quietly and without interruption for more than a year. LSA-C.C.P. art. 3658(2); LSA-C.C. art. 3454(2), now repealed; see also LSA-C.C. arts. 3449(2), now LSA-C.C. art. 3434, and 3487, now LSA-C.C. arts. 3435, 3436 and 3476. The species of possession required to acquire the right to possess is either corporeal possession or civil possession preceded by the corporeal possession of the plaintiff or his ancestors in title. LSA-C.C.P. art. 3660. In all cases, a person must possess as owner and for himself. Thus, to acquire the right to possess, "one must combine the intention of possessing as owner with the corporeal detention of the thing." Norton v. Addie, 337 So.2d 432, 436 (La.1976). Pitre v. Tenneco Oil Co., 385 So.2d 840 (La.App. 1st Cir.1980), writ denied 392 So.2d 678 (La.1980).***

The Louisiana law of possession and the jurisprudence interpreting it also provide that a person who possesses property in good faith under a deed translative of ownership is considered to possess to the extent of his title, provided he has corporeally possessed part of the property described in the deed. In such a case, the person is considered to be in constructive possession of the entire tract. However, when one possesses without title, he is required to show an adverse possession by enclosures. *Hill v. Richey, supra.* Corporeal possession required to maintain a possessory action when one has no title contemplates actual possession within enclosures sufficient to establish the limits of possession with certainty, by either natural or artificial marks, giving notice to the world of the extent of possession exercised. Hill v. Richey, *supra*; Gaulter v. Gennaro, *supra.****

Once it is established that a person has possessed property, as required by law, quietly and without interruption for more than a year, he has proven his right to possess. There is no need to show he acquired this right in the year immediately preceding suit, but only that he obtained the right at one time and that he has not lost it prior to the disturbance. Liner v. Louisiana Land and Exploration Company, 319 So.2d 766 (La.1975).

HOW THE RIGHT IS LOST

A person loses the right to possess immovable property either voluntarily, by transferring or abandoning the property; or involuntarily, by being evicted or expelled for more than a year or by acquiescing in a third party's usurpation of the property for more than a year. LSA-C.C. arts. 3447, 3448, 3449, now LSA-C.C. art. 3433. Pitre v. Tenneco Oil Co., *supra.*

A question often arises as to what type of activity by an adverse party will sufficiently interrupt a person's right to possess so as to usurp his possession and strip him of his right upon passage of more than a year's time. Not every disturbance is strong or long enough to interrupt another's right to possess. Disturbances which do not interrupt another person's right to possess may be challenged in court and the disturber cast for appropriate damages and other appropriate relief. But such minor disturbances will be insufficient, even if unchallenged within a year's time, to strip the right to possess from the person who presently has that right. See *Liner, supra,* particularly the per curiam opinion on rehearing, 319 So.2d 778; Pitre v. Tenneco Oil Co., *supra*; Plaisance v. Collins, *supra*; Richard v. Comeaux, 260 So.2d 350 (La. App. 1st Cir.1972); Yiannopoulous, 2 Louisiana Civil Law Treatise, Property, § 217, page 582 (2d Ed. 1980); and Work of the Appellate Court--1974-1975, Property, 36 La. L.Rev. 354 (1976).

Louisiana courts have indicated that for a disturbance to be sufficient to interrupt another's right to possess, the disturbance must bring home to the actual possessor the realization that his dominion is being seriously challenged. Pittman v. Bourg, 179 La. 66, 153 So. 22 (1934); Souther v. Domingue, 238 So.2d 264 (La. App. 3d Cir.1970), writ refused, 256 La. 891, 239 So. 2d 544 (1970); Hebert v. Chargois, 106 So. 2d 15 (La. App. 1st Cir.1958). In addition, the person with the right to possess must acquiesce in the interruption for more than a year without conducting any act of possession or without interfering with the usurper's possession. LSA-C.C. art. 3449(2), now LSA-C.C. art. 3434.

The single rule of law that can be fashioned from the foregoing is that the plaintiff, to win a possessory action, must show that he at one time acquired the right to possess and that he has not lost the right prior to the disturbance. Stated another way, "possessory protection is available to anyone who has previously acquired the right to possess and did not lose it in the year preceding the disturbance." Yiannopoulous, *supra*, ' 215, page 580; see also Tate, J., concurring in denial of rehearing in Liner, *supra*, 319 So. 2d 779, 782. In all cases, of course, suit must be filed within a year of the disturbance. LSA-C.C.P. art. 3658(4). A person who proves that he had the right to possess and that he has not lost it in the year prior to the disturbance has proved, concomitantly, that he is in possession of the property as required by LSA-C.C.P. art. 3658(1). See Liner, *supra*, and Plaisance v. Collins, *supra*, at 613.

DID MIRE HAVE THE RIGHT TO POSSESS?

The facts that the trial court found, and we agree, prove that Karl Mire acquired the right to possess. For some fourteen years, Mire, his family, and his friends have performed various acts of corporeal possession on the disputed tract. Upon purchasing Lot 6 in 1968, Mire moved onto the property, had the property surveyed, and erected visible boundaries which complemented natural boundaries. Other acts of corporeal possession were conducted on the property, each act corresponding to the different kinds of property involved. Certain cleared areas were used to build a barn and plant a garden. The more wooded areas were utilized for walking and hunting. The areas which were partially covered by water were used for fishing. The disputed property was also used to graze cattle and raise hogs. Mire also granted a lease to a portion of the disputed tract. Those areas on which no corporeal activities were conducted were enclosed within the natural and the artificial boundaries established by Mire.

The record is also clear that when Mire took possession of Lot 6 and the disputed portion of Lot 7 in 1968, Crowe, who had previously conducted activities on the property, abandoned his use of the property, as owner, until August, 1981.

DID MIRE LOSE THE RIGHT TO POSSESS?

Having found that Mire acquired the right to possess, and actually possessed, we must now determine whether any acts of Crowe were of sufficient strength to interrupt Mire's possession or usurp Mire's right to possess.

Unquestionably, Crowe committed a number of trespasses on the property. Crowe crossed Mire's property to get to his own camp, primarily because Crowe had enclosed his camp by selling the surrounding property which fronted roads. These trespasses, however, seem not to have been made with Mire's permission.

Crowe may also have conducted several disturbances, each of which would have entitled Mire to bring a possessory action, as Crowe hunted and fished on the disputed tract through the years. These isolated acts were insufficient to dispossess Mire, especially in light of the fact that Crowe had prior to the sale pointed out the now disputed area to Mire as being sold to Mire. See Plaisance v. Collins, *supra* at 616, where sporadic trapping, chicken farming, hunting, and leasing a house in the vicinity were held to be insufficient acts to dispossess the plaintiff.

Additionally, when plaintiff's lessee, John Buttrey, was advised by Crowe on August 16, 1981, that he must cease building a corral and developing the "hill", plaintiff instituted this possessory action on December 10, 1981, clearly within a year of the disturbance.

We are simply not convinced that any of the activities conducted on the disputed tract prior to the disturbance in August, 1981, interrupted the quiet and peaceable possession of Mire. Mire possessed the property as owner and conducted numerous activities which were consistent with the nature of the property in question. He never acquiesced in Crowe's claims to the property, and he brought this action when it became apparent that Crowe claimed ownership of the "hill". The trial court correctly determined that Mire proved his right to possession of the disputed area and that he did not lose this right in the year immediately preceeding this suit. The requisites for the possessory action were clearly established, and Mire is entitled to be maintained in possession.

Therefore, for the foregoing reasons, the judgment of the trial court is affirmed. Appellant is to pay all costs.

c. Disturbance in fact and disturbance in law; Prescription
C.C.P. arts. 3658(3) and (4)

A. N. YIANNOPOULOS, CIVIL LAW PROPERTY
§§ 337, 338 (4th ed. 2001)
(footnotes omitted)

§ 337. Disturbance in Fact and Law

A disturbance of possession may be one in fact or in law. A disturbance in fact is a physical interference with the possession of an immovable or of a real right that prevents the possessor from enjoying his possession quietly, or which throws an obstacle in the way of that enjoyment. It may thus be a mere disturbance, short of dispossession, or it may amount to an eviction. A disturbance in law is the execution, recordation, registry, or continuing existence of record of an instrument that asserts or implies an adverse claim to the ownership or possession of an immovable or of a real right, except in an action or proceeding adversely to the possessor of such immovable or right.

§ 338. Institution of Action within a Year from the Disturbance

The plaintiff in the possessory action must allege and prove that he has instituted the action within a year from a disturbance in fact, be it a mere disturbance short of dispossession, or an eviction.

In the case of a mere disturbance in fact, the possessor is still in possession of the immovable property but his right to demand maintenance in his possession and damages is lost by the liberative prescription of one year. In the case of an eviction, the possessory may not demand restoration in his possession after the lapse of one year either because his possession has been interrupted or because his right to demand restoration is lost by the liberative prescription of one year. In either case, the one year prescription begins to run from the commencement rather than the completion of the disturbance. The prescription for a disturbance in law, however, does not begin to run as long as the document asserting an adverse claim remains in the public records.

GILL v. HENDERSON
269 So. 2d 571 (La. App. 1st Cir. 1972)

ELLIS, J. This is a suit for a mandatory injunction in which plaintiff Dedrick Gill seeks to compel defendant Joseph Lawrence Henderson to remove a fence from around a certain five and one-half acre tract of land. From an adverse judgment, plaintiff has appealed.

This is the second suit between these parties relative to the said tract. In the first suit, a possessory action, Mr. Henderson was plaintiff and Mr. Gill defendant. The case was tried on its merits and judgment was rendered dismissing Mr. Henderson's suit. In the said suit, Mr. Gill did not reconvene alleging his own possession of the property, and no finding was made relative thereto. No appeal was perfected from the judgment, and it is final.

Thereafter, Mr. Henderson constructed a one strand barbed wire fence around the property, and Mr. Gill brought this suit to compel its removal. It is his position that Mr. Henderson, having lost the possessory action, must now bring a petitory action in which he would have the burden of proving his own title. Mr. Gill claims that by building the fence, Mr. Henderson is attempting to force Mr. Gill to bring a possessory or petitory action and thereby force him to assume the burden of proving his own possession, or the superiority of his title. Plaintiff claims that there is no law applicable to this situation, and that under the equity provision of Article 21 of the Civil Code, the court should protect his "right" not to bear the burden of proof.

We cannot agree. In the first place, only a losing defendant or defendant in reconvention in a possessory action can be compelled by law to bring the petitory action. Article 3662, Code of Civil Procedure. Since Mr. Gill did not reconvene and attempt to show his own possession of the disputed tract in the possessory action, the effect of the judgment in that suit was to find that Mr. Henderson was not in possession thereof. Mr. Gill's possession or lack thereof was not adjudicated.

In the second place, the provisions of Article 3663 of the Code of Civil Procedure make injunctive relief, such as is sought by plaintiff herein, available to a plaintiff in a possessory action, or to one who has been disturbed in the possession which he has enjoyed for more than one year of immovable property of which he claims the ownership, possession or the enjoyment. Nowhere has plaintiff claimed the ownership, the possession or the enjoyment of this disputed tract. He has alleged his title, but not that it includes the disputed tract. He has alleged certain acts of possession, but not that he enjoys the legal possession of the disputed tract. We think it clear from a perusal of the code provisions relative to the petitory and possessory actions, particularly Articles 3654, 3662, and 3663 of the Code of Civil Procedure, that one who wishes to enjoy the evidentiary benefits which accrue to the successful plaintiff in a possessory action, whether in a declaratory judgment suit, a suit for injunctive relief, or any other case in which ownership may be an issue, must bear the burden of proving himself to be the legal possessor of the property. Plaintiff herein has not done so, and we hold that, under the specific provisions of Article 3663 of the Code of Civil Procedure, he is not entitled to the relief sought herein. The judgment appealed from is therefore affirmed, at plaintiff's cost.

d. Possessory action against the state

TODD v. STATE
465 So. 2d 712 (La. 1985)
474   430

ON SECOND REHEARING

CALOGERO, J. The troubling issue in this case, whether a possessory action may be brought against the State of Louisiana, has produced contrary opinions in this Court originally and on first rehearing. Plaintiffs, who won in the lower courts, and who with minor exceptions prevailed in this Court on original hearing, only to lose on first rehearing, were granted a rehearing by this Court, the first that they have had reason to seek.

In the opinion written for the Court by this same author, rendered on November 28, 1983, we determined that a possessory action may be maintained against the state. However, we concluded that the successful plaintiff's right under La. Code Civ. Pro. art. 3662(2) to have the judge require that the losing defendant file a petitory action within a period not to exceed sixty days (where plaintiff has prayed for such relief) is not constitutionally permissible when the state is the loser in the possessory action.

After we granted a rehearing sought by the state, a differently constituted majority, with three dissents, reversed our earlier judgment and the judgments of the district court and the Court of Appeal and held that "one does not have a cause of action to maintain a possessory action against the state." That majority's reasons can be summarized as follows:

(1) The purpose of the possessory action is to protect the presumption of ownership as acquisitive prescription accrues.

(2) However, since state property can never be acquired by prescription,

(3) It would be a useless exercise to give judicial recognition to a plaintiff's right to possess against the state which would never be sufficient to acquire ownership.

(4) Furthermore, the strong public policy of the state to protect the wealth of its lands and minerals would not be served by distinguishing between public things and private things and permitting the possessory action against the state as relates to private things.

(5) Also, other remedies are available to the owner to protect the peaceful possession of his property whether disturbed by the state or by any other person.

(6) Therefore, one does not have a cause of action to maintain a possessory action against the state. Rehearing applicants have in brief countered a number of the underlying premises on which the majority relied on first rehearing. We now conclude that our original opinion was correct and should be reinstated; that a possessory action may be maintained against the state where the object of possession is a private rather than public thing.

Our reasons are more fully stated in our original opinion. Todd v. State, Dept. of Natural Resources, 456 So. 2d 1340 (La. 1983). Those reasons are adopted herein with one minor exception.

The fallacy of our opinion on first rehearing lies in the assertion that the purpose of the possessory action is simply to facilitate a continued possession while acquisitive prescription accrues, and in rendering a judgment based largely upon an ascertained or presumed public policy of the state, rather than appropriate constitutional and legal principles. We also conclude that the first rehearing majority's assertion that there are other adequate remedies available to an owner to protect the peaceful possession of his property is in some measure misleading.

PURPOSE OF THE POSSESSORY ACTION

The purpose of a possessory action is to protect possession. It is part of the well-conceived and long-standing system of real actions for the protection of possession and ownership of immovable property, adopted by the Legislature and recognized by the courts of this state. The concept of possession, established by our Civil Code, is designed as a *first step* in protecting ownership, whether acquired by acquisitive prescription, title, or otherwise. The series of real actions set forth in our Code of Civil Procedure has been carefully structured to establish an orderly procedure by which questions concerning possession, and subsequently ownership, can be determined. Thereunder, the status quo is maintained in order to promote peace and stability and to avoid resort to self-help when disputes arise as to ownership and possession of property.

Accordingly, a presumption is established by the Civil Code that a possessor is the provisional owner of the object of his possession until the true owner establishes his right. La. Civ. Code Ann. art. 3423. Should his possession be disturbed, he is entitled, by means of the possessory action, to be either maintained in or restored to his possession. La. Code Civ. Pro. Ann. art. 3655. The legislative reasoning in adopting this approach to the resolution of disputes over property is self-evident. In most cases, those in possession of land are the owners, not squatters attempting to acquire ownership through acquisitive prescription. Rather than requiring these rightful owners to carry the heavy burden of proof, and expense, in establishing ownership, the Legislature allows one who is disturbed in his possession and who claims ownership to bring a possessory action against any person who evicts him or disturbs his possession. La. Code Civ. Pro. Ann. art. 3658. Because of the difficulty of proving ownership, the law permits a person in possession (normally the owner) to set aside disturbances of that possession simply upon proof of the right to possess rather than upon proof of ownership.

We did of course note in our opinion on original hearing that:

"the "intent to possess" in a possessory action has been found to be similar in nature to that required of a person seeking to acquire property by prescription. City of New Orleans v. New Orleans Canal, Inc., 412 So. 2d 975 (La. 1982); Norton v. Addie, 337 So. 2d 432 (La. 1976); Liner v. Louisiana Land and Exploration Company, 319 So. 2d 766 (La. 1975); Note, 49 Tul. Law Review 1173 (1975). Admittedly, too, the possessory action is oftentimes but the "skirmishing ground for the impending contest as to ownership." Writ System in Real Actions, 22 Tul. Law Review 459 at 467 (1948). However, the fact that one action may in the usual course precede another does not mean that availability of the latter is a sine qua non of the former" (emphasis added)

In fact, the Civil Code clearly provides that "[t]he ownership and the possession of a thing are distinct." La. Civ. Code Ann. art. 481. And, as Justice Dennis pointed out in his dissent to the first rehearing,

"The right to posses is protected by the possesory action not merely for protection of the presumption of ownership inherent in possession, but also for protection of all rights attending possession. These rights include: (1) Present authority to detain and enjoy (until adverse ownership is proven), La.C.C. arts. 3421, 3422; (2) Transferability for value or otherwise, La.C.C. 3441; (3) Ownership of fruits gathered during possession and works built on the property possessed, La.C.C. arts. 485-486, 496-497; (4) Reimbursement for expenses incurred by the possessor which inure to the owner's benefit, id., La. C.C. arts. 527-528; and (5) the right to maintain possession until the owner fully reimburses the possessor, La.C.C. 529."

PUBLIC POLICY CONSIDERATIONS

According to our opinion on first rehearing, the strong public policy of the state to protect the wealth of its lands and minerals requires that all state lands be protected from contrary acquisition, and possession, since the possessory action was deemed to be nothing more than a prelude to ownership through acquisitive prescription, and resulted in the entitlement to certain fruits and revenues even in the event of ultimate eviction. That opinion's preoccupation with public policy, in our present view, is an inappropriate consideration in light of what we perceive to be controlling constitutional and statutory law. Nonetheless, our examination of the effects of permitting a possessory action against the state indicates that there is little basis for this concern. There is ample protection for the state's resources without stretching the existing law to exempt the state from the procedures designed by the Legislature to deal with questions of possession and ownership.

> The Civil Code does provide that possession involves the "detention or enjoyment of a corporeal thing." La. Civ. Code Ann. art. 3421. As part of its enjoyment, the possessor is entitled to the ownership of fruits which he has gathered and to the reimbursement of his expenses for fruits he is unable to gather if evicted by the owner. La. Civ. Code Ann. art. 486. The ownership of the fruits, however, is limited to a "good faith possessor," which includes only one who "possesses by virtue of an act translative of ownership and does not know of any defects in his ownership." La. Civ. Code Ann. art. 486 and 487. Clearly, a simple squatter or bad faith possessor, who *would* be eligible to acquire ownership of other than state owned property by means of 30 years acquisitive prescription, would not be entitled to retain the fruits produced on the lands owned by the state (or any other owner if challenged before passage of the thirty year acquisitive period). Such a limitation on the acquisition of fruits certainly alleviates some fears that a possessor of state lands would be entitled to enjoy significant economic advantage at the expense of the state.

Furthermore, some of the state's more valuable resources, i.e., timber and minerals, would not be classified as fruits, that benefit which would accrue to the good faith possessor of property, state owned or otherwise.***

In this same vein, we reaffirm our determination in the original opinion that the state shall not be subject to the requirement of La. Code Civ. Pro. art. 3662(2) that it assert any adverse claim of ownership in a petitory action within 60 days of the judgment of possession.***

LA. CIV. CODE. ANN. ART. 3422 AND ACQUISITION OF THE RIGHT TO POSSESS

Although not addressed in our first rehearing opinion, an argument which perhaps more than any other prompted the first rehearing grant with a consequent first change in the result in this case, originated with the contention in the dissent by the Chief Justice that "the acquisition of the right to possess is itself a kind of prescription which cannot run against the state." This notion is founded on both the language of La. Civ. Code Ann. art. 3422 and the substance of La. Code Civ. Pro. Ann. art. 3658(2), which provide that a possessor for over a year acquires the right to possess and to maintain a possessory action. Proponents equate the one year period before acquisition of the right to possess or ability to bring a possessory action with a prescriptive period running against the state. Of course, prescription against the state is prohibited by both La. Const. art. 12, § 13 and art. 9, § 4(B). However, we can ascertain little foundation for this position in either the Civil Code or jurisprudence of this state.

We point out that the term, "right to possess," was not found in any French text, the Louisiana Civil Code of 1870, the Louisiana Code of Practice, or the Code of Civil Procedure. The term first appeared in Justice Tate's concurring opinion in the denial of an application for rehearing in Liner v. Louisiana Land and Exploration Co., 319 So. 2d 766 (La. 1975) and was subsequently adopted by the redactors in a 1982 amendment to La. Civ. Code Ann. art. 3422. It was apparently devised in recognition of the "confusion [which] has resulted in Louisiana from the use of the word 'possession' in the Civil Code and in the jurisprudence to denote both physical control and the right to possess," the availability of a possessory action. Liner v. Louisiana Land and Exploration Co., 319 So. 2d at 781. Thus, the "right to possess" is little more than a shorthand method of saying that one has acquired the right to bring a possessory action. It does not involve any other consequence in Louisiana law and was never intended to alter the civilian scheme of real actions for the protection of possession and ownership of immovable property.

According to La. Civ. Code Ann. art. 3422, "[p]ossession is a matter of fact." La. Civ. Code art. 3423 provides that the possessor "is considered provisionally as owner of the thing," a presumption which apparently commences immediately (without delays, prescriptive or otherwise). Likewise, as soon as possession commences, the possessor may be entitled to fruits and reimbursements of certain expenses. La. Civ. Code Ann. art. 486. Thus, the fact of possession and its attributes are not contingent upon the running of any period of time nor is possession a right acquired by the running of time. It either exists or does not exist without regard to any notion of prescription.

Even the availability of the possessory action, furthermore, is not always delayed one full year from the beginning of possession. According to La. Code Civ. Pro. Ann. art. 3658(2), the requirement of possession for more than a year prior to disturbance is not applicable when the possessor is "evicted by force or fraud."

It should also be noted that the history of La. Code Civ. Pro. Ann. art. 3658 supports our conclusion that, in connection with the required one year of peaceful possession, prescription is not involved. The source of art. 3658 is art. 49 of the Code of Practice, which in turn corresponds to the 1806 French Code of Civil Procedure art. 23, and the official comment to Article 3658 assures us that no change has occurred in the law with the article's incorporation in the Louisiana Code of Civil Procedure. French commentators have explained that the requirement of one year's actual possession for the availability of the possessory action is an emphasis on continuity, which expresses the quality of possession, and the period takes into account the agricultural cycle of preparation, planting and harvesting. Such a period is no prescriptive right, but a procedural assurance of the fact of undisturbed possession.

DECREE

For the reasons expressed in our original opinion as well as those expressed hereinabove, the decree which we rendered in our original opinion is reinstated. The lower courts' judgments are affirmed except insofar as they "order [the state] to bring a petitory action against the plaintiffs to assert any claim of ownership that [the state] has to the property.... within sixty (60) days after this judgment becomes executory or be precluded thereafter from asserting the ownership thereof."

DIXON, C.J., dissents with reasons.
MARCUS, J., dissents and assigns reasons.
BLANCHE, J., dissents and assigns reasons.

CHAPTER V. OWNERSHIP
Civil Code arts. 477-532

1. CONTENT OF OWNERSHIP
Civil Code arts. 477-482

2 AUBRY ET RAU, DROIT CIVIL FRANCAIS 169-179
(an English translation by the Louisiana State Law Institute 1966)

CONCEPT OF OWNERSHIP

Ownership of Corporeal Things. In the proper sense, the term ownership *(droit de propriete)* expresses the idea of a complete legal power of a person over a thing. It can be defined as a right by virtue of which the thing is absolutely and exclusively subject to the volition and the actions of a person.

The powers inherent in a full ownership right cannot be taxatively enumerated. They can be summarized as follows: The owner can at will use or enjoy his property, dispose of it physically, perform all the legal transactions of which it is susceptible, and exclude all third parties from any participation in the exercise of his various powers over the property.

Although the ownership right is by its nature absolute, its exercise is subject to various restrictions imposed in public interest.

Secondly, the powers inherent in an ownership right must not be exercised so as to interfere with the property interests of others. This imposes certain limits which the property owners must not exceed in their mutual interest.

Finally, ownership may be modified by statutory or contractual servitudes. But because it is by its nature absolute and exclusive, it is presumed to be free of any servitude. It follows that one who claims a servitude on the land of another, has the burden of proving it, although he might in fact be in possession of this servitude.

In general the benefits of ownership are the same whether it bears on immovable or on movable property. However, law insured better the conservation of immovables than of movables. The owner of a movable cannot recover it from a third party purchaser in good faith unless he was dispossessed by loss or theft. Also, the law has been less exacting with respect to alienation of movables than of immovables.

Extension of the Term Ownership to Incorporeals. In its original meaning, ownership referred only to corporeals. But the term has been broadened to include the exclusive right to use and dispose of incorporeals...

Use, Transformation and Destruction of the Thing. The owner has the power to subject the thing belonging to him to any use compatible with its nature.

He is also authorized to receive all the profits, income or other benefits which the thing can produce or procure. This aspect of ownership is the basis for the right to fish or hunt on the owned land. By virtue of the same attribute, the owner may exploit a quarry, surface or subterranean mine on his land, and to search out for the purpose of exploitation sources of water, ordinary or mineral (art. 552.3).

Finally, the owner is free to change the nature of the thing, lessen its value or destroy it. He can change the mode of land cultivation, turn arable land into pasture or vineyard, or vice versa, cultivate forest land, and erect any structure above or below the surface, all the way to the limits of his land. (art. 55.,3). He can build a pond on it, using water sources originating on his land, rain water, or water flowing in from a higher land or a public road.

Although the exercise of these various rights of ownership is subject to the condition that it must not interfere with the ownership of another and, if the property involved has been classified as a historical monument, that it will not be violated (Laws of 30 March 1887 and 31 December 1913), the mere fact that the exercise deprives a third person of some advantage or benefit does not give a cause of action for damages.

Acts of Administration and of Disposal. Ownership includes the power to undertake any legal transactions of which the thing is susceptible. He can lease it, alienate it gratuitously or for consideration, and if the thing is an immovable, burden it with servitudes or mortgages. He can even give up his ownership by simply abandoning the property, without transfer to another person.

The power to alienate is of public order; the owner cannot, in principle, renounce it by contract; a prohibition to alienate imposed by the donor on the donee, or by a testator on a legatee, has only limited effect.

Exclusive Character of Ownership. The Right to Enclose One's Land. Common Pastures. The owner has the power to exclude all third persons from any use, enjoyment or disposal of his property and to take all convenient measures. He can, especially, surround his estate by walls, ditches or other enclosures, provided he respects the servitudes with which it is burdened (art. 647)....

The Perpetual Character of Ownership. The Court of Cassation has held that the ownership of an immovable is not lost because the owner has abstained for thirty years from any acts of enjoyment. It can be lost as a result of non-use only if another person becomes the owner through acquisitive prescription....

2. PATRIMONY
Civil Code arts. 3182, 3183, 3506(28)

A.N. YIANNOPOULOS, CIVIL LAW PROPERTY
§§ 191-200 (4th ed. 2001)
(footnotes omitted)

§ 191. The Classical Theory: Aubry and Rau

The civilian notion of patrimony *(patrimonium)* has its origin in Roman law. A general theory of patrimony, however, was first developed last century by Aubry and Rau. According to this theory that remains classical, the cohesion of the various values composing a person's patrimony and the resulting universality of rights and obligations is explained as an attribute of personality. In the words of Aubry and Rau, "the idea of patrimony is deduced logically from the idea of personality.... The patrimony is the projection of personality and the expression of the juridical capacity with which a person is invested."

From this precept, the authors derived a series of propositions: 1. *Only* natural and juridical persons may have a patrimony. The existence of a distinct patrimony is frequently the essential element and the justification of juridical personality. 2. *Every* person has a patrimony, even if it contains liabilities only. Exceptionally, however, a person may be deprived of his patrimony by a general confiscation as a penalty imposed by the state. 3. Every person has only *one* patrimony that is *inseparable* and *indivisible.* A living person, therefore, may not by inter vivos act transfer his patrimony to another person because this would annihilate the personality of the transferor. By way of exception, however, an ascendant may partition his property among his descendants and transfer to them all the individual elements of his patrimony.

§ 192. Objective Theory

The rigorously logical theoretic construct of Aubry and Rau has been subjected to severe criticism in France as being "fictitious, abstract, and abusively logical." Critics have pointed out that the bond between personality and patrimony has been exaggerated to the point of confusion of the two ideas and that the tenets of indivisibility and nontransferability of patrimony are contrary to both facts and law.

As a substitute for the questionable bond between personality and patrimony and in order to explain the cohesion of certain masses of assets and liabilities, modern authors expound the ideas of common destination and purpose. According to the so-called *objective theory,* a patrimony is an independent economic unit, a mass of assets and liabilities, tied inseparably until liquidation by the common destination and economic purpose of the elements which compose it.

This theory, though preferable in the light of contemporary conditions, is not compatible with the precepts of the Louisiana and French Civil Codes. It may simply be regarded as a rationalization of possible future developments. Legislation, jurisprudence, and doctrine in the two jurisdictions seem to admit that a person may have more than one patrimony and that each patrimony may be transferred by inter vivos juridical act. Nevertheless, the classical theory continues to have an important place in contemporary doctrine. Its abstract nature continues to be the object of criticism, but it has been countered, with good reason, that the suggested alternatives of common destination and purpose are no less abstract ideas.

§ 193. Legislative Foundation

In Louisiana and in France, the theory of patrimony rests on scattered provisions in the Civil Codes. Article 3182 of the Louisiana Civil Code, corresponding with Article 2092 of the French Civil Code, declares that "whoever has bound himself personally, is obliged to fulfill his engagements out of all his property, movable and immovable, present and future." Further, Article 3183 of the Louisiana Civil Code, corresponding with Article 2093 of the French Civil Code, declares that "the property of the debtor is the common pledge of his creditors, and the proceeds of the sale must be distributed among them ratably, unless there exist among the creditors some lawful cause of preference." Provisions concerning ownership, the property of absentees, and the matrimonial regime of community property may also be relied upon for clarification of the notion of patrimony.***

§ 194. Indivisibility of Patrimony; Patrimonial Masses

Under Louisiana and French law, a patrimony is a coherent mass of existing or potential rights and liabilities attached to a person for the satisfaction of his economic needs. Every person has a patrimony and only a person may have a patrimony.

In principle, the patrimony is indivisible. Exceptionally, however, a person may have two patrimonies or may have in his patrimony distinct patrimonial masses that are subject to special rules for purposes of administration and liquidation. This happened, for example, when under the regime of the Louisiana Civil Code of 1870 one accepted a succession under benefit of inventory, when one was an irregular heir or possesses the patrimony of an absentee, when a spouse living under the regime of community property has separate property, or when property is given or bequeathed for a special purpose. Further, under the maritime law, a shipowner's "fortune of the sea," that is, the ship and earned freight that may be abandoned to creditors for the purpose of limitation of liability, is likewise a distinct patrimonial mass within the shipowner's patrimony. Such patrimonial masses are distinct from the patrimony of a person, consist of particular assets and liabilities, and are destined to special purposes. They are often called "little patrimonies," and their very existence contradicts the classical theory. In deference to Aubry and Rau, however, it ought to be admitted that a person may have two or more distinct patrimonies only when the law allows it.***

In spite of the cohesion of the various elements of patrimony, the law recognizes merely rights in individual items rather than in the economic unit as a whole. Thus, unless the law provides otherwise, patrimonial assets may only be transferred by individual delivery, execution may be had on particular elements only, and, under the law of delictual obligations, protection is afforded to individual patrimonial rights rather than the universality. The patrimony as a whole, however, may become the object of an obligation because the right of the creditor bears on the person of the debtor rather than his patrimony.***

§ 195. Transferability of Patrimony

The patrimony, as a universality of rights and obligations, is ordinarily attached to a person until termination of personality. Thus, in principle, the patrimony is nontransferable by inter vivos act. In Louisiana and in France, an attempted inter vivos transfer of patrimony or of a fraction of it is ineffective as such but it may be a valid transfer of one's all existing individual assets. Exceptionally, however, a person's patrimony or a fraction thereof may be transferred by a marriage contract. The Louisiana and French Civil Codes authorize expressly the donation of present and future things by such a contract, and thus, in effect, an inter vivos transfer of patrimony subject to the uncertain term of the donor's decease and the condition that the donee or his descendants shall survive the donor.

Present individual patrimonial assets may be transferred by onerous title, but the transfer may be set aside by creditors. Present individual assets may also be disposed of by gratuitous title if the donor retains sufficient sums for his subsistence, subject to the rights of the donor's creditors to annul the donation and of his heirs to demand reduction of the donation to the extent that it infringes on the legitime.

All inter vivos transfers of patrimonial assets are, in principle, transfers by particular title. The recipient does not assume personal obligations of the transferor without stipulation to that effect and each thing must be delivered individually. However, according to jurisprudence, the acquirer of all of a person's present assets may be held liable for debts in certain cases and, under the Civil Code, the same result may be obtained in the cases of partition by ascendants and marriage contract.

Upon death, the patrimony of a natural person is transmitted to his heir who, in a figurative sense, continues the personality of the deceased. Under the Louisiana and French Civil Codes, the succession, that is, the patrimony of the deceased, is not a distinct mass of rights and liabilities subject to administration and liquidation but an indistinguishable part of the patrimony of the heir. The heir is thus personally bound to pay the debts of the deceased as if they were his own. However, the fiction of the continuation of the personality of the deceased has been discarded by the two codes in the case of succession under benefit of inventory. In such a case, the succession forms a distinct patrimonial mass in the patrimony of the heir.***

The fiction of the continuation of the personality of the deceased has largely faded away in Louisiana because administration has become the rule, and the succession has, in effect, become a mass subject to liquidation.***

§ 196. Composition of Patrimony; Assets and Liabilities

In France, the patrimony is composed of assets and liabilities that are susceptible of pecuniary evaluation.***

Assets are such as real rights, credits and accrued causes of action, even if they are exempt from seizure or exercise by creditors. Despite their great economic significance, civil liberties, family rights, rights pertaining to status, the moral right of a writer or composer to the products of his intellect, and the right of personality are considered in France to be extrapatrimonial rights. Likewise, a person's ability to work, in contrast with his right to earned salary, is not a patrimonial asset. In Louisiana, however, an author's interest in his unpublished letters and one's ability to work and enjoy the fruits of his labor have been held to be property rights. Further, Louisiana courts have held that one may have a property right in a will, in a name, or in an uncopyrighted design. However, one's interest in election to public office has been held not to be a property right.

The infringement of patrimonial as well as extrapatrimonial rights may everywhere give rise to a claim for damages, which, as an accrued cause of action, is property. Apart from the law of delictual obligations, certain extrapatrimonial rights are effectively protected by rules of public law.***

Liabilities are personal and real obligations, and, in general, claims of creditors against the patrimony of their debtor. In principle, the liabilities are inseparable from the assets. Thus, an heir inherits both unless he invokes the benefit of inventory. Since both assets and liabilities are susceptible of pecuniary evaluation, a balance statement is always possible. When the assets exceed the liabilities, the patrimony is solvent. When the liabilities exceed the assets the patrimony still exists but it is insolvent.

As an abstract entity, the patrimony is distinct from the elements that compose it. Assets and liabilities may increase or decrease but the patrimony remains the same in the sense that it retains its identity. This explains why unsecured creditors who have a right of pledge on the patrimony of their debtor may not, in the absence of fraud, pursue assets in the hands of transferees and also why they may obtain satisfaction from new assets that enter into the patrimony of the debtor. The general right of pledge does not bear on particular things nor on a stereotyped entity whether in favor of or against the interests of the creditors but on a universality of rights and obligations as it exists at the time of execution of a judgment against the debtor.***

§ 197. The Common Pledge of Creditors

In theory, the patrimony of a debtor consists of all his rights and obligations that are susceptible of pecuniary evaluation, namely, items that may be regarded as property in the broad sense. Realistically speaking, however, insofar as creditors are concerned, the patrimony of their debtor consists only of assets that may be seized at the time of execution of a judgment against him.***

In principle, creditors may exercise all patrimonial rights and actions of their debtor, with the exception of those that are strictly personal. Article 66, p. 272 of the Louisiana Civil Code of 1808 provided that "a creditor may exercise all the rights and actions of his debtor, except such as are exclusively attached to the person." This provision was suppressed in the 1825 revision as self-evident and unnecessary. When the proper occasions arose, Louisiana courts did not hesitate to affirm the principle that creditors may exercise all rights and actions of their debtor that are not strictly personal.

In this context, strictly personal means rights and actions which, though patrimonial in nature, are so closely connected with the personality of the debtor that they cannot be exercised by third persons. This legal determination is based on prevailing moral ideas and considerations of social utility. For example, Louisiana courts have held that the right of an heir to demand collation or reduction of an excessive donation, and the right of redemption of property sold by a debtor prior to his insolvency, are too personal to be exercised by creditors.

Contractual causes of action for the recovery of money or other things of value, and delictual actions for property damage are regarded in France as patrimonial assets susceptible of seizure by creditors. In Louisiana, the seizure of *pending* actions is authorized and regulated in detail in the Revised Statutes. The language of the applicable texts is sufficiently broad to cover any action; however, only actions involving pecuniary interests are contemplated. The statute ought to be interpreted in the light of the Civil Code and Louisiana jurisprudence according to which creditors may only seize actions that are not strictly personal.

Pending actions for slander and malicious prosecution, for damages resulting from wrongful attachment, and an action in revendication cumulated with a claim for damages, have been classified by Louisiana courts as patrimonial assets subject to seizure by creditors. Further, an action for lesion beyond moiety or rescission was allowed to be brought by creditors. Other decisions, however, indicate that claims deriving from contractual or delictual obligations may not be seized by creditors prior to the institution of suit by the debtor. It would seem that creditors should be allowed to seize or exercise any right of the debtor which may qualify as patrimonial unless this right is strictly personal.***

§ 199. Real Subrogation

Real subrogation is the substitution of a thing for another in a universality of assets and liabilities. Real subrogation takes place of right when a person has a single patrimony: anything acquired in exchange or as a consideration for the alienation of an element of the patrimony enters into the mass. When, however, a person has in addition to his patrimony one or more distinct patrimonial masses, question arises whether a newly acquired asset enters into his patrimony or into a distinct patrimonial mass.

The Code Civil and special legislation in France deal with real subrogation in isolated instances. These texts are not readily susceptible of generalization and application by analogy to other matters, and, for this reason, doctrine and jurisprudence have looked for guidance to the civilian tradition rather than legislation.

According to traditional civilian doctrine, real subrogation is a legal fiction by virtue of which a thing acquires the nature of another that was part of a universality: *subrogatum capit naturam subrogati* The measure and scope of subrogation is determined in the light of two maxims borrowed from the Glossators. By the first, as a consequence of the fungibility of the elements of patrimony, the price due as a consideration for the alienation of a thing belonging to a mass replaces of right the thing that has been disposed of. By the second, real subrogation does not apply to individual things unless its application is authorized by law or agreement. These maxims have been criticized as lacking rational foundation, as asserting an artificial relationship between fungibility and subrogation, and as arbitrarily confining the operation of real subrogation as a matter of right to situations in which a person has, in addition to his patrimony, a distinct patrimonial mass.

Modern French doctrine has discarded the idea that real subrogation involves a fictitious substitution of assets and has openly asserted that the nature or juridical quality of the substitute is not altered. A newly acquired asset merely serves the same purpose as the asset that it has replaced. The mechanical formulas of the Glossators have been abandoned, and real subrogation operates routinely when the destination of a thing or of a mass of things applied to a special purpose is to be preserved or when the restitution of a thing or of a mass is to be secured.

Things destined to a special purpose are regarded as representing a value rather than as individual objects. If a change in capital structure is desired or necessary, alienation is possible but anything acquired as a consideration thereof takes the place of the thing that has been alienated. For example, under the regime of community property, the price of a thing belonging to the separate property of a spouse takes the place of a thing alienated, the proceeds of a fire insurance policy are substituted for a thing damaged or destroyed, and an indemnity due for the expropriation for an immovable for public utility is substituted for the immovable. In these cases, subrogation is founded on the idea of *destination,* and its purpose is to prevent the confusion of a thing or of a mass applied to a special purpose with the rest of a person's patrimony. Subrogation takes place of right as to both individual things and things forming part of a mass without the need of an express legislative text or party agreement. Subrogation may be excluded, however, by directly applicable texts or it may be subject to certain conditions in the interest of third persons.

When a thing that is burdened with a mortgage or pledge is lost or damaged, the secured creditor may not obtain satisfaction from the proceeds of insurance or other indemnity due to the owner of the thing. However, since the thing securing the credit is applied to a special purpose, modern authors suggest that real subrogation ought to take place. Reform has been achieved by special legislation according to which, in indicated circumstances, the creditor's right of preference is transferred to the indemnity due. In the absence of contrary agreement, however, the creditor's right of preference is extinguished upon the payment of the indemnity to the owner of the thing.

Further, subrogation takes place of right when a person is under obligation to restore a universality of things. This happens, for example, when one possesses the property of an absentee, when one is an irregular or an apparent heir, and, generally, when one may be under obligation to restore the whole or a part of a succession. In these cases, subrogation is founded on the *origin* of assets rather than their destination. The price of a thing alienated, an indemnity due for the destruction or deterioration of things, and things acquired in exchange for others enter into the distinct patrimonial mass. There are no restrictions like those governing things that are applied to a special purpose, but civil code provisions applicable to irregular successions seem to confine subrogation to the price due for the sale of a thing and to the donee's action for the recovery of things given.

In these matters, the demand for restitution must bear on a universality rather than individual things. For reasons of fairness, however, French law has established two exceptions. Under the Commercial Code, when things are consigned to a merchant for deposit or in order to be sold on behalf of the owner, and the merchant after having sold them becomes insolvent, the owner may recover in full the price paid or any part of the price that is still due. Further, by virtue of special legislation, the owner of a leased immovable that has been destroyed by fire as a result of the negligence of the lessee, may recover the proceeds of insurance that are payable to the lessee.

Following the model of the French Civil Code, the Louisiana Civil Code has not articulated the principle of real subrogation. However, there are provisions in the Civil Code and in special legislation that presuppose this principle and provide for specific applications. Under the Civil Code, real subrogation takes place of right in the fields of usufruct, administration of an absentee's estate, recovery of an entire succession or a fraction thereof, and separate property of a spouse under the regime of community property. Under special legislation, subrogation takes place when a mortgaged immovable is damaged or expropriated. Courts have allowed subrogation as to partnership property. It would seem that as in France, subrogation should always be allowed as to things applied to a special purpose and as to things that one is bound to restore.

Real subrogation is particularly important in Louisiana for determination of the question whether property acquired by a spouse during the existence of a community property regime falls into the community or into the separate property of the spouse. In principle, property acquired during marriage forms part of the community of acquets or gains subject to exceptions established by legislation, and everything possessed by a spouse during the existence of the community is presumed to belong to the community. These provisions tend to exclude application of the principle of real subrogation to the mass of the separate property of a spouse, and, as a matter of fact, to augment the community at the expense of separate property.

Despite the wide delimitation of the mass of the community under the Louisiana Civil Code, the problem is to determine in each case which movables and immovables acquired with separate funds are substituted for the funds that have been expended. Under the regime of the Louisiana Civil Code of 1870, this determination depended on rules varying with the mode of acquisition of property and with the party claiming real subrogation, that is, the husband or the wife.

Subrogation took place of right in favor of either spouse in cases of acquisition of assets by exchange of separate property, partition of a succession, redemption of a tax sale, and acquisition of shares of a corporation by transformation of a separate partnership interest. In these cases, a thing was subrogated "in full right to that which was alienated: *subrogatum capit naturam subrogati."* Subrogation was excluded in cases of acquisition of immovable property by purchase or *dation en paiement* unless the presumption of community was rebutted.

A wife was always permitted to rebut the presumption of community by showing that "the funds constituting the price of the property were paraphernal funds, that they were administered by her, and that they were invested by her." Parol evidence was admissible for this purpose. A married woman did not need to declare in the act of purchase that the price was paid with her separate funds and that the acquisition was for her separate property. Such a declaration, if made, proved nothing. However, when the act of acquisition declared that the wife purchased an immovable with her own separate funds, her husband was estopped to deny the paraphernal nature of the funds if he had concurred in the act. When the price of the purchase was paid with fruits of the wife's separate property, the immovable fell into the community unless the wife had made a declaration of paraphernality.

A husband was allowed to rebut the presumption of community only if he had taken care to make in the act of purchase a double declaration that the property was bought with the proceeds of his separate property and the purchase was "for the purpose of replacing property sold *(pour servir de remploi)."* This rule, incorporating into Louisiana law Article 1434 of the Code Napoleon, was "not referable to any express article in the Code". It was established by jurisprudence. A double declaration merely permitted the husband to go forward with evidence to rebut the presumption of community. In the absence of such declaration, the presumption was irrebuttable, *juris et de jure,* and subrogation was excluded.

There is no longer room for the requirement of double declaration under the law of community property that is based on the principle of equal management. Under this law, the principle of real subrogation is expected to operate smoothly as to both the mass of the community and the separate property of either spouse. Moreover, real subrogation ought to take precedence over the presumption of community which is applicable only in the absence of real subrogation.***

§ 200. Enterprise

An enterprise is a mass of rights, interests, and relations destined to a determined purpose and organized as an economic unit by an entrepreneur. The purpose of an enterprise need not be the achievement of economic gain.

The notion of enterprise is known to Louisiana and French law, but neither the Louisiana nor the French Civil Code contain provisions regulating the incidents and function of an enterprise. In Germany, however, enterprise has been institutionalized in keeping with the exigencies of contemporary economic life and the need for regulation of certain legal relations concerning the mass as a whole.

An enterprise is similar to a patrimonial mass in that its elements constitute a universality which is not the object of a single right. It differs, however, from a patrimonial mass because an enterprise is comprised of interests and relations, such as clientele, good will, and business secrets, as well as potential sources of income, such as organization and advertising, whereas a patrimonial mass is composed exclusively of rights. Moreover, in contrast to a patrimonial mass, an unincorporated enterprise is an integral part of the patrimony of the entrepreneur. There is no distinction between the creditors of the entrepreneur and the creditors of the enterprise; all creditors may obtain satisfaction indiscriminately from the assets of the enterprise or from the patrimony of the entrepreneur and no one is entitled to preferential treatment.

An enterprise may not become the object of a real right and it may not be transferred without individual delivery of its elements. Its integrity, however, is protected from unauthorized or unlawful interference by the law of unfair competition. This has led certain courts and writers to conclude that the law recognizes the existence of a special right in the integrity of an enterprise. According to the traditional view, however, this alleged right is an incident of the entrepreneur's own right of personality. An invasion of this right may be set aside by injunction, and injuries may be compensated by an action for damages under the law of delictual obligations.

An enterprise may become as a whole the object of an obligation, such as a contract to sell, and in such a case the general law of sales is applicable by analogy. Provisions of law governing profits, fruits, and accession are likewise applicable by analogy to an enterprise. For example, certain incorporeals, such as trademarks, may be attached to an enterprise as accessories or component parts. When an enterprise is transferred, questions may arise as to the transferee's responsibility for debts. As between the parties, the matter is ordinarily governed by the agreement, but with respect to third persons the rights and liabilities of the acquirer of an enterprise are governed by directly applicable provisions of the German Commercial Code.

3. CO-OWNERSHIP
Civil Code arts. 480, 797-818

a. Ownership in Indivision

2(1) PLANIOL, TRAITE ELEMENTAIRE DE DROIT CIVIL 473-477
(an English translation by the Louisiana State Law Institute 1959)
(footnotes omitted)

A. GENERAL IDEA

Definition. A thing belonging to several co-owners is in indivision when the right of each owner bears upon the whole (and not upon a given part) of the thing held in common. The share of each is therefore not a tangible share but a portion expressed by a fraction: a third, a fourth, a tenth. It is the right of ownership that is divided among them. The thing is not. It is held in indivision. The right of each co-owner must be pictured as striking every molecule of the thing and as there encountering the right of the other co-owners for the portions belonging to them.

Theoretically, there is no limit to the number of co-owners. As a matter of fact most indivisions exist between a small number of persons. The shares of each may be equal or unequal. If there be no inequality, they may be as numerous as may be wished (citations omitted).

How Indivision Ends. The state of indivision is terminated by partition which attributes to each owner a divided share in the thing instead of the undivided share he previously had. The tangible share which is attributed to each owner should be of a value proportionate to that of the abstract share he had in the right of ownership applicable to the thing. The partition thus localizes the right of ownership. The co-owner obtains things that are less than the total thing but which offer the advantage of being clear cut ownerships, where the right of each is no longer limited by the coexistence of competitive rights. Partition is therefore a juridical act whose inherent function consists in terminating indivision by separating the thing into shares or lots.

Perpetual Indivision. There are instances where the indivision is destined to last forever and where application can never be made for partition. This is what is known as forced indivision. The cases where perpetual indivision may arise, are, theoretically speaking, exceptional and few in number. In fact, however, many examples may be cited.

Most common examples forced indivision always bears upon things which are destined to the common use of several pieces of property. Such are:

(1) The narrow streets, passages, alleys and courts that are common to several houses;

(2) The soil and certain parts of houses divided into stories by several owners (*infra* no. 2522) and

(3) The walls, hedges and other party enclosures. This is distinctly the most frequently recurring example of things held in indivision in perpetuity. It will be considered separately (nos. 2597 *et seq.*)***

Comparison of the Various Forms of Indivision. Under its original form, without fixed duration, indivision offered nothing but disadvantages. It interferes with the proper developments of property held in indivision. Every time one of the owners in indivision proposes an innovation or an improvement he runs the risk of being met by the resistance, the ill humor, the distrust of the others. And when this resistance arises it is invincible, because the slightest change requires that all agree to it. One of the co-owners cannot therefore, for example, change the mode of cultivation, because he is bound to respect the rights of the others which are equal to his. "He who has a companion has a master," said Loysel (*Instituts coutumieres,* no. 379). None of the co-owners can perform juridical acts alone (see as regards leasing, *Tribunal de la Seine,* Dec. 12, 1927, D.H. 1928. 159). Thus does the law earnestly desire a partition which will make each owner free. This is why it will not permit that co-owners agree to remain in indivision for more than five years.

Harrell, Problems Created by Co-ownership in Louisiana
32 Institute of Mineral Law 381, 382-93 (1985)

Louisiana generally recognizes only one form of joint ownership of land — that of simple, undivided co-ownership. Co-ownership, derived from Roman institutions, bears considerable resemblance to the tenancy in common prevailing in other American jurisdictions and is closer in effect to it than to the other common law forms of joint or co-tenancies. The fundamental principles which the courts have fashioned for co-ownership are simple and few in number.

1. A co-owner owns the entire property — but with his co-owners.
2. A co-owner may freely use the property for the purposes for which it is destined, but he may not interfere with the right of the other co-owners to the same enjoyment.
3. A co-owner may not, without unanimous consent of the others, modify or materially change the property or devote it to a use inappropriate to its destination.
4. A co-owner is entitled to share in the fruits, products or other revenues of the property in proportion to his undivided interest, whether or not he contributed to their production.
5. A co-owner is responsible for a proportionate part of the reasonable costs of maintaining or preserving the property.
6. A co-owner may require partition of the property at any time. Agreements not to partition the property are valid only under restricted circumstances and for limited periods.***

A co-owner may demand a partition at any time. No one can be compelled to hold property with another, unless the contrary has been agreed upon; and anyone has a right to demand the division of the thing held in common by the action of partition. Co-ownership is therefore essentially a voluntary relationship dependent for its existence upon the continued will of the owners. This has caused it to be seen as being in some respects analogous to a partnership. The relationship among co-owners has also been characterized as being essentially "quasi-contractual." Co-owners, unlike partners, are not fiduciaries for each other merely because of their ownership, although their agreements, such as those for the joint management or operation of the property, may create such a relationship. The liability of co-owners who contract with third persons relative to the property is joint, not solidary. A co-owner is not bound for the obligations of the other co-owners — not even for those debts incurred for the improvement of the co owned property.***

THE EXTENT OF A CO-OWNER'S UNDIVIDED INTEREST

The interests or shares of co-owners in the property do not have to be equal. The interest of a co-owner is determined from the nature of his acquisition, such as heirship, or from his agreement with the other owners. In the absence of an agreement, express or implied, a sale or other transfer of property to several persons is presumed to vest them with equal, undivided interests.***

PERSONAL ENJOYMENT OF THE PROPERTY

Each co-owner has an equal and correlative right to personally occupy and use all of the property without regard to the extent of his fractional interest if his activities are consistent with the destination of the property. He cannot be charged by his co-owners for such use. A few cases have suggested that a co-owner who exclusively occupies the property for a period of time may be responsible for the taxes and the costs of ordinary repairs occasioned by his use. These cases, however, appear to involve exceptional circumstances and are of dubious authority for the general proposition.

The courts will not regulate the ordinary use of the property by several co-owners, nor arbitrate disputes among them as to such matters. The remedy of co-owners is to partition the property if they cannot agree upon how the property is to be used. One co-owner may enjoin another from interfering with his lawful use of the property unless, perhaps, the interference is itself caused by lawful use of the property by his co-owners.

In a few cases, relief has been denied to a co-owner seeking to use the property jointly with another co-owner who has been exclusively enjoying it. The courts in these latter cases suggested that the injured party's remedy is to seek a partition. These cases involved situations where joint use of the premises was impractical and granting an injunction would only have prevented the party in possession from his continued enjoyment. Viewed from this perspective, the cases are consistent with those holding that a co-owner may be enjoined from interfering with the ordinary use of the property by other co-owners. Where joint use is pragmatically impossible and one co-owner has been permitted to exclusively use the property, ordering that co-owner to allow the others to use it also would prevent, rather than promote, its use. Refusing to intervene in such cases is consistent with the general principle of noninterference.

In summary, the law exercises only a form of negative control over the ordinary use of the property by co-owners. A co-owner may be prevented from interfering with the use of the property by the others. The courts will not, however, referee or settle disputes as to when or under what circumstances the various owners may use the land for ordinary purposes. If the co-owners cannot agree upon the manner or extent of their use, their remedy is to partition the property and terminate the relationship.

EXCEPTIONAL USES OF OR ALTERATIONS TO THE PROPERTY

The property may not be used in a manner incompatible with its destination, nor may it be materially modified or altered without the unanimous consent of the owners. The consent need not be written and the failure of an owner to object to such exceptional activities promptly after learning of them or any other indication of his acquiescence ordinarily constitutes a tacit consent to the activities.

The courts have been somewhat inconsistent in their treatment of an owner who does modify or alter the property without consent of his co-owners. He may be enjoined by the others from continuing in his activities. The basis for imposing other liability upon him and the circumstances under which he can be made to remove the improvements or restore the property to its original condition are uncertain. A few cases have likened him to a bad faith possessor and have imposed liability upon him consistent with that status. Other cases have, and more properly it is believed, recognized that his right to be on the property precludes him from being either a possessor or a trespasser as to his co-owners. These cases have simply held that by exceeding the scope of his rights he is liable to his co-owners for any damages he causes them. Under this approach liability has been imposed for diminution in value of the property as a consequence of his actions. He has not been required to remove his improvements, and, in at least one case, nonconsenting co-owners were actually held liable for their share of the enhanced value of the property caused by unconsented to improvements made by other co-owners.

There is a difference between a co-owner who exclusively occupies the premises, or who modifies or alters the property without consent of the other co-owners, but who also acknowledges he is a co-owner and a person who engages in the same activity because he claims ownership of the entire property, although he is actually a co-owner. For example, if A and B purport to acquire Arpent Noir from X, A's subsequent occupancy of the premises is obviously for himself and B. Since A's possession is precarious for B, both A and B are in possession. If it develops that X actually owned only an undivided 2/3 interest in the property and the other 1/3 interest was vested in Y, it is proper to say that A, B and Y are in fact co-owners. But it is also true that A is possessing both for himself and precariously for B and that both of them are possessing adversely to Y through A's activities on the land. It should also be obvious that the rights and obligations of A and B to each other might be based upon different principles than those regulating A and B's liability to Y should A, for example, construct a building on the land without the consent of B or Y or harvest crops from it.

RESPONSIBILITY FOR AND EXPENSES OF MAINTAINING AND PRESERVING THE PROPERTY

A co-owner may take such action and incur such expenses as are reasonably required to preserve, protect or maintain the property. Co-owners are responsible in proportion to their undivided interests for the costs necessarily incurred by any of them for this purpose.

LIABILITY FOR OTHER EXPENSES AND THE RIGHT TO SHARE IN PROFITS OR PRODUCTS

Although a co-owner may personally occupy and enjoy the property without cost or charge, the fruits, products or other revenues derived from the premises are deemed to belong to all the co-owners in proportion to their undivided interests. A co-owner has an absolute right to claim his share of profits derived from the land by the other co-owners even though he consented to the activities giving rise to the profits but refused to participate in or be responsible for their costs. The nonparticipating co-owner, however, may only claim the profits derived from the activity, and therefore, those co-owners receiving the revenues may deduct the reasonable costs of producing such revenues in accounting to him. A co-owner may not, however, make any charge for his personal services in producing or gathering the income. Thus, a co-owner may personally occupy the land and live in the house upon it without cost or charge until the other co-owners force a partition of the property. If, however, he leases the land to a third person, the other co-owners may claim from him their share of the rent. If the leasing co-owner employed a contractor to paint the house or repair the roof to keep or maintain the property in proper condition for leasing, he could offset the costs (assuming them to be reasonable) against the rent and he would only owe the other co-owners their share of the net revenues. If instead he bought the paint and roofing and applied or installed them himself, he could deduct the cost of the paint or supplies used on the job, but he could not charge the other co-owners for his labor or services.

Merely consenting to the exceptional activities of a co-owner is not equivalent to an agreement to participate in those activities and to bear a share of their costs. Nor does the fact that a co-owner is entitled to share in the fruits, products or other revenues derived from activities conducted on the land by other co-owners, of itself, impose personal liability upon him for the costs and expenses of production. Consequently, a co-owner cannot be charged with losses or expenses incurred by the other co-owners in conducting any activities on the land in which he has not agreed to participate, and he has an absolute right to refrain from engaging in such activities.

NOTE
Ownership in Indivision

Article 797 defines ownership in indivision as "[o]wnership of the same thing by two or more persons." As noted by Professor Harrell in the first paragraph of the preceding excerpt, ownership in indivision is the only form of co-ownership recognized in Louisiana (in contrast to the common law which recognizes several types of concurrent estates). Nevertheless, it should be noted that in Louisiana the co-ownership of spouses (and former spouses) in community property (and former community property) is subject to special provisions that derogate in numerous respects from the provisions applicable to ordinary co-owners. These special rules, found in chapter 2 of title VI of Book III of the Louisiana, are usually studied in a matrimonial regimes course.

NOTE
The Constituent Elements of Ownership

Since co-owners share every molecule of the co-owned thing, each co-owner holds all constituent elements of ownership: *usus* (use), *fructus* (fruits), and *abusus* (disposition). A co-owner's right to use the co-owned thing is addressed in articles 801-803; his right to fruits and products is described in article 798; and his right of disposition is governed by article 805. To what extent can a co-owner exercise these rights without consent of his co-owners?

Let's begin with *usus*. Article 801 recognizes the right of co-owners to agree upon the use and management of the co-owned thing. In the absence of an agreement by all co-owners, each "co-owner is entitled to use the thing held in indivision according to its destination." La. Civ. Code art. 802. Under article 802, the right of a co-owner to exercise the element of *usus* is not affected or limited by the extent of that co-owner's undivided interest. A co-owner of an undivided one-twentieth interest has the same right to exercise *usus* over the co-owned thing as a co-owner of an undivided nine-tenths interest. There are, however, two limitations on the right of each co-owner to use the co-owned thing. First, the right of a co-owner to exercise unilaterally the element of *usus* is limited to the thing's "destination"—meaning its historical use. The second limitation is the proscription against a co-owner preventing any other co-owner from similarly exercising the element of *usus*. La. Civ. Code art. 802. Finally, article 803 authorizes the court in limited circumstances to determine the use and management of the co-owned thing.

Since co-ownership strikes each molecule of the co-owned thing, a co-owner's right of *usus* extends to every molecule of that thing, so long as the co-owner's use is in accordance with the property's historical destination, and so long as he does not prevent any other co-owner from making the same use. The cases that follow explore the meaning of "destination" and the extent to which courts are willing to resolve disputes among co-owners over the use and management of the thing owned in indivision.

Now let's explore *abusus*. This is addressed in article 805, which differentiates between dispositions of the co-owned thing and of a co-owner's undivided interest in that thing. Any co-owner can "freely lease, alienate, or encumber" his undivided share of the co-owned thing without consent of his co-owners; however, all co-owners must consent to the lease, alienation, or encumbrace of the thing held in common.

Finally, there is the element of *fructus*. Pursuant to the principle of accession, will be explored in Chapter VI, *infra*, fruits and products produced by a thing belong to its owner unless the law recognizes the rights of another to them. La. Civ. Code arts. 483, 488. Article 798 provides that each co-owner shares in the fruits and products of the co-owned thing in proportion to his fractional interest. Thus, a co-owner of an undivided one-tenth interest would receive one-tenth of the fruits and products produced by the co-owned thing. Obviously, a co-owner's right to his proportionate share of fruits and products differs from his right of *usus*, pursuant to which he may use every molecule of the co-owned thing. It should be noted as well that article 798 permits a co-owner who has produced fruits or products from the co-owned thing to deduct his costs of production before making disbursements to his co-owners.

Fruits and products are different from each other. The production of fruits does not diminish the substance of a thing. La. Civ. Code art. 551. By contrast, the removal of a product diminishes the substance of the thing from which it is extracted. La. Civ. Code art. 488. Accordingly, the right to remove products does not fall within the scope of either *usus* or *fructus*; rather it falls within the scope of the element of *abusus*. Although the second paragraph of article 798 discusses the scenario in which one co-owner has produced fruits or products, this provision should not be interpreted as providing authorization for a co-owner to produce fruits or products without consent of the other co-owners. That authority will have to come from some other source, such as an agreement among the co-owners.

Whenever a co-owner produces fruits or products without consent of the other co-owners, any other co-owner may choose may assert his right to share in the fruits or products in proportion to their ownership. Of course, if a co-owner producing fruits or products were to spend more money producing them than they are ultimately worth, that co-owner would be out of luck. His right to allocate the costs of production to the other co-owners arises only as an offset against his co-owners' demand for their share of the fruits and products. If the costs of production exceed the value of the fruits or products, this loss is borne by the co-owner who acted unilaterally without consent of his co-owners.

The Louisiana Supreme Court recently examined the applicability of the "timber trespass" (also called "timber piracy") statute to co-owners in *Sullivan v. Wallace*, 51 So. 3d 702 (La. 2010). The timber trespass legislation imposes treble damages and attorney fees upon any person who cuts, fells, destroys or removes trees "growing or lying on the land of another, without the consent of…the owner…." La. R.S. 3:4278.1. The courts of appeal had been in disagreement over whether this statute applied to co-owners. The parties in *Sullivan* were former spouses who co-owned a 120-acre tract of land. During 1994 and 1995 the former husband cut and sold timber without the former wife's consent and without sharing any of the proceeds with her.

After learning of her former husband's actions, the former wife asserted a claim against him. Instead of relying upon her right as a co-owner to a proportionate share of fruits and products, she requested treble damages and attorney fees pursuant to the timber trespass statute. The supreme court rejected her claim for treble damages and attorney fees, holding that co-owners do not fall within the scope of the timber trespass statute. Focusing upon the statutory requirement that the timber be "on the land of another," and the language requiring the treble damages be paid to the owner of the trees, 51 So. 3d at 709, the court concluded that the statute does not apply to co-owners, whose rights are regulated by the co-ownership provisions in the Code, which allows each co-owner to share in fruits and products in proportion to his undivided interest in the thing from which the fruits or products were produced. The court bolstered its conclusion by making the following comment about the Code's provisions on co-ownership:

"[T]he legislature [in enacting the "piracy trespass" statute] surely was aware of the Civil Code's articles found in Title VII, Book II, governing ownership in indivision, which recognize the underlying principle that a co-owner would ordinarily act in his own economic self-interest with respect to his property."

51 So. 3d at 710.

LeBLANC v. SCURTO
173 So. 2d 322 (La. App. 1st Cir. 1965)

ELLIS, J. This appeal is before us challenging the correctness of a decision by the District Court of Terrebonne Parish which granted plaintiffs an injunction against defendant, enjoining and prohibiting the latter from in any way blocking a certain alley or interfering with the rights of plaintiffs to use the alley as a means of passage.

The plaintiffs, Mrs. Santa Scurto LeBlanc, wife of Edward N. LeBlanc, is the owner of an undivided one-third interest in certain real property in Houma. Sam Scurto owns another one-third and Mrs. Antonia Mule Scurto, widow of Charles Scurto, owns the final one-third. While the latter co-owner was made a party defendant, it does not appear from the record that she took any part in defending the suit or that she is involved in the dispute. The common property is situated at the intersection of Barrow and Main Streets, fronting 67.1 feet on Main and 115 feet on Barrow. It is fully developed and occupied by several small stores and shops, among them a shoe shop of which defendant Sam Scurto is the proprietor.

On the south end of this property there is, and has been for at least fourteen years, a 12 foot alley opening into Barrow Street and dead ending some few feet east of the parties' east boundary. The passage has been used extensively by the Philip Morris Furniture Company, the lessee of a store situated south of the litigants' property on property owned individually by Edward N. LeBlanc. Additional use was made of the alley by city garbage trucks.

On May 27, 1964, at about 9:00 A.M., defendant parked his car in this alley, effectively blocking it. Defendant did not often use the alley and claims to have done so on this occasion to facilitate the unloading of some parcels from his car into the shoe shop. Plaintiffs claim that defendant parked his car there in order to prevent them from using the alley and that such activity constitutes irreparable injury to their rights as co-owners to use the property.

It appears that the motive advanced by plaintiffs for the blocking of the alley is substantiated by the evidence. The testimony of Mrs. LeBlanc attributes to defendant statements to that effect. It is evident that there is considerable ill feeling between the parties and that the simple and infrequent blocking of the alley would not have led to the heated words and simple batteries which were freely exchanged between Mrs. LeBlanc and her brother, Sam Scurto, in the latter's shop while the alley was blocked. The record indicates that Sam Scurto acted as he did in an effort to persuade the LeBlancs to sell him their interest in the land and improvements occupied by his shoe store.

Regardless of the actual motives of the parties, this Court must determine the applicability of the injunctive process as between co-owners where one of the co-owners has acted to deliberately deny to the others the *equal* and *coextensive possession* of a designated portion of the common estate granted to each co-owner by the law of Louisiana.

It should be made clear at this point that plaintiffs are not seeking an injunction to prevent defendant from using the alley. No demand of that nature could be seriously proposed because of the obvious impossibility of protecting the equal rights of both parties by denying those rights to one. It is precisely this dilemma which impels the necessity of the provisions in our law giving to all co-owners a right to demand a partition of the property held in common.

What is sought by plaintiffs, and what was granted in the tribunal below, is an injunction prohibiting defendant from blocking the alley or interfering with the rights of plaintiffs to use the alley as a passageway. In other words, plaintiffs are before this Court seeking protection of their rights as co-owners, not a denial of those same rights to the defendant.

In determining whether or not injunctive relief is proper in cases of this nature, it is necessary to determine the use for which the common property is intended. In the case of Stinson v. Marston, 185 La. 365, 169 So. 436, the Supreme Court recognized that:

> The courts of this state have always recognized the right of a co-owner to use the property held in common *for the purposes for which it is destined,* such as the cultivation of farm lands of the sort involved in this controversy, Becnel v. Becnel, 23 La. Ann. 150; Toler v. Bunch, 34 La. Ann. 997; Moreira v. Schwan, 113 La. 643, 37 So. 542
>
> ***"The co-owner is further entitled to see that the property is preserved or maintained without deterioration; ***"(Emphasis added.)

Having established the use to which the common property is best suited, or is reasonably being put, the courts of this state will sanction injunctions between co-owners to prevent a waste of that property, or a denial of equal and coextensive possession by a co-owner. Thus, in Cotton v. Christen, 110 La. 444, 34 So. 597, the Court sanctioned an injunction between co-owners to prevent one from removing timber to the prejudice of the other, finding that such unauthorized removal was in the nature of a trespass on the rights of the other.

The alley in question was certainly used as an avenue of passage and not as a parking lot. There is evidence to indicate that the Philip Morris trucks loaded and unloaded in an area which did not interfere with the passage. However, even if these trucks do block the alley, it cannot be said that the blocking is deliberate and no showing has been made that they have ever refused passage to defendant. The deliberate blocking of the alley by the defendant to satisfy his desire for revenge or to induce some action on the part of his co-owner cannot be sanctioned.

It is apparent, therefore, that injunction does lie as between the co-owners in the instant situation. In using the common property for spite, or even for parking an unreasonable length of time to unload parcels, the defendant has converted its use from passage to parking. By parking as did the defendant co-owner in the present case practically all day, plaintiffs co-owners have been deprived of equal and coextensive possession and use of the common property. This is in the nature of a waste of the property just as surely as the cutting of trees is a waste. Except in situations where a co-owner is entitled to be maintained in possession against attacks by a co-owner out of possession, either has the right to demand of the other equal possession and coextensive use of any given spot within the common estate. If the defendant co-owner wishes to have *exclusive* possession of the common property or any part thereof, his remedy is by suit for partition. He cannot legally prevent equal and coextensive possession of the common property to his co-owner. The latter is entitled to be maintained in such possession. Gulf Refining Co. v. Carroll, 145 La. 299, 82 So. 277.

The defendant in this case has an equal right to an injunction against the plaintiffs to prevent them, or those tenants holding under them, from blocking the alley in such a manner as to destroy the equal and coextensive possession and use by all co-owners. However, such an injunction has not been sought by defendant. Such an action would clearly have defeated his purpose — the forcible filing of a partition suit by plaintiff or extra-judicial partition.

Counsel for defendant earnestly argues that even if plaintiffs sought to board up the windows and doors of the shoe shop, defendant would be without an injunctive remedy. While we do not propose to answer hypothetical questions, suffice to [sic] say that spiteful conduct on the part of a co-owner will not be tolerated on the pretense that he is simply exercising his equal and coextensive rights. Such conduct can be viewed in no other light than as constituting a waste of the property and a trespass on the rights of the co-owner.

The case of Juneau v. Laborde, 228 La. 410, 82 So. 2d 693, is inapplicable in the instant situation because that was a suit by a co-owner out of possession to recover rents and revenues from the co-owner in possession. The court correctly reasoned that the former co-owner could not prevent the latter from cultivating the land, and that the remedy for the co-owner out of possession was to seek a partition of the property. In the instant case neither co-owner is out of possession. The object of the instant litigation is not an accounting but an injunction to prevent the spiteful and wasteful use by one co-owner of a particular piece of the common estate and to enforce plaintiffs legal right to equal and coextensive possession and use of the passageway. If the defendant does not wish to remain in such possession with the plaintiffs co-owners, his remedy is by legal partition. The decision of the lower court is affirmed.

NOTE
Co-Owner Out of Possession

In *Juneau* v. *Laborde*, 228 La. 410, 82 So. 2d 693 (1955), the supreme court stated in dictum that a co-owner out of possession might be entitled to his share of the fair market value of the co-owned thing from a co-owner in possession if the former's demand for occupancy is refused by the latter. Such an award was granted in *Von Drake.* v. *Rogers*, 996 So. 2d 608 (La. App. 2d Cir. 2008).

SUCCESSION OF MILLER
674 So. 2d 441 (La. App. 4th Cir. 1996)

ARMSTRONG, J. This is an appeal from a judgment in a succession proceeding, authorizing the executor, Martin O. Miller II, to control access to the residence of the decedent, and the movables contained therein and elsewhere. Finding no error in the judgment of the trial court, we now affirm.

The decedent, Edna Kuntz Miller, died testate on August 22, 1994. One of her sons, Martin O. Miller II, was appointed executor pursuant to her statutory last will and testament. The decedent had been married once, to Martin O. Miller ("Mr. Miller"), who predeceased her. The couple had eight children born of the marriage, seven of whom survived her. The eighth child predeceased the decedent, but was survived by four children, all of whom survived the decedent.

At the time of the decedent's death, the seven surviving children each owned a one-sixteenth undivided interest, and the four children of the predeceased daughter, each a one-sixty fourth undivided interest, in a residence located at 24 Audubon Place, New Orleans, Louisiana, and the movables contained therein and elsewhere, by virtue of Mr. Miller's succession. Martin O. Miller II controlled the interest of one sister, Diane, who was an interdict, as her curator. The ownership interests of Mr. Miller's heirs was subject to the surviving spouse usufruct in favor of the decedent. Upon the decedent's death, they became owners in indivision of one-half of the property in question.

Because of concern about his personal liability as executor, on the advice of counsel, Martin Miller proposed a plan regarding access to the Audubon Place residence. He essentially gave the heirs two choices: (1) they could have access to the residence if they gave him reasonable notice, telling him how long they wanted access, access would be given only for a "reasonable time" and for a "legitimate purpose," and he or his designee would be present during the visit; or (2) the heirs could have unrestricted access to the house if they all released him from all personal liability. All heirs did not release him from liability so Martin Miller implemented the restricted access plan. The decedent's only other son, Pierre Valcour Miller ("Val Miller"), objected to the restricted access and filed a petition for injunctive relief, seeking to enjoin Martin Miller from interfering with his rights as a co-owner of the residence. The trial court denied relief. Approximately one week later, Martin Miller filed a "Motion To Determine Management of Property Held In Indivision."

At trial of the motion, Martin Miller testified that he was concerned about his personal liability should visitors to the residence, or heirs, remove movables from the residence or have an accident on the premises. The residence was appraised at $1,300,000.00 and, the contents, at $53,735.35. Martin Miller admitted that the Audubon Place residence and contents were insured for one million dollars and that all of the movables in the residence had been individually appraised. He said he had never refused anyone access to the residence under the plan and that Val Miller was the only heir who objected to the restricted access. Martin Miller also testified that there had been problems with Val Miller concerning the use of property co-owned by the heirs in Cameron and Vermilion parishes. He said Val Miller took two trailers and a bulldozer for personal use and had not returned them. He also said Val Miller had not been paying his share of the expenses to maintain this property. Martin Miller mentioned a check, in the amount of $1,130.75, from the State of Louisiana in reimbursement of money owed the late Mr. Miller's estate. Martin Miller said he sent the check to Val Miller for endorsement, with intentions of eventually sending it to all of the other heirs for signature. However, Val Miller would not sign the check, but instead, returned it to Martin. The check was eventually declared dead by the state. Martin Miller testified that the Audubon Place residence was listed for sale. A copy of an informational sheet from the real estate company was introduced into evidence.

A sister, Marian Miller Green, testified that she believed Martin Miller's restricted access policy was reasonable and that it would be chaos if everyone had unlimited access. She said it had been chaotic at the family-owned residence situated on the country property because one never knew how many people would be coming. Bed space was limited. On cross examination, she admitted there had been fewer beds than overnight visitors on only one occasion. She could not recall if Val Miller had been there on that occasion, nor could she recall Val Miller ever being associated with chaos.

Edward Rapier was the trustee of a trust established under the estate of the deceased daughter, Mildred Ann Miller Boulet, for Boulet's four children. Rapier said he agreed with Martin Miller's plan. He said as trustee he would not agree to hold Mann Miller harmless—it would violate his duty as a trustee.

Val Miller testified that he had tremendous sentimental associations with the Audubon Place residence. He lived there for twenty-two years and had continued to visit up to three times a week for thirty-three years until the death of his mother. Being a recovering alcoholic, he said is an extremely stressful time for him and it is being made more so by the actions of his brother in restricting his access to the residence. He believes as a co-owner, he has a right to unrestricted access to the home. He candidly admitted that he believed he has a right to take movables out of the residence without asking, possibly not returning the item(s) until another heir asks him to. However, he said he would agree not to take anything out of the residence and he would agree to hold Martin Miller harmless if he gave either himself or anyone else a key to the residence. He said he did not think he was legally required to get permission from the other co-owners before using the property.

Val Miller said he never interfered with the use of any of the Cameron or Vermilion Parish property by any of his co-owners. He introduced a letter into evidence wherein he requested that the co-owners voice any objection to his hosting a duck hunt bachelor party for his son at the country residence one particular fall weekend in 1993. He said one of his brothers-in-law drove the bulldozer into a canal years ago. He retrieved it after a period of time, intending to have it repaired, but discovered it would be too expensive. He still has the bulldozer in his possession and said none of the co-owners have ever asked for it. As for the two trailers, he said he uses those on the section of the country property he manages and that none of the co-owners has asked for them. He said he was not paying for the maintenance of the country property because he had paid the full cost of it for a period of time. As for the $1,130.75 check from the State of Louisiana, he said he did not feel it should have been simply endorsed by all heirs and negotiated as Martin Miller was attempting to do, rather, it should have been put through his father's succession. Val Miller introduced into evidence a letter from his sister, Judith M. Kavanagh, to Martin Miller's attorney, wherein Judith authorized the attorney to give any co-owner a key and alarm access code, and agreeing to hold Martin Miller harmless for any losses caused by a co-owner's access. Judith also indicated that she and her sisters might want to go through the decedent's clothing in the near future and that she might request a key and access code at that time. Val Miller seemed to believe the import of this letter was that Judith did not agree with Martin Miller's access policy.

The trial court heard this evidence and rendered judgment "pursuant to Louisiana Civil Code Article 803," giving Martin Miller control of the keys and alarm code to the residence, and decreeing that the co-owners could have access to the residence only if accompanied by the executor or his designee, "upon reasonable notice, for a reasonable time, and for a legitimate reason related to the administration of the succession and disposition of the home and the movables contained therein."

Appellant Val Miller claims the trial court had no authority to issue the ruling it did. The trial court rendered judgment, citing as authority, La.C.C. art. 803, which provides:

> When the mode of use and management of the thing held in indivision is not determined by an agreement of all the co-owners and partition is not available, a court, upon petition by a co-owner, may determine the use and management.

Val Miller argues that partition is available and, thus, C.C. art. 803 was not applicable. He cites La.C.C. art. 802 which states that a co-owner is entitled to use the thing but cannot prevent another co-owner from making use of it. He submits that La.C.C. art. 802 governs this case and that none of the co-owners can prevent him from using the property as Martin Miller is attempting to do. He argues that La.C.C. art. 803 is limited to a situation such as where the parties have agreed, in writing, not to partition property, for up to fifteen years, as provided for by La.R.S. 9:1112 and 9:1702.

Title VII of the Louisiana Civil Code, Ownership In Indivision, consisting of Articles 797 through 818, became effective in January 1991. There is scant jurisprudence interpreting these articles. La.C.C. art. 801 provides: "The use and management of the thing held in indivision is determined by agreement of all the co-owners." The code scheme envisions, first, the co-owners agreeing among themselves how to manage the property held in indivision. Martin Miller submits that if, for some reason the co-owners cannot agree on the use and management of the property, and a partition has not yet been ordered, then La.C.C. art. 803 authorizes a court, upon petition by another co-owner, to determine the use and management of the property.

Martin Miller, as co-owner (and as executor), and all of the co-owners in indivision, including Val Miller, agreed to list the residence with a real estate agent for sale and, at the time of trial, it was on the market. If the residence sold, a partition would have been unnecessary. Given that situation, no co-owner had sought a partition as of the time of trial. A court order of partition by licitation would simply have resulted in the residence being offered for sale, as it already had been. Pending that sale, we believe a trial court could determine the use and management of the residence, in the absence of an agreement between the co-owners. The alternative would be infighting among the co-owners pending the actual sale. We find that, as a practical matter, a partition was "not available" because it would have been a needless expense and unnecessary judicial procedure. Because the co-owners could not agree on the use and management of the thing among themselves pending the sale of the residence, the trial court had the authority to make that determination pursuant to C.C. art. 803.

Val Miller next questions the reasonableness of the trial court's determination of use and management. At one point in his testimony, Val Miller said he believed he had a right to use the residence as he so desired and to remove movables and possibly keep them until another co-owner asked for them. However, he subsequently stated that he would agree not to remove any item from the residence. Val Miller also gave some emotional testimony about his sentimental attachment to the family residence, which he had lived in for twenty-two years of his early life and frequently visited for more than thirty years thereafter. Nevertheless, the trial court, heard the evidence, observed the demeanor of the witnesses, and determined what it felt was the best use and management of the residence under the circumstances. We cannot say the trial court erred. For the foregoing reasons, we affirm the judgment of the trial court.

PROBLEM

Fred and Wilma, brother and sister, inherited Blackacre and a duplex from Uncle Lester. Since Uncle Lester's death two years ago, Fred has lived in the left half of the duplex, and Carl has lived in the east half (at a rental of $700 a month pursuant to a lease Carl entered into with Fred). Carl moved out yesterday, and Fred and Wilma got into a nasty argument this morning. Since Uncle Lester's death, Fred has maintained the duplex by cutting the grass regularly and making all repairs requested by Carl. Fred has also paid the annual property taxes. However, Fred has not shared with Wilma any of the rentals paid to him by Carl.

Blackacre is immovable property in Cameron Parish. For many years Blackacre has been surrounded by levees. According to Fred, the levees have been breached and are in need of maintenance and repairs to preserve their integrity and to prevent the encroachment of salt water. This morning Fred told Wilma that the levee repairs were necessary and that she needed to pay half of all repair costs. What are the parties' rights and responsibilities arising out of these facts?

NOTE
Authorized Unilateral Action by a Co-Owner

Title VII of Book II, entitled "Ownership in Indivision," was added to the Civil Code effective January 1, 1991. Although the Civil Code has always recognized ownership in indivision, prior to 1991 its only provisions on co-ownership regulated partition, which is the process by which co-ownership terminates. The addition of articles 797 through 806 in 1991 attempts to regulate the rights and duties of co-owners arising during the period in which they are co-owners. Professor Symeonides and Ms. Martin's article on the co-ownership title added in 1991, which is excerpted immediately following this note, provides a perspective on the then newly-enacted provisions. Inasmuch as Professor Symeonides was a member of the advisory committee that drafted the co-ownership title, the article furnishes the reader with the point of view of one of the drafters of these provisions. The excerpt which follows includes the authors' discussion of two codal provisions: article 800 and article 806. These provisions authorize unilateral action by a co-owner in specifically designated circumstances.

Symeonides & Martin, "The New Law of Co-Ownership: A Kommentar"
68 Tul. L. Rev. 69, 148-152 (1993)
(footnotes omitted)

THE FOLLOWING EXCERPT DISCUSSES CIVIL CODE ARTICLE 800

1. Unilateral Action: Rationale

Article 800 provides for one of the two instances of unilateral action authorized by the Act. Under this Article a co-owner may act to preserve the co-owned property, while under Article 802 he may make use of the property without the concurrence of his co-owners. These two rights form the inner core of ownership. Although the Act works several modifications of the concept of absolute ownership in order to accommodate the co-owners' needs, it leaves this core intact. The same is true in most civil law jurisdictions, although in some of them, to core is somewhat more expansive.

2. Classification of Acts and Distribution of Power

The Act draws a distinction between acts of preservation (Article 800), acts of management (Articles 801 and 803), and acts of disposition (Article 805). This classification reflects the French tripartite distinction between conservatory acts, acts of administration, and acts of disposition. Conservatory acts, addressed in Article 800, are acts that "tend to preserve a thing within a given patrimony, to prevent it from being destroyed, damaged, or lost for the owner." Acts of disposition, addressed in Article 805, are acts that "tend to divest the owner of his interest, to deprive him, in part or in whole, of a real or personal right." Finally, acts of administration, addressed in Articles 801 and 803, are acts that "exceed the limits of mere conservatory measures...and thus constitute a residual category." The classification of acts provides a mechanism for allocating power between involved parties--it "furnish[es] guidelines...for the determination of the authority of certain persons to act with respect to things under their ownership or control." For example, an usufructuary of nonconsumables is obligated to perform conservatory acts; may be able to perform acts of administration; and may not, ordinarily, perform acts of disposition.

The power of co-owners to act with regard to the common property is severely curtailed by the Act insofar as the Act prohibits unilateral acts by a co-owner other than acts of use or acts of preservation. Indeed, the Act requires unanimous consent or a court order for anything beyond these acts, including acts of administration, substantial alterations, and acts of disposition of the entire thing. In systems of special co-ownership such as partnerships and the matrimonial regime, as well as in foreign versions of simple co-ownership, the parties are accorded much broader powers....

3. Necessary Steps for the Preservation

Preservation implies some danger of decay, deterioration, or impending loss. The impending loss may be total or partial, physical or legal; however, the degree of imminence or gravity this danger must have is an open question. The Greek source provision speaks of "imminent peril," and the Swiss provision speaks of "imminent or increasing damage." The fact that no such words have been used in drafting the Louisiana provision suggests that a lesser standard might have been contemplated. "Preservation" also implies that the measures taken must aspire to preserve the thing rather than to alter either the thing or its economic purpose. The necessity of the measures, as well as their sufficiency and proportionality, should be judged objectively by the prudent man standard, rather than by the subjective standard of the acting co-owner.

4. Without Concurrence

At a minimum, this phrase means that the acting co-owner need not obtain consent of the other co-owners before taking action to preserve the property. A question that arises is whether a co-owner may take such action over the objections of his co-owners. In Greece and Germany, the prevailing interpretation of the corresponding civil code articles is that "without concurrence" includes "despite objection." Louisiana jurisprudence has also taken this position, and the same interpretation should be followed under the Act. The concurrence of the other coowners may be given in advance. However, such advance consent should not be taken as a waiver by the consenting co-owner of his own right to take measures necessary for the preservation of the thing.

5. Right or Duty to Act

The right conferred by Article 800 is assertable not only against the other co-owners but also against third parties. It confers on a co-owner the power to act in his own name and not necessarily to represent the other co-owners. There is some question as to whether this Article not only confers a right but also imposes a duty to act. Although the use of the word "may" implies only a right and not an affirmative duty, the answer to the question depends on Article 799. As previously explained the right becomes a duty only when the co-owner assumes the administration of the thing either on his own, as a negotiorum gestor, or by virtue of a court appointment or agreement of the parties.

6. The Right to Preserve the Property and the Doctrine of Negotiorum Gestio

The Reporter's comment to Article 800 distinguishes acts of preservation from situations of negotiorum gestio, stating that: "This is not unauthorized management of the affairs of another under Civil Code Article 2295 (1870) [Revised C.C. arts. 2992 and 2993]." This cryptic comment may signify an understanding that the provisions of the Act entirely displace the doctrine of negotiorum gestio. After all, the Act explicitly deals with all the issues that were previously handled under this doctrine. Article 799 provides a standard of care for all co-owners that is similar, though not identical, to the prudent administrator standard imposed on gestors by Article 2298 [Revised C.C. art. 2295]. In addition, Article 800 gives each co-owner the right to act unilaterally to preserve the property, and Article 806 provides the correlative duty of reimbursement. The measure of reimbursement provided for in Article 806 seems substantially the same as the "useful and necessary" measure provided for gestors in Article 2299 [Revised C.C. art. 2297]. Thus, it could be argued that there is no longer a need for the doctrine of negotiorum gestio in Louisiana's law of co-ownership. This is probably not a great loss, as the doctrine is generally not well understood. It may well be preferable to deal with coownership issues on the basis of ownership rather than on the basis of quasi-contractual principles.

The possibility also exists, however, that the doctrine of negotiorum gestio still applies in a residual fashion under reasoning similar to that applied in Moody v. Arabie. The Reporter's comment to Article 800 states only that, when a co-owner undertakes necessary acts for the preservation of the property, he is not acting as a gestor. This may simply signify that, in this circumstance, the rights of the acting co-owner are to be determined under the Act rather than under the principles of negotiorum gestio. However, neither the comment nor Article 800 addresses the situation in which a co-owner undertakes acts that go beyond mere acts of preservation.

Although the Act does not authorize a co-owner unilaterally to undertake such acts, the fact remains that when a co-owner does undertake such acts without objection from his co-owners, he is de facto acting as a gestor. The only question is whether this status should be recognized de jure. The Act itself contains no express language that would preclude this possibility.

THE FOLLOWING EXCERPT DISCUSSES CIVIL CODE ARTICLE 806

1. Necessary Expenses

Article 806 establishes a co-owner's right to be reimbursed for three categories of expenses: (a) "necessary expenses"; (b) "expenses for ordinary maintenance and repairs"; and (c) "necessary management expenses paid to a third person." This Article essentially codifies pre-Act jurisprudence, which had clearly recognized a co-owner's right to recover expenses incurred in preserving the co-owned property.

To give substance to the term "necessary expenses," the official comment to Article 806 refers to Professor Yiannopoulos's treatise on property. In his treatise, Professor Yiannopoulos describes the distinction made in civil law systems between necessary, useful, and luxurious expenses:

> Necessary expenses are those incurred for the preservation of a thing and for the discharge of private or public burdens, other than those incurred for ordinary maintenance and repairs. Useful expenses are those which, though not needed for the preservation of a thing, result in enhancement of its value. Luxurious expenses are those made for the gratification of one's personal predilections.

These distinctions become important with regard to good and bad faith possessors, because they provide the basis for reimbursement of the two types of possessors. The official comment to Article 806 cross references Article 527, which concerns necessary expenses. The comment to Article 527 cites cases holding that necessary expenses include property taxes and assessments, indispensable repairs and maintenance costs, and insurance costs. Cases are also cited for the proposition that the costs of ordinary maintenance and repairs do not constitute necessary expenses.

The right to incur, and be reimbursed for, necessary expenses was well established in the pre-Act jurisprudence on co-ownership. Several co-ownership cases have specifically addressed this issue. These cases are in accord with the cases cited above with regard to taxes, insurance, and indispensable repair costs, holding that such expenses are necessary.

Costs incurred by a co-owner in litigation necessary to preserve the property have also been considered necessary expenses. With regard to expenses for ordinary maintenance and repairs, however, the co-ownership cases have departed from the Code articles and cases concerning possessors, holding that such expenses are necessary expenses.

2. Expenses for Ordinary Maintenance and Repairs

The provision in Article 806 that allows for recovery of expenses incurred for ordinary maintenance and repairs applies when ordinary repairs are made pursuant to an agreement of all the co-owners under Article 801 or pursuant to a court order under Article 803. The provision may not prove particularly useful in these contexts, because many such agreements or court orders specifically provide for reimbursement. It will, however, be of use in some cases, such as situations in which co-owners have tacitly consented to ordinary repairs made by a co-owner.

Under pre-Act jurisprudence, ordinary repairs were considered to be acts of preservation that could be made by a co-owner without the concurrence of the other co-owners. Article 806's distinction between ordinary repairs and necessary expenses, however, could be read to overrule this jurisprudence. In this vein, it is worth noting that an earlier version of Article 806 referred to the right to reimbursement of "necessary expenses, including ordinary maintenance and repairs." It is unclear why the language was changed in the final version and whether such a marked departure from pre-Act jurisprudence was intended by the omission of the word including. Such a departure is undesirable, however, as it would deprive a co-owner of the right to engage in ordinary maintenance of his property. This would take away a right that is within the core rights of ownership. However, a prohibition of unilateral maintenance and repairs is not completely unreasonable in the context of the entire Act, which greatly limits the ability of co-owners to act in the absence of unanimous consent and pushes parties toward partition in the event of conflict.

3. Necessary Management Expenses Paid to a Third Person

This provision is in accord with pre-Act jurisprudence, which required reimbursement only for those management expenses paid to a third person. A co-owner may not, under Article 806 and pre-Act jurisprudence, demand reimbursement for his own services in managing the co-owned property. However, as noted by the official comment to Article 806, a co-owner may be entitled to recover reimbursement for his own management of the property "under a management plan adopted by agreement of all the co-owners, by judgment, or under the law of unjust enrichment."

4. Other Expenses: Unjust Enrichment and Negotiorum Gestio

The reference to the law of unjust enrichment in the last-quoted phrase indicates that, at least with regard to the management expenses referred to in that phrase, Article 806 is not intended to displace the general doctrine of unjust enrichment. It is unclear, however, whether the same is true for other categories of expenses not provided for in this Article.

The question is whether the enumeration of expenses for which the owner is entitled to reimbursement under this Article is exclusive or merely illustrative. For example, is reimbursement due for expenses that do not qualify as necessary but do qualify as useful in the sense that they enhance the value of the thing? Reimbursement for such expenses is clearly not due under Article 806. However, since this Article does not contain any prohibitory or restrictive language such as the word "only," it should not be read as prohibiting reimbursement if such reimbursement is available under another article of this Act or other statute, under the principles of negotiorum gestio, or under the general doctrine of unjust enrichment.

For example, a reimbursement of sorts is available under Article 798, which allows the producing co-owner to deduct his "costs of production" before giving to the other co-owners their share in the fruits and products of the thing. Similarly, as previously discussed, it is at least arguable that, in some instances, reimbursement might be due under the principles of negotiorum gestio even before resorting to the doctrine of unjust enrichment. Although there is some authority for the proposition that the doctrine of negotiorum gestio does not apply to co-owners, the courts have nevertheless applied it, both explicitly and implicitly, in the co-ownership context. One branch of the jurisprudence interpreting Article 2299, the Article providing the measure of reimbursement for gestors, has read the "useful and necessary" requirement of that Article conjunctively, requiring the expenses incurred to be both useful and necessary in order for reimbursement to be due. However, that jurisprudence is not immune from reexamination, because jurisprudence also exists to the contrary.

Finally, reimbursement for useful expenses may well be available under the general doctrine of unjust enrichment for any co-owner who meets the requirements of that doctrine. Although the Act covers much of the ground previously handled by the jurisprudence under the doctrine of unjust enrichment and thus displaces it to that extent, the Act does not displace the doctrine altogether. Unjust enrichment still remains a remedy in all cases for which the Act does not provide or imply otherwise.

5. Indirect Rent

Article 806 provides that "[i]f the co-owner who incurred the expenses had the enjoyment of the thing held in indivision, his reimbursement shall be reduced in proportion to the value of the enjoyment." As discussed above, this provision codifies pre-Act jurisprudence. The provision is essentially an indirect means of charging a co-owner rent for his personal occupancy of the co-owned property—it forces him to bear a portion of the cost of expenses attributable to the property of which he has exclusive enjoyment.

NOTE
Another Perspective on the Unilateral Power of a Co-Owner

In the past few years, at least two student commentators have criticized specific provisions in the co-ownership title in light of the jurisprudence that has developed since this title took effect in 1991. One commentator, who has focused specifically on articles 800 and 806, has identified problems the courts have encountered in their attempts to apply these articles, and has proposed and developed a legislative solution to these problems. The following excerpt is the author's brief summary of the flaws she has identified:

In a general sense, the broad nature of articles 800 and 806 are problematic in that a co-owner may affect a thing in which multiple persons have an interest without consulting the others first. In addition, the non-consenting co-owners will be further burdened with the reimbursement for such an expense. More specifically, however, the Louisiana rule is flawed in a number of less apparent ways. First, courts have had difficulty applying the current rule, particularly the vague term "necessary." Second, the ambiguities of article 800 have led to manipulation of the legislation by co-owners against their fellow co-owners. Finally, the provisions cause unnecessary risk in property investment, as the broad terminology used does not provide adequate notice of when reimbursement may be due.

Kristen E. Bell, Comment, "Preserving Your Pocket Book: Narrowing the Unilateral Power of a Co-Owner," 69 La. L. Rev. 139, 152 (2008).

b. Partition

Harrell, Problems Created by Co-Ownership in Louisiana
32 Institute of Mineral Law 381, 399-404 (1985)

The purpose of partition is to eliminate co-ownership. It can either be effected conventionally, through consent of all of the parties, or judicially, and against the will of some of them. In the latter case it may be accomplished either in kind, by dividing the property into lots and awarding each co-owner full ownership of one or more of them, or by licitation, that is, by selling the property at a public sale and dividing the proceeds among the owners in proportion to their interests.

CONVENTIONAL PARTITION

Conventional partition may be effected in any manner that ultimately vests full ownership of the property in a single person. It is ordinarily accomplished through a form of exchange by which each co-owner conveys his interest in part of the common property in exchange for the other co-owners' interest in another part so that each acquires full ownership of the part conveyed to him. Each party to the partition warrants to the others, in the absence of a contrary stipulation, against the disturbance or eviction each may suffer when the cause of the disturbance or eviction proceeds from a cause anterior to the partition. Conventional partition is generally subject to the rules prevailing for exchanges, which are in turn subject to the rules of sales. The parties may, of course, enter into any stipulation or condition in connection with a conventional partition which is not contrary to public policy.

JUDICIAL PARTITION

Judicial partition, as its name implies, requires the person seeking it to bring an action against the other co-owners. Judicial partition is accomplished in kind unless it is impracticable to do so in light of the rules regulating the matter. If the property cannot be partitioned in kind, partition by licitation (sale) is ordered. In that case, the property is sold at public auction, without appraisal, to the highest bidder. The rules prevailing for sale of property in execution of judgments otherwise apply. The court has some limited discretion in setting the terms and conditions of the sale.

When partition in kind is ordered, a notary is appointed by the court to carry it out. The law directs the notary to divide the property into discrete lots of substantially equal value. The various co-owners then draw for the lots in rotation. That is, the lots are assigned by chance, not by designation.

The Civil Code declares that partition in kind is the preferred method and that a sale or licitation of the property is to be ordered only when it is impossible to divide the property in kind or when its division would cause a loss to the co-owners. The rules regulating partition in kind have been so interpreted, however, as to make it impractical in all but the simplest of cases, notwithstanding the policy expressed in the Code of favoring it. The principal factors that prevent partition in kind are the following:

a. There must be as many lots as the least common denominator of the fractional ownership of the various parties.

b. The lots must be of substantially equal value, although minor variations in value may be compensated by ordering payment to equalize the discrepancy.

c. The aggregate value of the individual lots must substantially equal the value of the entire undivided property before the partition.

d. If there are mineral rights created by less than all the parties, the "surface" and "mineral" values of each lot must be proportionate to the value of the interests of the mineral and "surface" owners in the whole.

EFFECT OF PARTITION ON CHARGES OVER THE PROPERTY

Mortgages, servitudes, or other charges against the property created by all of the owners for their predecessors are unaffected by partition, conventional or judicial, whether it is in kind or by licitation.

If such charges were created by less than all of the co-owners, or their predecessors, partition generally has the following effect:

First, they are unaffected by a conventional partition.

Second, in the case of a judicial partition:

a. If the partition is in kind, the charges continue to burden the lots taken by the co-owners creating them. The lots taken by those who did not create the charges are transferred free of them.

b. If the partition is by licitation, the land is sold free of all the charges and the owners of such charges are relegated to a claim against the proceeds received from the sale which are attributable to the interests over which their charge rested. One exception to this rule is that if the property is purchased by a co-owner who had created the charge, then its burden continues uninterruptedly.

The policy of the rule applicable to licitation is obvious. If two people own land and one of them imposes a mortgage over it, or leases his 1/2 interest, a purchaser would hardly pay the full value for the property if the burden continues to rest against an undivided interest. More importantly, the purchaser in the licitation might even pay less than one-half the value of the land without the charges. Consequently, it may be impossible for the other co-owner to fairly obtain one-half of the intrinsic value of the property because of the existence of a burden or charge to which he has never consented.

NOTE
Lesion

The preceding excerpt describes conventional partitions and judicial partitions. A conventional partition is an agreement among co-owners that terminates co-ownership. The conventional partition is sometimes called a voluntary partition or an extrajudicial partition. Because an extrajudicial partition is a contract, it can be attacked on the same grounds as any other contract. Thus, a co-owner can annul an extrajudicial partition for any of the three vices of consent recognized by the Code: error, fraud and duress. See La. Civ. Code arts. 1948-1964.

In addition, an extrajudicial partition can be attacked for lesion. Article 814 states that an extrajudicial partition is lesionary "if the value of the part received by a co-owner is less by more than one-fourth of the fair market value of the portion he should have received." Assume that there are four equal co-owners (Al, Bob, Carol and Dick), that the co-owned thing is valued at $400,000, and that the part allocated to Al has a fair market value of $70,000. Is this partition lesionary with respect to Al?

Al should have received property valued at $100,000, but he received property valued at only $70,000. The fact that Al received property worth less than the amount he should have received does not mean the partition is lesionary, however, because the law tolerates a margin of twenty five percent. However, if the co-owner receives property valued below the 25% margin, the partition is lesionary. Here, the margin is $25,000, since that amount is 25% of $100,000. Thus, the partition is lesionary if Al receives property valued below $75,000. Since Al received property valued at only $70,000, the partition is lesionary, and can be attacked by Al. Liberative prescription on a co-owner's lesion action is five years. La. Civ. Code art. 1413.

THOMPSON v. CELESTAIN
936 So. 2d 219 (La. App. 4th Cir. 2006)

TOBIAS, J. This case involves a petition for partition of immovable property brought by Leona Thompson ("Thompson") against her former boyfriend/fiance Alfred L. Celestain, Sr. ("Celestain"), regarding the house that they purchased together in New Orleans in January 2001. Thompson and Celestain eventually ended their relationship, and Thompson moved out of the house.

On 29 July 2004, Thompson filed a petition to partition the property located at 4624 Eastern Street in New Orleans ("the property"). She alleged that she was the owner of an undivided one-half interest in the house and that the property was not susceptible to division in kind because the property included the land and the house. She prayed for partition by licitation of the immovable property. Along with her petition, she filed a descriptive list of assets and liabilities, listing the movable property in the house, as well as the mortgage on the property and the amount due on a VISA account. Celestain responded to the petition with his own descriptive list of assets and liabilities. His list differed from Thompson's regarding the value of many items of movable property; the liability for the debt of a VISA credit card; and further assigned ownership for each item of movable property to either himself or Thompson. On 7 December 2004, Celestain filed a motion to set a hearing on the petition to partition the property.

The hearing was set for 29 March 2005. Thompson was the only witness to testify on her behalf. She testified that she and Celestain purchased the house for $110,000.00 and that she tendered a $1,000.00 good faith deposit toward the purchase and an additional $26,462.28 as a down payment. She presented copies of an official check for $1,000.00 made payable to the realtor and an official check made payable to herself for $26,462.28. Thompson testified that after she and Celestain purchased the house, she made twelve or thirteen mortgage payments before she eventually moved out in August 2002. She did not present any cancelled checks to introduce into evidence in support thereof, but testified that she made the mortgage payments by money order and could not document the payments. She further testified that she paid for the installation of new windows at the house, costing her a total of $4,279.00. In conjunction with this testimony, she presented one copy of a money order made payable to the mortgage holder and two receipts for windows from LAS Enterprises.

Thompson also testified that she and Celestain had a VISA credit card account together, and that the balance on the account was $9,000.00. She testified that she and Celestain were both responsible for the charges on the account, and that he had agreed to pay for half of the charges on the account when they ended their relationship. He purportedly made a $5,000.00 payment on the account, but then withdrew $5,000.00 against the account by way of a counter check.

Celestain's testimony is at odds with Thompson's in many regards. Celestain testified that Thompson moved out during Mardi Gras 2001, and did not continue to reside there until August 2002 as she maintains. Further, Celestain denied that Thompson made the entire down payment on the property; he asserts that he put down $12,000.00 toward the purchase price. He further testified that he has made almost all of the mortgage payments on the property, and that Thompson made only one before she moved out. In support of his testimony, Celestain presented copies of canceled checks written on his personal checking account to the mortgage company, which totaled $12,453.58, representing fifteen mortgage payments. He also described and documented improvements he made to the property over the years, including replacing the front door, installing a hot tub, restoring a bathtub, plumbing repairs, and various other acts of maintenance on the property.

Celestain's son and brother were called to testify on his behalf. His son, Alfred Celestain, Jr., testified that he attended college in Baton Rouge, Louisiana from August 1999 through October 2003, frequently coming home to his father's house both on weekends and during the week. He testified that Thompson was no longer living at the house as of August 2001, but sometimes came by the house to shower and change clothes. He testified that Thompson and his father owned a white vehicle together of which Thompson retained possession after the break-up. Celestain's brother testified that Thompson had ceased living at the property sometime around Mardi Gras in 2001.

The trial court issued judgment on 6 April 2005 and issued detailed reasons for judgment. It awarded Thompson the following credits, totaling $24,042.20: $1,000.00 for the good faith deposit on the house; $13,081.14, representing one-half of the down payment on the property; $682.06 for one mortgage payment on the house; $4,279.00 for windows she had installed at the house; and $5,000.00 for the portion of the VISA credit card bill that Celestain admitted depositing the money to pay, but which he later withdrew from the joint account. The trial court awarded Celestain the following credits, totaling $48,025.60: $13,081.14 (one-half of the down payment); $25,463.60 for mortgage payments from August 2002 through the time of trial; the value of two windows installed at the house, calculated to total $713.17; and home repairs and improvements totaling $8,767.69. The judgment found that Thompson was indebted to Celestain in the amount of $23,983.40, with judicial interest due from the date of demand. It further found that the parties "have agreed to settle the jointly held real property" and conveyed Thompson's undivided interest in the property to Celestain.

Thompson appeals the judgment of the trial court, assigning six errors. Thompson maintains that the trial court erred in 1) ordering the transfer of Thompson's interest to Celestain instead of partitioning the property; 2) alternatively, if the transfer order was proper, failing to require Celestain to reimburse Thompson for her one-half undivided interest; 3) issuing a money judgment in favor of Celestain with interest accruing "from the date of judicial demand" when there was no judicial demand; 4) holding Celestain and Thompson to different evidentiary standards and burdens of proof; 5) requiring Thompson to reimburse Celestain for costs related to the Jacuzzi, when it was installed over her objections; and 6) failing to give Thompson a credit against maintenance costs to offset the benefit derived by Celestain who enjoyed sole use and occupancy of the house from August 2002 on.

Celestain argues that the parties negotiated extensively to divide the movable property between them, transfer title of the residential immovable property to Celestain, and to compensate Thompson for the value of her interest in the property. What was not intended by the parties, according to Celestain, was to proceed to a partition by licitation. Thus, although Celestain admits that the judgment as rendered by the trial court may be flawed in its computation of damages, he contends that it essentially reflects the will of the parties with regard to the disposition of the immovable property. As we discuss *infra*, we do not find this argument persuasive or in accordance with Louisiana law.

Under Louisiana law, a person may not be compelled to own property in indivision with another and may petition a court of competent jurisdiction to partition the property between its owners. La. C.C. art. 807; Ainsworth v. Ainsworth, 03-1626, p. 4 (La. App. 4th Cir. 10/22/03), 860 So. 2d 104, 109. If the property in question is not divisible in kind, such as a house, it must be partitioned by licitation and put up for sale at public auction. La. C.C. art. 811. The parties may agree, however, to a private sale at any time before the auction is held. La. C.C.P. art. 4607. Once the property is sold, the co-owners are entitled to a portion of the proceeds equal to their ownership share in the property, and further share according to their ownership interest in the liability for any mortgages or encumbrances on the property. La. C.C. art. 815.

The law does not, however, provide for the result reached by the trial court in this matter. In the absence of an agreement to privately sell the property or other stipulation regarding its ownership and transfer, the trial court was bound as a matter of law to order the property sold at auction with the proceeds to be divided between Thompson and Celestain, taking into account the credits and liabilities each party was entitled to with regard to the property. If, as Celestain argues, the parties intended for him to acquire Thompson's one-half undivided interest in the property with compensation to her for her interest, they may confect such an agreement prior to public sale. However, the evidence in the record on appeal does not preponderate to show that such an agreement was made, and an agreement to sell property in lieu of partition must be "definite and certain." Ainsworth v. Ainsworth, 860 So. 2d at 109, citing, Walker v. Chapital, 218 La. 663, 50 So. 2d 641 (1951). Otherwise, the trial court is bound to follow the Code of Civil Procedure and effect a partition by licitation. Because the trial court failed to follow the procedure outlined in the Code of Civil Procedure, it prematurely determined the amounts of reimbursements owed. Therefore, we vacate the judgment of the trial court and pretermit ruling on the remaining assignments of error.

As such, the judgment of the trial court is vacated and this matter is remanded to the trial court to proceed in accordance with law. Vacated; remanded.

MURRAY, J. (concurring). I agree that the trial court's judgment must be vacated in its entirety because the trial court made its factual findings in the context of ordering the transfer of one co-owner's interest in the property to the other co-owner, which transfer is not authorized by the law. However, I concur to emphasize that this court has not determined that the individual factual findings made by the trial court are manifestly erroneous, only that they were, as the majority states, "prematurely" made. Therefore, upon remand, the trial court may legitimately choose to reaffirm any of its prior factual findings that are not in conflict with partition of the property, which this court has determined to be the proper result in this case. Accordingly, I respectfully concur in the result.

NOTE
Comparison to Community Property Judicial Partition

If the parties in the preceding case had been a married couple living in community, judicial partition of their assets and liabilities would have been governed by La. R.S. 9:2801, a special partition statute applicable to spouses in a community property regime. Under that statute, the judge is empowered to allocate or assign community property to the spouses, and may even "order the parties to draw lots for the asset." La. R.S. 9:2801(A)(4)(e).

For another recent case examining the differences between the community property rules that govern spouses and the co-ownership rules that govern unmarried cohabitants, see Troxler v. Breaux, 105 So. 2d 944 (La. App. 5th Cir. 2012) (male cohabitant loses claim for items he purchased for female cohabitant's house).

BEN GLAZER COMPANY, INC. v. THARP-SONTHEIMER-THARP, INC.
491 So. 2d 722 (La. App. 4th Cir. 1986)

LOBRANO, J. On June 17, 1983, Jayne Album Glazer passed away. Her husband, Meyer Glazer, made arrangements to have her buried next to his mother and father in the family burial plot at the Gates of Prayer Cemetery in New Orleans. On June 19, 1983, Mrs. Glazer was interred.

Shortly thereafter, Abe Glazer, Harry Glazer, Pearl Glazer Horowitz (Meyer Glazer's siblings) and Ben Glazer, Inc. (collectively referred to as plaintiffs) sued Meyer Glazer (defendant) seeking: (1) to have the title to the burial plots recognized in Ben Glazer, Inc.; (2) to have the remains of Jayne Album Glazer exhumed and moved and (3) monetary damages for the burial without permission. Subsequent amended pleadings sought damages from Tharp Sontheimer Tharp, the funeral home that arranged Mrs. Glazer's funeral. Tharp Sontheimer third partied the Congregation Gates of Prayer, Inc., custodian of the cemetery grounds.

The trial court held that the burial plots were owned in indivision by the Glazer children (not the corporation) and ordered a partition by licitation. Tharp Sontheimer and the Congregation Gates of Prayer, Inc. were dismissed. The court reserved ruling on the issue of damages until after the ownership issue becomes final.

Meyer Glazer appeals contending that the partition should be in kind rather than by licitation. Plaintiffs filed an untimely answer to the appeal contending Ben Glazer, Inc. should be recognized as owner of the burial plots and seeking reversal of the dismissal of Tharp Sontheimer.***

The trial court's judgment ordered the partition by licitation of all seven burial plots, including the two occupied by the parents of plaintiffs and defendant. Presumably a sale to a third party of these plots could necessitate the exhuming of the remains of the person buried in those plots.

Exhumation is against public policy, is not favored in the law and should only be done on a showing of good cause. *Travelers Insurance Co.* v. *Welch,* 82 F.2d 799 (C.A. 5th, 1936); *Nolan* v. *Nolan,* 125 So. 2d 792 (La. App. 4th Cir. 1961). This Court will endeavor to follow public policy and reach a result which will allow the mortal remains of those buried in the subject plots to remain in their final resting place.***

Although we can understand the dilemma, and perhaps frustration of the trial judge in deciding this case, we nevertheless are of the opinion his judgment was in error.

There are seven burial plots, three of which are occupied. Two of the three contain the remains of the plaintiffs' and defendant's mother and father. The other contains the remains of defendant's wife. We would assume that the parties did not intend to partition the plots where their mother and father are buried. In any case, we decide that Civil Code Article 1303 [Revised Civil Code art. 808] prohibits the partition of those two plots because their use is indispensable to all of the owners in paying respects to their parents, and possibly religious worship.

Given the public policy against exhumation, the remaining five plots (including the one containing the remains of defendant's wife) should be partitioned in kind. However there are four co-owners, making that difficult, but not impossible. We decree that title to the plot containing the remains of defendant's wife be vested in defendant, Meyer Glazer. We decree that plaintiffs, Abe Glazer, Harry Glazer and Pearl Glazer Horowitz be vested with the title to one vacant plot each. The remaining plot, owned by all in indivision is not susceptible to being divided in kind, and therefore a partition by licitation of said plot is ordered.

Since we are unable to determine from the record which plots are occupied, and which are not, we remand to the trial court to make that determination and render a judgment in accordance with the opinion expressed herein. This matter is also remanded for a determination of damages, if any, that may be due plaintiffs because of the burial of Meyer Glazer's wife.

NOTE
Article 808—Indispensable Use of Co-owned Thing

In the preceding case, the court invoked pre-revision article 1303 [Revised C.C. article 808] as authority for rejecting a demand to partition the two plots where the co-owners' parents were buried. While it cannot be denied that the outcome reached by the court is just, the court was really applying Article 1303 by analogy because the text of the article as it then provided did not expressly support the court's ruling. Article 1303, the predecessor to article 808, had provided: "There can be no partition, when the use of the thing held in common is indispensable to the coheirs, to enable them to enjoy, or to derive an advantage from the portion of the effects of the succession falling to them, such as a passage to several houses, or a way common to several estates, and other things of the same kind."

The Louisiana Supreme Court had occasion to interpret article 1303 [Revised Civil Code art. 808] in one case, *Vuskovich* v. *Thome,* 498 So. 2d 1072 (La. 1986). That case was an action for partition of property (C-7) owned by two co-owners that was adjacent to two other parcels owned by one of the co-owners (C-8 and C-9). The trial court invoked article 1303 as authority for rejecting the partition demand. The supreme court reversed. Here is the court's analysis:

> Article 1303 [Revised Civil Code art. 808] has never been judicially interpreted. The article by its terms requires two elements: (1) the property sought to be partitioned must be owned in common, and (2) the common ownership must be indispensable to the enjoyment of other properties by the co-owners.***

> The trial judge's decision to apply Article 1303 [Revised Civil Code art. 808] was based on the theory that the common use of Lot C-7, C-8 and C-9, because of the peculiar configuration of the lots, was indispensable to the co-proprietors. However, Lots C-7, C-8 and C-9 were not *owned* in common, Lots C-8 and C-9 being owned solely by Joseph, and the requirement of common ownership, necessary for a determination of indivisibility of a tract composed of Lot C-7, C-8 and C-9, was missing.

> If Article 1303 [Revised Civil Code art. 808] is applicable to Lot C-7, the only property owned in common, the result is forced indivision in perpetuity. However, forced indivision is intended for things which are destined to the common use of *several* pieces of property. See M. Planiol, Traite Elementaire de Droit Civil § 2501 (Louisiana State Law Institute trans. 1959). When co-owned property is an indispensable accessory for two or more principal estates so that the principal estates are substantially less useful without the common use of the accessory property, the co-owned accessory property cannot be partitioned. 2 Aubry & Rau, Droit Civil Francais § 221(3) (7th ed. 1961, Louisiana State Law Institute trans.). Therefore, in order for Article 1303 to be deemed a bar to the partition of Lot C-7, the perpetual indivisibility of Lot C-7 must be indispensable to the co-owners to enable them to enjoy or to derive an advantage from *other* property. Here, Lot C-7 does not constitute accessory property which is indispensable to the enjoyment of two or more principal estates, and Article 1303 [Revised Civil Code art. 808] is not applicable.

> Furthermore, Article 1303 [Revised Civil Code art. 808] was intended as only a minor restriction on the right to partition. See Comment, Ownership in Indivision in Louisiana, 22 Tul.L.Rev. 611 (1948). Similar to the limitations on partition for fixed periods of time, the limitation expressed in Article 1303 [Revised Civil Code art. 808] should be strictly construed.

Article 808 was invoked in *Ivanhoe Canal Corp.* v. *Bunn,* 694 So. 2d 263 (La. App. 1st Cir. 1995). In that case, partition was sought by one of numerous co-owners of the Milling Tract, property through which the Ivanhoe Canal runs. Opposing the partition was Texaco, a co-owner of the Milling Tract who also held a long-term lease on nearby property (Ivanhoe Marine Base) which it used to support its oil and gas activities in the area. Vessels accessed the Ivanhoe Marine Base by means of the Ivanhoe Canal (pursuant to Texaco's rights a co-owner). Texaco successfully argued that partition of the Ivanhoe Canal was unavailable under article 808 because its use was indispensable to Texaco's enjoyment of the lease of the Ivanhoe Marine Base.

4. MODES OF ACQUIRING OWNERSHIP
Civil Code arts. 517-525; 3506(28)

1(2) PLANIOL, TRAITE ELEMENTAIRE DE DROIT CIVIL 510-512
(an English translation by the Louisiana State Law Institute 1959)

Various Classifications. The modes of acquiring may be classified in more than one way.

This may be done, first of all, according to the extent of the acquisition. From this point of view a distinction is drawn between the modes by universal and those by particular title. It may be done, according to the gratuitous or onerous nature of the mode of acquisition. And finally, it may be done with regard to the moment when the acquisitions are accomplished. Some take place through death and others, inter vivos.

Transmissions by Universal and by Particular Titles. Acquisition takes place by a universal title when it comprises the universality of the patrimony, or at all events, an aliquot part of it, that is to say a fraction as a third, a tenth, etc. It takes place by a particular title, when it applies to one or more given objects, considered individually, regardless of their number.

In universal transmissions, the acquirer or his successors are held for the debts and obligations of their author. He is bound for the entirety, if he has acquired the entire patrimony, or only for a part if he has acquired but a part. The division of the liabilities is in the same proportion as that of the assets. In transmissions by a particular title, the acquirer is not held personally for his debts, to any extent or for any fraction. He can be reached only by the right of following up of a mortgage creditor, exercising a real action against him (Comp. *supra* no. 304). This distinction is the corollary of the idea that a person's debts are a burden, not upon this or that particular piece of property, but upon his patrimony considered as an entirety. In order that there be responsibility for the debts, the acquisition must be of the entirety or of an aliquot part of the patrimony, considered as a juridical universality. The principle is set forth in two important texts. They are Arts. 2092 and 2903. And many are the applications made of this principle.

Acquisitions by Gratuitous And Onerous Titles. The acquisition is made by an onerous title, if the acquirer gives or promises anything in exchange for what he receives. Otherwise, it is made gratuitously. This distinction is of importance from several points of view, as regards the form of the alienation, the capacity of the persons who figure in it, and the question of whether or not disposal may be made of the thing. The repression of illicit or immoral conditions does not take place in the same way in the two kinds of transmissions. See Arts. 900 and 1172.

A. N. YIANNOPOULOS, LAW OF PROPERTY
Encyclopedia Britannica (1974)

Property rights may be acquired in a variety of ways: by the occupancy of things that belong to no one, by transfer from a previous owner or even by a nonowner, by operation of law, by the effect of judgments, and by acts of public authorities. For systematic purposes, distinction may be made between *original* and *derivative* acquisition of property rights. An original acquisition involves the creation of a new property right; it is independent of any pre-existing rights over the same thing. A derivative acquisition involves a transfer of a pre-existing right from one person to another.

The distinction between the two modes of acquisition of property rights is important in the light of the maxim, prevailing in most legal systems, that no one can transfer a greater right than one has. This means that, ordinarily, the transferor must be owner and must transfer the property as it may be burdened with rights of third persons. In a number of contemporary legal systems, the scope of the maxim has been narrowed by exceptions. Thus, under the laws of France and Germany, property rights in movables that are neither lost nor stolen may be transferred by a nonowner to a good-faith purchaser for value.

In American jurisdictions, analogous results have been reached by a so-called bona fide (good-faith) purchaser doctrine. Lands, as a rule, must be transferred by the true owner; yet, by way of exception, a good-faith purchaser may be protected in several legal systems if he has relied on entries in land registers or other public records. These problems do not arise in cases of original acquisition of property rights.

Original Acquisition. There is a variety of original modes of acquisition of property rights. For the purposes of this article, attention may be focused on occupancy, finding, accession, acquisitive prescription, expropriation, and the establishment of property rights by acts of public authorities.

Occupancy. Occupancy — namely, the taking of possession of things that belong to no one is perhaps universally recognized. In Roman law things without owner became the property of the first possessor. In contemporary legal systems, this mode of acquisition of property rights is largely limited to movable things, such as wild animals, birds, fish, and abandoned chattels. In times past, lands could also be acquired by mere occupancy or cultivation in various parts of the world; today, however, as a rule, the acquisition of property rights in lands is subject to license or grant by the state, which is supposed to hold title to all unclaimed lands. Akin to occupancy is the finding of lost things and the trove of a treasure. Lost things have an owner, but laws in various jurisdictions ordinarily attribute ownership to the finder after the lapse of a certain period of time or upon the completion of certain formalities, such as advertisements or reports to the authorities. Likewise, laws provide for the apportionment of a treasure trove between the finder and the owner of the property in which the treasure was hidden.

Accession. Accession is another broadly recognized mode of acquisition of property rights. It is based on the principle that the ownership of a thing, either movable or immovable, carries with it the right to whatever the thing produces and to certain other things that are united with it, whether naturally or artificially. Thus, the fruits of the earth, whether spontaneous or cultivated, and the increase of animals belong to the owner by right of accession. The ownership of the land carries with it the ownership of all that is directly above and under it, unless the contrary is established by provision of law or contract; therefore, buildings and other constructions erected by trespassers on the land of another become the property of the landowner. Detailed provisions in various legal systems deal with accession to movables, which, apart from the increase of animals, ordinarily takes place in cases of joining materials belonging to different owners; mixing grains or fluids; and, in cases of production of new things, bestowing labor on the materials of another person.

Acquisitive prescription. Acquisitive prescription, a civil law method of acquisition, is predicated on the possession of a thing over a designated period of time with the intention to own it. Acquisition of property rights in immovables ordinarily requires a longer period of possession than the acquisition of property rights in movables. The required period of time may also vary with the nature of possession; a good-faith possessor ordinarily acquires property rights in a shorter period of time than a bad-faith possessor. In common law jurisdictions, the institution of "adverse possession" performs the same function as acquisitive prescription. Technically adverse possession extinguishes the right of the previous owner and bars his remedy against the possessor; it does not confer title upon the adverse possessor. In all legal systems today, however, those in adverse possession are equally well protected and are able to transfer their rights to their heirs or administrators and such.

Expropriation. Expropriation of property for purposes of public utility, with or without compensation, is known in all contemporary legal systems. Even when made without compensation, expropriation is distinguishable from confiscation, the taking of property by the authorities arbitrarily or as a penalty for the violation of law. Ordinarily, constitutional provisions and other legislative texts insist upon notice and the payment of an adequate, fair, or just compensation to the owner for the expropriation to be valid, in effect, expropriation is made in favor of the state, its political subdivisions, or private utilities enjoying the so-called power of eminent domain because of the services they render to the general public. The possibility of expropriation in all legal systems indicates that property rights are not absolute.

Privileges conferred by public authorities. Finally, an original acquisition of property rights occurs when public authorities confer upon certain persons entirely new economic privileges or recognize privileges that had existed in fact but not in law. Examples are grants of property rights to lands of the public domain, including ownership and rights for exploitation of mineral resources; grants for the exploitation of natural resources, such as hydroelectric energy or radio waves; and patents, registered designs, trademarks, trade names, and copyright, which form so-called industrial or intellectual property.

Derivative acquisition. All legal systems establish methods for the acquisition of property rights by transfer from a previous owner. The transfer may be voluntary, as in the case of a last will and testament or an agreement between the previous owner and the transferee; it may be involuntary, as in the case of a judicial sale; or it may take place by operation of law, as in the case of intestate succession.

Sale. One of the most prevalent modes of acquisition of property rights is by the contract of sale. A sale involves the transfer of a thing for a sum of money or the promise of a sum of money; if the transfer is for something other than money, the transaction is technically designated as exchange. In legal systems of the French family and in common law jurisdictions, the contract of sale transfers the ownership of the things sold. Insofar as third persons are concerned, however, transfer of ownership may depend on delivery of movables or the recording of the title of immovables. In Roman law and in systems following the German Civil Code, however, the contract of sale merely involves a promise to transfer the peaceable possession of the thing sold; the actual transfer of property rights may depend on delivery or on compliance with certain formalities. In most legal systems, contracts of sale are free of any formalities and may be based on verbal agreement, but the rules of evidence may exclude the proof of certain verbal contracts if the object exceeds a specified value. Moreover, in most contemporary systems, the sale of immovable property must be recorded, either for its validity against third persons or for the actual transfer of rights.

Donation. Another prevalent mode of acquisition of property rights is by donation. Donations may be *inter vivos,* intended to take effect while the donor and the donee are living, or *mortis causa* that is, in contemplation of death. Donations of all sorts are ordinarily subject to strict requirements of form intended to ensure that their execution and the intent of the donor are genuine. *Mortis causa* donations are ordinarily contained in last wills and testaments, which must be executed everywhere in strict compliance with the requisite formalities. Formal requirements are usually dispensed with in cases in which the possession of tangible movables is transferred to the donee. As in the case of sales, the transfer of property rights may be effective as between the donor and the donee upon completion of a donation or it may require for its effect the delivery of movables and the recording of necessary documents.

Judicial sale. Another prevalent mode of acquisition of property rights is by judicial sale. Judicial sales take place in a variety of circumstances, such as in cases when the property of an insolvent debtor is seized and sold for the satisfaction of his creditors, when property is sold by the state or by its political subdivisions for the payment of tax claims, when property is judicially partitioned among co-owners, or when inherited property or that of a minor is sold by an administrator or tutor. Provisions of law ordinarily establish the requisite formalities and rules of substance for the validity of a judicial sale. As a derivative mode of acquisition, the judicial sale transfers to the acquirer only the property rights that the previous owner had.

Intestate succession. Finally, derivative acquisition of property rights takes place by operation of law in cases of intestate succession; that is, when a person dies without leaving a will. Rules of law in developed as well as primitive legal systems determine which rights are heritable and specify the order of succession, which varies with the culture and the structure of society. In Socialist legal systems, the devolution of property by inheritance tends to be restricted. In most other modern legal systems, death taxes have, to some extent, restricted the devolution of large fortunes, but the right of inheritance remains one of the fundamental precepts of law.

In civil law systems, the legal heirs of a deceased person are supposed to continue the "personality" of the deceased and to succeed to all of his rights and obligations that are considered to be heritable. Moreover, certain close relatives whether descendants, ascendants, or surviving spouses are entitled to a forced share of the estate, even against the will of the deceased. In common law systems, the property of an intestate is placed under the authority of an administrator who pays all debts and charges and who puts the legal heirs into possession upon completion of the administration. Although the concept of a forced share is foreign to common law, the children and surviving spouse share the estate of one who dies intestate. Modern legislation in a number of common law jurisdictions has also granted the spouse a right to elect what the law would allow her in the case of intestacy rather than accept the provisions of an unfavorable will.

NOTE
Louisiana's Bona Fide Purchaser Doctrine

Ownership of a movable is transferred voluntarily by a contract between the owner and a transferee purporting to transfer ownership. La. Civ. Code art. 518. The transfer is effective between the owner and the transferee according to their agreement. The transfer affects third parties when possession of the movable has been delivered to the transferee. Two consequences of this rule are spelled out in the article.

I.   If X sells a movable thing to Y but does not deliver, then X sells the same thing to Z and does deliver, Z owns the thing if he or she was in good faith, because the transfer by X to Y was not effective against Z.

II.   If M sells a movable thing to N but does not deliver, creditors of M can seize the thing while it remains in M's possession, because the transfer by M to N is not effective against M's creditors, who are third parties to that transfer.

In the situation where A conveys ownership of a movable thing to B, and delivers the thing to B, and B thereafter conveys ownership of that thing to C, and delivers it to C, article 518 would certainly appear to apply. However, A might not have been the true owner, which renders article 518 inapplicable. Or it might be that B conned A out of the thing, which renders uncertain the applicability of article 518. The Louisiana judiciary has evolved a doctrine to resolve disputes between A and C in these types of cases. This doctrine is often called the bona fide purchaser doctrine.

Under this doctrine, which is subject to exceptions, the relative innocence/negligence of A and C is determined, and ownership is awarded to the party who was less negligent. In the 1979 revision of this title, Louisiana's bona fide purchaser doctrine was overhauled and modified significantly. The key article in the revision was article 520, which provided for a "possession is title" rule. It had said: "A transferee in good faith for fair value acquires the ownership of a corporeal movable, if the transferor, though not the owner, has possession with the consent of the owner, as pledgee, lessee, depositary, or other person of similar standing." In the 1980 legislative session, article 520 was suspended, and in 1981 it was repealed.

The remaining articles have been left intact, resulting in an incomplete regulation of the topic. The general rule has been repealed while the exceptions and special rules have remained. The Code thus provides the following special rules for lost and stolen things, sales tainted by vices of consent, and sales of registered movables.

1. *Lost and stolen things.* If a thing is lost or stolen, the person having possession of it cannot transfer its ownership to another. The word "stolen" has its own definition in this context. Stolen means the true owner did not consent to the possession by another. Stolen does not mean the true owner voluntarily transferred ownership to another as a result of fraud. La. Civ. Code art. 521. Thus, if *D* loses a thing and *E* finds it, and *E* thereafter sells the thing to *F*, *D* will win because of article 521. The same result obtains if *E* steals the thing from *D*). Of course, the rule of article 521 is subject to the laws of acquisitive prescription.

There is an exception to the above rule. If a lost or stolen thing has been sold by authority of law, then the person to whom the thing was sold by authority of law will prevail against the former owner. La. Civ. Code art. 524. When the owner is able to recover the lost or stolen thing from the transferee (*i.e.,* in all cases except when it has been sold by authority of law), the owner must reimburse the transferee his or her purchase price if the transferee bought the thing in good faith from a merchant who customarily sells such things. La. Civ. Code art. 524.

2. *Vice of consent.* If an owner of a thing transfers ownership to someone ("transferor") in a transaction tainted with a vice of consent, and that someone thereafter transfers ownership to a third party ("transferee"), the third party gets ownership of the thing if he is in good faith and has paid fair value for the thing. La. Civ. Code art. 522. Good faith exists unless the third party "knows, or should have known, that the transferor was not the owner." La. Civ. Code art. 523.

Remember that fraud was expressly excluded from the category of lost and stolen things regulated by article 521. Fraud is covered by article 522, since fraud is one of the vices of consent. Vices of consent are the subject of chapter 4 of title IV of book III (arts. 1948-1965). Thus, if *S* sells his ring to *T* on credit, because *T* convinces *S* that *T* is really *X*, a rich woman, and if *T* thereafter sells the ring to *U* who is in good faith and pays fair value (*i.e,* is a bona fide purchaser), *U* will gets ownership over *S*.

3. *Registered movables.* Article 525 provides: "The provisions of this Chapter do not apply to movables that are required by law to be registered in public records." This article made more sense prior to the repeal of article 520, as the article envisions an exception to the "possession is title" rule of article 520. Without article 520, article 525 is unclear. Some cases have required the furnishing of a certificate of title for a valid transfer of a registered movable, but the cases are not all consistent.

4. *The general rule.* With the repeal of article 520, the Code does not have a general rule for cases covered by former article 520 and not covered by the special rules which remain. The pre-revision jurisprudence ought to remain relevant, under which the relative innocence/negligence of the two parties is weighed, and ownership is awarded to the less negligent party. However, at least one court of appeal has extended article 524 to situations that that would have been covered by repealed article 520. See Louisiana Lift & Equipment, Inc. v. Eizel, 770 So. 2d 859 (La. App. 2d Cir. 2000).

AUTOCEPHALOUS GREEK-ORTHODOX CHURCH OF CYPRUS v.
GOLDBERG & FELDMAN FINE ARTS, INC.
717 F. Supp. 1374 (S.D. Ind. 1989)

NOLAND, District Judge. In this case the Court is asked to decide the right of possession as between the plaintiffs, the Autocephalous Greek-Orthodox Church of Cyprus ("Church of Cyprus") and the Republic of Cyprus, and the defendants, Peg Goldberg ("Goldberg") and Goldberg & Feldman Fine Arts, Inc., of four Byzantine mosaics created in the early sixth century. The mosaics, made of small chips of colored glass, were originally affixed to and for centuries remained in a church in Cyprus, a small island in the Mediterranean. In 1974, Turkish military forces invaded Cyprus and seized control of northern Cyprus, including the region where the church is located. At some point in the latter 1970s, during the Turkish military occupation of northern Cyprus, the mosaics were removed from their hallowed sanctuary. The plaintiffs claim that the Church of Cyprus has never intended to relinquish ownership of the mosaics, that the mosaics were improperly removed without the authorization of the Church or the Republic of Cyprus, and that the mosaics should be returned to the Church. The defendants, on the other hand, claim that export of the mosaics was authorized by Turkish Cypriot officials, and that in any event Goldberg should be awarded the mosaics because she purchased them in good faith and without information or reasonable notice that they were stolen.

The Court concludes that because the place where the mosaics were purchased, Switzerland, has an insignificant relationship to this suit, and because Indiana has greater contacts and a more significant relationship to this suit, the substantive law of the state of Indiana should apply to this case.

I. HISTORICAL SETTING AND FACTUAL BACKGROUND

The facts established by the evidence presented are as follows:

A. The Mosaics of the Church of the Panagia Kanakaria

This case involves a dispute as to the ownership of four Byzantine mosaics. These four mosaics were originally part of a larger mosaic ("the original mosaic"). The original mosaic was affixed to the apse of the Church of the Panagia Kanakaria ("Kanakaria Church") in the village of Lythrankomi, Cyprus, in 530 A.D. Except for a unique quirk of fate, the original mosaic would have ceased to exist a thousand or more years ago. During the period of Iconoclasm (roughly the 8th century), government edicts mandated the destruction of religious artifacts so that such religious "images" would not be the subject of veneration. These iconoclast edicts were responsible for the destruction of religious artifacts so that such religious "images" would not be the subject of veneration. These iconoclast edicts were responsible for the destruction of many significant religious artifacts. The original Kanakaria mosaic is one of only six or seven Byzantine mosaics to survive the ravages of Iconoclasm and the passage of time.

The original Kanakaria mosaic depicted Jesus as a young boy seated in the lap of his mother, the Virgin Mary, who sat on a throne surrounded by a mandorla of light. The figures of Jesus and the Virgin Mary were bordered on each side by depictions of two archangels. This central composition was in turn bordered by a frieze containing the busts of the twelve apostles. The original mosaic was made of small pieces of colored glass referred to in the art world as tesserae.

As stated previously, the original mosaic was affixed to the apse of the Kanakaria Church in the early sixth century. Over the centuries, the mosaic has deteriorated. By 1960, all that remained of the original Kanakaria mosaic was the figure of Jesus, the bust of the North Archangel, and nine of the twelve apostles. Between 1959 and 1967, the mosaic was cleaned and restored under the sponsorship of the Department of Antiquities of the Republic of Cyprus, the Church of Cyprus, and Harvard University's Dumbarton Oaks Center for Byzantine Studies. With the knowledge gained in its efforts to restore the mosaic, Dumbarton Oaks published an authoritative volume on the Kanakaria Church and its art: The Church of the Panagia Kanakaria at Lythrankomi in Cyprus: Its Mosaics and Frescoes, authored by A.H.S. Megaw and E.J.W. Hawkins (1977).

The four mosaics at issue in this case were once a part of the original Kanakaria mosaic. These four mosaics depict the figure of Jesus as a young boy and the busts of the North Archangel, the apostle Matthew, and the apostle James. Each of the four mosaics measures approximately two feet by two feet.

This brief background enables one to understand the origin of the four mosaics at issue in this case and their invaluable and irreplaceable significance to Cyprus's cultural, artistic, and religious heritage. Had it not been for an unusual series of events, these four mosaics would probably have remained in the Kanakaria Church to this day — undisturbed in their deteriorating but readily recognizable state.

B. The Partition of Cyprus

Cyprus is an island located in the Mediterranean. The island covers 3,572 square miles and is smaller than the state of Connecticut. The population of Cyprus is approximately 696,000. The Cypriot population is comprised mainly of persons of either Greek or Turkish descent. Today, approximately 79 percent of the population is made up of persons of Greek descent, and approximately 18 percent of the population is made up of persons of Turkish descent. Historically, Greek Cypriots follow the Greek Orthodox faith; Turkish Cypriots follow the Muslim faith.

Cyprus was a British colony from 1878 to 1960, at which time it became an independent republic. In 1963, civil disturbances broke out between Greek Cypriots and Turkish Cypriots. United Nations peacekeeping forces were sent to Cyprus to restore order in 1964. The U.N. forces have remained in Cyprus even since.

On July 20, 1974, Turkish military forces invaded Cyprus. Turkish troops landed on the north coast of Cyprus and advanced to Nicosia. By late August, the Turkish forces had extended their control over the northern 37 percent of the island. This region has remained under Turkish military occupation since the invasion.

After the invasion, the Turkish military established in essence a puppet government in northern Cyprus called the "Autonomous Cyprus Turkish Administration." That government was succeeded in February 1975 by the "Turkish Federated State of Cyprus." In 1983, the Turkish Federated State of Cyprus was succeeded by the "Turkish Republic of Northern Cyprus." The Turkish Republic of Northern Cyprus is recognized as a legitimate government by only one nation in the world: Turkey. It is not recognized, nor has it ever been recognized, by the United States government. The United States government recognizes only the plaintiff Republic of Cyprus as the legitimate government of all the people of Cyprus.

The Kanakaria Church is located in the village of Lythrankomi, which is in an area of northern Cyprus now under Turkish military occupation. After the 1974 invasion, the Greek Cypriot population of Lythrankomi was "enclaved" by Turkish military forces. During this time the Greek Cypriots were denied many basic human rights, including freedom of movement, medical care, and the ability to earn a living. Many men from the village were arrested and detained in Turkish jails; there they received severe beatings by Turkish soldiers.

Despite the hardships that fell on the Greek Cypriot parishioners of the Kanakaria Church, religious services continued to be conducted in that church on a regular basis. In July 1976, the pastor of the Kanakaria Church, Father Antomis Christopher, was forced to flee to non-occupied southern Cyprus for fear of his life. The church itself was not physically damaged between the invasion in July 1974 and Father Christopher's departure in July 1976. By the end of 1976, all Greek Cypriots in Lythrankomi had vacated the village and had relocated to southern Cyprus, which is controlled by the plaintiff Republic of Cyprus. Their departure from northern Cyprus was not voluntary.

C. The Theft of the Mosaics

Since the 1974 Turkish invasion, the government of the Republic of Cyprus and the Church of Cyprus have generally been denied access to occupied northern Cyprus. However, since that time they have received reports from persons in the occupied area that several churches and national monuments have been looted and destroyed and that many mosaics, frescoes, and icons of those churches and national monuments have been stolen or destroyed. When Father Christopher fled occupied northern Cyprus in July 1976, the mosaics were still intact and affixed to the apse of the Kanakaria Church. Sometime between August 1976 and October 1979, the interior of the Kanakaria Church was vandalized and the mosaics were forcibly removed from the apse of the church. The mosaics were severely damaged during their removal. Neither the Republic of Cyprus nor the Church of Cyprus has ever authorized the removal or sale of the Kanakaria mosaics.

D. Cyprus's Efforts to Recover the Mosaics

As previously noted, since the Turkish invasion in 1974, the Republic of Cyprus has learned of the theft or destruction of much cultural property in Cyprus. Many churches, museums, and private collections have been looted, and other property has suffered destruction or loss. In some instances visitors who were allowed access to the occupied area would note such losses and report them to the Republic of Cyprus. It was through one such visitor that the Department of Antiquities first learned in November 1979 that the mosaics of the Kanakaria Church were missing. The Department is charged with the responsibility, among other things, of protecting church property which is either an antiquity or a national monument. The mosaics fall under this responsibility. Therefore, the Republic of Cyprus decided to seek recovery of the mosaics.***

E. The Mosaics Resurface

Goldberg is president and majority shareholder of Goldberg & Feldman Fine Arts, Inc. The co-owner of the company is George Feldman who serves as its vice president. Since becoming an art dealer in 1981, Goldberg has dealt almost exclusively in 19th and 20th century paintings, etchings, and sculptures. Goldberg is not, nor does she claim to be, an expert in Byzantine art.

On June 30, 1988, Goldberg flew to Amsterdam, The Netherlands, to inspect and possibly purchase for a client a painting by Amadeus Modigliani. The availability of a Modigliani painting for sale was brought to Goldberg's attention by Robert Fitzgerald, an art dealer from Indianapolis whom she "had known casually since 1980 or '81." Tr. 433. It was Fitzgerald who had located the purported Modigliani; he was to help facilitate the sale. In Amsterdam, Goldberg met Fitzgerald. Fitzgerald then took Goldberg to meet the owner of the painting. After inspecting the painting, Goldberg developed doubts "about being able to prove the authenticity of the painting." Tr. 438. At this point, the sale of the Modigliani painting fell through.

After the Modigliani sale fell through, Fitzgerald mentioned to Goldberg another deal. On July 1, 1988, Fitzgerald informed Goldberg that he was aware of four early Christian mosaics that were for sale. Later that day, Fitzgerald introduced Goldberg to Michel van Rijn, a Dutch art dealer, and Ronald Faulk, an attorney from California. Goldberg knew very little about van Rijn or Faulk. She was told, however, that van Rijn was once convicted in France for forging Marc Chagall's signature to prints of that artist's work and that he also had been sued by an art gallery "[f]or failure to pay money." Tr. 539. She was also aware that Faulk was in Europe to act as attorney for Fitzgerald and van Rijn.

At this July 1st meeting, van Rijn showed Goldberg photographs of the four Byzantine mosaics, and she immediately "fell in love" with them. Tr. 447. van Rijn told her that the seller requested $3 million for the four mosaics. She was also told that the seller was interested in selling the mosaics quickly because he "had recently become quite ill and had [a] cash problem." Tr. 457.

After arriving in Geneva, Faulk and Dikman met Goldberg in the free port area of the airport. This was the only time that Goldberg met Dikman. Dikman introduced himself to Goldberg and then left. In the presence of Faulk, Goldberg then inspected the four mosaics. Upon seeing the mosaics, she "was in awe" and wanted to buy them "more than ever." Tr. 486. She was concerned, however, about their deteriorating condition.

Goldberg testified that while she was in Geneva she inquired as to whether the mosaics had been reported as stolen or missing and whether any applicable treaties might prevent the mosaics from being imported into the United States. She testified that she contacted by telephone, the International Foundation for Art Research ("IFAR") in New York and UNESCO's office in Geneva. In addition, Goldberg claims she telephoned customs offices in the United States, Germany, Switzerland, and Turkey.

G. Goldberg Purchases the Mosaics

The sale and transfer of the mosaics was originally scheduled for July 5th; however, a delay in securing financing from Merchants prevented Goldberg from consummating the sale on that date. The $1.2 million from Merchants did not arrive at a bank in Geneva until July 7th. The $1.2 million was in $100 bills and was placed in two carrying bags. Of the $1.2 million, Goldberg kept $120,000 in cash, and gave the remaining $1,080,000 to Faulk and Fitzgerald for the purchase of the mosaics.
On July 8, 1988, Goldberg returned with the mosaics to the United States. Goldberg insured the mosaics for $1.2 million and declared their value at U.S. Customs to be $1.2 million. As previously noted, Goldberg paid $1.08 million for the mosaics.

H. Significant Events in Indiana

Goldberg intended to sell the mosaics. Beginning in the fall of 1988, she contacted at least two people in an attempt to market and sell the mosaics. By October 1988 Goldberg had discussed the sale of the mosaics with Dr. Geza von Habsburg, an art dealer operating out of Geneva and New York. In October of 1988 von Habsburg contacted Dr. Marion True of the Getty Museum in California and discussed whether the Getty would be interested in purchasing the mosaics.

The plaintiffs and their attorneys eventually learned that the mosaics were in Goldberg's possession in Indianapolis. The plaintiffs wrote to Goldberg requesting the return of the mosaics. Upon the defendants' refusal, the plaintiffs instructed their attorneys to file suit to recover the mosaics.***

Under Indiana law, the Court concludes that the plaintiffs have made credible and persuasive showings on the elements necessary for the replevin of personal property. The Indiana cases holding that a thief obtains no title to stolen property recognize a long-standing rule. The cases establish law which increases in precedential value over time. As the plaintiffs have proven their case for replevin, the Court concludes that possession of the mosaics must be awarded to the plaintiff Church of Cyprus.

III.   SWISS SUBSTANTIVE LAW

Assuming, *arguendo,* that Indiana substantive law does not apply in this case, the Court next considers the issues under Swiss law. Under Swiss law, a purchaser of stolen property acquires title superior to that of the original owner only if he purchases the property in good faith. Tr. 19 (von Mehren). A bad faith purchaser of stolen property never acquires title. *Id.* at 20. As Professor von Mehren explained at trial, to conclude that a purchaser did not act in good faith, a court must *either* find that the purchaser actually knew that the seller lacked title, *or* find that "an honest and careful purchaser in the particular circumstances would have [had] doubts with respect to the capacity of the seller to transfer property rights." *Id.* at 24.

Swiss law presumes that a purchaser acts in good faith. *Id.* at 26. However, a plaintiff seeking to reclaim stolen property may overcome this presumption. *Id.* To do so he must show that suspicious circumstances surrounding the transaction which should have caused an honest and reasonably prudent purchaser to doubt the seller's capacity to convey property rights. *Id.* If the plaintiff shows that the circumstances surrounding the transaction should have created such doubt, then the defendant purchaser has the burden of establishing his good faith. A purchaser establishes his good faith by showing that he took steps to inquire into the seller's capacity to convey property rights and that such steps reasonably resolved such doubt. *Id.*

1. Suspicious Circumstances

As previously set forth, under Swiss law, this Court must begin its analysis by presuming that Goldberg purchased the mosaics in good faith. The plaintiffs argue that they have overcome this presumption by showing that suspicious circumstances surrounded the sale of the mosaics sufficient to cause an honest and reasonably prudent purchaser in Goldberg's position to doubt whether Dikman had the capacity to convey property rights. Therefore, plaintiffs contend, Goldberg cannot rest on the presumption that she purchased the mosaics in good faith. The Court agrees. Many suspicious circumstances surrounded the sale of the mosaics.***

Conclusion

Regarding issues of credibility in this case, the Court finds that the evidence and testimony of the plaintiffs is more credible and persuasive. Indeed, in many instances the manner in which the defendants and associated individuals proceeded in this case reflects negatively on the credibility of the defendants' case.

As previously discussed, under Indiana law and in the alternative under Swiss law, defendant Goldberg never obtained good title to or any right to possession of the mosaics. The plaintiffs have made a proper showing in all respects for the return of the mosaics. The Court concludes that under the circumstances of this case, possession of the property at issue, and not money damages in lieu of return of the actual property, is the more appropriate remedy. Accordingly, the Court orders that the mosaics must be returned to the true and rightful owner, the Church of Cyprus.

CHAPTER VI. ACCESSION
Civil Code arts. 483-516

1. FRUITS AND PRODUCIS

See Civil Code arts. 482-489; A. N. YIANNOPOULOS,
CIVIL LAW PROPERTY §§ 26, 271- 274 (4ᵗʰ ed. 2001)

ELDER v. ELLERBE
135 La. 990, 66 So. 337 (1914)

O'NIELL, J. The plaintiff claims an undivided half interest in a tract of land described as the E 1/3 of W 1/2 of section 9, T. 21 N., R. 16 W., containing 160 acres, of which 135 acres is claimed by the defendant Ellerbe, and 25 acres is claimed by and in the possession of the defendant Producers' Oil Company. She also claims of the defendant Ellerbe, half of a certain bonus and of certain royalties received by him from the Standard Oil Company under a mineral lease.***

Judgment was rendered in favor of the plaintiff, recognizing her to be the owner of an undivided half of the entire tract of 160 acres, allowing her to recover from the defendant Ellerbe $10,125 being half of the bonus paid by the Standard Oil Company to Ellerbe for the mineral lease, and the further sum of $1,338.98, being half of the royalties accruing thereafter. Judgment was rendered in favor of Producers Oil Company against Ellerbe, in warranty for $666.67, being half of the purchase price of the 25 acres of the land in dispute. From this judgment all three defendants have appealed; and the plaintiff has answered, praying that the judgment against Ellerbe for $10,125, be increased to twice that sum.

This tract of 160 acres was purchased from the state of Louisiana by Ben Lewis under patent No. 630, dated the 11th of August, 1870. He sold it to C. W. Lewis and John H. Lewis jointly on the 26th of October, 1870. The plaintiff is the only surviving daughter and sole heir of C.W. Lewis, and there is no evidence of his having disposed of his undivided half of this land.***

The defendant Ellerbe contends that, even though the plaintiff be the owner of an undivided half of the land in contest, judgment should not have been rendered against him for half of the bonus and royalty collected from Standard Oil Company before the institution of this suit, because he was a possessor in good faith and was entitled to the fruits of the land.

In other words, the defendant contends that minerals are to be included in the definition of *fruits*. The sense in which the word "fruits" is used in this article of the Code, i.e. "the right which such a possessor has to *gather* for his benefit the fruits," does not suggest the meaning of minerals. It refers to what is produced and reproduced from time to time or in successive seasons. The fruits must be of things that are born and reborn of the soil. Dalloz, Baudry-Lacantinerie, No. 321.

It is well settled that a possessor in good faith must account to the owner of the land for the value of the trees or timber cut and removed from his land. In the case of Rives v. Gulf Refining Co., 133 La. 178, 62 South. 623, oil and gas beneath the surface of the earth, and not confined within a pipe or casing, were decreed to be a part of the realty, not subject to ownership separate from the land. The right of a possessor in good faith to gather for his benefit the fruits of the property of another, cannot be greater than the right of a usufructuary. "He has no right to mines and quarries not opened."

Our conclusion is that the defendant Ellerbe owes the plaintiff one-half of the price he received for permitting the Standard Oil Company to deplete this land of its mineral oil and gas. The fact that the plaintiff might have sued to annul the contract of lease between Ellerbe and the Standard Oil Company in so far as it affects her interest in the property does not defeat her right to recover half of the sum received by Ellerbe for the oil taken from the land owned by the plaintiff and defendant jointly.

We find no merit whatever in the appellee's prayer for an increase of the judgment against the defendant Ellerbe. For the reasons assigned, the judgment appealed from is affirmed at the cost of the appellants.

HARANG v. BOWIE LUMBER CO.
145 La. 95, 81 So. 769 (1919)

O'NIELL, J. This suit was brought to recover the value of forest timber cut and taken by the defendant from a tract of land of which the plaintiffs claim they are part owners. The claim of one of them was adjudged barred by the prescription of one year, and he did not appeal from the judgment. The other plaintiffs obtained judgment for a sum less than they sued for; and from that judgment, the defendant also appeals.***

Having come to the conclusion that the defendant was not the owner of the timber taken from the plaintiffs land, we take up now the only remaining question to be determined; that is, whether a possessor who, in good faith but without a valid title, cuts and takes away forest timber from the land of another, is liable for the value of the timber. We take it for granted — for there is no dispute of the fact — that the defendant was in good faith.***

In Leathem & Smith Lumber Co. v. Nalty, 109 La. 339, 33 South, 354, an erroneous interpretation of Dalloz & Vergefi, under article 550, Code Napoléon (No. 1), is given, to the effect that a possessor in good faith is not answerable to the owner for cutting and taking timber from his land. The French commentators, all excepting Marcadé, agree that it is only the "fruits" of the soil that the possessor in good faith need not account for; and that forest timber is not included in the terms "fruits."***

In Elder v. Ellerbe, we took occasion to say, too, that the right of a possessor in good faith, to gather for his own benefit the fruits or property belonging to another person, was not greater than the right of a usufructuary, in that respect; and that a usufructuary had no right to mines or quarries not opened. In that limitation of the rights of a possessor in good faith, we expressed the opinion of Laurent, and of all other French commentators except Marcadé, on similar provisions of the Code Napoléon.

Our conclusion is that the defendant, who, in good faith, but without a valid title, felled and took away the forest timber from the land of the plaintiffs, is liable for its value to the owners.

So far as the rulings in Banks v. Doughty, Hood v. Stewart, and Leathem & Smith Lumber Co. v. Nalty, relied upon by appellant, are in conflict with this decision; they are now overruled.

The amount of the judgment appealed from is not contested. During the trial, the parties to the suit, reserving all other contentions, admitted the quantity and value of the timber cut and taken by defendant from the land in context. The judgment appealed from is in accord with the admission. Judgment is affirmed.

2. ACCESSION IN RELATION TO IMMOVABLES
Civil Code arts. 490-506, 2695

a. The space above and below
Civil Code art. 490

SWISS CIVIL CODE

Art. 667. Ownership in land and soil reaches above and underneath into the air and the earth so far as the exercise of the ownership requires.

It embraces all buildings and plants as well as springs, subject to the legal restrictions.

LOUISIANA MINERAL CODE

Art. 5. Ownership of solid minerals

Ownership of land includes all minerals occurring naturally in a solid state. Solid minerals are insusceptible of ownership apart from the land until reduced to possession.

Art. 6. Right to search for fugitive minerals; elements of ownership of land

Ownership of land does not include ownership of oil, gas, and other minerals occurring naturally in liquid or gaseous form, or of any elements or compounds in solution, emulsion, or association with such minerals. The landowner has the exclusive right to explore and develop his property for the production of such minerals and to reduce them to possession and ownership.

Art. 8. Landowner's right of enjoyment for mineral extraction

A landowner may use and enjoy his property in the most unlimited manner for the purpose of discovering and producing minerals, provided it is not prohibited by law. He may reduce to possession and ownership all of the minerals occurring naturally in a liquid or gaseous state that can be obtained by operations on or beneath his land even though his operations may cause their migration from beneath the land of another.

b. Artificial accession
Civil Code arts. 491-498

See A. N. YIANNOPOULOS, CIVIL LAW PROPERTY
§§ 275, 276 (4th ed. 2001)

MARCELLOUS v. DAVID
252 So. 2d 178 (La. App. 3d Cir. 1971)

CULPEPPER, J. This is a suit for the return of a building and for damages caused by its wrongful removal from plaintiff's land. The district judge found the building was owned by the defendant, Coralie David, and hence rejected plaintiff's demand for return of the building and damages.....

This litigation arises out of an unusual set of circumstances. The defendant, Mrs. Coralie David, who is 80 years of age, was living alone in a house in the country and desired to move to the town of Breaux Bridge. Her only income was from Welfare and her only possession was this house. She proposed to various members of her family that if one of them would buy a lot in Breaux Bridge and pay for the expense of moving the house to the lot and installing a cesspool and then let her live there rent free for the remainder of her life, she would execute a will leaving the house to the owner of the lot. This proposal was finally accepted by defendant's niece, Gloria Jones Marcellous, wife of the plaintiff, George Marcellous. Plaintiff also agreed to the proposition and purchased two lots in Breaux Bridge to which the house was moved. It was placed on brick pillars, a cesspool was installed and attached to the plumbing, and George Marcellous painted the building. At about the same time, Coralie David executed a will leaving all of her property to plaintiff's wife.

Coralie David lived in the house rent-free for almost two years. During this time she made improvements to the building at a cost of about $1200. In 1969, difficulties arose between Coralie David and her niece. Finally, Mrs. David contacted her brother, Alex Lewis Jean, and requested that be help her move her house from plaintiff's lot. Alex purchased a lot, about two doors away, and had the house moved to it. This suit followed.

Essentially, plaintiff contends that he became the owner of the house when it was moved onto his lot, and that he can recover for its wrongful removal without his consent. On the other hand, defendant, Coralie David, contends she never lost her ownership of the house and had the right to move it.

The first issue to which we will address ourselves is plaintiff's contention that when the house was moved to his lot in Breaux Bridge, installed on brick pillars and a cesspool constructed and connected to the plumbing, it became immovable by nature and its ownership passed to the owner of the lot. Plaintiff cites C.C. Articles 464 and 506 [Revised C.C. arts. 462, 491] and the case of Lighting Fixture Supply Company, Inc. v. Pacific Fire Insurance Company of N. Y., 176 La. 499, 146 So. 35 (1933), for the proposition that buildings are immovable by nature and not susceptible of ownership separate from the land.

The issue is discussed in detail in Yiannopoulos, Civil Law of Property, Sections 43, 46 and 93. Under traditional civilian concepts, the ownership of land was not susceptible of horizontal division. However, Article 506 of the Civil Code of 1870 states that "All the constructions, plantations and works, made on or within the soil, are supposed to be done by the owner, and at his expense, and to belong to him, *unless the contrary be proved.* ***" (emphasis supplied). This language clearly contemplates the ownership of buildings separate from the land. Buildings are presumed to belong to the owner of the soil, but a person claiming the ownership of a building on the land of another can overcome that presumption by proof to the contrary.

The next question is whether Coralie David has sustained her burden of proving that she owned the house which was located on plaintiff's lot. Since she owned the house before it was moved to plaintiff's lot, she remained the owner unless she conveyed it to plaintiff. Plaintiff contends ownership of the house was transferred by an oral donation inter vivos. But buildings are immovable by nature, whether they belong to the owner of the ground or not, Cloud v. Cloud, 145 So. 2d 331 (La. App. 3d Cir. 1962); Meraux v. Andrews, *supra*; Buchler v. Fourroux, 193 La, 445, 190 So. 640 (1939); Yiannopoulos, Civil Law of Property, Section 46. Under C.C. Article 1536 [Revised C.C. art. 1541], every donation inter vivos of immovable property must be by an act passed before a notary public and two witnesses. In the present case, there was no written instrument whatever and hence there was no donation inter vivos of this house. The only thing in writing was the will executed by Coralie David leaving all property of which she died possessed to her niece, Gloria Marcellous. Of course, the will did not take effect since Coralie David is still alive, and, furthermore, the will could be changed by the testatrix at any time before her death, C.C. Article 1469.

Plaintiff also contends this is an onerous donation and that the rules peculiar to donations inter vivos do not apply, since in this case the value of the object given did not exceed by one-half that of the charges and services rendered by the donee, C.C. Article 1526 [Revised C.C. art. 1527]. Even assuming that there was an onerous donation, and that Civil Code Article 1523, [Revised C.C. art. 1526] requiring an act before a notary and two witnesses, does not apply, there remains the fact that the object given in this case was an immovable, the transfer of which must be in writing, C.C. Article 2275 [Revised C.C. arts. 1832, 1839]. There was no written transfer of the house.

We conclude the evidence shows the ownership of the house remained in Coralie David while it was located on plaintiff's lot. In consequence, Coralie David had the right to move the house from plaintiff's lot and his demand for its return and damages must be rejected.

It is noteworthy that the present litigation involves the parties to the transaction and not a third person relying on the public records. Prevot v. Courtney, 241 La. 313, 129 So. 2d 1(1961).....For the reasons assigned, the judgment appealed is affirmed.

GRAFFAGNINO v. LIFESTYLES, INC.
402 So. 2d 742 (La. App. 4th Cir. 1981)

BARRY, J. The trial judge's reasons for judgment present the factual background of this litigation and the basis for judgment which provides in pertinent part:

"This litigation began on August 22, 1974, when A. J. Graffagnino and Donald G. Perez, owners of the property at the corner of 8th Street and Causeway Boulevard in Metairie, filed a petition to enjoin the defendants, Lifestyles, Inc. and Murray P. Holmes, an officer of Lifestyles, from removing or disassembling a structure on the land. The defendants then answered, alleging that the structure is an "O'Dome", a dome-like building on a wooden platform supported by pilings and hooked up to electrical and water connections. The defendant, Murray, later testified at trial that the former owner of the property, Leeand, Inc., had allowed Lifestyles to place this demonstration model of the type of building it sells in return for keeping the grass cut. The defendants further alleged that the building is designed to be portable and therefore movable and its ownership did not pass when ownership of the land passed to the plaintiffs on December 20, 1973.

Defendants also alleged that Leeand had agreed in its arrangement with Lifestyles that it would retain ownership of the O'Dome and the right to remove it at the end of the lease and had informed the plaintiffs of this agreement before plaintiffs had bought the property.

"The defendant also reconvened against the plaintiffs for damages to the structure, which is now destroyed, in the amount of $15,000.00. The defendants also third-partied the former owner, Leeand and its president, Folse Roy, alleging that if the third party defendants had failed to notify the original plaintiffs, specifically the ownership of the structure separate from the land [sic], then the third party defendants are liable to defendants for the amount of their reconventional demand.

"The original plaintiffs' petition for an injunction has become moot since the building has subsequently been destroyed. The only issues now before this court concern the defendants' demands.

"The written act of sale by which Leeand conveyed the land to the plaintiffs on December 20, 1973, describes the property conveyed as 'Six certain lots of ground, together with all the buildings and improvements thereon...'. The property is described in the same manner in the mortgage and conveyance certificates.

"Art. 2276 [Revised C.C. art. 1839] of the La. Civil Code provides that 'neither shall parol evidence be admitted against what is beyond what is contained in the acts nor on what may have been said before, or at the time of making them, or since.' Other than in an action for reformation for mutual mistake, the sole exception to this general rule excluding parol evidence is that uncertain ties or ambiguities in the language may be clarified by parol evidence. Liberty Mutual Ins. Co. v. Ads, Inc., 357 So. 2d 1360 (4th Cir. 1978). In this case the wording of the contract of sale between Leeand and the plaintiffs is clear and unambiguous. Ownership of all buildings and improvements transferred with the land. The terms of the verbal agreement between Leeand and Lifestyles cannot be introduced to vary the terms of the contract of sale.

"It is agreed by all parties that Lifestyles did own the O'Dome and did lease the land from Leeand in July of 1973. Nevertheless, this lease was not recorded and the plaintiffs were not parties to it, so the plaintiffs acquired the property and buildings and improvements thereon free of obligations of the unrecorded lease regardless of the plaintiffs' actual knowledge of the situation. Art. 2276 [1870; now C.C. art. 1839]; McDuffie v. Walker, 125 La. 152, 51 So. 100 (La., 1909); Benoit v. Acadia Fuel & Oil Distributors, Inc., 315 So. 2d 842 (3d Cir. 1975). writ refused, 320 So. 2d 550 (La. 1975); American Creosote Co., Inc. v. Springer, 257 La. 116, 241 So. 2d 510 (La. 1970)."

"Therefore, <u>ownership of the O'Dome passed to the plaintiffs in the act of sale if it was a 'building or improvement', i.e., an immovable</u>. The Court believes that it is an immovable, a 'building or other construction' according to La. C.C. art. 464 (now C.C. art. 463, as revised by acts of 1978, No. 728), and the jurisprudence of this state.

"In Ellis v. Dillon, 345 So. 2d 1241 (1st Cir. 1977), the court held that a mobile home, sitting on its axle, hooked up to electrical wires and water pipes, was an immovable by nature. See the court's reasoning, at P. 1243.

"In Bailey v. Kruithoff, 280 So. 2d 262 (2d Cir. 1975), the court held that a fence was immovable by nature because it was embedded in the ground and because, unlike a movable, it had no identity as a fence when moved; it had identity only when constructed. See the court's reasoning, P. 264.

"While the O'Dome is designed to be portable, it is also designed to withstand storms and high winds. Therefore, when it is in use, it is designed to have a degree of permanency.

"The structure involved in this case was situated on a platform integrated into the ground with pilings. The structure remained so situated on the property for over a year in all kinds of weather, as the defendant, Holmes, testified that it was designed to do. It could be and was designed to be disassembled and transported easily, but it would lose its identity as a result. Furthermore, as the court held in Ellis v. Dillon, *supra*, the courts must determine what is a building or other construction qualifying as an immovable under Art. 464 (now art. 463, revised by Acts 1978, No. 728) in light of the social needs of the time. The O'Dome is designed to be easily portable, yet it is intended to be used as a dwelling. When used as a dwelling it is integrated with the soil and stationary. It is a movable only when disassembled, i.e., not in use. The <u>O'Dome on the plaintiff's property was therefore an immovable and therefore ownership of it passed to the plaintiffs</u> along with the land it occupied in the act of sale of <u>December 20, 1973.</u>

"Therefore, the court will dismiss Lifestyles' demands against A. J. Graffagnino and Donald G. Perez. The court is of the opinion that Leeand, Inc. was well aware of the fact that it did not own the building when it sold the land. Therefore, the court will order Leeand, Inc. to pay to Lifestyles, Inc., $8,000.00 representing the value of the building. <u>The court bases this recovery on the fact that Leeand, Inc. would be unjustly enriched if it was allowed to sell a building that was not their own and keep all the proceeds.</u>"

We agree that plaintiffs' petition for injunctive relief is moot and we fail to find abuse of discretion in the trial judge's determination that the O'Dome structure was immovable. Further, <u>Leeand's lease with Lifestyles was not recorded and plaintiffs were not privy to</u>

the lease, therefore, title to the immovable structure was legally transferred to plaintiffs at the time of the sale with Leeand.

We have difficulty with the lower court's holding that Leeand owes damages to Lifestyles because the O'Dome structure was transferred to plaintiffs when the sale was passed. The record shows that Leeand notified one of the plaintiffs in writing prior to the sale that Lifestyles owned the O'Dome structure, and it is abundantly clear that all parties to this litigation were aware that the O'Dome structure was owned by Lifestyles. Most importantly, Lifestyles was put on notice that Leeand was selling its property to the plaintiffs.

The act of sale included the standard verbiage "....together with all the buildings and improvements thereon...." and Leeand's only fault, if it be considered a fault, was in not noticing this language in the sale nor noting or requesting that the O'Dome structure be specifically excluded in the sale. However, Lifestyles had knowledge that the sale was pending, certainly was aware that its lease with Leeand was not recorded, yet did nothing to protect its acknowledged ownership of the structure. Lifestyles' apparent options included recordation of its written lease, or removal of the structure prior to the sale, or working out an agreement with the plaintiffs. We feel that Lifestyles' failure to protect itself constituted negligence and was the proximate cause for its subsequent loss and conclude that the district court judgment to the contrary was manifest error.

Accordingly, the judgment of the district court awarding damages in favor of Lifestyles, Inc. is reversed and set aside and in all other respects the judgment is affirmed. Costs of the appeal are to be paid by Lifestyles, Inc.

GUZZETTA v. TEXAS PIPE LINE CO.
485 So. 2d 508 (La. 1986)

DIXON, C. J. Plaintiffs-relators are co-owners in indivision of a tract of land on Bayou Lafourche in Lafourche Parish. In 1955 relators or their ancestors in title granted The Texas Pipe Line Company, defendant-respondent, a pipeline right of way for "the right to lay, construct, operate, maintain, inspect, repair, replace, change the size of, and remove a pipe line" for the transportation of oil, gas, petroleum or other substances. The stated consideration in the servitude agreement for the granting of these rights was $250.00.

Defendant constructed an eight inch pipeline running north to south across the plaintiffs' property for a distance of 1,061.90 feet, buried three feet below ground in low, marshy terrain. Around June of 1982 the defendant discontinued using this portion of pipeline. Plaintiffs asked the defendant to remove the pipeline, or to pay the costs of removal estimated at $12,000.00, and defendant refused.

Plaintiffs filed suit against the pipeline company asking for damages amounting to the costs of removal of the pipeline, which has not been removed as of this date. Both the trial court and the court of appeal determined that plaintiffs had no cause of action.

The court of appeal found that the servitude agreement was still in effect, because the agreement contained no applicable term or resolutory condition, and could only be extinguished by ten years nonuse under C.C. 753. Under the still valid agreement, the court noted that only the pipeline company was granted the right to remove the pipeline at its discretion and that accordingly the plaintiffs had no cause of action. We reverse.

The purpose of an exception of no cause of action is to determine the sufficiency in law of the petition. The exception is triable on the face of the papers, and the facts alleged by the plaintiff in the petition must be accepted as true. C.C.P. art. 927, Darville v. Texaco, Inc., 447 So. 2d 473 (La. 1984): Mayer v. Valentine Sugars, Inc., 444 So. 2d 618 (La. 1984); Haskins v. Clary, 346 So.2d 193 (La. 1977).

The general rule is that the exception of no cause of action must be overruled if the allegations of the petition admit to a reasonable hypothesis that the plaintiff has a cause of action for which any relief may be granted under the law. The exception may only be sustained where the allegations of the petition exclude every reasonable hypothesis that plaintiff has a cause of action under any evidence admissible in the pleadings. Darville v. Texaco, supra at 475.

The allegations of plaintiffs' petition do admit to the reasonable hypothesis that plaintiffs have a cause of action for which relief may be granted under the law. Although the cause of action which the petition does support will not provide plaintiffs with the remedy which they prefer, it may provide some relief in their situation. The plaintiffs' petition does not support a cause of action which would permit a suit to compel removal of the pipeline or payment of costs of removal of the pipeline from their property. But the petition does support a cause of action for a declaratory judgment that the servitude held by defendant has terminated, thus freeing their property from this encumbrance and restoring their full ownership of the land.

The court of appeal determined that the servitude agreement was still valid because it did not contain a term or resolutory condition and thus could only terminate upon expiration of a period of nonuse for ten years under C.C. 753. To the contrary, a resolutory condition was included in the contract and whether or not that resolutory condition was met, causing the termination of the servitude, is a factual determination which is not properly before a court on review of an exception of no cause to action.

The allegations of plaintiffs' petition, literally construed, indicate the assertion that defendant's servitude had terminated. Plaintiffs allege that defendant "abandoned" the pipeline, which could have triggered the resolutory clause in the contract: that The Texas Pipe Line Company only retained the rights under the agreement "so long as such pipe lines underground equipment or appurtenances thereof <u>are maintained</u>."[1] Whether or not any "abandonment" of the pipeline or right of way triggered the resolutory clause in the contract, terminating the servitude, is <u>an issue of fact</u> not properly resolved on an exception of no cause of action.

The allegation that the servitude has terminated <u>supports a cause of action</u> for a declaratory judgment that plaintiffs' land is no longer encumbered by this servitude. The allegations of plaintiffs' petition do not support a cause of action for either compelled removal or damages for costs of removal in this case.

Plaintiffs argue that the servitude has terminated, that defendant no longer has the right to keep its pipeline on plaintiffs' property, and that defendant must pay costs of removal of the pipeline since it refused to remove the pipeline on demand.

However, assuming as correct plaintiffs' allegation that the servitude agreement has terminated, in which case the contract between the parties is no longer in effect, Louisiana law provides that <u>ownership of an abandoned pipeline reverts to the owner of the land if the owners refuse to remove it within ninety days of demand</u>. C.C. 493; see also Yiannopoulos, Extinction of Predial Servitudes, 56 Tul. L. Rev. 1285, 1298 n. 88 (1982), citing Breaux v. Rimmer & Garrett, Inc., 320 So. 2d 214 (La. App. 3d Cir. 1975).

C.C. 493, the applicable code Article in this case, provides in part:

> "Buildings, other constructions permanently attached to the ground, and plantings made on the land of another with his consent belong to him who made them. They belong to the owner of the ground when they are made without his consent. When the owner of buildings, other constructions permanently attached to the ground, or plantings no longer has the right to keep them on the land of another, he may remove them subject to his obligation to restore the property to its former condition.

> "If he does not remove them <u>within 90 days</u> after written demand, the owner of the land <u>acquires ownership</u> of the improvements and <u>owes nothing</u> to their former owner."

Plaintiffs' allegation that the pipeline was "abandoned" must be construed in accord with the legal meaning of the word. In other words, plaintiffs are alleging that defendant has given up all <u>rights in relation to the pipeline</u>, and <u>not merely the right to use the pipeline</u>. Under this allegation plaintiffs' argument that the servitude terminated under the

---

[1] 'The term "abandon" has a specific legal meaning indicating more than mere discontinuation of use. C.C. 3418 provides that a "thing is abandoned when the owner relinquishes possession with the intent to give up ownership." Black's Law Dictionary provides that to abandon is "[to] desert, surrender, forsake or cede. To relinquish or give up with intent of never again resuming one's right or ....To give up absolutely; to forsake entirely; to renounce utterly; to relinquish all connection with or concern in; to desert...."

terms in the contract must be taken as true for the purpose of ruling on the exception of no cause of action.

Comment (b) to C.C. 493 points out that the second paragraph in this article fills a gap in the code, which previously had neglected to specify the rights and obligations between the owner of the improvements and the owner of the ground when their legal relationship terminated.[2] This paragraph may apply when a lease expires, when a predial or personal servitude is extinguished, or when a precarious possessor is given notice to vacate. It gives the owner of the improvements the right to remove them, but if he does not do so ninety days after written demand, the owner of the land acquires ownership of the improvements. It does not give the new owner of the improvements the right to compel removal by the old owner, nor to recover payment for the costs of removal.

Plaintiffs erroneously argued that they stated a cause of action to recover the costs of removal of the pipeline under C.C. 495, which provides that the owner of an immovable to which another attaches or incorporates things that become component parts of the immovable may have them removed at the expense of the person who made them. However, this provision only applies to things that become component parts of an immovable, and other constructions permanently attached to the ground are *not* component parts of a tract of land when they belong to a person other than the owner of the ground, as here. See C.C. 495 comment (c), C.C. 493 and C.C. 463. Accordingly, C.C. 495 and the remedy it provides are inapplicable to this case. See also Symeonides, Developments in the Law, 1982-1983: Property, 44 La. L. Rev. 505, 522 (1983). Under C.C. 493, the applicable article, plaintiffs' rights are clear, and they have no right to compel removal or costs of removal of the pipeline.

Plaintiffs would have no cause of action to recover the costs of removal of the pipeline even if the court finds, on remand, that the servitude agreement is still in effect. In such a case, defendant having proved that it had not *abandoned* the pipeline so as to trigger the resolutory condition to maintain the pipeline, but that it had only ceased to *use* the pipeline, the servitude would remain in effect until the actual abandonment of the pipeline or the expiration of ten years of nonuse under C.C. 753. Upon termination of the servitude for ten years nonuse, C.C. 493 would again apply, preventing plaintiffs from recovering costs of removal or compelling removal. Again, after the failure to remove the pipeline within ninety days of written notice, the ownership of the pipeline would revert to the plaintiffs.

---

[2] Even prior to the legislative correction of this oversight in the Civil Code, at least one court reached in part the result dictated by C.C. 493. In Breaux v. Rimmer & Garrett, *supra*, the court of appeal found that after extinction of a servitude, accessories such as a pipeline continue to belong to the owner of the accessories. However, if the property is abandoned, the landowner acquires ownership by accession. The court based this decision on former C.C. 3421 (reenacted without substantive change as C.C. 3418) which provides that: "He who finds a thing which is abandoned; that is, which its owner has let [left with the intention not to keep it any longer, becomes master of it in the same manner as if it had never belonged to anybody.

While plaintiffs cannot obtain the relief they prefer under Louisiana law, they are entitled, under the allegations of their petition, to pursue a suit declaring that the servitude has ended. If successful, this suit will at last unencumber their property and restore them to full ownership of their land.[3]

The judgment of the court of appeal sustaining the exception of no cause of action against plaintiffs is reversed, and the case is remanded to the district court for further proceedings; the liability for costs is to await further proceedings.

LEMMON, J. (concurring). I agree that La. C.C. Art. 493 is more applicable to the present case than La. C.C. Art. 495. However, Article 493 is silent as to the allocation of the cost of removal of constructions permanently attached to the ground, and the court should therefore look to the intention of the contracting parties.

The contract between the parties in the present case is also silent as to the expenses of removal of the pipeline at the termination of the servitude. It is therefore necessary to determine the intent of the parties by implication from the circumstances of the agreement and the conditions generally prevailing at the time.

There is a certain attraction to the idea that parties to a predial servitude generally contemplate that the land will be returned to its original condition at the termination of the servitude. However, the after-the-fact determination of the unexpressed intention of the parties turns on many considerations such as the character of the land at the time of the agreement, the location of the land, the type of construction to be undertaken by the servitude owner, and the effect of the construction on the landowner's ability to use the land at the termination of the servitude.

There is nothing in this case to suggest that any of the parties to the servitude agreement contemplated, at the time of the signing of the agreement, that the pipeline company would ever be expected to remove the pipeline which was to be buried three feet below the surface of the ground in a marshy area. I therefore conclude that plaintiffs are not entitled at the termination of the servitude to require the removal of the pipeline or to recover the cost thereof.

---

[3] This decision, of course, does not affect the duties and powers of the Commissioner of Conservation under R.S. 30:4(E)(2) to investigate and force corrective measures when an abandoned pipeline constitutes a hazard to the public's health or safety.

Symeonides, Developments in the Law, Property
47 La. L. Rev. 429, 444-452 (1986)

ACCESSION AND SERVITUDES

Article 493 of the Louisiana Civil Code provides in part that "[b]uildings, other constructions permanently attached to the ground, and plantings made on the land of another with his consent, belong to him who made them." Until 1984, this article did not provide for the fate of these improvements upon termination of the landowner's consent for their placement on his land. This gap was identified by this author in a previous symposium article which also suggested six alternative ways for judicially filling the gap. One year later, the gap was filled legislatively by Act 933 of 1984 which, among other things, added a new paragraph to Civil Code Article 493. This new paragraph provides that, upon termination of the landowner's consent,

> [t]he person who made the improvements may remove them subject to his obligation to restore the property to its former condition. If he does not remove them within 90 days after written demand, the owner of the land acquires ownership of the improvements and owes nothing to their former owner.

This provision, and Act 933 of 1984 in general, were discussed at length in another symposium article which identified several shortcomings of the new provision. Among other things, it was pointed out that

> [t]he fairness of the new provision depends on such factors as the facility and cost of removing the improvements, their bulk, and their relative value to the two parties. Although many combinations are possible, it seems that *in case of improvements which are valueless, yet costly to remove, the landowner is at the mercy of the builder, since he cannot force removal at the builder's expense.* But in the case of valuable but physically inseparable improvements, the landowner is unjustly enriched since he acquires ownership of the improvements without having to pay reimbursement.

GUZZETTA: THE CASE OF THE UNWANTED PIPELINE

Guzzetta v. Texas Pipe Line Co. involved the very fact pattern envisioned in the italicized portion of the above quotation. The improvement consisted of a pipeline buried in plaintiff's land on the basis of a servitude agreement with the defendant. Although the value of the pipe is not mentioned in the facts, it was presumably much lower than the $12,000.00 estimated cost of removal in 1986, and perhaps not much higher than the $250.00 plaintiff's ancestor had received in 1955 in consideration of the servitude. Asserting that the servitude had expired, the plaintiff landowner sought a judgment for damages amounting to the cost of removal. The court of appeal held that the servitude had not terminated, and consequently, the defendant had the right to keep the pipeline in plaintiffs land. The supreme court held that the servitude could have terminated, but since this was a factual question, it should be decided by the district court, to which the case was remanded for trial on the merits. The supreme court then went on to opine that "assuming as correct plaintiffs' allegation that the servitude agreement has terminated, Louisiana law provides that ownership of an abandoned pipeline reverts to the owner of the land if the owners refuse to remove it within ninety days of demand. C.C. 493.

The court presents this conclusion as flowing inevitably from a straightforward application of Civil Code Article 493. Whether this conclusion is inevitable, however, depends on the answer one gives to the following questions:

(a) whether one should resort automatically to the Civil Code provisions on accession without first scrutinizing the servitude agreement and trying to ascertain the implicit intent of the parties;

(b) whether this case should be decided on the basis of Civil Code Article 496 rather than Article 493; and

(c) whether, despite appearances, Article 493 encompasses improvements which, as in *Guzzetta,* neither party wants.

1. Abandonment and occupancy

Before exploring these questions, a few words may be necessary with regard to a secondary basis for the court's decision. In addition to Article 493, the court relied in part on, or at least cited with approval, *Breaux v. Rimmer & Garret, Inc.* *Breaux* had been based on former Civil Code Article 3421, which provided that "[h]e who finds a thing which is abandoned.becomes master of it in the same manner as if it had never belonged to anybody." In other words, the landowner was held to acquire ownership of the abandoned pipeline by means of occupancy.

It is worth recalling at this point that one of the essential elements of acquisition of ownership by occupancy is the taking of possession of the abandoned thing "*with the intent to own it.*" This requirement was satisfied in *Breaux* and previous decisions on which *Breaux* had relied. If only because they arose at a time when mineral exploration was at a peak and steel was scarce, all these cases involved *wanted,* not unwanted, pipelines. Indeed, the landowners in those cases had taken possession of the abandoned pipelines with the intent to own them. Obviously, this was not true in *Guzzetta,* the first such case of the oil glut era. If it were true that the pipeline company abandoned the pipeline, it was certainly not true that the landowner intended to own it. To forcibly make him the owner of the abandoned pipeline would be a grave misapplication of the law of occupancy.

2. *The intent of the parties*

In connection with the first question raised above, it should be recalled that most of the accession provisions of the Civil Code, and unquestionably the above quoted amendment of 493, are suppletive in character. These articles apply only with the parties have not provided otherwise in their agreement. Consequently, before resorting to Article 493, the agreement must be scrutinized with a view towards ascertaining the parties' intent on the issue of the eventual removal of the pipeline. In *Guzzetta*, the servitude agreement was silent on this issue. Obviously, however, silence does not necessarily entail lack of intent. For, according to Civil Code article 2054, "[w]hen the parties made no provision for a particular situation, it must be assumed that they intended to bind themselves not only to the express provisions of the contract, but also to whatever the law, equity, or usage regards as implied in a contract of that kind." Thus, the court should have first looked to these extra contractual sources, i.e., usages and equity, in order to infer the parties' unexpressed intent on the issue of the removal of the pipeline. Apparently believing it to be either unnecessary or fruitless, the majority did not undertake such an inquiry, either before or after resorting to Article 493.

In a concurring opinion, Justice Lemmon did undertake a similar inquiry, although he did not base it on Civil Code Article 2054. Justice Lemmon began with the assumption that "[A]rticle 493 is silent as to the allocation of the cost of removal of constructions permanently attached to the ground, and the court should therefore look to the intention of the contracting parties." Taken in context, Justice Lemmon's statement that Article 493 is silent on the issue was apparently intended to be confined to unwanted constructions, like the pipeline at stake, as distinguished from wanted constructions. However, as suggested earlier, one should look to the intent of the contracting parties even if Article 493 were not silent on the particular issue.

According to Justice Lemmon the intent of the parties should be determined "from the circumstances of the agreement and the conditions generally prevailing at the time." This determination "turns on many considerations such as the character of the land at the time of the agreement, the location of the land, the type of construction***and the effect of the construction on the landowner's ability to use the land at the termination of the servitude." Conspicuously absent from this indicative enumeration is any reference to the *value* of the construction to the two parties. Finding "nothing in this case to suggest that any of the parties contemplated, at the time of the signing of the agreement, that the pipeline company would ever be expected to remove the pipeline," Justice Lemmon agreed with the majority that the plaintiff landowner had no right to force removal of the pipeline at the defendant's expense.

Although lacking in detail, Justice Lemmon's approach was essentially correct as a matter of law. Because of its flexibility and deliberate vagueness, this approach is also preferable to that of the majority of the court. On the other hand, as a matter of equity, there remain some doubts about the fairness of the ultimate conclusion. Without an opportunity to see and evaluate the record, these doubts cannot be substantiated. Nevertheless, two factors should have been taken into account. The first is the ancient, civilian principle that *ownership is presumed to be free of burdens,* and that such burdens cannot be imposed by mere implication. While it is true that this principle contemplates primarily legal burdens, such as servitudes, it is broad enough to encompass physical burdens as well. Although recognizing "a certain attraction to...[this] idea," Justice Lemmon was apparently not convinced by it.

The second factor is that it is difficult to accept that, in a typical onerous transaction, the average landowner would agree to impose on his land such a heavy legal and physical burden for so little in return. Leaving aside the cost of the legal burden to the servient estate for the duration of the servitude, and discounting for inflation and similar factors, it should not be readily assumed that, for as little as two hundred and fifty 1955 dollars, the landowner would agree to impose on his land a physical burden the removal of which would cost twelve thousand 1986 dollars. The potential inequity of the *Guzzetta* decision becomes even more evident if one also considers the potential environmental hazards accompanying the presence of such a pipeline, not only to the landowner's own land, but also to the adjacent estates. Obviously, these arguments apply with equal force against the majority opinion.

3. Article 493 versus Article 495

Assuming for the moment that this case had to be decided under the law of accession, the second question is whether Article 493 or Article 495 is more pertinent.

The difference in the scope of these two articles has been explained in detail elsewhere. Suffice it to recall for the moment: that Article 493 applies to "buildings, other constructions permanently attached to the ground, and plantings," that is, improvements which, if owned by the landowner are classified as component parts of the land by Article 463, and as separate things by Article 464; that Article 495 applies to "things that become component parts of the immovable under Articles 465 and 466," and that, among them, the most pertinent to the case at hand are those described by Article 465 as "[t]hings incorporated into a tract of land.., so as to become an integral part of it." Thus, the answer to the above question hinges on whether the pipeline is classified as an "other construction permanently attached to the ground," in which case Article 493 would apply, or rather as an "integral part" of the ground, in which case Article 495 would apply.

The plaintiff had argued strenuously for the application of Article 495, which would enable him to have the pipeline removed at the defendant's expense. The court summarily dismissed the plaintiff's argument, reasoning that Article 495 "only applies to things that become component parts of an immovable, and other constructions permanently attached to the ground are *not* component parts of a tract of land when they belong to a person other than the owner of the ground, as here." Thus, without explanation, the court assumed that the pipeline was *not* "incorporated into [the] . . . land so as to become an integral part of it," but was rather in the category of "other constructions permanently attached to the ground." Opinions may reasonably differ as to whether this assumption is technically correct, but this may well be a secondary point in the long run. What is more regrettable in the long run is the loss of a good opportunity for a judicial delineation of the potentially overlapping scope of Article 493 and 463 on the one hand, and 495 and 465 on the other, and, more importantly, for an evaluation of the logic underlying these articles. Had the court engaged in such an evaluation, it would have discovered that there is simply no logic underlying these articles.

This absence of logic becomes more evident when these two groups of articles are juxtaposed, after having been translated into simple English. Here is how they would sound to the layman landowner:

> If a thing is incorporated into your land in such a way as to become an integral part of it, we call that thing a component part of your land (La. Civ. Code art. 465). This means that the thing is yours, whether or not you consented to its incorporation (La. Civ. Code art. 493.1). If, however, you consented to such incorporation, you may force the person who made it to remove the thing at his expense (La. Civ. Code art. 495), although the thing belongs to you and no longer to him.

> On the other hand, if the thing is not so incorporated into your land, but is merely attached to it permanently with your consent, then we do not call that thing a component part of your land (La. Civ. Code art 463, 464, 493 par. 1). Obviously, this means that the thing is not yours (La. Civ. Code art. 493 par. 1). Although it is not yours and you may not want to have it, it may somehow become yours, if the person who put it there does not want to remove it (La. Civ. Code art. 493 par.2 as interpreted in *Guzzetta).*

The layman should not be blamed for feeling perplexed by all of this. Nor should the court be blamed for creating this anomaly, but only for not detecting it. After all, it is a common secret by now that this entire area of the Civil Code resembles a pile of "cans of worms," and this author for one has had the misfortune of opening some of them. *Guzzetta* helps open yet another one.

Now that this anomaly has been revealed, the remaining question is how to eliminate it. A legislative intervention is of course conceivable, but, as with the last one, there is no guarantee that it will not lead to new anomalies. Thus, the only remaining avenue and the only one available to a court is judicial interpretation. This brings us back to *Guzzetta.* Since Article 495 was found inapplicable there, could not the problem be resolved judicially by a "creative" application or non-application of Article 493? This question is addressed below.

4. *Application of Article 493*

A "creative" interpretation of Article 493 could begin by drawing a distinction between "wanted" and "unwanted" improvements, and then by inquiring whether the article is applicable to both types of improvements. With regard to the first type, i.e., improvements which either *both* parties *or at least one* party wants, the answer would be clear and unavoidable: Article 493 would apply on all fours. With regard to the second type, however, i.e., improvements which, as in *Guzetta, neither* party wants, the answer would not be as categorical.

Article 493 does not address this question directly. In terms of literal interpretation, one could argue that, since the article does not on its surface distinguish between wanted and unwanted improvements, no such distinction should be made by judicial fiat. Nevertheless, as *Guzzetta* itself demonstrates, such interpretation may lead to potentially harsh results. It would therefore appear more equitable if the article were interpreted as simply being *silent* on the question of the removal of improvements which neither party wants. This latter interpretation would be more in line with the whole tenor of the 1984 amendment of the article and the background against which the amendment was drafted. It should be recalled at this point that *Babin v. Babin*, the case which caused the 1984 amendment of Article 493, involved wanted, not unwanted, improvements. Although the amendment employed language that is broad enough to encompass unwanted improvements, a fact for which it has been severely criticized by this author, it would be preferable to subject this language to a restrictive interpretation. Such an interpretation would be consistent with the cardinal principle that ownership is presumed free of burdens and would allow the court to focus more closely on the peculiarities of the particular case and to reach a more individualized and equitable solution. In this sense, Justice Lemmon's view that "Article 493 is silent" on the question is the more equitable approach in the long run, even though his final conclusion on the facts might not have been as equitable.

BROUSSARD v. COMPTON
36 So. 3d 376 (La. App. 3d Cir. 2010)

GENOVESE, J. In this contentious family feud over the ownership of a home and the property upon which it was built, the Defendants/Appellants, Theta Charles Compton, Woodrow Mays Compton, and Elva Fay Compton, appeal the trial court's judgment in favor of the Plaintiffs/Appellees, Peter Norman Broussard, Jr. and Patsy Compton Broussard. For the following reasons, we affirm the judgment of the trial court.

FACTUAL AND PROCEDURAL BACKGROUND

Peter Norman Broussard, Jr. (Peter Broussard) and Patsy Compton Broussard (Patsy Broussard) filed a Petition for Breach of Contract and Revocation of Donation against Theta Charles Compton (Theta Compton), Woodrow Mays Compton (Woodrow Compton), and Elva Fay Compton (Elva Compton). The Plaintiffs sought to revoke Theta Compton's donation to Woodrow Compton and Elva Compton of the property upon which the Plaintiffs built a home. The Plaintiffs asserted that they built the home on Theta Compton's property with her permission and with the understanding that she would donate to them the property upon which they built the home upon its completion.

The record indicates that in the early 1990s, Theta Compton owned a home located on Cemetery Road in St. Martin Parish, Louisiana, which she acquired from her mother,

Violetta Drake Charles (Violetta Charles). According to the Plaintiffs, they voluntarily assumed the responsibility of caring for Violetta Charles and maintaining her property. Theta Compton allegedly "offered to give the home and immovable property" to the Plaintiffs in consideration for the care and assistance which they gave to her mother, Violetta Charles. Tragically, in May of 1993, the house burned down, and Violetta Charles perished in the fire. Thereafter, the Plaintiffs allege that even though the home they were to receive was destroyed by fire, Theta Compton proposed an alternative to them. According to their petition, Plaintiffs allege:

> Theta Charles Compton offered to provide [money from the insurance proceeds] for the purchase of materials only for the construction of a house to be owned by [the Plaintiffs] in exchange for Peter Norman Broussard, Jr. clearing the immovable property owned by Theta Charles Compton of a burned out home previously occupied by Theta Charles Compton's mother, as well as other dilapidated buildings, junk vehicles[,] and overgrown trees and shrubs[,] and providing all of the labor and additional materials needed for the construction of a home to be owned by [the Plaintiffs], the said home to include a bedroom for Theta Charles Compton to reside in for the remainder of her life should she so desire. Theta Charles Compton also provided the immovable property where the home was to be built. As part of the contract and prior to the construction of the home[,] Theta Charles Compton had promised that she would donate the immovable property on which the home was constructed to upon completion of the home.

The Plaintiffs began constructing a house on the property in 1993. Construction was completed in 1995, and the Plaintiffs have lived in the home since before its completion. The Plaintiffs assert that "the home was built on the immovable property with the full permission and knowledge of Theta Charles Compton." However, the Plaintiffs contend that Theta Compton did not fulfill her promise to donate to them the property upon which the house was built. Specifically, the Plaintiffs assert that:

> At the beginning of 2001[,] Theta Charles Compton refused to honor her part of the contract and execute a donation of the immovable property to [the Plaintiffs] but[,] instead[,] wanted to donate the home which she did not own and the immovable property to Patsy Compton Broussard, Elva Fay Compton Bourda and Woodrow Mays Compton. [The Plaintiffs] refused to accept a one[-]third interest and demanded that Theta Charles Compton fulfill her contractual agreement to donate the immovable property to [the Plaintiffs].

Nevertheless, Theta Compton did subsequently effectuate a donation of the property at issue herein to Patsy Broussard's siblings, Woodrow Compton and Elva Compton, in February of 2001. The Plaintiffs claim that they "were unaware of the . . . donation . . . until March of 2007[,] when they received correspondence from Woodrow May[s] Compton." It was this correspondence which the Plaintiffs assert prompted their filing of the instant action in December of 2007.

The Plaintiffs' petition requests that the donation from Theta Compton to Woodrow Compton and Elva Compton be "revoked in so far as it includes the home and improvements made by [the Plaintiffs] and the immovable property for which they had contracted." It further declares:

> [The Plaintiffs] are entitled to . . . enforcement of the contract between them and Theta Charles Compton declaring [the Plaintiffs] to be the owners of the immovable property on which the home stands and the home built by them to be theirs with the right of Theta Charles Compton to live in the private bedroom and bath for the rest of her life.

> Alternatively, in accordance with Louisiana Civil Code Article 496 [the Plaintiffs] are entitled to the cost of the materials and workmanship, or current value or enhanced value of the immovable property.

> Alternatively, in accordance with Louisiana Civil Code Article 529 [the Plaintiffs] are entitled to remain in possession of their home until [they receive] reimbursements for the expenses and improvements to which they are entitled.

The Defendants countered with an Exception of No Cause of Action, Answer, and Reconventional Demand. In their answer and reconventional demand, the Defendants "admit that Theta Charles Compton permitted [the] Plaintiffs to reside on the property"; however, the Defendants denied ever acknowledging that the home was to belong to the Plaintiffs. The Defendants asserted their entitlement "to a reasonable credit for the value of [the] Plaintiffs' use and occupancy of the property in question." The Defendants also sought "an order . . . recognizing their ownership of the subject property and ordering [the Plaintiffs] to immediately surrender possession of the subject property to [them]."

On June 27, 2008, the Plaintiffs filed a First Supplemental and Amending Petition on Petition for Breach of Contract and Revocation of a Donation. In it, the Plaintiffs supplemented their demand against the Defendants, asserting:

> Alternatively[, the Plaintiffs] are entitled to be reimbursed for the improvements made to the property in excess of the $ 32,000.00 expended by Theta Charles Compton on the grounds of unjust enrichment in an amount to be determined at the time of trial because the improvements were made based upon the promises made by Theta Charles Compton that the immovable property would be donated to petitioners in the future.

Trial in this matter was held on September 25, 2008, and November 12, 2008, after which, the trial court took the matter under advisement. The trial court wrote Reasons for Judgment, dated December 17, 2008, wherein it ruled, in pertinent part:

> In this case, no act translative of ownership exists to the [P]laintiffs. Therefore, we must turn our attention to Article 497 of the Louisiana Civil

Code. This article provides for obligations from owner to possessor and possessor to owner when the possessor is a bad faith possessor. [Louisiana Civil Code Article] 497 provides that when construction, plantings, or works are made by bad faith possessors, the owner of the immovable may keep them or he may demand the demolition and removal at the expense of the possessor, and, in addition, damages for the injury that he may have sustained. If he does not demand demolition and removal, he is bound to pay at his option either the current value of the materials and of the workmanship of the separate improvements that he has kept or the enhanced value of the immovable. [La.Civ.Code art.] 497.

In the case before us, [D]efendants, Elva Compton and Woodrow Compton, sent a letter to [the Plaintiffs], requesting that they be evicted from the property. At no time did they request the removal of the construction. Therefore, this is a tacit acceptance of the construction on the property indicating that the owners of the property do not want its removal but would be bound to pay either the current value of the materials and of the workmanship of the separate improvements or the enhanced value of the immovable.

This also comports with the argument being made by [the Plaintiffs] that they are entitled to unjust enrichment.***

Therefore, in the instant action, all of the requirements of unjust enrichment have been met. There is an enrichment to Elva Compton and Woodrow Compton, that being the home built on the property; there is an impoverishment to the [Plaintiffs], that being the home they built and for which they have not been compensated. There is a connection between the enrichment and the impoverishment. The next requirement is that there must be an absence of justification of cause for the enrichment or impoverishment. In this case, the [Plaintiffs] had the verbal commitment from Ms. Theta Compton that they should build this home on the piece of property and it would be theirs. Therefore, although not a legal justification or cause, there was a moral justification and cause for them to do so. Finally, there must be no other remedy available to the [P]laintiffs. In this case, there is no other remedy available to the [Plaintiffs] to compensate them for their impoverishment. That being said, unjust enrichment is applicable to this case.

Considering the trial testimony of the certified land appraiser, Robert Braquet, the trial court determined that the home was valued at $ 220,000.00. The trial court then deducted $ 32,000.00 from that amount as a credit for the amount initially paid by Theta Compton for the construction of the home, thereby determining that the value of the enrichment was $ 188,000.00. Additionally, the trial court addressed the Defendants' request for a credit for the Plaintiffs' use of the home. The trial court stated:

[N]ot only was there no evidence presented as to the rental value for all those years, even if there were, the evidence at trial strongly indicates that the family supported the fact that the [Plaintiffs] lived there, had a room for Theta [Compton] to stay in when she desired, and maintained the surrounding property. At no time from 1993 until 2007 was any mention made that the [Plaintiffs] would owe any type of rent to the owners. There is evidence in the record, however, that Elva Compton and Woodrow Compton decreed in a letter to Patsy Broussard that $ 250.00 per month would be a fair sum for the maintenance of the home and the rental value of the home. Therefore, the Court will consider this as the rental value requested by Elva and Woodrow [Compton]. Therefore, the [c]ourt will award rental value to the [D]efendants from August 6, 2007, which was the date of the letter, until such time that the Broussards vacate the premises. The [c]ourt will grant a credit to the [D]efendants for this amount of money against the $ 188,000.00 owed by the [D]efendants to the [P]laintiffs.

On February 26, 2009, before the trial court's ruling was signed into judgment, the Defendants filed a Motion and Order for Reconsideration or New Trial. . . . The Defendants also asserted that the trial court erroneously applied La.Civ.Code art. 497 when "[u]nder the facts found by the [c]ourt, [La.Civ.Code] art. 493 should have been utilized by the [c]ourt to determine the rights and obligations of the parties." Finally, the Defendants disputed the trial court's calculations relative to the value of the home and the amount of rent owed.

On April 7, 2009, the trial court signed a judgment concomitant with its written Reasons for Judgment issued on December 17, 2008. Thereafter, the Plaintiffs filed a Motion and Order for Reconsideration or New Trial on April 21, 2009. In their motion, the Plaintiffs urged that, pursuant to La.Civ.Code art. 529, they be allowed to remain in possession of the home until they are reimbursed for the expenses and improvements. Therefore, the Plaintiffs sought the reconsideration of that provision of the trial court's judgment which ordered that they vacate the home. The Plaintiffs asserted that in accordance with their rights under La.Civ.Code art. 529, "the eviction is premature" and, therefore, the trial court should not have ordered them to vacate the home "until after [they] are reimbursed for the expenses and improvements."

A hearing on the parties' motions for reconsideration was held on May 6, 2009, after which, the trial court again took the matter under advisement. The trial court wrote Reasons for Judgment on the motions for reconsideration, dated June 5, 2009, wherein it ruled, in pertinent part:

Defendants argue that the [c]ourt should not have applied [La.Civ.Code art.] 497 and the principal [sic] of unjust enrichment but rather focused on [La.Civ.Code art.] 493. The [c]ourt has reviewed the memorandum submitted by the parties and the relevant law on this issue.

[Louisiana Civil Code Article] 493 states that when a building is built on the land of another with his consent, the structure belongs to the builder. When the owner of that structure no longer has a right to keep it on the land of another, he may remove it subject to his obligation to restore the property to its former condition; if it is not removed, the property owner has the right to demand by written notice that the house owner remove the house within 90 days. *Kibbe v. Lege, 604 So.2d 1366 (La.App. 3 Cir. 1992).*

Application of this Civil Code Article actually bolsters [the Plaintiffs'] position. The house was built on the [D]efendants' property with the consent of the [D]efendants; therefore, the house belongs to [P]laintiffs. Plaintiffs have a right to remove the home subject to an obligation to restore the property to its former condition. The [P]laintiffs have made no effort to exercise this right; therefore, [D]efendants then had the right to demand by written notice that the [Plaintiffs] remove the house within 90 days. Defendant[s] never did send [P]laintiffs a request for removal of the home. For these reasons, the house built by the [Plaintiffs] belongs to them and under [La.Civ.Code art.] 493, the result remains the same as in the reasons rendered previously by this [c]ourt.

The trial court denied the Defendants' Motion for Reconsideration or New Trial and granted the Plaintiffs' Motion for Reconsideration or New Trial. A judgment was signed by the trial court on June 18, 2008, which amended its previous judgment solely to grant the Plaintiffs "possession of the home until they are reimbursed for expenses and improvements in the amount of one hundred eighty[-]eight thousand ($188,000.00) dollars []" in accordance with La.Civ.Code art. 529. The Defendants appeal.***

LAW AND DISCUSSION

The Defendants, in brief, contend that the issues before this court are: (1) which Louisiana Civil Code Article applies to the instant case, La.Civ.Code art. 497 or La.Civ.Code art. 493; (2) whether the doctrines of unjust enrichment and quantum meruit are applicable to the claims and facts of this case; (3) whether La.Civ.Code art. 592 applies in order to grant to the Plaintiffs the right to retain possession of the home until they are reimbursed.

According to the Defendants, La.Civ.Code art. 493 applies and "[t]he only remedies that are available under Article 493 are for the owner of the structure to remove the structure, or he may abandon the structure to the landowner (after the appropriate actions are taken)." Thus, they contend that the trial court's ruling that the Defendants' owe the Plaintiffs $ 188,000.00 pursuant to the provisions of La.Civ.Code 497 is erroneous. We disagree.

The trial court determined that the Plaintiffs were bad faith possessors of the immovable property because they did not possess an act translative of title. Because the Plaintiffs are bad faith possessors, La.Civ.Code art. 497 contains the remedy available to "the owner of the immovable[.]" The trial court further concluded that the Plaintiffs legitimately believed that upon the completion of the building of their home, Theta Compton would donate the immovable property upon which it was built to them. Yet, when the Plaintiffs received a letter from the Defendants in 2007, they discovered that the immovable property had, instead, been donated to Woodrow Compton and Elva Compton, and not to them.

When correspondence, dated August 6, 2007, was received by the Plaintiffs, it contained the demand that the Plaintiffs contribute "$ 200.00 per month to be set aside as your contribution to the taxes and insurance beginning 1 September 2007." Clearly, the Defendants chose not to demand demolition and removal of the home; therefore, they became "bound to pay" the Plaintiffs as per La.Civ.Code art. 497.

Finally, the trial court denied the Defendants' Motion for Reconsideration or New Trial, wherein the Defendants argued that La.Civ.Code art. 493 was applicable in this matter, not La.Civ.Code art. 497. On appeal, the Defendants reiterate: "The facts of this case fit squarely within the four corners of [La.Civ.Code] art. 493. The only remedies that are available under *Article 493* are for the owner of the structure to remove the structure, or he may abandon the structure to the landowner . . . ." Though it applied La.Civ.Code art. *497*, the trial court, in its June 5, 2009 reasons, opined that the application of La.Civ.Code art. 493 would yield the same result as the application of La.Civ.Code art. 497. We agree.

Pursuant to La.Civ.Code art. 493, the Defendants had the right to make a written demand that the Plaintiffs remove the home. Instead, the Defendants sought to reap the rewards of the Plaintiffs' labor and evict them from the home they built on property which they legitimately believed would be donated to them. We find the trial court correctly determined that the same result would be reached if La.Civ.Code art. 493 were applied. The home, which belongs to the Plaintiffs, "remain[s] the property of he who made [it] . . ." as per La.Civ.Code art. 493.

Absent a finding that the trial court's conclusions were unreasonable, we find no clear error in the trial court's judgment and, therefore, affirm the trial court's judgment in favor of the Plaintiffs/Appellees, Peter Norman Broussard, Jr. and Patsy Compton Broussard.

DECREE

For the foregoing reasons, the judgment of the trial court is affirmed. Costs of this appeal are assessed against the Defendants/Appellants, Theta Charles Compton, Woodrow Mays Compton, and Elva Fay Compton. AFFIRMED.

NOTE

The court of appeal's analysis prompts a number of questions. If, as the court concluded, the Broussards still owned the house, then on what basis were they entitled to *any* remedy at all under the law of accession? Is it not the case that the remedies established by that law are, by definition, remedies for one who has lost ownership of the improvement to the owner of the underlying thing? Further, was the court correct in classifying the Broussards as "possessors" of the land (or was it the house?)? Did they not detain the land with the permission of the owner of the underlying immovable, Theta, and were they not on that account "precarious possessors", which is as much as to say "not possessors at all"? Are, in fact, the remedies provided by Article 493 the same as those provided by Article 497? Is it not clear that Article 493 provides one and only one remedy to the person who makes the improvement – the right to remove the thing – and one and only one remedy to the owner of the underlying immovable – to appropriate ownership of the improvement, free of charge, after proper notice and delay? Finally, even if Article 497 does apply, what would be the appropriate remedy? Those remedies are more varied that the court's opinion lets on: alongside the alternative of indemnity in the amount of "the current value of the materials and of the workmanship", which the court seems to acknowledge, there's also the alternative of indemnity in the amount of the "enhanced value of the immovable", about which the court's opinion is silent. Who is it who gets to choose from among the remedies for which the article provides? Is it the person who made the improvement (or the court itself?), as the court seems to have assumed, or is it the owner of the underlying immovable?

BRITT BUILDERS, INC. v. BRISTER
618 So. 2d 899 (La. App. 1st Cir. 1993)

REMY CHIASSON, Judge Pro. Tem. This is a devolutive appeal from a judgment denying claims for continuing trespass on a reconventional demand. The trial court rendered judgment in favor of the defendant/plaintiff in reconvention, Maureen Brister, and against the plaintiff/defendant in reconvention, James D. Britt. The trial court further dismissed Britt's main demand and ordered that he pays Ms. Brister $3,500 for damage to her property. Ms. Brister filed this appeal.

FACTS

Maureen Johnson Brister bought Lot 201 of Woodlands Subdivision, Baton Rouge, Louisiana, on March 1, 1984. Title to the lot was recorded on March 2, 1984. Ms. Brister bought this lot because it had an unusual shape and a large oak tree. She financed this purchase by paying $5,000 down and promised to pay $251.22 a month for ten years. Total purchase price of the lot was $20,500. On June 25, 1984, Britt Builders, Inc., a Louisiana corporation owned by James Britt, entered into a purchase agreement for Lot 201 with Five L Development Corporation, the same company that sold the lot to Ms. Brister. A title search was conducted by H. Matthew Chambers who did not discover that the lot was owned by Ms. Brister. Soon after Britt was told that the title was clear, he removed the large oak tree, poured a concrete slab for a residence, and began framing the walls. Cost of this work was $10,179. 76.

On July 10, 1984, Britt first learned that Ms. Brister owned the lot. Ms. Brister was immediately contacted; all work on the lot was stopped, and negotiations begun to mitigate damages. Two weeks later Britt filed suit against Ms. Brister seeking $12,000 in damages for the enhanced value to her lot. She answered and filed a reconventional demand, seeking damages associated with the cost of her lot, damages for trespass, mental anguish, and attorney's fees.

Trial was held on May 24, 1991. At trial several experts in real estate appraisal testified. Marvin R. McDaniel, II said that a treed lot should bring $2,000 to $2,500 more than an untreed lot. He estimated that the cost of removing the concrete slab was $8,000 to $10,000 and the lot had a present value of $14,000 to $15,000 with the slab on it. He said that anyone purchasing the lot and planning to use the slab would have the problem of no warranty and few people would want the lot with a slab on it.

Jim Wilson, a general contractor, testified that he gave Ms. Brister an estimate of $9,168 to remove the slab. He said that there was no salvage value to the slab and the job would require use of four or five trucks all day to remove the debris.

H. Matthew Chambers, the real estate lawyer who did the title search for Britt, said that he was hired June 20, 1984, to close the sale. He stated that a week to two weeks after he said the title was clear, he learned that Ms. Brister, and not the corporation which sold the lot to Britt, was the owner of Lot 201.

James Britt was accepted by the court as an expert in residential construction. He testified that he started building homes in 1965. He said that he did not know about the defect in the title before be began construction and he spent $400 to $500 to have the tree removed. He added that he bought the lot next to 201 hoping to negotiate a settlement and he was paid $8,816 by Chambers for the materials used in constructing the slab on Ms. Brister's lot.

Maureen Brister was the last witness. She said she had financed the purchase of the lot and she selected this lot because it was pie-shaped, on a curve, and had a large tree which she envisioned next to her bedroom. She and her family had prepared the lot for construction by cutting down five trees, hauling off debris, and mowing the grass. She had spent $1,630 clearing the lot. She said that she had spent the last seven years having to keep the lot clear because of liability and complaints by her neighbors. She also stated that she had no idea that construction began on her lot until Chambers told her, that she had asked Britt to remove the slab, and she could not understand why Britt was suing her for something he had put on her property. She claimed that her life has been on hold waiting for a resolution or her damages.

The court dismissed Britt's demands for $12,000 and assigned him costs of the trial. On the reconventional demand, the court awarded Ms. Brister $3,500, plus legal interest, for the destruction of the tree and clean-up of the lot. From that decision, Ms. Brister filed this appeal.

DETERMINATION OF GOOD FAITH, POSSESSION, END FAILURE TO AWARD FULL DAMAGES FOR TRESPASS

Ms. Brister argues that the court erred when it determined that Britt was a good faith possessor when he constructed the slab on her lot. She contends that she should not be fully precluded from her damages in trespass because these damages resulted solely from Britt's actions. She maintains that the construction of the slab on her lot, removal of the tree, and placement of debris and construction materials by Britt constituted legal trespass.

In his brief to this court Britt argues that he was in good faith when he bought Lot 201 and began construction. He contends that he enhanced the value of the lot by constructing $12,000 worth of improvements on it and he should be entitled to restitution for these improvements. However, this Court cannot consider changing the trial court's ruling against Britt because he neither appealed nor answered Ms. Brister's appeal. See La.C.C.P. art. 2133; Lamouisn v. Ankesheiln, 560 So.2d 459, 461 (La. App. 1st Cir. 1990).

Possession is the detention or enjoyment of a corporeal thing, movable and immovable, that one holds or exercises by himself or by another who keeps or exercises it in his name. La.C.C. art. 3421. A possessor is considered provisionally as owner of the thing he possesses until the right of the true owner is established. La.C.C. art. 3423. To acquire possession, one must intend to possess as owner and must take corporeal possession of the thing. La.C.C. art. 3424. Corporeal possession is the exercise of physical acts of use, detention, or enjoyment over a thing. La.C.C art. 3425.

One is presumed to intend to possess as owner unless he began to possess in the name of and for another. La.C.C. art. 3427. Possession is lost when the possessor manifests his intention to abandon it or when he is evicted by another by force or usurpation. La.C.C. art. 3433. Good faith is presumed. Neither error of fact nor error of law defeats this presumption. This presumption is rebutted on proof that the possessor knows, or should know, that he is not owner of the thing he possesses. La.C.C. art. 3481.

Buildings, other constructions permanently attached to the ground, and plantings made on the land of another with his consent belong to him who made them. They belong to the owner of the ground when they are made without his consent. La.C.C. art. 493. When constructions, plantings, or works are made by a possessor in good faith, the owner of the immovable may not demand their demolition and removal. He is bound to keep them and at his option to pay to the possessor either the cost of the materials and of the workmanship, or their current value, or the enhanced value of the immovable. La.C.C. art. 496.

When constructions, plantings, or works are made by a bad faith possessor, the owner of the immovable may keep them or he may demand their demolition and removal at the expense of the possessor, and, in addition, damages for the injury that he may have sustained. If he does not demand demolition and removal, he is bound to pay at his option either the current value of the materials and of the workmanship of the separable improvements that he has kept or the enhanced value of the immovable. La.C.C. art. 497.

In his ruling the trial court determined that Britt was a good faith possessor in light of Phillips v. Parker, 483 So. 2d 972 (La. 1986) and that Civil Code Article 496 governed the outcome concerning the slab. By so ruling, the court concluded that Ms. Brister would have been bound to pay, at her option, either the cost of the materials and of the workmanship, or their current value, or the enhanced value of her immovable. However, because Britt failed to present adequate proof of the amounts, the court refused to award him damages under Article 496.

This Court agrees with the determination that Britt was a good faith possessor. In *Phillips* our Supreme Court held that good faith is presumed and when an erroneous title search is made, the possessor who relied on that search should not be precluded from the same status given a good faith possessor who conducts no search. Phillips v. Parker, 483 So. 2d at 978-979. Britt was similarly situated when he placed reliance on a faulty title search and acted upon the advice of his attorney.

However, this Court's inquiry does not end simply because Britt was a good faith possessor under La.C.C. art. 496. The article itself speaks of enhanced value and Comment (c) to this article refers to improvements made to another's property. This comment states in pertinent part that all improvements made by a possessor in good faith on another's immovable belong to the owner of the immovable. The wording in both suggests that Article 496 is. intended to apply to buildings, other constructions, and plantings that improve and enhance the value of an immovable. The article does not speak of partial constructions that actually diminish the value of an immovable.

In the instant case the record reveals that the only person likely to benefit from the slab was Britt. He poured the slab to fit the configuration of his house plans. For Ms. Brister and any potential buyer of the lot, it would be necessary to use an unwanted and unwarranted slab that has no utility until a house is built on it or else spend eight to ten thousand dollars to remove the slab. The testimony clearly established that the slab diminished the value of the lot.

Therefore, this Court believes that the redactors of our Civil Code envisioned application of Article 496 when the owner of the immovable would be unjustly enriched by the efforts of a good faith possessor. They did not intend that the owner be burdened with partial constructions and unwanted works on his property that actually diminished its value. Further recourse is available to an owner in a situation such as this.

Article 2315 of the Civil Code provides in pertinent part that every act whatever of man that causes damage to another obliges him by whose fault it happened to repair it. The tort of trespass has long been recognized by courts throughout this state as a means to correct the damage caused when an owner is unjustly deprived of the use and enjoyment of his immovable.

The tort of trespass is defined as the unlawful physical invasion of the property or possession of another. Dickie's Sportsman's Centers, Inc. v. Department of Transportation and Development, 477 So.2d 744, 750 (La. App. 1st Cir.), writ denied, 478 So. 2d 530 (La. 1985). A trespasser is one who does upon the property of another without the other's consent. Williams v. J.B. Levert Land Company, Inc., 162 So. 2d 53, 58 (La. App. 1st Cir.), writ refused, 245 La. 1081, 162 So. 2d 574 (La. 1964).

A person injured by trespass is entitled to full indemnification for the damages caused. Where there is a legal right to recovery but the damages cannot be exactly estimated, the courts have reasonable discretion to assess same based upon all of the facts and circumstances. Damages are recoverable even though the tortfeasor acts in good faith. Versai Management, Inc. v. Monticello Forest Products Corporation, 479 So.2d 477, 484 (La.App. 1st Cir. 1985).

Damages for dispossession are regarded as an award of compensatory damages for violation of a recognized property right and are not confined to proof of actual pecuniary loss. Anguish, humiliation, and embarrassment are appropriate considerations. Owens v. Smith, 541 So. 2d 950, 955 (La. App. 2d Cir. 1989). Damages are recoverable for unconsented activities performed on the property of another, based on physical property damage, invasion of privacy, inconvenience, and mental and physical suffering. Beacham v. Hardy Outdoor Advertising, Inc., 520 So. 2d 1086, 1091 (La. App. 2d Cir. 1987).

In the instant case Britt did not dispute that he erected the concrete slab on Ms. Brister's property without her permission, nor does Britt claim to be owner of the property. Britt only occupied the lot as owner for two weeks, but the slab has remained on the lot seven years. Furthermore, the continued presence of the slab deprived Ms. Brister of the use and enjoyment of her property and diminished its value to her or other potential owners.

For the reasons herein stated, this Court concludes that under the circumstances of this case the trial court erred by determining that Article 496 of the Civil Code precluded full payment of damages resulting from a tort of trespass. Accordingly, the first and third assignments of error pertaining to trespass have merit.

QUANTUM

Ms. Brister claimed the following damages:

(1) Cost of removing the slab and removing the slab and repairing the lot	$ 9,168.00
(2) Interest paid on lot loan	13,000.00
(3) Destruction of tree	2,500.00
(4) Out of pocket lot expenses	1,630.00
(5) Inconvenience, invasion of privacy, mental anguish and emotional trauma (7 years at $2,000.00 per year for the continuing nature of the trespass)	14,000.00
(6) Loss of use of down payment ($5,000.00) on lot loan for 7 years at 6% per year	2,100.00

TOTAL $42,398.00 plus legal interest and court costs

In his oral reasons for judgment, the trial judge awarded Ms. Brister damages of $1,000 for trespass for cleanup of materials left on her lot when Britt constructed another house and $2,500 for removal of the tree. These awards are affirmed. However, the court committed error when it denied Ms. Brister's claims for the continuing trespass caused by the slab remaining on her lot. Accordingly, Ms. Brister is awarded an additional $9,168 for the removal of the slab. No other damages were sufficiently proven in the record.

DECREE

For the foregoing reasons, the judgment of the trial court rejecting Ms. Britt's claim for the cost of removing the slab as a continuing trespass is reversed. The awards for $1,000 for cleanup of construction materials and $2,500 for removal of the tree are affirmed. Judgment is rendered in favor of Ms. Brister and against James D. Britt for an additional $9,168 as damages in trespass for removal of the concrete slab, for a total award of $12,668, with legal interest thereon from date of judicial demand until paid. Mr. Britt is cast for all costs.

NOTE
Accession in Relation to Immovables in the Context of Lease

If the lessee of an immovable makes improvements to it, who owns the improvements - the lessee or the lessor? And what are the lessee's and the lessor's "remedial" rights / duties with respect to such improvements: can the lessee remove them, can the lessor have them removed at the lessee's expense, must the lessor reimburse the lessee? The answers to these questions depend, in the first instance, on the provisions of the lease agreement.

If the lease agreement addresses these issues, then that's the end of the matter: the agreement controls. Consider, for instance, the case of *Schulingkamp v. Heaton,* 455 So. 2d 1181 (La. App. 4th Cir. 1984), plaintiff had leased and used as his principal residence a boathouse situated on land water bottom owned by the Board of Commissioners of the Orleans Levee District. Under the terms of the lease, at which time the improvements would belong to the lessor. When the City of New Orleans imposed an ad valorem tax on the lessee, the claimed that the improvements belonged to the Levee Board and therefore were exempt from the tax. The court, relying on the terms of the lease agreement, held that the improvements belonged to the lessee and, for that reason, could be taxed.

But what if the lease agreement does *not* address these issues? Then they are resolved by the law of lease, specifically, by Civil Code article 2695. Take a close look at that article. How do the rules of ownership established by that article compare to those established by Articles 493, par. 1, and 493.1? How do the remedial rules established by that article compare to those established by Articles 493, par. 2, 495, 496, and 497?

c. Reimbursement for Expenses and Improvements
Civil Code arts. 485, 488

See A. N. YIANNOPOULOS, CIVIL LAW PROPERTY
§§ 275, 276 (4th ed. 2001)

VOIERS v. ATKINS BROS.
113 La. 303, 36 So. 974 (1903)

ON REHEARING

PROVOSTY, J. ***On behalf of Mrs. Voiers it is contended that a possessor in bad faith can claim compensation only for such improvements as are susceptible of being removed, and for such expenses as have been incurred in the preservation of the property; and that, as a consequence, nothing can be recovered for the following items: Cost of lake ditch, $923.25; cost of other ditching, $240; clearing timber, $101; clearing 80 acres of land, $640; digging and cementing three cisterns, $45.

This contention appears to us to be well founded. No one has a right knowingly to go upon the property of another, and cut down the timber, and dig ditches, etc. even from a good motive. If he does it, so much the worse for him; he has no claim to make.***

In the case of Gibson v. Hutchins, 12 La. Ann. 546, 68 Am. Dec. 772, this court said:

"The right of a possessor to recover of the true owner for ameliorations inseparable in their nature from the soil cannot, it appears to us, be recognized in any case, unless the possessor was at least a possessor in good faith, believing himself to be the owner. The mere possessor is presumed to have made such changes for his own amelioration, and to have received a sufficient reward in the immediate benefit which he reaps from the enhanced production of the soil. Perhaps the ditching will not suit the purposes for which he wishes to use the land. To place a real proprietor at the mercy of a possessor in bad faith, by requiring him to pay the latter, who has, without just authority, changed the face of the land for selfish purposes of his own, does not accord with those rules of law which give the dominion of the soil to the proprietor only, or to one who has a right to consider himself a proprietor for the time. An intruder may recover such expenses as are necessary for the preserving of the thing. A negotiorum gestor may recover what he has spent in doing the business necessary to be done for another, even without a mandate. It is a general rule of equity that no one should enrich himself at another's expense. But this doctrine must not be stretched so far as to let an intermeddler recover for willfully doing what was not necessary to be done, or what the owner might not wish to have done, and what the law did not require to be done. If an intermeddler goes to expense with the single view of benefiting himself, and reaps the benefit, he cannot demand a reimbursement for his time and trouble from the person upon whose property he has intruded, by suggesting that he, too, has been incidentally benefited."

In Cannon v. White, 16 La. Ann. 91, the court said:

> "The defendant, being thus a possessor in bad faith, owes indemnity, and is entitled, in law, to no other claim for his improvements than those stated in the three first sentences of the Civil Code, art. 508 [Revised C.C. arts. 491-498]."

That is to say, he has a right to remove his materials, if the owner does not elect to keep them. In that case nothing was allowed to the defendant for clearing land, except that he was not made to pay rent on the land which he had cleared.

In Wood's Heirs v. Nicholls, 33 La. Ann. 751, the court said:

> "As to improvements in their nature inseparable from the soil, such as ditching, wells, etc., he is not entitled to compensation."

In Breaux-Renoudet Lumber Co. v. Shadel, 52 La. Ann. 2098, 28 South. 292, the court said:

> "They can be regarded in no other light than as intruders on the land. Being such, they can neither claim to be paid the expenses they incurred in deadening the trees, nor the trees which they felled, nor their value. Civ. Code, art. 502 [Revised C.C. art. 486]. The expenses which they incurred were not such as were necessary for the preservation of the thing, and it may well be that the true owner may have preferred that the primitive forest should remain."

McDade v. Levee Board, 109 La. 625, 33 South. 628, and other like cases, where the possessor in bad faith was permitted to offset the claim for fruits and revenues by a claim for enhanced value resulting from land clearing and other improvements inseparable from the soil, militate in no wise against the foregoing. The claim for fruits and revenues is nothing more than a claim in indemnity for loss, and naturally may be defeated by proof that, instead of a loss, there has been a gain. The theory of these cases is well and fully expounded in the case of Wilson v. Benjamin, 26 La. Ann. 588, as follows:

> "The defendants set up another claim for $10,560 for the rent of the land, but as there was, previously to the sale in 1855, no privity of contract between them and the plaintiff, the case is not one of letting and hiring. Civ. Code art. 2639. The claim is one in the nature of damages for the wanton detention of the property; and, although the trespasser is not allowed to prefer a claim for the enhanced value of the soil attributable to his improvements, yet in the ad measurement of damages to which he is subject the benefit derived from such improvements becomes an important element. The

improvements, such as clearing a portion of the land, the whole of which was at the time a forest, and putting it in a high cultivation, were worth, independently of the buildings and constructions, fully the amount at which the detention of the property might be appraised."

Cases may be found here and there in our Reports where the strong magnet of equity has swerved the court from the straight line of the rule; where, as in the time of Pothier, while the rule was recognized to be one way, the practice was sometimes permitted to go the other way in cases appealing strongly to the sense of justice of the court. It is needless to refer to these cases. What may have been justifiable in the time of Pothier, under the guidance of general principles, is not permissible under the Code Napoléon or our Civil Code, which have drawn the line sharply between the two kinds of possession, and prescribed the rights of the possessor in bad faith.

While the evidence is of the scantiest, we shall accept it, in the absence of contradiction, and allow defendants the following items: Four double cabins, $450; shed at landing, $60; fencing and repairing fences, $102.50. This last item is properly classable as expenses for the preservation of the property, for which defendants are entitled to absolute judgment. The remaining two items, salary of W. H. Young, $200, and balance of improvements, $200, are too vague and uncertain. Neither the statement nor the evidence informs us what the improvements were, not what proportion of the time of Mr. Young was taken up by his overseeing the construction of the buildings and fences, for which part of his time alone defendants would have the right to recover.

It is therefore ordered, adjudged and decreed that the former decree of this court be reinstated, with the sole amendment that the defendants have judgment against the plaintiff for the sum of $102.50, with legal interest from judicial demand; and, in case the plaintiff elects to keep any of the buildings put upon the land in controversy by defendants, then that for any of the buildings so kept defendants have judgments against plaintiff for the estimated value thereof as follows: $112.50 for each cabin kept of the four cabins for which defendants have claimed $450, and $60 for the seed shed at the landing. Plaintiff to make her election in the premises before proceeding to the execution of the present judgment. The amounts thus allowed the parties on their respective demands to compensate each other pro tanto.

SANDERS v. JACKSON
192 So. 2d 654 (La. App. 3d Cir. 1966)

SAVOY, J. Plaintiff instituted a boundary action, to which defendants answered and also entered a plea of prescription.

The lower court overruled the plea of prescription and ordered a survey be made to establish the boundary. Thereafter, the survey and procés verbal of the court-appointed surveyor were homologated. As a result, the boundary line was established approximately fifty feet farther south, that line being plaintiff's south property line and defendants' north property line.

For the purposes of this appeal, the parties do not contest the above described actions of the lower court; they are not at issue on this appeal, and we will not discuss them further. They simply lay the foundation for the remainder of this opinion.

Thereafter, the defendants filed a petition seeking certain relief. The plaintiff answered and filed a reconventional demand, which was answered by defendants. The nature of these claims and cross-claims are as follows:

The defendants contend that:

(a) On the fifty-foot strip in question, defendants landscaped a distance of about 1000 feet back from the highway;

(b) Defendants also built a dam and a pond, and that the dam and part of the pond are within that strip of land;

(c) Those said improvements were made by defendants in good faith, believing that they were being placed on defendants' own land;

(d) Defendants are entitled to reimbursement for the reasonable value of the landscaping work, and are further entitled to be paid either the reasonable value of the dam and pond, or the cost of removal and relocation of same.

The plaintiff contends that:

(a) Defendants were not in good faith, having been prewarned that the property line in question was not necessarily in its correct location;

(b) Consequently, defendants are entitled to no reimbursement;

(c) Alternatively, if defendants were in good faith, plaintiff elects to reimburse the defendants only for the enhanced value of plaintiff's land;

(d) The value of plaintiff's land was in no way enhanced, and consequently, plaintiff owes defendants nothing;

(e) Likewise, with regard to the landscaping done by defendants;

(f) The presence of the dam depreciates the value of plaintiff's bottom land and interferes with the flow of water into a pond belonging to plaintiff, for which defendants should be held indebted in damages to plaintiff;

On those issues the lower court rendered judgment which denied plaintiff's claim for damages, denied defendants' claim for reimbursement or cost of relocation, gave judgment to plaintiff for a proportionate share of the money paid to defendants by the Department of Highways and assessed all costs of court against defendants, except to divide equally between the parties the cost of the survey to establish the boundary line.

From that judgment the defendants have appealed, and plaintiff has answered the appeal.

This Court finds that defendants were in good faith regarding placement of the dam and pond. While the defendants were aware that a formal survey had never been made, an old fence had been standing for a number of years about fifty feet north of the subsequently established boundary line. The size of the respective properties, ten acres each out of an original twenty-acre tract, was such that a discrepancy of fifty feet certainly would not have been apparent to the naked eye. The defendants' property was fairly heavily wooded up to the old fence, and plaintiff's property was relatively clear by comparison from the fence north, thus creating a visual situation tending to suggest the old fence as the boundary. Prior owners of defendants' land had, in past years, sold timber up to the old fence. While there had been prior conversations between plaintiff and defendants about the property line, the record does not reveal that there had been any unequivocal statements made or positions taken. Plaintiff purchased her tract in 1950; defendants purchased theirs in 1958; defendants' pond and dam were built about a year or so after their purchase; plaintiff's suit was not brought until 1962.

With the finding of good faith, the parties are thus placed under the provisions of the fourth paragraph of Civil Code Article 508 [Revised C.C. arts. 491-498], which provides that in the case of a third person evicted, but who has possessed in good faith, the true owner may either reimburse the value of the materials and the price of workmanship, or reimburse a sum equal to the enhanced value of the soil. With further reference to Civil Code Article 508 [Revised C.C. arts. 491-498], it also treats the subject of bad faith possessors. It is only they who can be assessed with damages.

With regard to whether plaintiff must reimburse defendants on either a value-price or enhanced value basis, we again feel that the lower court's judgment denying such claims was correct. While Mr. Jackson estimated his cost on the dam and pond, he had no records on which to substantiate it, and, in addition, a good part of the work was done without cost to him by a friend whom he assisted in various ways from time to time. The record further reveals that there was no enhanced value to plaintiff's property. Most of the dam and only a very small part of the pond lie upon plaintiff's land. Only one witness testified on the specific question of enhancement, Mr. George W. Black, Jr., a real estate man. He felt that there was no enhancement for the reasons that the property would bring the same price with or without the dam and pond and that what possible esthetic value there might be would be offset by a probable detriment to plaintiff's natural watershed caused by the dam. The lower court's judgment should remain undisturbed on this issue. Affirmed.

3. ACCESSION IN RELATION TO MOVABLES
Civil Code arts. 507-516

2 AUBRY ET RAU, DROIT CIVIL FRANÇAIS 265-266
(an English translation by the Louisiana State Law Institute 1966)

This subject was greatly developed by Roman jurisconsults. Today it has only limited practical importance because of the maxim *En fait de meubles, possession vaut titre* (with regard to movables, possession equals title). Only in cases where this maxim is inapplicable, we have to fall back on the provisions of Arts. 565 ff. which set out the right of accession with respect to movables.

These provisions are, however, alien to the case of a union of two movables, owned by different persons, but carried out by their mutual accord. The status of a thing so formed is regulated by the agreement of the parties.

The accession of one movable to another can take place in one of three principal forms: adjunction, transformation (*specification*) and commingling (*melange*) or fusion (*confusion*).

Adjunction is the union of two things belonging to different owners, so these things form a single whole, though each of them is a distinct and recognizable part of this whole. Adjunction is governed by Arts. 561-569: the owner of the principal thing generally becomes the owner of the whole, with the charge of paying to the owner of the accessory thing its value.

Transformation is that act of making a new thing with material belonging to someone else. In general and with the exception provided for in art. 571, the owner of the material may either claim the ownership of the new thing with the charge of reimbursing the cost of the labor, or claim compensation for his material or restitution of the same kind and quality of material (Arts. 570-576).

The special case where the transformer used in part his own material and in part the material of another is regulated by art. 572.

When two dry or liquid matters belonging to different owners are commingled or fused so they can not be separated without difficulty, the new thing so formed is in general, and with the exception indicated in art. 574, commonly owned by the two parties in proportion to the quantity, quality and value of the material each of them furnished, and must be auctioned for their common benefit (Arts. 573-575).

Law of 17 May 1960, amending Arts. 566, 570, 571, 572, 574 and 576 provides that the value of the material or the labor is to be determined as of the date of the reimbursement or auction.

In cases of accession not provided for by these statutory rules, the judges are to decide according to principles of equity, using as guides the specific solutions in the Code.

In all other cases of accession, any person who has used materials belonging to another without the knowledge of the owner, may be sentenced under circumstances, and independently from the restitution of the material or compensation for its value to full damages or, even, criminally prosecuted (art. 577).

AETNA BUSINESS CREDIT CORP. v. LOUISIANA MACHINERY CO.
409 So. 2d 1304 (La. App. 2d Cir. 1982)

SEXTON, J. Aetna Business Credit appeals a trial court judgment sustaining the defendant's motion for summary judgment, thereby upholding the defendant's vendor's privilege. We affirm.

The facts of the case are not in dispute. In March 1979, Irving Leasing Corporation owned two drilling rigs and accessory equipment including a Gardner Denver PY-7 Triplex pump. To finance the purchase of this equipment, Irving Leasing Corporation borrowed from Aetna Business Credit Corporation and then secured the loan with a chattel mortgage on all the equipment. The chattel mortgage was duly recorded.

Irving Leasing Corporation, which is in the business of leasing drilling equipment, leased the rigs along with various equipment including the Gardner Denver pump to Ram Drilling Company, a Louisiana corporation engaged in the drilling of oil wells. Some eight months later, while drilling a well in DeSoto Parish, Ram entered into an agreement on November 20, 1979, with the defendant for the purchase of a Model D353 Caterpillar engine to be used to power the Gardner Denver pump. This engine was a replacement for the engine contained on the pump at the time of lease. The new engine was mounted on the drilling platform upon which the pump was also mounted. The engine was then connected to the pump by a specially built drive device which Ram had fabricated for this purpose.

Ram's financial condition worsened and on February 6, 1980, the Caterpillar engine was repossessed by the defendant due to Ram's inability to pay. Ram acquiesced in the repossession.

After the defendant had repossessed the Caterpillar engine, the plaintiff filed suit against Irving and foreclosed on the two rigs and equipment including the Gardner Denver pump.

Plaintiff subsequently purchased this equipment at public auction. Plaintiff then filed this suit, claiming that the Caterpillar engine had, by the law of accession, become attached to the pump and/or rig in such a manner as to become the property of Irving Leasing Corporation and thus subject to the chattel mortgage executed by Irving. If not, then defendant's vendor's privilege is valid.

The trial court in considering defendant's motion for summary judgment described the "attachment" or "connection" of the Caterpillar engine and Gardner Denver pump as follows:

> ". . . the engine was attached to its own I-beam skid by eight bolts; and the skid was in turn bolted to a flat metal floor, upon which the pump was also affixed. This whole assembly of equipment, at the time of repossession, was sitting on the ground next to the drilling rig. Two rubber hoses supplied fuel to the engine. The drive assembly used consisted of two concentric drums; one was a small drum bolted to the flywheel *of* the engine and the other was a larger drum attached to the pump. The smaller drum fit inside the larger one without making any physical contact. Power from the engine was transferred to the pump when an 'air clutch' or inner tube was inflated between the two drums. Only when this device was inflated could the power from the engine be transferred to the pump by transferring motion from the small drum to the large drum. To remove the engine required only the disconnection of the two fuel lines, removal of the bolts from the skid and disconnection of the small concentric drum from the engine flywheel."

The trial judge found that defendant was easily able to remove the engine without damage to the pump, the drive device, or the engine itself. The trial court held that, "a complete piece of machinery such as this engine does not become merged with a pump simply by being mounted upon the same rack, or connected to a drive device of the type used here."

Plaintiff-appellant relies upon Roberts v. Williams, 99 So. 2d 392 (La. App. 2d Cir. 1957); McVay v. McVay, 318 So. 2d 660 (La. App. 3d Cir. 1975); Guaranty Bank and Trust Company v. Hoggins, 347 So. 2d 919 (La. App. 3d Cir. 1977) and General Motors Acceptance Corporation v. Madden, 331 So. 2d 882 (La. App. 2d Cir. 1976). These are all "automobile cases" in which the owner of an automobile authorized the replacement of parts necessary for the continued functioning of the vehicle. These parts included an engine, universal joints, and tires. These cases are prior to the reorganization of law in this area, but as the redactor's comments note, no change was made in the law of accession between movables. In each case it was found that when the parts were bolted on or otherwise affixed to the vehicle the parts became incorporated into the vehicle, and the law of accession was held to apply. In other words, the parts ceased to have an individual identity, but rather became part of the greater whole.

In this case Ram was only a lessee of the rig and pump. It was the owner of the engine, indicating an intent on Ram's part that any "attachment" of the Caterpillar engine and the Gardner Denver pump was temporary, lasting only as long as the lease was in effect.

The general principle of accession is defined is C.C. art. 482:

> "The ownership of a thing includes by accession the ownership of every-thing that it produces or is *united with it*, either naturally or artificially, in

accordance with the following provisions." (Emphasis added).

C.C. art. 150 carries forward this concept of a union in defining accession between movables:

> "When two corporeal movables are *united to form a whole,* and one of them is an accessory of the other, the whole belongs to the owner of the principal thing...." (Emphasis added).

Therefore ownership of movables by accession requires a permanent union between the things which, of course, must be determined on the facts of each case.

Automobile parts are designed to become united with an automobile. Thus there is a distinct difference between the replacement of universal joints and automobile engines and this case. Also, in *McVay, supra,* "the tire case," although the tires could be easily removed, they were united with the automobile as an accessory in a permanent sense. See C.C. art. 508.

In this case the attachment of this engine by the drive device and the fuel hose connections are of such a nature that each machine retains its separate identity. The requirement that movables must be "united to form a whole" requires something more permanent than the easily removable drive device which connected this pump and engine. We view the union here as temporary and tenuous rather than permanent.

We agree with the trial court's finding that due to the various uses of the engine, its characteristics, and the ease of disconnection it remained a distinct piece of machinery so that the law of accession does not apply. Therefore, plaintiff's chattel mortgage is inapplicable to the engine, and the defendant's vendor's privilege is valid.

For the reasons assigned, the trial court judgment is affirmed at plaintiff-appellant's costs. Affirmed.

INT'L PAPER CO. v. EAST FELICIANA PARISH SCHOOL BOARD
850 So. 2d 717 (La. App. 1st Cir. 2003)

KLINE, J. This is an appeal taken by International Paper Company (IP) from a summary judgment rendered in favor of East Feliciana Parish School Board (School Board) allowing it to levy and collect sales tax on parts and labor used in repairing IP's equipment in East Feliciana Parish. For the following reasons, we affirm.

FACTS AND PROCEDURAL HISTORY

Between January 1, 1994 and December 31, 1996, IP owned and operated a paper mill located in Mobile, Alabama. During that period, IP sent equipment used at its Mobile mill to be repaired at Woodyard Equipment and Supply Company, Inc. (WYESCO), located in East Feliciana Parish. According to IP, these repairs generally required the installation of new parts. After WYESCO completed the repairs, it returned IP's equipment to the Mobile mill on WYESCO trucks. . . .

Subsequently, the School Board conducted a tax audit of IP for the period of January 1994 through December 1996. The audit revealed that IP had not paid taxes in East Feliciana Parish for the repairs performed by WYESCO. Consequently, the School Board issued an assessment to IP on December 30, 1997, seeking collection of taxes in the amount of $15,421.64, penalties in the amount of $3,855.41, and interest in the amount of $4,217.76, for a total of $23,494.81. In its assessment, the School Board levied sales tax on the full cost of the repairs, including labor and the cost of the parts used in making the repairs.

On March 2, 1998, IP paid the assessment under protest and soon after filed suit for recovery of the amount paid. While IP subsequently admitted that the labor used in making the repairs was taxable in East Feliciana Parish, it disputed that the parts used in making the repairs were also taxable in the parish. Rather, IP contended that the repair parts constituted tangible personal property delivered outside the parish and, as such, was exempt from East Feliciana sales tax.

On September 10, 2001, IP filed a motion for partial summary judgment arguing that the School Board "lack[ed] authority to impose and collect sales taxes on the materials used in the repairs because WYESCO delivered the materials that it sold to IP at its mill in Mobile, Alabama." Subsequently, on October 1, 2001, the School Board filed a cross motion for partial summary judgment contending entitlement to levy and collect a sales tax on the materials used in the repairs. A hearing on the motions was conducted on November 26, 2001.

***IP's argument that the parts are exempt from sales tax in East Feliciana because they were delivered outside the parish must still fall. Under East Feliciana Parish Ordinance Section 15-31 the term "sale" is to be given the meaning ascribed to it in La. R.S. 47:301. Louisiana Revised Statute 47:301(12) defines "sale" as "any transfer of title or possession...of tangible personal property, for a consideration...." (Emphasis added.)

Ordinarily, tax laws are sui generis. South Central Bell Telephone Co. v. Barthelemy, 94-0499 at p. 6, 643 So. 2d at 1243. However, the courts have applied property law in tax contexts. City of New Orleans v. Baumer Foods, Inc., 532 So. 2d 1381, 1383 (La. 1988). In Exxon Corporation v. Traigle, 353 So. 2d 314, 316-317 (La. App. 1st Cir.1977), writ denied, 354 So. 2d 1385 (La. 1978), this court held that "tangible personal property" as it is used in the state sales tax law is synonymous with "corporeal movable property" as used in the Civil Code. . . .

Louisiana Civil Code article 461 defines corporeals as "things that have a body, whether animate or inanimate, and can be felt or touched." Louisiana Civil Code article 471 further defines corporeal movables as "things, whether animate or inanimate, that normally move or can be moved from one place to another." Under these definitions, the repair parts are clearly "corporeal movables" and thus qualify as "tangible personal property" under the relevant ordinance and statute. However, the analysis cannot end there, because La. C.C. art. 482 states that "the ownership of a thing includes by accession the ownership of everything that it produces or is untied with it either naturally or artificially." More specifically, La. C.C. art. 510 provides, in pertinent part, that "[w]hen two corporeal movables are united to form a whole, and one of them is an accessory of the other, the whole belongs to the owner of the principal thing." Accordingly, title to the repair parts (accessories) passed to IP when they were united to or incorporated in the equipment (principal thing) during the repair services wholly performed in East Feliciana Parish. See Roberts v. Williams, 99 So. 2d 392, 394 (La. App. 2 Cir. 1957).

Although we are unable to find any tax law cases applying the article on accession as it relates to corporeal movables, we are convinced that such an application is appropriate. We are buttressed in our opinion by several cases applying other germane property law articles to various tax law issues. See Exxon Corporation v. Traigle, 353 So. 2d 314, 317 (La. App. 1st Cir.1977), (court determined the applicability of state sales and services tax by classifying the property at issue under general property law) writ denied, 354 So. 2d 1385 (La. 1978); Showboat Star Partnership v. Slaughter, 00-1227 (La. 4/3/01), 789 So. 2d 554 (applying La. C.C. art. 466 to determine whether gaming equipment on a riverboat gaming vessel qualified as "component parts" under La. R.S. 47:305.1 A for sales tax exemption purposes); Clyde Juneau Company, Inc. v. Caddo-Shreveport Sales and Use Tax Commission, 28,433 (La. App. 2d Cir. 6/26/96), 677 So. 2d 610 (applying La. C.C. art. 466 to determine that corporeal movable repair parts became component parts of an immovable and thus, were exempt from sales taxes); City of New Orleans v. Baumer Foods, Inc., 532 So. 2d 1381 (La. 1988) (applying La. C.C. art. 467 to determine that corporeal movable equipment had not become immovable by declaration when use tax attached and thus the tax was correctly levied); Sales Tax Collector, St. Charles Parish v. Westside Sand Company, Inc., 534 So. 2d 454 (La. App. 5th Cir. 1988) (applying La. C.C. art. 468 on deimmobilization to determine that once removed from its natural source, sand becomes a corporeal movable and thus subject to sales tax) writ denied, 536 So. 2d 1240 (La. 1989).

As a consequence, the repair parts, as well as the labor, are subject to taxes in East Feliciana Parish.***

DECREE

For the foregoing reasons, the summary judgment granted in favor of the East Feliciana Parish School Board is affirmed. Costs of this appeal are taxed to International Paper Company.

CHAPTER VII. OCCUPANCY
Civil Code arts. 3412-3420

1 (2) PLANIOL, TRAITÉ ÉLÉMENTAIRE DE DROIT CIVIL 514-526 (an English translation by the Louisiana State Law Institute 1959)

Definition. Occupancy is a mode of acquiring a thing that belongs to nobody. It is done by the taking of possession with intent of becoming owner of the thing. This mode of acquisition therefore consists solely in the taking of possession. Nothing need be added to this to define it. But inquiry must be made regarding what things may be occupied and then the rules applicable to certain cases must be studied.

§ 1. Things Susceptible of Occupancy

Possibility of Occupancy. May occasions still arise in France where occupancy may take place when Arts. 539 and 713 declare that "that all vacant property and property that has no owner belong to the State?" If all property not under private ownership belongs to the State, then, under French Law, there is nothing without a master and occupancy fails because there is nothing to which it can apply. This view was sometimes advanced and principally by Zachariae. But his error has long since been corrected. The possibility of occupancy is shown by the history of the compilation of the Civil Code and by the presence in it of several articles that still speak of occupancy and regulate it.

Immovables. Occupancy is impossible as regards immovables forming part of the territory of France or of her colonies governed by the Civil Code, because there is never found there any immovable that is, strictly speaking, without a "master." Lands that have never been privately owned belong either to the public domain of the State or to that of the Departments. Those that have been or that are now private property can cease to be so only in two ways: (1) by escheat and (2) by voluntary abandonment.

The first case presupposes that a succession has been opened and that nobody claims it. It belongs to the State by virtue of art. 768. The second case happens much less frequently. In order to escape taxation, a person may abandon his land when it is unproductive.

Movables As regards movables, a sub-differentiation should be made between universalities of movables and isolated movable things. Universalities of movables cannot be found in a state of abandonment except in the form of a succession without heirs. They still belong to the State by right of escheat (art. 768). Therefore, as far as they are concerned, occupancy is impossible.

Isolated movables remain. There are two kinds of them that have no master. One kind has never had a master. Reference is made to game. The others have been abandoned by their master as *res derelictae.* It is for these kinds of movables and for them alone, that occupancy can still function at French Law. They are veritable *res nullius* and the first comer becomes owner of them by occupancy.

§ 1. Of Some Special Cases of Occupancy

A. Hunting

Case Where the Hunter Acquires the Game. The hunter becomes owner by occupancy of the game he has killed and of which he has taken possession, regardless of whether the act took place on his land or on the land of somebody else. It is true that Art. 1 of the law on hunting dated May 3, 1844 prohibits hunting on somebody else's land, without the consent of the owner or those who hold for him. This prohibition refers however to the hunter's entry upon the other's property and not to the taking of the game he kills. He is responsible in damages for the harm done by him, if he has caused any, he or his dogs. On the other hand, the owner who authorizes another to hunt upon [the owner's] land does not give [the hunter] the game he kills. This right flows from the nature of the law. All that the owner does is that he renounces his right to prevent third parties entering his land.

Case Where Game Is Not Acquired by Hunter. Results are not the same, that is, game does not become the hunter's property, if the hunting took place during the closed season. The law then attributes it to public welfare societies. (Art. 4 of the amended law of May 1, 1924). It has been held that such a provision established confiscation, that is to say a penalty, and that it assumes the previous acquisition of the game. The concept is subtle. Is not the non-acquisition of the game by the hunter the practical outcome? And, if it be true that the prohibition of hunting does not keep game from being something without a master and susceptible of ownership, does it not at least prevent the hunter from obtaining possession of it?

Mode of Occupancy of Game. The act from which the occupancy of the game results is not necessarily the manual seizure of the animal. It is universally admitted that the killed game, which the hunter has but to pick up, as well as the wounded game that is seized by the hunting dogs, belongs to the hunter. The rule goes still further. The game is deemed to have lost its natural liberty, when it is mortally wounded or when it is so closely pursued by the dogs that it cannot escape them (Dijon, Dec. 7, 1910, P. and S. 1911. 2.68). But when another person has taken possession of an animal that has been wounded or is being pursued, questions of fact that are hard to solve often arise in fixing the seriousness of the wound or the possibility of the animal escaping the dogs. Analogous difficulties arise when the animal has been shot, at the same time or successively, by two hunters, and when it is momentarily lost by him who had fired at it or pursued it, etc. The Court of Cassation has held that an owner may prevent a hunter entering his lands to seize game shot and wounded by the hunter (Cass., April 29, 1862, D. 62. 1. 449).

B. Fishing

State of the Legislation. The capture of fish and of other kinds of animals that live in water is still another case of occupancy in connection with which the Code (art. 715) refers to special laws. These "laws" include not only laws but decrees and even diplomatic agreements (for the North Sea, for the Lake of Geneva and for the Coast of Algeria, etc.). M. Hue gives a list of them (Vol. V, no. 10 to no. 13). These special texts, however deal solely with regulations and police measures and not with the acquisition of the product of fishing....

Fishing In Private Waters. Fishes in ponds or canals whose waters are private property are not animals without a master. They are the property of him who possesses the pond or canal where they live (art. 564). It follows, that he who seizes them without the owner's authorization, far from acquiring them by occupancy, is guilty of a veritable theft (see law of June 18, 1923).***

D. Of Treasures

What Is a Treasure. In order that a thing be deemed to be "a treasure" it must fulfill the four following conditions: (1) be movable, (2) be hidden, (3) be distinct from the thing enclosing it, and (4) and belong at the moment to nobody.

(1) In order that the thing be a "treasure," it must be movable. This provision is not found in the Code, which, on the contrary, uses the sweeping terms that "a treasure is anything hidden or imbedded" (art. 716). But the jurisprudence imposes this condition by applying the Roman definitions and by adhering to tradition (Pothier, *Domaine de propriété,* no. 64). It has accordingly been decided that a mosaic pavement of Roman times discovered by Lillebonne in 1870 was not a treasure and that art. 716 did not apply to it. The owner of the soil was declared to be the sole owner of it (Paris, Nov. 20, 1877, D. 78. 2. 197; Cass., Dec. 13, 1881, D. 82. 1. 55 Car. Dijon, May16, 1905, S. 1907. s. 41).

(2) The treasure is a thing hidden or imbedded. Thus a thing that has been mislaid, and has fallen upon the surface of the soil is not a treasure. It is a lost article (*infra,* no. 2583 *et seq.*). It makes no difference whether the treasure is found in a movable or in an immovable, although the law, contemplating the ordinary case, assumes that the treasure is found "in the ground." It is generally in the ground or in walls that treasures are usually hidden. But the formula that the law-maker uses must not be understood in a restricted sense. It sometimes happens that a treasure is found in a movable. Examples are: banknotes among the pages of an old book, gold coins or stones in the secret drawer of a desk, etc.

(3) The treasure is distinct from the container. This condition excludes precious substances found in the earth in their nature strata. They are not distinct from the land and they belong in their entirety to its owner.

(4) The treasure is a thing previously appropriated, but upon which nobody can any longer establish a right of ownership. If anyone appears, who succeeds in adducing the proof, a case of revendication of a movable then arises, which should be dealt with according to the general law. If the suit is successful, the [suspected] treasure cannot be acquired by occupancy.

Useless Conditions. Art. 716 seems to impose an additional condition. According to this text it would be necessary that the discovery of the treasure was [merely] the result of chance. This condition is useless as regards the definition of a treasure. The hidden thing, belonging to nobody, is still a treasure, even if excavations were undertaken to discover it because its existence was suspected. Chance, when it has brought about such a discovery, plays no part except in the attribution of the treasure. [Chance] has nothing to do with [the] definition [of treasure].

The same remarks apply to the treasure's antiquity. It is the usual characteristic of a treasure but . . . is not essential. [The treasure] may have been embedded recently. If nobody has a right to the thing discovered, it is a treasure. There is a contrary ruling set forth in an old decision of the Court of Bordeaux (1806) but its solution is generally attacked. See also Tribunal of Rennes, Dec. 3, 1900, under Cass., 1903. 1. 405.

§ 1. Occupancy of Things Having a Master

B. Acquisition of Things Lost

Definition of Things Lost. Under this are included all movable objects lost by their owner. Care must be taken not to confuse lost things with *res derelictae (supra,* no. 2198 *in fine).* A lost thing is not a thing without a master that may be acquired by occupancy. Its owner has not renounced his ownership. He often is aware that he has lost his thing. He would accordingly be entitled to bring an action in revendication, in as much as he has merely lost possession and French law has always recognized that a revendication will lie in the case of fortuitous loss *(supra,* nos. 2463 and 2469). But in most cases, the owner of a lost article cannot claim it because he does not know where it is. The wreck therefore definitively remains the property of the finder *(qui invenit).* So that the "finding" of lost things is deemed to be a mode of acquisition analogous to occupancy. The thing is as if it were without a master in as much as he cannot find it.

Title by Which Things Lost Are Acquired. By what title is this acquisition made? It is generally believed that it is based on occupancy. But it is an occupancy different from the normal case. True occupancy assumes that the thing acquired is a *res nullius* and things lost still have an owner who has not renounced his right. The title [to lost things] springs rather from usucapion (acquisitive prescription). In as much as the owner's right of revendication is reserved, the acquisition of ownership by the finder is not immediate. There is therefore no occupancy. The acquisition of ownership is derived from prolonged possession, that is to say from usucapion. If, due to the fact that no revendication is set up, this acquisition of ownership appears to be instantaneous, it is so merely in appearance. See in this sense, Commercial Tribunal Saint-Etienne, Nov. 8, 1898, D. 99.2. 331.

NOTE

Occupancy as a mode of acquiring ownership in Louisiana, as in France, is now confined to corporeal movables. Immovables and incorporeals (whether movable or immovable) cannot be *res nullius,* and the Louisiana Civil Code article defining occupancy appears to require that the thing "does not belong to anybody." La. Civ. Code art. 3412. However, as the treatise passage below indicates, in the twentieth century Louisiana asserted its ownership of much of the wildlife within the state in a series of legislative acts; see La. Civ.Code art. 3413, revision comment (b). Article 3413 recognizes the possibility of state ownership, but also indicates that wildlife may be subject to occupancy under "particular laws and regulations."

A. N. YIANNOPOULOS, CIVIL LAW PROPERTY
§ 58 (4th ed. 2001)
(footnotes omitted)

§ 58. Wildlife as a Public Thing

According to traditional civilian conceptions, wild animals, fish, and shellfish are *res nullius,* that is, they belong to no one in particular. Every one may acquire the ownership of such things by occupancy. In Louisiana, however, statutes declare that the state "owns" all wild quadrupeds and birds in the state and all fish and shellfish in the waters of the state.

The state ownership of wildlife is not a private ownership under the Civil Code; it is an ownership of a public law nature for purposes of conservation and regulation of rights in wildlife in the interest of all. This predominant feature sets out the limits of state ownership. Thus, concession of exclusive rights in wildlife to any private person would be hardly conceivable.

It is apparent in the light of the foregoing that state ownership of wildlife is a novel conception that does not fit the traditional conceptual framework. Though a "public thing," wildlife is not subject to public use; moreover, it is susceptible of private ownership. Upon compliance with rules and regulations concerning hunting and fishing, one may acquire the ownership of wild quadrupeds and birds, fish, and shellfish in accordance with the rules of the Civil Code governing occupancy.

LEGER v. LOUISIANA DEP'T OF WILDLIFE & FISHERIES
306 So. 2d 391 (La. App. 3d Cir. 1975)

HOOD, J. Alex Leger instituted this action against the Louisiana Wildlife and Fisheries Commission and Burton Angelle, in his capacity as Commissioner of the Louisiana Department of Wildlife and Fisheries, to recover damages for the loss of his 1973 sweet potato crop. The trial court rendered judgment sustaining defendants' exception of no cause of action, and plaintiff appealed.

Two important issues are presented. One involves an interpretation of R.S. 56:102. The other is whether plaintiff has alleged facts sufficient to show that defendants, through their employees, were negligent and thus liable to plaintiff for damages under Article 2315 of the Civil Code.***

The following are the pertinent facts alleged in plaintiff's original and supplemental petitions.

In March and/or April, 1973, plaintiff bedded potatoes on property in Avoyelles Parish for the purpose of planting a potato crop. The Red River began to flood in February, March and/or April of that year, and the flooding caused deer in that area to migrate toward the property in which plaintiff had bedded his potatoes. The deer ate Leger's plants during March, April and May, causing substantial damage to his 1973 potato crop. Upon first noticing the deer eating his potatoes, plaintiff called Tom Britt, an employee of the Louisiana Department of Wildlife and Fisheries, and told him that it would be necessary to kill the deer in order to save his 1973 sweet potato crop. In response to that call, Britt inspected the field of bedded potatoes, and he informed plaintiff that "he as agent of the Louisiana Department of Wildlife and Fisheries would institute prosecution for violation of Wildlife and Fisheries ordinances should petitioner kill any of the deer to save his crop." Leger could have saved his entire crop had he been able to shoot the deer which were eating his potatoes.

After setting out the above facts, plaintiff alleges several conclusions of law. He asserts, for instance, that Britt, in acting within the course and scope of his employment with the Louisiana Department of Wildlife and Fisheries, is legally responsible for the damage to his 1973 potato crop, and that the Department of Wildlife and Fisheries and Burton Angelle, as Commissioner, also are liable to him under C.C. art. 2315 for the damages he sustained.

Plaintiff also alleges that "by virtue of R.S. 56:102, the Louisiana Department of Wildlife and Fisheries is the owner of all wild birds and wild quadrupeds, which includes wild deer," and that "under Article 2321 of the Louisiana Civil Code the owner of an animal is answerable for the damages it caused and therefore, since the Department of Wildlife and Fisheries owned the deer which were eating petitioner's potatoes... they are legally responsible for the damage done to his 1973 potato crop." His pleadings conclude with allegations that Britt was at fault in several particulars, and that his acts are imputed to the Department of Wildlife and Fisheries.

The principal question presented is whether the Department is the owner of all wild quadrupeds found in the state, and if so is its ownership of such a nature that it is responsible under C.C. art. 2321 for the damages to plaintiff's crop caused by wild deer.

R.S. 56:102 provides, in part, that:

"The ownership and title to all wild birds and wild quadrupeds found in the state is declared to be in the State of Louisiana *in its sovereign capacity.* The title of the state to all such wild birds and wild quadrupeds, even though taken in accordance with the provisions & this Sub-part always remains in the state *for the purpose of regulating and controlling the use and disposition thereof. . .*"

Article 2321 of the Civil Code provides that the owner of an animal is answerable for the damage he has caused.

Plaintiff's argument, consistent with his pleadings, is that "since the Department of Wildlife and Fisheries owned the deer which were eating petitioner's potatoes, they are legally responsible for the damages done to his 1973 sweet potato crop." He relies on Harris v. Roy, 108 So. 2d 7 (La. App. 2d Cir. 1958); and Raziano v. T. J. James & Co., 57 So. 2d 251 (La. App. Orl. 1952).

The cited cases involved claims for damages allegedly caused by domestic animals owned by private parties. Neither of those cases required an interpretation of R.S. 56:102. No question was raised in either suit as to whether the State, or any of its agencies, ha[s] a proprietary interest in wild animals and if so, whether the state has a duty to control them and whether it can be held liable for damages done by those animals. The Harris and Raziano cases thus are not applicable here.

We have concluded that the wild birds and wild quadrupeds found in the state are owned by the State of Louisiana in its sovereign capacity, as distinguished from its proprietary capacity, and that it owns them solely as trustee for the use and common benefit of the people of the state. Because of its ownership in a sovereign capacity, and in the exercise of its police power, the state may regulate and control the taking and subsequent use of wild birds and wild quadrupeds, and the property rights which may be acquired in them. Lacoste v. Department of Conservation, 263 U.S. 545, 44 S.Ct. 186 (1924); Geer v. State of Connecticut, 161 U.S. 519, 16 S.Ct. 600 (1896); Foster-Fountain Packing Co. v. Haydel, 278 U.S. 1, 49 S.Ct. 1 (1928).

R.S. 56:102 has as its source Act 273 of 1926. We think the language used in that section of the Revised Statutes, and in other sections having the 1926 act as their source, compels the conclusion that the state's ownership is in a sovereign, and not a proprietary, capacity. Section 102, for instance, provides that the title to wild birds and quadrupeds is declared to be in the state "in its sovereign capacity," and that the title remains in the state "for the purpose of regulating and controlling the use and disposition thereof."

The Department of Wildlife and Fisheries, in the exercise of the state's police power, is given the duty of protecting wild birds and wild quadrupeds, of preventing the destruction of feeding and breeding grounds, of establishing game refuge[s] or preserves, and of regulating the taking, killing or transporting of wild birds and wild quadrupeds. R.S. 56:101 et seq.

The law specifically authorizes and provides rules for the taking or killing of wild birds and wild quadrupeds by private persons, and the appropriation of the birds and animals so taken to private use. It provides for the issuance of hunting and trapping licenses to private persons for that purpose. The Legislature clearly did not intend for Act 273 of 1926 (now R.S. 101 et seq.) to vest title to all wild birds and wild quadrupeds in the state, in its proprietary capacity, and thus make them items of state owned property, while at the same time authorizing private persons to take and appropriate that publicly owned property to their own private use.

We find nothing in the cited statutes or in the law which indicates that the state has a duty to harbor wild birds or wild quadrupeds, to control their movements or to prevent them from damaging privately owned property. If such a duty should be imposed on the state, then it would mean in many instances that the state would have to impound or confine some birds and animals, and they thus would cease to be wild creatures, but instead would be birds or animals which had been taken, possessed or harbored. It would mean in some cases that the state would have to restrict or interfere with the migration or other habits of our wildlife, or it would have to destroy them. We do not believe that the Legislature intended for any such duty to be placed on an agency or department of the state.

In Pavel v. Pattison, 24 F.Supp. 915 (D.C. W.D. La. 1938), the validity of a Louisiana statute regulating the trapping of fur-bearing animals or alligators was at issue. The court said:

> "It is well settled that the wild life, including animals, fish and fowl, is under the control of the State, which holds the title thereto in trust for all the people; that it may prohibit the taking, catching or killing of any or all of it; and that it may also, under proper conditions, confine these privileges to its own citizens."

The United States Supreme Court, interpreting another Louisiana statute in Lacoste v. Department of Conservation, *supra*, held:

> "The wild animals within its borders are, so far as capable of ownership, owned by the state in its sovereign capacity for the common benefit of all of its people. Because of such ownership, and in the exercise of its police power[,] the state may regulate and control the taking, subsequent use and property rights that may be acquired therein."

***It is for these reasons that we have concluded that the ownership of all wild birds and wild quadrupeds is vested in the state solely in its sovereign capacity, as trustee for the use and common benefit of the people of the state.

We also conclude that C.C. art. 2321 does not apply here, since the state does not own wild quadrupeds in its proprietary capacity and it does not harbor such animals. We think that article of the Civil Code applies only to the owner of an animal who owns or harbors it in a proprietary capacity. See Marsh v. Snyder, 113 So. 2d 5 (La. App. Orl. 1959). If the animal is owned or harbored, it is not a wild quadruped. In the instant suit the state did not harbor the deer which caused the damage and it did not own them in a proprietary capacity.

If the interpretation urged by plaintiff should be placed on R.S. 56:102 and Article 2321 of the Civil Code, it would follow logically that the state has the impossible duty of preventing damage to private property by all wild birds and wild animals, including such things as crows, sparrows, squirrels, rats and fox. We do not think these laws were intended to have such an effect.

Plaintiff argues further that [he] is entitled to recover damages from defendants under Article 2315 of the Civil Code because of fault or negligence on the part of defendants' employee, Britt, in refusing to permit plaintiff to shoot the wild deer which were damaging his crop. We find no merit to that argument.

R.S. 56:6 provides, among other things, that the Commissioner "shall protect and propagate, when possible, all species of birds and game of whatever description," and that he "shall rigidly enforce all law... relative to the protection, propagation, and selling of birds and game...." R.S. 56:124 (1) provides that no person shall "[t]ake... a wild deer at any time when driven to the high lands by overflow or high water." And, R.S. 56:139 provides criminal penalties for violation of the last cited section of the Revised Statutes.

Britt, as an employee of the Department, had no authority to allow plaintiff to shoot the wild deer which were damaging his crop, and he was not negligent in refusing to give plaintiff permission to do so. He simply informed plaintiff that he [Britt] would perform the functions which were delegated to him and the Department of Wildlife and Fisheries by law if plaintiff killed the deer, and Leger thereupon elected to not shoot the animals which were causing the damage.

We question whether Britt's permission to shoot the deer, in the event such permission had been given, would have exculpated plaintiff from criminal responsibility, if any such responsibility in fact would have attached to the shooting. In any event, the statement made to plaintiff by Britt did not constitute a proximate cause of the loss. Britt's legal duty would have remained the same, regardless of the response he made to plaintiff's request. Plaintiff could have proceeded to shoot the animals and then raise the legal questions in the event charges were preferred against him. He could have applied for a written permit from the Commissioner under R.S. 56:112. Or, he could have instituted proceedings seeking injunctive relief, a mandamus or a declaratory judgment. Whatever relief plaintiff might have sought, however, our holding here is that the statement made by Britt that he would discharge the duties imposed upon him and the Department by law did not constitute fault under C.C. art. 2315 or a proximate cause of the loss.

The Department, through Britt, also was not negligent in failing to control the wild deer and in preventing the animals from damaging plaintiff's crop. We have already pointed out that the Department of Wildlife and Fisheries has no duty to take those steps.

Our conclusion is that plaintiff's original and supplemental petitions fail to state a cause of action against defendants under either Article 2315 or Article 2321 of the Civil Code. The trial judge thus correctly sustained the exception of no cause of action filed by defendants.

On this appeal plaintiff argues that R.S. 56:124(1) is unconstitutional in that it denies plaintiff his constitutional right to defend his property (his potato crop) from threatened injury by wild deer. The cited section of the Revised Statutes prohibits the taking of a wild deer at any time when driven to the high lands by overflow or high water.

We have not considered plaintiff's attack on the constitutionality of this statute, because it was not pleaded or urged in the trial court. The attack on the constitutionality of that statute apparently was made for the first time in the brief which plaintiff filed on this appeal.***For the reasons herein assigned, the judgment appealed from is affirmed. The costs of this appeal are assessed to plaintiff-appellant.

QUESTION

The court declined to consider the plaintiff's attack on the constitutionality of La. R.S. 56:124(1) because he failed to raise it at trial. What would be the basis of the plaintiff's argument? Given the court's refusal to find liability in the Department and its agents, is the argument plausible?

HARRISON v. PETROLEUM SURVEYS, INC.
80 So. 2d 153 (La. App. 1st Cir. 1955)

TATE, J. Plaintiff-landowners appealed from judgment after trial on the merits dismissing their suits for muskrats killed and damages to muskrat lands allegedly caused by the geophysical explorations conducted thereon by Petroleum Surveys, Inc., defendant-appellee.

Such geophysical exploration operations consist of recording the subterranean reactions to explosions set off about 200 feet beneath the ground at a certain predesignated pattern of points situated over certain territory. The skilled interpretation of these recorded reactions may approximately indicate the presence or absence of mineral potentialities. In marshy country such as is here involved, the surveying, explosion, and recording crews are transported on "marsh buggies" — huge, heavy vehicles which churn through the marsh on two sets of two broad (4 feet wide each) wheels leaving tracks from 18 inches to four feet deep, depending on the softness of the marsh, and approximately twelve feet in width.

By stipulation between the parties, it is admitted that Petroleum Surveys employees did actually trespass specifically without authorization from plaintiff land-owners (hereinafter designated as "the Harrisons") on their property by operating their marsh buggies on approximately two acres of marsh land at the north west corner of [the Harrisons'] section, and by firing the shot in question at a depth of 172 feet, after sinking a pipe 190 feet deep. It is further expressly stipulated that this trespass was unintentional and was the result of an honest surveying error.

Petroleum Surveys produced three former employees in an effort to minimize the damage done to the two-acre strip. But taking into consideration that the location-point in question was one of many such shots taken on the day in question and over three years before trial, their testimony as to the use of two such marsh buggies to a depth into the Harrison's land of about 200 feet, leaving two tracks each about 50 feet wide or 100 feet in all, together with the testimony of the trapper, trapping supervisor, and owner of the land convinces us, as claimed, that Petroleum Surveys' operations completely crushed the two-acre tract in question and the muskrat-supporting 3-cornered grass growing thereon.***

The evidence presented describes the muskrat as a small (2 lb.) fur-bearing animal, living in marshy areas. It feeds on the roots of certain grasses, which it eats from tunnels under the ground dug by itself. The muskrat lives underground in nests, and prefers areas with ground firm enough to support grass, but not so firm as to impede its digging processes. It also prefers areas upon which certain types of grass grow, such as "3-cornered" grass. The male inhabits the nest with the female. An external manifestation of this nest may be a "muskrat hill," which may also indicate four or five or more such combined nests. The muskrat breeds monthly a litter of 2-4 kittens, constructing a new chamber to its nest for each such litter.***

We feel that the plaintiffs have established by a preponderance of the evidence that two-acre tract damaged by Petroleum Surveys was good muskrat land and could reasonably have been expected to produce through trapping operations an average of 100 muskrats per year. It is not seriously denied that over the last several years the landowner's net profit per muskrat pelt would be 57-58 cents.***

The chief defense to this action by Petroleum Surveys is its contention that by law the Harrisons had no cause of action for the damages alleged because as a matter of law the landowner has no property interest in the muskrats themselves while still untrapped. Muskrats, being wild animals, are owned by the State of Louisiana while still at large, R.S. 56:101, 56:102, 56:252; and wild beasts in general belong not to the landowner, but to the captor no matter upon whose land captured, Article 3415, C.C. [Revised C.C. art. 3413].

It was this contention the District Court sustained in dismissing the landowners' suit.

While the landowner does not own the muskrats situated on his property, he owns the exclusive right to take muskrats therefrom, Esmele v. Violet Trapping Co., 187 La. 728, 175 So. 471, Curran v. Jones, 163 La. 579, 112 So. 492, Rosenthal-Brown Fur Company v. Jones Frere Fur Company, 162 La. 403, 110 So. 630.

Defendant skillfully urges that these cases hold that only trespassers in bad faith are held liable for muskrats taken from another's land, and then only for the principle of restoring the fruits of unjust enrichment. Article 1963 [no corresponding article after Revision], Civil Code. Some language in these cases might be so construed. But the facts of the Curran and Rosenthal-Brown cases cited involve a determination of the measure to be used in the accounting by possessors under (what was subsequently held to be) inferior title to the true owners of the land for profits derived by the wrongful possessors during their possession thereof.

The Esmele case simply awards the true lessee the estimated profit on pelts taken by a wrongful trespasser (a trapping company) without discussion as to legal good or bad faith, see Esmele v. Violet Trapping Company, 184 La. 491, 166 So. 477 on merits. It is not authority for the proposition that the owner of muskrat lands cannot recover from the trespasser for damages occasioned thereby, but rather the contrary. The wrong or damage to the rightful possessor occasioned in the Esmele case was the wrongful trapping of muskrats by the trespasser on the lease-owner's muskrat land, and the trespasser was held in damages to the lease-owner for the estimated profits the lease-owner lost through the trespasser's wrongful act and not for profits on pelts taken by the trespasser. See 166 So. 479.

Negligence is a violation of a relative right, and trespass a violation of an absolute one: but, under Article 2315, C.C., either wrongful act entitles one injured thereby to recover the damages occasioned him thereby. Through this wrongful act (trespass) of Petroleum Surveys, the landowner has suffered provable damage and is entitled to recover therefor. While punitive damages may be recovered when the trespass is intention or willful or wanton, Nickerson v. Allen Brothers & Walley, 110 La. 194, 34 So. 410, see also Grandeson v. International Harvester Credit Corporation, 223 La. 504, 66 So. 2d 317 and, La. App., 61 So. 2d 550; only compensatory damages are awarded in unintentional trespasses as this. ...

The Harrisons sought recovery for (1) 500 muskrats killed in the ground by Petroleum Surveys' operations; (2) loss of 1,500 muskrats, over 15 years.***

Petroleum Surveys also urge that for this same reason, at least as pleaded, the Harrisons cannot recover damages, since they are seeking payment for 1,500 muskrats to be captured in the future, over fifteen years. But the petition pleads, Article 21: "That because of the destruction of said muskrat hills and the damages to the surface of the land, the land has become valueless for trapping purposes for a period of 15 years." Under Article 22, the petition originally itemized this damage as "loss of fur revenues for 15 years and damages to the land." In response to defendant's exception of vagueness, this itemization was further explained as loss of profits from 100 muskrats a year for 15 years. (The evidence indicates that muskrat lands are leased, not at so many dollars per acre, but at so much per cent of the price received for each muskrat subsequently trapped thereon during the life of the lease.)

Contrary to the contention of Petroleum Surveys that any recoverable damages could only have been pleaded at the restoral cost for the acreage, or the value of 3-cornered grass on the tract, we feel that plaintiffs have adequately pleaded the damage sustained by them through defendant's trespass. This damage is not only the value of the grass destroyed, but is really the damage to the property right representing the chief economic value of this small tract — its ability to produce muskrats in trapping operations, measured by the loss of muskrat revenues reasonably to have been expected therefrom had the trespass not occurred.

AWARD

In cases where although there is a legal right to recovery, an exact estimation of damages cannot be made, courts have discretion to assess same based upon all the facts and circumstances of the case, see, for instance, Brantley v. Tremont & Gulf Railway Company, 226 La. 176, 75 So. 2d 236, involving damages occasioned by causing overflow of minnow pond and loss of minnows therein. As previously discussed in detail, in evaluating the economic loss occasioned to the Harrisons by destruction temporarily of the value of this small tract for muskrat trapping purposes through defendant's unauthorized trespass, we feel an award based on loss of 100 muskrats per year, over a period of 8 years, at an average loss of profits to plaintiffs of 57 cents per muskrat, or $456 in all, will be a fair award under all the facts and circumstances as shown by the evidence herein.

For the reasons above assigned, the judgment of the District Court herein is reversed, and judgment is rendered in favor of plaintiffs, William H. Harrison, Walter J. Harrison, and Mrs. Lydia Harrison Knight, and against the defendant, Petroleum Surveys, Inc., in the full sum of Four Hundred Fifty-Six and No/100 Dollars, together with legal interest thereon from date of judicial demand until paid. Defendant-appellee is cast with all costs of this appeal and of these proceedings, including the expert fees fixed by District Court.

NOTES

1. The result in this case follows from paragraph two of article 3413; see revision comment (c).

2. The principle that captured wildlife belongs to the captor also appears in American common law, drawing on sources familiar to civil lawyers such as Justinian's Digest, Pufendorf, and Grotius. See *Pierson v. Post*, 3 Cai.R. 175, 2 Am. Dec. 264 (Supreme Court of New York, 1805).

3. Article 3414 of the Civil Code provides that the captor's ownership of the wildlife can be lost if the animal recovers its natural liberty and the captor does not take immediate steps to recapture it.

4. Two articles that follow indicate additional circumstances in which wild animals are considered to be privately owned, and thus not subject to occupancy. Wild animals in enclosures or, if aquatic, within private waters (whether artificially enclosed or not) are privately owned under article 3415. An exception is made for animals, including bees, that migrate naturally, without human encouragement, from one enclosure, to another. Article 3416 provides that tamed wild animals "are considered privately owned as long as they have the habit of returning to their owner." When they fail to return in a "reasonable time," article 3414 becomes applicable.

5. Domestic animals, on the other hand, are not subject to ownership by occupancy as long as they are privately owned; see La. Civ. Code art. 3417. This raises two questions: what animals qualify as "domestic"? And under what circumstances is a domestic animal not privately owned?

As to the first issue, according to Revision comment (d), "[d]omestic animals include those which are tame by nature, or from time immemorial have been accustomed to the association of man, or by his industry have been subjected to his will and have no disposition to escape his dominion." In contrast, "[w]ild animals comprehend those wild by nature, which, because of habit, mode of life, or natural instinct, are incapable of being completely domesticated and which require the exercise of art, force, or skill to keep them in subjection." Consider George the cat in *Peloquin v. Calcasieu Parish Police Jury, supra* Chapter 4. The Louisiana third circuit Court of Appeal in that case suggested that George might have been "a wild beast or animal" who "never had an owner" and thus was owned by the Peloquins immediately once they took possession of him, despite being a "pet cat," of the sort usually described as domestic. The court found it unnecessary to rule on that issue because mere possession still entitled the Peloquins to damages for conversion if the case against the defendants was proved. Comment (d) suggests, however, that the term "domestic" is used generically.

6. With regard to the second question above, in addition to res nullius, abandoned things—*res derelictae*—are subject to occupancy; see La. Civ. Code art. 3418. These corporeal movables were once owned, but the owner has given up possession with the intent to give up ownership. The person who takes possession of the abandoned thing with the intent to own it immediately becomes its owner through occupancy. The *Peloquin* court suggests that the plaintiffs may have become owners of George by this method of occupancy also. In *Charrier v. Bell*, 496 So. 2d 601 (La. App. 1ˢᵗ Cir. 1986), the court held that the Tunica-Biloxi tribe of

Native Americans had not abandoned tribal artifacts buried with the decedents at its ancient burial ground: "The intent to abandon res derelictae must include the intent to let the first person who comes along acquire them. Obviously, such is not the case with burial goods." The 1990 Native American Graves Protection and Repatriation Act, 25 U.S.C. §§ 3001 et seq., now pre-empts this area. However, the same result—recognition of Native American ownership—would obtain. See 25 U.S.C. § 3002 (Ownership), (a)(1) and (2)(A).

UNITED STATES v. PETER
178 F. Supp. 854 (E.D. La. 1959)

J. SKELLY WRIGHT, District Judge. The setting of this drama is the Lemmon Mattress Works, Hammond, Louisiana Miss Emily Baron, a local recluse, died in 1957 at the age of 82. A year later her mattress, after being locked up in her room since her death, is sold and sent to the Mattress Works for renovation. After the mattress ticking is removed and the cotton contents processed through the chopping machine, they are placed in the deodorizer box. There the cotton is subjected to an air blast which blows into the air $22,200 in gold certificates.·

Emily Baron was one of three children of Lucian Sebastian Baron, a wealthy resident of south Louisiana. Mr. Baron died in 1928. Up to the time of his death he was taken care of by his spinster daughter, Emily. A short time after her father's death, Emily moved in with her brother in his family home near New Orleans. She bought a mattress, the mattress in suit. She used the mattress in her brother's home until 1932 when she and her brother's family moved to Covington, Louisiana. She took the mattress with her.

Emily had built on her brother's acreage in Covington a separate house for her occupancy 30 feet from the home in which her brother and his family lived. In addition to the usual locks on the doors of this house, Emily also had a special lock placed on the door of her bedroom, for it was in that bedroom she kept the mattress.

Emily seldom left her little house and she allowed no one to enter her bedroom except she be present. She ordered her clothes by catalog and kept dormant bank accounts in several banks. As the years went by. Emily gradually lost her sight until at the end she was totally blind. On her death she left no will. Her bedroom was searched and $26,000 in Government bonds and $2,000 in cash was found in scattered places around the room. No one looked in the mattress.

Emily's legal heirs, one set of claimants here, were judicially placed in possession of all property of which she died possessed. In disposing of her property of little value (sic), her mattress was sold for $2.50 to Mr. and Mrs. John E. Cleland, another set of claimants

---

· Gold certificates were dollar bills that represented an amount of gold held by the U.S. Treasury. On the abandonment of the gold standard, they were replaced first by silver certificates, and later by the current Federal Reserve notes. — Ed.

in these proceedings. It was the Clelands who had the mattress picked up from the bedroom of Emily's old house and brought to the Mattress Works. They never saw their purchase. At the Mattress Works the mattress ticking was stripped off and the cotton contents processed as heretofore described. The gold certificates were found by Mr. John Lemmon, in charge of Lemmon's Mattress Works. Mr. Lemmon refused to make a claim for the gold certificates. He testified that they do not belong to him and that he does not want them.

The United States has brought this interpleader action, claiming the gold certificates, but agreeing to pay the rightful owner thereof their face value. See 31 C.F.R. 53.1. Only the heirs of Emily Baron and the Clelands have made a claim. The Clelands originally contended that when they purchased the mattress for $2.50, ownership of the $22,200 in gold certificates contained therein was transferred to them. When it appeared that this contention was obviously without merit, the Clelands decided that the gold certificates were in fact a treasure trove, and that, since the treasure was found in their property, it belonged to them. As authority for this lately conceived contention they cite Civil Code, Article 3423 [Revised C.C. art. 3420]. The heirs of Emily Baron rely on Civil Code, Article 3422 [Revised C.C. art. 3419], maintaining that the certificates were merely lost chattels belonging to their Aunt Emily and that, as her heirs, they own them.

The law of treasure trove has been the subject of much exhilarating conjecture but very little use. Under the early English common law, treasure belonged to the finder. 1 Bl.Comm. (Cooley's 4th ed. 1899) 296. The king soon took care of this detail, however, by promulgating a statute declaring that all treasure belonged to the royal sovereign. 4 Edw. 1, c. 2, 1 Pick.Stat. at L. 112 (1276).*

The Code Napoléon, 1804, Article 716, on which Louisiana Civil Code is largely based, provides that: "The ownership of a treasure belongs to the person who finds it. ..." But that same article provides further that: "A *treasure* is a thing hidden or buried in the earth, on which no one can prove his property...." The treasure trove article in the Civil Code, Article 3423 [Revised C.C. art. 3420], is but a restatement of the Code Napoléon. While the language may be garbled to some extent in translation, it is clear that under [the] Louisiana Civil Code as well as under the Code Napoléon the finder of treasure did not own it. He became the owner only if no one could prove that the treasure was his property.

The other Louisiana Civil Code article of relevance is Article 3422 [Revised C.C. art. 3419] which is entitled "Finding lost things," which provides that the finder of a lost article, the ownership of which is unknown, "remains master of it till he, who was the proper owner, appears and proves his right ***." This article has no counterpart in the Code Napoléon. No useful purpose will be served by distinguishing situations intended to be covered by this article from those under Article 3423 [Revised C.C. art. 3420], because it is clear to this Court that these gold certificates belonged to Aunt Emily and can now be rightfully claimed by her legal heirs under either article.

While ownership of the gold certificates in Emily Baron has not been proved to a mathematical certainty, the preponderance of the evidence shows that in all probability it was Emily who opened the mattress covering sufficiently to insert the certificates inside and crudely sewed the opening up. Emily coveted [sic] this mattress, as she did all of her possessions, from the time she first purchased it. When she first came to live with her brother after her father's death, there was a child in diapers in the family. At the time the air blast blew the gold certificates out of the deodorizer box, it also blew bits of diaper into the air, indicating the possibility that the diaper, before being chopped in the chopping machine, was the wrapper on the certificates. Not long after Emily presumably placed the certificates in the mattress, it became illegal to have gold certificates in one's possession. 33 C.F.R. 53.1. This may explain why Emily allowed her cache to remain in the mattress. It is also conceivable that as the years went on she forgot where she placed the certificates or perhaps even that she had them.

It is true that much of the above appears to be speculation. But considering all the circumstances of this case, and the obviously credible testimony of the members of the Baron family, carefully delineating the eccentricities of this recluse, this Court has the abiding conviction that the certificates did belong to Emily Baron and that her rightful heirs are entitled to their currency equivalent. Judgment accordingly.

NOTES AND QUESTIONS

1. The cache of gold certificates fulfills two of the requirements of the definition of treasure in article 3420, paragraph 2: They are movables hidden in another thing, in this case a movable. However, it fails the requirement of being hidden "for such a long time that its owner cannot be determined." What evidence is regarded by the court as sufficient to establish Ms. Baron's ownership of the certificates?

2. If Ms. Baron's ownership had not been established, who, under article 3420, would have owned the certificates?

3. The Native American burial artifacts in *Charrier v. Bell*, 496 So. 2d 601 (La. App. 1st Cir. 1986) (note 6, *supra* p.290) did not qualify as treasure, and therefore were not subject to ownership by occupancy upon discovery. The opinion, relying on French sources, distinguished funeral goods, intended to be permanently entombed with the decedent, from treasure, which is intended to be temporarily stored by hiding. In addition, the French sources offered the policy reason that "any contrary decision would...promote commercial speculation and despoilment of burial grounds."

4. The heirs of Emily Baron argued that the gold certificates were lost. Under article 3419, the present rule in the Code on "lost things," the finder is required to make a diligent effort to locate its owner or possessor of the cache and return it. He only obtains ownership of it if after three years the owner is not found. What constitutes a diligent effort? Does the article require that the effort must last for three years, or only that three years pass?

5. According to the third circuit Court of Appeal in the *Peloquin* decision, George the cat, that font of knowledge of occupancy law, was apparently considered by the trial court to have been "lost" when taken in by the Peloquins. What actions by the Peloquins might have sufficed to fulfill the requirements of present article 3419?

6. The *Exposé des motifs* to Titles XXIII and XXIV of Book III of the Civil Code (Occupancy, Possession and Prescription) points to the technical inconsistencies in the modes of acquiring property rights that are grouped together under the heading of Occupancy:

> Lost things are not res nullius. Therefore, one who takes possession of a lost thing does not acquire ownership by occupancy.... This mode of acquisition of ownership may be likened to the acquisitive prescription of three years under Article 3489....

> A treasure ... is not res nullius; nor is it a lost thing or an abandoned thing. Thus, strictly speaking, occupancy should not apply to treasure trove. Nevertheless, following civilian tradition, Article 3420 declares that one who finds a treasure in a thing that belongs to him or no one acquires ownership of the treasure; if the treasure is found in a thing belonging to another, half of the treasure belongs to the finder and half belongs to the owner of the thing in which it was found.

Exposé des Motifs, Titles XXIII and XXIV, Occupancy, Possession, and Prescription, 14 WEST'S LOUISIANA STATUTES ANNOTATED: CIVIL CODE ARTICLES 3278 TO 3472, 209, 210 (2007).

CHAPTER VIII. PRESCRIPTION -- GENERAL PRINCIPLES
Civil Code arts. 3445-3472

1. NOTION AND KINDS OF PRESCRIPTION
Civil Code arts. 3445-3461

BAUDRY-LACANTINERIE ET TISSIER, PRESCRIPTION Nos. 25-35
(an English translation by the Louisiana State Law Institute 1972)

Acquisitive prescription is a mode of acquiring ownership as a result of lawful possession over a certain period of time. Thus if I enter into possession of land belonging to my neighbor and hold it thirty years as if it were mine, the fact of my possession will become a legal title at the end of this period. If the former owner then claims his property, I can plead prescription and he will lose.

Liberative prescription is a mode of discharging a debt as a result of inaction by the creditor for a period of time stipulated by law. I owe a sum of money. My creditor fails to make any claim against me for thirty years. My debt is discharged. cIf he then sues me, I can plead prescription. Liberative prescription is not only a denial of action, but also a loss of remedy. In our law it brings about the extinction of the nonexercised right.***

The first impression which the definitions quoted above give is that of spoliation: the owner is deprived of his ownership, the creditor of his creditor's right. But we know in fact that prescription is an institution necessary for the sake of legal stability. The redactors put it at the end of the code since prescription consolidates all the rights established by the preceding titles.

There would be no stability without prescription. Owners would never be sure that they will keep their property; debtors would never be sure that they will not have to pay twice.

The reason no one would be certain to keep his property is that the proof of ownership would often be impossible. In order to prove my ownership and thereby prevail in an action in revendication against a usurper, it does not suffice for me to show that I have acquired by a title translative of ownership, such a sale, exchange, donation inter vivos or through a testament; I must prove that my author was owner, for he could transfer ownership to me only if he had it himself. *Nemo dat quod non habet.* To prove the title of my author, I must show the titles of everybody through whose hands the property has passed before he acquired it. If there is one person in the chain who was not owner, he could not transfer the full title and none of his successors could acquire it. Prescription simplifies all this. It eases the burden of proof by freeing the claimant from having to go back to an era when often no trace of his title can be discovered. All he has to prove is that he or his predecessors have been in possession for thirty years. Prescription also comes to the rescue of the owner who lost his documentary title. This can happen easily if it was a private instrument. The function of prescription does not seem less legitimate in this case than in the first one.

We have also said that, without prescription, a debtor who has paid would never be safe against another claim for payment. Indeed, the loss of the receipt or its deliberate destruction after a certain time makes it impossible for the debtor to prove that he has already paid, if the creditor comes again and demands the payment. Here, too, prescription will substitute for the missing document.

Thus, on the one hand, prescription consolidates or strengthens legitimate ownership titles which are not sufficient in themselves, or it replaces a lost documentary title; on the other hand it protects the debtor who has paid against the claim of a dishonest creditor who knows that the receipt has been lost or destroyed. Thus it gives security to individuals by protecting their patrimony against unjust claims. Here it is correct to say that prescription rests partially on a presumption of ownership or discharge. Domat states it in this manner: "All types of prescription which cause a right to be acquired or lost are based on the presumption that the person who enjoys a right must have some just title, without which he would not have been allowed to enjoy it for such a long period; that he who ceases to exercise some right has been deprived of it for some just cause; and that he who has failed to claim his debt for a long time has either been paid or has recognized that nothing is owed to him." Prescription then appears as providing evidence to support situations which have existed a long time, the legitimacy of which is being contested.

But all human institutions have some weakness. Prescription is no exception. In some cases it will make a usurper prevail over the real owner; or it will discharge a debtor who has not paid his debt. In these cases the thirty-year prescription results in a spoliation of the owner or of the creditor. Is it not a revolting injustice?

Let us not hasten too much to feel sorry for this owner or creditor, or to damn the possessor or the debtor who has enriched himself. First, we can at least say that the owner or creditor has been guilty of gross negligence. Why has the former waited thirty years without revendicating his property? Did this long silence not authorize the usurper to believe that the owner had renounced his right and thus sanctioned the usurpation by doing nothing about it? Is it not correct to say as did Roman law *"vix est enim ut non videatur alienare qui patitur usucapi?"* And what about the creditor? How to explain his long inactivity? Should the debtor not have thought after a certain time that the creditor had renounced his right? And if charges on real property are involved, is it not reasonable that they disappear if the failure to exercise them for a long time shows that they are not important for the entitled party?

On the other hand, after the long prescriptive period has run, the possessor or debtor who thinks that he will never be disturbed, no doubt bases his budgeting on his present resources. Moreover, the possessor acquiring by prescription may have made substantial improvements. Would it be just in all cases to honor the belated claim of the owner or creditor? "The law," says Troplong, "exploits his silence. It finds in it an element of amnesty in favor of the person who through thirty uninterrupted years of work, activity and, perhaps, worry, has sufficiently expiated the violation of an unclaimed right."

At any rate, even if prescription seems to lead in some rare cases to results contrary to equity, if it constitutes what Justinian called "*impium praesidium*," it can easily be forgiven in exchange for the great services it renders to society. Without it there would be no security in transactions, no stability in private estates, no peace among individuals, no order in the state. These were the thoughts which inspired the spokesman of the government when he stated, in the exposé of the legislative motives: "Of all civil law institutions, prescription is the most necessary for social order." At times, it can injure equity. But, in a larger sense, Bigot-Preameneu is right in saying that "in general, justice is done; an individual interest which might possibly be hurt, must give way to the necessity of maintaining social order."

This is the true and main foundation of prescription. The concept of presumed acquisition or discharge, as well as of the renunciation of the title holder of the prescribed interest, are only secondary and accessory motives. Domat wrote with regard to the predominant motive of social interest: "If there were no other reason favoring prescription than public interest in assuring the tranquility of possessors, it would be just in order to prevent a continuing uncertainty about ownership of things." Laurent expressed the same opinion: "After a certain lapse of time, possession should become the base of right. This represents more than a social interest; it is a question of existence. Hence society is entitled more than anybody else to oppose an individual, because society exists only where property is assured; and this does not happen unless possession is made secure. The title of the owner himself is, in its origin, nothing more than possession which society has sanctioned by giving it the authority of law. If ownership can be based on possession, it can be also acquired by possession against one who has ceased to possess."

We can say with Cujas: "*Usucapio damno est dominis, bono reipublicae.*" Cicero correctly called it "*finis solici tudinis ac periculi litium.*" It is also essential not to allow rights to be exercised indefinitely. "Let us imagine the state of a community where rights 10,000 years old could be claimed! This would be the main cause of trouble in matters of property. There would not be a single person or family outside the reach of an action which could put their social standing in question. This permanent state of insecurity would cause a continuous social upheaval. How could individuals and the community persist in such anarchy? Anybody who complains to have lost a right by prescription should be answered that the same institution has protected the obligations contracted by him or by his ancestors centuries ago. This is the compensation for the loss of right which affects a creditor: it generates the general security which his debtor counterclaims."

In terms of its social utility, prescription can be compared with the rule of res judicata. Their function is analogous. There comes a moment when it is necessary to say the last word, where the uncertainty of the law is more burdensome than injustice. "Everything must end," says Troplong; "the state has an interest in seeing that rights are not held in suspense for too long." Thiers wrote similarly, "it is necessary to have a fixed term whereby that which exists will be declared legitimate by the very fact that it exists; without this litigation would spread all over the face of the globe."

Distinguishing Acquisitive and Liberative Prescription

The Civil Code treats acquisitive and liberative prescriptions together. Pothier followed a system which seems to be more correct. He dealt with these prescriptions separately, dedicating to acquisitive prescription a special treatise, entitled "Prescription based on possession;" liberative prescription is discussed in a chapter of his treatise on "Obligations." The authors of the Civil Code thought that the two prescriptions have many points of contact. To eliminate numerous repetitions, they dealt with both in one title. But this system has the inconvenience of generating various difficulties when it comes to making distinctions between the rules common to both prescriptions and the special rules which are peculiar to each of them.

Having in mind these difficulties, we can state several important rules common to both prescriptions:

1) Provisions of Arts. 2220-2227 [LCC arts. 3445-3453] apply in general to acquisitive and liberative prescription. They define the rights to which prescription applies and those which are outside its reach; they define persons who can plead prescription and those against whom it can be pleaded; and they establish rules governing the renunciation of prescription.

2) The lapse of time is calculated in the same manner for prescription (Arts. 2260, 2261) [LCC arts. 3454-3456].

3) The suspension and interruption of both prescriptions is also governed by the same rules (Arts. 2243-2259) [LCC arts. 3462-3472].

4) Neither the acquisitive, nor the liberative prescription constitutes, before it is completed, a vested right (*droit acquis*) in terms of Art. 2 [LCC art. 6 & LRS 1:2], on the retroactivity of statutes. Consequently, a new statute can modify the rules governing the running of prescription, without any retroactive effect. The Court of Cassation stated that "until consummated, prescription does not create any vested right; until then the legislator is always in a position to change the statute."

35. But we must also point out the profound differences which separate the two prescriptions.

1) Acquisitive prescription is based essentially on possession. Liberative prescription, with the exception of several particular cases (prescription of mortgage; of an action to enter into possession of a decedent's estate), does not presuppose possession.

2) Acquisitive prescription can give both an action and provide a defense (exception) in favor of the prescribing party. Thus acquisitive prescription of an immovable allows me to bring both an action in revendication against a de facto possessor, if I have lost my possession; or, if I am in possession, to plead a peremptory exception against an action in revendication brought against me by the former owner. Liberative prescription, on the contrary, is merely a manner of defending against an action. Hence it gives, in general, only an exception.

3) The proper scope of liberative prescription is broader than that of acquisitive prescription. The latter can lead only to the acquisition of ownership or of real rights. And not even of all real rights: mortgage rights and discontinuous or nonapparent servitudes, are outside its reach. Liberative prescription applies to creditor's rights, to real rights other than ownership, to actions other than revendication.

NOTE
Retroactivity of Legislation

For the question of the constitutionality of legislation establishing a new prescription or altering an existing prescriptive period, see *Lott. v. Halley*, 370 So. 2d 521 (La. 1979), in which the Supreme Court declared:

It is well established that statutes of limitation are remedial in nature and as such are generally accorded retroactive application. State v. Alden Mills, 202 La. 416, 12 So. 2d 204 (1943); Shreveport Long Leaf Lumber Co. v. Wilson, *supra*; DeArmas, v. DeArmas 3 La. Ann. 526 (1848). However, statutes of limitation, like any other procedural or remedial law, cannot consistently with state and federal constitutions apply retroactively to divest a person of a pre-existing right. Orleans Parish School Board v. Pittman Construction Co., *supra*. Nonetheless, a newly-created statute of limitation or one which shortens existing periods of limitation will not violate the constitutional prohibition against divesting a vested right provided it allows a reasonable time for those affected by the act to assert their rights. Copper v. Lykes, 218 La. 251, 49 So. 2d 3 (1950); State v. Recorder of Mortgages, 186 La. 661, 173 So. 139 (1937). Moreover, the legislature is the judge of the reasonableness of the time and the courts will not interfere except where the time is so short as to amount to a denial of justice. Copper v. Lykes, *supra*. Finally, where an injury has occurred for which the injured party has a cause of action, such cause of action is a vested property right which is protected by the guarantee of due process. Barmaster v. Drainage District No. 2 of the Parish of St. Charles, 366 So. 2d 1381 (La. 1978).***

In the instant case, plaintiff's cause of action for damages vested on January 21. 1972, the date of Dr. Haley's alleged act of negligence giving rise to plaintiff's injuries. This was prior to enactment of La. R.S. 9:5628 which became effective September 12, 1975. Under the law in effect prior to that date, plaintiff's suit would have been timely filed. La. R.S. 9:5628 is a statute of limitation in that it prescribes fixed time periods for institution of medical malpractice suits. According to the general rule, statutes of limitation are accorded retroactive application. However, in the instant case, La. R.S. 9:5628 operates to eliminate plaintiff's vested right to sue on his pre-existing cause of action without providing a reasonable period following its enactment to assert his claim. Absent such a provision, we conclude that La. R.S. 9:5628 cannot be retroactively applied in the instant case because to do so would divest plaintiff of his vested right in his cause of action in violation of the due process guarantees under the state and federal constitutions. The court of appeal erred in holding otherwise.

a. Things Susceptible of Prescription

LOUISIANA CIVIL CODE

Art. 3485. Things susceptible of prescription

All private things are susceptible of prescription unless prescription is excluded by legislation.

LOUISIANA CONSTITUTION (1974)

Article 9, § 4. Reservation of Mineral Rights; Prescription

A. *Reservation of Mineral Rights.* The mineral rights on property sold by the state shall be reserved, except when the owner or person having the right to redeem buys or redeems property sold or adjudicated to the state for taxes.

B. *Prescription.* Lands and mineral interests of the state, of a school board, or of a levee district shall not be lost by prescription.

Article 12, § 13. Prescription Against State

Prescription shall not run against the state in any civil matter, unless otherwise provided in this constitution or expressly by law.

CITY OF NEW IBERIA v. ROMERO
391 So. 2d 548 (La. App. 3d Cir. 1980)

LABORDE, J. This appeal involves an eviction action filed by the City of New Iberia against Exalta Romero, Sr. based on a lease from the City to Romero. The lease covers a strip of land located in the City of New Iberia. The trial court, after sustaining Romero's exception of thirty (30) years acquisitive prescription, ordered dismissal of the City's eviction action. The City appeals. We affirm. We find no error in the trial court's ruling.

On January 14, 1980, the City of New Iberia filed a motion to evict Exalta Romero, Sr. from a strip of land located in New Iberia pursuant to a lease dated May 23, 1972. The City alleged that the lease was for a period of one (1) year and continued from year to year after the primary term.

Romero filed peremptory exceptions of 10 years liberative prescription, 30 years acquisitive prescription, and no right of action. He alleged that the property in question, Wana Alley, acquired by the City on April 3, 1903, was not being used for any public purpose, and had been abandoned by nonuse for a period in excess of ten (10) years. Romero further alleged that on April 26, 1940, he acquired a certain town lot bounded by Wana Alley and since that time has been in uninterrupted possession of that portion of Wana Alley described as "A" on the plat of survey of Alvin C. Badeaux, City Engineer, dated March 1972 and attached to the lease.

The City of New Iberia contends that since Romero executed a lease on May 23, 1972, he is a precarious possessor and may not acquire his lessor's property by prescription. Romero contends that the City has no standing to bring an eviction proceeding since he acquired ownership of the strip of land by 30 year acquisitive prescription prior to executing the lease on May 23, 1972.

In his reasons for judgment the trial court concluded that: "The exception of thirty year acquisitive prescription is sustained, and the City's eviction action will be dismissed."

In reaching the conclusion that Romero's plea of thirty years prescription was well founded, the trial court discussed two basic concepts which must be considered when acquisitive prescription arises involving a public body. We take the liberty of quoting in part from the trial judge's well-written opinion:

> ***First the state and its political subdivisions have a dual personality. They act as sovereign, and in a private capacity. (C.C. art. 450 Comments)

> Secondly, things under the civil law have been traditionally divided into three categories: Common, public and private. (C.C. art. 448)

Common things may not be owned by anyone (C.C. art. 449). Public things are those things which are owned by the state or its political subdivisions in their capacity as public persons. They include such things as streets and squares. (C.C. art. 450) Private things are things owned by private persons, or by the state or its political subdivisions in their capacity as private persons. (C.C. art. 453).

Two recent Court of Appeal (Third Circuit) cases recognized these distinctions and hold that acquisitive prescription may run against a public body as to private things it owns, but not as to public things. In the case of Town of Broussard v. Broussard Volunteer Fire Dept., 357 So. 2d 25 (1978) the Court held that acquisitive prescription as to the things in question ran against the municipality in favor of the Volunteer Fire

Department, as they were private things owned by the City in the capacity of a private person. According to the Court in *Broussard*, public property to which all inhabitants of a City are entitled in common, such as public streets and walks, is not subject to acquisitive prescription. Public property not used by the people in common, which is used for their benefit by the administrators of the City, is subject to acquisitive prescription.

An immediate precursor to the Broussard case was that of Prothro v. City of Natchitoches, 265 So. 2d 242 (La. App. 3d Cir. 1972), which was cited by defendant in an attempt to show that prescription does run against a city.

A careful reading of *Prothro* reveals that the Court impliedly followed the same logic later specifically endorsed in *Broussard*. The property involved was originally acquired

by the City for use in drilling water wells. Such a use falls into the category of administrative use defined in *Broussard*. As such, the property could not be considered "hors de commerce", and insusceptible of prescription, and the Court decided that the prescription did run against the City.

As previously discussed, a street a public thing owned by a political body in its capacity as a public person (C.C. art. 450, *supra*) and is consequently not susceptible of prescription. Both *Prothro*, and *Broussard*, *supra*, cited by defendant, are accordingly distinguishable from the instant matter in the sense that the property in dispute here was acquired by the plaintiff for use as a public street, but indistinguishable in the sense that the said property has not been put to use as a public Street since at least 1940, and probably never was. Indeed, the first evidence of any use at all by the City is its lease to defendant in 1972. This certainly demonstrates an intention to own as a private person, to put to administrative use, and not for the use of the people in common. In fact, the lease spells out that the property was not then being used for public purposes. The next question, then, is whether a thing acquired by a public body as a public thing but subsequently owned as a private thing is subject to acquisitive prescription. The answer is found in the case of Louisiana Highway Commission v. Raxdale, 12 So. 2d 631 (La. App. 2d Cir. 1943). In that case, the City of Alexandria had purchased property "as a street of said town," but had never used it as such, and in fact had never possessed it at all, vendors and their heirs having retained possession up to the time of the litigation. The argument was made that the property was a public acquisition and not subject to acquisitive prescription. The Court, relying on the principles announced above and on former C.C. art. 482, at page 635 ruled in effect that regardless of the character of the acquisition, if the thing is never used, or ceases to be used, as a public thing, it takes on the character of alienability and becomes subject to prescription. Former C.C. art. 482 (now arts. 449, 450 and 455) provides, inter alia, that things naturally susceptible of ownership but applied to some public purpose, resume their original quality as soon as they cease to be applied to such public purpose; and gives as examples of such things highways, roads, streets and public places.***

A remaining question on acquisitive prescription is whether the running of prescription is defeated by part of the property granted in 1903 being used as a public thing, since the evidence is that approximately half of it is being used by the public. The evidence is silent as to how long that part has been used by the public, but for purposes of argument, let us assume that it has been continuously since 1903. Such argument would not avail the City, because when the City uses a private thing, it is in the same position as a private person. Just as a private person is susceptible of losing only part of a piece of property through acquisitive prescription (by whatever method and for whatever reason), so is the City. In accordance with former C.C. art. 482, when any (part of whole) things naturally susceptible of ownership retains or resumes that quality, it may be prescribed against. The undersigned is aware of no authority to the contrary.

The evidence is clear and undisputed that defendant possessed adversely the property in dispute continuously from 1940 in such a manner as to acquire by prescription, until 1972. Thirty years had run prior to 1972, so the execution of the lease by defendant,

whatever he thought he was signing (he testified he thought it was some sort of partition agreement), is of no moment.

Neither can it be said that defendant renounced his acquisition through prescription by entering into the 1972 lease, thereby acknowledging ownership in plaintiff. The law is clear that such a renunciation must be express, absolute and unequivocal, and be so clear that it leaves no room for contrary interpretation. Porter-Wadley Lumber Co. et al v. Bailey, 110 F. 2d 974, USCCA(5), 1940; A.M. Ross v. Harvey Adams, 23 La. Ann. 621 (1871); Reconstruction Finance Corp. v. Ardillo, 200 So. 2d 687 (1941); C.C. arts. 3460, 3461; Traité Théorique et Pratique de Droit Civil, Vol. XXVIII, Nos. 1-815, at pages 44-45, Baudry-Lacantinerie & Tissier. That is obviously not the case here."

We find the trial judge's scholarly analysis of the instant case to be fully supported by the record. For the above and foregoing reasons the judgment of the trial court is affirmed....

b. Prescription and Peremption

NOTE

In *Pounds v. Schori*, 377 So. 2d 1195 (La. 1979), the Louisiana Supreme Court was required to consider the timeliness of an action that had been brought by the presumed father of a child to "disavow" his "paternity" of that child (see generally La. Civ. Code arts. 185 & 187). Though the plaintiff (the child's presumed father) acknowledged, first, that the applicable limitation period was only six months long, reckoning from the birth of the child, and, further, that his disavowal action had not been filed until sometime later than 6 months from his presumed child's birth, he contended that the running of the limitations period had been "interrupted" by virtue of another disavowal action that he had previously filed in another state, one that had been filed within the 6 month period (see generally La. Civ. Code art. 3462). In opposing that argument, the defendant (the child's mother) argued that inasmuch as the limitation period in question was one of "peremption" rather than "prescription", the running of the period was not susceptible of interruption, be it by the filing of an action or otherwise (see generally La. Civ. Code arts. 3458 & 3461). The Supreme Court agreed with the defendant. In explaining its decision, the court had this to say about the difference between "prescription" and "peremption":

> Our jurisprudence has long recognized a major distinction between a statute of limitations (prescription) and a peremption. It has been repeatedly held that prescription bars the remedy sought to be enforced and terminates the right of access to the courts for enforcement of the existing right. A peremptive statute, however, totally destroys the previously existing right with the result that, upon expiration of the prescribed period, a cause of action or substantive right no longer exists to be enforced....

> Recently, in Flowers, Inc. v. Rausch, La., 364 So.2d 928 (1978), we held that peremption is but a form or species of prescription possessing the differentiating characteristic that peremption does not admit of interruption or suspension. . . .

> In Flowers...we recognized that peremption is a common law term that has infiltrated our jurisprudence. We noted also that peremption is, in reality, the civil law equivalent of "forfeiture". We so held on the basis of 28 G. Baudry-Lacantinerie & A. Tissier, Traite Theorique et Pratique, De droit Civil, Secs. 38-39, Louisiana State Law Institute Translation . . . . In short, we adopted the Baudry-Lacantinerie & A. Tissier concept that there is little if any doctrinal difference between forfeiture and prescription.

> We reiterate the following pronouncement in Flowers...:

> There is indeed a difference between prescription and peremption as noted by the Court of Appeal and as pointed out in the Succession of Pizzillo, supra. Nevertheless we conclude that peremption is but a form of prescription, a species thereof, but with the characteristic that it does not admit of interruption or suspension, and we determine that the constitutional provision barring prescription bars prescription in all its forms, including peremption.

Id. at 1198-99.[14]

c. Contractual Freedom
Civ Code art. 3471, 3505-3505.4

NOTE

At issue in *Contours Unlimited v. Board of Commissioners*, 630 So. 2d 916 (La. App. 4th Cir. 1993), was the enforceability of a contract whereby the parties had purported to "shorten" the rather lengthy prescriptive period established by the applicable legislation – five years (see the Public Contracts Act, La.

---

[14] In the part of the supreme court's opinion that immediately follows that reproduced above, the court explained why, in its judgment, the limitation period applicable to the "disavowal" action was peremptive rather than prescriptive. Though the court's conclusion was entirely correct at the time, the legislature has since then changed the law. By the express terms of Civil Code art. 189, par. 1, revised in 2005, the limitation period applicable to the disavowal action is now prescriptive rather than preemptive.

R.S. 38:2189.1) – to just 30 days. The court of appeal refused to enforce the contract, reasoning as follows:

La Civil Code Article 3471 states:

"A juridical act purporting to exclude prescription, to specify a longer period than that established by law, or to make the requirements of prescription more onerous, is null." In light of the code article, we find that the provision in the Board's contract is a nullity. Contours is entitled to a 5-year prescriptive period as proscribed [sic] by law.

Was the court of appeal correct? In particular, did the court have a proper understanding of the concept of what "make[s] the requirements of prescription *more onerous*"?

In Act 88 of the Regular Session of 2013, the legislature added to the Civil Code a number of new articles pertaining to the "extension" of *liberative* prescription by contract. The new articles are 3505-3505.4. What effect do these new articles have upon the rule of Article 3471?

2. COMMENCEMENT OF PRESCRIPTION

1(2) PLANIOL, TRAITÉ ÉLÉMENTAIRE DE DROIT CIVIL 574-577
(an English translation by the Louisiana State Law Institute 1959)

RULES COMMON TO BOTH FORMS OF PRESCRIPTION

When Prescription Starts. The time of prescription commences, in principle, to run the day after the day of the entrance into possession. The day itself of the taking of possession does not count, because it is necessarily incomplete. Thus if the entrance into enjoyment took place April 7, 1897, the first day that counts for prescription would be the eighth. . . .

Exceptional Case. There are [certain] exceptions to the rule that causes prescription to run from the day after the day when possession commenced. The starting point must be postponed beyond this day [in these cases. One such case is that of "eventual rights".] . . .

. . . Commentators, even though they insist that prescription runs against . . . rights suspended by a condition, recognize that prescription does not run against merely eventual rights. These are such as a person may be called upon to exercise some day as the successor of a deceased person, in virtue of the law or a testament or by a donation of future things. The doctrinal writers explain the distinction they thus make between two kinds of rights. They say that the eventual right has not yet entered the patrimony of him who will have it one day. They add that the conditional right already figures in the patrimony in as much as it is transmissible under this form to the heirs of its holder. They insist that this right may be protected, by conservatory measures, while awaiting the accomplishment of the condition (Art. 1180. Comp. Dalloz, note 1900.2.305). Eventual rights, which have not yet come into existence and which can be neither transmitted nor defended are thus imprescriptible as opposed to conditional rights. . . .

Mode of Computing the Time. The delay applicable to acquisitive prescription is made up of a given number of years that are counted by days and not by hours (Art. 2260). It would be impossible, in most instances, to fix the hour when possession began....

The last year must be finished for the acquisition of prescription (Art. 2261). What is the last day of the term? It is that day of the final year which is the same day of the month as that of the taking of possession. Thus if possession was taken on April 7, 1897, the last of the prescriptive delay will be, according to the duration of the prescription; April 7, 1907 . . . or 1927. The anniversary day is necessarily included in the delay, because the initial day is not counted. . . .

This [final] day must be completed. [In contrast to the old law, which held that certain kinds of prescription, including acquisitive, accrued as soon as the final day *begins*], [m]odern law exacts that it be *terminated*. And thus is more logical.

2(1) PLANIOL, TRAITÉ ÉLÉMENTAIRE DE DROIT CIVIL 358-361 (an English translation by the Louisiana State Law Institute 1959)

Liberative prescription begins to run as soon as the action accrues, or, as Pothier said "the day on which the creditor could institute his demand." It cannot commence sooner, because the time given for prescription should be a time during which the action can be exercised, and one cannot reproach the creditor for not having acted at a time when he did not have the right to do so. Otherwise, it could happen that the right would be lost before it could be exercised, which would be as unjust as absurd . . . .

When the action depends on a suspensive condition, the prescription does not run until the condition happens. (Art. 2257, par. 1.). Traditional solution (Pothier No. 680). But the cause which retards the prescription does not exist in obligations subject to a resolutory condition, for the execution of it can be demanded immediately; the action would therefore be prescribed if the time of the prescription has elapsed before the accomplishment of the condition.. . .

The same reason exists for suspending prescription until the arrival of the term, and this is what the law has done (Art. 2257, par. 3). Up till then the creditor cannot claim his payment: his credit is not exigible.. . .

When a sum is payable in fractions at different terms, the prescription runs separately against each part of the debt, counting from the day when it comes due. This rule applies: (1) to the principal the reimbursement of which is payable by annuities or by fractions, to facilitate payment by the debtor; (2) to revenues (interest, rents, arrears, etc.) payable by installments; (3) to pledges and salaries payable at the end of the year or at various times of the year.

Imprescriptible Actions

Certain actions seem to escape all prescription and to perpetuate themselves indefinitely. In this class are included the action of partition; the action of boundary; the action to establish the right of passage in case of enclosure; the action to acquire rights to a party wail. These actions, in fact, are not extinguished by lapse of time; but it is not because of the effect of a veritable imprescriptibility, analogous to that of the ancient Roman actions. Their indefinite duration comes from the fact that their cause renews itself every day: they are never prescribed because at whatever time one places oneself, it is always the date after the fact which gives rise to them. What is the cause of the action of partition? It is the indivision. That state prolongs itself, and as long as it lasts it creates, every day, the principle of the action. . . .

DARBY v. DARBY
120 La. 847, 45 So. 746 (1908)

PROVOSTY, J.   The present matter has been brought before this court by writ of review to the Court of Appeal sitting for the parish of Iberia. Defendants having acquiesced in the judgment of the district court except as to the notes C, D, and E, and plaintiff not having appealed, or, so far as the record shows, filed an answer to the appeal, the only notes involved are the said three notes, and to them the Court of Appeal confined its judgment.

The said notes are dated respectively, January 1, 1899, January 15, 1900, and January 1, 1901, and are payable on demand. This suit to enforce their payment was filed November 25, 1905. Defendants pleaded the prescription of five years.

Defendants are sued as the heirs of Mrs. Coralie Darby, the marker of the notes, who was the mother of the plaintiff and of one of the defendants and the grandmother of the other defendants.

Plaintiff offered parol evidence to show that the notes were given to him in payment of his salary as agent and manager of the plantation of his mother; that at the end of each year she would give him a note; that she had the cash with which to pay, and would have paid if he had not preferred to take the notes, which were interest bearing and a good investment; that his mother knew that such was his motive, and always cautioned him to take good care of the notes, thereby recognizing them as due. This evidence is now relied on for showing interruption of prescription. It was objected to in so far as tending to prove the acknowledgment of the debt or a promise to pay it by the deceased, for the purpose of taking it out of prescription. The court reserved its ruling on the objection, and never made any; but, had it ruled on it, would, doubtless, have sustained it, as the Code forbids the reception of parol evidence to prove "any acknowledgment or promise of a party deceased to pay any debt or liability, in order to take such debt or liability out of prescription, or to revive the same after prescription has run or been completed." Article 2278 [Revised C.C. arts. 1832, 1847]. Except as tending to prove a continuing acknowledgment of the debt, the facts established by said evidence would not have the effect of either suspending or interrupting prescription; since a note is not rendered immune from prescription by the fact of its having been accepted by way of investment.

The next cause of interruption, or suspension, of prescription relied on by plaintiff is a written agreement entered into by him and his coheirs, including defendants, by which they made a partition of the estate, paid all the debts-excepting two, which they said were contested--and deposited in bank an amount of cash sufficient to pay whatever judgment might be rendered on the said contested debts, one of which was the debt now sued on. The agreement provided that suit should be brought within six months; and that the agreement should not "in any way prevent or affect any rights which the said Octave Darby may have to claim judicially of his coheirs any amount herein referred to as claimed by him."

This agreement does not contain a word intimating in the slightest degree a willingness on the part of defendants to waive any of their rights or defenses; but plaintiff contends that the clause limiting to six months his right to bring suit is pregnant with an agreement that during such six months prescription shall not run against him. Both of the lower courts took a different view, and we agree with them. The parties to the agreement guardedly provided that the agreement should not affect the rights of the parties except as expressly stipulated. Moreover, the agreement was entered into in June, 1905, when the notes C and D were already prescribed, and it contains no express renunciation of a prescription already accrued. Civ. Code, art. 2278 [Revised C.C. arts. 1832, 1847].

Both lower courts took the view that on a demand note prescription runs from demand, and not from the date of the note. In the case of Andrews v. Rhodes, 10 Rob. 52, this court decided the contrary, and that view has not been departed from, so far as we have been able to find; but, on the contrary, has been reaffirmed in the case of Harman v. Claiborne, 1 La. Ann. 342, where prescription was maintained in an action against the drawer of a check never presented for payment.

The underlying principle of the matter is that expressed by Judge Martin in the said Rhodes Case--that "prescription attaches to a right from the moment it may be exercised." This is so because from that moment the "silence" of the creditor begins, which, if it lasts long enough, operates the prescription. Civ. Code, arts. 3528, 3459 [Revised C.C. arts. 3447]. This is the principle of the decision of Wardwell v. Sterne, 22 La. Ann. 28, and Van Wickle v. Police Jury, id. 76, where prescription was held to run on a duebill from its date. Indeed, if a demand note were not prescriptible until demanded, the parties to it would have discovered a mode by which prescription would not run upon an obligation exigible immediately; and this, practically, would amount to the discovery of a mode by which prescription could be renounced in advance, or could by an agreement be prevented from running, although article 3460, Civ. Code, provides that such a thing cannot be.

In a case where the adjudicatee at a judicial sale was to pay the price "within fifteen days from notification of judgment fixing the order in which the creditors were to be paid," the Court of Cassation held that prescription ran from the moment of the adjudication; because from that moment the debt was an absolute unconditional debt. Glais v. Villebranche, 13 Juillet, 1846, J. du P. 1846, vol. 2, p. 741.

The decisions in other states, with a few hold that prescription on a demand note runs from the date of the note; and even in most of the few exceptions the decisions are influenced, more or less, by special facts [citations omitted].***

The judgments of the Court of Appeal and of the district court are therefore set aside in so far as condemning defendants to pay the notes C, D, and E and the costs of suit, and the suit of plaintiff is dismissed as to said notes; in other respects the said judgments are affirmed, and plaintiff is condemned to pay costs of suit.

RIEGER v. TIERNEY
265 So. 2d 279 (La. App. 4th Cir. 1972)

CHASEZ, J. Anthony J. Rieger, plaintiff herein, filed suit against the defendant, Robert J. Tierney, praying to be recognized as a one-half owner of the following described property:

> "A certain lot of ground together with all the buildings and improvements thereon, and all the rights, ways, privileges, servitudes, and advantages, thereunto belonging, or anywise appertaining, situated in the fourth district of this city, square 161 bounded by Camp, Ninth, Chestnut and Eighth streets. Said lot is designated by the letter C and measures 47' front on Camp Street by a depth of 124' 4''. Municipal nos. 3119-21 Camp Street."

Both parties are in substantial agreement on the facts of this case. The original negotiations for the purchase of the property were started by Mr. and Mrs. Anthony J. Rieger to provide a home for themselves and Mrs. William Tierney, the mother of Robert J. Tierney and Mrs. Anthony J. Rieger.

After consultations with the Home Building and Loan Assn. it developed that the Riegers did not have a sufficient amount of money to make the down payment of $2400.00.

Robert J. Tierney, a veteran, agreed to use his benefits under the (3.1. Bill to provide the required shelter. The Riegers put up $1200.00, which was sufficient to make the down payment when combined with the G.I. benefits supplied by Robert J. Tierney. The title to the property was taken in the name of Robert J. Tierney on the 1st day of May, 1947, and the property has remained in his possession ever since.

The Riegers made' monthly payments of $30.50, contending that this represented one-half of the monthly installment of $61.00 due the Homestead during the life of the Homestead loan. The Homestead note was paid in full in the latter part of December, 1964.

Prior to Tierney's acquisition of the Camp Street property hereinabove described, the Riegers had lived in rented premises along with Mrs. William Tierney, the mother of Mr. Robert J. Tierney and Mrs. Anthony J. Rieger. They were required to move from the rented premises when that house was sold and had difficulty in locating suitable rental quarters. These considerations broadened the search for a home and led to the subsequent purchase of the Camp Street property herein involved.

After the act of sale to Robert J. Tierney in 1947 Mrs. William Tierney moved into one side of the premises with the Anthony J. Rieger and Robert J. Tierney moved into the other side shortly thereafter. Mrs. William Tierney died in 1953. Plaintiff, Anthony J. Rieger, contends that he occupied one-half of the premises bearing municipal #3119 Camp Street in the City of New Orleans from the time the property was purchased until July 16, 1966, when he and his family were forced by Robert J. Tierney to leave the house.

Although plaintiff's suit was filed primarily to have him recognized as the co-owner of the above described property, in the alternative, he plead that he be reimbursed for all payments made by him to the Home Building & Loan Assn., as well as other expenses incurred in the purchase of the aforementioned property, and the cost of some repairs made thereto, aggregating the sum of $5358.83. He also demanded the issuance of a temporary restraining order and ultimately an injunction prohibiting Robert J. Tierney from assigning, selling, donating or otherwise encumbering the property.

Robert J. Tierney filed an answer denying all allegations of plaintiff's petition except that he admitted the act of sale by the Homestead to himself of the property involved; and by reconventional demand he alleged that he is the record owner of the property, that he never executed a counter letter or sold any interest therein or otherwise alienated any portion thereof.***

The court a quo tried the case on the merits. In its reasons for judgment, among other things, the court stated that it would consider the various payments of $30.50 per month made by Mr. and Mrs. Rieger as rent. It further stated that in its opinion the defendant had unjustly enriched himself to the extent of $1200.00, this amount representing the deposit of $450.00 for down payment, closing costs, etc., which the record discloses were made by Mrs. Rieger at the time the act of sale was passed in 1947. That the preliminary injunction issued on March 15, 1968 would be recalled and the permanent injunction would be refused; and also that the exception of prescription filed by Robert J. Tierney would be overruled.***

There is sufficient evidence in the record to warrant the finding of the court for the judgment in favor of the plaintiff, Anthony J. Rieger, for $1,200.00, interest and costs;

however, on March 20, 1972 Robert J. Tierney filed a plea of prescription in this court leveled at the judgment rendered in favor of Anthony J. Rieger against him for the sum of $1,200.00, interest and costs, and reflects that the alleged cause of action arose in 1947 and suit was not filed until 1968, and therefore any debt which the defendant Tierney might have owed to the plaintiff, Rieger, on the basis of a loan, contract, or quasi contract, has prescribed pursuant to Articles 3538 and 3544 of the Civil Code [Revised C.C. arts. 3494, 3499].

In our opinion this plea of prescription is sound and we must reverse the District Court's judgment in this respect.

The record discloses that plaintiff, Anthony J. Rieger, was aware of the fact, at least as far back as February, 1954, that the defendant, Tierney, did not recognize him as co-owner of any portion of the property involved herein and refused to sign a counter letter to that effect.

By letter dated February 22, 1954, Mrs. A. J. Rieger, through her attorney, Henry M. Robinson, requested the defendant to execute a counter letter to protect her alleged claim of one-half ownership in the property. From the record it appears that Tierney at all times refused to execute the requested document. Plaintiff, therefore, knew as of 1954 that the defendant would not acquiesce in this demand. As a result, plaintiffs claim for the return of $1,200.00 arose as of this date and prescription began to toll.

The applicable prescriptive period is ten years pursuant to C.C. Article 3544 [Revised C.C. art. 3499]. Therefore, since the plaintiff-appellee did not file his suit until March 4, 1968, the plea of prescription must be maintained. C.C. Article 3459 and Art. 3528 [Revised C.C. art. 3447].*** Reversed in part, affirmed in part, and rendered.

LEMMON, J. (dissenting). I disagree with the legal conclusion of the majority that the Riegers' claim for $1,200.00 has prescribed. There is no factual dispute that the Riegers advanced $1,200.00 at the 1947 act of sale, but in order to determine when liberative prescription commenced, the court must first determine the nature of the transaction which gave rise to the claim.

The Riegers testified that the bargain struck with Tierney in 1947 was a joint purchase of the residence, with the Riegers providing the cash necessary for the act of sale and Tierney furnishing the benefit of his "G.I. Bill." As part of this agreement Tierney obligated himself to subsequently execute a counter letter recognizing the undivided one-half ownership of the Riegers. Furthermore, the Riegers obligated themselves to pay one-half of the mortgage note for the entire term of the loan, which the undisputed evidence established that they did.

The trial judge apparently found as a fact that this was the agreement reached between the parties, since he found Tierney to be in bad faith, and the majority has also made this finding of fact. Accepting this factual finding, I would then legally classify this agreement as a verbal contract for the transfer of immovable property, which was unenforceable because the contract was not in writing. C.C. art. 2275 [Revised C.C. arts. 1832, 1839].

However, Tierney could have voluntarily fulfilled the agreement at any time by transferring title as agreed, and the Riegers had no right to sue for recovery of the $1,200.00 until Tierney breached the contract by refusing to deliver title. In my opinion no cause of action for restitution of the $1,200.00 arose in favor of the Riegers until Tierney breached the contract. Of course, prescription could not begin to run until the cause of action arose.

It is on this legal and factual determination of the date of occurrence of the breach that the majority and I differ. In my opinion the crucial determination is the date on which Tierney communicated to the Riegers that he refused to fulfill his agreement to execute a counter letter.

The majority relies upon a 1954 letter to Tierney from an attorney, who was a friend of the family, to establish the date of *Tierney's* refusal to execute a counter letter. The letter reads as follows:

> February 22, 1954.
> Mr. Robert J. Tierney 3121 Camp Street New Orleans, Louisiana.
> Dear Robert:
> In all fairness I believe it would be proper for you to execute a Counter-Letter in favor of your sister, Mrs. A. J. Rieger, to protect her one-half ownership in the property owned by you jointly.
>
> If you agree with this, will you telephone me and arrange to come in and sign the Courter-Letter [sic] which has been prepared for you.
> With best wishes, I am,
> Very truly yours,
> /s/ Henry M. Robinson
> Henry M. Robinson
> HMR:der
> B/c - Mr. Rieger

Tierney admitted receiving the letter, but stated that he did not understand the nature of the request. It is significant that Tierney did not testify that he refused to execute a counter letter upon receipt of the attorney's communication or at any other time. On the contrary, he testified that he never discussed a counter letter with the Riegers until after the loan was paid off in 1965.

The party asserting liberative prescription as a defense to a claim has the burden of proving when prescription began to run. If prescription did not begin to run until Tierney communicated his refusal to execute a counter letter, and he testified that he did not even discuss a counter letter until 1965, I believe that he has failed to prove that prescription began to run before then. Suit was filed on March 4, 1968. I do not believe that his simple failure to answer the 1954 letter was sufficient to sustain his burden of proof, especially in view of his positive testimony.

Neither is there anything in the Rieger's testimony which would establish an earlier commencement of prescription. Mrs. Rieger testified that her brother prior to the act of sale agreed to give them a counter letter, but that she did not press him for this document, being afraid of him because of his violent and brutal behavior on past occasions. After the Robinson letter in 1954 went unanswered, she consulted the homestead lawyer in 1958 to obtain his assistance in tactfully getting her brother to deliver the counter letter. A few years later, she consulted the same lawyer, who advised her that she had a "slim chance" to obtain title. The lawyer verified that this conversation was about 1966. I believe that Mrs. Rieger's continued efforts to secure assistance in obtaining the counter letter tend to prove, rather than disprove, that she was unaware of any unequivocal refusal by her brother to fulfill his agreement.

Finally, there is nothing in the record to show that Tierney ever treated the Riegers as anything but co-owners, since they paid their proportionate share of the mortgage note, taxes and insurance, performed repairs on the premises, and paid no rent or other consideration after the mortgage loan was paid off. There was therefore no reason for the Riegers to believe that Tierney would not eventually recognize their interest.

In my opinion the agreement for a joint purchase remained in effect until Tierney affirmatively breached it. As long as Tierney had the power to choose whether to perform or to breach the agreement and took no affirmative action, I would hold that prescription did not begin to accrue in his favor.

NOTE
Continuous Tort

For the doctrine of continuous tort, see *South Central Bell Telephone Co. v. Texaco*, 418 So. 2d 531 (La. 1982). The court declared:

Generally, the prescriptive period for damage to adjacent land commences when the damage becomes apparent and the injured party discovers who or what caused it. C.C. arts. 3537, 667; Dean v. Hercules, Incorporated, 328 So. 2d 69 (La., 1976). However, Dean did not consider the question of "continuing damages." 328 So. 2d at 73. See Di Carlo v. Landry & Dry Cleaning Service, 178 La. 676, 152 So. 327 (1934); Devoke v. Yazoo & M.V.R. Co., 30 So. 2d 816 (La.1947); Craig v. Montelepre Realty Co., 252 La. 502, 211 So. 2d 627 (1968); and Wilson v. Hartzman, 373 So. 2d 204 (4th Cir. 1979) writ refused 376 So. 2d 961. When the damaging conduct continues, prescription runs from the date of the last harmful act. Where the cause of the injury is a continuous one giving rise to successive damage, prescription dates from cessation of the wrongful conduct causing the damage.

3. INTERRUPTION OF PRESCRIPTION
Civil Code arts. 3462-3466

NOTE

Earlier versions of the Louisiana Civil Code, as does the French Civil Code even today, distinguished between two supposed modes of interrupting prescription, named, respectively, "natural" and "civil". The difference between the two, according to the few French legal scholars who have attempted to explain it, supposedly consists in this: that whereas "natural interruption" results from a "physical act" (namely, a "loss of possession"), "civil interruption" results from a "civil act" (either a suit by the prescribee against the prescriber or an acknowledgment of the prescribee's right by the prescriber). No scholar has yet even attempted to clarify, much less succeeded in clarifying, the concept "civil" in this context. One suspects that, for any number of reasons, the game is not worth the candle.

Be that as it may, the supposed distinction, in the end, fails to live up to its billing in at least one very important respect. It is billed as if it were part of the law that pertains to "prescription in general". That proposition, if accurate, would mean that natural as well as civil interruption applies to all forms of acquisitive prescription, "liberative" and "non-use" as well as "acquisitive". And therein is the rub. It turns out that only one of these modes of interruption – civil – applies to *all* forms of prescription. As for natural interruption, it applies only to *acquisitive* prescription. For these reasons, in this Chapter, which pertains to prescription in general, we will confine our attention to civil interruption.

a. Civil Interruption; Filing of Suit
Civil Code arts. 2097, 3462-3463

LOUISIANA CODE OF CIVIL PROCEDURE

Art. 561. Abandonment in trial and appellate court

A.   (1) An action is abandoned when the parties fail to take any step in its prosecution or defense in the trial court for a period of three years...

(2) This provision shall be operative without formal order, but, on ex parte motion of any party or other interested person by affidavit which provides that no step has been taken for a period of three years in the prosecution or defense of the action, the trial court shall enter a formal order of dismissal...

C. An appeal is abandoned when the parties fail to take any step in its prosecution or disposition for the period provided in the rules of the appellate court.

Art. 1067. When prescribed incidental or third party demand is not barred

An incidental demand is not barred by prescription or peremption if it was not barred at the time the main demand was filed and is filed within ninety days of date of service of main demand or in the case of a third party defendant within ninety days from service of process of the third party demand.

Art. 5059. Computation of time

In computing a period of time allowed or prescribed by law or by order of court, the date of the act, event, or default after which the period begins to run is not to be included. The last day of the period is to be included, unless it is a legal holiday, in which event the period runs until the end of the next day which is not a legal holiday.

A half-holiday is considered as a legal holiday. A legal holiday is to be included in the computation of a period of time allowed or prescribed, except when:

(1) It is expressed excluded;
(2) It would otherwise be the last day of the period; or
(3) The period is less than seven days.

NOTE

In *Levy v. Stelly*, 277 So. 2d 194 (La. App. 4th Cir. 1973), the court was presented with a rather complicated claim of "interruption" of liberative prescription. In that case, the plaintiff, a "personal injury" victim, filed not one, not even just two, but rather three suits to recover damages. He filed the first in state court, well within a year of the accident. But then, fearing that the action should have been brought in federal court, he filed a parallel action there. By then, more than a year had passed since the accident. Several months later, the first suit (that brought in state court) was dismissed. Then, concluding that his action should have been brought in state court after all, he filed a second action there. The federal suit was still pending.

The defendant met this new state court suit with an exception of prescription (see generally La. Civ. Code art. 3492). The plaintiff opposed the exception, arguing as follows: the first state court suit had interrupted prescription, so that the federal suit had been timely filed; the federal suit had interrupted prescription, so that the second state court suit had been timely filed (see generally La. Civ. Code art. 3462, sent. 1). In response, the defendant attacked the first premise of the plaintiff's argument, that is, that the first state court suit had interrupted prescription. Noting that that suit had eventually been dismissed, the defendant argued that the supposed interruptive effect of that suit had been "wiped out" (see generally La. Civ. Code art. 3463, sent. 2) and, not only that, had been wiped out "retroactively", so that the federal action had been prescribed.

The court of appeal rejected the defendant's "retroactivity" theory, explaining itself as follows:

> Prescription is interrupted by the filing of a suit, which provides the first notice to a debtor that a claim is being judicially asserted. . . . It is therefore logical that any issues as to interruption of prescription by suit should be determined as of the time of the filing of that suit.

> Using the time of filing as the test point, we observe that prescription was interrupted by the filing of the original suit, since the one year period provided by

C.C. art. 3536 had not yet elapsed. Likewise, at the time suit was filed in Federal court, that action was not subject to a dismissal based on prescription, since prescription remained interrupted by the pending suit.

Defendants argue, however, that C.C. art. 3519 literally prohibits us from now considering the first interruption. We disagree. As stated above, issues as to interruption of prescription are determined as of the time of the filing of the suit sought to be dismissed, and not as of the time of the filing of the exception.

We construe C.C. art. 3519 to apply prospectively to suits filed after a plaintiff abandons, voluntarily dismisses or fails to prosecute his demand. The purpose of the article is to prohibit the plaintiff from voluntarily dismissing his suit on a cause of action and later filing a second suit on the same cause of action. By taking away the benefit of the original interruption, the article prevents the plaintiff from claiming that a new prescriptive period commenced when he dismissed the suit which had previously interrupted prescription. The basic purpose of prescription-to provide legal stability-is thus fulfilled.

But in the case where a second suit is filed Prior to abandonment, voluntary dismissal or failure to prosecute the original demand, the interruption provided by the first suit is still viable at the time of the filing of the second suit, and the interruption remains viable after the dismissal because of the pendency of the second suit. In the present case there was never a time after the one year anniversary date of the accident when a suit asserting plaintiff's cause of action against defendants was not pending in some court.

We conclude that defendants cannot use the facts existing at the time of the filing of their exception to dismiss an action which was not prescribed when the suit was filed. A suit not prescribed when filed cannot later become prescribed by the subsequent dismissal of a previous suit on the same cause of action.

Id. at 195-96.

The defendant applied for a rehearing, arguing that the court's rationale and conclusion were inconsistent with those of an earlier opinion issued by the same court, one that involved a claim that the interruptive effect of a suit had been wiped out due to its "abandonment". The court rejected that argument, finding that the abandonment case was distinguishable:

On application for rehearing defendants cite Long v. Chailan, 196 La. 380, 199 So. 222 (1940) in support of their position. In the Long case plaintiffs abandoned their first suit by failing to take any steps in its prosecution for more than five years, although the suit was not dismissed until after the filing of another suit on the same cause of action. The court held that it was the abandonment, not the dismissal, which destroyed whatever effect the first suit had on the interruption of prescription.

In the present case the suit which interrupted prescription was active and viable when the second suit was filed.

While this application for rehearing was pending, another panel of this court held in Tug Alamo, Inc. v. Electronic Service, Inc., 275 So. 2d 419, (La. App. 4th Cir. 1973), involving similar circumstances:

> '* * * art. 3519 operates prospectively and the question of whether a claim is prescribed must be decided according to the circumstances at the time of its filing (or, if appropriate, service). Thus a suit filed after the first suit is dismissed is filed at a time when the first suit's interruption is considered as never having occurred and therefore prescription has accrued . . . . But a second suit filed before the first suit is dismissed is filed at a time when the interruption has occurred and therefore prescription has not accrued. And prescription cannot thereafter accrue, since the second suit itself interrupts (and suspends) the running of prescription.'

The application is denied.

Id. at 198. The supreme court thereafter denied writs, stating, "The Court of Appeal is correct." 279 So. 2d 203 (La. 1973).

b. Civil Interruption; Acknowledgment
Civil Code art. 3464

CARRABY v. NAVARRE
3 La. 262 (1832)

The facts are fully stated in the opinion of the court, delivered by PORTER, J.

This action is brought on a promissory note, given by the defendant in payment of a house and lot, purchased by her from Pierre and Antoine Carraby. The debt is secured by a mortgage of the property, which was the consideration of the note. The petition asks for judgment for the amount due, and for a sale of the mortgaged premises. *issue*

The answer admits the execution of the note, and avers, the defendant gave an order on the heirs of Fletcher, which was to be in full satisfaction of the price of the house and lot. To this defense is added, the plea of prescription.

There was judgment in the court of the first instance in favor of the plaintiff, and the defendant appealed.*** *Procedural hx.*

The term of the contract of sale accorded to the buyer, the right to extend the payments for two years, on paying interest at ten per cent, by installments every three months. The interest does not appear to have been paid, and it has been much debated at the bar, whether the failure of the defendant, to comply with the right of suspending the payment, did not leave the obligation in force from the expiration of the first three months. We need not examine this question, for on another ground, we think the exception cannot be sustained.

It is proved by testimony, which we are not authorized to reject, and which from all the circumstances of the case, we give credit to: that an agent of the plaintiff demanded payment of the defendant frequently since the year 1823, and that she answered by requesting him to have patience, "as she expected a sufficient sum from the estate of Fletcher, when settled, as would enable her to pay the price of the house and lot." By the Articles 3486, 3516, 3517 and 3518 [Revised C.C. art. 3462] of the Louisiana Code, prescription is interrupted by the acknowledgment of the debtor. A promise to pay a debt can be considered in no other light but an acknowledgment of its existence. But it has been contended, that by another article of the code, (3423) [Revised C.C. art. 3420] prescription not acquired, cannot be renounced, and this acknowledgment was made previous to the completion of the time necessary to the prescription, it can have no effect. We understand by the article last cited, that a man cannot renounce the right of pleading prescription, which may thereafter be acquired. But we do not understand, that the debtor may not renew his obligation, so as to make the time run from his acknowledgment and not from the date of the engagement. The law clearly repels the argument relied on, by using the word "interrupt." If the acknowledgment could only take effect after prescription was acquired, it might be renounced, but could not be interrupted. The latter act supposes the prescription progressing, and not accomplished.

It is, therefore, ordered, adjudged, and decreed, that the judgment of the District Court be affirmed with costs.

LOUISIANA REVISED STATUTES

R.S. 9:5807. Interruption of prescription on pledged obligations by payment on obligation secured by pledge. A payment by a debtor of interest or principal of an obligation shall constitute an acknowledgment of all other obligations including promissory notes of such debtor or his co-debtors in solido pledged by the debtor or his co-debtors in solido to secure the obligation as to which payment is made. In all cases the party claiming an interruption of prescription of such pledged obligation including a promissory note as a result of such acknowledgment shall have the burden of proving all of the elements necessary to establish the same.

4. SUSPENSION OF PRESCRIPTION
Civil Code arts. 3467-3472

LOUISIANA REVISED STATUTES

R.S. 9:5802. Fugitive from justice. Prescription does not run against the action of a citizen of this state against a former citizen or resident of this state who is a fugitive from justice and is without a representative in this state upon whom judicial process may be served.

Prescription begins to run from the day the fugitive returns to the state or from the day his power of attorney appointing a representative upon whom judicial process may be served is filed in the office of the clerk of court of the parish of his former residence.

R.S. 9:5803. Property adjudicated to state for non-payment of taxes. In all cases where immovable property has been, or may be, adjudicated or forfeited to the state for non-payment of taxes and has been or is subsequently redeemed by a purchaser in good faith and by just title, or by the heirs or assigns of such purchaser, prescription shall not be interrupted or suspended during the period that title is vested in the state. This Section shall not apply to or affect the three-year prescription provided by law for tax privileges, and in all cases where immovable property has been adjudicated to the state for non-payment of taxes, such property shall only be redeemed upon paying the amounts provided by law.

R.S. 9:5804. Immovable property of municipal corporation. Any municipal corporation owning alienable immovable property may prevent the running of prescription adquirendi causa against it in favor of any third possessor, by recording a notice with the clerk of court of the parish where the property is situated, or with the register of conveyances in the Parish of Orleans insofar as property in that parish is concerned. This notice shall contain a description of the property and a declaration that it is public property belonging to the municipality and the recording shall suspend the running of prescription during the time the ownership of the property shall remain vested in the name of the municipality.

The recordation of the written act by which a municipal corporation shall acquire alienable immovable property likewise shall be deemed sufficient notice in order to suspend the term of prescription.

CORSEY v. STATE DEPARTMENT OF CORRECTIONS
375 So. 2d 1319 (La. 1979)

TATE, J. The plaintiff Corsey was a prisoner at the state penitentiary. He sues the state department of corrections for personal injuries sustained on June 18, 1972. He did not file suit so as to interrupt prescription until June 25, 1974. Since this legal demand was made more than one year after the tortious injury was sustained, La. Civ. C. arts. 3536, 3537 [Revised C.C. art. 3492, C.C.P. art. 3658, C.C. art. 3426], His suit was dismissed as prescribed. 366 So. 2d 964 (La. App. 1st Cir. 1978).

We granted certiorari, 368 So. 2d 127 (February 23, 1979). We desired to consider whether prescription could run against the plaintiff (a prisoner within the total control of the defendant state agency) when, due solely to the defendant's negligence, the tort-caused physical and mental (brain) injuries to the plaintiff so mentally incapacitated him that he lacked any understanding of what had happened to him and of his possible legal remedies until July 1973, when he began to recover an awareness of the events and of his condition.

For the reasons set forth more fully below, we hold that, under these facts, prescription did not begin to run against the plaintiff until July 1973. Therefore, his legal demand of June 1974 was timely. In so holding, we rely upon the principle that prescription does not run against a party who is unable to act (a principle often denoted by the maxim *contra non valentem agere nulla currit prescriptio*). The principle is especially applicable in the present instance, where the plaintiff's inability to act is due to the defendant's willful or negligent conduct.

I

The specific issue before us is whether the year within which the plaintiff must bring his tort action for personal injuries negligently caused by the defendant, La. Civ. C. arts. 3536, 3537 [Revised C.C. art 3492, C.C.P. art. 3658, C.C. art 3493], is interrupted or suspended during the period in which, due to the defendant's negligent conduct, the plaintiff had incurred such mental incapacity as to be unable to assert a legal demand to recover for such injuries.

Article 3521 of our Civil Code [Revised C.C. art. 3467] provides, "Prescription runs against all persons, unless they are included in some exception established by *law* [*i.e.*, legislation]." (Italics ours). Despite the express statutory provision, our Louisiana jurisprudence has recognized a limited exception where in fact and for good cause a plaintiff is unable to exercise his cause of action when it accrues. French jurisprudence (despite an identical provision in the French Civil Code) likewise recognizes this exception. Comment, The Scope of the Maxim *Contra Non Valentem* in Louisiana, 12 Tul. L. Rev. 244 (1938); Planiol, Civil Law Treatise, Volume 1, Section 2704-05, Volume 2, Section 678 (LSLI translation, 1959).

The exception is founded on the ancient civilian doctrine of *contra non valentem agere nulla currit prescriptio*, predating and within the penumbras of modern civilian codes, and it has been recognized from Louisiana's earliest jurisprudence. Comment, 12 Tul. L. Rev. 244, cited above; Henson v. St. Paul Fire & Marine Ins. Co., 363 So. 2d 711 (La. 1978); Hyman v. Hibernia Bank & Trust Co., 139 La. 411, 71 So. 598 (1916); McKnight v. Calhoun, 36 La. Ann. 408 (1884); Quierry's Ex'r & Faussier's Ex'rs, 4 Mart. (*O.S.*) 609 (1817).

II

As the cited comment notes, 12 Tul. L. Rev. at 253-54, this court in Reynolds v. Batson, 11 La. Ann. 729, 730-31 (1856), authoritatively lays down the three categories of situations in which our early jurisprudence held that the principle *contra non valentem* applied so as to prevent the running of liberative prescription: (1) Where there was some legal cause which prevented the courts or their officers from taking cognizance of or acting on the plaintiff's action; (2) Where there was some condition coupled with the contract or connected with the proceedings which prevented the creditor from suing or acting; and (3) *Where the debtor himself has done some act effectively to prevent the creditor from availing himself of his cause of action.*

Modem jurisprudence also recognizes a fourth type of situation where *contra non valentem* applies so that prescription does not run: Where the cause of action is not known or reasonably knowable by the plaintiff, even though his ignorance is not induced by the defendant. (This principle will not except the plaintiff's claim from the running of prescription if his ignorance is attributable to his own willfulness or neglect; that is, a plaintiff will be deemed to know what he could by reasonable diligence have learned.).***

This fourth or more modern situation, which has been judicially characterized as a *contra non valentem* exception to the running of prescription, is generically similar to instances provided by statute where prescription does not begin to run until the claimant has knowledge of his cause of action. in these, the cause of action does not mature (so prescription does not begin to run) until it is known or at least knowable.

The fourth situation is thus generically somewhat distinguishable from the earlier three situations first recognized to justify exceptions to prescription on the basis of *contra non valentem*. In them (as in the present case, as we will show), the cause of action had accrued, but nevertheless the plaintiff was prevented from enforcing it by some reason external to his own will — the courts closed by wartime conditions, some contract or administrative condition preventing his access to the courts, or some conduct of the defendant which prevented him from availing himself of his judicial remedy.

In concluding our general discussion of the application of *contra non valentem,* we should finally note that the Louisiana jurisprudence, as does the French, distinguishes between personal disabilities of the plaintiff (which do not prevent prescription from running) and an inability to bring suit for some cause foreign to the person of the plaintiff (which does suspend its running).

Thus, a person whose ignorance of his cause of action or inability to assert it is the result of his own mental incapacity cannot claim the benefits of this rule unless he has been interdicted. Israel v. Smith, 302 So. 2d 392 (La. App. 3d Cir. 1974), cert. denied, 303 So. 2d 183 (La. 1974); Buvens v. Buvens, 286 So. 2d 144 (La. App. 3d Cir. 1973), Lassere v. Lassere, 255 So. 2d 794 (La. App. 4 Cir. 1972), cert. denied, 257 So. 2d 434 (La. 1972). Perrodin v. Clement, 254 So. 2d 704 (La. App. 3 Cir. 1971). *Cf.*, Vance v. Ellerbe, 150 La. 388, 90 So. 735 (1922).

Likewise, a plaintiff cannot invoke *contra non valentem* to escape the running of prescription based merely upon his inability to attend to his affairs because of his personal illness, Ayres v. New York Life Ins. Co., 219 La. 945, 54 So. 2d 409 (1951) at least when this illness arises independently of any fault on the part of the defendant.

III

In the present instance, we are not, strictly speaking, concerned with whether the plaintiff Corsey's cause of action had accrued or matured at the time of the incident, for it had: the damage was immediately discernable to a person of ordinary diligence and capacity. Nor are we concerned with his mental competency per se, since (as he was not interdicted) he is a person subject to having prescription run against his cause of action.

Here, however, unlike mere mental incompetency (which will not suspend prescription), the defendant's own tort has produced the plaintiff's mental and physical inability to file suit during the period of tort-caused incompetency. The values at issue are not similar to those which control in cases of mere mental incompetency; they are more analogous to those which permit invocation of *contra non valentem* to suspend prescription because the defendant has concealed information or has otherwise prevented the plaintiff from bringing the action within the prescriptive delay.

Due to the defendant's wrongful conduct, until July 1973 the plaintiff was unable because of the tort-caused mental incompetency to know he had a cause of action or to have the mental ability to pursue it. We hold that, consequently, prescription did not begin to run against the plaintiff (under the facts stipulated for purpose of the exception pleading prescription) until July, 1973.

The fault or wrongful conduct of the defendant which prevents the plaintiff from suing timely is a traditional *contra non valentem* reason to except the plaintiff's claim from prescriptive extinguishment. We find this principle here applicable.

It is true that the usual case in which *contra non valentem* was applied on this ground has involved conduct of the defendant preventing the plaintiff's pursuit of his claim — conduct separate from the wrongful conduct giving rise to the claim itself. We have not previously been confronted by a case in which the same wrongdoing that gave rise to the cause of action also made it impossible for the plaintiff to avail himself of his legal remedy because of the tort-caused mental incapacity. Nevertheless, we can discern no rational distinction which would justify us to apply *contra non valentem* in the former case, but not in the latter.

As Justice Provosty stated for this court in the Hyman v. Hibernia Bank & Trust, 139 La. 411, 417, 71 So. 598 (1916), an "exception must be recognized, we think, in a case like the present, where the inability of the plaintiff to act was brought about by the practice of the defendant. Otherwise, the defendants would be profiting by their own wrong — a thing inadmissible in law."

To permit prescription to run under the present facts would permit a defendant with custody and control over a person he had tortiously injured to profit by his subsequent laxity in medical treatment, when (as here stipulated) the injured person's recovery of mental faculties was retarded beyond the prescriptive period. The plaintiff in these circumstances is doubly helpless to file suit by virtue both of his mental incapacity and also of his removal from the solicitous attention of relatives and friends who might act in his stead.

SUMMERS, C.J. (dissents and files a separate opinion)***Does mental incompetence suspend prescription?

It is Corsey's position that when a defendant through negligence and willful and wanton conduct renders another disabled to such an extent that the injured person is unable to help himself, prescription is suspended until the helpless condition ends. In adopting this position plaintiff seeks to distinguish this case from the cases which have held that prescription does run against a plaintiff who is feeble-minded when the condition is unrelated to his claim; the distinction being that in the case at bar plaintiff's incompetence — mental and physical — was due to the fault of defendants.

It is a basic principle of Louisiana law announced in Article 3521 [Revised C.C. art. 3467] of the Civil Code that "[prescription] runs against all persons, unless they are included in some exception established by law."

Article 3522 [Revised C.C. art. 3468] contains an exception to this rule, providing that "[minors] and persons under interdiction cannot be prescribed against except in the cases provided by law." See also La. Civ. Code art. 3554 [Revised C.C. art. 3469]

In the decisions of this Court and the Courts of Appeal which have considered the exceptions created by Article 3522 [Revised C.C. art. 3468], it has been decided that mental incompetence alone is insufficient to qualify one as an interdict. Even commitment to an institution for the mentally incompetent does not supply the "interdiction" contemplated by Article 3522 [Revised C.C. art. 3468] which would suspend the running of prescription against one mentally incompetent. Interdiction must be pronounced in accordance with law.

In substance, the courts have held that this State must deal with a person alleged to be mentally incompetent or insane as a sane person, until the courts have interdicted him. The argument is that the law writer has advisedly used the word "interdict" in the technical sense of a judgment rendered contradictorily as distinguished from a person of unsound mind not formally interdicted. La. Code Civ. Pro. arts. 4541-4557.

The reasoning is said to be that where there has been a lawful interdiction, all persons are legally charged with knowledge of the incapacity; whereas, in cases of insanity or unsound mind not judicially declared, without the restrictions on civil rights imposed by interdiction, the validity of judicial proceedings, or, as in the case at bar, the timely assertion of rights by such an individual, would depend upon a determination of mental capacity in each case. Claims that physical incapacity or illness prevented the timely assertion of a person's rights have also been rejected. Cox v. Von Ahlefldt, 105 La. 543, 30 So. 175 (1900); Vance v. Ellerbe, 150 La. 388, 90 So. 735 (1922); Ayres v. New York Life Insurance Company, 219 La. 945, 54 So. 2d 409 (1951).

"Prescription is a manner of acquiring the ownership of property, or discharging debts, by the effect of time, and under the conditions regulated by law." La. Civ. Code art. 3457 [Revised C.C. arts. 3445, 3447]. Because of the general proposition that prescription runs against all persons, prescription is not suspended unless the conditions prescribed by law for suspension are fulfilled. The requirement of interdiction to suspend the prescription running against a cause of action is such a condition in this case. It has not been fulfilled and prescription is not suspended.

***There are obvious and well-recognized reasons for a high degree of certainty in the law of prescription. The passage of time dims the memory of witnesses, destroys evidence and imposes undue burdens upon litigants in their efforts to prepare their defense and reconstruct the facts as they existed in the distant past. When the legislature, in a tort case, fixes a one-year interval for filing suit it is because, in its wisdom, that is the time during which such a suit should be commenced. Courts should extend the time only in exceptional circumstances upon adequate authority.

In McClendon v. State through Dept. of Corrections, 357 So. 2d 1218 (La. App. 1978), the court reviewed the Louisiana cases on "contra non valentem" and concluded that since 1916 the cases have stressed the need for some concealment or misleading action on the part of a defendant before a plaintiff could avail himself of the doctrine.

Applying these tests and recognizing the reluctance of the Court to depart from the clear and certain rules of the Civil Code, it must be concluded that the doctrine of "contra non valentem" does not apply here. The injury complained of by plaintiff was susceptible of proof on the day the stabbing occurred, it having been made manifest from the outset. Moreover, defendants did nothing to conceal, mislaid or lull plaintiff into inaction.

5. RENUNCIATION OF PRESCRIPTION
Civil Code arts. 3444-3451

1(2) PLANIOL, TRAITÉ ÉLÉMENTAIRE DE DROIT CIVIL 601-604
(an English translation by the Louisiana State Law Institute)

§ 8. Of The Renunciation of Prescription

Prohibition of Anticipatory Renunciations. "One cannot renounce prescription in advance," says Art. 2220 [LCC art. 3449]. This prohibition is based upon the general interest that prescription offers. Prescription is a matter of public policy. Private agreements cannot derogate from it (Art. 6) [LCC art. 7]. If such a clause had been permitted it would soon have assumed a stereotyped form.

While it is easy to conceive of anticipatory renunciations of prescription in contracts and in matters of obligations, it is difficult to think of them in the domain of usucapion. One cannot grasp why and how a person, who acquires an immovable in good faith and under title, would contract not to avail himself of prescription, should the occasion arise. Such a renunciation seems to be even more unlikely in the case of a usurper who without a title takes possession of an immovable. The presence of this prohibition in the law, where it has no bearing as regards usucapion, springs from the perpetual and useless blending of the two kinds of prescription.

Possibility of Renouncing an Acquired Prescription. The law that prohibits anticipatory renunciations, authorizes, on the contrary, renunciations after the completion of prescription (Art 2220) [LCC art. 3449]. There is then but an individual interest involved. He, who is protected by prescription, may at his option, avail himself of it or he may renounce it. He merely does what he wants with his own right.

Renunciation is a unilateral act that does not require acceptance by the other party. It is moreover an act that is not solemn, that may be performed in any manner whatsoever. It may be done expressly or tacitly (Art. 2221) [LCC art. 3450]. Tacit renunciation flows from facts which imply an intention of abandoning an acquired right. It is obvious that courts should not hold that such intention exists by inferring it from equivocal acts, susceptible of another interpretation. Renunciations are never presumed (Civ. Cass., Jan. 31, 1927, D. H. 1927. 208).

Effect of Renunciation. The possessor who renounces prescription when it has run in his favor seems to divest himself of his right and to agree to an act translative of ownership in favor of somebody else. But this is so merely in appearance. As has already been seen (no. 2709) prescription does not take place by operation of law. It must be set up by the party. The Court cannot do so of its own motion [LCC art. 3452]. Consequently, if it be a means of acquiring, it is still necessary that use be made of it. When he, in whose favor prescription has run renounces it, he refrains from making use of a means that the law offers him to become owner. It may accordingly be said that he threw away an opportunity to acquire, that he refused to have a piece of property become part of his patrimony. It would, however be a mistake to say that he had alienated it, that he had transmitted the ownership to another. Art. 2221 speaks of the renunciation of prescription as "the abandonment of an acquired right." But this term "acquired" connotes merely the right to set up the plea of prescription. It is of this right, and not of the ownership which is not as yet acquired, that the possessor despoils himself by his renunciation.

Capacity. Even though the renunciation of an acquired prescription is not the juridical equivalent of an alienation, it nevertheless has the same practical effect. It deprives the person who makes it of the ownership of a piece of property which he could have definitively retained. Renunciation is therefore essentially dangerous. And thus does the law prohibit it to "him who cannot alienate" (Art. 2222) [LCC art. 3451].

The term "cannot" here includes the two questions of capacity (for him who acts as regards his own property) and of power (for him who acts as regards the property of another). Consequently, an incapable, even one having the administration of his property, such as an emancipated minor or a wife separated in property, cannot renounce prescription. And a tutor cannot do so without the same authorization he requires when the matter at issue is the alienation of an immovable.

Rights of Creditors of Person who Renounces. If the renunciation is made by an insolvent debtor in fraud of his creditor's rights there is no doubt about their right to have it annulled by means of the Paulian action (Art. 1167) [LCC 2036]. They will thus retain as security, the property whose ownership their debtor had acquired by prescription. This is but applying the general law. But it is held that Art. 2225 [LCC art. 3453] accords them a special advantage which consists in this: the creditors would be dispensed from proving the fraud. It suffices that they establish the proof of damage caused them by the renunciation. Such damage is usually manifest. The law says that creditors have a right to set up the prescription "even when the debtor renounces it." It does not require that there be fraud. The creditors accordingly will not have to prove that their debtor intentionally renounced the prescription in order to harm them. The success of their suit is thus made much easier than it would be if they had to fall back upon the general law. It is in this sense that Art. 2225 [LCC art. 3453] is interpreted by the great majority of commentators and courts.

This interpretation does not seem to me correct. The text of Art. 2225 [LCC art. 3453] was clearly taken from the following passage in Dunod de Charnage's treatise. He wrote: "If he who prescribes, neglected to avail himself of it, his creditors may do so, because prescription forms an acquired right of which a man cannot despoil himself to the detriment of his creditors." (Bk. 1, Chap. 14, page 110).

Here is therefore a case where the possessor omits setting up the plea based upon prescription and not a case where he, by a special act, renounces the prescription. If there were a renunciation made, a categorical text would be necessary to derogate from the general principles of the Paulian action and to dispense the creditors from proving the fraud. Such a derogative text does not exist in Art. 2226 [LCC art. 3453]. If the law had contemplated referring to a renunciation already made, it would have said: "even though the debtor had already renounced it." The use of the verb in the present tense shows that the lawmaker contemplated the mere fact of an abstention still lasting when the creditors intervened.

SUCCESSION OF SLAUGHTER
108 La. 492, 32 So. 379 (1902)

PROVOSTY, J. The opponent, J. H. Gardner, was holder of three notes of the de cujus,-one for $500, dated May 28, 1884, due 45 days after date, with 8 per cent. interest from date; another for $200, dated May 1, 1885, due 60 days after date, with 8 per cent. interest from date; and another for $75, dated May 31, 1889, due 60 days after date, with 8 per cent. interest from date,-all to the order of the opponent. No payment had been made on these notes, and they were long prescribed, when, on the 28th of July, 1900, the de cujus wrote a letter to the opponent, in which is found the following: "And my memorandum book tells me I owe you money. That I can pay. Difficult to pay you constant, never--failing friendship. I must plead bankruptcy for that." This excerpt is the only part of the letter having reference to any debt of the de cujus to the opponent. Five months later the de cujus gave the opponent a check for $1,000. Parol evidence being inadmissible to show the circumstances under which this payment was made, the payment stands as an isolated fact in the case. Parol evidence was admitted--and, we think, properly--to show that the three notes in question were the only debt due by the de cujus to the opponent. McGinty v. Succession of Henderson, 41 La. Ann. 384, 6 South. 658. The question is whether, under this condition of the facts, that part of the three notes not satisfied by the $1,000 payment was taken out of prescription. The renunciation of a prescription once acquired may be either express or tacit. Civ. Code, art. 3461 [Revised C.C. art. 3450]. The letter, standing by itself, amounts to nothing more than to an expression of ability on the part of the writer to pay some uncertain sum of money which his memorandum book told him he was owing the opponent. The payment of the $1,000, reduced to an isolated fact,-as it is by the exclusion of parol evidence to show the circumstances under which it was made,-amounts at most to an acknowledgment of the existence of the debt. The letter and the payment taken together amount to nothing more than to an acknowledgment of the existence of the debt. They neither expressly nor tacitly renounce the acquired prescription. A man may acknowledge his debt, and pay part of it, without renouncing the prescription acquired on it. Frellsen v. Gantt, 25 La. Ann. 477; Levistones v. Marigny, 13 La. Ann. 354; Blossman v. Mather, 5 La. Ann. 335; Utz v. Utz, 34 La. Ann. 754; Lackey v. Macmurdo, 9 La. Ann. 18 (dissenting opinion of Judge Ogden)....

It is ordered, adjudged, and decreed that the judgment appealed from be set aside, and that the opposition herein be dismissed, at the cost of the opponent in both courts.

HARMON v. HARMON
308 So. 2d 524 (La. App. 3d Cir. 1975)

FRUGÉ, J. This is a suit for payment of a loan made by the plaintiff, Alma Harmon, to her brother, Dr. Alfred E. Harmon. The defendant contends that the debt has prescribed and in the alternative that he is entitled to a set-off due to services rendered. The trial court granted judgment in favor of the plaintiff in the amount of $1,770. We amend and affirm.

It was stipulated by the parties that four loans totaling $2,300 were made by the plaintiff to the defendant between February 8, 1967, and February 7, 1968. It was further stipulated that payments totaling $250 were made by the defendant between May and October of 1972.

The record indicates that the loans were made by Alma Harmon to her brother while he was a senior in medical school and during the first year of his internship. There is no record of any payment or other activity concerning the loans prior to 1972. A phone call was made by plaintiff to defendant concerning the loans during which defendant agreed to begin making monthly payments of $50. Although the record does not conclusively establish when this call was made, it appears to have been made in 1972 since the monthly payments began in May of that year.

After the October 1972 payment the defendant discontinued the monthly payments apparently in response to a quarrel with his sister. In November of 1972 the defendant wrote a letter to his sister stating he would continue the payments if she would make apology to the girl friend of Doctor Harmon. The payments were never resumed and this suit was filed July 5, 1973.

The trial court rendered judgment in favor of the plaintiff in the amount of $1,770. The trial judge arrived at this figure by subtracting $250, for payments made, and $330, for services rendered Alma Harmon, from $2,350.

The main issue on appeal deals with prescription. Under Article 3538 [Revised C.C. art. 3494] of our Civil Code the action for payment on a loan prescribes in three years. The last loan made by the plaintiff was on April 7, 1968. Unless there was an interruption or suspension, this debt prescribed in 1971. There is no contention by the plaintiff that any interruption or suspension occurred during this three-year period.

We are therefore dealing with a renunciation of accrued prescription. Accrued prescription can be renounced under our jurisprudence, but it has been held that:

"A mere acknowledgment is not sufficient for the purpose, even if accompanied by payment on account of the debt. There must be a new promise to pay the debt in order to nullify an accrued prescription." Burdin v. Burdin, 171 La. 7, 129 So. 651, 655 (1930). See also Torrey v. Simon-Torrey, Inc., 284 So. 2d 130 (La. App. 3rd Cir. 1973), and cases cited therein.

Appellant contends that the trial court erred in overruling its exception of prescription in that he never renounced the prescription which had run in his favor by making a new promise to pay.

From the jurisprudence cited above it is clear that neither the partial payments made by the appellant nor his letter to his sister constituted a renunciation of prescription. Neither was accompanied by a new promise to pay the debt.

However, from the trial court's ruling we must infer that he held that a new promise to pay was made by the defendant during the telephone call made by plaintiff in 1972. The testimony concerning the call is disputed.

Alma Harmon testified that she called her brother to ask him to begin paying the loans and that she told him exactly how much he owed. According to her testimony her brother promised to begin paying $50 per month "until the amount was paid out, the money that he owed me."

Doctor Alfred Harmon admits that he promised to begin paying $50 a month to his sister but stated that the amount owed was not discussed. He denied any promise to pay until the amount of the debt was paid.

If the testimony of Alma Harmon is correct, there was a new promise to pay the debt by Dr. Harmon which would nullify the accrued prescription under the jurisprudence cited *supra*. If Dr. Harmon's testimony is correct, no new promise to pay the entire debt was made.

The trial court gave no written reasons for judgment. However, since neither the partial payments nor Dr. Harmon's letter constituted a renunciation of prescription, we must infer that the trial court accepted the testimony of Alma Harmon and found that there had been a promise to pay the whole debt by Dr. Harmon.

This finding is a finding of fact for which there is support in the record. We therefore find no manifest error in this holding and conclude that there was a renunciation of prescription by Dr. Harmon. Prescription began to run anew from the moment of renunciation, and since the suit was filed within three years of the renunciation prescription is no bar. We conclude that the trial court correctly overruled defendant's exception of liberative prescription.***

We note that the trial judge based his award of $1,770 on a loan amount of $2,350. From this loan amount he subtracted $250 for payments and $330 for services rendered to Alma Harmon. The parties stipulated that loans totaling $2,300 (not $2,350), and payments totaling $350 (not $250), were made. This was obviously a clerical error which can be noticed and corrected by this court [citations omitted].***Amended and affirmed.

NOTE
Renunciation of Prescription

An interesting recent case regarding the renunciation of prescription is *Blackstone v. Strother*, 10-1163 (La. App. 1 Cir. 5/6/11), 2011 WL 1938671.

In July 2007 Blackstone bought a tract of land which contained approximately 11.982 acres. After the purchase, he noticed that a barbed-wire fence encroached on the tract about twenty feet. Upon investigation, Blackstone learned that the Strothers were the record title owners of the adjacent tract, which they had bought in 1996. The barbed-wire fence encompassed one of their tracts and the disputed tract of land. Around September of 2007, a mandatary for Blackstone entered the property and placed survey markers and a corner post to extend the fence line to the surveyed property line. Strother removed the survey markers and corner post.

Blackstone filed a petitory action against Strother, claiming ownership and seeking possession of the disputed property. In his defense, Strother claimed that he and his ancestors-in-title had acquired ownership of the disputed property as a result of thirty-year acquisitive prescription. Blackstone countered this defense on a number of grounds, including that Strother (or, more precisely, Strother's ancestor-in-title, Fisher), assuming he had ever satisfied the requirements for acquired prescription in the first place, had later "renounced" it. In support of this theory,

Blackstone established that Strother's ancestor-in-title, a certain Fisher, after having conducted a survey of his land, had prepared an "act of correction", with a modified description of the land that excluded the disputed area, and had filed that act into the public records. The trial court rejected Blackstone's theory.

On Blackstone's appeal, the court of appeal affirmed the trial court's ruling. As the court of appeal noted, a renunciation of prescription has to be unequivocal, and only occurs when the intent to renounce is clear, direct, and absolute and is made manifest either by words or actions of the party in whose favor prescription as run. The word "renunciation", the court noted, was not used in the act of correction. Thus, the court found that it was not a clear, unequivocal, and absolute renunciation of the prescription that had run in the favor of Fisher.

LOUISIANA REVISED STATUTES

R.S. 9:5605. Actions for legal malpractice

A. No action for damages against any attorney at law duly admitted to practice in this state, any partnership of such attorneys at law, or any professional corporation, company, organization, association, enterprise, or other commercial business or professional combination authorized by the laws of this state to engage in the practice of law, whether based upon tort, or breach of contract, or otherwise, arising out of an engagement to provide legal services shall be brought unless filed in a court of competent jurisdiction and proper venue within one year from the date of the alleged act, omission, or neglect, or within one year from the date that the alleged act, omission, or neglect is discovered or should have been discovered; however, even as to actions filed within one year from the date of such discovery, in all events such actions shall be filed at the latest within three years from the date of the alleged act, omission, or neglect.

B. The provisions of this Section are remedial and apply to all causes of action without regard to the date when the alleged act, omission, or neglect occurred. However, with respect to any alleged act, omission, or neglect occurring prior to September 7, 1990, actions must, in all events, be filed in a court of competent jurisdiction and proper venue on or before September 7, 1993, without regard to the date of discovery of the alleged act, omission, or neglect. The one-year and three-year periods of limitation provided in Subsection A of this Section are peremptive periods within the meaning of Civil Code Article 3458 and, in accordance with Civil Code Article 3461, may not be renounced, interrupted, or suspended.

C. Notwithstanding any other law to the contrary, in all actions brought in this state against any attorney at law duly admitted to practice in this state, any partnership of such attorneys at law, or any professional law corporation, company, organization, association, enterprise, or other commercial business or professional combination authorized by the laws of this state to engage in the practice of law, the prescriptive and peremptive period shall be governed exclusively by this Section.

D. The provisions of this Section shall apply to all persons whether or not infirm or under disability of any kind and including minors and interdicts.

E. The peremptive period provided in Subsection A of this Section shall not apply in cases of fraud, as defined in Civil Code Article 1953.

6. EFFECTS OF PRESCRIPTION

1(2) PLANIOL, TRAITÉ ÉLÉMENTAIRE DE DROIT CIVIL 598-601
(an English translation by the Louisiana State Law Institute 1959)

§ 1. The Effects of Prescription

Acquisition of Ownership. When prescription is completed, the possessor becomes owner.***

Survival of Personal Actions. Acquisitive prescription is a mode of acquiring; it vests ownership; but it does not have the effect of liberating the debtors. Consequently, it does not prevent the owner from exercising the different personal actions he may have in restitution of his property from those who detained it. It is true that when the acquisitive prescription of thirty years has run, his actions will likewise be extinguished by the liberative prescription of thirty years at the same time that the ownership of the property will have been acquired; but his personal action in revendication may well survive the ten or twenty years required for the acquisitive prescription provided in Art. 2265. For example, if the alienation whereby the third party possessor is permitted to prescribe by ten years has been made by a lessee, the latter remains bound towards the original owner for the restitution of his property, and this obligation lasts for thirty years.

Retroactivity of Prescription. When prescription is completed, the possessor is deemed to be owner, not merely from the last day of the delay, but retroactively from the moment when the prescription began to run. This is readily understandable when the possessor has a title. The prescription merely consolidates this title. The possessor keeps the thing indefinitely as purchaser, donee, etc., just as if the act that permitted him to prescribe, had transferred ownership to him from the outset. The same effect takes place in the case of the thirty years prescription, even when the want of title is avowed or known. Prescription replaces the title.

CONSEQUENCES OF RETROACTIVITY. (1) The fruits collected by the possessor, even if he be in bad faith, remain with him indefinitely. They could have been claimed of him only accessorily in a revendication suit brought within the legal delays. The owner who has lost his main action has no right to retake the fruits;

(2) Third parties who had acquired from the possessor real rights upon the immovable (servitudes, mortgages, etc.) during the duration of prescription, find them retroactively consolidated. It is just as if they had been granted by the true owner and;

(3) If the possessor marries under the legal community system, the immovable which he was in process of prescribing at the time of marriage, will belong to the possessor personally. And this is true even if his spouse was merely in possession and the prescription was accomplished solely during the marriage. If the prescription were accomplished without retroactive effect, the acquisition of the ownership, by applying Art. 1401, par. 3, would be placed during the marriage and the immovable would be common to both spouses.

Necessity of Setting up Prescription. Prescription does not produce its effect by operation of law. The law says that: "a court cannot arise, *ex proprio motu,* the plea of prescription" (Art. 2223). Prescription must accordingly be set up by the possessor, that is to say formally set forth in his pleadings. The usual reserve habitually inserted in pleadings, "and for such other reasons of law as the court may apply of its own motion," is not sufficient. And the same thing may be said of raising the point merely in argument and not in formal pleadings (Cass., Nov. 16, 1886, S. 87. 1. 72).

The reason for this exaction is that prescription is based in the last analysis, upon a presumption. And it runs, counter to the truth, in certain cases. The law therefore leaves it to each individual conscience to decide whether or not to take advantage of this plea.

At What Moment Plea Should be Raised. It can be set up at any stage of the proceedings (Art. 2224), that is to say even on appeal, as long as the case is not closed by the court's formal declaration that "the case is heard." This is but an application of the general law. New pleas may be presented for the first time before the Appellate Court but not before the Court of Cassation.

It is well understood that the defendant loses the right of setting up prescription if, according to circumstances he may be deemed to have renounced it (Art. 2224). But the fact that no plea of prescription was set up, for the first time, before the trial court, does not deprive the possessor of the right of doing so on appeal.

Right of Possessor's Creditors. The possessor is not the only person who may set up the exception of prescription. His creditors have the same right as he has (Art. 2225). They may have a great interest in doing so. The property in connection with which prescription has been completed in favor of their debtor, may be the best security they have. If it were taken away from him by a plaintiff in revendication they may run the risk of not being paid. They may intervene in the suit in order to set up prescription, when their debtor fails to do so. The right thus accorded creditors is but an application of a general rule.***

2(1) PLANIOL, TRAITÉ ÉLÉMENTAIRE DE DROIT CIVIL 370-374
(an English translation by the Louisiana State Law Institute 1959)

§ 5. Effect of Prescription

General Notion. The prescription furnishes to the debtor and against the creditor a peremptory exception which is a means of defense permitting him to obtain the dismissal of the suit without paying anything.***

B. Normal Effect of the Exception of Prescription

Liberation of the Debtor. The Code treats of prescription as a means of liberating oneself (Art. 2219). It had already said (Art. 1234) that by the effect of prescription obligations are extinguished. The debtor therefore is discharged, and as we shall see farther on in studying the exceptional cases where it is otherwise, the creditor in general has no means of avoiding the loss which confronts him.***

Survival of a Natural Obligation. When it is pleaded, prescription has the effect of paralyzing the action of the creditor. Does it completely extinguish his right? No, at least according to the general opinion; there remains a natural obligation. One can hardly demonstrate the survival, to such an inferior degree, of the prescribed obligation. All that one can say is that the reasons on which prescriptions rest are satisfied when the right of action is withdrawn from the creditor. If the creditor is not really discharged, he remains bound in conscience to acquit his debt, and there is no reason for not recognizing that what remains of the obligation has the characteristics of a natural obligation. If the debtor changes his mind after a judgment declaring him acquitted of his debt because of its having been prescribed, and pays the debt, the intention of the parties would be uselessly misconstrued in making of such act a donation instead of a payment. If it is payment, there is a natural obligation, and such obligation can not only be acquitted, but may also be novated and secured.

CHAPTER IX. ACQUISITIVE PRESCRIPTION
Civil Code arts. 3473-3491

Comment, Acquisitive Prescription
The 1982 Revision of The Louisiana Civil Code
58 Tul. L. Rev. 618-641 (1983)
(citations omitted)

Overview of General Policy

Acquisitive prescription is defined in Louisiana Civil Code Article 3446 as "a mode of acquiring ownership or other real rights by possession for a period of time." This extra-judicial method of acquisition, which historically may be traced to the Twelve Tablets of Rome, continues to track closely the language of the French *Code civil.* The philosophical bases for the doctrine have been amply explored by French commentators, who generally have regarded prescription as "necessary for the sake of legal stability." Laurent, for example, reasoned that title to property is really "nothing more than possession which society has sanctioned." Hence, since ownership is itself based on possession, "it can also be acquired by possession against one who has ceased to possess." Baudry-Lacantinerie considered prescription to be similar to the rule of res judicata, in that both lend finality to otherwise fluctuating legal rights. As Thiers noted, "it is necessary to have a fixed term whereby that which exists will be declared legitimate by the very fact that it exists."

Acquisitive prescription applies to both movables and immovables. The lapse of time necessary to acquire ownership varies according to both the nature of the thing acquired and the existence of good faith and just title. Ownership and other real rights in immovables may be acquired in ten or thirty years; movables may be acquired in three or ten years.

1. IMMOVABLES: TEN YEAR PRESCRIPTION
Civil Code arts. 3473-3485

a. Just Title
Civil Code arts. 3483, 3484

NOTE
Just Title v. Good Title

Article 3483 of the Louisiana Civil Code describes the just title required for the ten-year acquisitive prescription of an immovable as a "juridical act" that would have been sufficient to transfer ownership or another real right in the thing if the transferor had been its true owner. It requires that the title be "written, valid in form, and filed for registry in the conveyance records in which the immovable is situated." Often, the title on which the possessor is founding his acquisitive prescription claim is part of a sequence of titles—a "chain of title"—involving a series of "ancestors in title." For example, in the case of *Clayton v. Rickerson*, 160 La. 771, 107 So. 569 (1926), the defendant possessor had obtained a title to the land in a purchase from Sissie Parham in 1904; she, in turn, had obtained her title from the heirs of William Parham, deceased, in 1903; the deceased Parham had obtained his title from John Boyet in 1881; Boyet had purchased the land by title from the estate of John Chapman in 1879. Chapman had title from an 1865 sale by Thomas Woodward in 1865; Woodward had purchased the land from George Peterson in 1855. Peterson was the original patentee of the land; that is, he had received his title from the state.

This chain of title back to the state was not perfect, however. Chapman's heirs claimed ownership via his succession. They pointed to an irregularity in Boyet's purchase of the land that not only made Boyet's title a nullity, but also, they asserted, disqualified it from being considered a "just title."

It was necessary for Rickerson to establish his ownership through acquisitive prescription; but could he use the prescription of ten years with Boyet's title in his chain? In finding for Rickerson, the court made clear that only a title relied on during the ten years of possession that Rickerson made the basis of his claim was required to qualify as a just title. "It is immaterial whether Boyet's title to this property was a nullity, or whether he had any title at all," the Supreme Court of Louisiana held. *Id.* at 774, 570. Nor could apparent defects in Sissie Parham's title alleged by the Chapman's heirs defeat Rickerson's claim. The title that had to be *"apparently* good, and of a kind calculated to induce belief in the possessor that it is perfect," was the title from Sissie Parham to Rickerson. *Id.*

WILKIE v. COX
222 So. 2d 85 (La. App. 3d Cir.)
cert. denied 254 La. 470, 223 So. 2d 873 (1969)

HOOD, J. This suit was filed originally as an action to quiet a tax title. It was instituted by B. B. Wilkie against the heirs of George W. Cox, deceased. The defendants filed an answer and a third party petition, impleading W. J. Colbert as a party to the suit, attacking the validity of the tax sale which plaintiff seeks to confirm, and alleging record title in defendants. Plaintiff impleaded Howard L. Raphiel as an additional defendant.

Thereafter a number of pleadings were filed by the parties, among which were pleas or exceptions of prescription filed by plaintiff Wilkie and by third party defendant Colbert. In these last mentioned pleadings, Wilkie and Colbert allege that they and their authors in title have possessed the property for more than ten years under a deed translative of title, and that they thus have acquired the ownership of the subject property by prescription of ten years acquirendi causa. Wilkie demands that he be recognized as the owner of the north one-half of that property, and Colbert demands that he be recognized as the owner of the south one-half of it.

At the trial, the case was treated as a petitory action, and all parties apparently concede that the issue presented here involves a determination of the ownership of the property. Plaintiff and Colbert contend primarily that they acquired record title to this tract of land by virtue of a 1941 tax sale, and alternatively that they acquired ownership of it by acquisitive prescription of ten years under the provisions of LSA-C.C. art. 3478 [Revised C.C. arts. 3473, 3474]. Defendants contend that they are owners of the property by record title, and that they should be recognized as owners of it.

The case was tried on its merits, and judgment was rendered by the trial court confirming the tax title, recognizing B. B. Wilkie and W. J. Colbert as owners of the property and enjoining the remaining defendants from claiming title to that property. The original defendants have appealed.

This tract of land, comprising about 40 acres, was homesteaded by George W. Cox some time prior to 1903, and a patent was issued to him by the United States on May 24, 1909. The property was assessed for taxes prior to the issuance of the patent, however, and it was adjudicated to the State of Louisiana at a tax sale held on July 2, 1904, for unpaid taxes due for the year 1903, under an assessment in the name of G. W. Cox. No question is raised in this proceeding as to the legality of that tax sale or as to the validity of the adjudication to the State at that time.

The property was not redeemed from the state until April 13, 1965, when a certificate of redemption was issued by the Register of the State Land Office certifying that it was

---

For an explanation of tax titles and the procedure for tax sales in Louisiana at the time *Wilkie* was decided, see Notes and Questions following this case, #1 — Ed.

- No one bought it?
or
- State didn't put it up for sale?

then redeemed to G. W. Cox. The property thus remained unredeemed for a period of almost 61 years, from July 1, 1904, until April 13, 1965.

In spite of the fact that the property had been adjudicated to the state on July 2, 1904, it was allowed to remain on the tax rolls for a number of years thereafter under assessments at various times in the name of "G. W. Cox," or "George Cox, Sr.," or "G. W. Cox, Sr." And, under those assessments, the same property was again adjudicated to the State of Louisiana on at least five other separate occasions for unpaid taxes due for the years 1904, 1909, 1920, 1921, 1922, 1923, 1924 and 1937.

Finally, at a tax sale held on June 18, 1941, this property was sold and adjudicated to "Howard L. Raphiel, Trustee," for unpaid taxes due for the year 1940, under an assessment in the name of G. W. Cox. Plaintiff Wilkie, and third party defendant W. J. Colbert, acquired record title to the property from or through Raphiel, the purchaser at the above mentioned tax sale. [Raphiel acknowledged that he had purchased the land for both himself and Colbert; Wilkie bought Raphiel's half-interest in 1962.] Both of those parties, Wilkie and Colbert, claim to be owners of the property by record title, and their claim of ownership by such a title, of course, depends upon the validity of the 1941 tax sale to Raphiel. One of the important issues presented on this appeal, therefore, is whether that tax sale to Raphiel is valid.

Defendants contend that the 1941 tax sale to Raphiel is an absolute nullity, because the property previously had been adjudicated to the state and it had not been redeemed prior to the time of that tax sale. They contend that under those circumstances the taxing officers of the state were without authority to assess and sell the property as belonging to the former owner, and that the tax sale thus is void.

Plaintiff concedes that the property had been adjudicated to the state for unpaid 1903 taxes, and that it had remained unredeemed up to the time of the 1941 tax sale. And, he admits that the taxing authorities thus were without power to assess and sell the property in 1940 and 1941 as belonging to the former owner. He contends, however, that defendants are now barred from asserting the invalidity of the 1941 tax sale by: [inter alia] ... the prescription of ten years acquirendi causa as provided in LSA-C.C. art. 3478 [3473, 3474].

Where property has been adjudicated to the state, and has not been redeemed in the time and manner provided by law, the taxing officers of the state are without authority to assess and sell the property for taxes as belonging to the former owner or any other person. The purported sale of property for unpaid taxes under those circumstances is an absolute nullity, and an interested party is not barred...from asserting the invalidity of such a sale [citations omitted].

In the instant suit the evidence shows that the property at issue here had been adjudicated to the state, and it had not been redeemed by the time of the 1941 tax sale. Under those circumstances, we conclude that the purported tax sale to Raphiel on June 18, 1941, is an absolute nullity ....

....We feel, however, that the provisions of LSA-R.S. 9:5803 are applicable in determining the issues raised by plaintiff's plea of prescription of ten years acquirendi causa.

The next important issue presented is whether plaintiff and Colbert have acquired the ownership of the subject property by prescription of ten years acquirendi causa, as provided in LSA-C.C. art. 3478 [3473, 3474] et seq.***

The evidence convinces us that the plaintiff and Colbert were in good faith, and that the possession which they, or their authors in title, have exercised has been sufficient to satisfy the requirements of LSA-C.C. arts. 3478-3498 [Revised C.C. art. 3473-3477, 3481-3485, 3426-3427, 3435-3436, 3441-3443]. The question remains, then, as to whether the 1941 tax deed is a "just title" sufficient to serve as the basis for claiming ownership by the acquisitive prescription of ten years.

Defendant contend[s] that since the 1941 tax deed is an absolute nullity, it cannot be construed to be a "just title," sufficient to serve as the basis for a ten year prescriptive title. We are unable to agree with that argument.

Even though a tax sale is invalid, this invalid deed may serve as the basis for the acquisition of an indefeasible title by prescription of ten years acquirendi causa under LSA-C.C. art. 3478, if the tax deed appears on its face to be valid and translative of title, and if the tax purchaser is in good faith and takes actual and notorious possession of the property [citations omitted].***

Defendants point out that under the provisions of Article 3497 of the Civil Code [Revised C.C. art. 3485] the ten year acquisitive prescription cannot be applied unless the object of it "be susceptible by its nature of alienation, and the alienation ... is not prohibited by law." They argue that the alienation or re-sale of the property was forbidden by law while it was in a condition of forfeiture to the state, and thus the ten-year prescriptive period could not run while plaintiff's author in title owned it. [citations omitted].

A similar issue was presented in Saucier v. E. Sondheimer Co., 212 La. 490, 32 So. 2d 900 (1947). There the property was adjudicated to the State for unpaid 1898 taxes. The good faith purchaser acquired and began possessing it in 1927. It was redeemed from the State in the name of the original tax debtor in 1941. The possessor then claimed ownership by ten years' acquisitive possession. Our Supreme Court held that Act 310 of 1936 (now LSA-R.S. 9:5803) enured to the benefit of the purchaser in good faith by just title, and that after the property was redeemed in 1941, the possessor was entitled to claim ownership of the property by prescription of ten years, computing his period of possession as beginning in 1927. See also Menefee v. Pipes, 159 So. 2d 439 (La. App. 2d Cir. 1964).

The pertinent portion of LSA-R.S. 9:5803 provides, "In all cases where immovable property has been, or may be, adjudicated or forfeited to the state for non-payment of taxes and has been or is subsequently redeemed by a purchaser in good faith and by just title, or by the heirs or assigns of such purchaser, prescription shall not be interrupted or suspended during the period that title is vested in the state."

We have held that plaintiff's author in title and Colbert were purchasers in good faith and by just title. It has also been shown that the property was redeemed from the 1904 adjudication to the state. We now conclude that LSA-R.S. 9:5803 inures to the benefit of plaintiff and Colbert now that the subject property has been redeemed, and that the prescription of ten years may be applied even though the property was in a condition of forfeiture to the state during a substantial part of the time while the parties possessed it.

We think plaintiff and Colbert have established ownership of the property by the prescription of ten years acquirendi causa. The judgment rendered by the trial court decrees, in part, that the tax title be confirmed and quieted. Since we have determined that the tax title was invalid, the judgment appealed from must be amended to eliminate that portion of the judgment which decrees that the tax title be confirmed and quieted.

The remaining portion of the judgment rendered by the trial court recognizes Wilkie and Colbert as being owners of the entire tract. The record indicates that Wilkie owns the north one-half and Colbert owns the south one-half of the subject property. These two parties appear to be satisfied with the judgment which was rendered, however, since neither has appealed or answered the appeal. We have decided, therefore, to affirm that portion of the judgment appealed from which recognizes Wilkie and Colbert as owners of the tract of land in dispute here.

For the reasons herein set out the judgment appealed from is amended by elimination of that portion of such judgment which decrees that the tax title from G. W. Cox to Howard W. Raphiel, dated June 23, 1941, be confirmed and quieted. All of the remaining portions of the judgment rendered by the trial court, and particularly that portion which decrees that B. B. Wilkie and W. J. Colbert are recognized as owners of the subject property and enjoins the remaining defendants from setting up any right, title or interest in or to any part or portion of said property, are affirmed. The costs of this appeal are assessed to defendants-appellants. Amended and affirmed.

On Application for Rehearing

CULPEPPER, J. (dissenting from the denial of an application for rehearing). I am now persuaded this case is controlled by the rule that a title which is an absolute nullity cannot constitute "just title" for purposes of the acquisitive prescription of ten years.

In our original opinion we correctly concluded that the 1941 tax sale, which is the foundation of Wilkie's title, is an absolute nullity. It is in contravention of LSA-R.S. 47:1955, which provides that property, unredeemed from a prior tax adjudication to the state, shall not again be sold while the property remains in a condition of forfeiture to the state....

However, we then proceeded to hold that the 1941 tax sale, although an absolute nullity, did constitute "just title" for purposes of the acquisitive prescription of ten years, under LSA-C.C. Article 3478 [Revised C.C. art. 3473, 3474].

Not one of the cases cited in support of this holding (see our original opinion) involved an absolute nullity. They concerned dual assessments, which in my view are relative nullities. Absolute nullities are those which are in derogation of public order and good morals, are never susceptible of ratification and cannot be prescribed. Relative nullities are those established for the interests of individuals. These are susceptible of ratification and may be prescribed against. See Nelson v. Walker, 250 La. 545, 197 So. 2d 619 (1967). The sale of property which belongs to the state is in derogation of public order and is an absolute nullity. The sale property under a dual assessment is merely in derogation of a law for the protection of the interests of individuals and hence is a relative nullity. On this basis, the cases cited in our original opinion are distinguishable.

Planiol, Civil Law Treatise, An English Translation by the Louisiana State Law Institute, Volume 1, Section 2662 expresses the view that a title which is an absolute nullity cannot be considered just title for purposes of prescription[, w]hereas, titles which are "merely annullable" can constitute just title. An example given by Planiol is a title tainted with "substitution," which is an absolute nullity because rigorously prohibited by our law. The author of the comment, Just Title In The Prescription of Immovables, 15 T.L.R. 436, at 442, also reaches the conclusion that absolute nullities, which are in derogation of public order, should never constitute just title.

Louisiana jurisprudence supports this view. In Hicks v. Hughes, 223 La. 290, 65 So. 2d 603 (1953) a clerk of court granted an order for the sale of succession property where the administrator had not complied with the statute that a request for such an order of sale be accompanied by a statement of the debts of the succession. The court held that the clerk of court had no jurisdiction to issue the order of sale; that the sale was an absolute nullity and could not be the basis of the acquisitive prescription of ten years.

Bulliard v. Davis, 185 La. 255, 169 So. 78 (1936) also involved a succession sale, which was an absolute nullity because the court was without jurisdiction of the res. The court held that such a sale could not form the basis of the prescription of ten years acquirendi causa.

In Boudreaux v. Olin Industries, 232 La. 405, 94 So. 2d 417 (1957), our Supreme Court recognized the rule of Hicks v. Hughes, supra, that "an absolutely null deed cannot form the basis for the acquisitive prescription of ten years" but then distinguished the Hicks case on the facts. In my view, judgment should be rendered for defendants appellants. For the reasons stated, I respectfully dissent from the denial of an application for rehearing.

NOTES AND QUESTIONS

1. *Tax sales and adjudication*: The failure to pay real property taxes in the year in which they were due could result in the sale of the real property to satisfy the tax bill under La. Const. Art. 7, § 25 at the time that *Wilkie v. Cox* was integrated. The real estate could be sold immediately for the amount needed to pay the tax debt. For a period of three years after the tax sale is recorded, the former owner or someone acting for him could redeem the property by paying the taxes owed, further taxes accrued, a penalty and interest. If the property was not sold immediately, it was adjudicated to the taxing authority—the State in this case. The three-year period for redemption did not begin to run while the adjudicated real estate was in State hands. In the *Wilkie* era, as long as title to the land remained in the taxing authority, the land could be redeemed. This was what the Cox heirs have attempted to do, to be denied on the ground that attempted purchasers at a later, invalid sale have acquired the land by acquisitive prescription.

2. The Third Circuit Court of Appeal's conclusion that although "the purported tax sale to Raphiel on June 18, 1941 is an absolute nullity," "the 1941 tax sale, although an absolute nullity, did constitute "just title" for purposes of the acquisitive prescription of ten years" is not the view of scholarly authorities, as Justice Culpepper indicates and the following note confirms:

Just Title and Absolute Nullity
A.N. Yiannopoulos

It is granted that an absolute nullity cannot be a just title for ten-year acquisitive prescription. A person holding such a title, however, may acquire the ownership of immovable property by the thirty-year acquisitive prescription, unless, of course, the property itself is insusceptible of prescription. See La.Civil Code arts. 2030, 3475.

It is also granted that the person holding property under an absolutely null title may convey the property to another person and the conveyance may be a just title. See Clayton v. Rickerson, 160 La. 771, 107 So. 569 (1926), *supra*. It is questionable whether the purchase of assets of the succession by the personal representative of the deceased is an absolute or a relative nullity. See La. Civil Code art. 2030; *cf.* Louisiana Civil Procedure arts. 3194, 3195; Succession of Lewis, 700 So. 2d 1002 (La. App.1st Cir. 1997) (purchase of succession property by co-executor who was also heir of the deceased); Succession of Hirt, 612 So. 2d 1054 (La. App. 4th Cir. 1993) (contract voidable rather than void).

Why must Wilkie assert this absolutely null title to be "just title" when his purchase was not at the tax sale itself, but from Raphiel?

3. Justice Culpepper observes, "Absolute nullities are those which are in derogation of public order and good morals.... Relative nullities are those established for the interests of individuals." Should a tax sale that is defective in its procedure automatically be categorized as an "absolute nullity," as the Third Circuit held in *Wilkie*?

b. Good Faith
Civil Code arts. 2502, 3475, 3480-3482

1(2) PLANIOL, TRAITÉ ÉLÉMENTAIRE DE DROIT CIVIL 580-582
(English translation by the Louisiana State Law Institute 1959)

Definition. The second condition requisite for prescribing by from ten to twenty years is good faith. Possessors in good faith are those who believe that he who transmitted the immovable to them was its legitimate owner. Good faith therefore consists in making a mistake regarding the alienator's ownership, when dealing with someone who is not the owner of the thing. The acquirer's good faith must be entire. If he had the slightest doubt regarding his author's ownership, he must be deemed to be in bad faith.

It is not necessary that the possessor be ignorant of the other defects that may exist in his title of acquisition. The alienator was, for example incapable. The alienation was made by a married woman acting without her husband's authorization. The alienation may be annulled upon the wife's petition and the purchaser knows this. This does not prevent him from being in good faith and of being able to have prescription of ten or twenty years run in his favor against the true owner, if he thought that the wife was the owner of the immovable sold by her. There are, in such a case, two vices in the alienation. There is the fact that she was not the owner of the thing. And there is the additional fact of her incapacity. The first gives rise to an action in revendication by the owner, and the second to an action in nullity in behalf of the alienator. As the sole objective of usucapion is to cause the first of these defects to disappear, it suffices that the acquirer was in ignorance of this vice. It makes no difference whether he was or was not aware of the second.

Proof of Good Faith. Good faith is always presumed (Art. 2268). It is therefore incumbent upon the possessor's adversary to prove that he knew of his author's want of right. This proof may be adduced in all possible ways. It is a question of fact (Civ. Cass., Feb. 15, 1927, Gazette du Palais, May 4, 1927).

At What Moment Good Faith Is Necessary. Good faith is necessary solely at the moment of acquisition (Art. 2269). It follows from this that bad faith, arising during the course of prescription by the discovery of the error, does not prevent the possessor from benefiting from the prescription of ten or twenty years. This is the Roman rule: *mala fides superveniens non impedit usucapionem* (Comp. Digest, B.XLI, Tit. 1 fr. 40, sec. 1).

BOARD OF COMMISSIONERS v. S.D. HUNTER FOUNDATION
354 So. 2d 156 (La. 1977)

TATE, J.   By this petitory action, the plaintiff levee district claims title to some 83 acres of land lying between Twelve Mile Bayou and a large tract of plantation property owned by the defendants. The trial court recognized the levee district's title to the acreage, but the court of appeal reversed. 342 So. 2d 720 (La. App. 2d Cir. 1977). It held that the defendants had acquired title to the disputed strips by ten years' acquisitive prescription.

We granted certiorari, 344 So. 2d 3 (La. 1977), primarily to review the intermediate court's finding that the defendants had acquired title by ten years' possession through acquisition in good faith and by just title. La.C.C. Art. 3478 [Revised C.C. arts. 3473, 3474].

We are particularly concerned with the issue of the good faith, La. C.C. Art. 3479(1) [Revised C.C. art. 3475], of a purchaser who acquired by an act of sale which expressly warranted title to some of the property purchased, but which was expressly without warranty as to other property conveyed by the same act of sale. As to the latter property, to which the seller had no title whatsoever, the issue concerns whether and to what extent the good faith of the purchaser is to be presumed. La.C.C. Art. 3481.***

Factual Context

The lands between the traverse line [of Soda Lake] and the bayou originally belonged to the federal government. The 1850 Swamp Land Grant Act, 43 U.S.C. Section 982, had allowed the states to select and take title to swamp and overflowed lands of the United States. See Madden, Federal and State Lands in Louisiana, Sections 3, 23, 43 (1973). Louisiana had taken title to certain of these lands in Caddo Parish, including the tracts presently in dispute. Act 74 of 1892. In 1901, by formal act, the state conveyed title to the plaintiff levee district [of] the tracts presently in dispute (along with all other acreage in the area lying between the bayou and the traverse line). The district has never transferred record title to these strips.

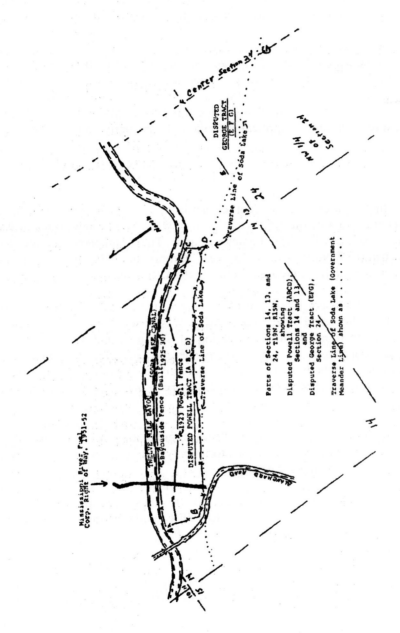

Principal Legal Issues

The defendants (The S. D. Hunter Foundation and the widow of S. D. Hunter) claim title . . . on the basis of acquisitive prescriptions of ten and thirty years. S. D. Hunter, their predecessor in title, had acquired the parent tracts of which these strips form part by acts of sale. . . . These acts conveyed the lands outside of the traverse line (which mark the limits of the former swamp land), with full warranty of title and with precise description. (It may here be added that Hunter's vendors had apparent record title to these other lands, which were south and west of the traverse line.)

However, the conveyance of the lands on the bayou side of the traverse line (i.e., north and east of it) were described differently in each of Hunter's acquisition deeds, as will be set forth more fully below. Also, as will be shown, the overflowed lands (i.e., the levee district property north and east of the traverse line, which was subject to periodic overflow from the bayou) were conveyed by warranty sales of a different nature than the express warranties applicable to the other property conveyed by the same deeds.***

I. THE DISPUTED GEORGE TRACT

In 1951, S. D. Hunter purchased the George tract from Walter George et al. The acts of sale conveyed "That portion of the Northwest Quarter (NW 1/4) lying South and West of the traverse line of Soda Lake (less 11 acres)" and "The Southwest Quarter (less 50 acres), all in Township 19 North, Range 15 West, comprising 223 acres." This was the George tract proper, to which the Georges held apparent record title.

The conveyance of *this* George-tract property (unlike the conveyance of the Disputed George Tract within the same deed, see below) was made "with full guarantee of title, and with complete transfer and subrogation of all rights and actions of warranty against all former proprietors of the property herein conveyed, together with all rights of prescription, whether acquisitive or liberative, to which the said vendors may be entitled." The vendors further reserved one-half of the mineral rights to this property.

After conveying the George tract proper with express and full warranty title, and reserving one-half of the mineral interests as to it (only), the deed continued (conveying the Disputed George Tract without warranty):

> "Vendors further declare that they do by these presents GRANT, BARGAIN, SELL, CONVEY AND DELIVER, without any warranty of title whatsoever, unto the said Vendee, the following described property located in Caddo Parish, Louisiana:

> "That portion of the Northwest Quarter (NW 1/4) of Section 24, Township 19 North, Range 15 West lying generally North of the traverse line of Soda Lake."

The Disputed George Tract was on the bayou (northerly) side of the traverse line of Soda Lake. Governmental plats and all transactions pertinent noted this line as marking the southerly limits of the levee district overflow lands conveyed to it by the State.

The Disputed George Tract was immediately adjacent to (northerly of) the other land in the Northwest Quarter of Section 24 to which the Georges held record title. However, as the court of appeal noted, the evidence reflects insignificant, if any, prior possession of this levee district land by the Georges or their predecessors in title.

Ten Years' Acquisitive Prescription

The sole arguable ground for the Hunter defendants' claim to title of the Disputed George Tract is based upon S. D. Hunter's possession of the tract for ten years after his alleged good faith acquisition by this 1951 sale. "He who acquires an immovable in good faith and by just title prescribes for it in ten years...." La.C.C. Art. 3478 [Revised C.C. arts. 3473, 3474].***

The plaintiff levee district concedes that a non-warranty sale may be a "just title" for purposes of acquisition of ownership by this prescription. Nevertheless, it contests the "good faith" of the purchaser, who in a single conveyance acquired certain lands with express warranty, but the disputed land (to which his vendors had no title and little, if any, possession) expressly without warranty, considering also that the deed reserved the vendor's mineral interest only to the warranted title and not to the disputed strip.

A possessor in good faith is one who has "just reason to believe himself the master of the thing which he possesses, although he may not be in fact...." La.C.C. Art. 3451 [Revised C.C. art. 3480]. Bad faith possession is possession as owner, but with the possessor having knowledge that he had no title or that his title is defective. La.C.C. Art. 3452 [Revised C.C. art. 3481]. "Good faith is always presumed in matters of prescription; and he who alleges bad faith in the possessor, must prove it." La.C.C. Art. 3481.

Excellent analyses of the jurisprudence on the issue, with comprehensive citation and summary, are set forth in Johnson, Good Faith as a Condition of Ten Year Acquisitive Prescription, 34 Tul. L. Rev. 671 (1960) and in the Comment, The Ten-Year Acquisitive Prescription of Immovables, 36 La. L. Rev. 1000, 1001-05, 1011 (1976). In describing the nature of good and bad faith, (then Professor) Johnson states, 34 Tul. L. Rev. 673-75 (footnote citations included in brackets where appropriate):

"Unlike moral good faith or moral bad faith, which is solely subjective, legal good faith or legal bad faith is both subjective and objective. Concisely stated, good faith or bad faith is a state of mind indicated by acts and circumstances. In other words, the good faith or bad faith of a particular purchaser must be determined by the particular facts of each case. (See Land Development Co. v. Schulz, 169 La. 1, 124 So. 125 (1929); Hall & Turner v. Mooring, 27 La. Ann. 596 (1875); Franz v. Mohr, 4 So. 2d 584 (La. App. 1941).) There is no rule of law that categorizes the acts and circumstances that will be considered in good faith as opposed to those acts and circumstances that will be considered in bad faith: the purchaser must acquire the property from one whom he has 'just reason to believe' to be the owner;***

"Having 'just reason to believe' is the same thing as having an 'honest belief' that the seller is the owner of the property which he is selling. 'Just reason to believe' means that the purchaser has reasonable grounds to believe that the seller is the owner of the property which is being transferred although there is a defect in the title. That is to say, if his grounds of belief are such that a man of ordinary business experience would say that the seller is the owner of the property, the purchaser is then in good faith [citations omitted]. On the other hand, if the purchaser has reason to doubt the validity of the title being acquired from the seller, he is in bad faith. To explain, the purchaser is in bad faith if he acquires the property when he knows that the seller does not own the property, or when the facts and circumstances are such that a man of ordinary business experience would say that the seller is not the owner of the property [citations omitted]."

EFFECT OF A PARTIAL NON-WARRANTY DEED ON THE PURCHASER'S GOOD FAITH

Our early jurisprudence held that a non-warranty sale of the vendor's right, title and interest in his property disclosed a defect in the title, thus putting the purchaser in bad faith (as well as defeating the just title requirement) [citations omitted]. The present jurisprudence, however, is that a quitclaim or non-warranty deed by itself is insufficient to place the purchaser on inquiry and make him a bad faith purchaser. In [Land Development Co. v. Schulz, 124 So. 125 (1929)], we stated, 124 So. 128:

"A stipulation in an act of sale that the seller does not warrant the title might be regarded as an indication that the seller lacked faith in his title, but it is not an indication that the buyer lacked faith in his title."

This last statement, however, is incomplete. If, aside from its non-warranty nature, the deed discloses a basis for doubting the vendor's ownership of the property conveyed, then the purchaser is not in good faith:

"Doubt as to ownership, or the right to alienate, is inconsistent with good faith, because doubt is the mean between good and bad faith. Good faith demands a firm and positive belief." Knight v. Berwick Lumber Co., 130 La. 233, 241, 57 So. 900, 903 (1912). The acquirer's good faith must be absolute. If he had the slightest doubt concerning his author's ownership, he must be deemed to be in bad faith. Planiol, Civil Law Treatise, Vol. 1, No. 2667, p. 581 (LSLI translation, 1959). See also Aubry & Rau, Property, Section 218, pp. 363-65 (2 Civil Law Translations, LSLI, 1966).

Thus, where a deed itself indicates that a seller may not own the entirety of the property conveyed, the buyer is not presumed (see La.C.C. art. 3481) to be a purchaser in good faith. Bel v. Manuel, 234 La. 135, 99 So. 2d 58 (1958). If the deed gives the purchaser notice of any fact which should "put a reasonably prudent person on guard, it then devolves upon him to pursue every lead and ferret out all the facts to the end that he may not purchase until he has complete information before him." Boyet v. Perryman, 240 La. 339, 352, 123 So. 2d 79, 83 (1960).

When other factors tend to show that the purchaser had knowledge of defects in the title, a quitclaim or non-warranty deed may, of course, be an indication of the purchaser's bad faith at the time of acquisition. Board of Com'rs of Port of New Orleans v. Delacroix Corp., 274 So. 2d 745 (La. App. 4th Cir. 1973); Board of Com'rs, Lafourche Basin Levee Dist. v. Elmer, 268 So. 2d 274 (La. App. 4th Cir. 1972).

In the present George deed, the sellers expressly warranted title to property south and west of the traverse line, but in the same deed conveyed land north of the traverse line (the Disputed George Tract) expressly "without any warranty of title whatsoever."

In our view, this circumstance alone should have been sufficient, under the jurisprudence cited, to raise doubt in the purchaser's mind as to the vendor's title to the non-warranted title, so as to defeat his good faith at the time of its acquisition. Board of Com'rs of Port of New Orleans v. Delacroix Corp., 274 So. 2d 745 (La. App. 4th Cir. 1973). (A contrary view was reached in Nugent v. Urania Lbr. Co., 16 La. App. 73, 133 So. 420 (2d Cir. 1931); but it is disapproved, since Delacroix represents the better view and is more consistent with the decisions of this court above cited.) [citations omitted].

We therefore find that Hunter was not a good faith purchaser of the Disputed George Tract at the time of his acquisition of it in 1951. The possession under the deed by him and his successors (1951-64) was not sufficient to afford prescriptive title by thirty years' possession without good faith. La.C.C. art. 3499 [Revised C.C. art. 3486]. (As earlier noted, the evidence does not suggest that his predecessors in title had possessed it at all, with the possible exception of an incident in 1942.)

Accordingly, since the Hunters did not acquire title to the Disputed George Tract by prescription, we hold that the plaintiff levee district is entitled to be recognized as owner of it, in accordance with its title.

[In addition, the court found that the Hunters did not acquire title to the Disputed Powell Tract on ground that they lacked continuous possession for sufficient years because of interruption of their possession by precarious possessors for the levee district.]

DECREE

For the reasons assigned, we reverse the judgment of the court of appeal, and we reinstate and affirm the judgment of the district court in favor of plaintiff, the Board of Commissioners of the Caddo Levee District, and against the defendants, the S. D. Hunter Foundation and Mrs. Milryn M. Hunter, recognizing the plaintiff's title to and ownership.***

MALONE v. FOWLER
228 So. 2d 500 (La. App. 3d Cir. 1969)

MILLER, J. Fred T. Malone, allegedly the owner of a small interest in a rural 15 acre tract of land located about 10 miles from Alexandria, sought to partition the property by licitation. Defendants were Andrew J. Fowler and some absent and unknown heirs listed as co-owners of the land.

The only issue before us concerns defendant Fowler's good faith under his plea of prescription, contending for ownership by ten years acquisitive prescription under C.C. Articles 3478 et seq. [Revised C.C. arts. 3473 et seq.].

The trial court handed down a well reasoned written opinion holding that Fowler's acquisition was not in good faith, and overruled his plea of prescription. Fowler has appealed, contending that the trial court was manifestly erroneous in making this factual determination.***

For the price of $100, Fowler acquired the property in dispute with the following description:

> " 'All of their rights, title, and interest in and to a certain tract, piece or parcel of land, together with all ways, means and privileges thereunto appertaining, lying, being and situated in the Parish of Rapides, State of Louisiana, and containing the quantity of fifteen (15) acres, more or less. Said tract of land is situated East of the Public Road leading from LeCompte to Lamourie and is bounded on the North by land formerly belonging to H. H. Hardy, commonly known as the William Wright Place, now the property of Mrs. Ernestine Drewett, on the South by the N. L. Stewart place, formerly property of W. A. Wiggins and now the property of Deal, on the West by the Public Road, and on the East or in the rear by property formerly belonging to Oran Dorsett, now the property of Edgar Fowler. The property herein conveyed is the same property that was sold by Miss Emily Carnal and others, to Sallie Jones, which sale is recorded in book 72 on page 403 of the Conveyance Records of Rapides Parish, State of Louisiana.' "

The deed was executed July 30, 1955 by Frances Tutt Howard and on August 8, 1955 by Evelina Fields West, both as vendors, and on April 27, 1956 by A. J. Fowler, as vendee. In August of 1955, Fowler paid the consideration and fenced the property and has maintained undisputed possession of the property from that time until this suit was filed in June of 1967.

Although on three separate occasions Fowler specifically denied that he prepared the description used in this deed (Tr. 88, 191, 196), Exhibit Engolio 1 establishes as a fact that Fowler did prepare the description.

The above quoted description refers to a deed "***to Sallie Jones, which sale is recorded in book 72 on page 403 of the Conveyance Records of Rapides Parish,***" and is in evidence as P-1. That deed shows that the property was purchased by Mrs. Jones on September 16, 1916 for the price of $250. There was no succession proceedings or deed to show how title passed from Salle Jones to Fowler's vendors, Frances Tutt Howard and Evelina Fields West.

Fowler testified that he was contacted by mail by these owners. They allegedly offered the land to him for $100, but he did not keep these letters. Fowler then contacted the attorney for Mrs. Howard. On June 12, 1955, Fowler sent the above quoted description along with these instructions:

> "***You send the deed to the woman in California (Mrs. Howard) after the one's there have signed it and when it comes back to you, send it on to me and deposit the draft there in your bank. When I see the deed is executed properly, as I am sure it will be if some notary over there doesn't do something wrong, then I will order the draft paid and you can distribute the money."

On the same day, June 12, 1955, Fowler again wrote the attorney stating in part:

> "***I have notified Evelina West that I must have a letter from them stating they are the owners of this 15 acres in "fee simple" as I do not desire to buy an interest in this property. She states that she and her niece Mrs. Howard, are the only owners. I have no reason to doubt this, since I do not know these people and cannot obtain a family history, and you say you cannot obtain one. I have asked her to put this in writing to me, and if I do not receive this information from her, I will not honor the draft."

On or about August 10, 1955, Fowler received a letter purportedly written by "Evalina," (Exhibit Fowler 3) stating:

> "New Orleans, La.   Aug. 8, 1955
> "Dear Mr. Fowler
>
> "I am sending you back the deed you sent me It is all signed like you said.
>
> "Francis signed it the 30th of July and I signed it today.
>
> "You asked about other owners, there are none. We are the only ones who have anything in that place.

"Francis is my sisters only child. We wrote you about selling the place because it is so far and the ones we had looking after it never sent us no money though I hear they rented the place.

"Sincerely,
"Evalina"

Fowler testified that the deed was forwarded to him with this letter and he attached the letter and envelope to the deed. But a letter from Mrs. Howard's attorney dated August 25, 1955 states that the attorney had the deed in his possession and would forward it to Fowler after Fowler sent the $100.

The handwriting and signature of "Evalina" on the letter does not in any way resemble the signature of Evelina Fields West on the deed. Appellant explains this by the fact that Evalina was then more than 80 years old and had friends to write letters for her. This is all the more reason why Fowler should have obtained an affidavit.

The trial court was impressed by the fact that prior to 1955, Fowler had completed two years of law school, having dropped out during his senior year. This establishes that Fowler was well informed on the Civil Code Articles here at issue and the requirement for good faith at the time of purchase. When Fowler was testifying, he stated that he knew "as much about successions and land matters as most attorneys" and can "check titles to the nth degree, and draw deeds". Tr. 195. He stated however that he did not have that much knowledge in 1955.

We find ample support for the trial court's factual determination that Fowler did not have "good faith" at the time of acquisition.

First, Fowler prepared a "quitclaim" type description commonly used to convey a vendor's undivided interest in property. Therefore, Fowler's vendors did not warrant to him that they owned the entire interest in the property. Adding importance to this basis for the trial court's decision is the fact that Fowler (three times) denied that he prepared the description. But it was established that he did.

Second, 15 acres of land located ten miles from a major city, fronting a major highway with ten acres of pasture land suitable for farming cotton, corn, hay, etc., which was worth $250 in 1916, must have been worth substantially more than $100 in the year 1955. In 1954, five acres planted to cotton yielded seven bales of cotton. The fact that these alleged owners of the entire "fee simple" were willing to sell "all their right, title and interest" for this small amount should cause Fowler to question their ownership of the en-tire tract. Fowler lived all of his life within 2¼ miles of the tract, and his brother owned an adjacent tract.

Third, it was not established to the trial court's satisfaction, nor ours, that the letter signed "Evalina" (Exhibit Fowler-3) was sufficient to give Fowler the "good faith" belief that he was acquiring the full interest in the 15 acres. The difference in signatures on the letter and on the deed (which according to Fowler arrived in the same mail) should have alerted him to some title problem. An affidavit of heirship should have revealed that these Parties owned only a 1/10 interest in the property. The fact that Fowler bought property that he knew was last titled to Sallie Jones from parties who did not have Jones in their name, should have alerted him to the need for succession proceedings or at least an affidavit of heirship. Again, the fact that Fowler required the letter shows that he was aware of some title problem.***

The trial court's findings of fact are supported by the evidence. The law was correctly applied, and the trial court's judgment is affirmed. All costs of this appeal are to be paid by defendant-appellant, Andrew J. Fowler.

PHILLIPS v. PARKER
483 So. 2d 972 (La. 1986)

LEMMON, J. This boundary action raises the question whether defendants were properly denied the status of good faith possessors of immovable property, for purposes of ten-year acquisitive prescription, simply because they obtained a title examination at the time of their purchase and the examining attorney failed to discover that the seller had already sold a portion of the property to another party. We conclude that, especially in the light of the 1982 revisions clarifying the Civil Code articles relating to acquisitive prescription, a party who obtains a title examination is not solely for that reason precluded from claiming the status of a good faith possessor in a plea of ten-year acquisitive prescription, but rather that the obtaining of a title examination and the information actually revealed by the examination are merely factors to be considered in the judicial determination of whether the presumption of good faith has been successfully rebutted.

FACTS

In 1947 G.R. Weaver, plaintiff's and defendants' common ancestor in title, acquired a tract of land containing 2.55 acres. Weaver eventually built a camp on a small portion of the lakefront property. In 1955 Weaver agreed to sell two lakefront lots from the remainder of the tract to defendants and to the McCuller brothers, who were plaintiff's immediate ancestor in title. The tract was not subdivided and contained no visible boundaries.

On August 22, 1955, Weaver executed two cash deeds by which he sold one lot to the defendants and one lot to the McCullers, each for the price of $750. When defendants went out to the property after the sale to mark off the lot, they learned that the property description in the deed did not describe the property they had intended to purchase, but instead described the part of the tract on which Weaver's camp was located. On advice of their attorney, defendants employed a surveyor, who surveyed the property defendants had intended to purchase, and an attorney, who examined the title to that property and expressed the opinion that Weaver had a good and valid title. Weaver then transferred to defendants by cash deed on October 7, 1955 the lot defendants had intended to buy, and defendants conveyed back to Weaver the lot purchased in error in August.

Defendants immediately cleared the property and built a camp. The following year they erected a fence in accordance with the survey, and they were in peaceful possession of the fenced property until 1982.

In the meantime the McCullers had conveyed their lot to plaintiff in 1972. When plaintiff desired to move a trailer onto her property in 1982, she discovered that the property described in her August, 1955 deed overlapped the property described in defendants' October, 1955 deed by thirteen feet. Her request that defendants remove the fence was apparently the first time that defendants learned that their fence was on plaintiff's property.

In this ensuing boundary action, defendants filed an exception of ten-year acquisitive prescription, claiming to have possessed since 1956, in good faith and under just title, all of the property located within the fence. At trial the only disputed issue relative to defendants' plea of acquisitive prescription was their good faith. The title examiner testified that he did not recall finding the August, 1955 sale from Weaver to the McCullers. Apparently defendants relied completely on the title examiner's written opinion that Weaver had a good and valid title to the lot which they purchased in October 1955.

The trial court overruled the exception of prescription, concluding that the defendants were in "legal bad faith" because they obtained a title examination which did not reveal the defect in their title. The court further determined that plaintiff was the owner of the disputed strip and fixed the boundary accordingly.

The court of appeal affirmed. 469 So. 2d 1102. The intermediate court first noted that the doctrine of legal bad faith, under which an error of law (such as an erroneous conclusion as to ownership rights) precluded a finding of good faith for purposes of acquisitive prescription, had been legislatively overruled by La.C.C. Art. 3481 (enacted by Acts 1982, No. 187), which provides that neither an error of fact nor an error of law defeats the presumption of good faith. However, the court concluded that the 1982 Civil Code revisions did not affect the theory of law that a purchaser who undertakes a title search of the public records is charged with knowledge of the defects in title that a reasonable person would acquire from a search of the public records. Citing *Martin v. Schwing Lumber & Shingle Co.,* 228 La. 175, 81 So. 2d 852 (1955), the court held that because of this theory of constructive knowledge, based on the public records doctrine, the defendants were not in good faith once they had undertaken through their attorney a search of the public records which should have revealed the overlap in the property descriptions.

We granted certiorari to determine, especially in the light of the 1982 revisions, the validity of a theory of law which deems a party to be a bad faith possessor simply because he obtained a title examination, even though the party acted reasonably by employing an attorney to examine the title to the property he intended to purchase and then reasonably relied on the opinion of the title examiner that the seller had a good and valid title to the property. 475 So. 2d 347.

The court of appeal (perhaps in reliance on some loose language in prior cases) has misconstrued the public records doctrine and has misapplied a questionable theory of constructive knowledge as conclusive of the determination of good faith of a possessor who obtains a title examination. It is therefore appropriate to review the public records doctrine and to analyze the effect of obtaining a title examination upon the determination of good faith under the 1982 Civil Code revisions.

THE PUBLIC RECORDS DOCTRINE

The law of registry is stated principally in La.R.S. 9:2721 and 9:2756 (formerly La. C.C. Art. 2266) as follows:

> "No sale, contract, counter letter, lien, mortgage, judgment, surface lease, oil, gas or mineral lease or other instrument of writing relating to or affecting immovable property shall be binding on or affect third persons or third parties unless and until filed for registry in the office of the parish recorder of the parish where the land or immovable is situated; and neither secret claims or equities nor other matters outside the public records shall be binding on or affect such third parties." R.S. 9:2721.

> "All sales, contracts and judgments affecting immovable property, which shall not be so recorded, shall be utterly null and void, except between the parties thereto. The recording may be made at any time, but shall only affect third persons from the time of the recording.

> "The recording shall have effect from the time when the act is deposited in the proper office, and indorsed by the proper officer." R.S. 9:2756.

The fundamental principle of the law of registry is that any sale, mortgage, privilege, contract or judgment affecting immovable property, which is required to be recorded, is utterly null and void as to third persons unless recorded. Redmann, The Louisiana Law of Recordation: Some Principles and Some Problems, 39 Tul. L. Rev. 491 (1965). When the law of recordation applies, an interest in immovable property is effective against third persons only if it is recorded; if the interest is not recorded, it is not effective against third persons, even if the third person knows of the claim. This principle is traceable to the decision in *McDuffie v. Walker*, 125 La. 152, 51 So. 100 (1909), in which the court held that the plaintiff, as purchaser of immovable property by recorded act, was entitled to recognition as owner in a petitory action against the defendant who had purchased the property seven years earlier and had immediately gone into possession, but had not recorded the deed. In response to the defendant's argument that the plaintiff had knowledge of the prior unrecorded sale, the court reiterated its decision in *Harang v. Plattsmier,* 21 La.Ann. 426 (1869) that actual knowledge is not the equivalent of registry, which is absolutely required in order for the sale to affect third persons.

Thus, the law of registry does not create rights in a positive sense, but rather has the negative effect of denying the effectiveness of certain rights unless they are recorded. The essence of the public records doctrine is that recordation is an essential element for the *effectiveness* of a right, and it is important to distinguish between *effectiveness* of a right against third persons and *knowledge* of a right by third persons. An unrecorded interest is not effective against anyone (except the parties). A recorded interest, however, is *effective* both against those third persons who have *knowledge* and those who do not have *knowledge* of the presence of the interest in the public records. From the standpoint of the operation of the public records doctrine, knowledge is an irrelevant consideration. Any theory of constructive knowledge which imputes knowledge of the contents of the public records to third persons forms no part of the public records doctrine.

Another element of the public records doctrine is the protection of third persons. La.R.S. 9:2722 provides that a third person is entitled to rely on the law of registry and is protected thereby. This protection of third parties has significance only when an interest which is required to be recorded is *not recorded,* because a third person under such circumstances can deal with the property in *reliance on the absence* of the interest from the public records, even if the third person has actual knowledge of the interest. Thus, the primary concern of the public records doctrine is the protection of third persons against *unrecorded interests.* The public records doctrine therefore has little applicability in the present case in which the claim of plaintiff's ancestor in title was recorded.

In the present case, the sale from Weaver to the McCullers included the disputed thirteen-foot strip, and recordation made the sale effective against third persons who thereafter dealt with that strip. Because of the recordation, plaintiff (as successor in title to the McCullers) had a superior title to the strip, and defendants did not obtain a valid title in their subsequent purchase from Weaver. The fact that defendants did not have *actual knowledge* of the recorded sale from Weaver to the McCullers did not bear one iota on the *effectiveness* of that sale. Moreover, as to the merits of the boundary action, defendants lost because the McCuller's recordation made the sale *effective* against any third persons who later dealt with that property and not because third persons (including defendants) had *constructive knowledge* of that recorded sale.

TITLE EXAMINATION AND THE GOOD FAITH POSSESSOR

The purpose of good faith acquisitive prescription is to secure the title of a person who purchases immovable property by a deed translative of title, under the reasonable and objective belief that he is acquiring a valid title to the property, and thereafter remains in peaceful possession of the property for more than ten years without any disturbance by the true owner. Acquisitive prescription plays an important social role by doing away with the insoluble problems that otherwise could arise if there was an unknown defect in the chain of title of a long-time possessor. 1 M. Planiol, Civil Law Treatise § 2645 (La. St. Law Inst. Trans. 1959). The redactors of the Civil Code therefore provided that a person who purchases immovable property under the required circumstances should eventually prevail in a title dispute with the owner who allows continuous, uninterrupted, peaceable, public and unequivocal possession for more than ten years without objection.

The law of registry is not involved in any way with the theory of acquisitive prescription that a party who reasonably believed he was acquiring valid title should be deemed to have a valid title after a certain period of possession in which the owner failed to object. The law of registry simply makes the true owner's recorded title effective against the good faith possessor until the period of time has elapsed by which the good faith possessor acquires a valid title by means of the required possession. The theory of constructive knowledge should also have no bearing on the determination from an objective standpoint of the good faith of a possessor of immovable property who claims acquisitive prescription. Nevertheless, inconsistent decisions prior to the 1982 revisions of the Civil Code imputed bad faith to certain possessors, irrespective of their objective good faith.

In the present case, the lower courts applied the theory of constructive knowledge to deprive defendants of the right to claim acquisitive prescription on the basis that they were not in good faith because their attorney failed to discover a prior sale by Weaver in the public records. If the constructive knowledge afforded by recordation of Weaver's sale to the McCullers would *absolutely* preclude a finding of good faith on the part of defendants who later purchased the same thirteen-foot strip from Weaver, then the theory of constructive notice would write ten-year acquisitive prescription completely out of the Code. Such a result is totally unacceptable. Equally unacceptable, from the standpoint of an objective determination of good faith, is the theory of constructive knowledge which precluded good faith possession only because the attorney employed by defendants examined the records and failed to find the prior sale. This result restricts good faith status to those possessors who purchased property without any attempt whatsoever to check the validity of the title, thereby penalizing a purchaser who employs a title examiner and rewarding one who doesn't. This theory places the purchaser in a dilemma, since it is imprudent in modern practice to purchase property without a title examination, but the obtaining of a title examination would forfeit any right to claim the status of a good faith possessor in the event of an ancient defect in title. The better approach, and the one we conclude is required by the clarification provided by the 1982 revisions, is that the good faith of the possessor should be determined by a consideration of all of the factors of the particular case relevant to the definition of good faith in the Civil Code, and not merely by any reference to the public records doctrine or to any theory of constructive knowledge.

La.C.C. Art. 3480, effective January 1, 1983, defines the good faith requirement in ten-year acquisitive prescription as follows:

> "For purposes of acquisitive prescription, a possessor is in good faith when he reasonably believes, in light of objective considerations, that he is owner of the thing he possesses."

The Comments to Article 3480 note that the definition of good faith was contained in former Article 3451 and that the new article changes the law. The Comments further note that while former Article 3451 was ambiguous and was sometimes construed as basing good faith on the subjective view of the possessor that he owned the thing possessed, the prevailing jurisprudence determined good faith in the light of objective considerations. *The new article codifies the prevailing jurisprudence.* The Comments also point out that the new article does not affect the public records doctrine and that any considerations involving a search of the public records should be addressed to the issue of whether the presumption of good faith in Article 3481 has been rebutted.

Even under the old law it was appropriate to determine good faith on the basis of objective criteria. Further, good faith is presumed under Article 3481, as it was under the old law. The legislative overruling of the doctrine of legal bad faith did change the law. See Comments to Article 3481. However, the problem in this case was not the application of the overruled doctrine of legal bad faith, but the misapplication of the theory of constructive knowledge to preclude the possessor (who was clearly in good faith on the basis of objective criteria) from claiming acquisitive prescription.

Perhaps the prior cases imputed knowledge of the public records to preclude good faith by possessors who obtained title examinations in order to prevent claims of good faith by purchasers to whom title defects had been privately communicated. Actual knowledge of a title defect at the time of purchase certainly precludes good faith. However, knowledge by a purchaser of title defects can be inferred from circumstances more relevant than the mere obtaining of a title examination. For example, a purchase by quit claim deed or at an extremely low price may be suggestive (but not conclusive) of knowledge of title defects which may rebut the presumed good faith of the purchaser. The age and nature of the title defect, and other such factors bearing on the likelihood of discovery, are also relevant to the determination.

The 1982 amendments, reiterating that good faith should be presumed and restricting to objective criteria the determination whether the presumption has been rebutted, have removed the questionable basis of prior decisions which imputed bad faith to certain possessors, regardless of their objective good faith, such as by imputing knowledge of the contents of the public records to those purchasers who employed title examiners or imputing errors of title examiners to their clients on the basis of agency. However, there was never any logical or compelling reason to deny a purchaser the status of a good faith possessor simply because the title examiner failed to discover a title defect. At worst, such a purchaser lacks objective good faith only as to the defects actually discovered in the title examination. As to defects that the purchaser's attorney failed to discover, the purchaser who relied on the seller's declaration and on the attorney's professional opinion should be in at least as good a position to claim the status of a good faith possessor from the standpoint of objective criteria, as a purchaser who conducted no title examination.

Here, defendants' good faith was presumed by operation of La.C.C. Art. 3481. Neither the deed nor the evidence at trial suggested any reason for defendants to doubt that Weaver was the owner of the property. Weaver had built a camp on a portion of the property he was selling to defendants, and he represented that he owned the property that was being sold. When the August sale mistakenly described the lot on which Weaver's camp was located, defendants consulted an attorney and then followed the attorney's advice by obtaining a survey and a title examination. Defendants then reasonably relied on the professional opinion of the attorney they had employed for that purpose. Moreover, the defect was a simple overlap in a nearly contemporaneous sale (which had no survey showing the exact location relative to defendants' property) that the examiner could easily have missed. Both defendants and the examiner testified that they were unaware of the overlap, and the examiner also pointed out the bad condition of the records in that parish at the time. It would truly be a distortion of the term "good faith" to decide that defendants lacked objective good faith under these circumstances, inasmuch as a reasonable man under like circumstances certainly would have believed that the seller had a valid title.

We therefore conclude that plaintiff has failed to carry her burden of rebutting, on the basis of objective criteria, the presumed good faith on the part of defendants.

Accordingly, the judgments of the lower courts are reversed, and defendants' plea of ten-year acquisitive prescription is sustained.

MARCUS, J., concurs in the result.

LOUISIANA REVISED STATUTES
R.S. 9:5630. Actions by unrecognized successor against third persons

A. An action by a person who is a successor of a deceased person, and who has not been recognized as such in the judgment of possession rendered by a court of competent jurisdiction, to assert an interest in an immovable formerly owned by the deceased, against a third person who has acquired an interest in the immovable by onerous title from a person recognized as an heir or legatee of the deceased in the judgment of possession, or his successors, is prescribed in two years from the date of the finality of the judgment of possession.

B. This Section establishes a liberative prescription, and shall be applied both retrospectively and prospectively; however, any person whose rights would be adversely affected by this Section shall have one year from the effective date of this Section within which to assert the action described in Subsection A of this Section and if no such action is instituted within that time, such claim shall be forever barred.

C. "Third person" means a person other than one recognized as an heir or legatee of the deceased in the judgment of possession.

D. For the purposes of this Section, after thirty years from the date of recordation of a judgment of possession there shall be a conclusive presumption that the judgment was rendered by a court of competent jurisdiction.

Added by Acts 1981, No. 721, § 1; most recent amendment, Acts 1988, No. 312, § 1.

LACOUR v. SANDERS
442 So. 2d 1280 (La. App. 3d Cir. 1983)

CUTRER, J. This is a suit for partition by licitation of approximately thirty acres of land located near Woodworth, Rapides Parish, Louisiana. Leah Maxine Jett Lacour, in her capacity as administratrix of the succession of her mother, Mary Ellen Scott Jett, sued Joseph E. Sanders claiming a one-half interest in a tract of land Sanders purchased from Ms. Lacour's father, Robert Jett, Jr. Sanders answered the suit pleading the affirmative defense of ten year acquisitive prescription. The trial judge rendered judgment recognizing Sanders as the owner of the disputed tract of land. Ms. Lacour appeals. We affirm.

The trial judge has favored us with excellent reasons for judgment and we will take the liberty of quoting from his statement of the facts and his discussion of the issues.

"Robert Jett, Jr. and Mary Ellen Scott were married in Grant Parish on September 1, 1932.... The property in dispute was acquired by Robert Jett, Jr. while married and living with Mary Ellen Scott by act of sale dated May 25, 1937.... About the time of the deed, Robert Jett, Jr. and Mary Ellen Scott Jett moved on this property and farmed it with their children and Ellen's children by her first marriage. In 1947 the Jett family moved about a mile away to a twenty-acre tract which Jett had purchased. The Jetts continued to farm the property, the subject of this lawsuit, until the death of Mary Ellen Scott on December 14, 1959.... Joe Sanders, the purchaser and possessor, testified that three or four years before Ellen Scott Jett died no one lived on the property.... Joe Sanders, his family, and the Jett family were friends for many years in a small community. The families attended the same church. The Jett children and the Sanders children played together and went to school together. Joe Sanders and his wife knew Mary Ellen Scott died on December 14, 1959. Both attended the wake.

"Shortly after the funeral, Robert Jett, Jr. married Willie Mae Williams. On July 9, 1960, Robert Jett, Jr. alone sold the property, subject to this lawsuit, to defendant, Joe Sanders.

"Shortly thereafter the Sanders family occupied a frame house, which they moved onto the property, and lived there until 1976, when they constructed on the property the brick veneer house in which they presently reside...Mr. Sanders further testified that he executed two mineral leases on the property. He executed a ten-year lease in 1970 and a five-year lease in 1982.... Mr. Sanders testified that from the date of purchase until the date of this trial he believed he was indeed the owner of the full 30.30 acres which he possessed as owner.

"To plaintiffs claim to be recognized as co-owners of an undivided one-half interest in the property, defendant has answered alleging ten years acquisitive prescription; estoppel, and ownership of his home. Defendant third partied his vendor, Robert Jett, Jr., who answered and third partied Ellen Scott's forced heirs, which issues were deferred for later hearing." (Reference to trial exhibits omitted.)

ISSUES

The determinative issue in this appeal is whether the trial judge's ruling, that Sanders had proven ownership of the property by prescription, is correct. Mr. Lacour also raised questions concerning equitable estoppel and the appropriateness of partition by licitation. Because of our resolution of the prescription issue it is not necessary that we discuss these other questions.

ACQUISITIVE PRESCRIPTION

Civil Code art. 3458 [Revised C.C. art. 3446], as it read at the time this suit was filed, defined acquisitive prescription as follows:

"The prescription by which the ownership of property is acquired, is a right by which a mere possessor acquires the ownership of a thing which he possesses by the continuance of his possession during the time fixed by law."

An immovable, such as the tract of land at issue in this case, can be acquired in full ownership, by the operation of acquisitive prescription, in ten years, if four criteria are met. These criteria are set out in Civil Code art. 3479. They are: (1) Good faith on the part of the possessor; (2) A title which shall be legal, and sufficient to transfer the property; (3) Possession during the time required by law; and (4) An object which may be acquired by prescription.

The trial judge, after enumerating the prerequisites of art. 3479, stated:

"This Court finds that Joe Sanders proved without contradiction that he exercised continuous and uninterrupted, peaceable, public and unequivocal possession as owner for more than ten years and with a legal title sufficient to transfer the property. Melancon v. Wood, 357 So. 2d 75 (4th Cir., 1978), [writ denied, 359 So. 2d 201 (La. 1978)], C.C. 3479, 3483, 3487, (C.C. 3475, 3476, 3483 as amended by Act No. 187 of 1982.)

"The final element to be determined for ten-year acquisitive prescription and the only element disputed by plaintiff is good faith on the part of Sanders....

"The Court in Melancon, *supra,* at page 77, held that to be in good faith, '...a possessor must have legitimately and reasonably believed that the person from who he acquired title was the true owner of the property.***

"Both Robert Jett, Jr. and Joe Sanders are uneducated... men who lived in the rural community of Woodworth. Sanders was ignorant of Louisiana community property laws.... The property in dispute is located in the Ashton [Community]. Furthermore, at the time of the sale Article 2404 of the Civil Code, the Head and Master rule, was in effect whereby the husband could transfer full interest in the community by onerous title without the permission of his wife.

"Plaintiff's position is that defendant is in bad faith because he knew of the death of Ellen Scott Jett. Plaintiff's contention is based upon Juneau vs. Laborde, 54 So. 2d 325 (1951) and Thibodeaux v. Quebodeaux, 282 So. 2d 845 (3rd Cir., 1973). These cases are inapposite. It is clear in these cases the vendee has knowledge of title defects.

"In Juneau, the vendee was warned against buying the property and told that the title was not good. In Thibodeaux, the vendee lived near the vendor. He was aware that the vendor acquired the property while married and sold it after the vendor's wife died. Equally, in Thibodeaux, *supra,* at page 850, the vendee was aware of the Louisiana community property laws and knew that '... when a man and a woman are married and they acquire property half is for the man and half is for the woman.' [This emphasis ours.] The Courts in the Juneau and Thibodeaux cases found the vendee's knowledge tantamount to an error in law which previously barred 10-year acquisitive prescription. This Court notes in passing that under the new law, Article 3481, neither error of law, nor error of fact defeats the right to acquire by ten-year acquisitive prescription.

"In this case, Sanders testified that several years prior to the sale, while Ellen Scott Jett was alive, he asked Robert Jett, Jr. to sell the property and Jett said no. Sanders testified he told Jett if he changed his mind to let him know. Sanders testified that in 1960, Jett came to him and said he wanted to sell.

"Joe Sanders' wife, Ola Marie Sanders, testified that Jett stated all of the children were willing to sell.... In her deposition at page 7 she was asked:

"Q. 'You thought that Robert Jett, Jr. could sell all the property in spite of the fact that his wife had died?'

"A. 'Well, I didn't think in those terms that way, but I thought after we had wanted to buy the property and he had come to us and say the children all had agreed and they wanted to sell the property and knowed we were looking for land, so, and after that, well, I...'

"Reading her entire deposition makes it clear that even Ola Marie thought Robert Jett could convey all of the property. Celestine Cole and Leah Maxine Jett LaCour, daughters of Robert Jett, Jr., testified that before the sale they told their father that they did not want to sell the property. It is clear that neither Jett nor his daughters conveyed this information to the Sanders. Additionally, after both Celestine and Leah received from their father $200.00 each as their portion of the proceeds from the sale, they still did not tell the Sanders of their opposition to the sale until this suit was filed twenty-two years later.

"Under Melancon v. Wood, 357 So. 2d 75 (4th Cir., 1978)... [Writ ref'd, 359 So. 2d 201 (La. 1978)], legal bad faith of the seller is not a relevant determination as to the issue of good faith by the purchaser. Additionally, the knowledge of the seller's lack of right or interest in the property is not imputed to the buyer, and the buyer's error in buying from the seller is an error of fact. The record is silent as to any information conveyed to Sanders which would place him on notice to inquire about his title. He remained a good faith possessor.

"A title examination would not reveal that Mary Ellen Scott Jett was deceased[;] thus the preparation of the act of sale by [the] attorneys [involved in the sale] would have been made in accordance with the facts set forth in the public records. Sanders testified he did not study and read the documents and that the lawyers prepared the deed and kept everything straight.

"It is abundantly clear that defendant Joe Sanders was a good faith possessor of the entire 30.30 acres in dispute and entitled to acquire full ownership under the acquisitive prescription of ten years and this Court so holds."

A careful review of the record before us and a thorough study of the jurisprudence of acquisitive prescription convinces us that the trial court's determination was correct. We find no error in the trial judge's actual findings or in his application of the law to those facts. The trial judgment shall be affirmed.

For the reasons assigned, the judgment of the trial court is affirmed. Plaintiff-appellant, Leah Maxine Lacour, is assessed with the costs of this appeal.

Symeonides, Error of Law and Error of Fact in Acquisitive Prescription 47 La. L. Rev. 429-444 (1986) (citations omitted)

I. Some Truisms about Errors and Prescription

Let us begin with some truisms: the reason a good faith possessor finds himself in the position of having to invoke the ten-year prescription is that he made the *mistake* of buying from someone who turned out not to be the owner of the property; one of the most important functions of the ten-year prescription is to cure such mistakes; and, if *all* mistakes were considered inexcusable, the institution of prescription would be largely unnecessary.

One of the bases of the ten-year prescription for immovables is the requirement that the possessor be in good faith at the time of his acquisition. The basis of his good faith is his *mistaken belief* in the seller's ownership. Whether founded on an error of law or an error of fact, this belief is thus the first necessary ingredient of good faith. If this belief did not exist, the possessor would not have bought the property, or if he had, he would not be in good faith. If this belief is not mistaken, then the possessor is the owner of the property and does not need prescription.

The second ingredient of good faith is the requirement that the possessor's belief in the seller's ownership be reasonable by objective standards. Viewed from the opposite angle, this process of evaluating the reasonableness of the possessor's belief is simply a process of evaluating the seriousness of his mistake and its impact on society in general. Depending on the circumstances, the possessor's mistake may be objectively justifiable or excusable, or it may be inexcusable. While the legislature may determine in advance which mistakes are excusable and which are not, the better solution is to leave this determination to the courts. This latter solution was adopted by the 1982 revision of the Civil Code provisions on acquisitive prescription.***

It is submitted that new Article 3481 has abolished not only the distinction between errors of law and errors of fact, but also the very notion that any type of error may be used to defeat the presumption of good faith in an *a priori* fashion, regardless of the circumstances of the particular case. As suggested elsewhere, despite the lack of a change at the surface, the new law has thus opened the door for re-examination of many other artificially constructed jurisprudential "rules" that over the years have undermined the presumption of good faith.***

II. Error of Law

[*Lacour v. Sanders*] involves an error of law.***Because it is essentially a trial court decision despite its affirmation by the higher courts, *Lacour* may not have much precedential value. Nevertheless, *Lacour* is worth discussing because it involves a recurring fact pattern, and because the result is intuitively equitable and probably in line with the philosophy of the new law. The court's reasoning, however, is a different matter. In fact, it would appear that, taken individually, none of the reasons advanced by the trial court would suffice to sustain its decision, at least under the pre-1983 jurisprudence.

For example, the possessor's lack of education might be important in satisfying the first level of inquiry, i.e., determining the possessor's subjective belief in his seller's ownership. Nevertheless, the *individual* possessor's level of sophistication should be rather secondary in the second level of inquiry, i.e., evaluating the reasonableness of this belief on the basis of the average, "reasonable-person" standards. Although the line between the two inquiries may not be as clear as one would prefer, what should be clear is that a below-average sophistication of the individual possessor may benefit him in the first but not the second inquiry, for the same reason that an above-average sophistication would harm him in the first but not the second inquiry (assuming, of course, he ever overcomes the first).

Similarly, it is largely irrelevant that the "head and master rule" was still in force at the time of the sale. In the first place, it is inconsistent first to sanction the possessor's ignorance of community property law, and then selectively to invoke on his behalf one particular rule from that law. More practically, however, the head and master rule was actually inapplicable to these facts. Had this rule been applicable, the buyer would have acquired full and immediate ownership of the property at the time of his purchase, and thus he would not need prescription. However, at the time of the sale, the seller was no longer the head and master of the community, since the community had been dissolved by his wife's death. Her children, of whose existence the buyer was fully aware, had already inherited her one half-interest in the property. It was their interest, not their mother's, that their father purported to sell.***

This unnecessarily liberal treatment of the possessor is also obvious in the court's statement that, because a title search would not have revealed that Mrs. Jett was deceased, the possessor's actual knowledge of her death was irrelevant. It may be true that, under some questionable though often repeated old jurisprudence, a buyer who had reason to doubt the seller's ownership, but did not conduct a title search, is imputed with constructive knowledge of the contents of the public records. To this author's knowledge, however, the reverse has not been true. A party who did not make a title examination may not claim the benefits accorded by law to a party who did make such examination. The court's reliance on the absence from the public records of any notation of Mrs. Jett's death and its willingness to disregard the buyer's actual knowledge of that death seem to echo, subconsciously perhaps, the rule of *McDuffie v. Walker,* that a buyer who relies on the public records acquires the seller's interest free of unrecorded interests of third parties, despite his own actual knowledge of such interests. The *McDuffie* rule, however, never meant that such actual knowledge has no bearing on the good faith of a buyer who has *not* relied on the public records.

Be that as it may, the only aspect of *Lacour* that is important in terms of future trends is its treatment of the error of law problem. To understand this problem one must go back to *Dinwiddie*, the leading error of law case. In that case, the possessor knew that his seller's biological ancestor had left predeceased children other than the seller. Nevertheless, being ignorant of the rule of Louisiana succession law of inheritance by representation, i.e., that the share of predeceased children is inherited by their own descendants, the possessor did not try to find out whether such descendants existed. Ac-cording to *Dinwiddie's* oft-parroted dictum, this error of law prevented the buyer from claiming the status of a good faith possessor, because "if he purchased and possessed under error of law, he *thereby* became a possessor in bad faith." Herein lies the court's own error, i.e., the *automatic* assumption that the possessor was in bad faith *because* of his error of law. What the court meant was that the buyer's belief in the seller's ownership was not reasonable, because at the time of the purchase, the buyer knew of facts — the existence of predeceased children — which would raise doubts in the mind of the average reasonable buyer about the seller's ownership. Although this conclusion might well have been correct under the circumstances, it should not have been reached without first addressing the intermediate and more pertinent question of whether the possessor's belief in the seller's ownership was reasonable in light of his erroneous assumptions about the law.

The *Lacour* court did slightly better in this respect in that it at least paused somewhat to consider this question. This aspect of *Lacour* appears in line with the philosophy of the new law. Nevertheless, the process by which the decision was reached, and perhaps the correctness of the ultimate conclusion, is a different story. The *Lacour* facts were strikingly similar to *Dinwiddie*. In *Lacour*, the buyer knew that the seller was married and that his deceased wife was survived by children who were, in fact, from a marriage other than that with the seller. In the absence of an error of law, these facts would be sufficient to raise doubts in the mind of the average buyer about the seller's right to sell the entire property, and to render his belief in the seller's ownership unreasonable. Should the buyer's error of law alter this conclusion? The court appeared all too ready to answer this question in the negative, without much scrutiny of the particular circumstances, and without any discussion of *Dinwiddie*. Unable to distinguish *Dinwiddie*, and apparently perceiving itself unable to overrule it, the *Lacour* court chose instead to disregard it.

Fortunately, *Dinwiddie* has been legislatively overruled by the new revision. This does not, however, automatically make *Lacour* a correct decision. The abolition of the error of law doctrine does not mean that an error of law has no bearing on the question of good faith. As said earlier, it simply means that, rather than automatically defeating good faith, an error of law becomes one of the many factors on the basis of which good faith will be determined. The buyer's belief in his seller's ownership must still meet the objective standards of reasonableness. The individual buyer's sophistication, if it happens to be below average, would seem almost immaterial in this determination. The question is not so much whether the individual buyer could honestly believe that he was buying from a full owner, but rather whether the average buyer could have reasonably harbored such a belief. In cases involving an error or ignorance of law, the reasonableness of that belief cannot be divorced from the status in the community at large of the particular legal rule whose ignorance is invoked. The more widely known a rule is to the community at large, the less likely it is that its ignorance by the particular buyer would be excusable, and vice versa. Although there may be room for disagreement, it would seem that, whether it pertained to community property, succession, or mandate law, the legal rule whose ignorance caused the error in *Lacour* is a rule that is widely known among Louisianians regardless of educational background.

III. Error of Fact

[*Phillips v. Parker*] involved a very common error of fact by the possessor: conducting a title examination but failing to discover a defect in the seller's title. In this case the defect was a mere thirteen-foot overlap with a neighbor's lot sold to the neighbor by the same seller in a previous but nearly contemporaneous sale. The title examiner, an attorney hired by the possessor's attorney, testified that he had missed the overlap.***

[1.] Time for a New Approach

(a) Title search and reasonableness

The development of the new approach must begin by reassessing, in light of contemporary practices, the role of a title search in determining good faith. One of the first jurisprudential rules to be affected by such a reassessment would be the rule which requires a title search only in suspicious circumstances. This rule seems to be based on the dated assumption that a title examination is the exception rather than the norm and is therefore not a required element of reasonableness. In light of contemporary practices, this assumption is unrealistic and unnecessarily liberal. If this premise is true, then a title examination should be viewed as one of the elements by which to evaluate the reasonableness of the possessor's belief in the seller's ownership. From this premise flow two corollaries: (a) that, in the absence of special circumstances, failure to conduct a title examination is a factor that normally points against rather than towards reasonableness; and (b) that the conducting of a title examination should weigh in favor rather than against a finding of good faith. Indeed, a title examination that fails to reveal any defect in the seller's title reinforces, not only the buyer's subjective belief in his ownership, but also his claim that such belief is reasonable by objective standards.

If both corollaries are accepted, then the above jurisprudential rule should be modified in both directions, i.e., (a) failure to conduct a title examination should be weighed against the possessor when evaluating the reasonableness of his conduct by objective standards; while (b) the conducting of a reasonably thorough title examination which failed to reveal any defects in the seller's title should be weighed in favor of the possessor in evaluating the reasonableness of his belief in the seller's ownership. It may well be that the system is not yet ripe for accepting the first modification. The second one, however, is long overdue, and may be implemented without the first. If this second modification were accepted there would be little room for the theory of constructive notice.

(b) Title search and the theory of constructive notice

In any event, even if both of the above corollaries were rejected together with their underlying premise, there would still be little reason for retaining the second rule described above, i.e., the rule that imputes the possessor who conducted a title search with constructive knowledge of the contents of the public records. In other words, even if a title examination is viewed as the exception rather than the norm in contemporary transactions, there would be little reason for either discouraging title searches in general, or for penalizing those buyers who, out of an abundance of caution, find it advisable to search the public records before they make their investment.

If the public records in Louisiana were in such perfect condition that any search of them would easily reveal whatever defects exist in the seller's title, then perhaps the theory of constructive notice would be somewhat realistic. As any title examiner would testify, however, the condition of Louisiana's public records leaves much to be desired. The only reason that would seem to render support for the theory of constructive notice might be the desire to prevent fraud or collusion between a title examiner and a possessor. To be sure, it is conceivable that a possessor who has actual knowledge of defects in the seller's title might use a title examination that shows no such defects as a shield against claims of bad faith. Nevertheless, this scenario is not very likely to occur. Speculators aside, one does not invest money because he hopes to acquire property ten years later by prescription, but rather because he believes that he is acquiring ownership immediately upon purchase. Furthermore, one cannot assume lightheartedly that a title examiner would endanger his reputation or livelihood by participating in a collusive scheme with the possessor. In any event, the judicial process is capable of detecting fraud where fraud exists. A remote possibility of fraud in some cases is no justification for penalizing everybody in all cases.

In sum, implicit in the theory of constructive notice is the notion that no mistake in a title search is tolerable. That such a notion is unrealistic, mechanistic, and consequently unfair is too obvious for argument. It is unrealistic because of the condition of the public records; it is mechanistic because it treats all mistakes alike, regardless of their gravity or the likelihood of their being avoided; and, consequently, it is unfair because it penalizes prudent innocent parties. The net result of this theory is to restrict the availability of the ten-year prescription to those imprudent innocent possessors who did not conduct a title search. This result alone makes the whole theory suspect. It is not suggested that a title search should automatically insulate possessors from a finding of bad faith, or that any title search should suffice for a finding of good faith. What is suggested instead is that, rather than preventing the inquiry into the reasonableness of the possessor's belief, a title search should become one of the objects of that inquiry. The possessor's actual good or bad faith should be determined, not by artificial fictions, but rather by evaluating, on a case by case basis, all of the surrounding circumstances, including the condition of the public records, the thoroughness of the particular title search, the competence and reputation of the title examiner, the type of title defect involved, the possibility of it being missed, and other similar factors. This is essentially the Supreme Court's approach in *Phillips*, described below.

[2.] The Phillips Approach

(a) Title search and reasonableness

In *Phillips*, the Supreme Court accepted, and successfully discharged, the challenge of restoring sanity and consistency to the law of good faith by reexamining the theory of constructive notice. The court recognized the absurdity of treating a possessor who made a title search worse than a possessor who did not. Although the court stopped short of requiring a title search as an element of reasonableness in good faith determinations, the whole tenor of the opinion suggests that the court ascribes to the view that, *if conducted,* a title examination is an element that reinforces rather than weakens the possessor's claim of good faith. A footnote in the court's decision suggests that the court may have more to say on this issue when the right case arises.***

(d) Title search and the law of mandate

One of the beneficial side-effects of *Phillips* is that it reduces the scope of another related jurisprudential rule: the rule which imputed the possessor with notice of whatever knowledge, actual or constructive, was obtained by his title examiner. With regard to *actual* knowledge received by the title examiner in the context of a title examination, this rule was, and remains, justified by the principles of the law of mandate, insofar as the title examiner is a true mandatary of the buyer. Without this rule, the possessor would be able to immunize himself from accusations of bad faith by simply delegating the title examination to someone else. Nevertheless, nothing in the law of mandate ever justified extending this rule to constructive knowledge imputed to the title examiner. As a result of *Phillips*, this rule would now be confined to defects actually discovered by the title examiner, whether or not those defects are actually communicated to the possessor.

A question still worth asking even after *Phillips* is whether the title examiner is actually the mandatary of the possessor or of someone else. In *Phillips*, the possessor had tried to raise this question by arguing that he had not "directly hired or paid" the title examiner. The court of appeal excluded such evidence as "irrelevant." This evidence would indeed be irrelevant, if, as it seems likely from the facts, the possessor's attorney were acting within his implied authority when he hired the title examiner, in this case, the title examiner would have become the possessor's mandatary, and his actual knowledge would be imputed to his principal, whether or not he was paid by him. On the other hand, if for some reason the title examiner cannot be characterized as the agent or subagent of the possessor, the law of mandate is inapplicable, and there is no basis for imputing the possessor with the acts or omissions of the title examiner. Such may often be the situation in a typical financed purchase where the title examiner is selected, paid, and controlled, not by the buyer, but by the finance company.

QUESTIONS

In his commentary "Error of Law and Error of Fact in Acquisitive Prescription," Professor Symeonides succinctly identifies two key elements of good faith for ten-year acquisitive prescription: (1) there must be a mistaken belief on the part of the possessor of the property that his author in title was its owner ("the possessor's subjective belief in his seller's ownership"); and (2) that belief must be "reasonable by objective standards." He then suggests that the "objective standards" to be employed require "evaluating the seriousness of his mistake and its impact on society in general," rather than the objective circumstances of the particular possessor that would support or discredit his claim of belief. According to Professor Symeonides, "The individual buyer's sophistication, if it happens to be below average, would seem almost immaterial in this determination." Consider the following hypothetical situations:

1. Professor C teaches Louisiana property law at a top-50 law school in Applewood, Louisiana, in the southeastern part of the state. She purchased Lot X from A for $2,000 in one cash payment in 1997. A said she had inherited Lot X from her late mother, M. Lot X lies directly east of a lot Prof. C owns, Lot Y; Prof. C built her home on Lot Y, and immediately upon purchasing Lot X enclosed the two lots within a single fence. Prof. C. had paid $10,000 for the empty Lot Y, which is the same size as Lot X, two years before purchasing Lot X. She is considering purchasing Lot Z, an empty lot the same size as Lot X directly west of Lot Y, for which the owners are asking $15,000.

Prof. C did not have a title search done before purchasing Lot X. Before she bought the lot, Prof. C's banker told her that A had only one sibling, a deceased brother, B. B had moved to the northwest corner of Louisiana, married and had a child, and had recently passed away.

Sgt. D has just arrived in Applewood, having recently returned to the U.S. from deployment in Iraq. He has evidence that he is the only child of A's brother, B, and that A and B's mother died without a will. Under Louisiana law, A and B would have inherited M's property in equal shares. B, who was divorced and had no other children, had left all his property to D by will, although under Louisiana law D would have inherited it anyway. D claims to own a half-interest in Lot X, and is asking market value of $7,500 for it. Could a claim by Prof. C that she owned Lot X by 10-year acquisitive prescription pass the subjective element of the Symeonides test of good faith? Could it pass the objective element?

2. L is a minimum-wage worker who loads delivery vans in Applewood's only industry, its water bottling plant. He has also purchased real estate included in M's estate from A, a small house on a lot, for $4000. The sale was contracted in 1997; A permitted him to pay over time, and he has now completed the payments. Like Prof. C, L did not have a title search done; A was a long-time member of L's church, and L trusted her. He knew that she had a brother, but A explained that B had told her he wasn't interested in their mother's real estate, and that A could have it all. L does not qualify as disabled, but he cannot read documents of any complexity and can barely write. He had been unable to complete high school because it was too

difficult. He thought $4000 was a good price; A said she was giving him a bargain because they belonged to the same church. In fact, this was a bargain price; comparable homes in the area cost $7500 in 1997. They now sell for $20,000. Sgt. D now makes a claim for a half interest in the land and house L bought on the same basis as his claim against Prof. C. Could a claim by L that he owned the house and lot by 10-year acquisitive prescription pass the subjective element of the Symeonides test of good faith? Could it pass the objective element?

3. Is the rationale underlying the acquisitive prescription of 10 years better served by treating Prof. C and L in the same way under the law, or by treating them differently? What objective measure of the reasonableness of a possessor's good faith subjective belief in his ownership would produce the latter result?

c. Possession
Civil Code arts. 936, 3476-3479, 3506(28)

1(2) PLANIOL, TRAITÉ ÉLÉMENTAIRE DE DROIT CIVIL 573-574, 584-586
(an English translation by the Louisiana State Law Institute 1959)

It has already been seen (No. 2286, par. 6) that the possession capable of leading to the acquisition of ownership is veritable possession, that which implies, besides the physical fact of detention, the intention of acting as master, or *animus domini*. It follows from this that precarious possessors or mere detainers, who possess in virtue of a title that obliges them to restore the thing to its owner (*supra* no. 2311 to no. 2318), cannot prescribe. Art. 2236 provides that these persons "never prescribe by any lapse of time whatsoever." Art. 2230 again confirms this provision by saying that "one cannot prescribe against one's title." This is true in the case of precarious detainers. They hold in virtue of a title that prevents them from prescribing.

The existence of a veritable possession is not sufficient. It is also necessary that this possession be free from any defect capable of making it useless (Art. 2229). Let it be not forgotten that there are but four such defects. They are discontinuity, violence, lack of public character and equivocality (see *supra* no. 2276).***

It is not necessary that the same person possess the immovable during the entire period required for prescription. The present possessor may count, besides his possession, that of his predecessors (Art. 2235). This is what is called the junction of possessions. This favor was necessary on account of the many mutations that take place in ownerships. Prescription would often be impossible if a person had to possess himself throughout the entire time required by law.

This taking of possession takes place in two different ways, depending upon whether the present owner is a successor by universal title or by a particular title. Art. 2235 does not draw this distinction. It seems to put all successors of every kind upon the same footing. But the differentiation results from the very nature of things.

The universal successor merely continues the deceased's possession (no. 2661). He succeeds to all of the latter's obligations as well as rights. It is thus not a new possession that begins but it is the deceased's possession that is transmitted to his heirs, with its virtues and its faults. Therefore if the deceased was a precarious possessor, his successor is necessarily a holder under the same title. He cannot prescribe as long as his precarious title has not been changed (no. 2320). If the deceased being in good faith, had a right to prescribe in from ten to twenty years, his heir may complete the prescriptive period within this delay, although he personally was in bad faith. On the contrary, if the deceased, being in bad faith, could not prescribe except by thirty years, his heir will be in the same position even if he personally is in good faith.

It is necessary that the preceding possession be itself one that could give rise to prescription. Thus if the preceding possessor was merely a precarious possessor, the purchaser, who commences an independent and useful possession, may prescribe, but naturally he cannot join to his possession that of his predecessor for the latter had nothing to pass on to him (Art. 2239).

Assuming that the preceding possessor was himself in the process of prescribing, several combinations may arise. If both of them were entitled to prescribe within from ten to twenty years, the new possessor would certainly have a right to consolidate the two possessions. The same result would obtain if neither of them was entitled to prescribe within these terms. In both cases, the thirty year period would be the only one available. In these two cases, the two successive possessions of the successor and of his author may be added together. They are of the same nature and of the same quality.

But if it be assumed that the two successive possessors are not in the same position from the standpoint of prescription, but one of them have a just title and being in good faith, complications arise. They are solved by this very simple rule: The years that apply to the thirty years prescription, which requires neither just title nor good faith, cannot be used in completing the prescription running from ten to twenty years. The latter prescription requires that both conditions exist. But, on the contrary, the years that have run in connection with this favored prescription may be counted in computing the thirty years of prescription. All that it requires is possession.

EXAMPLES: Where the vendor is a possessor in good faith, and the purchaser is in bad faith. If the ten years prescription has not run in favor of the vendor at the time of the sale, the purchaser cannot prescribe except upon the basis of thirty years, but he can count his author's years of possession.

Where the vendor was in bad faith but the purchaser in good faith, the latter can prescribe upon the basis of ten years but he cannot avail himself of his author's possession, because it applied solely to the thirty year period. In such a contingency, it might sometimes pay the purchaser to abandon his claim to the prescription of ten years in order to take advantage of the thirty years prescriptive period commenced by his author. This interest will come into play whenever the prescription has less than ten years to run before being completed. There is no doubt about the fact that he can then join his possession to that of his author to complete the thirty years. If the latter's possession would have applied to the shortened and privileged prescription it will *a fortiori* apply to the general prescription of thirty years.

Instance Where New Possessor is not the Successor of Preceding Possessor. In order that the tacking of possession be permissible it is necessary that the new possessor be the successor of the preceding one (Civ. Cass., Oct. 25, 1927, S. 1928. 1.47). Consequently the usurper who, without a title, takes possession of an immovable commences a new prescription. It links up with no other possession because such a person is the successor of nobody. And likewise, he who, by means of a revendication, takes an immovable from its possessor is not the successor of the person whom he evicts. He therefore cannot join this possession to his to protect himself, in his turn, against a revendication brought by a third party. Roman Law decided this point in a contrary sense. Its ruling was thus expressed: *"Si jussu judicis res mihi restituta sit, accessionem mihi esse dandam placuit"* (Digest, Bk. XLI, Tit. 2, fr. 13, § 1).

NOTE
What is Included in Ownership Gained
Through Acquisitive Prescription?

What is included in the ownership obtained by ten years' acquisitive prescription of a tract of land? In *Tremont Lumber Co. v. Powers & Critchett Lumber Co.*, 139 So. 12 (La. 1932), the state Supreme Court found that the plaintiff company had obtained not only the tract of land, but also the standing timber, with regard to which it had not exercised corporeal acts of possession. The tract first had been corporeally possessed through a lessee of Tremont's vendor, Louisiana Lumber Co., which had begun possessing in 1906 under a just title. After the lessee's departure, Louisiana Lumber and then its vendee Tremont possessed civilly. In 1927, the original owner's widow and heirs purported to sell the tract; a few months later, the defendant company purportedly bought the timber separately from the land from the family's vendee's vendee. (A separate estate in immovable timber, as Chapter III indicates, is recognized under art. 464.) Why would the timber be considered to have been possessed by the plaintiff, when the acts of corporeal possession with which his possession began had not involved the standing timber?

If the timber estate had been separated from the tract of land before Tremont had accumulated ten years of possession, should the result be the same? Should the result be the same for other rights that third parties could have affecting the tract of land (e.g., servitudes)?

BARTLETT v. CALHOUN
412 So. 2d 597 (La. 1982)

BLANCHE, J. This is a petitory action. The disputed property is a 300-acre tract of land located near the Black River in Catahoula Parish and owned at one time by W. C. Thompson and his wife. The Thompsons purportedly sold this tract to defendant, Stella Calhoun, on November 30, 1949. It appears from the record that thereafter the property was transferred by Ms. Calhoun to Grey Ramon Brown by act of sale dated December 10, 1949. Finally, in October of 1951, Ms. Calhoun re-purchased the property from Mr. Brown and it has remained in her possession since that date.

Plaintiffs, the alleged heirs of the Thompsons, filed this suit in 1977 seeking ownership and an accounting of revenue from the contested property. They challenge the validity of the November 30, 1949 act of sale, claiming that the Thompsons' signatures were forged.

Defendant moved for summary judgment, urging that because there was no issue as to a material fact, she was entitled to judgment as a matter of law. At the hearing on this motion, Ms. Calhoun contended that she had acquired the land in question by acquisitive prescription of ten years.

Plaintiffs argued that defendant, because of the alleged false signatures in the November 30, 1949 act of sale, was not in good faith. Defendant, in response to plaintiff's claim, urged that, even if she was in bad faith when she originally acquired the tract, she could take advantage of Grey Brown's (her transferee's) good faith, tack her subsequent possession to his, and own the property after the passage of ten years.

Both lower courts were of the opinion that the holding of Liuzza v. Heirs of Nunzio, 241 So. 2d 277 (1st Cir. 1970) was controlling in the instant case. When confronted with the identical issue, the court in Liuzza came to the following conclusion:

> In the very early case of Devall v. Choppin, 15 La. 566 (1840) the Supreme Court enunciated the proposition that if a successor showed that one of his authors was a possessor in good faith and had all the necessary ingredients for ten year prescription, he could acquire by such prescription even though he as well as an intermediary author possessed in bad faith. This interpretation has become the rule in our jurisprudence.

Accordingly, the trial and appellate courts held that, because Ms. Calhoun could rely on Grey Brown's good faith, it did not matter whether defendant was or was not herself in good faith. Concluding that plaintiff's challenge to Ms. Calhoun's plea of prescription did not bear on a material fact, summary judgment was rendered in favor of defendant. C.C.P. art. 966.

We granted writs to determine whether the lower courts' conclusion that defendant's status as a good or bad faith possessor was not a material fact was proper. In so doing, we re-evaluate the soundness of the jurisprudential rule which permits a bad faith possessor to tack his possession to that of his good faith author in order to acquire ownership by acquisitive prescription of ten years.

"Tacking," or the "joining of possessors," allows the present possessor to count, besides his own possession, that of his predecessor in order to prescribe. M. Planiol, Civil Law Treatise, Part 2, Sec. 2673 (12th ed. La.St.L.Inst. trans. 1959). As a result, it is not necessary that the same individual possess the immovable during the entire period required for prescription. This joining, or tacking, of possessions is authorized by C.C. art. 3493 [Revised C.C. arts. 3441, 3442], which provides:

> Art. 3493. The possessor is allowed to make the sum of possession necessary to prescribe, by adding to his own possession that of his author, in whatever manner he may have succeeded him, whether by a universal or particular, a lucrative or an onerous title.

By the word "author" this code provision contemplates the person from whom another derives his right, whether by universal title or by particular title. C.C. art. 3494 [Revised C.C. art. 3441]. Thus, it is imperative that a juridical link exist in order for a successor to acquire his predecessor's prescriptive rights. Though art. 3493 does not contain a separate provision for the universal successor as distinguished from the successor by particular title, we believe that a differentiation must exist due to the nature of these types of transfers.

The French commentators agree that the universal successor continues the deceased's possession and does not commence a new possession. 2 Aubry & Rau, Droit Civil Français Nos. 218 (7th ed. Esmein 1961), 2 Civil Law Translations at 365 (1966): Baudry-Lacantinerie & Tissier, Traité Théorique et Pratique de Droit Civil. Prescription Nos. 346, 347 (1924), 5 Civil Law Translations at 181 (La. St.L.Inst. trans. 1972). See also Griffin v. Blanc, 12 La. Ann. 5 (La. 1857). As noted by Planiol:

> The universal successor merely continues the deceased's possession (no. 2661). He succeeds to all of the latter's obligations as well as rights. It is thus not a new possession that begins but it is the deceased's possession that is transmitted to his heirs, with its virtues and its faults. Planiol, *supra*, Sec. 2674.

Because the universal successor's possession is nothing more than a continuation of the deceased's possession, he is bound by his author's good or bad faith and is powerless to alter the prescriptive rights transmitted to him. *Aubry & Rau, Sec. 218, supra; Planiol, Sec. 2674, supra.*

For instance, the decedent possessed with just title and in good faith an immovable belonging to another. He was thus in the process of prescribing ten to twenty years. His possession continues in favor of his heir with the same characteristics and the prescription will be completed at the end of ten or twenty years, commencing with the date when the decedent entered in possession. It is irrelevant that the heir is in bad faith at the moment when the possession is transferred to him.

The effect of vices in the possession will be always the same as if the possession continued for the benefit of the decedent. It follows that vices incurable with respect to the decedent cannot be cured by the heir. For instance, if the decedent was in bad faith from the beginning of his possession, his heir can prescribe only by thirty years although he is personally in good faith. Baudry-Lacantinerie, Sec. 348, *supra*.

Thus, it is evident that the provisions of C.C. art. 3482, which permit prescription to accrue after ten years as long as the possession is commenced in good faith, envisions only one possession and applies when property is transferred to a universal successor. Baudry-Lacantinerie, Sec. 351, *supra*. As far as the universal successor is concerned, it would be more accurate to leave out tacking and its connotations and describe the transaction as a mandatory substitution. Comment, "Tacking of Possession for Acquisitive Prescription", 8 La. L. Rev. 105 at 107-110 (1948).

Contrary to the universal successor, an individual who acquires by particular title commences a new possession which is separate and distinct from his author's possession. Aubry & Rau, Sec. 218, *supra*.

...This type of successor commences a new possession, completely distinct from that of his grantor. Here we have two mutually independent possessions. Baudry-Lacantinerie, Sec. 350, *supra*.

Though the particular successor can cumulate his and his author's possessions, *both* must have *all* the statutory characteristics and conditions required for the completion of prescription. Domat, The Civil Law in its Natural Order, Sec. 2226 (2d ed., Cushing trans. 1861); Aubry & Rau, Sec. 218, *supra*; Baudry-Lacantinerie, Sec. 350, *supra*. The implications of this limitation on a particular successor's right to tack are fully explained by Planiol:

> Assuming that the preceding possessor was himself in the process of prescribing, several combinations may arise. If both of them were entitled to prescribe within from ten to twenty years, the new possessor would certainly have a right to consolidate the two possessions. The same result would obtain if neither of them was entitled to prescribe within these terms. In both cases, the thirty year period would be the only one available. In these two cases, the two successive possessions of the successor and of his author may be added together. They are of the same nature and of the same quality.

> But if it be assumed that the two successive possessors are not in the same position, from the standpoint of prescription — but one of them

have a just title and being in good faith — complications arise. They are solved by this very simple rule: The years that apply to the thirty years prescription, which requires neither just title nor good faith, cannot be used in completing the prescription running from ten to twenty years. The latter prescription requires that both conditions exist. But, on the contrary, the years that have run in connection with this favored prescription may be counted in computing the thirty years prescription. All that it requires is possession.

EXAMPLES: Where the vendor is a possessor in good faith, and the purchaser is in bad faith: If the ten years prescription has not run in favor of the vendor at the time of the sale, the purchaser cannot prescribe except upon the basis of thirty years, but he can count his author's years of possession.

Where the vendor was in bad faith but the purchaser in good faith, the latter can prescribe upon the basis of ten years but he cannot avail himself of his author's possession, because it applied solely to the thirty year period. In such a contingency, it might sometimes pay the purchaser to abandon his claim to the prescription of ten years in order to take advantage of the thirty years prescriptive period commenced by his author. This interest will come into play whenever the prescription has less than ten years to run before being completed. There is no doubt about the fact that he can then join his possession to that of his author to complete the thirty years. If the latter's possession would have applied to the shortened and privileged prescription it will *a fortiori* apply to the general prescription of thirty years. Planiol, Sec. 2676, 2677, *supra.*

It is our opinion that this statement properly explains the restraints placed on a successor's right to join his possession with his author's possession for purposes of acquisitive prescription. Accordingly, any language to the contrary in previous opinions of this Court or of the courts of appeal must be disregarded. E.g. see Liuzza v. Heirs of Nunzio, *supra*; Devall v. Choppin, 15 La. 566 (1840); Liquidators of Prudential Savings and Homestead Soc. v. Langermann, 156 La. 76, 100 So. 55 (1924); Brewster v. Hewes, 113 La. 45, 36 So. 883 (1904); Wheat v. Bear and Thayer Hardwood Co. Inc., 15 La. App. 306, 131 So. 307 (1930); Vance v. Ellerbe, 150 La. 388, 90 So. 735 (1922); Jackson v. D'Aubin, 338 So. 2d 575 (La. 1976).

Applying this civilian principle to the present case, it is evident that Ms. Calhoun's status as a possessor is essential to her claim of acquisitive prescription of ten years. Defendant, as a purchaser, is a successor by particular title. If she was in good faith when she re-acquired the property in 1951, she could cumulate the requisite ten years on her own, or tack her possession to that of her good faith author. On the other hand, if defendant was in bad faith she could not avail herself of Grey Brown's good faith and become owner of the land in question after the passage of ten years. Though she could still tack her possession to that of her author's for thirty-year acquisitive prescription, the institution of this suit in 1977 would interrupt her possession and preclude her claim of ownership. See C.C. art. 3518 [Revised C.C. art. 3462].

However, both lower courts were of the opinion that defendant's status as a possessor did not present a material fact. As a result, it was never determined whether the pleadings, depositions, admissions of fact or affidavits established a genuine issue as to this material fact. This determination is to be made on remand.

Accordingly, the summary judgment rendered in defendant's favor is reversed, and the case is remanded to the district court for further proceedings in accordance with law.

2. IMMOVABLES; THIRTY YEAR PRESCRIPTION
Civil Code Arts. 3486-3488

a. Possession as Owner

THERIOT v. BOLLINGER
172 La. 397, 134 So. 372 (1931)

ST. PAUL, J. This is an action to declare plaintiff the owner of a certain nine acres of land in Caddo parish, and more fully described in the petition. Defendant's sole and only title to this property is derived, through mesne conveyances, by a patent from the state issued in 1849. And plaintiff's sole and only title is derived from one Creasie Howard and her husband, alleged to have been in possession for more than 30 years.

The evidence shows that Creasie Howard and her husband went into possession and fenced the lands in 1892, or more than 30 years before she sold to plaintiff. It further shows that she and her husband were in public possession as squatters. But squatters possess in their *own* name, since they do not possess in the name of and for another. Rev. Civ. Code, art. 3488 [Revised C.C. art. 3427]. Hence they may acquire by the prescription of 30 years.

The evidence tends to show that for some years one of defendant's lessees built a gas well on the extreme northern portion of the land in controversy, within a few feet of the boundary, which well was afterwards abandoned. But this interruption covered only a small and undermined [sic] area, and we do not think it sufficed to deprive plaintiff of the benefit of their prescription.

DECREE

The judgment appealed from is therefore reversed, and it is now ordered that there be judgment in favor of plaintiff, Rell S. Theriot, and against defendant, S.H. Bollinger, recognizing plaintiff as the owner of property described in the petition, and enjoining defendant from claiming same or in any way disturbing plaintiffs possession thereof; and for costs of both courts against defendant.

CORTINAS v. PETERS
224 La. 9, 68 So. 2d 739 (1953)

McCALEB, J. Plaintiff is demanding a specific performance of an executory contract made with defendant on May 20, 1949, in which the latter promised to purchase from him five lots of ground in Square No. 1010 of the Third District of the City of New Orleans for $2500. Defendant refused to comply with the agreement on the ground that plaintiff's title to the property is not valid and merchantable. Plaintiff, on the other hand, maintains that he and his ancestors in title have been in open, corporeal and public possession of the land for more than 30 years prior to the filing of this suit and, therefore, have acquired the lots by the prescription provided by Article 3499 of the Civil Code [Revised C.C. art. 3486].

After hearing evidence in support of the prescriptive title, the trial judge found for plaintiff and granted him the relief requested. Defendant has appealed.

It appears from the record that plaintiff bought the five lots on May 5, 1949, for $1000 cash (just 15 days before defendant agreed to purchase them for $2500) from one Joseph W. Sheldon, who declared in the act that he had acquired the property by adverse possession as owner for a period in excess of 30 years, having taken corporeal possession in the year 1918 and having remained in continuous and uninterrupted possession thereafter.

It is upon this declaration of ownership that plaintiff rests his claim to a merchantable title. In support thereof, he produced three witnesses, besides himself, who asserted that the entire Square No. 1010 in the Third District of New Orleans had been enclosed by a fence prior to the year 1918, when nineteen of the lots were owned by a corporation known as Quaker Realty Company and that it had been continuously used as a truck farm and for grazing purposes. It was also shown that, in August of 1918, the nineteen lots (together with other property) were sold by Quaker Realty Company to Interstate Bank & Trust Company of New Orleans. At the time of that sale and for some time thereafter, Sheldon was General Sales Manager of the real estate department of the Interstate Bank. Mr. Sheldon, who is stated to be 94 years of age and infirm, did not testify at the trial and the only evidence respecting his prescriptive title was given by his son, Joseph W. Sheldon, Jr. This witness declared that he remembered the transaction in 1918, when Quaker Realty Company sold the 19 lots in Square No. 1010 to Interstate Bank & Trust Company; that his father took possession of the whole square (the 19 lots purchased and the 5 lots in question) for the bank and that, in 1921, he acquired the 19 lots in Square 1010 from the bank as his own and took possession of the entire square for himself. On cross-examination, he gave the following testimony:

"Q. *** Did your father hold that property as his own or as the owner for himself or for the Interstate Banking & Trust Company?

"A. It was for Interstate, but in 1921, he took that property as his own."

This answer is destructive of plaintiff's alleged prescriptive title to the lots in suit. In order to sustain a claim of ownership by adverse possession of 30 years it is not only essential that the possession be continuous and uninterrupted during all that time; it must be public and unequivocal "and under the title of owner." Article 3500 Civil Code [Revised C.C. arts. 3435, 3436, 3486]. In the case at bar, Sheldon's possession of the lots in 1918 was not as owner but, admittedly, as agent for the Interstate Bank. Hence, he was a precarious possessor under Articles 3441, 3489, 3490 and 3510 of the Civil Code [Revised C.C. arts. 3438, 3477] and could not become an adverse possessor in the ab-sence of a showing that he manifested such an intention by some unequivocal act of hostility which was brought to the attention of the bank. See Arnold v. Sun Oil Co., 218 La. 50, 48 So. 2d 369 and authorities there cited.

The fact that Sheldon acquired 19 of the lots in Square No. 1010 from the bank in 1921 cannot of itself aid him in the establishment of a prescriptive title to the five other lots, which he was holding as agent for the bank, in view of Article 3489 of the Code [Revised C.C. art. 3438] providing that "when a person's possession commenced for another, it is supposed to continue always under the same title, unless there be proof to the contrary." And even if we were to rule that the testimony of Sheldon's son concerning his father's possession of the lots was sufficient to show that his holding became adverse to the bank in 1921, when he bought the other nineteen lots in the square, the title pleaded by plaintiff would nonetheless be invalid as the 30 year prescription had not yet accrued on June 13, 1949, when this suit was filed.

The judgment appealed from is reversed and the suit is dismissed at plaintiff's cost.

QUESTIONS

If Sheldon was possessing the five lots not included in Interstate Bank's title for the Bank from 1918 without ever performing acts sufficient to show that he was possession for himself, who owns the lots? If, as his son maintained, Sheldon began to possess the lots adversely to the bank in 1921, who owns the lots?

HUMBLE v. DEWEY
215 So. 2d 378 (La. App. 3d Cir. 1968)

HOOD, J. This is a petitory action instituted by Mrs. Elizabeth Fuller Humble and Mrs. Catherine Fuller Stark against T. J. Dewey, Sr. Plaintiffs demand judgment decreeing them to be the owners of a six-acre tract of land in Beauregard Parish. Defendant answered claiming title by acquisitive prescription of thirty years to the western portion of that tract, comprising about four and one-half acres.

Judgment was rendered by the trial court in favor of plaintiffs, declaring them to be owners of the subject property and directing defendant to remove fences from it. Defendant has appealed.

Plaintiffs have record title to the entire six-acre tract of land. The sole issue presented on this appeal is whether defendant's possession has been sufficient to give him a 30-year prescription title to the western portion of that tract.

J. W. Duckworth purchased the subject property from J. D. Bailey in 1927. He moved into a residence building located on the property and began occupying it as his home about that time. The residence building in which Duckworth lived was destroyed by fire in 1931, and no one has lived on the property since that time. Duckworth sold the entire six-acre tract to A. A. Fuller in 1939. Fuller died in 1950, leaving as his sole survivors his widow and the plaintiffs in this suit, the latter being his only children. Plaintiffs later acquired the interest of the surviving widow, and according to the public records they now are the sole owners of the property.

For the past 40 years defendant Dewey has lived with his family on a two-acre tract of land which is located immediately north of and adjacent to the property which is in dispute here. A public road separates the defendant's home place from the subject six-acre tract of land.

During the spring of the year 1932, or about one year after the Duckworth residence had been destroyed by fire, defendant planted and raised a crop of corn and beans on the six-acre tract. The property was under fence at that time. Defendant testified, however, that in 1932 he was "ordered" by the nephew of a former owner to take down the existing fence, that pursuant to that order he removed the wire from that fence, and that immediately thereafter he constructed another fence on the same posts around the entire six-acre tract of land. He raised corn and cotton on the property until 1938, and for several years thereafter he raised garden crops on a small portion of the tract and he used the rest of it for pasturage purposes. Later he stated that he fenced off the eastern part of the land because it was "poor," and since that time he has used only the western part of it for crops and pasturage purposes. The portion which he has continued to use comprises about four and one-half acres.

Defendant concedes that he has never acquired title to the disputed tract of land. He testified that there was a financial "panic" in 1931 and 1932, that he was having difficulty in providing food for his family, and that after the subject property became vacant in 1931, he began raising crops on it. He stated, "I just went over there and went to plowing and nobody didn't come tell me to get off, and I didn't ask nobody."

Dewey testified that he did not know who owned the property when he began farming it, that he thought it was owned by Jeff Bailey, and that he did not know that Bailey had sold it to Duckworth in 1927 or that Duckworth had sold it to Fuller in 1939. He stated, "I couldn't say who it belonged to, hadn't nobody come around there and told me to get off." Defendant also testified that Duckworth owed an account to him at defendant's grocery store about the time the house burned down, and that Duckworth had told him, "Son, if I had any dealings with that property or anything about it you can have my part for what I owe you." He acknowledged, however, that he knew that such a statement by Duckworth did not given him legal title to the land and that he did not own the property when he began using it.

Defendant has never paid any taxes on the property[;] all taxes which were levied against the property since 1932 having been paid by the record title owners.

In 1959, a neighbor named Hardee Myers contacted the husband of one of the plaintiffs, and through him Myers obtained verbal permission from the plaintiffs to use the eastern portion of the six-acre tract for pasturage purposes. He explained that the reason why he contacted plaintiffs and obtained their permission to use the land was because he thought they were the owners of the property. He did not ask Dewey for permission. Immediately after obtaining this permission, Myers informed defendant Dewey of the agreement, and Dewey replied, "O.K., just fix a good fence." Myers thereupon constructed a fence around the east one and one-half acres of the original tract, and he has been using it since 1959.

In 1962, plaintiffs had an opportunity to sell the property. They authorized the prospective purchaser to look over the land, but Dewey refused to let him go on the premises. Plaintiffs contend that that was the first indication they had that Dewey was claiming ownership of the property. The husband of one of the plaintiffs thereupon contacted defendant personally and demanded that he either lease the property from plaintiffs or vacate it. Defendant refused to comply with either of these demands, stating that he "was going to try to hold that land." Plaintiffs also demanded that defendant remove the fences which he had placed on the property, and they gave him two weeks within which to do so. Defendant did not comply with that demand.

About two months after the first oral request had been made to lease or vacate the property, plaintiffs contacted the City Marshal of Merryville, who prepared for them a letter addressed to defendant formally requesting that he remove the fences which he had constructed on the property so plaintiffs could complete the sale of it. This letter was signed by plaintiffs and was sent to defendant.

Mrs. Stark, one of the plaintiffs, testified that her father, A.A. Fuller, and Dewey had been "good friends" during her father's lifetime, and that Dewey's daughter had been the other plaintiff's (Mrs. Humble's) best friend. She stated that she and her sister had assumed that their father had "let Mr. Dewey use the land," and that nothing had occurred which caused them to question Dewey's motives until 1962, when he refused to allow a prospective purchaser to go on the land. Immediately after this occurred, of course, they made a demand on defendant that he remove the fences and that he lease the property from them or vacate it.

The trial judge concluded that defendant had failed to establish that he had possessed the subject property for thirty years "under the title of owner." He stated in his reasons for judgment that, "it did not appear that the people in and around Merryville knew the defendant claimed to be the owner," and that "the defendant's intent to claim as owner first became known less than eight years ago and after the death of A.A. Fuller." Judgment was rendered, therefore, rejecting defendant's demand that he be decreed to be the owner of a part of that property by prescription of thirty years.

The ownership of immovables may be acquired by the acquisitive prescription of thirty years without any need of title or possession in good faith. LSA-C.C. art. 3499 [Revised C.C. art. 3486]. The possession on which this prescription is founded must be continuous and uninterrupted during all the time, and it must be public and unequivocal, and under the title of owner. LSA-C.C. art. 3500 [Revised C.C. arts. 3435, 3436].

LSA-C.C. art. 3436 [Revised C.C. arts. 3421, 3424] provides that: "To be able to acquire possession of property, two distinct things are requisite: (1) The intention of possessing as owner. (2) The corporeal possession of the thing."

In order for a possessor to successfully claim the ownership of immovable property under a plea of thirty years acquisitive prescription, he must establish not only that there has been corporeal possession of the property for the required period of time, but also that there was a positive intention to take and commence possession of the property as owner. LSA-C.C. arts. 3436, 3499, 3500, 3503 [Revised C.C. arts. 3421, 3424, 3486, 3487]; Stille v. Schull, 41 La. Ann. 816, 6 So. 634 (1889) [additional citations omitted].

In some cases, we think the intention to possess as owner may be inferred from the surrounding facts and circumstances. We believe, however, that ordinarily the intent to possess as owner should not be inferred unless the actions of the possessor or the surrounding facts and circumstances are sufficient to reasonably apprise the public, and the record title owner of the property, of the fact that the possessor has the positive intent to possess as owner.

The burden of proof to establish the facts essential to support a plea of thirty years acquisitive prescription rests on the party who makes the plea. Chapman v. Morris Building & Land Improvement Ass'n, 108 La. 283, 32 So. 371 (1902) [additional citation omitted].

We agree with the trial judge that the evidence in the instant suit fails to establish that defendant Dewey intended to possess the subject property as owner when he commenced his possession in 1932. The evidence shows, we think, that he began cultivating and using the property without any intention of possessing it as owner. When he first began to use the property he intended merely to raise some small crops on it until the owner instructed him to discontinue doing so. He occupied the land, therefore, merely by the suffrage of the landowner. It is clear that at some later date he had a change of heart, and did decide to possess it as owner. The trial judge concluded that this intention to possess as owner occurred less than eight years ago. Our conclusion is that the evidence fails to show that the defendant had the positive intent to possess as owner for the required period of thirty years, and that he thus has failed to establish ownership by acquisitive prescription.

Defendant argues, however, that the fact that he went into possession of the property creates a presumption that he possessed as master and owner. He relies on LSA-C.C. art. 3488 [Revised C.C. art. 3427] which provides:

> "As to the fact itself of possession, a person is presumed to have possessed as master and owner, unless it appears that the possession began in the name of and for another."

The above quoted article relates specifically to prescription of ten years, but in view of the provisions of LSA-C.C. art. 3505 [Revised C.C. art. 3488] we think it also must be applied to prescription to thirty years. See Theriot v. Bollinger, 172 La. 397, 134 So. 372 (1931).

We agree with defendant that the fact that he went into possession of the subject property created a presumption that he possessed it as owner. This presumption is subject to rebuttal, however, and we think the defendant's own testimony, considered with the surrounding facts and circumstances, rebuts and overcomes that presumption.

Defendant has failed to establish that he has acquired a thirty year prescriptive title to the property, and we thus find no error in the judgment which was rendered by the trial court. For the reasons herein set out, the judgment appealed from is affirmed. The costs of this appeal are assessed to defendant-appellant. Affirmed.

NOTES AND QUESTIONS

1.   The *Humble* court characterizes Dewey as physically detaining the property without the intent to possess as owner for most of the time on which he bases his acquisitive prescription claim. What testimony of the defendant and "surrounding facts and circumstances" support the court's finding that the presumption of the intent to possess as owner has been overcome? What other ways of characterizing Dewey's possession would make it equally ineffective for acquisitive prescription?

2 .   Is the intent to possess as owner to be evaluated by subjective or by objective means?

3 .   The issue in this case resembles that in *Harper v. Willis, supra,* Chapter IV. How do the facts differ? Which presents a stronger case for finding lack of intent to possess as owner?

b. Precarious Possession

FRANKS PETROLEUM, INC. v. BABINEAUX
446 So. 2d 862 (La. App. 2d Cir. 1984)

HALL, J. In this concursus proceeding brought by the operator of producing gas units, the district court resolved the dispute between two sets of record co-owners, identified as the "Group A defendants" and the "Group B defendants," by holding that the Group A defendants had acquired full title to the properties involved by acquisitive prescription based on adverse possession by them and their ancestors for more than 30 years after notice of such adverse possession to the Group B defendants and their ancestors. From judgments recognizing the Group A defendants and those holding under them as entitled to the mineral and/or royalty interests involved, the Group B defendants appealed. Finding that the issues were correctly resolved by the district court in its comprehensive, studious reasons for judgment, we affirm.

On appeal, the appellants urge that the trial court erred in holding that a recorded ex parte judgment of possession sending the Group A defendants into possession of the properties involved constituted sufficient notice that their possession was as owners and adverse to the Group B defendants, and that the court erred in failing to find that the only actual notice of adverse possession was given in 1950, less than 30 years prior to the commencement of this litigation.

The property was acquired by C. C. Colvin and his brother, John A. Colvin, in 1874. The Group A defendants are the heirs of C. C. Colvin and his wife. The Group B defendants are the two children of one of the 10 children of John A. Colvin and his wife. The widow and all the other heirs of John A. Colvin executed quitclaim deeds of their interests in the properties to the Group A defendants in 1937 and 1938. The quitclaim deeds recited that C. C. Colvin purchased the interest of John A. Colvin in the property, and paid for the interest, but that the deed was lost or destroyed and was not recorded. The consideration for the quitclaim deeds was stated to be the consideration paid by C. C. Colvin to John A. Colvin and the vendors acknowledged that John A. Colvin received full payment.

The trial court correctly found that C. C. Colvin and then his heirs exercised full and complete possession of the property from as early as 1900 through the time this litigation was commenced by living on the property, farming it, growing timber, making timber sales, selling sand and gravel, having the property surveyed, marking boundaries, and the like. The trial court also correctly found that the evidence was insufficient to support any possession whatsoever by John A. Colvin or his heirs. These findings are not seriously questioned on appeal.

There is in evidence a timber deed dated in 1899 by which C. C. Colvin sold timber on the subject property. John A. Colvin signed as a witness to the timber deed.

In 1937, a judgment of possession was rendered in the Succession of C. C. Colvin and his wife, and was duly recorded, in which their heirs were recognized as the owners of the "whole interest in and to" the subject property.

In 1950 appellants were specifically told in a conversation with one of the C. C. Colvin heirs that John A. Colvin had sold his interest in the property, the deed was lost, and that [the appellants] did not own any interest in the property. However, they had earlier knowledge that other heirs of John A. Colvin had quitclaimed their interest, and they were approached to sign papers to get the property "straight."

Subsequently, the heirs of C. C. Colvin partitioned the property, purporting in the recorded instrument to deal with the full interest in the property.

Appellants urge that the possession of their co-owners must be regarded as possession on behalf of all the co-owners of the property, and that such possession did not become adverse to them until they were given actual notice in the 1950 conversation, less than 30 years prior to their asserting their claim to title. Appellants particularly urge that the trial court erred in holding that the ex parte judgment of possession served as notice to them of the adverse nature of the possession of their co-owners.

Particularly applicable to the issues in this case are C.C. Arts. 3439 and 3478:

> C.C. Art. 3439: "A co-owner, or his universal successor, commences to possess for himself when he demonstrates this intent by overt and unambiguous acts sufficient to give notice to his co-owner.
>
> "Any other precarious possessor, or his universal successor, commences to possess for himself when he gives actual notice of this intent to the person on whose behalf he is possessing."
>
> C.C. Art. 3478: "A co-owner, or his universal successor, may commence to prescribe when he demonstrates by overt and unambiguous acts sufficient to give notice to his co-owner that he intends to possess the property for himself. The acquisition and recordation of a title from a person other than a co-owner thus may mark the commencement of prescription.
>
> "Any other precarious possessor, or his universal successor, may commence to prescribe when he gives actual notice to the person on whose behalf he is possessing that he intends to possess for himself."

These Civil Code articles were adopted by Act 187 of 1982, effective January 1, 1983. The provisions are new, but as noted in the comments thereto, do not change the law. See prior Articles 3512 and 3515.

The well-settled jurisprudential general rule is that an owner in indivision cannot acquire by prescription the rights of his co-owners in the property held in common. Possession by one co-owner is generally considered as being exercised on behalf of all co-owners. It is equally well settled that an exception to the general rule is recognized in those instances where the possessing co-owner gives notice to the other co-owners that he intends to possess as owner adversely and contrary to the common interest. Under such circumstances, one owner in common may prescribe against a co-owner provided such possession be clearly hostile and notice be given thereof. *Givens v. Givens,* 273 So. 2d 863 (La. App. 2d Cir. 1973).

Under Civil Code Articles 3439 and 3478 and the jurisprudence, actual notice to other co-owners of the possessing co-owner's intent to possess for himself is not necessary. Actual notice is required in the case of other precarious possessors, but not in the case of co-owners.

In determining whether a particular case falls within the exception rather than the general rule, mere occupancy, use, payment of taxes, and similar acts of possession will not suffice to constitute notice of adverse possession to an 'owner in common. However, where a co-owner possesses under a recorded instrument apparently conveying title (even though the purported conveyance is invalid), the recorded instrument, together with the acts of possession, constitutes notice to other co-owners and the possession is then regarded as hostile to the interests of the other co-owners, rebutting the presumption that possession is for the benefit of all co-owners. *Givens v. Givens, supra.*

Civil Code Article 3478's provision that the acquisition and recordation of a title from a person other than a co-owner may mark the commencement of a prescription is illustrative, not exclusive. Recordation of an instrument translative of title is only one example of overt and unambiguous acts sufficient to give notice to co-owners.

A recorded instrument may constitute notice to co-owners even though it is not translative of title. Thirty years acquisitive prescription is founded upon possession, not a deed translative of title. The function of the recorded instrument is simply to serve as an overt manifestation that a co-owner exclusively possessing is doing so by virtue of his claim to exclusive ownership. It is objective evidence that he possesses adversely to those who may claim to be his co-owners. *Dupuis v. Broadhurst,* 213 So. 2d 528 (La. App. 3d Cir. 1968). In *Dupuis,* a partition, not translative of title, coupled with active and open possession for 30 years, was held to negate the presumption that the possessing owner was possessing for other co-owners. Likewise, in *Minton v. Whitworth,* 393 So. 2d 294 (La. App. 1st Cir. 1980), the language of a recorded partition was held to be a clear indication that the parties thereto considered themselves to be the owners of the full interest in the property and to constitute notice to co-owners that subsequent possession of the property was adverse and hostile to their interests.

A recorded invalid donation was held to constitute adequate notice in Givens, *supra*, and a simulated sale was given the same effect in *Detraz v. Pere,* 183 So. 2d 401 (La. App. 3d Cir. 1966).

It was not error for the trial court to hold that the recorded ex parte judgment of possession which purported to send the C. C. Colvin heirs into possession of the "whole interest" in the subject property was an act of notice to the other record co-owners of the intended adverse possession of the C. C. Colvin heirs. *Boyet v. Perryman,* 240 La. 339, 123 So. 2d 79 (La. 1960), relied on heavily by appellants, is not applicable. That case held only that an ex parte judgment of possession does not purport to be a transfer of title and cannot serve as a basis for 10 years acquisitive prescription. It has no relevancy to the issue of notice of adverse possession as between co-owners and 30-years acquisitive prescription based on adverse possession.

Perhaps more significant than the judgment of possession are the declarations contained in the quitclaim deeds recorded in 1937 and 1938. The declarations serve as notice to the other co-owners that the C. C. Colvin heirs were possessing as owners for themselves and adversely to the John A. Colvin heirs under a lost or destroyed deed from John A. Colvin. This declaration was joined in by John A. Colvin's widow and all of his heirs except the appellants.

There is also evidence that the appellants were aware, prior to the 1950 conversation mentioned previously, of the claim by the C. C. Colvin heirs to full ownership of the property and their exclusive possession as full owners.

The intent of C. C. Colvin and his heirs to possess for themselves was demonstrated by overt and unambiguous acts sufficient to give notice to their co-owners, marking the commencement of acquisitive prescription more than 30 years prior to the commencement of this litigation. These acts included the actual physical acts of possession described earlier in this opinion, the timber deed by C. C. Colvin which was witnessed by John A. Colvin, the recorded declarations contained in the quitclaim deeds, the recitals of the recorded judgment of possession, and communications among the family which indicate an awareness on the part of appellants of their co-owners' intent to possess for themselves, all commencing or occurring more than 30 years ago. The judgment of the district court recognizing appellees' acquisition of the interests of appellants by 30 years acquisitive prescription is correct.

The appellants initially pled the invalidity of the quitclaim deeds on the grounds of lack of or insufficiency of consideration. Although this issue was not addressed in the trial court's reasons for judgment, the judgment rejecting in full appellants' demands for recognition of an ownership interest in the property had the effect of rejecting their claims in this respect. No formal specification of error is directed to this issue, but appellants, in brief, ask that the issue be decided on this appeal, and the plaintiff, in brief, has responded. Suffice it to say that the appellants have failed to demonstrate or establish that the consideration recited in the quitclaim deeds was not accurately stated or sufficient to support the transfers made in acknowledgment of the prior transfer by their ancestor for money consideration and to comply with the vendors' natural obligation to execute the disposition their ancestor and former owner had made. See C.C. Arts. 1758 and 1759. For the reasons assigned, the judgment of the district court is affirmed at appellants' costs.

QUESTIONS

1. This case discusses the difference between the "actual notice" required for precarious possessors and the "overt and unambiguous acts sufficient to give notice" for co-owners for these to begin possessing for themselves. Why might the legislature have made such a distinction in the requirements?

2. Why must the *Franks* court assert that the example in Civil Code article 3478 is illustrative, not exclusive, to find for the plaintiffs, who have a recorded judgment of possession and quitclaim deeds from J.A. Colvin's widow and eight of his ten children?

3. The language of the example in article 3478 is permissive ("may") rather than mandatory ("shall"). What does the court rely on in deciding to apply it in this case?

COCKERHAM v. COCKERHAM
16 So. 3d 1264 (La. App. 2d Cir. 2009)

OPINION

DREW, J. In this dispute over the ownership of an 80-acre tract of land located in Bienville Parish, John L. Cockerham, Jr. ("Junior") and Melissa Cockerham ("Melissa") appeal a judgment recognizing the ownership interests of others, including the petitioner, Clarence Cockerham ("Clarence"). We affirm.

FACTS

The property at issue is a tract measuring approximately 80 acres and is described as follows:

> The South Half of the Southwest Quarter (S/2 of SW/4), Section 13, Township 15 North, Range 8 West, Bienville Parish, Louisiana.

The property was at one time owned by Mose Henry Cockerham ("Mose"), who attempted to perfect a homestead certificate on the property in 1946. Mose died intestate in 1949. . . . Jim Mose Cockerham was married first to Hannah Reaves Cockerham, and born of the marriage were four children: Mose, Currie Mae Cockerham Jack ("Currie Mae"), Currie D. Cockerham Mingo ("Currie D."), and Gene Cockerham. Gene Cockerham ("Gene") is Clarence's father. Jim Mose Cockerham's second marriage was to Drucilla Boston Cockerham, and one child, John L. Cockerham ("John"), was born of the marriage. Junior is one of John's twelve children. Jim Mose Cockerham died in 1924.

In the judgment of possession filed in Mose's succession in 1953, Gene, Currie Mae, and Currie D. were each recognized as the owner of a 7/24 interest in the property, and John was recognized as the owner of a 1/8 interest in the property. . . . In the judgment of possession rendered in Gene's succession in 2007, Clarence was recognized as the owner of an undivided 1/2 interest in an undivided 7/24 interest in the property and in the funds deposited in the court registry relating to the expropriation lawsuit.

In October of 2003, Clarence filed a petition for declaratory judgment and/or petitory action against Junior and his wife, Melissa. Clarence noted an attempted donation of the entirety of the tract from John and his wife, Clara, to Junior and Melissa on October 30, 1993. Clarence was concerned that defendants might try to claim ownership of the property through 10-year acquisitive prescription, so he averred that this suit would interrupt prescription under La. C.C. art. 3462. Clarence prayed that the court render a judgment declaring his ownership interest in the property and that no acquisitive prescription had accrued to the benefit of Junior and Melissa.

[The defendants, Junior and Melissa,] asserted that their ancestors in title, John and his wife, had acquired the property by cash sale deed, and that they had acquired ownership of the property by both 10-year and 30-year acquisitive prescription.

Neither Junior nor Melissa testified at trial. Junior was unavailable because he was inmate in a Texas prison. Melissa chose not to attend the trial. The trial court found in favor of Clarence and recognized the ownership of the property as follows:

- A 3/24 interest was owned by Junior and Melissa from John.
- A 7/24 interest was owned by the heirs of Gene (Clarence owned one-half of this 7/24).
- A 7/24 interest was owned by the heirs of Currie D.
- A 7/24 interest was owned by the heirs of Currie Mae (Clarence owned 3/48 of this 7/24, and John and Melissa each owned 1/48 of this 7/24).

All funds on hand and all funds held in the court registry from an expropriation lawsuit involving a pipeline on the property were ordered distributed to the co-owners.

Junior and Melissa have appealed.

DISCUSSION

Junior and Melissa argue on appeal that the trial court erred in finding that they had not acquired the property through acquisitive prescription of either 10 years or 30 years.

Acquisitive Prescription of 10 years

Ownership and other real rights in immovables may be acquired by the prescription of 10 years. La. C.C. art. 3473. The requisites for the acquisitive prescription of 10 years are possession of 10 years, good faith, just title, and a thing susceptible of acquisition by prescription. La. C.C. art. 3475.

The purpose of good faith acquisitive prescription is to secure the title of a person who purchases immovable property by a deed translative of title, under the reasonable and objective belief that he is acquiring a valid title to the property, and thereafter remains in peaceful possession of the property for more than 10 years without any disturbance by the true owner [citations omitted].

For purposes of acquisitive prescription, a possessor is in good faith when he reasonably believes, in light of objective considerations, that he is owner of the thing he possesses. La. C.C. art. 3480. The trier of fact must ascertain in the light of objective considerations whether a reasonable person in the position of the possessor could believe himself to be the owner. Comment (c) to art. 3480. Although good faith is presumed, this presumption is rebutted on proof that the possessor knows, or should know, that he is not owner of the thing he possesses. *See* La. C.C. art. 3481.

A just title is a juridical act that is sufficient to transfer ownership or another real right. La. C.C. art. 3483. The act must be written, valid in form, and filed for registry in the conveyance records of the parish in which the immovable is situated. *Id.*

In a 1963 cash deed, Rufus Lacy purported to convey the property to John. The evidence at trial did not reflect how Rufus Lacy may have acquired the interests of all co-owners. We cannot find that Lacy had anything to convey. Having received a 3/24 interest in the property in 1953, John should have known that Lacy did not own the property which he was attempting to convey to him in 1963. Accordingly, John was in bad faith, and acquisitive prescription of 10 years is not available to him.

Acquisitive Prescription of 30 Years

Ownership and other real rights in immovables may be acquired by the prescription of 30 years without the need of just title or possession in good faith. La. C.C. art. 3486. The possession must be continuous, uninterrupted, peaceable, public, and unequivocal. La. C.C. art. 3476.

The general and well-established jurisprudential rule is that an owner in indivision cannot acquire by prescription the rights of his co-owners in the property held in common. Possession by one co-owner is generally considered as being exercised on behalf of all co-owners [citations omitted].

It is equally well settled that an exception to the general rule is recognized in those instances where the possessing co-owner gives notice to the other co-owners that he intends to possess as owner adversely and contrary to the common interest. Under such circumstances, one owner in common may prescribe against a co-owner provided such possession be clearly hostile and notice be given thereof [citations omitted]. Actual notice to other co-owners of the possessing co-owner's intent to possess for himself is not necessary.

In determining whether a particular case falls within the exception rather than the general rule, this court has held that mere occupancy, use, payment of taxes and similar acts of possession will not suffice to constitute notice of adverse possession to an owner in common.

This exception to the general rule is reflected in La. C.C. arts. 3439 and 3478. Article 3439 provides that a co-owner, or his universal successor, commences to possess for himself when he demonstrates this intent by overt and unambiguous acts sufficient to give notice to his co-owner. Article 3478 provides that a co-owner, or his universal successor, may commence to prescribe when he demonstrates by overt and unambiguous acts sufficient to give notice to his co-owner that he intends to possess the property for himself. Article 3478 additionally provides: "The acquisition and recordation of a title from a person other than a co-owner thus may mark the commencement of prescription." La. C.C. arts. 3439 and 3478 were adopted by Act 187 of 1982. As noted in the comments to these articles, the provisions are new, but do not change the law.

The issue becomes whether the 1963 deed from Lacy to John marked the commencement of prescription as contemplated by La. C.C. art. 3478. That an attempted conveyance is invalid is unimportant when determining whether a co-owner has given notice that he intends to possess for himself....:

> A recorded instrument may constitute notice to co-owners even though it is not translative of title. Thirty years acquisitive prescription is founded upon possession, not a deed translative of title. The function of the recorded instrument is simply to serve as an overt manifestation that a co-owner exclusively possessing is doing so by virtue of his claim to exclusive ownership. It is objective evidence that he possesses adversely to those who may claim to be his co-owners. Dupuis v. Broadhurst, 213 So. 2d 528 (La. App. 3d Cir. 1968). In *Dupuis*, a partition, not translative of title, coupled with active and open possession for 30 years, was held to negate the presumption that the possessing owner was possessing for other co-owners. Likewise, in Minton v. Whitworth, 393 So. 2d 294 (La. App. 1st Cir. 1980), the language of a recorded partition was held to be a clear indication that the parties thereto considered themselves to be the owners of the full interest in the property and to constitute notice to co-owners that subsequent possession of the property was adverse and hostile to their interests.

A recorded act purporting to convey an interest in property in and of itself will not always constitute notice to the other co-owners. Otherwise, La. C.C. art. 3478 would read that the acquisition and recordation of a title from a person other than the co-owner "shall mark" the commencement of prescription, instead of "may mark" the commencement. The recorded instrument is not to be read in isolation. As noted by this court:

> [W]here a co-owner goes into and continues possession under a recorded instrument apparently conveying title, **even though the purported conveyance may be invalid**, the recorded instrument **together** with the acts of possession constitute notice to other co-owners. The possession is then regarded as hostile to the claims of the other co-owners, rebutting any presumption that possession is for the benefit of all co-owners [citations omitted].

In Franks Petroleum, Inc. [v. Babineaux, 446 So. 2d 862 (La. App. 2d Cir. 1984)], numerous recorded instruments served to give notice to co-owners of adverse possession. One such instrument was a judgment of possession in the succession of C. C. Colvin, one of the two brothers who originally owned the property, in which C. C. Colvin's heirs were recognized as the owners of the whole interest in the property. The other instruments were quitclaim deeds from the widow and most of the heirs of John Colvin, the other brother, in which they recited that C. C. Colvin had purchased John Colvin's interest in the property, but that the deed had been lost and not recorded.

In Succession of Seals, 243 La. 1056, 150 So. 2d 13 (1963), Henry Seals, who was single at the time, purchased a tract of land. Henry died intestate, survived by his brothers and mother. One brother, Stokes, acquired from Henry's widow any interest that she had in the tract, which was sufficient to give notice that he was to possess the property as sole owner. Stokes immediately moved onto the property and exercised acts of possession and ownership, such as farming, selling timber, and executing mineral leases.

In Givens v. Givens, 273 So. 2d 863 (La. App. 2d Cir. 1973), a purported sale of land from mother to son ... served as notice to other co-owners that the son was possessing adversely to their interests. In Detraz v. Pere, 183 So. 2d 401 (La. App. 3d Cir. 1966), a simulated sale from father to son was sufficient to give the required notice to co-owners....

Immediately prior to the execution of the 1963 deed, John was not in the position of co-owner; rather, John purportedly had no ownership interest whatsoever at the time as Lacy was conveying interest in all of the property. Furthermore, based upon the evidence presented at trial, Lacy in fact had no interest to convey. In the cases cited above, all the vendors or donors, except the widow in *Succession of Seals*, had some actual or future ownership interest that they were attempting to convey.

Even if the 1963 deed gave notice [to the plaintiff] of commencement of prescription, it was not followed by acts that were consistent with adverse possession. In addition, any adverse possession was interrupted by the acts of co-owners.

It is undisputed that John moved his family onto the property in the 1950s and raised his family there. However, the act of moving onto the property and establishing a home there would have been prior to the marking of commencement of acquisitive prescription by the 1963 deed.

What is apparent from the evidence presented at trial is that although John's branch of the family resided on the property, it was still considered by his siblings and their descendants as belonging to all of them.

Clarence and the other Cockerhams often met at the property for family reunions, holidays, and activities centered around family-related events. They would normally meet for a reunion or homecoming on the property in early June, and Clarence, who was 51 years old at the time of trial, could recall not meeting there only three years. The reunions usually lasted a weekend, but the family members may have gone to the property for a week to visit with relatives. Family members also sometimes took vacations there. Junior constructed a pavilion on the property in 1998 to be utilized for family events.

Clarence . . . used the property as his home address while attending Grambling State University. He would sometimes stay on the property during the summer when not in school. During his summertime visits, he would play and occasionally work on the property, helping John harvest pulpwood. When Clarence was younger, his father would stay during his summer visits, but as Clarence grew older, he would stay there on his own.

Clarence thought of the property as a "family home." He said that over the years there had been discussions about other family members building homes on the property. The only home on the property was where John and his family lived. The house had been rebuilt and repaired after several fires.

Clarence related that in conversations with family members during reunions when John and Junior were present, the property was discussed as being family property, and neither John nor Junior ever objected.

Clarence testified that neither John nor Junior ever indicated that they were attempting to claim the property as their own. Family members could freely come and go on the property. Clarence first thought that Junior was considering himself to be the sole owner when he received a call from Junior in October or November of 2002 asking that he sign off on Gene's undivided interest in the property.

...[A]round the time of the reunion held in June of 2003[,]Clarence and other family members received a letter and checks, some of which were for $700, from Junior. Junior wrote in the letter about the property's history and listed the amounts of money that he had spent on the property since 1991. Of particular note, Junior wrote that the property had been lost in the 1940s because of unpaid taxes, and that Gene told John in the 1950s to redeem the property for John's family, and that he (Gene) wanted no part of the property except to be able to come there and know it was still in the family. Junior also wrote that 60 acres were placed in his name in 1993, the remaining 20 acres were sold in

1994 but these 20 acres were bought back in 1998 by him as a sole owner, and that the checks represented benefits from these 20 acres.

The letter included a "by laws for family fund" stating that $ 2,000 would be set aside for a family fund and asked each recipient to add to the family fund. The "by laws" further stated that trees would be ready to cut in several years from the 60 acres for a profit, and they were open to suggestions, presumably about what to do with the profits. Clarence stated that although the letter contained references to the property as family property, he thought of it as the first written declaration that anyone intended to possess the property as sole owner.

A note accompanying the $ 700 check sent to Clarence's mother stated that it was a "gift off of the place." ...Each check stated in the memo section that it was for a "gift." No additional checks were ever sent by Junior; the checks were never cashed.

Clarence decided to do a title search of the property after receiving the check and letter from Junior. The paragraph in the letter stating that his father told John to redeem the property so he could have a home was what spurred his interest in inquiring about the land's ownership. Clarence discovered the 1963 deed when he checked the public records.

...At the 2003 reunion, Clarence noticed that many trees had been cut down and that natural gas residue storage tanks had been placed on the property. Clarence, who has been employed by a gas company for over 30 years, estimated that it would have taken about one to three months to erect those tanks.

When Clarence was younger, he would help John harvest pulpwood to make money for the summer. ...When Junior wrote in the 2003 letter that in 1998 he paid $ 15,000 to plant pine trees "for future profit for the family," Clarence thought "family" meant the entire Cockerham family.

Clarence stated that other family members outside of John's branch had given money for the upkeep and maintenance of the property. For instance, Gene had paid taxes on the property. They also occasionally gave financial assistance to John and to John's son Charles Jackson, who had recently started living on the property. Clarence gave a $100 check in September 2007, a $75 check in October 2007, and a $75 check in November 2007 to Jackson. Clarence gave this money to Jackson to help him pay bills on the property since Junior was now in prison.

Clarence agreed that the only things actually done to the property were done by John or Junior, although he believed decisions about the property were discussed between his father and John because he heard some of these discussions.

Patricia Cockerham is Junior's niece. Her mother was John's daughter. She was 51 years old at the time of trial. Patricia testified that she was born and raised on the property. Her grandparents helped raise her, and as she got older, she returned to the property for holidays, vacations, and when her mother thought she needed her grandparents' influence. When she was growing up, she spent entire summers at the property.

Patricia testified that after John had died and her grandmother had been moved to a nursing facility in Castor, there was a period when nobody lived on the property. The extended family discussed that they needed someone to look after the property, so it was agreed that when different family members were in the area, they would check on the property. Help was not rendered exclusively by John's branch of the family; it was rendered by whoever was available.

Patricia made contributions for the care and upkeep for the property, and she was aware that Clarence and other members of the family did likewise. For example, when nobody was living at the property, she arranged to have the grass cut. Patricia testified that family members had constructed other buildings on the property, such as storage buildings and a washroom.

Patricia had discussed with her grandfather about building a log cabin on the property. She recalled that he never raised an objection about these plans. Patricia did not remember John or Junior ever saying during the reunions that they were exclusive owners of the property.

Patricia testified that the first time Junior indicated that he considered himself the exclusive owner of the property was through the check and letter that she received at the 2003 reunion. Prior to that, she had never received any notice from John or Junior that they were possessing the property as sole owners.

Patricia always thought of the property as belonging to and as a home for the extended Cockerham family. She disagreed that John and his wife, Junior, and Charles Jackson were the only adults who had lived on the property. She recalled that her Uncle Don and his wife had lived there for about a year in the late 1970s or early 1980s.

In the expropriation proceeding, Steven Yancey testified as an expert in the examination of land titles. He testified that his conclusion was that Gene owned a 7/24 interest, Currie Mae owned a 7/24 interest, and Currie D. owned a 7/24 interest in the property. He also concluded that Junior owned a 3/24 interest on 60 acres of the property that had been donated by his father, but because there was no succession proceeding for John, he could not conclude with any certainty about Junior's interest in the remaining 20 acres. He based his conclusion upon the judgment of possession in the succession of Mose Henry Cockerham, and the patent from the State to the heirs of Mose Henry Cockerham. We concur.

A legal description of the property was attached to the judgment rendered in the expropriation proceeding in 2007. The exhibit listed the Cockerhams as having unknown ownership interests. The exhibit also referenced a 1998 conveyance of 20 acres of the property from John's wife to Junior, and a 2004 conveyance of 60 acres of the property from Junior.

[D]efendants presented no witness testimony at trial other than the proffered testimony. Exhibits offered by defendants were the 1963 deed and a May 1995 affidavit filed into Bienville Parish records in which it was stated that the affiants were unaware of anyone other than John's family possessing any of the property in the prior 30 years.

Based upon our review of the record, we cannot conclude that the trial court was manifestly erroneous in recognizing the ownership interests in the property of Clarence and other members of the Cockerham family in addition to Junior and Melissa.

DECREE

With appellants to bear the costs of this appeal, the judgment is affirmed.

QUESTIONS

1. The court rejects Junior's claim that his ancestor John obtained full ownership of the land via ten-year prescription because despite his just title (from Rufus Lacy), he is not in good faith. What leads the court to conclude that John was not in good faith? Can you offer another explanation of his behavior?

2. Why were the activities of Junior and his ancestor in title John inadequate to demonstrate "by overt and unambiguous acts sufficient to give notice to his co-owner" that they intended to possess for themselves?

Symeonides, Prescription by Co-owners
46 La. L. Rev. 683 (1986)

According to Civil Code Articles 3439 and 3478, co-owners possessing precariously for other co-owners may rebut the presumption of precariousness by showing something less than actual notice, namely, "overt and unambiguous acts sufficient to give notice." But, according to old jurisprudence which continues to be relevant, "mere occupancy, use, payment of taxes, and similar acts of possession will not suffice to give notice of adverse possession to an owner in common." This jurisprudence was reaffirmed by *Jenkins v. Blache*, and *Boase v. Edmonson*. Civil Code Article 3478, provides further that the recordation by a co-owner of a "title from a person other than a co-owner" is an "overt and unambiguous act sufficient to give notice to [the other] co-owner that [the recording co-owner] intends to possess...for himself" and "thus may mark the commencement of prescription." Obviously, the only prescription that is possible here is the 30 year prescription, since the recording co-owner is unlikely to be in good faith. The jurisprudence, both old and new, has uniformly held that the "title" contemplated here need not be a "just title" of the kind needed for the ten year prescription. Thus, the recordation of a partition deed, a donation invalid as to form, and a simulated sale were held sufficient to rebut the presumption of precariousness by the recording co-owner, although none of the above deeds qualify as "just title," i.e., title "translative of ownership." To this list *Frank Petroleum, Inc. v. Babineaux* adds the recordation of an *ex parte* judgment of possession which sends the co-owners into possession of the entire property rather than half of it.

Tax sales seem to be an entirely different matter. The old jurisprudential rules on the subject may be summarized as follows: The adjudication to one co-owner of the entire property at a tax sale does not divest the other co-owners of their interest in the property, but operates simply as a payment of the taxes on their behalf. The adjudicatee co-owner is, of course, entitled to reimbursement, but he cannot become owner by prescription of either ten or thirty years. The same rule applies when the co-owner redeems the property within the redemptive period from a third-party adjudicatee at the tax sale, but not when the redemption occurs after the expiration of the redemption period. In *Boase v. Edmonson,* Mrs. Edmonson redeemed the property from a third party who had bought it one month earlier at a tax sale and had recorded his purchase. Following *Golson* and *Grizzaffi,* the court held that the redemption of the property within the redemption period by Mrs. Edmonson operated "for the benefit of all of her co-owners. Thus, her act was not an act of possession adverse to her co-heirs and for her exclusive interest. Consequently, prescription was not triggered and she was not entitled to recover in a possessory action."

From Adverse to Precarious

When the possessor acknowledges that he is possessing on behalf of someone other than himself, he not only interrupts the running of prescription, but also renders his subsequent possession precarious. In *Briggs v. Pellerin,* the defendant rendered his possession precarious by acknowledging before witnesses that the fence enclosing his property was erroneously placed at a point beyond the limits of his title, thus enclosing partly the land of his neighbor. But in *Nugent v. Franks,* the erroneously placed fence was believed by the parties on both sides (who were cousins) as being on the correct bound-ary. Relying on the statutory presumption that "one is presumed to possess as owner," the court concluded:

Neither the fact that Benton and Chancie were cousins and friendly neighbors who did not concern themselves with the exact location of a surveyed boundary, nor the fact that the location of such a boundary was not known to them carries the implication that Bunton Rushing's possession was anything other than as owner to the visible boundaries of the property possessed by him.

In *Comeaux v. Davenport,* the plaintiff signed a lease from the record owners of the disputed property, after having possessed it adversely as owner for twenty-three years. Had this lease been valid, it would have constituted an acknowledgment capable of not only interrupting the plaintiff's prescription of twenty-three years, but also of preventing prescription from running again by rendering the plaintiffs subsequent possession precarious. However, after expressing "serious misgivings regarding the validity of plaintiff's consent" because he could not read and did not know what he was signing, the court declared the lease invalid because, of the two co-owners named as lessors in the lease document, only one had signed it.

In *Williams v. McEacharn,* the defendant was allowed to testify, over the hearsay objections of plaintiff's attorney, that plaintiff's ancestor, who had died long before the trial, had acknowledged orally that he was possessing more land than his title called for, and that he had asked defendant's permission to continue possessing as before. Apparently relying on this testimony, the trial court found that plaintiff's ancestor's possession was precarious. The court of appeals reversed this finding as manifestly erroneous because:

> No evidence of any farm lease was produced at trial to show that the Chocklins rented the property from anyone.

> The lengthy undisturbed use of the enclosed disputed property by the Chocklins without paying rent to anyone is a strong circumstance indicating their intent to possess as owners.

Plaintiff is entitled to the strong legal presumption provided in CC art. 3427... because the Chocklins did not commence their possession in the name of or for another. The testimony of Malcolm McEacharn that Abner made a declaration against his interest in 1967 long after Chocklin had possessed this property for more than thirty years is not sufficient to rebut the presumption of possession as owner... which possession as owner is also established by the lengthy use of the property.

A more direct way of reaching this result would be to say that, since it was made "long after...,thirty years" of possession, this declaration is governed by Civil Code Article 3490 which provides that "with respect to immovables *renunciation* of acquisitive prescription must be express and in *writing.*"

Ramsey v. Pace contains the following statement:

> The exercise of corporeal possession by Pace's mineral lessee, Marshall Exploration, over the five acres in question inures to Pace, notwithstanding Ramsey's testimony that he gave *verbal* permission to Marshall to so operate. Marshall's exercise of this corporeal possession can better be attributed to its mineral lease from Pace because Ramsey's lease to Marshall *excluded* the 10 acres.

It should be recalled, however, that Ramsey was found by the court to be Pace's precarious possessor. Therefore, even if Marshall's corporeal possession were to be attributed to Ramsey, this would probably not amount to the "actual notice" required by Article 3439 thus converting his precarious possession to possession as owner.

c. Tacking of Possession

NOEL v. JUMONVILLE PIPE AND MACHINERY COMPANY
245 La. 324, 158 So. 2d 179 (1963)

HAMLIN, J. This matter concerns a certain irregular-shaped tract of land, containing 38.88 acres, lying both north and south of the state highway and the Texas & Pacific Railroad in Ascension Parish near the Iberville Parish line.

Jumonville Pipe and Machinery Company, Inc. (hereinafter referred to as Jumonville), instituted these proceedings in the form of a petitory action.***

The record reflects the following transactions relating to McManor Plantation (the ancestral and present home of Frank S. Noel), which adjoins the instant property:

1. December 22, 1914, acquisition by Frank S. Noel's father, Robert E. Noel, from Emile Legendre.
2. January 17, 1920, sale by Robert E. Noel to Dr. Isaac Benson.
3. December 16, 1920, sale by Dr. Isaac Benson to Robert E. Noel.
4. December 16, 1937, judgment of possession in Succession of Robert E. Noel, in the proportions of one-third to Lillian Easton Noel, Widow of Robert E. Noel, and one-twelfth each to Juanita Noel Joffrion, Frank Noel, R. Everett Noel, Wilfred Noel, Easton Noel, Meredith Noel, Lillian Noel Wood and Eloise Noel Hall.
5. August 20, 1945, donation of her undivided interest by Lillian Easton Noel, Widow of Robert E. Noel, to her eight children.
6. August 27, 1945, sale of their interests by Mrs. Robert E. Noel, Juanita Noel Joffrion, R. Everett Noel, Wilfred Noel, Meredith Noel, Easton Noel, Eloise Noel Hall and Lillian Noel Wood to Frank S. Noel.
7. December 18, 1945, sale of a one-half interest by Frank S. Noel to J. Meredith Noel.
8. March 17, 1953, sale of his undivided one-half interest by J. Meredith Noel to Frank S. Noel.

The property which forms the subject matter of this suit and lies adjacent to McManor Plantation is not mentioned in any of the above transactions; it is unquestioned that Jumonville is the record owner.

We have carefully read the testimony of record and agree with the findings of the trial judge that there is ample evidence to show that Robert E. Noel and thereafter Frank S. Noel continuously possessed the disputed property for a period of thirty years commencing from December 16, 1920, when Dr. Isaac Benson sold to Robert E. Noel. The record actually shows that Robert E. Noel manifested acts of possession and acts of ownership immediately after his original purchase in 1914. He continued such acts after reacquiring McManor Plantation in 1920 until his death in November, 1937. Frank S. Noel continued the conduct of his father; he managed McManor Plantation and possessed the disputed property from the time of his father's death until the time of trial in the district court. Acts of possession and ownership consisted of the building of fences, farming and cattle grazing, and requesting that certain neighbors refrain from hunting on the land.

We find no necessity for reiterating the testimony of the numerous witnesses who appeared on behalf of plaintiff and defendant. Later in this opinion, a determination will be made as to whether Frank S. Noel's possession satisfies the requirements of West's C.C. Article 3500 [Revised C.C. arts. 3435, 3436, 3486], and whether he can tack to his possession that of his ancestors in title.

C.C. Article 3500 [Revised C.C. arts. 3435, 3436, 3486] provides that the prescription of thirty years is founded on continuous and uninterrupted possession which must be public and unequivocal, and under the title of owner. The trial judge found that plaintiff herein met the requirements of said Article 3500 [Revised C.C. arts. 3435, 3436, 3486]; he concluded as follows:

"Certainly in view of the civil law doctrine of 'le mort saisit le vif,' there was 'a succession of relationship' between the possession of the late Robert E. Noel and his son Frank S. Noel, 'created *** by operation of law' and existing in fact. As the court understands that doctrine, the heirs succeed to all of the rights of the decedent at the very moment of death, and without the passage of the slightest moment of time. This being true, there was 'no interval for the constructive possession of the true owner to intervene, such two possessions are blended into one, and the limitation period upon the right of such owner to reclaim the land is thereby continued.'

"Furthermore, the idea that one who sells according to his title thereby abandons his material detention of the excess beyond his title is rather theoretical. The average layman knows little or nothing of the legal description of his property; he only knows it as he sees and possesses it. On the other hand the notary who simply copies the legal description as given in the title is likely to know very little about the area which his client actually possesses. Although all of the transfers among the heirs of Robert E. Noel as set forth above were made according to the title by which he acquired, and without any specific mention of any additional area possessed beyond the title, nevertheless, in each instance, the legal description of the property is prefaced by the statement that what is being conveyed is 'A certain sugar plantation known as McManor Plantation; situated in the parish of Ascension, State of Louisiana, on the right bank of the Mississippi River at about one league above the town of Donaldsonville....' The evidence shows that the Noels have always considered the subject property as a part of McManor Plantation and have always treated it as such. There was certainly never any intention to abandon either their possession or claim of ownership with regard to the area in dispute, nor did any such abandonment occur in fact.

"In view of these considerations, and in view of the doctrine of 'le mort saisit le vif,' the court concludes that the present litigant, Frank S. Noel, is entitled to tack to his possession that of his father, Robert E. Noel. The two possessions constituting in reality one continuous possession extending for a period in excess of thirty years, and that possession meeting, in the opinion of the court, all of the requirements of Article 3500 [Revised C.C. arts. 3435, 3436, 3486], the plea of thirty years prescription will be maintained."

The Court of Appeal, relying in great part on the case of Stutson v. McGee (241 La. 646, 130 So. 2d 403), found that there was no privity of contract between Frank S. Noel and his predecessors in title; that, consequently, the possession of Frank S. Noel's authors could not be "tacked on" to his own possession for the purpose of establishing possession for the thirty year period prescribed in Article 3499 [Revised C.C. art. 3486].... The Court concluded that having failed to establish possession in himself for thirty years, Frank S. Noel had not discharged the burden of proving possession sufficient to maintain his plea of prescription. ...

On rehearing, the Court of Appeal reinstated its original decree; it held that Frank S. Noel's attempt to invoke the provisions of Article 852 [Revised C.C. arts. 794, 796] for the first time in his application for rehearing was prohibited by the procedural rules and requirements obtaining under our jurisprudence and laws, and stated, "It is clear beyond question that after having pitched his title on prescription predicated upon alleged 30 years adverse possession without expressly alluding to either Article 852 or 3499 ...[Revised C.C. arts. 794, 796, 3486], appellee, in the court below, limited and restricted his efforts to an attempt to establish title pursuant to Article 3499 [Revised C.C. art. 3486]."***

We are primarily concerned with the principle of "Tacking On" as it applies to acquisitive prescription under C.C. Article 3499 [Revised C.C. art. 3486] and related articles, and our findings herein will be based on these articles.

In the case of Stutson v. McGee, 241 La. 646, 130 So. 2d 403, the defendant George McGee was and had been in possession of the disputed property for a few months short of thirty years. Prior to his possession, the property had been possessed by W. A. Davis and his heirs. McGee purchased adjacent property from the Davis heirs and continued the possession of the Davis heirs of the controversial land. This Court sustained plaintiff's contention that since there was no privity of title respecting the disputed property between defendant and his vendors, the possession of the latter could not be tacked to provide the requisite thirty years; we stated:

"Unquestionably a person may actually possess an immovable for 30 years without any title and, by that means, acquire ownership thereof. Revised [1870] Civil Code Articles 3499 and 3503 [Revised C.C. arts. 3486, 3487]. But if he has to add to his possession that of his vendor for effecting the accrual of such period he is governed by Revised Civil Code Articles 3493 and 3494 [Revised C.C. arts. 3441, 3442], contained in that part of our Civil Code which deals with the ten year acquisitive prescription, and those provisions clearly disclose that they may be availed of only if the person seeking to 'tack' possesses under some kind of title.***

"Since this defendant himself did not possess the disputed tract for 30 years, and inasmuch as he is not permitted to 'tack' the possession thereof held by his vendors of the adjacent lands to that which he has enjoyed, the plea of prescription was correctly overruled."

The instant case can be differentiated from the Stutson case; therein the Court was considering the question of privity with respect to possession and prescription as it affected a vendor-vendee relationship.***

When Robert E. Noel died in 1937 (he had possessed the disputed property for seventeen years) his eight children were his legal heirs, being called to his succession by operation of law.... Being seized of the succession of their father, the children were authorized to continue the possession of the disputed property as if there had been no interruption ...; it being necessary for them to continue the possession for thirteen years before ownership could be asserted.... (citations omitted)* * *

Immediately after his father's death, Frank S. Noel continued the possession of the disputed property. He testified that he operated McManor Plantation and the disputed property as a unit on behalf of his mother and his brothers and sisters.

The evidence preponderates that the possession was in the capacity of ownership in the Noels....No adverse possession nor hostility was ever expressed by Frank S. Noel's brothers and sisters [citations omitted].

Up until the sale of McManor Plantation by his co-heirs to him, on August 27, 1945, Frank S. Noel's interest in McManor Plantation and in the possession of the disputed property was at all times undivided.***

A natural conclusion follows that when Mrs. Robert E. Noel and seven of her children divested themselves of their interest in McManor Plantation by sale to Frank S. Noel on August 27, 1945, those seven children gave up their undivided interest in the possession of the herein disputed property (this possession they had never asserted). Frank S. Noel remained in control of the whole possession; as stated *supra*, he possessed the disputed property as owner up until the time of trial in the district court.

The sale of December 18, 1945 by Frank S. Noel to his brother J. Meredith Noel was the sale of "the undivided half" of McManor Plantation, and the Act of Sale described McManor Plantation. Frank S. Noel has never divested himself of his undivided interest in McManor Plantation. There is no evidence of record to the effect that J. Meredith Noel ever exercised any right of possession on the disputed property or disturbed the possession of Frank S. Noel thereon between December 18, 1945 and March, 1953.

While the property which forms the subject matter of this suit is not specifically described in any of the transactions hereinabove recited, nevertheless, the property which was intended to be transferred and which was actually transferred and delivered is described as "A certain sugar plantation known as McManor

Plantation, situated in the Parish of Ascension, State of Louisiana,...," which in fact included the property in controversy. We note that each transfer not only conveys all the rights, ways, servitudes and privileges, but also conveys the advantages and appurtenances belonging to McManor Plantation.

We, therefore, conclude that the foregoing transfers complied with C.C. Article 3493 [Revised C.C. art. 3441] et seq., and that Frank S. Noel is entitled to tack his possession to that of his ancestors and authors in title. In this connection, it is pertinent to observe that these views are supported by Articles 2673 and 2674, Planiol's Traité Élémentaire de Droit Civil, Volume 1, Part 2, Page 584 [quotations omitted].

For the reasons assigned, the judgment of the Court of Appeal, First Circuit, is reversed and set aside; the judgment of the trial court is affirmed and reinstated....

McCALEB, J. (dissenting). Assuming, without necessarily conceding, that plaintiff has the right to tack to his own possession his father's adverse possession of the 38 acres in contest, I fail to perceive how, under the facts stated in the majority opinion plaintiff has acquired more than an undivided 1/12th interest in the land by the 30-year acquisitive prescription.

According to the facts, plaintiff's father possessed adversely from 1920 until his death in 1937, or for 17 years. Plaintiff succeeded to his father's possession in 1937, but only to the extent of an undivided 1/12th interest as a co-owner with his mother and brothers and sisters. This character of possession continued until 1945, during which year plaintiff acquired, by donation from his mother and by purchase from his brothers and sisters, their outstanding interests in McManor Plantation. But this acquisition by donation and purchase did not transfer to plaintiff the right of adverse possession of his mother and brothers and sisters to the 38 acres in dispute. This is because the instruments of transfer did not contain a description of the 38 acres and, therefore, under the well-settled jurisprudence, the adverse possession of the donor and vendors cannot be tacked to plaintiff's possession to change or increase his adverse interest or possession from an undivided 1/12th to an exclusive possession of the whole. See Stutson v. McGee, 241 La. 646, 130 So. 2d 403 and the many authorities there cited.

Thus, plaintiff's adverse possession has never exceeded the undivided 1/12th interest in the right of possession he inherited from his father and, by tacking his father's possession to his own, he would be entitled at the most to be recognized as having acquired by the 30-year prescription an undivided 1/12th interest in the land in contest, if, and only if, one co-owner-possessor may maintain an action of this sort without the joinder of the other co-owners as parties plaintiff.

Whether or not this can be countenanced, I am not at all certain. However, the law is well established that a co-owner in possession is a precarious possessor, as defined by Article 3490 of the Civil Code [Revised C.C. art. 3477], and that one possessing in such quality cannot prescribe against his co-owner. Liles v. Pitts, 145 La. 650, 82 So. 755; Hill

v. Dees, 188 La. 708, 178 So. 250 and the cases there cited.

Indeed, it was held in Satcher v. Radesich, 153 La. 468, 96 So. 35, that the possession of a vendor, which was not *exclusively* as owner, but for his co-heirs, could not be added to the possession of his vendees to establish prescription. Whether the reverse of that situation, which appears in this case, would be governed by the same rule I am not prepared to say at this time. However, one conclusion is perfectly evident and that is that plaintiff cannot tack his mother's and brothers' and sisters' possession to his own so as to entitle him to a complete prescriptive title to the land in contest.

It is to be observed that the majority opinion, in an apparent effort to take this matter out of the well-settled jurisprudence of the many cases involving tacking of possession, to which we strictly adhered in Stutson v. McGee, has construed the deeds herein under which plaintiff acquired the interests of his mother and his brothers and sisters as transferring to him a *title* to the 38 acres in contest as well as the acreage comprising McManor Plantation which is particularly described in the deeds. It is said that this is true because the deeds declare that the property conveyed is generally described as "A certain sugar plantation known as McManor Plantation ***" which necessarily included all acreage possessed by the donor and vendors even though they had no title to part of the acreage.

In concluding thus the majority has completely overlooked the legal effect of the fact that the deeds contain a particular description of the lands conveyed which description omits the property in dispute. The jurisprudence relative to the construction of such deeds is likewise well established. It is, of course, the general rule that the particular description must prevail over the general description when there is a conflict between them. See Snelling v. Adair, 196 La. 624, 199 So. 782 and the many authorities there cited.

But, even if there is good reason to suppose that the donor and vendors in this case were attempting to transfer their possession of the 38 acres to plaintiff, this does not suffice. For, under Civil Code Articles 3493 and 3494 [Revised C.C. arts. 3441, 3442], a *title* to the land must be transferred, in order for the vendee to tack the possession of his vendor to his own. If this is not so, then all the jurisprudence laid down in the past is meaningless. In one of the landmark cases on the subject, Sibley v. Pierson, 125 La. 478, 51 So. 502, the court put it thus in the syllabus it wrote:

"Where one possesses beyond his title, but sells according to his title, the vendee cannot, for the purposes of the prescription of 30 years, adquirendi causa, tack to his own possession that of his vendor of the property which is not included in the deed by which he acquires; there being no privity between him and his vendor with respect to such possession."

That is exactly this case. In my opinion, it is incorrect in law and in fact to conclude that the deeds herein evidence the conveyance of any sort of *title* by the vendors to the 38 acres, which are not included in the description. The law is well settled that a deed which does not include a particular description of the disputed property does not translate a *title* to such property which will serve as a basis for a plea of acquisitive prescription of ten years by adverse possession. Bendernagel v. Foret, 145 La. 115, 81 So. 869; Hunter v. Forrest, 195 La. 973, 197 So. 649; Pierce v. Hunter, 202 La. 900, 13 So. 2d 259 and cases there cited.

The same rule applies as to tacking under Civil Code Articles 3493 and 3494 [Revised C.C. arts. 3441, 3442]. There must be a *title* translative of the property in order for the purchaser to tack the possession of his vendor. I respectfully dissent.

SANDERS, J. (dissenting). At issue here is the ownership of a 38-acre tract of land in Ascension Parish. The defendant is the record owner. However, the majority opinion has sustained the prescriptive title of the plaintiff-relator under Article 3499 [Revised C.C. art. 3486] of the Louisiana Civil Code, by permitting him to add to his own possession that of his mother, brothers, and sisters so as to cumulate the required 30 years adverse possession.

It is well settled that in order to tack, or add, possessions for the 30-year acquisitive prescription there must be a juridical link between the possessors as to the particular property. A purchaser may avail himself of the possession of his vendor only if he received a title to the property from the vendor. Civil Code Arts. 3493, 3494 [Revised C.C. arts. 3441, 3442], Stutson v. McGee, 241 La. 646, 130 So. 2d 403; Sibley v. Pierson, 125 La. 478, 51 So. 502.

As a basis for its decision under the foregoing rule, the majority makes the following finding concerning the conveyances to plaintiff-relator from his mother, brothers, and sisters:

"While the property which forms the subject matter of this suit is not specifically described in any of the transactions hereinabove recited, nevertheless, the property which was intended to be transferred and which was actually transferred and delivered is described as 'A certain sugar plantation known as McManor Plantation, situated in the Parish of Ascension, State of Louisiana ***' which in fact included the property in controversy. We note that each transfer not only conveys all the rights, ways, servitudes and privileges, but also conveys the advantages and appurtenances belonging to McManor Plantation."

I cannot agree to this finding. The parties to this proceeding concede that the plaintiff-relator "at no time acquired by written instrument, nor did he or any heir ever transfer by written instrument, *any part or interest* in the property which is the subject of this suit, viz., the 38.88 acres." (Italics mine). However, irrespective of the concession, the instruments of conveyance reflect that the 38-acre tract was not included in the transfers. In these instruments, the parties transfer McManor Plantation as described in detail, according to section, township, range, and acreage. No land in Section 6, where the property in dispute is located, is described or conveyed.

However, to support its finding that the conveyances included the transferor's interest in the disputed property, the majority points to the following language, which follows the detailed description:

"Together with all the rights, ways, servitudes, privileges and advantages belonging to said plantation and all of the buildings and improvements thereon and belonging and appurtenances thereof."

Clearly, this language has reference to predial servitudes, which are owed to one estate by another. See Arts. 646-659, Civil Code [646-654, 741]. It does not, and cannot, convey the additional tract of land. Moreover, neither the ownership, nor a claim to the ownership, of the 38-acre tract can be considered a servitude, privilege or *advantage belonging to said plantation.*

Inasmuch as there is no juridical link between plaintiff-relator and his mother, brothers, and sisters as to the property in controversy, he cannot utilize their possession for purposes of acquisitive prescription.

I, of course, assume at this time that the plaintiff succeeded to his father's possession to the extent of an undivided 1/12th interest and that his prescriptive title to this interest has been shown. For the foregoing reasons, I respectfully dissent.

NOTE
Juridical Link for Tacking of Possession

The decision in *Noel v. Jumonville* gives rise to serious legal questions. Is the holding that Frank S. Noel acquired the ownership of the 38.88 acres of land by acquisitive prescription contrary to law, as the dissenting Justices maintain? Do these Justices miss some thing in their legal reasoning? *Cf.* La. Civil Code arts 940, 941, 852 (1870); present Articles 794, 3486.

Admittedly, Frank S. Noel's title to the McManor Plantation did not include the 38.88 acres. Frank's claim of ownership of those acres rested, exclusively, on acquisitive prescription of thirty years. Frank alone had not possessed the 38.88 acres for thirty years. However, Frank and his father, Robert E. Noel, together had been in possession of the disputed land for more than thirty years. The question was, therefore, whether Frank could tack his possession onto that of his father's.

According to the Civil Code and well-settled Louisiana jurisprudence, tacking of possession is predicated on the existence of a juridical link between successive possessors of the same property. In inter vivos transfers of property, the juridical link is an act translative of ownership, such as a sale, exchange, or donation, conveying property. See *Stutson v. Magee*, 241 La. 646, 130 So. 2d 403 (1961). Such a juridical link between Frank and his father was missing and, at first blush, the majority opinion seems to be contrary to former article 3493 and present articles 3441 and 3442 of the Louisiana Civil Code.

However, this is not the end of the inquiry. Quite apart from the requirements for the tacking of possessions under former article 3493 and present articles 3441, 3442 of the

Louisiana Civil Code, possession may also be tacked by possession beyond one's title within visible bounds or by virtue of universal succession. See former articles 852, 940, 941 and present articles 794, 936, 3441, and 3442. These provisions supply the requisite juridical link for tacking of possession in addition to tacking under former article 3493 and present article 3441 and 3442 of the Civil Code.

Possession is heritable, and Frank, as heir of his father, continued his father's possession of the 38.88 acres within visible bounds. Therefore, Frank could tack his possession onto his father's possession under former articles 852 or 940 and 941 of the 1870 Civil Code. He would be able to do the same under present articles 794, 3441, and 3442.

However, Frank was not the only heir of his father. Robert E. Noel's succession devolved in indivision to all his children, including Frank's siblings. Should, then, the 38.88 acres also belong in indivision to Frank's coheirs? Note that Frank's mother and all co-heirs had transferred to Frank their undivided interests in the McManor Plantation. Did those transfers include interests in the 38.88 acres? See *Noel v. Noel*, 312 So.2d 134, 136 (La. App. 1st Cir. 1975).

BROWN v. WOOD
451 So. 2d 569 (La. App. 2d Cir. 1984)

HALL, J. Plaintiffs filed a petitory action against defendants to establish their ownership of a tract of land in Caldwell Parish. The trial court awarded judgment in plaintiff's favor and defendants have appealed. We affirm in part, reverse in part, and remand.

Plaintiffs in this cause are Donald R. Brown, Charlotte Brown Hislop, Beulah Howell Brown, and Henry Brown. Defendants are husband and wife, Charles and Vera Wood. In this petitory action filed June 3, 1982, the plaintiffs, Browns, sought legal recognition of their ownership of the Boeuf River riverfront tract to which they held the record title. In a decision rendered June 15, 1983, the trial court awarded judgment in plaintiff's favor, recognizing the Browns as owners of the tract in question and ordering defendants, the Woods, to surrender possession of that property.

The tract at issue, approximately 5 acres in Section 18, Township 14 North, Range 5 East, is located between the southern bank of the Boeuf River and other property held by the Woods under record title, and is traversed by Louisiana Highway 133. The following diagram illustrates the situation

The tract in question is part of a larger tract which was deeded to Dr. S.H. Brown, plaintiffs' ancestor in title, in 1904. The same tract was sold by Dr. Brown to Ernest "Buddy" Oliveaux and Tray Ritchie in 1936. In 1944, the tract was purchased at a sheriff's sale by Erwin and Cecil Brown, the sons of the then deceased Dr. S. H. Brown. Cecil and Erwin Brown have both since died intestate, and the four instant plaintiffs are their heirs. Plaintiffs Donald Brown and Charlotte Brown Hislop are the children and sole heirs of Cecil Brown. Plaintiffs Beulah Howell Brown and Henry Brown are the widow and son, respectively, of Erwin Brown, and his sole surviving heirs. Upon the deaths of Cecil and Erwin, the four instant plaintiffs acquired record title to the tract in question via intestate succession. Thus, plaintiffs are the record owners of the contested property.

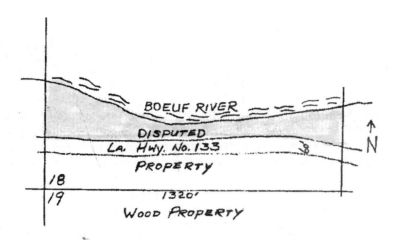

In 1956, defendants Charles and Vera Wood purchased from Ernest "Buddy" Oliveaux a plot of land in Section 19 immediately to the south of the disputed tract. The deed from Buddy Oliveaux to the Woods did not include or encompass the contested tract. However, subsequent to the 1956 conveyance to the Woods of the property abutting the south end of the contested river front acreage, the Woods performed various acts of corporeal possession on the disputed tract. In 1981, the Woods acquired a quit claim deed to that part of the Brown tract lying north of the highway from the Oliveauxs.

Ownership of immovable property under record title may be eclipsed and superseded by ownership acquired under prescriptive title. Under the general code provisions on acquisitive prescription, a possessor lacking good faith and/or just title may acquire prescriptive title to land by corporeally possessing a tract for 30 years with the intent to possess as owner. Such possession confers prescriptive title upon the possessor only when it is continuous, uninterrupted, peaceable, public and unequivocal, and confers title only to such immovable property as is actually possessed. C.C. Arts. 3424, 3476, 3486, 3487, 3488. Alternatively, under Civil Code Art. 794, a title holder may acquire more land than his title calls for by possessing property beyond his title for 30 years without interruption and within visible bounds. Such a title holder may attain the thirty year possessory period which is necessary to perfect prescriptive title in the absence of good faith and just title by "tacking" on the possession of his ancestor in title. C.C. Arts. 794, 3442. Possession is only transferable by universal title or particular title, and thus privity of contract or estate is an essential prerequisite to tacking. C.C. Art. 3441.

The legal principles which govern tacking under Civil Code Article 794 are in some respects different and distinct from the principles which govern tacking under Civil Code Articles 3441 and 3442 (formerly embodied in Articles 3493-3496). Article 794 deals with *boundary* prescription, strictly speaking, while Articles 3441 and 3442 provide general rules which refer in broader terms to acquisitive prescription of property, generally.***

Under Article 794, the privity of title between the possessor and his ancestor in title need *not* extend to the property to which the possessor asserts prescriptive title; under Article 794, the juridical link, or written instrument which passes to the possessor from his ancestor in title need not encompass or include the particular property to which the possessor claims prescriptive title. On the other hand, it is generally conceded under the *general* tacking provisions of Articles 3441 and 3442 and their statutory pre-cursors, that tacking is only allowed with respect to property that is included and described in the juridical link between the possessor's ancestor in title and the possessor himself.

Simply stated, under Art. 794 (old Art. 852), one may utilize tacking to prescribe *beyond title* on adjacent property to the extent of visible boundaries, but under the general prescriptive articles, Arts. 3441 and 3442, tacking may be utilized to prescribe *only to the extent of title.* As was succinctly stated by former Justice, then Judge Tate, in Stanford v. Robertson, 144 So. 2d 747, 750 (La. App. 3d Cir. 1962),

"Under C.C. art. 3499, the possession of the predecessors in title cannot be added to that of the present possessor, unless the title of the present possessor includes the property in dispute, else there is no privity of estate such as is necessary to make up the thirty years adverse possession '*as owner*'. On the other hand, under C.C. Art. 852, the tacking of successive possessons up to the established visible bound between two estates is permitted, whether or nor the land in dispute is included within the title description of the party pleading prescriptive title under this article." (Citations omitted).

However, when correctly viewed, there still must be *some* juridical link to effectuate tacking under *either* species of tacking, whether it is Article 794 or Articles 3441 and 3442.

The fact that Article 794 envisions that tacking requires *some* juridical link or privity of title between the possessor and his ancestor is clear. That statute affords prescriptive title only in instances where there has been thirty years of possession by the possessor "and his ancestors *in title.*" (Emphasis added). The fact that Art. 794 envisions tacking only where there is privity of title is therefore clear from the fact that this Article expressly authorizes tacking not in terms of a *predecessor in possession,* but in terms of an *"ancestor in title. "*

In summary, tacking allows one to prescribe beyond title under Art. 794, and *not* under Articles 3441 and 3442; but nevertheless some juridical link, or some title privity in contract or estate, is required before tacking is allowed under *either* Articles 3441 and

3442 or 794. [citations omitted]***

Privity of estate or contract is essential to tacking possessions for the theoretical reason that absent such privity succeeding possessions of the same tract are legally viewed as merely unconnected acts of trespass. In the absence of privity, acts of adverse possession by different possessors "can be construed only as a series of trespasses." Upon the termination "of each of these acts the possession returns, by operation of law, to the record owner of the property." Roberson v. Green, *supra,* at 447. See also, Buckley v. Catlett, *supra*; Emmer v. Rector, *supra;* Sibley v. Pierson, *supra.*

Privity of title denotes a relationship which "may be created by a deed, as in a sale, by an act, such as a donation, or by operation of law, as in a succession." Note, Immovables—Thirty-Year Acquisitive Prescription—Tacking, 38 Tul. L. Rev. 575, 577 (1964). See also, Stutson v. McGee, *supra;* Emmer v. Rector, *supra*; Harang v. Golden Ranch Land & Drainage Co., 79 So. 768 (La. 1918). Privity of title, at least with respect to immovable property, cannot be created by verbal transactions, and as a general rule cannot be proved by parol evidence. As was stated by the Supreme Court in *Stutson v. McGee:*

"In our research..., we have carefully examined numerous other Louisiana authorities; but in none has any language been found which tends to support the contention of this defendant that, for the purpose of effecting an accrual of the 30 years' prescription, possession alone can be transferred by mere actions or by verbal agreement and that the transfer may be shown by parol evidence. 130 So. 2d at 407."

In the instant suit, it was stipulated by the parties at trial that the Browns had perfect record title to the tract at issue: the Brown's chain of title extended back in unbroken sequence to the sovereign, such title having been ultimately derived from a patent deeded to a private citizen by the United States Government. Since the Browns thereby established by stipulation that they held perfect record title to the property, the burden of proof in this petitory action shifted to the Woods to establish by a preponderance of the evidence that they had acquired prescriptive title to the tract. Verret v. Norwood, 311 So. 2d 86 (La. App. 3d Cir. 1975), app. den., 313 So. 2d 842 (La. 1975); Clayton v. Langston, 311 So. 2d 74 (La. App. 3d Cir. 1975); Tinney v. Lauve, 280 So. 2d 588 (La. App. 4th Cir. 1973).

In discharging their burden of proving prescriptive title, defendants, the Woods, may not rely on the code provisions conferring prescriptive title to immovable property upon ten years good faith possession since defendants have proven neither just title nor a good faith belief in ownership with respect to the tract in question. C.C. Arts. 3473-3485. Since they may not avail themselves of the good faith prescription of ten years, the Woods must prove that they have satisfied the above-stated requirements of 30 years prescription.

One of the most fundamental requirements of 30 years prescription is of course the requirement that possession continue for 30 years. C.C. Art. 3486. However, the Woods themselves have only performed possessory acts on the disputed tract since 1956. The Browns interrupted the Woods' possession and acquired prescription by filing suit in 1982. C.C. Art. 3462. Thus, the Woods did not accumulate the necessary 30 years of possession in the 26 year period between 1956 and 1982.

Since it is clear that the Woods themselves did not possess the disputed tract for the required 30 year period, they must tack the possession of the Oliveauxs onto their own possession in order to achieve the requisite 30 year period. The Woods accordingly contend that the Oliveauxs possessed the disputed tract for many years prior to the Woods' possession; they further contend that by tacking their own possession to that of the Oliveauxs, they have accumulated the 30 years of possession necessary to acquire prescriptive title.

The Woods are entitled to tack on the possession of the Oliveauxs. Although their 1956 deed from Oliveaux was not filed into evidence, it is clear from several references in the record that Oliveaux conveyed by deed to the Woods the NW/4 of the NW/4 of Section 19, less a portion thereof, which tract Oliveaux had acquired from Brown several years earlier. It does not appear that plaintiffs dispute this fact or that any issue was made of it at trial. The trial court's written reasons for judgment state: "The record at trial shows that the Woods acquired the adjacent property on March 9, 1956 by deed from Earnest Oliveaux, husband of Enolua Curry." The briefs filed on behalf of the plaintiffs in the trial court and this court contain reference to the defendants' ownership of the adjacent property to the south. Consequently, there exists the juridical link or privity of title which is essential to tacking.

The Woods also established the required 30 years possession by them and their ancestor in title to part of the disputed tract. The section line between Sections 18 and 19 is located at varying distances of only about 50 to 150 feet south of the curving highway. Oliveaux and then the Woods lived on the tract to which they had record title in a house located on the south side of the highway for more than 30 years prior to the time this suit was filed. In addition to maintaining their front yard to the highway, they maintained the balance of the property along the highway for raising crops and for pasture. The highway, and a fence along the south side of the highway, served as a visible north boundary of the property possessed by them as part of their home place. It appears that their possession extended to extensions of their east and west boundaries. The Woods and their ancestor in title, Oliveaux, possessed for more than 30 years, without interruption, within visible bounds, more land than their title called for, that is, the narrow strip between their north property line and the highway.

There is also considerable evidence of their possession north of the highway, between the highway and the river. However, there is contrary evidence and considering the contradictory evidence as to that strip, we defer to the trial court's finding that the Woods failed to carry their burden of proof as to possession of that part of the disputed property north of the highway.

The Woods also stake their claim to tacking upon a quit claim deed to that part of the disputed tract lying north of the highway, executed by the Oliveauxs in favor of the Woods. However, this quit claim was not executed until 1981, at which time as the trial court duly noted "this controversy was already boiling," and a dispute between the parties as to the tract in question had already fomented. We agree with the trial court that, under these circumstances, a quit claim deed executed in 1981 does not effectuate tacking with respect to a piece of property that was conveyed in 1956. In so holding, we are influenced by the Supreme Court's position that a juridical act confected under such circumstances is suspicious.

As was stated in Stutson v. McGee, 130 So. 2d at 407, "In a further endeavor to substantiate the claim of privity between himself and his predecessors in possession this defendant introduced a document styled an "Act of Correction and Confirmation" executed, after this suit was filed, by three of the seven persons then interested as vendors and which purported to show an intention to convey the disputed property. Because that instrument was belatedly confected we entertain serious doubt that it was admissible in evidence, for seemingly to approve such a practice in aid of the accrual of the acquisitive prescription might well provide a method for the perpetration of fraud."

However our view in this regard is not based solely on *Stutson.* Our position is predicated as well upon the *a priori* nature of tacking itself. Tacking, by its very nature, combines such possession of the ancestor in title *which has accrued immediately prior to the transfer of the property* with the possession of the possessor *which accrues immediately subsequent to the transfer.* It is the time of the transfer itself which constitutes the "day of reckoning" in computing the periods to be tacked. The possessory period of the ancestor in title *which has accrued immediately prior to transfer of title* is added to the possessory period of the succession in title which has accrued *immediately subsequent to transfer of title.* Thus, at the time the quit claim was confected, the ancestor, Oliveaux, had no accrued possession to transfer. In the strictest sense, privity may not be retroactively established subsequent to a transfer of possession. Privity of title must exist at the time possession is transferred, else there is no succession *under title* to the rights of the predecessor.***

We simply hold that this quit claim, which the trial court found embodied a spurious intent, which was executed while litigation was in the offing, and which involved a tract of land not adjacent to the title property of the party seeking to tack, is insufficient to establish privity for the purposes of tacking under C.C. Art. 794.***

The district court judgment is correct insofar as it recognizes the plaintiffs as the owners of that part of the disputed tract north of the highway, and the judgment is affirmed to that extent. Insofar as the judgment of the district court recognizes the plaintiffs as owners of that part of the disputed tract south of the highway, it is reversed and set aside. The defendants are recognized as the owners of that part of the disputed tract south of the highway which adjoins the property of which they are record owners. The action is remanded to the district court for entry of a judgment in accordance with this decision, which judgment should describe the property involved as required by C.C.P. Art. 1919. Costs of these proceedings, including the costs of appeal, are assessed equally to the plaintiffs and defendants. Affirmed in part, reversed in part, and remanded.

NOTE
Special Acquisitive Prescription: Acquiring Blighted Property Under La. Rev. Stat. 9:5633

In addition to the forms of acquisitive prescription described in the Code, the Legislative may establish acquisitive prescription by means of statutes. La.R.S. 9:5633 provides a three-year acquisitive prescription period, without the need for just title or good faith, to obtain ownership of immovable property located within a municipality having a population of three hundred thousand or more; the property must have been declared or certified blighted after an administrative hearing. The lengthy and complex requirements for prescribing on such property appear in the statute's paragraphs A. through K., providing safeguards for original owners, while at the same time opening the door for possessors who remediate such property to ac-quire its ownership, or at least repayment for their efforts.

In *Mouledoux v. Skipper*, 104 So. 3d 585 (La. App. 4 Cir. 2012), Louisiana's fourth circuit appellate court provided the first reported opinion interpreting 9:5633, which had been in existence since 1995. In that case, the plaintiff's property was located at 6470 General Diaz Street in the Lakeview area of New Or-leans, which had been inundated with flood waters following Hurricane Katrina. The defendant lived directly across the street from Mouledoux's house. As the court observed, "most other neighbors had either torn down their homes or restored them," but Mouledoux's property "remained virtually untouched." On October 16, 2009, her house was adjudicated blighted and a public nuisance. Despite the plaintiff's knowledge of the adjudication, she took "no visible steps" to remediate the property's condition. Beginning on July 7, 2010, the defendant, Mr. Skipper, advised by legal counsel, took the requisite steps under the statute to obtain legal possession, which included notifying Ms. Mouledoux and the adjoining landowners of his intentions by certified mail. He then remediated the property. As a result of his repairs to the house, Skipper obtained recission of the adjudication of blight, and the City waived the fines that had accrued during the owner's neglect.

On March 24, 2011, Ms. Mouledoux filed a possessory action and in addition for a temporary restraining order against Mr. Skipper. Ultimately, she amended her petition to demand damages as well. The trial court's judgment in favor of Ms. Mouledoux, though it did not award damages, recognized her as in possession of the property and awarded the defendant reimbursement for less than half of his expenses. In doing so, the appellate court observed, the trial court judgment was "contrary to the plain language of the statute"; the statute recognized the remediator in compliance as legal possessor of the property and mandated fuller reimbursement. The appellate court reversed in part and remanded to the trial court to "appoint appraisers" in accordance with the statute to calculate Mr. Skipper's reimbursement. In addition, the court found that Mr. Skipper was entitled to reimbursement of attorney's fees and costs incurred in obtaining the authorization to remediate the house; these were also to be determined on remand. The appellate court affirmed the trial court's order that Skipper had a right of first lien and privilege on the formerly blighted property.

The statutory prescription in 9:5633 offers far less leeway for judicial interpretation than the prescriptions in the Civil Code. Throughout its discussion, the fourth circuit stressed that the lower court's errors lay in substituting its own interpretations for the "clear and unambiguous" language of the statute.

3. MOVABLES
Civil Code arts. 524, 3489-3491

McKEE v. HAYWARD
710 So. 2d 362 (La. App. 1st Cir. 1998)

SHORTESS, J. William Campbell Hayward (Hayward) and Helene Reuss Hayward (Mrs. Hayward) had four children: William C. Hayward, Jr., Douglas S. Hayward, John R. Hayward, and Helene Hayward Renken (Renken). Renken predeceased her parents, leaving one daughter, Joan Renken McKee. Douglas was executor of his mother's estate and trustee of her trust. He is also president of Germania Plantation, Inc., (Germania), which owns the family plantation. For years William, Douglas, John, and Joan have been squabbling. In 1985 they agreed to settle their differences and entered into a written agreement. They did not abide by the terms of that agreement, however, and at least nine lawsuits resulted. Nine suits were consolidated at the trial court level, four of which were dismissed before trial. The remaining suits were tried jointly.***

Douglas has appealed the portions of the trial court's judgments that direct him ... to deliver certain property to Joan. ...

The property in dispute includes two paintings and leaves that convert a square dining table into a larger oval table, as well as a watch chain and fob. Joan contends her great-grandmother, Bertha Spor Reuss (Reuss), bequeathed the paintings and the table to her mother, Renken. Joan was Renken's only child and inherited all her property. Douglas, however, contends he owns the paintings and leaves, either through a bequest from his mother of all Germania Plantation furnishings or, alternatively, through acquisitive prescription. He does not contest Joan's ownership of the watch chain and fob but claims he has no knowledge of their whereabouts.

Joan testified her mother inherited the table and paintings from Reuss, but after Joan's father died and the family was forced to move to a smaller house, many of their furnishings, including the paintings and table leaves, were moved to Germania. Douglas testified he "may have influenced" his mother not to give the paintings back because he wanted them. They are currently hanging in the house where Douglas resides. Douglas also has possession of the table leaves, although Joan has the square center portion of the table. Douglas contends the table and paintings belonged to his mother and he inherited them from her. Alternatively, he contends his mother owned the paintings and table through acquisitive prescription as they have been at Germania Plantation since approximately 1959.

Title to movables may be acquired through prescription of three years by a good-faith possessor or ten years by a bad-faith possessor. The party asserting acquisitive prescription has the burden of proving all facts essential to support it.[1] One essential element of a claim of acquisitive prescription is the intent to possess the property as owner; mere physical possession is insufficient.[2] Furthermore, possession for the convenience of another gives the possessor neither legal possession nor the right of prescribing.[3]

The trial court obviously believed Joan's testimony that Mrs. Hayward was holding the paintings and table leaves at Germania for Renken's convenience. The court rejected Douglas's plea of prescription, holding the property belonged to Renken and thus could not be bequeathed to Douglas by his mother. This is a factual determination; it cannot be disturbed by the appellate court unless it is manifestly erroneous or clearly wrong. We find no manifest error in this factual determination.

Douglas does not dispute Joan's claim to the watch fob and chain, which were bequeathed to Renken by Hayward. According to Joan's uncontroverted testimony, the chain and fob were last seen about a week before Renken's death in 1981. Renken, on her deathbed, asked Douglas and her mother to visit her and bring the chain and fob, which they did. Douglas showed them to Renken, then put them back in his pocket and left. He testified he does not know what happened to them, but stated that if he could find them, he would give them to Joan.

The trial court ordered Douglas to give Joan the table leaves and paintings within sixty days of the date the judgment in this case becomes final. If he fails to do so, the judgment authorizes Joan to search Germania for those items at a time of her choosing. The court also ordered that Joan be permitted to conduct a search at a time of her choosing, accompanied by a deputy sheriff, for the watch chain and fob. Douglas contends this order invades his privacy.

Louisiana Civil Code article 4 provides that when no rule for a particular situation can be found in legislation or custom, a court is bound to proceed according to equity, resorting to justice, reason, and prevailing usages. A trial court has great discretion in fashioning an equitable remedy, but it may do so only when there is no express law applicable.[4] Douglas admitted at trial that the paintings were hanging on the wall of his home and the table leaves were also in his home. If he defies the judgment and secretes the property, he will be in contempt of court. Because there is a remedy at law if he refuses to deliver the property to Joan within the time set by the court, the trial court committed legal error in fashioning an equitable remedy, and that portion of the judgment must be reversed.

---

[1] Phillips v. Fisher, 93-928, p. 3 (La. App. 3d Cir. 3/2/94), 634 So. 2d 1305, 1307 *writ denied*, 94-0813 (La. 5/6/94), 637 So. 2d 1056.
[2] Id; Sterling v. Estate of Vicknair, 93-594 (La. App. 5th Cir. 1/12/94), 631 So. 2d 463, 464.
[3] Jeanfreau v. Jeanfreau, 182 La. 332, 162 So. 3, 5 (1935).
[4] Wier v. Glassell, 216 La. 828, 44 So. 2d 882 (1950).

The watch chain and fob are a different story, however. Douglas disclaimed knowledge of their whereabouts, but when last seen, they were on their way to Germania in Douglas's pocket. The trial court fashioned an equitable remedy by ordering that Joan be allowed to search the property accompanied by a deputy. These suits have been pending before the trial court for years, and the court appeared thoroughly familiar with the parties involved. The court obviously felt this order was necessary to achieve the objective of returning the watch fob and chain to Joan. This trial court faced an uncommon problem that required an uncommon solution. It did not abuse its discretion.

NOTE AND QUESTION

1. Why does "possession for the convenience of another give[] the possessor neither legal possession nor the right of prescribing"?

2. The uncertainty of the location of McKee's watch fob and chain illustrates the principal problem that the owner of a movable may have recovering it from a possessor: unlike a tract of land or a building, the movable is not likely to remain where the owner left it when another takes possession of it.

SUCCESSION OF WAGNER
993 So. 2d 709 (La. App. 1st Cir. 2008)

GUIDRY, J. These consolidated appeals arise from the successions of a husband and wife who died approximately nine months apart. . . .

Louis and Leila Wagner (the Wagners) were married on April 23, 1937, and had two children, Warren and Faye Wagner. Following Louis Wagner's death on May 22, 2001, Warren filed a petition for probate of his father's last will and testament, which named him as universal legatee and executor of his father's estate. While that succession was still under administration, Leila Wagner died on March 3, 2002. Except for a $100,000.00 bequest to a grandson, Leila left her entire estate to Faye. Subsequently, Faye opened her mother's succession with a petition for probate and was appointed as executrix thereof. The two successions were later consolidated, although the consolidation order specifically provided they would continue to be administered separately. Several issues arose in the proceedings regarding the classification of certain properties as being either community or separate in nature and as to the validity of certain donations made by Louis and Leila to one or the other of their children.

[T]he trial court rendered judgment, dated July 12, 2004, declaring a 1999 donation of gold coins by Louis Wagner to Warren to be a nullity based on the courts findings that the coins were community in nature and Leila Wagner did not consent to the donation. Leila Wagner was recognized as the owner of and sent into possession of one-half of the coins. . . .

By authentic act dated August 27, 1999, Louis Wagner donated to his son, Warren, certain gold coins having a value at that time of approximately $450,000.00. The coins were purchased by Louis Wagner, at Warren's suggestion, in 1997 and 1998. According to Warren's testimony, his father told him he purchased the coins with his separate funds.

Nevertheless, he concealed the donation from his wife and asked Warren to do the same. Warren admitted that he complied with his father's request.

Louisiana Civil Code article 2349 provides that, except for usual and customary gifts, "[t]he donation of community property to a third person requires the concurrence of the spouses ...." Additionally, La. C.C. art. 2353 provides that, when the concurrence of a spouse is required by law, as in the case of true donations, the alienation of community property by one spouse without the consent of the other is relatively null, unless the other spouse has renounced his right to concur [citations omitted]. In this case, it is undisputed that Leila Wagner did not consent to the donation of the gold coins. Nor was there any evidence that she had renounced her right to concur in transactions alienating community property.***

Finally, Warren also maintains he acquired ownership of the gold coins by three-year acquisitive prescription. Under La. C.C. art. 3490, title to movables may be acquired through prescription of three years by a good-faith possessor. To establish three-year acquisitive prescription under article 3490, one must establish: (1) possession as owner for three years; (2) in good faith; (3) under an act sufficient to transfer ownership; and (4) without interruption. The party asserting acquisitive prescription has the burden of proving all facts essential to support it. Moreover, mere physical possession is insufficient.

Warren relies on the authentic act of donation executed by his father to satisfy the requirement of an act sufficient to transfer ownership. He further asserts the good faith requirement was met because he in good faith believed the coins were his father's separate property, since his father said they were purchased with separate funds and listed them as separate property on the gift tax return he filed in connection with the donation. Warren maintains his belief was reasonable since he knew his father had separate assets, having previously inherited a substantial amount of property from his brother. Finally, he contends he has also met the requirement of three years possession, since he has been in continuous possession of the gold coins since the donation occurred in 1999.

In denying Warren's claim of acquisitive prescription, it is clear the trial court concluded the essential element of good faith was absent. The court noted in particular that Warren and his father "actively concealed" the donation of these community assets from Leila Wagner. The court was of the opinion that a fraud had been committed against her regarding the coins and stated that it would not allow "the co-conspirator [Warren] to benefit from his concealment."

A trial court's determination of whether a person acted in good faith is a factual finding which cannot be disturbed in the absence of manifest error [citations omitted]. Under the manifest error standard of review, a district court's reasonable evaluations of credibility and reasonable inferences of fact should not be disturbed on review, even though the court of appeal is convinced that had it been the trier-of-fact, it would have weighed the evidence differently. As the trier-of-fact, a trial court is charged with assessing the credibility of witnesses and, in so doing, is free to accept or reject, in whole or in part, the testimony of any witness. When factual findings are based upon determinations regarding the credibility of witnesses, the manifest error standard demands that great deference be accorded to the trier-of-facts findings [citations omitted].

In the instant case, the trial court rejected Warren's testimony that he in good faith believed the coins were purchased with his father's separate funds. The courts determination is supported by the fact that while purportedly asserting the coins were his separate property, Louis Wagner nevertheless asked Warren not to reveal the donation to his mother. Warren complied with this request and concealed the donation from his mother. Even after his father's death, Warren failed to disclose the donation of the coins until he was compelled to do so by discovery requests in these proceedings. Moreover, since he personally wrote the check, Warren was well aware that at least some of the coins were paid for by a check drawn on a community checking account. In light of these circumstances, we find no manifest error in the trial courts conclusion that Warren lacked good faith. Since good faith is an essential element for acquisitive prescription under article 3490, he failed to establish ownership of the coins by three years' acquisitive prescription.

QUESTION

Suppose the movables in the preceding cases had been taken not by a family member who admitted to having them, but by a thief; can the thief obtain ownership by acquisitive prescription in bad faith if he retains possession for ten years? The case that follows illustrates that problem.

LIEBER v. MOHAWK ARMS, INC.
64 Misc. 2d 206, 314 N.Y.S. 2d 510 (1970)

J. ROBERT LYNCH, J. The defendant moves for summary judgment. The facts are undisputed.

In 1945 the plaintiff, then in the United States Army, was among the first soldiers to occupy Munich, Germany. There he and some companions entered Adolph Hitler's apartment and removed various items of his personal belongings. The plaintiff brought his share home to Louisiana. It included Hitler's uniform jacket and cap and some of his decorations and personal jewelry.

The plaintiff's possession of these articles was publicly known. Louisiana newspapers published stories and pictures about the plaintiff's collection and he was the subject of a feature story in the Louisiana State University Alumni News of October, 1945. There is some indication that the articles were occasionally displayed to the public.

In 1968 the collection was stolen by the plaintiff's chauffeur, who sold it to a New York dealer in historical Americana. The dealer sold it to the defendant who purchased in good faith. Through collectors' circles the plaintiff soon discovered the whereabouts of his stolen property, made a demand for its return that was refused, and commenced this action seeking the return.

The defendant resists and asks summary judgment on the ground that the plaintiff cannot succeed in the suit since he "never obtained good and legal title to this collection," that "the collection properly belongs to the occupational military authority and/or the Bavarian Government."

This defense, title in a third party, was at one time effective ([N.Y.] Code Civ. Pro., § 1723; Civ. Prac. Act, § 1093). But it did not survive the enactment of CPLR 7101 of which provides for the recovery of a chattel by one who has the superior right to possession. (Bulman v. Bulman, 57 Misc 2d 320; see also Practice Commentary, McKinney's Cons. Laws of N. Y., Book 78, CPLR 7101.) In proposing the elimination of this defense, the draftsmen of the CPLR sought to prevent the very thing being attempted by the defendant here....

The question presented by an action to recover a chattel is "whether or not a plaintiff has such title in the cause of action so that a recovery or satisfaction by it will protect the defendant from the claims of third parties" (Bulman v. Bulman, *supra*, p. 321). Applying this test we find that the plaintiff must recover possession of the chattels. The defendant, despite its good faith, has no title since its possession is derived from a thief (Uniform Commercial Code, § 2-403; Bassett v. Spofford, 45 N. Y. 387). The plaintiff's possession prior to the theft and since 1945 is unquestioned. He further benefits from Article 3509 of the Louisiana Civil Code [Revised C.C. art. 3491] which provides that when "the possessor of any movable whatever has possessed it for ten years without interruption, he shall acquire the ownership of it without being obliged to produce a title or to prove that he did not act in bad faith."

The cases cited by the defendant have no applicability to actions to recover a chattel under the Civil Practice Law and Rules. Summary judgment is granted to the plaintiff.

NOTES AND QUESTION

1. The *Lieber* case differs from many cases of movables looted by soldiers during wartime, or stolen in other circumstances, in two ways: the American soldier's possession of the loot was publicized, and the heirs of Hitler showed no interest in recovering it. Consider the following more typical scenario: Alphonse's family owns a tomb in one of New Orleans' famous above-ground cemeteries. In 1988, when theft from these cemeteries was rife, a 19th-century marble statue of an angel that stood in front of the slab opening into the tomb was stolen. Alphonse and his family searched diligently for the statue, but did not locate it until 2008, when it turned up at the estate auction of a well-known New Orleanian's art collection. The decedent's heirs had proof that their ancestor had purchased it from a French Quarter dealer in antiquities. It had stood in the sculpture garden of the decedent's home from 1990 until it was sent to be auctioned with the rest of his collection. Should the interests of Alphonse and his family prevail over the interests of the collector's heirs? Why or why not?

2. In *Keim v. Louisiana Historical Association Confederate War Museum*, 48 F.3d 362 (8th Cir. 1995), the purchaser of a civil war flag brought an action for declaratory judgment that he was the owner of the flag. The museum brought a counterclaim asserting the right to possession of the flag. The United States Court of Appeals for the Eighth Circuit held that the museum's counterclaim was time barred and that the purchaser had acquired ownership by acquisitive prescription. More than sixteen years had passed since the museum learned of the flag's whereabouts and the purchaser had possession of the flag during that time. The court stated that under the law of all three states in which relevant transactions had occurred (Louisiana, Virginia, and Nebraska), the museum's action had prescribed. The court further applied Louisiana law on the acquisitive prescription of movables to find that the purchaser had acquired ownership of the flag.

CHAPTER X. PROTECTION OF OWNERSHIP; REAL ACTIONS

1. PETITORY ACTION
La. Civil Code arts. 526, 530-532

LOUISIANA CODE OF CIVIL PROCEDURE

Art. 3651. Petitory action

The petitory action is one brought by a person who claims the ownership, but who is not in possession, of immovable property or of a real right therein, against another who is in possession or who claims the ownership thereof adversely, to obtain judgment recognizing the plaintiff's ownership.

Art. 3652. Same; parties; venue

A petitory action may be brought by a person who claims the ownership of only an undivided interest in the immovable property or real right therein, or whose asserted ownership is limited to a certain period which has not yet expired, or which may be terminated by an event which has not yet occurred.

A lessee or other person who occupies the immovable property or enjoys the real right therein under an agreement with the person who claims the ownership thereof adversely to the plaintiff may be joined in the action as a defendant.

A petitory action shall be brought in the venue provided by Article 80(1), even when the plaintiff prays for judgment for the fruits and revenues of the property, or for damages.

Art. 3653. Same; Proof of title; immovable

To obtain a judgment recognizing his ownership of immovable property or real right therein, the plaintiff in a petitory action shall:

(1) Prove that he has acquired ownership from a previous owner or by acquisitive prescription, if the court finds that the defendant is in possession thereof; or

(2) Prove a better title thereto than the defendant, if the court finds that the latter is not in possession thereof.

When the titles of the parties are traced to a common author, he is presumed to be the previous owner.

Art. 3654. Proof of title in action for declaratory judgment, concursus, expropriation, or similar proceeding

When the issue of ownership of immovable property or of a real right therein is presented in an action for a declaratory judgment, or in a concursus, expropriation, or similar proceeding, or the issue of the ownership of funds deposited in the registry of the court and which belong to owner of the immovable property or of the real right therein is so presented, the court shall render judgment in favor of the party:

(1) Who would be entitled to the possession of the immovable property or real right therein in a possessory action, unless the adverse party proves that he has acquired ownership from a previous owner or by acquisitive prescription; or

(2) Who proves better title to the immovable property or real right therein, when neither party would be entitled to the possession of the immovable property or real right therein in a possessory action.

NOTE

Article 80(1) has been reorganized since the last revision of art. 3652; the appropriate venue can be found in either art. 80 A. (1) or art. 80 B. of the Louisiana Code of Civil Procedure.

a. Proof of Ownership
La. Civil Code arts. 530-532

1) Ownership Good "Against the World"

See A. N. YIANNOPOULOS, CIVIL LAW PROPERTY
§ 263 (4th ed. 2001)

DESELLE v. BONNETTE
251 So. 2d 68 (La. App. 3d Cir. 1971)

CULPEPPER, J. This is a petitory action. From an adverse judgment, defendant appealed.

Plaintiff alleges in his petition, and defendant admits, that defendant is in possession of the disputed property. The issue is whether plaintiff has sustained his burden under C.C.P. Article 3653(1) to "make out his title" against a defendant in possession.

In dispute is plaintiff's title to a narrow strip of land, approximately 65 feet in width and 600 feet in length. This strip is located between the old and the new routes of the highway which runs generally north and south from Marksville to Hessmer and thence on to Bunkie. The new highway is west of and approximately parallel to the route of the old one.

The plaintiff, James J. Deselle, is the owner of a 12-acre tract of land which fronted on the east side of the old highway, which was abandoned in about 1920. The strip in dispute lies between plaintiff's land and the new highway.

The defendant, Paul D. Bonnette, is the owner of the property on the west side of the new highway, across from the strip in dispute. Defendant contends the strip is included in his title and that he and his ancestors in title have been in possession for many years.

Previous to 1911, the property of plaintiff, the property of defendant and the strip in dispute were part of a 48-arpent tract owned by Alcide A. Chatelain on both sides of the old highway. In 1911, Chatelain sold the 12 acres lying east of the old highway to Marius Deselle, plaintiff's ancestor in title. In 1916, Chatelain sold the 36 acres lying west of the old Marksville-Hessmer highway to Isaac Gauthier, defendant's ancestor in title. When the old highway was abandoned in about 1920, the new highway was located approximately 65 feet west of the previous route. The strip of land between the old and new highways is that which is in dispute.

Plaintiff's chain of title from the common author is as follows:

(1) Sale from Alcide A. Chatelain to Marius Deselles on September 30, 1911 conveying "about 12 arpents, more or less; and being all the lands belonging to vendor on the east side of the public road leading from Marksville to Bunkie."

(2) Act of exchange on September 27, 1926 from Marius Deselles to Wade Deselles conveying "12 arpents and being all the land belonging to the vendor on the east side of the public road leading from Marksville to Bunkie *** being the same acquired by the vendor herein from Alcide A. Chatelain ***" (No mention is made of the fact that the highway location was changed in 1920.)

(3) Sale on February 1, 1945, from Wade J. Deselles to James Deselles conveying an undivided one-half interest in "12 acres, more or less, bounded *** and west by public road, said property having been acquired by vendor during the existence of the community of acquets and gains between him and Lonie McCoy, now deceased, and the other undivided half interest presently belonging to purchaser herein, he having inherited same from the estate of his deceased mother, the said Lonie McCoy."

As shown by plaintiff's above delineated chain of title, Marius Deselle acquired in 1911 only 12 arpents lying east of the old Marksville-Bunkie road, which was abandoned in about 1920. Hence, in the exchange in 1926, Marius Deselle conveyed to Wade Deselle valid title to only the 12 acres lying east of the old abandoned highway and did not convey valid title to any portion of the strip in dispute which lies west of the old abandoned highway.

Since Wade Deselle did not acquire valid title to any portion of the strip in dispute, he could not convey valid title to an undivided one-half interest in the strip to the plaintiff, James Deselle, in the 1945 sale.

As to the undivided one-half interest which plaintiff contends he inherited from his mother, Mrs. Lonie McCoy Deselle, there is no other proof in the record of the title to this interest except the statement in the 1945 deed from Wade Deselle to James Deselle. Under this statement, plaintiff's mother's title was no more extensive than that of his father and did not include the strip in dispute. Hence, there is not sufficient proof that plaintiff has valid title to an undivided one-half interest in the strip through inheritance from his mother.

C.C.P. Article 3653 [1960] provides:

"To obtain a judgment recognizing his ownership of the immovable property or real right, the plaintiff in a petitory action shall:

"(1) Make out his title thereto, if the court finds that the defendant is in possession thereof; or

"(2) Prove a better title thereto than the defendant, if the court finds that the latter is not in possession thereof."

Comment (a) under Article 3653 states that the words "make out his title" are taken from Article 44 of the Code of Practice, and are intended to have the same meaning as given to them under the jurisprudence interpreting the source provision. Jurisprudence under Code of Practice Articles 43 and 44 establishes the rule that in a petitory action against a defendant in possession the plaintiff must make out his title to the property claimed and must recover upon the strength of his own title and not upon the weakness of the defendant possessor's, Blevins v. Manufacturer's Record Publishing Co., 235 La. 708, 105 So. 2d 392 (1957) and the cases cited therein. Furthermore, in such an action defendant's title is not at issue until plaintiff has proved an apparent valid title in himself, Albritton v. Childers, 225 La. 900, 74 So. 2d 156[.] Where both plaintiff and defendant trace their titles to a common author, plaintiff is not required to prove his title beyond the common author, Gaylord Container Corp. v. Stilley, 79 So. 2d 109 (La. App., 1st Cir. 1955) and the cases cited therein.

Applying C.C.P. Article 3653 and the cited jurisprudence to the present case, it is obvious that plaintiff has not proved a valid title under the chain of conveyances delineated above. Furthermore, plaintiff does not seek to establish ownership by acquisitive prescription. Hence, it is clear that plaintiff has not proved a valid title as against the defendant who is in possession.

The district judge recognized that plaintiff did not prove a valid title back to the common author. However, he held that under the facts of the present case the plaintiff need only establish a better title than the defendant. In so holding, the court relied on cases decided before the adoption of the new Code of Civil Procedure in 1960[; these cases] held that if the defendant in a petitory action has possession without a title translative of ownership, the plaintiff need only establish a better title than defendant, Kernan v. Baham, 45 La.Ann. 799, 13 So. 155 (1893); In re St. Vincent de Paul Benevolent Association of New Orleans, 175 So. 140 (Orl.App. 1937)[.]

Applying this jurisprudence to the present case, the district court held that the defendant, Paul Bonnette, had no title translative of ownership since his 1943 deed of acquisition from J. Ledoux Bonnette described the property as "located on the Marksville-Hessmer blacktopped highway, and containing 36 acres, more or less, and described as being bounded *** east by said highway leading from Marksville to Hessmer ***" The district court reasoned that since the old highway, abandoned in 1920, was never blacktopped, the highway referred to is necessarily the new highway which is blacktopped, and therefore defendant's title does not cover any portion of the strip in dispute located east of the new highway route. The district judge then went on to hold that since plaintiff's deed of acquisition from Wade Deselle in 1945 did cover the strip in question and defendant's 1943 deed of acquisition did not, plaintiff had a better title than defendant.

Although the district judge's position is respectable, it is our view that the jurisprudence on which be relies has been legislatively overruled by the new Code of Civil Procedure[.] C.C.P. Articles 3651-3653 are new and make important procedural changes in the real actions which existed under the prior Code of Practice and the jurisprudence.

Under Article 43 of the Code of Practice, it was required that the petitory action be brought "against the person who is in the actual possession of the immovable." Jurisprudence developed the "action to establish title" where neither plaintiff nor defendant were in possession, and there was a conflict in the cases as to whether plaintiff's burden in such an action was to prove a valid title or simply to prove a better title than defendant. The Code of Civil Procedure broadens the petitory action to include both the prior petitory action and the action to establish title. Under Article 3651 the petitory action is brought "by a person who claims the ownership, but who is not in possession, of immovable property or of a real right, against another who is in possession or who claims the ownership thereof adversely."

Under the Code of Civil Procedure, defendant's possession, or lack of it, determines the burden of proof imposed on the plaintiff in a petitory action. Article 3653 provides that if the defendant is in possession plaintiff must "make out his title," but if the defendant is not in possession the plaintiff need prove only a better title than the defendant. The relevant possession is defined in Article 3660 as "corporeal possession *** or civil possession *** preceded by corporeal possession." No distinction is made between the situation where defendant possesses without a title translative of ownership and the situation where the defendant possesses with such a title. Hence, it is our view that the prior jurisprudence making this distinction, and on which the trial judge relied, is no longer a part of our law.

Of course, comment (a) under Article 3653 indicates that the words "make out his title" are intended to have the same meaning as given to them under the jurisprudence interpreting the source provision. But, apparently, the redactors were thinking of the mainstream of jurisprudence rather than of technical exceptions. Be that as it may, the comment is not a part of the text and cannot be taken to establish exceptions when the text establishes none. From the viewpoint of policy considerations, there might be some merit to the idea that a person with a defective title ought to prevail over a possessor who has no title at all. But if such an exception were allowed to prevail in the light of the text of Article 3653(1), which is clear and unambiguous, a chaotic situation would arise. The burden of proof would no longer be allocated in the light of the defendant's possession as Article 3653(1) and (2) requires.

Having concluded that plaintiff's petitory action must be dismissed, we do not reach the question of defendant's title. Our jurisprudence is established that in a petitory action against a defendant in possession the title of the defendant is not at issue until plaintiff has proved a valid title in himself, Dupuy v. Shannon, 136 So. 2d 111 (3d Cir. 1961) and the authorities cited therein. For the reasons assigned, the judgment appealed is reversed and set aside....

PURE OIL COMPANY v. SKINNER
294 So. 2d 797 (La. 1974)

BARHAM, J. We granted writs (285 So. 2d 541 (La. 1973)) to review the decision of the Court of Appeal on the issue of a plaintiff's burden of proof in a real action when defendant is the possessor of the property in controversy. Defendants, the relators in these cases, contended in their writ applications that the decisions of the Court of Appeal (284 So. 2d 608, 284 So. 2d 614 (La. App. 2d Cir. 1973)) conflict with that of the Third Circuit in Deselle v. Bonnette, 251 So. 2d 68 (La. App. 3d Cir. 1971), wherein it was held that in a petitory action against a defendant in possession, a plaintiff must make out his title to the property in dispute without regard to the title of the party in possession.

The Court of Appeal in the instant cases held that respondents, the parties claiming title or ownership of the disputed land against adverse claimants in possession without a deed translative of title, did not have to prove a title good against the world but only had to prove better title than relators.

The issues in the instant cases were first presented for consideration in 1961 when The Pure Oil Company, which had oil, gas and mineral leases covering the disputed property from both claimants, instituted a concursus proceeding by depositing royalties attributable to the property in controversy in the registry of the court and citing both relators and respondents to assert their respective interests. Subsequent to the institution of the concursus proceedings, respondents instituted a boundary action against the relators and, by stipulation, the parties agreed that judgment rendered in the concursus proceedings would be determinative of the issues in the boundary action.

The one and one-half acres tract of land, the ownership of which is the subject of the controversy, is claimed under two chains of title. It was established in the lower courts to their satisfaction, and to ours, that neither respondents nor relators have valid record title to the property in dispute.

Code of Civil Procedure Article 3654 provides:

"When the issue of ownership of immovable property or of a real right is presented in an action for a declaratory judgment, or in a concursus, expropriation, or similar proceeding, or the issue of the ownership of funds deposited in the registry of the court and which belong to the owner of the immovable property or of the real right is so presented, the court shall render judgment in favor of the party:

(1) Who would be entitled to the possession of the immovable property or real right in a possessory action, unless the adverse party makes out his title thereto; or

(2) Who proves better title to the immovable property or real right, when neither party would be entitled to the possession of the immovable property or real right in a possessory action."

The record in this case establishes, and it is undisputed, that the relators have possessed the property in question since 1947. Therefore it is clear that the burden of proof placed on respondents is greater than that provided in Code of Civil Procedure Article 3654(2), the burden of proving a better title. The statutory imposition of a higher burden of proof than simply proving better title when an adverse claimant is in possession of disputed land leads to the inevitable conclusion that respondents' burden was to "make out his title thereto." In other words, respondents were required to prove valid record title, to show title good against the world without regard to the title of the party in possession. C.C.P. Arts. 3653, 3654. See 2 A. Yiannopoulos, Louisiana Civil Law Treatise, § 137 (1967); 35 Tul. L. Rev. 541, at 547 (1961). This respondents have failed to do. The record reveals that there is a 16-year break in the title of the respondents from 1858, when an entry by Charles M. Cawthoon from the United States Government is recorded, to 1874, when conveyance of the subject property from Jeremiah Payne to Elizabeth J. Colvin was recorded.

Upon oral argument, in response to an inquiry by the Court, respondents contended that they had established acquisition of prescriptive title to the property in dispute prior to 1947, when relators entered into possession of the tract in dispute. The state of the record, however, does not support this contention of respondents and there is no holding by the lower courts to this effect. Respondents, therefore, have not established either valid record title or prescriptive title to the property in dispute.

Hutton v. Adkins, 186 So. 908 (La. App. 2d Cir. 1939), the case relied upon by the Court of Appeal for the holding that relators were required only to prove better title than respondent who was in possession without a deed translative of title, is hereby overruled.***

SUMMERS, J. (dissenting). The only fault, if it can be considered such, in the chain of title asserted by the Skinners is a missing link between the original entry from the United States Government by Charles M. Cawthoon in 1858 and a deed from Jeremiah Payne to Elizabeth J. Colvin in February 1874, a period of sixteen years....

After 1874 the links in the Skinner chain of title are complete. Their ownership was never brought into question until the Simontons enclosed the disputed one and one-half acres in 1947....

[T]he majority is ... in error when it imposes upon the Skinners, plaintiffs in a petitory action, who are out of possession, claiming title as against the Simontons who are possessors without title, the obligation *"to prove a valid record title, to show title good against the world without regard to the title of the party in possession."* Under this stringent requirement the majority has held that the break in the chain of the Skinner title from 1858 to 1874 denies them the title requisite to maintain their petitory action.

The requirements of proof of title imposed upon a plaintiff in a petitory action were not changed by the enactment of Article 3654 of the Code of Civil Procedure. Under that article the possessor is entitled to be maintained in possession unless the adverse party "makes out his title" to the immovable or real right in question. Article 3653 (1) of the Code of Civil Procedure utilizes the identical language....

As the comments to Article 3653 make clear,

"When the defendant is in possession, this article makes no change in the law. The words 'make out his title' are taken from Art. 44 of the Code of Practice, and are intended to have the same meaning as given to them under the jurisprudence interpreting the source provision." ***

To impose the requirement of a title perfect against the whole world, when no better title is asserted to oppose the plaintiff's title in a petitory action, is virtually to require the impossible in some cases, as this case illustrates. Undoubtedly no complete chain of title can be established by the Skinners, for the deeds needed to complete the chain between 1858 and 1874 were lost. In many instances, as we all know, court houses have burned and the deeds needed to complete chains of title are nonexistent. The invalidity of the Skinner title upon which the majority relies is the sixteen-year break in the chain between 1858 and 1874. Otherwise the title is in all respects good and valid. In my view the Skinners have not only made out an "apparently valid" title, they have established a good, valid and perfect title against every title opposed to it.

To permit a possessor to occupy one's property for more than a year, and then compel the owner to came forth with a complete chain of title, perfect in all respects, to oust the possessor is entirely unsupported by the statutes or decisions of this Court. Such a rule is certain to create many problems seriously impairing stability of titles in this State. I respectfully dissent.

NOTES AND QUESTIONS

1. *Procedural terminology*: A *concursus* proceeding is one in which someone who does not claim a thing in his possession, but who is uncertain as to which of multiple claimants has a right to it, brings in the various claimants in order to have the court determine to whom the thing should be delivered. It is similar to the common law proceeding of interpleader. The *relator* is the party at whose behest a writ is issued, in this case the appellant; and the *respondent* is the party who contends against an appeal, the appellee in this case.

2. In his dissent in *Pure Oil*, Justice Summers protested that the amended article was not intended to change the burden of proof imposed on the plaintiff in a petitory action against a defendant in possession. He quoted the comment to the article, which stated "this article makes no change in the law." What was the *Deselle* court's response to that argument in the prior case?

3. The confusion sparked by the 1960 Code of Civil Procedure's retention of the phrase "make out his title" for the plaintiff's burden of proof in a petitory action against one in possession was quelled not only by the *Pure Oil* opinion, but by a revision of those articles in 1981, as the case after the following note explains.

NOTE
The Publician Action

Suppose that Alphonse pays Gaston $20,000 for Arpent Noir, believing him to be its owner. Gaston does not, in fact, have good title to the tract. After Alphonse has farmed Arpent Noir for seven years, he is called to active duty by the Louisiana National Guard and deployed with his unit in Iraq. He returns from an 18-month tour of duty in Iraq to find that Beatrice has usurped Arpent Noir. She has no semblance of a title to the tract; she is a squatter. However, she has possessed it corporeally for over a year.

Under present Louisiana law, Alphonse has no mechanism for recovering possession of Arpent Noir from Beatrice. While he had been possessor of Arpent Noir with the right to possess, he has now been ousted by Beatrice. She is now the possessor of Arpent Noir with the right to possess—and thus the right to be maintained in possession if Alphonse should bring the possessory action against her in court.

The petitory action would likewise be of no avail to Alphonse, since he does not satisfy the requirements of either method of acquiring ownership of the tract: by transfer of title from an author who could demonstrate an unbroken chain of title back to the sovereign, or by acquisitive prescription of either ten or thirty years. Alphonse would be in the same position if he had bought from anyone whose chain of title contained a gap, however small, resulting from whatever cause; a gap caused by the condition of the public records, occupying a few years in a two-hundred-year-old title, would defeat his claim of ownership. He could not prove his ownership by title, and would not have enough time in possession to establish ownership by acquisitive prescription. He faces what medieval European lawyers called the *probatio diabolica*[1] (the devil's proof) for its notorious difficulty: proof of ownership, accomplished either by "an unbroken chain of transfers from the owner or by acquisitive prescription."[2]

The inequity of treating Alphonse's claim to Arpent Noir as inferior to Beatrice's despite his years of work on the tract was not lost on the ancient Romans whose property law is the ancestor of Louisiana's. The Roman praetor Publicius created the *actio Publiciana*, probably in the first century B.C.E., as a remedy.[3] The Publician action permitted a former possessor who had been in the process of acquiring ownership through acquisitive prescription to maintain an action for ownership against a mere squatter.[4] The action protected these possessors, both those who acquired from the owner of the tract but who could not prove their ownership because of some defect, and good faith possessors who acquired under just title from a non-owner. It did so by dispensing them from the requirement of the full passage of time in

[1] A.N. YIANNOPOULOS, PROPERTY: THINGS—REAL RIGHTS—REAL ACTIONS, Louisiana Civil Law Property Series vol. 2, § 256 (4 ed. 2001).
[2] Id.
[3] Id.
[4] See Susan Talley Rodwig, *Symposium: Louisiana Property Law Revision: The Civil Code Articles on the Protection of Ownership*, 55 TUL. L. REV. 192, 216 (1980).

order to maintain their claims against an adverse claimant. In effect, under the Publician action, Alphonse would be treated by the court as having completed the time-in-possession requirements for acquisitive prescription in his action against Beatrice.[5] The modern Greek civil code offers this protection to one who was in the process of attaining ownership through acquisitive prescription "against a later possessor 'without lawful or putative title.'... [T]he Greek Publician action extends the protection of ownership to a nonowner."[6] France also included a remedy similar to the Publician action in its modern code, protecting as owner a plaintiff without valid title, but with a prior possession that is "legally preferable" to the possession of the defendant.[7]

In Louisiana during the nineteenth and most of the twentieth century, the courts interpreted the proof required of a plaintiff with title who could not prove ownership by an unbroken chain of title originating with the true owner, and in the process of prescribing, in a manner that protected him from a possessing squatter. Relying on the French jurist Pothier,[8] courts imposed two different types of proof, their choice depending on the position of the defendant. Against a defendant with a title, the plaintiff had to prove ownership by an unbroken chain of title or by an acquisitive prescription that met all the Code requirements. If, however, the defendant whose later possession had ousted the plaintiff was a squatter who had no title, the plaintiff was merely required to demonstrate *better* title than the defendant. Thus, defects in the plaintiff's title could be overlooked, avoiding the need for him to complete acquisitive prescription. This position was not abandoned until the two cases above, *Deselle v. Bonnette* and *Pure Oil Co. v. Skinner,* decided in the early 1970s. The following commentary illuminates the problematic policy underlying that abandonment:

Douglas Nichols, *Comment: The Publician Action*,
69 TUL. L. REV. 217, 240-243 (1994)

C. Should Louisiana Reinstate the Publician Action?

The injustice of *Pure Oil Co.* shows the *probation diabolica* at work in Louisiana. Nevertheless, Louisiana courts have followed *Pure Oil Co.,* although often reluctantly and critically. If a Publician action is to be restored to Louisiana, it is through the legislature that the reform should come.

D. Vigilantibus Iura Succurrunt

The Publician action is favored by our visceral reaction to the apparent wrongfulness of the trespasser's actions. The trespasser is depicted as someone who opportunistically preys upon defects in another's title, rather than asserting a better claim of his own. However, an

---

[5] See Douglas Nichols, *Comment: The Publician Action*, 69 TUL. L. REV. 217, 224-235 (1994).
[6] Id. at 237.
[7] Yiannopoulos, op. cit. at sec. 257.
[8] In a seminal 1835 case, the Louisiana Supreme Court cited Pothier to the effect "that although regularly the action of revendication can be maintained only by the owner, it may sometimes be maintained by one who is not the real owner, but was in the way of becoming so, when he lost the possession. For he who was in possession in good faith, in virtue of a just title, and lost the possession before the period required for prescription, can recover it in a petitory action, from one who is in possession without title." Nichols, op. cit. at 238, quoting Bedford v. Urquhart, 8 La. 241, 246 (1835).

equally visceral argument can be based on the plaintiff's slothfulness. The plaintiff's disregard for his own affairs permits a trespasser to gain a foothold on the property. Civilians capture this argument with the maxim: laws come to the aid of the watchful.

In fact, civilians should be familiar with the *vigilantibus iura succurrunt* argument; they have seen it in the context of acquisitive prescription. Acquisitive prescription has been criticized for despoiling an owner of his property. This invasion of the right of ownership traditionally has been justified by the owner's long neglect of his affairs. We lack sympathy for the former owner because prescription accrues only after the passage of decades.

While ownership is lost only by extreme neglect, the right to possess is lost after only one year. Any culpability for losing the right to possess is trivial in comparison. Moreover, under the current state of the law, loss of possession amounts to loss of ownership for plaintiffs with breaks in their title, no matter how ancient the defect. In no other area of the civil law can ownership be lost so quickly.

Thus, the relative rapidity with which the right to possess can be lost limits the capacity of the *vigilantibus iura succurrunt* argument to taint the Publician plaintiff. In contrast, the defendant of the Publician action is identical to a person who ordinarily would acquire ownership by prescription only after the passage of thirty years. Therefore, the *vigilantibus iura succurrunt* argument of acquisitive prescription can be applied by analogy to the Publician defendant.

The defendant of the Publician action lacks just title to the property. In the context of prescription, acquisition of ownership by this person has been criticized as sanctioning the actions of a spoliator. Without just title, however, this person only acquires ownership after the passage of thirty years. The passage of such a long period of time, in essence, redeems the spoliator in our eyes. The Publician defendant would require the same redemption.

It might be counted against the Publician action that it could be used to evict a defendant who has possessed the disputed property for twenty-nine years. This result appears, and is, very harsh. However, the result is consistent with the principles of acquisitive prescription, which do not grant ownership to a possessor without just title in twenty-nine years. Under the current state of the law, the spoliator may gain a sort of ownership in only one year because of the *robation diabolica*. The Publician action restores harmony to the law.

2. Proposed Louisiana Publician Action

The Publician action, like acquisitive prescription, is a mechanism for stabilizing title. It cures lost records and allocates ownership where it intuitively lies. Prior to *Pure Oil Co.*, Louisiana courts unknowingly captured the Publician action in the *Bedford* rule. Because of its eloquence and efficiency, the *Bedford* rule is used as the basis for the proposed revision to Civil Code Article 531, which would restore the Publician action to Louisiana.

Art. 531 (PROPOSED). Proof of ownership of immovable

> *One who claims ownership of an immovable against another in possession must prove that he has acquired ownership from a previous owner or by acquisitive prescription. One who had possession of an immovable in good faith and under just title shall prevail against a possessor who has no title. If neither*

party is in possession, he need only prove better title.

V. CONCLUSION

The Publican action is a modern legal construct rooted in the study of Roman law. The Publican action is used in France and Greece to permit one who first possessed immovable property in good faith and under just title to prevail in a revendicatory action against a trespasser, despite defects in the plaintiff's title.

By adopting the proposed revision to Civil Code Article 531, the legislature would restore the Publician action to Louisiana and reinvigorate an old but auspicious line of Louisiana jurisprudence. The achievement of Louisiana courts before *Pure Oil Co.* should not be underestimated. These courts developed a rule of law that captured the principles of the Publician action in language more eloquent than that of Roman-law scholars.***

In the process of revising Chapter 4 of Book II, "Protection of Ownership," Professor A.N. Yiannopoulos proposed a revision of article 531, which Nichols reproduced in the passage included above.[9] Such a revision would have relieved Alphonse, the ousted possessor, of the *probatio diabolica* by legislatively overruling *Pure Oil*. Professor Yiannopoulos' suggestion was not accepted by the Council of the Louisiana Law Institute for inclusion in the revision that was sent to the legislature. As a result, the present Code preserves the outcome of *Pure Oil*. Thus Alphonse, if he could not prove a perfect chain of title, is left with no recourse in the courts against Beatrice, even though her title to the property is not merely inferior to his, but non-existent.

WEAVER v. HAILEY
416 So. 2d 311 (La. App. 3d Cir. 1982)

CULPEPPER, J. This is a petitory action. The plaintiff, L. C. Weaver, claims ownership by record title of one acre of land of which defendants, the Haileys, are in possession. The Haileys filed an answer alleging ownership by the acquisitive prescriptions of 30 years and 10 years of the 40 acres in which plaintiff alleges the one acre in dispute is located. But defendants prayed only that plaintiff's demands be rejected. They did not file a reconventional demand for recognition of their ownership. The district judge recognized the Haileys as the owners of the 40 acres less and except the one acre in dispute, and he recognized the plaintiff, L. C. Weaver, as owner of the one acre. The defendants appealed.

The substantial issues are: (1) Did the plaintiff sustain his burden of proving ownership by record title to the one acre in dispute? (2) Since defendants have not prayed for recognition of their ownership by acquisitive prescription and have not filed a reconventional demand, is the issue of their ownership before us? (3) If the issue of defendants' ownership is before us, have they proved acquisitive prescription of 10 years as to the one acre in dispute?

---

[9] Nichols, op. cit., text accompanying footnote 186. Nichols "[a]dapted [it] with only a slight change to harmonize the proposed sentence with the surrounding text." Id. at fn. 186.

The first issue is whether the plaintiff in this petitory action against defendants in possession sustained his burden of proving ownership by record title. This is the first case to reach the appellate courts since the adoption, effective January 1, 1980, of the following articles of our Civil Code on Protection of Ownership:

Art. 531. Proof of ownership of immovable

One who claims the ownership of an immovable against another in possession must prove that he has acquired ownership from a previous owner or by acquisitive prescription. If neither party is in possession, he need only prove a better title.

Art. 532. Common author

When the titles of the parties are traced to a common author, he is presumed to be the previous owner.

C.C.P. Article 3653 (1), referred to in Comment (b) under Civil Code Article 531 above, was amended by Act No. 256 of 1981 as follows:

Art. 3653. Same; proof of title; Immovable

To obtain a judgment recognizing his ownership of immovable property or real right therein, the plaintiff in a petitory action shall:

(1) Prove that he has acquired ownership from a previous owner or by acquisitive prescription, if the court finds that the defendant is in possession thereof; or

(2) Prove a better title thereto than the defendant, if the court finds that the latter is not in possession thereof.

When the titles of the parties are traced to a common author, he is presumed to be the previous owner.

Before the 1979 amendments to the Civil Code and the 1981 amendment to the Code of Civil Procedure, as set out above, it is clear the controlling jurisprudential rule was that stated in Pure Oil Company v. Skinner, 294 So. 2d 797 (La. 1974), i.e., that the plaintiff in a petitory action against a defendant in possession must prove ownership good against the world regardless of defendant's lack of title. Under that rule, the plaintiff in the present case has not sustained his burden of proving title good against the world. He has deraigned his title only back to the 1946 sale from Robert Richard to H. L. Weaver. He has not deraigned his title back to the sovereign, nor has he proved title back to a common author, nor has he proved ownership by acquisitive prescription.

The only question is whether the legislature intended to overrule Pure Oil v. Skinner, *supra*, when it adopted Civil Code Articles 531 and 532 in 1979 and amended Code of Civil Procedure Article 3653 (1) in 1981. We have no difficulty in concluding that the legislature did not intend to overrule Pure Oil Company v. Skinner.

An understanding of the legislative intent in making these changes begins with the difference between the words "ownership" and "title." Ownership is defined in the Civil Code as follows:

Art. 477. Ownership; content

Ownership is the right that confers on a person direct, immediate, and exclusive authority over a thing. The owner of a thing may use, enjoy, and dispose of it within the limits and under the conditions established by law.

The word "title" is not defined in our Codes. It is used in different senses. A. N. Yiannopoulos, Louisiana Civil Law Treatise, Vol. 2, Property, 2d ed., Section 192, at page 518 discusses C.C. Article 531 as revised in 1979 and explains the different uses of the word "title":

"The first sentence of Article 531 of the Louisiana Civil Code has the same meaning as Article 3653(1) of the Louisiana Code of Civil Procedure which declares that the plaintiff in the petitory action, in order to recover, must "make out his title", if the court finds that the defendant is in possession of the immovable property or of the real right. The word "title" is used in Louisiana legislation and jurisprudence in at least three different senses. It may mean an act translative of ownership, such as a sale, donation, or exchange; it may mean an instrument evidencing ownership or another real right, such as a partition or a judgment; or it may simply mean ownership of a thing or a valid claim to a real right other than ownership. Thus, an act of sale or an act establishing a predial servitude is a title; a judgment recognizing one's ownership or other real right is likewise a title; and the owner of a thing or a person entitled to a real right has title to the thing or to the real right. It is apparent that the word "title" in Article 3653(1) of the Louisiana Code of Civil Procedure means ownership or a valid claim to a real right other than ownership. A plaintiff in a petitory action thus "makes out his title" when he proves his ownership of the immovable property or that he is entitled to the real right he claims."

***In 1974, the Louisiana Supreme Court in Pure Oil Company v. Skinner, *supra*, decided that the word "title" in C.C.P. Article 3653 (1) meant "ownership." The court held that the plaintiff in a petitory action against a defendant in possession was required to prove a perfect record title back to the sovereign, since he had not proved ownership by acquisitive prescription. No common author was involved. The only missing link in the plaintiff's record title was between the years 1858 and 1874. Chief Justice Summers wrote a strong dissent, joined by Justice Marcus, in which he took the position that the redactors of the Code of Civil Procedure of 1960, and in particular Henry G. McMahon, did not intend the word "title" to mean "ownership." Nevertheless, the majority in Pure Oil v. Skinner held to the contrary.

Following Pure Oil Company v. Skinner, *supra*, a question arose in the Courts of Appeal as to whether the common author rule was still viable. Clayton v. Langston, 311 So. 2d 74 (La. App. 3d Cir. 1975) held that where both plaintiff and defendant in a petitory action traced their record titles to a common ancestor, this satisfied the Pure Oil v. Skinner requirement of proof of title "good against the world." Tenneco Oil Company v. Houston, 372 So. 2d 1194 (La. App. 2d Cir. 1979), affirmed on other grounds, 372 So. 2d 1194 (La. 1979), held to the contrary that proof of title back to a common author did not satisfy Pure Oil Company v. Skinner. It became clear that legislation was needed to solve the common author problem, and to make it clear that the word "title" in C.C Article 3653 (1) actually meant "ownership."

From this explanation, it is clear that when the legislature adopted in 1979 Civil Code Article 531, requiring that the plaintiff in a petitory action against a defendant in possession must prove that he has acquired "ownership from a previous owner," it intended to retain the rule in Pure Oil Company v. Skinner, not overrule it. The intent was to require that such a plaintiff prove he had acquired "ownership from a previous owner," i.e., an owner who had a perfect record title back to the sovereign, or ownership by acquisitive prescription. Article 532 solved the common author problem, by stating that "when the titles of the parties are traced to a common author, he is presumed to be the previous owner."

If there was any doubt as to the legislative intent in adopting Articles 531 and 532 in 1979, such doubt was put to rest when the legislature followed by adopting in 1981 the amendment to Code of Civil Procedure Article 3653 (1), which removed the troublesome clause "make out his title," and inserted instead the provision that the plaintiff must "prove that he has acquired ownership from a previous owner or by acquisitive prescription." This amendment to the Code of Civil Procedure was necessary to conform to the new Civil Code Articles 531 and 532.

Our conclusion as to the intent of the legislature is supported by A. N. Yiannopoulos, Louisiana Civil Law Treatise, Vol. 2, Property, 2d. ed., Section 192 at page 517:

> *Defendant in possession; proof of ownership.* Article 531 of the Louisiana Civil Code, as revised in 1979, declares: "One who claims the ownership of an immovable against another in possession must prove that he has acquired ownership from a previous owner or by acquisitive prescription. If neither party is in possession, he need only prove a better title." This provision is new but does not change the law. It is directly applicable to claims of ownership of immovables, and, by analogy, to claims of other real rights in immovable property.

Ownership of immovable property may be acquired either by an unbroken chain of transfers from a previous owner or by acquisitive prescription of ten or thirty years. A real right other than ownership may be acquired by virtue of a grant from the owner of the immovable burdened by the right, by a valid chain of transfers from a person who acquired such a real right, or by acquisitive prescription. In a sense, proof of acquisition of ownership or other real right in one of these manners establishes a title good against the world.

Also supporting our view is the Comment, 55 Tul. L. Rev. 192 (1980).

We are aware that the Comments under Civil Code Articles 531 and 532, adopted in 1979, did not appear in Act No. 180 of 1979, are not part of the articles, and were added pursuant to the joint rules of the senate and house of representatives. Nevertheless, we find these comments correctly imply the intent of the legislature was to retain the rule in Pure Oil Company v. Skinner, *supra*, not to legislatively overrule it.

Having reached this conclusion, it is clear that in the present case the plaintiff has not sustained his burden of proving ownership.

DEFENDANTS' FAILURE TO PRAY OR FILE A RECONVENTIONAL DEMAND FOR RECOGNITION OF OWNERSHIP

As stated above, the defendants filed an answer alleging ownership by 10 years acquisitive prescription, but they prayed only that plaintiff's suit be dismissed. Moreover, they did not file a reconventional demand. There is a procedural problem as to whether we can recognize defendants' ownership, even if they have proved it. In Clayton v. Langston, 311 So. 2d 74 (La. App. 3d Cir. 1975), we decided in a similar case that under C.C.P. Article 862 we could render judgment granting "the relief to which the party in whose favor it is rendered is entitled, even if the party has not demanded such relief in his pleadings and the latter contained no prayer for general and equitable relief." Under the authority of Clayton v. Langston, we could render judgment in the present case recognizing defendants' ownership of the one acre in dispute if they have proved it.

Defendants' Proof of Ownership by Ten Years Acquisitive Prescription

*** In the present case the defendants were in the required good faith. Mr. and Mrs. Lee Roy Halley believed they were acquiring ownership of the property described in their deed from Mallett in 1953. Since they were in good faith at the time of their purchase of the property, it is of no consequence that they subsequently learned H. L. Weaver claimed one acre.

There is a serious question as to whether condition #2 of Article 3479 is satisfied. The title, i.e., the act of sale, by which Mr. and Mrs. Lee Roy Halley acquired in

1953 describes the property as the "SW/4 of the SW/4 of Section 26, Township 12 North, Range 7 West, less one acre, being 39 acres, more or less." The question is whether the act of sale transfers the one acre excepted. The trial judge reasoned that since Mr. Lynn Weaver testified the SW/4 of the SW/4 of said Section 26 is a regular section containing approximately 40 acres, the sale of the 40 acres "less one acre, being 39 acres, more or less" did not convey the one acre in dispute. ***

We also note that there is a serious question as to whether the one acre in dispute could be described with sufficient certainty to render judgment recognizing defendants as owners thereof. There is no survey in the record showing that the fence is located on the boundary lines of the SW/4 of the SW/4 of said Section 26 and along the west side of the Ashland-Creston highway. Thus, there may be a question as to whether the one acre in dispute, as described in plaintiff's petition, is actually located inside defendants' fence around their 32 acres.

As to that portion of the trial court judgment which recognizes the defendants as the owners of 39 acres, we note that the 39 acres is not in dispute, and its ownership should not be adjudicated in these proceedings.

DECREE

For the reasons assigned, the judgment appealed is reversed and set aside. It is now ordered, adjudged and decreed that judgment be rendered herein in favor of defendants and against the plaintiff dismissing plaintiff's suit. All costs in the trial and appellate courts are assessed against the plaintiff-appellee.

NOTES AND QUESTIONS

1. *Procedural terminology*: A *reconventional demand* is the device by which a defendant, rather than simply defending himself against the plaintiff's claim, requests something further from the court. In this case, had the Haileys gone beyond attacking the plaintiff's claim of ownership to request recognition of their ownership of the acre in dispute, or damages, or both, that plea would have constituted a reconventional demand. It is analogous to a counterclaim in common law. To *deraign one's title* is to vindicate or prove it.

2. The Third Circuit, consistently with its prior jurisprudence, determines that it has the power to find that the Haileys have ownership, even though they have not pleaded it, provided that the Haileys had proven their ownership in the course of the case. What is lacking in the Haileys' proof of ownership?

3. Fact pleading and its consequences: The label by which a litigant characterizes an action in his pleadings does not bind the courts will treat it that way, or limit the remedies available. The Weaver court declared that, had the evidence of location of the disputed acre been clear, La. C. Civ. Pro. 862, quoted in the case, gave the court the power to render judgment for the defendants recognizing their ownership, even though they had demanded neither such relief nor general and equitable relief. This principle results from Louisiana's adoption of "fact pleading" in La. C. Civ.

Pro. 854, which begins "No technical forms of pleading are required." In Reynolds v. Brown, 84 So.3d 655 (La. App. 5 Cir. 2011), the appellate court upheld a trial court ruling that the plaintiff, who had filed a possessory action, was in her facts claiming ownership rather than possession. Therefore her suit was a petitory action. Because she had failed to prove all of the elements necessary to succeed in a petitory action, her claim for the removal from the lot she purported to own of a trailer and its attached structure, both belonging to her uncle, was denied. In affirming, the appellate court explained:

> Louisiana is a fact pleading state that values substance over form and does not require the use of magic titles or terminology as a threshold requirement for validly pleading an action. Courts should look through the caption of pleadings in order to ascertain their substance and to do substantial justice to the parties. The trial court has a duty to recognize the true nature of the pleadings. Because our civil procedure is based on fact pleading...the courts must look to the facts alleged to discover what, if any, relief is available to the parties.

Accord, Rodessa Oil and Land Co. v. Perkins, 104 So.3d 52 (La. App. 2 Cir. 2012): In that case, the plaintiff originally filed a boundary action; the defendant responded with a possessory action. The plaintiff then converted that action to a petitory action under La. C. Civ. Pro. 3651, admitting the defendant's possession. Plaintiff then filed for, and was granted, a summary judgment below, on the basis that it had a title and that defendant had not asserted ownership of the disputed land. The court of appeal reversed that judgment. Though the defendant did not use the specific term "acquisitive prescription" in his answers to petitions, he had asserted facts—over 30 years of possession with boundaries--that tended to support a claim of ownership acquired by prescription. Thus, a disputed issue of material fact precluded summary judgment.

BAKER v. ROMERO
55 So. 3d 1035 (La. App. 3d Cir. 2011)

KEATY, J. Plaintiff, Lyn Baker, appeals a judgment dismissing her petitory action against Defendants, Rogerist Romero and Carol Romero, and granting their possessory action on the basis that Baker did not meet her burden of proof regarding her claim of ownership of the subject immovable property while the Romeros established as a matter of law their right to possess the property. For the following reasons, we affirm.

FACTS AND PROCEDURAL HISTORY

According to a Cash Sale Deed (the Deed) recorded on July 26, 2006, Baker acquired the "right, title and interest" in a forty-foot strip of property located in the Toledo Bend Reservoir in Sabine Parish (the Property) from six of her relatives for the purchase price of $10. Shortly thereafter, Baker, through her attorney, mailed a certified letter to the Romeros, owners of land adjacent and contiguous to the Property, to inform them that she had recently acquired the Property and would be having it surveyed in the near future. This litigation ensued after the Romeros would not allow the surveyor hired by Baker to have access to the portions of the Property contained within the land that they owned. [After Baker commenced litigation against the Romeros, they reconvened, asserting that they and their ancestors in title had possession for more than a year, and that they were title owners of the disputed tracts of land. However, they permitted Baker to have the land surveyed. After the survey, Baker moved for summary judgment, which the trial court denied. Baker then amended her petition, requesting recognition of her ownership of the disputed tracts, using the survey as evidence that the land was in her title.]

A bench trial took place on Baker's petitory action. . . . In a written judgment, the trial court found that:

1. Plaintiff did not meet her burden of proof to establish ownership of the subject immovable property as a matter of law,

2. Defendants have been in statutory possession of the subject property since 1988, and

3. Plaintiff's Motion for Summary Judgment promptly and properly converted Defendants' possessory action pleaded in their Reconventional Demand to a viable and justiciable petitory action.

Accordingly, judgment was rendered in favor of the Romeros and against Baker dismissing her petitory action. The Romeros' possessory action was granted because the trial court found that they had established as a matter of law the right to possess the Property.

Baker timely filed a motion for new trial wherein she argued that due to the Romeros' last minute abandonment of their claims of ownership of the Property, her burden of proof changed from that of proving better title than that of the Romeros to proving title good against the world. As a result, she requested that the case be re-opened to allow her to introduce additional documentary evidence in order to meet her newly heightened burden of proof.

Following a hearing, the trial court granted Baker's motion for new trial. The matter was retried. . . .

In a written judgment signed on July 19, 2010, the trial court found that Baker did not meet her burden of proof regarding her claim of ownership of the Property as a matter of law. As a result, the trial court affirmed the prior judgment rendered on August 18, 2009; rendered judgment in favor of the Romeros and against Baker, dismissing Baker's petitory action; granted the Romeros' possessory action on the basis that they had established their right to possess the Property as a matter of law; and ordered that costs be equally divided between the parties.

Baker is now before this court on appeal, asserting the following assignments of error. First, Baker claims that the trial court erred in failing to make the Romeros the plaintiffs in the petitory action concerning the Property by virtue of their answer and reconventional demand wherein they pled possession and ownership of the Property.

Plaintiff further claims that the Romeros' possession claims were waived upon their making a claim of ownership. Accordingly, Baker submits that the trial court should have granted her motion for summary judgment when the Romeros failed to present any proof of title in opposition to her motion. Second, Baker asserts that although she should not have had to bear the burden of proof in the petitory action, she did establish her title in an unbroken chain back to Wyatt Speight, a man whom the same trial court declared to be the judicial owner of the same land in 1919. Thus, according to Baker, the trial court did not have to apply the harsh evidentiary standard set forth in Pure Oil Co. v. Skinner, 294 So.2d 797 (La. 1974). Instead, the trial court should have applied the supreme court's holding in Badeaux v. Pitre, 382 So.2d 954 (La. 1980) and held that Baker met her burden of proof because she established title that was apparently good. Third, Baker contends that even if she was the proper plaintiff in the petitory action and the *Pure Oil* standard was properly applied, the trial court incorrectly read *Pure Oil* to include "a requirement that every title chain in a petitory action trace itself to a government transaction." Had the trial court correctly applied *Pure Oil*, Baker argues, she would have been entitled to a declaration of her ownership of the Property because she proved better title to the Property than the Romeros, who admittedly have no title to it.

DISCUSSION

Louisiana Code of Civil Procedure Article 3651 defines a petitory action as "one brought by a person who claims the ownership, but who is not in possession, of immovable property or of a real right therein, against another who is in possession or who claims the ownership thereof adversely, to obtain judgment recognizing the plaintiff's ownership." Thereafter, La. Code Civ.P. art. 3653 provides that:

> To obtain a judgment recognizing his ownership of immovable property or real right therein, the plaintiff in a petitory action shall:
>
> (1) Prove that he has acquired ownership from a previous owner or by acquisitive prescription, if the court finds that the defendant is in possession thereof; or
>
> (2) Prove a better title thereto than the defendant, if the court finds that the latter is not in possession thereof.
>
> When the titles of the parties are traced to a common author, he is presumed to be the previous owner.

On the other hand, the code of civil procedure defines a possessory action as "one brought by the possessor of immovable property or of a real right therein to be maintained in his possession of the property or enjoyment of the right when he has been disturbed, or to be restored to the possession or enjoyment thereof when he has been evicted." La. Code Civ. P. art. 3655. "In the possessory action, the ownership of title of the parties to the immovable property or real right therein is not at issue." La. Code Civ. P. art. 3661.

Fortunately, the Louisiana Code of Civil Procedure contains provisions to govern situations where the parties involved in a matter concerning the ownership of or real rights to immovable property alter their positions during the course of litigation involving the property. Louisiana Code of Civil Procedure Article 3657 provides, in pertinent part, that:

> The plaintiff may not cumulate the petitory and the possessory actions in the same suit or plead them in the alternative, and when he does so he waives the possessory action. If the plaintiff brings the possessory action, and without dismissing it and prior to judgment therein institutes the petitory action, the possessory action is abated.

> When, except as provided in Article 3661(1)-(3), the defendant in a possessory action asserts title in himself, in the alternative or otherwise, he thereby converts the suit into a petitory action, and judicially confesses the possession of the plaintiff in the possessory action.

In Pure Oil, 294 So.2d 797, the issue concerned the plaintiff's burden of proof in a petitory action when the defendant is in possession of the property in controversy. The supreme court held that those claiming title or ownership of disputed land in the possession of others are "required to prove valid record title, to show title good against the world without regard to the title of the party in possession. C.C.P. Arts. 3653, 3654." *Id.* at 799.

Badeaux, 382 So.2d 954, likewise involved a petitory action brought by a claimed owner of a tract of land against a person possessing the land; however, the defendant was found to have been a precarious possessor in that he possessed the land not on his own behalf but rather on behalf of and with the permission of another. *See* La. Civ. Code art. 3437. That being the case, the supreme court held that the plaintiff had met his burden of proof in his petitory action by proving that he had acquired the tract of land by thirty-year acquisitive prescription. *Id.* In doing so, the supreme court noted:

> Although it be true that the plaintiff in a petitory action, must succeed on the strength of his own title, and not on the weakness of his adversary's, yet, when the latter has no title at all, he cannot, as a trespasser, take advantage of any defect in the former's muniments of title. In such cases, a title apparently good, is all that is required to maintain the petitory action." Zeringue v. Williams[,] 15 La. Ann. 76 [(La. 1860)].

Id. at 956.

ASSIGNMENT OF ERROR NUMBER ONE

Baker contends that the trial court erred in failing to make the Romeros the plaintiffs in the petitory action after they asserted possession and ownership of the Property in their answer and reconventional demand. In addition, she insists that the Romeros' possession claims were waived pursuant to La. Code Civ.P. art. 3657 when they made a claim of ownership of the Property. The Romeros counter that after the Property was surveyed, they acknowledged that they no longer had a claim of ownership and instead were claiming possession of the Property. Moreover, the Romeros claim that because Baker did not assert in the trial court that they should have been the plaintiffs in the petitory action, she should be precluded from asserting that argument for the first time on appeal.

In their answer and reconventional demand, the Romeros assert that they are the title owners of ten tracts of land and that they and their ancestors in title have possessed the Property for well over one year without interruption. Their prayer for relief requests that judgment be rendered recognizing their right to possession of the Property. Moreover, the Romeros stipulated at the June 19, 2009 hearing that they did not have title to the Property and were instead alleging good faith possession of the Property.

Ultimately, the Romeros did not claim ownership of the Property and thus did not waive their possession claims. In addition, because Baker did not allege in the trial court that the burden of proof in the petitory action should have shifted to the Romeros, she cannot make that argument for the first time on appeal. *See* Uniform Rules--Courts of Appeal, Rule 1-3; Guilbeaux v. Times of Acadiana, Inc., 94-1270 (La. App. 3d Cir. 8/9/95), 661 So. 2d 1027, writ denied, 95-2942 (La. 3/29/96), 670 So.2d 1238. The trial court was correct in not making the Romeros the plaintiffs in the petitory action. Baker's first assignment of error lacks merit.

ASSIGNMENT OF ERROR NUMBER TWO

Baker next contends that the trial court erred in applying the *Pure Oil* standard and requiring that she prove title good against the world. She argues that the trial court should have instead applied the La. Code Civ. P. art. 3657 standard and simply required that she prove title better than that of the Romeros, as was done in Badeaux, 382 So.2d 954, a supreme court decision rendered after *Pure Oil*. The Romeros insist that the trial court properly and appropriately applied the *Pure Oil* standard and that *Badeaux* is not applicable to this matter. In support of their argument, they rely on Aymond v. Smith, 476 So.2d 1081, 1084 (La. App. 3d Cir. 1985), wherein this court held that:

> When the defendant in the petitory action . . . is in possession, the plaintiff in the petitory action . . . must rely on the strength of his own title and not the weakness of that of his adversary, and the title of the defendant in the petitory action is not at issue until the plaintiff has proved valid title in himself.

Aymond, which was decided by this court eleven years after the supreme court handed down the Pure Oil decision and four years after it handed down the Badeaux decision, began as a possessory action brought by a plaintiff who claimed that the defendant had disturbed his possession of a one acre tract of land. In answer to the petition, the defendant denied the plaintiff's possession, claiming that he owned the land through title or thirty-year acquisitive prescription. We noted that, in claiming ownership of the disputed property, the defendant converted the possessory action into a petitory action in which he became the plaintiff with the burden of proving "ownership either by an unbroken chain of valid transfers from the sovereign or an ancestor in title common with the defendant or by acquisitive prescription." *Id.* (citations omitted). We further noted that "[i]f the plaintiff in the petitory action should fail and be unable to make out his title good against the world, his demands must be rejected and his case dismissed even if the defendant in the petitory action has no title to the property." *Id.* at 1084 [citations omitted].

Considering our prior decision in Aymond, we cannot conclude that the trial court erred in requiring Baker to prove title good against the world. Moreover, we agree that Baker's reliance on Badeaux is misplaced given the fact that the defendant in that petitory action was a precarious possessor who possessed the disputed property with the permission of its owner. Here, Mr. Romero testified that when he purchased the tract of land in 1987, he believed that he was getting all of the property within certain boundaries; there were no markers around the forty-foot strip, *i.e.*, the Property now at the center of this litigation. Mr. Romero further testified that no one had ever given him any indication that they owned the Property until he got the letter from Baker in 2006 seeking to survey the Property which she claimed to have recently purchased. Baker's second assignment of error is without merit.

ASSIGNMENT OF ERROR NUMBER THREE

Finally, Baker asserts that even if she was the proper plaintiff in the petitory action and Pure Oil was properly applied, the trial court erred by reading into it a requirement that her title chain be traceable to a government transaction. The Romeros counter that the trial court properly applied the law of Pure Oil and Aymond and correctly held that the July 8, 1885 sheriff's tax sale deed upon which Baker relied was "not a transfer of title 'with a sovereign grant as its origin.'"

In dismissing Baker's petitory action and granting the Romeros' possessory action on the basis that they established their right to possess the Property, the trial court, referring to the burden established in Pure Oil, noted the Latin phrase "Dura Lex, Sed Lex" which means "the law is harsh, but it is the law." Nevertheless, the trial court recognized that although it had been heavily criticized, Pure Oil remained the law of this state and it was "duty-bound to apply it." Citing Aymond, the trial court reasoned that "[a] tax sale bespeaks prior private ownership, thus the evidentiary destination to a sovereign grant, the originating transfer upon which all title to the tract is founded, has not been reached."

The trial court went on to state:

>   Ownership back to a common ancestor in title, another route to prove
> ownership, does not apply here as Defendants claimed only possession of the
> subject tract, thus no possibility of a common author. The remaining
> alternative to prove ownership, acquisitive prescription, was neither pleaded
> nor argued and the court is prohibited from doing so sua sponte. La. Civ.
> Code art. 3452.

...We are convinced that the trial court properly applied the law to this matter and that
Baker simply failed to meet the requisite burden of proof. Baker's final assignment of
error lacks merit.

DECREE

For the foregoing reasons, the judgment of the trial court is affirmed in entirety. All
costs of this appeal are assessed against the plaintiff, Lyn Baker. Affirmed.

2) Proving Better Title

a) Neither Party in Possession

KELSO v. LANGE
421 So. 2d 973 (La. App. 3d Cir. 1982);
cert. denied 426 So. 2d 174 (La. 1983)

STOKER, J. This is a petitory action in which neither plaintiffs nor defendants are
in possession. The trial court held that the plaintiffs "established the best claim to
the property, and that judgment should be rendered declaring them to be the owners of
the property in question." From a judgment to that effect the defendants appealed.
We reverse.

The property consists of approximately 164.65 acres of low marsh land located in
the Rapides Parish, Louisiana....

The property was acquired by one George Y. Kelso on August 5, 1876, from Robert
P. Hunter through an act of cash sale which is recorded in Rapides Parish, Louisiana.
This George Y. Kelso's marital status is not set forth in the act of sale.
Plaintiffs and defendants both claim the property through persons bearing the name
George Y. Kelso. This case presents a unique issue because neither set of parties can
trace a record title to the George Y. Kelso who purchased the property. Neither set can
establish ownership by prescription. The facts show that in all likelihood the property

has never been occupied and has perhaps never been possessed in the legal sense, at least for any appreciable period of time.

The plaintiffs are descended from a George Y. Kelso who married Felonese Kelso on April 20, 1887. Defendants claim through a George Y. Kelso who married Mar[ie] L. Baillio on November 10, 1869....

The plaintiffs, descendants of Felonese Kelso and the George Y. Kelso she married, either reside in Rapides Parish or show origins and close family connections in Rapides Parish. Some of the plaintiffs testified. The defendants are all located out of Louisiana and none of them testified. In fact, the defendants produced no testimonial proof and relied solely on documentary evidence.

The George Y. Kelso who married Felonese Kelso died in 1901 and her husband died in 1914. Marie L. Kelso died in 1921 and her husband died in 1900. The plaintiff-descendants of Felonese Kelso deny any knowledge of the existence of a George Y. Kelso who was married to Marie L. Baillio until just prior their bringing of this petitory action. The thing which sparked the action was the discovery by plaintiffs that the public records contained certain transactions and succession proceedings in which defendants or their ancestors (actual or in title) figure and which affected the 164 acres of property which is the subject of the litigation.

Plaintiffs have had minimum contact with the property and there is no evidence that defendants have ever had any physical contact with the property. The indifference to the property in previous years may possibly by explained by the fact that the land is marsh land completely enclosed by other lands owned by others, and there is no ready access to it. Moreover, the property is split by Bayou Boeuf, a major drainage stream which flows diagonally across the property.

From a factual standpoint the general facts of the case are as follows:

1. In 1876 an unidentified George Y. Kelso bought the property through a recorded act of sale.

2. After the 1876 purchase there is no recorded act translative of title (ownership) of the property out of the unidentified George Y. Kelso.

3. Neither of the parties can prove ownership through prescription. Although the defendants claim 30 years acquisitive prescription, there is no evidence of corporeal possession such as would begin prescription.

4. Both sets of parties claim their alleged ancestor in title is the George Y. Kelso who purchased in 1876, but there is no concrete evidence to support the claim of either party.

5. Plaintiffs deny any kinship with the Kelso who is the ancestor of the defendant set of Kelsos. There is no evidence or suggestion that the two George Y. Kelsos of plaintiffs

and defendants were ever married twice.

6. The Succession of George Y. and Felonese Kelso does not dispose of nor mention the property but the Succession of Marie A. Mitchell, the starting point of defendants' title, does purport to dispose of the property. An affidavit in the succession alleges that Marie A. Mitchell was a daughter of George Y. Kelso and Marie L. Kelso.

7. George Robert Kelso, Jr., the grandson of George Y. Kelso of the plaintiffs, testified that in the middle 1940's he helped Irion LaFargue, a surveyor, survey the property while his father, George Robert Kelso, was present. The elder George Robert Kelso was a petitioner in the Succession of the George Y. Kelso who married Felonese. Such a survey was in fact made on August 19, 1944.

8. The elder George Robert Kelso paid the taxes on the property several times, according to George Robert Kelso, Jr.'s testimony, but stopped when told someone else was paying them.

9. Mr. Kirby Joseph Gleason, a son-in-law of the plaintiffs' George Y. Kelso, testified that his wife attempted to pay taxes but was prevented on one occasion after being informed that someone else was paying them.

10. Mrs. Katie Kelso Swift testified that her father told her that her grandfather, who was George Y. Kelso of the plaintiffs, said he bought the property in question.

11. It was stipulated at trial that since 1920 tax notices on the property were sent to persons in the defendants' family.

12. Several acts which encumbered or alienated the property were introduced by the Marie Kelso group which indicates that they have regarded the property as their own: a timber sale dated June 16, 1916; a mineral lease dated May 3, 1922; the January 3, 1951, judgment in the Succession of Marie A. Mitchell, daughter of Marie Kelso, which devolved upon Patricia Nichley, Marie Mitchell's daughter, a one-half interest in the land; a September 6, 1957, sale by Patricia Nichley to Constance L. Lange of 5/8 interest in the land; a September 3, 1968, right-of-way grant from Constance Lange to Rapides Parish.

THE BURDEN OF PROOF

This is a petitory action where neither party claims to be or is in possession and the burden of proof in such an action is set forth in Civil Code article 531 which reads as follows:

Art. 531. Proof of ownership of immovable

One who claims the ownership of an immovable against another in possession must prove that he has acquired ownership from a previous owner or by acquisitive prescription. If neither party is in possession, he need only prove a better title.

And Code of Civil Procedure article 3653, which reads as follows:

> Art. 3653. Same; proof of title; Immovable
>
> To obtain a judgment recognizing his ownership of immovable property or real right therein, the plaintiff in a petitory action shall:
>
> (1) Prove that he has acquired ownership from a previous owner or by acquisitive prescription, if the court finds that the defendant is in possession thereof; or
>
> (2) Prove a better title thereto than the defendant, if the court finds that the latter is not in possession thereof.
>
> When the titles of the parties are traced to a common author, he is presumed to be the previous owner.

The trial court decided this case in favor of the plaintiffs, the Felonese Kelso group, on the basis of finding that they had "established the best *claim* to the property in question." (Emphasis supplied.) As noted in the codal articles quoted above, the burden of proof which plaintiffs bore at the trial of this case was to prove a *better title* to the property than that of the defendants. Hence, the first thing which plaintiffs must have proven was that they have a title.

As recently noted by Judge Culpepper of this court in *Weaver v. Hailey*, ... the word "title" is not defined in our codes. That case did not deal with a petitory action in which neither party was in possession of the property in dispute. Therefore, the case was governed by the 1979 adoption of Civil Code articles 531 and 532 and the 1981 amendment of Code of Procedure article 3653. In their present form, where the defendant is in possession, these articles refer to "ownership" rather than "title". In *Weaver v. Hailey*, it was concluded that "title" was equivalent to "ownership". If the same meaning is applied in the case before us, in which neither party is in possession, it would result in construing the burden of plaintiffs as proving "better ownership". Such a theoretical concept would appear to us to be somewhat strained or obscure. Therefore, we think it was significant that the Legislature retained the word "title" in providing for the contingency of both parties in a petitory action being out of possession whereas it focused on the word "ownership" in providing for the contingency of the defendants being in possession.

PLAINTIFFS FAILED TO ESTABLISH IDENTITY WITH 1876 GEORGE Y. KELSO VENDEE

Although we mention the conceptual difficulties discussed above, such discussion provides little aid in our resolution of this case. Whether we focus on "title" or "ownership," our inquiry is the same. The last record title holder is that George Y. Kelso who purchased the property on August 5, 1876, whose marital status was not mentioned and whose act of sale is on record in the records of Rapides Parish. The practical burden of plaintiffs is to establish an identity between that George Y. Kelso and the George Y. Kelso who married Felonese Kelso, from which union they descended. There is no evidence of such an identity.

Presumably, the George Y. Kelso who bought the property in 1876 is deceased. If plaintiffs could show that fact and also that they are descendants of that George Y. Kelso, they would be in a position to seek a judgment of possession evidencing their *ownership* of the property in question. Aside from such opposition as they might draw in such a proceeding from the present defendants, plaintiffs are unable to establish any identity between their ancestor George Y. Kelso and the 1876 vendee George Y. Kelso.

All that plaintiffs have shown is a tradition among some family members to the effect that their biological ancestor named George Y. Kelso had at some time purchased the property. They have not proved this ancestor and the 1876 vendee, George Y. Kelso, are one and the same.

The plaintiffs not only have no record title to the property in question, they have not proved ownership through inheritance from the 1876 vendee, George Y. Kelso. They have not produced any evidence to show that their biological ancestor, George Y. Kelso, ever treated the property as his. They have not shown, for instance, that he used it, paid taxes on it, or left any records pertaining to it. Most damaging to plaintiffs is the fact that those of his descendants who handled the succession of the biological ancestor failed to list the property in his succession.

For the foregoing reasons, we conclude that plaintiffs have not proved any title to the property, much less a better title than any title defendants may have. Defendants have not shown any act translative of title out of the 1876 vendee, George Y. Kelso. Likewise, they have not shown ownership through proof of identity between the 1876 vendee, George Y. Kelso, and the person of the same name who married Marie L. Kelso. Defendants did not reconvene and request that they be declared owners of the property. On the state of evidence, we are not disposed to consider this question even in the absence of a prayer for such relief, as was done in *Weaver v. Hailey*, supra, following *Clayton v. Langston*, 311 So. 2d 74 (La. App. 3d Cir. 1975). Nevertheless, defendants' evidence is considered as evidence adverse to plaintiffs' case. This is not to say that defendants should prevail over plaintiffs and we make no pronouncement on that question. What we do say is that it is a fact to be considered against plaintiffs that there appears to have been at least one other George Y. Kelso whose descendants have seen fit, as early as 1916, to treat the property as their own.

For all we know there may have been three George Y. Kelsos. Conceivably, the 1876 vendee of the property was not biologically related to plaintiffs or the Kelsos in the defendant line.

For the foregoing reasons, the judgment of the trial court is reversed and judgment is now rendered in favor of defendants and appellants rejecting the demands of plaintiffs and appellees. The costs of court, including the costs of this appeal, are assessed to plaintiffs-appellees.

NOTES AND QUESTIONS

1. What sort of evidence, according to the *Kelso* case, is insufficient for a plaintiff to establish *better* title than that of a defendant out of possession? What sort of evidence did the court indicate would have satisfied it?

2. If the plaintiff decided to establish the right to possess the property, and began using it to do so, could the defendant force him to leave?

3. This case is unusual in that the court has no evidence before it that the disputed tract of land has ever been possessed by anyone. Notice that the defendants did not file a reconventional demand asking for recognition of their title. What facts in the record recounted by the Court suggest starting points for the defendants to investigate if they want to prove that they have better title to the property in a petitory action?

b) Common Ancestor in Title

GRIFFIN v. DAIGLE
769 So. 2d 720 (La. App. 1st Cir. 2000)

PARRO, J. In this petitory action, Charles E. Griffin, II, appeals a trial court judgment declaring that the title to his property extends only to the center of the "public road," being Morris Road. We reverse, render, and remand.

FACTUAL AND PROCEDURAL BACKGROUND

This case involves a dispute over the meaning of the words "public road" in a 1941 partition document, in which property formerly owned by Green D. Spillman was divided by his heirs into five lots. Both parties in this lawsuit trace their titles to the disputed properties to this partition document, which described the boundaries of the partitioned properties with reference to the "public road" lying between and alongside them. The parties stipulated that the "public road" that is the source of the controversy was reworked and renamed between 1932 and 1935. The new name is Morris Road, and it generally tracks the roadbed of the former road, which was known as the

New Hope-Whitaker Springs Road. In the area involved in this dispute, Morris Road lies somewhat west of the former roadbed. The current location of Morris Road was in place and used as a public road when the partition agreement was executed and filed of record in 1941....

The title to the portion of Griffin's property at issue can be traced to a tract on the west side of the road in Section 55. This tract became (Lot One) in the 1941 partition and became the property of Leslie R. Spillman. The partition document describes this property, in pertinent part, as "thirteen acres, more or less, and bounded on the North by Highway No. 258, and by lands of Leslie R. Spillman, on the East by the Public Road, on the South by lands of Charles Griffin [the plaintiff's grandfather], and on the West by State Highway No. 258."***

The controversy involves the small stretch of "public road" forming the boundary between the southern portion of Lot One on the west side of the road and the northern portion of Lot Two across from it on the east side of the road. In 1998 the defendants, Donald Hugh and Geraldine Bourgeois Daigle, purchased property on the east side of the road .... The title to the portion of their property at issue is traced back to Lot Two of the partition, which in that document became the property of Llewelyn Spillman. A survey performed in connection with this purchase depicts the centerline of the old public road as the Daigles' western property line where their property... lies across the road from the property Griffin acquired from his grandfather. However, according to this survey, the Daigles' western property line does not continue to track the old public road north of the section road. Rather, the line shifts about thirty feet due west... and proceeds northward along the centerline of the present public road. The present public road, Morris Road, lies to the west of the old road at this point. Therefore, the portion of the Daigles' property located between the centerline of the old road and the centerline of the new road encroaches on property claimed by Griffin under his title traced back to Lot One. The recordation of this survey and transfer document to the Daigles is the first documented indication that ownership of property between the two roads is claimed by the Daigles or their ancestors in title.

Griffin bought the Lot One property and a small one-acre parcel just north of it in 1985. The property description for this purchase shows his property is bordered on the east by the "public road (New Hope-Whitaker)." The clarifying parenthetical first appeared in Griffin's chain of title in 1955, when Leslie R. Spillman sold the property he had received in the partition to his brother. In that document, the property is described, in pertinent part, as:

> largely triangular in shape more particularly described as bounded: North by State Highway 258; South by C. E. Griffin; East by Public Road (New Hope-Whittaker); West by State Highway 258, containing Fourteen (14) acres, more or less, being a portion of the Green Davis Spillman property acquired by Vendor from the Estate of the Former.

The reference to the New Hope-Whitaker Springs Road is included in all subsequent conveyances in Griffin's chain of title. Based on this description, Griffin claims his property extends to the centerline of the old roadbed, the New Hope-Whitaker Springs Road, rather than to the centerline of the present public road, which is Morris Road. On a survey recorded by Griffin in March 1998, the eastern boundary of his property is shown as the centerline of the old public road. When Griffin became aware of the Daigle purchase in November 1998 and the survey upon which their property description was based, he took the steps that ultimately culminated in this lawsuit.

Griffin's suit asked for a declaratory judgment in his favor declaring him the true and lawful owner of the property described in the petition, amending the Daigles' purchase document to clarify that the western boundary of their property is the centerline of the old road, and enjoining any further acts that might constitute a cloud on his title or a trespass on his property. ...[At the trial court level, Griffin agreed to a stipulation, and the lower court entered judgment, that this case was to be regarded as a petitory action.][1]

APPLICABLE LAW

The petitory action is one brought by a person who claims the ownership, but who is not in possession, of immovable property, against another who is in possession or who claims the ownership thereof adversely, to obtain judgment recognizing the plaintiff's ownership. To obtain a judgment recognizing his ownership of immovable property, the plaintiff in a petitory action must: (1) prove that he acquired ownership from a previous owner or by acquisitive prescription, if the court finds that the defendant is in possession of the property; or (2) prove a better title thereto than the defendant, if the court finds that the latter is not in possession thereof. Therefore, the first issue that must be determined in a petitory action is the question of current possession. The defendant's possession, or lack of it, determines the burden of proof imposed on the plaintiff. See LSA-C.C.P. art. 3651, Official Revision Comments (a). When the titles of the parties are traced to a common author, he is presumed to be the previous owner. LSA-C.C.P. art. 3653; LSA-C.C. arts. 531 and 532.

The possession required to put the more onerous burden on the plaintiff is the same possession required to initiate the possessory action or to establish acquisitive prescription. LSA-C.C.P. art. 3660. ...

ANALYSIS

... As required by the statutes and developed by the jurisprudence, the burden of proof on Griffin depends on whether or not the Daigles were in possession of the property. The trial court did not address that issue at all. In fact, it does not appear from the court's reasons for judgment that it actually utilized the substantive and procedural law pertaining to petitory actions. Yet it is clear from Griffin's petition and from the stipulated judgment that this case does fall within the parameters of such an action. Under this circumstance, we find legal error in the trial court's judgment. Having found manifest error and legal error, this court must conduct a de novo review of the record.

The first step in that review is to examine the seminal issue of whether the Daigles were in possession of the property at issue. Mr. Daigle testified that he simply assumed the western boundary of the property he purchased extended to Morris Road. He had looked at that portion of the property and noticed an old fence with what appeared to be a drainage area between the fence and Morris Road. He did not do anything on the property at issue.

Helen Spillman Miller, who sold the property to the Daigles, stated that years ago when she was growing up there, she had regularly crossed the disputed area to get to her father's garden at the back of the property. However, Ms. Miller said she had moved away after World War II and did not return to the area until 1991. She also testified that after Griffin bought the property across the road in 1985, members of her family continued to cross that area for access to her property; in particular, her sons used it when they hunted there. However, when Ms. Miller identified the gap in the fence from a photograph, it appeared that the spot she had identified as the access path was not within the disputed portion of the property. Rather, it was located at a spot further south where the old roadbed and new roadbed coincided. Therefore, this area of passage was not within the disputed portion. Ms. Miller also said that in 1994, some timber was harvested on her property and the logging truck pushed through the old fence and took the lumber out through the disputed area. Griffin confronted her about this situation when it occurred and asked her to sign a servitude agreement. She did not sign it, but instead re-installed fencing along the old fence line. She located a gate for access to her property south of the disputed portion, where the property touches Morris Road.

Her son, Andrew Miller, said there was a crossing in the disputed area that he and his brother used to go to the back of the property .... They had used this as a right-of-way about a dozen to two dozen times, the last time about two years before the trial. However, after the logging truck pushed through that area, his mother re-fenced it along the old fence line; they then accessed the property through the gate on Morris Road.

Ms. Miller's brother, W. D. Spillman, also testified. He said he advised his sister not to sign the servitude agreement, because she, not Griffin, owned that property. Neither he nor his sister put up any posted signs, and he did not recall seeing the ones Griffin had put up in the disputed area. Mr. Spillman acknowledged that an old fence on his sister's property was behind the old road and had been there for as long as he could remember. He said there was no room to erect a fence along the new roadbed. Mr. Spillman described the old roadbed as looking more like a ditch, with trees and bushes growing up in the middle of it. However, for some time there had been an entrance that the Spillman family used to go back and forth across the disputed property to get to the back of their property. This entrance did not drain well, so the gate was installed at its present location on Morris Road. He said his sister's property became overgrown every year and he would burn it off all the way to the edge of Morris Road. Mr. Spillman admitted that Griffin complained to him about this several times, because Griffin did not want any burning on the portion he claimed to own. About eight years earlier, the fire had spread to an old barn and Mr. Spillman had pushed the remnants and debris into the old roadbed. Griffin also complained to him about this, and Mr. Spillman recalled that his response was, "Well, Charles, I didn't push it but half way, but the property isn't yours to start with."

Griffin testified that he was upset by the trespass on his property in 1994 when the logging truck cut through the fence.... Other than the logging truck incident, he knew of no acts of possession by the Spillmans or Millers. Griffin said he did not want his property burned because it looked bad and because he had planted some cypress, walnut, and oak trees in the old roadbed. When the old barn burned, Mr. Spillman pushed it only as far as his half of the old roadbed. Griffin said the gap [used as a passageway] described by Mr. Spillman and the Millers was not in the area in dispute, which was bounded alongside the old roadbed for its entire length by an old wire fence. In March 1998, Griffin recorded a survey clearly showing the old roadbed as the eastern boundary of his property.

From the facts presented, we are unable to conclude that the Daigles had possession of the property in dispute. It is clear that the Daigles' predecessors possessed the property up to the fence line, which was east of and alongside the old roadbed. Although a party with a just title who possesses a portion of his property is presumed to possess to the full extent of the area specifically described in his title, it is the extent of the Daigles' title that is at issue here. It is because the area between the two roadbeds is not specifically described that this case is before us. Therefore, this presumption does not assist in establishing the Daigles' or their predecessors' possession of the disputed property. Furthermore, it is not clear from the testimony of Mr. Spillman or the Millers that their sporadic entrance through property beyond the fence line fell within the area that is actually in dispute in this case, rather than at a point south of the disputed property. Mr. Spillman's burning of the fields that sometimes encroached on the disputed area seems less an intentional act of ownership than an unintentional failure to control the burning. Indeed, his statement that he only pushed the burned barn debris "half way" into the old roadbed supports an inference that he recognized Griffin claimed ownership of the other half of the roadbed, even if he did not agree with that claim. Certainly since 1985, when Griffin bought his property, he has consistently challenged anyone else's attempts to use or possess that area. It is obvious that no one else had the full enjoyment of the disputed property, because every time anyone attempted to do anything there, Griffin interfered. Ultimately, a disturbance in law occurred some months before the Daigles bought the property, when Griffin filed the survey that clearly depicted his claim to ownership of the disputed area. Therefore we find the evidence of possession by the Daigles and their predecessors was insufficient to establish that they had continuous, uninterrupted, peaceable, public, and unequivocal possession of the disputed area.

Because we conclude the Daigles have not shown they are in possession of the property, Griffin bears the burden of proving better title to the disputed area. ("Better title") is a slippery concept. A commentator has remarked:

> The difficulty in defining an expression as nebulous as better title has proven almost insurmountable. No definition can fully account for the infinite variety of factual situations that arise when parties attempt to trace titles from records that date from over one hundred years ago and that often prove inaccurate.

Camille B. Poche, Comment, *Better Title: An Examination of the Burden of Proof in Louisiana Petitory Actions*, 67 Tul. L. Rev. 511, 540 (1992).

In some cases in which title is traced back to a common author, the courts have concluded that the more ancient title is the better title. *See* LSA-C.C. art. 532, Revision Comments--1979, comment (a); *Williamson v. Kelly*, 520 So. 2d 868, 872 (La. App. 3d Cir. 1987), *writ denied*, 522 So. 2d 562 (La. 1988). However, in the case we are reviewing, the common author was the estate of Green D. Spillman, and the transfer to both parties' ancestors in title occurred simultaneously in the act of partition. Therefore, this case cannot be resolved by reference to that principle. In other cases, the term "better title" has been applied when neither party has a perfect title, but the property description in one title is more precise than that of the other. *See Gore v. Ronaldson*, 200 So. 2d 46 (La. App. 1st Cir.), *writ denied*, 251 La. 68, 203 So. 2d 87 (1967); *Tinney v. Lauve*, 280 So. 2d 588 (La. App. 4th Cir. 1973). However, in this case the dispute arises because of the use of a single term in both chains of title--the "public road." Therefore one title in this case is no more precise than the other. Yet another general rule is that where there are differences between the textual description of the property conveyed and the description shown on a plat of survey, the plat of survey will control and govern the conveyance. *Gore*, 200 So. 2d at 51; *Hayward v. Noel*, 225 So. 2d 638 (La. App. 1st Cir.), *writ refused*, 254 La. 857, 227 So. 2d 595 (1969). However, this general rule has no application when the map or plat is not prepared as a survey of the property and possesses none of the dignity or attributes or indicia of accuracy generally identified or associated with a survey of property. *Gore*, 200 So. 2d at 51. Therefore, this rule also provides little guidance in our case, because the map attached to the partition is a rough sketch with a fair degree of accuracy, but not precise enough to answer the question of which "public road" was meant in the partition.

The cardinal rule to be followed in construing a title document that is uncertain because of ambiguity is to ascertain the intention of the parties from the entire language of the document. The intentions of the parties must be gathered from an inspection of the instrument itself, without the aid of extrinsic evidence, if possible. If the description is so ambiguous as to leave doubt as to the parties' intent, the court may resort to extrinsic evidence as an aid in construction. *Williams v. Hawthorne*, 601 So. 2d 672, 676 (La. App. 2d Cir. 1992). Looking first at the partition document itself, there is little to assist in determining the intent of the parties. As noted, there is only one line drawn on the map attached to the partition document, and only one "public road" is mentioned in the document. Yet, we know that two roads, one old and one new, existed when this document was executed. Therefore, we must look to extrinsic evidence as an aid in construction.

We note first that the documentary evidence establishes that the major portion of the "public road" referenced in the partition document had to be the old road, because this was an existing boundary for adjoining properties that could not be altered by the partition. By referring to only a singular "public road," the major portion of which had to be the old road, it is logical to infer that the entire boundary line described as the "public road" refers to the old road. Had the parties meant otherwise, it seems the document would have differentiated between the two roads. To a limited extent, the partition map is helpful here, because it shows only a single, straight line as the "public road." It does not depict a second roadbed or a jog to another roadbed along a portion of the boundary.

Second, we find persuasive evidence of intent in the parenthetical in Griffin's chain of title that follows the words, "public road" with the words, "New Hope-Whitaker." The parties have stipulated that the old road was known by this name. This clarification was added to the property description when Lot One was transferred by Leslie R. Spillman to his brother in 1955. True, this occurred fourteen years after the partition, but it is the first transfer of title to occur after the partition and it is a transfer from one of the original participants in the partition to another of the original participants. Obviously, Leslie R. Spillman and his brother believed the intent of the partition document they signed was to set the eastern boundary of Lot One at the centerline of the old road.

Third, we note that the parties to the partition were similarly imprecise with reference to another public road. The partition document states that Lot One is bounded on the west by "State Highway No. 258." According to the evidence, State Highway No. 258 no longer carried that designation when the partition document was executed. It had also been re-worked in the mid-1930's and its new name was State Highway No. 421. Yet the text of the partition document and the attached map show this highway by its former name. This use of the historical name for the state highway supports the inference that the parties were also referring to the historical New Hope-Whitaker Springs Road when they used the words "public road" in the partition document.

Finally, we note that when transferring title to immovable property, it is customary to use exactly the same language as was used in the preceding transfer of the same property. This makes it clear that exactly the same property is being transferred. If any deviation in location is intended, the language is changed. In the transfers of the Lot One property before the partition, the property description referred to State Highway No. 258 and the "public road" as two of the boundaries. In the partition, the description of Lot One was not changed at all, but repeated that terminology. The continued use of these historical designations supports the inference that the parties meant to describe and convey the exact same property in the partition. This being so, the eastern boundary of Lot One should be the old public road.

Based on this evidence in the record, we conclude that Griffin met his burden of proof and established "better title" to the disputed property. Therefore, the judgment of the trial court must be reversed and judgment rendered declaring Griffin the owner of that property. Additionally, because the act of cash sale to the Daigles and the attached survey incorrectly show Morris Road as the western boundary of a portion of the Daigles' property, these documents must be reformed to show the correct property description and must be recorded to clear the cloud on Griffin's title.

CONCLUSION

For the foregoing reasons, the judgment of the trial court is reversed, and judgment is rendered in favor of Griffin, declaring the "public road" that forms the eastern boundary of his property is the center of the old roadbed, the New Hope-Whitaker Springs Road.

NOTES AND QUESTIONS

1. In footnote 5 of the opinion, the appellate court observed, "As previously noted, the parties stipulated and the court entered judgment that this matter was to be regarded as a petitory action. However, Griffin asked for a judgment declaring his ownership rights, and presented facts at trial suggestive of his possession of the property at issue. By stipulating that this matter is petitory in nature, he effectively abandoned his claims of possession, because the petitory action may only be brought by a party not in possession of the property. Had this stipulation not been entered, Griffin could have proceeded under an action for declaratory judgment and still maintained his claim of possession. See LSA-C.C.P. art. 3654; A. N. Yiannopoulos, Louisiana Civil Law Treatise: Property, § 261, at 516 (3d ed. 1991)." If Griffin had not abandoned his claims of possession, what advantages would he have obtained in the litigation with the Daigles?

2. For the declaratory judgment action by which one in possession may bring an action to establish ownership, see La. C.C.P. arts. 1871-1883 and, for the burden of proof, 3654. In footnote 7, the court also points out that the case "could also have been treated as a boundary action." See infra for the boundary action.

3. The court provides a useful list of "general rules" that are used to determine who has better title when both parties derive their titles from a common author, as is the case here. What justifies the use of each of the first three rules?

4. Given the "Pure Race" nature of the Louisiana Public Records doctrine, is it accurate for a court to conclude that when "title is traced back to a common author, the more ancient title is the better title"?

NELSEN v. COX
2012 WL 2154253 (La. App. 1ˢᵗ Cir. 6/13/2012)
(unpublished opinion)

CARTER, C.J. This is a dispute between certain heirs of Henry Burton Nelsen (the Heirs), represented by Shirley Nelsen, executor of the estate of Henry Ellis Nelsen (the plaintiff), and the defendants, Bruce D. Cox, Tangipahoa Development, L.L.C., and Lonesome Properties, L.L.C., concerning the ownership of real property (the property) located in Tangipahoa Parish.

The plaintiff claims that the Heirs are the record owners of the property, as evidenced by an Amended Judgment of Possession signed on June 24, 2009, filed in the record of the matter entitled "Succession of Henry Burton Nelsen," ... in the conveyance records of Tangipahoa Parish....[and] that the defendants caused to be recorded in the conveyance records of Tangipahoa Parish two documents that place a cloud on the Heirs' title: 1) a quitclaim deed indicating that on March 12, 2007, Elvira Artigue Nelsen Simmons (Elvira) conveyed the property to Tangipahoa Development (represented by Bruce D. Cox, member) [for a stated consideration of $500]; and 2) a cash sale indicating that on March 27, 2007, Tangipahoa Development conveyed the property, together with two other properties, to Lonesome Properties (also represented by Bruce D. Cox, member). Although plaintiff's petition is titled as one to quiet title, the allegations and prayer for relief seek judgment recognizing the Heirs "as the sole and only owners in perfect ownership" of the property, and therefore sets forth a petitory action.

The defendants answered the petition, asserting the affirmative defense of good faith possession.... The defendants maintained that Lonesome Properties acquired the property pursuant to a valid conveyance in authentic form, as did its predecessor in title, Tangipahoa Development. Finally, the defendants alleged that Elvira had acquired full ownership of the property pursuant to a valid judgment of possession signed April 11, 1989, and recorded April 25, 1989, as part of the succession of her husband, Henry Burton Nelsen.

The defendants later amended their answer and filed a reconventional demand, asserting that Lonesome Properties had "physically detained, enjoyed and possessed publicly the full extent" of the property since it was acquired from Tangipahoa Development on March 27, 2007. Further, the defendants maintained that Lonesome Properties had legal possession of the property by virtue of more than ten years of good faith possession, pursuant to Louisiana Civil Code article 3473, and thirty years of possession, pursuant to Louisiana Civil Code article 3486. In calculating the length of time Lonesome Properties had possessed the property, the defendants included the terms of possession of Lonesome Properties' ancestors in title, Tangipahoa Development and Elvira, pursuant to Louisiana Civil Code article 3442. To calculate the thirty-year possession, Lonesome Properties also included the possession of Henry Burton Nelsen. Lonesome Properties prayed for judgment recognizing it as the "rightful owner" of the property.

The trial court granted the plaintiff's motion for summary judgment, confirming and quieting the title of the Heirs and recognizing the Heirs "as the sole and only owners in perfect ownership" of the property. The Clerk of Court of Tangipahoa Parish was ordered to make a notation of the trial court's judgment on the quit-claim deed and the cash-sale documents in the conveyance records. The judgment further dismissed all claims of the defendants.

The defendants appeal, alleging that the trial court erred in granting the motion for summary judgment, because the plaintiff failed to meet her burden of proving an unblemished title to the property dating back to the sovereign and that genuine issues of material fact remain in dispute regarding whether Lonesome Properties and its ancestors in title possessed the property for the requisite prescriptive period.

After *de novo* review, we find that the plaintiff was entitled to summary judgment as rendered by the trial court. In a petitory action, the plaintiff has the burden of proving that the Heirs acquired ownership from a previous owner. *See* La.Code Civ. Proc. Ann. arts. 3653 and 3654; La. Civ.Code Ann. art. 531. When the titles of the parties are traced to a common author, the common author is presumed to be the previous owner. La.Code Civ. Proc. Ann. art. 3653; La. Civ.Code Ann. art. 532. Here, Henry Burton Nelsen is the common author-in-title and, contrary to the defendants' assertion, the plaintiff need not prove title to the sovereign. Rather, the plaintiff can establish the Heirs' apparent title to the property by setting forth an unbroken chain of valid transfers from their uncle, Henry Burton Nelsen.... The plaintiff established the Heirs' apparent record title through: 1) an "Amended Judgment of Possession" signed on June 24, 2009, declaring the Heirs to be the sole owners of the property, which was identified as the separate property of Henry Burton Nelsen, and placing the Heirs in possession; and 2) the March 12, 1942 act of sale in which Robert R. Reid sold the property to "[Henry] B. Nelsen, single never married, resident of the Parish of Tangipahoa, State of Louisiana." The March 1942 act of sale shows that Elvira never had an ownership interest in the property, because the April 1989 judgment in her husband's succession transferred only property acquired during their marriage.

The summary judgment evidence further establishes that the defendants cannot prove that they acquired the property by ten-year acquisitive prescription, because they cannot show that Lonesome Properties, Tangipahoa Development, and Elvira each had just title and was in good faith, or that there were ten years of continuous, uninterrupted, peaceable, public, and unequivocal possession of the property. *See* La. Civ.Code Ann. arts. 3475 and 3476. Heir Francile Nelsen Ortiz stated in an affidavit that in March 2006, she was informed by a letter from attorney Robert Tillery that defendant Bruce D. Cox wanted to purchase the property from the Heirs. The letter from Tillery was attached to Ortiz's affidavit, in which it was stated that the property was part of the 44.26 acres that Cox was attempting to purchase from Elvira and that the property "was subject to a possible claim of ownership in the name of ... Henry Nelsen." The plaintiff also presented the affidavit of heir Janice Nelsen Stark, who referenced email correspondence to her from Cox, in which Cox wrote in November 2006 that "although I do not expect to have a problem with your [A]unt Elvira[,] she must sign and agree that she has no interest in the property." These factors are sufficient to establish that defendants' possession did not commence in good faith. In fact, the absence of good faith on the part of Bruce D. Cox is obvious.

Unlike ten-year acquisitive prescription, ownership of immovable property can be acquired by prescription of thirty years of possession without the need of a just title or good faith. La. Civ.Code Ann. art. 3486. However, the record establishes that the defendants cannot establish the requisite possession, which would require tacking the possession of both Elvira and Henry Burton Nelsen, the common author-in-title. *See* La. Civ.Code Ann. arts. 3442 and 3476.

CONCLUSION

For the above reasons, we affirm the summary judgment entered in favor of the appellee/plaintiff, Shirley Nelsen, executor of the estate of Henry Ellis Nelsen, and the dismissal of the reconventional demand of the appellants/defendants, Tangipahoa Development, L.L.C., Lonesome Properties, L.L.C., and Bruce D. Cox.

PARRO, J., concurs.

b. Imprescriptibility of the Petitory Action
La. Civil Code art. 481

The petitory action is imprescriptible. See La. Civil Code art. 481; *id.* art. 3502, Comment (c); Buckley v. Catlett, 203 La. 54, 13 So. 2d 384 (1943); Yiannopoulos, Civil Law Property 544 (3d ed. 1991). This means that the defendant in a petitory action may not raise the peremptory objection of *liberative* prescription; he may, however, raise the peremptory objection of *acquisitive* prescription.

2. REVENDICATORY ACTION
Civil Code arts. 518-519, 521-525, 530

A. N. YIANNOPOULOS, CIVIL LAW PROPERTY
§§ 347, 350-355 (4th ed. 2001)
(footnotes omitted)

§ 347. Real Actions

The law of property accords to the owner of a corporeal movable, and to one having a real right in it, a *revendicatory action* for the recovery of the movable in the hands of any unauthorized person. This action is *real* because it tends to protect or enforce a real right.***

Provisions in the Louisiana Civil Code deal with or presuppose the recovery of movables by the revendicatory action, that is, an action brought by the owner of a corporeal movable for the recognition of his ownership and delivery of possession. Article 526 of the Civil Code, declares: "The owner of a thing is entitled to recover it from anyone who possesses or detains it without right and to obtain judgment recognizing his ownership and ordering delivery of the thing to him." This provision expresses a rule inherent in the Louisiana Civil Code of 1870 that has been only partially expressed in the Louisiana Code of Civil Procedure and in Louisiana jurisprudence. Article 526 applies to all things movable or immovable, but an action for the recovery of an immovable is a petitory action under the Code of Civil Procedure, whereas an action for the recovery of a movable is an innominate real action.***

Article 60 of the Louisiana Code of Practice made an allusion to the "revendication" of a movable. The Code of Civil Procedure, however, has no corresponding provision. Ownership of movables is ordinarily determined under the Code of Civil Procedure in a proceeding commenced by a writ of sequestration. This is an effective remedy for the protection of the ownership as well as possession of movables. Recovery in such a proceeding may be based on a contractual or a property right.***

§ 350. Availability and Nature of the Revendicatory Action

Article 526 of the Louisiana Civil Code, which applies to both movables and immovables, makes it clear that the dispossessed owner of a movable may bring the revendicatory action against a possessor or detentor for the recognition of his ownership and recovery of the movable.

Under the regime of the Louisiana Civil Code of 1870, courts experienced analytical difficulties in cases involving revendication of movables. The question of the nature of the action for the recovery of movables in kind proved particularly perplexing. Such an action is not a real action under the Code of Civil Procedure because it is not one brought "to enforce rights in, to, or upon immovable property." Nor is it a personal action, because it is not one brought "to enforce an obligation against the obligor, personally and independently of the property which he may own, claim, or possess." An action for the recovery of movables in reality is an innominate real action, "fully recognized in the French jurisprudence from which we derive our system of practice."

Occasionally, an argument drawn from the nature of the revendicatory action had been advanced to challenge its availability under procedural law. In a case involving a claim for the recovery of certain movables that plaintiff had allegedly purchased, defendant argued that such an action was a possessory action inapplicable to movables. The court, however, properly maintained the action on the ground that plaintiff had established his ownership. In another proceeding for the recovery of movables allegedly removed by defendant from plaintiff's premises, defendant argued that the action must be either possessory or petitory and, therefore, plaintiff had no cause of action because such an action is restricted to immovable property. In the light of procedural provisions defining petitory and possessory actions, defendant's argument had some merit. Defendant, however, had overlooked the fact that the revendicatory action for the recovery of a movable has persisted through the centuries as an innominate real action. The court properly allowed recovery of the movables on the authority of a multitude of cases "in which the owner recovered possession of the property from the possessor."

§ 351. Plaintiff and Defendant

Ordinarily, plaintiff in the revendicatory action is the dispossessed owner of a movable; defendant is anyone who possesses or detains the movable without right. However, according to Article 530 of the Civil Code a present possessor of a corporeal movable is presumed to be its owner, and a previous possessor of such a movable is presumed to have been its owner during the period of his possession. Relying on these presumptions, a present or previous possessor may bring the revendicatory action against a detentor, and a previous possessor may bring the same action against the possessor of a lost or stolen movable.

The possession of movables is not protected by a distinct possessory action under the Code of Civil Procedure. However, one may, without claiming the ownership of a movable, bring an innominate civil action to enjoin a disturbance of his possession or to be restored in his possession. The nominate possessory action under Article 3655 of the Code of Civil Procedure applies to immovable property only. This may reflect some misunderstanding of the redactors as to the purpose of possessory protection. If the purpose of the possessory action were merely to determine the position of the parties as plaintiff and defendant in a subsequent petitory action and thereby allocate the burden of proof of ownership, such an action is unnecessary because the possession of a movable is readily ascertainable. However, the purpose of the possessory action is also to provide a speedy remedy for the determination of a claim to possession independently of the question of ownership. Such a proceeding is equally desirable in certain circumstances as to both movables and immovables.

An action for the recovery of the possession of a movable by an owner or other person having a real right is clearly admissible in Louisiana as a revendicatory action. A person entitled to the possession of a movable by virtue of a contractual right, such as a lessee or a depositary, may bring an appropriate personal action for the recovery of the movable. A possessor without title may bring an action for the recovery of the movable he possesses against a thief, finder, or usurper, by relying on the presumptions of Article 530 of the Civil Code. However, the thief, finder, or usurper of a movable may not bring an action against another possessor for the protection of his possession.

§ 352. Lost or Stolen Things

The owner of a lost or stolen thing may reclaim it in the hands of the finder or of the thief as well as in the hands of any acquirer who purchased it in good faith for fair value. However, the owner is bound to reimburse the purchase price if the possessor purchased the movable in good faith at public auction or from a merchant selling similar things. In all cases, the purchaser of a lost or stolen thing in good faith has a remedy against his vendor. If a lost or stolen thing has been sold by authority of law, the former owner may not recover it from the purchaser; in such a case, the revendicatory action is excluded.

Under the Civil Code, a thing is stolen when one has taken possession of it without the consent of the owner. A thing is not stolen when the owner delivers it to another as a result of fraud. In such a case, there is consent though vitiated by fraud. Under Article 520 of the Civil Code, the person who practiced the fraud could transfer the ownership of the movable to an acquirer in good faith for fair value. It was otherwise under the regime of the Louisiana Civil Code of 1870. The owner of a movable could reclaim it in the hands of a good faith purchaser for value if it was sold by one in violation of a confidential relationship with the owner or obligation toward him.

A fortiori, a thing is not stolen when the owner transfers its ownership to another person as a result of fraud. The transferee may further transfer ownership to an acquirer in good faith for fair value. The annulment of the title of the party who practiced the fraud will not result in annulment of the title of his transferee. A transferee of a corporeal movable in good faith for fair value "retains the ownership of the thing even though the title of the transferor is annulled on account of a vice of consent."

It was the same under the prior law as to things purchased by a dishonored check. Louisiana courts liberalized the rules of sales and held that the original purchaser acquired the ownership of the movables although the vendor did not receive payment or was dispossessed as a result of fraud practiced by the purchaser. The solution is consistent with the rule that the unpaid vendor may not exercise his right of dissolution when the movables sold are no longer in the possession of the purchaser.

§ 353. Burden of Proof

The plaintiff in the revendicatory action has the burden of proof of his ownership, and if he fails to carry this burden the action is dismissed. Ordinarily, plaintiff must prove that he has acquired the movable by a transfer from a previous owner, by accession, or by acquisitive prescription. In certain circumstances, however, plaintiff may prove his ownership by virtue of the presumptions of Article 530.

The defendant may always rely on the presumption of Article 530(1), first sentence, according to which the present possessor of a movable is presumed to be its owner. The plaintiff may rebut this presumption on proof that he was prior possessor and that he lost the possession of the movable as a result of loss or theft. In such a case, plaintiff may rely on the presumption of Article 530(1), second sentence, according to which the prior possessor of a corporeal movable is presumed to have been owner during the period of his possession. The burden then shifts and the defendant, in order to be allowed to retain the movable, must prove that the plaintiff was never its owner, or, if he was, he lost his ownership. If the plaintiff can not prove that he lost the possession of the movable as a result of loss or theft, he may not rely on the presumption of prior possession and ownership.

The presumptions of ownership under the first paragraph of Article 530(1) do not apply in favor of a precarious possessor, such as a lessee or a depositary. Thus, the plaintiff in the revendicatory action is entitled to recover the movable if he proves that the defendant is his lessee or his depositary. In such a case, the plaintiff may rely on the presumption of his present possession and ownership. If the precarious possessor lost the thing, or if it was stolen from him, the owner may reclaim it in the hands of a finder, thief, or subsequent transferee.

§ 354. Defenses

A possessor may defend the revendicatory action on the basis of a personal or real right that he may have for the enjoyment and possession of the movable. He may thus claim that he is entitled to retain the movable by virtue of a contract with the owner or by virtue of his usufruct or ownership.

The revendicatory action will fail if the defendant has acquired the ownership of the movable by acquisitive prescription, by accession, by transfer from the owner, or, exceptionally, by a transfer from a non-owner....

When the movables are no longer in the possession of the defendant, the revendicatory action abates; the owner, however, may have a personal action for damages or unjust enrichment against the former possessor of the movable.

§ 355. Judgment; Accounting

The successful plaintiff in the revendicatory action is entitled to judgment recognizing his ownership and ordering the delivery of the movable to him. He is also entitled to the fruits and products of the movable in accordance with Articles 485, 486, and 488 of the Civil Code. The possessor may be entitled to reimbursement for expenses. In such a case, he is also entitled to retain the thing until he is reimbursed.

SONGBYRD v. BEARSVILLE RECORDS, INC.
104 F.3d 773 (5th Cir. 1997)

WIENER, Circuit Judge. The late Henry Roeland Byrd, also known as "Professor Longhair," was an influential New Orleans rhythm-and-blues pianist and composer, and is widely regarded as one of the primary inspirations for the renaissance of New Orleans popular music over the last thirty years. His numerous hits included original compositions such as "Tipitina" and "Go to the Mardi Gras," as well as his famous renditions of Earl King's "Big Chief." After achieving modest commercial success as a local performer and recording artist in the 1940's and 1950's, Byrd fell on hard times during the 1960's. His fortunes began to change for the better in 1970, however, when New Orleans music aficionado Arthur "Quint" Davis, along with others, founded the New Orleans Jazz and Heritage Festival ("Jazz Fest"). Needing talented performers for Jazz Fest, Davis located Byrd in 1971 working in an obscure record store in New Orleans and transformed him into a perennial star attraction of the Jazz Fest and other venues from that time until his death in 1980.

Soon after Byrd's first performance at Jazz Fest, Davis, acting as the pianist's manager, and Parker Dinkins, an attorney, arranged for Byrd to make several "master recordings" at a Baton Rouge recording studio known as Deep South Recorders. These master recordings consist of four reels of 8-track tape which could be "mixed" to produce either demonstration tapes or final recordings suitable for the production of records, cassettes, and compact discs. According to SongByrd, several demonstration tapes produced from these master recordings found their way to Bearsville Records, Inc., a recording studio and record company located in Woodstock, New York and operated by Grossman. Impressed by the demonstration tapes, Grossman apparently arranged with Davis and Dinkins for Byrd and another New Orleans musician to travel to Bearsville's studio for a recording session.

For reasons that are unclear but not material to this appeal, the Bearsville recording sessions proved unsatisfactory. For equally unclear reasons, Davis and Dinkins wanted Grossman to be able either to listen to or play for others the full version of the Baton Rouge master recordings. In furtherance of this desire, Davis and Dinkins caused the four "master recording" tapes to be delivered to Grossman in New York. According to the as yet unrefuted affidavit of Davis, these tapes were delivered to Grossman, "as demonstration tapes only, without any intent for either Albert Grossman or Bearsville Records, Inc. to possess these aforementioned tapes as owner." Also for reasons as yet not explained by either party, the tapes remained in Grossman's possession for many years thereafter.

Acting on behalf of Davis and Byrd in 1975, Dinkins wrote two letters to Bearsville—the first addressed to a George James, the second to Grossman himself—requesting that Bearsville return the master recording tapes. Bearsville made no response whatsoever to Dinkins' letters (or at least has not introduced any evidence of a response). Dinkins, for reasons as yet unknown, did not press his request any further.

After Albert Grossman's death in the mid 1980's, Bearsville Records, Inc. was dissolved, but Grossman's estate continued to do business as "Bearsville Records." Even though it no longer signs artists or promotes their products, Bearsville Records still operates a recording studio which it leases to record labels and third parties; it also licenses a catalog of recordings by artists originally under contract with Bearsville Records, Inc. Acting in this latter capacity, Bearsville licensed certain of the Byrd master recordings to Rounder Records Corporation of Cambridge, Massachusetts (Rounder) for an advance against royalties.

In 1987, Rounder released Professor Longhair, Houseparty New Orleans Style:

The Lost Sessions, an album that contained 11 songs or "tracks" made from Byrd's original Baton Rouge master recordings. This release garnered Byrd a posthumous Grammy Award for Best Traditional Blues Album of 1987. The liner notes of the Rounder album make hardly any reference to Bearsville and no reference whatsoever to the contractual agreement between Rounder and Bearsville. Bearsville Records also licensed certain of the master recordings to another record company, Rhino Records (Rhino). According to SongByrd's petition, Rhino released an album, titled "Mardi Gras in Baton Rouge," featuring seven tracks from the Baton Rouge master recordings.

In 1993, SongByrd, Inc. was incorporated and commenced business as successor-in-interest to the intellectual property rights of Byrd and his deceased widow, Alice Walton Byrd. In 1995, SongByrd filed this lawsuit in state court in New Orleans against Bearsville Records, Inc. SongByrd's "Petition in Revendication" sought a judgment (1) recognizing its ownership of the master recordings, (2) ordering return of the recordings, and (3) awarding damages. The court held that SongByrd's action was barred by liberative prescription and also rejected SongByrd's argument that at all times Bearsville has been only a precarious possessor and therefore prescription has never commenced to run. SongByrd timely filed its notice of appeal from the district court's ruling.

ANALYSIS

B. Applicable Law—Erie-Bound

1. Special Louisiana Erie Considerations

The basis of our jurisdiction, and that of the district court, to decide the instant case is diversity of citizenship, under which a federal court's obligation is to apply substantive state law. In Louisiana this obligation has special dimensions because of our unique Civilian tradition. We remain ever aware of the late Judge Rubin's caution to federal Erie courts applying Louisiana Civil law to steer clear of the common law principle of stare decisis and to apply instead the distinctly Civilian doctrine of jurisprudence constante:

Because of the reviewing power of [Louisiana] appellate courts, the [Louisiana]trial judge may pay great respect to the decisions of these courts. He is not bound to do so, however, because the doctrine of stare decisis does not apply. Instead, each judge, trial and appellate, may consult the civil code and draw anew from its principles. Interpretation of the code and other sources of law is appropriate for each judge. The judge is guided much more by doctrine, as expounded in legal treatises by legal scholars, than by the decisions of colleagues.... Instead of stare decisis, the rule is one of deference to a series of decisions, jurisprudence constante.

Emphatically elaborating on the proposition that Erie "does not command blind allegiance to [any] case on all fours with the case before the court," now-Chief Judge Politz wrote that:

If anything, this flexibility is even greater when a federal court sits as a Erie court applying the Louisiana civil law. In such cases, "the Erie obligation is to the [Civil] Code, the 'solemn expression of legislative will.'" Shelp, 333 F.2d at 439 (quoting the very first article of the Louisiana Civil Code). The Louisiana Supreme Court has taken great pains to "plainly state that ... the notion of stare decisis, derived as it is from the common law should not be thought controlling in this state." Ardoin v. Hartford Acc. & Indem. Co., 360 So.2d 1331, 1334 (La.1978). While case law in the State of Louisiana is acknowledged as "invaluable as previous interpretation. ..." [id. at 1335], it is nonetheless properly regarded as "secondary information." Id. at 1334.

2. Prescription

The central issue in the instant appeal is whether plaintiff's action is time-barred. The answer to this question depends on whether the applicable period of limitation—prescription in Louisiana; statute of limitations in the common law—is liberative or acquisitive. As shall be seen from our analysis of the pertinent provisions of the Louisiana Civil Code and from "legal treatises by legal scholars," the applicable type of prescription is acquisitive....

C. Revendicatory Actions Are Imprescriptible

SongByrd contends that the district court erred when it determined that SongByrd's action seeking recognition of its ownership interest in the master recordings, return of those recordings, and damages, has prescribed under Louisiana law. The district court's memorandum order held that SongByrd's action had prescribed under Louisiana Civil Code Articles 3499 and 3492 regardless of whether SongByrd's claims were based in contract, quasi-contract, or tort. In so doing, the district court implicitly characterized SongByrd's action as a "personal action" arising from these areas of law. This characterization of SongByrd's action constitutes the first and fundamental error committed by the district court and led to its first erroneous holding.

As explained by Professor A N. Yiannopoulos in his treatise on Louisiana property law, actions seeking recognition of ownership or enforcement of the rights thereof, whether in movable or immovable property, are not personal actions; they are "realactions." Such real actions, otherwise known as "revendicatory actions," are expressly authorized by the Louisiana Civil Code. As the official comments to the Code make clear, there are two kinds of revendicatory action, depending on the object of the ownership interest that the plaintiff seeks to have recognized: (1) a "petitory action" for the recovery of immovable property (real estate), and (2) an "innominate real action" for the recovery of movable property (personalty). Further, any "incidental demand for damages made in an action for the recovery of an immovable [or a movable] does not affect the classification of the main demand as a real action."

It follows from this basic dichotomy that, as the Civil Code specifically provides liberative prescription periods for all manner of personal actions (including delictual, contractual and quasi-contractual actions), "[l]iberative prescription does not bar real actions seeking to protect the right of ownership." The rationale for this distinction is that "[u]nder our Civil Code, ownership can never be lost by the failure to exercise it—only by the acquisition of ownership by another through possession sufficient to acquire it through an acquisitive prescription." Thus, it is well established in Louisiana that the petitory action (for the protection of immovables) is not barred by liberative prescription. The same rule applies to the revendicatory action brought to assert or protect the right of ownership in movable property because it, too, is a real action, not a personal one. On this point Professor Yiannopoulos' Louisiana Civil Law Treatise could not be clearer:

An action that is grounded on a wrongful act, that is, an offense or quasi-offense, is subject to the prescription of one year and an action grounded on quasi-contract is subject to the prescription often years. The revendicatory action [for the recovery of movable property] is imprescriptible; however, such an object is without object when the defendant has acquired the ownership of a movable by the acquisitive prescription of three or ten years.

Despite this obvious truism of Civilian doctrine, a number of older Louisiana decisions overlooked or disregarded it and, just as the district court did here, applied either one-year or ten-year periods of liberative prescription on the erroneous assumption that the revendicatory action is personal in nature, either delictual or quasi-contractual.

Nevertheless, a 50-year old Louisiana Supreme Court case, Faison v. Patout, appears to be the most recent pronouncement on point, and it supports our reading of the Civil Code and Professor Yiannopoulos' reading as well. In Faison, Mrs. Hypolite Patout executed a manual donation of her jewelry to her two daughters. Following the donor's death, one of her sons, Sebastian Patout, suggested to his sisters that it was unsafe for them to keep this jewelry in one sister's bedroom; so, with his sisters' permission, Sebastian put the jewelry in his bank safety deposit box. Sebastian died some twelve years later, whereupon his widow removed the jewelry from the safety deposit box and refused to give it to the sisters. In the sisters' suit to recover the jewelry, the trial court held, and the Louisiana Supreme Court agreed, that the sisters were the true owners. More significant to our consideration today, the Patout defendants (children of Mrs. Hypolite Patout's sons) had pled liberative prescription under Louisiana Civil Code Article 3544 (1870). They contended that their aunts' action was personal and thus had prescribed because more than ten years had elapsed between the time the property left the aunts' possession and the time suit was filed. Rejecting this contention, the Supreme Court wrote:

There might be some merit in a plea of prescription if Sebastian Patout had possessed the property for himself and the other heirs, and adversely to [his sisters], but the record convinces us that he was acting as depository for his two sisters, these plaintiffs, and that his possession of the property was for their benefit--for them, and not in his own name or right.

Counsel for defendants is in error in his contention that the ten-year [liberative] prescription under Article 3544 commenced to run in March 1931 [when Sebastian took possession of the jewelry]. [Acquisitive] [p]rescription began to run when plaintiffs were first denied delivery of this jewelry in June 1942, after the death of their brother, Sebastian Patout, and this suit was filed in December 1942, about six months later.

In thus rejecting the defendants' plea of liberative prescription, the Louisiana Supreme Court clearly recognized that the concepts of precarious possession and acquisitive prescription applied to this action for the recovery of movable property, even though the court did not use these terms of art. The facts in Faison are closely analogous to the situation before us today, and the holding of the Louisiana Supreme Court in Faison—the most recent pronouncement by the highest court of the state—is instructive despite being non-binding due to the inapplicability of the common law doctrine of stare decisis.

In sum, even though some decisions of the Louisiana Supreme Court have treated actions for recovery of movables as personal (delictual and occasionally as quasi-contractual), other decisions of that court have found that such actions are properly considered to assert claims of ownership and therefore are subject only to acquisitive prescription. Despite its age, Patout is still the most recent Louisiana Supreme Court pronouncement on point, and it so held. But regardless whether the most recent pronouncement of the Louisiana Supreme Court supports our analysis of the Civil Code and that of Professor Yiannopoulos, there is simply no jurisprudence constante on the question. It follows, then, that our Erie-bound decision to follow the plain wording and indisputable structure of the Louisiana Civil Code and Professor Yiannopoulos' analysis is either supported by or at least does no violence to Louisiana's jurisprudence as a secondary source of law. To the extent that our decision today may constitute an "Erie guess," we take additional comfort in the observation that almost 60 years have passed since the Louisiana Supreme Court last applied liberative prescription to actions claiming ownership or possession of movable property—a span of years attributable at least in part, we assume, to the broad reliance in recent decades on Professor Yiannopoulos' doctrinal work on this subject.

As SongByrd's "Petition in Revendication" sought recognition of its purported ownership interest in the Baton Rouge master recordings and recovery of possession of those recordings, and only incidentally sought damages resulting from Bearsville's contravention of SongByrd's alleged ownership interest, we hold that, as a fundamental matter of Louisiana property law, SongByrd's action is not subject to liberative prescription.

D. Termination of Precarious Possession and Actual Notice

This foundational holding does not end our analysis in the instant case, however. In addition to its failure to characterize SongByrd's suit as a real action and its concomitant error in applying the rules of liberative prescription, the district court also missed the mark in its treatment of SongByrd's assertion that Bearsville was and is only a precarious possessor. To situate the concept of precarious possession in its proper Civilian context, we again return to basics. As Professor Yiannopoulos explains, a defendant in possession (such as Bearsville) may defend a revendicatory action for the recovery of movable property by (1) asserting some right, be it personal or real, to possess the movable, or (2) claiming that he is in fact the owner of the movable by virtue of, e.g., a transfer from the owner, acquisitive prescription, or some other mode of acquiring ownership. No such defenses have been proffered by Bearsville; but if, on remand, it should assert the defense of acquisitive prescription, the district court will have to address SongByrd's contention—made both in its original petition and in opposition to Bearsville's motion to dismiss—that Bearsville is and always has been nothing more than a precarious possessor.

Under the Civil Code, the concept of "precarious possession" is defined within Title XXIII of Book III, "Of the Different Modes of Acquiring the Ownership of Things," as "the exercise of possession over a thing with the permission of or on behalf of the owner or possessor." A precarious possessor is presumed to possess for another, but precarious possession may be terminated or converted to possession on one's own behalf in either of two specific ways. First, a precarious possessor who is a co-owner (or his universal successor) may terminate his precarious possession, and thus begin to possess for himself alone, only when he demonstrates his intent to possess for himself by "overt and unambiguous acts sufficient to give notice to his co-owner." Second, a precarious possessor who is not a co-owner is held to a higher standard and only "commences to possess for himself when he gives actual notice of this intent to the person on whose behalf he is possessing."

In the instant case, then, should Bearsville assert that it acquired ownership of the master recordings by acquisitive prescription of either three or ten years, pursuant to Louisiana Civil Code Articles 3489-91, it will have to overcome SongByrd's assertion, so far supported by Quint Davis' affidavit, that Davis and Dinkins delivered the master recordings to Bearsville intending only for Bearsville to possess the tapes precariously. Bearsville may, of course, assert that (1) it was never a precarious possessor, or (2) even if it was a precarious possessor initially, at some point it terminated its precarious possession and began to possess for itself. Either way, Bearsville will have the burden of proving facts sufficient to support such a defense....

CONCLUSION

For the reasons stated above, we reverse the district court's grant of summary judgment in favor of Bearsville and remand the case for further proceedings consistent with this opinion.

NOTES AND QUESTIONS

1. On remand, the District Court on its own motion transferred SongByrd's action to the Northern District of New York. That court granted summary judgment for the defendants on the ground that action was time-barred under New York law. The judgment was affirmed on appeal in *SongByrd v. Estate of Grossman*, 206 F.3d 172 (2d Cir. 2000). The court held that Louisiana lacked jurisdiction over the estate of Grossman, and that the action accrued under New York law when the company began using master tapes as its own. Therefore, the action was time-barred.

2. If Louisiana law had applied to the merits of this case, what results would be possible, and what assumptions would underlie each of them?

SOUTHEAST EQUIPMENT CO. v. OFFICE OF STATE POLICE
437 So. 2d 1184 (La. App. 4th Cir. 1983)

GULOTTA, J. In this case involving the sale of a stolen movable, we are confronted with the competing possessory rights of a true owner and an innocent purchaser. From a judgment recognizing the purchaser's superior right to possession, the owner appeals. We affirm.

According to the stipulated facts, Southeast Equipment Co., Inc. (Southeast) purchased, in good faith, a stolen 1979 Caterpillar Loader for $54,000.00 from C. Ogle, through his agent Hattaway International, Inc. (Hattaway). Hattaway is a corporation that customarily sells heavy equipment such as this loader, but Ogle is not. Ogle had consigned the loader to Hattaway for sale.[10]

About two weeks after the sale, the Louisiana State Police seized the machine from Southeast, pursuant to a search warrant alleging it was stolen. Southeast thereafter filed this mandamus action against the State Police to demand return of the machine. J.W. Conner and Son Construction Co. (Conner), owner of the loader at the time it was stolen, intervened and also sought possession.

The trial court rendered judgment ordering the State to return the machine to Southeast as a "good-faith possessor" until Conner reimbursed Southeast the $54,000.00 purchase price. The trial judge reached his decision based on C.C. Art. 524, which states in pertinent part:

---

[10] The stipulation does not state that Southeast was a "good faith" purchaser. The stipulation states: "Southeast did not know that the loader was stolen or that Hattaway could not sell it." See also C.C. 523 for a definition of good faith. Conner acknowledges in brief, however, that Southeast purchased in "good faith."

"The owner of a lost or stolen movable may recover it from a possessor who bought it in good faith at a public auction or from a merchant customarily selling similar things on reimbursing the purchase price."

According to the trial judge, Southeast had a "greater right" to the movable because C.C. Art. 524 is an "exception" to C.C. Art. 521, which provides that a person "who has possession of a lost or stolen thing may not transfer its ownership to another."

Citing C.C. Art. 521 and C.C. Art. 2987, Conner contends, on appeal, that neither the suspected thief Ogle, nor his agent, Hattaway, could transfer ownership of the stolen movable. Conner argues that C.C. Art. 524 has no application because Southeast purchased the machine from Ogle, who is not a "merchant customarily selling" heavy equipment. We disagree.

C.C. Art. 524 does not expressly require that the "merchant customarily selling similar things..." be the apparent owner of the thing sold; it specified that the good faith purchaser buy it "from" the merchant. We interpret this language to encompass not only direct sales of movables from the merchant's own inventory, but also consignment sales, as in our case, where the merchant is acting as an agent on behalf of someone else who purports to be the owner.

Under our interpretation of C.C. Art. 524, the *sine qua non* for application of the article is a dealing between the good faith purchaser and a merchant customarily selling similar things. We conclude that if such a merchant conducts the sale, C.C. Art. 524 applies, whether the merchant is acting as apparent owner or only as an agent for another. This interpretation is consistent with the legislative recognition of the need for balancing the rights of a good faith purchaser and an owner, and comports with the preservation of security of transactions.

We are further persuaded to reach this conclusion by the ambiguous wording of the act of sale in our case. Hattaway's printed "BILL OF SALE ——EQUIPMENT" contains the following warranty of title to Southeast, the "Grantee":

To have and to hold all and singular the said goods and chattels to said Grantee, his successors and assigns. The undersigned covenants with said Grantee that undersigned is the lawful owner of said chattels; that they are free from encumbrances; that undersigned has a good right to sell the same; that undersigned will warrant and defend same against the lawful claims and demands of all persons.

WITNESS the hand and seal of the seller, this 28th day of October, 1981.

HATTAWAY INTERNATIONAL, INC.
Agent for Witness
Owner: C. Ogle . . ., Seller
Accepted by purchaser By David Hattaway, President

Address P.O. Box 20555
City and State Orlando, Fla. 32814
Hattaway International Form No. 022

white copy to buyer — yellow copy to seller

Although the bill of sale is signed by Hattaway as "Agent for Owner: C. Ogle...", it conveys an impression that Hattaway is the "undersigned" who is selling the machine and warranting the title. Ogle did not sign the bill of sale. A copy of the sales agreement between Hattaway and Ogle, which would have further clarified Hattaway's status as agent, was not incorporated in the sale document. Under these circumstances, Southeast could justifiably have believed that it was dealing with an established heavy equipment seller who had a right to sell the loader. Accordingly, we conclude that Southeast purchased the stolen movable "from a merchant customarily selling similar things," and "in good faith" within the meaning of C.C. Art. 524.

We are mindful of the competing equities between the true owner and the good faith purchaser who are both innocent victims. Nonetheless, interpreting the language of C.C. Art. 524, we must give effect to the Legislature's apparent intent to weigh the equities in the purchaser's favor under these circumstances. Conner's recourse may be against Hattaway or any other party responsible for the loss.

Having so concluded, we affirm the judgment of the trial court.

REDMANN, C.J. (dissenting). The basic posture of this suit is that Southeast Equipment, a Louisiana corporation, demands mandamus against the Louisiana state police to return to Southeast a 1979 Caterpillar 950 Loader, serial no. 81J12566, that the police seized under a warrant. The affidavit by Trooper First Class Joseph Mura in support of that warrant's issuance recites that

"On 11-13-81 ... Sgt. P. Hamburger was contacted by one Det. Perry Young of the Hillsbourgh County S[heriff's] O[ffice], Tampa, Florida. Det. Young advised that he had received information from one J. B. Cole W/M 38, of 501 E. Cooper St., West Memphis, Arkansas, that a 1979 Caterpillar Model 950 front end loader serial #81J12566 was located in the New Orleans area at [a described location]. Det. Young further advised that said pellicle was reported stolen on 10-28-81 [the date of Southeast's purchase of it in Florida from Hattaway as, purportedly, agent for Ogle]. ... At approximately 4:50 p.m. this date [of the seizure] affiant telephonically contacted Mr. Cole. Subject identified himself as the general manager of the Razorback Concrete Co. of 501 E. Cooper West Memphis Arkansas. Mr. Cole stated that on 11-03-81 [six days after Southeast's purchase and the report of the theft] he had sent one E. J. Hart W/M 49 head mechanic of Razorback Concrete to New Orleans to inspect the above front end loader in order to purchase same. Mr. Hart did go and returned with his report on the vehicle and its serial No. 81J12566. Mr. Cole in the morning hours of 11-13-81 [the date of the affidavit, warrant and seizure] while in the process of purchasing said vehicle, contacted the Rosier Co. of Tampa FL., the original seller of said vehicle. Rosier representatives advised that a vehicle of the description of the above front end loader had been stolen several weeks previously from the J. W. Conner and Son Construction Co. of Tampa, FL. Mr. Cole advised that a short time later he was contacted by Det. Perry Young and reconfirmed the serial no. of said equipment."

If Razorback Concrete in Arkansas so easily learned that it was a stolen loader that Southeast was trying to peddle just six days after buying it in Tampa, why did not Southeast learn that it was a stolen loader that Hattaway was trying to sell (apparently the same day it was reported stolen). (As an aside, one wonders why professional seller Hattaway, which proclaims itself "The Company Founded on Integrity," did not know that the loader was stolen.)

The stipulation that Southeast did not know that the loader was stolen[11] is not a stipulation that Southeast was in good faith for purposes of La. C.C. art. 524. Art. 521 declares one in good faith "unless *he knows, or should have known,* that the transferor was not the owner." (Emphasis added.) There is no stipulation that Southeast

---

[11] The intriguing question of La. C.C. 524's application to one who *in good faith* bought from a merchant, knowing the merchant to be the agent for a non-merchant owner, need not be decided, because Florida law governs this case (and Southeast is not in good faith for Louisiana law purposes anyway). But one may note the importance of articles 2505 and 3013 in the overall scheme of the Louisiana Code.

Art. 2505 entitles a buyer, in case of loss of the thing because of a third person's claim ("eviction"), to recover the price from the seller, "[e]ven in case of no warranty...."

On the other hand, art. 3013 provides that an agent has no responsibility "to those with whom he contracts [except] when he has bound himself personally, or when he has exceeded his authority without having exhibited his powers [of attorney]."

Thus the merchant would appear to be liable to return to the buyer the price of a stolen thing if the merchant were the seller, but not if the merchant were but the agent of the seller.

The legislature by the 1979 revision of the property articles did not intend to shield professional sellers from responsibility for selling stolen items, for that article is substantially identical to its source, art. 3507 as worded in 1870, and thus presumably not in conflict with article 2505 of the 1870 Code. The professional seller would thus owe the restitution of the price to the good faith buyer under art. 2505 (and thus the owner who pays it to the buyer under art. 524 would be entitled to reimbursement from the seller by legal subrogation to the buyer's right against the seller, C.C. 2161 (3)).

But if the professional seller who sells as agent can escape liability to the buyer to reimburse the price because of art. 3013's general rule that the agent is not personally liable, the result would be that an owner who was forced to repay the price to the buyer under art. 524 would not get reimbursement by subrogation to the buyer's right against the professional seller. The inconsistency would be that the courts would tell the owner (a) you must repay the buyer from "merchant, agent for X" under art. 524 because the buyer bought not from X but from the merchant, but (b) you cannot recover from the merchant because the buyer did not buy from the merchant but from X.

The intriguing question stated deserves a firmer factual foundation before being decided than that present here, where Southeast is not shown to be a good faith purchaser.

should not have known that the loader was stolen. Judging from the quoted affidavit, the least that can be said is that Southeast does not appear to be a good faith purchaser.

Thus, even if Louisiana law governed the effect of the Florida sale of a thing stolen in Florida from a Florida owner, the judgment appealed from should be reversed and there should be judgment for the owner.

NOTES

1. You might want to review the overview of Louisiana's bona fide purchaser doctrine in Chapter V, *supra*.

2. What remedy does the original owner have once this decision is final? Is that less satisfactory than recovery of the object itself?

2. *Southeast Equipment v. State Police* illustrates the reluctance of appellate courts to overturn a factual finding of good faith from the trial court, even when there are factors, as the dissent suggests, that raise doubts as to that finding. See *Britt Builders v. Brister, supra* Chapter VI, for a similar situation.

3. BOUNDARY ACTION
Civil Code arts. 784-796

A. N. YIANNOPOULOS, CIVIL LAW PROPERTY
§§ 282-290 (4th ed. 2001)
(footnotes omitted)

§ 282. Boundary and Boundary Markers; Fixing the Boundary

A boundary is the line of separation between contiguous lands. This line is ordinarily marked on the ground by natural or artificial objects called boundary markers.

Ordinarily, the boundary of contiguous lands is certain and marked on the ground. However, the markers may have been wrongly placed, may have been removed, or may have been destroyed. Occasionally, the line of separation between contiguous lands is certain but has never been marked on the ground. For example, the owner of an estate containing one hundred acres may have sold fifty acres to one person by directions and courses and the remaining fifty acres to another person but the purchasers never took care to separate their estates by boundary markers. At times, the line of separation between contiguous lands is itself uncertain or disputed. For example, the owner of an estate containing one hundred acres may have conveyed to one person the "north half" of his estate and to another person the "south half," or he may have conveyed to one person the "highlands" and to another person the "lowlands." Further, one of the contiguous landowners may have possessed for a long period of time within visible bounds more land than his title calls for and may dispute the validity of a line of separation established by titles.

In these circumstances, owners of, and persons having real rights on, contiguous lands have claims for the fixing of the boundary. The fixing of the boundary may involve merely determination of the line of separation, if it is uncertain or disputed; placement of markers on the ground if the line of separation is certain but markers were never placed, were wrongly placed, or are no longer to be seen; and determination of the line of separation and placement of markers on the ground if the line of separation is uncertain or disputed and markers were never placed, were wrongly placed, or are no longer to be seen.

The boundary may be fixed either judicially, that is, by a boundary action, or extrajudicially by a boundary agreement. The two modes of fixing the boundary will be discussed separately.

§ 283. Boundary Agreements

The boundary is fixed extrajudicially when adjoining landowners determine the line of separation between their lands by a written agreement, with or without reference to markers on the ground. Thus, owners of contiguous lands may enter into a written agreement designating the boundary between their lands with reference to markers on the ground, utilizing for this purpose natural monuments, fences, trees, posts, or other boundary markers. However, owners of contiguous lands may also enter into a boundary agreement that merely designates on paper the line of separation between their lands. In such a case, either of them may subsequently demand that the line be marked on the ground in accordance with the agreement.

A boundary agreement may in fact confirm an existing boundary or convey ownership to a neighbor up to the line fixed in the agreement. In the last case, the boundary agreement is an act translative of ownership having the effect of compromise. When filed for registry in the appropriate conveyance records, the agreement is effective toward third persons in the same way as any other contract affecting immovable property. . . .

Annulment of boundary agreement; liberative prescription. If the parties to a boundary agreement that determined the line of separation between their lands *with reference to markers on the ground* made an error as to the location of the line, as to the location of the markers, or both, the boundary agreement may be a relative nullity. This happens when the error is sufficient to support the recission of a compromise. In such a case, a party may institute an action for the annulment of the boundary agreement within five years "from the time the ground for nullity either ceased, as in the case of incapacity or duress, or was discovered, as in the case of error or fraud." However, contractual actions other than those governed by Article 2032 are subject to the ten-year liberative prescription of Article 3499 of the Louisiana Civil Code.

Comments (b) and (c) under Article 795 of the Louisiana Civil Code state that if the parties or the surveyor committed an error in the location of the line of separation, or the markers, or both, "the error may be rectified by the court unless the agreement is no longer assailable as a result of the ten-year prescription." These comments refer to the ten-year prescription under Article 3544 of the Louisiana Civil Code of 1870 that was in force at the time of the 1977 revision of the laws governing boundaries. Further, these comments contemplate the rectification of boundaries by an action for the reformation of the boundary agreement, that is, the correction of erroneous descriptions in accordance with the actual intent of the parties to the agreement. In Louisiana, an action for the reformation of an instrument is "an equitable remedy and lies only to correct mistakes or errors in written instruments when such instruments, as written, do not express the true contract of the parties." Such actions were subject to the ten year liberative prescription of Article 3544 of the 1870 Code that commenced to run against the person seeking reformation from the time he discovered the error or should have discovered it by the exercise of due diligence.

...Accordingly, an action for the annulment of a boundary agreement for errors that suffice for the rescission of a compromise is subject to a five-year liberative prescription under Article 2032. However, it would seem that an action for the rectification of a boundary is still subject to a ten-year liberative prescription under Article 3499 of the Louisiana Civil Code (corresponding with Article 3544 of the Louisiana Civil Code of 1870). That prescription applies to all personal actions unless otherwise provided by legislation....

If the parties to a boundary agreement determined correctly the line of separation between their lands *without reference* to markers on the ground, and, subsequently, markers were incorrectly placed by one of the contiguous owners alone or by both of them but not in accordance with the prior agreement, the placement of the markers may also be corrected. In these circumstances liberative prescription is immaterial because the mere placement of markers on the ground is not a contract. Correction, however, is excluded when a contiguous owner has acquired ownership up to the visible bounds by thirty years' possession. The words "or not in accordance with the written agreement fix-ing the boundary" in Article 796 of the Civil Code necessarily contemplate a fixing of the boundary on paper, that is, without reference to markers on the ground.

Acquisitive prescription: When markers are placed by one of the contiguous owners alone, or by two contiguous owners without a written boundary agreement, the boundary is not fixed. A demand for a judicial or extrajudicial fixing of the boundary is, therefore, proper. The mere passive failure of a contiguous owner to object to the location of a fence or other marker, or the informal acquiescence by contiguous owners to a jointly erected fence, does not constitute a fixing of the boundary. If the markers were placed wrongly, they will be removed unless a contiguous owner and his ancestors in title have possessed up to them without interruption for thirty years.

The existence of a recorded boundary agreement does not preclude the running of acquisitive prescription in favor of an adverse possessor. The line of separation, whether or not marked on the ground, may be altered in favor of a possessor in good or in bad faith in accordance with the rules of the Civil Code governing acquisitive prescription. The ten-year acquisitive prescription is pertinent when a neighbor possesses in good faith and under just title more land than his ancestor owned under a boundary agreement the ancestor had made. There is no ten-year acquisitive prescription by possession under an erroneous or formally defective survey made amicably between adjoining owners in an effort to fix their boundary. If such a survey is made a part of a boundary agreement, the error of the surveyor in the location of the line of separation is the error of the parties that may be rectified unless the liberative prescription has accrued. If the survey is not a part of the agreement, the error of the surveyor is immaterial insofar as the ten-year acquisitive prescription is concerned. In either case, the agreement conveys ownership up to the boundary designated by the parties and there is no room for acquisitive prescription up to the same line.

§ 284. Judicial Fixing of the Boundary

The boundary between tracts of land held by private persons is fixed judicially by the boundary action, a nominate real action under the Code of Civil Procedure.***

§ 285. Nature of the Boundary Action

A boundary action is distinguishable from a petitory action, a possessory action or an action for declaratory judgment. In contrast with a possessory action, the boundary action may be brought by a possessor without regard to the requirements of Article 3658 of the Code of Civil Procedure. In contrast with a petitory action which is brought for the recognition of one's ownership of an immovable or of a real right, the boundary action is brought for the fixing of the boundary between contiguous lands. The court does not merely render a judgment recognizing plaintiffs' ownership of a disputed strip of land but also determines the line of separation between the contiguous lands with reference to markers on the ground. One who claims the ownership of a strip of land adjoining the land of a neighbor may bring the petitory action or the action of boundary, or he may cumulate the two. It is true that the burden of proof is different in each of the two actions but when ownership is claimed the proof of ownership is the same. Finally, in contrast with an action for declaratory judgment which is brought for the declaration of "rights, status, and other legal relations," the action of boundary is brought to "fix" the boundary.

§ 288. Effect of Titles, Prescription, and Possession

After considering the evidence, including the testimony and exhibits of a surveyor or other expert appointed by the court or by a party, the court renders judgment fixing the boundary between the contiguous lands in accordance with the ownership or possession of the parties. Possession is, of course, material when none of the parties establishes his ownership of the strip of land in dispute.

The ownership of immovable property may be proved by title, that is, an unbroken chain of transfers from a previous owner, or by acquisitive prescription. If both parties rely on titles only, the boundary shall be fixed according to titles.***

If either or both parties rely on acquisitive prescription, "the boundary shall be fixed according to limits established by prescription rather than titles." Thus, a party that has possessed the strip of land in dispute for ten years in good faith and under just title will be entitled to a line of separation along the limits of his title. Further, if a party and his ancestors in title possessed for thirty years without interruption within visible bounds more land than their title called for, the boundary shall be fixed along these bounds.

When the parties rely both on titles and acquisitive prescription, and a party proves acquisitive prescription, the boundary shall be fixed according to lines established by prescription rather than titles. If neither party proves acquisitive prescription, the boundary shall be fixed according to titles.

When one party relies on title and the other party on acquisitive prescription, the party relying on title will prevail unless the adversary establishes his ownership by acquisitive prescription. When neither party proves ownership, the boundary shall be fixed according to limits established by possession. The judgment in such a case ought to fix merely the boundary rather than determine the ownership of one of the parties up to the line of separation between the contiguous lands.***

§ 290. Liberative Prescription; Rectification of Boundary

The action of boundary is imprescriptible. For the same reasons that no one is bound to hold an estate in indivision, no one is bound to leave the limits of contiguous lands undetermined. Thus, the boundary action may not be dismissed on the basis of a peremptory exception of liberative prescription. As one is always permitted to bring an action for partition; likewise one is always permitted to demand that the limits of his property be ascertained and fixed. However, an action of boundary may be dismissed on the basis of a peremptory exception of acquisitive prescription, as when the limits of contiguous lands are actually fixed by possession within visible bounds for over thirty years.

When the boundary is judicially fixed, there is no action to rectify the boundary established by a final judgment. Such a judgment is res judicata and may not be attacked for error. It may be attacked for fraud only but within one year from the date of its rendition.

LOUISIANA CODE OF CIVIL PROCEDURE

Art. 3691. Boundary action

An action to fix the boundary is an ordinary proceeding.

Art. 3692. Appointment of surveyor by court; duties of surveyor

The court may appoint a surveyor to inspect the lands and to make plans in accordance with the prevailing standards and practices of his profession indicating the respective contentions of the parties.

Art. 3693. Evidence; judgment

After considering the evidence, including the testimony and exhibits of a surveyor or other expert appointed by the court or by a party, the court shall render judgment fixing the boundary between the contiguous lands in accordance with the ownership or possession of the parties.

ALCUS v. ELLISER
310 So. 2d 663 (La. App. 1st Cir. 1975)

BARNETTE, J. This litigation involves a boundary dispute between owners of contiguous estates. They acquired titles respectively which had derived from the same prior owner. The plaintiffs' title is to all the "swampland" in a certain described portion of a section, being 35 acres more or less, and the defendant's deed conveys to him all the "highland" in the same described portion of section, being 15 acres more or less.

This suit was filed by plaintiffs as a boundary action to have the line separating the two estates judicially determined and for an accounting of revenues received by defendant from that portion of the disputed land upon which they allege defendant has wrongfully erected certain improvements.

A judgment was rendered by the trial court in favor of plaintiffs recognizing the two-foot elevation contour line as the boundary. The judgment further ordered the court-appointed surveyor to physically mark that line across the property and make due return thereof. The defendant was allowed 30 days after homologation of the surveyor's proces verbal to account for all revenues received from that portion of the land below the determined two-foot contour line. The judgment made no reference to the exceptions of no right of action and of prescription which defendant had pleaded. The defendant has appealed.***

There is no dispute between Alcus and Elliser relative to their respective deeds of acquisition of the properties claimed but there is issue between them as to the location of the boundary separating the two properties described.

The plaintiff, Alcus, owns:

Thirty-five (35) acres of *swampland* situated in the East Half of the Southwest Quarter of the Southwest Quarter (E/2 of SW¼ of SW 1/4) of Section Fourteen, Township Nine South, Range Four East (emphasis added).

The defendant, Elliser, owns, by virtue of a deed executed June 10, 1941, the following described property:

Fifteen (15) acres, more or less of *highland,* situated in the East Half of Southwest Quarter of Southwest Quarter (E/2 of SW¼ of SW 1/4) of Section 14, Township 9 South, Range 4 East, *containing all the highland* in said East Half of Southwest Quarter (E/2 of SW ¼ of SW 1/4) of Section 14, Township 9 South, Range 4 East.

A strip of land 15 feet wide on West side of Northeast Quarter of Southwest Quarter (NE¼ of SW 1/4) of Section 14, Township 9 South, Range 4 East, running North to gravel highway (emphasis added).

The above descriptions are confusing and partially incorrect in that they aggregate 50 acres more or less, "situated in" the East half of the Southwest Quarter of the Southwest Quarter (E/2 of 5W¼ of SW¼). This described fractional section contains at most only 20 acres. All of the 15 acres, more or less, of *highland* described in the Elliser deed lies wholly within this 20 acres. Most of the Alcus land lies to the west of this 20 acres and only 5 acres at most lies in the area described. It is within this approximately five acres that the disputed boundary lies. The maps filed in evidence indicate this to be in the extreme southern portion of the above-described 20 acres. The Amite River Diversion Canal constructed in 1959 cuts off the southwest corner of the 20 acres described thus reducing the disputed area to something less than five acres.

This action was brought properly under almost identical articles of the Civil Code and the Code of Civil Procedure.***

Alcus employed Alex Theriot, Jr., a Civil Engineer, in 1967 to make a survey of the land in question to locate and determine the property line between the Alcus property and that owned by Elliser within the twenty acres above described. The result of his survey, which fixed the boundary along the two-foot contour line, is shown by Exhibit P-2 filed in evidence. It is dated December 20, 1967. This suit was filed August 19, 1971. On August 23, 1971, an order was signed appointing Mr. Theriot to "*** inspect the property described in the foregoing petition, to survey the same and report thereon, in writing, to the Court, according to law."

Pursuant to that order, Mr. Theriot: "Revised [his December 20, 1967 survey made for Alcus] to show gravel lane, sheds, frame camps and trailers existing as of August 10, 1973."

It is significant, we think, that the survey which actually fixed the boundary along the two foot contour was made in 1967, not pursuant to the court order, but for a private client, now the plaintiff in this case. No boundary survey was made after the Court appointment. Mr. Theriot merely updated the survey made for Alcus by indicating improvements which had been made the property after December 1967.

During the course of the trial below (January 14, 1974) more than two years after the appointment of Mr. Theriot as the Court surveyor, counsel for defendant, Elliser, objected to Theriot's appointment on the basis that the survey which he had made fixing the boundary was not done pursuant to the Court's appointment, but on behalf of the plaintiff and that he could not therefore be an impartial surveyor.***

The objection to Mr. Theriot's appointment based on his possible conflict of interests as the expert employed by the plaintiff appears to have substantial merit. This does not imply any reflection on Mr. Theriot's integrity or professional competence. But irrespective of the merit or timeliness of the objection, his survey could not be accepted as the basis of the Court's judgment for the reason that it was not made in accordance with the strict requirements of law.***

His testimony at the trial of the case was in large measure an attempt to justify his predetermined location of the boundary. It is significant also that his selection of the two foot contour was made not from an inspection of the property, but after consultation with professors at L.S.U. and other people in his line of work having knowledge of the lower elevation of land. After selecting the two foot contour he computed the acreage and found it to be 15.3 acres in the portion described in the Elliser deed. This further convinced him of the accuracy of the boundary selected.

The judgment of the trial court now before us on this appeal, after judicially recognizing the boundary to be the two-foot contour, then orders the surveyor to survey and mark that line on the ground.

This we think puts the cart before the horse. It is the purpose of the survey to provide the Court with impartial guidance to assist it in reaching a judicial determination of the boundary between the two estates. Here the Court made that judicial determination primarily upon the result of a private expert's survey and then ordered the surveyor to stake out that line and thereafter file his procès verbal for homologation. This reverse order of procedure does not follow the requirements of law enacted for the exclusive purpose of regulating boundary actions. There is no alternative than to remand for further proceedings in strict conformity with the regulatory articles of the Civil Code and Code of Civil Procedure. [citations omitted].

Our opinion should not be interpreted to mean that the two-foot contour may not ultimately be found to be the boundary between the two estates. It may be, but its location should be made from evidence to be determined from an examination of the land with the purpose of drawing a line of demarcation between the "highland" and the "swampland" without regard to a specific or predetermined contour.

The construction of the Amite River Diversion Canal, depositing a large amount of spoil from the excavation, has materially altered and obscured natural land marks. This will make the surveyor's task very difficult in his search for physical evidence existing before the construction. Man-made as well as natural markings have evidentiary value, for certainly no better guide could be found than the line of demarcation which the adjoining landowners themselves accepted and established as evidenced by the limits of their possession long before the canal was constructed.

We are of the opinion that the appointment of Mr. Theriot as the Court Surveyor was improper in view of his predetermined boundary under employment by the plaintiff. It is not necessary to discuss the timeliness of the objection to his appointment since the procedural requirements of the Code Articles, *supra*, were not followed. We will remand for the appointment of another surveyor and further proceedings.

The exceptions of no right of action and prescription based on Mr. Elliser's alleged possession are referred to the merits for trial on remand. The issue raised by these exceptions cannot be resolved until the boundary between the "highland" and the "swampland" has been determined. The question of possession addresses itself to counsel to whom is reserved the right to introduce further evidence as may be deemed appropriate when the new survey has been completed....

SKILLMAN v. HARVEY
898 So. 2d 431 (La. App. 1st Cir. 2004),
cert. denied **897 So. 2d 610 (La. 2005)**

McCLENDON, J. Plaintiffs filed this action to establish a boundary line between the contiguous properties of plaintiffs and defendants. Defendants reconvened asserting a different boundary line and seeking damages for trespass. The trial court rendered judgment in favor of defendants. For the reasons that follow, we reverse the judgment of the trial court.

FACTS AND PROCEDURAL HISTORY

On August 3, 2001, plaintiffs, William B. Skillman and Ernest E. Skillman, filed a boundary action against defendants, Melba L. Harvey, Jr., James Ford Harvey and Rosemary Harvey Jackson. The Skillmans asserted that on December 31, 1976, they purchased the following described property in East Feliciana Parish:

> Tract lying, being and situated in the Parish of East Feliciana, Louisiana, Town of Jackson, with all of the buildings and improvements thereon, containing 29 acres, more or less, described as: commence at vendor's gate in the field; run east to Keller's line; thence run north on Keller's line to the Clinton and Jackson public road; then west down said public road towards Jackson to a point opposite said gate first mentioned, thence

south to place of beginning, LESS right of way of the Jackson railroad through said described tract of land.

The Skillmans further asserted that the Harveys are the record title owners of the adjoining tract of land described as follows:

A certain tract or parcel of land, together with all buildings and improvements thereon and all rights, ways, privileges, servitudes and prescriptions appurtenant thereto or in anywise appertaining, lying, being, and situated in the Parish of East Feliciana, State of Louisiana, and containing thirty (30) acres, more or less, bounded on the North by Jackson Railroad, East by Klein and Peterson, and South and West by East Louisiana State Hospital.

The eastern edge of the Harvey property abuts the western edge of the Skillman property. The Skillmans asserted that because the reference points in the property description no longer exist, a dispute has arisen between plaintiffs and defendants as to the boundary lines of their respective properties. Based on the knowledge of the location of the eastern, northern and part of the western boundaries of the Skillman property, and the fact that the property description reflects twenty-nine acres, more or less, the Skillmans sought to have the remainder of the western boundary and the location of the southern boundary determined in accordance with a survey performed by Curtis M. Chaney for GWS Engineering, Inc. The Skillmans asserted that the survey accurately reflects the boundary between the Skillman and Harvey properties based on physical evidence and historical title documents.

The Harveys filed an Answer and Reconventional Demand on November 5, 2001, asserting that the common boundary between the properties is an existing fence, painted line, and old railroad embankment, and sought to have the boundary fixed along said line. The boundary line as requested by the Harveys is set farther north than that requested by the Skillmans. At issue, therefore, are nine acres claimed by both parties. The Harveys additionally sought treble damages for timber cut by the Skillmans on the nine acres of disputed property.

Trial of the matter was held on July 16, 2003. Reasons for Judgment were issued on August 20, 2003, in favor of the Harveys, finding that they proved ownership of the nine acres by possession. Judgment fixing the common boundary up to the disputed fence line was signed on September 4, 2003. Plaintiffs appealed.

On appeal, the Skillmans raise three assignments of error:

1. The trial court erred in holding that plaintiffs failed to establish the boundary of their property by title where clear title records were introduced into evidence without objection and the boundary of the Skillman property was established according to the calls set forth by Louisiana law.

2. The trial court erred by holding that defendants gained ownership of the disputed portion of the Skillman property by acquisitive prescription where the property has never been cleared or used for any consistent purpose that could possibly establish open, notorious and adverse possession sufficient to establish ownership under Louisiana law.

3. The trial court erred by awarding the defendants $14,000.00 for timber which the plaintiffs cut on property which plaintiffs own and to which they have a good title.

DISCUSSION

In a boundary action, the court shall fix the boundary according to the ownership of the parties; if neither party proves ownership, the boundary shall be fixed according to limits established by possession. LSA-C.C. art. 792. Additionally, LSA-C.C.P. art. 3693 provides that after considering the evidence, including the testimony and exhibits of a surveyor or other expert appointed by the court or by a party, the court shall render judgment fixing the boundary between the contiguous lands in accordance with the ownership or possession of the parties.

The Louisiana Supreme Court has established that in cases where boundary questions exist, the legal guides for determining the location of a land line in property descriptions, in order of their importance, are: natural monuments, artificial monuments, distances, courses, and quantity, the controlling consideration being intention of the parties. *City of New Orleans v. Joseph Rathborne Land Co.,* 209 La. 93, 109-10, 24 So. 2d 275, 281 (La. 1945); *Meyer v. Comegys,* 147 La. 851, 857, 86 So. 307, 309 (La. 1920).

The survey in this matter was conducted by Wayne Sledge, a licensed surveyor with GWS Engineering, Inc., who was qualified as an expert land surveyor at trial, and testified that when performing the survey, his surveyors inventoried the entire area to collect as much data as possible. Thus, it was necessary to survey the Harvey property in conjunction with the Skillman property. Mr. Sledge testified that in this case, there were no remaining natural or artificial monuments, nor were there distances or bearings given in the deeds. Therefore, according to the rules of surveying, and going through the hierarchy of calls, it was necessary to use the last call, the call of quantity. The titles called for twenty-nine acres, more or less, in the Skillman tract, and thirty acres, more or less, in the Harvey tract. Mr. Sledge testified that based on the results of the survey, the Skillmans would have 28.94 acres and the Harveys would have 30.31 acres, which is very consistent with the historical title documents.

Mr. Sledge further testified that Curtis Chaney, who was his survey coordinator between 1996 and 2001, made the original survey in 2000. In 2002, when Mr. Sledge saw that this matter was going to trial, he reconstructed the original survey since Mr. Chaney was no longer with the firm. Mr. Sledge testified that he agreed with the southern boundary as established by Mr. Chaney.

Mr. Chaney testified by deposition. He testified that he surveyed the property in 2000 at Ben Skillman's request to determine the property lines of the Skillman tract. He was provided copies of the historical title documents. The starting point in the Skillman's property description was the vendor's gate, which no longer existed. He testified that initially he was unsure where the western line of the Skillman property was located, so he contacted Mr. Skillman for permission to contact the adjacent landowner to discuss the survey and obtain additional information. Mr. Harvey showed him some maps and other information. Thus, utilizing the east and west boundaries, Mr. Chaney testified that he projected the line south to encompass the twenty-nine acres called for in the deed, using quantity as the only available call.

Aditionally, Charles R. St. Romain, a registered land surveyor and Administrator of the State Land Office, retained in part by the Harveys to confirm the survey prepared by Mr. Chaney, admitted on cross-examination that Mr. Chaney's survey was accurate as to the mathematical calculations and configurations.

A survey predicated on sound surveying principles should be accepted unless the record shows it is incorrect. *Liner v. Terrebonne Parish School Bd.,* 519 So. 2d 777, 780 (La. App. 1 Or. 1987), *writ denied,* 521 So. 2d 1173 (La. 1988), *cert. denied,* 488 U.S. 827, 109 S. Ct. 79, 102 L. Ed. 2d 55; *Fallin v. Pesnell,* 27,814, p. 8 (La. App. 2d Cir. 1/24/96), 667 So. 2d 581, 585. We find that the survey correctly established the southern boundary of the Skillman property according to title. Further, with regard to intent, the parties clearly intended that the Skillman property would comprise twenty-nine acres, more or less, and the Harvey property would contain thirty acres, more or less. Thus, the trial court erred when it determined that neither party showed ownership as reflected by titles. The Skillmans have proven that they owned the disputed property based on the strength of their own title.

We also find that the trial court was clearly wrong in finding possession by the Harveys of either ten or thirty years. Ownership of immovable property may be acquired by prescription of thirty years without the need of just title or possession in good faith. LSA-C.C. art. 3486. If a party and his ancestors in title possessed for thirty years more land than called for in the title without interruption and within visible bounds, the boundary shall be fixed along those bounds. LSA-C.C. art. 794....

The Skillmans established that their family has owned the twenty-nine acres since 1902 and that they bought it from their mother, Helen Klein Skillman, in 1976. Ben Skillman testified that since he purchased the property, he has paid property taxes, placed two mortgages and entered into a mineral lease on the twenty-nine acres.

The Harveys established that M.L. Harvey, Sr. acquired his thirty acres in 1968. James Harvey testified he occasionally rode a horse with his father to the back of the property to check on the timber. Leroy Harvey testified that he has walked the property but not all the way around the perimeter. Two witnesses on behalf of the Harveys also testified that in 1996 and 1997 they leased 30 acres from the Harveys for bow hunting.

Mr. St. Romain, the surveyor hired by the Harveys, was asked to look for any evidence of possession along or near the property lines or within the properties. He testified that he found evidence of an old fence, painted trees and angle irons which indicated possession along the disputed fence line. On cross-examination, however, Mr. St. Romain conceded that fences are not necessarily external boundaries and therefore do not necessarily indicate possession.

Based on the above, we are unable to conclude that the Harveys proved their own possession of the nine acres for thirty years. Occasional hunting is insufficient to constitute actual corporeal possession. *Norton v. Addie, 337* So. 2d 432, 436 (La. 1976). Also, the occasional acts of walking or riding the property are not the type of acts to constitute open, notorious and adverse possession. LSA-C.C. art. 3476. Furthermore, with regard to the old fence on the railroad line, the evidence is undisputed that the Harveys did not maintain the fence as their own. The evidence clearly shows that it was the Skillmans' tenants who maintained the fence in question. The only evidence presented as to the identity of the original builder of the fence was that the fence was built to keep the livestock of the Skillmans' tenants from falling or getting trapped in the lower, heavily-wooded area south of the fence line, not to establish a boundary. While we recognize the difficulty in showing possession of heavily-timbered property, we simply cannot find sufficient evidence of possession that included the disputed nine acres.

With regard to ten-year possession, the party claiming ownership of property has the burden of proving the four requisites for ten years acquisitive prescription: (1) possession for ten years; (2) good faith; (3) just title; and (4) a thing susceptible of acquisition by prescription. LSA-C.C. art. 3475. Because we find that the Harveys failed to present sufficient evidence of just title or sufficient evidence of possession, the claim of ten-year acquisitive prescription also fails.

Accordingly, we determine the southern and lower western boundaries of the Skillman property to be that described in the GWS Engineering, Inc. survey, attached hereto and made a part hereof as Appendix 1, originally dated October 18, 2000, and revised on November 10, 2000 and May 2, 2002, by G. Wayne Sledge, land surveyor, wherein the Skillman property contains 28.74 acres and the Harvey property contains 30.31 acres.

Having found the disputed nine acres to be part of the Skillman tract, we also reverse the trial court's award of $ 14,000.00 to the Harveys for the value of the timber cut by the Skillmans on the disputed property.***Because both parties benefited from the fixing of the boundary, we assess the costs equally. *Smith v. Overton*, 417 So. 2d 872, 877 (La. App. 1st Cir. 1982).

NOTES AND QUESTIONS

1. *Procedural terminology:* The *peremptory exception* referred to in *Alcus v. Elliser* is a defense denying that any ground for the action exists. The surveyor's *procès verbal* is his written report in proper legal form of what he has found in his role as an officer of the court. *Homologation* is court approval of that document.

2. What is the reason that Chaney's survey, prepared for the plaintiff in *Skillman v. Harvey*, can serve as the basis for a judgment in the latter's favor, while the Theriot survey prepared for the plaintiff in *Alcus v. Elliser* cannot because "It is the purpose of the survey to provide the Court with impartial guidance to assist it in reaching a judicial determination of the boundary between the two estates"?

NOTE
The Limits on the Value of a Survey or Plat in
Boundary Determinations

In *Skillman v. Harvey*, the first circuit Court of Appeal stresses the reliance placed on a survey "predicated on sound surveying priniciples" in determining a disputed boundary, and in *Roy v. Belt* the third circuit refers to "the basic rule of property law that, where there is a conflict between a worded description and a survey, the survey prevails." In *Bourgeois v. Linden Interest*, 84 So.3d 715 (La. App. 3 Cir. 2012), the third circuit, citing *Lamson Petroleum Corp. v. Hallwood Petroleum, Inc.*, 824 So.2d 1194 (La. App. 3 Cir. 2001), references "the jurisprudentially accepted rule that when a property description conflicts with a plat or survey, the plat or survey prevails." The *Linden* court explained, though, that the rule was not without exception. "[A] plat or survey **normally** prevails over a conflicting property description," it stated, but the *Lamson* court itself had added a qualification: the general rule is not applicable when "it is very obvious that a [plat or] survey is wrong."

Linden furnishes some guidance for determining whether the plat or survey is wrong. The language of the property descriptions in that case described the boundary between the two tracts, East Linden and West Linden, created in a partition in 1951. The boundary was there described as lying between two points (Y and A2), not as a straight line, but as turning southwest along a canal and along the middle of the road running between the two tracts. The plat differed from the property descriptions in depicting the boundary as a straight line running between points Y and A2. Moreover, the civil engineer who had drawn the plat stated in a later report that the straight line depicted on it was not authorized and he had not surveyed it at the time the plat was drawn. Yet the trial court had used the straight line on the plat to fix the boundary between the East and West Linden tracts, basing its decision on the acreage listed on the plat. The appellate court reversed that decision as "manifestly erroneous." Instead, it determined that the boundary was fixed "along a canal and the center line of a road dividing West Linden and East Linden Plantations" because "this was clearly the intention of the parties when the 1951 partition transpired." The court noted: "[T]his result is also harmonious with the jurisprudential guide for determining a boundary. A canal is either a natural or an artificial monument. A road is an artificial monument. According to the value assigned when fixing a boundary, both warrant more value than a straight line between A2 and Y, which is a course, or acreage, which is a quantity."

NOTE
The Jurisprudential Background of Article 794

Article 794 of the Louisiana Civil Code rests on the authority of *Opdenwyer v. Brown*, 155 La. 617, 99 So. 482 (1924). Plaintiff brought action against an adjoining neighbor seeking to establish the boundary between the two properties. Plaintiff placed in evidence his title and claimed that the defendant had taken land belonging to plaintiff. Defendant answered and pleaded the prescription of 10 and 30 years. The court found that, indeed, defendant had taken possession of land that was included in plaintiff's title and that the defendant and his ancestors had long *possessed* beyond the limits of their titles. For more than 50 years before the filing of the suit those from whom defendant derived title had possessed as far as a certain "gully" or water course, considerably into plaintiff's land, on the edge of which they had set up a fence which marked the limit of their possession and served as the boundary between their property and the property of plaintiff. On these findings, the court held that the public interest requires that boundaries established for more than 30 years should not be disturbed. In the course of its opinion, the court declared:

"The sanctity which all nations have at all times attached to land boundaries is a part of general history. The Romans even *deified* such boundaries under the pseudonym of the god "Terminus", who had neither feet nor arms, so that *he could not move.* This was symbolic of their jurisprudence; and that jurisprudence is ours.***

Let us then take a case of boundaries. Say that A. buys a tract of land bounded on the north by the line X, and that C. acquired the adjoining tract bounded on the south by the same line X. The former then builds his fence or wall N feet north of the line X; that is to say, on the land of C. After 25 years have elapsed, A. sells to B. his tract of land, describing it as bounded on the north by the lands of C., and B. goes into possession of the whole tract up to the fence or wall aforesaid. Five years after that being 30 years after the fence or wall was set up, C. brings an action to fix the boundary between his property and that of B. And this is what C.C. art. 852 (1870) [794, 796] says...***

It will be observed that in such a case the holder of the junior title may retain any quantity of land "beyond his title" which he or those under whom he holds may have possessed for 30 years.***It is our firm conviction that the public interest requires that boundaries established for more than 30 years should not be disturbed; and we think the law so provides."

LOUTRE LAND AND TIMBER COMPANY v. ROBERTS
63 So. 3d 120 (La. App. 2d Cir.),
cert. denied 76 So. 3d 1177 (La. 2011)

CLARK, J. We granted certiorari to determine whether the court of appeal erred in reversing the trial court's judgment and in recognizing the defendant as the owner of a disputed tract of property. For the reasons that follow, we find the laws on acquisitive prescription require reversal of the court of appeal's ruling, and we remand for the determination of issues pretermitted on appeal.

FACTS AND PROCEDURAL HISTORY

The instant litigation involves a dispute over a tract of land that lies between two contiguous pieces of property that are owned by two separate owners. The Marie Wilson

Morgan family owned an 80-acre tract that was described as the "Section 3 Tract" in a recorded deed dating back to 1943.[1] As evidenced by the same recorded deed, the Morgan family also owned twenty acres located adjacent to the Section 3 Tract, lying in the SW/4 of Section 2. The combined land is hereinafter referred to as the "100 Acres." The Wilton A. Roberts family owned the tract of land that was described as the "Section 10 Tract" in a recorded deed.[2] Title to the Section 10 Tract passed from Dorothy Harbour to Wilton A. Roberts and Rebecca Jane Roberts in 1964. Subsequently, Edward W. Roberts ("Roberts"), the defendant, inherited his parents' interests in the property. The Section 3 Tract is immediately north of the Section 10 Tract, and the "Ideal Boundary" between these two tracts is the governmental section line, separating the SE/4 of the SE/4 of Section 3 Tract and the NE/4 of the NE/4 of Section 10.

A fence, running from east to west, however, is located in the middle of the Section 10 Tract and has been present for well over thirty years. The amount of land lying north of the fence to the Ideal Boundary is approximately 15 acres of property and is hereinafter referred to as the "Disputed Tract."[3] The record establishes (and no one contests) that the Morgan family adversely possessed the Disputed Tract for more than thirty years via actual acts of corporeal possession.

On July 29, 2002, the Succession of Marie Wilson Morgan ("the Succession") sold the following land to Loutre Land and Timber Company ("Loutre") through a full warranty deed, entitled "Act of Sale":

> The South Half of the Southwest Quarter of the Southwest Quarter (S-1/2 of SW-1/4 of SW-1/4) of Section 2, Township 16 North, Range 8 East, Franklin Parish, Louisiana, and the East Half of the Southeast Quarter (E-1/2 of SE-1/4) of Section 3, Township 16 North, Range 8 East, Franklin Parish, Louisiana, consisting of 100 acres, more or less, including all crop base acres.

Additionally, the deed transferred "all rights of prescription, whether acquisitive or liberative, to which said vendor may be entitled." Loutre paid the Succession $75,000.00. The deed was recorded on August 5, 2002.

After conducting a survey and confirming the Disputed Tract was included in the 1964 title he inherited from his parents, Roberts sought to obtain a quitclaim deed from the Succession ("the Quitclaim Deed") to recognize his right to the land. The Succession's attorney, Daniel Wirtz, indicated he believed the Succession had sold the Disputed Tract to Loutre and, therefore, had nothing to transfer to Roberts. However, on January 29, 2003, the Succession ultimately executed the Quitclaim Deed in favor of Roberts in exchange for $3,000.00. The Quitclaim Deed was recorded on February 27, 2003, and conveyed to Roberts [land that would have included the Disputed Tract, if the Succession had still owned it].

Subsequently, in June 2003, Roberts entered the Disputed Tract and "bush hogged" a path in an effort to erect a new fence to establish the boundary described in the Quitclaim Deed. In doing so, he destroyed pine seedlings that had been planted along the fence by

Loutre and created ruts in the land. Loutre filed suit, contending it owned the Disputed Tract insofar as it tacked the possession of its ancestor, the Morgan family. In its petition for damages, Loutre asserted claims for trespass and property destruction. Roberts answered and filed a reconventional demand, arguing he owned the Disputed Tract and should be compensated for loss of rental income.

On October 7, 2004, Loutre filed a motion for partial summary judgment, asking the trial court to recognize the fence as the proper boundary. Finding Loutre to be the rightful owner of the property by virtue of acquisitive prescription, the trial court entered judgment in favor of Loutre on June 2, 2005. After a trial on the merits to determine the amount of damages, the trial court awarded Loutre $15,250.00.

Roberts appealed the grant of the partial summary judgment and the amount of damages. The court of appeal found there was a genuine issue of material fact regarding the intent of the Succession and Loutre as to what land was actually being transferred pursuant to the full warranty deed. Accordingly, the court of appeal found summary judgment was inappropriate and remanded the matter to the trial court to conduct a trial on the issue of intent. Loutre Land and Timber Co. v. Roberts, 42,918 (La. App. 2d Cir. 4/16/08), 981 So.2d 775, writ denied, 08-1422 (La. 10/31/08), 994 So.2d 535.

On remand, the trial court heard testimony and accepted evidence relative to the intent of the Succession and Loutre in executing the Act of Sale. The trial court ruled in favor of Loutre, finding the parties intended to convey all of the land north of the fence, including the Disputed Tract. Recognizing Loutre as the owner, it then awarded it $17,750.00 in damages. Both Loutre and Roberts appealed.

The court of appeal reversed the judgment of the trial court and remanded the case to fix the boundaries in accordance with the parties' surveys. Loutre Land and Timber Co. v. Roberts, 45,355 (La. App. 2d Cir. 8/4/10), 47 So.3d 478. In reaching this conclusion, the court of appeal held that the fact the Succession was the "ancestor in title" to both Roberts and Loutre placed the issue outside the scope of a typical boundary action when one party claims acquisitive possession and the other relies on title. Accordingly, it conducted an analysis under "something other than [Civil Code] Article 794" in order to rank the competing transfers.[4] The court of appeal began by acknowledging the Morgan family's possession extended beyond thirty years and, thus, the Succession acquired the right to sell the property via acquisitive prescription. Next, the court of appeal recognized that Loutre continued the possession by virtue of planting the seedlings. Thus, it classified Roberts as an adverse possessor due to his act of bush hogging the land. Pursuant to La. Civ. Code art. 3654,[5] then, Roberts was required to show "he had acquired ownership from a previous owner." Ultimately, by turning to the public records doctrine, the court of appeal found Roberts satisfied this burden. In particular, it found the Quitclaim Deed to Roberts specifically described the Disputed Tract while the Act of Sale to Loutre did not. As such, the deeds represented separate transfers of differently described immovables. Further, the court of appeal noted that Roberts was a third party to the transfer between the Succession and Loutre, and he could have concluded that the Succession intended to sell the 100 acres separate from the Disputed Tract. Under the law of registry, then, it determined Roberts' deed was superior to Loutre's deed. Finally, the court of appeal dismissed Roberts' claims for damages, finding no support in the record to justify an award.

Judge Moore dissented, finding La. Civ. Code art. 794 clearly governed and mandated a ruling different from that reached by the majority. He agreed that the Morgan family possessed the property for more than thirty years; therefore, the Succession acquired the right to sell it to Loutre. However, he disagreed that the public records doctrine had any relevance and opined that to the extent it could somehow trump acquisitive prescription, the doctrine would not work in favor of Roberts. Rather, the Act of Sale that conveyed 100 acres "more or less . . . together with all rights of prescription, whether acquisitive or prescriptive, to which said vendor may be entitled" clearly evidenced the intent by the Succession and Loutre to transfer all of the property north of the fence, including the Disputed Tract. Because (1) the Act of Sale conveyed the property to Loutre and (2) a quitclaim deed can only convey whatever interest the seller actually has in the property, the Succession had nothing to sell when it executed the Quitclaim Deed in favor of Roberts. Thus, nothing was transferred to Roberts. Additionally, Judge Moore believed the majority ignored the manifest error standard by failing to give credit to the trial court's credibility determinations that led it to find such intent indeed existed.

Loutre filed a writ application in this court, contending the court of appeal committed error. We granted certiorari to determine who is the rightful owner of the Disputed Tract. *Loutre Land and Timber Co. v. Roberts*, 10-C-2327 (La. 1/7/11), 52 So.3d 879.

APPLICABLE LAW

"To acquire possession, one must intend to possess as owner and must take corporeal possession of the thing." La. Civ. Code art. 3424. "The possessor must have corporeal possession, or civil possession preceded by corporeal possession, to acquire a thing by prescription. The possession must be continuous, uninterrupted, peaceable, public, and unequivocal." La. Civ. Code art. 3476. "Ownership and other real rights in immovables may be acquired by the prescription of thirty years without the need of just title or possession in good faith." La. Civ. Code art. 3486. "For purposes of acquisitive prescription without title, possession extends only to that which has been actually possessed." La. Civ. Code art. 3487.

"When a party proves acquisitive prescription, the boundary shall be fixed according to limits established by prescription rather than titles. If a party and his ancestors in title possessed for thirty years without interruption, within visible bounds, more land than their title called for, the boundary shall be fixed along these bounds." La. Civ. Code art. 794. "Possession is transferable by universal title or by particular title." La. Civ. Code art. 3441. "The possession of the transferor is tacked to that of the transferee if there has been no interruption of possession." La. Civ. Code art. 3442.

In Marks v. Zimmerman Farms, LLC, 44,279, pp. 11-12 (La. App. 2d Cir. 5/20/09), 13 So.3d 768, 774-75, the Louisiana Second Circuit Court of Appeal succinctly explained tacking as it relates to La. Civ. Code art. 794:

> The legal principles which govern tacking under La. C.C. art. 794 are in some respects different and distinct from the principles which govern tacking under La. C.C. arts. 3441 and 3442. La. C.C. art. 794 deals with boundary prescription, strictly speaking, while La. C.C. arts. 3441 and 3442 provide general rules which refer in broader terms to acquisitive prescription of property, generally. Brown v. Wood, [451 So.2d 569 (La. App. 2d Cir. 1984), writ denied, 452 So.2d 1176 (La. 1984)].

In *Brown v. Wood, supra,* this court noted that tacking under La. C.C. art. 794 is different from tacking under the general tacking provisions of La. C.C. arts. 3441 and 3442 in the following respect:

> Under Article 794, the privity of title between the possessor and his ancestor in title need not extend to the property to which the possessor asserts prescriptive title; under Article 794, the juridical link, or written instrument which passes to the possessor from his ancestor in title need not encompass or include the particular property to which the possessor claims prescriptive title. On the other hand, it is generally conceded under the general tacking provisions of Articles 3441 and 3442 and their statutory precursors, that tacking is only allowed with respect to property that is included and described in the juridical link between the possessor's ancestor in title and the possessor himself.

Simply stated, under Art. 794 (old Art. 852), one may utilize tacking to prescribe beyond title on adjacent property to the extent of visible boundaries, but under the general prescriptive articles, Arts. 3441 and 3442, tacking may be utilized to prescribe only to the extent of title.

DISCUSSION

The record establishes that the Morgan family corporeally possessed the Disputed Tract for more than thirty years, prior to the sale of the land to Loutre. The possession was continuous, uninterrupted, peaceable, public, and unequivocal. Thus, the Succession was legally entitled to sell the land. The Succession then executed the Act of Sale with Loutre, transferring the 100 acres "more or less," "together with all rights of prescription, whether acquisitive or liberative, to which said vendor may be entitled." This full warranty deed, then, served as the juridical link. As explained above, the deed is not required to include the particular property to which the possessor claims prescriptive title, namely, the Disputed Tract. Rather, La. Civ. Code art. 794 allows a party to tack onto the possession of its ancestor in title if the possession occurs without interruption. If the combined possession spans thirty years, the party is entitled to have the boundary fixed along the visible bounds of the possession. Loutre, by planting the pine seedlings along the fence, continued the possession of the Succession, making the fence the proper boundary line. As such, the trial court correctly determined Loutre is the proper owner of the Disputed Tract. The inquiry ends after this straightforward application of La. Civ. Code 794.

The court of appeal, however, felt "something other than *794* must be considered" because the Succession was the seller to both parties. We find nothing in Louisiana's codal or jurisprudential authority to justify this assertion or to require an analysis under the public records doctrine. However, even if it could be argued that the Act of Sale to Loutre was required to include a specific description of the Disputed Tract, we find the language in the deed to be sufficiently particular. Namely, the Act of Sale conveys "more or less" the 100 acres together with all acquisitive prescription rights to which the seller was entitled. It is clear from the four corners of the deed that the Succession was selling all of its interests in the property.

Additionally, this exact issue of intent was decided by the trial court on remand. The Succession's attorney, Daniel Wirtz, unequivocally testified that the parties intended to convey all the land north of the fence, including the Disputed Tract. Roberts attempted to discount this testimony by suggesting Wirtz's memory of the sale was less than accurate. In particular, Roberts asserted the file on the matter had been destroyed; Wirtz could not correctly recall the amount of the consideration tendered in exchange for the Quitclaim Deed; and he could not remember who received the proceeds of the Quitclaim Deed. Furthermore, Roberts presented testimony in an attempt to show that the parties acknowledged the amount paid was $750.00 per acre for a total of $75,000.00. Thus, the parties must have intended to sell only the 100 acres. Ultimately, the trial court, after weighing the evidence and making credibility determinations, decided that both the Succession and Loutre intended to sell all of the property north of the fence. The court of appeal erred, then, by not giving deference to the trial court's factual finding on this issue without mention or application of the manifest error standard of review. Rather, the court of appeal simply noted ". . . [t]he Succession could have intended to sell the Disputed Tract and the 100 Acres separately to different parties." This speculation ignores the significant fact that a trial occurred to determine this very issue and a factual finding was made by the trial court.

Thus, we conclude that La. Civ. Code art. 794 does not require particular title to the Disputed Tract in order to convey the accompanying acquisitive prescription rights to that land. Rather, the continued possession of the land to the fence's boundary by the Succession and Loutre for over thirty years mandates a finding that Loutre owns the Disputed Tract. In fact, because the law operates in favor of Loutre in the absence of a particularized description of the land, the Act of Sale would have required a clause *excluding* the Disputed Tract if that had been the parties' intent. Even if the law could be read to require a deed's inclusion of all the land subject to transfer, the language of the Act of Sale was specific enough to effect a transfer of the Disputed Tract. Lastly, even if the language lacked specificity, the trial court made a factual determination that the parties intended to include the Disputed Tract, and, without a finding of manifest error or clear abuse, the court of appeal was not authorized to disturb that finding.

DECREE

For the foregoing reasons, we reverse the ruling of the court of appeal and remand the matter to the court of appeal to rule on the assignments of error asserted by Loutre, which were necessarily pretermitted by the court of appeal's ruling. Reversed and remanded.

NOTES

1. The *Loutre* holding was of no avail to the plaintiff in *Taylor v. Dumas*, 2013 WL 1976236 (La.App. 2d Cir 5/15/2013). The appellate court distinguished it from *Loutre*, finding that Taylor was unable to prove that the land beyond title that she claimed to own through the acquisitive prescription of her ancestors in title had not been possessed by them with the intent to own. In fact, they had tolerated the defendant's construction of a new fence that excluded them from the disputed tract and later quitclaimed to Dumas any ownership interest in it.

2. The Louisiana Supreme Court's holding in *Loutre Land and Timber Co. v. Roberts* that "La. Civ. Code art. 794 does not require particular title to the Disputed Tract in order to convey the accompanying acquisitive prescription rights to the land" provided the basis for a decision establishing a disputed boundary in *Jackson v. Herring*, 86 So.3d 9 (La. App. 2 Cir. 2012). In that case, the defendants erected a fence that barred the plaintiff from access to the disputed property, on which a house was located. A survey showed that property to be located within the defendants' lot. Yet the plaintiff prevailed, establishing that her ancestors in title had possessed beyond their title within the visible bounds of the house and an old fence line for more than 30 years, obtaining ownership of the disputed area by acquisitive prescription. Though the plaintiff's petition was captioned a petitory action, the court remanded for fixing of the boundary in accordance with the requirements of La. Civ. Code 794. It explained:

> The petitory and boundary actions are not mutually exclusive; rather, they are "mutually complementary," with the petitory action seeking a "judicial determination of the plaintiff's ownership," and the boundary action seeking a "judicial localization of this ownership on the ground." Symeon Symeonides, *Ruminations on Real Actions*, 51 LA. L. REV. 493, 511 (Jan. 1991). Issues of title and ownership may be decided in a boundary action....Title prescriptions may be pled in boundary actions and boundary prescriptions in title suits.

ROY v. BELT
868 So. 2d 209 (La. App. 3d Cir. 2004)

SULLIVAN, J. Lillia Roy and her children, Constance Roy, Catherine Roy, Sheldon Roy and Lillia Roy, filed a boundary action against The Law Enforcement District of Avoyelles Parish, Louisiana (Sheriff Belt). They amended their petition to add a claim for inverse condemnation. After a trial, judgment was rendered in favor of Sheriff Belt, establishing Bayou Savage as the boundary between these respective properties and denying the Roys' claims for inverse condemnation. For the following reasons, we reverse that judgment and remand for a determination of the appropriate damages.

FACTS

The Roys and Sheriff Belt own adjoining properties situated in Avoyelles Parish. In 1978, 1986, and 1992, Sheriff Belt or his predecessor built three buildings which the Roys claim encroach upon their property. The chain of title for both properties is derived from a common ancestor in title, J. Clifton Cappel, who acquired 100 arpents, more or less, from Clarence LaFargue on February 24, 1896. In February 1904, November 1904, and February 1906, Pierre Poret purchased three parcels of land from Mr. Cappel totaling 29.5 acres. Sheriff Belt's title derives from this chain of title. In 1906, Louis Coco purchased 34.42 acres from Mr. Cappel, and in 1956, Van L. Roy, the Roys' husband and father, purchased 32.5 of those 34.42 acres from Ernest M. Coco, Louis' transferee. The Roys' title derives from this chain of title.

The Roys contend that the boundary between their property and Sheriff Belt's property is north of Bayou Sauvage,[12] while Sheriff Belt contends that the boundary is the center of the bayou.

Pierre Poret's first acquisition from Clifton Cappel was on February 26, 1904, when he purchased four acres. He next acquired ten acres on November 23, 1904. Then, by sale dated February 20, 1906, he acquired an additional 15.5 acres from Mr. Cappel. The southern boundaries of these properties are described as: "Bounded . . . South and East by Vendor"; "South by Vendor and Mrs. Victor Moreau"; and "South by vendor," in the respective deeds.

In the transfers from Mr. Cappel to Louis Coco, Louis to Ernest Coco, and Ernest to Van L. Roy, the northern boundary is described as: "bounded on the north by W.S. Edwards, F. Moreau, and Poret"; "bounded on the north by W.H. Edwards, P. Gauthier, L.P. Gremillion, and P.L. Poret"; and "bounded on the north by Pierre L. Poret and northwest by Emeric G. Laborde," respectively.

On April 20, 1964, a Judgment of Possession was signed in the Succession of Pierre L. Poret and Eliza Bordelon Poret. That same day, the Porets' heirs partitioned their parents' property, dividing it into lots and drawing for designated lots; however, one lot, Lot 6, was not allotted and remained owned in indivision by the heirs. The southern boundary of the property is described in each document, in part, as "Bayou Moreau." In conjunction with the Judgment of Possession and the partition, a plat was prepared by surveyor, Ralph L. Gagnard, which was recorded and referenced in the property descriptions used in both of these documents. This survey, dated March 28, 1964, depicts a line along a fence/tree line in the southern portion of the survey. South of this line is a wooded area through which a bayou runs. The land situated south of the

---

[12] Documents in the chain of title refer to Bayou Moreau, Bayou Savage, and bayou. Surveys of the properties depict a Bayou Sauvage and an unnamed bayou. Witnesses testified that Bayou Moreau and Bayou Sauvage are probably one and the same. For ease of discussion and consistency throughout our opinion, the term "bayou" is used.

bayou is labeled "Van L. Roy." The property between the fence/tree line and the bayou is not labeled.

In 1974, the Poret heirs sold Lot 6 to Charles A. Riddle, Jr. and Patrick E. Lemoine. The act of sale by four of the five Poret heirs references the 1964 Gagnard survey and describes the property as being bounded "on the south by the Estate of Van Roy (formerly Ernest Coco), on the East by Estate of Van Roy (formerly Ernest Coco) and T & P Railway." The sale by the fifth Poret heir only references the 1964 survey. Some time after the sale, Mr. Riddle and Mr. Lemoine began clearing the wooded area between the fence and the bayou. At that time, a portion of the fence along the tree line was removed. Remnants of the fence were found when the surveys were conducted for this litigation.

In August 1976, Mr. Lemoine and Mr. Riddle's wife and heirs entered into an option to purchase with the Avoyelles Parish Police Jury (Police Jury), which provided for the sale of six acres situated in Lot 6, described as "bounded on the south by Van L. Roy and/or

Rudolph Haydel." The judgment of possession in Mr. Riddle's succession describes the Riddles' interest in Lot 6 by referencing Mr. Gagnard's 1964 survey and stating the property was bounded on the south by the "Estate of Van L. Roy," yet the November 15, 1976 sale of the property describes the southern boundary as "Bayou Sauvage." In connection with this sale, Mr. Gagnard prepared a survey of these six acres, which are situated east of what is now Government Street. This survey differs from the 1964 survey as the calls and distances along the southern portion of this acreage are on the bayou, not the fence/tree line north of the bayou.

Thereafter, on May 18, 1978, and June 22, 1978, Mr. Gagnard surveyed another portion of Lot 6 also owned by the Riddles, which is situated west of Government Street. These surveys are similar to the March 28, 1964 survey as they depict the southern boundary of the Poret property as being north of the bayou; the bayou is not even depicted on the June 1978 survey.

In March 1989, the Riddles sold an eleven acre tract to Sheriff Belt. The property, which is also west of Government Street, is depicted on a survey dated January 19, 1989 prepared by Jessie Lachney, a registered surveyor, who is Sheriff Belt's expert in this matter. The survey is of the same property depicted on Mr. Gagnard's May 1978 survey and, like that 1978 survey, the southern boundary is shown north of the bayou.

On March 24, 1989, Mr. Lachney surveyed the Avoyelles Parish Jail Facilities[,] which [are] east of Government Street. Unlike Mr. Gagnard's 1964 and 1976 surveys and his own 1978 survey of the property on the west side of Government Street, this survey depicts the bayou as the southern boundary. Mr. Lachney testified that he recognized the differences between Mr. Gagnard's 1964 and 1976 surveys of this property, but he chose to follow the later survey.

In Mr. Lachney's opinion, the bayou is the southern boundary of the Poret property. He explained that he believes the line north of the bayou in Mr. Gagnard's 1964 survey was a traverse line. He testified that a traverse line is a line sometimes used as a "working line" or to indicate a stream, bayou, or river. On cross-examination, he admitted that he did not know there was no reference in the Poret chain of title to the southern boundary of the property being a bayou and that he did not attempt to confirm whether the acreage calculated by Mr. Gagnard for Lot 6 on his 1964 survey extended to the center line of the bayou. He also admitted there is nothing on Mr. Gagnard's 1964 survey which specifically indicates that the line north of the bayou is a traverse line. However, he identified three facts which indicated to him that the bayou is the southern boundary: 1) Mr. Gagnard showed the bayou on the survey; 2) there was no land hook showing that the Roy property south of the bayou extended north of the bayou; and 3) the survey conflicts with the Judgment of Possession. He testified that, when he prepared the 1989 survey of the area east of Government Street, he noticed the difference between the 1964 survey and the 1976 survey, but he relied on the 1976 survey, believing Mr. Gagnard had a different intent when he prepared the latter survey. However, he did not explain what that difference may have been. He concluded that the line on the 1964 survey was not the property line because Mr. Gagnard's later surveys differed in that respect.

James Townsend surveyed the Roys' property and testified as their expert. He testified that he was informed by the Roys before he began his work that they believed their property extended north of the bayou. After surveying the property at issue, he advised the Roys that the jail encroached on 0.90 acres of their property. He explained that he used the 1964 Gagnard survey to begin his work and relocated the calls and distances on that survey. At trial, he identified those calls and distances on his survey. He further testified that he reviewed all of the deeds in the Roys' name and did not find any deed which defined their northern boundary as the bayou; however, he admitted he did not run the chain of title on Sheriff Belt's property. In Mr. Townsend's opinion, the 1964 Gagnard survey does not depict the southern boundary of Lot 6 extending to the center of the bayou, noting there is a difference in acreage in the 21.36 acres designated on that survey for Lot 6 and the actual acreage to the bayou, 24.76 acres.

Sheriff Belt filed a third party claim against the Police Jury, which in turn filed a third party demand against the Riddles and the Lemoines.

Following the trial of this matter, the trial judge recused himself, and the [Louisiana S]upreme [C]ourt appointed another judge to decide the case. After reviewing the record, the judge determined that the boundary between these properties is the center of the bayou, finding it was the "historical boundary" between them. The Roys appeal, assigning two errors: the determination of the boundary and the trial court's failure to award them damages.***

DISCUSSION

The Boundary Action

The burden of proof in a boundary action is divided. *Russell v. Producers' Oil Co.* (La. 1918), 143 La. 217, 78 So. 473; *Carroll v. Holton* (La. App. 1st Cir. 1985), 472 So. 2d 212. In a boundary action, the Civil Code instructs the court to "fix the boundary according to the ownership of the parties; if neither party proves ownership, the boundary shall be fixed according to limits established by possession." La.Civ.Code art. 792. "When both parties rely on titles only, the boundary shall be fixed according to titles. When the parties trace their titles to a common author preference shall be given to the more ancient title." La.Civ.Code art. 793. Lastly, La.Code Civ.P. art. 3693 instructs, "After considering the evidence, including the testimony and exhibits of a surveyor or other expert appointed by the court or by a party, the court shall render judgment fixing the boundary between the contiguous lands in accordance with the ownership or possession of the parties."

Evidence of possession by the Roys, the Lemoines and Riddles, and the Porets was presented at trial. However, the evidence presented showed only sporadic activities on the disputed property by these parties or their representatives, which were insufficient to satisfy the possession requirements in a boundary action. *See Martin Timber Co. v. Taylor,* 187 So. 2d 196 (La. App. 3d Cir. 1966); *William T. Burton Indus., Inc. v. McDonald,* 346 So. 2d 1333 (La. App. 3d Cir. 1977). As political subdivisions of the state, neither Sheriff Belt nor his predecessor in title, the Police Jury, can acquire property through acquisitive prescription. *King's Farm, Inc. v. Concordia Parish Police Jury,* 97-1056 (La. App. 3d Cir. 3/6/98), 709 So. 2d 953, *writ denied,* 98-1450 (La. 9/18/98), 724 So. 2d 748. Therefore, acquisitive prescription had to have accrued prior to the 1978 purchase of the property by the Police Jury to benefit Sheriff Belt. As discussed above, it did not.

We find the best evidence of the boundary between these properties, as reflected by the parties' titles, is Mr. Gagnard's 1964 survey which depicts the southern boundary of Sheriff Belt's property north of the bayou. ... We have been mindful throughout our review of the basic rule of property law that, where there is a conflict between a worded description and a survey, the survey prevails. *Casso v. Ascension Realty Co.,* 195 La. 1, 196 So. 1 (La. 1940). *See also Lamson Petroleum Co. v. [Pg 8] Hallwood Petroleum, Inc.,* 99-1444 (La. App. 3d Cir. 5/24/00), 770 So. 2d 786, *writ denied,* 2000-2568 (La. 11/27/00), 775 So. 2d 448. This is particularly true with respect to the Poret Judgment of Possession and partition and the 1964 survey, which is the first survey of all of Pierre Poret's property.

Reviewing the evidence, especially the conflicting surveys and the conflicting expert testimony, we found the following evidence persuasive. No property description in either chain of title prior to the Poret Judgment of Possession and partition designates the bayou as a boundary. The 1976 conveyance by the Poret heirs and the 1978 option to purchase in favor of the Police Jury describe the southern boundaries of those properties as property owned by Van L. Roy[,] not [as] a bayou. There is no indication by Mr. Gagnard on the 1964 survey that the disputed line is a traverse line and not the boundary line. The acreage of Lot 6 on Mr. Gagnard's 1964 survey is calculated as 21.36 acres; if the bayou was the southern boundary of Lot 6, the acreage would be 24.76 acres. Last, but perhaps most important, are the differences between the surveys of the property west of Government Street, where the boundary is depicted north of the bayou, and the surveys of property east of Government Street, where the bayou is depicted as the boundary. These differences are illogical and inexplicable in light of the fact that these properties were contiguous until Government Street, which is fifty feet wide, was dedicated.

Inverse Condemnation

Our determination of the boundary, coupled with the nature of the permanency of the encroachments on the Roys' property, requires that we address the Roys' claims of inverse condemnation. In *Williams v. City of Baton Rouge*, 98-1981, 98-2024, pp. 6-7 (La. 4/13/99), 731 So. 2d 240, 246, the [Louisiana S]upreme [C]ourt addressed the concept of inverse condemnation, explaining:

> "Since a taking or damaging of property may in fact occur without expropriation proceedings by a public body through *oversight or lack of foresight*, there must be some proceeding whereby an owner may seek redress when his property is damaged or taken without the proper exercise of eminent domain." *Reymond* [*v.* State, 255 La. 425, 231 So. 2d 375, 383 (La.1970)] (emphasis added). "Such an action is often referred to as 'inverse condemnation', and our Article 1, Section 2, and Article 4, Section 15, support a proceeding in the nature of inverse condemnation by such an affected property owner." *Id.*

In order to determine whether property rights have been "taken" under La. Const. Art. 1, Sec. 4, which provides that property shall not be "taken or damaged" by the state or its political subdivisions except for public purposes and with just compensation paid to the owner, the court must (1) determine if a right with respect to a thing or an object has been affected; (2) if it is determined that property is involved, decide whether the property has been taken or damaged in a constitutional sense; and (3) determine whether the taking or damaging is for a public purpose under Article 1, Sec. 4. *Constance v. State ex rel. Department of Transp. & Dev.*, 626 So. 2d 1151, 1157 (La. 1993); *State Through Dept. Of Transp. and Development v. Chambers Investment Co., Inc.*, 595 So. 2d 598 (La. 1992).

The Roys' property has been "taken" as the Avoyelles Parish Jail is built on 0.90 acres of it, and they are entitled to inverse condemnation damages. The compensation for landowners in inverse condemnation proceedings is the same as in expropriation cases: the owner is entitled to market value of his property and severance damages. *Gray v. State Through Dep't of Highways*, 250 La. 1045, 202 So. 2d 24 (La. 1967). The value of appropriated property is fixed as of the date of its appropriation. *Bd. of Levee Comm'rs of Orleans Levee Dist. v. Aurianne*, 229 La. 83, 85 So. 2d 39 (La. 1955); *Jacobs v. Kansas City, S. & G. Ry. Co.*, 134 La. 389, 64 So. 150 (La. 1913). Interest accrues on that value from the time of the taking. *A. K. Roy, Inc. v. Bd. of Comm'rs for Pontchartrain Levee Dist.*, 238 La. 926, 117 So. 2d 60 (La. 1960).

Earl Waltman, a real estate appraiser, appraised the Roys' property. He testified at trial regarding his appraisals which he conducted in December 2001 and April 2002. The buildings which encroach on the Roys' property were built in 1978, 1986, and 1992; hence, there were three appropriations. Accordingly, this matter must be remanded for a determination of the value of each piece of property at the time it was appropriated and whether the Roys are entitled to severance damages.

Landowners are also entitled to recover damages under La.Civ.Code art. 2315 for mental anguish, loss of use, loss of enjoyment, irritation, anxiety, discomfort, and embarrassment when their property is appropriated. *Williams*, 731 So. 2d 240. The Roys were not aware of the appropriation of their property until 1996. Constance Roy was the only plaintiff who appeared and testified at trial. She testified that she moved from the property in 1986. On the issue of damages, she testified that she did not like it that someone had taken something which belonged to her. We find this insufficient to justify an award of damages under La.Civ.Code art. 2315. The other plaintiffs did not appear and testify at trial; therefore, they did not bear their burden of proof on this issue.

Costs

The general rule is that fixing a boundary is beneficial to both parties and the costs should be shared equally. *Deshotel v. Lachney*, 465 So. 2d 974 (La. App. 3d Cir. 1985). Accordingly, we assess the costs for the boundary action equally between the Roys and Sheriff Belt. All costs associated with the inverse condemnation proceeding are assessed to Sheriff Belt.

Disposition

The judgment of the trial court is reversed. The boundary between the Roys' property and Sheriff Belt's property is found to be that depicted on surveys prepared by Ralph Gagnard dated March 28, 1964 and James Townsend dated September 16, 1996. This matter is remanded for further proceedings to determine the Roys' damages for their property which was appropriated....

NOTES AND QUESTIONS

1. Even if the Avoyelles Parish had been able to prove thirty years in possession, it could not have successfully argued Art. 794 to acquire ownership up to the visible boundary of the bayou because the political subdivisions of the state cannot exercise acquisitive prescription. What policy rationale underlies this prohibition?

2. The court observes that "the basic rule of property law [is] that, where there is a conflict between a worded description and a survey, the survey prevails." However, this case presents the court with two conflicting surveys. What factors does the appellate court consider in determining the Gagnard survey to be the "best evidence" of the boundary between the properties?

3. *Inverse condemnation* of property taken by a governmental entity without the due process guarantees of formal eminent domain proceedings is a cause of action under the takings clauses of both the state and the Federal constitutions. See *Palazzolo v. Rhode Island*, 533 U.S. 606, 611-14 (2001).

PART II: DISMEMBERMENTS OF OWNERSHIP

INTRODUCTION:
DISMEMBERMENTS OF OWNERSHIP

A.N. YIANNOPOULOS, CIVIL LAW PROPERTY
§§ 201, 203, 217 (4th ed. 2001)
(footnotes omitted)

§ 201. Rights; Patrimonial and Extrapatrimonial

***According to a rigorous traditional classification, patrimonial rights are either personal or real. This dichotomy can be fully grasped only in the light of the civilian tradition that distinguishes sharply between the law of property and the law of obligations. A real right is a right that a person has in a thing, a matter of property law. A personal right is a right that a person has against another person to demand a performance, a matter of the law of obligations. In that light, despite certain similarities, the two species of rights appear to be of a different nature. According to appearances, a usufructuary and a lessee seem to have the use and enjoyment of a house in much the same way. But, technically, the usufructuary has a right in the enjoyment of a house; the lessee has a right against the owner of a house to let him enjoy it. One has a *real right* and the other *personal right.*

The notion of real rights as a systematic generalization is firmly established in all western systems of law though its content and precise meaning may differ in each system.***

§ 203. Louisiana Law

The Louisiana Civil Code has incorporated either expressly or by implication certain assumptions, maxims, and doctrinal ideas that form the substratum of the civilian tradition. The distinction of rights into patrimonial and extrapatrimonial, and the division of the former into personal and real are inherent in the Code and may be formally established by reference to specific provisions.

A *personal* right may be defined as the legal power that a person (obligee) has to demand from another person (obligor) a performance consisting of giving, doing, or not doing a thing. The Louisiana Supreme Court has declared that "a personal right ... defines man's relationship to man and refers merely to an obligation one owes to another which may be declared only against the obligor." As in France, obligations in Louisiana ultimately result in financial responsibility of the obligor. His entire patrimony may be seized and sold for the satisfaction of the obligee's claim.

All obligations may be reduced to the same pecuniary denominator, whether they are money obligations from their inception or are converted into claims for damages for nonperformance. This homogeneity of all obligations carries practical consequences that become apparent in concursus proceedings. When the value of the property seized is insufficient to satisfy all creditors, satisfaction will be proportionate to approved claims. Among all holders of personal rights money is the common measure of satisfaction.

Real rights are an established category of important patrimonial interests. The term real rights is employed in the Civil Code, in the Code of Civil Procedure, and in Louisiana jurisprudence. Yet, it has not been legislatively defined and for this reason the classification of a right as real may be a controversial issue. A definition of real rights and a determination of their juridical nature would furnish criteria for the classification of rights as personal or real. In turn, classification would entail practical consequences ranging from the applicability of the rules governing prescription of nonuse to the availability of the possessory and petitory actions and the effect of the right as against a particular person or against the world.

Definition of real rights and determination of their juridical nature have been made in Louisiana decisions. The Supreme Court has declared that "the term 'real right' under the civil law is synonymous with proprietary interest, both of which refer to a species of ownership. Ownership defines the relation of man to things and may, therefore, be declared against the world." The use of the term proprietary interests may be confusing. The Supreme Court apparently intended to define real rights as dismemberments of ownership. This definition accords fully with historical development's within the civilian tradition and with French doctrine and jurisprudence. According to the prevailing view in France that has been followed in Louisiana by an unbroken line of decisions, "the rights of use, enjoyment, and disposal are said to be the three elements of property in things. They constitute the *jura in re.*" Within certain broad limits, these elements are susceptible of further subdivision.

There can be no simple answer to the question which rights are real in Louisiana. The answer necessarily presupposes two steps of analysis: first, identification of rights generally recognized as real; and second, determination of other rights that function in a way similar to the established real rights. In both instances, it might be interesting to verify conceptual generalizations by the test of functional analysis.

The distinction between personal and real rights is fundamental in civil law systems. The character and content of the correlative obligations that real rights generate, and the power of a person entitled to a real right to derive economic advantages from the thing directly, suffice to establish this distinction. But differences apart, real rights and personal rights are not such pure concepts as to exclude the existence of several categories of rights that partake of the nature of both and, therefore, defy accurate classification. These rights structurally appear to be personal rights but functionally exhibit characteristics common to real rights. Of that nature are, in the first place, the so-called real obligations *(obligations reeles, obligationes propter rem).* An example of a real obligation is the duty imposed by Article 746 of the Civil Code on the owner of a servient estate to construct at his expense works necessary for the exercise of a servitude. This duty to render a performance resembles a personal obligation. But in contrast with a personal obligation that generates full personal responsibility, the obligor is not bound with his entire patrimony. He is merely bound as owner of a particular immovable, and he may avoid the obligation to make necessary works by abandoning or alienating the immovable. Doctrinal writers also classify as an obligation *propter rem* the debt owed to the mortgagee by one acquiring an immovable subject to mortgage. The acquirer of the immovable is not personally responsible for the payment of the debt, but if it is not paid he must suffer the consequences of a forced sale. His responsibility is limited to this immovable and is based on his ownership.

Certain personal rights have acquired characteristics traditionally associated with real rights. Thus, the contract of lease may be asserted against the lessor's successor in title, and, by virtue of the right of retention, unsecured creditors may obtain preferential treatment. A creditor who is in possession of a thing belonging to his debtor is entitled to keep it until the indebtedness is paid. Conversely, real rights are frequently interwoven with personal rights and liabilities. An abusive or abnormal exercise of the right of ownership gives rise to an obligation for the repair of the damages caused to neighbors; and a lawful exercise of the right of ownership, as when one claims a thing from a possessor in good faith, may generate an obligation for compensation of expenses.***

§ 217. Numerus Clausus — Louisiana Law

Article 487 of the Louisiana Civil Code of 1870 declared that: "There may be different kinds of rights to things: (1) A full and entire ownership; (2) A right to the mere use and enjoyment; and (3) A right to certain servitudes due upon immovable estates."

The provision had been derived from Article 543 of the French Civil Code. Its meaning was explained in the *Expose des Motifs* accompanying the promulgation of the Code Civil: "These are actually the only modifications of which ownership is susceptible in our political and social organization; there cannot be any other species of rights in things: one has either a complete and perfect ownership which includes the right to enjoy and to dispose of; or one has a simple right of enjoyment without being able to dispose of the land; or, finally, one has only the right to claim predial servitudes on the property of another; servitudes which cannot be established but for the use and utility of an estate; servitudes which do not entail any affirmative duties of the person; servitudes, finally, which have nothing in common with the feudal tenures that have been destroyed forever."

These declarations are indicative of the intent of the legislature that Article 487 of the 1870 Code ought to be interpreted as listing *all* permissible dismemberments of ownership. However, it is apparent that the enumeration of real rights was incomplete as it included only the so-called principal real rights. Mortgage, pledge, and accessory real rights were not mentioned in Article 487. Therefore, the provision could only be interpreted as illustrative of permissible real rights.

Since the Code did not expressly determine the question whether one may create new forms of real rights or work modifications of the incidents of recognized real rights, French courts and writers have suggested a variety of solutions. However, according to the view that has prevailed in France, parties may in their exercise of contractual or testamentary freedom create new forms of real rights or modify the rules governing the recognized real rights within limits set by considerations of public policy. Louisiana courts, influenced by this view and determined to accommodate legitimate demands for flexibility in matters of property law, have taken certain liberties with the text of Article 487.

In a leading decision, the Louisiana Supreme Court quoted extensively from Toullier and other commentators and adopted the view that, in principle, the parties to a contract may create real rights "apart and beyond" those regulated in the Civil Code, subject to close judicial scrutiny in the public interest. As in France, however, and perhaps for the same reasons, little use of this facility has been made in practice. The most important examples of new forms of real rights created by parties in the exercise of their contractual freedom are mineral rights, limited personal servitudes, and building restrictions.

Louisiana courts have been advisedly cautious. They have repeatedly declared that "the modifications of the right of property under our laws are few and easily understood, and answer all the purposes of reasonable use. It is incumbent on courts to maintain them in their simplicity." They have also stated that the general idea of property under Roman law and under our system is "that of simple, uniform and absolute dominion. The subordinate exceptions of use, usufruct, and servitudes are abundantly sufficient to meet all the wants of civilization, and there is no warrant of law, nor reason of policy for the introduction of any other."

Article 476 of the Louisiana Civil Code is based on Article 487 of the 1870 Code but employs more precise terms. It declares: "One may have various rights in things: (1) Ownership; (2) Personal and predial servitudes; and (3) Such other real rights as the law allows." As under the prior law, ownership may be dismembered, and real rights created within limits prescribed by public policy. Article 476 does not open "the door to an unregulated brood of real rights;" parties may create only such real rights as legislation or customs allow.

Perpetual restraints on alienation have always been and remain invalid. Personal and predial servitudes may not, in principle, involve affirmative duties imposed on the owner of the servient estate. Building restrictions, however, may involve affirmative duties that are reasonable and necessary for the preservation of a general plan for subdivision development. As a matter of fact, all modifications of the right of ownership in Louisiana fall, with the exception perhaps of building restrictions which are *sui generis* real rights, within the categories of personal and predial servitudes. Joint tenures and the common law doctrine of estates are not recognized in Louisiana. Express trusts, however, are governed by the Louisiana Trust Code which has successfully integrated useful common law institutions with the precepts of the Civil Code.

CHAPTER XI. PREDIAL SERVITUDES; GENERAL PRINCIPLES
Civil Code arts. 646-654

A. N. YIANNOPOULOS, PREDIAL SERVITUDES
§§ 3-12 (3d ed. 2004)
(footnotes omitted)

§ 3. Predial Servitudes: Definition

According to Article 646 of the Louisiana Civil Code, a predial servitude is "a charge laid on a servient estate for the benefit of a dominant estate. The two estates must belong to different owners." The definition indicates that a predial servitude is a real right burdening an immovable, that the creation of such a right requires the existence of two immovables belonging to different owners, and that this right is for the benefit of an immovable rather than a person. The definition makes no reference to the purpose or content of a predial servitude. This omission is quite natural because, in contrast to other real rights that have a single purpose or content, predial servitudes may serve a multitude of purposes and may have a variable content. Reference in the Code to the purpose or content of a predial servitude would be impractical. One might only state in a general way that a predial servitude either confers certain advantages of use without exhausting the utility of the burdened immovable or deprives the owner of the burdened immovable of certain specified prerogatives of his ownership.

Language in the Louisiana and French Civil Codes indicates that predial servitudes are due to an estate rather than to the owner of an estate. This apparent *personification* of the so-called dominant estate has its roots in Roman sources. Roman jurisconsults have used colorful expressions, such as *servitus praedii magis quam personae videtur. jus hauriendi non hominis sed praedii est, jus fundi, fundus fundi servit,* and *servitus praedio videtur,* which might be taken to mean that the right of a servitude belongs to the dominant estate, a thing.

According to modern analysis, however, things may not be subjects of rights; rights belong to persons only. Therefore, legislative declarations in Louisiana and in France that predial servitudes are due to an estate must be taken as metaphors; they merely mean that predial servitudes are not attached to a particular person but they are due to anyone who happens to be owner of the dominant estate. Other civil codes have eliminated analytical inaccuracies and provide expressly that predial servitudes are due to the owner of the dominant estate.

The German Civil Code contains a precise but cumbersome definition of predial servitudes *(Grunddienstbarkeiten)*. These servitudes are charges laid on a tract of land in favor of the owner of another tract of land which confer on the latter certain advantages of use or exclude the doing of certain acts on the burdened land or prohibit the exercise of a right arising out of the ownership of the burdened tract of land in relation to the other tract of land. The definition is cumbersome because it includes reference to the purpose or content of predial servitudes.

In Greece, Article 1118 of the Civil Code declares that a predial servitude is a real right, burdening an immovable in favor of the owner of another immovable, which confers on the latter a certain advantage. Article 1119, referring to the purpose or content of a predial servitude, specifies that the owner of the burdened immovable must tolerate certain uses by the owner of the other immovable or must refrain from the exercise of certain prerogatives of his ownership.

In the civilian literature, the estate burdened with a predial servitude is designated as "servient" *(praedium serviens);* the estate for the benefit of which (or for the benefit of the owner of which) the servitude is established is designated as "dominant" *(praedium dominans,)*. In France, the redactors of the Code Civil avoided these expressions in an effort to wipe out the memory of reprobated feudal tenures. They resorted to descriptive statements, such as "the estate for which the servitude has been established," "he who has a right of servitude," and "the estate which owes the servitude." Occasionally, however, reference is made in the French Civil Code to "the subject estate" or to the "servient estate." The redactors of the Louisiana Civil Codes of 1808, 1825 and 1870 likewise avoided reference to the "servient" or the "dominant" estate. This was quite unnecessary, because feudal tenures have never had a place in Louisiana law. The terms servient and dominant estate could have been used in the text of the Civil Code for the sake of brevity. This has been done in the 1977 legislation.

§ 4. Content of Predial Servitudes

According to Article 651 of the Louisiana Civil Code, predial servitudes may impose on the owner of the servient estate the duty either "to abstain from doing something on his estate or to permit something to be done on it." Corresponding provisions in foreign civil codes indicate that the content of a predial servitude may be the toleration of certain activities on the servient estate *(pati, servitus in patiendo)*, the prohibition of certain material acts *{non facere, servitus in non faciendo)*, or the restriction of certain rights belonging to the owner of the servient estate by virtue of his ownership. On principle, predial servitudes nowhere involve affirmative duties for the owner of the servient estate.

Predial servitudes involving toleration of certain activities on the servient estate may be for the use of that estate for certain purposes, for example, rights of way, aqueducts, or support of structures; or they may be for the taking of certain materials, as earth, stones, water, or wood. The taking of mineral substances, however, ordinarily forms the object of rights other than predial servitudes. In Louisiana, servitudes for the taking of minerals, such as oil and gas, are *sui generis* real rights in the nature of limited personal servitudes rather than predial servitudes.***

Servitudes involving prohibition of material acts may exclude the erection of a building on a vacant lot, building in a style other than one agreed upon, building above or below a certain height, and the use of the servient estate as a pasture or as an industrial establishment. In Louisiana, restraints on the use of property may either take the form of *sui generis* real rights or they may be veritable predial servitudes. Everywhere, the use of immovable property is partly governed by zoning and building ordinances, *i.e.,* by rules of public law.

Predial servitudes may, finally, exclude certain rights that the owner of the servient estate would be entitled to exercise by virtue of his ownership. For example, the owner of the servient estate may be deprived of his right to drain waters into an estate situated below or of his right to diffuse reasonable quantities of smoke, heat or noise. Conversely, the owner of the servient estate may be bound by virtue of a predial servitude to tolerate an excessive emission of smoke, heat, or noise from the dominant estate, which, without the servitude, he would be entitled to suppress.

Predial servitudes, however, may not exclude the performance of juridical acts affecting the servient estate; thus, a prohibition of alienation or partition may not form the content of a predial servitude. The question whether a predial servitude may involve prohibition of a competing business on the servient estate is still largely unresolved.

§ 5. Prohibition of Affirmative Duties

It is a principle of civil law that predial servitudes may not involve affirmative duties for the owner of the servient estate. Article 651 of the Louisiana Civil Code thus declares that "the owner of the servient estate is not required to do anything." This is a rule of public policy which may not be derogated from by juridical act, unless the law provides otherwise.

The matter has been discussed extensively in Louisiana & Arkansas Railway Co. v. Winn Parish Lumber Co. A purchaser of timberlands had agreed, as a part of the consideration for the sale, to have the tonnage arising from the manufacture of timber transported by the railway of the seller. A clause in the contract provided that "all the obligations and conditions herein contained are declared to extend to and be binding upon the legal representatives and assigns of the parties hereto." In an action brought by the seller for the enforcement of the tonnage agreement, the defendant invoked Articles 655 and 709 of the Louisiana Civil Code of 1870 and argued that the contract "cannot be so enforced, because that would be to establish a servitude upon the land and the owner, consisting, as to the latter, *infaciendo"*

The Louisiana Supreme Court held that the obligation assumed by the vendee "created, not a servitude, either upon the property or upon the vendees, but a real obligation, other than servitude, as to the property and the vendees, which passes with the title, and also a personal obligation as to the vendees." Upon rehearing, however, this holding was repudiated. The court stated that a decision on the question whether the tonnage stipulation constituted a real obligation was "unnecessary" because the original purchaser was still owner of the land. The court indicated that the contract established *valid personal* obligations but found that the defendant had not violated such obligations. Turning to the question of the validity of the tonnage agreement as a real obligation, the court admitted that such an agreement suggests "a return to feudal times when the lord of the manor held the small farmers under his control and domination" but refrained from expressing an opinion "upon this very weighty matter" because this matter commended itself to the legislature then in session.

In a monumental separate opinion, based on an exhaustive analysis of the historical sources of the Louisiana Civil Code, Justice Provosty dissented from the holding that determination of the validity of the tonnage agreement as a real obligation was unnecessary. He concluded that real rights and real obligations are synonymous and that all innominate land charges are servitudes. Hence, the tonnage stipulation was invalid as it purported to establish a reprobated servitude *infaciendo.*

The principle that servitudes may not involve affirmative duties for the owner of the servient estate admits an exception as to certain incidental duties necessary for the exercise of a servitude. Thus, the title of the servitude may provide that the owner of the servient estate shall be charged with the duty to keep his estate fit for the purposes of the servitude or that he shall maintain in good state of repair works necessary for the use and preservation of the servitude. Further, the law may impose certain affirmative duties on the owner of the servient estate. Thus, Article 700(2) of the Louisiana Civil Code declares that unless the title provides otherwise, the owner of an estate burdened with a support "is bound to keep the wall fit for the exercise of the servitude." This provision, and corresponding provisions in the Civil Codes of Germany and Greece, reflect solutions reached by Roman jurisconsults. Roman law recognized a remarkable exception to the principle that servitudes may not involve affirmative duties for the owner of the servient estate. The servitude *oneris ferendi,* a right to have one's wall supported by a neighbor's wall, imposed on the neighbor the duty of keeping his wall in repair.

In connection with natural and legal servitudes, the law implies that the owner of the servient estate is charged with the duty to keep his estate fit for the purposes of the servitude. For example, the owner of an estate owing a natural servitude of drain may be compelled to remove, at his expense, underbrush choking the flow of the waters, and a riparian proprietor may be under obligation to cut trees on the banks of a stream in order to keep the channel deep for the exercise of servitudes relating to navigation.

All incidental affirmative duties of the owner of the servient estate qualify as land charges or real obligations; accordingly, the owner of the servient estate may be relieved of these duties upon abandonment of the burdened property to the owner of the dominant estate.

The owner of the servient estate may bind himself by a personal obligation to perform certain affirmative duties in connection with a predial servitude. These obligations may be heritable, but they are not transferable to a successor by particular title without express stipulation to that effect. Whether a juridical act is intended to create a personal obligation, a permissible predial servitude, a *sui generis* real right, or a reprobated servitude *infaciendo,* may be a question of contractual or testamentary interpretation.***

§ 6. Nature of Predial Servitudes

According to civilian analysis, predial servitudes are real rights on the land of another *(jura in re aliena).* The owner of the dominant estate does not "own" the servitude, because it is only corporeal things that may be owned. Nor does he own the part of the servient estate that is burdened with the servitude. Article 658 of the Louisiana Civil Code of 1870 declared: "The part of an estate upon which a servitude is exercised, does not cease to belong to the owner of the estate; he who has the servitude has no right of ownership in the part, but only the right of using it." This provision has not been reproduced in the 1977 legislation because it is self-evident.

The analytical distinction between predial servitudes and ownership carries significant legal consequences. Thus, the ownership of an immovable may not be lost by nonuse, but predial servitudes are extinguished if not exercised during the requisite prescriptive period. Further, the owner of an immovable may use it as he sees fit, but the owner of the dominant estate must use his right in accordance with the purpose of the servitude. Therefore, when one has the right to use an immovable, it is important to determine whether his right is ownership or merely a predial servitude. If one has a title, determination of the nature of the right is a matter of contractual or testamentary interpretation. If one has no title, the nature of the right is determined in the light of all pertinent facts. There is no legal presumption in France or in Louisiana for the determination of the question whether a person uses an immovable by virtue of ownership or by virtue of a predial servitude.

In Louisiana and in France, predial servitudes are immovable real rights, that is, incorporeal immovables. Although predial servitudes do not confer a right of ownership, they are immovable property governed, in principle, by the laws applying to *immovables*. Indicatively,. Article 722 of the Louisiana Civil Code declares that predial servitudes are established "by all acts by which immovables may be transferred," and Article 742 of the same Code declares that "the laws governing acquisitive prescription of immovable property apply to apparent servitudes." Further, when property burdened with a predial servitude is expropriated for public utility, the owner of the dominant estate is entitled to compensation for the taking of his property.

Certain rules governing immovable property are not applicable to incorporeal immovables. For example, Louisiana courts have refused to allow an action for lesion incurred by the owner of the servient estate as a result of the conveyance of a predial servitude. Moreover, as incorporeals, predial servitudes may be subject to special rules. They are susceptible of quasi possession rather than possession, and they are transferred without actual delivery. According to Article 722 of the Louisiana Civil Code "delivery of the act of transfer or use of the right by the owner of the dominant estate constitutes tradition."***

Predial servitudes, according to the Romanist tradition, are inherent qualities of estates: *praediis inhaerent.* They may not exist independently of the dominant or of the servient estate. Once they are established, the rights of predial servitudes may not be alienated or seized separately from the dominant estate to which they belong. On the contrary, any alienation, seizure, or encumbrance of the dominant estate includes predial servitudes established in its favor: *ambulant cum dominio.* Conversely, an alienation, seizure, or encumbrance of the servient estate is made subject to existing rights of servitudes. Thus, changes in the ownership of the two estates are immaterial; the person who happens to be owner of the servient estate is bound to suffer the exercise of the right of servitude by the person who happens to be owner of the dominant estate.

These principles have been expressly incorporated into the Louisiana Civil Code. Article 650 declares: "A predial servitude is inseparable from the dominant estate and passes with it. The right of using the servitude cannot be alienated or encumbered separately from the dominant estate. The predial servitude continues as a charge on the servient estate when ownership changes."

There are no precisely corresponding provisions in the French, German, or Greek Civil

Codes. Nevertheless, it is clear that predial servitudes are rights which cannot exist independently of the dominant or of the servient estate. According to French doctrine and German legislation predial servitudes are component parts of the ownership of an immovable. And in Greece, though not component parts, predial servitudes are regarded as accessory rights inherent in immovables.

§ 7. Things Susceptible of Predial Servitudes: Immovables

According to Article 646 of the Louisiana Civil Code, predial servitudes may be established on an estate for the benefit of another estate. Question thus arises as to the meaning of the word *estate* which is a translation of *heritage,* occurring in the French text of the Civil Code of 1808 and 1825 as well as in the French Civil Code.

It is well-settled in France that the word *heritage* in Article 637 of the Code Civil refers exclusively to tracts of lands and buildings. These are the only immovables that may be burdened in France with a predial servitude or for the benefit of which a predial servitude may be established. Standing timber, immovables by destination, and incorporeal immovables are not susceptible of predial servitudes. According to French law, standing timber and immovables by destination are parts of an immovable by nature rather than distinct immovables; hence, they may neither be burdened nor benefited by a predial servitude. Incorporeal immovables, *i.e.,* rights which the law classifies as immovables, are insusceptible of predial servitudes by their nature; predial servitudes involve the exercise of material acts which relate to corporeal things only. It follows that there can be no servitude on another servitude *(servitus servitutis non potest).*

The word estate in Article 646 of the Louisiana Civil Code means a distinct corporeal immovable. This is made clear by Article 698 of the same Code which indicates that predial servitudes may be established on, or for the benefit of, distinct corporeal immovables. These were in 1870 — and still are under the 1977 legislation — the only immovables susceptible of servitudes. It follows that constructions other than buildings, though classified as immovables under the Civil Code, are not susceptible of predial servitudes because they are not distinct immovables; and the same is true of incorporeal immovables. Timber estates and individual apartments, however, qualify by virtue of special legislation as distinct corporeal immovables; hence, predial servitudes may be established on, or for the benefit of, timber estates and individual apartments.***

§ 8. Servitudes on Public Property

Predial servitudes may be established on, or for the benefit of, immovable property of private persons as well as immovable property of the state and its political subdivisions.

In Louisiana and France, things of the state and its political subdivision are distinguished into private things public things. Private things do not differ in nature from things held by private persons and ought to be subject to all the rules of the Civil Code governing predial servitudes. This idea is generally followed in France.

Private things of the state and its political subdivisions. In Louisiana, the Constitution, legislation, and jurisprudence have worked out exceptions from the general rules of the Civil Code with respect to the alienation and prescription of things owned by the state. Thus, private things of the state must ordinarily be alienated in accordance with certain formalities and may not be lost to the state by prescription.

It follows that private persons may acquire servitudes on private things of the state only by title and in accordance with the applicable formalities governing alienation of state property. The acquisition of servitudes on such property by prescription is excluded. Private things of municipalities, on the other hand, are subject to the general rules governing prescription; this property may be burdened with servitudes in favor of private persons by title as well as by the effect of acquisitive prescription.

Public things of the state and its political subdivisions. According to Article 723 of the Louisiana Civil Code, servitudes may be established "on public things, including property of the state, its agencies and political subdivisions." Some of these servitudes arise from the natural situation of lands, as drainage through public waterways; others arise by operation of law, as servitudes of public use, dealt with elsewhere; and still others are purely conventional. Conventional servitudes on public things of the state and its political subdivisions may not be acquired by acquisitive prescription; they may be created by title only.

Servitudes for the use or enjoyment of public things may be granted by the authorities or reserved by the owner upon dedication of a thing to public use. These servitudes are ordinarily established by a franchise, which, in order to be valid as a title for the creation of a servitude, must conform with certain special formalities and substantive requirements. The extent to which servitudes in favor of private persons may interfere with the public use of private things is subject to judicial review within the limits of a broad administrative discretion.

In the absence of a title, works that obstruct the use of public things may be removed at the expense of the persons who built or own them and "the owner of the works may not prevent their removal by alleging prescription or possession." A building that merely encroaches on a public way without preventing its use and which cannot be removed without causing substantial damage to its owner, shall be permitted to remain. But, in this case, if it is demolished for any cause, the owner shall be bound to restore to the public the part of the way upon which the building stood.

It is generally accepted in France that property of the public domain may be burdened with servitude-like rights in favor of private persons. Some of these rights correspond to the destination of public things. Of this kind are rights of passage, of ingress and egress, of lights and view, and of drainage, that owners of immovables have over adjacent public lands or waterbodies—subject to the applicable administrative regulations. Other servitude-like rights are merely compatible with the destination of public things, and are accorded by the administration. Of this kind are subterranean passageways, overpasses, and bridges connecting properties separated by a highway, a railway, or a canal. There is no general agreement in France on the precise classification of these rights. Some courts consider these rights to be servitudes; other courts, under the influence of the doctrine developed by Aubry and Rau, avoid reference to servitudes and prefer to speak of *sui generis* rights. Commentators classify these rights as administrative servitudes.

The rights of adjoining owners over things of the public domain are protected in France against invasion by third persons by analogous application of the rules governing protection of servitudes. Vis-a-vis the administration, however, the rights of adjacent owners are somewhat precarious; the authorities may, in the interest of the general public, suppress or restrict the rights of adjacent owners by abandoning a right of way, relocating it, or by undertaking the execution of public works. The adjacent owners may recover compensation for damages suffered as a result of the construction of public works; and, in cases of abuse of administrative discretion, they may resort to the courts for the annulment of prejudicial administrative acts.***

§ 9. Essential Features of Predial Servitudes

According to traditional civilian precepts which have been incorporated into modern civil codes, predial servitudes are characterized by a number of *essential* features.

In the first place, it is necessary that there be two different estates, that is, a servient and a dominant estate. No servitude may be imposed on an estate in its own favor; nor may a predial servitude be imposed on a person in favor of an estate; and, if a servitude is imposed on an estate in favor of a person rather than of another estate, it is a personal servitude.

Second, it is necessary that the two estates "belong to different owners." A partnership possesses distinct juridical personality; therefore, a predial servitude may be established on the land of one of the partners in favor of land belonging to the partnership. The requirement that there be two different owners is fulfilled. Further, a private corporation created by a public corporation possesses a distinct juridical personality; therefore, the property of the private corporation may be burdened with a servitude in favor of the agency of the state. But property belonging to the state may not be burdened with a servitude in favor of the state or of a state agency; the requirement that there be two different owners is not met.

In Louisiana and in France, if the two estates belong to the same person, the application which the owner makes of one to the advantage of the other is not called a servitude, but a destination of the owner *(destination dupere defamille)*. The destination of the owner involves an exercise of the prerogatives of ownership rather than of a right of servitude. This is expressed in the maxim *nemini res sua servit* (no one has a right of servitude in his own things), which has been incorporated into the Civil Codes of Louisiana, France and Greece. The maxim refers to situations in which two estates belong in their entirety to the same owner. Thus, the co-owner of an estate held by undivided shares may have a right of servitude on an estate of which he is the sole owner; and, conversely, the sole owner of an estate may have a right of servitude on an estate in which he has an undivided interest. The maxim that no one may have a right of servitude on his own things has been abrogated in Germany by the Civil Code.

Third, it is necessary that there be "a benefit to the dominant estate." This principle of utility, expressed in the adage the *servitus utilis esse debet,* sets the outer limits of party autonomy in the field of predial servitudes. The law will allow contractual or testamentary freedom to the extent that a servitude may serve a useful purpose; unreasonable whims of parties, serving no socially useful purpose, may not give rise to predial servitudes. The utility to be derived from the servitude need not be economic; it may be merely esthetic. Further, the utility need not exist at the time of the contract; a mere "possible convenience or a future advantage suffices to support a servitude." But, if there is proof that the servitude "cannot be reasonably expected to benefit the dominant estate," it will be decreed null.

The utility of the servitude must derive from the servient estate and must be attributed to the person who, at any given time, happens to be owner of the dominant estate. If the utility is attributed to a designated owner, the servitude is personal rather than predial. For example, a servitude in favor of a named owner of an estate for the enjoyment of a swimming pool or of a tennis court in another estate is a limited personal servitude; but the same stipulation in favor of an estate, or any owner of that estate gives rise to a predial servitude.

Further, a right of passage stipulated for the benefit of a designated person is a limited personal servitude, whereas a right of passage stipulated for the benefit of an estate is a predial servitude. Likewise, the prohibition of certain activities on an estate, for example, the prohibition of erecting a building on a certain lot, may be a limited personal servitude or a predial servitude, depending on whether the advantage is attributed to a designated person or to an estate.

§ 10. Non-essential Features of Predial Servitudes

Servient and dominant estates are ordinarily located in the same geographical area. Neither contiguity, however, nor vicinity are conditions essential to the existence of a servitude under modern Civil Codes. It suffices that the two estates are so located as to allow "one to derive some benefit from the charge on the other." Accordingly, certain species of servitudes, as those for the extraction of materials from the ground or for the maintenance of an aqueduct, are ordinarily imposed on estates located far away from the dominant estate.

Predial servitudes are perpetual in the sense that, if properly used, they do not terminate upon the lapse of any period of time. The perpetuity of predial servitudes is a consequence of their qualification as inseparable component parts of the ownership of an immovable. Nevertheless, perpetuity is not an essential feature of predial servitudes because they may be stipulated for a term or under a suspensive or a resolutory condition. It was otherwise in Roman law, which required that servitudes have a perpetual cause (*causa perpetud*).

In modern legal systems a predial servitude may be established for the satisfaction of temporary needs of the dominant estate and the utility to be derived from the servient estate may be exhaustible. If there is no longer need for a servitude, or if the utility of the servitude is exhausted, the servitude may be declared terminated; but there is no reason to exclude the validity of the servitude in advance if future events are certain to cause the termination of the servitude.

§ 11. Indivisibility of Predial Servitudes

Predial servitudes are indivisible. Article 652 of the Louisiana Civil Code declares that "a predial servitude is indivisible. An estate cannot have upon another estate part of a right of way, or of view, or of any other servitude, nor can an estate be charged with a part of a servitude."

The principle of indivisibility of predial servitudes carries significant practical applications, especially in the field of mineral servitudes. At this point, attention is focused merely on the consequences of the division of the dominant or of the servient estate. Division may result from a juridical act of the owner, such as sale or partition; it may also result from judicial or administrative action, as adjudication or expropriation.

Article 656(3) of the Louisiana Civil Code of 1870 spoke of a sale only, but this was merely an illustration of possible methods of division. Article 652 of the Louisiana Civil Code has a much broader scope. It indicates that if the dominant estate is divided, by whatever means, "every acquirer of a part has the right of using the servitude in its entirety." Nevertheless, the division of the dominant estate may not result in the placing of an "additional burden ... on the servient estate." Each acquirer of a part is entitled to use the servitude in its entirety but the use made by all of the acquirers may not exceed the limits of the use previously made.

For example, the quantity of water or wood due by the servient estate remains the same, even if the needs of the dominant estate have increased as a result of its division. And if the servitude was one of a right of way, all acquirers of parts of the dominant estate "are bound to exercise that right through the same place." If the water, wood, or right of way available is not sufficient for the satisfaction of the new needs, the use of the servitude must be apportioned among the various acquirers of parts. If, on the other hand, after the division of the dominant estate, the servitude is useful only for a part, the servitude is extinguished as to the parts for which it is no longer useful. This is provided for expressly in the German and Greek Civil Codes. The same solution is suggested by doctrinal writers in France and ought to be followed in Louisiana.

Neither the Louisiana Civil Code nor the French Civil Code provides expressly for the consequences of the division of the servient estate. Nevertheless, on principle as well as in the light of a proper interpretation of pertinent provisions in the two Codes, it is clear that the division of the servient estate does not affect adversely the interests of the owner of the dominant estate. Insofar as these interests are concerned, the servitude remains the same. This does not mean that each part of the divided estate is necessarily burdened with the servitude; determination of this matter depends on the purpose of the servitude and the circumstances of each case.

For example, a servitude of light or of view on a vacant lot is not modified at all by the division of the servient estate; the servitude is now due by each part. It is the same in the case of a servitude for the taking of sand, earth, or stones from a borrow pit or a quarry; after the division of the borrow pit or of the quarry, each part will have to furnish a proportionate quantity of earth, sand, or stones. But if a servitude of right of way or of a right to draw water from a well was localized on a certain part of the servient estate, the division of this estate will result in the release of the servitude as to parts which are no longer needed for the exercise of the servitude. Similar solutions are reached in Germany and in Greece in the light of provisions in the Civil Codes of the two countries dealing with the division of the servient estate.

The principle of indivisibility of predial servitudes does not exclude division of the advantages resulting from predial servitudes, provided, of course that these advantages are susceptible of division. For example, the right of taking a certain number of loads of earth from the land of another, or of sending to pasture a certain number of animals on the land of another, may be divided among several estates entitled to the servitude. Thus, if a servitude for the pasturage of one hundred heads of cattle exists in favor of an estate belonging to two owners, each of them may be attributed the right to send to pasture fifty animals. Limitations on the use of the servitude, however, do not constitute division of the servitude or of the advantages of the servitude. The limitation of the use to "certain days or hours.. .is still an entire right," and not part of a right.

Article 654 of the Louisiana Civil Code and corresponding Article 639 of the French Civil Code, establish a tripartite classification of predial servitudes into natural, legal, and voluntary or conventional. Natural servitudes are those that arise from the natural situation of estates; legal servitudes are those imposed by law; and voluntary or conventional servitudes are those established by juridical act, prescription, or destination of the owner.

Article 659 of the Louisiana Civil Code of 1870 seemed to indicate that conventional servitudes could arise only from "contract between the respective owners." However, this was merely an example of the methods available for the creation of conventional servitudes, because Article 743 of the same Code specified that servitudes could be established by *all acts* by which property could be transferred. Hence, there should be no doubt that under the regime of the 1870 Code conventional servitudes could be established, as they may under the 1977 legislation, by contracts as well as unilateral juridical acts.

The tripartite classification of servitudes has been subjected to vivid criticism in France. In the first place, critics have observed that the division of servitudes into natural and legal is arbitrary; both kinds of servitudes are legal in the sense that they arise by operation of law and are imposed by directly applicable legislative texts. Predial servitudes, like personal servitudes, should thus be divided into legal and conventional. This criticism has been answered by the observation that natural servitudes are not, strictly speaking, imposed by the law; the law merely takes cognizance of certain natural situations of fact. In contrast, legal servitudes are solely creatures of the law and are imposed in the light of policy considerations.

Second, critics have observed that, from the viewpoint of accurate analysis, natural and legal servitudes involve limitations on the content of ownership rather than veritable servitudes. It is often impossible to determine which is the dominant estate, in whose favor a legal servitude is established, and which is the servient estate owing the servitude. Moreover, in practice, the word servitude is ordinarily reserved for conventional servitudes; thus, the vendor of an immovable may well declare that his immovable is free of servitudes although it may be burdened with natural or legal servitudes. This criticism is "difficult to answer." In the German and Greek Civil Codes, the concepts of natural and legal servitudes have thus given way to the idea of limitations on the content of ownership.

It seems that the redactors of the French Civil Code grouped together natural, legal, and conventional servitudes as a matter of convenience, in their concern to alter pre-revolutionary conceptions as to the nature of the charges imposed by law on the ownership of immovable property. In medieval French law, limitations on the right of ownership were regarded as personal obligations founded on a quasi-contract of vicinage. The redactors of the Code Civil wished instead to classify these limitations as real obligations founded on directive applicable texts. As real obligations, these limitations on the right of ownership could be, on principle, subject to the rules governing conventional servitudes. Thus, disputes concerning limitations on the right of ownership could be resolved in the venue available for conventional servitudes; and the owner of the burdened immovable could exonerate himself of these obligations by abandoning his immovable. Yet, vestiges of the old conceptions may still be found in the Code Civil and in the Louisiana Civil Code of 1870. In both Codes, obligations arising from the vicinity of estates are designated as "obligations contracted without any agreement," arising from the "authority of the law." In deference to the tradition, and in light of practical considerations, the tripartite division of servitudes has been maintained in the 1977 legislation.

CHAPTER XII. NATURAL SERVITUDES
Civil Code arts. 655-658

LOUISIANA REVISED STATUTES

38:218. Diversion of natural drain prohibited. No person diverting or impeding the course of water from a natural drain shall fail to return the water to its natural course before it leaves his estate without any undue retardation of the flow of water outside of his enclosure thereby injuring an adjacent estate.

Whoever violates this Section shall be fined not less than twenty-five dollars nor more than one hundred dollars or imprisoned for not less than ten days nor more than thirty days, or both.

BROUSSARD v. CORMIER
154 La. 877, 98 So. 403 (1923)

THOMPSON, J. The plaintiff and the defendant are owners of adjoining farms in section 11, township 11 south of range 4 west. The plaintiff owns the southeast quarter, and the defendant the north half, of said section. The land is of the same general character — low semi- marsh, with about the same elevation and possessing little natural drainage. For many years the properties have been cultivated in rice.

In 1918 there was an extraordinary amount of rainfall, which, with the irrigation waters, overflowed the two estates, as well as the surrounding country, to such an extent as to cause great damage and destruction to the rice crops.

This suit is the result of the condition produced by the exceptional and abnormal rainfall of that year. Its purpose is to enforce the legal servitude which the plaintiff claims is due his estate by that of the defendant to receive all of the surplus waters which naturally fall on his estate.

The petition alleges that the surplus water which fall on the plaintiffs land, when left unhindered and unobstructed, naturally flow north onto and across the land of defendant, which is alleged to be the lower estate. It is further alleged that the defendant has obstructed the natural flow of water by closing and building up an old levee which runs along the dividing line of the two properties east and west.

A mandatory injunction was issued, after hearing on a rule nisi, which directed the sheriff to make openings in the levee so as to permit the free passage of the waters from plaintiffs land into a ditch which the defendant had constructed on his own land, and by means of which ditch the waters from defendant's land ultimately were emptied into the low or marsh lands northwest of the defendant's property. The injunction, however, was bonded by the defendant on the same day, and was never executed.

The defendant in his answer admits the construction of the levee between the two properties, but denies that his property owes any servitude of drain to the property of plaintiff. It is alleged that the natural flow of water from the plaintiffs land is not in a northerly direction over the defendant's land but is in a westerly direction where there exists a sufficient drain for plaintiffs' property which was left open and was not obstructed by the defendant. It is alleged further that the only drain in a northerly direction is a private ditch constructed by defendant at a heavy expense and which traverses defendant's property in a northerly course and empties into a larger drain ditch constructed by one Ritchie to drain his own property.

On a final hearing there was judgment recognizing the servitude in favor of plaintiff under certain conditions which will be noticed later, and making the injunction perpetual.

Objection was made to the right of the judge to issue a mandatory injunction in a case like this, even after hearing on a rule nisi. We think the ruling of the court was correct. The general rule is that an injunction will issue only in its prohibitory form, but when a defendant obstructs a plaintiff in the enjoyment of a real right, as by fencing a common passageway or building a levee across a drainage course, the latter is entitled to a prohibitory injunction restraining the disturbance and to a mandatory injunction for the removal of the obstruction or to undo what has been illegally done [citations omitted].

There is no dispute as to the legal principles applying in suits of this character under ordinary conditions. The Code [Revised C.C. art. 655] grants a servitude of drain in favor of the upper estate against the lower estate by which the lower estate is burdened with receiving the waters which run naturally from the estate situated above; provided, of course, the industry of man has not been used to create that servitude. The lower proprietor is not at liberty to raise any dam or make any other work to prevent this running of water.

And the proprietor above can do nothing whereby the natural servitude due by the estate below may be rendered more burdensome. But with this modification: That the owner of the superior or creditor estate may make all drainage works which are necessary to the proper cultivation and to the agricultural development of his estate. To that end he may cut ditches and canals by which the water running on his estate may be concentrated and their flow increased beyond the slow process by which they would ultimately reach the same destination. But the upper proprietor cannot improve his lands to the injury of his neighbor by cutting ditches or canals. or do other drainage works by which the waters will be diverted from their natural flow and concentrated so as to flow on the lower lands at a point which would not be their natural destination [citations omitted].

It is to be observed that both of the estates under consideration are the more valuable for raising of rice. In the earlier history of that agricultural industry in this state, dependence was had entirely upon Providence or the rain for the necessary water to grow the rice. In the more recent years the work of man has established an artificial irrigation system of canals, ditches, and levees, by means of which water is collected, and the rice fields are flooded at pleasure during the growing season, and the waters released therefrom when the time for harvest approaches. Each of these estates was provided with such instrumentalities by which the necessary water for irrigation, as well as the natural normal rainfall, was collected, cared for, and disposed of for many years prior to this suit without complaint on the part of the owner of either estate as to inadequate drainage, obstructed drainage, or improper artificial drainage. And it is a fact not disputed that the plaintiff has committed no act to make the servitude of the defendant more burdensome, further than was necessary to the proper cultivation of his land in rice; and the works for that purpose did not increase the volume of water that would naturally flow onto the defendant's land in seasons of normal rainfall.

It was the unusual rainfall of 1918, as already stated, which caused the plaintiffs land to overflow, and doubtless the same situation and condition will occur again with a like amount of rain. And this would be the case without the artificial appliances for irrigation purposes.

The plaintiff, however, occupied no worse position than did the defendant and other rice planters in that section of country. After all, we are not very greatly impressed with any serious difference in the legal rights of the parties by reason of any increase of water on account of or resulting from the artificial flooding of the farms. The defendant does not claim that to open up the ditch in question will impose an increased burden on his estate during normal rainy seasons. His sole contention is that his estate owes no servitude of drain whatever to plaintiffs land.

As we have heretofore stated, the two estates have practically the same elevation; still there is a slight difference of a few inches, especially when the surrounding estates, south and east, are taken into consideration. There were four engineers and several other witnesses who testified in the case, and while there is a divergence of opinion among them, we think a decided preponderance of the testimony shows that the tendency of the bulk of the water from rainfall, when not impeded or restrained, is to flow north onto the property of defendant with a slight variation to the west. The district judge, after hearing all of the witnesses, found this to be true. Without going into the details of the evidence, it is sufficient to say that we approve that finding.

If the natural drain was west and not north, as contended for by the defendant, there would, it seems to us, have been no occasion for the defendant to maintain the levee south of his ditch and next to the line of plaintiffs property. The levee was obviously constructed to protect the ditch and property of defendant from the waters flowing from plaintiffs land.

The judgment rendered by the district judge requires the defendant to remove the levee or a portion thereof near the center of the south line of defendant's property sufficient to allow the free flow of water from plaintiffs land, or to be permitted to be opened a passageway to the ditch which should allow the waters to flow at all times when the said ditch or the double levees are not being used to their fair capacity for the removal of water from the defendant's land, and when the drainage from the plaintiffs land to the northwest is being used by the plaintiff to its fair capacity. The judgment is manifestly fair and just and equitable, alike to both parties, and we can discover no sufficient reason for changing the same in favor of either party.

ADAMS v. TOWN OF RUSTON
194 La. 403, 193 So. 688 (1940)

PONDER, J. In this suit the plaintiff is seeking an injunction to restrain the town of Ruston and its employees from causing or permitting waste water emptied from the town's swimming pool to flow across and damage his land.

The plaintiff owns a tract of land located in the town of Ruston. The town owns and operates a concrete swimming pool which has a capacity of between 450,000 to 500,000 gallons of water. The town owns the property on which the swimming pool is located. Between the town's property and the plaintiffs property there is a highway and a tract of land owned by Raymond Heard. There is a small branch or natural drain that runs through the town's property near the swimming pool across the property of Raymond Heard and under the Dixie Overland Highway and across the plaintiffs property. Once a week during the summer the swimming pool is emptied into this ditch or natural drain from the swimming pool through a 14-inch outlet. It requires from an hour to an hour and a half to empty the water from the swimming pool. The point where the water enters the ditch is approximately 450 feet south of the plaintiffs south boundary line. The plaintiff instituted this suit seeking a judgment to enjoin the town of Ruston from emptying the water into the ditch or natural drain and permitting it to flow across and damage his land. The plaintiff alleged that if the town is permitted to continue discharging the water from the swimming pool it will damage him to extent of total loss and thereby cause him irreparable injury. He alleged that the present value of his land is not less than $10,000 and that it has already been damaged by this water to an amount in excess of $5,000. The town answered the plaintiffs petition, the case was duly tried and the lower court rendered judgment rejecting the plaintiffs demands. The plaintiff has appealed.

The record does not show how many acres are contained in the plaintiffs land. The land was unimproved at the time the plaintiff bought it and no improvements have been placed on it. The plaintiff testified that when he purchased the property some twenty years ago that he could step across the ditch or drain, but that it is now from six to eight feet wide. He estimated that 75 per cent of the eroding that has taken place in the ditch since the pool was built has been caused by the water emptied from the swimming pool. A witness for the plaintiff testified that it was his opinion that the flow of water from the swimming pool across the plaintiffs property damages it. The mayor of the town of Ruston testified that the swimming pool was constructed in the year 1931 at a cost of $27,500 and that it is kept open and in operation about three and a half months each year. He testified that the pool is emptied on an average of about fifteen times per year. He further testified that the plaintiff has never made any complaint either to him or the town council of any injury or damage the water from the pool was causing his land until thirty days before this suit was filed and that that complaint was made in a letter from the plaintiffs attorney. A witness for the town, who is an Assistant Professor of Engineering at Louisiana Tech, testified that from scientific tests he had made the amount of water discharged from the swimming pool into the ditch each year is only one-tenth of the amount that flows through it from the natural drainage from rainfall. He testified from actual tests made by him that the water emptied from the swimming pool picked up and carried away only one-half of one cubic foot of soil and that on the basis of this experiment in a year's time the water from the swimming pool would erode seven and one-half cubic feet of soil which would only carry away seventy-five cubic feet of soil from the plaintiffs land in ten years.

The plaintiff contends that the natural drainage servitude imposed upon his property in favor of the defendant's property by [Revised C.C. art. 655], is being made more burdensome by the discharge of the water from the swimming pool and that he is entitled as a matter of right to an injunction to protect his property from such additional injury and damage.

The record shows that when the swimming pool is emptied into the drainage ditch that the drainage ditch does not overflow but the water is confined solely within the ditch. From a preponderance of the testimony the damage caused the plaintiff is negligible which can be adequately compensated in money. While the natural servitude of drainage through plaintiffs property has been made slightly more burdensome on account of the water from the swimming pool flowing across the property, the damage is of such a negligible character that it would not entitle the plaintiff to an injunction as a matter of right. Under the doctrine laid down in the case of Young v. International Paper Company, 179 La. 803, 155 So. 231, 233, the question presented is one that addresses itself to the discretion of the court. In the case of Young v. International Paper Company, *supra*, the court stated:

"Plaintiff has asked for an injunction to abate the alleged nuisance. The trial court, under all of the facts before it, refused to grant the injunction. The granting of it was discretionary. Plaintiffs land is hardly susceptible now to any damage that the water may cause it, and, if such should occur, it may be easily compensated in money. To enjoin defendant from using the stream to take off its waste water, and thereby deprive it of its only means of doing so, is virtually to close down mills costing several millions of dollars to prevent some possible damage, of no particular moment, on land, which has but slight value, save possibly for mineral purposes."

In City of Harrisonville, Mo., v. W.S. Dickey Clay Mfg. Co., 289 U.S. 334, 53 S.Ct. 602, 603, 77 L. Ed. 1208, it was said in a suit to enjoin the pollution of a creek by sewage from a city that:

"Thus, the question here is not one of equitable jurisdiction. The question is whether, upon the facts found, an injunction is the appropriate remedy. For an injunction is not a remedy which issues as of course. Where substantial redress can be afforded by the payment of money and issuance of an injunction would subject the defendant to grossly disproportionate hardship, equitable relief may be denied although the nuisance is indisputable. This is true even if the conflict is between interests which are primarily private."

The plaintiff can be adequately compensated for his damage and he is not entitled to an injunction herein.

The defendant urges in his answer that since the plaintiff has stood by for eight years and permitted the water from the swimming pool to be drained across his land that the plaintiff is estopped from claiming an injunction. Since we have arrived at the conclusion that the injury or damage is so negligible, it is unnecessary for us to consider this contention.

In the case of McFarlain v. Jennings-Heywood Oil Syndicate, 118 La. 537, 538, 43 So. 155, cited by the plaintiff, the demand was for damages and did not involve injunctive relief. Ogden v. Police Jury of East Baton Rouge Parish, 166 La. 869, 870, 118 So. 65, and Chandler v. City of Shreveport, 169 La. 52, 124 So. 143, cited by the plaintiff were cases where water was diverted to such an extent that the injury or damages were of an aggravated nature. In fact, they were of such nature that it practically destroyed the usefulness of the property over which the water flowed. Neither of the cases cited is authority to the effect that where the damage caused to the property is negligible and can be adequately compensated in damages that such causes irreparable injury and warrants the issuance of an injunction. For the reasons assigned, the judgment is affirmed at appellant's cost.

BRANSFORD v. INT'L PAPER TIMBERLANDS OPERATING CO.
750 So. 2d 424 (La. App. 2d Cir. 2000)

WILLIAMS, J. The plaintiff, Camille S. Bransford, appeals a summary judgment rendered in favor of the defendant, International Paper Timberlands Operating Company, Ltd. ("IP Timberlands"). The district court found that the defendant did not have a duty to remedy naturally occurring conditions on its land that obstructed drainage and caused flooding of plaintiff s property. For the following reasons, we affirm.

FACTS

The plaintiff, Camille S. Bransford, and IP Timberlands own adjacent tracts of land in Webster Parish, Louisiana (referred to herein as the "Bransford Tract" and the "Timberlands Tract" respectively). Surface water from the plaintiffs land naturally drains across the defendant's property. In December 1991, the plaintiff, who is an elderly widow, gave to her son, James Bransford ("Bransford"), the power of attorney to manage her properties, including the Bransford Tract, which contains timber.

On and around the Bransford Tract, beavers had built dams which caused flooding in some areas of the property. In late 1995, Bransford began efforts to destroy and remove the beavers and their dams. During the summer of 1996, Bransford learned that flooding had also occurred on that part of the Bransford Tract contiguous to the Timberlands Tract. Subsequently, Bransford entered the Timberlands Tract and observed a beaver dam, which was apparently preventing drainage from plaintiffs land. Bransford did not attempt to dismantle the dam.

The plaintiff filed a petition for damages, alleging that the defendant's failure to remove beaver dams on its property caused flooding of plaintiffs land and the loss of timber. The case was removed to the United States District Court for the Western District of Louisiana, where the defendant filed a motion for summary judgment. Subsequently, the case was remanded to the 26th Judicial District Court, which held a hearing on the summary judgment motion.

For the purposes of the motion for summary judgment, IP Timberlands conceded that beaver dams built on its property had obstructed the natural drainage from the Bransford Tract, causing flooding of the plaintiffs land and damage to the timber. IP Timberlands does not dispute that there is a natural servitude of drainage between the two contiguous tracts of land, and that its parcel is the servient estate to the Bransford Tract.

Following the hearing on the motion, the trial court found that IP Timberlands did not have an affirmative duty to remedy conditions of a purely natural origin, and determined that such a duty would place an unreasonable burden on rural landowners. The district court granted the defendant's motion for summary judgment, dismissing plaintiffs claims. Consequently, the court did not address the defendant's prescription argument. The plaintiff appeals the judgment.

DISCUSSION

The plaintiff contends the district court erred in granting the motion for summary judgment. Plaintiff argues that the defendant, as owner of the servient estate, is liable for damages due to its failure to remove beaver dams, which prevented drainage and contributed to flooding of plaintiff s dominant estate.

Summary judgment shall be rendered if the pleadings, depositions, answers to interrogatories, admissions on file, and any affidavits, show that there is no genuine issue of material fact and that the mover is entitled to judgment as a matter of law. LSA-C.C.P. art. 966. Appellate courts review summary judgments *de novo* under the same criteria that govern the district court's consideration of whether summary judgment is appropriate. *NAB Natural Resources* v. *Willamette Industries, Inc.,* 28,555 (La. App.2d Cir. 8/21/96), 679 So. 2d 477.

A predial servitude is a burden on a servient estate for the benefit of a dominant estate, with each having different owners. LSA-C.C. art. 646. Generally, the owner of the servient estate is not required to do anything. His obligation is to abstain from doing something, or to permit something to be done, on his estate. He may be required by convention or by law to keep his estate in suitable condition for the exercise of the servitude due to the dominant estate. LSA-C.C. art. 651. A predial servitude may be a natural servitude, which arises from the natural situation of estates. LSA-C.C. art. 654.

Pursuant to the natural servitude of drainage, an estate situated below is bound to receive the surface waters that flow naturally from an estate situated above, unless the flow was created by an act of man. LSA-C.C. art. 655. The owner of the servient estate may not do anything to prevent the flow of water. The dominant estate owner may not act to render the servitude of drainage more burdensome. LSA-C.C. art. 656.

In the present case, the plaintiffs claim for damages is not based on the defendant's control of the beavers, but is based on the defendant's ownership of the servient estate, which is subject to a servitude of drainage for the benefit of the Bransford Tract. The defendant does not dispute the fact that the flooding of plaintiffs land was caused by beaver dams located on the Timberlands Tract.

In support of her argument that defendant is liable for damage caused by the flooding, plaintiff cites authority from another jurisdiction. In *Illinois Central R.R. Co.* v. *Watkins,* 671 So. 2d 59 (Miss. 1996), the railroad modified a natural drain and constructed a culvert to allow the flow of surface water. The culvert became obstructed by beaver dams, which prevented drainage and caused flooding of Watkins' land, damaging his crops. Watkins notified the railroad, which cleared the blockage. However, the culvert became blocked by beaver dams a second time and was cleared. Watkins sued for damages alleging that the railroad had negligently maintained its property. The court determined that the railroad had a duty to maintain its culvert, which became blocked by a dam, that the railroad knew of the condition and allowed it to remain, and that these facts supported the jury's finding that the railroad was negligent.

The factual situation in *Watkins* can be distinguished from that in the present case. Here, the defendant did not build a structure which modified or blocked the drainage area. Nor is there evidence that defendant was aware of the presence of beaver dams blocking the flow of water until being informed of this fact by Bransford after the flooding had occurred. Thus, the *Watkins* case does not provide persuasive authority for the plaintiffs argument.

In evaluating the defendant's duty as the servient estate owner, we must apply the provisions of the previously cited codal articles. Pursuant to Article 656, defendant was required to refrain from taking any action which would prevent the natural flow of water from the Bransford Tract. Article 651 obligated defendant to either abstain from doing something or permit something to be done on the Timberlands Tract, but defendant was "not required to do anything." The record shows that the defendant did not take any action to impede the natural flow of water from the plaintiffs land. Nor is there evidence that defendant refused to permit plaintiffs representative from acting in connection with the servitude.

The plaintiff contends that her property damage was caused by defendant's failure to remove the beaver dams from the Timberlands Tract. However, this court has previously provided for an award of damages only under circumstances in which the owner of the servient estate has acted directly to obstruct or interfere with the servitude of drainage. See *Tool House, Inc.* v. *Tynes*, 564 So. 2d 720 (La. App. 2d Cir.), *writ denied*, 568 So. 2d 1087 (La. 1990); *Cole* v. *Mott*, 351 So. 2d 1326 (La. App. 2d Cir. 1977). The record demonstrates that defendant did not act to prevent the flow of water from the plaintiffs land. Consequently, defendant is not liable for property damage caused by the flooding of the Bransford Tract.

The plaintiff also argues that the codal articles impose upon defendant the affirmative duty to remove naturally occurring obstructions which prevent the natural drainage from the Bransford Tract. We recognize that Article 651 provides that a servient estate owner may be required by convention or law to keep his estate in suitable condition for the exercise of the servitude. In addition, we are aware that in the case of *Brown* v. *Blankenship*, 28 So. 2d 496 (La. App. 2d Cir. 1946), this court affirmed a judgment ordering the owner of a servient estate to remove underbrush and other debris which accumulated over time and obstructed the natural drainage of water from the dominant estate.

However, in the present case, the plaintiff has not sought such injunctive relief. Thus, we will not address the issue of whether the defendant could have been compelled to remove the beaver dams which were preventing the natural drainage from the Bransford Tract. We note that in its brief, the defendant acknowledges that plaintiff would have been entitled to enter the Timberlands Tract in order to maintain the servitude of drainage by removing the obstructions.

Based upon this record, we cannot say the district court erred in granting the defendant's motion for summary judgment. The plaintiff's assignment of error lacks merit.

CONCLUSION

For the foregoing reasons, the district court's judgment granting the motion for summary judgment is affirmed. Costs of this appeal are assessed to the appellant, Camille Bransford. Affirmed.

POOLE v. GUSTE
261 La. 1110, 262 So. 2d 339 (1972)

TATE, J. The essential issue concerns the plaintiffs', the Pooles', claim that their estate enjoys a servitude of drain into and through a canal which is on the adjacent property of the defendants, the Gustes.

The Gustes built levees which both previous courts found prevented the flow of the surface water from the Poole property into the canal on the Guste property. Upon finding that the Poole estate was owed a servitude of drain by the Guste estate, the trial court issued a mandatory and prohibitory injunction ordering the defendants Guste to cease obstructing the drainage and to remove their levees in two places. The court also awarded damages. The court of appeal affirmed. 246 So. 2d 353 (1971).***

As the excellent analysis of the evidence by the previous courts shows in more detail, the preponderant evidence proves the following relevant facts:

1. The parties own adjacent tracts of land. Relevantly to present purposes, the Pooles (plaintiffs) own Section 30, and the Gustes (defendants) own Section 29. The Poole Section 30 is west of the section line boundary, and the Guste Section 29 east of it.

2. In 1916, by agreement of the ancestors in title of the parties, the "Dendinger Canal" was constructed, approximately 30 feet wide and 6 or 7 feet deep. Pertinently to present purposes, it is situated in the Guste land, just east of the section line between Section 30 (Poole) and Section 29 (Guste). This north-south canal empties at its south end into the Main (or Bedico) Canal. The latter flows east-west and empties into streams which eventually flow into Lake Pontchartrain, which is 1 to 2 miles below the present tracts.

3. Prior to the construction of the Dendinger Canal, the natural drainage of the surface waters on the portion of the Poole tract in Section 30 was southeasterly into and across the Guste property in Section 29. This drainage was of rainwater, other waters draining onto the Poole property from the north, and tidal overflow water. (The latter, at high tide, after the Canal was built, flowed onto the Poole land from the south (through the Dendinger Canal) and from the west (from a natural creek.) When the tide ebbed, the waters then drained southeasterly from the Poole land into the Dendinger Canal.) As the trial court noted, a reasonable inference from the evidence is that much of this pre-Canal drainage occurred at a draw or natural drain at a place we designate as the "bridge site." (This place of drain is more particularly

designated in the trial court judgment.)

4. The Dendinger Canal was constructed in accordance with a written agreement in 1916 by the ancestors in title of both parties. By this agreement, the canal was constructed within Section 29 (Guste) for the purposes of affording the Pooles' predecessor in title (Dendinger) the free use of the canal to transport timber down the canal for a period of (only) ten years, i.e., until 1926. The evidence further shows that this agreement was not renewed and that, in fact, the predecessor owner of the Poole estate ceased using the canal for timber-floating purposes after 1924. From 1924 on, the sole function of the canal was for drainage purposes (aside from its occasional use for fishing and recreation by members of the public).

5. After the construction of the Dendinger Canal in 1916, the principal change in drainage was that surface waters from the Poole tract flowed into and down the canal instead of *across* the surface of the Guste land. The drainage into the Dendinger Canal occurred principally at the place called that "bridge site" or "the gap."

6. (When the Dendinger Canal was dug, the dirt was thrown on the west bank of the canal, forming a "spoil bank." When the canal was constructed, a gap was left in this spoil bank; when a road was constructed on top of the spoil bank, a bridge was built at this gap. The gap left a clear avenue of drainage from the Poole property into the Dendinger Canal, the spoil bank preventing southeasterly drainage formerly occurring at other places along the boundary section line.

7. In 1965, the defendants (who had purchased the property in 1959) constructed a 7 feet high, north-south levee along the section line between Sections 29 and 30 (i.e., between the Poole property and the Dendinger Canal). This levee used the old spoil bank as a base; but, in constructing the levee, the Gustes filled in the gap at the bridge site through which water had formerly drained from the Poole land, thus completely blocking off the latter's property from the Dendinger Canal. (Actually, in building the levee, the Gustes constructed it partially on Poole property.)

The Dendinger Canal remained, but the Gustes now use it as part of their internal drainage system for the improvement of their tract of use in intensive agricultural cultivation. A levee was also constructed across the south end of the Dendinger Canal, closing it off where it had formerly emptied into the Main (Bedico) Canal. (The Gustes did so in order to prevent the tidal flow of water from that canal into their property. A new interior canal was dug.. .just inside of and parallel to this south levee to facilitate the internal drainage of this improved tract.)

Under the well-supported findings of fact by the trial and intermediate courts, these courts correctly found that the estate of the plaintiffs Poole enjoys a servitude of drain onto the estate of the defendants Guste and through it (via the Dendinger Canal) to the Main (or Bedico) Canal to the south of both properties. The servitude due by the Guste estate to the Poole estate is in part a natural servitude of drain, Civil Code Article 660 [Revised C.C. art. 655], and in part a "conventional" servitude of drain acquired by acquisitive prescription, Civil Code Articles 709 and 765 or 3504 [Revised C.C. arts. 697, 740, 742].

A *natural* servitude of drain is due by a servient (or "below") estate to receive the waters which run naturally from a dominant (or "above") estate, Civil Code Article 600 [Revised C.C. art. 605]. A *conventional* servitude of drain (the right "of passing water *collected in pipes or canals* through the estate of one's neighbor," Article 714 [no corresponding article after Revision] may be created by contract, Article 709 [Revised C.C. art. 697], or, being continuous and apparent, may be acquired by prescription.

In the present case, the Poole estate is owed a conventional servitude of drain onto the Guste estate at the bridge site and through the Dedinger Canal on the Guste property. This results from drainage into the canal at this point, and the canal's use for this purpose without title, for a period well in excess of thirty years before the construction, in 1965, of the Guste levees which obstructed the Poole drainage into and through the Guste estate.   This servitude was, at the least, acquired by the thirty-years' acquisitive prescription provided by Article 3504 [no corresponding article after Revision]. In so holding, we expressly do *not* determine:

(1) Whether the period of thirty years' prescriptive use necessary for acquisition under Article 3504 [no corresponding article after Revision] commenced in 1916, when the canal was first used for drainage purposes (although expressly created for timber-floating purposes *only),* or instead in 1926, when the contractual right of the Poole estate to use the canal (i.e., for timber-floating purposes) terminated;

(2) Whether the conventional servitude acquired by prescription might, also, have been acquired under Article 765 [Revised C.C. arts. 740, 742] by the ten-years' simple unopposed and uninterrupted use following termination of the timber-floating servitude in 1926, see Levet v. Lapeyrollerie, 39 La. Ann. 210,1 So. 672 (1887)... or whether, since use was without title, thirty years' acquisitive use under Article 3504 [no corresponding article after Revision was required, Comment, Acquisitive Prescription of Servitudes, 15 LaX.Rev. 777 (1955);

(3) To what extent the servitude of drain from the Poole property onto the Guste estate at the bridge site is a natural servitude of drain under Article 660 [Revised C.C. art. 655] (being the use of a natural drain — which, at least before the Dendinger Canal spoil bank, was not created by the industry of man—) through which surface waters were passed onto the Guste estate, not increased in volume (although some waters were perhaps diverted into drainage at that point rather than at others nearby), Nicholson v. Holloway Planting Co., 255 La. 1, 229 So. 2d 679 (1969), Broussard v. Cormier, 154 La. 877,98 So. 403 (1923); and to what extent, if any, such more burdensome use of the natural servitude of drain exceeded or was contrary to it, Articles 660, 790 [Revised C.C. arts. 655, 754], Planiol, Civil Law Treatise, Volume 1, Section 2903 (Louisiana State Law Institute translation, 1959), so as to alter it or substitute for it a conventional servitude created by acquisitive prescription, Articles 765, 790 [Revised C.C. arts. 740, 742, 754], Johnson v. Wills, 220 So. 2d 134 (La. App. 3d Cir. 1969), certiorari denied 254 La. 132, 222 So. 2d 883 (1969), noted 30 La.L.Rev. 192-93 (1969).

We should at this point note that we find no support in the Civil Code, the jurisprudence, or the commentators for the contentions of the defendants Gustes (a) that the timber-floating servitude of 1916 cannot be enlarged beyond its original use by acquisitive prescription, nor that (b) the Poole land cannot be the dominant estate and the Guste property the servient estate unless we find that overall! (i.e., as between the 5000-

acre Guste tract and the 2000-acre Poole property), irrespective of individual patterns along particular points of the boundary, one estate is upper to the other.

Having found the Poole estate is due a servitude of drain by the Guste estate, the previous courts correctly held the plaintiffs Poole, as owners of the dominant estate, to be entitled to injunctive relief requiring the defendants Guste, as owners of the servient estate, to remove the obstacles they had erected to the drainage of waters from the dominant through the servient estate. Articles 660, 777 [Revised C.C. arts. 655, 748] [citations omitted].

The trial court thus correctly granted a mandatory injunction ordering the Gustes to remove their levees at (1) the bridge site leading from the Poole tract onto the Guste tract and (2) at the south end or mouth of the Dendinger Canal (since otherwise the Dendinger Canal would not drain the Poole property as before.)

The defendant Gustes further contend that, even if the Poole property is due a servitude of drain by the Guste estate, the plaintiff Pooles are not entitled to the equitable remedy of injunctive relief. The defendants' argument is based upon limitations to the remedy of equity recognized in common-law jurisdictions, based on the historical use in them of injunctions by the chancery court where the damage-remedy in the regular courts was inadequate. Cf. James, Civil Procedure, Section 1.4 (1965). These doctrines are not necessarily applicable to Louisiana, with its different civilian procedural background, and where the injunction has historically been recognized as a remedy available to protect possession of property, Cf. La.C.Civ.P. Art. 3663(2), including (see cases previously cited) the continued use of a servitude of drain over another's land.

In further urging that injunction does not lie, the defendant Gustes likewise suggest that equity does not require the issuance of a mandatory injunction which would compel them to spend large sums of money to remedy their disturbance of the Poole drainage. Young v. International Paper Co., 179 La. 803,155 So. 231 (1934), cited in support, held that, where negligible further harm would be caused by reason of continuing drainage of wastes into a servient estate (whereas to cease such waste would cause the industrial plant to close and thus cause grossly disproportionate hardship to the drainer), injunctive relief would be denied. See also Adams v. Town of Ruston, 194 La. 403, 193 So. 688.

The relegation of a landowner to compensatory damages instead of to injunctive relief for violation of his property right was permitted, so far as we know, in only the two cited cases concerning very exceptional situations, 27 La.L.Rev. 440 (1967), 22 La.L.Rev. 316 (1962), 3 La.L.Rev. 28 1-82 (1941), and never so as to deny protection of a servitude due by a servient estate to a dominant estate. See Esnard v. Cangelosi, 200 La. 703, 8 So. 2d 673 (1942), noted 5 La.L.Rev. 141 (1941). In any event, the substantial damage here caused the dominant Poole estate by the blocking of drainage from it, and its substantial interference with the right of the Pooles to use their own property for their own purposes (the profitable growing of timber), Article 667, make inappropriate any consideration here of whether such a balancing of the equities is ever permissible to deny an owner protection of his property right by, in effect, granting his offending neighbor the right to pay damages instead of terminating such neighbor's continuing disturbance.

We further find unsupported by any authority the defendant Gustes' contentions (a) that recognizing the property rights of the dominant estate (thus causing them to lose at least some of the most profitable estate (thus causing them to lose at least some of the most profitable use of their own servient estate) violates due process or equal protection guarantees of the state and federal constitutions, (b) that they are entitled to cause this damage to the Poole estate in order to protect their own (the Guste) property from tidal flow, and (c) that the Pooles should be denied relief because, by their improving and reconstructing a rice irrigation canal (the Peters Canal) on their own property, they could furnish proper drainage from their own property instead of through the Guste property as they were entitled because of the servitude of drain.

The court of appeal affirmed the trial court award to the plaintiffs Poole of $4,511.37 for timber damages sustained through the obstruction of the drainage. We find no error in this award, under the facts set forth in the opinions of the previous courts, and in their finding that suit for such damages was timely brought within a year of the time the Pooles learned of the damage, Article 3537 [Revised C.C. arts. 3492,3493].

For the foregoing reasons the judgments of the trial court and of the court of appeal are affirmed. The defendants are to pay all costs of these proceedings.

SUMMERS, J. (dissenting). Many important factual aspects of this case have not been mentioned in the majority opinion. After the use of the canal for floating logs was discontinued in 1924, the canal became clogged to such an extent in places that cattle could walk across it. It served no drainage function at the time relators acquired the property in 1959. One of the Poole witnesses agreed with this. He said the only flow water in the canal at the time the levee was built consisted of tidewater and standing water caused by rain falling directly into the canal.

This fact, in my opinion, destroyed any servitude of drainage, if one was in fact ever acquired. A servitude of drain is not such unless it serves a drainage function.

What has not been emphasized in the majority opinion, and what is of such overriding significance in this case, is the fact that the greatest part of the lands involved are tidal overflow lands. A detailed investigation of the land and a review of the tidal overflow history of the area, including past hurricane surges, revealed that during the years 1961-1965, the lands involved were subject to flooding on 237, 195, 148, 218 and 259 days for each of the respective years. A protection levee with a crown elevation of 6 or 7 feet was recommended.

It was established by uncontradicted expert testimony that to open the levee system at the points ordered by the trial court and court of appeal would open the Guste property to flood water and render it useless, or by moving the levee at an expenditure of $50,000 flooding could be avoided.

At the same time, unimpeached expert testimony established that a canal on the Poole property called the Peters Canal, immediately adjacent to the float-road canal, would perform the identical function as the float-road canal since it too opened to the Bedico Canal and thence to Lake Pontchartrain, if only the Pooles would open their own unused Peters levee at one point. But the court of appeal and this Court refused to recognize this fact or require the Pooles to alleviate a problem partially of their own making. Because of the refusal of the Pooles to open this levee at nominal costs, 5,000 acres of Guste property must remain unproductive or the expenditure of $50,000 is necessary. I fail to see the equity of this result. Adams v. Town of Ruston, 194 La. 403, 193 So. 688 (1940);

Young v. International Paper Co., 179 La. 803,155 So. 231 (1934).

Important, too, is the fact that no court has reached a conclusion as to the over-all dominance between the two estates. Rather their opinions seem to be concerned more with individual points along the boundary line between the Poole and Guste properties.

Article 660 of the Civil Code [Revised C.C. art. 655] is concerned with servitudes which originate from the natural situation of the places..

This article of the code as interpreted by this Court in Broussard v. Cormier, 154 La. 877, 98 Co. 403 (1923), and more recently in Nicholson v. Holloway Planting Co., 255 La. 1, 229 So. 2d 679 (1969), convinces me that the over-all dominancy between two large estates is the controlling factor and not isolated points of drainage disproportionately small to the whole property. Where these isolated points create drainage problems the proprietor above (assuming the Poole property to be the superior estate) should be compelled to adjust the drainage within his estate and absorb the problem within the estate itself. He should not be permitted to impose upon his neighbor such a hardship as this case presents.

Visual inspection, upon which reliance was placed, is not reliable where the question of drainage concerns large, flat, tidal overflow, marshy areas. The only reliable testimony in these cases is duly qualified expert opinion based upon detailed evaluation studies and other supporting data. The only testimony in this latter category was expressed by Robert Berlin, surveyor admitted by the Pooles to be "eminently qualified," who was shown to be an expert in the use and interpretation of aerial photography.

He undertook an over-all drainage study, in the course of which he prepared one large aerial photograph whereon he super-imposed the elevation data and general direction of drainage of the two properties. In his opinion the Guste estate was the dominant estate and the direction of drainage was south and westerly. By contrast, the surveyor presented on behalf of the Poole interest was never asked which estate was dominant. His testimony concerned drainage at isolated points along the boundary.

In these circumstances the Guste property as the dominant estate owes no obligation to the Poole property except to "do nothing whereby the natural servitude due by the estate below may be rendered more burdensome." La. Civil Code art. 660 [Revised C.C. art. 655]. This the Gustes have not done. To the contrary they have relieved the Poole property of any water flow from the Guste property.

Even assuming that the Guste property is the servient estate, the exceptional circumstances of this situation demand a contrary result. In Mailhot v. Pugh, 30 La. Ann. 1359 (1878), the defendant conceived a plan for the defense of his plantation from floods which this Court considered intelligent and systematic. He wanted, and sought, the cooperation of the neighboring plantation owner in the construction of a common system of protection levees but the plaintiff refused, just as the facts of this case disclose that the Gustes sought the cooperation of the Pooles. Defendant then built a protection levee between the two estates and plaintiff sued for damage to his crop caused by the water the levee threw back on his property. In this context the broader question of the servitude of drain owed to an upper estate was presented. Our predecessors, relying upon Dalbon contre Graveson of the French tribunals, quoted from the decision, saying:

The owner of the lower ground has the right to build dikes or other works to guarantee his property against inundation [sic], even though he aggravates thereby the damage which may be caused to the superior proprietor. (Translation supplied.)

The Court then observed that the French court in its opinion explains that the principles governing such cases are different from those regulating natural servitudes, and that works to guard against inundations [sic] of one's property from floods or torrents (hurricane surges) are regulated by other principles than those which regulate natural servitude (La. Civil Code art. 660) [Revised C.C. arts. 655, 656]. Everyone can preserve his property from floods even though the works will surely damage his neighbor, the court continued on French authority. Journal du Palais, 1813, p.384; Duvernoy contre Sarnpso, Idem. 1861, p. 888.

Quoting from Chardon, treating the obligations of the proprietor, the court recognized that all works may be executed which are judged appropriate to guard properties, against flood disasters whether it be by dikes or other structures. And the failure of the neighbor to do likewise makes his damage due to his indolence and not to the vigilance of the proprietor who erects protective works. Summarizing, the court noted:

So Demolombe, reiterating what had been taught by his predecessors with striking unanimity, that a proprietor has a right to protect himself from damage by an overflow by the erection of works of his own land, even though they should cause the overflow to be more hurtful to his neighbor.

Demolombe was again quoted. He observed that it was inconceivable that the law would impose upon proprietors the obligation to let their property be damaged by floods without being able to do anything about it. These principles, he wrote, which allow the proprietor to protect his lands conform with reason and equity and have always been recognized in the ancient Roman and French jurisprudence and were at that time consecrated by unanimous accord. Tome 11, No. 30.

What these authorities so wisely expound is that the law of drain servitude does not and cannot apply to flat marsh and swamp where tide is the prevailing cause of water flow. The reason for this should be obvious. Tidal waters alternately rise and fall. Consequently these waters run both ways, in and out of the lands so affected. Drainage laws on the other hand were enacted to govern the flow of water in one direction. The rule of Article 660 [Revised C.C. arts. 655, 656] cannot apply to lands periodically and so frequently subject to overflow and inundation by storm and tide.

The vast reaches of lowlands, swamp and marsh which dominate the coastal regions of Louisiana can never be protected against the frequent surges of hurricanes or the ravages of floods by wind or tide and turned to agricultural or industrial uses under the narrow view the Court articulates today. It is an unrealistic application of the law detrimental to a substantial area of our State. Despite the fact that this case lends itself so well to the sound rule of law expounded by the jurisconsults and tribunals of France, no reference to that position has been made by the majority. I respectfully dissent.

NOTE

In *Freestate Industrial Development Co.* v. *T. & K, Inc.*, 209 So. 2d 568, 571 (La. App. 2d Cir. 1968), the court declared: "An owner whose waters flow by natural drains onto lands of his neighbor may cut ditches to concentrate and speed the flow of water beyond the slow natural process by which they would ultimately reach their destination. Of course, this rule is qualified to the extent that the alternation or change in method must not cause any greater quantity to flow than before."

In *Wood* v. *Gibson Construction Co.*, 313 So. 898, 901 (La. App. 2d Cir. 1975), the court indicated that the owner of the upper estate "may breach his obligation under Civil Code Article 660 [Revised C.C. arts. 655, 656] to refrain from rendering the natural servitude of drainage more burdensome, without causing a greater quantity of waterflow." The court, however, did not reach this question. Plaintiff had brought suit seeking by mandatory injunction to compel a subdivision developer to prevent unnatural drainage onto his property. A judgment granting an injunction was reversed by the court of appeal on the ground that plaintiff had failed to prove that he was threatened with irreparable injury, loss, or damage. For a critique, see The Work of the Louisiana Appellate Courts for the 1974-1975 Term, 36 La. L. Rev. 335, 350-351 (1976). See also David v. Dixie Rice Agricultural Corp. 379 So. 2d 62 (La. App. 3d Cir. 1980); Elliot v. Louisiana Intrastate Gas Corp., 336 So. 2d 295 (La. App. 3d Cir. 1976) (mandatory injunction without need to prove irreparable harm).

CHAPTER XIII. LEGAL SERVITUDES
Civil Code arts. 659-696

1. LEVEES AND RIVER ROADS
Civil Code art. 665

A. N. YIANNOPOULOS, CIVIL LAW PROPERTY
§§ 88, 89 (4th ed. 2001)
(footnotes omitted)

§ 88. The Levee Servitude

Lands fronting navigable rivers have been burdened in Louisiana, apart from the servitude of public use under Article 456 of the Civil Code, by the servitude under Article 665 for the construction and maintenance of levees. The constitutionality of Article 665 has been questioned, but repeatedly affirmed. This article applies "only to navigable rivers or streams. Lakes are not included."

The burden for the construction and maintenance of levees affects lands that were part of a riparian tract at the time of severance from the sovereign, even if they are not riparian at the time of appropriation. In the past, the converse was also true. Lands that were not a part of a riparian tract at the time of severance from the sovereign but were riparian at the time of appropriation were burdened by the levee servitude. However, beginning with Delaune v. Board of Commissioners, the Louisiana Supreme Court, in a series of decisions, adopted a more restrictive view and "effectively overruled" the prior jurisprudence. As a result, lands that were not part of a riparian tract at the time of severance from the sovereign but were riparian at the time of the taking were not burdened by the levee servitude. Such lands could be expropriated for levee construction but could not be appropriated under Article 665 of the Louisiana Civil Code.

The property taken must be "within the range of the reasonable necessities of the situation, as produced by the forces of nature, unaided by artificial causes."

The levee board enjoys discretion to appropriate lands away from the site of levee construction. Failure to appropriate lands near the site "does not in and by itself constitute palpable abuse" of privilege. Landowners have the burden of proof that the taking should be shifted to someone else's property. The levee board is not "required to come forward and justify its present action," but the levee must be necessary for the control of the flood waters of the river to which the land is riparian.

Originally, landowners in Louisiana were required to construct and maintain levees at their own expense. In the last part of the nineteenth century, however, the legislature established levee districts under the authority of levee boards authorized to build and maintain levees at public expense. While originally no compensation was due for taking lands for the construction of levees, the Louisiana Constitution of 1898 accorded landowners in the Orleans Levee Board district a right of action for the value of property taken for levee construction. Subsequently, Article 16, Section 6 of the 1921 Constitution provided that all lands and improvements actually used or destroyed for levee or levee drainage purposes "shall be paid for at a price not to exceed the assessed value of the preceding year; provided, that this shall not apply to batture, nor to property the control of which is vested in the state or any subdivision thereof for the purposes of commerce."

The exclusion of compensation as to batture and property under the control of the state or of a political subdivision was justified on the ground that "such property was for all practical purposes already forever lost to the owner" by virtue of the servitude of public use. Owners of property taken or destroyed by levee boards, which was neither batture nor under the control of a political subdivision, namely, owners of property lying above the ordinary high water mark landward, had a claim for compensation at a price not exceeding the assessed value of the preceding year. The ownership of the lands used or destroyed for levee purposes remained in the riparian landowner, because the lands were not "expropriated" but merely "appropriated" for levee construction and the payment was an indemnity for the public use.

The burden of the servitude under Article 665 of the Civil Code has been diminished by the Louisiana Constitution of 1974. Under this constitution, the only exception to the principle that property may not be taken except for public utility and with just compensation is for "appropriation of property necessary for levee and levee drainage purposes." However, the constitution declares that lands and improvements actually used or destroyed for levees or levee drainage purposes "shall be paid for as provided by law," with the exception of "batture or property the control of which is vested in the state or in a political subdivision for the purpose of commerce." Article 16, Section 6 of the 1921 Constitution, including its measure of payment, was continued as a statute until the enactment of legislation establishing a new measure of compensation.

Following the constitutional mandate the legislature enacted a statute which provides that "All lands, exclusive of batture, and improvements hereafter actually taken, used, damaged or destroyed for levee or levee drainage purposes shall be paid for at fair market value to the full extent of the loss." Batture may still be taken without compensation according to the statute and the Louisiana Constitution.

§ 89. Public Use of Batture

The word *batture* occurs in the Louisiana Constitution, in statutes, and in jurisprudence. A study of Louisiana legal texts and jurisprudence leads to the conclusion that batture has three meanings. In the first sense batture refers to lands of alluvial origin formed by imperceptible deposits of material or by receding waters on the banks of a river; it has the same meaning as accretion. In a second sense, the word batture refers to land formations in the bed of a river, that is, in an area below the ordinary low water mark. In a third sense, the word batture is used to denote the natural bank of a river, that is, the area between the ordinary low and ordinary high stage of the water.

Determination of the meaning of the word batture is important in a variety of contexts, including acquisition and apportionment of alluvial lands among riparian proprietors, acquisition of such lands by the transferee of a riparian estate, compensation for the taking of riparian lands for the construction of river roads, public works, and levees, and recognition of private ownership of alluvial lands free of any public servitudes. In determining these matters, Louisiana courts have attributed to the word batture different meanings for different purposes.

Under the regime of the Louisiana Civil Code of 1870, batture could be *appropriated,* that is, taken without compensation, for the construction of river roads, levees, navigation facilities, and other public works. In this respect, no distinction was made between batture and other lands. The Louisiana Constitutions of 1898 and 1921, however, diminished the burden of the levee servitude except as to batture. Levee boards could appropriate batture without any indemnity but they were bound to pay the riparian owner an indemnity for the taking of other lands. The Louisiana Constitution of 1974 has further strengthened the principle that private property may not be taken or damaged for public purposes without just compensation, subject to the exception that batture may still be appropriated without indemnity for "levee and levee drainage purposes." It would seem that all other riparian servitudes may be exercised by the state or its political subdivisions only upon payment of just compensation for the taking of batture or other lands. The distinction between batture and other lands may thus be pertinent today only for the exercise of the levee servitude.

For purposes of interpretation of Article 665 of the Louisiana Civil Code and Article 16, Section 6 of the Louisiana Constitution of 1921, the Louisiana Supreme Court has consistently defined batture as the area between ordinary low and ordinary high stage of the water of a navigable river. This is, of course, the definition of the *natural* bank of a river, as distinguished from the definition of the second paragraph of Article 457 of the 1870 Code. Thus, levee boards were, and continue to be, bound to pay an indemnity for land between the ordinary high water mark and a levee actually used or destroyed for levee purposes. This application of the word batture has been adopted by the United States Supreme Court. However, in cases involving taking of the bank of a navigable river for the construction and maintenance of roads under Article 665 of the Civil Code, or for the construction and maintenance of navigation facilities under Article 863 of the 1870 Code, the word batture was used broadly at times to denote the alluvial origin of the lands in question and, at other times narrowly to denote the area between the ordinary low and ordinary high stage of the water.

The owner of batture within the limits of a municipality may institute an action for the recognition of his ownership free of public servitudes of "so much of the batture as may not be necessary for public use." Depending on facts and circumstances, Louisiana courts have either granted or refused such demands. It was early established that servitudes of public use burden lands from the edge of the water to a levee established according to law. Property on the land side of such a levee, or of a bulkhead constructed by the public authorities, ceases to be the bank of a river and is freed of all public servitudes. In the absence of such works, land above the ordinary high water mark is likewise freed of all public servitudes. In such cases, the word batture is used broadly to denote accretions, and is used narrowly the area between the ordinary low and ordinary high stage of the water, that is, the natural bank.

NOTE
The Levee Servitude

The historical development of the Levee servitude is expounded by Judge Overton in *Mayer v. Board of Commissioners for Caddo Levee District,* 177 La. 1119, 150 So. 295 (1933):

"In the early days of this state, the levees were built and maintained solely at the joint expense of the front proprietors, and were diminutive constructions compared with present-day levees. Gayare's History of Louisiana, vol. 2, p. 2; Ward v. Board of Levee Commissioners, 152 La. 158, 166, 167 92 So. 769, 772. The construction of levees came under public supervision as early as 1808. See Act of February 15 (No. 1) of 1808, and Ward v. Board of Levee Commissioners, *supra.*

"To illustrate the size of levees in the early days as compared with the levees of to-day, even after their construction came under public supervision, and as late as 1829, we may refer to Act 31 of that year, the second section of which specifies the number of feet wide the base of each levee should be, depending on the depth of the water to be held back by the levee, as well as the number of feet its height and the width its summit should be. Where the levee was to hold back water of the depth of one foot, and not more than 3 feet, the base was required to be 5 feet wide for each foot in height, and, where the levee was to hold back more than 6 feet of water — the greatest depth specified — the levee was required to have a base of at least 8 feet for every foot in height. The summit of each levee was required to be of the breadth of one-third of its base, and the general requirement was made that every levee should be of such height that, after the settling of the earth, it would be one foot above the level of the water at its highest. By section 3 of the act, at places where the bank was apt to cave, it may be observed, in passing, the levee was required to be constructed at least one arpent from the water's edge, and in places where this condition did not exist at a distance of at least 60 feet therefrom. In both instances the measurement was required to be from the summit of the bank of the river.

"Pretermitting reference to Article 312 of the Constitutions of 1898 and 1913, which affected the Orleans levee district alone, up to the promulgation of the Constitution of 1921, the public authorities, in taking advantage of the servitude for levee purposes, and in the proper exercise of the police power, upon which power the servitude may be said to rest, paid nothing to the owner of the land for such part of his land as was taken for levee purposes, or for such part as was thrown outside of the levee...

"It appears, therefore, from the foregoing, that whatever section 6 of Article 16 of the Constitution of 1921 may give to the owner of land, subject to the servitude for levee purposes, is in the nature of a gratuity. It is a payment made by the agency of the state — the levee district — for what already belonged to the state at the time of the adoption of the Constitution. The Constitutional Convention of 1921 was evidently prompted, in adopting the provision, to lessen, so far as the means of the public authorities would permit, the burden of the servitude resting on lands, bordering on navigable streams, and growing out of the necessities of the situation. Care should be taken, therefore, not to carry the spirit of the provision beyond its clear intendment, and thereby render, perhaps, the state unable to discharge its duty of protecting a large part of the public from inundation...

"When Article 457 [Revised C.C. art. 456], defining the banks of rivers, was carried into the Civil Code of 1870, levees, comparatively speaking, were small affairs, and were generally constructed close to the river, say between 60 feet and an acre or two. The levees could then serve with some degree of exactness as the banks of the river, and may do so, in many instances, now. Today, however, the levees are usually built much larger, and not infrequently some distance from the natural bank of the river. As for example (though this would seem to be an extreme case) in Wolfe v. Hurley (D.C.) 46 F. (2d) 515, the levee was set back 4 or 5 miles from the river. To apply the code definition of the banks of a river, and thereby make, with the aid of Article 453 of the Civil Code [Revised C.C. arts. 450,452], all land lying between the levee and the river a part of the bed of the river, and a public thing, no longer available for private use, without reservation or qualification, to present methods of building levees, would be going further, we think, than the Legislature ever intended by its enactment."

DELTIC FARM AND TIMBER CO. v. BOARD OF COMMR'S
368 So. 2d 1109 (La. App. 2d Cir. 1979)

HALL, J. The defendant, Board of Commissioners of the Fifth Levee District, appeals from a judgment awarding plaintiffs, Deltic Farm and Timber, Inc. et. al, and Anderson-Tully Company, full value compensation for land taken by the Levee Board for levee construction, maintenance or repair along the right descending bank of the Mississippi River in Madison Parish.

The land was appropriated by the Levee Board in 1970 in connection with the Cabin Teele Louisiana Riverside Enlargement and Berms project. In 1972, the plaintiffs filed suit alleging the property was not subject to appropriation and seeking recovery of damages based on the full value of the land taken. Alternatively, plaintiffs sought to recover the assessed value of the land. Tenders of the assessed value of the land were refused. The case was tried on documentary evidence and stipulated facts. It was stipulated that the issues were to be decided under the 1921 Constitution and statutes applicable at the time of the taking. The amount of plaintiffs damages based on actual value ($63,300 to Deltic, et. al and $25,212 to Anderson-Tully) were stipulated. The trial court held that the property was not subject to the levee servitude, was not subject to appropriation, and that damages based on full value were due. Judgment was rendered in favor of plaintiffs for the stipulated amounts.

The legal issue in this case is whether the property of plaintiffs which the Levee Board appropriated for levee construction and maintenance purposes is subject to the levee servitude provided by Civil Code Article 665 and therefore subject to appropriation by the Levee Board, in which case the Levee Board would owe the landowners only the assessed value of the property under Article 16, § 6 of the Louisiana Constitution of 1921.

The Levee Board contends that the property is subject to the servitude because it is presently riparian, that is, it fronts on the Mississippi River. The landowners contend the property is not subject to the servitude because it was not riparian at the time the property was severed from the public domain and because the existence of the servitude depends on the riparian nature of the property at the time of severance.

The facts are that the property appropriated lies in sections which did not front on the river at the time of severance. These sections were patented to parties other than the parties to whom the sections fronting on the river were patented. Over the years the river has changed course, eroding away the sections which originally fronted on the river so that the river now abuts parts of plaintiffs' property located in the back sections.

The plaintiffs rely primarily on a line of cases beginning with Delaune v. Board of Commissioners, 230 La. 117, 87 So. 2d 749 (1956), which cases, the plaintiffs contend, hold that property is subject to the levee servitude only if the property was riparian at the time the property was severed from the public domain. Cases following Delaune are Board of Commissioners for Pontchartrain Levee District v. Baron, 236 La. 846, 109 So. 2d 441 (1959); A. K. Roy, Inc. v. Board of Commissioners, 237 La. 541, 111 So. 2d 765 (1959); Jeanerette Lumber and Shingle Co. v. Board of Commissioners, 249 La. 508,187 So. 2d 715 (1966); Thomas v. Board of Commissioners for Pontchartrain L. Dist, 208 So. 2d 163 (La. App. 4th Cir. 1968); Hathorn v. Board of Commissioners, 218 So. 2d 335 (La. App. 3d Cir. 1969) writ ref. 253 La. 881, 220 So. 2d 461(1969); Grayson v. Commissioners of Bossier Levee District, 229 So.2d 139 (La. App. 2d Cir. 1969); and Taylor v. Board of Levee Commissioners of Tensas Basin L.D., 332 So. 2d 495 (La. App. 3d Cir. 1976).

The Levee Board contends that the servitude exists on all property that is presently riparian regardless of whether the property was riparian at the time of severance. It relies on the earlier cases of Wolfe v. Hurley, 46 F.2d 505 (W.D. La. 1930) aff. per curiam, 283 U.S. 801, 51 S.Ct. 493, 75 L. Ed. 1423 (1931) and Board of Commissioners of Tensas Basin Levee 1) 1st. v. Franklin, 219 La. 859, 54 So. 2d 125 (1951) appeal dismissed 342 U.S. 844, 72 S.Ct. 80, 96 L. Ed. 638 (1951) and some of the more recent cases cited by plaintiffs. The Levee Board distinguishes the cited cases, pointing out that in none of those cases was the property taken presently riparian. The Levee Board argues that those cases stand only for the proposition that where the property taken is not presently riparian it nevertheless can be subject to the servitude if it was riparian at the time of severance.

Riparian property (property adjacent to a navigable stream) subject to the levee servitude (an ancient servitude codified in Civil Code Article 665) may be appropriated (as distinguished from expropriated) for levee purposes. Article 16, Section 6 of the 1921 Constitution provided for payment for lands used or destroyed for levee purposes at a price not to exceed the assessed value. Use of property subject to the levee servitude for levee purposes is not a taking of private property for which compensation is due under either the Louisiana or Federal Constitutions, the compensation provided by Article 16, Section 6 being a mere gratuity. The rationale of decisions upholding the constitutionality of appropriation for levee purposes is that the levee servitude was reserved to the public at the time riparian property was severed from the public domain and that title to such riparian property is held subject to the servitude, Eldridge v. Trezevant, 160 U.S. 452, 16 S.Ct. 345, 40 L. Ed. 490 (1896) is the leading United States Supreme Court decision on the subject. Dickson v. Board of Commissioners of Caddo Levee Dist., 210 La. 121, 26 So. 2d 474 (1946) contains an excellent discussion of the history of the levee servitude, as does Hebert v. T. L. James & Co., 224 La. 498, 70 So. 2d 102 (1953). An authoritative discussion appears in 40 Tul. L. Rev. 233.

Dickson held:....No grants of lands were ever given without a specific reservation being made therein for the common use of the public of all rights to the shores of rivers and bayous upon which they might front. 26 So. 2d p. 478.

Despite the repeated contention in numerous litigations that Article 665, imposing this servitude on riparian lands, controverts the constitutional guarantee in both the state and federal Constitutions that no one can be deprived of his inalienable rights of property without due process of law, it has been consistently held by this court and by the Supreme Court of the United States that such constitutional requirements relate to the right of expropriation and do not have the effect of abrogating our law giving the state authority to appropriate land upon which rights for the construction of levees, roads, and other such public works have always been reserved. 26 So. 2d p. 479.

And however unfair it may seem to the owners of this type of land they are without right to complain because their acquisition of such land was subject by law to this ancient servitude and the private mischief must be endured rather than the public inconvenience or calamity. 26 So. 2d p. 479.

Following *Wolfe* and *Franklin* which seemed to recognize the levee servitude as affecting non-riparian property, the Louisiana Supreme Court reverted to a more restrictive view, effectively overruling *Wolfe* and *Franklin* in a series of decisions beginning with *Delaune*. *Delaune* enunciated a two-prong criteria for determining whether property is subject to the levee servitude:

(1) The property must have been riparian when severed from the public domain; and

(2) The property taken must be within the range of the reasonable necessities of the situation as produced by the forces of nature unaided by artificial causes.

These criteria have been repeated and applied in *Baron, Roy, Jeanerette, Thomas, Hathorn, Grayson* and *Taylor*.

Delaune also held: This servitude, as explained in Dickson v. Board of Commissioners, comes into existence at the time the property bordering on the navigable stream is separated from the public domain. Accordingly, in order to ascertain whether a particular property appropriated for levee purposes is subject to a servitude, it is essential to trace title to the original grant *when the land itself does not actually front on the stream.* 87 So. 2d p. 754 (emphasis supplied).

The Levee Board seizes upon and stresses the underlined language found in the *Delaune* opinion and some of the subsequent cases which indicates it is only necessary to determine if property was riparian at time of severance where the property is not presently riparian. It is correctly pointed out that in none of the cited cases did the land abut the navigable stream at the time of taking, as does the land in the instant case. Defendant points out that for flood control purposes, it is important that the servitude exist and be exercised along the present course of the river as it changes and shifts and argues that other servitudes, such as the use of banks and for roads, and ownership rights, shift with the shifting course of a river.

Our view is that to impose the levee servitude and appropriation without compensation on property that was not riparian and subject to the levee servitude at time of severance would constitute the taking of private property without due compensation in violation of both the Louisiana and Federal Constitutions. We find nothing in the history of the servitude, as disclosed by the cited cases and articles, which indicates the servitude was reserved beyond the limits of riparian concessions. *Delaune* specifically recognizes that a state statutory or constitutional provision "does not and could not for obvious constitutional reasons, burden land already separated from the public domain with a servitude."

The language in the cited decisions on which the Levee Board relies does not mean, as the Levee Board contends, that the levee servitude exists not only on lands riparian at the time of severance but also exists on lands riparian at the time of taking. That was essentially the holdings of *Wolfe* and *Franklin* which have been effectively overruled. What we understand the court to have meant in those cases, in which it was dealing with land not riparian at the time of taking, was that even though the land did not presently front on a navigable stream, it would nevertheless be subject to the levee servitude if it was riparian at time of severance.

The importance to the public safety and welfare of the levee system and of changes in the levee system as the course of the river changes cannot be denied or underestimated. However, taking of private property without due compensation cannot be constitutionally justified under the police power of the state alone. *Eldridge* v. *Trezevant* so held.

We hold, as did the trial court, that property which was not riparian at the time of severance is not encumbered by the Article 665 levee servitude and is not subject to appropriation for levee purposes, even though it may be riparian at the time of taking due to changes in the course of the navigable stream due to natural causes.

The property involved in this case was not riparian at the time of its severance from the public domain. It is not subject to the levee servitude anti appropriation. Plaintiffs are entitled to full compensation for its damages caused by the Levee Board's use of their property. The judgment of the district court awarding such damages is correct and is affirmed, at appellant's costs.

NOTE
The River Road Servitude

For the scope of the river road servitude, see *Lyons v. Hinckley,* 12 La. Ann 655 (1856). For the extent of the river road servitude under Articles 665 and 666 of the Civil Code, see *Hebert* v. *T.L. James & Co.,* 224 La. 498, 70 So. 2d 102 (1953). There was on plaintiffs property a well-traveled graveled road, approximately thirty feet wide, and the state attempted to expand and pave that road so that it would measure seventy-five feet wide. The landowners demanded compensation for the extra width taken and the state argued that no compensation was due because the land was burdened by the river road servitude. The Louisiana Supreme Court rejected the state's argument on the ground that the proposed road exceeded the limits of the servitude contemplated by Articles 665 and 666 of the Civil Code.

2. OBLIGATIONS OF NEIGHBORHOOD
Civil Code arts. 667-669

HIGGINS OIL & FUEL CO. v. GUARANTY OIL CO.
145 La. 233, 82 So. 206 (1919)

PROVOSTY, J. The plaintiff holds an oil lease of a tract of land adjoining another tract of which the defendant holds a lease of the same kind. The plaintiff sunk a well on its tract, and was drawing oil from it by means of a pump at the rate of some 124 barrels a day, when defendant sunk a well on its tract approximately 400 feet from plaintiffs well. This well of defendant proved a nonproducer, and was abandoned. Through some underground communication it lets air into the radius affected by plaintiffs pump, thereby reducing the suction power of the pump, and as a consequence reducing markedly its production. By closing this dry well, which may be done with no trouble or expense by simply putting back the plug that has been taken out, the capacity of plaintiffs pump is at once restored. Defendant refuses to close it; and plaintiff brings this suit to compel defendant to do so, and also to recover the damages suffered up to now, and continuingly being suffered, as the result of the reduced production of the pump. The petition of plaintiff alleges these facts, and that, while plaintiffs pump is thus being prevented from working to its full capacity, the pumps which are being used by other parties on all the adjoining tracts of land are depleting the reservoir of oil which lies under the lands of mat locality.***An exception of no cause of action was sustained below, and plaintiff has appealed.

The articles of our Code bearing upon the matter are the following:

"Art. 491 [Revised C.C. art. 477]. Perfect ownership gives the right to use, to enjoy and to dispose of one's property in the most unlimited manner, provided it is not used in any way prohibited by laws or ordinances."

"Art. 505 [Revised C.C. art. 490]. The ownership of the soil carries with it the ownership of all that is directly above and under it.

"The owner may make upon it all the plantations, and erect all the buildings which he thinks proper, under the exceptions established in the title: Of Servitudes.

"He may construct below the soil all manner of works, digging as deep as he deems convenient, and draw from them all the benefits which may accrue, under the modifications as may result from the laws and regulations concerning mines and the laws and regulations of the police."

"Art. 666 [Revised C.C. art. 659]. The law imposes upon the proprietors various obligations towards one another, independent of all agreements; and those are the obligations which are prescribed in the following articles."

"Art. 667. Although a proprietor may do with his estate whatever he please, still he cannot make any work on it, which may deprive his neighbor of the liberty of enjoying his own, or which may be the cause of any damage to him."

"Art. 668. Although one be not at liberty to make any work by which his neighbor's buildings may be damaged, yet every one has the liberty of doing on his own ground whatsoever he pleases; although it should occasion some inconvenience to his neighbor."

"Art. 2315. Every act whatever of man that causes damage to another obliges him by whose fault it happened to repair it."

This last article can be but of little assistance in the case, for it applies only to a person who is at fault, or, in other words, who has committed, or is committing, a wrong; and the question in the case is whether the defendant is "at fault."

The provision of Article 667, that the owner may not make any work on his property "which may be the cause of any damage to" his neighbor is found under the title "Of Servitudes," and hence apparently is one of the exceptions to which Article 505 [Revised C.C. art. 490] refers, and hence would seem to be a limitation upon Article 505 [Revised C.C. art. 490].

It is also apparently in direct conflict with the provision of Article 491 [Revised C.C. art. 477] that "ownership gives the right to enjoy and dispose of one's property in the most unlimited manner." The line of demarcation between what an owner may do with impunity and what he may not do without incurring liability is drawn by Article 668 between what is a mere inconvenience and what causes a real damage. But that cannot be the meaning; for very evidently an owner cannot be debarred from the legitimate use of his property simply because it may cause a real damage to his neighbor. It would be contrary to the fundamental legal principle according to which the exercise of a right cannot constitute a fault or wrong, and, besides, every damage is real; an unreal damage cannot be damage.

We cannot reconcile these contradictions, or gather the true meaning or scope of these articles, from the articles themselves, but, for ascertaining this true meaning, must resort to the works of Pothier and Toullier, whence these articles were derived by the framers of our Code.

Pothier, in his second appendix to his work on Partnership (Paris Ed. 1835) vol. 3 says:

At page 549:

> "Neighborhood is a quasi contract which creates reciprocal obligations between the neighbors; that is to say, between the owners or possessors of contiguous estates."

And at page 556:

> "The laws of good neighborhood forbid me to cause anything to pass from my estate to that of my neighbor which may damage him; but they do not prevent me from depriving him of some convenience which he derives from my estate. For instance, if he derives light from my estate, I may, by raising a building on my estate, deprive him of this light."

And in his general introduction to his treatise on Customs, volume 10 of same edition, he says:

At page 40:

> "Ownership may be defined to be the right to dispose of a thing as one pleases, provided the rights of others are not thereby infringed, or some law violated."

At page 41:

> "The rights here alluded to as not to be infringed upon are not only those which others may at some future time be entitled to have in the estate, but also those of the owners or possessors of neighboring estates. Although ownership gives to the owner the power to dispose of his estate as be pleases, he nevertheless cannot do what the obligations of neighborhood do not allow him to do to the prejudice of his neighbors."

And in his treatise on Ownership, volume 8 of same edition, he says at page 117, No. 13:

"We have defined ownership to be the right to dispose at one's pleasure of a thing; and we have added, without, however, infringing the rights of others.***Among these rights are those of owners and possessors of neighboring estates. The owner of an estate, howsoever perfect his ownership may be, cannot injure these rights, and, in consequence, cannot do that within his estate which the obligations arising from neighborhood do not allow him to do therein to the prejudice of his neighbors."

***The Code Napoleon not containing a provision corresponding with the said provision of Article 668, Demolombe, basing himself upon the definition of ownership as giving the right to use, enjoy, and dispose of one's property in the most unlimited manner, and upon the principle that one who but exercises a right he has cannot be at fault, concludes that, even though what is done is simply for the purpose of injuring the neighbor, with no benefit to the owner, the neighbor has no right to complain; but the author adds that the contrary doctrine "which is very ancient," is generally admitted. Des Servitudes, Nos. 66 and 648.

Laurent, De La Propriete, vol. 6, p. 186, No. 138, says:

"The science of jurisprudence requires as much precision as the imperfection of language will allow of. The laying down of principles so vague as to open the door to conclusions evidently false ought to be avoided. In our present discussion, the word 'damage' ought to be discarded, and the expression infringement of right' adhered to: no doubt, a damage results from such infringement of right, but the sole fact of there being a damage does not suffice for giving rise to an action. And this is, at bottom, the doctrine which has been consecrated by the decisions of the courts."

And again at page 183, No. 136:

"We come to another formulation of the principle, precisely as Pothier formulates it: The right of the owner is limited only in so far as it comes in conflict with some equal right of another owner. Hence, in order that he should have to repair a damage caused by him in the exercise of his right, it does not suffice that be should have caused the damage, but some right of the neighbor must have been thereby infringed. If he does not infringe some right of the neighbor, though he causes damage, he is not held to any reparation."

"It is then a settled principle that a person who uses his own right without infringing the right of another owes no reparation for the damage he may cause. But the application of that principle gives rise to more than one difficulty. If the owner who uses his right does it through malice, from a desire to injure, without any profit to himself, will he be held bound to repair the damage he causes, although he does not infringe any right? There is an ancient maxim inscribed in Roman laws which says that we must not favor the perversity of men. Now, would it not be to encourage this perversity if a right were allowed to be used for the sole purpose of injuring another. Perhaps another maxim, equally inscribed in the Roman laws, will be invoked, according to which what one does in the exercise of one's own right cannot injure one, in this sense that the person acting is not held to repair the injury. But can it well be said that to exercise ones s right for the sole purpose of causing injury is the exercise of one's right? Why are rights sanctioned by law? Because they are faculties which are necessary to enable us to fulfill our mission on this earth. Is it our mission, forsooth, to do evil for the mere pleasure of doing evil? And does the legislator owe protection to him who employs for doing evil a right which has been accorded to him as an instrument for intellectual and moral development? Conscience answers with the Roman jurisconsults: *'Malitiis hominum non est indulgendum.'*

"And that has been the view taken by the courts. An owner constructs a building which cuts off his neighbor's light. In so doing he but exercises a right he has, and therefore owes no reparation of the damage he causes to the neighbor. But he does more; he erects in front and almost against the window of his neighbor, part of which is already masqued by the new building, a dummy chimney, beginning on the roof, resting on the rafters, at the extreme corner of the gable end of the building, and which cuts off all the light from the window. The court of Colmar ordered the suppression of the dummy chimney. It acknowledges that the owner can, in strictness, abuse of his property, but on one condition, that he does not do it for the purpose of injury. Rights are serious things and must be used seriously. Beyond that serious use there is no right but only wickedness, and justice cannot sanction an act prompted by malevolence.

"An owner constructing works on his land diminishes the volume of a spring the benefit of which his neighbor has been having. He is within his right. If he thereby causes an injury to his neighbor, the latter cannot complain; for he has not the absolute ownership of the waters. But, if it has been by malice that the works have been undertaken, for the sole purpose of injuring the neighbor, we have no longer the exercise of a right, but spitefulness, and he who abuses malignantly of his right ought to repair the damage he causes. This was the decision of the court of Lyons in the following case: A mineral spring spreads over several tracts. One of the owners sets up a pump for getting a larger quantity of the water, not for using it, but for pouring it, in pure waste, and we will add, through spite, into a dyer. The court condemned him in damages, but without ordering the suppression of the pump. We think that in the latter connection the court was too conservative. From the moment that an act can be characterized as illicit the owner can no longer invoke any right of ownership; now an unlawful act should disappear."

On the point of an owner not being allowed through pure spite or wantonness to do something on his property injurious to his neighbor, we find but one dissenting voice among the French law-writers and decisions. It is Demolombe, who, in his work on Servitudes (volume 12 of the Paris ed. of 1859, at pages 139 and 140), says:

"No. 647.*** Digging a well on one's own property, although it may cause the neighbor's well to go dry, is none the less a permitted act; this result is a purely fortuitous event; strictly speaking, it is less an actual damage the neighbor suffers as that he ceases to enjoy an accidental, casual, provisional profit, on which he had no right to depend.

"And this principle is now generally recognized.

"No. 648. We must add, however, that generally a very important qualification is applied to that principle, which it is contended would be no longer applicable if the owner, in constructing on his land some work the effect of which is to deprive the neighbor of an advantage he has been enjoying, did so for no other purpose than to injure this neighbor with no benefit to himself.

"This modification, indeed, appears to be as ancient as the principle itself, and we invariably find it coupled with the principle in the works of the Roman jurisconsults (L. 1, paragraph 12, f.f de aqua), and of our ancient authors (citing long list), and in the decisions of the courts (citing decisions).

"This modification, despite its traditional ancientness, appears to us to be inadmissible.

"The text of Article 644 is formal; it is in the most absolute manner that an owner may use or enjoy his property.

"Legally no account can be required of him of his motives; there is here a bar which precludes the making of any allegation that he has acted from malice."

From Carpentier and Du Saint:

"If it is found that an owner who has dug his soil has been prompted in doing so simply by the desire to injure his neighbor, the court can abate what has been done." Carpentier and Du Saint, Rep. du Droit Francais, vo. Eaux, p. 435, No. 145, citing numerous authorities.

From these excerpts it is clear that cases like the present are not to be decided by the application of any broad or inflexible rule, but by a careful weighing of all the circumstances attending them, by diagnosing them, to use the expression of Baudry-Lacantinerie and Chauveau, with the aid and guidance of the two principles, that the owner must not injure seriously any right of his neighbor, and, even in the absence of any right on the part of the neighbor, must not in an unneighborly spirit do that which while of no benefit to himself causes damage to the neighbor.

Defendant does not contest the right of plaintiff to get out of its land all the oil it possibly can, and by means of a well, but contests plaintiffs right to do this by means of a pump, because a pump sucks the oil from under defendant's land. The argument is that plaintiff may appropriate the oil passing from defendant's land to plaintiffs provided the oil passes, or flows, from the one tract to the other "naturally," that is, by gravity, and not as the effect of the use of artificial means.

So far as artificiality is concerned, we do not see the difference between a well and a pump; both are artificial; both cause the oil to flow from the neighbor's land; and both produce that effect by creating a vacuum which the oil from the neighbor's land comes in to fill. In both cases the oil flows from the neighbor's land by gravity. The fact that some of the oil which plaintiffs pump is producing may come from defendant's land can make no difference; for in the case of a flowing well so close to the boundary line that one-half of its product would to a reasonable certainty be known to be coming from the adjoining tract the owner of this tract would hardly, we imagine, claim either the ownership of one-half of the oil or the right to close the well; and the reason would be that an owner of land does not own the fugitive oil beneath it so as to have the right to follow it after it has left his land.

Plaintiffs right to operate this pump would appear, therefore, to be clear, and that defendant's well, or air pipe is seriously interfering with the operation of the pump is one of the facts alleged in the petition which for present purposes must be taken for true.

Were defendant leaving this well open for some purpose of utility other than the supposed utility of preventing the drainage of the oil from under defendant's land, a different case might perhaps be presented; but the allegation, which must be taken for true, is that leaving this well open is of no benefit to defendant. It will be noted that this action of defendant in leaving this well open has the effect not merely of preventing plaintiff from drawing the oil under defendant's land, but also from under plaintiffs own land; so that an unquestioned right of plaintiff is being interfered with.

Were this result brought about by the mere inaction of defendant, plaintiff could not complain. An owner is not bound to do anything to save his neighbor from loss. The only restriction upon him is that he abstain from doing anything that may cause a loss. In the present case defendant is not charged with mere inaction, but with the action of having bored this well and thereby opened a vent for the air to penetrate where it causes injury.

In last analysis the case must turn upon whether plaintiff has the right to operate the pump in question, and whether, if plaintiff has that right, defendant may interfere with it with no benefit to itself, but simply to hinder plaintiff.

In the case supposed above of a well so near the boundary line as to be deriving one-half of its product from the adjoining land, we do not suppose there would be any dispute as to the right of the adjoining owner to interpose a partition between the two tracts of land so as to prevent the escape of oil from his land. Unquestionably he could build a wall for preventing the wild animals on his land from escaping; and oil comes much nearer forming part of the realty than the wild animals do. And if an owner may thus protect himself by means of a partition or wall, why not by any other kind of work on his land. So that, if land, we should be clear that plaintiff would have no good ground for complaining. But for all that is known, no oil is being drawn out of defendant's land, while to a certainty defendant is directly and seriously interfering with plaintiffs right to operate for oil and is doing so with no benefit to itself. The judgment appealed from is therefore set aside, the exception of no cause of action is overruled, and the case is remanded for trial.

NOTE
Abuse of Right

In the preceding case, the court recognizes two principles: "the owner must not injure seriously any right of his neighbor, and, even in the absence of any right on the part of the neighbor, must not in an unneighborly spirit do that which, while of no benefit to himself causes damage to the neighbor." These principles underlie the abuse of right doctrine. The following excerpt from Professor Yiannopoulos' article explains the role that the *Higgins* decision played in the development of Louisiana's abuse of rights doctrine.

Yiannopoulos, "Civil Liability for Abuse of Right: Something Old, Something New" 54 La. L. Rev. 1173, 1176-1180 (1994)

The abuse of right doctrine made its debut in Louisiana jurisprudence in 1919. In *[Higgins]*, a landmark opinion, Justice Provosty, one of Louisiana's great jurists, formulated the tenets of liability for abuse of the right of ownership on the basis of civil code provisions and French authorities....

Justice Provosty's opinion was largely ignored by courts and writers for almost half a century. By the beginning of the third quarter of the twentieth century, however, a virulent renaissance of the civilian tradition was sweeping juridical thinking in the state and the abuse of right doctrine was rediscovered by the Louisiana Supreme Court in *Hero Lands Co. v. Texaco, Inc.* An oil company had constructed on its right of way servitude a high pressure pipeline for the transmission of natural gas. The pipeline was located along the boundary of adjoining property at a distance of fifteen feet. The owner of the adjoining property filed suit against the oil company seeking damages for the diminution of the value of his property, caused by the location of the pipeline in close proximity to the boundary. Since plaintiff had not accused defendant of negligence, intentional misconduct, or operation of the pipeline in violation of Article 669 of the Louisiana Civil Code, the trial court sustained defendant's exception of no cause of action, and the court of appeal affirmed. The Louisiana Supreme Court, however, reversed. In a per curiam opinion, the court explained its judgment overruling defendant's exception of no cause of action: "[W]e have remanded for trial on the merits to determine if the proof in support of these allegations entitles plaintiff to recovery of damages for the fault of defendant under the theory of abuse of right as expressed by Louisiana Civil Code articles 667 and 668." In a concurring opinion, Justice Barham declared:

> [T]he majority here recognizes that Louisiana adopts as a general theory or principle of law that in all areas of legal relationships a legal right can be exercised in such a manner as to constitute a legal abuse. An abusive use of a legal right may be enjoined or may give rise to damages.

Justice Barham also suggested that the abuse of ownership theory found in Article 667 of the Louisiana Civil Code "by analogy and extension . . . can be applied to contractual, delictual, and legal relations other than ownership of property." This suggestion was followed by the court in *Morse v. J. Ray McDermott & Co.* Plaintiff, a former employee who had been laid off by the defendant during an economic downturn, had participated in certain deferred compensation plans. These plans provided for forfeiture of a worker's interest upon termination of the employment unless the employer, at its discretion, waived the forfeiture. McDermott opted not to waive and caused Morse to forfeit the deferred compensation. In a suit by Morse for the recovery of benefits under the plans, the court held for the plaintiff. In the reasons for judgment, the court declared:

> [T]he exercise of a right (here, to discharge an employee while opting not to waive the nontermination requirement) without legitimate and serious interest, even where there is neither alleged nor proved an intent to harm, constitutes an abuse of right which courts should not countenance ....

> Thus, the otherwise permissible exercise of a legal right to discharge, in the situation where the employer has the discretion to obviate the harsh forfeiture consequence and chooses not to do so, is transformed from a legal right to an abuse of that right.

Two years later, the Louisiana Supreme Court engaged in a scholarly discussion of the abuse of right doctrine and established certain criteria for its application. Plaintiff, a lessor, sought to evict a lessee on the ground that the lessee had sublet the property without the lessor's consent. The defendant answered that this was no ground for eviction because the plaintiff had abused his right to withhold consent to the sublease. The court found for the plaintiff:

> The withholding of consent to a sublease was for a relatively brief period of time, not done for the sheer sake of exercising the right, but done for the purpose of attempting to carry on actual good faith negotiations for cancellation of the lease, in which the lessor had a serious and legitimate interest under the circumstances....

Subsequently, in another case in which the lessor had allegedly abused his right to consent to a sublease, the court held for the defendant and articulated four criteria, at least one of which must be met for liability under the Louisiana doctrine of abuse of right. These criteria have been constantly and ceremoniously repeated in Louisiana decisions that may have achieved the status of a *jurisprudence constante*:

> To justify the application of the doctrine of "abuse of rights," one of the following must exist:
>
> (1)   the exercise of rights exclusively for the purpose of harming another or with the predominant motive to cause harm;
>
> (2)   the non-existence of a serious and legitimate interest that is worthy of judicial protection;
>
> (3)   the use of the right in violation of moral rules, good faith or elementary fairness; or
>
> (4)   the exercise of the right for a purpose other than that for which it was granted.

YOKUM v. 615 BOURBON STREET, L.L.C.
977 So. 2d 859 (La. 2008)

KIMBALL, J. We granted certiorari in this matter to review the Court of Appeal's ruling that Defendant in this matter, 615 Bourbon Street, L.L.C., as owner and lessor of the premises upon which its lessee operates the bar "The Rock," is not liable to the plaintiffs for the alleged excessive noise associated with the loud music played by the bar, and is therefore entitled to summary judgment. For the reasons that follow, we find that the Court of Appeal erroneously concluded under the facts of this case that the defendant/owner and lessor of this property cannot be held responsible for the actions of its lessee under Article 667 of the Louisiana Civil Code. Accordingly, the Court of Appeal's decision affirming summary judgment is reversed, and the case is remanded for further proceedings.

FACTS AND PROCEDURAL HISTORY

Peterson M. Yokum is the owner of and resides at the premises located at 723 Toulouse Street in the French Quarter in New Orleans, Louisiana, with his wife, Polly Elizabeth Anderson. The property located at 723 Toulouse Street is zoned "Vieux Carre Commercial District-2 Mixed Residential" ("VCC-2"). The entity 615 Bourbon Street, L.L.C. is the owner and lessor of the premises located at 615-617 Bourbon Street. On October 15, 2003, 615 Bourbon Street, L.L.C. executed a commercial lease of property with O'Reilly Properties, L.L.C. ("O'Reilly"), leasing the premises located at 615-617 Bourbon Street in New Orleans, Louisiana, to O'Reilly to be "used exclusively for legitimate, commercial, purposes ...".*** O'Reilly thereafter began operating the bar The Rock on the premises owned by 615 Bourbon Street, L.L.C.

Plaintiffs, Mr. Yokum and Ms. Anderson, allege that they have been subjected to loud and ongoing live entertainment conducted at the bar known as The Rock, located at 615-617 Bourbon Street, beginning as early as 2003, which has prevented the proper quiet enjoyment of their home.***In their [Petition for Damages and Declaratory and Injunctive Relief], plaintiffs allege that defendant 615 Bourbon Street, L.L.C. d/b/a The Rock, located within the "Vieux Carre Entertainment District" ("VCE") "owns and operates a bar between the hours of 3:00 p.m. and 3:00 a.m. with live amplified music and entertainment at 615/617 Bourbon Street, New Orleans, Louisiana" with noises that "are sufficient to cause physical discomfort and annoyance to Peter Yokum and Polly Anderson, and any person of ordinary sensibilities, and constitute a nuisance."*** [P]laintiffs assert in their Petition that defendants in this instance are in violation of Louisiana Civil Code articles 667 and 669, relating to nuisance.***

[Defendant asserted in the memorandum in support of its Motion for Summary Judgment that plaintiffs' allegations of noise ordinance violations and the creation of a nuisance arise out of the operation of the business known as The Rock. Defendant further argued in its motion that "[t]he petition contains no allegations whatsoever which would impose liability upon 615 BOURBON STREET, L.L.C., in its capacity as lessor of the premises, and it is further submitted that liability, if any, would arise only out of the operation of La. Civil Code Articles 667 and 668." Defendant therefore asserted that "the issue is thus raised whether or not 615 BOURBON STREET, L.L.C., as lessor, has any liability whatsoever to its neighbors for the use of its premises by a lessee....

Plaintiffs opposed defendant's Motion for Summary Judgment on April 13, 2006, asserting that...articles 667, 668, and 669 of the Louisiana Civil Code dictate that 615 Bourbon Street, L.L.C., as owner of the leased premises, cannot escape liability as a lessor based upon its lease of the property to O'Reilly Properties, L.L.C. Moreover, plaintiffs stated that through the certified letters sent to 615 Bourbon Street, L.L.C. and The Rock individually, 615 Bourbon Street, L.L.C. had knowledge of the noise nuisance emanating from its premises and took no action to cease and desist or to reduce the noise....

Following a hearing on April 21, 2006, the trial court granted defendant 615 Bourbon Street, LL.C.'s Motion for Summary Judgment, dismissing the plaintiffs' claims against 615 Bourbon Street, L.L.C, with prejudice, and denied the defendant's Motion for Sanctions, in a written judgment signed April 28, 2006. The record does not reflect any written reasons for judgment from the trial court, nor does the record contain a transcript of the hearing.

Plaintiffs appealed to the Court of Appeal, Fourth Circuit, on September 26, 2006....Plaintiffs...argued at the Court of Appeal that under articles 667, 668, and 669 of the Louisiana Civil Code, 615 Bourbon Street, L.L.C. is, as owner of the subject property, a "proprietor" and is therefore burdened with a legal servitude in favor of its neighbors, plaintiffs Mr. Yokum and Ms. Anderson. Plaintiffs therefore asserted that the existence of a lease does not extinguish the legal servitude or the duties defendant in this matter owes to them as neighbors.***

In an opinion issued on June 20, 2007, the Court of Appeal, Fourth Circuit, affirmed the trial court's grant of summary judgment and dismissal of plaintiffs' claims against 615 Bourbon Street, L.L.C, with Judge Cannizzaro dissenting. In its decision, the Court of Appeal reasoned that although the plaintiffs' appeal is based on the obligations of vicinage arising out of articles 667, 668, and 669 of the Louisiana Civil Code, because the Court of Appeal could find no cases imposing liability upon the owner lessor of property under Louisiana Civil Code article 667 for the acts of its lessee, it declined to do so in this matter. Specifically, the court stated that "[i]n view of the numberless owner-lessor-lessee relationships known to exist in this State, it would be most extraordinary for owner-lessor liability for acts of the lessee under La. C.C. art. 667 to be *res nova* if it were the purpose of that Code article to impose such liability." Yokum v. 615 Bourbon Street, L.L.C., 06-1057, p. 2 (La. App. 4th Cir. 6/20/07); 960 So. 2d 1283,128.***

We granted certiorari in this matter to review the Court of Appeal's ruling that summary judgment in favor of defendant was appropriate because defendant 615 Bourbon Street, L.L.C., as lessor owner in this matter. is not the person actually responsible for the existence of the noise complained of, and therefore, there is no basis in law for holding the lessor/owner liable under Louisiana Civil Code article 667. We disagree with the Court of Appeal's reasoning, as our review of Louisiana law and its long-standing jurisprudence regarding this matter dictates a different conclusion. For the reasons set forth below, we find that the Court of Appeal's decision below was in error, and therefore reverse its ruling affirming summary judgment in favor of defendant, and remand the case to the trial court for further proceedings.

DISCUSSION

Because the Court of Appeal affirmed summary judgment based upon its conclusion that defendant/lessor 615 Bourbon Street, L.L.C. is not responsible for the actions of its lessee under Louisiana Civil Code article 667, we must first examine article 667 and its application to owner lessors. From that determination, we must then decide whether summary judgment in favor of defendant 615 Bourbon Street, L.L.C. in this instance is appropriate.

Louisiana Civil Code Article 667

It is a "general principle of law, that owners may use their property as they please, with the exception that they do no injury to others," under the theory of "sic tuum utere ut alium non laedas." Boatner v. Henderson & Al., 5 Mart, (n.s.) 186 (La. 1826); see also Borgnemouth Realty Co. v. Gulf Soap Corp., 212 La. 57, 31 So. 2d 488, 490 (1947). As courts have recognized, Louisiana law does impose certain limitations on ownership, with one instance being through predial servitudes. A predial servitude, provided for in Article 646 of the Louisiana Civil Code, is a "charge on a servient estate for the benefit of a dominant estate."***

[A]rticles 667, 668, and 669, found in the same Title of the Louisiana Civil Code governing "Predial Servitudes," establish certain limitations on the scope and extent of the right of ownership in immovable property. Inabnet v. Exxon Corp., 93-0681, p. 9 (La. 9/6/94); 642 So. 2d 1243, 1250-1 ("Articles 667-669 place limitations on the rights of owners by setting out principles of responsibility applying the doctrine of *sic utere tuum ut alienum non laedas*, which requires an owner to use his property in such a manner as not to injure another.") Thus, the referenced limitations set forth in articles 667, 668, and 669 of the Louisiana Civil Code are limitations on ownership imposed by law. Predial Servitudes, Yiannopoulos, 4 Louisiana Civil Law Treatise, §§ 33, 34 (West 2004). Further, this Court has previously found that the corresponding rights and obligations of neighboring proprietors, arising from that relationship between proprietors, are principally governed by Louisiana Civil Code articles 667, 668, and 669. Inabnet v. Exxon Corp., 93- 0681, p. 8 (La. 9/6/94); 642 So. 2d 1243,125.***

[O]ur discussion focuses primarily on Louisiana Civil Code article 667, as we are faced with the issue of whether or not a "proprietor" owner and lessor can be responsible for the actions of its tenant/lessee. Article 667, originally enacted in 1808, was subject to the significant tort reform undertaken by the Louisiana Legislature in 1996. *See* Acts 1996, 1st Ex.Sess., No. 1, § 1. The language contained in Article 667 regarding strict or absolute liability for ultrahazardous activity was most heavily affected by the amendments, as this Court has so recognized:

> Article 667 now clearly articulates that the only cognizable ultrahazardous activities are "pile driving" and "blasting with explosives." Any other activities besides the two the article specifically lists are not ultrahazardous for purposes of article 667. Thus, to qualify for the absolute liability standard, the plaintiff must show that the activity complained of is either "pile driving" or "blasting with explosives."

Suire v. Lafayette City-Parish Consolidated Government, et al., 04-1459, p. 13 (La. 4/12/05); 907 So. 2d 37,49.

Notably, the 1996 amendments to article 667 also incorporated the requirement that a proprietor or landowner be responsible for damages to an aggrieved neighbor "only upon a showing that he knew or, in the exercise of reasonable care, should have known that his works would cause damage, that the damage could have been prevented by the exercise of reasonable care, and that he failed to exercise such reasonable care," thus shifting the absolute liability standard to a negligence standard similar to that set forth in La. C.C. art. 2317.1 and the 1996 amendments to Articles 2321 and 2322. The 1996 amendments to article 667 did not change *who* could be held liable under the article, namely, the "proprietor"; rather, it changed the theory of liability under which the proprietor could be held responsible. As a result, in order for a proprietor/landowner to be held responsible for damages allegedly caused by works or actions on his property, it must be shown that the proprietor/landowner knew or should have known that the "works" on his property would cause damage, and that the damage could have been prevented by the exercise of reasonable care.

The term "proprietor" as used in Article 667, while commonly interpreted to refer to landowners, "has been expansively interpreted by the courts to apply not only to a landowner, but also to a person whose rights derive from the owner." Inabnet v. Exxon Corp., 93-0681, p. 12 (La. 9/6/94); 642 So. 2d 1243, 1251 (citing Lombard v. Sewerage and Water Bd. Of New Orleans, 284 So. 2d 905 (La. 1973) and Ferdinand F. Stone, *Tort Doctrine in Louisiana: The Obligations of Neighborhood,* 40 Tul.L.Rev. 701, 711 (1966)). As mentioned previously, certain limitations are imposed upon proprietors through Article 667: "although a landowner may use and enjoy his property as he sees fit, Article 667 provides that he may not exercise his right in such a way as to cause damage to his neighbors." State Through Dep't. of Transp. & Dev. v. Chambers Inv. Co., 595 So. 2d 598, 604 (La. 1992). Furthermore, this Court has also stated that "the proprietor is likewise responsible not only for his own activity, but also for that carried on by his agents, contractors and representatives with his consent and permission."

Not only has the term "proprietor" been expanded from its traditional meaning of simply "landowner," the "work" to which Article 667 refers includes not only constructions but also activities that may cause damage. This Court stated in Chaney v. Travelers Ins. Co., that "our view will not accept the proposition that a proprietor is responsible for damage to a neighbor for a 'work,' that is, a structure on his premises which harms his neighbor *without imposing a like responsibility for harmful activity"* 259 La. 1, 249 So. 2d 181, 186 (1971) (emphasis added). We further stated that "[i]t is not the manner in which the activity is carried on which is significant; it is the fact that the activity causes damage to a neighbor which is relevant." *Id.* Thus, we find that the alleged excessive noise emanating from the defendant's leased premises in this instance falls within the concept of "work" as contemplated by Louisiana Civil Code article 667, in that it is an activity that could be harmful to neighboring proprietors.

Article 667, setting forth limitations imposed upon the *ownership* of land, is directly applicable to a proprietor landowner who may also be a lessor of its property, as the act of lease by the landowner is a right which is derived from ownership of the property. La. C.C. art. 2673 ("All things, corporeal or incorporeal, that are susceptible of *ownership* may be the object of a lease, except those that cannot be used without being destroyed by that very use, or those the lease of which is prohibited by law." (emphasis added)). Thus, because article 667 dictates, and this Court has previously established, that a proprietor/landowner can be responsible for the works or actions on its property that may cause damage to neighboring proprietors, we find the Court of Appeal's reasoning in this matter erroneous. Merely because a proprietor/landowner utilizes his right as a property owner to lease his property to another does not eradicate his or her responsibilities and obligations, set forth above, as a landowner. Moreover, under the Court of Appeal's rationale, even an owner/lessor with full knowledge of the potentially harmful effects of the lessee tenant's activities on its property would have little or no responsibility to protect the public and his neighbors from his lessee tenant's harmful activities. As a result, the Court of Appeal's interpretation creates a virtual immunity for landowners, allowing them to remove themselves from potential liability for damages that arise out of the ownership of their property by simply establishing a lease on their property.

We therefore find the Court of Appeal was incorrect in its assertion that a mere lack of jurisprudence imposing liability upon an owner or proprietor for the actions of its lessee which cause damage out of a lessee's use of the premises equates to a finding that an owner is not responsible for the actions of its lessee. More specifically, as shown above, it is well-settled that a "proprietor," which at its very basic meaning is a landowner, can be responsible for damages for any "work" under Article 667 of the Louisiana Civil Code, which this Court has clearly stated includes not only constructions but also activities, performed on its land that may cause damage to neighboring proprietors.

We do not venture to specifically find that 615 Bourbon Street, L.L.C., as owner and lessor of the subject premises, is responsible for the alleged damages caused in this particular instance, as that issue is not specifically before the Court. As discussed above, we decide today only that the Court of Appeal was erroneous in its conclusion that a proprietor/landowner/lessor may not be responsible for the actions of its lessee under article 667 of the Louisiana Civil Code. Because we find that an owner lessor can be responsible for damages caused by its lessee tenant under article 667 of the Louisiana Civil Code, we therefore conclude the Court of Appeal was in error in affirming summary judgment in favor of defendant 615 Bourbon Street, L.L.C.***

NOTE
Yokum Casenote

For an in-depth examination of *Yokum*, see Gina Palermo, Comment, "Waking the Neighbors: Determining a Landowner's Liability for Rowdy Tenants Under Louisiana Law," 70 La. L. Rev. 1339 (2010).

a. Injunctive Relief

FUSELIER v. SPALDING
2 La. Ann. 773 (1847)

KING, J. The plaintiff obtained an injunction prohibiting the defendant from burning a brick kiln, which the latter had erected near her dwelling house in the town of St. Martinville, alleging that the security of her premises, and the health of herself and family, would be endangered, if the defendant were permitted to execute his purpose. The injunction was perpetuated in the court below, and the defendant has appealed. We think that the judge did not err. The plaintiff had a clear right to invoke the aid of a court in this form, to protect from an impending danger, and the health of herself and family from being impaired. The evidence, in our opinion, shows that the kiln could not have been burnt in the position where it stood without exposing the premises of the plaintiff, which were all of wood, to danger from fire, besides seriously incommoding, if not injuring the health, of the occupants. Judgment affirmed.

FREDERICK v. BROWN FUNERAL HOMES, INC.
222 La. 57, 62 So. 2d 100 (1952)

ON APPLICATION FOR REHEARING

PONDER, J. In this suit the plaintiffs sought to enjoin the establishment or operation of a funeral home in a purported residential section of the Town of Covington. The trial court granted a preliminary injunction. The defendant was granted a devolutive appeal and applied to this court for writs which were granted. This court issued a writ of certiorari with a stay order and ordered the plaintiffs to show cause why the relief sought in the defendant's application for writs should not be granted. Upon hearing of the rule, this court recalled the writs and remanded the cause for trial on the merits. A rehearing is now submitted for our consideration.***

Our main concern in granting the rehearing was whether or not the provisions of Articles 667, 668 and 669 of the Civil Code were properly interpreted in the majority opinion in arriving at the conclusion that the operation of the funeral home was a nuisance in fact or per accidens. As we take it the majority opinion is to the effect that the funeral home became a nuisance because of its location and enjoined its operation before it was established. According to the record the funeral home was not in operation at the time the suit was filed and tried.

On reconsideration we have arrived at the conclusion that the injunction should be set aside. Articles 667, 668 and 669 of the Civil Code, governs us in this controversy.***

In the case of Borgnemouth Realty Company, Limited v. Gulf Soap Corporation, 212 La. 57, 65, 31 So. 2d 488,490, this court stated:

> "From the point of view of their nature, nuisances are sometimes classified as nuisances per se or at law, and nuisances per accidens or in fact. A nuisance at law or a nuisance per se is an act, occupation, or structure which is a nuisance at all times and under any circumstances, regardless of location or surroundings. Nuisances in fact or per accidens are those which become nuisances by reason of circumstances and surroundings." 46 C.J. 648, Section 5. See, also, 39 Am.Jur. 289, Section 11. As pointed out in the latter authority, "The difference between a nuisance per se and a nuisance in fact lies in the proof, not in the remedy. In the case of a nuisance per se, the thing becomes a nuisance as a matter of law. Its existence need only be proved in any locality, and the right to relief is established by averment and proof of the mere act. But whether a thing not a nuisance per se is a nuisance per accidens or in fact depends upon its location and surroundings, the manner of its conduct, or other circumstances. In such cases, proof of the act and its consequences is necessary. The act or thing complained of must be shown by evidence to be a nuisance under the law, and whether it is or is not a nuisance is generally a question of fact."

We have carefully considered the opinion handed down in the case of Moss v. Burke &

Trotti, Inc., 198 La. 76, 87, 3 So. 2d 281, 285, and have reached the conclusion that the pronouncement made therein is a proper interpretation of our code articles, viz.: "In the absence of legal zoning prohibition any business establishment may be established or located in a residential district, however it may affect the property values, unless by its very nature, its operation shall physically annoy the inhabitants."

The operation of a funeral home is a lawful enterprise, Moss v. Burke & Trotti, Inc., *supra*, and under the provisions of Article 667 of the Civil Code the defendant has a right to do with his estate as he pleases provided he does not cause damage to his neighbor. As pointed out in the majority opinion the operation of a funeral home is not a nuisance per se and it is impossible for us to state at this time whether it would be operated in such a manner as to result in a nuisance. Mere inconvenience to an adjoining property owner would not necessarily constitute a nuisance. Article 668 of the Civil Code. There is no zoning ordinance or police regulation prohibiting the establishment of such an enterprise in any portion of the town and the evidence fails to show that the custom of the place would prohibit same. From a careful reading of the aforementioned Articles of the Civil Code, it is apparent that, unless the establishment and operation of the funeral home is prohibited by rules of police or custom of the place, it cannot be enjoined prior to its operation and then only if it is operated in such a manner as to cause damage to those living in neighboring houses.

The case of Osborn v. City of Shreveport, 143 La. 932, 79 So. 542, 3 A.L.R. 955, is only authority for what it held, that an ordinance prohibiting undertaking shops except on the business streets of the city is valid, and whatever else was said is purely obiter dicta and of no controlling effect in the case at bar.

This court has on numerous occasions refused to enjoin the establishment or erection of a lawful business simply on the ground that it might be conducted so as to become a nuisance. Bell v. Riggs & Bros., 38 La.Ann. 555; Lewis v. Sandell, 118 La. 852, 43 So. 526; Canone v. Pallet, 160 La. 159, 106 So. 730; Graver v. Lepine, 161 La. 97, 108 So. 138.

In Bell v. Riggs & Bros., cited *supra*, 38 La.Ann. 555, 556, this court said:

> "The rule is founded in reason and firmly established by authority that injunction will not lie against a prospective nuisance except in cases where its establishment will occasion imminent danger or irreparable injury, or at least where there is no question that the proposed erection will be a nuisance violative of legal right. Wood, Law of Nuisances, para. 103,104."

Likewise in Lewis v. Sandell, cited *supra*, 118 La. 852, 859, 43 So. 526, 529, the court held "that a lawful business not yet in existence and not a nuisance per se could not be enjoined on the face of the papers until evidence had been adduced to establish same."

Again in Canone v. Pallet, cited *supra*, 160 La. 159, 162, 106 So. 730, and Graver v. Lepine, cited *supra*, 161 La. 97, 100, 108 So. 138, 139, this court held: "A lawful business is never a nuisance per se, and no one has the right to prevent the establishment of such business for fear that it might be conducted so as to become a nuisance." Citing ample authority to support the statement.

While the common-law authorities relied upon and cited by the plaintiffs may be persuasive, they are not decisive of the issue in view of our code articles and jurisprudence.

For the reasons assigned, it is now ordered that the rule be discharged, and the preliminary writ of injunction dissolved. The case is remanded to be tried on the merits consistent with the view herein expressed. Plaintiffs-respondents to pay all costs incurred in this court; all other costs are to await the final disposition of the case.

ON REHEARING

HAWTHORNE, J. (dissenting). There was presented for our consideration originally and on rehearing only one question: Is a funeral home by its very nature such a business that when located in a strictly residential area its operation will so annoy and inconvenience the residents that they will be deprived of the enjoyment of their homes? There was then and there is now no disagreement on the general law relative to nuisances, which, as far as I can see, is all that is discussed in the opinion on rehearing. In that opinion there is no discussion at all of the extent of annoyance and inconvenience that a funeral home in a residential area will cause the adjoining residents or landowners.

If the answer to the question presented by this case is in the affirmative, the establishment of the business would be prohibited under Civil Code Articles 667, 668, and 669 upon proof that the district is strictly residential, and under the courts' authority to issue injunctions the respondents would be entitled to injunctive relief. If the answer to this question is in the negative, they have no right to interfere with the use that relator proposes to make of its property. I can only conclude from the lack of discussion of the real question in the opinion on rehearing that the reasons given for answering it in the affirmative on original hearing are unanswerable. I cannot believe that the average person in this jurisdiction is any less sensitive to the depressing effects of a funeral home than is the average person in the common-law jurisdictions where it has been concluded that as a matter of fact funeral homes are by their very nature so depressing that their close proximity deprives one of the enjoyment of his home and that they can be enjoined when they seek to intrude themselves into an exclusively residential district.

The Code provisions in my opinion do not make the relator's privilege of using its property as it pleases any more important than the respondents' right to use and enjoy their premises. A comparative evaluation of the conflicting interests in this case has convinced me that the gravity of the annoyance and inconvenience that will be caused to the respondents by the business that the relator proposes to establish is such that the relator ought to be enjoined if the respondents can show that the district is exclusively residential. I respectfully dissent.

ROBICHAUX v. HUPPENBAUER
258 La. 139, 245 So. 2d 385 (1971)

SUMMERS, J. Plaintiffs are two neighboring property owners and two tenants all occupying dwellings near defendant Huppenbauer's horse stable located at 1618 Annette Street in the city of New Orleans. This suit was brought to permanently enjoin defendant from operating the stable or keeping horses on the premises. After trial, judgment was rendered enjoining defendant as prayed for. On appeal to the Fourth Circuit the judgment was affirmed. 231 So. 2d 626. On defendant's application we granted certiorari limited to the contention that the Court of Appeal erred "in applying a positive injunction totally prohibiting defendant's operations, instead of limiting them in scope or manner." 256 La. 64, 235 So. 2d 94.

Defendant uses the stable in connection with his business of providing horse drawn carriages for hire by tourists in the historic French Quarter or Vieux Carre Section of the city. The stables are about one mile from the French Quarter. These carriages are vestiges of a bygone era adding color and character to a section which is one of the city's outstanding attractions to visitors and tourists. Fifteen men are employed in the business of maintaining the horses at the stables and driving the carriages. The stable has been in operation for many years, even beyond the memory of the participants at the trial.

The lot, where the stable is located and where the horses are kept, has a frontage of 32 feet on Annette Street and runs 90 feet back into the block. All but 15 feet of this front portion is occupied by a dwelling house in which one of defendant's employees resides, the fifteen-foot strip being used as a driveway. Behind this front portion the lot widens to 64 feet and extends back an additional 100 feet into the block. The horses are principally stabled, fed, washed and exercised on this 64 by 100 foot section.

For a short time prior to acquiring the stables in July 1968, defendant kept horses there under arrangement with the owner. When he acquired the property in August 1968, however, the Director of the Bureau of Public Health Sanitation, Charles J. Miramon, filed an affidavit charging violations of city ordinances regulating the harboring of rats and the removal of manure. At that time, according to Miramon, the stable did not comply with the standards prescribed by the Bureau, and it was a health menace.

Later, in September and October 1968, while these charges were pending in the Municipal Court, defendant's stable was inspected by James Bryant and Harold Clark, Sanitarians in the Bureau of Public Health, who found the stable free of any condition violative of the city's ordinances or their regulations. On the basis of these inspections, the charges were dismissed.

This suit for injunction was then filed and the case was tried on February 27, 1969, resulting in the injunction. Plaintiffs' petition charges that the use of the premises at 1618 Annette Street as a stable results in the deposit of manure on the lot which is responsible for nauseous odors, flies and insects and creates a stench, all of which infest the neighborhood and permeate the houses nearby.

At the trial, plaintiffs' witnesses, who lived very near the stable, some as close as four feet, testified that from eight to eighteen horses are kept there. Rats and flies, particularly horseflies, breed in the manure and urine deposited by the animals. These pests are prevalent on the lot and swarm onto the adjoining property endangering the health and destroying the peace and tranquility of plaintiffs' homes. Noxious odors remain in the neighborhood. At times the horses drop manure on the street and sidewalk as they move to and from the stable. And when it rains the manure runs from beneath the gate of the horse lot onto the sidewalk and into the gutters in front of the nearby houses. The departure and arrival of the carriages, waste disposal vehicles and the animals cause noises and disturb the plaintiffs' sleep and repose.

Plaintiffs rely upon Article 669 of the Civil Code to support their claim that the nuisance resulting from the stable should be abated.*** [After determining that Article 669 was only partially applicable—to nauseous smells only—the court resorted to common law notions of nuisance.]

Nuisances by their nature are nuisances per se or at law, and nuisances per accidens or in fact. A nuisance at law or a nuisance per se is an act, occupation, or structure which is a nuisance at all times and under any circumstances, regardless of location or surroundings. Nuisances in fact or per accidens are those which become nuisances by reason of circumstances or surroundings.***

[The court then concluded that a stable is not a nuisance per se; thus, whether it is a nuisance is a question of fact determined by its location, construction, and the manner in which it is conducted.] [A] stable in close proximity to a residence, in a residential section of the city, and kept in such a condition that it is unsanitary, and from which noxious and offensive vapors, fumes, smells, odors, and stenches arise during a period of twelve months, and enter into and spread and diffuse themselves over the adjoining residential property, is such a nuisance as will sustain an action.***[The court concluded that the stable was a nuisance because of the manner in which it had been operated, but that the defendant could continue his operations so long as he complied with certain mandates and restrictions. The court then ordered the defendant to spray the ground with disinfectants and deodorizers, to cover feed bins, to remove wastes daily, to limit the number of horses to ten, and to keep the premises drained.]

BARHAM, J. (concurring). I concur in the result which affords the defendant an opportunity to take corrective measures to abate the severe inconveniences caused the plaintiffs, his neighbors, because of his operation of a stable. However, I am of the opinion that the result should have been reached solely by the application of the civil law, more particularly Civil Code Article 669, without resort to common law authority or terminology.

I reiterate that Article 669 does not establish a servitude, for it does not provide for a dominant and a servient estate, and in fact, contrary to the servitude law, even provides redress for those in the same house and upon the same estate against their neighbors. 1 Pt. 2 Planiol, Treatise on the Civil Law (La. State Law Institute tr. 1959) No. 2906. However, I find the article vital and most functional in expressing the activities of men upon property they own, hold, occupy, or use which become impermissible by causing insupportable inconvenience to neighbors.

The majority's error in holding Article 669 of the Code of 1870 not to be illustrative because of the omission of the pertinent phrase from it and from corresponding Article 665 of the Code of 1825 results from failure to examine the *French* text of Article 665 of the 1825 Code. While the "other different inconveniences" is omitted from the English text of that article, the French text is the same as that of our 1808 Code, and contains the words: "*** *et les autre differentes incommodites qu'un voisinpeut causer a Vautre***"* See 3 Pt. 1 Louisiana Legal Archives: Compiled Edition of the Civil Codes of Louisiana (1940), p. 385.***

In Chretien v. Theard, 2 Mart.(N.S.) 582 (1824), it was said that the two texts of an article should be made to harmonize if possible, and that if one presented a more enlarged meaning or sense than the other, that version should be adopted, for in this way both texts could be given full effect.

We are required to hold that the 1825 Code, like the 1808 Code, included the "other different inconveniences" in the article. We need not inquire why the phrase was omitted from the English text in that Code, although the most obvious reason is that it was an error or oversight in translation. Reasonable men should agree that the 1870 Code, which is in English only, merely incorporated the English text of the 1825 article. The express language of the Legislature used in the Codes of 1808 and 1825 as well as our jurisprudence requires us, then, to find that "smoke" and "smell" as contained in the 1825 article were merely illustrative and that all other insufferable inconveniences were included; and that the 1870 text following the exact language of the English text of 1825 carries with it the same interpretation: That smoke and smell are merely illustrative and that we are required to exercise control over other inconveniences.

Moreover, our jurisprudence has established that our courts do have the power to protect neighbors from all insufferable inconveniences and not merely from those two named in Article 669, and the result reached by the majority holding here is the same. Among the many cases which have considered other inconveniences alleged to be insufferable to neighbors are Froelicher v. Oswald Ironworks, 111 La. 705, 35 So. 821 (1903) (noise, smoke, and odor); Froelicher v. Southern Marine Works, 118 La. 1077, 43 So. 882 (1907) (noise, steam, odors, vibrations); Perrin v. Crescent City Stockyard & Slaughterhouse Co., 119 La. 83, 43 So. 938 (1907) (noisome gases and vapors); Tucker v. Vicksburg, S. & P. Ry. Co., 125 La. 689, 51 So. 689 (1910) (soot, cinders, coal, and dust; air poisoned by gases; odors and vapors; noises including the screeching, rumbling, and bumping of the turntable); Orton v. Virginia Carolina Chemical Co., 142 La. 790, 77 So. 632 (1918) (pollution of a stream with poisonous acid and the air with poisonous gases); Dodd v. Glen Rose Gasoline Co., 194 La. 1, 193 So. 349 (1939) (flare burning waste gases and arcading heat, noise, sand, and impurities); McGee v. Yazoo & M.V.R.

Co., 206 La. 121, 19 So. 2d 21(1944) (smoke, gases, soot, cinders); Devoke v. Yazoo & M.V.R. Co., 211 La. 729, 30 So. 2d 816 (1947) (obnoxious smoke including gases, soot, and cinders). There are numerous other decisions from this court and the several Courts of Appeal which have considered many other by-products of men's activities for determining insufferable inconveniences to neighbors. Much of the jurisprudence has cited common law without resort to the Civil Code, a few cases have cited Article 669, and some cases have cited no authority. It is clear that the jurisprudence has constantly and consistently included the "other different inconveniences" even though our present Code article does not contain that phrase.

There is no question, then, that the words "smoke" and "smell" in our present Code article must be interpreted as being illustrative of the "other different inconveniences which one neighbor may cause to another." In accord with the Chretien and Straus cases, this court should prefer the French text of the 1825 article as more enlarged and inclusive than the English text, and realize that it was the intent of the redactors to carry into the 1825 Code the 1808 article unchanged. An obvious error of omission in the English version of the 1825 article was perpetuated when this version was adopted into our 1870 Code. We should therefore, in the instant case, grant the plaintiffs the relief sought under our Civil Code Article 669 according to "the rules of the police" and "the customs of the place," and need not resort to common law concepts or to the common law terminology of nuisance per se and nuisance per accidens. I concur in the result.

TATE, J. (dissenting).... I respectfully dissent from our modifying the injunction. In view of the strong evidence supporting these decrees of the previous courts, we should not disturb their considered judgment that the neighbors should have relief—that, because of the unavoidable intolerable stench, noise, and pest attracting filth resulting from this stable, its continued operation on this narrow lot in this thickly settled neighborhood should be enjoined.

HILLIARD v. SHUFF
260 La. 384, 256 So. 2d 127 (1971)

SANDERS, J. The plaintiff, Francis Hilliard, sued to enjoin Elden Ray Snuff from maintaining four above ground fuel storage tanks on his property adjacent to the Hilliard residence. The Fifteenth Judicial District Court held that plaintiffs evidence failed to establish a nuisance and denied injunctive relief. The Third Circuit Court of Appeal affirmed. 241 So. 2d 56. We granted certiorari to review the judgment of the Court of Appeal. 257 La. 454, 242 So. 2d 577 (1971).

The facts of the case are clear. Hilliard owns a tract of land in a commercial area north of Interstate Highway 10 near Crowley, Louisiana. He and his family live on the plot.

The defendant, Shuff, holds an adjoining four-acre tract under lease. He uses the site for a truck stop, including a service station, a restaurant, and a car wash. Gasoline and diesel fuel sales average 3,000 gallons per day.

In order to meet the demand for motor fuel, Shuff installed four used, above ground storage tanks within 5 feet of Hilliard's property and about 150 feet from his residence. The tanks have a combined capacity of 58,800 gallons. He uses the tanks to store 25,200 gallons of gasoline and 33,600 gallons of diesel fuel. Both gasoline and diesel fuel are volatile. They generate high internal tank pressures.

The tanks were neither designed nor built for the storage of gasoline and diesel fuel. As constructed, they were designed for the storage of crude oil only. Crude oil is much less volatile than either gasoline or diesel fuel and generates no excessive pressure.

Because of the higher pressures of gasoline and diesel fuel, the tanks were vented. The vents, however, operate by releasing fumes, which are flammable and dangerous. The record reflects that they can be ignited by a random spark.

Defendant recognized the danger by posting the following warning sign on the tanks: *Flammable and dangerous. No smoking within 50 feet.* In testimony, defendant's own expert inferred that an ignition hazard existed within 20 feet of the tanks. The record is clear that the zone of danger extends well into the Hilliard property.

Plaintiff contends that the maintenance of these tanks deprives him of the use of 45 feet of his property and poses a threat to his residence. He seeks to have the tanks moved to another portion of defendant's property or placed underground.

Plaintiff relies upon the following articles of the Louisiana Civil Code: 667-669 [articles omitted]

These code articles control the disposition of the case. The storage of basic fuels, a lawful activity, does not, without more, violate these articles. Phrased in terms of *nuisance,* the storage of such fuel does not constitute a nuisance per se. See Canone v. Pallet, 160 La. 159, 106 So. 730 (1926); Crump v Carnahan, 155 La. 648, 99 So. 493 (1924); Galouye v. A. R. Blossman, Inc., La. App., 32 So. 2d 90 (1948). When, however, the storage of fuel creates a substantial hazard to the adjoining property, the use of the property runs counter to the code articles. In determining whether the storage creates a substantial hazard to the adjoining property, the court must consider such factors as location, structure of the storage tanks, quantity of fuel stored, operational procedures, as well as the surrounding circumstances. See Robichaux v. Huppenbauer, 258 La. 139, 245 So. 2d 385 (1971); Borgnemouth Realty Co. v. Gulf Soap Corporation, 212 La. 57, 31 So. 2d 488(1947); Devoke v. Yazoo & M.V.R. Co., 211 La. 729, 30 So. 2d 816 (1947): Froelicher v. Oswald Ironworks, 111 La. 705, 35 So. 821 (1903).***

Defendant's use of crude oil tanks for the storage of gasoline and diesel fuel within a few feet of plaintiff s property offends these principles. The hazard created is not limited to structures, but threatens the physical security of the Hilliard family and others lawfully upon the premises.

As the dissenting judge in the Court of Appeal noted, the plaintiff cannot safely operate an automobile, truck, tractor, or even a power mower on his property within the danger zone.

That the plaintiff was aware that the tanks were being erected and made no complaint creates no bar to injunctive relief under the circumstances. The record does not reflect that plaintiff then had knowledge that, because of their improper design, they would create a hazard to his property.

A violation of the code articles relating to the use of property, however, requires no automatic injunction to remove the tanks. Robichaux v. Huppenbauer, *supra*. Injunction is an equitable remedy and should be carefully designed to achieve the essential correction at the least possible cost and in-convenience to the defendant.

We note, as did the Court of Appeal, that the defendant made a substantial investment in the erection of the tanks. The record fails to reflect whether some corrective action short of removal or underground placement is feasible. Under these circumstances, a remand to the trial court for the reception of further evidence relative to methods of correction will best serve the interest of justice.

For the reasons assigned, the judgment of the Court of Appeal is reversed, and an injunction, both mandatory and prohibitory, is granted on such terms and conditions as the district court may find necessary after the reception of further evidence. For the determination of the terms and conditions of the injunction, the case is remanded to the Fifteenth Judicial District Court for further proceedings consistent with the views herein expressed. All costs are assessed against the defendant.

BARHAM, J. (dissenting). ***While I am of the opinion that the phrase "other different inconveniences" should be read into...article [669] '(see my concurrence in Robichaux v. Huppenbauer, *supra)* so as to include the type of activity involved here, I find this article inapplicable since there is no proof in this record to support a finding of the existence of an insufferable inconvenience — a nuisance.

Although I conclude that plaintiff failed to establish factually and legally that these tanks storing gasoline and Diesel fuel were a nuisance, I do not conclude that the plaintiff is not entitled to relief. I am of the opinion that relief should be granted in this case — not just partial relief as allowed by the majority, but total relief in the form of a permanent injunction prohibiting the defendant from storing gasoline and Diesel fuel in this manner at this particular location. The relief to which the plaintiff is entitled is provided by the rule of property announced in Article 667 of the Civil Code, reading as follows:

> "Although a proprietor may do with his estate whatever he pleases, still he can not make any work on it, which *may* deprive his neighbor of the liberty of enjoying his own, or which *may* be the cause of any damage to him." (emphasis supplied.)

Under this rule of property there exists a servitude in favor of an estate upon the adjoining estate. Since the above ground storage of gasoline and Diesel fuel in these renovated oil storage tanks presents a substantial hazard which "may" deprive the plaintiff of the enjoyment of his land or "may" cause him damage, injunctive relief is warranted. The dominant estate (here the plaintiffs) has a right to require the servient estate (the defendant's) to remove any work which threatens the enjoyment of his land or threatens to cause him damage. The exercise of this servitude does not depend on the *subjective* test of whether the owner or occupier of the dominant estate is in fact disturbed in his use and enjoyment of his land, nor does it depend upon proof of actual damage. The only requirement is an *objective finding* of probability that the owner of the dominant estate may at some time be deprived of enjoyment of his property or suffer damage because of the work made upon the servient estate. In the case at hand the expert and other testimony clearly establishes the objective determination which entitles the plaintiff to relief.

Article 667 is a valuable rule of property which establishes a legal servitude prohibiting the making of works on the servient estate which may damage the dominant estate. Its provisions are modified only by the language of Article 668 which excepts those *kinds* of encroachments upon the full enjoyment of an estate that are mere inconveniences. Reymond v. State, Through Department of Highways, 255 La. 425, 231 So. 2d 375. It protects from possible deprivation of or damage to *a real right.* Article 668 makes certain that the legal servitude of Article 667 protects only from a work which may occasion "real damage" and not from a work which "occasions only an inconvenience." Inconveniences are regulated by Article 669, and are to be determined according to ordinance or to the custom of the place. Unlike the abatement of these inconveniences, abatement of encroachments on the servitude established by Article 667 does not depend upon neighborhood environment and practice or custom and regulations, but is mandated upon legal request.

Danger from fire and explosion which may be caused by the maintenance of a work on a neighboring estate is not a mere inconvenience. Just as excavations made upon the servient estate may be corrected before the land and the buildings of the dominant estate subside and fall, so may a work which threatens the dominant estate with fire and explosion be abated.***

Since the plaintiff has not shown that he suffers from a nuisance, an insufferable inconvenience, I fail to see how he has established any right for relief under Article 669. Plaintiff does, however, have a right to immediate and full abatement of the encroachment upon his legal servitude under Article 667. For these reasons I respectfully dissent, being of the opinion that the plaintiff is entitled to the full injunctive relief sought.

NOTE
What is "Mere Inconvenience"?

In *Critney* v. *Goodyear Tire & Rubber Co.,* 353 So. 2d 341 (La. App. 1st Cir. 1977), the court held that escaping polyvinyl chloride into neighboring property was not a mere inconvenience. An injunction was issued because "the continuous encroachment on the property of plaintiff with polyvinyl chloride by Goodyear would be to permit irreparable injury which should not be tolerated." The court declared that "irreparable injury includes an injury, whether great or small, which ought not to be submitted to, and which, because it is so large or so small or is of such constant or frequent occurrence, cannot receive reasonable redress in a court of law." What is your conclusion? Any critique?

b. Actions for Damages

A. N. YIANNOPOULOS, PREDIAL SERVITUDES
§§ 39, 43 (3d ed. 2004)
(footnotes omitted)

§ 39. Liability Without Negligence

Historically, Articles 667, 668, and 669 of the Louisiana Civil Code have imposed responsibility for damage caused to property and injuries to persons in the neighborhood. These articles, however, did not specify whether responsibility is founded on fault. However, Article 667 of the Louisiana Civil Code, was amended in 1996, to establish liability on grounds of fault and exceptionally liability without regard to negligence for damage caused by certain specified ultrahazardous activities.

Because, according to traditional notions, civil responsibility is ordinarily founded on fault one might have expected Louisiana courts to require intentional misconduct or negligence for responsibility under Articles 667, 668, and 669 of the Louisiana Civil Code of 1870. Louisiana courts, however, have consistently declared since the end of the nineteenth century that the responsibility under these articles is "absolute" or "strict," in the sense that it does not depend on a showing of negligence or intentional misconduct.

In a leading case, the Louisiana Supreme Court declared that "it has been universally recognized that when, as here, the defendant, though without fault, is engaged in a lawful business, conducted according to modern and approved methods and with reasonable care, by such activities causes risk or peril to others, the doctrine of absolute liability is clearly applicable." And, in another case, the same court declared that an activity "which causes damage to a neighbor's property obliges the actor to repair the damage even though his actions are prudent by usual standards. It is not the manner in which the activity is carried on which is significant; it is the fact that the activity causes damage to a neighbor which is relevant. This being ascertained, it remains only to calculate the damage which ensued."

From the viewpoint of accurate analysis, it is preferable to assert that the responsibility under Articles 667, 668, and 669 was "without negligence." Strictly speaking, the responsibility under Article 667 is not an example of absolute or strict liability, because the abusive exercise of a right is fault within the meaning of Article 2315 of the Civil Code. It is only the responsibility under Article 669, likewise imposed without regard to negligence, that may be regarded as a species of responsibility without fault.

There is an easy explanation why Louisiana courts adopted a broad view as to the scope of responsibility under Articles 667, 668, and 669. If these articles were interpreted to impose liability merely for intentional misconduct and negligence, they would be largely unnecessary. The general principle of Article 2315 would suffice to establish responsibility for blameworthiness-fault. In a modern society, however, certain harms ought to be compensable even in the absence of blameworthiness. For a long time courts were unwilling to accomplish this end by tampering with the terms of Article 2315. They grasped instead at Articles 667, 668, and 669 which furnished a ready vehicle as they did not mention fault.

For a while, it was thought that responsibility without negligence was imposed on landowners only. Gradually, however, the confining terms of Articles 667, 668, and 669 were eroded and liability without negligence under these articles was imposed on persons other than landowners. Once this was accomplished, broadening of the terms of Article 2315 to include liability for ultrahazardous activities without regard to negligence was a logical solution.

One should not conclude that the broadened notion of fault under Article 2315 rendered the notion of liability without negligence under Articles 667, 668, and 669 unnecessary. The two sets of provisions could overlap in part but continued to establish distinct grounds of responsibility. Article 2315 establishes responsibility under the law of delictual obligations for all injuries to persons and property. Articles 667, 668, and 669 established, specifically, responsibility without negligence for certain kind of damage and injuries in the framework of vicinage under rules of property law. It is conceivable that liability could rest on either ground exclusively or on both cumulatively. A plaintiff could satisfy the terms and conditions of both sets of articles and could have two distinct causes of action for a single recovery, one resting on precepts of the law of obligations and the other on precepts of the law of property; or he could have a cause of action either under Article 2315 or under Articles 667, 668, and 669.

Since ultrahazardous activities give rise to a cause of action under Article 2315, reliance on Articles 667, 668, and 669 in such cases was unnecessary. However, Articles 667, 668, and 669 could furnish the sole basis of recovery in cases in which there was no fault under Article 2315.

The view that Articles 667, 668, and 669 imposed under certain circumstances liability without negligence conforms with considerations of policy and is compatible with the civilian tradition. By way of exception to the principle of responsibility based on fault-blameworthiness, Roman law imposed on landowners responsibility without negligence for damage caused by buildings, and landowners had at their disposal the *actio de effusis et dejectis* for damage resulting from excessive or harmful emissions. Further, courts in France have imposed on landowners responsibility without negligence for damage caused to neighbors without the benefit of provisions corresponding with Articles 667, 668, and 669 of the Louisiana Civil Code. In sister states, common law courts have developed the notions of ultrahazardous activities and nuisance to reach comparable results.

While the responsibility under Articles 667, 668, and 669 of the Civil Code may be with or without regard to negligence, a landowner or other user of immovable property is not responsible for all his acts that cause damage or insufferable inconvenience to neighbors. Indeed, there are certain harms that go uncompensable. Question thus arises where a line of demarcation between those works and activities that constitute a lawful exercise of ownership and those that give rise to civil responsibility may be drawn. This matter is explored in the following Sections.

§ 43. Acts and Works

Articles 667, 668, and 669 of the Louisiana Civil Code apply, according to their own terms, to works and operations. Specifically, Articles 667 and 668 declare that a proprietor is responsible for "works" that cause damage to a neighbor, and Article 669 declares that the works of an "operation" that cause inconvenience to neighbors may be tolerated or must be suppressed, depending on ordinances and local customs.

For a long time, Louisiana courts have understood Articles 667, 668, and 669 to apply to constructions as well as activities on an estate that cause damage or insufferable inconveniences to persons in the neighborhood. In Reymond v. State, Department of Highways, however, a divided Louisiana Supreme Court held that Articles 667 and 668 were inapplicable to the activities of man and that they were only applicable to structural damage caused by constructions. This interpretation was founded on the text of Domat, the apparent source of the provisions. The literal interpretation of the text of Domat, expounded by the majority opinion, is undoubtedly correct. The examples furnished by Domat, indeed, refer to "constructions" rather than "acts."

Question arises, however, whether the text of Domat ought to control in the interpretation of the word "work" in Articles 667 and 668 of the Louisiana Civil Code. In the light of all historical evidence, the redactors of the Civil Code used the text of Domat to express an idea common to all sources they inspected, namely, that a landowner may not use his property in an unneighborly fashion. Moreover, the word "work" in these articles is a translation of the French "ouvrage," which means both constructions and the doing of a job.

Limiting the meaning of the word "work" to constructions might thus be contrary to the intent of the redactors, and it would certainly be contrary to the pronouncements of an impressive Louisiana jurisprudence. While the literal interpretation of Articles 667 and 668 in the light of their historical derivation might leave room for the view that the word work means merely constructions, a teleological interpretation of the same articles leads to the conclusion that the word work ought to include acts. As a matter of policy, it is preferable to assert that Articles 667 and 668 apply to all situations in which constructions or activities cause unwarranted harm to property or persons. The contrary view would eliminate a most important basis of civil responsibility in the framework of vicinage.

In Chaney v. Travelers Insurance Company, the Louisiana Supreme Court had the opportunity to reexamine the proper interpretation and scope of application of Articles 667 and 668 of the Civil Code. Plaintiff brought action against parish authorities and a contractor and his insurer for the recovery of damages to his dwelling house. He alleged that works undertaken for the improvement of a canal by the parish and its contractor necessitated the use of heavy equipment in close proximity to his house, and that vibrations caused the interior sheetrock to crack near doors and windows. The contractor argued that plaintiff could not recover because neither negligence nor other fault had been shown on the part of the parish or its contractor; and that responsibility without negligence under Articles 667 and 668 of the Civil Code could not arise because these articles are inapplicable when activities, as distinguished from *constructions,* cause damage to adjacent owners. Justice Summers, writing for the majority, repudiated the narrow interpretation of Articles 667 and 668 in the Reymond decision and attributed to these articles their broad historical meaning which includes damage caused by constructions as well as damage caused by activities on neighboring property.

RIZZO v. NICHOLS
867 So. 2d 73 (La. App. 3d Cir. 2004)

AMY, J. Plaintiffs, husband and wife, sought recovery for damage that occurred after the defendant changed the natural drainage of water across the plaintiffs' property. The trial judge determined that the defendant had notice that construction activities at this particular location would cause such drainage problems and that the defendant's activities were a cause-in-fact of the water damage to the plaintiffs' property. The trial judge awarded the plaintiffs actual damages as well as damages for inconvenience and mental anguish. From this judgment, the defendant appeals. For the following reasons, we affirm.

FACTUAL AND PROCEDURAL BACKGROUND

According to the record, Jasper and Mary Rizzo, plaintiffs herein, moved into a house on Brooks Boulevard in Alexandria, Louisiana, in November 2001. At the time, and for several months thereafter, the Rizzos' property was located next to a vacant lot. Mr. Rizzo testified at trial that when it rained, the water that fell on his and the adjoining properties was channeled into a lower area that ran across the adjacent property and drained into the street. The record further indicates that Heath Nichols, defendant herein, purchased the vacant lot contiguous to the Rizzos' in June 2001. Mr. Nichols began construction of a duplex apartment shortly thereafter, whereupon the Rizzos' property allegedly began to flood. Mr. Rizzo filed the instant suit for damages on October 30, 2002, and a bench trial was held in the matter on April 29, 2003.

Mr. Rizzo testified at trial that until Mr. Nichols began construction on the duplex, his-

Mr. Rizzo's-property never flooded after it rained. However, Mr. Rizzo noted, after construction, the natural drainage across Mr. Nichols's property was disrupted, and Mr. Rizzo began to have problems with standing water. He approached Mr. Nichols about the drainage problems, and he recalled that Mr. Nichols agreed to "look into it." Mr. Rizzo testified that he approached Mr. Nichols two or three more times after their initial conversation to repeat his request that he do something about the flooding, but Mr. Nichols took no further action. At trial, Mr. Rizzo advanced the theory that Mr. Nichols had built the duplex "up," at a higher elevation than the surrounding land, thereby causing Mr. Rizzo's property to be the low spot where water collected after a rain. Mr. Rizzo testified that the standing water had damaged the shed that stood behind his house and that he eventually had to install a catch basin at the back of his property to ameliorate the drainage problem.

The trial judge issued written reasons for judgment on June 20, 2003, in which he observed that the primary issue for determination in the matter was whether Mr. Nichols knew or was aware that construction on his property would cause damage and whether he could have prevented that damage by the exercise of reasonable care. The trial judge noted that Mr. Nichols admitted at trial that he had discussed the drainage issue with two plumbers but had not taken any action. As such, the trial judge concluded, Mr. Nichols had notice that his activities would cause damage to the Rizzos' property. The trial judge likewise concluded that the construction on Mr. Nichols's property was a cause-in-fact of the damage to the Rizzos' property. Accordingly, the trial judge awarded the Rizzos damages in the amounts of $2,175.00 for construction of a catch basin; $750.00 for repairs for water damage to the shed; $2,000.00 in inconvenience damages for the loss of use of the shed, loss of use of the yard, and standing water on the property; and $2,000.00 general damages for mental anguish. Mr. Nichols appeals the trial judge's findings.

DISCUSSION

Mr. Nichols advances the following assignments of error on appeal:

1. The trial court erred in its determination that Mr. Nichols knew that constructing the duplex on his property would cause flooding on the Rizzos' property.

2. The trial court erred in awarding damages of $2,175.00 for the installation of a catch basin on the Rizzos' property.

3. The trial court erred in awarding damages of $750.00 for repairs to the water damage in the Rizzos' shed.

4. The trial court erred in awarding inconvenience damages of $2,000.00 for the Rizzos' loss of use of the shed, loss of use of their yard, and for the standing water on their property.

5. The trial court erred in awarding general damages of $2,000.00 for the

Rizzos' mental anguish.

The present appeal involves the obligations of vicinage, set forth in Articles 667-669 of our Civil Code.***

In the present appeal, Mr. Nichols argues that testimony elicited at trial establishes that he neither knew nor could have known that the construction activities on his property would cause flooding and damage to the Rizzos' property. Mr. Nichols maintains that although he knew that water stood on his property after a heavy rain, he did not know that said standing water would cause damage. In support of his assertion that he was unaware of the consequences of building on his property, Mr. Nichols points out that "standing water is common throughout the entire neighborhood" and that he "employed a reputable contractor, who built the duplex [on Mr. Nichols's property] in accordance with local codes and regulations."

According to the record of the proceedings below, Mr. Rizzo testified that he had informed Mr. Nichols of the drainage problem soon after construction began. Mr. Nichols's testimony confirmed that Mr. Rizzo had approached him during construction and that he had contacted two plumbers about remedying the situation. However, the record indicates that Mr. Nichols did nothing further to provide a solution to the disrupted drainage pattern occasioned by his activities. Instead, the record reflects that Mr. Rizzo installed a catch basin on his property in an attempt to remedy the situation.

Where an aggrieved party seeks recovery under the law of vicinage for damage occasioned by a neighboring landowner's activities, that party must demonstrate a causal link between the damage sustained and the neighboring landowner's action or inaction. Haworth v. L'Hoste, 95-0714 (La. App. 4th Cir. 11/30/95), 664 So. 2d 1335, *writ denied,* 96-408 (La. 3/29/96), 670 So. 2d 1235.

At trial, Mr. Elbert Wiggins, the previous owner of the Rizzos' property, testified that his land never flooded during the five years that he lived there; instead, he noted, water drained from his property through the lower-lying area that ran across the adjacent vacant lot, now owned by Mr. Nichols. Mr. Rizzo likewise testified that before Mr. Nichols began construction, his property never flooded, and water drained in the manner described by Mr. Wiggins. Mr. Rizzo introduced into evidence photographs of his land, taken before construction activities commenced next door, which showed the low-lying area on the adjacent property. He then introduced photographs of his property after construction began in which standing water covered substantial portions of his yard and surrounded his shed. Additional photographs, taken of Mr. Nichols's duplex after its completion, show that the duplex was built at a higher elevation than the surrounding land, as indicated by the dirt and sod sloping downward from the building to the level of Mr. Rizzo's property.

We find no manifest error in the trial judge's determination that Mr. Nichols knew that the activities on his property would cause damage to the Rizzos' property and that he could have prevented such damage by the exercise of reasonable care. Moreover, we find no manifest error in the trial judge's determination that the construction activities undertaken by Mr. Nichols disrupted the natural drainage of his and the Rizzos' respective properties and that these activities were the cause-in-fact of the Rizzos' damages. This assignment is without merit.

DAMAGES

In addition to general damages, a plaintiff in a vicinage cause of action may recover damages for mental anguish, discomfort, irritation, anxiety, and loss of use and/or enjoyment of his property. Branch v. City of Lafayette, 95-298 (La. App. 3d Cir. 10/4/95), 663 So. 2d 216. A trial court is afforded great discretion in fixing damages in accordance with its factual determinations in a case, and an appellate court may not disturb such awards absent a clear abuse of this discretion. Arnold v. Town of Ball, 94-972 (La. App. 3d Cir. 2/1/95), 651 So. 2d 313.

With respect to the catch basin, Mr. Nichols argues on appeal that the Rizzos paid "an excessive amount" for it and that the trial court's award of $2,175.00 for its installation is excessive. Mr. Nichols proposes that this same catch basin could be installed for $1,000.00. Moreover, Mr. Nichols argues that four properties benefit from the catch basin, and he should not be required to "bear the entire expense."

Regarding the award of $750 for repairs to the water-damaged shed, Mr. Nichols claims that the evidence presented at trial fails to establish conclusively that the shed sustained damages. Mr. Nichols points out that none of the boards in the shed were rotten.

Mr. Nichols further argues that the award of $2,000.00 for inconvenience is not warranted because the Rizzos' land is low-lying and because an "unusual amount of rain fell in 2002."

When we examine the record, we find that the trial judge did not abuse his vast discretion in awarding the Rizzos damages for the installation of the catch basin, for repairs to the shed, and for inconvenience. The evidence presented at trial clearly supports such awards. These assignments of error lack merit.

With respect to recovery for mental anguish, a panel of this court noted in Begnaud that such damages are appropriate:

(1) when property has been damaged by an intentional or illegal act; (2) where property is damaged by acts for which the tortfeasor will be strictly or absolutely liable; (3) when property is damaged by acts constituting a continuous nuisance; (4) when property is damaged at a time in which the owner thereof is present or situated nearby and the owner experiences trauma as a result. [Citations omitted.]

Begnaud, 721 So. 2d at 555 (quoting Kolder v. State Farm Ins. Co., 520 So. 2d 960, 963

(La. App. 3d Cir. 1987)).

Regarding the award of $2,000.00 for mental anguish, Mr. Nichols claims that such an award was inappropriate because the Rizzos failed to prove that any of the four considerations listed in *Begnaud,* above, were applicable.

Mr. Rizzo testified at trial that the standing water on his property kept him from venturing into his back yard and proved a breeding ground for mosquitoes. He also testified that the shed would often be unusable for a week's time after the water receded. Moreover, Mr. Rizzo testified that the condition of his property caused tension between him and his wife. Based upon our review of the record, we find no abuse of discretion on the part of the trial judge in awarding $2,000.00 to the Rizzos for mental anguish due to damage to their property. This assignment is without merit.

DECREE

For the foregoing reasons, the judgment of the trial court is affirmed. All costs of this proceeding are assigned to the defendant-appellant, Heath Nichols. Affirmed.

NOTE
Liberative Prescription

What is the prescriptive period for a suit for damages under articles 667-669? That issue was resolved by the Louisiana Supreme Court in *Dean* v. *Hercules,* 38 So. 2d 69 (La. 1976). Here is an excerpt from that opinion.

An action for damages for a violation of article 667 is most closely associated with an action for damages based on C.C. 2315 et seq. Indeed, it can be said that a violation of article 667 constitutes fault within the meaning of article 2315....Therefore, the prescriptive period in an action for damages for a violation of article 667 should be one year....However, while the applicable prescriptive period for an action for damages for a violation of article 667 is one year, the one year period cannot necessarily be reckoned from the date of the occurrence. In modern technology damages from industrial emissions and the like may not become apparent until some years after the occurrence. Additionally, it might be impossible for the injured party to know what or who caused the damage, until an investigation can be made after the damage in fact becomes apparent. In such cases, the prescriptive period would run only from the date the damage becomes apparent [quote omitted].

c. Encroaching Buildings
Civil Code art. 670

THOMPSON v. HEMPHILL
438 So. 2d 1124 (La. App. 2d Cir. 1983)

HALL, J. This dispute between brothers-in-law involves certain structures located on adjoining tracts of land on Smith Street in West Monroe. A schematic diagram of the property involved is reproduced below.

Tracts Nos. 1 and 2 were previously owned as community property by L. H. and Alice Hemphill, defendant's parents and plaintiffs in-laws. Upon the Hemphills' divorce, as part of the community property settlement, L. H. Hemphill acquired Tract No. 1 and Alice Hemphill acquired Tract No. 2. A store building was located on each of the tracts, with a common wall between the buildings located on the property line. Gas pumps were located on Tract No. 1 and gas storage tanks servicing the pumps were located on Tract No. 2. Plaintiff-appellant, William D. Thompson, purchased Tract No. 1 from L. H. Hemphill in 1976. Defendant-appellee, Lamar Hemphill, purchased Tract No. 2 from Alice Hemphill in 1978. Plaintiff acquired Tract No. 3 in 1979 from a Mrs. Gresham.

Friction arose between plaintiff and defendant in July 1980 over plaintiffs continued use of the underground gasoline storage tanks located on Tract No. 2. A survey revealed that Hemphill's store building encroached slightly onto Thompson's Tract No. 3. A signpost set in concrete related to Hemphill's store was determined to be located on Tract No. 3. A truck body or trailer which Hemphill placed on a concrete slab or concrete blocks in 1978 and which he used as a workshop was found to encroach on Tract No. 3.

On August 1, 1980 plaintiff filed suit seeking injunctive relief, removal of the encroachments, and damages for trespass and loss of business revenue. A temporary restraining order restraining Hemphill from interfering with Thompson's use of the gasoline storage tanks was issued, but lapsed when the rule for a preliminary injunction was continued and not tried. Plaintiff abandoned his claim for injunctive relief after building new storage tanks on his own property.

After trial on the merits, pursuant to written reasons for judgment, the trial court rendered judgment (1) granting defendant a predial servitude for that part of his permanent building and trailer which encroaches on plaintiffs property, Tract No. 3; (2) awarding plaintiff compensation in the amount of $150 for the servitude granted to defendant; (3) awarding plaintiff $500 for gasoline belonging to him which defendant would not let plaintiff remove from the underground storage tanks, provided however that defendant could relieve himself of the payment of the $500 by allowing plaintiff to remove the gasoline; (4) awarding defendant $250 as damages for his attorney fees incurred in connection with the temporary restraining order which the court found to be wrongfully issued; and (5) ordering defendant to remove all litter, debris, and other objects surrounding the trailer. Although not expressly mentioned in the judgment, plaintiff's demand for damages to a fence torn down by the defendant was rejected, as was his demand for damages in the form of lost revenue allegedly caused by defendant's refusal to let him obtain gasoline from the gasoline storage tanks.

The plaintiff appealed, specifying that the trial court erred in granting the predial servitude for the encroachment of the trailer, in awarding an insufficient sum as compensation for the servitude, in failing to award damages for the destruction of the fence, in failing to award plaintiff damages for lost revenue, in awarding attorney fees for the wrongful issuance of the temporary restraining order, in failing to render judgment establishing the boundary between Tracts Nos. 1 and 2, and in failing to grant a new trial. The defendant did not appeal or answer the appeal.

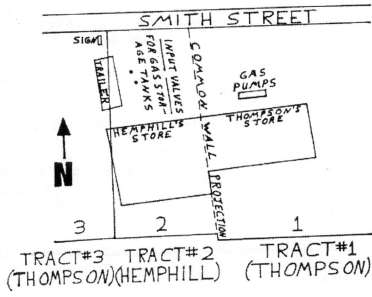

SERVITUDE FOR ENCROACHMENT

Plaintiff does not question the servitude granted by the trial court insofar as it concerns the building located on Tract No. 2 which encroaches slightly onto Tract No. 3. However, plaintiff contends there is no authority for the trial court's action in granting a servitude for the encroachment of the trailer because the trailer is not a "building" for which an encroachment servitude may be granted by the court under C.C. Art. 670. The defendant argues, on the other hand, that the truck trailer placed on a concrete slab and used as a workshop is a building or an "other construction" under C.C. Art. 463 for which an encroachment servitude may be granted under C.C. Art. 670 or the general equitable principles of C.C. Art. 21 [Revised C.C. art. 4].

Regardless of whether this particular structure can be classified as a building for which an encroachment servitude may be granted under C.C. Art. 670, it is our view that the trial court abused its discretion in granting the servitude for the trailer encroachment.

Prior to the revision of the Civil Code articles on predial servitudes in 1978, effective January

1, 1979, the Civil Code provided no express remedy for the situation where a landowner in good faith constructed a building or other structure of a permanent nature which encroached upon adjoining property. Recognizing the sometimes harsh and inequitable result of requiring a landowner in good faith to demolish or remove a structure in such a situation, the courts on occasion turned to C.C. Art. 21 [Revised C.C. art. 4] in seeking an equitable solution to the problem. See Morehead v. Smith, 225 So. 2d 729 (La. App. 2d Cir. 1969); Porterfield v. Spurgeon, 379 So. 2d 56 (La. App. 3d Cir. 1979). In the revision of the Civil Code articles, C.C. Art. 670 was designed to grant to the courts express discretionary authority to reach an equitable solution by granting a predial servitude for the encroachment with payment of compensation to the adjoining landowner whose property is burdened by the servitude, Article 670 allows a court, in the sound exercise of its discretion, to avoid a situation in which a good faith landowner, in order to remove an encroachment, would be required to demolish or destroy the utility of a building which encroaches, perhaps only slightly, onto adjoining property.

Here, the structure involved, whether or not it be considered a building, is an old truck body placed on a concrete slab or blocks. The structure encroaches substantially onto the adjoining property in that at least one-half of it is located on the adjoining property. There is no evidence that the trailer is attached in any permanent manner to the concrete on which it rests. There is ample space on the defendant's property to relocate the trailer without encroachment onto the plaintiffs' property. There is no reason why the trailer could not be moved off of the plaintiffs' property without undue expense and without impairing the utility of the structure. Under these circumstances the grant of a servitude, thereby encumbering the adjoining landowner's property in a substantial manner for an indefinite period of time, is not warranted.

The granting of the servitude was an abuse of the court's discretion. The judgment will be reversed and set aside insofar as it grants a predial servitude for the encroachment of the trailer and judgment will be rendered ordering the defendant to remove the trailer from the plaintiffs property.

COMPENSATION FOR SERVITUDE

Plaintiff-appellant contends that the amount awarded for the encroachment servitude, $150, is insufficient. The thrust of this contention is diminished by the fact that the extent of the servitude is reduced substantially in accordance with the conclusions reached in the previous section of this opinion. The $150 award seems reasonable for the slight encroachment of the store building on plaintiffs property, and will not be disturbed.

Decree

For the reasons assigned, the judgment of the district court is reversed insofar as it grants to the defendant a predial servitude for that part of the trailer which encroaches on plaintiffs property and the judgment is amended to strike the words "and trailer" in the fourth adjudicating paragraph of the judgment.

NOTE
Article 670 Invoked in Other Contexts

In *Winingder* v. *Balmer,* 632 So. 2d 408 (La. App. 4th Cir. 1994), a neighbor built a fence on her own property, in close proximity to the adjacent neighbor's house. The court found that the fence, as built, restricted drainage, that the fence constituted a fire hazard as it denied access to the neighbor's property by utilities servicemen and egress, and that it also caused structural damage to the neighbor's wooden house by accumulation of humidity, leaves, and debris. The trial court granted a servitude to the neighbor under Article 670 of the Louisiana Civil Code for a reasonable width on account of prior encroachments. The house of the neighbor, indeed, encroached on the property of the neighbor who built the fence. The court of appeal affirmed the trial court's decision that the fence violated Article 667 of the Louisiana Civil Code, stating: "[A]lthough, in principle, a landowner may use and enjoy his property as sees fit, ... he may not exercise his right in such a way as to cause damage to his neighbors. Balis, Civil Law Property 87 (3d ed. 1955) (in Greek), and other authorities." *Id.* at 414.

In *Hayes v. Gunn,* 2013 WL 1749388 (La. App. 3d Cir. 4/24/2013), a mother, who owned the property next door to her daughter and son-in law (hereinafter "the couple"), granted them oral permission to construct part of their covered carport on her land. She also permitted them to use her land as a driveway to access the carport. The mother sold her property to a third party who refused to allow the couple to cross her land. Additionally she demanded that the encroaching carport be removed. The couple filed suit seeking (unsuccessfully) judicial recognition of their right to the encroachment and to cross the land. The couple invoked article 670 as a basis of their alleged right, but the court swiftly and correctly rejected their claim, inasmuch as the couple failed to meet the threshold requirement of a good faith that they owned the land on which their building encroached.

In *Lafargue v. Barron,* 2012 WL 602173 (La. App. 1st Cir. 2/10/2012), *cert. denied* 90 So. 3d 437 (La. 2012), defendants, the owners of property, constructed an addition thereon which violated the Broadmoor subdivision restrictions (to which their property was subject). [Building restrictions will be explored in Chapter XV, *infra.*] Under the restriction, no building could be erected any nearer to the side property line than five feet. The defendants' addition was three feet, six inches from the side property line. Plaintiff filed suit seeking to require the defendants to remove the portion of the addition that violated the restriction. Defendants unsuccessfully relied upon article 670 as authority for the court's discretion to allow the encroaching building to remain in spite of the subdivision restrictions. The court briskly dismissed defendants' argument, noting that defendants' situation did not involve a building that encroaches upon an adjacent estate, thus rendering article 670 inapplicable. Accordingly, the court ordered the defendants to bring their addition into compliance with the subdivision restrictions.

3. COMMON ENCLOSURES
Civil Code arts. 673-688

A. N. YIANNOPOULOS, PREDIAL SERVITUDES
§§ 68-71 (3d ed. 2004)
(footnotes omitted)

§ 68. Conditions for building a wall

Under Article 673, one is entitled to take, under certain conditions, up to nine inches from the land of an adjoining neighbor for the construction of a partition wall and, additionally, up to one and one-half inches for the plastering without any payment to the neighbor. This right belongs to the landowner and to a person acting under his authority, whether by virtue of a real right as a usufructuary or by virtue of a personal right as a lessee. According to an early Louisiana decision, this right is also accorded to a person who possesses land for himself.

The exercise of the right given by Article 673 is subject to certain requirements. The person exercising the right must be the first to build on a tract of land not surrounded by walls. This condition is easily met when the adjoining property is vacant, but questions of interpretation arise when there are fences, buildings, or other constructions on the neighboring estate. One does not have a right under Article 673 if his neighbor has already taken advantage of this provision and has built a partition wall of the type contemplated. But one has the right to build a wall under Article 673 if his neighbor has merely built a fence or a wooden wall on or at the property line. Likewise, the existence of a house or of a brick or stone wall more than nine inches away from the boundary does not preclude exercise of the right granted to a neighbor by Article 673. If the brick or stone wall is within the nine inch servitude, exercise of the right under Article 673 may be excluded, but question remains whether the wall may become one in common by application of Article 676.

No more than one-half of the wall may rest on the land of the neighbor. If more than one-half of the thickness of the wall is taken from the land of the neighbor, the wall encroaches to that extent, and the neighbor is entitled to the remedies that the law provides against encroachment.

The right under Article 673 is given to one who builds a wall with "solid masonry at least as high as the first story." Iron columns are not a wall within the contemplation of this article. An early Louisiana decision indicates that a neighbor may enjoin one who attempts to build a wall with materials other than stones or bricks. Article 673, however, does not forbid the use of heavy timbers to make a firm and smooth basis for the foundation of a brick or stone wall.

It has been held in France that any form of solid construction satisfies the requirements of Article 661 of the Code Napoleon, which corresponds with Article 684 of the

Louisiana Civil Code of 1870, even if the materials were unknown at the time of the redaction of the code. Thus, the use of reinforced concrete is allowed. A similar solution ought to prevail in Louisiana because reinforced concrete is solid masonry.

The thickness of the wall may not exceed eighteen inches, not including the plastering. The foundation of this wall, however, under the land of each neighbor, may extend as far as it is necessary for solid construction. The Louisiana Supreme Court has declared in a leading case that "when the Code authorized the proprietor to rest one-half of an 18-inch wall on the land of his neighbor, it necessarily included authority to rest such wall upon the center of a foundation adequate to support it, and therefore extending a greater distance upon the land of each."

Exercise of the right given by Article 673 does not require the consent of the neighbor. If the neighbor objects, entry into his land may be secured by injunction. Parties may modify by agreement the conditions of Article 673, but, according to an early decision, parol evidence is not admissible. A wall built under Article 673, without the neighbor's contribution, is a private wall: it belongs to the neighbor who built it, but it may become common at any time by application of Article 674 of the Civil Code.

§ 69. Distinction between Articles 674 and 676

Articles 674 and 676 of the Louisiana Civil Code establish legal servitudes whereby a landowner may, under certain conditions, acquire the co-ownership of a wall that his neighbor has built on or at the boundary. The rights that the two articles confer are imprescriptible. It has been said that the right given to an adjoining landowner to make a private wall common is, in effect, a right of expropriation though not for private utility; it is given in the general interest, that is, for the conservation of land, labor, and materials.

A private wall that a neighbor has built on the boundary in compliance with Article 673 may become common by application of Article 674. This article declares that the neighbor who has refused to contribute to the raising of the wall preserves the right of making the wall common, in whole or in part, by paying to its owner "one-half of the current value of the wall, or of the part that he wishes to make common." If the person who built first did not take advantage of the legal servitude established by Article 673 but located the wall on his own land at the boundary, the wall that he built may become common by virtue of the legal servitude established by Article 676. This article declares: "When a solid masonry wall adjoins another estate, the neighbor has a right to make it a common wall, in whole or in part, by paying to its owner one-half of the current value of the wall, or of the part that he wishes to make common, and one-half of the value of the soil on which the wall is built."

This provision is based on Article 684 of the Louisiana Civil Code of 1870 but changes the law in two respects: it deletes the proviso at the end of the source provision and specifies that the landowner who wishes to make an adjoining wall common is bound to pay one-half of the *current* value of the wall or of the part that he wishes to make common.

Article 684 of the Louisiana Civil Code of 1870 accorded to a landowner the right to make common a wall built by his neighbor at the property line, "if the person who has built the wall has laid the foundation entirely upon his own estate." The purpose of this proviso was to draw a clear distinction between a wall straddling the property line, built under Article 675 of the Louisiana Civil Code of 1870, and a wall at the property line, contemplated by Article 684 of the same Code. In French, it reads: *"si celui qui a fait le mur I 'a fait porter entierement sur son heritage",* which ought to be translated "if he who has built the wall has made it to rest entirely on his own estate." The mistranslation was early noticed by Louisiana courts, and the English text has been "practically nullified. ... It is, indeed, so absurd and so incongruous that it is difficult to see how any other view could be taken of it." It was thus established that Article 684 did not require that the foundation of the wall be entirely on the land of the person who built it, courts having taken judicial notice that "a high wall cannot be erected on the line of a lot on our farms and alluvial soil without the projection of the foundation on the adjacent land." The condition of the article was satisfied when the base of the wall at the ground level was located "entirely on one property."

The right that Article 676 confers on an adjoining neighbor applies to walls exclusively. Other types of enclosures may be held in common by virtue of agreements or by application of the presumptions of Articles 685 and 686 of the Civil Code. The walls that Article 676 contemplates are of the same nature as those built under Article 673, namely, walls of solid masonry. When an adjoining owner brought suit to compel his neighbor to cede the co-ownership of a wooden wall at the boundary, the court rejected the demand on the ground that "the side of a wooden house is not a party wall held in common. It is not a wall at all." French jurisprudence and doctrine interpreting the corresponding provision of Article 661 of the Code Civil are in accord.

All walls built with solid masonry, as bricks or stones, are susceptible of becoming common, whether they are located in towns or in the country, and whether they separate houses, yards, or gardens. The law encourages co-ownership of walls because it allows an interested neighbor to acquire as much or as little as he needs and to make the wall common in whole or in part of its height and length. According to French doctrine and jurisprudence, which ought to be relevant for Louisiana, acquisition of the co-ownership of a wall is excluded in two situations only: (1) when a wall belongs to the public domain, because the property of the public domain is inalienable and (2) when the owner of the wall enjoys servitudes of light and view on adjoining property, because a regime of co-ownership of the wall would be incompatible with these real rights.

The law accords the right to make an adjoining wall common to every neighbor, even to one who has abandoned his right to the wall in order to avoid contribution for repairs or rebuilding. In such a case, if he wishes to reacquire the co-ownership of the wall, he must pay one-half of its current value and one-half of the value of the soil on which the wall rests. It has been suggested in France that the co-ownership of a wall may be acquired not only by a landowner but also by persons enjoying real rights on the land of another, such as usufructuaries or purchasers under a contract of rent of lands.***

Article 676 of the Louisiana Civil Code presupposes an "adjoining" wall, namely, a wall located along its entire length at the boundary line. If a wall is removed, even a fraction of an inch from the boundary, Article 676 excludes the possibility that this wall may ever become common. Moreover, the existence of this wall would exclude application of Article 673 because the premises would be surrounded by a wall. Thus, for all practical purposes, the common wall servitude is limited to the two situations provided for expressly in the Code, namely, when neighboring estates are not surrounded by walls or when there is a wall at or on the property line. The existence of a wall near the property line effectively precludes the creation of a partition wall as a common enclosure.***

§ 70. Use of adjoining wall; payment

A landowner who wishes to use an adjoining wall belonging to his neighbor should first obtain the owner's permission or demand that the wall be made common. One who has not contributed to the raising of the wall "has no right, without the owner's consent, to make any use thereof whatever; and the most simple structure, leaning against or attached to the wall, is a violation of the right of the owner." The owner of the wall may protect his ownership against unauthorized interference by all procedural means, including injunctions and personal as well as real actions. Quite frequently, however, the owner of the wall allows the works to be completed and then proceeds against his neighbor for reimbursement on the ground that the wall in question has been treated as one in common.

The owner of the wall is entitled to demand reimbursement if his neighbor, or a person acting under him, such as a lessee, makes "any use at all" of the wall or if he derives from it an advantage of use other than what is "merely a natural or necessary consequence or incident of the proximity of the wall, provided the benefit or advantage is not the result of any act on his part." The neighbor may thus render himself liable to the owner of the wall without making full use of the rights accorded by Article 680 of the Civil Code to the co-owner of a wall. Indicatively, it has been held that the use of a wall to support the roof, floors, and walls of a building renders the neighbor liable for one-half of what he, by such use, has treated as common. When the roof of a building "flashes" into the neighbor's wall, when a neighbor's wall is used for lateral support of a building as well as a means of preventing a roof from leaking, or when a shed rests on the wall, there is likewise sufficient use to render the neighbor liable to the owner of the wall.

The use of a wall to enclose the side of a building, with minimal or no connection at all with the wall, has proved to be a troublesome question. In an early case, the court declared that a neighbor "by attaching the roof of this shed, whether by tar, paste or nails, to the wall in question, and building against it in such a manner that it served to exclude the rain, and prevent the access of thieves or intruders ... there was an exercise of the right of making this wall one in common." In another case the court declared, "when a neighbor uses an adjoining wall as a wall or protection to enclose his building, ... he must pay one-half of the value of the wall used by him at the moment of using it." But in a case in which there was ample evidence that the neighbor did not derive any benefit from the presence of the wall, and in a case in which the use of the wall was a mere trifle, the neighbor was exonerated from responsibility.

§ 71. Cost and value of the wall

The amount of reimbursement due to the owner of the wall, that is, the price for the acquisition of the co-ownership, varies according to whether the wall is built on the land of the neighbor at the property line or on the boundary. For a wall built by the adjoining neighbor on his own land, Article 676 requires reimbursement of one-half of the current value of the wall or of its part that is made common and reimbursement of one-half of the value of the soil occupied by the wall. For a wall built on the boundary, Article 674 merely requires payment to the owner of the wall of one-half of the current value of the wall or of the part that the neighbor wishes to make common. There is no requirement for the payment of one-half of the value of the soil occupied by the wall because the wall rests in equal proportions on the adjoining estates.

Article 684 of the Louisiana Civil Code of 1870 required reimbursement of one-half of the "value" of the adjoining wall made common, whereas Article 676 of the same Code required reimbursement of one-half of the original construction "cost" of a wall built on the boundary. The difference in the measures of compensation, "value" on one hand and "cost" on the other, was noticed by Louisiana courts. The difference was, of course, inconsequential in cases in which value and original construction cost were the same, and in such cases courts tended to use the two terms indiscriminately. The difference became material, however, in cases in which the current value of a wall was either lower or higher than its original construction cost, namely, when the value of the wall had either depreciated or appreciated.

When the value of a wall, at the time it was first used by the neighbor, was less than the cost of construction, Louisiana courts typically awarded value rather than cost. This was accomplished by a narrow construction of Article 676 of the 1870 Code. The courts declared that the neighbor was bound to pay half the cost of the wall whenever he undertook to make it a wall in common. "But it is only on his refusal to contribute that he is held to be so bound; and, before refusing, he must certainly have an opportunity of assenting; he must be asked to contribute—he must, at least, be notified, and have an opportunity of contributing to the common cost of the wall, and of seeing that no useless expense is incurred for negligence, extravagance, or want of skill and that the work, is substantially and thoroughly executed. If, when called upon, he should refuse to contribute, or pay no attention to the notice, which amounts to the same thing, then and in that case the law binds him to reimburse his neighbor half the cost, whenever he makes use of the law." Because Article 676 of the 1870 Code did not apply in the absence of a demand to contribute, the matter of the amount of reimbursement was determined by application of "general principles" and by analogy from Article 684 of the same Code. Only one case was found in which a neighbor was asked to contribute and refused, and the court therein actually awarded the cost of construction. There was no indication, however, that the cost of construction differed from the value of the wall. In another case, although plaintiff had failed to prove that notice of the demand for contribution had been received by his neighbor, the court awarded him the construction cost on the ground that he "had shown that the work was done at a reasonable figure, after soliciting bids therefor, and that defendant made use of said wall within seven or eight months after it was reconstructed."

When the value of the wall at the time it was first used by the neighbor was more than the cost of construction, Louisiana courts consistently awarded cost rather than value. These decisions were based on the ground that a neighbor should not be held to a greater degree of responsibility than one who refused to contribute to the raising of a wall. In an effort at reconciliation of conflicting past determinations, the Louisiana Supreme Court declared that "a party who converts his neighbor's wall into a 'wall in common' must pay half of the replacement value, or present value, of the wall, unless he contends that, not having refused to contribute to the original cost of construction, he prefers to pay half of the original cost of construction, and, in that event, the burden of proof is on him to show what was the original cost of construction." In most instances, this was an impossible burden to carry, and the neighbor was bound to pay the value of the wall. Under this interpretation a neighbor preferably should refuse to contribute to the raising of the wall. Should he ever decide to make the wall one in common, he had a good chance to limit his liability to whichever was the lesser amount, original cost or current value of the wall.***

JEANNIN v. DeBLANC
11 La. Ann. 465 (1856)

SPOFFORD, J. We adopt the following opinion of the District Judge:

"The defendant, availing herself of the provisions of Art. 671 of the Civil Code [Revised C.C. art. 673], rested one-half of her wall on the ground of the plaintiff; the wall is shown to be thirteen inches thick. The plaintiff did not contribute and has not contributed, in any manner, to the building of said wall. Since the construction of the wall, the defendant has caused certain openings to be made in it, consisting of grated windows in the second story, and of ventilators below the ground flooring. The plaintiff alleges that the defendant had no right to make said openings in the wall thus constructed, and that in so doing, she usurps the right of view upon his premises to his injury and damage. Therefore, he prays that the defendant be condemned to close the said openings at her proper cost, and to the pay the plaintiff damages in the sum of $600, with costs, & c.

There is no question of servitude presented by the pleadings and evidence, since it is conceded that the plaintiff may at any time close the apertures and grated windows by making the wall a wall in common; but, in so doing, the plaintiff would have to pay one-half of its value.

The defendant contends that, until the wall is made common, it is her exclusive property, and that she has therefore a right either to pull it down altogether, or to make apertures in it, as she pleases. It appears to me that this view of the case is correct; indeed, if the exclusive right of property is conceded to the defendant, it seems to be a necessary consequence; and the only limitations placed upon this right of property, in the Code, are those having reference to the right of making such a wall common, and to the restricted use of it after it is made common."

These views, which led the court below to give judgment for the defendant, are supported by the text of the Code.***

It follows that, until the plaintiff pays the defendant one-half the cost of the wall it cannot be a wall in common, but remains the exclusive property of the defendant, though resting one half upon the plaintiffs land.

And it being the exclusive property of the defendant, it follows that she may open or shut apertures in it, at her pleasure, subject only to the police regulations of the city.

In this she exercises not a right of servitude, but a right of property.

But the plaintiff says that the judgment should, at least, be so amended as to recognize his right to shut the apertures by erecting a wall or enclosure opposite to them.

By the same right that the defendant builds a wall with apertures, undoubtedly the plaintiff may build one facing it without apertures, if it shall so please him. *"In suo pariete potest quisfenestrosfucere vicino etiam invito; vicinus contra aedificando eos obscurare potest."*

But, as this right of the plaintiff is not put in controversy by the pleadings, so it is not barred by the judgment. Judgment affirmed.

4. ENCLOSED ESTATES
Civil Code arts. 689-696
La. R.S. 9:1254

a. The "Article 689" Right of Passage

ROCKHOLT v. KEATY 256 La.
629,237 So. 2d 663 (1970)

BARHAM, J. In this suit plaintiffs seek a right of passage over the defendant's property for their land which became landlocked as a result of an expropriation for Interstate 12 in East Baton Rouge Parish by the State of Louisiana through the Department of Highways. The plaintiffs originally owned a 35.521-acre tract, but after the expropriation in full ownership of a 300-foot strip through the tract, their property was left in two separated segments, a southern portion of 10.308 acres and a northern portion of 17.954 acres. It is the northern portion of the property which is involved in this litigation. This tract, trapezoidal in shape, is surrounded on the west by the lands of the defendant and by Keaty Place Subdivision, on the north by Drusilla Place Subdivision, on the east by the land of Coastal Rentals Corporation, and on the south by the state highway, Interstate 12. (See map which is our composite, not drawn to scale, of maps contained in the transcript.)

Relying upon Civil Code Articles 699 [Revised C.C. arts. 689, 691] et seq., the plaintiffs alleged that their property was enclosed, and that they were entitled to a right of passage over the estate of their neighbor, the defendant Thomas S. Keaty, to the nearest public road. In their petition they recognized that Interstate 12 is the public road nearest to their property, but because it was a controlled-access highway, part of the National System of Interstate and Defense Highways, access to it had been denied in accordance with state and federal law. The right of passage sought is approximately 50 feet in width and crosses defendant's land at the corner bordering Interstate 12. This passage would give access not upon a public road but only to other property of plaintiffs at a point about 746 feet from Drusilla Drive, a public road. At the time of the filing of this suit there was no road on this other property to Drusilla Drive. However, this route is urged by plaintiffs to be the "shortest legally permissible and feasible passage to a public road" when cost, convenience, and practicality are considered.

The exception of no cause of action and the motion for summary judgment filed by defendant were sustained by the district court, and plaintiffs' suit was dismissed. On appeal taken by the plaintiffs the Court of Appeal affirmed the judgment of the district court. 226 So. 2d 76. Both courts held that Article 699 [Revised C.C. arts. 689, 691] of the Code is not applicable. They concluded that property is not "enclosed" within the meaning of the article when that property borders a highway, even though the highway is access controlled and allows neither ingress or egress. Both courts cited and relied upon the case of English Realty Company, Inc., v. Meyer, 228 La. 423, 82 So. 2d 698 (1955).

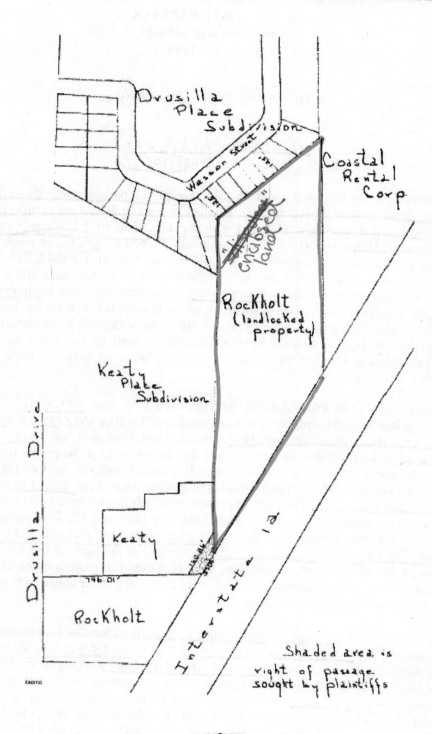

Article 699 [Revised C.C. arts. 689, 691] of our Civil Code grants private rights of way for roads of necessity.**

This article and its predecessors in our earlier Codes are based upon Code Napoleon Article 682. In 1881, however, the French article was amended to allow a right of passage also to the owner of an estate whose way to the public road was insufficient for the exploitation of his land. Planiol makes the following comment about the 1881 amendment:

> "In order to solve certain difficulties created by the original draft of the law, the 1881 law made these two rulings: (1) An estate must be deemed to be enclosed, not only when it has no issue upon the public road, but if it has merely an insufficient issue *** (2) The exploitation of the heritage of which the old law spoke must be deemed to apply to industrial exploitation as well as agricultural exploitation. These two solutions were however generally accepted before 1881." 1 Pt. 2 Planiol, Traite Elementaire de Droit Civil (Transl. La.State Law Institute, 1959), § 2920.

Planiol's comment is important for recognizing that the granting of the right of passage to enclosed estates for insufficient ingress and egress, as well as for no ingress and egress, was allowed prior to the 1881 amendment — that is, under the parent article of our Article 699 [Revised C.C. arts. 689, 691]. See 2 Fuzier-Herman, Code Civil Annote (1936), annotation under Article 682, pp. 208-209, cases Nos. 68, 71,72,79, 81, and 82.

Article 699 [Revised C.C. arts. 689,691] of our Civil Code has also been amended, but for a different purpose. In 1916 the article was changed to include right of passage for lack of access to railroads, tramroads, or water courses and the right to build a railroad or tramroad as well as a road. The amendment also added: "*** according to circumstances and as the exigencies of the case may acquire [require]." The purpose of this amendment was to allow construction of the proper facility needed in a particular case according to the circumstances and the exigencies of the case.

It is apparent that the French under their provision for passage from enclosed estates have from the beginning decided each case under its particular circumstances and have refused to reach for absolute legal pronouncements which would effect a restricted application of the law. We cannot be blind to the great change in the nature of land in our country and the needs of the people in regard to land since the adoption of our original provision. The open country and estates then in existence have rapidly disappeared, and the problems of access to estates for full utilization of them have become more complex.

Additionally, estates surrounding enclosed lands may by the very nature and method of their development pose problems in affording access to the enclosed lands not foreseen or contemplated by the adopters of the Code article. The situation which brings this case to our attention — that is, the development of public roads, freeways, and expressways which necessarily deny access to abutting property owners — is of recent vintage.

Although the English Realty Company case said that the State had no right to deny abutting property owner's access to a highway, it is now legislatively well settled that the State or its political subdivisions may deny such property owners access to certain public roads. See La. R.S. 48:301 et seq.; 23 U.S.C. 111. We also distinguish that case from the matter before us. The English Realty case cannot extend beyond the holding applicable to its particular facts. There the plaintiff purchased property *after* the building of an overpass and with knowledge of the limited accessibility afforded a portion of his property because of the highway construction. He then sold off various parcels of land until the remaining portion did not have adequate ingress and egress for a trucking business. The court in the English Realty case refused to let the plaintiff benefit from Article 699 [Revised C.C. arts. 689, 691], holding that the enclosure was "...not a direct consequence of the location of the land but of the act of the party seeking the relief."

In the instant case plaintiffs' property is enclosed by reason of the superior power of the State to expropriate property and to build non-access highways along and through the property of individuals. Our interpretation of Article 699 [Revised C.C. arts. 689, 691] leads us to the conclusion that plaintiffs' property has become "enclosed" within the contemplation of the article because of expropriation and the construction of a non-access public road.

The argument is made that the compensation paid by the Highway Department in the expropriation suit fully compensated plaintiffs for their loss of ingress and egress, and that they should not be entitled to invoke Article 699 [Revised C.C. arts. 689, 691]. The loss of access was noted by the court in the expropriation suit, and some compensation for it was included in the amount awarded. Although we are not able to determine whether the award was for full compensation as though the parcel was totally landlocked forever, such a determination is not necessary. We are of the opinion that public policy would dictate that such land as is here involved, located in a desirable and strategic area, should not be taken out of use and commerce.

While Article 699 [Revised C.C. arts. 689, 691] has been generally accepted as designed to benefit the landowner so he could produce profit for himself and obtain full utility of his land, it must now be deemed also to offer protection of public interest. As land becomes less available, more necessary for public habitation, use, and support, it would run contrary to public policy to encourage land locking of such a valuable asset and forever removing it from commerce and from public as well as private benefit.

We have found enclosures as required by Article 699 [Revised C.C. arts. 689, 691], and we must now determine whether the particular relief for passage sought by these plaintiffs is granted by law. The nature of the passage is governed "...according to circumstances and as the exigencies of the case may acquire [require]." The right of passage granted is to "the nearest public road," subject to indemnification for damages occasioned to the neighbor or neighbors. Article 700 [Revised C.C. art. 692] provides:

"The owner of the estate, which is surrounded by other lands, has no right to exact the right of passage from *which of his neighbors he chooses.*

"The passage shall be generally taken on the side where the distance is the shortest from the enclosed estate to the public road.

"Nevertheless, it shall be fixed in the place least injurious to the person on whose estate the passage is granted." (Emphasis supplied.)

The passage sought by the plaintiffs here is not to a public road but to other land of the plaintiffs on which there is no public road. The record reflects that there are numerous points of abutment where passage to a public road may be obtained, the shortest being a distance of approximately 125 feet. Plaintiffs contend that these latter properties are subject to building restrictions which would negate the possibility of obtaining passage across them, and that therefore the route here sought is the "legally" shortest and most feasible. We are not impressed with this contention. These restrictions alone would not be controlling of a landowner's right to obtain passage from enclosed land across neighboring property. We find (1) that plaintiffs do not seek passage to a pubic road as required by the Code and (2) that there are shorter, more direct, and more feasible routes of passage to public roads.

Under the express language of Civil Code Article 700 [Revised C.C. art. 692] plaintiffs are not entitled to the relief sought against this defendant. The plaintiffs' right in regard to passage over the property of other abutting landowners is not before us and must await adjudication in a suit to which these others are parties.

The judgments of the Court of Appeal and the district court are affirmed, but for the above stated reasons.

DICKERSON v. COON
71 So. 3d 1135 (La. App. 2d Cir. 2011)

STEWART, J. The defendant, Joan Terry Coon, individually and as Independent Executrix of the Succession of Henson S. Coon, Jr. (hereafter "Coon"), appeals a judgment granting a right of passage in favor of the plaintiffs, Steven Ralph Dickerson and Marcia Jeanette Simmering Dickerson (referred to jointly as "Dickerson"). Coon asserts that the trial court committed manifest error in placing the servitude along the shortest route and in failing to award damages. We find no manifest error by the trial court in fixing the servitude along the shortest route, but we do find that the trial court erred in failing to award damages for the value of the timber that will have to be removed from Coon's land.

FACTS

On March 11, 2008, Dickerson filed a petition seeking a right of passage for an enclosed estate described as follows:

> The Southwest Quarter of Northeast Quarter, Section 28, Township 17 North, Range 1 East, Ouachita Parish, Louisiana, containing 40 acres, more or less.

The nearest public road is Guyton Loop Road, part of which is located on neighboring property owned by Coon and described as:

> The Northeast Quarter of Southwest Quarter and Northwest Quarter of Southeast Quarter, Section 28, Township 17 North, Range 1 East, Ouachita Parish, Louisiana.

Dickerson asked that the right of passage be located along an existing logging road that begins at Guyton Loop Road and runs through Coon's land north of the road up to the southwest corner of his land. Alternatively, Dickerson asked the court to select the shortest route from Guyton Loop Road to the southwest corner of his property.

Dickerson attached to the petition plats and surveys detailing a 15–foot wide servitude over both the logging road and the shortest route. These two routes are in the same general area of the Coon property. According to calculations based on the attachments, the distance along the logging road is 2,433.67 feet, and the route contains 0.272 acres. The distance along the shortest route is 1,433.96 feet and contains 0.242 acres.

In answer, Coon asserted that the area of the logging road is the highest point of elevation on his land. He claimed that establishing a right of passage along the logging road would bisect the property and disturb the hunting club, which leases the acreage. Coon asserted that his acreage is used to grow timber, whereas the Dickerson acreage is at a lower elevation, subject to frequent flooding, and best described as a marsh for most of the year. Coon proposed an alternative right of passage along the north boundary of his westerly tract. Coon asserted that the boundary route would provide access to Dickerson's marshy acreage without bisecting his best land or disturbing the hunting club. Dickerson had previously rejected this route.

The main issues at trial concerned the location of the right of passage and damages, if any. That the Coon property was the servient estate and owed a right of passage for the benefit of Dickerson's enclosed estate was not disputed. The trial court recognized three possible options for location of the right of passage: (1) the shortest route; (2) the existing logging road; and (3) the border or west side/north side route proposed by Coon. After hearing the evidence and viewing the properties and areas of the proposed routes in person, the trial court ordered that the right of passage be fixed along the shortest route. The trial court found that the other two options had "pros and cons of equal weight" but that the first option, the shortest route, was clearly in line with the codal provisions governing rights of passage.

Judgment was rendered September 22, 2010, granting Dickerson the right of passage across the shortest route on Coon's land from Guyton Loop Road to the southwest corner of Dickerson's enclosed estate. The judgment did not mention any award of damages to Coon. Each party was ordered to bear its own costs and pay one-half the court costs.

Mr. Henson S. Coon, Jr., died on July 28, 2010. For purposes of the appeal, his wife, Joan Terry Coon, was appointed Independent Executrix for his succession and recognized as the defendant in lieu of the deceased.

DISCUSSION

Location of the Right of Passage

***La. C.C. art. 689 permits the owner of an estate with no access to a public road to claim a right of passage over neighboring property to the nearest public road. The owner of the enclosed estate "is bound to indemnify his neighbor for the damage he may occasion." Id.

La. C.C. art. 692, which governs location of the right of passage, instructs that the owner of the enclosed estate may not demand a right of passage at the location of his choice. Rather, it "generally shall be taken along the shortest route from the enclosed estate to the public road at the location least injurious to the intervening lands." La. C.C. art. 692.

The use of "generally" in La. C.C. art. 692 indicates that there are exceptions to the shortest route requirement. The circumstances of each case will determine the location of the servitude. *Anderton v. Akin*, 493 So.2d 795, 797 (La.App. 2d Cir.1986), writ denied, 497 So.2d 1014 (La.1986). Upon determining which estate will be burdened with the right of passage, courts usually engage in a balancing test to determine where on the servient estate the right of passage should be located. (Citations omitted.)

However, departure from the general rule requiring location of the right of passage along the shortest route "must be supported by weighty considerations." A.N. Yiannopoulos, 4 La. Civ. Law Treatise, Predial Servitudes § 97, (3d Ed.2004). While courts will normally grant a right of passage that is least injurious to the servient estate, other factors such as distance, degree of injury to the servient estate, practicability, and cost weigh in the decision of where to locate the right of passage. Id.

Instruction on fixing the right of passage is found in *Anderton*, 493 So.2d at 798, which explains that while the right of passage should be fixed at the point least injurious to the servient estate, the matter of its location is not to be left to the "caprice or option" of the party who must grant the servitude. The court must also be mindful of the rights that the law affords the dominant estate owner. As such, a right of passage that is "extremely circuitous, impracticable, and expensive" should not be selected because it is less burdensome to the servient estate owner. *Anderton*, supra, citing *Wells v. Anglade*, 23

So.2d 469 (La.App. 1st Cir.1945), citing *Littlejohn v. Cox*, 15 La.Ann. 67 (La.1860).

Coon argues that the trial court erred in fixing the passage along the shortest route rather than along the boundary route, which would be least injurious. Coon asserts that the evidence proves that both the logging road and the shortest route would be injurious. Both routes would divide the 55 acres north of Guyton Loop Road into about a 45–acre tract east of the servitude and a 10–acre tract west of the servitude. Also, either route would bisect the 55 acres at its crown (area of highest elevation), which Coon considers a prime area for building a house.

The possibility that grandchildren might one day build a house on the property and the concern that the passage dividing the property might prevent them from doing so was expressed by the defendants' son, Henson S. Coon, III, ("Henson") in his testimony and by the defendant, Henson S. Coon, Jr., ("Mr. Coon") in his deposition, which was introduced into evidence in lieu of his testifying. Coon's expert appraiser, A.J. Burns, Jr., agreed that fixing the passage along the shortest route or the logging road would bisect the property and diminish that area's desirability as a house site.

In his deposition, Mr. Coon stated that he inherited the land from his father, had owned it for 50 years, had harvested timber, and had leased it to a hunting club for the last 17 years. He recalled that when his father purchased the property, there had been a house site in the area of the logging road. His son Henson believed there may have been a home on the property about 100 years ago. Mr. Coon also recalled that the logging road was used for a while to access an oil well on the property. About five years before Dickerson bought the land, Mr. Coon had allowed a lumber company that was harvesting timber from what is now Dickerson's land to use the logging road.

We are not persuaded by the argument that the shortest route is injurious to Coon's land because it divides the 55 acres north of Guyton Loop Road at its crown and might prevent the use of that area as a home site. Coon has owned the property for over 50 years without residential development on it. There are no plans for future development. Mr. Coon and Henson merely expressed the desire that descendants might one day build a house on the property. If the servitude interferes with any future development, the servient estate has the right to demand relocation of the servitude to a more convenient location at his expense. La. C.C. art. 695. Also, nothing in the record shows that a passage along the shortest route would interfere with the hunting club which leases the Coon property.

Steven Dickerson testified that he purchased his property, which consists of 25 acres of wetland and 15 acres of timberland, in March 2008 for recreational purposes and for a timber investment. He estimated that he would need access to the property once per week to transport tools and materials either by foot, utility vehicle, or a light truck. He has no plans to erect a permanent structure or run utilities to the property. He requested the logging road because it was comparable to the shortest route, would require limited work to make passable, and no timber would have to be cleared. However, he had no strong objection to the shortest route even though it would require him to clear timber and bring in dirt to make a passage. He explained that the boundary route would require him to clear even more timber, to bring in even more dirt, and to contract engineering work to address an area where water collects along the route.

Darryl James Rayner, Jr., a dirt contractor and owner of R & R Dirt, L.L.C., testified as an expert in road maintenance and construction on behalf of Dickerson. Rayner prepared cost estimates for constructing a passable 15–foot wide servitude along the three proposed routes. Rayner testified that it would cost $997.50 to make the existing logging road passable and would require about 45 cubic yards of dirt to fill holes and shape the roadway. Construction of a passable roadway along the shortest route would cost $4,457.50, for excavation work, installation of a drainage pipe, and dirt work to fill the area of the roadway. Construction of a passable roadway along the Coon boundary route would cost $11,220.00, and would require the setting of two drainage pipes, excavation work, and 650 cubic yards of dirt for spreading and filling along the passage.

Gregory Hebert, a professional forester, testified as an expert in timber on behalf of Dickerson and conducted a timber assessment for the shortest route and the boundary route. He did not assess the area of the logging road because he did not expect there would be a need to remove much timber in an area where a passage already existed. He determined the value of the timber along the boundary route to be $643.60, and the value of the timber along the shortest route to be $291.43.

Considering cost and practicability, this court, if sitting as the trier of fact, may have selected the existing logging road which historically had been used as a passage and is in close proximity to the shortest route. However, we cannot conclude that the trial court's selection of the shortest route is unreasonable or that reversal is warranted. The law favors the shortest route, and departure from the general rule favoring the shortest route is not supported by "weighty considerations." The shortest route will provide direct access from the Dickerson's tract to the nearest public road. Making a passable roadway along the shortest route will involve considerably less expense than doing so along Coon's proposed boundary route. From our review of the record, we find the fixing of the right of passage along the shortest route to be neither manifestly erroneous nor clearly wrong.

Damages

Coon also argues that the trial court erred in failing to address and award damages. Coon seeks damages totaling $16,891.43 for a servitude along the shortest route.

The trial court's judgment is silent as to the issue of damages. When a judgment is silent as to a party's claim or demand, it is presumed that the trial court denied the relief sought. *TSC, Inc. v. Bossier Parish Police Jury*, 38,717 (La.App.2d Cir.7/14/04), 878 So.2d 880. Based on this principle of law, we find that the absence of any mention of damages in the judgment equates to a denial of damages.

La. C.C. art. 689 provides that the owner of an enclosed estate who claims a right of passage over neighboring property is "bound to indemnify his neighbor for the damage he may occasion." This provision recognizes that the owner of the servient estate "may" receive "damage" requiring indemnification by the owner of the dominant estate. *Greenway v. Wailes*, 41,412, p. 12 (La.App.2d Cir.8/1/06), 936 So.2d 296, 303. The Greenway opinion explains that "damage" under La. C.C. art. 689 does not mean compensation based on the appraised value of the servient property as though the fixing of the right of passage is an expropriation or taking of the property. The right of passage is a legal servitude, a limitation on ownership established by law for the benefit of the general public or particular persons. La. C.C. art. 659. This limitation on ownership is for the "common utility" of adjacent properties and has been part of this state's policy regarding ownership of land since statehood. *Greenway*, supra, at 41,412, p. 12, 936 So.2d at 303, and provisions cited therein. Moreover, the right of passage for the enclosed estate "has been a limitation on ownership of immovables since our earliest civil code." Id.

The burden is on the owner of the servient estate to prove the amount of damage resulting from the servitude of passage. *Bailey v. McNeely*, 2005–629 (La.App.3d Cir.12/30/05), 918 So.2d 1124. Burns, Coon's expert real estate appraiser, testified as to the damages he believed would be due for the "taking" or use of the right of passage. He valued the right of passage at $2,000 based on comparable sales of "rye grass and easements" and what he learned from talking to others who had negotiated such things. Next, he determined that the 55–acre tract, which he valued at $146,000, would suffer a 10 percent diminution in value when burdened with the right of passage. Thus, he assessed damages in the amount of $14,600. He likened these damages to severance damages. Burns believed that a right of passage along the shortest route, or even the logging road, would diminish the desirability of the area for building a house. Based on Burns' testimony and the timber value attributed to the shortest route by Dickerson's timber expert, Coon seeks damages in the amount of $16,891.43.

Dickerson's expert appraiser, Richard K. Moore, could not come up with any damages or calculate any loss to Coon's property from use of a right of passage along the shortest route, or even the logging route. He believed there to be enough acreage in the area of the crown to have a home site set back from the roadway. Thus, any damage from use of the right of passage would be minimal.

When expert testimony differs, the trial court must determine the more credible evidence. *ScenicLand Const. Co., LLC v. St. Francis Medical Center, Inc.*, 41,147 (La.App.2d Cir.7/26/06), 936 So.2d 247. The effect and weight to be given to expert testimony depends on the underlying facts and rests within the broad discretion of the trial court. Id. In deciding to accept the opinion of one expert and reject the opinion of another expert, the trial court can virtually never be manifestly erroneous. Id.; *Fox v. Fox*, 97–1914 (La.App.1st Cir.11/6/98), 727 So.2d 514, writ denied, 99–0265 (La.3/19/99), 740 So.2d 119.

By denying damages, the trial court must have accepted the expert appraisal testimony offered by Moore and rejected Burns' testimony. This finding is supported by *Greenway*, supra. Burns' assessment of damages was based on his view of the right of passage as a taking for which compensation is due rather than as the exercise of a limitation on ownership that already burdened Coon's property. The trial court could have reasonably credited Moore's opinion that there would be sufficient acreage for both a homesite and roadway in the area of the shortest route and that there would be no damage resulting from use of the right of passage. Also, Burns improperly valued the right of way by comparison with sales of easements. La. C.C. art. 689 refers to indemnification for damages that may be occasioned; it does not provide for compensation to the owner of the servient estate for the right of passage.

Though we find no error in the trial court's failure to award damages based on the testimony of Coon's appraiser, we do find that the record establishes damages in the amount of $291.43 based on the value of the timber that will have to be removed from the area of the servitude. We find that this amount, $291.43, should have been awarded to Coon, and amend the trial court's judgment accordingly.

CONCLUSION

For the reasons explained, we affirm the judgment of the trial court fixing the servitude of passage along the shortest route. We amend the judgment to award damages of $291.43 for the removal of timber in the area of the passage. Each party is to bear his own costs on appeal. Amended in part, and affirmed as amended.

b. The "Article 694" Right of Passage

PATIN v. RICHARD 291 So. 2d 879
(La. App. 3d Cir. 1974)

WATSON, J. Plaintiff, Austin J. Patin, is the owner of a camp in the community of Holly Beach, Cameron Parish, Louisiana. Mr. Patin's camp is located on a lot measuring 50' wide and 135' deep. His camp faces the Gulf of Mexico on the south and is bordered on the north by the property of defendant, Dennis S. Richard. To the north of Mr. Richard's property is the property of Harold Savoie. Both Mr. Richard and Mr. Savoie also have camps on their property. Mr. Savoie's property is 50' wide and 27 1/2' deep. It is bordered on the north by the nearest public road, Louisiana Highway 92, Johnson's Bayou Road. All three property owners are bordered on the east by the property of Mr. A.J. (Bebe) Reaux, whose property extends from the highway to the Gulf. To the west of the three property owners is a strip of land owned by Mr. Richard, which runs between the highway and the Gulf. On this property are three camps which Mr. Richard rents.

These three camps are built close to the eastern property line leaving about 18' between them and the camp that Mr. Richard uses personally. The western part of Mr. Savoie's property has been used by Mr. Richard to gain access to his personal camp. Plaintiff Patin was also in the habit of using the western part of Mr. Savoie's property and the western part of Mr. Richard's property to obtain access to his camp. This arrangement existed for many years until the Richards and the Patins became involved in a series of disputes involving the Patins or their guests blocking the Richard's driveway. Two employees of the Cameron Parish Sheriffs department were called on several occasions to move cars from the Richard's driveway. Mr. Richard then built a fence on the southern boundary of this property cutting off Mr. Patin's customary access to his camp. There is a beach road to the south of Mr. Patin's property, but it is often under water and generally does not offer satisfactory passage for vehicles.

After Mr. Richard constructed his fence, plaintiff Patin filed this suit alleging that his camp property is an enclosed estate; that the shortest and most direct route from his enclosed estate to a public road is across the property of defendant Richard; and that he and his ancestors in title have used a driveway across defendant Richard's land in excess of 35 years. He asked that he be granted right of passage and that the amount of the damage caused by the servitude to defendant Richard be fixed.

The trial court, after hearing the witnesses and viewing the property in question, denied plaintiff the servitude requested and dismissed his suit. The trial court found that the right of passage requested would seriously inconvenience Mr. Richard in the use and enjoyment of his property. Further, the trial court pointed out that it was impossible to grant a passage to the public road, since such a passage would have to cross Mr. Savoie's property as well as that of Mr. Richard and Mr. Savoie was not made a party to the suit. The trial court also stated that plaintiff could use the adjoining property of Mr. Reaux (his brother-in-law) almost as easily as that of defendant Richard. Mr. Patin has in fact been using this property to gain access to his camp during these proceedings. The court stated in its written reasons for judgment that the right of passage requested .... would restrict defendant's right to the use and enjoyment of his own property. The use of the Reaux property "... would create a far less burdensome imposition upon that owner with no measurable difference in convenience as far as plaintiff is concerned."

The trial court's description of the properties (stipulated to be correct by the parties) and the trial court's sketch of the area in question are reproduced here as they appear at TR. 41 and 42. [description omitted].

It was stipulated between the parties that their property was owned by a common ancestor in 1949. When land is enclosed as a result of sale or partition, C.C. art. 701 [Revised C.C. art. 694] applies.

The trial court did not apply this article of the code "...because from the descriptions themselves it is obvious that all the property that surrounds plaintiff has a common ancestry. Whatever obligation is owed under Article 701 [Revised C.C. art. 694] by any lot adjacent to plaintiffs is owed equally by all the other adjacent lots," (TR. 44-45).

Plaintiff Patin has appealed from the adverse judgment of the trial court, alleging that the trial court erred in failing to grant him a servitude of passage over the already existing driveway leading from the nearest public road to his enclosed estate. Plaintiff also argues in brief that it was not necessary to name Mr. Savoie as a party defendant, because Mr. Savoie has not objected to plaintiff passing over his land and making him a party defendant would be a vain and useless act.

We believe that the trial court's interpretation of C.C. art. 701 [Revised C.C. art. 694] does not take into account the phrase "upon which the right of passage was before exercised". This phrase indicates that the land which owes the servitude is that upon which it has existed in the past. Mr. Savoie, an attorney in Lafayette, stated in his disposition, introduced into evidence by plaintiff, that the western side of his property and the western side of Mr. Richard's property had been used as a passage by "whoever the owners were at different periods of time," (TR. 22). They all used the western side or followed the western line of that lot and they would back and park on the south side of their various camps to leave the distance between their camp and the fence as an access to the rear property and not to block whoever was at the end." (TR. 23, 24). He also stated that his property, that of Mr. Richard and that of Mr. Patin were all at one time part of a tract 50' wide and 230' deep owned by the Constantin family, and that all three lots were acquired from this family at about the same time.

We are convinced that in the instant case a predial servitude of passage exists as to plaintiffs property through the operation of C.C. art. 701 [Revised C.C. art. 694]. The burdened estates are those of Mr. Savoie and defendant Richard. All three of these owners have been aware of the existence and exercise of this servitude of passage. Defendant Richard has made no allegation of prescription for nonuse. It is noteworthy that, although Mr. Richard denies plaintiff a right of passage on his land, he himself claims a right of passage on the land of Mr. Savoie; defendant Richard, like plaintiff Patin, having an enclosed estate.

An examination of Mr. Richard's deed, introduced into evidence as P-8, at TR. 13 and 14 shows that the right to pass or right-of-way that he claims is not in his deed. His right of passage, like that of plaintiff Patin, exists only through the operation of C.C. art. 701 [Revised C.C. art. 694]. What defendant Richard denies to plaintiff he claims himself from Mr. Savoie; any right of passage belonging to defendant Richard would belong equally to plaintiff.

The trial court felt that Mr. Savoie was a necessary party to this suit. Since Mr. Savoie has always recognized the right of passage of his two neighbors to the south, it would be a pointless thing to make him a party to this suit. It would cause Mr. Savoie trouble and expense to no purpose and might add another brand to the flame of contention between these neighbors. Since this servitude already exists as a matter of law, the only one who should be a necessary party is the one who contests the servitude and that is defendant Richard.

Further, when Mr. Richard bought his land the right of passage existed and he was aware of it. As he stated, he would not have bought the property if it had not had a right of way across Mr. Savoie's land and the Patins were using the right of way across his land "... since I bought that land." (TR. 155). It is not a case of his property being burdened with a right of way of which he was unaware when he acquired it.

We realize that the record shows some lack of cooperation by the Patins and their guests. Recognizing that plaintiff has a right of passage under C.C. art. 701 [Revised C.C. art. 694] does not give him the right to block Mr. Richard's driveway and otherwise hinder Mr. Richard's enjoyment of his property. If the Patins do not refrain in the future from such activities, defendant Richard could ask that the location of the servitude be changed as provided by C.C. art. 703 [Revised C.C. art. 695] in order to make it less inconvenient to him.

It is necessary to reverse the judgment of the trial court and to recognize a passage. Bandelin v. Clark, 7 La. App. 64 (La. App. 1 Cir. 1927). The Civil Code indicates that a way must be provided for both pedestrian and vehicular passage. C.C. art. 702 [Revised C.C. art. 690]; Bourg v. Audubon Park Commission for City of New Orleans, *supra*. Defendant's lot is small and we believe the passage should be as narrow as could be safely traversed by one automobile. The legal maximum width of an automobile in this state is 96 inches (or eight feet). R.S. 32:381. We conclude that a passage of twelve feet would be reasonable under the circumstances. Reversed and rendered.

DOMENGEAUX, J. (dissenting). I agree with the majority as to its holding with regard to the plaintiff Austin Patin being entitled to a right of passage over the estate of his neighbor, the defendant Dennis Richard, but respectfully disagree as to the applicability of C.C. Article 701 [Revised C.C. art. 694] to the facts of the case.

In my opinion Civil Code Article 701 [Revised C.C. art. 694] is clear and should be read in context with the preceding Articles 699 and 700 [Revised C.C. arts. 689, 691, 692], all under the subsection of the Code dealing with the servitude of the right of passage and of way which is imposed by law.

Article 699 [Revised C.C. arts. 689, 691] states that the owner of an enclosed estate may claim the right of passage on the estate of his neighbor(s) to the *nearest* public road, etc. Article 700 [Revised C.C. art. 692] further indicates that the passage theretofore mentioned in Article 699 [Revised C.C. arts. 689, 691] should generally be taken on the side of the subservient estate where the distance is the *shortest* from the enclosed estate to the public road, but that nevertheless, it should be fixed in the place least injurious to the owner of the estate owing the servitude.

Article 701 [Revised C.C. art. 694], in my opinion, gives a limited exception to this rule that the right of passage is to be suffered by the neighboring estate which affords the shortest and most direct route to a public road. Under Article 701 [Revised C.C. art. 694] the subservient land owner is bound to furnish a *gratuitous* passage, but only when the requisites of the article are met. First, there must be a land owner, etc. who has sold, etc. a portion of his estate which in so doing encloses that sold portion with no way to a public road. Second, the landowner must have *reserved a remaining portion* of the land (third) over which a right of passage had before been exercised. See Brown v. Terry, 103 So. 2d 541 (La. App. 1st Cir. 1958); Bourg v. Audubon Park Commission for City of New Orleans, 89 So. 2d 676 (La.App.Orl. Cir. 1955).

None of the requisites are present under the factual situation in our case. Herein, the plaintiff Austin Patin, the defendant Dennis Richard, and Harold Savoie are owners of adjacent lots at Holly Beach in Cameron Parish which were once a single tract of land owned by a person named Constantin. At a common sale in 1949 Constantin disposed of the lots to (a) Lawrence Savoie, who sold it to his son Harold in 1957, (b) Clarence Savoie, a cousin of Lawrence Savoie and ancestor in title through several buyers finally to the defendant Richard by sale in 1970, and (c) Paul Miller, ancestor in title to plaintiff Patin by sale in 1967. Camps were built on the properties as far back as 1949 with a passageway along the western edge of said lots which had been used by the camp occupants to get to the nearest public road from that date until the present dispute, wherein defendant Richard built a fence along the southern boundary of his property thereby cutting off plaintiffs customary access to his camp. Thus it was only after a common sale to the three aforementioned parties that any of the lots became enclosed and a right of passage was exercised. Therefore, I am of the opinion that Article 701 [Revised C.C. art. 694] is inapplicable.

In addition, I respectfully suggest that the distinction made by the majority between Civil Code Article 701 [Revised C.C. art. 694] and Articles 699 and 700 [Revised C.C. arts. 689, 692] [i.e. that Articles 699 and 700 are concerned with fixing a right of passage where there has been none before, while Article 701 [Revised C.C. art. 694] concerns itself where a passage has existed before] is without merit.

I agree, as aforementioned, that Article 701 [Revised C.C. art. 694] is applicable only where a theretofore right of passage had existed, in addition to the other two requisites. But a perusal of the jurisprudence indicates to this writer that the following cases have applied Articles 699 and 700 [Revised C.C. arts. 689, 692] in establishing a right of passage over a *theretofore used* right of way. Pittman v. Marshall, 104 So. 2d 230 (La. App. 2d Cir. 1958), Martini v. Cowart, 23 So. 2d 655 (La. App. 2d Cir. 1945).

However, to reiterate, I am in complete agreement that plaintiff should be granted a right of passage over those land(s) which will afford the shortest route to a public road. C.C. Arts. 699, 700 [Revised C.C. arts. 689, 692]; see also Vermilion Parish School Board v. Broussard, 263 La. 1104, 270 So. 2d 523 (1972); Mays v. Rives, 267 So. 2d 792 (La. App. 2d Cir. 1972). But this should be determined under Articles 699 and 700 [Revised C.C. arts. 689, 692] and the plaintiff is obliged to indemnify his neighbor(s) in proportion to the damage sustained.

Although without so holding, the trial judge concluded plaintiff could use the adjoining property of his neighbor, A.J. Reaux (not made a party defendant) almost as easily as that of defendant, and that such use would create less of an imposition upon Reaux than on the defendant. However, admittedly, the shortest route by about 35 or 40 feet is over defendant Richard's land as well as that of Harold Savoie. In addition said passageway has been used for almost a quarter of a century. I do not interpret Articles 699 and 700 [Revised C.C. arts. 689, 692] or the jurisprudence thereon to mean, as apparently the trial judge concluded, that the passageway shall be fixed upon the person's land whom will be least injured or inconvenienced by the fixing. The articles clearly reflect that it is to be fixed upon the estate over which the distance is shortest to the public road. It is then that the question of the least injurious place comes into consideration. See C.C. Art. 700 [Revised C.C. art. 692].

But as noted by the trial judge, passage cannot in fact be granted to the nearest public road inasmuch as Harold Savoie was not made a party to this suit. See Vermilion Parish School Board v. Broussard, *supra;* Rockholt v. Keaty, 256 La. 629, 237 So. 2d 663 (1970). Without Savoie being made a party all we could grant is a passage to the nearest *neighbor* which is not provided for in the aforementioned articles. However, it is clear from the record that Harold Savoie is very agreeable to the continued use of the passage way over the western edge of his lot. Therefore I think it appropriate to remand the case first so as to allow Savoie to be made a party hereto, and also with instructions to the district judge to fix the right of passage and its width; (from a reading of the articles, jurisprudence related thereto, and the facts herein, the only place where the passageway could be fixed is where it has been for the past 22 or 23 years) and to set damages occasioned by Richard and Savoie.

c. The "Article 693" Exception

LeBLANC v. THIBODEAUX
615 So. 2d 295 (La. 1993)

CALOGERO, C.J. We granted a Writ of Review in this case to determine whether C.C. article 689 applies (enclosed estate has right of passage over neighboring property) when an estate becomes enclosed as a result of an act of partition, and a right of passage reserved in the act is not utilized thereafter for more than ten years.

The case involves a 72 arpent tract of marsh land that was once part of a single larger tract, owned by Charles Dugas and Edmonia Thibodeaux. In 1929, after the deaths of both Dugas and Thibodeaux, their five children partitioned the single tract of land except for the part that constituted the 72 arpent tract. The five children continued to hold the latter in indivision. The act of partition granted a right of passage from the 72 arpent tract over land which in the partition went to two of the five children, Emma and Eva Dugas.

The district court found that the conventional servitute had prescribed. The LeBlancs did not appeal that finding. In a separate proceeding instituted by the LeBlancs against Thibodeaux, the trial judge addressed the issue of whether the LeBlancs had an enforceable claim to a legal right of passage. He first determined that the LeBlancs were not entitled to a gratuitous right of passage under C.C. art. 694. He found that because the tract "was never partitioned and remains to this day in indivision," it "was never alienated by sale, exchange, or otherwise," and furthermore "this right of passage was [not] exercised prior to the 1929 partition or subsequently." In effect, the trial judge found that the tract was not alienated property which had become enclosed because of the partition, but rather property which had been owned in indivision by the five co-owners both before and after the act of partition.

The trial judge nonetheless found that the LeBlancs were entitled to a right of way under C.C. art. 689, which provides that the owner of an estate with no access to a public road may claim a right of passage over neighboring property to the nearest public road by indemnifying his neighbor for the damages the right of passage may occasion. Furthermore, although there was a conventional servitude granted in the 1929 act of partition, this did not change the fact that the property, after 1929, had no natural access to a public road and had therefore become enclosed in that year. The enclosed property was thus entitled to a C.C. art. 689 legal servitude following the partition.

The trial judge determined that the LeBlancs' right to claim passage over neighboring land was unaffected by the fact that the act of partition also created a conventional right of passage (later lost through non-use). The judge further determined that the 1929 right of passage had never been used. What's more, the LeBlancs and their ancestors had not committed any voluntary act or omission, distinct from the partition, that had enclosed the estate. Rather, it was the act of partition itself which had enclosed the estate; and the estate remained enclosed thereafter. In addition, the trial judge noted that the right to a legal servitude of passage does not prescribe. Finally, the trial judge noted that Rockholt v. Keaty, 256 La. 629, 237 So. 2d 663 (La. 1970) had determined that it was against public policy to encourage land locking of property. Accordingly, the trial judge held that the LeBlancs had a right to a Revised C.C. art. 689 legal right of passage, with the corresponding obligation "to indemnify his neighbor for the damages he may occasion."

The Court of Appeal reversed. That court agreed with the district court that the LeBlancs were not entitled to a gratuitous right of passage under C.C. art. 694. But they reversed the district court's finding that a right of passage came into existence by virtue of C.C. art. 689. The court of appeal found that the 1929 partition had created a right of passage, although it was not utilized thereafter by the LeBlancs. They concluded that the estate had not become enclosed until the conventional servitude was lost through nonuse for ten years, that this loss of the servitude through nonuse was a voluntary act or omission (over the ten year period) which triggered C.C. art. 693, with the consequence recited in that article that "the neighbors are not bound to furnish a passage to him or his successors."

The dispositive question in the case is whether the court of appeal was correct in deciding that the estate had not become enclosed until the conventional servitude, which was created in the 1929 act of partition, was lost after ten years of nonuse. We conclude differently from the court of appeal on this point; the land became enclosed when the act of partition was passed. The 1929 Act of Partition was a well written legal document. In detailing how the 810 arpent tract of land (approximately 700 acres) was to be divided, the act of partition explained in great detail which part of the large tract each of the five children was to receive. The 72 arpent tract of land came into existence by virtue of the partition. After the act divided the bulk of the property among the children, the undivided 72 arpent tract remained as the only part owned in indivision. Consequently, that tract, a distinct parcel of land, was created and became simultaneously enclosed, as a result of the voluntary partition of the single large tract, not by the loss of the conventional servitude of passage ten years later.

The Civil Code addresses the right of passage in Book II, Things and the Different Modifications of Ownership; Title IV, Predial Servitudes; Section 3, Right of Passage. Section 3 includes eight articles, C.C. art. 689 through 696. The articles were revised in 1977. Civil Code Article 689 details the legal right of passage. It allows an owner of an estate that has no access to a public road to claim a right of passage over neighboring property to the nearest public road provided that the owner pays indemnity for the damage he causes. Articles 690, 691, and 692 address the extent of, constructions allowed on, and location of the passage. Complementing Article 689 is Article 694 which provides a gratuitous right of passage when property alienated or partitioned thereby becomes enclosed. According to that article, passage is to be furnished gratuitously by the owner of the land on which the passage was previously exercised.

Article 693, the article which is pivotal in resolving this case, came into being for the first time in 1977. It is essentially an exception to the obligation of a neighbor to provide passage to an estate that becomes enclosed, and it is triggered by a voluntary act or omission of an owner. Article 695 deals with relocation of a servitude. Finally, Article 696 deals with the prescriptibiliry of the right of indemnity against the owner of the enclosed estate — the right may be lost — while specifying that accrual of prescription has no effect on the right of passage.

Article 693 brings to the statutory scheme a certain tension, if not ambiguity. By virtue of articles 689 and 694 an enclosed landowner is entitled to a right of passage irrespective of how the enclosure came to pass. If the owner of the enclosed estate simply has no access to a public road, he must indemnify his neighbor for the damage he causes — art. 689. If a partition (or alienation) causes the enclosure, passage is to be gratuitously furnished — art. 694. Yet, art. 693 relieves a neighbor of the obligation to furnish a right of passage if there has been a voluntary act or omission on the part of the landowner who is demanding the right. Therein lies the possible conflict.

The pertinent question for us, regarding art. 693, are whether and to what extent, if at all, art. 693 has changed the law, and just what type of voluntary act or omission of the owner is required to excuse the neighbor of enclosed property from furnishing passage. Helpful in discerning the redactors' intent in revising the articles on the right of passage are the transcripts of the Louisiana Law Institute: Revision of the Code Book II of the Louisiana Civil Code of 1870 (meetings held on June 6-7 and June 27-28, 1975), which contain discussions regarding the revisions of the articles on the right of passage. Also directly pertinent is the section of Professor Yiannopoulos's treatise on property which addresses the same Civil Code articles.

The drafters apparently contemplated that article 693's exception would negate the right of passage otherwise afforded by art. 689 where the enclosure has been created by the owner's sale of his access property, for the entire focus of their discussion was on how the law would affect vendors. Their statements demonstrate that this article was drafted primarily to address a vendor's voluntary act or omissions, where the vendor fails to reserve a right of passage after his land becomes enclosed as a result of his sale of adjoining property. According to the article, the vendee, in this instance, will be relieved of the obligation to supply passage if his vendor, through his own voluntary act of selling part of his property, has neglected to, or chosen not to reserve a right of passage over the land.

Professor Yiannopoulos addresses article 693 at Chapter 5, titled "Enclosed Estates: The Right of Forced Passage". In a brief discussion of the article, he points out that

"[a]rticle 693 declares that if an estate becomes enclosed as a result of a voluntary act or omission, such as the sale of a part of an estate that furnishes access to a public road, the neighbors are not bound to furnish a passage to the owner who enclosed himself and his successors."

We believe that a reasonable interpretation which respects C.C. articles 689 and 694 while giving effect to C.C. art. 693, the exception to the right of passage added to our law in 1977, is to apply C.C. art. 693's "voluntary act or omission only to instances where the enclosed estate's owner has caused his dilemma by selling off his access property, or at the least by not applying art. 693 where the voluntary "alienation" which causes the enclosure is a partition, which is governed by C.C. art. 694 and C.C. art. 689.

How and if the article is applicable to voluntary acts or omissions beyond an owner's creating his own enclosure by selling off access property is problematic. It is simply unnecessary for us to resolve that question here. This interpretation is not only consistent with the thinking of the redactors but it respects the strong public policy of this state which is to discourage land-locking.

For the foregoing reasons we conclude that the district judge was correct when he decided that the plaintiffs are entitled to a legal right of passage.

For the above reasons the judgment of the court of appeal is reversed and that of the district court is affirmed. The case is remanded to the district court to determine the location of the right of passage and to fix the amount of indemnity (for the damages to be occasioned) which the plaintiffs owe the defendant. Reversed; remanded to the district court.

LEMMON, J. (concurring). The seventy-two-arpent tract was not enclosed after the 1929 partition because of the servitude of passage established in the act of partition. The tract became enclosed when the servitude of passage prescribed because of non-use ten years later. Nevertheless, La.Civ.Code art. 693 does not deprive plaintiffs of the right to claim passage over his neighbor's property in this case. As the majority states, Article 693 was designed to prevent an owner from claiming passage across his neighbor's land when the enclosure results from the owner's voluntary act of selling or partitioning part of the property without reserving a right of passage. Here, plaintiffs reserved a right of passage from the tract that would otherwise have become enclosed by the partition and did not voluntarily enclose themselves. The enclosure occurred ten years later when the servitude lapsed by operation of law.

In my view the failure to use the servitude for ten years was not the type of voluntary act or omission contemplated by Article 693. Therefore, plaintiffs are entitled to claim passage under La.Civ.Code art. 689.

QUESTION

How should the following fact pattern be resolved under the Code?

Pat was given land in 1965 by his mother. The sale also contained a right of passage over an adjacent lot to the highway. In 1992 Pat's mother sold additional land to Pat and Dan that contained the same right of passage as the 1965 sale (this 1992 land was co-owned). Pat and Dan partitioned the land. Subsequently, Pat lost a large portion of his land due to a Sheriff's sale for the failure to pay a creditor, and he now only retains a small enclosed piece of land. Pat seeks a right of passage over Dan's land. Is this allowed under article 689? See what the fourth circuit held in *Petrovich v. Trabeau*, 780 So. 2d 1258 (La. App. 4th Cir. 2001).

d. The Relationship Between Articles 689 and 694

STUCKEY v. COLLINS
464 So. 2d 346 (La. App. 2d Cir. 1985)

HALL, J. Defendant, Richard Collins, appeals from a judgment granting plaintiff, Robert O. Stuckey, an unimpeded right of passage 30 feet in width across a narrow strip of defendant's property for access to a public road. On appeal, defendant urges that since plaintiff acquired his enclosed property by purchase from a vendor whose property had access to a public road, plaintiff is entitled to a C.C. Art. 694 gratuitous servitude across his vendor's property and, consequently, is not entitled to a C.C. Art. 689 servitude across defendant's property. Plaintiff argues principally that access across the vendor's property is impractical because the property which must be crossed to get to the public road is low and swampy and the construction of a road already exists from plaintiffs property to and across defendant's land and is the shortest route to the road with the least inconvenience to adjoining properties.

STATEMENT OF THE FACTS

On November 16, 1981, Harvey Willis purchased a tract of land containing approximately 41.5 acres, and divided the tract into lots as shown on a recorded subdivision plat, a copy of which is attached to this opinion as an appendix. He then proceeded to sell several of the lots. One of these lots, Lot 3, was sold to plaintiff Robert Stuckey on December 10, 1981. Since the lot had no access to a public road, the deed conveying the lot granted a servitude of passage over Lot 1 which was still owned by

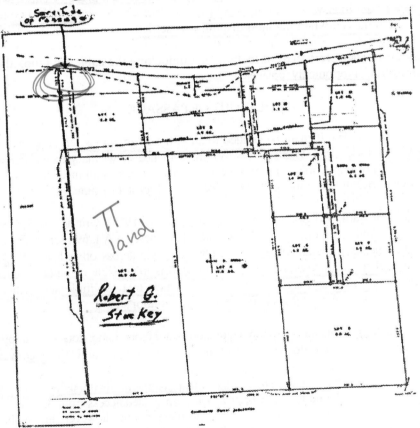

Willis. Although the deed purportedly granted a passage all the way to Highway 148, the nearest public road, the narrow strip of land immediately adjacent to the highway was not owned by Willis, but by defendant Richard Collins.

Before Stuckey purchased Lot 3, Willis cleared a passage all the way to the highway. Collins did not protest this action apparently because Collins and Willis had discussed exchanging land owned by Collins, including the small strip adjoining the highway, for other land owned by Willis. This exchange never took place.

Stuckey used the passage both before and after purchasing Lot 3 in order to enter and exit his property. Although he testified that he knew Collins owned land near the highway, Stuckey stated that he did not know that Collins owned the strip across the front of the cleared passage. Stuckey became aware that Collins owned the strip when Collins decided to erect a barrier across the front of the passage in order to protect himself from what Collins perceived as a threat to his ownership of the land.

Collins and Stuckey agreed to make the barrier across Stuckey's passage one which could be opened and closed. Collins then erected two wooden posts on each side of the passage at the point where it joined the highway, and locked a piece of cable between the posts. A key to the lock was given to Stuckey. The barrier was supposed to be temporary, and was to be removed when the land dispute was settled.

Stuckey eventually grew tired of locking and unlocking the cable, and took the cable down. However, Collins quickly replaced it.

THE RIGHT OF PASSAGE

Under these facts plaintiff may be entitled to an Art. 694 gratuitous servitude across the land owned or formerly owned by Willis.[1] However, the evidence shows that passage across that land is impractical if not impossible. The passage would have to cross an area that holds water, is boggy and swampy, and the construction of a road would "cost a fortune."

Langevin v. Howard, 363 So. 2d 1209 (La. App. 2d Cir. 1978), writ denied 366 So. 2d 560 (La. 1979), cited and relied on by appellants, holds that where an Art. 694 servitude is available, an enclosed owner is not entitled to an Art. 689 servitude across other land. We hold now, however, that where passage across the vendor's land is impossible or highly impractical, an enclosed owner, even though legally entitled to an Article 694 servitude across his vendor's property, may seek an Art. 689 servitude across a neighbor's land.

The instant case presents an exceptional situation. On the one hand, construction by Stuckey of an alternate passage would "cost a fortune"; on the other hand, the inconvenience to

---

[1] The requirements of Article 694 are met to the extent that the original tract owned by Willis did border on the public road, and could theoretically have provided access from Stuckey's lot to the highway at the time the lot was purchased. At the present time, however, the applicability of Article 694 is questionable for two reasons. First, the article specifically provides that passage shall be furnished by the owner of the land on which "the passage was previously exercised." In the present case passage from Stuckey's lot has never been exercised over the land of Willis. There is no previously existing road. Thus, strict adherence to the wording of the article arguably indicates the article's inapplicability to the situation at hand. See Fuller v. Wright, 464 So. 2d 350 (La. App. 2d Cir. 1985), decided this day. Second, Willis no longer owns any of the lots sold from the original tract. Thus, the question arises whether the obligation of Willis to furnish passage to Stuckey was transmitted to Willis's successors.

Collins of allowing Stuckey a right of passage is minimal since a road already exists, since only about 1/100 of an acre of Collins' land is affected, and since the affected land is located at an extreme corner of Collins' unfenced property.

Although the importance of not imposing a burden of forced passage on neighboring lands will be controlling in the majority of enclosure cases arguably falling under Article 694, the growing recognition of the importance of fully utilizing land dictates that a balancing of interests approach should be employed to a limited extent on a case-by-case basis. The Louisiana Supreme Court in *Rockholt* v. *Keaty*, 237 So. 2d 663 (La. 1970), when discussing the policies behind Article 699 (now Article 689), stated:

> "As land becomes less available, more necessary for public habitation, use, and support, it would run contrary to public policy to encourage land locking of such a valuable asset and forever removing it from commerce and from public as well as private benefit."

The court also noted:

> "It is apparent that the French under their provision for passage from enclosed estates have from the beginning decided each case under its particular circumstances and have refused to reach for absolute legal pronouncements which would effect a restricted application of the law."

A balancing of interests is apparent in French Civil Code Article 684 which, like Article 694 of the Louisiana Civil Code, addresses the situation in which an estate becomes enclosed as the result of the division of a larger tract of land by sale, exchange, or partition. While both articles provide for passage over the lands which composed the original tract, French Civil Code Article 684 provides that when sufficient passage cannot be made over the lands which composed the original tract, Article 682 of the French Civil Code shall apply. Article 682 corresponds with Article 689 of the Louisiana Civil Code. Thus, under the French Civil Code, Article 682 rather than Article 684 is applied in the exceptional case in which sufficient passage may not be established over the divided lands. Similarly, under the facts of the present case, Article 689 of the Louisiana Civil Code should apply instead of Article 694; Article 694, even if otherwise applicable, provides an insufficient remedy.

In this case, the shortest and only practical route from plaintiffs property to the public road is across a narrow strip at the end of defendant's property which lies between the right of way granted by plaintiffs vendor and the public road. The road is in existence and was constructed and used for a period of time with the consent of and without interference by defendant. Inconvenience and damage to defendant is minimal. Construction of a road across the property formerly owned by plaintiffs vendor would be impossible or highly impractical and economically unfeasible. Under these circumstances, the trial court correctly granted plaintiff a servitude across the defendant's land under Art. 689.

IMPEDIMENT TO PASSAGE

Under the facts of this case, plaintiff is entitled to the servitude without the impediment of the posts and cable erected by defendant. The cable serves no purpose other than as an impediment. An owner entitled to an Art. 689 servitude for passage to a public road may be subjected to some inconvenience where the servient estate owner has a fence and gate. See Pittman v. Marshall, 104 So. 2d 230 (La. App. 2d Cir. 1958). But unlike the factual situation in *Pittman* where the plaintiffs estate was used for agricultural purposes, the Stuckeys' estate is being used as a place of residence. Because the route from the road to the Stuckeys' house is a quarter of a mile long and passes through a wooded area, visitors to the residence apparently have no way to directly alert the Stuckeys of their presence at the highway. Utility company employees who need to read meters or check lines are similarly hindered. Furthermore, Stuckey testified at trial that the ground near the cable had washed down to red clay which became very slick when rain fell. Once one stopped a vehicle in order to get out and open the cable, it was very difficult to get the vehicle moving again. Another factual difference between *Pittman* and this case is that the gates in *Pittman* served the necessary purpose of enclosing livestock. But here the posts and cable are not part of a fence and were erected, according to defendant's own testimony, simply to assert and delineate his ownership of the property crossed by the road, and serves no useful purpose. Under these circumstances, the impediment to use of the passage is unreasonable and is not warranted. See C.C. Art. 690.

INDEMNITY TO DAMAGES

Under C.C. Art. 689, plaintiff is bound to indemnify defendant for the damage occasioned. Damages were not made an issue at the trial of the case, probably because of the posture of the pleadings at the time the case went to trial. Defendant should not be precluded from claiming damages, and we will amend the judgment to reserve defendant's right to claim indemnification of any damages sustained.

DECREE

For the reasons assigned, the judgment is amended to reserve defendant's rights to seek indemnity for damages sustained, and as amended, is affirmed.

NOTE
What are the Requirements for Article 694?

1. Although the court in the preceding case speculated that the plaintiff Stuckey might have been entitled to a gratuitous servitude under article 694, it nonetheless recognized plaintiff's entitlement to a servitude of passage under article 689 (which required plaintiff to indemnify defendant for damages sustained). If the court had found that plaintiff was definitely entitled to a right of passage under article 694, could the court still find that plaintiff nonetheless had satisfied the requirements of article 689?

2. In footnote 1, the court lists two reasons why the court believes it is questionable whether

Stuckey could have asserted a right of passage under article 694. With respect to the first reason, do you believe that the language of article 694 should be applied strictly? Why or why not? The court cites *Fuller* v. *Wright*, 464 So. 2d 350 (La. App. 2d Cir. 1985), a suit in which the trial court ordered defendant to remove a gate he had placed across a road over which plaintiffs claimed a right of passage pursuant to article 694. In affirming the trial court, the court of appeal in *Fuller* stated:

> Having shown that a definite *roadway* existed and had been used before and after the 1962 partition, these plaintiffs are and have been entitled to the exercise of their C.C. art. 694 servitude rights. Under these circumstances it is not necessary to fix the location of the servitude before granting an injunction to protect interference of plaintiffs' use of this roadway. Compare Estopinal v. Storck's Estate, 44 So. 2d 704 (Orl. App. 1950); Marceaux v. Reese, 36 So. 2d 504 (La. App. 3d Cir. 1978), where injunction was denied because there was no previous exercise of the right over a fixed route.

464 So. 2d at 352-53.

3. With respect to the second reason cited in footnote 1 as to whether Stuckey can assert a right of passage under article 694, the court states: "Willis no longer owns any of the lots sold from the original tract. Thus, the question arises whether the obligation of Willis to furnish passage to Stuckey was transmitted to Willis's successors." Consider the applicability of the following reading to this issue.

QUESTIONS

How should the following fact patterns be resolved under the Code?

FACT PATTERN ONE

Pat (vendor) sold a portion of his land to Dan (vendee). Pat's retained portion of land was enclosed and he did not retain a right of passage in the sale. Pat now seeks a gratuitous right of passage over Dan's land. Can Pat do this? See what the third circuit held in Spotsville v. Herbert & Murrell, Inc., 698 So. 2d 31 (La. App. 3d Cir. 1997)

FACT PATTERN TWO

Blackacre became enclosed in 1953 when the landowner granted the Blackacre Police Jury permission to construct Brandon Ditch, which subsequently enclosed Blackacre. The Brandon Ditch benefited the surrounding properties by allowing drainage. In 1997 Dan gave Pat permission to use a road located on Dan's land to access Pat's enclosed estate. In 1999 Dan changed the locks on the gate that allowed Pat to access his land. Does Pat have a case for a statutory right of passage? If so is it gratuitous or will Pat have to indemnify Dan? Did the acts in 1953 of allowing Blackacre Police Jury to dig Brandon Ditch bar Pat from seeking a legal right of passage under article 693? See what the third circuit held in *Walker Louisiana Properties v. Broussard*, 813 So. 2d 487 (La. App. 3d Cir. 2002).

FACT PATTERN THREE

Dan was the landowner of an enclosed estate. The only access to a public highway was by using Merritt Mountain Road, which is located on Pat's land. Pat claims that Dan knowingly and voluntarily bought property that was enclosed and that he should not be entitled to a legal right of passage. Does Pat have a claim to rid his property of all servitudes? See what the third circuit held in *Griffith v. Cathey*, 762 So. 2d 29 (La. App. 3d Cir.), *cert. denied* 771 So. 2d 85 (La. 2000).

A.N. YIANNOPOULOS, PREDIAL SERVITUDES
§ 103 (3d ed. 2004)
(footnotes omitted)

§ 103. Article 694: Enclavement From Alienation, Exchange, or Partition

The right to demand a gratuitous passage under Article 694 of the Louisiana Civil Code may be asserted by universal successors or particular successors of the acquirer of an estate that became enclosed as a result of partition or alienation of lands. The new owner of an estate that became enclosed as a result of partition or voluntary alienation may claim a gratuitous passage from a coparcener of his author, from the person who voluntarily transferred to his author the enclosed estate, or from the universal or particular successors of those persons. A Louisiana court observed aptly: "The change in ownership of either or both of the estates does not terminate the landed or predial servitude. Anyone who acquires either of the estates after the legal servitude comes into being takes such tract subject to the servitude already established."

In Patin v. Richard, by a common act of sale, a landowner subdivided his property into three distinct lots, referred to as "A," "B," and "C," and sold each to a different purchaser. The owners of the three lots at the time of litigation were particular successors of the original acquirers, namely, their vendees or transferees. As a result of the subdivision and sale, lots "B" and "C" became enclosed; lot "A" was the only one communicating with the public road. Since the time of the sale, the owners of lots "B" and "C" had been using an unpaved driveway on lot "A" for exit into the public road. When the owner of lot "B" forbade the owner of lot "C" to use the driveway on lot "B" for exit into the public road through lot "A", the owner of lot "C" brought suit against the owner of lot "B", claiming a right of passage. If lots "A," "B," and "C" were still in the hands of the original purchasers, there should be no doubt that plaintiff, owner of lot "C," was entitled to a gratuitous right of passage over lots "B" and "A." However, question arose whether the obligation to grant a gratuitous passage had been transmitted to the subsequent purchasers of lots "B" and "A." In a well-reasoned opinion, the court granted a gratuitous passage rather than a passage for indemnity on the lots of subsequent purchasers.

In Dallas v. Farrington, the Louisiana Supreme Court wrote the requirements of the public records doctrine into the provisions of Article 694 of the Civil Code. Property that was alienated became enclosed as a result of the alienation, and the vendor was bound to furnish a gratuitous passage to the purchaser in accordance with Article 694 of the Civil

Code. However, the vendor sold his lands to his son, and the question arose whether the purchaser of the enclosed estate could exercise his rights under Article 694 of the Civil Code against a particular successor of the vendor. In the opinion of the Louisiana Supreme Court, the purchaser of an enclosed estate is precluded by the public records doctrine from asserting against a particular successor of the vendor the claim for the creation of a conventional servitude of passage under Article 694 of the Civil Code when there is nothing in the public records showing that the particular successor acquired an estate bound to provide a gratuitous passage.

If the recorded act of sale provides for a gratuitous passage on the lands of the vendor, a purchaser of the enclosed estate may claim that passage against all successors of the vendor. However, if the act of sale is silent as to the gratuitous passage, the vendor may convey his property to a subsequent purchaser free of the legal obligation to furnish a gratuitous passage! This solution involves a misapplication of the public records doctrine and a misunderstanding of Article 694 of the Civil Code.

Article 694 imposes on the owners of lands which before the partition or alienation furnished access to a public road a *legal* obligation to provide, after the partition or alienation, a gratuitous passage to that road. The legal obligation, implied in partitions and alienation that result in the enclavement of lands partitioned or alienated, has been imposed on coparceners in favor of other coparceners and on transferors in favor of transferees in order to prevent claims for passage against neighbors under Article 689 of the Louisiana Civil Code. Indeed, coparceners in the case of partition, and transferors in the case of a sale or other alienation, should not be allowed to shift the burden of passage on their neighbors.

The public records doctrine applies to acts which according to law must be filed for registry in order to have effect against third persons. This doctrine, however, does not apply to burdens imposed by law, including legal servitudes and legal obligations. The legal obligation imposed on coparceners and transferors of lands by Article 694 of the Civil Code should be enforced against subsequent purchasers without any recordation and without regard to the public records doctrine. In holding otherwise, the Louisiana Supreme Court apparently confused the *legal* obligation to provide a gratuitous passage under Article 694 of the Civil Code with the fixing of a *conventional* passage in compliance with that obligation.

CHAPTER XIV. CONVENTIONAL SERVITUDES
Civil Code arts. 697-77

1. CONTRACTUAL AND TESTAMENTARY FREEDOM
Civil Code art. 697

A. N. YIANNOPOULOS, PREDIAL SERVITUDES
§§ 105-110 (3d ed. 2004)
(footnotes omitted)

§ 105. Public Policy

In all legal systems under consideration, contractual and testamentary freedom in the field of property law is limited by rules of public policy enacted in the general interest. Apart from general limitations, however, the creation of conventional servitudes is subject to special rules that are not susceptible of modification by agreement of the parties.

Article 697 of the Louisiana Civil Code declares that predial servitudes "may be established by an owner on his estate or acquired for its benefit." This provision reproduced the substance of Article 709 of the 1870 Code and did not change the law. The source provision, corresponding with Article 686 of the French Civil Code, declared that "owners have a right to establish on their estates, or in favor of their estates, such servitudes as they deem proper; provided, moreover, that services imply nothing contrary to the public order." There is no directly corresponding provision in the German or in the Greek Civil Code but, as under the present text of the Louisiana Civil Code, limitations on contractual and testamentary freedom obtain from the legislative definition of predial servitudes.

The reason the redactors of the French Civil Code felt compelled to spell out the limits of contractual and of testamentary freedom in connection with the creation of predial servitudes may be properly understood in the light of historical developments. In Roman law, a predial servitude was a charge laid on an estate in favor of another estate, namely, a real right on an immovable belonging to another owner (*Jus in re aliena*). In medieval French law, however, predial servitudes evolved into feudal tenures, burdening lands as well as persons. Thus, the tenant of the servient estate owed certain personal duties to the owner of the dominant estate and occupied toward him a position of social inferiority. These feudal institutions were wiped out by the Revolution; and, in giving expression to the new social order, the redactors of the Code Civil sought ways to insure that the old tenures would not be resurrected. The best assurance in that regard would be the elimination of real rights other than full ownership and the suppression of contractual freedom in the domain of property law. Yet, there was a legitimate demand for the recognition of real rights other than full ownership, and one of the fundamental precepts of the new legislation was freedom of the will.

Faced with these contradictory demands, the redactors of the Code Civil struck a happy balance. Contractual and testamentary freedom in matters of property law ought to be respected, provided that the limits of public policy are not transcended. Thus, neither feudal tenures may be resurrected nor interests be created contrary to Article 686 of the Code Civil. Within these broad limits individuals may modify the provisions of the Code by dismembering their ownership as they see fit and by establishing "such servitudes as they deem proper."***

§ 106. Services May Not Be Imposed on a Person

In the absence of contrary provision of law, predial servitudes may not involve performance of affirmative duties by the owner of the servient estate. For example, the owner of the servient estate may not be bound by virtue of a predial servitude to cultivate the dominant estate. Such duties, though, may properly form the object of personal obligations. A predial servitude is a dismemberment of ownership, a real right by virtue of which the owner of the dominant estate is entitled to exercise certain prerogatives of ownership on the servient estate; correspondingly, the owner of the servient estate is merely charged with the duty to tolerate the acts of the owner of the dominant estate.

The law prohibits affirmative duties that are intended to be the main object of the servitude; it does not exclude the imposition of certain incidental duties that may be necessary for the exercise or preservation of a servitude. Thus, parties may stipulate that the owner of the servient estate shall be charged with the duty to keep his estate fit for the purposes of the servitude or that he shall maintain in good state of repair certain works on his land needed for the use or preservation of the servitude. Moreover, the owner of an estate burdened with a servitude of support must keep his constructions fit for the exercise of the servitude at his expense, unless the contrary is stipulated. French jurisprudence goes further still: the owner of the servient estate may be charged with the duty to produce certain materials, such as coal needed for a factory on the dominant estate, or to generate and transmit electricity. In these circumstances, the duties imposed on the owner of the servient estate form real, rather than personal, obligations that are transferable to particular successors without stipulation to that effect.

The prohibition of personal services, other than those regarded as incidental for the use or preservation of the servitude, applies to both conventional and legal servitudes. In the case of legal servitudes, however, the law may impose on the owner of the servient estate certain affirmative duties that could hardly be regarded as incidental. Thus, in France, owners fronting public streets may be charged with the duty to plant trees, forest owners may be required to keep safety zones for protection against fires, and homeowners may be charged with the duty to uplift the facade of buildings. In Louisiana, riparian landowners were in the past charged with the duty to keep levees in a good state of repair, and they are still bound to keep the banks of navigable waterways free of growing vegetation.

§ 107. A Predial Servitude May Not Be Imposed in Favor of a Person

According to civilian precepts that have been incorporated in modern civil codes, predial servitudes may not be established in favor of named persons; they must be stipulated in favor of anyone who happens to be the owner of the dominant estate. Further, rights that have no direct relationship with the use of the dominant estate may not be predial servitudes.

In Roman law, the creation of a predial servitude was subject to the requirements that there be two estates, and that the servitude be for the use or benefit of the estate in favor of which it was established. A right that had no direct relationship with the use of the dominant estate could not be a predial servitude. Thus, the right to take a walk, or to collect fruits or flowers, on the land of another could not be stipulated as a predial servitude; it could properly be a usufruct or a right of use, because the beneficiary could derive the contemplated advantage whether he was owner of an estate or not. The right to take certain materials from an estate could be a predial servitude or a usufruct, depending on whether the contemplated advantage was attributed directly to an estate or to a person. For example, the right to take dirt needed for the marketing of the agricultural products of the dominant estate in ceramic containers could be stipulated as a predial servitude. If, however, the dirt was needed for the operation of a pottery, the servient estate could be burdened only with a usufruct because the advantage was attributed to the owner of the manufacturing establishment.

The formulas used by Roman jurisconsults are reflected in the language of Article 686 of the French Civil Code which declares that services may not be imposed "in favor of the person, but only ... in favor of an estate." French commentators of past generations have interpreted the provision literally to mean that predial servitudes must be advantageous to the dominant estate rather than its owner. Modern authors, however, have observed that the contrast between the dominant estate and its owner is "unintelligible," since rights benefit persons rather than things. Accordingly, the legislative declaration that predial servitudes must confer an advantage on the dominant estate ought to be taken as a metaphor. It merely means that predial servitudes may not be stipulated in favor of a named person but must be stipulated in favor of anyone who happens to be owner of the dominant estate. Modern civil codes have obviated such analytical difficulties by providing expressly that predial servitudes must confer an advantage on the owner of the dominant estate.

In addition to prohibiting services in favor of a named person, Article 709 of the Louisiana Civil Code of 1870 gave expression to the traditional idea that rights having no direct relationship with the use of the dominant estate may not be predial servitudes. The same idea is expressed in the legislative definition of the content of predial servitudes in the Civil Codes of Germany and Greece. Traditional ideas incorporated in modern civil codes, however, must be interpreted in the light of contemporary conditions without regard to the narrow applications sanctioned by Roman jurisconsults. Accordingly, all kinds of rights that have a direct relationship with the use of an immovable may be predial servitudes. The rights to take a walk, to collect fruits or flowers, to enjoy a swimming pool or a tennis court, and to use certain facilities on the land of another may have a direct relationship with the use or exploitation of an immovable; hence, they may be predial servitudes.

Question has arisen whether fishing or hunting rights may be predial servitudes. According to the prevailing view in France and in Greece, these rights involve a strictly personal gratification for the beneficiary; hence, they may not be predial servitudes. Nevertheless, argument may be made that the French, Greek, and Louisiana Civil Codes allow the creation of fishing or hunting servitudes in favor of the owner of an estate destined to the pursuit of fishing or hunting operations. In Germany, however, the creation of hunting servitudes is forbidden by special legislation, whereas fishing rights may form the object of real charges under applicable local laws.

In Louisiana fishing or hunting rights may form the object of a limited personal servitude. These rights may be leased for extensive periods of time; and, since the lease is not affected by subsequent changes of ownership, the lessee is adequately protected. The question of the availability of predial servitudes for fishing or hunting purposes, therefore, has mostly academic significance.

Questions whether restraints on trade and on the use or alienation of immovables may form the object of predial servitudes are discussed in the following sections.

§ 108. Prohibition Against Competition

Reasonable restraints on trade, such as prohibitions against competition and agreements providing for the delivery of certain quotas of natural, agricultural, or industrial products, may undoubtedly establish personal obligations between the contracting parties. Modern demands of business and finance, however, have given rise to the question whether such stipulations may also form the object of predial servitudes imposed on, or in favor of, lands destined to commercial or industrial use.

Louisiana courts have not been faced squarely with the issue whether prohibitions against competition may validly be stipulated as predial servitudes.***Prohibitions against competition should not be allowed to restrict the use of lands in Louisiana; existing economic needs may be amply satisfied by means of personal obligations.

In France, courts have taken the view that contracts not to compete may not give rise to predial servitudes. The beneficiary of the prohibition against competition is the owner of a commercial or industrial establishment rather than the estate on which the establishment is located; moreover, there is no direct relationship between the purpose of the intended servitude and the use of the dominant estate. Thus, prohibitions against the extraction of materials from the ground in favor of competing establishments have been held to create rights other than predial servitudes; and an obligation assumed by the vendor of lands not to sell other lands for the purposes of a competitive business has been held to be a personal obligation.***

§ 109. Quota Requirements

Agreements providing for the purchase or sale of certain quotas of agricultural or industrial products may not form the object of predial servitudes. These agreements involve the performance of affirmative acts and may properly form the object of personal obligations only.***These contracts do not establish predial servitudes in Germany because, in addition to imposing affirmative duties contrary to law, they contemplate the prohibition of juridical acts rather than purely physical acts; moreover, they limit one's freedom to do business, which is an attribute of personality rather than of land ownership.***

§ 110. Restraints on Alienation of Immovables

According to traditional civilian precepts, juridical acts imposing restraints on the alienation of immovable property give rise to personal obligations only. These obligations are enforceable against the original and his universal successors, namely, heirs, universal legatees, or legatees under universal title. Third persons, and particular successors of the obligor, i.e., buyers, donees, or legatees of particular things, are not bound to respect the relationship between the obligor and obligee, unless, of course, they are made parties to it by their own consent. As a rule, therefore, transfers of immovable property by particular title ought to be valid in spite of the violation of restraints on alienation imposed by juridical acts.

This traditional approach attributes excessive significance to the general interest in the free alienability of property. It fails to recognize that, at least in exceptional circumstances, the general interest in the free alienability of property should be balanced against the interest of individuals to dispose of their property under modifications that contemporary needs dictate. Indeed, in the framework of a well-defined public policy, individuals may have legitimate claims for the enforcement of reasonable restraints on alienation against anyone and in the annulment of unauthorized transfers of immovable property. This may be accomplished in civil law jurisdictions either by straining the notion of personal obligations or by attributing to restraints on alienation the character of real rights, which, by their nature, are effective against anyone. In common law jurisdictions, Chancery courts faced with the problem of the validity of restrictions concerning use of lands among persons other than the original contracting parties gradually fashioned old institutions of contract law into a doctrine of covenants running with the land.

In a leading decision, *Queensborough Land Co. v. Cazeaux*, the Louisiana Supreme Court declared that a restriction of limited duration on the landowner's right to alienate property to persons of a particular race was valid and enforceable as a charge on the land. The three elements of the right of ownership the usus, fructus. and abusus, the court reasoned, are susceptible of subdivision within certain limits prescribed by rules of public policy. Thus, whereas absolute or perpetual restraints on alienation are invalid, restraints of limited duration imposed by persons having a substantial interest are valid and enforceable against any acquirer of the land with notice. Restrictions on the right to alienate property to persons of a particular race, religion, or nationality are a deprivation of the equal protection of laws under the United States Constitution and are no longer valid; but certain reasonable restraints on alienation imposed on other grounds may still give rise to real rights in Louisiana.

In case of an impending violation, the restraint may be enforced by an action for injunction brought by the person who imposed the restraint or by persons in whose favor the restraint was imposed. After violation, depending on the facts and circumstances of each case, a proper plaintiff may demand damages, resolution of the original transfer of the property, or merely annulment of the alienation made in violation of the restraint.

In cases involving inter vivos or mortis causa donations of immovables subject to reasonable restraints on alienation, annulment of the alienation made in violation of the restraint rather than resolution of the donation ought to be the rule. Presumably, a donor who imposes a restraint on alienation wishes that the property remain in the patrimony of the donee. Hence, resolution of the donation would be contrary to the intention of the donor and the best interest of the donee.

In France, restraints on alienation may not be stipulated as predial servitudes because the advantage of the restraint is attributed to a person rather than an estate. According to well-settled jurisprudence, however, which has no direct foundation in the Code Civil, restraints of limited duration, imposed by a person having a legitimate interest, are effective against third persons in the sense that any alienation in violation of such a restraint is a relative nullity.***

2. KINDS OF SERVITUDES
Civil Code arts. 706,707

A. N. YIANNOPOULOS, PREDIAL SERVITUDES
§§ 13,14,16 (3d ed. 2004)
(footnotes omitted)

§ 13. Apparent and Nonapparent Servitudes

Article 707 of the Louisiana Civil Code, corresponding with Article 689 of the French Civil Code, declares that predial servitudes "are either apparent or nonapparent." Apparent servitudes are those that are perceivable by exterior signs, works, or constructions; such as a roadway, a window in a common wall, or an aqueduct. Nonapparent servitudes are those that have no exterior sign of their existence, such as the prohibition of building on an estate or of building above a particular height.

This division of servitudes was developed in medieval French law as a sub-classification of continuous and discontinuous servitudes. In the Louisiana Civil Code of 1870, however, the division of servitudes into apparent and nonapparent was independent of any other division, and the same is true under the French Civil Code and the 1977 Louisiana legislation. There is no corresponding division of servitudes in the Roman, German, and Greek legal systems.

The classification of a particular servitude as apparent or nonapparent depends on facts and circumstances rather than on the nature of the servitude. Thus, a servitude of right of way may be apparent or nonapparent. If the right of way is exercised over an arid tract of land, without a trace, the servitude is nonapparent; if it is exercised on a paved road or a railway track, the servitude is apparent. Likewise, if the pipes of an aqueduct are buried into the ground, the servitude is nonapparent; if the pipes are visible, the servitude is apparent. Certain kinds of servitudes are apparent almost by necessity; for example, servitudes of view on common walls, of drip, of support, and servitudes for the maintenance of a levee. Other kinds of servitudes are nonapparent almost by necessity; for example, negative servitudes, building restrictions in a subdivision, and prohibitions of building on a neighboring estate.

The practical significance of the division of predial servitudes into apparent and nonapparent relates to the rules governing the creation of servitudes. Nonapparent servitudes may be acquired by title; apparent servitudes may be acquired by title, by destination of the owner, or by acquisitive prescription.

§ 14. Affirmative and Negative Servitudes

Article 706 of the Louisiana Civil Code declares that predial servitudes are either affirmative or negative. Affirmative servitudes are defined as those "that give the right to the owner of the dominant estate to do a certain thing on the servient estate." Such are servitudes that confer on the owner of the dominant estate the right to take certain materials from the servient estate or to use that estate for certain purposes, including passage, drain, and support. Negative servitudes are those "that impose on the owner of the servient estate the duty to abstain from doing something on his estate." Such are servitudes that deprive the owner of the servient estate of certain prerogatives of ownership; they prohibit certain material acts, such as the erection of a building on a vacant lot or the use of an estate as a commercial establishment, or they exclude the exercise of a certain right, such as to drain waters on an estate situated below.

The division of servitudes into affirmative and negative is important in Louisiana in light of the rules governing commencement of the prescription of nonuse. This prescription begins to run for affirmative servitudes "from the date of their last use" and for negative servitudes "from the date of the occurrence of an event contrary to the servitude."***

§ 16. Continuous and Discontinuous Servitudes

According to the Romanist tradition predial servitudes are distinguished into continuous and discontinuous.***The Louisiana Civil Code of 1870, following the model of the French Civil Code, declared that predial servitudes "are either continuous or discontinuous." This provision has been suppressed by the 1977 legislation. Thus, the distinction of predial servitudes into continuous and discontinuous is now merely doctrinal in Louisiana; it does not carry any legal consequences.***

3. ACQUISITION OF SERVITUDES
Civil Code arts. 708-743

a. Acquisition by Title
Civil Code arts. 708-739

BURGAS v. STOUTZ
174 La. 586,141 So. 67 (1932)

LAND, J. Mrs. Vincent Pizzolata owned a lot in Square 379, Seventh district of the city of New Orleans, bounded by Dublin, Apple, Belfast, and Dante streets. This lot was designated by the letter "X" on a plan of Adloe Orr, civil engineer, dated November 22, 1920, and formed the corner of Dublin and Apple streets. It measured 60 feet front on the former street and a depth of 90 feet on the latter street.

Thereafter, Mrs. Pizzolata subdivided lot "X" into lots "A" and "B," and another lot into lot "C," in a survey made by A. J. Oilveira, civil engineer, dated October 20,1922. A later survey by the same engineer, dated February 25, 1929, and showing the location of lots "A" and "B," is filed in the transcript at page 55. September 13,1923, Mrs. Pizzolata sold lot "A" to the Security Building & Loan Association, and, on the same day, the association conveyed this lot to the plaintiff, Morris Burgas.

In the sale by Mrs. Pizzolata to the association, and in the sale by the association to plaintiff, the following stipulation appears:

> It is distinctly agreed and understood between the parties hereto that the purchaser, its successors and assigns, shall have the privilege of using the paved driveway in the rear of the property hereinabove described, which paved driveway is part of Lot "B" belonging to the vendors herein.

The above stipulation was recorded in the conveyance records of the parish of Orleans in the following language:

> Purchaser (omitting "successors and assigns") has the privilege of using the paved driveway in the rear of the above property, which driveway is part of Lot B belonging to the vendor herein.

December 7,1923, Mrs. Pizzolata sold lot "B" to the Fidelity Homestead Association. On the same day the homestead transferred this lot to Walter Clark. On August 20, 1925, Clark reconveyed the property to the homestead, and on the same day the homestead deeded the property to defendant, Henry L. Stoutz.

It is admitted that, at the date plaintiff purchased lot "A," together with the privilege of using the paved driveway on lot "B," Mrs. Pizzolata owned lots "A" and "B," and that the paved runways mentioned in the petition and shown on three photographs, marked "Plaintiff 5, 6, and 7," had been laid. Tr. 54.

It is also admitted that the runways were built by Mrs. Pizzolata prior to the time she disposed of either lot "A" or lot "B." Tr. 54. It is further admitted that Henry L. Stoutz, defendant, had notified Morris Burgas, plaintiff, that he (Stoutz) was about to build a fence which would impair and destroy the use of the paved driveway. Tr. 54.

It was upon the receipt of this notification that the present suit for an injunction was brought by plaintiff. A preliminary injunction was issued, and, after hearing on the merits, was made permanent by judgment of the lower court, in which was fully recognized the right of plaintiff to use the driveway in dispute in this case, as delineated by red ink lines on a blueprint of survey made by A. J. Oliveira, civil engineer and surveyor, dated February 25,1929, and in which was also reserved the right of plaintiff to claim whatever damage, loss, or injury that may have been occasioned to him by defendant herein. From this judgment defendant has appealed.

1. Defendant attacks the recorded stipulation as to the right of passage granted to plaintiff on the ground that it is insufficient, as it does not state the length or width of same.

This particular ground of attack is without merit, since the paved runways are located as physical objects on the surface of lot "B," the property of defendant, as shown by photographs filed in evidence, and the length and width of same are easily ascertainable. That which can be made certain is considered in law as certain.

2. The second ground of attack by defendant is that a servitude of passage, a discontinuous servitude, cannot be acquired by destination de pere de famille, and parol evidence is inadmissible.

It is true that a right of passage is a discontinuous servitude, and can be established only by title. R. C. C, arts. 727 [no corresponding article after revision] and 766 [Revised C.C. art. 739].

The destination made by the owner is equivalent to title only with respect to continuous apparent servitudes, such as aqueducts, drain, view, and the like. RC.C. arts. 727 [no corresponding article after revision] and 767 [Revised C.C. art. 741]. As the right of passage in this case depends upon contract, we must look to the terms of the contract in order to determine if they are sufficient to vest title in plaintiff.

In the original deeds from Mrs. Pizzolata to the Security Building & Loan Association, and from the association to plaintiff, Morris Burgas, the privilege of using the paved driveway on the property of defendant is expressly granted to "the purchaser, its successors and assigns." Since the purchasers of lot "A," stipulating the servitude of passage over lot "B," owned by defendant, acquired it as owners of lot "A," and for then-successors and assigns, it is clear that the right became real and is a predial servitude, and not a right merely personal to the individual and expiring with him. R.C.C. art. 757 [Revised C.C. art. 734].

In the titles to lot "A" of the Security Building & Loan Association, and of plaintiff, Morris Burgas, as recorded, the servitude is granted only to "the purchaser," or the owner of the property. The acts establishing the servitude do not declare that the right is given for the benefit of an estate. It must then be considered, as declared in article 755

[Revised C.C. art. 732] of the Civil Code, whether the right granted be of real advantage to lot "A," or merely of personal convenience to the owner.

As stated in article 756 [Revised C.C. art. 733] of the Civil Code: "If the right granted be of a nature to assure a real advantage to an estate, it is to be presumed that such right is a real servitude, although it may not be so styled."

In our opinion, the right of passage over lot "B," granted to the purchasers of lot "A," is of real utility to the latter property, which is a 50-foot corner lot fronting on Apple street, and is not incumbered with a driveway; thereby giving to lot "A" more free space either for building or for flowers, or for a garden, and making the property more desirable and valuable. See map, Tr. p. 55 and photographs, Tr. p. 53.

It is also significant that the right of passage over lot "B" was not given to a named individual, but to "the purchaser," the owner of lot "A," thereby connecting the servitude with the property as a real advantage to it, and not as a mere matter of convenience to a particular person and terminating with him. As the granting to plaintiff of the right of passage over lot "B" is of real benefit to lot "A," our conclusion is that such right is a real servitude.

Since the creation of a real servitude is a form of alienation, defendant contends that the recorded stipulation as to the right of passage over lot "B," owned by defendant, is too vague, uncertain, and indefinite in description to be a notice to a purchaser in good faith.

At the risk of repetition, we quote this recorded stipulation again, which is as follows: "Purchaser has the privilege of using the paved driveway in the rear of the above property, which driveway is part of Lot B belonging to the vendor herein."

The survey of lots "A" and "B," found at page 55 of the transcript, shows conclusively that there is but one paved driveway on lot "B," and that this driveway is indicated by a red line drawn next to lot "A," owned by plaintiff.

As the driveway consists of paved runways, as shown by the runways themselves in place, as well as by the photographs filed at page 53 of the transcript, it is idle for defendant to contend that the description of these runways as located "in the rear" of lot "A" is erroneous and misleading, since there is only one set of paved runways on lot "B," and this driveway is particularly described in the stipulation creating the right of passage as being "a part of Lot "B."

Manifestly, this was sufficient recorded notice to have placed defendant on inquiry, and to have enabled him to have ascertained the true facts of the case before purchasing lot "B."

Besides, as held in Schneidau v. New Orleans Land Company, 132 La. 264, 61 So. 225, the law in this state has for many years been that an act of conveyance is effective against third persons as soon as deposited for record in the recorder's office. The original deeds in this case, deposited in the recorder's office, show conclusively that the servitude of passage over the driveway on lot "B" was granted to the purchaser, its successors and assigns, and was therefore a real servitude.

Under the circumstances of the case, we are of the opinion that it is unimportant that, in the chain of title from Mrs. Pizzolata to defendant, the servitude of right of passage in favor of lot "A," owned by plaintiff, is not mentioned, especially as plaintiffs title antedates that of defendant, and both have purchased from a common author. Judgment affirmed.

RCC PROPERTIES, L.L.C. v. WENSTAR PROPERTIES, L.P.
930 So. 2d 1233 (La. App. 2d Cir. 2006)

DREW, J. Wenstar Properties, L.P., appeals from a judgment invalidating a predial servitude in favor of an estate owned by Wenstar. We reverse and render.

FACTS

In 2002, AZT Winnsboro La., Inc., (AZT) sold a tract to Wenstar. A Wendy's restaurant is currently operating on the Wenstar property (the dominant estate). In the "Act of Cash Sale and Servitude," AZT, the vendor, granted to Wenstar, the vendee, a servitude in the following language:

> Vendor also grants to vendee a predial servitude in favor of the Property prohibiting the use of the property adjacent to the Property that is owned by Vendor and described on Exhibit A attached hereto and made a part hereof (hereinafter, Vendor's Adjacent Property) or any part or parcel thereof for a restaurant with a drive-thru pick-up window, the primary business of which is the sale of hamburgers, hamburger products or chicken sandwiches (or any combination thereof). For the purposes of this servitude and restriction, a restaurant has the aforesaid products as its primary business if fifteen percent (15%) or more of its gross sales, exclusive of taxes, beverage and dairy product sales, consists of sales of hamburgers, hamburger products or chicken sandwiches (or any combination thereof). This servitude and restriction shall burden Vendor's Adjacent Property for a period of twenty (20) years from the date of this act of sale; provided, however, that this servitude and restriction shall terminate at such time that the Property is no longer used as a Wendy's restaurant or if operation of a Wendy's restaurant ceases on the Property for a continuous period of three (3) months.

In 2004, AZT sold the adjacent property (the servient estate) to R.C.C. Properties, L.L.C. R.C.C. subsequently received an offer to purchase this tract from Hannon's Food Service of Vicksburg, Inc., which intended to build a KFC (Kentucky Fried Chicken) franchise on the property. Hannon's agreed to purchase the property only if R.C.C. could obtain a satisfactory release of the servitude.

In February 2005, R.C.C. filed a petition for a declaratory judgment asking the district court either to invalidate the servitude or declare it inapplicable to the R.C.C. property. R.C.C. subsequently added Hannon's and Wendy's International, Inc., as defendants.

The court held a trial in July 2005 and heard testimony from several witnesses. Among the witnesses was Bobby Hannon, chairman of Hannon's, who explained that a KFC restaurant serves several types of chicken sandwiches and that any KFC built on the R.C.C. property would serve these sandwiches. Hannon also stated that "the deal would be off as far as he was concerned if the servitude binding the property was found to be valid.

Edward Buchner, III, a certified public accountant from Vicksburg who handled Hannon's business, also testified. Buchner reviewed Hannon's sales figures for Hannon's KFC restaurants to determine what percentage of KFC restaurant sales consisted of chicken sandwiches. For 2003, chicken sandwiches amounted to 1.77% of total sales; for 2004, the percentage was 1.81%, and for the first six months of 2005, the percentages were January-1.91%; February-4.87%, March-14.18%, April-11.2%, May-10.8%, and June-6.7%.

Pete Subowicz, a field director for real estate for Wendy's International, testified that he negotiated this predial servitude with the original property owner when Wenstar acquired its Winnsboro property. He explained that deed restrictions limiting competition are a "pretty common standard" in the fast food industry. The servitude defined "primary business" as the sale of hamburgers, hamburger products or chicken sandwiches "if fifteen percent (15%) or more of its gross sales, exclusive of taxes, beverage and dairy product sales, consists of sales of hamburgers, hamburger products or chicken sandwiches (or any combination thereof)." In his view, a particular restaurant that wanted to locate on the servient estate would have to establish that its hamburger and chicken sandwich sales did not exceed 15%, as described above. In his view, that restaurant would have to establish that fact by submission of national sales records, then regional sales records and sales records of existing restaurants. Subowicz admitted that the existing predial servitude would not prohibit the construction of a KFC store provided the KFC owners could demonstrate that its sales of the proscribed sandwiches was less than 15%. Subowicz testified Wendy's International would never agree to the release of a predial servitude.

The court subsequently issued reasons for judgment stating its intent to invalidate the servitude in its entirety. The court stated, in part:

> This Court understands that predial servitudes are to be strictly construed, and any doubts as to the extent or exercise of rights created by such servitudes should be resolved in favor of the servient estate. This Court believes that this predial servitude is unclear and ambiguous. It is not clear as to what time period the chicken sandwich sales are to be measured. Is it one week, one month, one quarter or one year? It is also unclear how the determination is to be made. Does the owner of the dominant estate have the right to examine the books and records on demand or must legal action be taken, or does the owner of the servient estate have a duty to provide those records on a weekly, monthly, quarterly, or annual basis? Since the servitude is silent as to both the time period and manner of showing compliance, this Court must determine the servitude to be ambiguous. Since servitudes are not favored and are to be strictly construed, any ambiguity is to be assessed

against the dominant estate.

The court also noted that it did not consider the parol evidence presented by the parties regarding the intent when the servitude was negotiated and effected. On August 12,2005, the court signed a judgment invalidating the servitude.

DISCUSSION

In Blanchard v. Rand, 34,442 (La. App. 3/2/01), 781 So. 2d 881, writs denied, 1-0897, 01-0931 (La.6/1/01), 793 So.2d 193,194, this court explained that a predial servitude is a real right burdening an immovable. To have a predial servitude requires two different tracts belonging to different owners. A predial servitude is due to the estate rather than the owner of the estate and is a charge on the servient estate for the benefit of the dominant estate. La. C.C. art. 646.

La. C.C. art. 697 provides:

> Predial servitudes may be established by an owner on his estate or acquired
> for its benefit.

> The use and extent of such servitudes are regulated by the title by which
> they are created, and, in the absence of such regulation, by the following
> rules.

A predial servitude restricting or prohibiting commercial use of property is a negative, nonapparent servitude which may be acquired only by title. La. C.C. arts. 706, 707, 739; Mardis v. Brantley, 30,773 (La. App. 2d Cir. 8/25/98), 717 So. 2d 702, 704, writ denied, 98-2488 (La. 11/20/98), 729 So. 2d 563. Once the document creating the servitude is recorded in the public records, the restriction is binding on subsequent owners who acquire the servient estate without further mention of the restriction in the act conveying the servient estate. Mardis, *supra*.

La. C.C. art. 730 provides:

> Doubt as to the existence, extent, or manner of exercise of a predial
> servitude shall be resolved in favor of the servient estate.
> La. C.C. art. 749 provides:

> If the title is silent as to the extent and manner of use of the servitude, the
> intention of the parties is to be determined in the light of its purpose.

When a predial servitude is created by title, the intention of the parties to place a charge on one estate for the benefit of another estate, and the extent of the charge, must be expressed on the face of the title document and cannot be inferred or implied from vague or ambiguous language. Mardis, *supra*. Servitudes claimed under title are never sustained by implication; the title creating them must be express as to their nature and extent, as well as to the estate that owes them and the estate to which they are due. Williams v. Wiggins, 26,060 (La. App. 2d Cir. 8/17/94), 641 So. 2d 1068.

We disagree with the trial court's finding that the servitude was invalid because the method of measuring "primary business" described by the servitude was ambiguous. The servitude in favor of Wenstar's property is a conventional predial servitude. The original vendor, AZT, and purchaser of the dominant estate, Wenstar, clearly intended to create a predial servitude restricting the use of the servient estate still owned by AZT.

The instrument transferring the property to Wenstar was entitled "Act of Cash Sale and Servitude." The intent of the proprietor to create a servitude must clearly appear on the fact of the document. Blanchard, *supra*. This instrument specifically stated a "predial servitude" was granted in favor of the property acquired by Wenstar. The "predial servitude" bound the adjacent property by prohibiting a certain use of the remaining property owned by AZT, the vendee. The title document clearly reflected the intention of the parties to create an obligation in favor of the dominant estate. Blanchard, *supra*. The extent of the charge on the servient estate is the prohibition against using the servient estate "for a restaurant with a drive-thru pick-up window, the primary business of which is the sale of hamburger products or chicken sandwiches (or any combination thereof)." The servitude is effective as written. The trial court erred as a matter of law in invalidating the servitude; therefore, we make a *de novo* review of the record.

Having found that the predial servitude is binding on the servient estate, we find that the trial court's concerns about the practical implementation of the servitude were perceptive. In particular, the method by which the "primary business" of the servient estate should be measured is unclear. The yearly totals of Harmon's KFC chicken sandwich sales for 2003 and 2004 were well underneath the 15% specification in the title, as was the average for 2005, but in three months of 2005, chicken sandwich sales approached 15% of Harmon's sales revenues.

Because the "primary business" measurement is related to the manner of use of the servitude, we look to the intent of the parties in creating the servitude. The trial court refused to consider parol evidence to determine that question. However, the intent of Wenstar and AZT in creating the servitude is apparent from the face of the title. Wenstar intended to prevent a competitor in the fast-food hamburger or chicken sandwich business from opening a restaurant next to the Wendy's. Toward that end, the servitude created by the parties defined the level of competition that would trigger the restriction.

Hannon's KFC sales figures, as recited at the hearing, showed that the revenues from chicken sandwiches sold at Hannon's other KFC restaurants never equaled or exceeded 15% of total restaurant sales. Although the future is uncertain, the only evidence presented showed that the "primary business" trigger in the servitude was never reached by the other Hannon's restaurants in the past. Interpreting the servitude in light of La. C.C. art. 730, the servitude does not prohibit the construction or operation of a KFC restaurant at this location.

We are not called upon to decide what result may obtain should the KFC, or any other restaurant, later have a revenue mixture that triggers the "primary business" measure in the servitude. We note that doubt as to the manner of exercise of a predial servitude is resolved in favor of the servient estate. La. C.C. art. 730. The intention of the parties in light of its purpose is used to determine manner of use of the servitude. La. C.C. art. 749. Considering the contingent nature of Hannon's agreement to buy the property from R.C.C. and Hannon's testimony that a valid servitude would result in the deal being off, it is unlikely that a decision will be necessary on how to determine 15% of the proscribed sales figures.

As requested in R.C.C.'s pleadings, this decision is limited to the finding that a valid predial servitude exists in favor of the dominant estate (specifically described in footnote #1). The trial court judgment, which declares the predial servitude (quoted above) "invalid and of no effect as to the entirety of the Servient Estate" (specifically described in footnote # 2), is reversed.***

NOTE
Restraints on Competition

Reread section 108 of Professor Yiannopoulos' treatise that is reproduced supra. Should the court in the preceding case have ruled against R.C.C. on the basis that the contested provision imposed a restraint on competition that is permissible as a personal obligation but not as a predial servitude, or as any other real obligation? Compare the preceding case with the following excerpt from SPE FO Holdings, LLC v. Retif Oil & Fuel, LLC, 2008 WL 754716 (E.D. La.) 3/19/08, in which Judge Lemmon addressed the question of whether noncompetition agreements can create real rights:

> The Restrictions do not establish a real right of a predial servitude or building restrictions that would bind a successor in title. The issue is whether the Restrictions, which attempt to restrict competition, can affect real rights. While reasonable restraints on competition may establish personal obligations between the contracting parties, prohibitions against competition may not constitute real rights in Louisiana.

> In Leonard v. Lavigne, 245 La. 1004, 162 So. 2d 341, 343 (La. 1964), the Supreme Court of Louisiana construed the following stipulation in a recorded lease which stated that:

>> [Lessors bound] themselves, their heirs and assigns not to sell or lease all or part of the adjoining premises owned by them to any other person, firm or corporation for the purposes of engaging in a competitive business with this lessee.

> The adjoining premises were subsequently sold by the lessor to the third person without mention of the restriction in the act of sale. When the new owners started erecting a competitive business on their land, the lessee sought an injunction. The Supreme Court held that the stipulation did not create a restriction that ran with the land but rather the clause gave rise to a personal obligation. The Supreme Court concluded:

>> The stipulation in the contract of lease does not create a real obligation upon the land itself, but is clearly an obligation the lessors placed upon themselves.

> As Professor Yiannopolous explains, prohibitions against competition should not be allowed to restrict the use of lands in Louisiana; existing economic needs may be amply satisfied by means of personal obligations. The Leonard case supports this view.

> The United States Court of Appeal for the Fifth Circuit, construing Louisiana

law, treated the issue similarly when affirming a district court's summary judgment that certain provisions in a lease did not create real rights that were binding on a successor in title. In Solo Serve, a leaseholder of space in a shopping center sued his landlord's successor in title for failing to honor lease provisions when available space was leased to an off track betting facility. While affirming the district court's summary judgment in favor of the landlord, the Fifth Circuit disagreed with the district court's finding that the alleged breached lease provisions were restrictive covenants. Construing similar state cases, the Fifth Circuit noted "public policy concerns about the potential anticompetitive effect of such covenants justified a strict construction limiting the scope of such anticompetitor covenants."

In this case, the court must subject the Restrictions to strict construction because they purport to restrict competition. The Restrictions in this case were recorded and attempt to preclude competition, but were not included in the Marshall's Deed conveying the property to SPE. Recordation of a lease does not create rights that do not exist, nor does recordation make valid restrictions which are not. Even if the Restrictions had been made part of the Marshall's Deed, the Restrictions do not constitute a predial servitude or a building restriction, as defined by the Louisiana Civil Code.

Accordingly, the court grants summary judgment that the Restrictions do not create a real right as against the Dunn St. property.

LANGEVIN v. HOWARD
363 So. 2d 1209 (La. App. 2d Cir. 1978)

JONES, J. The defendant appeals from a judgment recognizing a legal predial servitude 50 feet in width and 1,537 feet in length across his land in favor of a 1.1 acre tract owned by plaintiff.***

The property involved in this litigation was included in a 1955 partition of the Kent tract as shown on the following plat which was attached to the partition.

The lot now owned by the plaintiff is sketched in the northwest corner of Tract F as shown on the plat of the partition and the lots owned by the defendant and Turk are identified by inscribing their names on the plat.

In the Kent partition of Tracts A, B, C, D, E and F as shown on the plat, the parties reserved ownership in indivision of a 50 foot wide strip running north and south through the approximate center of the partitioned tracts as a right of way to the Primitive Baptist Church public road located along the south line of the partitioned property. The partition contained with reference to this strip the following stipulation:

"Appearers herein have not partitioned a strip of land, hereinafter described, and continue to hold in indivision for the use and benefit of all appearers as an access road for the purpose of ingress and egress to the tracts herein described. It is understood that this reservation is not to be construed as establishing an easement or right of way in favor of the public generally, but is private in nature and ownership. Said strip of land is described as follows..."

The parties to the partition failed to pay the taxes on the 50 foot strip and were divested of ownership of this strip at a tax sale in 1960. In 1969 Turk acquired the ownership of Tract F. In 1972 the defendant acquired ownership of Tracts B, E and the 50 foot strip, in 1973, following defendant's completion of his home on Tract E, he employed Turk to construct a 10 foot driveway down the approximate center of his 50 foot tract from its south line bordering the Primitive Baptist Church Road to his home located on Tract E. Defendant paid Turk the sum of $1,000 for this work.

In 1975 Turk decided to sell two lots in the northwest corner of Tract F adjacent to the east line of the 50 foot strip and pursuant to this plan, he had a survey made of each lot. Turk contemplated the use of the driveway which he had constructed on the 50 foot strip as the access route to the public road for the future owners of these two lots. One of these lots was .74 of an acre located in the northwest corner of Tract F, which Turk sold to V plaintiff on August 6, 1975. The other lot was adjacpt to and immediately to the south of it. Turk had arranged to sell the second lot on the same day that he sold the plaintiff his lot, however, the proposed vendee died prior to the sale. for the first time with defendant his plan to sell two lots in the northwest corner of Tract F and use the driveway constructed on the 50 foot strip as access for the purchasers of these lots to the Primitive Baptist Church road. Turk advised defendant of his ownership claim to a portion of the right of passage over the 50 foot strip as a result of the Kent partition. Turk at this time gave defendant *back* $200 of the $1,000 that he had received from defendant for construction of the driveway. The $200 was given to defendant in the form of Turk's check which contained a notation on the face of it "use of driveway." Defendant accepted the check and cashed it. While Turk and defendant recognized that the check was a reimbursement to defendant of a portion of his $1,000 paid for the construction of the driveway, their understanding of the rights that were acquired for these two lots by this payment is in dispute. At the time of these negotiations defendant was unaware that one of the lots had already been sold to plaintiff.

Plaintiff moved a house trailer on his lot in October of 1975 and commenced the use of defendant's driveway. In May of 1977 defendant advised plaintiff to make arrangements for other access to his lot because defendant owned the 50 foot strip unencumbered by any right of passage. In the first week of July defendant proceeded to obstruct plaintiffs passage from his lot to the driveway located on the 50 foot strip. Defendant installed posts along the east line of the 50 foot strip, two of which were at a point on plaintiffs west line where his individual driveway entered the 50 foot strip. This interfered with easy access from the plaintiffs lot to the driveway located on the 50 foot strip.

Plaintiff instituted this action on July 8 wherein he sought judicial declaration of the existence of a right of passage on the 50 foot strip from the Primitive Baptist Church Road to his lot in the northwest corner of Tract F. Plaintiffs suit first contended his lot had a servitude of passage to the public road created by the 1955 Kent partition. Plaintiff alternatively argued that if there was no servitude in favor of his lot as a result of the Kent partition, then one was created on the defendant's driveway by the 1975 $200 check transaction between Turk and defendant... The issues presented are:

$200 CHECK TRANSACTION

Servitudes are established by all acts by which property can be transferred. C.C. Art. 743 [Revised C.C. art. 722]. Creation of a servitude is an alienation of a part of the property. C.C Art. 731 [Revised C.C. art. 708]. Conventional predial servitudes and personal servitudes affecting immovable property which are created by agreement between the parties must be in writing. Art. 2440 [citations omitted].

Plaintiff contends the $200 check with the notation on the face of it, "use of driveway" given by Turk payable to defendant and by him endorsed and cashed, constitutes the required written grant of the servitude. The writing on the check does not describe the 50 foot strip belonging to the defendant.

Plaintiff contends that parole evidence is admissible to supply the description of the servient estate. The rule that parole evidence is admissible to make clear a vague description requires the writing to sufficiently identify the property so that the property involved in the transaction can be determined by the writing rather than from the parole evidence [citations omitted].

On the check the only word referring to the servient estate is "driveway" and this falls far short of giving any written information upon which a determination of the servient estate could be made. For this reason no parole evidence was admissible for the purpose of providing the description of the servitude.

Plaintiff argues that the check given by Turk to defendant creates a personal servitude by the operation of the doctrine of stipulation *pour autrui* in favor of the plaintiff over the defendant's driveway. The creation of a personal servitude over real property creates an interest in the property and for this reason must be in writing. *Newman v. Gumira,* [77 So. 2d 899 (La. App. 1955]. Because the check contains no writing describing the property subject to the personal servitude nor referring to it with sufficient certainty to justify the admission of explanatory parole evidence, it cannot form the basis for a personal servitude in favor of plaintiff.

VERBAL SERVITUDE

The rule that transfers of interest in immovable property must be in writing is subject to the exception that a verbal transaction is binding upon the grantor who confesses it when interrogated under oath. C.C. Arts. 2440 [no corresponding article after revision] and 2275 [Revised C.C. arts. 1832, 1839].

Plaintiff contends the defendant admitted during the trial he accepted the check in payment for a permanent servitude over the 50 foot strip in favor of the lot which Turk had conveyed to the plaintiff. A fair evaluation of the totality of the defendant's testimony establishes he admitted under oath only that he agreed for the plaintiff to use the driveway for a period of two years in consideration of the receipt of Turk's check. The defendant testified that any longer right of passage upon his 50 foot strip could be obtained only by negotiation in the presence of his wife and such right would have to be put in a written document prepared by an attorney.

The testimony of Turk and his wife about the circumstances surrounding the delivery of the check to the defendant is not admissible under C.C.Art. 2275 [Revised C.C. arts. 1832, 1839] for the purpose of establishing the admissions of the defendant about his verbal transfer of the servitude. Only the admissions of the grantor are effective against him. Testimony from witnesses to the verbal transaction attempting to establish the verbal immovable property transaction is inadmissible [citations omitted]. The two year personal servitude created by the defendant by his admissions under oath commenced on August 14,1975, and had expired in November 1977 when this case was tried below and therefore it cannot justify an adjudication of a servitude over defendant's driveway, nor the continuation of the injunction against the defendant contained in the trial court judgment. For the reasons assigned, we amend the trial court judgment and hold the plaintiff has no right of passage upon the defendant's property.

b. Acquisitive Prescription
Civil Code arts. 740,742

PALOMEQUE v. PRUDHOMME
664 So. 2d 88 (La. 1995)

MARCUS, J. On January 12, 1994, Dr. F.E. Palomeque filed a petition for injunctive relief to prohibit Paul E. Prudhomme from bricking over windows in the common wall between Dr. Palomeque's condominium at 422 Chartres Street and Prudhomme's property at 420 Chartres. Dr. Palomeque alleges that his condominium has acquired servitudes of light and view over Prudhomme's estate.

The properties at 420 and 422 Chartres Street were originally constructed in 1834 for Philippe Auguste Delachaise as two buildings in a row of three, four-story brick buildings. There is no evidence as to how or when the buildings were reduced to their current state, but today the Prudhomme property at 420 Chartres is but one story high while the condominium building at 422 Chartres is two stories high. On August 21, 1974, the Maison-Chartres Condominium Association acquired 422 Chartres and converted the building to condominiums with two units on the second floor. Architectural drawings by Leonard Reese Spangenberg, Jr., dated April 20, 1972 and created in anticipation of the condominium project, show ten windows in the common wall. At the time of trial there were only six functional windows. Two additional windows were apparent from the exterior but were sheetrocked over on the interior. Based on these discrepancies, the trial judge found that the windows were not preexisting but rather were placed in the common wall as part of the conversion project in 1974.

In 1981 Paul Prudhomme purchased the one-story building at 420 Chartres, which now provides K-Paul's Restaurant with office space, a test kitchen and a garage facility. Prudhomme first applied to the Vieux Carre Commission ("Commission") for approval of a second story addition in 1985. This project requires the bricking up of the windows at 422 Chartres. The Commission granted a six month permit but no work was done until 1991, when, with Commission approval, Prudhomme began the process of strengthening the failing facade. The second floor facade was added at that time.

In July 1993, Prudhomme's architect met with Andrew McCollam and Dr. Palomeque, owners of the second floor units, regarding Prudhomme's plan to close the windows. No agreement was reached, and Prudhomme went forward with his efforts to obtain another permit. In the meantime, on September 20, 1993, Andrew McCollam sold the front unit to Dr. Palomeque, who continued to oppose Prudhomme's efforts to enclose the second floor of 420 Chartres. A few days later the Commission approved the permit. Dr. Palomeque's action for injunctive relief followed.

A temporary restraining order was granted, and after a hearing, a preliminary injunction was granted. However, after a trial on the merits, the trial judge denied the permanent injunction and held that servitudes of light and view cannot be acquired by acquisitive prescription. Dr. Palomeque appealed. The court of appeal affirmed, finding that, even if acquisitive prescription were applicable, Dr. Palomeque did not have the requisite ten years of good faith. On application by Dr. Palomeque, we granted certiorari to review the correctness of that decision.

The issues presented for our consideration are: (1) whether servitudes of light and view can be acquired by acquisitive prescription; and (2) if so, whether servitudes were acquired in this case.

Apparent servitudes may be acquired by title, by destination of the owner, or by acquisitive prescription. La. Civ.Code. art. 740. Nonapparent servitudes may be acquired by title only. La. Civ.Code art. 739. Therefore, we must determine whether the servitudes of light and view are apparent or nonapparent servitudes.

Civil Code Article 707 defines apparent servitudes as those "that are *perceivable by exterior signs, works, or constructions;* such as a roadway, a window in a common wall, or an aqueduct." (emphasis added). Nonapparent servitudes are those "that have no exterior sign of their existence; such as the prohibition of building on an estate or of building above a particular height."

A window in a common wall is clearly an exterior sign of a servitude because a co-owner of a common wall may not make any openings in the wall without the consent of his neighbor. La. Civ. Code art. 681; A. N. Yiannopoulos, Predial Servitudes § 135, at 390-91 (4 Louisiana Civil Law Treatise 1983) (hereinafter Yiannopoulos, Predial Servitudes. Thus, by definition, a servitude of light or view in a common wall is apparent and can be acquired by acquisitive prescription. Yiannopoulos, Predial Servitudes § 135, at 390-93. Nonetheless, Prudhomme argues that, even in a common wall, the servitudes of light and view cannot be apparent because they are equivalent to a prohibition against building, a nonapparent servitude. This argument is without merit. The servitudes cannot be equated. A servitude of prohibition of building is much more onerous in that it prevents the owner of the servient estate from building any constructions on his estate. With servitudes of light and view the owner of the servient estate may still build on his property; he is only prevented from raising constructions that would obstruct the light or view. This prohibition against obstructions is merely an accessory right to the servitudes of light and view. La. Civ.Code arts. 701, 703; see also, A. N. Yiannopoulos, Creation of Servitudes by Prescription and Destination of the Owner, 43 La. L. Rev. 57, 61-65 (1982).

Thus, we hold that the servitudes of light and view in a common wall are apparent servitudes which encompass the right to prevent the servient estate from building obstructions to the light and view. As apparent servitudes, the servitudes of light and view may be established by acquisitive prescription. La. Civ. Code art. 740.

This brings us to the second question presented: Did Dr. Palomeque acquire servitudes of light and view by acquisitive prescription often years.

Prior to the 1977 revision of the law on predial servitudes, controversy existed as to the requisites for ten year prescription. Article 765 [no corresponding article after revision] and 3504 of the Civil Code of 1870 [cf. Revised C.C. art. 742], the articles in effect at the time, provided:

> Article 765: "Continuous and apparent servitudes may be acquired by title, or by a possession often years...."

> Article 3504: "A continuous apparent servitude is acquired by possession and the enjoyment of the right for thirty years uninterruptedly, even without a title or good faith."

The interrelation of these code articles is an unresolved matter. See, Comment, Acquisitive Prescription of Servitudes, 15 La. L. Rev. 777 (1955). The earliest decisions required that the possessor have just title and be in good faith in order to acquire a servitude by ten years possession. Kennedy v. Succession of McCollam, 34 La. Ann. 568 (1882). However, subsequent decisions required only ten years and good faith. Blanda v. Rivers, 210 So. 2d 161 (La. App. 4th Cir. 1968). Still others effectively wrote Article 3504 out of the Code by requiring no more than ten years of possession, regardless of good faith or just title. Levet v. Lapeyrollerie, 39 La. Ann. 210 (1887).

In 1977, these code articles were replaced by Article 742 which read as follows:

> The laws governing acquisitive prescription of immovable property apply to apparent servitudes. An apparent servitude may be acquired by peaceable and uninterrupted possession of the right for ten years in good faith and by just title; it may also be acquired by uninterrupted possession for thirty years without title or good faith, (emphasis added).

According to the Revision Comments, this article was based on a combined reading of Articles 765 and 3504 and was intended to overrule all contrary jurisprudence. In 1982, the code article on just title was also amended. That article now requires that just title be written, valid in form and recorded in the conveyance records of the parish in which the immovable is situated. La. Civ.Code art. 3483.

Dr. Palomeque argues that these revisions to the law of predial servitudes are not applicable here and that under the pre-1977 law, he is not required to establish just title. Blanda v. Rivers, 210 So. 2d 161 (La. App. 4th Cir. 1968). This argument is without merit. Section 7 of Act No. 514 which enacted the 1977 revisions provides:

The provisions of this Act shall apply to all predial servitudes, including those existing on the effective date of this Act; but no provision may be applied to divest already vested rights or to impair the obligation of contracts.

In order for a right to be vested it must be absolute, complete, unconditional, and independent of a contingency; the mere expectation of a future benefit or contingent interest in property does not create a vested right [citations omitted]. On January 1, 1978, the effective date of Act No. 514, Dr. Palomeque's predecessors had been possessing these servitudes for approximately four years. The right to the servitudes was contingent on continued possession without interruption for six more years. Consequently, Dr. Palomeque had no vested right in these servitudes which would prevent the application of the 1977, or even the 1982, revisions.[1]

Predial servitudes are in derogation of public policy because they form restraints on the free disposal and use of property. Therefore, servitudes are not entitled to be viewed with favor by the law and can never be sustained by implication [citations omitted]. Any doubt as to the existence, extent or manner of exercise of a predial servitude must be resolved in favor of the servient estate. La. C.C. art.730; McGuffy v. Weil, 240 La. 758, 125 So. 2d 154,158 (1960).

Applying the revised law on acquisitive prescription of servitudes, Dr. Palomeque must establish that he has possessed the right for ten years in good faith and with just title. La. Civ.Code art. 742. The trial judge found that the windows were created in 1974. Based on the record, this finding is not clearly wrong. Thus, the ten years of adverse possession have been conclusively established. However, the requirement of just title is more problematic for Dr. Palomeque.

Just title is a juridical act sufficient to transfer ownership or another real right. It must be written, valid in form and filed for registry in the conveyance records of the parish in which the immovable is situated. La. Civ. Code art. 3483. As applied to servitudes, Article 3483 requires that the possessor have a title that would have established a servitude if it had been granted by the owner of the servient estate. Yiannopoulos, Predial Servitudes § 137, at 396. Because Dr. Palomeque has no agreement with the servient estate, he argues that his titles to the two condominium units serve as just title for these servitudes. In setting forth the description of the properties to be conveyed in the acts of sale, the descriptions commence with the following standard language:

That certain piece of ground or portion of ground, condominium parcels, units and/or apartments, common elements and limited common elements, together with all the buildings and improvements thereon, and all the rights, ways, privileges, servitudes and

---

[1] Counsel for Dr. Palomeque conceded during oral argument before the court of appeal that the evidence would not sustain a plea of thirty years acquisitive prescription. Thus the court considered only ten year prescription. The court found that the creation of an opening in the common wall without permission of the co-owner is intrinsically an act of bad faith, and in the alternative, if Dr. Palomeque's predecessors had built the windows with permission, the possession would have been precarious and would not give rise to a claim of acquisitive prescription. Consequently, Dr. Palomeque's claim failed and the court was able to pretermit the questions of whether Dr. Palomeque had just title and whether servitudes of light and view can be acquired by acquisitive prescription. 94-0847 c/w 94-1942 (La. App. 4th Cir. 2/23/95), 650 So. 2d 1264.

appurtenance thereunto belonging or in anywise appertaining, situated on....

This boilerplate language has been used in every deed transferring these condominiums since their development in 1974.

Clearly, the language in question would be too ambiguous and imprecise to establish servitudes of light and view by title. Even if this language were used in an agreement with the servient estate, it could not establish servitudes of light and view. For a servitude to be created by title, the instrument must be express as to the nature and extent of the servitude. Because servitudes are so disfavored, an ambiguous agreement to establish a servitude is unenforceable. "Where the language is insufficient to convey ownership of property which belongs to the grantor, it cannot be sufficient to create just title in property which does not in fact belong to the grantor." Williams v. Wiggins, 26,060 (La. App. 2d Cir. 9/17/94), 641 So. 2d 1068,1073.

Nonetheless, Dr. Palomeque argues that this language is sufficient to constitute just title for purposes of acquisitive prescription. We disagree. Even assuming this language could transfer a preexisting right, under no circumstance would this ambiguous language create a servitude. Therefore, it cannot suffice for just title [citations omitted].

Moreover, "just title in acquisitive prescription is not required only as an element of showing good faith. It represents a separate condition. Hence it must exist in reality; the possessor's belief in its existence is insufficient, no matter how plausible." 2 Aubry & Rau, Droit Civil Francais § 218, no. 311, at 363 (La.St.L.Inst.trans. 7th ed. 1961). Dr. Palomeque may not rely on his belief, no matter how justifiable, that the condominium association had a right to install windows in a common wall. He must show more than that; he must show a written, recorded act that would have created a servitude had it been granted by the owner of the servient estate. If this language were considered sufficient for the purposes of just title, the just title requirement would be rendered meaningless, resulting in the requirement of only good faith and ten years. In 1977, the Louisiana legislature took very specific steps to overrule Blanda and its progeny. To hold otherwise would be to undermine those revisions. Lacking the requisite just title, the only way Dr. Palomeque could acquire servitudes of light and view is by accrual of thirty years of uninterrupted possession which he admittedly does not have.

Accordingly, we hold that the language in Dr. Palomeque's deeds is insufficient to constitute just title to a servitude under Civil Code article 3483. Having found that Dr. Palomeque lacks just title, we need not reach the issue of good faith.

DECREE

For the reasons assigned, the judgment of the court of appeal is affirmed. All costs are assessed against Dr. F.E. Palomeque.

RYAN v. MONET
666 So. 2d 711 (La. App. 4th Cir. 1995)

PLOTKIN, J. Elizabeth H. Ryan appeals a preliminary injunction that permits Alexandra Monett to maintain four window unit air conditioners on the side of her building at 2708 Coliseum Street that extend beyond the property line onto appellant's adjacent property at 2700 Coliseum Street. We amend the injunction to require appellee to remove these air conditioners, and we remand for further proceedings.

Ryan and Monett own adjacent estates at 2700 and 2708 Coliseum Street, respectively. Both lots contain buildings that were constructed over a century ago. The foundation of the building at 2708 Coliseum was built on the boundary between the estates. On March 21, 1958, a predecessor in title to Ryan executed a document that purported to create a servitude of overhang, which document states:

> [Ryan's predecessor in title] hereby recognizes the existence of a servitude of overhang over his said property in favor of the said adjoining property more particularly described hereinafter, to the extent of one foot (1') by the cornice of the main building of said property and eight inches (8") by the roof thereof, and does therefore hereby grant, donate, confirm, transfer and deliver, in favor of said adjoining property, a servitude of overhang to the extent hereinabove mentioned over and above his said property, the same to be continued in full force and effect in favor of said adjoining property for as long as the aforesaid building designated as Municipal No. 2708 Coliseum Street. New Orleans, Parish of Orleans, State of Louisiana, shall continue in existence as presently located, but to terminate upon the removal thereof;

Monett acquired 2708 Coliseum in December 1971 and reacquired it for use as rental property in March 1993 by dation en paiement from Mary Hart and her husband George O. Lillich Jr. Ryan owns and resides at 2700 Coliseum.

On March 7, 1995, Ryan sought an injunction to compel Monett to remove four air conditioners that extended over the property line and to remove a spout that had been added to a gutter of 2708 Coliseum that drained onto a garden at 2700 Coliseum. Ryan also sought damages from trespass by Monett's workers. On April 25, 1995, the trial judge, after reviewing the pleadings and affidavits, issued a preliminary injunction that required Monett to relocate the spout to its original position, to give reasonable notice to Ryan when Monett's workers would enter Ryan's yard, and authorized Monett to maintain no more than four window unit air conditioners that extended over the property line. The preliminary injunction is appealed only with regard to the air conditioners.

The trial judge stated the following in his reasons for judgment:

> Since these homes were built prior to the lifetime of the present litigants, it is obvious that predial servitudes exist in favor of the property at 2708 Coliseum Street and that these predial servitudes have been acquired by prescription in excess of thirty years.

With respect to the location of the window units projecting onto the plaintiffs property, the Court cites C.C. Article 647 for the proposition that a servitude may exist although the benefit need not exist at the time the servitude is created and that a possible convenience or a future advantage suffices to support a servitude.

In other words, air conditioning units did not exist at the time the property at 2708 Coliseum Street was erected. Nevertheless, the fact that the house was located on the property line, has continued to exist beyond ten years and that the window units are necessary in order to enjoy the property at the present time means that the servient estate—2700 Coliseum Street—must accept the overhang of the air conditioning units.

Also. C.C. Articles 743 and 744 provide for the accessory rights and necessary works in order to use the servitude.

On appeal, Ryan contends that the judge erred in the application of Civil Code Articles 647,743-744, and the law of acquisitive prescription.

A charge on 2700 Coliseum Street to tolerate the overhang of existing window unit air conditioners from the adjacent property for the benefit of 2708 Coliseum Street would be an apparent, affirmative predial servitude, which can only be acquired by title, destination of the owner, or by acquisitive prescription. See La.C.C. arts. 646. 697, 706-707, 740. Because there has been no allegation of common ownership that might implicate destination of the owner, we must consider only whether any such servitude has been created by title or by acquisitive prescription and, if created, not extinguished by nonuse.

The only "title" that is purported to have created a servitude is the March 21, 1958 agreement. A conventional servitude may be created by any juridical act sufficient to establish a real right in immovable property. See La.C.C. art. 708; see also A. N. Yiannopoulos, Louisiana Civil Law Treatise vol. 4, Predial Servitudes § 112 (1983). Because we interpret this agreement as not intending to create a servitude that would encompass the air conditioners, it is not necessary to decide, nor can it be determined from the record, whether this agreement is a juridical act sufficient to establish a real right in immovable property, or whether the effectiveness of this agreement against third persons was maintained in accordance with the public records doctrine.

A document purporting to create a predial servitude is interpreted in accordance with both the general rules of contract construction as well as in accordance with specific rules of construction for instruments that purport to create servitudes. Yiannopoulos, supra, § 128. A court must determine the intent of the parties, resolving any doubt as to the existence, extent, or manner of exercise of the purported servitude in favor of the servient estate. La.C.C. arts. 697, 730, 749, 2045, 2057. Assuming that the March 21, 1958 instrument validly created a servitude, it is clear, by reading the unambiguous language in favor of the servient estate, that this servitude was intended only to authorize the roof to extend eight inches, and the cornice to extend a foot, over the property line.

Neither do we agree with the trial judge that air conditioners were a future benefit intended by the parties and authorized by Civil Code Article 647, nor that air conditioners are authorized by Articles 743 and 744 as necessary or accessory rights to this servitude. Article 647 provides in part:

> There must be a benefit to the dominant estate. The benefit need not exist at the time the servitude is created; a possible convenience or a future advantage suffices to support such a servitude.

Without deciding whether an overhanging air conditioner can be considered a future advantage under Article 647, the precise language of the instrument, which defines the type and extent of overhang to be permitted, does not permit the inference that the parties intended any future advantage. Articles 743 and 744 provide:

> Art. 743. Accessory rights
> Rights that are necessary for the use of a servitude are acquired at the time the servitude is established. They are to be exercised in a way least inconvenient for the servient estate.

> Art. 744. Necessary works; cost of repairs
> The owner of the dominant estate has the right to make at his expense all the works that are necessary for the use and preservation of the servitude.

Window unit air conditioners cannot be considered necessary under Article 743 to the continued overhang of the roof and the cornice. Moreover, the owner of the dominant estate is free to install a central air- conditioning unit on the other side of the property, obviating entirely the need for window units and causing less inconvenience to the servient estate. Likewise, Article 744 does not authorize air conditioners, which are not necessary to the use and preservation of the overhanging roof and cornice.

Apparent predial servitudes may also be created by acquisitive prescription and extinguished by nonuse. See La.C.C. arts. 740, 742. 753; see also Yiannopoulos, *supra,* §§ 134,163. The trial judge found it obvious that, because the building at 2708 Coliseum had existed on the property line for more than a century, predial servitudes must have been acquired by prescription. The trial judge may be correct that some servitudes have been acquired; however, the question to be resolved is whether a servitude permitting the overhang of the air conditioners has been acquired by prescription. The record is insufficient to support the finding that such a servitude has been acquired.

Civil Code Article 740, enacted by Act 1977, No. 514, § 1, changed the law by abandoning the requirement that an apparent servitude also be considered continuous to be acquired by prescription. La.C.C. art. 740 comment (a). This change is not retroactive. Id. Because we find that no servitude permitting the overhang of the window unit air conditioners has been created under the new law, which is broader than the old, it is not necessary to precisely determine the times at which the air conditioners were in place, or to determine whether the requirement of continuity under the old law was satisfied.

Civil Code Article 742 provides in part:

> An apparent servitude may be acquired by peaceable and uninterrupted possession of the right for ten years in good faith and by just title; it may also

be acquired by uninterrupted possession for thirty years without title or good faith.

The type of possession necessary to create such a servitude is unauthorized use that infringes on the ownership of the servient estate. Yiannopoulos, supra, § 138. Civil Code Article 753 provides:

> A predial servitude is extinguished by nonuse for ten years. Nonuse commences for an apparent, affirmative servitude from the date of last use. See La.C.C. art. 754; see also Yiannopoulos, supra, § 163. The only evidence regarding the length of time the air conditioners have been in place is the following: By affidavit, Lillich stated that air conditioners were there when he began to manage the property in 1983, although he conceded that particular window units may have been replaced between 1983 and 1993; and from photographic evidence, it is apparent that four air conditioners are still there.

Assuming without ruling that this possession suffices for purposes of acquisitive prescription, we find the appropriate prescriptive period to be thirty years. Although no evidence has been presented to rebut the presumption of good faith, neither has any evidence been presented to establish just title. Monett suggests that after a century just title must be present, but cites no authorities supporting the presumption of just title. The only "title" appearing in evidence is the instrument dated March 21,1958. This document on its face does not purport to describe or convey any property right that would authorize the placement of the window units. Without just title, the soonest this servitude could be created by prescription appears from the only evidence before this Court to be some time in the year 2013, if prescription had not been interrupted by the filing of this suit.

Monett contends that "cooling system platforms" were in place as early as 1971. It is not necessary to decide whether these suffice to commence possession for the purpose of acquisitive prescription; this still would not establish thirty years uninterrupted and peaceable possession.

Monett also contends that when the original owners built these houses over a century ago, a servitude was created. Monett claims that Ryan was aware that the building at 2708 Coliseum was built on the property line when she purchased 2700 Coliseum and suggests that Ryan should be barred by Civil Code Article 670 from complaining of this "encroachment" because a reasonable time has passed. The trial judge appears not to have accepted Monett's argument under Article 670. In essence, Monett asserts that Ryan should be estopped from bringing this suit by her own acts and the acts of her predecessors in title. Estoppel, however, is not one of the methods enumerated in the Civil Code for the creation of a predial servitude, and resort to equity under the facts of this case is neither authorized by the Code nor appropriate under the circumstances.

Instead, the trial judge articulated his decision on the basis of acquisitive prescription; Civil Code Articles 647, 743-744; and the notion that the addition of window unit air conditioners might be the justifiable growth in use of an existing servitude. We find the record insufficient to support the conclusion that a servitude, which would permit Monett to extend window unit air conditioners over the property line onto Ryan's estate, was created by either convention or by acquisitive prescription. Even if we assume the existence of an underlying servitude of some sort, we cannot find that Monett has acquired the additional right to extend window units over the property line before acquisitive prescription has accrued. Additional rights cannot be acquired by use except by acquisitive prescription. See Yiannopoulos, supra, § 136.

Accordingly, we amend the injunction to require Monett to remove all window unit air conditioners that extend over the property line between 2700 and 2708 Coliseum Street within thirty days after any final judgment in these proceedings, and we remand for further proceedings in accordance with this opinion. All costs of this proceeding are assessed to appellee.

GOODWIN v. ALEXANDER
105 La. 658, 30 So. 102 (1901)

MONROE, J. Plaintiffs own a frame house on Washington avenue, between St. Charles avenue and Carondelet street, in New Orleans, which stands about six inches within the line which divides their lot from that of the defendant. The house has been standing in its present position for more than 30 years, and during that time had had a window the sill of which is about six feet from the ground, with blinds opening out, in the side next to the defendant's, so that the blinds, if opened more than six inches, pass over the defendant's property. We infer that there was some trouble between the parties, or, perhaps, between the defendant and the plaintiffs' tenant, prior to the occurrence out of which this suit arises. But in January, 1899, the defendant caused a frame or screen con-sisting of two pieces of scantling, about 10 feet long and 4 feet apart, with boards nailed across their upper ends for a distance of about 2!/2 feet, to be fixed in the ground upon the line of her property, and immediately in front of the plaintiffs' window, for the purpose, and with the effect, of preventing the opening of the blinds, and of cutting off the view into her premises through said window.

This screen, either when originally put up, or shortly after, leaned about 3 1A inches in the direction of the plaintiffs' house, so that, while the base was 6 inches away, the upper end came within an inch of the window blinds. In fact, it is said that it at first touched the blinds, but we are not satisfied that such was the case. Later on, in November, 1899, the screen was straightened up, and has since stood entirely on or within the defendant's line. In the meanwhile, in March, 1899, plaintiffs brought this suit, in which they claim to have acquired a servitude of light and view, through the window in question, by reason of the prescription of 30 years; and they claim, as damages, $10 per day from January 6, 1899, the date at which the screen was erected, and $1,000 as "punitive and vindictive" damages; and they pray that said screen be removed, and that defendant be restrained from interfering with their enjoyment of the said servitude claimed by them. On behalf of the defendant, there is an exception of no cause of action and a general denial. The tenant now occupying the plaintiffs' house testifies that since the screen was put up she has demanded, and has obtained, an abatement of $2 per month in the rent. Such is the case as presented by the record.

ON THE MERITS

"The ownership of the soil carries with it all that is directly above and under it." Rev. Civ. Code, art. 505 [Revised C.C. art. 490]. "The prohibition of building above a particular height," is a continuous, nonapparent servitude, which "can be established only by title; immemorial possession itself is not sufficient to acquire it." Id. arts. 728, 766 [Revised C.C. arts. 707, 739]. No servitude of light and view, such as plaintiffs claim to have acquired by prescription, can include this servitude of "prohibition," which cannot be so acquired. 1 Mourlon, p. 861; 8 Laurent, p. 54; Oldstein v. Association, 44 La. Ann. 492, 10 South. 928. In Jeannin v. DeBlanc, 11 La. Ann. 466, Mr. Justice Spofford, as the organ of this court, said: "By the same right that defendant builds a wall with apertures, undoubtedly, the plaintiff may build one, facing it, without apertures, if it shall so please him." So, in this case, by the same right that the plaintiffs' authors built the house now owned by them with apertures overlooking the adjoining lot, undoubtedly the owners of the adjoining lot might, or may, build a house, or any other structure, facing those apertures, if it shall so please them; and this last-mentioned right is never barred by prescription. Plaintiffs' claim for damages has no other foundation than the fact that for a while the screen erected leaned. 3!/2 inches over the line, and we are unable to discover that any damage was sustained on that account. The main complaint is that the screen, whether perpendicular, or leaning, as it was, cuts off the light and view, and prevents the opening of the blinds, and this complaint is unfounded in law. Judgment affirmed.

LOUISIANA MINERAL CODE

Art. 159. Mineral rights not established by acquisitive prescription

Mineral rights may not be established by acquisitive prescription.

Comment

Article 159 articulates the holding of Savage v. Packard, 218 La. 637, 50 So.2d 298 (1950). It is also reflective of Article 766 of the Civil Code, which provides that "continuous nonapparent servitudes, and discontinuous servitudes, whether apparent or not, can be established only by a title," adding that "immemorial possession itself is not sufficient to acquire such servitudes."

c. Destination of Owner
Civil Code arts. 739,741

ALEXANDER v. BOGHEL
4 La. 312 (1832)

The facts are stated in the opinion of the court, delivered by PORTER, J. A right of service is contested in this case; both parties claim title under a common vendor. While owner and possessor of both lots, a house stood on that sold to the defendant in such a situation, that the roof projected over the lot then vacant and now in possession of the plaintiff, and caused the rain water to drip or fall on it. The defendant was the first purchaser. At the time the plaintiff bought, the house stood in the position it now does.

The defendant sets up a right to the service, and pleads prescription. The cause was decided in his favor on the latter ground, in the court of the first instance. The plaintiff appealed.

It is contended on the part of the plaintiff, that the fact of the house standing in the situation it does is no evidence of servitude. The common vendor being owner of both lots at the same time, could not owe a servitude to himself.

It is true, no man can owe a servitude to himself. The legal maxim is nemini res sua servit jure servitutis. But according to an express provision of the code of Louisiana in force at the time the defendant purchased —"if the proprietor of two estates, between which there exists an apparent sign of service, sell one of said estates, and if the deed of sale be silent respecting the service, the same shall continue to exist actively or passively, in favor of, or upon the estate, which has been sold." C. Code, 140, 57.

When the proprietor of the two lots sold to the defendant, and remained silent, that which he retained was burdened with the service. He could not have resisted the exercise of the right; and it is almost unnecessary to say, that he could not transfer to another that which he had not himself.

It is, therefore, ordered, adjudged, and decreed, that the judgment of the District Court be affirmed, with costs.

TAYLOR v. BOULWARE
35 La. Ann. 469 (1883)

MANNING, J. The defendant was the owner for several years of the two adjoining lots on Camp street numbered 469 and 471. He built a brick building of two stores and an attic, with a two-story wing, on No. 471 in 1855, and a cottage of one story and attic on No. 469 in 1865. The houses were two and half or three feet apart.

The brick house was built with windows in the side towards lot No. 469, in which were the usual sashes, and these were covered by Venetian blinds with movable or revolving slats. When the defendant built the cottage, he nailed boards across these windows on the outside, thus preventing the opening of the Venetian shutters, and shutting out the view over the cottage lot, and excluding light and ventilation from that side of the brick house. These boards had remained for about fifteen years, viz., from 1865, when the cottage was built, to 1880, when he sold the brick house and lot to the plaintiff. They were there when the plaintiff took possession in the same condition as when first put there.

Mrs. May bought in April, 1880, for five thousand two hundred and fifty dollars cash, but Boulware was to remain in possession until first of September following. A few days after she went into the occupancy of the brick house, she gave Boulware notice to remove the strips of board from across the window blinds, so that the shutters might be opened and closed at her pleasure, and if it was not done in forty-eight hours, that she would have them removed. He refused to remove them, and she had it done. Thereupon he had screens erected on his own lot, No. 469, opposite the windows of No. 471, to protect the adjoining cottage from view. The tenant of his cottage had promptly complained as soon as the windows were opened, and notified defendant that he would be compelled to move if the windows were not closed as before. These windows were in the upper story and gable end of the attic and overlooked the cottage and the lot No. 469.

The object of the present suit is to compel the defendant to remove these screens, and for the recovery of fifteen hundred dollars as damages, suffered and to be suffered, from deprivation of light and air, and twelve hundred dollars additional for depreciation in the value of the brick house, from the assertion by the defendant of his pretended right to shut out light and air from that side of the house; and in the event the Court should hold that the defendant rightfully closed the windows and erected the screens, then the plaintiff claims such right was a non-apparent vice and defect in the property, for which a reduction in the price of twelve hundred dollars should be allowed, for which sum judgment is prayed.

The plaintiff also complains of a water pipe fastened to the wall of her house, leading from the cottage; and of two sheds on the cottage lot that overlap the dividing line one inch or more, which sheds are fastened to the weather boards of the rear of her building; and a gutter runs across the line a foot or more; and the front gate-bell is fastened to her property; and two iron staples for supporting a clothes-line are driven into her wall; all these things being for the convenience of the cottage lot, and cause her five hundred dollars damage. She prays for removal of all of them.

The defendant justifies the erection of screens for the protection of his cottage, charges the plaintiff with a trespass in illegally and tortiously opening the windows which had been closed for fifteen years continuously, and demands two thousand dollars as damages therefor, and prays that the windows be closed as before. The answer passes by the complaints of the two iron staples, and id genus omne, in contemptuous silence.

The provisions of the Code on the matter are: If the owner of two estates, between which there exists an apparent sign of servitude, the same shall continue to exist actively or passively in favor of or upon the estate which has been sold. Rev. Civ. Code, Art. 769 [Revised C.C. art. 741].

Servitudes are either visible and apparent, or non-apparent. Apparent servitudes are such as are perceivable by exterior works, such as a door, a window, an aqueduct. Non-apparent servitudes are such as have no exterior sign of their existence, such for instance as the prohibition of building on an estate, or of building above a particular height. Ibid., Art. 728 [Revised C.C. art. 707].

The destination made by the owner is equivalent to title with respect to continuous apparent servitudes. By destination is meant the relation established between two immovables by the owner of both, which would constitute a servitude if the two immovables belonged to two different owners. Ibid., Art. 767.

There does not seem to be room for doubt that there existed an apparent sign of servitude in the windows when the defendant sold to the plaintiff, and the deed is silent respecting it. Not only is the deed silent, but the defendant was reticent to all to whom he should have spoken of the barred windows, if barring them was supposed by him to have the significance he now claims for it. No one, examining a house with a view to purchase or occupancy, and seeing the Venetian blinds with a board nailed across them on the outside, would think, or have reason to think, that this obstruction to opening them was permanent. It does not alter the case that these windows had been thus closed fifteen years or other considerable time. The defendant had the right to close them when he did, for he was owner of both lots, and he could have taken them away, and made that side of his house an unbroken surface of brick, and had he done so before Mrs. May's purchase, she could not have complained. But instead of doing that, he left the windows and blinds, perceptible on the exterior and from the interior, with all appearance of destination to use, save only the immediate present use was prevented by an obstruction that in appearance was temporary. Very great stress is laid, both by defendant and by the Judge below, on the circumstance of the slats of the Venetian blinds having been "reversed," by which they seem to mean the slats were turned up.

Venetian blinds are turned up or down every day as occasion requires. The object in having the slats rolling or movable is to turn them either way, and the way in which they are turned depends upon the object to be accomplished. These windows cannot be seen from the street, but of course the plaintiff saw them from within when she examined the house, and it is urged that as the "blinds were reversed" and a board nailed across the outside, she was bound to notice that condition. We take for granted she did notice it, and that is precisely why we think she had a right to believe she would have light and air through the windows, for she could not see, from within, the board nailed across the outside, and if she did see it while outside most likely regarded it as a precaution of safety. The real estate agent who negotiated the sale for Boulware examined the house, passed all the openings inside, and did not notice the boards, nor did Boulware mention to him that the windows were closed permanently, and not intended to be reopened. The servitude was visible and palpable as in Durel vs. Boisblanc, 1 Ann. 407; see also Alexander vs. Boghel, 4 La. 312; Barton vs. Kirkman, 5 Rob. 16.

The identical question here presented came before the Court in Lavillebeuve vs. Cosgrove, 13 Ann. 323. Six months before Cosgrove bought, the plaintiff Lavillebeuve closed a window which had existed in the partition wall from the time when the wall was built, by nailing heavy planks across the Venetian blinds of the window on the outside. The planks were there when Cosgrove bought, and he took them away and reopened the window. Lavillebeuve brought the action to have the window closed, and sounding in damages for a trespass, and contended that Cosgrove acquired the property as it was at the time of his purchase and because the window was then closed by boards, it must remain boarded up in perpetuity, and the removal of the boards was a trespass. The Court held otherwise saying, it is pretended the servitude was lost by barring up the window, but it was not. The Code expressly provides, in order that the tacit release of a servitude may be inferred from the permission given, by the owner of an estate to which it is due, for the erection of works which prevent the exercise of it, it is necessary that the works thus constructed be of a permanent and solid kind, such as an edifice or walls, and that they present an absolute obstacle to every kind of exercise of the servitude. Civ. Code, Art. 820 [no corresponding article after revision]. There can be no question of prescription in the case at bar since Boulware owned both lots up to the sale to Mrs. May, and he cannot prescribe against himself.

Nor can the servitude be claimed to have been extinguished. Among other means of extinguishing servitudes is such a change taking place that the thing subject to the servitude cannot be used. Civ. Code, Art. 783 [Revised C.C. arts. 751, 753, 765, 770, 771, 773, 774], And as an example of a change which does not extinguish the servitude the French writers say, thus a window, an aqueduct, preserves the right of servitude, although it is not used. Toullier, L.31, T.4, c.3, No. 709; 2 Demolombe des Servitudes, p. 488 et seq.

But it does not follow as a corollary, if Mrs. May has a right to open the windows for light and air that the defendant's screens cannot remain to obstruct the view into his lot. She has a right to such light and ventilation as may be obtained by the removal of the board from the outside of the windows, but the screens are equally necessary to protect his cottage property from intrusive eyes. There can be no doubt that the defendant could build another story to his cottage, which would obstruct the view from the brick house as much as the screens.

As to the other branch of the case, it seems certain from the proof that the water pipe, and iron staples, et cetera, are servitudes upon the plaintiffs property due to or in favor of the defendant's lot, established by the latter when owner of both, and existing at the time of the plaintiffs purchase. The Judge below so found, and he also rejected the money demands of both parties.

It is therefore ordered and decreed that the judgment of the lower court is affirmed in this respect, viz: rejecting the demands of both parties for damages, and disallowing the plaintiffs demand for the removal of the staples, and sheds, and gutter, etc., and in this respect that it be amended, so that the plaintiff have judgment recognizing her absolute right of servitude in all the windows as claimed, and in this other respect that it be reversed, wherein the removal of the screens is ordered and the defendant's claim to have certain of the windows enclosed and the boards again nailed across the blinds is recognized, which claim is now rejected, the costs of appeal to be paid by the parties in equal parts.

ON REHEARING

The plaintiff claims that so much of the judgment of the lower court as was in her favor cannot be disturbed because the appellee did not pray any amendment. No prayer for amendment had then been filed, but the defendant acted on that suggestion and filed an answer praying the amendment he desires. This answer was not filed until nearly two months after the plaintiffs petition for rehearing. Of course it comes too late.

It is also claimed by the plaintiff that she cannot exercise the right of servitude in the windows unless she is permitted to open the shutters fully and entirely, but we held, while the defendant could not again enclose the windows and nail boards across the shutters, she was entitled only to such light and ventilation from the windows as may be obtained by the removal of the boards from across the shutters, which does not imply that she may fully open them. If she may fully open the shutters, the defendant could not erect a second story upon his cottage which would obstruct her view, but we held that he could, and we said it to illustrate the extent of that servitude in the windows which she had.

The removal of the boards from across the shutters enables the plaintiff to move the slats up or down at pleasure, and to open the shutters even partially, but not to spread them "wide open," and thus obtain an unrestricted view upon and over the defendant's lot and cottage.

It is therefore ordered and decreed that the judgment of the lower court, ordering the screen opposite the window marked B to be removed, remain unaltered, and that plaintiffs right of servitude in the windows does not extend to opening the shutters fully and entirely, but only so far as was prevented by the boards nailed across them, and that so much of our former decree as is inconsistent herewith is set aside, and that the defendant pay the costs of appeal.

PHIPPS v. SCHUPP
45 So. 3d 593 (La. 2010)

CIACCIO, Justice ad hoc. We granted certiorari in this matter to determine whether the court of appeal erred in affirming the district court's grant of summary judgment in favor of the defendants, Cynthia Nelson Schupp and Roland Lawrence Cutrer, Jr. Specifically, we must consider whether the existence of a concrete driveway, which extends from an enclosed parcel of land through an adjacent property to the nearest public road and which existed when the common owner of the properties sold one of the parcels, is an exterior sign evidencing the common owner's intent to create a predial servitude. For the reasons discussed herein, we conclude the defendants failed to carry their burden of proof that there is no genuine issue of material fact as to whether the existence of the driveway evidences the common owner's intent to create a servitude by destination of the owner. Therefore, the summary judgment rendered in favor of the defendants is vacated and the case is remanded for further proceedings.

FACTS AND PROCEDURAL HISTORY

Located in Orleans Parish, "Lot F" is bounded by Exposition Boulevard and Audubon Park to the West, Patton Street to the North, and other residential properties to the South and East. In 1978, the common owner, Richard Katz, subdivided the land into two lots: 543 Exposition Boulevard, which is located in the northernmost section of the parcel directly adjacent to Patton Street, and 541 Exposition Street. When 541 Exposition Boulevard was sold separately, it had no direct access to a usable public street other than through 543 Exposition Boulevard to Patton Street, the nearest public road. Although 541 Exposition Boulevard has frontage on Exposition Boulevard, the boulevard is not a public road. Rather, it is a walkway adjacent to Audubon Park and is not designated for vehicular passage. Therefore, 541 Exposition Boulevard is an enclosed estate, as its only access to Patton Street is through 543 Exposition Boulevard. At the time the common owner sold 541 Exposition Boulevard, he left in place a paved driveway that extended from a garage located on 541 Exposition Boulevard through 543 Exposition Boulevard to Patton Street.

In 1978, the common owner appears to have sold 541 Exposition Boulevard to First Homestead and Savings Association, which subsequently sold the property to Michael Botnick. The plaintiff in this matter, Roger Phipps, and his wife, Evanthia Phipps, purchased the property from Mr. Botnick in 1982, and the Phipps have resided at that address for over 24 years. Mr. Phipps alleges throughout that time he has possessed, exercised, and used the driveway as a right of passage from his property through 543 Exposition Boulevard to Patton Street. Mr. Phipps concedes he has not used the driveway for vehicular passage since 2003, when the enclosure of a carport in the backyard of 543 Exposition Boulevard blocked the driveway and prevented vehicular access to his garage. However, Mr. Phipps has continued to use the unobstructed portion of the driveway for walking access to and from Patton Street.

On June 13, 2006, defendants Cynthia Schupp and Roland Lawrence Cutrer, Jr., who reside at 543 Exposition Boulevard, began erecting a fence across the alleged pedestrian right of passage, thereby completely preventing Mr. Phipps from accessing Patton Street. In response, Mr. Phipps filed a possessory action in which he sought to have his alleged right of passage recognized and to have the carport enclosure and fence that block the alleged right of passage removed.

The defendants filed an Exception of No Cause of Action, which was denied by the district court. Subsequently, the defendants filed a Motion for Summary Judgment. Mr. Phipps opposed the motion, contending the existence of the driveway at the time the common owner sold one of the parcels evidences the creation of a servitude by destination of the owner in accordance with La. C.C. art. 741. The district court granted the defendants' Motion for Summary Judgment, finding Mr. Phipps was unable to demonstrate "intent evidenced by exterior signs," as required by La. C.C. art. 707, because the mere existence and use of the driveway does not constitute a predial servitude.

The court of appeal affirmed the district court's grant of the defendants' Motion for Summary Judgment, agreeing that under 730 Bienville Partners Ltd. v. First Nat. Bank of Commerce, 596 So.2d 836 (La.App. 4 Cir.1992), writ denied, 600 So.2d 642 (La.1992), proof of the common owner's intent to create a servitude goes beyond the existence of the contested pathway itself and must be proven by other exterior signs. Finding Mr. Phipps was unable to prove the existence of exterior signs evidencing a predial servitude, the court of appeal concluded he failed to carry the requisite burden of proof.

Mr. Phipps now appeals to this court, asserting the defendants would require a predial servitude be evidenced by title even though La. C.C. art. 741 provides a predial servitude may be created by destination of the original owner. He also contends the lower courts ignored the material facts evidencing the common owner's intent to create a servitude, including (1) the fact that the common owner left the visible concrete driveway in place when the two estates ceased to belong to the same owner; (2) the fact that the common owner did not provide an express provision stating an apparent servitude was not created, as required by La. C.C. art. 741; and (3) the fact that a gate attached to 543 Exposition Boulevard, which could block the right of passage on the driveway, was locked and unlocked by a key delivered to Mr. Phipps when he purchased 541 Exposition Boulevard. Additionally, Mr. Phipps avers intent is a subjective fact, that exterior signs may serve as circumstantial evidence of the common owner's intent to create a servitude, and that facts regarding intent should be construed in the light most favorable to the non-movant on summary judgment. Thus, Mr. Phipps maintains the lower courts erred in granting the defendants' Motion for Summary Judgment.

DISCUSSION

A motion for summary judgment shall be granted "if the pleadings, depositions, answers to interrogatories, and admissions on file, together with the affidavits, if any, show that there is no genuine issue as to material fact, and that mover is entitled to judgment as a matter of law." La. C.C.P. art. 966(B); Jones v. Estate of Santiago, 03-1424, p. 4 (La.4/14/04), 870 So.2d 1002, 1005. The summary judgment procedure is favored in Louisiana and is designed to secure the just, speedy, and inexpensive determination of actions. La. C.C.P. art. 966(A)(2); Jones, 870 So.2d at 1005. Appellate courts review summary judgment de novo, using the same criteria that govern the trial court's consideration of whether summary judgment is appropriate, and in the light most favorable to the non-movant. Yokum v. 615 Bourbon Street, L.L. C., 07-1785, p. 25 (La.2/26/08), 977 So.2d 859, 876. Thus, appellate courts must ask the same questions the trial court does in determining whether summary judgment is appropriate: whether there is any genuine issue of material fact, and whether the mover is entitled to judgment as a matter of law. Hood v. Cotter, 08-0215, p. 9 (La.12/2/08), 5 So.3d 819, 824.

The initial burden of proof remains with the mover to show that no genuine issue of material fact exists. La. C.C.P. art. 966(C)(2); Jones, 870 So.2d at 1006. If the mover has made a prima facie showing that the motion should be granted, the burden shifts to the non-moving party to present evidence demonstrating that a material factual issue remains. Id. The failure of the non-moving party to produce evidence of a material factual dispute mandates the granting of the motion. La. C.C.P. art. 966(C)(2); Jones, 870 So.2d at 1006. Summary judgment usually is not appropriate for claims based on subjective facts such as motive, intent, good faith, knowledge, and malice. Id. However, this court has acknowledged "summary judgment may be granted on subjective intent issues when no issue of material fact exists concerning the pertinent intent." Smith v. Our Lady of the Lake Hospital, Inc., 93-2512, p. 28 (La.7/5/94), 639 So.2d 730, 751.

The defendants note that, under La. C.C. art. 730, "doubt as to the existence, extent, or manner of exercise of a predial servitude shall be resolved in favor of the servient estate." Palomeque v. Prudhomme, 1995-0725, p. 7 (La.11/27/95), 664 So.2d 88, 93. They contend since it is questionable whether the common owner intended to establish a predial servitude by leaving the driveway in place, this issue should be resolved in their favor. However, the defendants in this instance utilize the summary judgment procedure to seek relief. Therefore, in order to determine if there is doubt as to whether the driveway was intended to serve the enclosed estate, we must view the record and all reasonable inferences that may be drawn from it in the light most favorable to the non-movant, Mr. Phipps. See, Hines v. Garrett, 2004-0806, p. 1 (La.6/25/04), 876 So.2d 764, 765. For the reasons discussed below, considering this matter in the light most favorable to the non-movant, we find issues of material fact exist concerning the intent of the common owner to create a predial servitude. Therefore, the district court's awarding of summary judgment was not appropriate.

Although the lower courts and the parties failed to refer to La. C.C. art. 689, we must address this article, as it has bearing on the outcome of the case, and thus, should have been considered by the lower courts. La. C.C. art. 689 provides, "The owner of an estate that has no access to a public road may claim a right of passage over neighboring property to the nearest public road. He is bound to indemnify his neighbor for the damage he may occasion." A "public road" is any place that is open to vehicular traffic by members of the general public, even if the public is unlikely to use the road except to go to a particular place, and maintained by the public. Bardfield v. New Orleans P.B. Railroad, 371 So.2d 783, 786 (La.1979).

Passage from an enclosed estate to a public road is necessary in order for city services, such as a fire department, garbage collection, and sewage services, to access the property. Furthermore, passage to the public road keeps the enclosed estate in commerce because, without such access, it is unlikely any prospective purchaser would want to buy the property from the owner of the enclosed estate. See, Vermilion Parish School Bd. v. Broussard, 263 La. 1104, 270 So.2d 523, 525 (1972) (holding a servitude which the owner of an estate surrounded by other lands may impose on neighboring property to gain access to a public road is provided not only for the benefit of the landowner by permitting full utility of his land, but also to benefit the public by keeping valuable property in commerce.) Applying La. C.C. art. 689 to the instant matter, we find genuine issues of material fact exist as to whether Mr. Phipps, as the owner of an estate that has no access to a public road, has the right to claim a right of passage over neighboring property (543 Exposition Boulevard) via the driveway to the nearest public road (Patton Street).

Next, we address Mr. Phipps' argument that a predial servitude came into existence when the common owner sold one of the parcels and left the driveway in place. Predial servitudes are either apparent or nonapparent. La. C.C. art. 707. Apparent servitudes are those that are perceivable by exterior signs, works, or constructions; such as a roadway, a window in a common wall, or an aqueduct. Id.; Palomeque, 664 So.2d at 91. Nonapparent servitudes are those that have no exterior sign of their existence; such as the prohibition of building an estate or of building above a particular height. La. C.C. art. 707; Palomeque, 664 So.2d at 91. Apparent servitudes may be acquired by title, by destination of the owner, or by acquisitive prescription. La. C.C. art. 740; Palomeque, 664 So.2d at 91. Destination of the owner is a relationship established between two estates owned by the same owner that would be a predial servitude if the estates belonged to different owners. La. C.C. art. 741; 730 Bienville Partners Ltd., 596 So.2d at 839. When the two estates cease to belong to the same owner, unless there is express provision to the contrary, an apparent servitude comes into existence of right and a nonapparent servitude comes into existence if the owner has previously filed for registry in the conveyance records of the parish in which the immovable is located a formal declaration establishing the destination. La. C.C. art. 741; 730 Bienville Partners Ltd., 596 So.2d at 839.

In the matter before us, Mr. Phipps solely contends an apparent servitude came into existence by destination of the owner in accordance with La. C.C. art. 741. He asserts the lower courts erred in determining there is no genuine issue of material fact as to whether the existence of the driveway, which was left in place when the common owner sold 541 Exposition Boulevard, is an exterior sign evidencing the common owner's intent to create a predial servitude. We agree.

In granting the defendants' Motion for Summary Judgment, the district court relied upon the court of appeal's decision in 730 Bienville Partners Ltd. v. First Nat. Bank of Commerce, in which the court stated:

... the common owner must intend to create an apparent servitude and such intent must be evidenced by exterior signs which are consistent with the nature and extent of the servitude claimed. Any doubt concerning the Aexistence, extent, or manner of exercise of a predial servitude shall be resolved in favor of the servient estate.@ 596 So.2d 836, 839 (La.App. 4th Cir.1992), writ denied, 600 So.2d 642 (La.1992).2

In 730 Bienville Partners Ltd., Lot K was located in between and adjacent to the St. Louis Hotel, which faced Bienville Street, and a parking garage, which faced Iberville Street. Although all three properties were at one time owned by the same parties, the hotel and Lot K eventually were owned separately from the garage. The St. Louis Hotel and the owners of the parking garage entered into an agreement whereby the hotel patrons would be allowed to park their cars in the garage. Eventually, the hotel terminated its contract with the parking garage and formed a parking agreement with another garage located on Iberville Street. However, the hotel patrons continued driving through Lot K and the adjacent parking garage until the owners of the garage placed a metal blockade between Lot K and the garage. As a result, the New Orleans Fire Department ordered the removal of the blockade because it violated the fire code.[3]

The hotel filed a petition to enjoin the owners of the garage from implementing the blockade, asserting the existence of an apparent servitude by destination of the owner in favor of the hotel and Lot K through the parking garage. The district court determined a servitude did not exist, and therefore, denied the request for an injunction. The court stated:

[Parcel K's doorway] has been used over the [past] several years as a means of ingress and egress between the garage and the hotel pursuant to the lease of spaces in the garage to the hotel. These parking spaces were used for the hotel's employees and guests. Id. at 838.

Furthermore, the district court found the "designation of a doorway as a fire exit" or "the use of property pursuant to a lease" does not create a servitude. Id.

The court of appeal affirmed the district court, holding:

[a]ppellants failed to prove that the former common owners of the

---

[2] It is important to note the district court in the instant matter failed to recognize 730 Bienville Partners Ltd., unlike the matter before us, was not decided on summary judgment. Rather, that case was decided after the district court considered the evidence presented pursuant to a full trial on the merits.

[3] The court of appeal noted its holding had no bearing on the apparent fact that the door between the parking garage and Lot K was a fire exit for the hotel. 730 Bienville Partners Ltd., 596 So.2d at 840. During the preliminary injunction proceedings, the parties stipulated "the door is a designated fire door." Id. The court of appeal stated any restriction by the plaintiff on use of the door had to be consistent with the stipulation and comply with the Fire Prevention Code. Id. The court of appeal further concluded use of door as a designated fire exit does not create a servitude of general passage through the parking garage to Iberville Street. Id.

property...intended to establish a servitude of passage through the Garage to and from Iberville Street. Historical use of the door and interior signs and works show that pedestrian traffic from the Garage via the door was conditioned on the Hotel parking cars in the Garage. There is no evidence to support the appellants' contention that the Garage was intended as a path for persons to enter or leave the Hotel via Iberville Street. Id. at 840.

The instant matter is distinguishable from 730 Bienville Partners Ltd. because in that case, there were no exterior signs indicating the existence of an apparent servitude, such as signs directing foot or vehicular traffic from Iberville Street through the parking garage to the passage in Lot K. Rather, all signs evidencing a possible right of passage were located within the interior of the garage.[4] According to La. C.C. art. 707, an apparent servitude, such as a servitude created by destination of the owner, must be evidenced by the presence of exterior signs, such as a roadway, in order for an apparent servitude to exist. In the case before us, it is conceivable that the paved driveway is a perceivable exterior sign--a "roadway"--contemplated by La. C.C. art. 707. After all, the driveway visibly extends from Mr. Phipps' garage through the defendants' property to the nearest public road. Therefore, issues of material fact remain as to whether the driveway's location suggests it was intended to serve the enclosed estate as a right of passage to the nearest public road.

In addition, the court of appeal in 730 Bienville Partners Ltd. did not discuss any argument set forth by the plaintiffs that the hotel had no access to a public road other than through the alleged right of passage. In fact, the hotel has frontage on Bienville Street, a public road. Therefore, considering the facts as set forth by the court of appeal in 730 Bienville Partners Ltd., that matter was not governed by La. C.C. art. 689, which allows the owner of an estate that has no access to a public road to claim a right of passage over neighboring property to the nearest public road. Although the court of appeal in 730 Bienville Partners Ltd. noted the plaintiffs asserted an apparent servitude of passage existed in favor of the hotel and Lot K through the parking garage, the court did not state the plaintiffs averred the hotel's only access to the nearest public road was through the parking garage. In contrast, in the matter before us, Mr. Phipps argues his only access to the nearest public road is through 543 Exposition Boulevard. The fact that such a right of passage is required in order for Mr. Phipps to have access to the nearest public street brings the instant matter within the ambit of La. C.C. art. 689. Moreover, the lower courts in 730 Bienville Partners Ltd. noted use of the passage from the parking garage to Lot K was conditioned on the hotel parking cars in the garage pursuant to the parking lease. Such is not the case in the instant matter.

Additionally, the defendants maintain because Mr. Phipps could not refer to any "writing, title, survey, or other exterior sign that evidenced the common owner's intent to create an apparent servitude," the common owner did not intend to create a servitude by

---

[4] Photos in evidence in 730 Bienville Partners Ltd. revealed an illuminated sign above the passageway door which read "The Saint Louis Hotel." Also, a sign on the garage's interior wall indicated the door was an entrance to the Louis XVI Restaurant, which was located inside the hotel. Furthermore, signs on Parcel K's side of the passageway read "To Parking" and "Exit." The court of appeal also noted Iberville Street was visible from Parcel K, and the door can be seen from Iberville Street. Additionally, decorative light fixtures adorned each side of the hallway in Parcel K leading to the passageway door. Finally, the garage wall near the passageway was painted to match the walls surrounding the door. 730 Bienville Partners Ltd., 596 So.2d at 839.

destination. The defendants concede that an express provision is not required to create a servitude by destination of the owner, but they contend had it existed, it would have shown the common owner intended for the driveway to serve 541 Exposition Boulevard. We find the defendants' argument is without merit, as La. C.C. art. 741 does not require an express provision in order for a servitude by destination of the owner to exist.

Moreover, the common owner did not provide an express provision that a servitude by destination was not created when he sold 541 Exposition Boulevard. Under La. C.C. art. 741, the common owner must disavow the existence of a predial servitude when both estates cease to belong to him, or an apparent servitude comes into existence as of right. The defendants maintain the common owner expressly disavowed any encumbrance of the 543 Exposition Boulevard property in the 1983 Act of Sale.[5]   However, the common owner did not place an express provision denying the apparent servitude in the property descriptions of either estate when he subdivided the property in 1978 and sold one of the parcels. Thus, it is plausible that a servitude by destination of the owner came into existence as of right in 1978 at the moment the common owner alienated one of the properties. As such, genuine issues of material fact remain regarding this issue.

In addition, Mr. Phipps asserts a key provided to him by the seller (Mr. Botnick) that locks and unlocks a gate that crosses the concrete driveway is additional evidence of the common owner's intent to create a servitude. The key also unlocks and locks the doors to 541 Exposition Boulevard (including a front door, a side-rear door, and a gate that fronted Exposition Boulevard) and garage doors. If the common owner provided the key to Mr. Botnick, who then gave it to the Phipps, then it would appear the common owner did intend for the driveway running through 543 Exposition Boulevard to serve 541 Exposition Boulevard. Thus, the existence of the key and the nature of its alleged use also raise questions of material fact as to the common owner's intent to create a servitude by destination of the owner.

Additionally, in order to have received permission from the New Orleans City Planning Commission to subdivide the land, and thus, to sell the property in separate parcels, the common owner must have intended to provide the enclosed estate access to the nearest public road. According to the public records of the city of New Orleans, a 1950 subdivision regulation[6] required all parcels of land in a subdivision to have frontage on a public street. Subsequent regulations in 1999[7] augmented this requirement. We must

---

[5]The 1983 Act of Sale provides. "By reference to the certificates of the Register of Conveyances and Recorder of Mortgages in and for the Parish or County of Orleans annexed hereto it does not appear that said property has been heretofore alienated by the seller or that it is subject to any encumbrance whatever."

[6]The 1950 Subdivision Regulations promulgated by the New Orleans City Planning Commission provide, in pertinent part:
Section 4 Standards of Design; (d) Street and Alley Widths; (3) Where it is desirable to subdivide a tract of land, which because of its size or location, does not permit an allotment directly related to a normal street arrangement, there may be established one or more "Places." Such a "Place" may be the form of a court, a deadend street, or other arrangement; provided, however, that proper access shall be given to all lots from a dedicated "Place" (Street or Court).
[7]The 1999 Subdivision Regulations promulgated by the New Orleans City Planning Commission provide, in pertinent part:
Article 5. Design Standards and Principles of Acceptability; Section 5.1. General Principles of Acceptability; 5.1.4. Access to Lot. No subdivision will be approved by the Commission unless it creates a lot or parcel having its principal frontage and access from an officially approved street or

assume that because the Planning Commission approved the common owner's request to subdivide his land, he must have complied with the 1950 subdivision regulation, thereby intending both parcels to have access to the nearest public road (Patton Street).[8]

Finally, we address the defendants' contention that Mr. Phipps' possessory action has prescribed because he did not bring this action within one year from the alleged disturbance of possession, namely, the enclosure of the carport in 2003, which obstructed vehicular passage along the driveway. To maintain a possessory action the possessor must allege and prove: (1) he had possession of the immovable property or real right therein at the time the disturbance occurred; (2) he and his ancestors in title had such possession quietly and without interruption for more than a year immediately prior to the disturbance, unless evicted by force or fraud; (3) the disturbance was one in fact or in law, as defined in Article 3659; and (4) the possessory action was instituted within a year of the disturbance. La. C.C.P. art. 3658; Chaney v. State Mineral Bd., 444 So.2d 105, 107 (La.1983). Disturbances of possession which give rise to the possessory action are of two kinds: disturbance in fact and disturbance in law. La. C.C.P. art. 3659; Mary v. H-Tide Realty, Inc., 202 So.2d 457, 459 (La.App. 4 Cir.1967). A disturbance in fact is an eviction, or any other physical act which prevents the possessor of immovable property or of a real right therein from enjoying his possession quietly, or which throws any obstacle in the way of that enjoyment. La. C.C.P. art. 3659; Mary, 202 So.2d at 459. A disturbance in law is the execution, recordation, registry, or continuing existence of record of any instrument which asserts or implies a right of ownership or to the possession of immovable property or of a real right therein, or any claim or pretension of ownership or right to the possession thereof except in an action or proceeding, adversely to the possessor of such property or right. La. C.C.P. art. 3659; Mary, 202 So.2d at 459.

In the matter before us, the defendants assert the enclosure of the carport in 2003 was a disturbance in fact that triggered the one-year prescriptive period during which Mr. Phipps was required to file suit in order to maintain a possessory action. The defendants argue if a predial servitude existed in favor of the enclosed estate, its primary purpose was to serve as a vehicular passage between 541 Exposition Boulevard and Patton Street. Because Mr. Phipps did not bring this action until 2006 (when passage by foot was obstructed by erection of the fence), the defendants maintain Mr. Phipps' right to bring a possessory action has prescribed. We disagree.

A partial use of the servitude constitutes use of the whole. La. C.C. art. 759; See, Dupont v. Hebert, 2006-2334 (La.App. 1 Cir. 2/20/08), 984 So.2d 800, writ denied, 2008-0640 (La.5/9/08), 980 So.2d 695 (holding use of a portion of a servitude of passage by the dominant property owner was sufficient to interrupt the prescription of nonuse, although it was possible that no one used the unpaved portion of the servitude to access the rear of the dominant property owner's property since the servient property owner moved there). A predial servitude is indivisible. La. C.C. art. 652; Cathcart v. Magruder, 2006-0986 (La.App. 1 Cir. 5/4/07), 960 So.2d 1032, 1039. An estate cannot have upon another estate part of a right of way, or of view, or of any other servitude, nor can an estate be charged with a part of a servitude. La. C.C. art. 652; Cathcart, 960 So.2d at

---

place, public or private;
Section 5.5. Lots. Every lot of land hereafter created shall have its principal frontage on and access from an officially approved (public or private) street or place.

[8]It is important to note the subdivision regulations are consistent with La. C.C. art. 689, which grants the owner of an enclosed estate a right of passage over neighboring property to the nearest public road.

1039.

In light of La. C.C. art. 759, we find Mr. Phipps' partial use of the servitude as a walkway, after vehicular passage was obstructed in 2003, constitutes use of the entire servitude. Therefore, Mr. Phipps' possession of the servitude was not disturbed until 2006, when he could no longer use the driveway in any capacity. Furthermore, in accordance with La. C.C. art. 652, the servitude is indivisible, and thus, its use for vehicular purposes cannot be considered separate from its use as a passage by foot. Because Mr. Phipps filed suit within one year of when the entire servitude was obstructed, his possessory action has not prescribed.

CONCLUSION

Genuine issues of material fact exist concerning whether an apparent servitude was established by destination of the common owner. For the reasons assigned, the summary judgment rendered in favor of Cynthia Nelson Schupp and Roland Lawrence Cutrer, Jr., is hereby vacated and the case is remanded for further proceedings. Vacated and remanded.

d. St. Julien Doctrine

A. N. YIANNOPOULOS, PREDIAL SERVITUDES
§ 147 (3d ed. 2004) (footnotes omitted)

§ 147. Expropriation; St. Julien doctrine

Conventional servitudes may also be created in civil law systems by modes not regulated in civil codes. Such a mode is the expropriation of a servitude for public utility. Ordinarily, entities having the power of expropriation enjoy discretion to expropriate the ownership of immovable property or merely a servitude. When a servitude is expropriated, the owner of the immovable property is entitled to receive an indemnity for the value of the servitude taken and severance damages. The servitude established by expropriation may be permanent or temporary.

When land sought to be expropriated is burdened with a servitude, the expropriating authority must expropriate both ownership and servitude. The person entitled to the servitude is a party to the expropriation proceeding and has a right to an indemnity for the taking of his property. When the land sought to be expropriated is subject to a recorded lease, the leasehold interest must likewise be expropriated. If there is an unrecorded lease, the indemnity of expropriation is apportioned between the lessor and the lessee in proportion to the value of the interest of each. In such a case, there is no separate expropriation of the leasehold interest.

In Louisiana, servitudes may not be created by estoppel. In the past, however, a judicially created estoppel, known as the St. Julien doctrine, allowed entities having the power of expropriation to acquire servitudes by unopposed use and possession of another's land for some public purpose. The landowner could no longer sue for damages or for the removal of works but merely for the value of the servitude taken.

For acquisition of a servitude by the St. Julien doctrine there was no need for a prescriptive period. Occupancy of the land with the knowledge, consent, or acquiescence of the owner sufficed. In the absence of consent or acquiescence by the owner of the property, the St. Julien doctrine is inapplicable. The action for recovery of the value of the servitude was subject to a ten year prescription. The action for the value of the servitude taken is personal. A subsequent purchaser of the land has no right of action for indemnity in the absence of express assignments.

In Lake Inc. v. Louisiana Power & Light Co., the Louisiana Supreme Court prospectively overruled the line of decisions establishing the St. Julien doctrine. The court gave convincing reasons for the abandonment of the "deviant and conflicting jurisprudence and for return to the Civil Code provisions governing the establishment of servitudes."

Subsequently, the Louisiana legislature enacted Act No. 504 of 1976, now R.S. 19:14. The act provides that—when the state, its political subdivisions, or private corporations having power of expropriation take, in good faith, possession of the immovable property of another person and construct on, under, or over it facilities with the consent or acquiescence of the landowner—a presumption arises that the landowner waived his right to receive just compensation prior to the taking; in such a case, the landowner's remedy is an action for determination whether the taking was for a public and necessary purpose and for just compensation. The 1976 Act did not overrule legislatively the Lake decision. Thus, St. Julien is not resurrected; it is merely un-dead, feeding on servitudes established prior to Lake.

It has been held that the St. Julien doctrine and R.S. 19:14 are inapplicable "absent a good faith belief of authority to take possession of the property and the "consent and acquiescence" of the property owner to those actions."

R.S. 19:14 does not determine the liberative prescription governing claims for damages for the taking of a servitude in accordance with the statute. Certain courts have applied to claims under R.S. 19:14 the two year prescriptive period of R.S. 19:2.1(B) In Howard v. Louisiana Power & Light Co., however, the court held that the two year prescription of R.S. 19:2.1(B) applies only when private property has been expropriated for public purposes, and this prescription does not apply when property is "appropriated" for public purposes under the St. Julien doctrine.

R.S. 13:5111 establishes a three year prescriptive period for claims against the state arising from the taking of property (other than through an expropriation proceeding." This prescription may be applicable to claims for the unauthorized taking of a servitude by the state. However, it has been held that the three year prescriptive period begins to run from the date of discovery of the taking.

LOUISIANA REVISED STATUTES

R.S. 19:14. Possession of property; removal of facilities; objection; waiver

A. In any case where the state or its political corporation or subdivision has actually, in good faith believing it had authority to do so, taken possession of privately owned immovable property of another, and constructed facilities upon, under or over such property with the consent or acquiescence of the owner of the property, such owner shall be deemed to have waived his right to contest the necessity for the taking and to receive just compensation prior to the taking, but he shall be entitled to bring an action for such compensation, to be determined in accordance with the provisions of R.S. 19:9, for the taking of his property or interest therein, the just compensation to be determined as of the time of the taking of the property, or right or interest therein, and such action shall proceed as if the state, its political corporation or subdivision had filed a petition for expropriation as provided for in R.S. 19:2.1.

B. In the case where any corporation referred to in R.S. 19:2 has actually, in good faith believing it had the authority to do so, taken possession of privately owned immovable property of another and constructed facilities upon, under or over such property with the consent or acquiescence of the owner of the property, it will be presumed that the owner of the property has waived his right to receive just compensation prior to the taking, and he shall be entitled only to bring an action for judicial determination of whether the taking was for a public and necessary purpose and for just compensation to be determined in accordance with R.S. 19:9, as of the time of the taking of the property, or right or interest therein, and such action shall proceed as nearly as may be as if the corporation had filed a petition for expropriation as provided for in R.S. 19:2.1.

C. The provisions of Subsection A of this Section shall apply only to privately owned immovable property over which the state or its political corporation or subdivision has exercised actual possession in good faith for ten years and has completed construction of facilities upon, under, or over such property. The provisions of this Section shall not be deemed to authorize the acquisition of any interest in privately owned immovable property adjoining such facilities, including but not limited to a servitude, right of use, or any right of passage across or access to the private immovable property adjoining such facilities.

4. RIGHTS OF THE OWNER OF THE DOMINANT ESTATE
Civil Code arts. 744-750

HYMEL v. ST. JOHN THE BAPTIST PARISH SCHOOL BOARD
303 So. 2d 588 (La. App. 4th Cir. 1974)

SCHOTT, J. Plaintiffs instituted these injunction proceedings to prevent defendant from interfering with their use of a right-of-way. In answer defendant denied it impeded the use of the servitude. After trial plaintiffs were awarded a judgment for only part of the relief they sought and they have appealed.

Plaintiffs are the owners of a tract of ground in St. John the Baptist Parish. This tract which they cultivate as sugar cane farmers is directly to the rear of a smaller tract owned by defendant which has constructed and is operating a public school on the tract. Plaintiffs and defendant derive their respective titles from a common ancestor in title, Willie Hymel. When Willie Hymel sold the smaller tract to the defendant in 1963, he reserved a servitude in the following words:

> There is hereby reserved by vendor for himself, his heirs, successors, and assigns, a right of way 25 feet in width along the westerly line of the above property to afford ingress and egress in favor of the property situated south of the herein conveyed property.

The Succession of Willie Hymel later sold to plaintiffs the rear tract together with the servitude. A surveyor employed to examine the situation noted on a plot of survey the location, dimensions and elevations of various encroachments on the right-of-way. They consisted of a chain-link fence across the width of the servitude in the front, an overhang of the school roof, encroaching on the right-of-way by 1.7 feet in the front and increasing to 2.9 feet in the rear for a distance of 70 feet and at a height of 9.5 feet above ground level; three drop inlets, extending from 2 inches above the natural ground to 11 inches above, all connected with an underground drainage pipe on the east side of the right of-way near the school building and on the west side a drainage ditch 3 feet wide and 3 feet deep extending entirely along the length of the property line, located entirely within the right-of-way and one foot inside the line. Other testimony established that school automobiles were regularly parked on the front portion of the right-of-way.

Plaintiff, Lynn Hymel, testified that the right-of-way is not used constantly but is used to some extent; that the amount of use fluctuates with the various agricultural seasons, such as planting time, cultivation time and harvest time; that the vehicles using the passage are cane cutters, about 13 feet in height and 10 feet in width, cane haulers or trailers about the same size and tractors of various sizes including one used as a three row tractor with draw boards and having a width of at least 20 feet; that all of the right-of-way is necessary for plaintiffs' use; and that various obstacles in the right-of-way prevent two of his vehicles from passing abreast on the servitude from the front of the school building to the rear.

The trial court, recognizing plaintiffs' right-of-way, permanently enjoined defendants from interfering with plaintiffs' peaceful use of it as follows:

(a) The barrier fence across the entire right of way is to be removed.

(b) The parking of vehicles on and across said right of way is to cease and said vehicles are to be parked elsewhere.

(c) The building overhang is to remain as is and defendant school board is not required to remove same, provided that said plaintiff shall have no interference and peaceful use of said right of way subject to said use bearing in mind that the safety of the school children shall be accorded by plaintiffs in the use of said right of way and specifically at no time shall two vehicles, namely, cane cutters pass side by side.

(d) That in accordance with (c) supra the defendant school board is to abandon (by covering up) or remove and cover up said drainage devices currently in use or on said right of way with an end in view to separate defendants property from the right of way with a small ditch or swale in order to afford drainage.

(e) Furthermore, it is ordered adjudged and decreed that the defendant school board strongly consider the installation of a fence separating their property from the right of way in question in order to afford a workable solution with plaintiffs use or their right of way and to afford the maximum degree of safety to the school children.

Each party is to bear his own respective court costs.

Plaintiffs appeal from sub-section (c) and (d) of this judgment and from that portion taxing costs. They specify errors in that the trial judge did not order the removal of the overhang, in that he exceeded his authority in enjoining them from using the right of way as they see fit, and in not taxing court costs, including the expert witnesses' fee against the defendant.

In denying plaintiffs' prayer that defendant be ordered to remove the overhang the trial judge gave the following reasons:

> As far as the building overhang, it is not of such a degree that would warrant removal. The evidence preponderates that said right of way can be used without same impeding said use. The court will not order the overhang removed. To do so would cast an unreasonable burden upon a situation of which the free use of the servitude can be had without forcing removal of the overhang.

Our discussion of the problem begins with C.C. Art. 777 [Revised C.C. art. 748] which provides:

> The owner of the estate which owes the servitude can do nothing tending to diminish its use, or to make it more inconvenient.

> Thus he cannot change the condition of the premises, nor transfer the exercise of the servitude to a place different from that on which it was assigned in the first instance.

Yet if this primitive assignment has become more burdensome to the owner of the estate which owes the servitude, or if he is there by prevented from making advantageous repairs to his estate, he may offer to the owner of the other estate a place equally convenient for the exercise of his rights, and the owner of the estate to which the servitude is due cannot refuse it.

Defendant contends that under this article plaintiffs have the burden to prove that the overhang has diminished the use of the servitude or made it more inconvenient and that they failed to carry this burden. Defendant relies on evidence which demonstrated that the servitude was used only sparingly and at particular times of the year for the passage of agricultural vehicles and that with the removal of the other impediments, plaintiffs will experience no difficulty whatsoever in the passage of their equipment through the right-of-way. While it may be that two of the larger vehicles may not pass abreast of each other in the area where the school building is located, the testimony is that there is never an occasion when two such vehicles must pass abreast because the servitude is so sparingly used.

On the basis of these facts and the rationale in Kaffie v. Pioneer Bank & Trust Company, 184 So. 2d 595 (La. App. 2d Cir. 1965), Appeal after Remand 204 So. 2d 54 (1967), Writ Refused, 205 So. 2d 605 (1968), defendant contends that a result in its favor is clearly indicated. We do not agree and hold that the trial court erred in this part of his judgment.

When the right-of-way "is the result of a contract, its extent...is regulated by the contract." C.C. Art. 722 [Revised C.C. art. 705]. It is only where the contract does not designate the width of the right-of-way that its extent is subject to interpretation based upon previous use of the servitude. C.C. Art. 780 [Revised C.C. art. 749]. Pursuant to these articles there could hardly be any doubt that plaintiffs are entitled to clear passage at ground level for the full width of 25 feet. Nor is mere a sound basis for a distinction as to encroachments above ground level.

While the Civil Code provides that ownership of soil carries with it ownership of all that is directly above it, Art. 505 [Revised C.C. art. 490], we have no code authority for the proposition that a right of passage or right-of-way confers the right to all that is above the soil. It seems that Art. 722 [Revised C.C. art. 705] in defining right-of-way as a servitude by virtue of which one has the right to pass on foot or in a vehicle or to drive beasts or carts through the estate of another implies that the right-of-way does include something above ground level, at least sufficient to accommodate such things as carts and vehicles.

The expressed purpose of the right-of-way in this case was to provide plaintiffs' ancestor with ingress and egress from the property to the rear of defendant's property. The uncontroverted evidence is to the effect that plaintiffs property was always used for sugar cane production and that plaintiffs' sugar cane cutter and their trailer used for hauling the cane are 13 feet high. These are precisely the vehicles and cart spoken of in C.C. Art. 722 [Revised C.C. art. 705]. Plaintiffs' ancestor reserved a 25 foot right-of-way to accommodate his equipment and they are now being made to suffer a reduction of their right-of-way. Surely this is a clear cut violation of the spirit if not the letter of the law embodied in the code articles cited.

The trial court's reasoning that the overhang "is not of such a degree that would warrant removal" is not consistent with C.C. Art. 777 [Revised C.C. art. 748] which provides that the owner "can do nothing tending to diminish'" the servitude's use. The word "tend" means to move or extend in a certain direction or to be disposed or inclined. It cannot be said that defendant's construction of their overhang well below the height of plaintiffs equipment is not even inclined to diminish plaintiffs' use of the servitude, when as a fact plaintiffs are prevented from using from 6.8% of the right-of-way on one end of the overhang to 11.6% on the other end for a distance of 70 feet.

We therefore conclude that there is no basis for permitting defendant to construct any obstacles within the 25 foot roadway at such height which might impede the passage of any equipment regardless of its height, and plaintiffs are entitled to an order to defendant to remove the encroaching overhang.

As the remainder of paragraph c of the judgment, it limits the plaintiffs in the use of the right-of-way by requiring that it cannot be used in any way detrimental to the safety of the school children and specifically at no time shall two vehicles, namely cane cutters, pass side by side. There was no issue raised herein that plaintiffs were using the servitude in any manner which may create a hazard to the school children. As a matter of fact, their testimony evidences the reverse situation. Plaintiffs, being fearful that they may in some fashion damage either the school board property and presumably thus endanger the children, have hesitated to use the property in full, and have been using other means of egress and ingress to their farmlands because of these considerations. Although we appreciate the concern of the trial judge, we believe the inclusion of the vague restriction of use without regard to safety of the school children goes beyond the pleadings and the issues of this case. Likewise, the restriction against two vehicles passing side by side has no basis in the pleadings or the evidence. Even so it would be inconsistent with the nature of plaintiffs' right-of-way to impose limitation on its use not found in the contract which created it.

Finally, the trial judge's concern that defendant's removal of the overhang would be "an unreasonable burden" is not supported by any evidence as to the scope or cost of such work.

Accordingly, the judgment appealed from will be amended so as to delete the entirety of paragraph c and to order defendant to remove that part of the overhang of its building which encroaches upon plaintiffs' right-of-way.

While plaintiffs appealed from paragraph (d) of the judgment they specify no error in this connection and we are unable to perceive any inconvenience or harm suffered by plaintiffs from that portion of the judgment. Reversed in part, affirmed in part.

BOUTALL, J. (dissenting in part). I dissent from that portion of the opinion requiting the School Board to remove its roof overhang. ***In the present case, the servitude was used only occasionally, and the trial court found as a fact that the right of way can be used without the overhang impeding its use. The record supports this finding. The trial court concluded that to order the overhang removed "would cast an unreasonable burden upon a situation of which the free use of the servitude can be had without forcing removal of the overhang." I agree with this conclusion and therefore respectfully dissent.

RYAN v. SOUTHERN NATURAL GAS COMPANY
879 F.2d 162 (5th Cir. 1989)

W. EUGENE DAVIS, Circuit Judge. Southern Natural Gas Company (SNG), which was granted a servitude to property owned by appellees' ancestors, challenges the district court's judgment against it for the loss and deterioration of approximately 330 acres of marshland. The district court found that the marsh damage was due to appellant's failure to dam a pipeline canal it constructed on plaintiffs property. Because the servitude agreement absolved SNG from the obligation to dam the canal appellant owed no duty to apples to do so. We therefore reverse and render the judgment entered by the district court.

I

In 1956, SNG obtained a servitude agreement from several ancestors of the plaintiffs^pplesycollectively the "Harrisons"). Pursuant to the written agreement, SNG constructed a pipeline canal on two portions of the Harrisons' land, which we refer to as the southern strip or strip I and the northern strip or strip II. The agreement required SNG to backfill the pipeline canal in the northern strip and allowed the canal in the southern strip to be left open. The agreement specifically prohibited SNG from backfilling the southern strip.

Consistent with its contractual obligations, when SNG built the pipeline canal in 1956, it did not backfill or dam that part of the canal running through the southern strip. In 1978, the Harrisons' attorney wrote to SNG complaining that erosion had taken place along the spoil banks of the canal in the southern strip, causing it to widen beyond the right-of-way. The Harrisons also complained that failure to dam the southern part of the canal was allowing the tide to flow into and out of the canal and marsh, resulting in saltwater damage to a large area of the marsh beyond the right-of-way. The Harrisons requested that SNG dam or plug the canal. SNG refused.

In 1986, the Harrisons filed this action to recover for (1) land lost due to erosion and widening of the canal and, (2) "extended marsh loss" allegedly caused by the change of the ecological makeup of the marshlands because of increased tidal flow in and out of the canal. The Harrisons sought damages under theories of negligence, strict liability and breach of the servitude agreement. The district court found that the Harrisons' contract claim had prescribed, but allowed the Harrisons to recover from SNG under a negligence theory; the court found that SNG's negligent failure to dam the canal caused the canal banks and the marshland top soil to erode. The court awarded the Harrisons damages both for the loss of thirty-nine acres of land due to the widening of the canal and for the cost of stabilizing the surrounding marshland to prevent further deterioration.

SNG appeals the adverse judgment against it; the Harrisons, by way of cross-appeal, contend that the trial court erred in finding that SNG was not strictly liable for the loss.

II

The initial issue confronting us is whether the servitude agreement between SNG and the Harrisons absolved SNG of any duty to dam the canal.

When a servitude is established by contract, the extent and mode of using the servitude is regulated by the contract. See Ogden v. Bankston, 398 So. 2d 1037, 1040-41 (La. 1981). A written agreement is the law between the parties and must be interpreted and enforced according to its terms. La.Civ.Code art. 1983; Massie v. Inexco Oil Co., 798 F.2d 777, 779 (5th Cir. 1986) (Applying Louisiana law). The duty of SNG to plug or backfill the pipeline canal in question was defined by its contract with the Harrisons:

[T]he Grantee [SNG] is given the right to use the right of way granted above for the purpose of constructing a canal or ditch,...and which canal or ditch, may, at [SNG's] option, be left open insofar as [the southern strip] is concerned.... The canal or ditch constructed by the Grantee will not be backfilled upon completion of construction at any other time by [SNG].

The plain words of the contract gave SNG the option to leave the canal "open." This obviously gave SNG the right to refrain from damming the canal. The Harrisons argue that irrespective of the language of the contract, Article 745 of the Louisiana Civil Code establishes a general duty by the servitude owner to avoid unreasonable damage. We disagree. Any duty imposed on the servitude owner by Article 745 is subject to thE provisions of the written servitude agreement between the parties.

Article 697, Louisiana Civil Code, makes it clear that the duty imposed on the servitude owner by Article 745 to avoid unreasonable damage to the dominant estate is subject to the provisions of the instrument creating the servitude: "The use and extent of such servitudes are regulated by the title by which they are created, and, in the absence of such regulation, by the following rules." Also, Article 774 (the predecessor Article to Article 745), which was in effect in 1956 when the servitude was created, explicitly recognized the ability of the parties to contractually alter the duty owed by the servitude owner. We conclude therefore that any duty SNG had under Article 745 did not include the duty to dam the canal because SNG was relieved of that specific duty under the servitude agreement.

We reach a similar conclusion with respect to the Harrisons' claim under Louisiana Civil Code Article 667, which imposes a strict duty on proprietors to avoid work on their property that may cause damage to their neighbors. Assuming without deciding that the relief afforded by Article 667 is available to the Harrisons, as the owners of the dominant estate, against SNG, the servitude owner, we know of no reason the parties cannot contractually modify the duty SNG would owe the Harrisons under that Article. Article 729 of the Louisiana Civil Code provides: "Legal and natural servitudes may be altered by agreement of the parties if the public interest is not affected adversely." Thus Article 667 cannot be the source of any duty upon SNG to dam the canal when the parties dispensed with that duty in their agreement. See Butler v. Baber, 529 So. 2d 374, 382 (La. 1988) (Dennis, J. concurring).

The Harrisons call our attention to an SNG memo, written around the time the servitude agreement was executed, in which the SNG representative stated, "I was greatly surprised that we were able to talk Captain Harrison out of making us construct several dams or plugs, which I believe would have cost us at least $25,000." The Harrisons argue that this memo tags SNG with culpability in declining to place dams in the canal when it rally expected it would be required to do so. But in our view, this memo is more detrimental than helpful to the Harrisons' position. It demonstrates that the contracting parties turned their attention to whether SNG would be required to construct dams in the canal and SNG was successful in negotiating an agreement that relieved it of this responsibility.

Our conclusion that the servitude agreement relieved SNG of any duty to dam the canal resolves this case and makes it unnecessary for us to discuss the remaining issues. Accordingly, the judgment of the district court is reversed and the case is remanded for entry of a take-nothing judgment in favor of SNG. Reversed and remanded.

NOTE

Plaintiff, the South Central Bell Telephone Company, had a right of passage servitude on defendants' property. The defendants constructed a shed on their property over the telephone company's underground cable, and refused to allow plaintiff entry to repair the cable for fear that the repairs would damage the shed. Plaintiff filed a suit for injunction prohibiting the defendants from interfering with plaintiffs entry into defendant's property and ordering the removal of the shed. The court rendered judgment enjoining the defendants from interfering with or obstructing the entry of the plaintiff on the property subject to the servitude and refused to order the removal of the shed in the absence of a showing, by the plaintiff, that the shed interfered with or obstructed the use of the servitude. South Central Bell Telephone Co. v. Demster, 303 So. 2d 280 (La. App. 1 st Cir. 1973).

5. EXTINCTION OF SERVITUDES
Civil Code arts. 751-774

VINCENT v. MEAUX
325 So. 2d 346 (La. App. 3d Cir. 1975)

HUMPHRIES, J. This is an appeal by defendants-appellants from an adverse judgment granting plaintiff the right to use water from a deep water well.

Walter Vincent, plaintiff-appellee, flied suit for a declaratory judgment seeking to have his rights under a 1941 partition agreement determined. A certain tract of land was partitioned into three lots. In 1941 the use of a deep water well, located on lot L3, was reserved for lots LI, L2 and L3. The Act of Partition contained the following stipulation:

> "It is further agreed and understood that the deep water well located on
> tract number three is reserved for the use and benefit of lots LI, L2 and L3.
> The owner of either of said lots enjoying the right of use of said well for
> irrigation purposes when so desired or upon necessity."

The plaintiff-appellee is the owner of lot L2. Lloyd Abshire and Lena J. Abshire (wife of David Meaux, Jr.) own lot LI. Agnes Vincent Hebert is the owner of lot L3.

This conventionally created right is a servitude. The servitude created is a real servitude. Revised C.C. Art. 646 divides servitudes into two kinds — personal and real. In this case the servitude is a real or predial or landed servitude because the act creating it specifically provides that it is for the benefit of the other estates. The act creating the servitude did not grant it to a particular person.

David Meaux, Jr. claims an interest in the well. He claims that he purchased Lloyd Abshire's interest in the well. There is no explanation in the record regarding this supposed transaction. Certainly he can not purchase Abshires interest in the well unless he purchases the land as well. The servitude was created in favor of an estate and not in favor of one particular individual.

The deep water well in question is located on lot L3 which is owned by Mrs. Hebert. Mrs. Hebert disclaims any interest in the well. She claims that she verbally gave her interest in the well to Ovey Abshire, father of Lena and Lloyd Abshire. This is not explained in the record.

In 1951 the well dried up due to a lowered water table. In this year Ovey Abshire employed a contractor to re-dig the well. Not only was the well dug deeper but steel casing for wooden cypress casing was substituted. Following this Ovey Abshire claimed all interest the well.

Subsequent to the partition, plaintiffs lessees, with one or two years exception, planted crop on his land and used the well in question for irrigation purposes. Prior to 1951 the plaintiff did not pay anything for procurement of water from the well located on lot L3. After 1951 the plaintiff was required to pay x/i of his crop for the use of water from the well on lot L3.

Plaintiff-appellee contends that he should have the free and uninhibited use of the well pursuant to and by virtue of the servitude created in the 1941 act of partition. Defendants-appellants contend that the object of the servitude ceased to exist in 1951 when the well dried and hence the servitude was extinguished. The defendants also contend that the servitude has been extinguished by the 10 year prescription period of non-usage provided by C.C. Art. 789 [Revised C.C. art. 753]. Defendants contend that by paying for the use of the well the servitude was not used in the mode intended at its inception and hence the prescriptive period has run. In order to have kept the servitude viable, it was necessary for the plaintiff to have used it at least once every ten years since its creation in 1941. The evidence revealed that although the plaintiff never personally planted his land or used the well for irrigation purposes, there was never a period often years wherein his lessees did not use the land and well. This was sufficient to interrupt the running of prescription. C.C. Art. 793 [Revised C.C. art. 757] provides that the servitude may be preserved by persons other than the owner.

> "To preserve the right of servitude and prevent prescription from running against it, it is not necessary that it should be exercised exclusively by the owner to whom it is due, or by those who use his rights or who represent him directly, as the usufructuary, the lessee or tenant, the attorney in fact or agent. It suffices if the servitude has been exercised by workmen employed by the owner or by his friends, or those who come to see him."

The question becomes whether the paying for the water is a "use" of the servitude. The servitude was the use of a well. The servitude was used whenever plaintiff, through his lessees, used the well for irrigation purposes. The payment for the water from the well does not obviate the fact that the well, and hence the servitude, was indeed used and prescription interrupted.

The defendants-appellants also advanced the proposition that the servitude ceased to exist when the original well became dry. As authority of their contentions they cite C.C. Articles 783-786 [Revised C.C. arts. 751, 752] which deal with the destruction of the estate which owes the servitude. It is the position of the defendants that the deepening of the old well did not re-establish the servitude.

The well existing in 1941 ceased to be functional due to a lowered water table. Drilling on the same site, defendants' ancestors lowered the original well shaft to a point which was concurrent with the then existing water table and set a new and different type of casing. This did not create a new well. It was a re-establishment of the thing. Although the Civil Code does not, except in rare circumstances, impose an affirmative duty upon the owner of the servient estate to do work to keep the object of the servitude usable, neither does it prohibit him from so acting. The tenor of Articles 772-775 [Revised C.C. arts. 744, 745, 746] indicates that the redactors of the Code sought to make preservation of the servitude, through necessary works, as convenient as possible. The deepening of the well by the defendants' ancestors was "works necessary to use and preserve the servitude." C.C. Art. 772 and 773 [Revised C.C. art. 744].

We are of the opinion that the servitude was not extinguished by the destruction of the object of the servitude, nor was it extinguished by ten years of non-usage. Plaintiff was the beneficiary of the servitude created in 1941 and maintained through the years. He is entitled to the use of that servitude.

This Court is also of the opinion that plaintiff would be unjustly enriched if he were not compelled to pay his pro rata share of the costs of the operation, maintenance and preservation of the well. The cost of work necessary for the preservation and use of the servitude must be shared by those persons to whom the servitude is due. C.C. Art. 773 [Revised C.C. art. 744].

We must remand this case to the trial court as an indispensable party was omitted from the proceeding below. C.C.P. art. 641. Mrs. Agnes Vincent Hebert, the owner of the lot upon which the well is located must be a party even though she sought to disclaim any interest therein. Her interest, however, is very much at issue. C.C. Art. 654 [Revised C.C. art. 650] provides:

> "Servitude is a right so inherent in the estate to which it is due, that the faculty of using it, considered alone and independent of the estate, can not be given, sold, let or mortgaged without the estate to which it appertains, because it is a servitude which does not pass to the person but by means of the estate."

Mrs. Hebert sought to divest herself of her interest in the well without divesting herself of the estate, an act clearly contrary to the Code. Remanded.

TILLEY v. LOWERY
511 So. 2d 1245 (La. App. 2d Cir. 1987)

MARVIN, J. In this action to construe a 1974 "Right of Way" agreement and counter letter that did not specify the exact location of the right of way, the plaintiffs, who are the dominant estate owner and his assignees, appeal a judgment declaring that the 1974 agreement created a predial servitude of passage which was extinguished by the 10-year liberative prescription of nonuse.

The facts were stipulated. We find no error of law and affirm. C.C. Arts. 705, 706, 753.

The litigants owned interests in adjacent tracts of land separated by a bayou in Bossier City at the intersection of Foster Road and I-20. The servient estate fronted more than 200 feet on Foster Road but the 60-foot servitude affected only the southernmost 200 feet of the frontage. The agreement and counter letter obligated the dominant estate owner to build a bridge across the bayou. The pertinent part of the agreement stated that

> The parties.... have agreed to create a servitude of drive, as limited herein, across a portion of [their respective lands and for Plaintiff Kemmerly to] build a bridge across [the bayou] to afford ingress and egress to his property from Foster's Road....

> Said servitude of drive shall be only 60 feet... along Foster Road ... in a direct line on the KEMMERLY property a sufficient distance in order to bridge [the] Bayou. The parties... will, at a future date, stipulate the exact location of this servitude as it affects the property.

The counter letter relieved Kemmerly of the obligation to maintain the bridge in the event he elected to dedicate it to public use. The counter letter, which was last executed May 10, 1974, related the agreement to the counter letter in its opening paragraph by stating that "The undersigned entered into a servitude of drive executed [on certain dates].

The litigants stipulated that

—adequate consideration was paid by Kemmerly for "the right of way" and by the other plaintiffs to Kemmerly for "the assignment of the right of way";

—neither Kemmerly nor any of his successors in title ever requested defendants to specify the location of the servitude;

—the   60-foot location of the   servitude within the 200-foot area   owned by [defendants] was never designated; and

—the servitude has never been used.

Plaintiffs contended that the servitude was not created when the right of way agreement was executed, but was to be established only when the exact location was designated; that the provision for specifying the exaction location is a condition which suspended the agreement; and that prescription did, or could, not begin to run until the location was specified.

Defendants contended the agreement to specify the exact location of the servitude was not a suspensive condition but was intended to evidence the location of the servitude for public record purposes and that plaintiffs were not prevented from using the servitude.

The trial court found that the agreement created the servitude, not merely an obligation to establish the servitude at a later date, and that the provision for specifying the exact location did not delay the time when prescription would begin. The court concluded the servitude had been extinguished since it was not "used" for the 10 years after the agreement was executed in 1974.

ESTABLISHMENT OF SERVITUDE; BEGINNING OF PRESCRIPTIVE PERIOD

A servitude of passage, or right of way, is an affirmative predial servitude which is extinguished by nonuse for ten years. C.C. Arts. 705, 706, 753. If the servitude has been used, prescription begins to run from the date of the last use. C.C. Art. 754. If it has never been used, prescription begins to run from the date the servitude is established and its exercise is possible. Yiannopoulos, Predial Servitudes, 4 Louisiana Civil Law Treatise § 164 (1983), citing De La Croix v. Nolan, 1 Rob. 321 (La. 1842). See also Chicago Mill and Lumber Co. v. Ayer Timber Co., 131 So.2d 635 (La. App. 2d Cir. 1961).

The owner of the dominant estate has the burden of proving his use of the servitude during the 10-year prescriptive period. C.C. Art. 764; Craig v. Finnazzi, 159 So. 2d 732 (La. App. 4th Cir. 1964).

A conditional obligation is one dependent upon an uncertain event. If the obligation may not be enforced until the uncertain event occurs, the condition is suspensive. C.C. Art. 1767. Courts do not construe stipulations in a contract as suspensive conditions unless the express contract language compels such construction. Cahn Elec. Co., Inc. v. Robert E. McKee, Inc., 490 So. 2d 647 (La. App. 2d Cir. 1986).

Here, neither the contractual provision for designating the exact location of the servitude in writing, nor any other language in the contract, indicates that the parties intended that the servitude would be created only when its exact location was designated. The agreement consistently refers to the servitude as having been created:

> In consideration of the granting of the servitude of passage across the [defendant's] property the said Kemmerly has paid [$100 and other good and valuable consideration], the receipt of which is hereby acknowledged.

> Nothing herein contained will be interpreted to exclude the right granted herein to KEMMERLY, his successors and assigns, running with the

property described above as owned by him, to create rights of passage from his property [north] to Highway 80 or [east] to Foster's Road across his property and [across the servitude created herein] (emphasis added).

Although the right of way agreement does not specify the exact location of the servitude, it is sufficient as a title document by which this type of servitude is created. See J. C. Trahan, Drilling Contractor, Inc. v. Younger, 169 So. 2d 15 (La. App. 2d Cir. 1964), and cases cited therein.

Even had defendants not agreed to designate the exact location, plaintiffs could have required defendants to designate the location. See C.C. Art. 750. Plaintiffs could have made the location certain by using the servitude for the purpose and to the extent allowed by the agreement. Thalian v. Younger, supra. Defendants were never asked to designate the exact location. The uncertainty about where the 60-foot servitude would be located within the 200-foot frontage on Foster Road does not preclude a finding that the servitude was established by the 1974 agreement.

If the title is silent as to the extent of the servitude, the intention of the parties is to be determined in light of the servitude's purpose. C.C. Art. 749. Since we have no testimony about the intent of the contracting parties, we must discern their intent from the agreement as a whole and from the counter letter. C.C. Art. 2045, 2050, 2053.

The 1974 agreements detail the rights and obligations involving the servitude and support the conclusion that the parties intended to create a servitude in 1974, and not merely an obligation to create the servitude at a later date. Compare Chicago Mill, supra, in which prescription for nonuse began with a sale clearly expressing a mineral reservation and not with an earlier surface lease and option to purchase stipulating that the lessor would retain the mineral rights if the option were exercised. Also compare Kavanaugh v. Frost-Johnson Lumber Co., 149 La. 972, 90 So. 275 (1921), in which the parties to a timber deed agreed to create a servitude of passage for removal of timber but did not contemplate or intend that the servitude would come into existence until it was needed to remove the timber. The agreement under construction here is not an accessory to any other contract such as a timber deed.

Finally, C.C. Art. 730 provides that doubt as to the existence, extent, or manner of exercise of a predial servitude shall be resolved in favor of the servient estate. If the trial court perceived any doubt about when the servitude was created, it properly resolved the doubt by finding that the servitude was established in 1974 and was extinguished by the time plaintiffs filed their action more than 10 years later. The judgment appealed, at appellants cost, is affirmed.

ASHLAND OIL COMPANY, INC. v. PALO ALTO, INC.
615 So. 2d 971 (La. App. 1st Cir. 1993)

LOTTINGER, C.J. This is an appeal by Ashland Oil Company Inc. and International Minerals and Chemical Corporation of a judgment terminating their pipeline right of way. The trial court found, on Palo Alto's reconventional demand, that the servitude had not been used within the 12-month prescriptive period provided for in the contract.

Appellants seek to have their servitude enforced and the public records reformed to erase a survey error indicating that the servitude did not completely traverse Palo Alto's lands.

FACTS

In 1980, James Lawn, an employee of Fred, Bacon & Davis Construction Company, acting as agent for Ashland Oil Company and International Minerals and Chemical Corporation (joint venturers, both hereinafter referred to singularly as Ashland), began negotiating with the landowners along a 26 mile long route for a pipeline right of way, from Agrico Chemical Company's plant near Donaldsonville to Ashland's plant near Plaquemine. Ashland's plant was the former Hercu-Fina plant, now styled the "Allemania" plant, which would produce methanol. The plant could produce approximately 100 million gallons per year when Ashland purchased it, but it was determined that a pipeline feeding carbon dioxide (CO_2) to the plant could boost production to 130 million gallons per year. During negotiations with Palo Alto's president, Arthur Lemann, Jr., Mr. Lawn learned that any right of way across Palo Alto's lands would be conditioned upon an agreement restricting use of the pipeline to the transportation of CO_2 and that there would be a shortened term for the prescription of non-use of 12 months, as opposed to La. Civil Code Article 753's 10-year prescriptive period.

After haggling over the price, the parties agreed to the servitude and confected an agreement providing that the servitude granted to Ashland was:

[A] non-exclusive right of way and servitude to construct, lay, maintain, operate, repair, remove and replace below ground, one single pipeline ... for the transportation of carbon dioxide in either its gaseous or liquid state, through lands which [Palo Alto] owns, situated in the Parishes of Iberville and Ascension....

Following the grant of servitude language, were numbered conditions for use of the servitude, the sixth of which provided:

This agreement shall be null and void and of no effect if [Ashland] shall fail to construct, complete and put into actual operation said pipeline described herein across said right of way within twenty-four months from the date hereof... It is fur-ther agreed and understood that after the said pipeline shall have been constructed and put into operation, should [Ashland] fail to use the same for the purposes herein provided for a period of twelve consecutive months, then and in that event the within right of way agreement shall be terminated....

The Allemania plant and pipeline were used as planned until July, 1984, when methanol production became unprofitable for Ashland. The plant was mothballed and the pipeline was pressurized with nitrogen to prevent its corrosion during the time it was unused. However, in order to prevent the 12-month prescriptive period from accruing, Ashland had crews at the Agrico and Allemania plants run CO_2 through the line on a 11 1A month basis, beginning in April, 1985. The CO_2 was fed into the line at Agrico and run through it under pressure to Allemania, where it was simply vented into the atmosphere. This procedure was repeated in two additional years, until Ashland began selling Agrico's C02 to Georgia Gulf via the pipeline in 1988 and, later, again began to produce methanol in January, 1989.

Ashland, additionally, visually inspected the route of the right of way to ascertain that no encroachments or potentially disruptive activities occurred on or near the servitude and pipeline. Ashland considered these activities, and the nitrogen injections, maintenance in compliance with the language of the servitude grant. Ashland contends that all of these activities sufficiently constitute the specified "use" of the pipeline such as would interrupt the running of the 12-month prescriptive period.

ASSIGNMENTS OF ERROR

Ashland assigns as error the trial court's action in:

1. Permitting parol evidence to be admitted to explain the terms, provisions and conditions of a written contract which was, on its face, unambiguous;

2. Finding that the servitude at issue had not been "used" as provided by the written agreement and by the intention of the parties;

3. Adding terms to the contract which were not contained within the agreement and making performance of the contract more onerous including that the gas transported by the pipeline had to be used for production of methanol or some other purpose, the use of the pipeline was dependent upon the operation of the plant, that certain quantities of certain types of gas had to be transported through the pipeline;

4. Shifting the burden of proof concerning the occurrence of a resolutory condition in the contract from the plaintiffs to the defendants;

5. By failing to reform the Servitude Agreement to reflect the intention of the parties to show that the servitude was to extend completely across the lands of Palo Alto.

DISCUSSION

We will consider assignments of error 1 and 2 together as each is intimately involved with resolution of the other. Ashland asserts that the trial court erred in looking beyond the language of the contract granting the servitude to determine that the intent of the parties required Ashland to do more than it did to use its servitude.

It has long been the law in this state that to use a servitude, so as to interrupt prescription, requires one to use it in the manner contemplated by the grant of the servitude [citations omitted]. Reference must therefore be made to the object of the grant, not for the purpose of determining whether there has been a breach of any obligation, but to determine whether there has been such use as to interrupt prescription.

This directive need not be viewed as an exception to the rule that parol evidence is inadmissible to negate or vary the contents of this contract. See La.Civ.Code Article 1848. Where, as here, the language of the contract granting the servitude is broadly and generally worded, a determination of the object of the grant does not depend upon the admission of parol evidence, because it can readily be seen that any pipeline servitude to transport gas from one location to another must have as its purpose a use other than that availed of here. Cf. Robert Investment Co., Inc. v. Eastbank, Inc., 496 So. 2d 465 (La. App. 1st Cir. 1986). Therefore, we find, even if the trial court did erroneously admit and rely upon such evidence, that use of parol evidence in this case was irrelevant and harmless. Accordingly, in Broussard, the Court stated that in the case of a mineral servitude, where the exploiting, though begun, has been stopped or abandoned at a depth at which there was no reasonable hope of discovering minerals in paying quantities, the use is not such as to interrupt prescription. 135 So. at 3. In Goldsmith, the Court concluded that geophysical exploration of the premises for the purpose of determining the indication of minerals underlying the surface will not interrupt prescription. 182 So. at 523. In Harrington, the Court did find that prescription had been interrupted where a mineral lessee drilled carefully, taking numerous core samples for testing, and stopped drilling only when he had reached the frontiers of geological knowledge circa 1938. The Court specifically noted that the well "was not drilled as a mere gesture by the mineral owners to preserve a servitude, but by the owner of a mineral lease under an obligation to substantially develop with due diligence." 192 So. at 518. It is important to note, that although these decisions were based on former La.Civ.Code Articles 796-800 (repealed in 1977), the Articles relied upon pertained to use of a servitude that was less than allowed or called for in the title creating it. Thus, they applied where the manner of use was inconsistent with a broadly or generally worded grant of a servitude. See La. Civ e Article (759, Comments (b) and (c); La.Civ.Code Article 761. We can see, there¬fore, that Ashland erroneously relies upon the following language, found in Professor Yiannopoulos' treatise on predial servitudes in 4 Louisiana Civil Law Treatise 449.

If the title does not establish an exclusive manner of use, the use of the servitude in a different manner from that which is designated or appropriate ought to interrupt the prescription of nonuse.

Ashland asserts that this language supports its contention that any use of the pipeline involving the running of CO_2 from one end of the pipeline to the other is use of the servitude comporting with the object of the grant of the servitude. However, this sentence must be read in conjunction with the sentence preceding it, wherein Professor Yiannopoulos states:

The use of a servitude for over ten years in a manner different from that which is appropriate for the servitude ought to result in extinction of the original servitude by nonuse, if the title establishes an exclusive manner of use. (Emphasis added) Id.

In this case the title did establish an exclusive manner of using the pipeline; it is "for the transportation of carbon dioxide in either its gaseous or liquid state, through lands which [Palo Alto] owns." (Emphasis added). The servitude is not used, as Ashland asserts, merely by running CO_2 through the line. This would be "a mere gesture by the [pipeline] owners to preserve a servitude," Lynn v. Harrington, 192 So. at 518, which practice has been repudiated in our law. Thus, we find, as did the trial court, that Ashland did not use its servitude for at least twelve consecutive months between July, 1984, and January, 1989. This finding compels the conclusion, under the contract, that the servitude was prescribed for nonuse. This determination obviates consideration of Ashland's third, fourth, and fifth assignments of error, and we pretermit them.*""""Therefore, the judgment of the trial court is affirmed at appellants' costs.

FOIL, J. (dissenting). I disagree with the majority in this case. The majority affirms the trial judge in holding that the servitude ended because of prescription, in that it was not used in the manner contemplated by the grant of the servitude. Ashland, the servitude owner, in 1980, at the outset of the servitude, transported CO_2 through the pipeline servitude to its plant to produce methanol. Ashland stopped producing methanol at the plant in 1984. From that time until 1989, Ashland ran CO_2 through the line approximately once each year to keep the servitude alive, but the CO_2 was merely vented into the atmosphere at the end of the line rather than used to produce methanol. Ashland began producing methanol again in 1989. The servitude agreement stated the servitude would terminate if Ashland failed to use it "for the purposes herein provided" for a period of 12 consecutive months. The purposes of the servitude specified in the contract of servitude were to "lay, maintain, use, and to transport gas through the lands" of Palo Alto. There was no requirement that Ashland was to continue producing methanol in order to keep the servitude alive. I would reverse the trial court's finding that the servitude had prescribed, and remand the case for further proceedings.

NOTE
Public Policy

Consider the applicability of Civil Code article 3471 to the preceding case. It provides: "A juridical act purporting to exclude prescription, to specify a longer period than that established by law, or to make the requirements of prescription more onerous, is null." Did the provision discussed in the preceding case "make the requirements of prescription more onerous" by reducing the prescription of non-use to twelve months?

BROOMFIELD v. LOUISIANA POWER & LIGHT COMPANY
623 So. 2d 1376 (La. App. 2d Cir. 1993)

NORRIS, J. Louisiana Power and Light ("LP&L") appeals a judgment denying its reconventional demand for injunctive relief and declaring that its power line servitude on the Broomfields' property was lost by 10 years of nonuse. For the reasons expressed, we affirm.

FACTUAL BACKGROUND

The property in question sits on the east side of U.S. Highway 167 near Dodson in Winn Parish. The highway right-of-way extends 50' each way from the centerline of the road. The record does not say when it was built, but a barbed wire fence now stands on the east boundary of the highway right-of-way.

By eight separate instruments executed in 1955, LP&L acquired its powerline servitude from the then-owners of the property. Three of the instruments specified that the servitude would be 16' wide, measured from the edge of the highway right-of-way, and would run parallel with and adjacent to the east side of the highway. These three instruments also granted LP&L the right to construct, operate and maintain electric transmission lines, including poles, wires and other appurtenances, and "to trim and cut trees and other growth so as to keep the wires cleared upon, over and across" the property. The other five instruments did not state the width of the servitude, but at the hearing for preliminary injunction Mr. W.R. Roberts Jr., LP&L's senior right-of-way agent, testified that the original servitude was 16' Supp., 4. These five instruments also gave LP&L the right to trim not only foliage on the servitude itself but "to cut any trees that in falling would reach the wires." In accord with these instruments, LP&L installed an 8 Kv. transmission line. The poles supporting this line sat a foot or two to the east of the highway right-of-way, inside the fence and on the subject property.

By five separate instruments dated 1956, 1959 and 1967, Mr. and Mrs. Broomfield bought the property. Mrs. Broomfield testified that when they did so, the transmission line and poles were inside the fence. In May 1968 the Broomfields applied to LP&L for electric service. To provide this LP&L added a pole, which it refers to as a "dual purpose" pole, along the powerline. This pole diverted a service line across the servient estate to the Broomfields' house and also helped to hold up the transmission line.

In 1972, to service a plant north on Hwy. 167, LP&L decided to upgrade its transmission line to 13 Kv. According to Mr. Roberts, this required an extra 15' of servitude to maintain line clearance from the trees. LP&L asked the property owners along the highway to grant this, and all agreed except the Broomfields, with whom LP&L could not come to terms. LP&L installed the new line, but moved its existing transmission poles a few feet to the west, in front of the Broomfields' property. After this, the transmission line and all its supporting poles have stood outside the fence and off the servitude area. The service pole, however, remains inside the fence, without holding up the transmission line. It supports only the service line to the Broomfields' house. Since 1972, no transmission line has passed over, or transmission pole stood upon, the servitude area.

The only point of genuine dispute at trial was what the parties did over the next 16 years. The Broomfields planted a large stand of pine trees several feet back from the fence. See the photos, Ex. LP&L-7 in globo. These obviously grew and the limbs would tend to reach the transmission line. Mr. Roberts testified that his men inspected the entire line once or twice a year and never found, until January 1988, that the trees posed any danger to the line. R.p. 55. Mrs. Broomfield, however, testified that LP&L did nothing, and it was her husband who trimmed the branches and cleared the brush periodically to protect the line. R.p. 49.

After the freeze of January 1988, LP&L sent a crew to trim pine branches along the line. Although the Broomfields protested, the crew trimmed branches from several of their trees. Mrs. Broomfield claimed that 38 trees were thus "damaged," though LP&L's timber expert, Mr. Merlin Smith, counted that only 26 trees were trimmed. LP&L's maintenance foreman, Mr. Jerry Smith, admitted that the crew trimmed the entire 16' servitude plus a little beyond. R.p. 57. Mrs. Broomfield called the sheriff when LP&L showed up to do some more trimming. Mr. Broomfield had a heart attack and died about two weeks later.

PROCEDURAL HISTORY

Mrs. Broomfield and her children filed suit in January 1989 seeking damages for the trimmed trees. LP&L reconvened, seeking an injunction to keep the Broomfields from interfering with their tree trimming, or a declaratory judgment to interpret the 1955 servitude agreements. In March 1989, after a hearing, the trial court granted LP&L a preliminary injunction, but allowed it to cut only "directly above and west of the Broomfield fence and around the service pole." R.p. 17. LP&L then moved for a partial summary judgment to declare that it could trim and cut the entire 16' servitude area. Summary judgment was not pursued; trial on the merits was held in February 1991.

By written reasons the trial court took up the reconvention first. The court quoted the 1955 servitude agreements; these granted LP&L the right to construct "transmission lines, including poles, wires and other appurtenances." However, the court found that poles are really just an accessory to the right to transmit electric power. Hanks v. Gulf States Util., 253 La. 946, 221 So. 2d 249, 251 (1969). The court found that the one service pole on the servitude area of the Broomfields' property since 1972 did not amount to use of the servitude for 10 years. La.C.C. art. 753. The court also rejected any application of the doctrine of St. Julien v. Morgan La. & Texas R., 35 La. Ann. 924 (1883), because LP&L did not prove the requisite occupation of the Broomfields' property. Finally, the court dismissed the Broomfields' principal claim, finding inadequate proof of damages.

Strictly speaking, the judgment only rejects LP&L's claim for injunctive relief and declaratory judgment (as well as the Broomfields' claim for damages), but in effect it declares the servitude lost to nonuse. LP&L has appealed.

APPLICABLE LAW

A predial servitude is defined as a charge on a servient estate for the benefit of a dominant estate. La.C.C. art. 646. A predial servitude is extinguished by nonuse for 10 years. La.C.C. art. 753. Under current law, a powerline servitude is defined as an "affirmative servitude" as it gives the owner of the dominant estate the right to do a certain thing, transmit electricity, on the servient estate. La.C.C. art. 706. For an affirmative servitude, prescription of nonuse begins to run from the date of its last use. La.C.C. art. 754. Under prior law, a powerline servitude was classified as a "discontinuous servitude," as it required an act of man to be exercised. La.C.C. art. 727 (1870); Lake v. Louisiana Power & Light, 330 So. 2d 914 (La. 1976). The nonuse of a discontinuous servitude began "from the day they ceased to be used." La.C.C. art. 790 (1870). In the instant case the servitude agreements were executed and the alleged nonuse began under the old law, and the alleged nonuse accrued after the new law took effect in 1978. La. Acts 1977, No. 514. Strictly speaking, the new law cannot be applied retroactively. See Daniel v. Department of Trans. & Dev., 396 So. 2d 967 (La. App. 1st Cir.), writ denied 400 So. 2d 1385 (La.1981). Under either scheme, however, nonuse is measured from the date of last use of the servitude, and the issue presented is whether LP&L's activity since 1972 amounts to use.

A partial use of the servitude constitutes use of the whole. La.C.C. art. 759. However, the use of a right that is only accessory to the servitude is not use of the servitude. La.C.C. art. 761. The lead case for defining the nature of a powerline servitude is Hanks v. Gulf States Util., supra. There the property owners granted a utility company the right to build "poles, frames or towers *** with lines of wires" for the transmission of electricity. Although this entitled the utility company to erect an H-frame transmission line, for over 10 years the company maintained only a single-pole transmission line on the servient estate. The property owners argued that the utility lost the right to construct an H-frame tower because of nonuse. The Supreme Court found the utility's conduct sufficient use of the servitude to block prescription of nonuse. "The right to transmit electric power is the servitude." Id., 221 So. 2d at 251 (emphasis in original). By contrast, poles, frames and towers are "merely types of supporting structure for transmission lines or other transmitting devices." Id. In McGuire v. Central La. Elec. Co., 337 So. 2d 1070 (La. 1976), the Court held that the right to enter the servient estate to cut and trim trees and shrubs for clearance is only an accessory to the grant of the servitude to transmit electricity. Id., at 1073.

Doubt as to the existence, extent or manner of exercise of a predial servitude shall be resolved in favor of the servient estate. La.C.C. art. 730.

DISCUSSION

On appeal LP&L urges that it has used, or at least partially used, its servitude because the "dual purpose" service pole and service line to the Broomfields' house has been present on the servitude area since 1968. LP&L also argues that it has maintained clearance over the servitude property in conjunction with the transmission of electric power and this amounts to use of the servitude, even though the precise location of the line is not on the servient estate. LP&L finally cites public policy considerations that militate against requiring it to prove "that someone passed over every square foot at least once in ten years." We would note that LP&L never did anything to evidence an intent to abandon its servitude over the Broomfields' property.

The trial court was not plainly wrong to dispose of LP&L's first argument and find that the service pole and line to the Broomfields' house was not in fact use of the servitude. Four of the eight servitude instruments state that the purpose is to "construct 8 Kv. line along U.S. Hwy. No. 167," and the others label it the "Dodson-Winnsboro Tie-Line." Since 1972 LP&L has not maintained such a north-south transmission line, either of 8 or 13 Kv. on the servitude property. Admittedly, between 1968 and 1972 the "dual purpose" pole could have been considered part of the transmission line, but it is doubtful that since 1972 this pole has satisfied the manner of exercise contemplated in the servitude instruments. La.C.C. art. 730. Moreover, it is definitely not an "integral" or essential part of the 13 Kv. line, thus distinguishing the case of Brooks v. New Orleans Pub. Serv. Inc., 370 So. 2d 686 (La. App. 4th Cir.), writ denied 373 So. 2d 512 (La. 1979), relied on by LP&L in brief. In Brooks, the guy pole was found to be an integral part of the transmission line.

For the second argument, LP&L urges us to adopt the reasoning that although it transmitted electricity off the servitude area since 1972, it continued to utilize that area for clearance purposes, thereby maintaining its servitude. The gist of the argument is that their acts of maintaining clearance on the 16' strip constituted use of the servitude. Safety concerns require adequate clearance around an uninsulated line. See Levi v. Southwest La. Elec. Membership Coop., 542 So. 2d 1081 (La. 1989). Mr. Roberts, the senior right-of-way agent, testified that LP&L likes to have a 30' clearance on each side of its 13 Kv. lines. R.p. 53. By moving the line outside the Broomfields fence in 1972, LP&L made 20' of clearance between the powerline and the east edge of the servitude line. If the right to transmit electric power includes the right to transmit it safely, the argument runs, then maintaining the necessary clearance is an exercise of the right, even if the actual line is off the servitude area. LP&L adds that it should not be penalized with nonuse simply because it never, until January 1988, had to physically create a clearance on the servitude.

We do not agree. The definition of a predial servitude requires it to be a charge on a servient estate. La.C.C. art. 646. The right to transmit electricity is the basis of the servitude. Flanks v. Gulf States Util., supra. It is obvious that LP&L has not transmitted electricity on the servient estate in a manner consistent with the servitude instruments since 1972. This point is critical because of the distinction between the servitude itself and its accessory rights.

While we recognize the safety considerations cited by LP&L, we must hold that the right to maintain reasonable clearance around a powerline is merely an accessory of the servitude. McGuire v. Central La. Elec. Co., supra. Use of an accessory right does not constitute use of the servitude itself. La.C.C. art. 761.

The Revision Comments to art. 761 give an example that is precisely on point:

> [I]f one who has the servitude of drawing water from the well of his neighbor passes over the servient estate and goes to the well without drawing any water during the period required for prescription, he will lose the servitude because the passage is merely accessory to the right of drawing water.

The fundamental flaw in LP&L's position is that, as the district court found, there has been no exercise, upon the servient estate, of the principal right to transmit electricity since 1972. Without this, LP&L's claim to have exercised the accessory right of clearance is as unavailing as that of the water-drawer in the Comment. Performing some acts on the servient estate will not block prescription unless the principal servitude right is also exercised thereon. LP&L's argument lacks merit. The further claim of public policy considerations does not alter this conclusion.

Although LP&L does not specifically contest it on appeal, the trial court further found that the proven use of the servitude was not sufficient to activate the St. Julien doctrine. St. Julien, supra; La.R.S. 19:14. On the record presented, this finding is not manifestly erroneous. For the reasons expressed, the judgment is affirmed. Costs are assessed to Louisiana Power and Light.

THOMPSON v. MEYERS
34 La. Ann. 615 (1882)

BERMUDEZ, C.J. This is a petitory action by the plaintiffs, who claim to have the ownership of a real right to which certain real estate is subjected indefinitely.

The object of the suit is to have it judicially declared that the plaintiffs, as owners of a certain contiguous piece of property, have a right of way, or passage, to a named street, through a certain strip of ground, in the possession of the defendants. The plaintiffs, besides, claim $6,000 damages.

The main defense is, that if the right to the servitude ever existed, it was extinguished by the non-usage of the same during ten years.

From a judgment in favor of the plaintiffs, this appeal is taken.

The evidence clearly establishes that, when the original plaintiff, Mrs. Thompson, purchased the lot described in her petition, she was entitled to a right of way, such as was claimed, at the institution of this suit, through the spot in question.

It appears that in 1841, the whole property comprising that of plaintiffs and that of defendants, was owned by the same person, who caused it to be divided into lots, for the common benefit of which the alley was established, the title to each lot, subsequently sold, mentioning this important appendage or accessory.

It is established that the alley was used by Mrs. Thompson, up to 1863, for domestic purposes, and that it has not been used by those subsequently in possession of her property, since 1864. This suit was instituted in 1878.

We have considered the testimony of a lady neighbor, witness for the plaintiff, which is to the effect that the alley was open in 1869 and 1870, when she had occasion to go through it after her son, who had a habit of climbing Mrs. Thompson's fence to go to the grocery store, at the opposite corner of the square, not kept on Mrs. Thompson's lot.

That testimony is merely the result of hearsay, and is outbalanced by that of almost every witness heard in the case, which shows that the alley was boarded up in 1864, and that the man who kept the grocery had moved from it some twelve years before the action was brought. Even if her testimony stood uncontradicted, it could not prove interruption of the prescription set up, because the act to do so, must be done, if not by the person entitled to the use, or by persons representing at least by one going to and from his premises for the ordinary legitimate purposes for which the alley was provided. Neither the act of the witness, nor that of her son crossing the alley, was done in the exercise of the right of way, primitively consented. They were the unauthorized acts of strangers, not within the original intendment of the grantor and grantees, and contrary to the purpose in view. They cannot be considered as done with the sanction, or for the benefit of Mrs. Thompson, and should be viewed as the clandestine acts of intruders and trespassers, not done "a l'occasion du fonds." Pardessus des Serv. II, No. 302, 308; Dalloz Serv. Sec. 7, Art. 1. § 1, No. 1: Laurent 409; Sirey, C. N. 706, No. 24; Dalloz, 1860, 3 Juillet; Duranton, V. p.674, No. 684; Demolombe xii, No. 995.***

In presence of the defense of non-user, and particularly of the evidence in support, which establishes facts affirmatively, the plaintiffs, in order to recover, should have, if not primarily established, adduced at least in rebuttal, proof of use of the alley, by herself, "or by some one under her authority, in her name. Up to a period clearly within the ten years preceding her action, she has not done so. (Powers v. Foucher) 12 M. 70; C.C. 804; (De La Croix v. Nolan) 1 R. 321; (Baker v. Pena) 20 A. 52.

The Code distinctly provides that a right to a servitude is extinguished by the non-usage of the same during ten years, which, for discontinuous or interrupted servitudes, are meant such as need the act of man to be exercised, such as the right of passage, drawing water, pasture and the like, (citations omitted).***

We think that the plaintiff has failed to make out her title to the use and enjoyment of the alleyway, and that her claim thereto was improperly recognized.***

6. PROTECTION OF SERVITUDES
C.C.P. arts. 3653-3664

LOUISIANA IRRIGATION AND MILL CO. v. POUSSON
262 La. 973, 265 So. 2d 756 (1972)

DIXON, J. Petitioner, Louisiana Irrigation and Mill Company, sought an injunction prohibiting defendant, James W. Pousson, from interfering with a described "lateral aqueduct servitude." The described servitude was a canal about thirty feet wide utilized to conduct water from a main irrigation canal known as the "Abbott-Duson Canal." The Abbott-Duson Canal, in turn, carried water about fourteen miles from Bayou Des Cannes. The lateral canal involved in this litigation crossed the lands of several owners including lands owned by the defendant. There is no allegation that plaintiff possessed the canal un-der color of title. Plaintiff alleges that the defendant dug his own irrigation well and began pumping water into plaintiffs canal, and by using the canal for irrigation purposes, disturbed the plaintiffs rights of possession.

In responsive pleadings, the defendant claimed to be the owner and the possessor of all canals involved in this litigation, particularly for more than one year prior to the institution of plaintiff s suit and for more than one year prior to the disturbance alleged by plaintiff.

The trial court overruled exceptions and denied the motion to dissolve, and, after trial on the rule for preliminary injunction, rendered judgment enjoining the defendant from interfering with plaintiffs use of the irrigation canal. The Court of Appeal reversed, deciding that plaintiff lacked the requisite possession to support injunctive relief under C.C.P. art. 3663. 252 So. 2d 151.

The Court of Appeal concluded that the "quasi possession" of the servitude claimed by the plaintiff had not been continuous for the year prior to March 20, 1970, the date found to be the beginning of the disturbance of the possession by defendant. Its ruling was confined to a portion only of the canal (252 So. 2d 151,155) as it crossed the lands of the defendant, since the plaintiff might have been in possession of other portions of the canal which crossed lands owned by other persons.

We agree with the conclusion of the Court of Appeal: before plaintiff can obtain an injunction under C.C.P. art. 3663(2) it must have been in possession of the immovable or real right for a year before the disturbance.

From the evidence the Court of Appeal found that the lateral canal involved was used by the plaintiff to furnish water to rice farmers for the purpose of irrigating rice crops for many years prior to 1967 (with the exception of the lower end of the canal, which was not constructed until 1965). Plaintiff maintained the levees and outlets, and ran water through the canal during the rice irrigation season, which normally begins in March and might extend through July in each year.

In 1962 the defendant, through whose land portions of the canal pass, dug his own well and constructed his own irrigation canal, paralleling a portion of plaintiff s canal. From 1962 until 1967 defendant irrigated his rice from his own well and from the canal which he constructed.

Plaintiff corporation is in the business of irrigating lands planted to rice, and furnishes water to farmers in return for a share of the rice crop. The canal involved in this suit was not used in 1967, since plaintiff had no contracts to furnish water to farmers adjacent to that canal in that year. Rice fields are rotated. Some of the fields for which plaintiff would have furnished water were planted to soybeans. In 1967, while defendant irrigated his own fields from his own well, some of the water from the canal which the defendant had constructed escaped and wet the bean crop of one of the owners of land through which the canal passed. Thereupon, defendant switched from his canal to plaintiffs unused canal, the one involved in this suit.

In 1968 plaintiff used a short portion of the canal here involved. In that year, the defendant again used a major portion of plaintiff s canal to carry his own water to irrigate his own rice crop.

In 1969 plaintiff used the entire canal, and its use was exclusive. Plaintiff first began pumping water through the canal for the 1969 season on May 12, 1969. This factual conclusion by the Court of Appeal gave plaintiff "every benefit of the doubt."

The 1967 and 1968 usurpation of the lateral canal by defendant clearly resulted in a loss of possession by plaintiff. Possession is lost "when the possessor of an estate allows it to be usurped and held for a year, without, during that time, having done any act of possession, or interfered with the usurper's possession." C.C. art. 3449 [Revised C.C. art. 3434]. Plaintiffs possession again commenced on May 12, 1969, continuing through the 1969 season. On March 20, 1910 defendant again occupied the lateral canal, pumping water from his own well into the canal to irrigate his own crops and that of others.

Plaintiff contends that the Court of Appeal erred in finding that the plaintiff did not have possession of the canal for one year preceding the disturbance by the defendant on Marsh 20,1970.

The arguments of the plaintiff are without substance. We find the evidence adequately supports the Court of Appeal in its factual findings, both as to the nature and extent of plaintiffs possession, and the open adverse possession of the defendant.***

BARHAM, J. (dissenting). We are here concerned with the question of whether the plaintiff can maintain a possessory action with the ancillary right to injunctive relief under Code of Civil Procedure Article 3663. We are unable to determine from the record before us the nature of the disputed right to the irrigation canal. We are dealing with an unusual real right not specifically defined by law. If it were a pure servitude, we would very likely be required to determine in a petitory action that the ownership of it could be established only by title and could not be acquired by prescription. See La. Civ.Code Arts. 765, 766 [Revised C.C. arts. 739, 740, 742]. But it is unnecessary to determine the ownership of the right in this possessory action. While it is clear the plaintiff and its ancestors in title have possessed the right for more than 50 years under the belief that they were the owners, I find nothing in the record which would lead me to believe that the defendant ever exercised any acts of possession or quasi-possession with the belief and intent of owning the immovable right until one month before suit was filed. The record does indicate that some of the land upon which the canal lies is owned by defendant, but much of the land which the canal crosses is owned by others. The record establishes simply that the defendant during the rice seasons of 1967 and 1968. by sufferance, used parts of the canal in question to irrigate his rice crop.

The majority here and the Court of Appeal below have both cited Civil Code Article 3432 [Revised C.C. art. 3421] as the basis for determining the nature of the required possession of incorporeal immovable rights That article says:

> Possession applies properly only to corporeal things, movable or immovable.

> The possession of incorporeal rights, such as servitudes and other rights of that nature, is only a quasi possession, and is exercised by the species of possession of which these rights are susceptible. (Emphasis mine.)

The record is replete with evidence that portions of rice canals are not used for the flow of water during periods of two or three years while the ground, once planted in rice and flooded by the canals, lies fallow so that the soil content may be repleted. This has been the custom of rice farmers and irrigation canal operators for many, many years. It is only when the rice crop is rotated back to the plots which have been left unused that the canals are needed again, by the companies for supplying water and by the farmers for flooding their rice fields. Nevertheless the canals are maintained to some extent between the periods of flowage use.

The fact that the plaintiff did not use portions of this irrigation canal for water flowage in 1967 and 1968 is of no moment since in those years there were no lands needing water from this canal to flood their rice crop. When the plaintiff company used all the disputed portion of the canal during the entire rice season of 1969, it continued the species of quasi-possession of this incorporeal right by which it had maintained its possession for over 50 years. This use constituted the exercise of that species of possession of which the right was susceptible. Here the right is simply the use of a large ditch which carries water three or four months of some years, does not carry in the remaining months, and in other years never carries water. I therefore conclude from the facts established and from the express language of the Code that plaintiff has maintained continuous possession for over 50 years, including the one year immediately preceding this suit as required by Article 3449(2) of the Civil Code [Revised C.C. art. 3434].

There is no merit in defendant's claim that he possessed for one year before suit.

Possession in law implies a right to enjoy linked to the right of ownership. La. Civ.Code Art. 3434) [Revised C.C. art. 3422]. Although one may possess without being the true owner (Art. 3435 [no corresponding article after revision], he may not acquire possession unless he has the "intention of possessing as owner" (Art. 3436(1)) [Revised C.C. art. 3424]. "This intention of retaining possession is always supposed, where a contrary intention does not appear decidedly...." La. Civ.Code Art. 3443 [Revised C.C. art. 3432]; see also Art. 3492 [Revised C.C. art. 3443]. One who possesses without color of title or in bad faith must possess as "master," as owner, in order to disturb the previous possessor or to establish legal possession in himself. La. Civ.Code Art. 3452 [Revised C.C. art. 3481]. For a possessor in bad faith to use civil possession for a continuation of his corporeal possession there must be vestiges of works erected by him. La. Civ.Code Art. 3502 [no corresponding article after revision]. There is no proof that such was the case here, and defendant cannot claim that any civil possession by him continued his two or three months' activity carried on in 1967 and 1968.***conclusion must be, from the facts in this record, that for the year preceding this suit the plaintiff possessed in the capacity of master and owner and is therefore entitled to maintain the possessory action. Plaintiff possessed in the only manner by which the right of possession could be exercised and to the extent necessary to preserve possession of that particular right. The corporeal acts of the defendant from March to July in 1967 and March to July in 1968 on a portion of the canal were not performed in the belief that he was the owner. It is clear from the record that the defendant meant to possess adversely as owner only when he interfered with plaintiffs possession just prior to the suit in 1970. There was no continuous corporeal adverse possession as owner by the defendant in 1967 or 1968; he merely used, without intent to claim as owner, a portion of plaintiffs unneeded and unused canal during those years.***

It is not difficult to make a positive determination under the law that the plaintiff has a right to maintain this possessory action and the ancillary injunctive proceedings. However, the real right here considered is of such a special kind that I would be hesitant to resort to laws which did not contemplate this particular right. These irrigation canals, vital to one of the most important agricultural enterprises of Louisiana, have existed in a large area of our state for many, many years with a particular and peculiar quality not assignable to servitudes or other particularized real rights. They have been utilized in most cases without title and by mutual consent of landowners and irrigation companies. Numerous contracts between rice farmers and suppliers of water have been drawn over the years which in many particulars do not meet the legal requirements for title to other real rights. This manner of exercising the right has continued for such a long period that it has become the custom of the place. It is the custom, as previously noted, for these canals to be managed and maintained by companies even though portions of them lie unused during the years when adjacent lands are not planted to rice because of crop rotation or legal allotment of acreage. In the present case every witness testified that the right to use the canal had belonged to and been exercised by the plaintiff, and that it was the custom to contract with the plaintiff when water was needed in particular portions of the canal for irrigation of the rice lands.

In my opinion this record supports a finding that under the Civil Code and the Code of Civil Procedure plaintiff continually possessed the right to operate the irrigation canal for many years until disturbed in that possession by the defendant's cutting of the canal levee in April of 1970, shortly before suit, and that therefore the plaintiffs possession satisfies the requirements for the possessory action of Civil Code Articles 3454, 3455, and 3456 [Revised C.C. art. 3423] and Code of Civil Procedure Articles 3655, 3658, and 3663. Moreover, when we resort to custom, natural law, and received usages as well as analogy to the law affecting similar rights, it is clear that plaintiff has established its right to maintain that action. I respectfully dissent.

KIZER v.LILLY
471 So. 2d 716 (La. 1985)

WATSON, J. Plaintiff, Goldie Hause Kizer, brought this possessory action, alleging possession of a servitude of passage on a twenty foot gravel roadway located on the northwestern boundary of land owned by defendant, Fred Lilly, Jr. According to her petition, the road offered Kizer's estate its "only access to a public highway," Louisiana Highway 412, and Lilly disturbed her use of the servitude by erecting a fence at the junction of the gravel road and Louisiana Highway 412. Kizer began using the servitude in the 1930's and its use by her and her lessees had allegedly been quiet and uninterrupted until defendant's fence was built on May 23,1984.

The trial court overruled an exception of no cause of action by defendant. The Court of Appeal, First Circuit, granted a writ and ordered that judgment be entered sustaining defendant's exception of no cause of action, citing Broussard v. Booth, 446 So. 2d 974 (La. App. 3d Cir. 1984). A writ was granted to consider the question. 457 So. 2d 1 (La., 1984).

C.C. art. 740 provides:

> Apparent servitudes may be acquired by title, by destination of the owner, or by acquisitive prescription.

The comments under this new article note that it changes the law by allowing prescriptive acquisition of apparent discontinuous servitudes but state that the provision is not retroactive. A right-of-way over a paved roadway was an apparent discontinuous servitude. Assuming good faith and just title for purposes of the exception, the prescriptive period for the acquisition of an apparent servitude would be ten years. C.C. art. 742. Professor A. N. Yiannopoulos has discussed the effect of C.C. art. 740:

> The 1977 revision broadened the availability of acquisitive prescription by dispensing with the requirement of continuity. According to revised Article 740 of the Civil Code, apparent servitudes may be created by prescription, even though they may have been

considered discontinuous and therefore insusceptible of creation by prescription under the 1870 Code. Thus, in contrast with the 1870 Code, a right of passage exercised over a railroad track, a paved road, or any other construction regarded as an exterior sign of a servitude may be created by prescription. However, Article 740 may not be applied retroactively. Therefore, the possession of a servitude that would be discontinuous under the 1870 Code does not give right to prescriptive rights except from the effective date of the new legislation. 43 La.L.Rev. 58, 59.

Under the 1870 Code, the servitude of passage over the gravel road would be an apparent one. C.C. art. 728. The gravel road would constitute an apparent exterior work. Under the 1870 Code, a servitude of passage is discontinuous. C.C. art. 727. The distinction between continuous and discontinuous servitudes has been criticized. See Yiannopoulos, supra, at p. 60. It was nonetheless firmly embedded in the Civil Code until the 1977 revision and C.C. art. 740 is not retroactive.

Plaintiffs possession was disturbed on May 23, 1984, and her possessory action, alleging quiet and uninterrupted possession for the preceding year, comes within the amended code articles on occupancy and possession effective January 1, 1983. She and her lessees allegedly exercised a servitude of passage, a quasi-possession, on the road for over a year immediately prior to the disturbance. C.C. art. 3421. According to C.C. art. 3421, the rules governing possession apply by analogy to the quasi-possession of incorporeals. Thus, the possessory action is available to quasi-possessors.

C.C. art. 3435 provides that discontinuous possession has no legal effect. However, the new code definition of discontinuous possession is that which is "not exercised at regular intervals." C.C. art. 3436. Plaintiffs petition alleges that she and her lessees have used the gravel road as access to her land "on a regular basis," i.e., at regular intervals. Therefore, her possession has not been discontinuous.

Plaintiffs petition meets the requirements of a possessory action under C.C.P. art. 3658 as follows:

To maintain the possessory action the possessor must allege and prove that:
(1)   He had possession [quasi-possession] of the immovable property or real right therein at the time the disturbance occurred;

(2)   He and his ancestors in title had such possession [quasi-possession] quietly without interruption for more than a year immediately prior to the disturbance, unless evicted by force or fraud;

(3)   The disturbance was one in fact or in law, as defined in Article 3659; and

(4)   The possessory action was instituted within a year of the disturbance.

In addition, quasi-possession of a servitude must be exercised "with the intent to have it as one's own." However, there is a presumption that one intends to possess as owner, and intent may be alleged generally, rather than with particularity. See Mayer v. Valentine Sugars, Inc., 444 So. 2d 618 (La., 1984). Intent to own the servitude can be inferred from plaintiffs petition. Louisiana has fact pleadings and it is not necessary to plead the theory of the case in a petition. Any doubt as to the sufficiency of a cause of action should be resolved in favor of petitioner. Weber v. H. G. Full Stores Co., 210 La. 977, 29 So. 2d 33 (1946). Since plaintiffs petition meets the requirements of C.C.P. art. 3658, the court of appeal erred in sustaining defendant's exception of no cause of action.

Therefore, the judgment of the court of appeal is reversed, the exception of no cause of action is overruled, and the matter is remanded to the trial court for further proceedings according to law. Reversed and remanded.

LEMMON, J. (concurring). The threshold issue is whether the possessor of a servitude which is susceptible of acquisition by acquisitive prescription may acquire the right to be maintained in possession by the passage of a period of more than one year, but less than the period required for acquisitive prescription. A second issue is whether plaintiff alleged sufficient facts to establish that she qualified as a possessor entitled to use the possessory action. Not at issue at this state of the proceeding, but a problem underlying the determination of the present issues, is the effect and the value of a judgment which the plaintiff receives in a possessory action to maintain possession of a servitude.

RIGHT TO USE POSSESSORY ACTION TO MAINTAIN POSSESSION OF A SERVITUDE

Implicit in the recognition of the right to acquire an apparent servitude by prescription is the recognition of the right to possess the servitude. The Code of Civil Procedure, since its adoption in 1960, has authorized the possessory action for the possessor of immovable property or of a real right therein. Article 3655. The possession necessary for a possessory action is corporeal possession, which is the exercise of factual authority with the intent to own the thing. Of course, one cannot exercise true corporeal possession of a servitude because one cannot exercise physical control over an incorporeal. Nevertheless, one may exercise a right of servitude by means of material acts and of constructions such as fences, buildings and roads. 2 Yiannopoulos, Louisiana Civil Law Treatise — Property § 211 (2d ed. 1980).

The more difficult concept is that of continuous possession which is essential for both acquisitive prescription and possessory protection. Arguably, an apparent servitude is continually possessed when it is used regularly according to the nature of the servitude. See La. C.C. Art. 3436. Professor Yiannopoulos observed:

> Under the 1977 legislation, question may still arise as to the availability of possessory protection of the right to possess a nonapparent servitude or a servitude which under the regime of the Louisiana Civil Code of 1870 would be classified as discontinuous. It is submitted that under the 1977 legislation the possessory action is available for the protection of the right to possess servitudes created by title as well as all servitudes that may be acquired by acquisitive prescription. Thus, apparent servitudes, regardless of their classification as continuous or discontinuous under the prior law, or as affirmative or negative under the 1977 legislation, are susceptible of possession and may be protected by the possessory action. For example, a right of passage evidenced by exterior works may be acquired under the 1977 legislation by ten or thirty years" acquisitive prescription and the owner

of the dominant estate may bring the possessory action for the protection of his right to possess such a servitude.

2 Yiannopoulos § 214.

Therefore, a cause of action exists for a possessor of an apparent servitude to protect his right to possess the servitude by means of the possessory action.***

THE EFFECT OF A JUDGMENT IN THE POSSESSORY ACTION

The most difficult problem in this case is that a decision on the narrow issue presented here raises more questions than it answers. The lurking question in the present case involves the effect and the value of the judgment that a plaintiff receives in a possessory action to maintain possession of a servitude.

The possessory action protects only the right to possess the servitude, which is different from the right of servitude itself. The issue of the right of servitude is beyond the scope of a possessory action involving a servitude, just as the issue of ownership or title is beyond the scope of a possessory action involving immovable property. When the plaintiff prevails in a possessory action involving immovable property, he is entitled to be maintained in his possession until another party claims ownership of the immovable property and proves his title thereto. However, when the plaintiff prevails in a possessory action involving a servitude, he is entitled to be maintained in possession until another party claims ownership of the immovable property allegedly burdened by the servitude and proves that he owns the immovable property free of the claimed servitude.

The true effect of a judgment in a possessory action involving a servitude placing the burden of proof on the owner to prove no servitude has ever been established — may be of little value to the plaintiff in this case. In an action to declare the property free of the claimed servitude, the owner will have to prove that no servitude has been established by title, by destination, or by acquisitive prescription. See La. C.C. Art. 740. In the present case, neither title nor destination is mentioned in the petition, and defendant in brief asserted that there was no acquisition by title or destination. Moreover, there can be no acquisitive prescription in this case, because La. C.C. Art. 740 (which provided for the first time the right to acquire by acquisitive prescription an apparent servitude previously classified as discontinuous) did not become effective until 1978, only six years before this suit was filed.

While these thoughts go beyond the holding of this case, such an analysis was necessary for a conceptual examination of this case's narrow issue in perspective. I have written these inconclusive thoughts for whatever value they may have to the parties in future proceedings.

DIXON, C.J. (dissenting). Under the facts alleged in plaintiff's petition and supplemental pleading, she may avail herself of two avenues for stating a cause of action. First, plaintiff claims that she has acquired a right of quasi-protection of a predial servitude over a gravel road. Second, she apparently contends that her estate is enclosed and therefore she is entitled to a legal right of passage over the gravel roadway. Under either of these theories plaintiff has failed to state a cause of action; therefore the decision of the court of appeal should be affirmed.

QUASI-POSSESSION OF A RIGHT OF PASSAGE

The basic requisites for a possessory action are stated in Article 3658 of the Code of Civil Procedure. In order to acquire the right of possession which is necessary to bring a possessory action, the possessor must intend to be the owner of the real right which he claims. C.C. 3424. According to Professor Yiannopoulos, in order to maintain a possessory action, the possession must manifest "the factual authority over a thing with the intent to own it." 2 La. Civ. Law Treat. (Yiannopoulos) 2d Edition § 211 at page 564. Under Article 3424, the possessor attempting to bring a possessory action is required to show a clear and unequivocal intent to use the property or the real right as his own. The decisions of the courts of appeal are in accord with this interpretation of C.C. 3424. Cf. Humble v. Dewey, 215 So. 2d 378 (La. App. 3d Cir. 1968); McCoy v. Toms, 384 So. 2d 518 (La. App. 2d Cir. 1980); William T. Burton Industries, Inc. v. McDonald, 346 So. 2d 1333 (La. App. 3d Cir. 1977). See, for example, Thevenet v. Clause, 302 So. 2d 649 (La. App. 3d Cir. 1974), discussed in 49 Tul. L. Rev. 1173,1178:

***Regardless of a party's subjective intent, he will not be allowed to maintain a possessory action unless he clearly manifested his intent to possess as owner through his acts of possession. This result advances the objective of not permitting a precarious possessor to bring a possessory action and further insulates the true owner from the danger of being prescribed against without his knowledge.

In her petition, plaintiff alleges that she possessed a predial servitude on a gravel road which paralleled the boundary of Fred Lilly's property, for one year prior to the disturbance. Her possessory allegations are based on her contention that she and her lessees regularly used the road for ingress and egress to her property. Nowhere in her petition or supplemental petition does plaintiff allege facts which indicate that she or her lessees intended to acquire a predial servitude over the roadway. Plaintiffs mere intermittent passage over the gravel road without more, is not sufficient to show an intent to become owner of a real right to use the road. Plaintiffs alleged acts of possession were equivocal in nature and did not express an intent to own a right of passage. Such acts are without legal effect. C.C. 3435, 3436.

BLANCHE, J. (dissenting). Plaintiff does not allege any fact that her possession of the right of passage over the defendant's land is that of owner, either by title, destination of the owner, or by acquisitive prescription. If she claims the right of passage through destination of the owner, I agree with the Chief Justice's dissent that she has not alleged any facts so as to state a cause of action and should be given leave to amend.

On the other hand, if plaintiff claims his right of passage through acquisitive prescription, her suit must surely be dismissed because it would be impossible for her to possess such a right as owner. Prior to the amendment to C.C. art. 740, an apparent servitude classified as discontinuous as in the case before us could not have been acquired through acquisitive prescription. Since the 1978 amendment apparent servitudes, whether continuous or discontinuous, can be acquired by 10 or 30 year prescription. La. C.C. art 742. However, since only 6 years have elapsed from the 1978 amendment to the filing of this suit, no servitude of passage exists and the plaintiff therefore cannot claim to possess as owner that which does not even exist.

Plaintiff has been given one chance to amend to state a cause of action by the trial court and has again failed to state a cause of action. Nevertheless, I would not object to giving the plaintiff another chance to amend. For the above and foregoing reasons, I respectfully dissent.

Symeonides, Developments in the Law, Property The Hypothetical Aftermath of Kizer, 46 La.L.Rev. 655,675-680 (1986)

The first question is whether, in the negatory action, the plaintiff should have to prove ownership of the part of the land over which the claimed servitude is exercised. The reason this question is asked is because the direct objective of a negatory action is to determine the existence or nonexistence, validity, and scope of the claimed servitude, rather than the ownership of the underlying land. Yet, for obvious reasons, title to such land must be a prerequisite for bringing the negatory action. A person who does not assert title to the allegedly servient estate should have no right or standing to complain about burdens thereon. But title and ownership may be two different things. A title may be a "perfect" title, in which case it is ownership, or according to the old expression "good against the world," or it may be something less than perfect, i.e., merely a "just title" or a "better" title. It is submitted that, in a negatory action, the plaintiffs burden should not be to prove perfect title or ownership, but rather a "better title" as this term is used in Civil Code Article 531 and Code of Civil Procedure Article 3654. The reason has to do with the defendant's lack of possession and title. The defendant, i.e., the person exercising the claimed servitude, is in quasi-possession of the incorporeal thing we call a servitude, but is not in possession of the corporeal immovable over which the claimed servitude is exercised. A person exercising a servitude of drawing water quasi-possesses the servitude, but does not possess the land on which the well is located. This distinction may be more difficult to detect in a case like Kizer involving a servitude of passage which is exercised through acts similar or identical to acts by which corporeal property is possessed. The distinction is nevertheless important, and the very fact that Mrs. Kizer claimed only quasi-possession of the servitude rather than possession of the strip of land over which the passage was exercised is, at least, an implicit acknowledgment that she did not [intend to] possess the strip itself. If a true petitory action, or an action for a declaratory judgment, were to be brought against Mrs. Kizer, the plaintiffs burden of proof would be to prove "better title" rather than ownership. There is no reason why this burden should be increased in a negatory action where, after all, the ownership of the strip is not even the primary issue. A "better title" should suffice, and, in this case any title by the plaintiff is a "better title", simply because, by definition, the defendant has no title at all. The reasons the defendant cannot have title to the strip is because, if he had such a title, he could not claim a servitude in the first place. Neminem res sua servit (One cannot have a servitude on his own land).

The second question is whether, after having proved his title, i.e., prima facia ownership of the [allegedly servient] estate, the plaintiff should also have to prove that the estate is not in fact servient, or, as Justice Lemmon put it, "free of the claimed servitude." An affirmative answer to this question would mean that the plaintiff would be required to prove a negative proposition. In an 1822 case, Justice Porter resolved the similar question of the burden of proving the use of a servitude for purposes of the prescription of nonuse by placing the burden on the owner of the dominant rather than the servient estate. Citing a provision of the Siete Partidas, Justice Porter said that "where the affirmative involves a negative, the burden of proof is thrown on the opposite party, because a negative cannot be proved." This solution was subsequently codified in what is now Article 764 of the Civil Code and should apply by analogy here, supported also by the general civilian principle that ownership is presumed to be free of burdens. Thus, the burden of proving that a servitude came into existence should rest with Mrs. Kizer, not Mr. Lilly. This solution is supported by the weight of doctrinal authority, including Yiannopoulos, Planiol and Ripert, and Aubry and Rau. According to these authorities, because ownership is presumed to be free of burdens, the burden of proving the existence of the claimed servitude rests with the defendant rather than the plaintiff in the negatory action. Aubry and Rau, as well as Planiol and Ripert, state expressly that "[i]t is the same when the defendant obtains judgment in a possessory action that maintains him in the possession of the servitude."

If this analysis is accepted, Justice Lemmon's misgivings about "the effect and the value of the judgment that a plaintiff receives in a possessory action to maintain possession of a servitude" become more understandable, and so does the reluctance of some other members of the court and of the lower courts to allow the possessory action in the first place. For, if this plaintiff is later sued in a negatory action he can draw virtually no procedural advantages from his prior victory in the possessory action. The contrast with a similarly situated possessor of corporeal property is obvious. As Professor Yiannopoulos explains:

> A possessor of a corporeal immovable who has satisfied the requisites of Article 3658 of the Code of Civil Procedure will remain in possession unless the owner of the immovable proves his ownership in a petitory action. In contrast, the possessor of a servitude who has satisfied the requisites of Article 3658 of the Code of Civil Procedure will eventually be evicted unless he proves the existence of the servitude. This is not an odd proposition. The possessory action protects the possession of an immovable, whether corporeal or incorporeal, and presupposes the existence of the thing possessed. The existence of a corporeal immovable is hardly ever in dispute but the existence of an incorporeal immovable must be proven by the plaintiff who claims that he is entitled to its possession.

Whatever the reasons and need for a different treatment between possessors and quasi-possessors, its detrimental effects on the efficiency of the system should not be disregarded. It would certainly be more efficient in both questions, that is, the quasi-possession of the servitude and its existence, could be resolved in one proceeding. Two solutions come to mind, but there are certainly more and probably better ones. The first, is to merge the possessory action for the protection of a servitude into the confessory action, that is, the innominate real action that seeks a judgment declaring the existence of the claimed servitude, rather than its mere exercise in fact. This solution would, in effect, amount to a compulsory waiver of the possessory action and a requirement that the person claiming the servitude prove its existence at the outset, in order to have any chance for judicial protection. This solution must be rejected because, among other things, it reduces to zero the effect of quasi-possession, thus depriving the plaintiff of an important tactical weapon. The second solution is to merge the defense to the possessory action into the negatory action. Unlike the previous solution, this one does not essentially deprive the defendant of the options he has under the current system. The defendant could, as under the present system, defend the possessory action either by denying the plaintiffs quasi-possession, or by denying the existence of the servitude and asserting his own title, in which case he converts the action into a negatory one and judicially confesses the quasi-possession of the plaintiff. The difference lies in the fact that, under this tentatively suggested solution, the defendant would have to assert his title, if, after having denied the plaintiff quasi-possession, the plaintiff was able to prove its exercise for the requisite year. The fact that, as suggested earlier, the defendant need only prove title rather than ownership, explains why the suggested solution does not put the defendant in a worse position than he is under the current law. If he has a title, he would prevail, unless the plaintiff proves the existence of the servitude. If he has no title, he is not a proper object of judicial solicitude, and, in any event, he would not prevail even under the current scheme. To recapitulate, the suggested solution would work as follows: A person exercising a servitude would have the same options in protecting its enjoyment as he has under the current law. He could file either the confessory action, in which case he has the burden of proving the existence of the servitude, or he could file a possessory action, in which case he has the burden of proving quasi-possession of the servitude for a year preceding the disturbance. In the latter situation, his opponent, the defendant, must assert and prove his title, and if he fails to do so he should be precluded from litigating the issue in a subsequent proceeding against the same plaintiff. If the defendant proves his title, the burden would shift back to plaintiff who would have to prove the existence of the servitude. The difference between this solution and the current system is that a defendant who is defeated on the issue of quasi-possession of the servitude is forced to initiate the discussion of— though not to prove the servitude's existence in one and the same proceeding rather than waiting to do so in a second proceeding. Since, as explained earlier, the burden of proving the servitude's existence remains with the plaintiff, the defendant's position remains essentially the same, while the system's efficiency is enhanced.

NOTE
Power of State and Political Subdivisions

The state and its political subdivisions may grant to private persons exclusive rights of use and enjoyment over public things. In such a case, the grantee may be in possession of a real right that is protected by the possessory action. Parkway Development Corp. v. City of Shreveport, 142 So. 2d 151 (La. 1977).

CHAPTER XV. BUILDING RESTRICTIONS
Civil Code arts. 775-783

1. GENERAL PRINCIPLES

A. N. YIANNOPOULOS, PREDIAL SERVITUDES
§§ 191-195, 199-200 (3d ed. 2004)
(footnotes omitted)

§ 191. Scope of this Chapter

Mostly due to the inadequacy of building and zoning ordinances to meet demands for the preservation and enhancement of property values, landowners and developers of land have, since the turn of the century, imposed restrictions limiting the future use of lands to certain specified purposes, prohibiting the erection of certain types of structures, or specifying the type and value of buildings that may be erected. In order to afford protection in appropriate cases, Louisiana courts have developed a body of law dealing with "building restrictions" as sui generis real rights, distinct and distinguishable from predial servitudes. In France, courts in order to reach comparable results had to strain the notion of personal obligations. In Germany and in Greece building restrictions as sui generis real rights may not be established by private persons; the matter is governed by rules of public law.***

§ 192. Nature of Building Restrictions

Building restrictions are charges on immovable property imposed "in pursuance of a general plan governing building standards, specified uses, and improvements." The nature of these charges is determined by Article 777 of the Louisiana Civil Code; they "are incorporeal immovables and real rights likened to predial servitudes." This provision codifies Louisiana jurisprudence and does not change the law.

The determination of the nature of building restrictions gave rise to analytical difficulties under the regime of the 1870 Code. According to one line of decisions, building restrictions were likened to non-apparent predial servitudes under Article 728 of the Louisiana Civil Code of 1870. This classification could properly apply to building restrictions involving prohibition of material acts in favor of a dominant estate; it could not apply to building restrictions involving affirmative duties.

In a second line of cases, building restrictions were termed real obligations following the land in the hands of any acquirer. This classification was thought to rest on Article 2012 of the Louisiana Civil Code of 1870. According to accurate analysis, however, real obligations are merely the passive side of real rights. Building restrictions have always given rise to real rights and correlative real obligations. The owner of an immovable in a subdivision has always been able to protect and enforce his real rights against other owners of immovables burdened with the correlative real obligations, and vice versa. Building restrictions, therefore, should not be properly classified as merely real obligations.

In a third line of cases, building restrictions were classified as covenants running with the land. This common law terminology derived from institutions so foreign to civil law property that its continued use could only result in confusion. The common law doctrine of covenants running with the land dates back to the time when common law courts refused to recognize the assignability of contractual rights and obligations. The development of the doctrine brought about a set of technical and sometimes artificial rules designed to determine the existence of "privity of estate" whenever a covenant "touches and concerns" land. Some of these rules have been subjected to criticism in modern times as inapposite to contemporary demands. It would have certainly been a mistake for Louisiana courts to adopt that doctrine, with all its historical coloring and artificialities, when they could turn to the Civil Code for simpler solutions.

Preferably, building restrictions should be classified as sui generis real rights akin to predial servitudes. This view has been adopted in the 1977 revision. Accordingly, building restrictions are regulated by Articles 775 through 783 of the Civil Code as well as "by application of the rules governing predial servitudes to the extent that their application is compatible with the nature of the building restrictions."

Like predial servitudes, building restrictions are "property rights." Nevertheless, a Louisiana court has held that landowners in a subdivision are not entitled to compensation for the taking of their rights to enforce building restrictions on an immovable expropriated for public utility. Consistent theory points to the opposite conclusion, but the determinative issue is whether the constitutional guarantees against taking apply to this kind of property right.

§ 193. Creation of Building Restrictions; General Plan

Building restrictions are ordinarily imposed by developers of land who intend to subdivide their property into individual lots destined for residential, commercial, or industrial uses. Article 775 of the Louisiana Civil Code defines building restrictions as charges imposed "by the owner of an immovable" in pursuance of a general plan governing building standards, specified uses, and improvements. Individual landowners, however, may also enter into agreements designed to restrict the uses of their respective properties in accordance with a general plan. Article 776 of the Louisiana Civil Code declares that building restrictions may be imposed "by the owner of an immovable or by all the owners of the affected immovables."

Agreements among landowners imposing restrictions on their properties in the framework of subdivision planning constitute "building restrictions," that is, sui generis real rights. But unlike restrictions imposed by a developer of land that do not qualify as predial servitudes due to the absence of a dominant estate, restrictions imposed by individual landowners may qualify as predial servitudes.

In the absence of subdivision planning, agreements among landowners imposing restrictions on individual lots may give rise to personal rights, limited personal servitudes, or predial servitudes. Because the laws governing building restrictions as sui generis real rights differ in certain particulars from the rules governing predial servitudes, question may arise as to the precise nature of the rights created by agreement among landowners. This is a matter of contractual interpretation resolved in light of the facts of each case and in accordance with the intent of the parties.

In the past, building restrictions were inserted by developers of land in each individual act of transfer of property in a subdivision. Building restrictions are now ordinarily contained in recorded notarial acts or are annexed to recorded plats of subdivisions. Individual transfers of property then incorporate by reference the recorded acts or plats.

The creation of building restrictions as sui generis real rights is subject to the requirement that there be a general plan that is "feasible and capable of being preserved." In the absence of such a plan, building restrictions are not sui generis real rights. Therefore, when restrictions are imposed by stipulations inserted in individual acts of sale, care should be taken to impose uniform restrictions on most, if not all, individual lots in the subdivision. Failure to make the restrictions uniform or insert them in a substantial number of sales may vitiate a contemplated general development plan. In these circumstances, the stipulations intended to establish building restrictions may create predial servitudes, limited personal servitudes, or merely personal obligations.

By analogy to nonapparent servitudes, building restrictions must be created by title. Article 776 of the Louisiana Civil Code declares that building restrictions "may be established only by juridical act." Hence, they may validly be established by declaration of intent made in the act of sale to the present owner or to an ancestor in title, or in a separate document.

In order to be effective against third persons, instruments establishing restrictions must be filed for registry in the conveyance records of the parish in which the immovable property is located. By virtue of the public records doctrine, an acquirer of immovable property burdened with recorded restrictions is bound by them. The restrictions need not appear in the act by which the present owner acquired the property nor in his chain of title. It suffices that the document establishing the restrictions was filed for registry in some form at the time the original subdivider conveyed the property to the ancestor of the present owner.

In the absence of recorded restrictions at the same time of the first sale by the subdivider, the property is transferred free of restrictions; and if, after the first sale, the subdivider imposes blanket restrictions by a recorded declaration of intent, the successors of the original acquirer are not bound by these restrictions....

§ 194. Protection and Enforcement of Building Restrictions

As real rights burdening immovables in favor of other immovables, building restrictions have an active side (right) and a passive side (real obligation). The active side is the real right of each landowner to enjoy his property without any violation of building restrictions. The passive side is the duty of each landowner whose property is burdened by building restrictions to do nothing in violation of the restrictions. It follows then that an action for the protection and enforcement of building restrictions may be brought against any violator by any person entitled to these "property rights." Quite apart from property theory, however, building restrictions established by agreement among landowners may also involve personal obligations. In such a case, a landowner may have recourse to both contractual and property actions.***

Building restrictions may be enforced by a variety of actions. They are ordinarily enforced by actions for injunctive relief brought by the original developer or by landowners in a subdivision. Article 779 of the Louisiana Civil Code, declares that building restrictions may be enforced "by mandatory and prohibitory injunctions without regard to the limitations of Article 3601 of the Code of Civil Procedure." Accordingly, injunctive relief need not be predicated on a showing of irreparable harm or injury.

Persons violating building restrictions may be forced to cease activities in contravention thereof or to remove objectionable structures. An injunction need not be sought while an objectionable structure is being constructed; however, if defendant relies on representations made by the plaintiff that he will not object to violations, the plaintiff may be estopped. Plaintiff may resort to summary process, but no injunction will issue to restrain minor, insignificant, or merely technical violations.

Apart from the injunctive process, persons violating building restrictions may be sued for damages. Article 781 of the Louisiana Civil Code clearly contemplates an action "for damages on account of the violation of a building restriction" grounded on contractual fault. When building restrictions form part of a contract that has been violated, the parties may have recourse to all sorts of remedies under the law of conventional obligations. For example, an obligor under a contract imposing building restrictions may be sued by the obligee for specific performance or for dissolution of the contract.

Contractual remedies are not available to landowners in seeking to enforce restrictions against violators with whom the landowners are not in a contractual relationship. The same landowners, however, may be entitled to claim affirmative injunctive relief which, in effect, is equivalent to specific performance. Further, if the violation of a building restriction satisfies the elements of delictual responsibility for damage to property, if it constitutes an abuse of right, or it amounts to a disturbance of possession, landowners may demand protection of their property rights under the general law.

§ 195. Affirmative Duties

In contrast to predial servitudes which, in principle, may not impose affirmative duties on the owner of the servient estate, building restrictions may impose on owners of immovables "affirmative duties that are reasonable and necessary for the maintenance of the general plan."

Whether affirmative duties are reasonable and necessary depends on the facts of each case. If the restrictions are founded not on substantial reason but on a mere caprice, and are of a character to tie up property to the detriment of the public interest, they will not be sustained. Provisions that each purchaser of a lot in a subdivision shall automatically become a member of a corporation formed to provide maintenance of the common grounds, and that each member shall be subject to an annual assessment, have been enforced as reasonable and necessary. Nevertheless, Louisiana courts have held that an action for the collection of assessments is a personal action subject to the ten-year liberative prescription.

§ 199. Effect of Zoning Ordinances

Zoning ordinances neither terminate nor supersede existing building restrictions. A parish or city ordinance enacted after a restrictive plan has been validly established and recorded cannot interfere with that plan. Further, the zoning of a restricted residential area as commercial does not prevent the enforcement of existing restrictions; it may merely give rise to an inference that the general plan has been abandoned in the area. The converse, however, is not necessarily true. Zoning ordinances affecting previously unrestricted areas involve a valid exercise of police power and exclude the freedom of landowners to establish building restrictions that are forbidden by the public acts.

In Oak Ridge Builders, Inc. v. Bryant, the court held that an ordinance zoning an unrestricted area as commercial establishes merely a permissive use of property within the zone. Since individuals are free to derogate from permissive rules of law, restrictions limiting the area to residential uses were valid and binding.

§ 200. Matters of Interpretation

Article 783 of the Louisiana Civil Code declares that doubt "as to the existence, validity, or extent of building restrictions is resolved in favor of the unrestricted use of the immovable." This provision codified Louisiana jurisprudence according to which instruments establishing building restrictions are subject to strict interpretation, and accords with the principle established in Article 730 of the Louisiana Civil Code. Because building restrictions are rights akin to predial servitudes, juridical acts establishing building restrictions are interpreted in favorem libertatis. Therefore, when there is doubt as to the intent of a person to impose restrictions, or as to the existence of a general plan, the doubt is resolved in favor of the owner whose property is allegedly restricted.

Apart from the rule of strict interpretation, documents establishing building restrictions are subject to the general rules of the Louisiana Civil Code governing the interpretation of juridical acts. Words used are to be understood in the common and usual signification; terms of art or technical phrases are to be interpreted according to their received meaning. Accordingly, if the document provides that the property shall be used for residential purposes only, churches may not be erected. In Wright v. Griggs, the subdivision plan provided that "[n]o lot shall be used except for residential purposes." Purchasers of a lot in the subdivision wished to use that lot solely as a road way for access to their properties that were located outside the subdivision. A majority of the court held that such use of the lot violated the residential use restriction.

If commercial establishments are excluded, the erection of an advertising billboard sign or the use of the property as a parking lot violates the restriction; and if the document requires that only single residences be erected, multiple dwellings or apartment houses are forbidden.

Within certain limits, restraints on the use of immovables may be given in the form of predial servitudes; limited personal servitudes; personal obligations; or building restrictions, that is, sui generis real rights in the framework of subdivision development. In the presence of ambiguities, the question of which type of right the parties have established may also be a matter of interpretation.

Question has arisen whether a "single family dwelling" restriction is violated when a building is used as a community home for mentally retarded persons. Louisiana courts have held that a "single family dwelling" restriction is not violated by the use of a house as a community home for mentally retarded persons. Courts have relied on R.S. 28:381(5) which defines community homes for the retarded as "single family units." This legislation has been considered to be an exercise of the state's police power; therefore, it can affect pre-existing restrictions without violating Article 1, Section 23 of the Louisiana Constitution which prohibits the enactment of laws impairing the obligation of contracts. The Louisiana Supreme Court has held that R.S. 38:478(C) is constitutionally infirm, as it requires approval of local authorities for the use of sites as community homes for retarded persons in violation of the equal protection clauses of the United States and Louisiana Constitutions. The same court has also held that R.S. 28:381(8) was not intended by the legislature "to override a local ordinance adopted in non-discriminatory terms at an unsuspicious time. The legislature arguably expressed in Chapter 5 a public policy...but that public policy cannot be extended to apply to single family residential districts in the absence of express legislation."

a. Validity and Nature of Building Restrictions
La. Civ. Code arts. 775-779, 783
La. R.S. 9:1141.1 through 9:1149.7

COSBY v. HOLCOMB TRUCKING, INC.
942 So. 2d 471 (La. 2006)

VICTORY, J. We granted this writ application to determine whether the court of appeal erred in reversing a trial court determination that this action to enforce a building restriction had not prescribed. After oral argument, we requested further briefing on whether the applicable building restrictions form part of a general plan as required by Louisiana Civil Code Article 775. Upon further review of the record and the applicable law, we reverse the judgment of the court of appeal and reinstate the judgment of the trial court on the original grounds upon which this writ was granted. The trial court's determination that this action was fried within the two-year time period because the violations of the building restrictions were not noticeable until 2001 was not manifestly erroneous.

FACTS AND PROCEDURAL HISTORY

In 1982, William Monroe King, Jr. and his wife Shirley Martin King developed Wedgewood Acres Subdivision ("Wedgewood Acres") in rural Livingston Parish. Contemporaneously with that development, the Kings established building restrictions for Wedgewood Acres, and on December 15, 1982, they filed the restrictions in the Livingston Parish public records.

Two years later, the Kings, along with other family members, Darron and Michele King, developed four rural tracts of land adjoining Wedgewood Acres along Ben Fuglar Road (the "Front Lots") in Livingston Parish. As part of that development, the Kings established a building restriction agreement expressly stating that with the exception of the set-back restrictions, "[a]ll other restrictive covenants shall be exactly as provided in the restrictive covenants for Wedgewood Acres Subdivision as per said [recorded] restrictions." On May 22, 1984, the Kings filed this second restrictive covenant agreement in the Livingston Parish public records.

The provisions of the restrictive covenants pertinent to the present case are:

1. All tracts are hereby designated as residential, and they shall be used for none other than residential purposes. No building shall be erected, altered, placed or permitted to remain on any tract, other than one single-family dwelling, not to exceed two and one-half stories in height, with the usual and appropriate out buildings, enclosed barns, and private garage and/or carports designed to house no fewer than two automobiles.***

7. No house trailers, buses, commercial vehicles or trucks shall be kept, store[d], repaired, or maintained on any lot, servitude or right-of-way in any manner which would detract from the appearance of the subdivision. No structure of any temporary character, trailer, basement, tent, shack, or other out-building shall be allowed on any tract for a prolonged period of time so as to detract from the appearance of the subdivision, unless approved by developer.***

16. No building or structure shall be used to operate any commercial activity on any tract, and no commercial activity shall be conducted from any lot in this subdivision, unless approved by developer.

In 1985, Harry and Joyce Holcomb acquired Lot "P" in Wedgewood Acres, but never built on the property. On January 9, 1985, William M. King, Jr., individually, executed an authentic act wherein he: (1) "grant[ed] permission to [Harry H. Holcomb, Jr.] to enter through public access and park on his premises his truck used in his profession;" (2) permitted him to "maintain this truck for normal maintenance but cannot enter into commercial maintenance in any form;" and (3) allowed him "to construct and maintain a permanent structure for the housing of this truck as long as it is built to other subdivision restrictions and does not detract in any manner from the appearance of the subdivision. Detraction from the general appearance of the subdivision shall be determined by the developer." In exchange, Holcomb agreed "not to haul loads in excess of 50 thousand pounds into Wedgewood Acres except pre-sold loads to other landowners."

Subsequently, on June 18, 1992, the Holcombs exchanged Lot "P" for one of the Front Lots on Ben Fugler Road. Harry Holcomb testified no search of the Livingston Parish public records was made prior to the exchange. In 1993, the Holcombs constructed a home on the newly exchanged lot and approximately four years later, they constructed a 40' x 40' steel outbuilding on their lot for use in connection with their trucking company, Holcomb Trucking, Inc. Traditionally, the Holcombs serviced their vehicles at a shop they leased in Livingston Parish. After the construction of the steel building on their lot along Fugler Road, they terminated this shop lease and started bringing trucks onto their Fugler Road lot for maintenance and service. He testified that none of the trucks are regularly parked at the residence and only general maintenance and minor vehicle repairs, i.e., oil changes, truck lubrication, and brake adjustments, are conducted in the shop. Additionally, the Holcombs also regularly use pressure washers to wash down at least one truck per weekend outside the shop on their property.

On February 20, 2002, eight of the Holcombs' neighbors filed these proceedings, alleging the Holcombs keep, store, repair and maintain one or more commercial vehicles and operate a commercial business on their property in violation of the 1984 restrictive covenants. The neighbors further claimed the continuing disturbance to the neighborhood caused by the Holcombs' trucking business violates the provisions of La. C.C. art. 667.***

The Holcombs responded to the petition with peremptory exceptions of no right of action and prescription. After conducting a contradictory hearing at which evidence was introduced, the trial court overruled the peremptory exceptions. After a trial on the merits on the defendants' violation of the building restrictions, the trial court granted a preliminary injunction, prohibiting the Holcombs from bringing commercial vehicles or trucks on their property in the Front Lots and from engaging in commercial activity on the property, excepting specified business communications.

The Holcombs appealed, seeking review of several issues, including the trial court's denial of their peremptory exception of prescription. Applying article 781, the appellate court found no reasonable factual basis for the trial court's finding the Holcombs' activities were not noticeable and apparent to the public until the spring of 2001 and reversed the trial court's denial of the Holcombs' peremptory exception of prescription. Cosby v. Holcomb, 03-2423 (La. App. 1st Cir. 12/17/04), 890 So. 2d 35 (unpublished opinion). Accordingly, it found the plaintiffs' suit filed on February 20, 2002, "over four years after 'the commencement of a noticeable violation'" was time-barred and the Holcombs' property was freed of the pertinent restrictive covenants that had been violated. Id. We granted the plaintiffs' writ application. Cosby v. Holcomb, 05-0470 (La. 5/6/05), 901 So. 2d 1078.

DISCUSSION

In 1977, the Louisiana Legislature enacted a new Title V of Book II of the Louisiana Civil Code regulating building restrictions. Accordingly, Articles 775-783 of the Louisiana Civil Code now define and govern building restrictions. Because prior to 1977 the Civil Code did not specifically address building restrictions, these new articles generally codified the existing jurisprudence.

Building restrictions are defined as "charges imposed by the owner of an immovable in pursuance of a general plan governing building standards, specified uses, and improvements." La. C.C. art. 775. "The plan must be feasible and capable of being preserved." La. C.C. art. 775. "The law is clear that building restriction clauses constitute real rights, not personal to the vendor, and inure to the benefit of all other grantees under a general plan of development, and are real rights running with the land; and that the remedy of the other grantees to prevent a violation of the restrictions by another is by injunction." Oakbrook Civic Ass'n, Inc. v. Sonnier, 481 So. 2d 1008, 1010 (La. 1986) (citing Edwards v. Wiseman, 198 La. 382, 3 So. 2d 661 (1941)). "Building restrictions may impose on owners of immovables affirmative duties that are reasonable for the maintenance of the plan." La. C.C. art. 778.

When this case was filed and argued to the lower courts and to this Court, there was no dispute that the building restrictions constituted a general plan of development which was properly filed and which gave constructive knowledge of its contents to all prospective purchasers. The defenses presented by the Holcombs in their peremptory exceptions were that a certain plaintiff had no right to pursue an action based on the restrictive covenants applicable to the Front Lots, and that the plaintiffs' action had prescribed. On appeal, the only issues raised by defendants other than the above issues, were that King granted them a waiver from the restrictive covenants and that the trial court erred in granting an injunction if the injunction was based on La. C.C. Arts. 667, 668, and 669. Sua sponte, this Court asked the parties to brief the issue of whether the restrictive covenants constituted a general plan in light of Le Blanc v. Palmisano, 43 So. 2d 263 (La. App. Orl. 1949), which held that a restrictive covenant did not run with the land because whether or not property could be used for commercial purposes was "contingent entirely upon the caprice" of the developer.

After further review, we find that this appellate court case is not dispositive and that the mere fact that certain restrictions can be waived by the developer does not ipso facto make the restrictive covenants unenforceable as such. For instance, in an analogous case, we explained as follows:

> There is a conflict in the circuit courts as to whether a building restriction requiring approval of construction plans by a neighborhood committee, when no guidelines or very general guidelines for approval are provided, is enforceable in this state. The Fourth and Third Circuits have held that such restriction is unenforceable because it is too vague, indefinite and ambiguous. Lake Forest, Inc. v. Drury, 352 So. 2d 305 (La. App. 4th Cir.1977), writ denied, 354 So. 2d 199 (La. 1978); Community Builders, Inc. v. Scarborough, 149 So.2d 141 (La. App. 3d Cir.1962). The Second Circuit and the First Circuit, until the instant case, have upheld such a provision, determining the validity of the enforcement by the reasonableness of the committee's actions. Jackson Square Towne House Homes Ass'n, Inc. v. Mims, 393 So.2d 816 (La. App. 2 Cir.1981); 4626 Corp. v. Merriam, 329 So. 2d 885 (La. App. 1st Cir.), writ refused, 332 So. 2d 800 (La. 1976). The majority of the states which have considered the issue have held that covenants requiring submission of plans and consent before construction are valid and enforceable, even though they vest the approving authority with broad discretionary powers, so long as the authority to consent is exercised reasonably and in good faith.

> We think that the applicable rule in the instant case should be that where the power is granted to a committee to approve or disapprove the erection of a building based on a standard of whether it conforms to the harmony of external design and location in relation to the surrounding structures and topography, such a standard is not ambiguous and is enforceable, provided that the authority is exercised reasonably and in good faith.

Oakbrook, supra at 1011-12.

While the restrictions in Oakbrook dealt with the discretion to approve of construction plans by a neighborhood committee, and some of the restrictions in this case arguably deal with the discretion to approve of certain types of commercial activity by the developer, the relevant issue in both cases is whether the fact that certain of the restrictions are not absolute and are subject to the discretion of a third party negates the finding of a general plan. In Oakbrook, this Court found that as long as the discretionary power is exercised reasonably and in good faith and is based on a standard that is unambiguous, the restrictions were enforceable.

In this case, plaintiffs' complaint is that the Holcombs are bringing commercial trucks onto their property and servicing them there. Section 7 of the building restrictions provides that "[n]o ... commercial vehicles or trucks shall be kept, store[d], repaired, or maintained on any lot, servitude or right-of-way in any manner which would detract from the appearance of the subdivision." This restriction is not subject to the discretion of the developer at all; therefore whether it constitutes part of a general plan is not at issue. Section 16 also appears to have been violated by the Holcombs' servicing of their trucks on their property. Section 16 provides that "[n]o building or structure shall be used to operate any commercial activity on any tract, and no commercial activity shall be conducted from any lot in this subdivision, unless approved by developer." There may be disagreement on whether the phrase "unless approved by developer" applies to both phrases in this sentence, or just the second phrase. However, whatever commercial activity may or may not be allowed based on the discretion allowed the developer, there is no doubt that such commercial activity cannot include keeping, storing, repairing, or maintaining commercial vehicles or trucks in such a manner as would detract from the appearance of the subdivision. Thus, not only did no party allege to the lower courts or to this Court that the building restrictions did not constitute a general plan, the activity complained of in this case, servicing and maintaining commercial trucks on the property in a manner which detracts from the appearance of the subdivision, was not subject to the discretion of the developer in any event and is strictly prohibited. Thus, we need not consider this issue further.***

[In the remainder of the opinion, the court addressed "whether the court of appeal correctly applied the appropriate standard of review in reversing the trial court's factual determination that this case had not prescribed." The court found that a reasonable factual basis existed for the trial court's findings, and that the trial court was neither clearly wrong nor manifestly erroneous. The court then concluded that there was "a reasonable factual basis for the trial court's finding that a noticeable violation first occurred in 2001 and therefore, the case has not prescribed."]

DECREE

For the reasons stated herein, the judgment of the court of appeal is reversed, the judgment of the trial court is reinstated, and the case is remanded to the court of appeal for consideration of the remaining assignments of error consistent with the reasoning of this opinion. Reversed and remanded to the court of appeal.

KNOLL, J. (dissenting). With all due respect to my colleagues, I dissent. In my view the building restrictions in this case fall far short of a real right running with the land. The building restriction's prohibition against the operation of commercial activity on the tract, as well as the proscription against the storage, repair or maintenance of commercial vehicles or trucks, was left entirely to the whim or caprice of the developers which renders a general plan ineffective, and ignores the requirements of La. Civ.Code Ann Art. 775.

The majority skirts this issue and frames the issue as to whether the commercial activity "detracts from the appearance of the subdivision, [which] was not subject to the discretion of the developer in any event and is strictly prohibited." I find resolving the issue in this manner troubling and an incorrect approach to this case. While the issue of whether the building restrictions constituted a general plan was not raised in the lower courts, in my view we cannot engage in a proper analysis on any issue raised concerning building restrictions unless the building restrictions constitute a valid general plan that is a real right running with the land. The majority's feigned attempt to analyze this case under an "appearance of the subdivision" is internally inconsistent when the alleged offending appearance is commercial activity that is prohibited by the building restrictions unless allowed at the whim of the developers. I find this approach unreasonable and ignores the dictates of La. Civ.Code Ann. Art. 783, which requires us to resolve doubt as to the existence, validity or extent of building restrictions in favor of the unrestricted use of the immovable.

The existence of a general plan that is "feasible and capable of being preserved" is a threshold requirement for the creation of building restrictions as sui generis real rights. La. Civ.Code Ann. Art. 775. Without such a plan, building restrictions are simply not sui generis real rights. See McGuffy v. Weil, 240 La. 758, 125 So. 2d 154 (1960). Failure to provide for the uniformity of the restrictions may vitiate a general development plan. See Murphy v. Marino, 60 So. 2d 128 (La. App. 1st Cir. 1952).
In Murphy, the court stated:

It is our understanding of the law that in order to create a binding covenant running with the land in a subdivision, and enforceable by any purchaser of property therein, there should be a uniform plan of restriction applicable to the subdivision as a whole, or to a particular part of the subdivision, known to each purchaser and thereby, by reference or implication, forming a part of his contract with the subdivider....

26 Corpus Juris Secundum, Deeds, § 167, pages 552 and 553, covers the above point as follows:

A general building scheme may be defined as one under which a tract of land is divided into building lots, to be sold to purchasers by deeds containing uniform restrictions.*** In determining whether land is included in a building scheme, doubts are to be resolved in favor of the free use and enjoyment of the property and against restrictions.*** The right to enforce restrictions imposed pursuant to a general scheme must be universal or reciprocal, that is, the same restrictions must apply substantially to all lots of like character or similarly situated, and the scheme must be incorporated in all the deeds.

Murphy, 60 So. 2d at 130. See also Richard v. Broussard, 378 So. 2d 959 (La. App. 3d Cir. 1979) (finding a building restriction did not exist because the original landowner did not have an orderly subdivision plan); Herzberg v. Harrison, 102 So. 2d 554 (La. App. 3d Cir. 1958) (holding that "[b]uilding restrictions are valid and enforceable where inserted in deeds in pursuance of a general plan devised by the ancestor in title to maintain certain building standards"); In re: Congregation of St. Rita Roman Catholic Church, 130 So.2d 425 (La. App. 4th Cir. 1961 (restrictions on 40 percent of the lots does not constitute a general plan).

Particularly germane is LeBlanc v. Palmisano, 43 So. 2d 263 (La. App. Orl. 1949). In LeBlanc, property owners in the Claiborne Gateway Subdivision sued the defendant, requesting injunctive relief to prohibit him from erecting a tourist court on property he owned in the subdivision in violation of a title restriction or covenant running with the land. The particular restriction at issue provided:

> No building shall be constructed to cost less than two thousand dollars. No commercial property shall be permitted to be constructed or occupied as such on this property except by written consent of the [developer] Claiborne Avenue Extension Realty Company, Inc.

In its affirmation of the trial court's denial of the plaintiffs' application to restrain the defendant from erecting commercial buildings on the property, the appellate court stated:

> The law is clear that building restriction clauses constitute real rights, not personal to the vendor, and inure to the benefit of all other grantees under a general plan of development, and are real rights running with the lands; and that the remedy of the other grantees to prevent a violation of the restrictions by another is by injunction. Queensborough Land Company v. Cazeaux et al., 136 La. 724, 67 So. 641, L.R.A.1916B, 1201, Ann.Cas.1916D, 1248; Hill v. Wm. P. Ross, Inc., 166 La. 581, 117 So. 725 and Ouachita Home Site & Realty Co. v. Collie et al., 189 La. 521, 179 So. 841, Edwards v. Wiseman, 198 La. 382, 3 So. 2d 661, 663.

> In our opinion, however, a casual reading of this restriction indicates that it is not a covenant running with the land, but is a personal covenant between the vendor, Claiborne Avenue Extension Realty Company, Inc., and Henry M. Rahders, the predecessor in title of defendants.

> A covenant runs with the land when not only the original parties or their representatives, but each successive owner of the land, will be entitled to its benefit, or be liable, as the case may be, to its obligations. It is so called when either the liability to perform it or the right to take advantage of it passes to the assignee of the land. Real covenants relate to realty and have for their main object some benefit thereto, inuring to the benefit of and becoming binding on subsequent grantees, while personal covenants do not run with the land. Whether or not certain property in this subdivision shall be used for

commercial purposes is contingent entirely upon the caprice of the Claiborne Avenue Extension Realty Company, Inc., and, therefore, this covenant did not run with the land for the benefit of the purchasers or grantees of property in this subdivision.

LeBlanc, 43 So.2d at 265-66 (Emphasis added).

In the present case, two of the building restrictions at issue closely parallel the covenant found unenforceable in LeBlanc because the restriction did not constitute a general plan governing building restrictions for the subdivision.*** Although contained in one numbered paragraph of the building restriction, paragraph 7 contains two separate restrictions. First, the opening sentence addresses house trailers, buses, commercial vehicles or trucks and states they "shall [not] be kept, store [d], repaired, or maintained on any lot, servitude or right-of-way in any manner which would detract from the appearance of the subdivision." Then, the concluding sentence considers a structure of any temporary character, trailer, basement, tent, shack, or other out-building and provides that they "shall [not] be allowed on any tract for a prolonged period of time so as to detract from the appearance of the subdivision, unless approved by developer." Considering the separate topics contained in paragraph 7, it is evident from a clear reading of the provision that it is only the latter provision that the developer may exempt.

No such interpretation is needed for the provision of paragraph 16 of the building restriction. Clearly, with the approval of the developer, a building or structure, as provided in paragraph 16 of the building restrictions, may be used to operate a commercial activity on any tract in this subdivision.

Clearly, the same holding in LeBlanc is applicable here. Whether or not certain property in the Front Lots may be used for commercial purposes as contemplated in paragraph 16 is contingent entirely upon the caprice of William M. King, Jr., his wife, Shirley Martin King, and the two other family members who developed the Front Lots on Fugler Road. Similarly, as provided in the second sentence of paragraph 7, the developer may allow a temporary structure, trailer, basement, tent, shack, or other out-building. Considering the provisions of La. Civ.Code Ann. Art. 775, these provisions of the building restrictions failed to constitute real rights because they did not foste· the development of this property in pursuance of a general plan capable of being preserved. Therefore, these covenants did not run with the land for the benefit of the purchasers or grantees of property in this subdivision.

It cannot be denied that the provisions of Paragraph 1 ("All tracts are hereby designated as residential, and they shall be used for none other than residential purposes,") and the opening sentence of Paragraph 7 ("No house trailers, buses, commercial vehicles or trucks shall be kept, store[d], repaired, or maintained on any lot, servitude or right-of-way in any manner which would detract from the appearance of the subdivision.") conflict with paragraph 16 which clearly gives the developer the right to approve a commercial use of the property. Such a conflict, however, calls into operation the general rules of construction.*** Considering the irreconcilable difference created in this building restriction as regards commercial activity and giving recognition to the dictates of La. Civ.Code Ann. Art. 783 to resolve doubt as to the existence, validity, or extent of building restrictions in favor of the unrestricted use of the immovable, I conclude these building restrictions relative to commercial activity do not constitute a general plan as required in La. Civ.Code Ann. Art. 775. As provided in paragraph 16, the developer may approve commercial activity on any tract despite the declaration in paragraph 1 that "[a]U tracts are ... designated as residential." Thus, I find the plaintiffs may not enforce the provisions of paragraphs 1 and the first sentence of paragraph 7 pertaining to commercial trucks and vehicles, as they do not constitute a real right.

Building restrictions are a means of insuring the lasting aesthetic and monetary value of property. They involve a scheme or plan of which all prospective purchasers are aware. Chambless v. Parker, 38,276 (La. App. 2d Cir. 3/3/04), 867 So. 2d 974, 978; 4626 Corp. v. Merriam, 329 So. 2d 885 (La. App. 1st Cir.), writ denied, 332 So. 2d 800 (La. 1976). A cursory reading of the building restrictions in the present case would have alerted any prospective purchaser that the developer reserved the right to approve any of the subdivision lots for commercial use. In this regard, I further find the majority's reliance on Oakbrook Civic Ass'n v. Sonnier, 481 So. 2d 1008 (La. 1986), misplaced and factually distinguishable. Although this Court approved the use of neighborhood committees to approve certain construction plans in Oakbrook, in the present case the Kings reserved to themselves, in the restrictions, the option of granting a variance for commercial use, which reservation clearly negated a finding of a general plan as required by the pertinent provisions of the civil code. This vastly differs from the procedure approved in Oakbrook.

For the foregoing reasons, I would affirm the court of appeal on other grounds, dismiss the plaintiffs' action based upon the violation of building restrictions, dissolve the preliminary injunction granted in the trial court, and remand the matter to the trial court for consideration of the issues related to the plaintiffs' contention that they are also entitled to damages and the issuance of an injunction grounded on the law of nuisance.

NOTE
Cosby on Remand

On remand, the court of appeal rejected the Holcombs' remaining assignments of error, including the claim that developer William King had granted the Holcombs a waiver from the building restrictions. Cosby v. Holcomb Trucking, Inc., 2007 WL 1300810 (La. App. 1st Cir. 5/4/07) (on original hearing), and 2007 WL 2193549 (La. App. 1st Cir. 8/1/07) (on rehearing).

b. Types of Restrictions; Residential Use

OAK RIDGE BUILDERS, INC. v. BRYANT
252 So. 2d 169 (La. App. 3d Cir. 1971)

FRUGE, J. This action is a suit for a permanent injunction brought by Oak Ridge Builders, Inc., and some 13 property owners of a subdivision, seeking to enjoin the defendant from operating a beauty parlor in her home. The injunction was sought on the ground that the operation of a beauty parlor violates restrictive covenants applicable to the subdivision property.

Following a trial on the merits, judgment was rendered in favor of the plaintiffs in accordance with the oral reasons assigned by the District Court on September 30, 1970. Written reasons were handed down and the defendant was restrained and enjoined from operating a beauty parlor on her property in Cherry Hill Subdivision, No. 2, Lake Charles, Louisiana. The court held that the defendant, Mary Louise Bryant, was in violation of recorded restrictive covenants. The court also overruled a plea of prescription filed by the defendant. Subsequently, defendant perfected the instant appeal. We affirm.

This appeal has three issues for our consideration. These issues are: (1) Do the recorded restrictive covenants (which admittedly apply to the defendant's premises) forbid a business activity of the nature in which Mrs. Bryant is engaged? (2) If Mrs. Bryant has been doing business in violation of the restrictive covenants, are the plaintiffs precluded from enjoining her because she has been doing so far more than two years? R.S. 9:5622(A). (3) Does a valid zoning ordinance, causing an area to be zoned commercial, prevent the subsequent establishment of restrictive covenants, limiting the area to residential buildings?

The appellant contends that her activities were not in violation of the restrictive covenants in the subdivision. Appellant contends that for her business to be in violation of the restrictive covenants, the business activity in which she was engaged would have to be a noxious or offensive one.

Paragraph 7 of the recorded instrument containing the various building restrictions governing the subdivision reads:

"No noxious, offensive, unsanitary, unsightly or unusually noisy activity or business may be carried on upon any lot, nor shall anything be done thereon that might be considered a nuisance to the neighborhood."

The appellee takes the position that this paragraph forbids noxious, offensive or unsanitary activities, or any kind of business activity. We think when the instrument is read as a whole, that it makes it clear that the entire subdivision is limited to single family, residential dwellings, and prohibits the carrying on of any business activity as such.

Another portion of the instrument in question, Paragraph 1, reads:

"No structure shall be erected, altered, placed or permitted to remain on any residential lot hereinabove described other than one detached single family dwelling and shall not exceed two and one half stories in height with a private garage or carport and other outbuildings incidental to residential use."

In Plauche v. Albert, 42 So. 2d 876 (La. App. 1st Cir., 1949), the court interpreted a restrictive provision which read:

"No building shall be erected on any part of the property hereinabove described other than a single family dwelling and a garage or out-house, to be used in connection with the said single family dwelling."

It was held that this restriction prohibited the use of a structure as a warehouse. In light of the entirety of the instrument establishing the restrictive covenants, we hold that a business activity as such on any of the premises covered by these covenants is restricted and prohibited.

The next question for our determination is whether or not the activity in which Mrs. Bryant is engaged is a business, and if it is, for how long has Mrs. Bryant been operating this business?

Mrs. Bryant is a licensed beauty operator under the laws of Louisiana. She apparently has been fixing ladies' hair in her home since 1967. Mrs. Bryant testified that here was a part-time business prior to the first part of 1970, but that now it is a full-time business. She apparently told her next-door neighbor early in 1970 that she was opening a beauty parlor in her home, and in February of 1970 her home was licensed as a beauty parlor by the State of Louisiana.

Mrs. Bryant's activity prior to 1970 amounted to having only one customer at a time, or occasionally two, in her home.

In his written reasons for judgment, the trial judge stated:

"Mrs. Bryant's home was licensed as a beauty parlor by Louisiana in February of 1970. She stated she bought bigger dryers and put in a shampoo bowl. Prior to February, 1970 she fixed her customers' hair in her combination 'L' shaped living room. She also testified she bought a beauty chair last year. She also admitted that she kept no business records prior to 1970, and made no income tax returns from her activities for the years '67, '68, and '69. *** There was no telephone listing to indicate it was a business place. The Court concludes that while Mrs. Bryant did have a number of people come to her home to have their hair fixed, her activities were not of such a nature to constitute a business that would toll prescription."

We are of the opinion that when, early in 1970, Mrs. Bryant had her home listed as a beauty parlor and licensed as such, and began the full-time operation of a beauty parlor, with full equipment in her home, she began operating a business on the premises in violation of the restrictive covenants in the subdivision.

Where building restrictions or covenants are violated, it is clear that the parties within a subdivision may have that activity enjoined and may enforce the restrictive covenants. However, if the violation continues for more than two years, prescription will bar any attempt to enforce the provisions or restrictive covenants. R.S. 9:5622(A) [Revised C.C. art. 781]

The trial court held that Mrs. Bryant's activities between 1967 and 1970 did not amount to the operation of a business so as to toll the running of prescription. We think that the conclusion is eminently correct.

The appellant's third contention is that, since an area of which the subdivision is a part was zoned commercial in 1956 by a valid city ordinance, no subsequent restrictive covenants can be made which would limit a portion of the area zoned commercial to residential housing only. The appellant has cited no authority for this contention, and we consider the question to be res nova.

The property was acquired by the appellant in 1964. The restrictive covenants were established in her deed of acquisition, subsequent to the adoption of the 1956 zoning ordinance.

The appellee contends that since the present zoning ordinance was adopted on March 6, 1968, and the restrictive covenants were filed of record October 22, 1964, the subsequent zoning of the property so as to permit the establishment of commercial operations could not alter the previously established covenants.

When adopted, the 1968 ordinance stated that it was not intended that the ordinance should interfere with any covenant or other agreement previously established except where the ordinance imposed a greater restriction upon the land than that imposed by such covenants or agreements. The appellant admits that the law does not allow a zoning ordinance to change an already existing covenant. Insofar as the 1968 ordinance is concerned, it cannot be given the effect of destroying or rendering invalid the restrictive covenants validly established and recorded in 1964.

The portion of the appellant's argument, which we consider res nova, and upon which no authority has been cited, is the appellant's contentions that the 1956 ordinance, by permitting commercial establishments in an area of which the subdivision is a part, should supersede any subsequently established covenants or agreements which impose a greater restriction upon the use of the property within that area. The appellant argues that this court should, as a policy matter, rule that individuals or groups of individuals should not be allowed to impose greater restrictions upon the use of the land within municipalities that are established by municipal zoning ordinances.

We reject this contention. The 1956 zoning ordinance established a permissive use for the land within that zone. Individuals by their contracts may derogate from the permissive provisions of the law. The vendor of the property in question, in 1964, had the right to establish restrictions upon the use of the land which would enhance and increase the value of the land and make it more desirable. Nothing in our law prohibits the establishment of such covenants or agreements. Additionally, we consider that the restrictions placed upon the use of the property by the covenants established in 1964 motivated and influenced those persons who acquired the property at that time to purchase this property, because of the guarantee that it would be used only for residential purposes. Thus, we are of the opinion that restrictive covenants established in 1964 were valid and binding at that time and continue to be valid and binding today.

We hold that the recorded, restrictive covenants in question here forbid a business activity of the nature in which Mrs. Bryant is engaged on any of the premises covered by the covenants, and that this suit seeking to enjoin these activities was filed before the two-year prescriptive period established by R.S. 9:5622(A) [Revised C.C. art. 781]. We further hold that the restrictive covenants, as established, are valid and binding. For the above and foregoing reasons, the judgment of the District Court is affirmed. All costs to be paid by the defendant-appellant.

2. ESTABLISHMENT OF BUILDING RESTRICTIONS
La. Civ. Code art. 776
La. R.S. 9:1141.1 through 9:1141.9

NOTE
Louisiana Homeowners Association Act (LHAA)

Civil Code article 776 makes clear that unanimity is required to establish a building restriction. Unanimity is easily achieved when the owner of an immovable establishes a building restriction thereon in a juridical act. For example, a subdivision developer who has not yet sold any lots in the subdivision may establish building restrictions thereon by a unilateral juridical act since at that point in time he owns the entire subdivision. If prior to selling any lots in the subdivision, the owner properly records the juridical act establishing the building restrictions, the restrictions will be effective against all persons who purchase individual lots. *Cosby v. Holcomb Trucking, Inc., supra,* involves a building restriction created in this manner.

Article 776 also addresses the establishment of a building restriction on immovables owned by different persons. In such a case, a building restriction may be established by agreement of all owners of the affected immovables. For an example of building restrictions created in this manner, see *Diefenthal v. Longue Vue Foundation, infra.*

In 1999, the Louisiana legislature enacted the "Louisiana Homeowners Association Act" [hereinafter referred to as "the LHAA"], 1999 La. Acts, No. 309, § 2, adding La. R.S. 9:1141.1 through 9:1141.9, eff. June 16, 1999. The LHAA created different rules that govern the establishment and termination of building restrictions that satisfy the LHAA's concept of a "residential planned community." The provisions of the LHAA are found not in the Code but in the "Civil Code—Ancillaries," meaning Title 9 of Louisiana' Revised Statutes. The only reference to the LHAA in the Code is in article 783, which states that, in the event of a conflict between the codal provisions on building restrictions and the provisions of the LHAA, the latter provisions supersede the Code.

When then does a building restriction satisfy the criteria of the LHAA? The LHAA applies to "existing and future residential planned communities whose declarations have been duly executed and filed for registry." La. R.S. 9:1141.3(A). The key, then is the phrase "residential planned community," which is defined as "a real estate development, used primarily for residential purposes, in which the owners of separately owned lots are mandatory members of an association by virtue of such ownership." La. R.S. 9:1141.2(7).

This definition of a residential planned community has two key components. The first requirement is that the property to be affected by the building restriction be a residential real estate development. The second requirement is that the residential real estate development must impose mandatory membership in an "association" upon each owner of property in the development.

What then is "an association"? An association means a homeowner's association created by "any instrument, however denominated, that establishes or regulates, or both, a residential planned community, and any amendment thereto." La. R.S. 9:1141.2(4). The homeowner's association is "a nonprofit corporation, unincorporated association, or other legal entity..., whose members consist primarily of lot owners, and which is created to manage or regulate, or both, the residential planned community." La. R.S. 9:1141.2(5).

If the requirements of the LHAA are satisfied, then the establishment and termination of building restrictions for the residential planned community are governed by the LHAA to the extent that its rules conflict with the Civil Code. With regard to building restrictions regulated by the LHAA, unanimity of all owners is not necessarily required for their establishment. In contrast to Civil Code article 776, the relevant LHAA provision permits the "community documents" (defined in La. R.S. 9:1141.2(3)) to provide for the manner in which building restrictions may be established, amended or terminated. La. R.S. 9:1141.6(B). In the absence of a provision in the community documents governing their establishment, "[b]uilding restrictions may be established by agreement of three-fourths of the lot owners." La. R.S. 9:1141.6(B)(1).

The case that follows does not concern the LHAA (which had not yet been enacted in 1979). Rather, it concerns a case predating the enactment of the LHAA and of the building restrictions title in the Code. Thus, the court's only guide posts were the then-existing predial servitude provisions and the growing body of jurisprudence, some of which had been heavily influenced by the common law doctrine regulating what are called running covenants. *Richard* is a good example of a court adapting existence legislation to this rapidly growing area of law. We will consider the provisions of the LHAA further in connection with the amendment and termination of building restrictions.

RICHARD v. BROUSSARD
378 So. 2d 959 (La. App. 3d Cir. 1979)

STOKER, J. This is an action for declaratory judgment. Plaintiff, Patrick F. Richard, seeks a decree declaring that certain property purchased from John Elmer Jagneaux is free from any restrictive covenants. The restrictive covenant in Question was purportedly placed upon the land in 1968 by insertion in a deed by plaintiff's ancestor in title, Robert Joseph Broussard, Jr., who sold to Jagneaux. Robert Joseph Broussard, Jr. is the sole defendant in this case.

The issue presented by this appeal is whether the trial judge erred in his determination that there was a valid building restriction in effect on plaintiff's property which prohibited the use of that land for commercial purposes.***

FACTS

The defendant was the owner of a large tract of property located in the town of Church Point, Louisiana. The facts in this case are somewhat limited. However, the parties entered into a stipulation of facts. Admitted through the stipulation is a sketch of a long, rectangular piece of property located between four streets which allegedly contains properties which defendant began to subdivide in 1954. This sketch was introduced and appears in the record as exhibit "A". For the sake of clarity we have attached to this opinion a sketch abstracting the pertinent information shown on exhibit "A". As will be seen, an alley runs the length of, and parallel to, two of the streets for approximately three-quarters of the length of the block. A series of lots of varying widths front on the streets shown as David Street and the unmarked street which we take to be Main Street. Most of these lots appear to be approximately 200 feet in depth between parallel lines running from either David or Main Street back to the alley. The alley ceases to run through the block when it reaches the unsold land retained by Broussard.

No overall or general plan of subdivision restrictions was imposed on the entire subdivision, if such it can be called. Restrictive covenants were inserted in the instruments conveying lots to individual purchasers of certain lots; however, this was not done in all cases. Under the stipulation, it appears to be agreed that a prohibition against any use other than residential was included in all sales subsequent to 1954.

The deed transferring title from the defendant to John Elmer Jagneaux contained the following language: "It is understood and agreed by and between the parties to this sale that the...property shall be and remain residential property; that this stipulation shall be valid and binding upon the executors, administrators, heirs, successors and [word indistinct] of purchaser, and shall be enforced by the proper legal action.

The description in the deed from Broussard to Jagneaux reads as follows:

> A certain lot or parcel of land together with all buildings and
> improvements thereon and thereon belonging, if any, situated in the town of

Church Point, Acadia Parish, Louisiana, having a width of 125.2 feet fronting on South Main Street, and measuring 188.7 feet on its Southern Boundary, and running along a 55 foot street right-of-way not yet opened, and measuring 126.2 feet on its rear and/or Eastern boundary and measuring 188.5 feet on its Northern Boundary, bounded now or formerly on the North by Wade Leger; on the East by South Main Street; on the South by 55 foot unopened street right-of-way; and on the West by Mrs. Robert Broussard, et al, as per plat of survey made for John Elmer Jagneaux by W. H. Jarrell, Jr., dated July 2, 1968, which is attached hereto and made a part hereof.

The plat made by W. H. Jarrell, Jr. referred to above is not attached to the copy of the deed in evidence. However, we take the language to mean that the survey was of the property conveyed rather than a subdivision of the whole.

On December 28, 1972, plaintiff purchased this same tract of land from Mr. Jagneaux, which was then described within the deed as follows:

"A certain piece, parcel or lot of ground situated in the Corporation of the Town of Church Point, Acadia Parish, Louisiana on the S/W side of Main Street and measuring 125.2' fronting on Main Street; 188.5' on the N/W Boundary Line: 126.2' on the S.W Boundary Line and 188.7' on the S/E Boundary Line, and is bounded now or formally N/E by Main Street; N/W by Wade Leger; S/W by Alley or property of Shirley Bergeron and S/E by Robert Street."

The stipulation of fact between the parties opens with the following recitation:

We have prepared a map which we will introduce — We don't know if it is a survey(,) but it is a scale drawing of the block of land in question(,) and it has been colored in various colors and markings.

After that prefatory statement the parties indicate the character of each parcel of land within the block.

According to the stipulation, the property lying in the southeastern corner of Broussard and David Street, consisting of two lots of 50 and 82 foot frontages on Broussard, and marked through with a "X," were sold by parties other than defendant and his ancestors. The second classification of sales consists of property marked in yellow on the official exhibit and indicated by diagonal lines on our exhibit. These tracts constitute some five parcels of property, two fronting on David Street and three fronting on Main Street, which were sold prior to 1954 with no restrictions on them whatsoever.

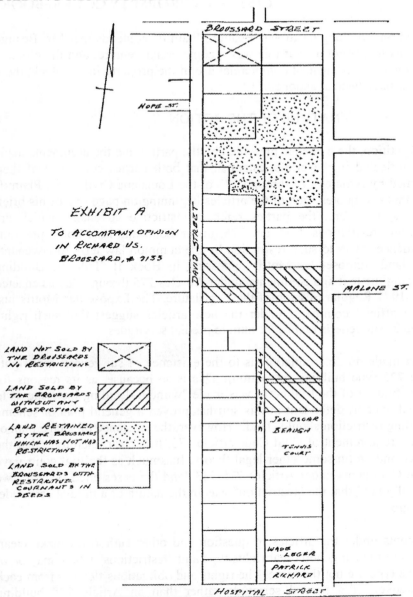

EXHIBIT A

TO ACCOMPANY OPINION
IN RICHARD VS.
BROUSSARD, # 7133

A third classification of property within the block consists of property near the northern end of the block fronting both on David Street and Main Street which has never been alienated by the Broussard family. This property has no restrictive covenants on it. All other individual plots of ground shown on the sketch were sold subsequent to 1954 and each of the acts conveying them contain a restriction to residential use similar to that quoted above which appears in the act of sale transferring title from the defendant to Jagneaux.

The trial evidence indicates that a plot belonging to Joseph Oscar Beaugh fronting approximately 200 feet on Main Street near the southern portion of the property has a tennis court located on it belonging to Mr. Beaugh. Plaintiff contends that Mr. Beaugh rented the use of this tennis court, that this was a commercial venture, and therefore, if viable restrictions ever existed against commercial use of the property in the block, these restrictive covenants have been abandoned.***

NATURE OF THE ACTION

The plaintiffs petition, the evidence presented by the parties and the arguments made in this appeal, as reflected in the briefs, establish that both parties conceived of their rights being governed by Articles 775 through 783 of the Louisiana Civil Code. Plaintiff specifically states this and quotes each of the articles beginning on page one of his brief. Under these articles, therefore, the parties refer to restrictive covenants which are designated as building restrictions, C.C. art. 775, under Louisiana law. Some previous Louisiana jurisprudence refers to such restriction by the common law term of covenants running with the land. Expose des Motifs appearing in Book II, Title V, Building Restrictions preceding the text and comments, under Articles 775 through 783 as enacted by Act 170 of the 1977 Regular Session of the Legislature. The Expose des Motifs just mentioned and the official comments under the new articles suggest that such rights should be classified as sui generis real rights akin to predial servitudes.

The trial court made no determination as to the existence of sui generis real rights (that is an Article 775 type building restriction). This is so because, as its reasons for judgment state, the finding of the trial court was made "without deciding the issue as to whether the original vendor, defendant in this suit has proved a general plan or scheme upon which a building restriction should stand." However, the existence of such a plan or scheme is a specific requirement of Civil Code article 775. It is clear, therefore, that the trial court based its finding on some other legal theory. Inasmuch as the trial court gave as its authority the Comments under Articles 775-783 "and the cases cited therein," we assume that it actually held that the "restriction" was in the nature of a predial servitude. With this we can agree.

As the Comments under the articles in question and other authorities make clear, building restrictions of the sui generis real rights type and "restrictions" which may be of the predial servitude type are not the same. The rights and obligations flowing from each are different. Moreover, if a predial servitude rather than an Article 775 building restriction is involved, the restriction is enforceable by the vendor only and not by owners of other titles which may contain the same type of restriction. Lamana-Panno-Fallo, Inc., v. Heebe, 352 So. 2d 1303 (La. App. 4th Cir. 1977); In Re Congregation of St. Rita Roman Catholic Church, 130 So. 2d 425 (La. App. 4th Cir. 1961) and Murphy v. Marino, 60 So. 2d 128 (La. App. 1st Cir. 1952).

In this declaratory action defendant Broussard, the seller, defends on the ground that since 1954 he has sold lots according to a general plan. In his brief his position and alternative position are set forth as follows:

In this case, all lots sold by defendant since 1954 have contained a residential restriction. Defendant contends that the pattern developed does in fact evidence a general plan of development devised to maintain certain building standards, and therefore, the restriction contained in plaintiffs title is a covenant running with the land, enforceable by defendant and the owners of other lots in the subdivision similarly restricted. If the Court should find, however, that this is not a covenant running with the land, then the restriction is enforceable only [by] the creator, the defendant herein. The jurisprudence is clear that defendant has the right to enforce the restriction in either instance.

Plaintiff appears to agree with defendant to the extent of conceiving of the issue as whether lots were sold according to a general plan. Plaintiff contends there was none. Alternatively, plaintiff contends that if there was a plan, the restriction against commercial use has been abandoned. It appears to us that the parties are entitled to have these issues adjudicated.***

HAS THE PROPERTY BEEN DEVELOPED ACCORDING TO GENERAL SUBDIVISION PLANS?

As was previously noted above, the evidence in this case is not extensive. Although we are reluctant to make assumptions, from the meager evidence in the record there is every indication that the Broussard property has not been subdivided according to any general plan. The course followed by defendant and his parents appears to be desultory and unplanned. The course followed appears to be quite contrary to the situation where a subdivision is formally planned, subdivided into lots from the beginning, platted by a surveyor, staked off into lots and offered for sale as such. On the contrary, the description of the property in the deeds to Jagneaux and the plaintiff would indicate that the property as a whole was never surveyed into lots at one time, but that the defendant and his parents simply sold property as the occasion arose. This gives rise to lots of varying widths. Moreover, at the northern end of the property there is no evident scheme or plan at all with reference to the large block of property still held by defendant, or by him or other members of his family.

This is not to say, or to hold, that it is necessary to impose restrictive covenants on a subdivision as a whole prior to the selling of the individual lots. It is quite possible to create valid subdivision restrictive covenants by simply inserting them into individual acts of sale. This was observed in Gwatney v. Miller, (371 So. 2d 1355 (La. App. 3d Cir. 1979)) as follows:

> The fact alone that restrictive covenants are inserted into individual acts of sale does not establish that they were not intended to pursue a general plan of development for the subdivision. Rather the uniformity or consistency of the restrictions must be examined in order to determine the original intentions of the subdivider. See Yiannopoulos, Real Rights: Limits of Contractual and Testamentary Freedom, 30 La. Law Rev. 44 (1969) at p. 64.

The observations on this point of Professor Yiannopoulos referred to in the Gwatney case read as follows:

> In the past, building restrictions were inserted by developers of land in each individual act of transfer of property in a subdivision. Today, however, building restrictions are ordinarily contained in recorded notarial acts or are annexed to recorded plats of subdivisions. Individual transfers of property then incorporate by reference the recorded acts or plats.

> The creation of building restrictions as sui generis real rights is subject to the requirement that there be a general plan that is feasible and capable of being preserved. Thus, when restrictions are imposed by stipulations inserted in individual acts of sale, care should be taken to impose uniform restrictions on most, if not all, individual lots in the subdivision. Omission to make the restrictions uniform or to insert them in a substantial number of sales may be taken to indicate failure of a general development plan. In these circumstances, the stipulations establishing the restrictions may create personal obligations rather than sui generis real rights.

In the case of In re Congregation of St. Rita Roman Catholic Church, 130 So. 2d 425 (La. App. 4th Cir. 1961) the Court said:

> Building restrictions, such as those in question, are valid and enforceable where inserted in deeds in pursuance of a general plan devised by the ancestor in title to maintain certain building standards; such restrictions inure to the benefit of all other grantees under a general plan of development, and are real rights running with the land, which the grantees or their successors in title may enforce by injunction. (Citations omitted.)

> However, where restrictive covenants do not appear in chains of title of half the lots of a subdivision, for which no general plan of subdivision or restrictions had been recorded, as obtains here, such restrictions will not be enforced as covenants running with the land against any of the grantees of original subdivider [sic] or their successors. (Citations omitted.)***

Where the restriction is not a covenant running with the land, it is personal to the creator of the restriction. (Citation omitted.)

With respect to the property involved in this declaratory action before us, an examination of the exhibit depicting the layout of the lots and the characterization of the various portions, it is not possible to discern any general plan of development. It is simply a strip of property lying between two streets permitting the selling off of lots at random fronting on the two streets. The Broussard interests have apparently provided for an alley which leads from the southernmost street, shown as Hospital Street, through the middle of the strip to that block of property still held by the Broussards. This irregular block of property (indicated as shaded in dots) is completely unburdened by the kind of restrictive covenants which have been inserted in conveyances of the properties since 1954. In fact, it is entirely unrestricted. While it may be granted that there appears to be some system of including the restrictive covenants in all sales since that date, the lots which were sold prior to 1954 although only five in number, include one lot which appears to be approximately 100 feet in width fronting on David Street. Another appears to have a frontage of 290 feet on Main Street. Therefore, insofar as total square footage is concerned, a considerable block of property which is unrestricted separates that group of restricted lots lying to the south of it from those lying to the north of it. The same may be said of the property retained by the Broussards, as it separates a number of restricted lots restrictions lying to its south from restricted lots to the north of it.

In addition to the random width in frontage of the properties which have been sold, there appear to be properties which may have been retained as side streets which do not bear any relationship to any orderly subdivision plan.

In view of all of the foregoing, we are unable to find that plaintiffs property is a "subdivision" which has been developed in accordance with a general plan governing building standards, specified uses, and improvements. It may well be that additional evidence might have disclosed such a plan. However, such evidence is not in the record.

IS THE RESTRICTION TO RESIDENTIAL USE INSERTED IN THE ACT OF SALE FROM BROUSSARD TO JAGNEAUX A PREDIAL SERVITUDE ENFORCEABLE BY BROUSSARD AGAINST SUBSEQUENT OWNERS?

Above we quoted from defendant Broussard's brief setting forth his alternative argument. This alternative argument is as follows:

> If the Court should find, however, that this lot is not a covenant running with the land, then the restriction is enforceable only [by] the creator, the defendant herein. The jurisprudence is clear that defendant has the right to enforce the restrictions in either instance.

We hold that defendant is correct in this alternative argument. McGuffy v. Weil, 240 La. 758, 125 So. 2d 154 (1960); Clark v. Reid, 122 So. 2d 344 (La. App. 2d Cir. 1960); and Yiannopoulos, Civil Law of Property, Volume 1 of Louisiana Practice, Section 104, page 310.

The restriction in question was established by title. It was inserted as an agreement in the act of sale between defendant as seller and the first purchaser, Jagneaux. It was stated "that this stipulation shall be valid and binding upon," among others, "successors of purchaser, and shall be enforced by proper legal action."

Two estates are involved, and it is clear that the restriction is in favor of the property of Broussard from which Jagneaux's lot taken. New Article 731 of the Civil Code provides that a "charge established on an estate expressly for the benefit of another estate is a predial servitude although it is not so designated." Act 514 of the 1977 Regular

Session of the Legislature. The Comment under the article states that it reproduces the substance of Article 754 of the Louisiana Civil Code of 1870 and does not change the law.

ART. 733. PREDIAL SERVITUDES

Art. 733. When the right granted be of a nature to confer an advantage on an estate, it is presumed to be a predial servitude.

New Article 653 states in its second paragraph that the "predial servitude continues as a charge on the servient estate when ownership changes." This article reproduces Old Article 563 and 654 which are to the same effect.

The case of McGuffy v. Weil, supra, is solid authority for our holding here. The facts of that case are parallel to those of this case except that only one lot had been sold from the parent estate or lot. The discussion of theory in that case is fully sufficient to establish that plaintiffs property in the case before us is burdened with a predial servitude which defendant may enforce. The narrow holding (in the reasons for judgment) of the trial court was that the language in the sale from defendant to Jagneaux "created a building restriction running with the land into the hands of successive buyers," and further that "there exists on said property a building restriction, restricting it to residential use only, the same being valid and enforceable against plaintiff." The judgment, very brief in form, denied plaintiff the declaratory relief of freeing his property from the residential restriction use and decreed "that the building restriction contained in plaintiffs title is valid and enforceable against plaintiff (emphasis supplied). We affirm this judgment.

This litigation is between plaintiff and defendant only. The former is owner of the servient estate and latter of the dominant estate. Our affirmance of the trial court's judgment affects the parties to this suit only. We make no adjudication as to the rights of holders of other lots purchased from defendant and make no comment thereon.

For the foregoing reasons we affirm the judgment of the trial court. Costs of this appeal are assessed to plaintiff-appellant.

NOTE
Illegal Restrictions

Restrictions forbidding the sale of property to persons of a particular race, religion or nationality violate the equal protection clause of the United States Constitution. See, e.g., Roy v. Ducote, 399 So. 2d 737 (La. App. 3d Cir. 1981) (declaring unconstitutional a restriction forbidding the construction of dwellings financed by a "Farmers' Home Administration interest credit loan, or by the Federal Housing Authority 235 T of HUD programs").

3. TERMINATION OF BUILDING RESTRICTIONS

a. Termination by Agreement of Owners
La. Civ. Code art. 780

A.N. YIANNOPOULOS, PREDIAL SERVITUDES
§ 196 (3d ed. 2004)
(footnotes omitted)

§ 196. Termination of Building Restrictions; Agreement of Owners

Building restrictions may terminate according to the terms prescribed in the act that establishes them, by agreement of owners of the lands affected by the restrictions, by a liberative prescription of two years, and by abandonment of the subdivision plan or of particular restrictions. Building restrictions may also terminate in accordance with the rules of the Civil Code governing extinction of predial servitudes to the extent that their application is compatible with the nature of building restrictions.

Article 780 of the Louisiana Civil Code, declares that building restrictions terminate "as provided in the act that establishes them." Persons imposing building restrictions are free to prescribe rules for termination, provided that these rules are not contrary to the public order. Provision may be made for termination of the restrictions upon the lapse of a period of time or upon the happening of an event; moreover, provision may be made for termination of the restrictions by agreement among the landowners in whose favor the restrictions were imposed and for the procedures by which this consent is to be obtained.

In the absence of pertinent provisions in the act that established the restrictions, owners of the area affected by the restrictions may terminate them by agreement. Article 780 of the Louisiana Civil Code, as enacted in 1977, declared: "Building restrictions terminate as provided in the act that establishes them. In the absence of such provision, owners representing more than one-half of the land area affected by the restrictions may terminate by agreement, for the whole or a part of the restricted area, building restrictions that had been in effect for at least fifteen years."

The second sentence of Article 780 of the Louisiana Civil Code was amended in 1980 and 1983 to read: "In the absence of such provision, building restrictions may be amended or terminated for the whole or of a part of the restricted area by owners representing more than one-half of the land area affected by the restrictions, excluding streets and street rights-of-way, if the restrictions have been in effect for at least fifteen years, or by agreement of both owners representing two thirds of the land area affected and two thirds of the owners of the land affected by the restrictions, excluding streets and street rights-of-way, if the restrictions have been in effect for more than fifteen years." These clumsy amendments to Article 780 of the Louisiana Civil Code have confused the distinct and distinguishable matters of termination and amendment of building restrictions. An "amendment" of building restrictions may actually involve termination of existing restrictions, an imposition of new restrictions, or both. However, the requirements for the termination of building restrictions and for the termination of existing restrictions were not the same.

It was correctly suggested that Article 780 contemplated amendments that lessen restrictions on property. When a purported amendment results in the imposition of new restrictions or in expansion of existing restrictions, all owners of the affected immovables should consent. However, Article 780 was again amended in 1999 to read: "Building restrictions may be amended, whether such amendment lessens or increases a restriction, or may terminate or be terminated, as provided in the act that establishes them. In the absence of such provision, building restrictions may be amended or terminated for the whole or a part of the restricted area by agreement of owners representing more than one-half of the land area affected by the restrictions, excluding streets and street rights-of-way, if the restrictions have been in effect for at least fifteen years, or by agreement of both owners representing two-thirds of the land area affected and two-thirds of the owners of the land affected by the restrictions, excluding streets and street rights-of-way, if the restrictions have been in effect for more than ten years."

In order to have effect toward third persons, an agreement that terminates building restrictions must be filed for registry in the office of the parish recorder or register of conveyances (Orleans Parish) in which the immovable property is located. R.S. 9:5622, repealed in the 1977 revision, provided for recordation of the agreement in the conveyance and mortgage records. No reason has been ascertained as to why the legislature thought it necessary to require recordation in the mortgage records. Recordation in the conveyance records is sufficient.

DIEFENTHAL v. LONGUE VUE FOUNDATION
865 So. 2d 863 (La. App. 4th Cir.), cert denied, 869 So. 2d 883 (La. 2004)

MURRAY, J. This is an action for declaratory and injunctive relief seeking to enforce restrictive covenants prohibiting commercial use of the properties fronting Garden Lane, one of the premiere residential neighborhoods in the City of New Orleans. The owners of the seven residences fronting Garden Lane (the "Residents") filed this action against Longue Vue Foundation and Longue Vue House and Gardens Corporation ("Longue Vue"). Longue Vue is the owner of a historic house, museum and gardens situated on several acres on the border of the City of New Orleans and Metairie; its northern boundary is Garden Lane.

This is the third time in the last thirty years that Longue Vue (or its prior owners) has been sued by its Garden Lane neighbors. All three cases have involved attempts to enjoin Longue Vue from expanding the commercial use of its Garden Lane property. The first suit, filed in 1973, was based on alleged violations of a commercial use restriction imposed by a 1931 Act on the Garden Lane properties. That suit was resolved by a 1977 settlement agreement, which relaxed the commercial use restriction, but only as to Longue Vue and only as to certain limited activities (the "1977 Agreement"). The second suit, filed in 1988, was based on alleged violations of the 1977 Agreement. That suit was litigated and was ultimately resolved by the Louisiana Supreme Court's decision in Diefenthal v. Longue Vue Management Corp., 561 So. 2d 44 (La. 1990).

In 2000, the Residents filed the instant suit based on alleged violations of the 1931 Act, the 1977 Agreement, and the 1990 Diefenthal decision. In this suit, the Residents seek to enjoin Longue Vue's plans to convert an adjoining, former Garden Lane property (the "Brint Property") into a parking facility; to hold parties and other functions on its site....From the trial court's judgment granting the Residents' motion for summary judgment and their request for injunctive relief, Longue Vue appeals. For the reasons that follow, we affirm that judgment.***

FACTUAL AND PROCEDURAL BACKGROUND

In 1922, Longue Vue's prior owners, Edgar and Edith Stern, acquired a 250 by 500 feet lot at the end of Garden Lane from Dr. Charles Eckhardt....On February 16, 1931, Mr. Stern and the other six then owners of the properties fronting Garden Lane entered into an authentic act imposing certain restrictions on their respective properties....Included among the restrictions imposed by the 1931 Act not only was a commercial use restriction, but also were restrictions on the types of buildings that could be erected, the number of dwellings on each lot, the size of buildings, the size of the lots, and the amount of setback....

Collectively, the restrictions "constitute^] a general plan of development and were properly filed, thus giving constructive knowledge of their contents to all prospective purchasers." Diefenthal, 561 So.2d at 51. Addressing the duration of the restrictions, the 1931 Act provides:

> [A]ll the above servitudes, reservations, restrictions, covenants, conditions and real obligations are valid and binding under the law of Louisiana without any limitation of time, but that in the event it should be held that said covenants can only be made under the law of Louisiana for a limited time, then and in that event each of such covenants is to be binding for a period of fifty (50) years from this date.

***In the 1960's, Mrs. Stern decided, despite the 1931 Act's commercial use restriction, to open her residence and surrounding gardens to the public and to convert her residence into a public museum. In 1973, her neighbors responded by filing suit, alleging her attempts to expand the public use of the property violated the 1931 Act.

The parties settled that first suit by entering into the 1977 Agreement, pursuant to which each side gave up something. The neighbors agreed to relax the commercial use restriction of the 1931 Act, but only as to the Longue Vue property and only as to certain uses. Simply stated, the parties agreed that Longue Vue's "gardens may be opened to the public for viewing, the house and other outbuildings may be used for museum purposes within the ordinary meaning of that word, and the Playhouse may be used for meetings, limited to three nights per week, of nonprofit groups." Diefenthal, 561 So. 2d at 54. In turn, Mrs. Stern agreed that Garden Lane would remain a private road [as provided for in the 1931 Act] and that the public generally would not use it for access to Longue Vue; rather, she was required to construct a public entrance for access to Longue Vue. This public entrance was subsequently constructed on Bamboo Road. The 1977 Agreement also provided that a majority of the other property owners could agree to erect a barrier or gatehouse at the Garden Lane entrance and to station a guard there to enforce the terms of the agreement and to share the costs pro rata.

Also in the 1970's, around the time of her husband's death, Mrs. Stern attempted to donate the property to, among others, the New Orleans Museum of Art. This attempted donation was blocked because of a conflict with municipal zoning ordinances. Although the City Council passed an ordinance allowing any residence with four acres to be opened as a museum, Mrs. Stern's efforts to donate the property failed. Diefenthal, 561 So. 2d at 47. Consequently, she created and funded Longue Vue to operate the museum. Upon her death in 1980, Longue Vue became the owner of the property.

In 1987, Longue Vue began to host large, loud parties and other functions frequently on the property. In 1988, the neighbors commenced a second suit seeking declaratory and injunctive relief based on Longue Vue's violations of the 1931 Act and 1977 Agreement. In 1990, the second suit was resolved by the Louisiana Supreme Court's decision in Diefenthal.

In Diefenthal, the Court framed the issue as whether Longue Vue, "a museum located adjacent to a residential neighborhood, can allow use of its facility for large, outdoor functions which allegedly violated restrictive covenants governing use of the property." 561 So. 2d at 46-47. Holding that it could not, the Court reasoned that "[t]he stately Longue Vue residence may have been transformed into a museum, but it is nevertheless bound by and must recognize the constraints of its location." 561 So. 2d at 57. Those constraints were the restrictions set forth in the 1931 Act, as amended by the 1977 Agreement. (For ease of reference, we refer to that bundle of property restrictions in the 1931 Act and 1977 Agreement collectively as the "Restrictions.") Although the Court also stated that the large, outdoor functions created a nuisance, the Court based its decision on Longue Vue's past violations of the Restrictions and reinstated the trial court's judgment interpreting those Restrictions and granting injunctive relief.

Three events have occurred since the Diefenthal decision. It is these three events, which are detailed below, that have prompted the present suit. First, on June 9, 1998, Longue Vue purchased #14 Garden Lane (the Brint Property), which abutted the property Longue Vue already owned. As a result, Longue Vue became the owner of more than one-half of the Garden Lane property, excluding streets and street rights-of-way, subject to the Restrictions.

The second event occurred in December 1999, when Longue Vue applied to the City of New Orleans for a conditional use permit. This permit would allow Longue Vue's expansion of the property associated with its museum and gardens and its construction of museum-related improvements, including parking facilities. The permit also provided for a re-subdivision, which would allow Longue Vue to incorporate the Brint Property into the existing Longue Vue site. The Master Plan submitted to the City provided for demolishing the Brint residence and constructing a parking lot on part of the property. It further provided for erecting a fence across Garden Lane at the edge of the former Brint Property to prevent Longue Vue visitors from using Garden Lane as a means of ingress or egress, absent an emergency. This small, one hundred feet segment of Garden Lane that Longue Vue proposes to enclose is located in front of the Brint Property and surrounded on all three sides by property now owned by Longue Vue. (This small segment of Garden Lane is referred to in this litigation as the "End Strip.") The Master Plan also provided that Longue Vue would construct a turnaround, for the Residents* use, where Garden Lane meets the End Strip.

After a hearing, the City Planning Commission denied Longue Vue's request, concluding that to grant it "would destabalize and lessen the property values of a beautiful neighborhood" and would lead to "future demolitions in the neighborhood as well as commercial encroachment." Overruling the Commission's decision, the City Council on February 17, 2000 approved Longue Vue's application and passed Ordinance No. 19591, which embodied that approval. On March 28, 2000, former Mayor Marc Morial approved and returned the Ordinance.

The third triggering event occurred on February 17, 2000, when Longue Vue executed an Act of Termination. Because the validity of this Act of Termination is the core issue presented in this case, we quote its key recitals; to wit:

• The Subject Longue Vue Property and other parcels of immovable property owned by other persons...are the subject of certain restrictions established by an act...dated December 16, 1931, and registered in...Orleans Parish, Louisiana, as amended by an act ..dated April 18, 1977, and registered in...Orleans Parish, Louisiana (collectively, the "Restrictions") (for ease of reference, the Subject Longue Vue Property and the Other Restricted Property are collectively referred to as the "Restricted Property").

• To the extent that they apply, the Restrictions are building restrictions under Louisiana Civil Code articles 775 et seq.

• The Restrictions state that they are "without any limitation of time, but that in the event it should be held then [sic] said covenants can only be made under the law of Louisiana for a limited time, then and in that event each of such covenants is to be binding for a period of fifty (50) years from this date."

• The Restrictions specify no means for termination and have been in effect for at least 15 years.

• Pursuant to Louisiana Civil Code article 780, as owner of more than one-half of the Restricted Property, Longue Vue hereby terminates the Restrictions in their entirety.

The Act of Termination was recorded in the conveyance records on April 24, 2000. Meanwhile, in April 2000, shortly after the City passed the Ordinance, but prior to the recordation of the Act of Termination, the Residents commenced this suit seeking to enjoin Longue Vue's plan to convert the Brint Property into a parking facility, to hold functions on its property, and to close in the End Strip. The Residents contend that Longue Vue's plans are in violation of the 1931 Act, the 1977 Agreement, and the 1990 Diefenthal decision. After learning of Longue Vue's Act of Termination, the Residents filed an amended petition challenging the Act of Termination and seeking a declaration that it is void and without effect.

To place this rather complex property dispute in context, we briefly outline the Residents' claims as set forth in their original and amending petitions; to wit:

• The 1931 Act creates predial servitudes by its literal terms, and La. C.C. art. 780 does not apply to servitudes. The predial servitudes as they pertain to the Brint Residence (and the Residents alike) in the 1931 Act were not relaxed by the 1977 Settlement, and those servitudes prohibit the use of the Brint Residence for commercial purposes or for any use other than as a private residence. Accordingly, Longue Vue may not use the Brint Residence as a parking lot for a public museum and gardens.

• Even if the 1931 Act could be deemed to create "building restrictions," Article 780 (as it replaces La. R.S. 9:5622) cannot be applied retroactively to the 1931 Act to impair the Residents' vested contract and property rights.

• The 1977 Agreement in any event does not contain "building restrictions," and Article 780 does not apply to it, and it cannot be terminated unilaterally by Longue Vue.

• Longue Vue answered alleging that it entered into and recorded the Act of Termination pursuant to La. C.C. art. 780. As a result, Longue Vue asserts that neither the Restrictions in the 1931 Act, as amended by the 1977 Agreement, nor the 1990 Diefenthal decision interpreting those Restrictions are binding on its use of its property. The Residents and Longue Vue separately filed cross motions for summary judgment.***

ANALYSIS

***The trial court framed the issue presented as whether, as a matter of statutory construction, Article 780, as enacted by La. Acts 1977, No. 180, effective January 1, 1978, could be retroactively applied to the building restrictions created by the 1931 Act, as amended by the 1977 Agreement. Finding it could not, the trial court cited La. Acts 1977, No. 170, § 7, which provides:

> The provisions of this Act shall apply to all building restrictions, including those existing on the effective date of this Act; but no provision may be applied to divest already vested rights or to impair the obligation of contracts.

La. Acts 1977, No. 170, § 7. Based on the above provision, the trial court reasoned that to apply Article 780 to the 1931 Act and 1977 Agreement would impair the parties' contractual rights. The trial court thus concluded that Article 780 could not be retroactively applied to terminate the Restrictions, stating:

> At the time the contract was confected all parties would have to agree to terminate. Therefore, each had an obligation to continue the contract until all agreed to its termination. Conversely, each had a right to prevent its termination. To apply Article 780 retroactively would be to impair, deny or release parties from their contractual obligations or rights.

The Residents argue that the trial court's decision is correct and that our analysis should end here. Longue Vue counters that the trial court erred in refusing to find Article 780 applicable and its Act of Termination valid, and offers two arguments in support of its position. First, it argues that the application of Article 780 to the Restrictions is not a retroactive application of the law. In support of this position, Longue Vue cites the following civilian formula for determining when a law is being retroactively applied: "A law is retroactive when it goes back to the past either to evaluate the conditions of the legality of an act, or to modify or suppress the effects of a right that have already been realized. Apart from this there is no retroactivity, and a law may modify the future effects of facts or acts that have preceded it without being retroactive." 4 A.N. Yiannopoulos, Louisiana Civil Law Treatise: Predial Servitudes § 2 (2nd ed.1997. Longue Vue contends that, because the Restrictions did not provide a method for their termination, the parties' contractual rights will not be impaired by if Article 780 is applied to provide for same.***

Although retroactive application of Article 780 (or its predecessor, La. R.S. 9:5622) to the Restrictions, which were enacted in 1931, and amended in 1977, raises a constitutional issue, we find it unnecessary to resolve that issue in order to decide this case.***Resolution of the retroactivity issue is not essential to the decision of this case. Even assuming Article 780 applies, the Act of Termination is invalid.

Reviewing the trial court's ruling on summary judgment de novo, we find that the validity of the Act of Termination hinges on an analysis of two of the recitals in the Act of Termination; namely:

• The Restrictions are building restrictions under Louisiana Civil Code articles 775 et seq. (the "Classification issue").

• The Restrictions specify no means for termination and have been in effect for at least 15 years (the "Termination Provision issue").

The Classification issue poses the question whether the Restrictions are building restrictions, as Longue Vue contends, or predial servitudes, as the Residents contend. If the Restrictions are predial servitudes, the concurrence of all the property owners is required to terminate them. Whereas, if they are building restrictions, men Article 780 may apply to allow a majority landowner to terminate them.

The Termination Provision issue poses the question whether the provision in the 1931 Act addressing the duration of the Restrictions constitutes a contractual termination provision under Article 780 (and its predecessor La. R.S. 9:5622). We separately address these two issues.

BUILDING RESTRICTIONS VERSUS PREDIAL SERVITUDES

[In this part of the opinion, the court analyzed the 1931 Act, and the 1977 Agreement, and the 1990 Diefenthal decision interpreting those agreements and concluded that the parties intended to create building restrictions.]

LEGISLATIVE HISTORY OF ARTICLE 780

Analysis of the Termination Provision issue requires that we trace the legislative history of Article 780. In 1960, the Legislature amended La. R.S. 9:5622 to add a provision similar to that presently found in Article 780. Particularly, the provision authorized owners of a majority of the property to terminate restrictions that had been in effect for at least fifteen years when the agreement creating such restrictions made no provision for terminating them; it provided:

Stipulations in deeds and title to land providing for building restrictions which are inserted in pursuance of a general subdivision plan devised by a common ancestor in title to establish certain use and building standards, constituting covenants running with the land, and wherein no provision is made for terminating the effective date of said restrictions, may be terminated in the following manner:

(1)By agreement of owners of a majority of the square footage of land in said subdivision to terminate and end said restrictive covenants as of a definite date, provided said agreement will not be effective unless said restrictive covenants will have been established a minimum of 15 years prior to the date of termination of said restrictive covenants; and

(2)Any agreement purporting to comply with this statute shall be recorded in the conveyance and mortgage records of the Parish in which the land is located.

La. R.S. 9:5622(A)(as amended by La Acts 1960, No. 448).

In 1977, as part of the legislative codification of building restrictions, the Legislature moved this provision to La. C.C. art. 780; it provided:

> Building restrictions terminate as provided in the act that establishes them. In the absence of such provision, owners representing more than one-half of the land area affected by the restrictions may terminate by agreement, for the whole or a part of the restricted area, building restrictions that have been in effect for at least fifteen years.

La. C.C. art. 780 (as enacted by La. Acts 1977, No. 170). The comments to this article state that "[t]his provision reproduces the substance of La. R.S. 9:5622. It does not change the law." La. C.C. art. 780, comment (a). The comments further provide that "[b]uilding restrictions may terminate according to terms prescribed in the act that created them, under rules enacted by special legislation (R.S. 9:5622 as amended), or under rules adopted by the jurisprudence." La. C.C. art. 780, comment (b). Still further, the comments state:

> Persons imposing building restrictions may, in the exercise of their freedom of will, prescribe rules for termination, provided, of course, that these rules imply nothing contrary to public order. Thus, provision may be made for termination of the restrictions upon the lapse of a period of time or upon the happening of an event.

Id. (citing Bruce v. Simonson Investments, Inc., 251 La. 893, 207 So.2d 360 (1968)).

In 1980, the Legislature amended Article 780 by adding the highlighted language:

> Building restrictions terminate as provided in the act that establishes them. In the absence of such provision, owners representing more than one-half of the land area, excluding streets and their rights-of-way, affected by the restrictions may amend or terminate by agreement, for the whole or a part of the restricted area, building restrictions that have been in effect for at least fifteen years.

La. C.C. art. 780 (as amended by La. Acts 1980, No. 310).

In 1983, the Legislature again amended Article 780, rewriting it to provide:

> Building restrictions terminate as provided in the act that establishes them. In the absence of such provision building restrictions may be amended or terminated for the whole or a part of the restricted area by agreement of owners representing more than one-half of the land area affected by the restrictions, excluding streets and street rights-of-way, if the restrictions have been in effect for at least fifteen years, or by agreement of both owners

representing two-thirds of the land area affected and two-thirds of the owners of the land affected by the restrictions, excluding streets and street rights-of-way, if the restrictions have been in effect for more than ten years.

La. C.C. art. 780 (as amended by La. Acts 1983, No. 129).

Subsequently, the Louisiana Supreme Court in Brier Lake, Inc. v. Jones, 1997-2413 (La. 4/14/98), 710 So. 2d 1054, construed the provisions in Article 780 as authorizing only amendments that lessen the restrictions on property. In 1999, the Legislature responded by revamping Article 780; that amendment expressly states that "[t]he provisions of this Act legislatively overrule the case of Brier Lake, Inc. v. Jones, 97-C-2413 (La. 4/14/98); 710 So. 2d 1054, are remedial, and shall apply both prospectively and retroactively." La. Acts 1999, No. 309. The parties agree that the latter amendment is not relevant to the instant dispute involving an attempt to terminate building restrictions.

With that legislative background in mind, we turn to the issue of whether the provision in the 1931 Act addressing the duration of the Restrictions constitutes a form of contractual termination provision under Article 780 (and its predecessor La. R.S. 9:5622). As quoted above, the 1931 Act addresses the duration of the restrictions by providing as follows:

> [A]ll the above servitudes, reservations, restrictions, covenants, conditions and real obligations are valid and binding under the law of Louisiana without any limitation of time, but that in the event it should be held that said covenants can only be made under the law of Louisiana for a limited time, then and in that event each of such covenants is to be binding for a period of fifty (50) years from this date.

In the Diefenthal decision, the Supreme Court addressed the impact of the above provision, apparently under Article 780, stating that "[e]ven though that [1931] agreement was binding for a term of 50 years, its terms were renewed by incorporation into the 1977 agreement." 561 So. 2d at 51 n. 6. The Residents translate the Court's statement to mean that the 1977 Agreement incorporated the 1931 Act and that the fifty-year term in the 1931 Act commenced anew in 1977, extending the term of the Restrictions until 2027. On the other hand, Longue Vue contends that this argument overlooks the fact that the fixed duration provision of the 1931 Act only applies if there is a finding that the agreement cannot have an unlimited duration. Continuing, it contends that since no such finding has ever been made, the fifty-year fall-back provision has never become operable and is therefore irrelevant. We disagree.

Although there has been no express determination that building restrictions cannot be binding in perpetuity, the Supreme Court's statement in Diefenthal implicitly found the provision for unlimited duration was invalid and the fifty-year provision was operable. Moreover, the early jurisprudence on building restrictions recognized the invalidity of perpetual restrictions on the use of property; under that jurisprudence the view was that "whereas absolute or perpetual restraints on the alienation or use of immovable property are invalid, reasonable restraints of limited duration imposed by persons having a substantial interest are valid and enforceable against any acquirer of the land with notice." Acts 1977, No. 170, Expose des Motifs, Title V: Building Restrictions (citing Queensborough Land Co. v. Cazeaux, 136 La. 724, 67 So. 641 (1915)).

The Legislature implicitly recognized that building restrictions could not be binding in perpetuity by amending La. R.S. 9:5622 in 1960 to provide for termination by the majority owners after fifteen years. Likewise, the above legislative history of Article 780 evidences the Legislature's intent that building restrictions be subject to some type of contractual limitation on their term. If the parties fail to provide some contractual mode of termination, the Legislature has provided one for them in Article 780 (and its predecessor La. R.S. 9:5622). In so doing, however, the Legislature has recognized the freedom of parties to contractually agree and has made the special legislative provision applicable only if the act that established the restrictions failed to provide a mode of termination.

One such mode of termination that the parties may contractually agree upon is a provision for termination "upon the lapse of a period of time or upon the happening of an event." La. C.C. art. 780, comment (b). Recognizing the validity of such provisions, the jurisprudence has held that when the parties contractually agree to a fixed term, "the statute [is] inapplicable because provision is made in the covenants for terminating the effective date of the restriction. A termination date is not necessary." Robinson v. Morris, 272 So. 2d 444, 447 (La. App. 2d Cir. 1973). The Residents contend that the 1931 Act's fifty-year provision is such a contractual provision. They contend that "[t]he 1931 agreement meets this requirement by providing that if the covenants cannot be valid 'without any limitation of time,' then they will be binding for at least 50 years." They further contend that "when the 1931 agreement was 'renewed' by incorporation into the 1977 settlement, the 50-year period in the 1931 agreement was also 'renewed' by the 1977 settlement, and the covenants in the 1931 agreement thus remain binding upon Longue Vue until at least 2027." We find that argument persuasive.

Because building restrictions constitute real rights on property, the only way in which the Restrictions can be amended before the expiration of the fixed term is with the consent of all the landowners. See Simonson Investments, 251 La. at 900, 207 So. 2d at 363 (noting that building restrictions are a species of predial servitude and that normally "all owners of lots to which the servitude is due must give consent to achieve a full discharge of the servitude"); see also Mackey v. Armstrong, 97-30054 (La. App. 2d Cir. 12/30/97), 705 So. 2d 1198.

Concluding, we hold that Longue Vue's Act of Termination is invalid. We further hold that the Restrictions may not be terminated without the consent of all the landowners until April 18, 2027, fifty-years from the date of the 1977 Agreement. Having so held, the separate issue of Longue Vue's entitlement to close off the End Strip is now moot.

DECREE

For the foregoing reasons,...we affirm the judgment of the trial court granting summary judgment in favor of the owners of the seven residences fronting Garden Lane.

NOTE
LHAA

As noted by the fourth circuit in the preceding case, the legislature revamped Civil Code article 780 in 1999 in response to *Brier Lake, Inc. v. Jones,* 710 So. 2d 1054 (La. 1998). 1999 La. Acts, No. 309. As explained in an earlier note, Act 309 also enacted the Louisiana Homeowners Association Act (LHAA), La. R.S. 9:1141.1 *et seq.,* which applies to any "residential planned community," defined in the LHAA as "a real estate development, used primarily for residential purposes, in which the owners of separately owned lots are mandatory members of an association by virtue of such ownership." La. R.S. 9:1141.2(7).

Building restrictions in residential planned communities are governed by the LHAA, which derogates from the Civil Code in a number of respects, including rules governing their establishment. As explored in a previous note, Civil Code article 776 requires unanimity to establish a building restriction. By contrast, the LHAA permits the community documents to provide rules for establishing restrictions. The default rule applicable when no such rules have been promulgated requires agreement of three-fourths of the owners to establish a building restriction. Thus, under the LHAA, it is easier to create a building restriction than it is under the Civil Code's applicable provision.

Additional differences between the Civil Code and the LHAA exist regarding amending and terminating building restrictions when the act that creates the restrictions fails to provide therefor. Civil Code article 780 was explored in the preceding case. La. R.S. 9:1141.6(B), the default LHAA rules on amending and terminating restrictions, provides:

(2) Existing building restrictions may be made more onerous or increased by agreement of two-thirds of the lot owners.
(3) Existing building restrictions may be made less onerous, reduced, or terminated by agreement of more than one-half of the lot owners.

Hence, under the LHAA it is not only easier to establish a building restriction than provided for in the Code, it is also easier to amend or terminate a building restriction than it is under the Code. With regard to amendments, a curious difference exists between the LHAA and the Code. Civil Code article 780 was revised in 1999 in an effort to eliminate any distinction between the percentage of agreement among owners required to amend a building restriction in order to make that restriction more onerous and the percentage of agreement required to amend a building restriction in order to make that restriction less onerous.

Assuming the legislature succeeded in eradicating any difference in article 780's treatment of each type of amendment for building restrictions governed by the Civil Code, the LHAA (which was created by the same legislation that revised article 780) expressly distinguishes between an amendment of a building restriction that makes the restriction more onerous and an amendment that makes the restriction less onerous. The former type of amendment is treated in the same manner as the establishment of a building restriction, La. R.S. 9:1141(6)(B)(2), while the latter type is treated in the same manner as the termination of a building restriction. La. R.S. 9:1141(6)(B)(3).

b. Termination by Liberative Prescription
La. Civ. Code art. 781

A.N. YIANNOPOULOS, PREDIAL SERVITUDES
§ 197 (3d ed. 2004)
(footnotes omitted)

§ 197. Prescription of Building Restrictions

Article 781 of the Louisiana Civil Code declares that "no action for injunction or for damages on account of the violation of a building restriction may be brought after the lapse of two years from the commencement of a noticeable violation." However, the two-year prescription under Article 781 does not merely bar actions for enforcement of building restrictions as sui generis real rights; it extinguishes building restrictions in the same way that the prescription of nonuse extinguishes predial servitudes. Accordingly, all actions based on principles of property law for the enforcement of building restrictions become without object after accrual of the two-year prescription. Actions for the enforcement of restrictions that qualify as personal obligations are not affected by the prescription of Article 781 of the Civil Code. These actions are subject to the ten-year liberative prescription that bars personal actions.

The two-year prescription begins to run from the commencement of a noticeable violation rather than from the day the plaintiff acquires knowledge of the violation. Ordinarily, the prescription commences when the violation of the restriction is neither secretive nor clandestine. An activity conducted on a modest scale may not be noticeable or may not be a violation at all; but the same type of activity, if expanded, may become a noticeable violation.

Article 781 of the Louisiana Civil Code establishes a liberative prescription rather than preemption. Accordingly, the prescription by be interrupted by acknowledgment. Upon accrual of the prescription, the immovable on which the violation occurred "is freed of the restriction that has been violated." Determination of the restriction that has been violated is a matter of both statutory and contractual interpretation.

When restrictions exclude the use of property for commercial purposes, the question may arise whether activities in violation of the restrictions free the property from all restrictions relating to commercial use or only from the particular type of commercial use that has been practiced.

Louisiana courts have held that when an owner uses his property for commercial purposes contrary to restrictions during a period in excess of two years, the property is freed of all restrictions pertaining to commercial use; therefore, the landowner is entitled to enlarge his business and even to conduct a business of a different nature. It has been suggested, however, that the law "can hardly be taken to mean freedom from the whole commercial restriction, but only freedom to the extent that there had been a two-year unopposed violation." According to sound doctrine and jurisprudence, the mere prescription of one type of restriction on a particular lot does not free that lot of other types of restrictions, nor does it free other lots from the type of restriction that has been violated. Nonetheless, the prescription of a type of restriction may be indicative of the abandonment of the entire development plan or of a particular restriction.

HIDDEN HILLS COMMUNITY, INC. v. ROGERS
869 So. 2d 984 (La. App. 3d Cir.),
cert denied 874 So. 2d 158 (La. 2004)

GREMILLION, J.   In this case, the plaintiff, Hidden Hills Community, Inc., appeals the judgment in favor of the defendant, Frank Rogers, Jr., finding that he was not in violation of their restrictive covenant. Rogers...asserts the peremptory exception of prescription...for the first time on appeal. For the following reasons, we reverse and remand.

FACTUAL AND PROCEDURAL BACKGROUND

Hidden Hills is a community surrounding a lake. The developers of Hidden Hills adopted a set of restrictions and affirmative duties in order to maintain the community in the manner it deemed fit and recorded them in the records of the Clerk of Court for the Parish of St. Landry. Article 17 of the Restrictions provides that lots must be kept "reasonably neat and clean." In September 2001, Hidden Hills filed a Petition for Declaratory Judgment seeking to enforce the above restriction and to have the trial court determine if Rogers' property was "reasonably neat and clean" in accordance with the subdivision restrictions. It further sought to assess Rogers with a $200.00 per day fine in accordance with the rules. Rogers filed an Exception of No Right of Action urging that Hidden Hills did not have the authority to bring the lawsuit. The trial court dismissed the exception. After a trial on the merits in February 2003, the trial court found that Rogers' "presentation in his decoration and landscaping do not violate the covenants as written." Hidden Hills thereafter filed a Motion for New Trial, which was denied. Hidden Hills now appeals.

ISSUES

Hidden Hills' sole assignment of error is that the trial court committed manifest error in finding that Rogers' property did not violate the Act of Amended Restrictions of its community. We shall review the trial court's decision in that regard.***

PRESCRIPTION

Rogers urges, for the first time on appeal, that Hidden Hills' claims against him have prescribed...pursuant to La.Civ.Code art. 781.

La.Civ.Code art. 781 states:

> No action for injunction or for damages on account of the violation of a building restriction may be brought after two years from the commencement of a noticeable violation. After the lapse of this period, the immovable on which the violation occurred is freed of the restriction that has been violated.

Rogers claims that the suit is prescribed because several of the residents had begun noticing his unusual manner of decoration as early as 1998. To wit, he states:

> 1. Bobby Broussard testified that in 1998 he was aware that his home was colored a light pastel, he had noticed bones on the trees, his sidewalks had been painted in a striped fashion, the bottom of his house was painted in a checkerboard fashion, and he had items hanging from his trees.

> 2. Alvin Guidroz testified by the time he finished construction on his house in 1997, Rogers had life rafts, resin plastic chairs painted florescent colors and umbrellas and different colored carpet on his lawn.

We disagree and do not find these things were enough to qualify as the commencement of a noticeable violation. We hold that bright and unusual paint choices as well as fluorescent painted lawn chairs do not meet the standard of not "reasonably neat and clean." The testimony below reveals that the massive accumulation of various objects in Rogers' yard did not become a noticeable violation until late 2000, when the residents of the community began to report it to the Hidden Hills Board of Directors as a violation of the covenant. This assignment of error is dismissed as being without merit.***

REASONABLY NEAT AND CLEAN

We will not set aside a trial court's finding of fact in the absence of error or unless it is clearly wrong. Rosell v. ESCO, 549 So. 2d 840 (La. 1989).*** Restrictive covenants are governed by La.Civ.Code arts. 775 et seq. as they are building restrictions. La. Civ. Code art. 775 defines building restrictions:

Building restrictions are charges imposed by the owner of an immovable in pursuance of a general plan governing building standards, specified uses, and improvements. The plan must be feasible and capable of being preserved.

Further, "[b]uilding restrictions may impose on owners of immovables affirmative duties that are reasonable and necessary for the maintenance of the general plan." La. Civ. Code art. 778. The affirmative duty in question under the "MAINTENANCE" heading of the Rules and Restriction and/or by-laws of Hidden Hills Community, Inc., states:

> Lots, both occupied and unoccupied, are expected to be kept in a reasonably neat and clean condition, with grass not to exceed 18 inches in height. Upon complaint by other members, the offending member's lot may be mowed or cleaned at the direction of a member of the board and charges for the work shall be presented for payment to the offending property owner.

After reviewing the evidence, particularly the photographs, we find that the trial court's finding that Rogers' property was "reasonably neat and clean" was not reasonable. WEBSTER'S NEW COLLEGIATE DICTIONARY 212 (10TH ED.1993) defines "clean" as "free from dirt or pollution." It is synonymous with words such as "immaculate," "spotless," and "unsullied." WEBSTER'S COLLEGIATE THESAURUS 140 (1976). It is in contrast with words such as "grubby," "messy," "slovenly," and "foul." Id. "Neat," on the other hand, is defined as "free from irregularity," and "marked by tasteful simplicity." WEBSTER COLLEGIATE DICTIONARY 775 (10TH ED.1993). When used as an adjective, it means, "plain, pure, unadulterated, undiluted and unmixed," or "manifesting care and orderliness." Webster's Collegiate Thesaurus 545 (1976). It is synonymous with words such as "orderly," "shipshape," "tidy," "trim," "uncluttered," and "well-groomed." Id. Words that contrast "neat" are "disheveled," "disorderly," "sloppy," "slovenly," "unkempt," "untidy," "lax," and "remiss." Id.

Bobby Broussssard testified that he began building a home in the Hidden Hills subdivision in 1997, three houses down from Rogers' home. He stated that, at the time his house was completed, in 1998, Rogers' home was colored a light pastel, and there were multi-colored rings in Mardi Gras colors around his trees and bushes. However, he stated that, later that year, Rogers began hanging bones from trees, painting stripes on his sidewalk and a checkerboard pattern on the bottom of his house. By mid-1999, Broussard testified he began hanging more items from trees and placing toilets on his lawn. Broussard, who is President of the Hidden Hills Landowner Association, testified that he began receiving complaints from neighbors in late 2000. He stated that the board had a meeting on March 23, 2001, and Rogers was served on March 25, 2001, with a notice of the violations giving him thirty days to remove boards which were restricting the right of way and lines that were in the lake. Broussard testified that the boards were removed from the lake, but the lines were back on.June 6, 2001, and the boards were back in a right of way on June 7, 2001.

Broussard testified that none of the items hanging from the trees have been removed and that, in fact, Rogers has added to the collection with jugs, flags, streamers, and concession stand looking items. He then reviewed with counsel a series of pictures depicting the conglomeration of objects that Rogers has placed on his property.

Frank Rogers, Jr., testified that he bought the lot in Hidden Hills in June 1986, and began "decorating" his property sometime in 1997, beginning with painting the bottom portion of his house several different colors. However, at this time, the front of his house remained yellow with green shutters. Rogers testified that, over the years, he began "touching up a little bit here and there with a lot of different colors." He testified that the white plastic bleach jugs he has hanging from string between trees are birdhouses, although he has not cut out any holes for the birds. He further testified that, since the institution of the lawsuit, he has added more political signs, jugs, surveyor tape, and triangular banners typically used at car dealerships. He also testified that he has around four or five displays of bundled up empty chlorine bottles strung together hanging from the trees, which he says serve as birdhouses. Rogers has also added a peanut machine, a cash register machine, TVs, pieces of ladders, non-working satellite dishes, snow cone advertisements, a sign that says "rice and gravy," and cow skulls with deer horns and bull horns in them or a telephone sitting on top.

Deanna Cobb, Rogers' immediate next-door neighbor, testified that she has lived in the house next door since 1997. She stated that Rogers' property began to substantially change sometime in November 2000. Cobb testified that Rogers painted his shrubs assorted colors, painted rings around the trees, and painted animal horns and hung them from the trees. He continued adding items to the exterior of his property such as: dishwashers, weedeaters, lawnmowers, squirrel traps, vacuum cleaners, and telephones strung from the trees. Cobb testified that the next thing to occur, following her March 2001 complaint to the board, was a "plastic explosion," which included long pieces of triangular banners, plastic bottles hung from trees, flagging tape banners, political signs, food signs, real estate signs, home loan signs, PVC pipe, rope, television sets, computer monitors, and a plastic grandfather clock. She also noted a screen door suspended in the air, and a glove six or seven feet high in the air on PVC pipe with the middle finger pointing toward her property. Cobb testified that there are in excess of one thousand jugs on Rogers' property, and that he runs his sprinklers all night which cause the jugs to hit each other and make noise all night long.

Alvin Guidroz, who lives across the lake from Rogers' property, testified that he purchased his lot in 1995, and started building in 1997. He stated that, at this time, Rogers' home was neat and well kept, through to 1998. Guidroz testified that, after he moved into his house, he started noticing little changes here and there but nothing to be concerned about. However, he testified that it escalated to the hundreds of jugs, tapes, and assorted sundry items.

While the testimony in this case is brief, the photographic evidence tells the story. Rogers' property evidences thousands of plastic chlorine bottles hung in every which way on his property, brightly painted shrubs, hundreds of political signs, banners, caution tape, and flagging hanging everywhere. It can only be called a veritable junkyard, but brighter and more noticeable as many of the items, such as the white plastic jugs, are suspended from lines run across the trees.

The definition of neat referred to by the trial court, was "clean and in good order; trim, tidy." WEBSTER'S NEW WORLD DICTIONARY 905 (3rd Ed. 1994). Using this definition, the trial court found that Rogers' property was "reasonably neat and clean" and not in violation of the covenant. We disagree with our learned colleague. Not only do we find that the property is not "clean and in good order: tidy, trim," we find that it is not "immaculate," "spotless," nor "unsullied." To the contrary, it is "grubby," "messy," "slovenly," and even "foul." The property is certainly not "free from irregularity" or "marked by tasteful simplicity." It is not "plain, pure, unadulterated, undiluted, and unmixed" nor does it "manifest care and orderliness." It is, on the other hand, "disheveled," "disorderly," "sloppy," and "unkempt."

Further, we find that the term "reasonably neat and clean" is not ambiguous in the context used. In drafting the restrictive covenants, the redactors clearly meant to prohibit certain uses to one's property. It would be virtually impossible to draft a set of covenants that would consider all conceivable offending uses of property, notwithstanding the fact that no one would have dreamed up this instant offending use of property.

We acknowledge that "one person's trash is another person's treasure," however, a reasonable person cannot claim that the Rogers' property is neat and clean. He argues that the term "neat and clean" actually describes his property and argued at oral argument that the jugs and other objects are strung in a geometrical manner which should be pleasing to the eye. In a word, that is absurd. Accordingly, we reverse the trial court's finding that Rogers' property was not in violation of the restrictive covenant. We shall not address the penalty assessment, but shall remand this case to the trial court for a determination whether a penalty should be assessed under the restrictive covenants and, if so, how much.

CONCLUSION

The judgment of the trial court finding that the defendant-appellee, Frank Rogers, Jr., did not violate the plaintiff-appellant's, Hidden Hills Community, Inc., restrictive covenant is reversed and this matter is remanded to the trial court for a determination of the penalty assessment. All costs of this appeal are assessed to Rogers. Reversed.

BAYOU TERRACE ESTATES HOME OWNERS ASS'N, INC. v. STUNTZ
97 So. 3d 589 (La. App. 1st Cir. 2012)

GUIDRY, J. A homeowner appeals a judgment enjoining her from operating a business out of her home. While the appeal of this matter was pending, the homeowner filed a peremptory exception urging the objection of prescription with this court. For the following reasons, we overrule the exception and affirm the judgment appealed.

FACTS AND PROCEDURAL HISTORY

Bayou Terrace Estates is a subdivision located in Ascension Parish for which the Bayou Terrace Estates Home Owners Association, Inc. ("the Association") was created pursuant to the Louisiana Homeowners Association Act, La. R.S. 9:1141.1–1141.9, to manage and regulate the residential planned community.   On July 12, 2010, the Association filed a petition for injunctive relief against Jessica Stuntz, a homeowner in the subdivision, to enforce a building restriction that prohibits the commercial use of lots contained in the subdivision. In the petition, the Association asserted that Ms. Stuntz operated a business known as "Ink Girl Studio" out of her home, by which she provided art lessons and painting parties for which she was paid. Pursuant to the petition filed by the Association, the trial court issued a temporary restraining order (TRO) ordering Mrs. Stuntz to "cease operation of the business known as Ink Girl Studio or any other commercial studio on the property located in Bayou Terrace Estates." The trial court also set a date for a hearing on the issuance of a preliminary injunction, following which it held the matter should be set for a hearing for a permanent injunction and the operation of the TRO was extended to the date of the hearing for the permanent injunction.

A hearing for permanent injunctive relief was set for October 22, 2010; however, prior to that date, the Association filed a joint motion for contempt and motion in limine against Mrs. Stuntz for her failure to comply with the TRO ordering her to stop the operation of her business in the subdivision and for her failure to provide certain discovery responses. Thereafter, Mrs. Stuntz filed an answer to the petition for injunctive relief and the matter proceeded to a bench trial, which convened on November 30, 2010. Following the hearing, the trial court ruled in favor of the Association, holding that the art lessons Mrs. Stuntz provided in her home is "a commercial enterprise" and immediately enjoined Mrs. Stuntz "from operating a commercial enterprise in her home at 13445 Bayou Terrace, St. Amant, Louisiana, in Bayou Terrace Estates." The trial court declined to find Mrs. Stuntz in contempt, but left the petition open to allow the Association to re-urge contempt in the event Mrs. Stuntz continued to provide art lessons in her home.

It is from this judgment that Mrs. Stuntz appeals, and on appeal, Mrs. Stuntz has filed a peremptory exception urging the objection of prescription.

DISCUSSION

Subdivision restrictions governing the use and maintenance of lots contained within the Bayou Terrace Estates subdivision were first established by the contractor that created the subdivision, Achord Construction, Inc., in 1991. The original restrictions provided that the property comprising the subdivision could "be used only for residential and campsite purposes, all commercial or other activities incompatible with the same are prohibited." Over the years, the restrictions were amended and restated, and in August 2006, four contiguous subdivisions combined, amended, and restated the restrictions to apply to all four of the subdivisions, including both filings of the Bayou Terrace Estates, in a document titled, "Amended Act of Restrictions for the Bayou Terrace Estates Subdivision, Bayou Terrace Estates Subdivision, Second Filing, Canal Bank Subdivision, First Filing, and Canal Bank Subdivision, Second Filing," filed as Instrument # 00645571 with the Ascension Parish Clerk of Court.

At issue in this appeal is the interpretation and application of restriction 5.1.1 under the section titled, "GENERAL COVENANTS, OBLIGATIONS AND RESTRICTIONS," which provides:

> Except as otherwise provided in paragraph 5.1.2 [relative to storage buildings, garages, and other out-buildings used for storage purposes], all Lots shall be used solely for single family residential purposes, and no more than one single family residence shall be built upon any Lot. The use of a Lot for other forms of residential use or for commercial, institutional, medical, retail, religious or commercial storage uses of any kind is strictly prohibited. The foregoing shall not be interpreted to prohibit a personal office from being located within the residence.

On appeal, Mrs. Stuntz contends that the trial court erred in finding that the art lessons she gives are a commercial enterprise. As she argues in her brief, she is "carrying on her profession in her home and...not operating a business, trade, industry, or commercial enterprise as generally understood."

At trial, Mrs. Stuntz testified that she moved into the subdivision in October 2006, and that she provided art lessons in her home since moving into the subdivision. As she explained:

> It's no more than just a group. Art lessons, basically. Sometimes it's a group of people that know each other and they're actually celebrating something, like a birthday... so we call it [a] painting party. It's an art lesson done in a group form and they come, sometimes they come to me, sometimes I go to them, different locations....[B]ut they can come and arrange by appointment. I walk them through, usually, is one painting. Like, they're to choose a painting ahead of time that they want to try to do their own version of, and I help them do that.

Mrs. Stuntz admitted that she is "compensated" for the lessons she provides, and explained that the amount she charges depends on what the person wants to paint, because she provides the supplies. So the larger the painting, the more supplies she must provide, such as a larger piece of canvas, which cost more. However, when asked if she were just selling the canvases and paint, Mrs. Stuntz replied, "I'm selling my services to teach art"; but included in the amount she charges are the costs of the art supplies. While Mrs. Stuntz at one point characterized the lessons she gives as "[i]t's more like we have people over than it is a business," she admitted the lessons are not a personal party that she and her husband give for people they know, but the lessons are "part of my income."

At her art parties, Mrs. Stuntz testified that she could accommodate a group of up to sixteen people in her home, but on her website, she limits the groups to up to ten persons. She also stated that the lessons are open to the general public and that she does not have any restrictions on who she allows in her home for the lessons.

Building restrictions are charges imposed in pursuance of a general plan governing building standards, specified uses, and improvements and may impose on owners of immovables affirmative duties that are reasonable and necessary for the maintenance of the general plan. La. C.C. arts. 775 and 778. Generally, doubt as to the existence, validity, or extent of building restrictions is resolved in favor of the unrestricted use of the immovable. See La. C.C. art. 783. However, the provisions of the Louisiana Homeowners Association Act, La. R.S. 9:1141.1, et seq., supersede the Civil Code articles on building restrictions in the event of a conflict. La. C.C. art. 783. Regarding interpretation of building restrictions on property regulated by a homeowners association, La. R.S. 9:1141.4 provides that "[t]he existence, validity, or extent of a building restriction affecting any association property shall be liberally construed to give effect to its purpose and intent." Fern Creek Owners' Association. Inc. v. City of Mandeville, 08–1694, p. 11 (La.App. 1st Cir.6/30/09), 21 So.3d 369, 377.

While Mrs. Stuntz argues that the art lessons she provides are not in violation of restriction 5.1.1, the Association, as explained by the Board president, Frank Coates, takes a different position. Mr. Coates testified that the Board views restriction 5.1.1 as prohibiting "no commercial business being conducted out of a home, and that any services rendered at that home and someone paying for these services at that residence or location is strictly prohibited." Additionally, Judy Grounds, who holds the position of treasurer with the Board, explained that Mrs. Stuntz's activities violate restriction 5.1.1 because she has customers come to and performs services out of her home, as opposed to simply having a personal office that does not interfere with the operations of the subdivision.

Although personal office is not defined or described in the Association restrictions, our review of cases involving similar restrictions on the commercial use of residential property reveals that mere administrative or managerial activities, or even insubstantial provision of services in the home, have been found not to violate the intent of such provisions. See Schwab v. Kelton, 405 So.2d 1239, 1245 (La.App. 1st Cir.), writ denied, 407 So.2d 749 (La.1981). Moreover, Mrs. Stuntz's actions of providing art lessons in her home are clearly more analogous to those cases in which the activities of the homeowners were found to be in violation of "residential use only" restrictions. See Ellis v. Dearing, 435 So.2d 1107 (La.App. 1st Cir.), writ denied, 441 So.2d 765 (La.1983); Mulberry Association, Inc. v. Richards, 369 So.2d 185 (La.App. 4th Cir.), writ denied, 371 So.2d 1345 (La.1979); Oak Ridge Builders. Inc. v. Bryant, 252 So.2d 169 (La.App. 3d Cir.), writ denied, 259 La. 945, 253 So.2d 384 (1971); Woolley v. Cinquigranna, 188 So.2d 701 (La.App. 4th Cir.1966).

The issuance of a permanent injunction takes place only after a trial on the merits, in which the burden of proof must be founded on a preponderance of the evidence. Thus, the standard of review for the issuance of a permanent injunction is the manifest error standard. Fern Creek Owners' Association, Inc., 08–1694 at p. 10, 21 So.3d at 376. Considering the evidence presented and jurisprudence interpreting similar restrictions on the commercial use of residential property, we cannot say that the trial court erred in granting a permanent injunction based on its finding that the art lessons provided by Mrs. Stuntz violated restriction 5.1.1.

While this appeal was pending, Mrs. Stuntz filed a peremptory exception raising the objection of prescription directly with this court. In the exception, Mrs. Stuntz argues that even if the art lessons she conducts in her home are considered a commercial enterprise, the Association should be precluded from enforcing restriction 5.1.1 and denied injunctive relief based on the liberative prescription provided under La. C.C. art. 781. That article states:

> No action for injunction or for damages on account of the violation of a building restriction may be brought after two years from the commencement of a noticeable violation. After the lapse of this period, the immovable on which the violation occurred is freed of the restriction that has been violated. [Emphasis added.]

Louisiana Code of Civil Procedure article 2163 allows an appellate court to consider a peremptory exception filed for the first time in that court, if pleaded prior to a submission of the case for a decision, and if proof of the ground of the exception appears of record. Thus, the exception is properly before this court.

As previously stated, Mrs. Stuntz testified that she has been giving art lessons in her home since moving into the subdivision in October 2006. Moreover, she has maintained several websites, wherein she advertises the art lessons she provides, since 2002. Accordingly, Mrs. Stuntz asserts that the Association should be barred from enforcing restriction 5.1.1 and receiving injunctive relief because she has openly been providing art lessons in the subdivision in excess of the two-year prescriptive period contained in La. C.C. art. 781.

For the purpose of La. C.C. art. 781, some activity which is noticeable and apparent must occur on the lot, and at that point, the two-year prescriptive period commences. Investment Management Services, Inc. v. Village of Folsom, 00–0832, p. 7 (La.App. 1st

Cir.5/11/01), 808 So.2d 597, 604. Moreover, it has been observed that La. C.C. art. 781 has been interpreted and applied to provide that:

> The two-year prescription begins to run from the commencement of a noticeable violation rather than the day the plaintiff acquires knowledge of the violation. Ordinarily, the prescription commences when the violation of the restriction is neither secretive nor clandestine. An activity conducted on a modest scale may not be noticeable or may not be a violation at all; but the same type of activity, if expanded, may become a noticeable violation.

A.N. Yiannopoulos, Predial Servitudes § 197 at 455, in 4 Louisiana Civil Law Treatise (3d ed.2004) (footnotes omitted).

With these principles in mind, mere advertisement, without some correlating, noticeable activity on the immovable property at issue, would be insufficient to commence prescription under La. C.C. art. 781. Furthermore, we decline to hold that mere maintenance of a website or advertisement on the internet is sufficient to establish a noticeable violation.

Other than her assertion of the maintenance of various websites to advertise her services since 2002, Mrs. Stuntz's testimony at trial reveals that the earliest her actions of providing art lessons in her home became noticeable was in the fall of 2009. At trial, Mrs. Stuntz identified several members of the subdivision who had taken or were taking art lessons in her home, but she could not recall any member taking a lesson in her home before 2009. She explained that "[a]t that point[,] I wasn't aggressively marketing. It was all on the website, but it was very passive." She also admitted that in fall 2009, she handed out postcards in the subdivision and placed a sign in her yard advertising her art lessons. When she received the letter from the Association Board in March 2010, indicating that she was in violation of the subdivision restrictions regarding the posting of signs and parking, in addition to restriction 5.1.1, Mrs. Stuntz stated she immediately removed the sign and made arrangements for parking. The Association filed its petition for injunctive relief on July 12, 2010, prior to the lapse of two years from the fall of 2009, when Mrs. Stuntz's actions of providing art lessons in her home became noticeable.

Thus, the Association's action for injunctive relief to enforce restriction 5.1.1 is not prescribed, and, accordingly, we overrule the exception.

CONCLUSION

For the foregoing reasons, we affirm the trial court's finding that the art lessons given by Mrs. Stuntz in her home is a commercial enterprise in violation of the subdivision restrictions of the Bayou Terrace Estates Homeowners Association. Accordingly, we affirm the permanent injunction issued by the trial court. Moreover, finding that prescription has not accrued, we overrule the peremptory exception based on prescription filed by Mrs. Stuntz. All costs of this appeal are cast to the appellant, Jessica Stuntz. Affirmed.

c. Termination by Abandonment of Plan or of Restriction
La. Civ. Code art. 782

A.N. YIANNOPOULOS, PREDIAL SERVITUDES
§ 198 (3d ed. 2004)
(footnotes omitted)

§ 198. Abandonment of Plan or of Restriction

According to Article 782 of the Louisiana Civil Code, building restrictions terminate "by abandonment of the whole plan" or by "a general abandonment of a particular restriction." Abandonment, like prescription, does not merely bar the right of action for the enforcement of restrictions; it extinguishes the real right.

Abandonment of the general plan is ordinarily predicated on a great number of violations of all or most restrictions. Upon abandonment of the plan, all restrictions fall and the use of the property is free for all purposes. General abandonment of a particular restriction is predicated on a sufficient number of violations of that restriction in relation to the number of lots affected by it.

A limited number of violations in a remote part of the subdivision does not constitute abandonment of the restriction. If a restriction requires that a building should face a certain street, or should be erected a number of feet from the property line, only violations on property subject to the same restrictions are considered in determining the question of abandonment.

When the violations are sufficient in number to warrant the conclusion that a particular restriction has been abandoned, the property is freed from that restriction only. Thus, a change in the neighborhood from residential to commercial does not affect restrictions relating to the setback from property lines. Changes in the vicinity of the restricted area, but not within it, are without effect on the validity of building restrictions in the subdivision.

ROBINSON v. DONNELL
374 So. 2d 691 (La. App. 1st Cir. 1979)

LANDRY, J. This appeal by defendants E. C. Donnell, Jr., Earl Gatlin, and Titan Pipeline, Inc. (Appellants) is from judgment declaring only a portion of Tract A, Beau Village Subdivision, free of restrictive covenants, it being Appellants' contention that the entire area of Tract A was freed of restrictions because of a general abandonment of the recorded limitations on use. We reverse that portion of the trial court judgment which held a portion of the property to be still subject to the recorded restrictions. There is virtually no dispute as to the salient facts. On September 30, 1965, defendant Donnell, as owner of a certain tract of land situated in Livingston Parish partly within the municipal limits of Denham Springs, recorded a document entitled "Restrictive Covenants Beau Village Subdivision." The property to which the covenants applied was described in detail, following which description Donnell, as sole owner, declared:

> ***that he does hereby impose the following restrictions on all of said property, which restrictions shall be binding upon all purchasers, their heirs, successors and assigns, and any subsequent sale or transfer of said property shall be subject thereto, although not set forth therein;

> The first restriction states that all lots in the subdivision are designated as residential lots. Restriction nine recites that no structure of a temporary nature, or trailer, shall be used on any lot at any time as a residence either temporarily or permanently.

On January 17, 1966, Donnell caused to be recorded a plat of Beau Village Subdivision (Beau Village), dated November 4, 1965. The plat showed a subdivision, into 35 lots, of part of the property described in the previously recorded restrictive covenants. The map also showed the remaining and larger portion of the property as unsubdivided and designated said portion "Tract 'A' (Un-subdivided)," hereinafter referred to as Tract A.

On December 6, 1967, Donnell granted a borrow pit lease on part of Tract A to T.L. James Company. Pursuant to said lease, T. L. James removed dirt from an 8-acre area within Tract A for use in construction of adjacent Interstate Highway 12 (1-12). The excavation resulted in the creation of an artificial 8-acre lake.

On March 31, 1969, Donnell sold all of subject property to Donnell Industrial Maintenance, Inc., which subsequently became Titan Properties, Inc.

On January 30, 1974, Titan leased the lake to Cooper Marine Service, Inc. (Cooper) for a period of twelve months commencing February 1, 1974, for the purpose of demonstrating, testing, and storing motor boat equipment.

The lease expressly provides that the property leased is to be used exclusively for the lessee's business in the testing and demonstrating of boating equipment, that is, only by Cooper's employees and customers and not by the public at large. The lease further recites that Cooper shall construct a launch ramp, access to which shall be kept blocked by a fence and gate to be locked at all times when not in use. Upon expiration, the lease was extended indefinitely, each party having the right of cancellation upon thirty days notice. Since acquiring the lease, Cooper has continuously used, and is presently using, the lake and adjacent land area as a site for testing and demonstrating boats and boating equipment. It is also shown that for some years Cooper has maintained a large sign on Tract A, situated such that it is readily visible to motorists traveling upon 1-12, which sign advertises the lake as Cooper's testing and demonstration site. In July, 1977, Cooper placed a mobile home trailer on Tract A near the lake, which trailer Cooper has apparently used as an office. It is conceded that access to the lake is through the streets fronting on the lots which have been developed for residential use in Beau Village.

Plaintiffs filed this action August 5, 1977, alleging violation of recorded restriction number nine, which prohibits placing a trailer in Beau Village. Plaintiffs prayed for injunctive relief from said violation and also for an injunction prohibiting future violations of the restrictions. Defendants reconvened praying for judgment declaring Tract A free of all the recorded restrictions.

The trial court rendered judgment enjoining any future use of Tract A in violation of the restrictions and ordered the removal of the trailer in question, but held that Appellants are permitted to use the lake for the purpose of testing and demonstrating boats and also to use the small area on which Cooper's sign is located for advertising purposes.

Appellants contend the trial court erred in: (1) failing to hold that Tract A was never covered by the restrictions because it was shown as unsubdivided on the recorded map of Beau Village; (2) failing to hold that if Tract A was subject to the restrictions, it has since been freed therefrom because (a) it was no longer susceptible of development for residential purposes, and (b) the permitted non-conforming use for over two years prior to suit has effected an abandonment of the original plan for residential development thereof, thus freeing Tract A from all restrictions; (3) mandating removal of the trailer; (4) prohibiting use of Tract A for any purposes other than demonstrating and testing boats and maintaining a sign indicative of such use; and (5) refusing Appellants a new trial despite rendition of judgment before completion of the record as requested by the trial judge.

Tract A has never been subdivided. It has been fenced off from the area embracing the initial subdivision into 35 lots shown on the recorded plat of Beau Village. Pursuant to the restrictions, Tract A could not be subdivided into lots because it is shown on the plat as unsubdivided and the restrictions prohibit resubdivision of lots differently from the subdivision indicated on the recorded plat. Conversion of eight acres of Tract A into a lake has altered considerably the nature of the remaining portion of said parcel.

It is conceded that the remainder of Tract A located outside the lake and situated outside the limits of Denham Springs, cannot be subdivided in compliance with municipal regulations; that it is therefore ineligible under said regulations to receive municipal utility connections and service; and that the municipality is the most readily available source of utility services. It is stipulated that Donnell, as an expert contractor, would testify that it is not economically feasible to subdivide the remainder of Tract A into residential lots without an available connection to municipal utilities. It is also stipulated that Jim Carpenter, an expert real estate appraiser, would testify on behalf of plaintiffs that the remainder of Tract A is capable of development as residential lots.

The viability and applicability of building restrictions are governed by well established statutory and jurisprudential rules. Foremost among these is the precept that the law favors unrestricted use of real property. Harper v. Buckelew, 355 So. 2d 68 (La. App. 1st Cir. 1978).

Doubt as to the existence, validity, or extent of building restrictions is resolved in favor of the unrestricted use of immovable property. C.C. Article 783.

An action for injunction or damages for violation of a building restriction must be brought within two years from commencement of a noticeable violation. When the violation has continued for two years without objection, the immovable on which the violation occurred is freed of the violated restriction. C.C. Article 781. Building restrictions are terminated by abandonment of the restrictive plan as a whole, or by a general abandonment of a particular restriction. Abandonment of an entire plan of development frees the affected area of all restrictions. Abandonment of a particular restriction frees the area of the abandoned restriction only. Article 782.

Abandonment of a restriction occurs when violations transpire which constitute a subversion of, or a significant change in, the original scheme of development envisioned by the subdivider and which result in a substantial change in the intended nature of the subdivision. East Parker Properties, Inc. v. Pelican Realty Company, 335 So. 2d 466 (La. App. 1st Cir. 1976).

Because we find there has been a subversion of the developer's original intent to convert the entire area shown on the recorded plat of Beau Village, dated November 4, 1965 (apparently including Tract A), into a residential subdivision, we deem it unnecessary to pass upon the issue of whether Tract A was subject to the restrictions involved herein. We assume, solely for purposes of deciding the abandonment issue, that Tract A was subject to the restrictions.

It is significant that Tract A has remained unsubdivided since recordation of the original plat of Beau Village. Equally noteworthy is the fact that Cooper's lease restricts use of the lake to commercial purposes and precludes its use by the public at large. This of course precludes use of the lake by residents of Beau Village for recreational purposes. We find that the evidence preponderates in favor of the conclusion that the area of Tract A outside the lake is not likely to be developed into residential sites because of the unavailability of municipal utilities. While there is some evidence that the remainder of Tract A could possibly be developed into residential sites with utilities supplied by other than municipal sources, it also appears that such a method of development would be considerably more costly and therefore less attractive to a developer.

We find that in this instance there has occurred a subversion of and a significant change in, the original plan of development of Beau Village resulting in a substantial change in the initially intended nature of the subdivision. More precisely, we find an abandonment of the intent to develop the area of Tract A as residential.

It is ordered, adjudged and decreed that the judgment of the trial court be and the same is hereby reversed and judgment rendered herein decreeing Tract A, Beau Village

Subdivision, as shown on the plat of said subdivision dated November 4, 1965, by J.C. Kerstens & Associates, Consulting Engineers, recorded January 17, 1966, records of Livingston Parish, be and the same is hereby declared and adjudged free of all restrictive covenants affecting Beau Village Subdivision and recorded September 30, 1965, records of Livingston Parish; all costs of these proceedings to be paid by plaintiffs-appellees in equal portions.

GWATNEY v. MILLER
371 So. 2d 1355 (La. App. 3d Cir. 1979)

Plaintiffs instituted this action against the defendant, Joseph Miller, seeking to enjoin him from using a 2.935 arpent tract of land owned by him for storage of various pieces of "street fair" equipment. The 2.935 arpent tract owned by defendant forms part of a larger tract of land known as the "Oak-crest Plantation Subdivision" and is hereafter referred to as lot 26.

Plaintiffs allege that defendant's use of lot 26 for the purpose of storing this equipment is violative of a restrictive covenant which was placed on the land by the plaintiffs' and defendant's ancestors in title.... Following trial on the merits, the court issued a permanent injunction enjoining defendant from storing his street fair equipment on lot 26 and rejecting plaintiffs' demands for damages and attorney's fees. Defendant has appealed, urging that the trial court erred in its issuance of the permanent injunction. Plaintiffs have neither appealed nor answered the appeal. The substantial issues on appeal are:

I. DO THE PLAINTIFFS HAVE A RIGHT OF ACTION TO ENFORCE THE RESTRICTIVE COVENANTS SET FORTH IN THE DEED WHEREBY DEFENDANT ACQUIRED LOT 26?

The record reveals that lot 26, along with each of the lots owned by plaintiffs, originally formed part of an 82.15 acre tract of land owned by Lucien Hulin, Jr., Lewis C. Picard and Raywood J. Meyers. All the plaintiffs (with the exception of George Gwatney) purchased their lots directly from Messrs. Hulin, Picard and Meyers. Mr. Gwatney and the defendant acquired their lots from Elmer Brown, who had purchased them from the original owners. Nine restrictive covenants, identical in form and content, were incorporated into each act of sale for the lots purchased by plaintiffs. These restrictive covenants were likewise incorporated into defendant's act of sale for lot 26. Restrictive covenant number 6 which appears in each such deed reads as follows:

> "The purchaser named in the Act of Sale to which this Exhibit is attached, hereby binds and obligates himself, his heirs, successors or assigns not to use or permit to be used any house or houses erected or to be erected on the property described in the said Act of Sale either directly or indirectly, for

trade or business of any form or for any purpose other than that of a residential purpose."

Defendant contends that plaintiffs do not have a right of action to enforce the restrictive covenants on his property. He contends that insofar as the restrictions were not originally devised for the purpose of pursuing a general building plan or scheme for the area, they are purely personal obligations which can be enforced by the vendor-developer alone. Without specifically addressing defendant's exception of no right of action, the trial court apparently found no merit to defendant's contentions. We agree.

In support of his position, appellant relies upon the following jurisprudence: Murphy v. Marino, 60 So. 2d 128 (La. App. 1st Cir. 1952); Lamana-PannoFallo, Inc. v. Heebe, 352 So. 2d 1303 (La. App. 4th Cir. 1977) and In Re Congregation of St. Rita Roman Catholic Church, 130 So. 2d 425 (La. App. 4th Cir. 1961). In Murphy, supra, the court stated:

"It is our understanding of the law that in order to create a binding covenant running with the land in a subdivision, and enforceable by any purchaser of property therein, there should be a uniform plan of restriction applicable to the subdivision as a whole, or to a particular part of the subdivision, known to each purchaser and thereby, by reference or implication, forming a part of this contract with the subdivider. As stated before, that situation did not exist in the case of the Steele Place Subdivision.

In Murphy the court concluded that the restrictive covenants sought to be enforced had not been created pursuant to a general building plan or scheme, noting at the outset that the restrictions had not been uniformly imposed on the lots in the subdivision and had, in many instances, been amended or changed completely. In the instant case, however, appellant failed to produce any evidence at trial to indicate that the restrictive covenants imposed on the lots within Oakcrest Plantation Subdivision had not been uniformly imposed, or had been amended or changed by the subdivider. On the contrary, defendant's act of sale, as well as each of the plaintiffs' acts of sale reveal that the restrictive covenants for all these lots are identical.

In the case of Lamana-Panno-Fallo, Inc. v. Heebe, supra, the court found that the restrictive covenants sought to be enforced were unenforceable because they had been abandoned. In dicta, the court did state that the restrictions had not been made pursuant to a general subdivision plan; however it did not discuss the facts which formed the basis for this conclusion. Therein the court stated:

"The restrictive covenants in the title did not come into being as one overall or general plan of restrictions imposed upon the entire subdivision, but instead, restrictive stipulations were inserted in the initial title deeds from the owner and developer... to purchasers...." at pg. 1304.

The fact alone that restrictive covenants are inserted into individual acts of sale does not establish that they were not intended to pursue a general plan of development for the subdivision. Rather the uniformity or consistency of the restrictions must be examined in order to determine the original intentions of the subdivider. See Yiannopoulos, Real Rights: Limits of Contractual and Testamentary Freedom, 30 La L. Rev. 44 (1969) at p. 64.

In the case of In Re Congregation of St. Rita Roman Catholic Church, supra, the court found that the covenant sought to be enforced was a purely personal obligation, stating:

> [W]here restrictive covenants do not appear in chains of title of half the lots of a subdivision, for which no general plan of subdivision or restrictions had been recorded, as obtains here, such restrictions will not be enforced as covenants running with the land against any of the grantees of original subdivider or their successors. Herzberg v. Hamson, La. App., 102 So. 2d 554. The cited case, from our First Circuit Court of Appeal (1958) contains an exhaustive and clear review of our jurisprudence establishing this principle.

Where the restriction is not a covenant running with the land, it is personal to the creator of the restriction, in this case Interstate Land Co., whose existence is unknown or unaccounted for herein. Murphy v. Marino, La. App., 60 So. 2d 128 at pg.428.

In St. Rita Roman Catholic Church, the subdivider included the building and use restrictions in dispute into only 60% of his acts of sale. In the instant case, defendant has failed to produce any evidence to establish that a similar factual situation exists. We find, therefore, that the jurisprudence relied upon by appellant on this issue is not supportive of this position, and that he has failed to produce any evidence to refute the plaintiffs' contention that the area has been developed pursuant to a general building plan or scheme.

We conclude that the building and use restrictions which were uniformly incorporated into plaintiffs' and defendant's acts of sale were devised for the purpose of maintaining a general plan of development for the area, and therefore constitute real rights which inure to the benefit of all other grantees under said plan of development. Plaintiffs, therefore, clearly have a right of action to enforce the restrictive covenants on lot 26. We find this position to be further supported by the express terms of the covenants themselves. Restriction number nine provides:

> 9. These covenants and restrictions are to run with the land and shall be binding on all parties and all persons claiming under them.

We find no merit to this assignment of error.

II. DID JOSEPH MILLER VIOLATE THE RESTRICTIVE COVENANTS TO WHICH HIS LAND WAS SUBJECT?

The record reveals that Mr. Miller is in the business of operating a "street fair" for schools and churches in the Lafayette area. The equipment used for the fair, i.e., rides, concession stands, billboards, etc., is owned by Mr. Miller. The defendant also owns anumber of trucks, including two tractor-trailers, which he uses to transport this equipment to and from fair sites. When defendant's fair is not "on location," he stores the trucks and the equipment on lot 26, on which is also situated the mobile home in which he and his family reside. There is no evidence that Mr. Miller has ever charged admission for entrance onto his property, or conducted the fair or operated any of the equipment for direct financial gain while it was situated on lot 26. He uses the land to store the equipment, and while it is so situated, he inspects it for mechanical problems and makes any necessary repairs or improvements to it. There is not dispute that when the defendant purchased this lot, he did so subject to several restrictive covenants.

Plaintiffs allege that defendant has violated and continues to violate restrictive covenant number six which we have previously quoted.

In its written reasons for judgment granting the preliminary injunction the trial court stated:

> ***"The intent of Provision No. 6 leaves little room for reasonable minded persons to differ. The provision is clearly meant to preclude all commercial endeavors from the land affected by the covenant.
>
> In this regard, the court finds the use of the land made by the defendant falls within the scope of the restriction intended by the grantor."***

In the case of LeBlanc v. Bowen, 238 So. 2d 369 (La. App. 4th Cir. 1970) a tract of land which was situated adjacent to property subject to a residential restrictive covenant sought by plaintiff to be enforced was being used by a trailer sales company for commercial purposes. On occasion the trailer sales company would partially park its trailers on defendant's property and would use a roadway on defendant's property to transport its trailers back and forth from the highway. The court determined that such activities on defendant's property were within the scope of a restrictive covenant which provided that:

> "No commercial establishment, nor dairy, nor noxious or offensive establishment shall be erected or maintained thereon;..."

We have examined all of the building and use restrictions which apply to Mr. Miller's property and find that the clear intent of the subdividers was to maintain the lots exclusively for residential purposes. We find the appellant's contention that restriction number six governed solely the use to which "houses" on the lots were employed (and not the use to which the land itself was employed) to be untenable. To construe this restriction so as to preclude commercial activities only when such are conducted from "houses" would clearly subvert the subdividers' intention to maintain an area purely residential in character. A lot which is being used to store a "street fair" — albeit immobilized — is nevertheless being employed to further a commercial enterprise. The clear import of the restrictive covenant is not simply to prevent lot owners from transacting business or exchanging money for goods or services while occupying the land, but rather to maintain the visual aesthetics of the area and to keep away the ordinary manifestations of commercial activities such as signs, trucks and nonresidential structures. The covenant precludes using the property, either directly or indirectly, ". . . for trade or business of any form OR FOR ANY PURPOSE OTHER THAN THAT OF A RESIDENTIAL PURPOSE." The record reflects that defendant stores numerous trucks (including two tractor-trailers), a "merry-go-round," a "spook house," concession stands and various other rides, attractions and billboards on lot 26. While this equipment is so situated, he repairs, maintains and makes improvements on it. We find that such activity does not constitute a "residential purpose" within the intendment of restriction number six. We therefore agree with the trial court that the storage and/or repair of this equipment while it is located on lot 26 violates the restrictive covenant to which such lot is subject.

III. HAS THE RESTRICTIVE COVENANT PRECLUDING NON-RESIDENTIAL USE OF LOT 26 BEEN ABANDONED?

The defendant contends that restriction number six, precluding nonresidential use of lot 26, cannot be enforced because it has been abandoned. In support of this contention, appellant has produced several photographs allegedly depicting violations of this restriction within the subdivision. The trial court apparently found that the defendant failed to establish an abandonment of this restrictive covenant although it did not specifically address the issue in its reasons for judgment. We agree, and likewise find no merit to this assignment of error.

It is not every violation of a building restriction which will constitute its abandonment. Insubstantial, technical or infrequent violations which do not manifest an intent to subvert the original plan or scheme of development will not constitute an abandonment of the restrictions. However, when the property owners can be regarded as having abandoned the plan of development which the restrictions were intended to implement by virtue of their acquiescence to frequent and numerous violations thereof, such restrictions are con¬sidered abandoned. Edwards v. Wiseman. 198 La. 382, 3 So. 2d 661 (La. 1941). [additional citations omitted].***

Whether there has been acquiescence in violations of subdivision restrictions sufficient to defeat enforcement of the restrictions depends upon the circumstances of each case, including particularly the character, materiality and number of the violations. Guyton v. Yancey, 240 La. 794, 125 So. 2d 365 (La. 1960). As a result of the alleged abandonment of the restriction in dispute a substantial change in the intended nature of the subdivision must take place [citations omitted].

The record reveals that among the plaintiffs, Alton Pitre sells real estate from his home; Lawrence Harry sells shrimp from his home; William Menard sells tomato plants which are grown on his property; Raymond Jeoffroy advertises his concrete business in the yellow pages using his home telephone number; and, Jeanette Francez parks a school bus on her property when she is not driving it for a living. Assuming arguendo that each of these activities constitutes a violation of building and use restriction number six, we do not find that these few violations manifest an intention to abandon the plan of development which the restriction was originally intended to implement. The record reveals that Mr. Harry and Mr. Menard make only periodic sales to other neighbors of their goods, and do not rely on these periodic sales for a living. After examining all the evidence in the record, including photographs submitted by appellant, we are unable to find any outward manifestation of nonresidential activities taking place on these lots where the alleged violations are taking place. We do note that one property owner has a sign on his lot reading "puppies," and that he presumably has puppies for sale on the property. However, we find that the character of these technical violations fails to establish a general intent to substantially change the intended nature of the subdivision from that of a purely residential area. We therefore find no manifest error in the trial court's determination that the evidence failed to establish an abandonment of the building restriction herein sought to be enforced.

For the above and foregoing reasons, we affirm the judgment of the trial court. All costs of these proceedings are to be paid by appellant.

CHAPTER XVI. LIMITED PERSONAL SERVITUDES
Civil Code arts. 639-645

1. GENERAL PRINCIPLES

A. N. YIANNOPOULOS, PERSONAL SERVITUDES
§§ 8:1, 8:3 through 8:5 (5th ed. 2013)
(footnotes omitted)

8:1. Scope of this chapter

Article 533 of the Louisiana Civil Code declares that there are two kinds of servitudes: personal servitudes and predial servitudes. A personal servitude is a charge on a thing for the benefit of a person whereas a predial servitude is a charge on an immovable for the benefit of another immovable belonging to another owner. Article 534 of the Louisiana Civil Code specifies that there are three types of personal servitudes: usufruct, habitation, and rights of use. Articles 630 through 645 of the Louisiana Civil Code govern the personal servitudes of habitation and rights of use. In contrast, Articles 626 through 645 of the 1870 Code dealt with the personal servitudes of "use" and habitation.

The 1976 Revision suppressed the personal servitude of "use" as a nominate real right and established the quite different category of "rights of use". The removal of the detailed provisions referring to "use" is a recognition that this servitude had little, if any, practical significance. However, if an owner wishes to establish a real right in favor of another person for a portion of the fruits of a thing, he "may create a usufruct on a divided or undivided part of a thing, a legacy of revenues, or a right of use.

This Chapter is devoted to an analysis of the Louisiana law governing limited personal servitudes, that is, habitation and rights of use. For purposes of comparison, brief discussion will be undertaken of the corresponding institutions of property law in the legal systems of France, Germany, and Greece. Further, because personal servitudes of "use" created under the regime of the Louisiana Civil Code of 1870 may still be in existence, the pertinent provisions of that Code will be discussed at the end.

8:2. Notion of limited personal servitudes

Limited personal servitudes are real rights that confer on a person limited advantages of use or enjoyment over an immovable belonging to another person. They constitute an intermediary category between usufruct and predial servitudes. Like usufruct, they are charges on property in favor of a person rather than an estate; like predial servitudes, they are necessarily charges on an immovable belonging to another owner and are confined to certain advantages of use or enjoyment. Thus, they are both "personal" and "limited".

The qualification of limited personal servitudes as real rights is not a contradiction in terms. The word "personal" in the Louisiana Civil Code is used in many contexts with different meanings. In connection with the classification of servitudes as personal or real, the qualification of a servitude as "personal" indicates that the servitude is in favor of a person rather than an estate. In connection with the division of rights into personal and real, the word "personal" indicates an obligation as contrasted to a real right.

In connection with the question of the transferability of rights, personal or real, the words "personal," "strictly personal," or "exclusively personal" indicate that the qualified right may exist in favor of a designated person and that it is nontransferable. Thus, both personal and real rights may be strictly personal or exclusively "personal". Admittedly, this terminology is confusing and it might be analytically preferable to speak of personal or predial servitudes, obligations or real rights, and transferable or nontransferable rights.

Articles 630 through 638 of the Louisiana Civil Code govern specifically habitation, and Articles 639 through 645 of the same Code govern rights of use, that is, limited personal servitudes. However, under the 1976 Revision, habitation is a nominate limited personal servitude. The notion of limited personal servitudes is sufficiently broad to accommodate not only habitation but all real rights that confer on a person a specified use of an immovable less than full enjoyment. Accordingly, mineral rights, such as servitudes, leases, and royalties, may also be classified as limited personal servitudes.

The notion of limited personal servitudes is relatively modern as a theoretic construct; however, in Roman law and in the legal systems of Louisiana, France, Germany, and Greece, there have long been species of real rights that could be classified as limited personal servitudes. The traditional rights of usufruct, use, and habitation, do not, and should not, exhaust the category of personal servitudes. The needs for exploitation of wealth by means of rights to things, and the demands for a measure of contractual freedom in the field of property law, have led to systematization of the rules governing limited personal servitudes in the Civil Codes of Louisiana, Germany, and Greece. In France, however, usufruct, use, and habitation are the only species of personal servitudes dealt with in the Code Civil. Limited personal servitudes, to the extent that they are recognized, reflect ingenious efforts by courts and interested parties to accommodate contemporary demands in the framework of traditional institutions.

8:3. Freedom to create limited personal servitudes; legislation

***Article 639 of the Louisiana Civil Code declares that a limited personal servitude "confers in favor of a person a specified use of an estate less than full enjoyment." This provision, in accord with continental civil codes, authorizes a charge on an estate in favor of a person that does not exhaust the utility of the immovable; if it does, it establishes a usufruct rather than a limited personal servitude.

8:5. Incidents and function of limited personal servitudes

The Louisiana Civil Code contains few provisions dealing directly with the incidents and function of limited personal servitudes. Article 645 declares, generally, that a limited personal servitude is regulated by application of the rules governing usufruct and predial servitudes to the extent that their application is compatible with the notion of a limited personal servitude. Recourse to the rules governing usufruct and predial servitudes is, of course, unnecessary as to matters regulated in Articles 639 through 644 of the Louisiana Civil Code. These articles take precedence over the rule of analogy established in Article 645.

Article 641 of the Louisiana Civil Code declares that a limited personal servitude may be established "in favor of a natural person or a legal entity." In contrast with the right of habitation that may be established in favor of a natural person only, all other limited personal servitudes may be established in favor of a juridical person, such as a partnership or a corporation. Further, in contrast with a right of usufruct that may be established in favor of a juridical person for a period not to exceed thirty years, a limited personal servitude may be established in favor of a juridical person without any time limitation.

According to Article 642 of the Louisiana Civil Code, the grant of a limited personal servitude "includes the rights contemplated or necessary to enjoyment at the time of the creation as well as rights that may later become necessary, provided that a greater burden is not imposed on the property unless otherwise stipulated in the title." This article was derived from corresponding articles in the German Civil Code and in the Greek Civil Code.

Article 643 of the Louisiana Civil Code establishes the principle that a limited personal servitude is a transferable right unless transfer is excluded by provision of law or juridical act. This provision differs from corresponding provisions in the German Civil Code and in the Greek Civil Code because in those codes a limited personal servitude is a nontransferable right in the absence of contrary provision. By way of exception, habitation, though a limited personal servitude, is neither transferable nor heritable in Louisiana.

In accordance with the principle of transferability, a limited personal servitude that is established in favor of a natural person is a heritable right unless the contrary is provided by law or contract. Thus, a right of passage stipulated in favor of a person may continue to be exercised by his universal or particular successors. Further, if a limited personal servitude is established in favor of a juridical person, such as a corporation or a partnership, it is not extinguished at the dissolution of that person; it continues to exist in favor of its successor or in favor of the person to whom the right may have been assigned.

2. TYPES OF LIMITED PERSONAL SERVITUDES

Rights of Use
Civil Code arts. 639-645

SUSTAINABLE FORESTS, L.L.C. v. HARRISON
846 So. 2d 1283 (La. App. 2d Cir. 2003)

DREW, J.   Sustainable Forests, L.L.C. ("Sustainable"), appeals a judgment recognizing its "forest road" right of passage across defendants' land, but prohibiting members of Sustainable's lessee, Grand Bayou South Hunting Club, from using the road. Noticing *sua sponte*, the peremptory exception of no right of action which had been denied by the trial court, we sustain the exception and grant Sustainable leave to amend its suit.

FACTS AND PROCEDURAL HISTORY

Sustainable brought this action against Jack Keith Harrison and Leisa Miller Harrison (the "Harrisons") to prevent the Harrisons from interfering with Sustainable's use of a road right-of-way across their rural tract of land. The Harrisons objected to the use of the road by hunters crossing their tract in Section 3 to access Sustainable's land in Section 4. The hunters possessed hunting leases from Sustainable.

Sustainable characterized its suit as a possessory action and sought injunctive relief. Sustainable's petition asserts as the basis of its claim, a 1963 road grant (hereinafter the "Servitude Deed") from the Harrisons' predecessor-in-title, Olan B. Davis, to Sustainable's predecessor-in-title, International Paper Company ("IP"). The Servitude Deed described the property now owned by the Harrisons and identified, on an attached plat, a 12-foot right-of-way. The Servitude Deed granted IP "an easement for the construction and maintenance of a forest road across" the Davis tract in Section 3.

Sustainable's petition next asserts a 1998 deed (hereinafter the "1998 Deed") from IP to Sustainable conveying the land in Section 4 along with many other tracts of land. Sustainable claimed that on the basis of these title instruments, IP and Sustainable had been in open and continuous possession of the servitude of passage across the Harrison Tract.

In response to the suit, the Harrisons filed certain exceptions, including the exception of no right of action. The Harrisons pointed out to the court that IP's 1998 Deed to Sustainable did not specifically describe the 12-foot right-of-way. Therefore, it was urged that the ownership right of the disputed servitude remained in IP. The ruling on the exception was deferred to the trial of the case, and at the close of trial was rejected by the trial court.

After the bench trial, the Harrisons prevailed, nevertheless, on the merits of their defense concerning the limited scope of the "forest road" created by the 1963 Servitude Deed. Citing the Civil Code articles for the interpretation of predial servitudes, the trial court found that at the time of the 1963 transaction, IP acquired the road for its timber operations in Section 4 and not for hunting leases on that property. The trial court concluded:

Therefore, the term "forest road" would not have included hunters. The only way that hunting rights could be included would be by more specific language or by acquisitive prescription.

The trial court also found that there was insufficient evidence supporting Sustainable's alternative claim of acquisitive prescription under Civil Code Article 760 of an expanded use of the servitude across the Harrisons' tract. Sustainable now brings this appeal.

DISCUSSION

The resolution of this dispute begins with the characterization of the right which was created by the Servitude Deed. The 1963 instrument is entitled "Grant of Roadway Easement." It grants to IP "an easement for the construction and maintenance of a forest road across" the land of Harrison's predecessor-in-title, Davis. The agreement further twice references the right as a right-of-way. The 1963 instrument additionally provided that a one-year period of non-use, instead of the usual ten-year prescription of non-use, would result in the extinction of the servitude.

Most significantly and overlooked by the parties and the trial court, the Servitude Deed does not describe a dominant estate; it only describes a servient estate. There is nothing in the public records describing IP's land in Section 4 as the dominant estate. From the descriptions of Sustainable's land acquired from IP and the Harrisons' tract as set forth in the petition, and as shown on the plat exhibit in the record, the IP/Sustainable tract is not contiguous to the Davis/Harrison tract. Therefore, although contiguity is not necessary for the creation of a predial servitude (La.C.C. art. 648), its absence in this case may explain why there is no dominant tract described in the 1963 instrument.

In the absence of a description of a dominant estate in the title instrument, this conventional right of passage and access in favor of IP falls within the category of personal servitudes, which the Civil Code defines as a "right of use." La. C.C. art. 639, et seq. In 1963, when the servitude was created, such right of use, although not expressly addressed in the Civil Code, had been recognized in the jurisprudence as a real right. Simoneaux v. Lebermuth & Israel Planting Co., 155 La. 689, 99 So. 531 (1924). The right of use may confer only an advantage that may be established by a predial servitude, such as this right of passage. La. C.C. art. 640. The right of use is a transferable right which the initial grantee may convey to others. La. C.C. art. 643. Nevertheless, the right of use is not a predial servitude because of the absence of a dominant estate, and the distinction between these separate rights is critical in this case.

The 1998 Deed from IP to Sustainable describes large tracts of land, including a large tract in Section 4, which apparently is the land to which the disputed road provides access. The 1998 Deed, however, does not describe IP's right to the personal servitude created in the 1963 Servitude Deed. For this reason, Harrison pled the exception of no right of action in the trial court. The trial court denied the exception, however, apparently in reliance upon the principle set forth in Civil Code Article 650, which is applicable to predial servitudes. Article 650 provides, in pertinent part:

A predial servitude is inseparable from the dominant estate and passes with it. The right of using the servitude cannot be alienated or encumbered separately from the dominant estate.

Under Article 650, since a prior recorded grant of a predial servitude for a right of passage evidences the dominant estate status of a tract listed therein, the predial servitude's benefit is an accessory and passes with the sale of the dominant estate without mention of the prior grant of the predial right of passage. Nevertheless, when the right of passage is granted as a right of use to a juridical person, there is no dominant estate from which the principle of Article 650 may thereafter operate. The person who owns the right of use may convey that right by a deed identifying either the initial deed of origin of the right of use or a description of the land burdened by the right of use, which in this case would be a description of the 12-foot portion of the Harrisons' tract.

In this case, IP has not conveyed its right of use created by the 1963 Servitude Deed to Sustainable. Sustainable's assertion of those two recorded instruments as the basis for its suit therefore demonstrates its lack of right to assert the right of passage across the Harrisons' tract. The exception of no right of action assumes that the petition states a valid cause of action for some person and questions whether the plaintiff in the particular case has a legal interest in the subject matter of the litigation. Louisiana Paddlewheels v. Louisiana Riverboat Gaming Commission, 94-2015 (La. 11/30/94), 646 So. 2d 885, 888. Pursuant to La. C.C.P. arts. 927 and 2164, we choose to notice the peremptory exception, which was rejected by the trial court, and render judgment in this matter on that basis. Moreover, in accordance with La. C.C.P. art. 934, since the grounds for Sustainable's no right of action may be removable depending upon the scope of Sustainable's purchase agreement with IP, our judgment sustaining the exception shall allow Sustainable thirty days from the finality of this judgment to amend its suit and allege its title to the right of use.

Finally, while Sustainable has characterized this action as a possessory action in which title is normally not the issue (La.C.C.P. art. 3661), such characterization does not change our view regarding Sustainable's lack of a legal interest in the subject matter of this litigation. The jurisprudence holds that even though the grantee of a servitude or other real right possesses both for himself and the landowner, he also possesses in another sense for himself alone and may bring a possessory action against the landowner from whose ownership his right is derived. Parkway Development Corp. v. City of Shreveport, 342 So. 2d 151 (La. 1977); Faust v. Mitchell Energy Corp., 437 So. 2d 339 (La. App. 2d Cir. 1983). This is somewhat of a different slant upon the more traditional possessory action which pits a possessor of land against another possessor or record title holder of the land. To the contrary, this suit centers on the scope of the original 1963 title instrument. Moreover, the record does not show that Sustainable's intermittent use of the road for over one year prior to this suit was sufficient adverse possession to the Harrisons, who, also had the use of the road during the same period. Sustainable's possessory action is against the admitted landowner whose tract is burdened by the asserted servitude as alleged in its petition and therefore rests upon the 1963 Servitude Deed and its 1998 Deed from IP. Finding that the 1998 Deed did not convey the disputed right of use, we hereby grant the peremptory exception of no right of action subject to Sustainable's right to amend under La. C.C.P. art. 934.

DECREE

With costs of this appeal assessed equally to both parties, the peremptory exception of no right of action is GRANTED, and this matter is REMANDED for Sustainable's right to amend.

McCORMICK v. HARRISON
926 So. 2d 798 (La. App. 2d Cir. 2006)

PEATROSS, J. This appeal by Plaintiff, Dr. George M. McCormick, II, arises from the denial of McCormick's petition to terminate a servitude that Defendant, Donald Harrison, claimed to exist in his favor. For the reasons stated herein, we affirm.

FACTS

This is a dispute over a servitude of use for a private horse racetrack in Bossier Parish. Harrison owns a two-acre tract in Bossier Parish that he purchased from Danny and Susan Payne. When the Paynes acquired the property in 1993 from Gilbert and Nancy Ciavaglia and Plum Hill Training Center, Inc., the Paynes acquired the following rights:

As additional consideration, Vendor grants to Vendee a non-exclusive servitude of usage of a 5/8 mile horse race track located in the East Half (E1/2) of Section 27, T19N, R12W, Bossier Parish, Louisiana, which servitude shall include the right to gallop and exercise at all reasonable times, a maximum of fifteen (15) horses stabled at Vendee's barn located on the above described track (sic) of land; provided that Vendee shall pay Vendor $100.00 per month maintenance fees for any month that any of Vendee's horses are exercised on said 5/8 mile track.

The 1995 deed conveying the property from the Paynes to Harrison included this language:

Included in this transfer are all of vendor's rights under that certain non-exclusive servitude of usage of a 5/8 mile horse track located in the East half

(E1/2) of Section 27, Township 19 North, Range 12 West, Bossier Parish, Louisiana, as set forth in the Cash Deed from Gilbert A. Ciavaglia et al. to Danny W. Payne et al., recorded under registry number 561809, Conveyance Records of Bossier Parish, Louisiana.

The horse track described in the 1993 and 1995 deeds is located on McCormick's property, a much larger tract immediately to the northeast of Harrison's tract. McCormick purchased this tract from Lifeline Nursing Company ("Lifeline") in September 2004. Lifeline purchased the tract from the Ciavaglias in 1999. Neither the plaintiff's deed nor the deed from the Ciavaglias to Lifeline mentioned the horse track or the servitude.

From the time when Harrison purchased his property in 1995 until 1999 when the Ciavaglias sold the track to Lifeline, Harrison exercised his horses on the track. Harrison paid the Ciavaglias $100 for each month he used the track; the payments were made at irregular intervals. After the Ciavaglias sold the property containing the track to Lifeline, Harrison did not use the track because Lifeline objected to Harrison's use of the track.

When Lifeline sold the property to McCormick, Harrison decided to use the track. Without contacting McCormick, on October 26, 2004, Harrison's employee exercised a horse on the track without interference. On October 28, 2004, Harrison's employee attempted to use the track, but McCormick's son arrived and asked him to leave. The employee complied, but the next day Harrison's employee returned to exercise another horse on the track, accompanied by a deputy sheriff. McCormick or his representative again asked Harrison's employee to leave, and that was the last time Harrison tried to use the track. Harrison did not attempt to pay McCormick $100 for the use of the track at any time; he testified that he was asked to leave, not to pay $100. It is not clear from the evidence adduced at trial whether the horse that Harrison trained at the track was stabled at Harrison's barn.

In December 2004, McCormick filed a rule to show cause in the district court asking for a declaratory judgment to decide the parties' rights to the track. Specifically, McCormick asked the court for a judgment declaring that the servitude was extinguished. Harrison answered the rule and brought a reconventional demand asking for damages because of McCormick's refusal to allow Harrison to use the track.

At trial, the parties disagreed about the condition and usefulness of the track. McCormick, who had been a horse trainer for many years, said that the track was unusable and "totally unsafe for horse or rider" because a previous owner of the property had plowed over the track and had brought up subsurface rocks. Harrison, also an experienced horseman, agreed that the track was unsuitable for running horses, but said that the track was "fine for a horse that you're just breaking or colts to be broke and go on."

After considering the evidence, the court signed a judgment on September 2, 2005, incorporating reasons for judgment. The court concluded that the servitude held by Harrison was a personal servitude that was still in existence. The court declared that Harrison was entitled to continue to use the track so long as he paid McCormick $100 per month, in advance, for the use of the track. The court also held that Harrison did not owe McCormick for the month of October 2004. Finally, the court denied Harrison's demand for damages. McCormick took a suspensive appeal.

DISCUSSION

The trial court found the servitude established by the Paynes' deed to be a personal servitude of right of use, and we agree with that characterization. By use of the terms "vendor" and "vendee," the parties made clear their intent that the servitude ran in favor of persons and not estates. La. C.C. arts. 533, 534, 639; Sustainable Forests, L.L.C. v. Harrison, 37,152 (La. App. 2d Cir. 5/22/03), 846 So. 2d 1283. Limited personal servitudes are real rights that confer on a person limited advantages of use or enjoyment over an immovable belonging to another. Swayze v. State, DOTD, 34,679 (La. App. 2d Cir. 9/17/01), 793 So. 2d 1278, writ denied, 01-3136 (La. 2/1/02), 808 So. 2d 342, citing Yiannopoulos, 3 Civil Law Treatise § 223 (4th Ed.2000). Such rights are transferable. La. C.C. art. 643.

Right of use servitudes are regulated by the rules governing usufruct and predial servitudes to the extent that these rules are compatible with the servitude of right of use. La. C.C. art. 645. Doubt as to the existence, extent or manner of exercise of a servitude must be resolved in favor of the estate claimed to be burdened by the servitude. La. C.C. art. 730; St. Andrews Place, Inc. v. City of Shreveport, 40,260 (La. App. 2d Cir. 11/4/05), 914 So. 2d 1203; Mardis v. Brantley, 30,773 (La. App. 2d Cir. 8/25/98), 717 So. 2d 702, writ denied, 98-2488 (La. 11/20/98), 729 So. 2d 563.

A servitude may terminate in several different ways. For example, if that part of the servient estate that is burdened with the servitude is permanently and totally destroyed, the servitude is extinguished. La. C.C. art. 751. Although there was some evidence through McCormick's testimony that the horse track was in an unusable condition, the trial court accepted Harrison's testimony that the track remained useful for a limited purpose. A servitude may also end due to nonuse for a period of ten years. La. C.C. arts. 752-756. In this case, less than ten years had elapsed since Harrison used the track prior to his attempts to use it during McCormick's ownership.

In brief, McCormick urges that the servitude terminated because Harrison did not pay McCormick $100 for the use of the track in October 2004. Again, the evidence shows that, in October, Harrison used the track one day without interference and thereafter attempted twice to use the track only to be turned away. The evidence does not show that Harrison or his employee offered to pay for the use of the track, nor does the evidence show that McCormick or his representative demanded payment of the $100. The agreement creating the servitude specifies only that "Vendee shall pay Vendor $100.00 per month maintenance fees for any month that any of Vendee's horses are exercised on said 5/8 mile track." The agreement *does not* specify when or where payment is to be made.

We find no support in the civil code for the argument that a right of use servitude terminates upon the failure of the holder of the right to pay an installment. We have considered La. C.C. art. 749, which provides:

> If the title is silent as to the extent and manner of use of the servitude, the intention of the parties is to be determined in the light of its purpose.

This article, however, is intended to govern the scope of the servitude itself. The manner and place of payment for the servitude or right of use, at least in this instance, are not closely related to the purpose of the right, so the purpose of the right does not provide guidance for resolving this dispute.

Instead, the allowable delay for making the payment may be examined under the law of obligations. La. C.C. art. 1777 provides:

> A term for the performance of an obligation may be express or it may be implied by the nature of the contract.
>
> Performance of an obligation not subject to a term is due immediately.

La. C.C. art. 1778 provides:

> A term for the performance of an obligation is a period of time either certain or uncertain. It is certain when it is fixed. It is uncertain when it is not fixed but is determinable either by the intent of the parties or by the occurrence of a future and certain event. It is also uncertain when it is not determinable, in which case the obligation must be performed within a reasonable time.

Under the terms of the right of use, the holder of the right is entitled to use the track, but must pay the owner for each month when the track is used. We construe the nature of the contract to imply a monthly term for payment; the intent of the parties, as best as may be determined, was that the owner would be paid monthly in those months when the payor used the track. The specific time for payment-in particular, whether payment should be made at the beginning or the end of the month-however, is not determinable.

We note that the trial court's judgment provides that, prospectively, the maintenance fee must be paid *in advance* of Harrison's exercise of his use of the track. This portion of the trial court's ruling was not appealed and, therefore, we will not review this finding. In any event, we conclude that, although Harrison was able to use the track once in October, twice later that month the owner refused to allow him the use of the track. The obligation of the owner of the track was to allow the holder of the right of use to exercise his right without interference. *Cf.* La. C.C. art. 748. Since

McCormick refused to allow Harrison to use the track in accordance with the terms of the right of use, McCormick lost the right to demand that Harrison pay for October because McCormick did not fully perform his obligation. La. C.C. art. 1758(B)(1). Thus, we reject McCormick's argument that the servitude was extinguished by Harrison's failure to pay. For the foregoing reasons, the judgment of the district court is affirmed at the cost of George M. McCormick, II. Affirmed.

b. Habitation
Civil Code arts. 630-638

See A. N. YIANNOPOULOS, PERSONAL SERVITUDES
§§ 8:11 through 8:14 (5th ed. 2013)

GONSOULIN v. PONTIFF
74 So. 3d 809 (La. App. 3d Cir. 2011)

PICKETT, J. The defendant, Michelle Pontiff, appeals a judgment of the trial court evicting her from a home owned by the plaintiff, Gwen Gonsoulin.

STATEMENT OF THE CASE

In June 1992, Michelle Pontiff and her husband purchased a house at 104 Citron Drive in Youngsville, Louisiana. By the end of that year, they could no longer afford the house, and Pontiff and her husband executed a dation en paiement in favor of Gwen Gonsoulin, Pontiff's mother, on December 22, 1992. Pontiff continued to live in the house, even after she divorced her husband.

In April 2010, Gonsoulin served a notice of eviction on Pontiff through a justice of the peace court. Pontiff filed an exception, answer, and reconventional demand alleging that the amount in dispute was greater than the subject matter jurisdiction of the justice of the peace court, and the case was removed to the Fifteenth JDC. Pontiff argued that Gonsoulin had granted a right of habitation in favor of Pontiff which entitled Pontiff to use of the home until Pontiff's death. Gonsoulin claimed that she never executed such a document. The case proceeded to trial.

At trial, Pontiff admitted that she could not produce a document granting her a right of habitation. No such document had been recorded in the conveyance records of Lafayette Parish. Pontiff claimed that her mother actually executed two documents, one in Gonsoulin's living room, and one at the Lafayette Parish Assessor's office, but that both had been lost or destroyed. Because a right of habitation is a real right and must therefore be in writing, she sought to prove the existence and contents of these documents by resorting to La.Civ.Code art. 1832, which states:

> When the law requires a contract to be in written form, the contract may not be proved by testimony or by presumption, unless the written instrument has been destroyed, lost, or stolen.

Following a hearing, the trial court found that Pontiff had proven that Gonsoulin executed a document at the assessor's office purporting to establish a limited right of habitation to Pontiff for the purpose of receiving a homestead exemption on the property. The court found, however, that the cause of the granting of the right of habitation was illicit and unconstitutional, and therefore the document was a nullity. The trial court granted Gonsoulin a judgment evicting Pontiff from the house. Pontiff now appeals.

ASSIGNMENTS OF ERROR

Pontiff alleges three errors by the trial court:

1. The district court erred, as a matter of law, when it held that granting a Homestead Exemption was unconstitutional and unlawful.

2. The district court erred, as a matter of law, in failing to find an alternate true cause under Civil Code articles 1970 and 1967, which is valid and lawful.

3. The district court erred in finding a limited Right of Habitation, as a matter of law, when no limitation exists in the forms provided by the Tax Assessor's Office.

DISCUSSION

"Habitation is the nontransferable real right of a natural person to dwell in the house of another." La.Civ.Code art. 630. "The right of habitation is established and extinguished in the same manner as the right of usufruct." La.Civ.Code art. 631. A conventional usufruct is established by a juridical act. See La.Civ.Code art. 544. Because the object of the right of habitation is necessarily immovable property, it must be in writing, and will have effect on third parties only after it is filed for registry. See La.Civ.Code art. 1839.

At the trial, Pontiff attempted to prove that Gonsoulin's attorney prepared and Gonsoulin executed a right of habitation in favor of Pontiff, but that Gonsoulin had lost or destroyed that document. The trial court did not find evidence to support the existence of this document, and Pontiff abandons this contention by not assigning as error that part of the trial court's ruling.

Likewise, Gonsoulin does not appeal the finding of the trial court that she executed a document at the Lafayette Parish Assessor's office. It is clear that until 2000, the Lafayette Parish Assessor allowed residents to take advantage of the homestead exemption by executing a form document granting a "right of use of habitation" to the occupants of a house. When a new assessor was elected in 2000, he ended this practice and destroyed the forms.

The question raised in this appeal is the effect of this document. Pontiff introduced two forms into the record, both with the same operative language:

> BE IT KNOWN, that on this ___ day of _____ before the undersigned Notary Public and witnesses personally appeared _____ _____ a resident of Lafayette Parish, Louisiana who says as follows:
>
> _____ occupies a residence at _____ in the city of Lafayette, Louisiana, on property owned by _____ Affiant described as being LOTS _____ to the City of Lafayette, Louisiana.
>
> I hereby certify that no rent in any form is collected on this property. Since there is no rent collected, Affiant does hereby grant unto the said _____ the right of use of habitation of said property allowing him to claim Homestead Exemption under the laws of the State of Louisiana.

In her first assignment of error, Pontiff argues that the trial court erred in finding that the cause of the contract was unlawful. The supreme court discussed cause in Baker v. Maclay Properties Co., 94–1529, p. 14 (La.1/17/95), 648 So.2d 888, 895–96:

> LSA–C.C. art. 1966 provides that an obligation cannot exist without a lawful cause. Cause is the reason that a party obligates itself. LSA–C.C. art. 1967. The cause of an obligation is unlawful when the enforcement of the obligation would produce a result prohibited by law or against public policy. LSA–C.C. art. 1968. A contract is absolutely null when it violates a rule of public order, as when the object of a contract is illicit or immoral. A contract that is absolutely null may not be confirmed. LSA–C.C. art. 2030. Persons may not by their juridical acts derogate from laws enacted for the protection of the public interest. Any act in derogation of such laws is an absolute nullity. LSA–C.C. art. 7. See Holliday v. Holliday, 358 So.2d 618 (La.1978).

It is clear from the testimony of Conrad Comeaux, the current assessor of Lafayette Parish, and Vicky Domingue, a long-time employee of the assessor's office, that the effect of filing this document was that the property was listed as exempt from property taxes. As owner of the land, Gonsoulin was clearly not entitled to claim a homestead exemption in this property. See La. Const. Art. VII, Sec. 20. The trial court did not err in finding that the cause of the contract was illegal.

In her second assignment of error, Pontiff claims that there was a valid alternative cause. We are not persuaded by the argument that the effect of the "right of use of habitation" had a legitimate cause, as Gonsoulin wanted to avoid the payment of taxes, and Pontiff has paid the property taxes instead of Gonsoulin since 2000. The clear purpose of the document was to exempt the house from property taxes, not find someone else to pay them. The fact that Pontiff, who paid no rent for over eighteen years, paid the property taxes since 2000 is not dispositive of the issue before us. Furthermore, there is no validity to the argument that in 1996 Gonsoulin executed a document that met the requirements of Article VII, Section 20(A)(4) and therefore the cause of the contract is licit. First, that provision of the constitution applies very clearly to usufructs, not a right of habitation. Second, Section 20(A)(4) was not added to the Louisiana Constitution until 2004. See Acts 2004, No. 929. This assignment of error strains credulity.

Finally, we find no error in the trial court's finding that there was a limited right of habitation. "When the words of a contract are clear and explicit and lead to no absurd consequences, no further interpretation may be made in search of the parties' intent." La.Civ.Code art. 2046. In the absence of the actual document executed by Gonsoulin, Pontiff introduced the forms used by the assessor's office. The forms very clearly state that "the right of use of habitation" is granted "allowing him to claim Homestead Exemption." The trial court found that the words of the document are clear and explicit and lead to no absurd consequences. We find no error in that determination.

CONCLUSION

The judgment of the trial court is affirmed. Costs of this appeal are assessed to Michelle Pontiff. Affirmed.

NOTE
Duties of Holder of Right of Habitation

When a right of habitation is conferred upon property that is burdened by a mortgage, is the holder of the right of habitation liable for payment of the debt? In *Succession of Firmin*, 938 So. 2d 209 (La. App. 4th Cir. 2006), the court held that the person having the right of habitation is not required to pay anything. Here is an excerpt from the opinion:

The Executrix relies on paragraph (b) of the Revision Comments-1976 to La. C.C. art. 630 for the proposition that where the Louisiana Civil Code articles on habitation are silent, then the right of habitation is governed by the code articles on usufruct. La. C.C. art. 630 defines the term "habitation" as the "nontransferable real right to dwell in the house of another." Paragraph (b) of the Revision Comments-1976 to La. C.C. art. 630 states that habitation is a charge on property in favor of a person and therefore, the personal servitude of habitation is "akin to usufruct," which is also a charge on property in favor of a person. The language does not connote, as the Executrix asserts, that where the Louisiana Civil Code articles on habitation are silent, the articles on usufruct apply.

The Executrix relies on La. C.C. art. 632 to support her position because it states that "[t]he right of habitation is regulated by the title that establishes it." Additionally, "[i]f the title is silent as to the extent of habitation, the right is regulated in accordance with Articles 633 through 635." The Revision Comments-1976 to La. C.C. art. 632 state in paragraph (b) that if an agreement exceeds the limits on the rules governing the right of habitation, then another right is created. Paragraph (b) further states that, if, for example, a person is given the right to receive the fruits and dispose of the fruits of a house in addition to the right of habitation, then a usufruct is created, and all of the laws concerning usufruct would be applicable to the right to receive and dispose of the fruits.

The Executrix interprets paragraph (b) as applying the laws of usufruct relating to paying the mortgage on the family home because the will did not dictate who should pay the mortgage. This is without merit. La. C.C. art. 632 states that only when the title establishing the extent of the right of habitation is silent, the right is regulated in accordance with La. C.C. articles 633 through 635, which are contained in the chapter of the Louisiana Civil Code on the right of habitation, not in the chapter on usufruct. If Mr. Firmin's will had granted Mrs. Firmin rights that exceeded those of habitation such that a usufruct was established in favor of Mrs. Firmin, the provision in paragraph (b) relating to the laws of usufruct would become operative. Mr. Firmin's will did not establish a right beyond that of habitation. Therefore, the provision in paragraph (b) relating to the law of usufruct is inapplicable in this case.

La. C.C. art. 636 states the obligations of a person with the right of habitation. If the person occupies an entire house, that person is liable for "ordinary repairs, for the payment of taxes, and for other annual charges *in the same manner as the usufructuary.*" (Emphasis added). Therefore, the articles on usufruct provide instruction on the manner in which a usufructuary is required to make ordinary repairs, to pay taxes, and to pay annual charges.

The manner in which a usufructuary is liable for ordinary repairs is set forth in La. C.C. arts. 577- 583. The manner in which a usufructuary is liable for the payment of taxes and the payment of annual charges is set forth in La. C.C. art. 584, which provides that the usufructuary is required to pay the annual charges, such as property taxes, that are imposed while the usufructuary enjoys the use of the property. Paragraph (d) of the Revision Comments-1976 to article 584 makes it clear that the annual charges to which La. C.C. art. 584 refers are "annual public charges." There is nothing in La. C.C. arts. 577-583 or in La. C.C. art. 584 that refers to mortgage payments. Thus, these articles are not applicable in this case. Mrs. Firmin's obligations relating to the repair of the family home and the payment of taxes and annual charges on the home are governed by the provisions of Mr. Firmin's will and the provisions of La. C.C. art. 636.

3. RULES OF INTERPRETATION—PREDIAL OR PERSONAL SERVITUDE?
La. Civ. Code arts. 730-734

A. N. YIANNOPOULOS, PREDIAL SERVITUDES
§§ 128, 131-133 (3d ed. 2004)
(footnotes omitted)

§ 128. Rules of interpretation

Contracting parties dealing with immovables do not always take care to designate, by its proper name, the kind of right they intend to establish. They use instead descriptive language. Consequently, questions frequently arise whether an instrument was intended to transfer ownership, to establish a dismemberment of ownership, or to impose merely personal obligations. The resolution of these questions is a matter of interpretation governed by the general rules of construction of juridical acts as well as by rules applicable specifically to instruments that purport to create servitudes.

A cardinal rule of contractual interpretation is that the intention of the parties governs. This intention "must be determined from the stipulations in the entire instrument, with a view to giving effect to all of the provisions therein contained and thereby avoid neutralizing or ignoring any of them as surplusage." If the instrument is ambiguous, extrinsic evidence to prove the kind of right that the parties intended to create is admissible. Precise technical terms are not necessary to create a predial servitude; nor is the use of the word "servitude" sacramental. For example, a provision granting "the privilege of using" a driveway has been held to be sufficient to create a predial servitude of passage. The parties to a contract may even use common law terminology and still validly establish a predial servitude under the civil law. On the other hand, use of the word servitude or of equivalent expressions is not determinative in the presence of dispositions that are irreconcilable with the notion of predial servitudes.

Another cardinal rule of interpretation is that a doubt "as to the existence, extent, or manner of exercise of a predial servitude shall be resolved in favor of the servient estate." This rule incorporates into Louisiana law the civilian principle that ownership is presumed to be free of burdens and that any doubt as to a burden must be resolved in favorem libertatis. The Louisiana Supreme Court has repeatedly declared that "servitudes are restraints on the free disposal and use of property, and are not, on that account, entitled to be viewed with favor by the law."

It follows that "servitudes claimed under titles, are never sustained by implication— the title creating them must be express, as to their nature and extent, as well as to the estate which owes them, and the estate to which they are due." In the past, there was an apparent derogation from the rule that servitudes may not be sustained by implication when the owner of a tract of land subdivided it into lots, designated on a map or survey of the subdivision streets or roads, and then sold property with reference to the map or survey; he thereby created by a title a servitude of passage over the streets or roads shown on the map or survey.

In Bart v. Wysocki, the court declared: "The intent to establish a servitude must clearly appear from the face of the instrument purporting to establish the servitude" and that a statement in an act of sale that the property is subject to a servitude already extinguished does not establish a new servitude. In Robert Investment Company v. Eastbank, Inc., a site plan, attached to an act of sale, designated an area for "future parking." This was held to be insufficient to create a predial servitude. The requisite express intent to create a servitude was missing. In Becnel v. Citrus Lands of Louisiana, Inc., the court held that a servitude had been established although the recorded plan of a subdivision was merely marked "Reserved for Road." The holding was based upon the fact that a road on the reserved land was actually built and used for many years.

In France servitudes may be exceptionally established by implication when the parties to transactions necessarily contemplate the creation of a servitude. The sale of an enclosed timber estate includes, by necessary implication, a servitude of passage for the cutting of timber.

In Germany and in Greece, contractual intent to create a predial servitude may be implied. Thus, when the owner of two contiguous tracts containing structures needed for the exercise of a servitude sells one of them, a servitude may come into existence by implication.

§ 131. Real right or personal obligation

When contracting parties do not specify in their agreements the kind of right they intended to create, question may arise whether they intended to create a real right, such as a predial servitude or a personal servitude, or merely a personal obligation. This question is resolved in Louisiana by application of Articles 731 through 734 of the Civil Code that furnish rules of interpretation as to the kinds of rights created by juridical acts in the absence of express designation. These articles have no equivalents in the Civil Codes of France, Germany, or Greece; they derive from the 1825 revision of the Louisiana Civil Code and the treatise of Toullier.

Article 731 of the Louisiana Civil Code declares that a charge "established on an estate expressly for the benefit of another estate is a predial servitude although it is not so designated." Thus, when a right of passage is expressly reserved "for the benefit and advantage of the property," a predial servitude is clearly established; but when the act establishing the servitude either does not declare that the right is given for the benefit of an estate or declares that the right is given to the owner of an estate, determination of the question whether the parties intended to create a predial servitude or another right is to be made in accordance with Articles 732 through 734 of the Civil Code.

Article 732 provides that, when the act establishing the servitude "does not declare expressly that the right granted is for the benefit of an estate or for the benefit of a particular person," the nature of the right is determined according to Articles 733 and 734. Article 733 declares that when the right granted "be of a nature to confer an advantage on an estate, it is presumed to be a predial servitude." Article 734 declares that when the right granted "is merely for the convenience of a person, it is not considered to be a predial servitude, unless it is acquired by a person or owner of an estate for himself, his heirs, and assigns."

§ 132. Predial servitude or personal obligation

An instrument may create a predial servitude or merely a personal obligation. In a typical case, an act of sale stipulated that "the purchaser, its successors and assigns, shall have the privilege of using the paved driveway in the rear" of the vendor's property. The act had been recorded, but the words "its successors and assigns" were omitted from the public records. A subsequent purchaser of the vendor's property, relying in part on the omission of the words "its successors and assigns," argued that the recorded act had established merely a personal obligation. The court found that the act of sale, as originally executed, established a predial servitude because the right of passage was acquired by the purchaser as owner of an estate and for his successors and assigns. But since the act, as recorded, granted the right of passage to the purchaser only and did not declare that the right was given for the benefit of an estate, the court felt that determination of the issue ought to be made in the light of the tests furnished by the pertinent provisions of the Civil Code. In the opinion of the court, the right of passage was of real utility to the property; it gave to it "more free space either for building or for flowers, or for a garden" and made the property "more desirable and more valuable." The court bolstered its conclusion that the act, as recorded, established a predial servitude by the observation that the right of passage was not given to a named individual but to the purchaser, "thereby connecting the servitude with the property as a real advantage to it, and not merely as a mere matter of convenience to a particular person and terminating with him."

The question whether property is burdened with a predial servitude or is used by virtue of a personal right may also arise in the absence of any title. It is to be resolved likewise by application of Articles 730 through 734 of the Civil Code.

§ 133. Predial servitude or limited personal servitude

An instrument may not only raise the question whether the contracting parties intended to create a predial servitude or a personal obligation; it may also raise the question whether the contracting parties intended to create a predial servitude or a limited personal servitude.

Articles 639 through 645 of the Louisiana Civil Code deal with limited personal servitudes (rights of use). Article 639 declares that a limited personal servitude is a real right that confers "in favor of a person a specified use of an estate less than full enjoyment." This provision, in concert with corresponding provisions in modern civil codes, authorizes a charge on an estate in favor of a person that does not exhaust the utility of the immovable; if it does, the charge establishes a usufruct rather than a limited personal servitude.

Under the regime of the Louisiana Civil Code of 1870, question arose whether interested parties had the freedom to create by will or by agreement personal servitudes other than usufruct, use, or habitation because these were the only ones regulated by the Code. Articles 755 through 758 of the 1870 Code seemed to indicate that contracting parties could create either predial servitudes or merely personal obligations. However, according to the prevailing view, these articles, in addition to furnishing rules for the interpretation of juridical acts, authorized by clear implication the creation of limited personal servitudes as well as the creation of predial servitudes and personal obligations. Toullier, whose text was closely followed by the redactors of the Louisiana Civil Code of 1825, had originally expounded the view that personal servitudes other than usufruct, use, and habitation were forbidden and that rights of enjoyment that did not qualify as predial servitudes or as usufruct, use, and habitation were necessarily personal obligations. The author, however, revised this view in the third volume of his treatise and concluded that a real right of enjoyment could validly be stipulated in favor of a person rather than an estate, and this right would bind all subsequent acquirers of the property. This right would not be a predial servitude because it would terminate with the life of the grantee. Nor would it be a personal service forbidden by Article 686 of the Code Civil, corresponding to Article 709 of the Louisiana Civil Code of 1870.

The expression "personal to the individual" in Articles 757 and 758 of the Louisiana Civil Code of 1870 did not mean that if a right was not a predial servitude it was necessarily a personal obligation binding only the parties to the agreement. The right could also be a limited personal servitude, which, according to Article 758, expired with the life of the grantee in the absence of contrary stipulation. If the right were necessarily a contractual right of enjoyment, there was no reason why it ought to terminate with the life of the grantee, because obligations are, in principle, heritable.

Quite apart from the Civil Code, Louisiana statutes have long provided for the creation of servitudes in favor of public utilities and governmental agencies. These servitudes do not conform with the definition of predial servitudes in the Civil Code because they are not charges laid on an estate in favor of another estate; nor do they conform with the definitions of usufruct and habitation. Like predial servitudes, these rights are transferable to heirs and assigns and their duration is unlimited; like usufruct and habitation, these rights are charges laid on an estate in favor of a person. They are limited personal servitudes, namely, real rights of enjoyment established in favor of a person, governed by the rules pertaining to both predial and personal servitudes.

The Louisiana Supreme Court did not hesitate to give full effect to limited personal servitudes under the regime of the 1870 Code. In Parkway Development Corporation v. City of Shreveport, the court declared that the grant of a right of way in favor of a railroad was "a limited personal servitude." And in Farrell v. Hodges Stock Yards, Inc., the court found that a similar right of way in favor of a railroad "was not a predial servitude but a limited personal servitude, governed by the rules of predial and personal servitudes, applied by analogy.

CHAPTER XVII: USUFRUCT
Civil Code arts. 535-629

1. GENERAL PRINCIPLES
Civil Code arts. 535-549

A.N. YIANNOPOULOS, PERSONAL SERVITUDES
§§ 1:1 through 1:6, 1:9 (5th ed. 2013)
(footnotes omitted)

§ 1:1. Usufruct; definition

In accord with contemporary civilian doctrine, Article 535 of the Louisiana Civil Code declares: "Usufruct is a real right of limited duration on the property of another. The features of the right vary with the nature of things subject to it as consumables or nonconsumables." This provision is an original one of the 1976 Revision.

Under Article 535 of the Civil Code, usufruct is a *real right* regardless of whether the property subject to the right is a movable or an immovable. Legal usage in the state tends, incorrectly, to associate the term "real right" with a right in immovable property. Real rights, however, may attach to both movables and immovables. The rights of pledge, ownership, and usufruct of movables have all the characteristics of real rights. Restricted use of the term "real rights" with respect to immovables is meaningful in the framework of the Louisiana Code of Civil Procedure, because the nominate real actions are exclusively available for the protection of immovable property. The usufruct of movables, though a real right, is protected by the revendicatory action rather than the nominate real actions of the Code of Civil Procedure.

The real right nature of usufruct distinguishes usufruct from leases and personal rights for collection of fruits or revenues. Usufruct is a real right of *limited* duration; it expires, necessarily, upon the death of the usufructuary. This feature distinguishes usufruct from rents of lands and rights of superficies.

Article 534 of the Louisiana Civil Code of 1870 declared that there are two kinds of usufruct: perfect usufruct and imperfect or quasi usufruct. Perfect usufruct was the usufruct of nonconsumable things "which the usufructuary can enjoy without changing their substance, though their substance may be diminished or deteriorated naturally by time or by the use to which they are applied; as a house, a piece of land, furniture and other movable effects." Imperfect usufruct was the usufruct of consumable things "which would be useless to the usufructuary if he did not consume or expend them, or change the substance of them, as money, grain, liquors." The definition of usufruct in revised Article 535 of the Louisiana Civil Code has made unnecessary the use of the terms "perfect usufruct" and "imperfect usufruct." A usufruct of consumables is the same as an imperfect usufruct and a usufruct of nonconsumables is the same as a perfect usufruct.

The classification of things as consumables or nonconsumables controls the features of the usufruct. In principle, classification depends on inherent characteristics of things and is made according to objective criteria. According to Article 536 of the Louisiana Civil Code, consumable things are "those that cannot be used without being expended or consumed, or without their substance being changed, such as money, harvested agricultural products, stocks of merchandise, foodstuffs, and beverages." The provision is based on the second paragraph of Article 534 of the Louisiana Civil Code of 1870. Louisiana courts that interpreted the source provision classified as consumables: money, promissory notes, certificates of deposit, negotiable instruments to the bearer, bales of cotton, and stocks of merchandise.

Article 537 of the Louisiana Civil Code declares that nonconsumable things. are "those that may be enjoyed without alteration of their substance, although their substance may be diminished or deteriorated naturally by time or by the use to which they are applied, such as lands, houses, shares of stock, animals, furniture, and vehicles." The provision is based on the first paragraph of Article 534 of the Louisiana Civil Code of 1870. Under the regime of that Code, Louisiana courts had held that shares of stock were nonconsumables.

Parties may, in the exercise of contractual freedom, treat certain nonconsumable things as consumables. Thus, at least in France, the usufructuary may acquire ownership of nonconsumables subject to the usufruct by an estimation-sale.

§ 1:2. Usufruct of nonconsumables; definition

Article 539 of the Louisiana Civil Code declares that if the things subject to usufruct are nonconsumables, "the usufructuary has the right to possess them and to derive the utility, profits, and advantages that they may produce, under the obligation of preserving their substance." The provision is based on Article 533 of the Louisiana Civil Code of 1870. Substantially similar definitions are employed in the French, German, and Greek Civil Codes. These definitions apply merely to usufruct properly so-called (perfect usufruct or usufruct of nonconsumables).

The grantor may relieve the usufructuary of the obligation to preserve the substance of a thing; for example, the grantor may confer on the usufructuary authority to sell the thing. In such case, the usufruct of nonconsumables may be converted at the option of the usufructuary into a usufruct of consumables with the usufructuary's right of enjoyment attaching to the proceeds of the sale.

§ 1:3. Usufruct of consumables; definition

Real rights for the enjoyment of things under the obligation of preserving their substance may properly be established on nonconsumables only.[1]

When a right of enjoyment bears on a consumable, a thing which is extinguished or is intended to be extinguished by the first use, the obligation of preserving its substance would contradict the very possibility of enjoyment. For such a thing the right of enjoyment (*jus utendi*) would be meaningless without the power of disposition (*jus abutendi*).

Usufruct of consumables was unknown in early Roman law. When a usufruct was established under universal title and the mass of the succession included consumables, the usufructuary could take possession of the nonconsumables only. In the early years of the Empire, however, a Senatus Consultum whose date remains uncertain provided that a testamentary usufruct could be established on all kinds of things. On the basis of that legislation Roman jurists and Romanist scholars in the successive centuries developed the notion and incidents of the usufruct of consumables.

Following the Romanist tradition, Article 534 of the Louisiana Civil Code of 1870 covered the usufruct of consumables under the rubric of imperfect usufruct. Such was the usufruct of things, "which would be useless to the usufructuary, if he did not consume or expend them, or change the substance of them, as money, grain, liquors." Provisions in the French, German, and Greek Civil Codes establish likewise the notion of usufruct of consumables and regulate its incidents.

According to Article 538 of the Louisiana Civil Code, if the things subject to usufruct are consumables, the usufructuary becomes owner of them. As owner, the usufructuary may consume, alienate, or encumber the things as he sees fit. At the termination of the usufruct, he is bound to pay the naked owner either the value that the things had at the commencement of the usufruct or deliver to him things of the same quantity and quality. The first sentence of Article 538 is based on Article 536 of the Louisiana Civil Code of 1870 and the second sentence of that article is based on Article 549 of the same Code.

A usufruct of nonconsumables may, under certain circumstances, be converted into a usufruct of consumables. This may happen, for example, when the usufructuary has been granted authority to dispose of nonconsumables at his discretion. If the usufructuary elects to exercise his authority, the usufruct attaches to the proceeds of the disposition. Further, when things of a succession are sold by the usufructuary or by the personal representative of the deceased for the satisfaction of creditors, the usufruct attaches to the cash residue remaining after the payment of debts. And, when nonconsumables are converted into money as a result of expropriation for purposes of public utility or liquidation without any act of the usufructuary, the usufruct becomes one of consumables by operation of the principle of real subrogation.

In a case decided under the regime of the Louisiana Civil Code of 1870, the Louisiana Supreme Court held that when the usufructuary converts nonconsumables into money without right or authority the usufruct does not become imperfect. The court meant that the usufructuary did not acquire ownership of the proceeds and that his liability to the naked owner was not limited to the value of the things at the time of the conversion plus interest from the date of termination of the usufruct. If the usufructuary alienates nonconsumables without having the right to do so, he violates the obligation to preserve the substance of the things. Accordingly, his usufruct may terminate by application of Article 623 of the Louisiana Civil Code, and, upon termination, the usufructuary will be "answerable for the losses resulting from his fraud, default or neglect."

A usufruct of consumables differs from a usufruct of nonconsumables because the usufructuary acquires ownership of the things and the naked owner becomes a general creditor of the usufructuary. The risk of deterioration or loss of these things is borne by the usufructuary that as owner is also entitled to any capital appreciation resulting from a successful investment.

Usufruct of consumables is rarely established under particular title. It is frequently brought about in cases of universal succession in which the patrimony of a deceased person includes both consumables and nonconsumables. Certain prevalent forms of usufruct of consumables are discussed in Chapter 2, §§2:34, 2:39 *infra*. The obligation of the usufructuary to account at the end of a usufruct of consumables is discussed in Chapter 6, §6:18 *infra*.

§ 1:4. Things susceptible of usufruct

According to Article 544 of the Louisiana Civil Code and corresponding Article 581 of the French Civil Code, usufruct may be established "on all kinds of things, movable or immovable, corporeal or incorporeal." The provision reproduces the substance of Article 541 of the Louisiana Civil Code of 1870.

The German Civil Code and the Greek Civil Code regulate in detail the usufruct of things, namely, the usufruct of corporeal objects, movable or immovable, that are susceptible of appropriation. Additional provisions in the two codes authorize the creation of usufruct of an entire patrimony or a fraction thereof as well as the usufruct of rights, namely, the usufruct of incorporeal objects in commerce that are not things. These provisions regulate certain incidents of such kinds of usufruct and declare that in the absence of contrary indication the rules governing usufruct of things apply by analogy to the usufruct of rights and the usufruct of patrimonies. In contrast with predial servitudes and limited personal servitudes that may burden immovables only and concern certain aspects of use or enjoyment, a usufruct under the two codes exhausts the utility of an object, movable or immovable, corporeal or incorporeal.

Usufruct may bear in all jurisdictions on copyrights, claims or credits, leases, partnerships, business enterprises, and, in France and in Louisiana on another usufruct. Generally, any corporeal or incorporeal that is capable to produce an economic advantage may be burdened by a usufruct.

The usufruct of rights has been said to involve a doctrinal anomaly. Under the schemes of the German Civil Code and the Greek Civil Code and prevailing doctrine in France, the word "ownership" applies to corporeal objects exclusively. Exceptionally, however, rights of intellectual property have been qualified in recent years as "ownership". The usufruct of incorporeals implies that the "ownership" of an incorporeal may be dismembered, when at the same time it is asserted that incorporeals cannot be "owned"!

That doctrinal anomaly does not involve practical consequences. The "ownership" of incorporeals might solve a number of problems and might result in more effective protection of rights. The usufruct of incorporeals is a necessary concession of theory to practical necessity. In Louisiana, one frequently speaks of ownership of rights, and the difficulty is entirely obviated.

§ 1:5. Usufruct as an incorporeal

According to Article 540 of the Louisiana Civil Code "usufruct is an incorporeal thing." The same classification obtains in France, even in the absence of a corresponding provision in the Code Civil. In Germany and Greece usufruct is a right, and, therefore, not a thing.

In France and in Louisiana usufruct may be an incorporeal movable or an incorporeal immovable, depending on the nature of the things that are subject to usufruct. The classification of rights as movables or immovables has been avoided in both the German and the Greek Civil Code.

§ 1:6. Conventional and legal usufruct

A usufruct may be created by a juridical act or by operation of law. Article 544 of the Louisiana Civil Code declares: "Usufruct may be established by a juridical act either inter vivos of mortis causa, or by operation of law. The usufruct created by juridical act is called conventional; the usufruct created by operation of law is called legal." A conventional usufruct established by a bilateral juridical act, whether onerous or gratuitous, is designated as a contractual usufruct, and a usufruct established by a testament is designated as a testamentary usufruct.

Following the French model, Civil Codes, doctrine, and jurisprudence in other civil law jurisdictions establish a distinction between conventional usufruct and legal usufruct. However, in Germany and in Greece all usufructs are conventional. The various methods of creation and incidents of each kind of usufruct in Louisiana, France, Germany, and Greece are discussed in §§1:11, 1:12, 1:28, 1:29 *infra*.

§ 1:9. Usufruct in divided shares and usufruct in indivision

According to Article 541 of the Louisiana Civil Code, usufruct may be conferred "on several persons, in divided or undivided shares." Similar provisions may be found in other civil codes. When usufruct is conferred in indivision to two or more persons, the right of enjoyment is a single right, shared by the co-usufructuaries in proportion to their shares. Under the regime of the 1870 Code, the question whether a right of survivorship was granted in favor of the persons named as usufructuaries was a matter of contractual or testamentary interpretation. Therefore, depending on the interpretation placed on a contract or a testament, each interest could terminate at different periods, and a share to a usufruct in indivision could be united with the naked ownership upon the death of each usufructuary or could inure to the benefit of the remaining usufructuaries.

The need for contractual or testamentary interpretation to determine rights of survivorship has been minimized by Article 547 of the Louisiana Civil Code. This article declares that when a usufruct is conferred in undivided shares in favor of several usufructuaries "the termination of the interest of one usufructuary inures to the benefit of those remaining, unless the grantor has expressly provided otherwise."

a. Usufruct of Consumables and of Non-Consumables
Civil Code arts. 536-539

LEURY v. MAYER
122 La. 486, 47 So. 839 (1908)

LAND, J. Plaintiff instituted this suit to be recognized as the owner of an undivided half interest in 20 shares of the capital stock of the Bank of Baton Rouge, represented by certificate No. 127 issued to the defendant, and for a partition by licitation of said shares and dividends accrued thereon.

Plaintiff is the only child of J.E. Leury and Hannah Leury, who were married in Baton Rouge on November 1, 1880. Plaintiff was born on November 4, 1881. Mrs. Leury died in Baton Rouge on August 17, 1893. On December 8, 1891, J. E. Leury acquired 20 shares of stock in the Bank of Baton Rouge, as evidenced by certificate No. 127. On October 27, 1893, a few months after the death of his wife, Leury transferred said certificate to the defendant.

The certificate was community property, and on the death of Mrs. Leury her undivided half interest therein was inherited by the plaintiff.

The defendant pleads the prescription of 3 and 10 years, and contends that the surviving husband, as usufructuary, had the legal right to sell the stock.

The last contention comes first in logical order, and is founded on the premise that the usufruct of shares of stock is an imperfect or quasi usufruct, under Civ. Code, arts. 534, 536, 549 [Revised C.C. arts. 536-538, 629]. The first article defines an imperfect usufruct to be one of the things which would be useless to the usufructuary, if he did not consume or expend them or change the substance of them, "as money, grains, liquors." Articles

536 and 549 [Revised C.C.arts. 538, 629] provide that the imperfect usufruct transfers the ownership to the usufructuary, so that he may consume, sell, or dispose of them as he thinks proper, subject to the obligation of returning the same quantity, quality, and value to the owner, or their estimated price, at the expiration of the usufruct.

It is obvious that bank stock does not fall within the purview of article 534, Civ. Code [Revised C.C. arts. 536, 537], but represents an investment of money for the purpose of producing revenue. In such a case the usufructuary is entitled only to the fruits, as in the case of "rents of real property, the interest of money, and annuities." Articles 544, 545 [Revised C.C. arts. 550, 551]. The argument that in the case at bar the usufructuary had the right to sell the stock because it was not producing a revenue is not only unsound in law, but unsupported by the facts of the case. Within a few years the stock had doubled in value, and 60 days after the sale to the defendant the first dividend was declared. Since the date of the sale the defendant had collected $1,495 in dividends, or $47.75 for each share of the par value of $50. At the date of the trial below the stock was worth $317.76 per share.

The plaintiff's father was entitled to all the dividends declared up to the date of his death, January 30, 1896, though they may not have been collected by him. Article 547, Civ. Code [Revised C.C. art. 556].

It does not appear that J.E. Leury was ever confirmed and qualified as tutor of his minor son, Louis F. Leury. But even had the father qualified as tutor, he could not have sold at private sale the interests of his minor son in the stock in question without an order of court issued upon the advice of a family meeting. Act No. 21, p. 17, Laws 1890.

The judgment below recognized the plaintiff as the joint owner with the defendant of 20 shares of the capital stock of the Bank of Baton Rouge, as evidenced by certificate No. 127, together with the accrued dividends; and ordered that said interest in and to the said ownership in said bank be sold at public auction according to law for the purposes of effecting a partition between the plaintiff and the defendant, and referred the parties to a notary for the purpose of completing said partition, reserving their rights as against each other in any claim growing out of the above ownership in said bank; the same to be settled and determined in the partition.

The complaint of appellant is well founded as to the sale of the accrued dividends, amounting to $1495.44, which have already been collected by the defendant. The only dividends which can be sold are such as have not been declared and paid by the bank. As already stated, the defendant is not accountable for dividends collected prior to the death of J.E. Leury, on January 30, 18%.

It is therefore ordered that the judgment appealed from be amended by restricting the partition sale to the stock plus dividends which have not been heretofore declared and paid, and by ordering the defendant to account in the partition for all dividends received by him on the stock in dispute since January 30, 18%; and it is further ordered that said judgment as thus amended be affirmed, and that plaintiff pay the costs of appeal.

NOTE

In *Vivian State Bank v. Thomason-Lewis Lumber Co.*, 162 La. 660, 111 So. 51 (1926), the Supreme Court was required to resolve a question regarding the prerogatives of a usufructuary of nonconsumables. Mr. Thomason, husband of Mrs. Thomason, bought a certificate of deposit (CD) from Vivian State Bank (VSB). Though the CD was made out in his name only, it nevertheless qualified as "community property". A few years after Mr. Thomason died, Mrs. Thomason "rolled over" the old CD into a new CD and, after doing that, "pledged"[24] the new CD to VSB to secure repayment of a loan that she and others were then taking out from VSB. The new CD was made out in the name of "the estate of Mr. Thomason". In time, Mrs. Thomason and the other borrowers defaulted on the loan, whereupon VSB sued Mrs. Thomason to enforce its pledge on the new CD. In her defense, Mrs. Thomason argued that the pledge was invalid because she had lacked the power to pledge the CD. The Supreme Court, affirming the district court, rejected that argument, relying on the following rationale. Because the original CD was community property, Mrs. Thomason had owned ½ of it from the get go. La. Civ. Code art. 2336. After Mr. Thomason died, she acquired a "legal usufruct" over what had theretofore been his ½ of the CD. La. Civ. Code art. 890. Because a CD is, in effect, money, which is a consumable par excellence, this usufruct was an "imperfect usufruct" (now known as a "usufruct of consumables", CC art. 538). As the imperfect usufructuary of her husband's half of the original CD, she enjoyed the "ownership" thereof. In the end, then, she owned both halves, that is, *all* of the original CD. As the owner of the whole CD, she was, of course, free to do with it whatever she wanted, including using it to acquire something else (the new CD) and pledging that "something else" to secure her debts.

b. Contractual and Testamentary Freedom
Civil Code arts. 545-548, 1522

SUCCESSION OF GOODE
425 So. 2d 673 (La. 1982)

LEMMON, J. This case involves the validity of a testamentary disposition. The issue is whether the contested legacy constituted a prohibited substitution.

The testator died in 1978, leaving no ascendants or descendants and being survived by a half brother and the descendants of a predeceased half sister. He left an olographic will, which provided for several specific dispositions, but no residuary legacy. The contested legacy provided as follows:

> "Fifth: All oil & gas royalty interest payments owned by me shall be paid to Pauline Egbert Parker for as long as she might live. After her death the amount of any payments shall be equally divided between my nieces and nephews and Linda Cosby Paine."

---

[24] A "pledge" is "a contract by which one debtor gives something to his creditor as a security for his debt." CC art. 3133. This contract gives the creditor an "accessory" real right in the thing pledged, rather like the right conferred by a "mortgage".

After the will was probated, the opponents of the will filed a petition to annul the testament. The case was tried on stipulated facts, and the trial court held that the legacy was a prohibited substitution. The court of appeal affirmed. 395 So. 2d 875.

We granted certiorari to review those holdings. 401 So. 2d 359.***

Prohibited Sub reas...

As noted in the Report by the Louisiana State Law Institute to Accompany the Proposed Louisiana Trust Code, a prohibited substitution must contain (1) a double disposition in full ownership of the same thing to persons named to receive it, one after the other, (2) a charge to preserve and transmit the thing, imposed on the first beneficiary for the benefit of the second, and (3) the establishment of a successive order that causes the thing to leave the inheritance of the burdened beneficiary and to enter into the patrimony of the substituted beneficiary. See also Baten v. Taylor, 386 So. 2d 333 (La. 1979). Nevertheless, the disposition of a usufruct is not prohibited, nor is the disposition of successive usufructs. See C.C. Art. 1522 and 546.

In the present case the proponents of the will contend there was no express double disposition in full ownership and no express charge on the first beneficiary to preserve and transmit the property to a second beneficiary. They urge that we construe the testator's words as intending to separate his royalty interest in the property from the payments attributable to that interest, so that either (1) he intended to bequeath the payments to named beneficiaries by successive usufructs, while allowing the naked ownership of the royalty interest to pass by intestacy, or (2) he intended to bequeath a life usufruct to Pauline Parker and the naked ownership to the other named legatees.

On the other hand, the opponents contend there were no words such as "use," "usufruct," "naked ownership," "enjoyment" or "use and benefit" indicative of the testator's intention to create the institutions of usufruct and naked ownership. Further citing the principle that a testator is presumed to have intended to dispose of all of his property, the opponents argue against construing the disposition as creating successive usufructs, while allowing the naked ownership to pass by intestacy.

When a landowner or servitude owner grants a mineral lease on property which is subject to a previously existing royalty interest and the lessee obtains production from the leased property, the royalty owner participates in the payments for minerals produced under the lease. See R.S. 31:80, codifying prior jurisprudence. But when the lease expires, the royalty interest remains in existence.

Although a layman, the testator (whose royalty income averaged more than $10,000 monthly) was undoubtedly aware of the difference between the royalty interest which he had acquired in one transaction and the payments he subsequently received, on account of that ownership, after the property was leased and production was obtained. Significantly, in drafting his will without benefit of counsel, he used the word "payments", and the deliberate use of that word suggests an intent to distinguish between the legal right he had originally acquired (royalty interest) and the income which subsequently flowed from that right. He could have left his royalty interest to Pauline Parker, thereby giving her both the right and the income currently flowing therefrom, but he chose to give her the royalty *payments*. While this disposition could reasonably be construed as a legacy of the royalty interest itself, it also could reasonably be construed as a legacy to Pauline Parker of the payments made on account of the royalty interest and a legacy to the other named legatees of the ownership of the royalty interest itself.[25]

In interpreting testaments, courts should principally seek to ascertain the intention of the testator, without departing from the proper signification of the testamentary terms. C.C. Art. 1712. Furthermore, when testamentary language is subject to two reasonable interpretations, courts should choose the interpretation which validates the will rather than the one which invalidates it, as long as that interpretation does not violate the testator's intent.

Here, the testator clearly intended for Pauline Parker to receive the payments made on account of his royalty interest in the property until her death and for the other named legatees to receive the payments thereafter in equal proportions. The law permitted him to accomplish this intention by giving the usufruct to one and the naked ownership to the others. While his uncounseled language did not expressly provide for the establishment of the legal institutions of usufruct and naked ownership, neither did the language expressly provide that both sets of legatees were to receive the royalty interest in full ownership or that the first legatee was to preserve it for the other legatees. This disposition can therefore be interpreted with equal reasonableness as the bequest of a life usufruct of the royalty interest to Pauline Parker and of the naked ownership to the other named legatees, and that interpretation accords completely with the testator's apparent intent, while making the testament valid. Accordingly, we interpret the testamentary disposition as establishing the enforceable legal institutions authorized by C.C. Art. 1522.

In cases such as the present one, an appropriate solution is to give effect to the testamentary disposition by construing it as a valid usufruct-naked ownership legacy, rather than as a prohibited substitution, when the testator does not expressly outline all of the details of a prohibited substitution.[26] E. Nabors, An Analysis of the Substitution-

---

[25] The word "payments" is also used in the disposition to Linda Paine and the nieces and nephews, which arguably weighs in favor of a finding of successive usufructs, once the court determines that the testator intended to distinguish between royalty interest and payments. However, the separate gifts of a usufruct and the naked ownership *are* probably closer to the uncounseled testator's actual intention, and we place significance on the use of the word "payments" primarily to demonstrate the testator's intent to distinguish between royalty interest and payments, rather than to determine which gift was intended for each legatee.

[26] The author of this opinion points out that even if the testator intended the legacy as a disposition of the royalty interest in full ownership to both sets of legatees, Pauline Parker was not charged with the obligation to preserve the property and to return it to a third person, which is one of the essential elements of a prohibited substitution as defined by *C.C.* Art. 1520. In the author's view, a disposition by which a legatee is given full ownership of property for his life and charged to transmit the *residue* of the property at his death is a valid substitution which is not prohibited by C.C. Art. 1520, because it does not contain the essential charge to preserve and

Usufruct problem under Articles 1520 and 1522 of the Louisiana Civil Code, 4 Tul. L. Rev. 603 (1930); A. Yiannopoulos, 3 Louisiana Civil Law Treatise — Personal Servitudes § 15 (2d ed. 1978). This interpretation achieves the laudable goal of validating testamentary dispositions, whenever the language may reasonably be construed so as to make the disposition valid and to achieve the testator's clear purpose, without frustrating the purpose of the prohibition against substitutions.[27] This interpretation also accords with Justice Dennis' suggestion in *Baten v. Taylor,* above, that pre-Trust Code jurisprudence concerning prohibited substitutions be reassessed in the light of the legislative amendments harmonizing substitutions with French doctrine and with the rule that penal and prohibitory laws should be strictly construed.

Accordingly, the judgments of the lower courts are reversed, and the petition to annul the probated testament is dismissed. Costs in all courts are assessed to the opponents.

CALOGERO, J. (concurring) The majority opinion is correct in finding that there is not here a prohibited substitution. Presented with the tough job of interpreting the will to ascertain the intent of the testator, the majority in my view comes up with the more reasonable conclusion when it finds that the testator wanted his wife's sister-in-law (Mrs. Pauline Egbert Parker) to have the royalty interest payments for the rest of her natural life with the seven other legatees (six nieces, nephews, and one Linda Cosby Paine) enjoying the mineral interest, in particular the payments following Mrs. Parker's death, and the mineral interest in its entirety. It is the preferable interpretation of the will that Mr. Goode did not intend that there be usufructs spanning successively the life of Mrs. Parker and the lives of seven variously aged younger people, with the naked ownership of the mineral interest property at the usufructs' terminations devolving upon his legal heirs. Incidentally those legal heirs are the six nieces and nephews and the testator's half brother, respondent James Philip Goode, who was named in the will as executor and as custodian of the family heirlooms.

As I see it, the testator, in effect, gave Pauline Egbert Parker a legacy of revenues from specified property, a "kind of usufruct", one which, under La. C.C. 609, "terminates, upon the death of the legatee unless a shorter period has been expressly stipulated." Incidentally, La. C.C. art. 609 with its reference to a "kind of a usufruct" appears in § 5 of Chapter 2 of Title III (Personal Servitudes) a section relating to the *termination* of usufructs, not in the earlier sections (§ 1, § 2, § 3, § 4) of Chapter 2, Title III which govern the principles of usufruct and the rights and obligations of the usufructuary and the naked owner. As I interpret the code articles there is no contemplation that the legacy of revenues, a "kind of usufruct", be governed by the articles relating to the obligations of

---

render. J. Tucker, Substitutions. Fideicommissa and Trusts in Louisiana Law: A Semantical Reappraisal, 24 La. L. Rev. 439, 489; A. Yiannopoulos, above; Succession of Walters, 259 So. 2d 12 (La. 1972), Barham, J., Concurring; Crichton v. Succession of Gredler, 235 So. 2d 411 (La. 1970), Sanders, J, Dissenting.

[27] 'The purpose of the prohibition is to prevent attempts to tie up property in perpetuity. However, C.C. Art. 1482 accomplishes that objective by limiting capacity to receive gifts to persons conceived at the time of the donation or the death of the testator

a usufructuary of money and consumable things (La. C.C. art. 536 which appears in § 1 of Chapter 2 of Title III); neither is a return of the revenues at the end of the "kind of usufruct" contemplated. As noted in comment (d) under La. C.C. art. 609:

> (d) Louisiana courts have declared that the intention of the legislature "was, not to make such bequests as the 'annuities' usufructs in reality, for there is no transfer of possession to the usufructuary, but to make them quasi-usufructs, only for the purpose of limiting their duration." New Orleans v. Baltimore, 13 La. Ann. 162 (1858) (decided under the corresponding Article 602 of the 1825 Code). See also Succession of Ward, 110 La. 75, 24 So. 135 (1903). This correct interpretation that a legacy of revenues does not necessarily establish a real right of enjoyment in favor of the legatee was followed in Peyton v. Hammonds, 125 So. 2d 491 (La. App. 2d Cir. 1960). For these reasons I concur.

DIXON, C.J. (dissenting). I respectfully dissent. This legacy seems to be that contemplated by our new (1976) C.C. 609:

> "A legacy of revenues from specified property is a kind of usufruct.. Such a "kind of usufruct" is probably one of "consumable things.., such as money..." (C.C. 536) for which the usufructuary must account at termination (C.C. 538). The first "kind of usufruct" terminates with the death of the first usufructuary, and then goes to nieces, nephews and Linda Paine. Since there is no residuary legatee, the naked owners of the royalty are the testator's heirs, who will probably consider the matter of security for the usufruct, which was not waived by the grantor. (C.C. 573).

BLANCHE, J. (dissenting). I respectfully dissent. The bequest containing the mineral interest created a double disposition in full ownership, as well as a charge to preserve and transmit.***

Because the testator failed to create a usufruct in favor of the named legatees, any payments received by Ms. Parker during her lifetime are indistinguishable from the royalty that produces them. Consequently, the "payments" which are to be divided upon Ms. Parker's death are synonymous with the real right from which they are derived. Though there is no express charge placed upon Pauline Parker to preserve and transmit any payments she actually receives, future payments to the nieces, nephews and Linda Paine are dependent solely upon the preservation and transmission of the income producing interest. Thus, Ms. Parker is charged to preserve and transmit the royalty interest. Accordingly, the court of appeal was correct in its conclusion that the contested disposition constituted a prohibited substitution.

The strained interpretation of the contested bequest by the majority clearly hinders the objectives of C.C. art. 1520. The prohibition against substitutions prevents the testator from keeping property out of commerce and controlling the distribution of family wealth by adhering the future order of succession. The bequest in dispute prevents the free alienation of the royalty interest and attempts to preserve the wealth generated by this real right. Though it is not likely that the existence and nature of mineral royalty interests were ever contemplated by the redactors of our Civil Code, the considerations which led to the prohibition against substitutions ought to apply with equal force to mineral interests.

WATSON, J. (dissenting). The will contains what is clearly a prohibited substitution. This conclusion is pointed up by the difficult and strained interpretation by which the majority attempts to find otherwise. I respectfully dissent for these reasons and also for the reasons assigned by Justice Blanche.

On Rehearing

DIXON, C.J. ***On original hearing this court was divided on the validity of the will's provision, and those upholding the provision were divided on which rights of ownership devolved to the nieces, nephews and Linda Cosby Paine. We granted rehearing to reconsider these questions.

In the interpretation of a legacy, our first task is to determine the intention of the testator. C.C. 1720. The trial court in written reasons found that the testator had attempted to make a bequest to Mrs. Parker during her lifetime and upon her death a bequest to other named legatees. This was considered to be a classic example of a prohibited substitution. The court of appeal, in examining the words of the testator, noted the absence of the terms "use" or "use and benefit" which would have suggested that a usufruct had been created, and determined that the testator was bequeathing a royalty interest and not merely payments made on account of a royalty interest. The court of appeal, therefore, also found a prohibited substitution.

Within the context of the Civil Code, the creation of a usufruct divides the rights of ownership between two or more persons for a period of limited duration. C.C. 535. The usufructuary generally has the right to the use of the property and to the fruits which it may produce, while the naked owner alone has the right to alienate the property. C.C. 561 directs that the rights of the usufructuary and the naked owner in mines and quarries are governed by the Mineral Code. Upon termination of the usufruct, the rights of the usufructuary and the naked owner are reunited.

As the Civil Code directs use of the Mineral Code only for the respective rights of the usufructuary and the naked owner, and not for the establishment or termination of a usufruct, the question of whether a usufruct has been created and when it will end must be determined under the Civil Code and relevant jurisprudence. However, our application of the Civil Code is clearer after examining the applicable provisions of the Mineral Code, R.S. Title 31.

Much of the difficulty in this case arises from the nature of the underlying asset (the mineral right) and the future payments which it generates (the royalty payments), and whether the two may be considered separately or are so united that they may not be distinguished....

With the exercise of the rights of use and enjoyment by the usufructuary, the minerals subject to the right become depleted, but the right itself is not diminished. The right to share in production remains. The usufruct of a mineral royalty is a usufruct of a nonconsumable though its value is dependent on a consumable resource — a resource which may be completely consumed during the term of the usufruct. But the attributes of ownership of the royalty right have been divided, and the naked owner stands ready to receive full ownership upon termination of the usufruct. The division of attributes of ownership of the royalty right is further clouded by the lack of rights and duties incumbent on a mineral royalty owner. Where there is a usufruct of a mineral royalty, the only readily apparent right is to receive royalty payments if and when production exists, with no corresponding duties.

Since there is so slight a difference between a full owner and a usufructuary of a mineral royalty, whether full ownership has been transferred or only a usufruct has been created is difficult to determine from analyzing the end result of any act of transfer or bequest. The language used in the transfer may be important in determining the intent.

The testator chose the word "payments" when describing the subject of his bequest. He did not choose the words "use" or "use and benefit" which would have clearly shown an intention to confer a usufruct on the named legatees. This is not, however, fatal to the validity of the bequest as a usufruct. What is required is a manifestation of the will of the testator to confer less than full ownership to the legatee. In bequeathing the "payments" rather than the "royalty interest," the testator fully described the benefits that would flow to a usufructuary of a mineral royalty. Since the case was submitted to the trial court on stipulated facts, there was no record developed below which would indicate the existence of any expertise of the decedent in the area of mineral rights. The stipulated facts are silent on the matter, but the death certificate filed into the record indicates the decedent was a retired independent oil operator. C.C. 1713, requiring a court to give a saving construction to a will whenever possible, encourages us to believe the testator understood the difference between a royalty payment and a royalty interest, and deliberately donated the payments and not the interest.

The testator again used the word "payments" when describing his bequest to the nieces, nephews and Linda Cosby Paine, who were to receive the payments, if any, upon the death of Mrs. Parker. Because of the identity of the language used, we find the same intent on the part of the testator, that is, to grant a usufruct of the mineral royalty to this second set of legatees. Successive usufructs are expressly provided for in the Civil Code in Article 546. To hold otherwise strains the clear meaning of the words chosen by the testator. See C.C. 1712.

Finding successive usufructs in this will, where there is no mention by the testator of the disposition of the naked ownership and no residuary legatee, the naked ownership falls intestate. Under these circumstances, this is not an inconceivable result. At oral argument on the rehearing of this case, opponents of the validity of the will's fifth provision suggested that both at the time the will was written and at the time of death of the testator, the payments being received by the testator were around $300 per month and the royalty was not the substantial asset that it later became. It is not unreasonable that the testator did not make a specific bequest of a residual right in a depleting asset that may not have been anticipated to have any value at the death of his last niece or nephew many years later.[1] In any event, the slight prospect that the right would still have been valuable at a distant point in the future is not a sufficient basis for a present construction of the will that would completely ignore the testator's expressed intention to bequeath the payments to the named legatees.

Further, the lack of a termination point of the rights of the second set of legatees is not determinative of the kind of legacy they received under the will. C.C. 609 provides that:

> "A legacy of revenues from specified property is a kind of usufruct and terminates upon death of the legatee unless a shorter period has been expressly stipulated."

This article, read in conjunction with C.C. 547 providing that where there are several usufructuaries the termination of the interest of one usufructuary inures to the benefit of those remaining, fixes the termination of the usufruct granted to the second set of legatees at the death of the last remaining legatee, at which point the usufruct and the naked ownership will be reunited into full ownership, whether or not there is any value remaining in either.

For the foregoing reasons, we hold that the fifth provision of the will of Ronald Bruce Goode creates successive usufructs[2] in favor of Pauline Egbert Parker, and, upon her

---

[1] 'That the testator may have believed that the payments would diminish over time may be inferred from the language of the bequest. With regard to Pauline Parker, the first usufructuary, the language used was: "*All..,* payments owned by me shall be paid..." while the second set of legatees was to divide: "...the amount of *any* payments.. ." (Emphasis added).

[2] The matter of security for the usufruct, though not before the court in this case, was mentioned in preceding dissenting and concurring opinions. Whether the payments bequeathed are considered legacies of revenues under C.C. 609 or as usufructs with the rights and obligations of the usufructuary and naked owner controlled by the provisions of the Mineral Code, there is probably no obligation on the legatees for either security or an accounting. Comment (d) to Article 609 states that the legacies of revenues are only a "kind of usufruct" that does not transfer possession to the legatee but only a personal non-heritable right to receive the revenues. Such a bequest is considered a quasi-usufruct only for the purpose of limiting their duration, and as such these quasi-usufructs are not burdened with the obligations of a usufructuary. However, there appears to be no prohibition to the creation of a usufruct over revenues that would require both security and an accounting. Specifically relating to usufructs involving minerals, C.C. 561 provides that the rights of the usufructuary and of the naked owner are governed by the Mineral Code. Comment (a) makes it clear that the article is intended to apply to both their respective rights and obligations. Within the Mineral Code, R.S. 31:194, amended by 1975 La. Acts No. 589, § 2, expressly provides: "... a usufructuary of a mineral right is not obligated to account to the naked owner of the... mineral right for the production or the value thereof or any other income to which he [usufructuary] is entitled."

death, in favor of the testator's nieces, nephews and Linda Cosby Paine. The naked ownership of the mineral royalty devolves to the intestate heirs.

The judgments of the lower courts are reversed, and the petition to annul the probated testament is dismissed, all at the cost of respondent, James Philip Goode, Sr.

CALOGERO, J., concurs in part, dissents in part and assigns reasons.
DENNIS, J., concurs.
BLANCHE, J., dissents for reasons previously assigned.
WATSON, J., dissents.

c. Partition of the Usufruct and of the Naked Ownership
Civil Code arts. 541-543.

SMITH v. NELSON
121 La. 170, 46 So. 200 (1908)

MONROE, J. The mother of the plaintiffs, being then the widow of Michael Smith, married the defendant, Nelson, and some years later executed a will whereby she bequeathed to her three major children (issue of her marriage to Smith) the property acquired during the first community, and to her surviving husband the property acquired during the second community, and further declared that:

> "Should my children claim the legitime, then I give and bequeath to my said husband the usufruct of all the property, movable and immovable, that was acquired during our marriage," etc.

The testatrix died in 1897, and upon the joint petition of the legatees thus mentioned her will was ordered to be executed, and the petitioners were put in possession — the children in full ownership of the property of the first community and "as owners of an undivided one-half of the property *** belonging to the second community, subject to the usufruct thereof in favor of *** Nelson;" and Nelson "as the lawful surviving husband in community of his deceased wife and as owner of the undivided half of the community of his deceased wife *** and as owner of the individual half of the community property *** and as the usufructuary of the other undivided half thereof." In September, 1906, the present suit was instituted by the two surviving Smith heirs, who allege that the third heir (a brother) is dead, leaving minor children; that the stepfather has remarried, and has thereby "lost the usufruct by operation of law;" that he and they and the minor children of their deceased brother own the property acquired by the second community (consisting of $900 in cash and certain real estate) in common; that they are unwilling to hold the same in indivision and desire a partition; that the stepfather has collected the revenues thereof since April 15, 1897 (the date of the judgment putting him and them in possession).

Wherefore they pray that an inventory and appraisement be made; that a special tutor be appointed, and a family meeting held in behalf of the minors: that the parties be cited, and that there be judgment ordering the sale of the real estate, and against "Nelson for such sum as may be found due for rents and revenues collected by him; and that said parties be referred to Charles A. Butler, notary public, to effect a final partition." The minors, made defendants, practically join the plaintiffs in their demands.

The defendant, Nelson, pleaded the exceptions, "no cause of action," res judicata, estoppel, and prescription, and, reserving his rights with respect thereto, answered, alleging that, should the sale of the property be ordered, he is entitled to the usufruct of the proceeds, or to one-third of said property in full ownership. The judge a quo at first held that plaintiffs were entitled to have the property sold for the purposes of a partition, defendant to enjoy the usufruct of the proceeds; but a new trial was granted, which resulted in a judgment dismissing the suit. Plaintiffs have appealed.

OPINION

In the opinion heretofore handed down it was held that as the usufruct enjoyed by Nelson was established by the will of his deceased wife, and by the judgment ordering its execution and putting him in possession, it is not affected by his remarriage.

The law which confers the right to the partition of a "thing held in common" has no application to those who hold, respectively, the fragments of a dismembered title to the same immovable property, for the reason that in such case, the title being dismembered, each part is a distinct thing, held by a different owner, and there is no "thing held in common." It is clear, therefore, that as between plaintiffs, as owners of an undivided interest in the naked title to the property in question, and defendant, as usufructuary (of such interest), there is no basis for this action. If it be said that plaintiffs and defendants are owners in common, of the naked title, and that, the property being indivisible in kind, plaintiffs have a right to compel the sale of such naked title in order to effect a partition, the answer is that a sale of that kind would have the effect, as to the undivided half interest in the property of which defendant has the perfect ownership, of permanently dismembering his title, so that the naked ownership would become vested in the purchaser whilst the usufruct would remain in the defendant, and he would thereby be deprived of the right to transmit to his heirs the most valuable part of his estate. There is no doubt that, as between those in whom the naked ownership alone is vested, a partition may be enforced in kind, where the property can be divided or by licitation, where it is not susceptible of division in kind, and this, notwithstanding that it may be burdened with a usufruct. And so (Civ. Code, art. 605) [Revised C.C. art. 603]:

> "The owner may mortgage, sell, or alienate the thing subject to the usufruct, without the consent of the usufructuary, but (observe) "he is prohibited from doing it in such circumstances and in such conditions as may be injurious to the enjoyment of the usufructuary."

The rule applicable to the situation here presented is stated by a French writer as follows, to wit:

> "If the universality of the property is burdened with a usufruct, the existence of the usufruct will not prevent the heirs from provoking, between themselves, a partition as concerns the naked property. But they cannot compel the usufructuary to participate in the partition and to consent to a sale of the immovables, acknowledged indivisible, reserving his rights to the proceeds." Aubry & Rau, p. 512.

The suggestion that the entire property, including the usufruct of the whole, may be sold in order to effect the partition demanded by plaintiffs, is obnoxious to the objection thus stated, and need not be further considered. The fact is plaintiffs have not prayed for a sale of the naked ownership, or for a sale of the property subject to the usufruct. They have proceeded upon the theory that the usufruct ceased when defendant entered into a second marriage, and have prayed merely that the property be sold to effect a partition; and, it having been ascertained that the usufruct did not cease, the superstructure of the case falls with the foundation. We may remark, in conclusion, that, it having been conceded that the property here in question is not susceptible of division in kind, we have not felt called upon to express an opinion upon the question whether, if it were divisible in kind, a partition of the naked ownership might not be enforced, and we do not wish to be understood as conveying any intimation to the contrary.

The conclusions stated, of course, dispose of all questions as to plaintiffs' rights with respect to their interest in the money of which defendant has the imperfect usufruct. For the reasons thus given, the judgment appealed from is now affirmed.

2. RIGHTS OF THE USUFRUCTUARY
Civil Code arts. 550-569

GUENO v. MEDLENKA
238 La. 1081, 117 So. 2d 817 (1960)

McCALEB, J. This is a suit for a declaratory judgment. Plaintiffs, Leonie Medlenka Gueno, Albert J. Gueno, Jr. and Donald J. Gueno, and their mineral lessee, Charles B. Wrightsman, seek a declaration that Leon Medlenka, who owns a usufruct on part of their land, has no right or interest in the oil, gas or other minerals thereunder and, therefore, was without authority to grant a mineral lease to the other defendant, Bryant A. Fehlman.***

From the foregoing, it is seen that this case presents for decision the question of the respective interests of a usufructuary and a naked owner in undiscovered oil, gas and other fugacious minerals under the land subject to the usufruct and also as to which one, if either, has the right to lease the property for purpose of exploration for and production of oil, gas and other minerals.

Initially, it must be determined whether the creation of a usufruct on land carries with it a right in the usufructuary to search for and reduce to his possession the oil and gas which may lie under the surface.

The usufruct of land is specifically designated by Article 534 of the Civil Code [no corresponding article after Revision] to be a perfect usufruct. Since minerals such as oil and gas are a part of the land itself (see Federal Land Bank of New Orleans v. Mulhern, 180 La. 627, 157 So. 370, 95 A.L.R. 948), it follows that they cannot be used by a usufructuary of land if such use will alter their substance. However, oil and gas have no use unless their substance is altered and, therefore, it is apparent that the usufructuary of land cannot use any oil or gas which exists under the land, and by a parity of reasoning, he does not have the right to explore for these minerals and withdraw them from the land. The usufructuary of land, having only a perfect usufruct, has only the right to the natural fruits of the land and such civil fruits as are described and treated in Articles 544 through 554 of the Civil Code [Revised C.C. arts. 538, 550-551, 554-556, 559-561, 563-565, 569, 629]. The right to consume the substance of the land is not permitted, save in the exceptional instance hereinafter pointed out.

Article 551 of the Civil Code [Revised C.C. art. 560] declares, in substance, that the usufructuary has the right to draw all the profits which are usually produced by the thing subject to the usufruct; he may cut trees on the land or take from it earth, stones, sand and other material for his own use provided he acts as a prudent administrator and does not abuse the right accorded. However, Article 552 [Revised C.C. art. 561], which the trial judge found applicable to the case, restricts the right of the usufructuary to the enjoyment and proceeds of mines and quarries in the land subject to the usufruct. "*** if they were actually worked before the commencement of the usufruct; but he has no right to mines and quarries not opened".

That exploration for oil and gas is mining within the meaning of our law is no longer an open question. [citations omitted].

Articles 544 and 545 [Revised C.C. arts. 550, 551], depended on by counsel, declare that the natural and civil fruits of the thing subject to the usufruct belong to the usufructuary and also confer upon him ownership of the produce, the rents and revenues of the land. But, here again, there must be excluded, from the fruits and products to which the usufructuary is entitled (see also Article 547 and 551) [Revised C.C. arts. 556, 560], the products derived from mines which are not opened before the commencement of the usufruct, as they are expressly excepted by Article 552 [Revised C.C. art. 561]. This is recognized by the well-respected French Commentator, Planiol, in Vol. 1, No. 2794 of his Traité Elementaire De Droit Civil, as translated by the Louisiana Law Institute, in commenting on Article 598 of the Code Napoléon, which is substantially identical with our Article 552 [Revised C.C. art. 561]. He observes:

"What is extracted from a mine or quarry is not a product of the soil. No earth produces a mineral, sand or limestone. It is the soil itself that is taken out and sold piece by piece. The exploitation of a mine or quarry leads inevitably to its exhaustion. Nevertheless, on account of the abundance of materials, the custom is to look upon what is withdrawn as a product. This is what the Code does. It classifies these products as fruits. It attributes them to usufructuaries because they are income upon which owners live.

"The law however imposes a condition to the granting of this right to usufructuaries. It is the same as the one already mentioned in connection with tall forest trees. The mine or quarry must already have been opened before the commencement of the usufruct. Usufructuaries may therefore continue an exploitation that has already begun. They may not themselves start it when it has not yet been commenced."

Being of the opinion that the usufructuary is without right to the minerals which may be produced from the land subject to the usufruct after it has commenced, the next question to be determined is whether the naked owner has the right to search for the minerals during the existence of the usufruct and to reduce them to his possession.

We think that Article 552 [Revised C.C. art. 561], in withholding from the usufructuary any right to mines and quarries not opened, necessarily recognizes that the naked owner retains, as an incident to his ownership, the right to open a new mine on the land subject to the usufruct and to the products derived from the mining operations. This is indicated by Planiol in No. 2795, Vol. I of the Treatise above referred to.*** Again, in dealing with the obligation of the usufructuary to respect the owner's habits, Planiol states in No. 2819, Vol. I, under the sub-heading "Exploitation of Quarries and Pits," that the usufructuary cannot exploit deposits of materials classified as quarries, pits, or turbaries except when their exploitation had already commenced when his usufruct opened.

Thus, it is seen that the right of the owner to explore for minerals remains unaffected by the fact that the land is burdened with a usufruct, save and except that these rights may not be exercised in a manner detrimental to the usufructuary's right of possession and use. Hence, we approve the ruling of the district judge that the plaintiffs' lease to Wrightsman is valid and enforceable.

The judge, while upholding plaintiffs' mineral lease, declared that their lessee's rights were subordinate to the usufructuary rights of Medlenka, in view of the obligations imposed on the landowners, set forth in Section 4 of Chapter 1 of Title III of the Civil Code, Articles 599 [Revised C.C. art. 557] et seq., and he therefore decreed that the lessee could not enter on the surface of the land subject to the usufruct without first obtaining Medlenka's consent.

In their answer to the appeal plaintiffs complain of this ruling and we believe that there is merit in their contention that the subordination of the exercise by plaintiffs of their rights to the usufructuary's right of possession and enjoyment of the land may well be contrary to our public policy. It is true, of course, that the Civil Code imposes upon the owner the following obligations: to deliver the thing to the usufructuary (Article 599) [Revised C.C. art. 557]; that he must neither interrupt nor in any way impede the usufructuary in the enjoyment of the property or impair his rights (Article 600) [Revised C.C. art. 605]; that, while he may make alterations on the premises, he must not do so in such a way as to worsen the condition of the usufructuary (Article 601) [Revised C.C. arts. 605, 606]; that he may not create any new servitude on the property unless it be done in such a manner as to be of no injury to the usufructuary (Article 603) [Revised C.C. art. 605] and that, although he may sell or alienate the thing without the usufructuary's consent, he is prohibited from doing it in such circumstances as may be injurious to the enjoyment of the usufructuary (Article 605) [Revised C.C. art. 603].

While the usufructuary is entitled to a substantial compliance by the owner with the aforementioned obligations, the owner has certain basic rights which be is also entitled to exercise, these rights being coextensive and concurrent with, not subordinate to, the usufructuary's right of enjoyment and use. One of the rights which the owner retains is the right of exploration for minerals. His quality as owner vests in him the right of entering the premises for certain purposes, i.e., to make alterations thereon (Art. 601) [Revised C.C. arts. 605, 606] and he may even create a new servitude on the land (Art. 602) Revised C.C. art. 604] provided in each case that it be done in such a manner as to be of no injury to the usufructuary. Therefore, in entering the land for mineral exploration purposes, the owner does not become a trespasser and does not require the consent of the usufructuary in order to exercise this right. The usufructuary, not having any right to explore for minerals, is not a necessary party to a mineral lease and neither may he prevent the owner's lessee from entering the property for exploration purposes nor may he object to such explorations as long as this right is exercised in such a way as to not unreasonably interfere with his use of the land.

In this connection, it is to be borne in mind that it is contrary to the public policy of this State to hold property out of commerce and this Court has consistently applied the liberative prescription of ten years in dealing with the exercise of mineral rights. Hence, it would not be reasonable to conclude that the usufructuary's consent was required in order for the owner to conduct mineral operations on the land as long as the operations do not to any substantial extent interfere with the usufructuary's enjoyment of the property— for to so hold would vest in the usufructuary a veto right not accorded by law and permit him to keep the mineral rights out of commerce during the entire life of the usufruct. In case the owner or his lessee does interfere and injures the usufructuary in his rights, "*** he (the owner or his assignees) shall be bound to make good the losses and damages which may result." Article 601, Civil Code [Revised C.C. arts. 605, 606].

Accordingly, the judgment appealed from is amended by deleting therefrom the declaration that the oil, gas and mineral lease granted by plaintiffs to Charles B. Wrightsman is subordinate to the usufructuary rights of deffendant, Leon Medlenka, and does not confer upon the lessee any rights of entry on the surface of the land subject to the usufructuary rights of Leon Medlenka without the consent of said Medlenka. In all other respects, the judgment appealed from is affirmed at defendants' costs.

LOUISIANA MINERAL CODE

Art. 188. Mineral rights not included in usufruct of land except as specifically provided

Except as specially provided in Articles 189 through 191, the usufruct of land does not include the landowner's rights in minerals.

Art. 189. Conventional usufruct may include enjoyment of mineral rights

A conventional usufruct, including one created by a donation inter vivos or mortis causa, may by express provision include the use and enjoyment of all or a specified portion of the landowner's rights in minerals.

Art. 190. Usufructuary of land entitled to enjoyment of mines or quarries worked; exception

A. If a usufruct of land is that of parents during marriage, or any other legal usufruct, or if there is no provision including the use and enjoyment of mineral rights in a conventional usufruct, the usufructuary is entitled to use and enjoyment of the landowner's rights in minerals as to mines or quarries actually worked at the time the usufruct was created.

B. If a usufruct of land is that of a surviving spouse, whether legal or conventional, and there is no contrary provision in the instrument creating the usufruct, the usufructuary is entitled to the use and enjoyment of the landowner's rights in minerals, whether or not mines or quarries were actually worked at the time the usufruct was created. However, the rights to which the usufructuary is thus entitled shall not include the right to execute a mineral lease without the consent of the naked owner.

Art. 191. When oil and gas wells and lignite operations considered open mines

A. As applied to oil and gas, the principle stated in Article 190 means that if at the time a usufruct is created minerals are being produced from the land or other land unitized therewith, or if there is present on the land or other land unitized therewith, a well shown by surface production test to be capable of producing in paying quantities, the usufructuary is entitled to the use and enjoyment of the landowner's rights in minerals as to all pools penetrated by the well or wells in question.

B. As applied to lignite or another form of coal, the principle stated in Article 190 means that if at the time a usufruct is created the land has been included in a mining plan, the usufructuary is entitled to the use and enjoyment of the landowner's rights in minerals as to all seams proposed to be developed in the mining plan provided the following requirements are satisfied:

(1) Lignite or another form of coal has been discovered as the result of acts committed on the land or due to acts providing a reasonable basis of proof of the discovery of the mineral.

(2) A mining plan for the ultimate production of lignite or other forms of coal, together with a permit issued by the responsible government official, is filed in the conveyance records of the parish or parishes in which the land is located.

(3) Actual mining operations have begun on land included in the plan, although such operations need not be conducted on the land subject to the usufruct.

Art. 192. When usufructuary of land entitled to grant lease

If the land subject to the usufruct, or any part thereof is subject to a lease granted by the landowner prior to the creation of the usufruct, the usufructuary is entitled only to royalties on actual or constructive production allocable to him under Article 191. If such a lease terminates, or if the land or any part thereof is not under lease at the time the usufruct is created, the usufructuary's right of use and enjoyment includes the right to execute leases as to any rights to which he is entitled under Article 190 and, accordingly, to retain bonuses, rentals, or other payments, or the proportionate part thereof, allocable to payments, or the proportionate part thereof, allocable to his interest under Article 191. Such a lease executed by the usufructuary may not extend beyond the period of his usufruct.

Art. 193. Nature of usufruct of a mineral right

One who has the usufruct of a mineral right, as distinguished from the usufruct of land, is entitled to all of the benefits of use and enjoyment that would accrue to him if he were the owner of the right. He may, therefore, use the right according to its nature for the duration of his usufruct.

Art. 194. Usufructuary not obligated to account to naked owner

A usufructuary of land benefiting under Article 190 or 191 or a usufructuary of a mineral right is not obligated to account to the naked owner of the land or of the mineral right for production or the value thereof or any other income to which he is entitled.

Art. 195. Right of naked owner of land to enjoyment of minerals

If a usufruct of land does not include mineral rights, the naked owner of the land has all of the rights in minerals that he would have if the land were not subject to the usufruct. The rights may not be exercised in coal or lignite which is to be produced through surface mining techniques without first obtaining the consent of the usufructuary. If the usufructuary is entitled to the benefits provided in Article 190 and 191, the rights of the landowner are subJect thereto.

Art. 196. Obligations of naked owner arising from enjoyment of rights in minerals

In enjoying the right recognized by Article 195, the naked owner is entitled to use only so much of the surface of the land as is reasonably necessary for his operations, but he is responsible to the usufructuary or those holding rights under him for the value of such use and for all damages caused by the naked owner's mining activities or operations. If the activities or operations are conducted by one to whom the naked owner has granted a mineral right, the naked owner and his grantee are liable in solido for damages suffered by the usufructuary or those holding rights under him.

NOTE
Usufruct over Minerals

1. Like royalties, delay rentals and bonuses deriving from a mineral lease are not fruits but products which belong to the naked owner. See *King v. Buffington*, 240 La. 955, 126 So. 2d 326 (1961). See also La. Civil Code art. 488. However, for purposes of community property, royalties, bonuses, delay rentals, and shut-in payments deriving from mineral leases are assimilated to fruits. See La. Civil Code arts. 2339, 2343.

2. Article 192 of the Louisiana Mineral Code accords to the usufructuary the "right to execute leases as to any rights to which he is entitled under Article 190," if a lease granted by the landowner terminates or if the land or any part thereof is not under lease at the time the usufruct is created. This article refers clearly to the first paragraph of Article 190, that is, 190A, which was enacted into law at the same time as Article 192. Question arises, however, whether Article 192 also refers to the second paragraph of Article 190, that is 190B, which was enacted in 1986.

Under Article 190B, if the usufruct of land is that of a surviving spouse, whether legal or conventional, and there is no contrary provision in the instrument creating the usufruct, the usufructuary is entitled to the use and enjoyment of the landowner's rights in minerals, whether or not mines or quarries were actually worked at the time the usufruct was created. However, the rights to which the usufructuary is thus entitled do not include "the right to execute a mineral lease without the consent of the naked owner." Argument may be made that Article 190B, being the latest expression of legislative will, has impliedly repealed the provisions of Article 192 to the extent that they refer to the usufruct of a surviving spouse and that the surviving spouse cannot any longer execute *any* lease without the consent of the naked owner. However, argument may also be made that the surviving spouse, like any other usufructuary, still has the right to execute leases under Article 192 as to mines that were opened at the time of the creation of the usufruct and that the consent of the naked owner is required for leases when mines were not opened at the time of the creation of the usufruct.

KENNEDY v. KENNEDY
699 So. 2d 351 (La. 1997)

On Rehearing

KNOLL, J. We granted rehearing in this case to revisit the issue of a usufructuary's right to harvest timber from a previously unmanaged tract of land. The facts of this case are laid out in detail in the original opinion. Helena Kennedy, the 91 year old usufructuary of a 143 acre tract of mature loblolly pine trees, sought a declaratory judgment authorizing a clear-cut on the tract. James Kennedy, the 70 year old naked owner, opposed the clear-cut.

Ordinarily, the right of the usufructuary extends only to the fruits of the thing subject to the usufruct. La.Civ.Code art. 550. On account of their slow growth and high value, trees are usually considered to be capital assets rather than fruits. In the case of an ordinary tract of land, the usufructuary may cut trees only for his personal use or for the improvement or cultivation of the land. La.Civ.Code art. 560. The revision comments to Articles 551 and 560 suggest that the continuous production of a "tree farm" or "regularly exploited forest" may be regarded as fruits, and thus belong to the usufructuary.

However, we find that the designation of the timber as "fruits" or "products" is irrelevant in the instant case, since the right of a usufructuary to harvest trees from timberland is governed by a specific article, La.Civ.Code art. 562, which states:

> When the usufruct includes timberlands, the usufructuary is bound to manage them as a prudent administrator. The proceeds of timber operations that are derived from proper management of timberlands belong to the usufructuary.

La.Civ.Code art. 13 provides that where two statutes deal with the same subject matter, they should be harmonized if possible. However, if there is a conflict, the statute specifically directed to the matter at issue must prevail as an exception to the statute more general in character. State ex rel. Bickman v. Dees, 367 So. 2d 283, 291 (La. 1978). Article 562 is a new provision, added in the revision of the Civil Code articles on usufruct in 1976. It provides for a different disposition of the proceeds of timber operations on timberland than from cutting trees on ordinary land. Since Article 562 is specifically directed to timberland, it must be treated as an exception to the general rules of usufruct.

Two factual issues are raised under Article 562, namely, whether the tract is "timberland" and what constitutes "proper management" of that particular tract.

Put simply, the central issue in the case sub judice is whether land containing valuable timber which has never been exploited or the subject of forestry management constitutes "timberland" for the purposes of the application of Article 562. Restated, does La.Civ.Code art. 562 require prior timber operations on the property for the land to be construed as "timberland"? As noted by Justice Kimball in her dissent in our original opinion, this exact issue was considered by the drafters of the 1976 revision of the law of usufruct. The original draft of Article 562, prepared by the Louisiana State Law Institute, stated:

> If the usufruct includes lands that *were regularly exploited for timber* at the time of the creation of the usufruct, and if there is no provision concerning the use and enjoyment of the landowner's rights in timber, the usufructuary is entitled to continue the operations of the owner; but he has no right to commence timber operations without the consent of the naked owner. (Emphasis added).

This original version of the article was intended to adapt the "open mines" policy for the usufruct of minerals to the usufruct of timberlands. Nevertheless, upon a motion by Prof. Joseph Dainow, this draft of the article was rejected in favor of the more flexible "prudent management" standard found in Article 562 today. The language requiring regular exploitation or continuing timber operations was removed.

La.Civ.Code art. 11 provides that the words of a law must be given their generally prevailing meaning, and that words of art and technical terms must be given their technical meaning when a law involves a technical matter. "Timber" is defined by La.Civ.Code art. 562, Comment (c) as trees which, if cut, would produce Lumber for building or manufacturing purposes. The term "timberland" is defined in Webster's Third New International Dictionary as "land covered with forest and especially with marketable timber."

The expert witnesses also supplied definitions of "timberland" as applicable to forestry operations. Mr. Lewis Peters, Mrs. Kennedy's forestry expert, defined "timberland" as "land that's capable of producing commercial forest products," while Mrs. Kennedy's other expert, Mr. Richard Freshwater defined "timberland" as "land with or without timber capable of growing timber in commercial quantities." Mr. Gary Wade agreed that "timberland" is "any land that has some type of timber growth on it, be it merchantable or not merchantable."

"Timberland" is distinguishable from land which has been regularly managed and exploited for timber, which is best defined by the term "tree farm." The defining characteristic of a "tree farm" as stated by this court is "the land's ability, through proper management techniques such as selective thinnings and plantings, to provide sustained yields." Succession of Doll v. Doll, 593 So. 2d 1239, 1249 (La. 1992). Mr. Peters noted that the term "tree farm" was "sort of like a trademark" and that "it's a designation that's given to landowners that apply and meet the requirements of the American Forestry Association whose ... under whose umbrella the tree farm system was created." The 143 acre tract is not a "tree farm," as it has never been managed, and is unable to produce a sustained yield of timber in its present state.

Under both the general definition and under the technical definition supplied by the foresters, the 143 acre tract is "timberland." For this tract not to be classified as "timberland," this court would have to create an alternative legal definition or term of art, requiring that the tract be regularly managed or exploited for timber prior to the initiation of the usufruct, making "timberland" synonymous with "tree farm." We decline to do so, especially since this would substantively reenact the original version of La.Civ.Code art. 562, which had been rejected by the Louisiana State Law Institute.

The second issue before us is whether Mrs. Kennedy's plan to clearcut the tract constitutes proper management or prudent administration of the tract. This is clearly an issue to be decided by the trier of fact. After a two day trial in which each party called two forestry expert witnesses, the trial court adopted the expert opinion of Mrs. Kennedy's forester, Mr. Lewis C. Peters, on the proper management of the tract.

Mr. Peters noted that the tract consisted of an even aged stand of mature and over mature loblolly pine, whose age was between sixty and seventy-five years. He testified that the life span of loblolly pine trees was between eighty and one hundred years. Mr. Peters stated that thirty acres in the southwest corner of the tract contained trees younger than those found on the remainder of the tract. Mr. Peters noted that undesirable hardwood species were beginning to succeed the pines on the tract, and he opined that because the tract had not been previously managed it would be difficult to rehabilitate. Mr. Peters testified that the most prudent approach would be to harvest the merchantable timber on the majority of the tract, including the hardwoods, and replant the site with genetically superior seedlings. He stated that it would not be prudent to simply cut the larger pines since the smaller trees were the same age. He opined that the smaller trees were so old and suppressed that they would not respond to the removal of the larger trees. Mr. Peters outlined the risks associated with allowing the older pine trees to remain on the tract, noting that the trees were rapidly approaching the end of their life span, that they were vulnerable to insect attack, and that they could attract endangered species, thus preventing their harvest. Mr. Peters recommended that some hardwoods be left along watersheds and streams to prevent erosion and encourage wildlife. With respect to the thirty acre portion of the tract containing the younger trees, Mr. Peters recommended a selective cut of only the larger trees.

Obviously, what constitutes "proper management" of timberland will vary depending on the species, condition, size, location, age, and density of the timber on the tract. The trial court was presented with several expert opinions on the prudent administration of this particular tract, and was well informed about the several available alternatives. The trial court's acceptance of Mr. Peters' recommendations as the most prudent course of management of the property was reasonable, and we find no manifest error in its decision to accept Mr. Peters' expert opinion.

It is apparent from the findings of the trial court that prior to the initiation of the usufruct, the 143 acre tract had not been properly managed to provide sustained yields, and that selective thinnings and plantings on the tract would do little to rehabilitate the tract. Because the tract had been neglected for so long from a forestry standpoint, leaving some of the trees standing placed the entire stand of timber at risk of infection, infestation, destruction by the elements, and succession by less desirable species. These risks greatly outweighed any benefits that could accrue by leaving the smaller trees. The trial court reasonably concluded that the most prudent management of the tract called for a clear-cut of the majority of the tract, followed by replanting with genetically improved seedlings.

Had this tract been a properly managed "tree farm" prior to the initiation of Mrs. Kennedy's usufruct, it is unlikely that her plan to clear-cut the tract would be considered prudent. However, we recognize that under certain circumstances, such as those found in the present case, a clear-cut may be warranted. The prudent administrator/proper management standard is a flexible one, and we are unwilling to hold that as a matter of law clear-cutting will never constitute the proper management of timberland.

Accordingly, under Article 562, Mrs. Kennedy is entitled to the proceeds of the prudent management plan proposed by her foresters and approved by the trial court. The judgment of the court of appeal, limiting Mrs. Kennedy's timber activities to a selective cutting from the thirty acre stand of younger trees is reversed, and the judgment of the trial court is reinstated.

JOHNSON, J. (dissenting). I respectfully dissent. La.C.C. Art. 560 provides: The usufructuary may cut trees growing on the land of which he has the usufruct and take stones, sand and other materials from it, but only for his use or for the improvement or cultivation of the land.

This case presents an area of land that has not been improved or cultivated in many years. As a result, many of the trees have reached their prime and others are near maturity. It is evident that some type of maintenance is needed to preserve this land for both the naked owner and the usufructuary. When the parties cannot agree as to the management plan, the courts must approve a plan. In this case, the majority approved a clear cut plan.

The experts have testified that selective cutting of the timberlands is far more prudent. This land is capable of producing commercial timber if properly maintained. The ecological aspects warrant a selective cutting and not a clear cut of the land. To follow the majority's plan would mean that the fruits of the land are being dissipated. La.C.C. Art. 562 provides:

> "When the usufruct includes timberlands, the usufructuary is bound to manage them as a prudent administrator. The proceeds of timber operations that are derived from proper management of timberlands belong to the usufructuary. The statute is clear that "timber operations should not deplete the substance of the land. The interests of the naked owner are protected by the prohibition of waste and by the obligations of the usufructuary to act as a prudent administrator and to preserve the substance of the property subject to the usufruct." See comments La.C.C.P. Art. 562.

A clear cut of the land will affect the substance of the property and therefore, deny the naked owner the protection that the statutes in this regard afford him. Clearly, prudent management of the land requires that it be selectively cut in order to preserve the substance of the land.

NOTE
Usufructuary's Right to Fruits

One of the rights given to the usufructuary is the right to all fruits[1] produced by or derived from the things that are subject to the usufruct. La. Civil Code art. 550. The usufructuary's right to fruits commences on the effective date of the usufruct, La. Civil Code art 554, and ends when the usufruct terminates, La. Civil Code art 628. For this reason, it is important to determine whether any given fruit of the thing that will be, still is, or once was subject to a usufruct is produced by or derived from that thing during the existence of the usufruct. If it is produced or derived during this period, the usufructuary gets ownership of that fruit and need not account for it at termination of the usufruct to the naked owner. Until the fruit is produced by or derived from that other thing ("the base thing"), the so-called fruit is not a distinct thing but merely part of the base thing that is producing it or from which it will be derived. The point in time at which the fruit becomes a thing distinct from the base thing is sometimes called accrual. The rules for accrual of fruits depend upon whether the fruit is a natural fruit or a civil fruit.

"Art. 555. Nonapportionment of natural fruits

"The usufructuary acquires the ownership of natural fruits severed during the existence of the usufruct. Natural fruits not severed at the end of the usufruct belong to the naked owner.

"Art. 556. Apportionment of civil fruits

"The usufructuary acquires the ownership of civil fruits accruing during the existence of the usufruct.

"Civil fruits accrue day by day and the usufructuary is entitled to them regardless of when they are received."

NATURAL FRUITS HYPOTHETICAL

Assume that the creator of the usufruct owns an apple orchard. One day before the usufruct commences, the ripe apples are picked and placed in crates. The crated apples are sold for $1,000 on the day after commencement of the usufruct. During the existence of the usufruct, the usufructuary picks, crates and sells the apples for $10,000. At termination of the usufruct, the trees are full of ripe apples. The day after the usufruct terminates, these apples are picked, crated, and sold for $500. What are the rights of the usufructuary under these facts?

---

[1] A fruit is defined as a thing that is "produced by or derived from another thing without diminution of its substance." La. Civil Code art. 551.

The usufructuary gets ownership of all fruits that accrue during the usufruct. Natural fruits accrue when they are severed. Thus, the usufructuary gets to keep the $10,000 for those apples picked during the usufruct, and need not account to the naked owner at termination. The apples that are still on the trees at termination are still part of the tree and have not accrued. Thus, the usufructuary has no right to the $500 received in the sale of these apples. The fruits that were picked and crated before commencement of the usufruct are not fruits accruing during the usufruct, so the usufructuary cannot claim them as fruits. Since these fruits accrued before commencement of the usufruct, they are distinct from the trees, and the usufruct over the apple orchard does not give the usufructuary any right to them or the $1,000 received for them.[2]

CIVIL FRUITS HYPOTHETICAL

Assume that Mom and Dad own a condominium in Jefferson Parish, and that it is community property. They enter into a lease with a tenant for a five year term, commencing January 1, 1985. The tenant is to pay annual rental of $9,600 on the last day of the year. Dad dies on March 31, 1986 and Mom dies on September 30, 1989. Assuming that Mom has a legal usufruct over all community property, and that the tenant pays rental as per the contract, what are the rights and responsibilities of Mom's estate to the naked owners (who of course will be Dad's descendants)?

First of all, one-half of all rentals are owned by Mom by virtue of her community property interest in the condo. La. Civil Code arts. 797 and 2369.2. Insofar as Dad's one-half interest in the condo is concerned she has a usufruct over it. As usufructuary, she gets ownership of all fruits that accrue during the usufruct, and civil fruits accrue day by day, regardless of when the money is actually received. Therefore, Mom, as usufructuary, is entitled to only part of the rentals for 1986, viz., those amounts attributable to April through December. Mom is entitled to all of the rentals for 1987 and 1988, and she is entitled to only part of the rentals for 1989, viz., those amounts attributable to January through September. As to the 1986 rentals attributable to January through March (when Dad was alive), these fruits accrued before commencement of the usufruct, and thus became a thing distinct from the condo. Nonetheless, these revenues are community property, La. Civil Code art. 2338, and thus Mom has a usufruct over them. Since money is a consumable, Mom owns this money but must account to the naked owners at the end of the usufruct. As to the 1989 rentals attributable to October through December (after Mom died), these fruits accrued after termination of the usufruct and thus go to the naked owners. Plugging numbers into the answer, we first segregate out Mom's one-half interest that she receives under community property law. $9,600 breaks down to $800 a month, so only $400 a month represents Dad's one-half interest (which is owned by the naked owners and is subject to the legal usufruct in favor of Mom).

---

[2] Note, however, that if the usufruct had been conferred over *all* property owned by the creator of the usufruct, then the usufructuary's usufruct would have extended over the apples as well as the orchard. Since apples are consumbles, the usufructuary would have owned the crated apples but would have had to account to the naked owner at termination of the usufruct, either by paying $1,000 to the naked owner (which presumably is the value of the apples at commencement of the usufruct) or by replacing them with apples of the same quantity and quality. La. Civil Code art 538.

YEAR	MONTHS	AMOUNT	TREATMENT
1986	Jan. - March	$1,200	consumable - Mom has usufruct of it and must account for it
	April – Dec.	$3,600	fruit - Mom owns; need not account it
1987	all 12	$4,800	fruit - Mom owns; need not account for it
1988	all 12	$4,800	fruit - Mom owns; need not account for it
1989	Jan. - Sept.	$3,600	fruit - Mom owns; need not account for it
	Oct. - Dec.	$1,200	belongs outright to dad's descendants

Recapping, Mom must account for $1,200. She received a total of $13,000 in fruits during the usufruct which she owns and need not account for. When the rental is paid on December 31, 1989, the naked owners must pay to Mom's estate $3,600 as rentals accruing during the usufruct to which Mom is entitled.

3. LEGAL POWERS OF THE USUFRUCTUARY
Civil Code arts. 539, 550, 566, 567, 2716
Cf. Civil Code arts. 588 through 568.3

NOTE
Introduction to *Sparks*

The following case explores the legal powers of a usufructuary over a nonconsumable as to which he has not been expressly granted the right of disposition. La. Civ. Code art. 539, 567, and 568. This case does not apply to a usufructuary's disposition of a nonconsumable pursuant to an express grant of disposition. See generally La. Civ. Code arts. 568-568.3. A lease granted by a usufructuary with the express power of disposition is governed by article 568.2.

SPARKS v. DAN COHEN CO.
187 La. 830, 175 So. 590 (1937)

O'NIELL, C.J. This is a suit to have a contract of lease adjudged terminated by the death of the lessor, who had only the *life* usufruct of the property. The plaintiffs are the owners of the property. They are the six sons and daughters and a grandson, the latter representing a deceased son, of R.J. Nelson, deceased. The plaintiffs acquired title to the leased property, which is a store building in the city of Monroe, as a legacy from their uncle, James L. Nelson. He died in 1908, and in his will he bequeathed his estate to the seven children of his deceased brother, R.J. Nelson, and bequeathed the usufruct of the estate to his widow, Mrs. Martha Nelson. She leased the store to the Dan Cohen Co., Inc., defendant in this suit, on February 1, 1934, for the term of five years, at the rental of $200 per month, with the privilege of renewal for an additional term of five years at $300 per month, at the option of the lessee. Mrs. Nelson was then 92 years of age. She died on the

23rd of April, 1936. Four days after her death, the parties who are the plaintiffs in this suit, as owners of the property, served a written notice on the Dan Cohen Company, as lessee, that the lease was terminated by the death of Mrs. Nelson, who had only a life usufruct of the property. The Dan Cohen Company, after considerable correspondence and discussion, denied that the lease was terminated by the death of the lessor, and insisted that the lease should continue to the end of the term stipulated. Thereafter, the parties who are the plaintiffs in this suit, and who were collateral heirs of Mrs. Martha Nelson, inheriting one-eighths of her estate, joined in a petition with the other collateral heirs of Mrs. Nelson, inheriting seven-eighths of her estate, to be recognized as her heirs at law, and to be sent into possession of her estate unconditionally and without the benefit of inventory. An ex parte judgment was rendered accordingly. Thereafter, the parties who are the plaintiffs in this suit, as owners of the leased premises, served a formal demand on the Dan Cohen Company to vacate the leased premises; and, upon the company's refusal to vacate, the owners brought this suit.

The defendant, before answering the petition, filed a plea, termed a plea of estoppel and of no cause or right of action, to the effect that the plaintiffs, by accepting their share of the succession of Mrs. Martha Nelson, unconditionally and without the benefit of inventory, assumed all of her obligations, and particularly the obligation of warranty, to defend the lessee's possession of the leased premises for the full term of the lease. In that connection, the defendant averred that the contract of lease, on the part of Mrs. Nelson, was an unqualified or unconditional contract of lease for the term stipulated. The averment had reference to the fact that Mrs. Nelson was not referred to in the lease as the usufructuary of the property, and did not sign the lease as usufructuary, but was referred to in the lease merely as "hereinafter called lessor," and signed her name without any designation, either as owner or usufructuary of the property. Hence the defendant pleaded that the plaintiffs were estopped by their unconditional acceptance of the succession of the lessor, and had no right of action to contest the lease. The plea was overruled. The plaintiffs then filed a supplemental petition, averring that the Dan Cohen Company, and its members and authorized representatives who acted for the company in negotiating for the lease, were informed by the parties representing Mrs. Nelson, that she did not own the property but had only an usufruct, which would terminate at her death. In their supplemental petition, the plaintiffs set forth all of the letters that had passed between them and the Dan Cohen Company, between the date of the death of Mrs. Nelson and the time when they and the other collateral heirs of Mrs. Nelson accepted her succession. The purpose of disclosing this correspondence was to show that, before the owners of the property, and the lessee, had come to such an impass in their attempt to settle the controversy, that [sic] a lawsuit was inevitable.

After the supplemental petition was filed, the defendant answered the suit, and admitted all of the material allegations of fact, except the allegation that the defendant was informed or knew, before or at the time of entering into the contract of lease, that Mrs. Nelson was only the usufructuary, or that she was not the owner, of the property. On the contrary, the defendant averred that none of the members or representatives of the company was informed or knew, previous to the death of Mrs. Nelson, that she was only the usufructuary, or was not the owner, of the leased premises. The defendant reiterated the plea that the plaintiffs, by accepting unconditionally their interest in the succession of Mrs. Nelson, assumed all of her obligations, and particularly the obligation to warrant and defend the lessee's possession of the leased premises to the end of the term stipulated in the lease.

After hearing the case on its merits the judge decided in favor of the plaintiffs, declaring the lease terminated by the death of the lessor, and allowing the plaintiffs $300 per month rent thereafter, and ordering the defendant to deliver possession of the leased premises to the plaintiffs. The defendant has appealed from the decision. The plaintiffs, answering the appeal, pray for an increase of the allowance of rental to $350 per month, as prayed for in their petition.

The defense of this suit is based entirely upon the doctrine that, if an heir accepts unconditionally, and without the benefit of inventory, the succession of the person from whom the heir has inherited, he thereby makes himself liable for all of the obligations of the deceased, including his obligations of warranty, and is therefore debarred from suing to recover from a third person property which the deceased sold under a warranty deed. The doctrine is recognized in the following cases, cited by counsel for the defendant, viz: Stokes v. Shackleford, 12 La. 170; Smith v. Elliot, 9 Rob. 3; Cochran v. Gulf Refining Co., 139 La. 1010, 72 So. 91 So. 837. In all of these cases, except Cochran v. Gulf Refining Co., which will be explained hereafter, the obligation was a warranty of title in an act of sale. Such a warranty obligation, of course, is not extinguished by the death of the warrantor, but survives as an obligation of his succession. But the obligation of a lessor, to warrant and defend the lessee's right of possession of the leased premises, survives as an obligation of the succession of the lessor, in the event of his death before the expiration of the term of the lease, only in cases where the lessor claimed ownership of the leased premises. Article 2730 [Revised C.C. art. 2716] of the Civil Code declares that a lease made by one having only the usufruct of the property ends when the right of usufruct ceases, and that the lessee has no claim against the heirs of the deceased usufructuary, for indemnification, if the usufructuary made known to the lessee that he, the lessor, had only the usufruct — and not the ownership of the property. In Cochran v. Gulf Refining Co., the lease was not an ordinary lease, for the occupancy of the house or tract of land, but was an oil and gas lease. The widow of the lessor, or "grantor," as he was called, owning a half interest in the land and having the usufruct of the other half interest, granted extensions of the time in which the lessee should begin drilling wells. She died before the last extention of the lease expired; and her four daughters accepted her succession unconditionally and partitioned the leased property in kind, and permitted the lessee to drill three wells on the land within the extended term of the lease. Thereafter, two of the daughters, one of whom had sold a part of the land that was allotted to her in the partition, sued to annul the lease in so far as it affected their lands; and it was held that, by accepting the succession of their mother unconditionally, they had assumed her obligation to warrant and defend the possession of the lessee. In the decision in that case the court regarded the oil and gas lease more as a sale of a real right than as an ordinary lease for the occupancy of a house or land. It had been said, in Rives v. Gulf Refining Co., 133 La. 178, 62 So. 623, 624, referring to oil and gas leases. "There is scarcely any comparison between them and the ordinary farm or house lease."

***The law that governs this case is in Articles 555, 606, and 2730 of the Civil Code [Revised C.C. arts. 567, 607, 2716], *viz*:

"555 [Revised C.C. art. 567]. The usufructuary may enjoy by himself or lease to another, or even sell or give away his right; but all the contracts or agreements which he makes in this respect, whatever duration he may have intended to give them, cease of right at the expiration of the usufruct."

"606 [Revised C.C. art. 607]. The right of the usufruct expires at the death of the usufructuary."

"2730 [Revised C.C. art. 2716]. A lease made by one having a right of usufruct, ends when the right of usufruct ceases.

"The lessee has no right to an indemnification from the heirs of the lessor, if the lessor has made known to him the title under which he possessed."

A lease made by an usufructuary, therefore, "ceases of right at the expiration of the usufruct," whether the lessor informed the lessee, or failed to inform him, before or at the time of making the lease, that he, the lessor, was only the usufructuary, and not the owner, of the property. It is the right of the lessee to be indemnified by the heirs of the lessor, if the lessor is only the usufructuary and if he dies before the expiration of the term of the lease, that depends upon whether the lessor failed to make known to the lessee that he the lessor, was not the owner but only the usufructuary of the property. That is the precise language and meaning of Article 2730 of the Civil Code. An usufructuary cannot, by failing to disclose to a lessee that he, the lessor, is, not the owner but only the usufructuary of the property, deprive the owner of his right under the law which says that such a lease "ceases of right at the expiration of the usufruct." The second paragraph of Article 2730 [Revised C.C. art. 2716] is intended to protect one who leases property from an usufructuary under the belief on the part of the lessee that the lessor is the owner of the property. The reason for that is given in Article 2682 of the Civil Code, thus: "He who lets out the property of another, warrants the enjoyment of it against the claim of the owner."

The judge who tried this case says in the written reasons for his decree that the evidence convinced him that the members and representatives of the Dan Cohen Company were informed when they were negotiating for the lease that Mrs. Nelson was not the owner but only the usufructuary of the property. On behalf of Mrs. Nelson, the negotiations were carried on by a son-in-law of one of the plaintiffs in this suit, the son-in-law being the president of a national bank in Monroe; and by the husband of one of the plaintiffs, the husband being in charge of the making of leases for Mrs. Martha Nelson; and by a son of one of the plaintiffs, the son being a practicing attorney at law in Monroe. All of these representatives of Mrs. Nelson testified that the parties representing the Dan Cohen Company in the negotiations were informed that Mrs. Nelson was not the owner but had only the life usufruct of the property. The negotiations on the part of the Dan Cohen Company were carried on by the president and another executive of the company, and by a prominent real estate agent, doing business in New Orleans, who was employed as broker by the Dan Cohen Company to negotiate for the lease. The broker went to Monroe and opened the negotiations with the bank president, representing Mrs. Nelson, more than three months before the lease was signed. The president of the Dan Cohen Company came from Cincinnati to Monroe to lend his aid to the negotiations; and the other executive of the company, whose duties included the obtaining of leases for the company, came to Monroe two or three times during the negotiations. The Company testified that they were not informed at any time before the death of Mrs. Nelson that she was not the owner of the property but only the usufructuary. It is not casting any reflection upon this testimony to say that the testimony for the plaintiffs is corroborated by the strong presumption that they and Mrs. Nelson would not have withheld from the lessee such important information. The testimony for the plaintiffs on this subject is corroborated also by the fact that the public records in the conveyance office in Monroe disclosed that Mrs. Martha Nelson had not the ownership, but only the life usufruct of the property of which the Dan Cohen Company was negotiating to obtain a lease.***The judgment is affirmed.

ON APPLICATION FOR REHEARING

PER CURIAM. In the petition for a rehearing, the defendant, appellant, directs our attention to an inaccurate — if not erroneous — statement of the law in the opinion rendered in this case. The statement which was intended to be made was that, although the obligation of warranty in an act of sale is not extinguished by the death of the warrantor, but survives as an obligation of his succession, the obligation of a lessor, to warrant and defend the lessee's right of possession of the leased premises, survives as an obligation of the succession of the lessor, in the event of his death before the expiration of the term of the lease, only in cases where the lessor claimed or pretended to be the owner of the leased premises — not in cases where the lessor claimed to be — as was in fact — only the usufructuary of the leased premises. Instead of saying "only in cases where the lessor claimed ownership of the leased premises," we said "only in cases where the lessor owns the leased premises." Although what followed after that expression explained it thoroughly, we have substituted for the word "owns" the words "claimed ownership of" — which makes the statement of the law more exact — without affecting the purport of the opinion originally rendered. The petition for a rehearing is denied.

4. OBLIGATIONS OF THE USUFRUCTUARY
Civil Code arts. 570-602

a. Inventory and Security:
Civil Code arts. 570-575

SUCCESSION OF WATSON
517 So.2d 276 (La. App. 1st Cir. 1987)

CHIASSON, J. This is an appeal from a judgment of the trial court ordering the executor to post security in the amount of $30,000.00 within ten (10) days from service of the order.

The appellant, John Milton Watson, is the testamentary executor of the Succession of Frances Doyle Watson. The decedent left an olographic will in which she bequeathed the forced portion of her estate to her daughter, Sylvia Watson; her son, John Earl Watson; and her granddaughter, Laurie Watson. Sylvia and John Earl Watson are children of decedent's marriage to John Milton Watson, her surviving spouse, testamentary executor and appellant herein. Laurie Watson is the only child of Sidney Watson, a predeceased son by appellant. The decedent left the disposable portion of her estate to appellant and gave him a usufruct for life over the forced portion. She also named appellant as executor of her estate and relieved him of the obligation of furnishing security.

The decedent's will was admitted to probate. Subsequently, Sylvia and Laurie Watson filed a petition seeking to compel appellant, as the executor of the estate, to furnish security. After hearing, the trial court rendered judgment ordering appellant to post security in the amount of $30,000.00. Appellant has perfected this appeal.

The primary question is whether appellant can be compelled to furnish security even though in her will the decedent dispensed with the requirement that be furnish security. The olographic will provided as follows: "I hereby name, appoint and constitute my husband, John Milton Watson, executor of this will, with seizin on my estate from the moment of my death, and dispense him from furnishing security."

The trial court held that La.C.C.P. art. 3154 is mandatory in nature, requiring only a finding that the applicant for security is a forced heir; thereafter the discretion afforded the trial court is in determining the amount of security. Appellees/petitioners in this case are the daughter and granddaughter of the decedent. Appellee Laurie A. Watson's father predeceased his mother, the decedent, and therefore represents her father in the succession under La.C.C. art. 822. Appellees are forced heirs under the provisions of La.C.C. arts. 1493 and 1495.

We agree with the trial court. Although decedent dispensed with the requirement that the executor of her estate furnish security, La.C.C.P. arts. 3163-3154 are applicable.

Article 3153 of the Code of Civil Procedure provides that a person named by the testator as executor is not required to furnish security except when required by the testament or as provided in Articles 3154 through 3155. La.C.C.P. art. 3154 provides that:

> Forced heirs and the surviving spouse in community of the testator may compel the executor to furnish security by an ex parte verified petition therefor. If the court finds that the petitioner is a forced heir, or the surviving spouse in community, it shall order the executor to furnish security, within ten days of the service of the order, in an amount determined by the court as adequate to protect the interest of the petitioner.

The trial court correctly found that the petitioners in this matter are forced heirs and are therefore entitled to compel the executor to furnish security. It is immaterial to the case *sub judice* that the executor is also the surviving spouse in community and thus a usufructuary. Art. 3154 provides authority for the forced heirs to compel the surviving spouse acting in the position of *executor* to furnish security even though the forced heirs (as issue of the marriage between surviving spouse and decedent) may not be able to compel the surviving spouse in the position of usufructuary to provide security. See La.C.C.P. art. 3154.1. The right of the forced heirs to compel the executor to furnish security is not abrogated simply by virtue of the executor also being a usufructuary who may not be required to do so.

Decree

For the above and foregoing reasons the judgment of the trial court is affirmed. Costs are to be paid by appellant.

b. Repairs, Preservation Efforts, and Charges:
Civil Code arts. 577-585

SUCCESSION OF CRAIN
450 So. 2d 1374 (La. App. 1st Cir. 1984)

PONDER, J. Appellant, a residuary legatee and former provisional administratrix, appealed the judgments holding the succession liable for one-half of the cost of repair and maintenance of the family home and for all the estate tax penalties and interest amounts.

The issues are: (1) whether the succession or the usufructuary should bear the costs of repair and maintenance of the family home and (2) whether the testamentary executrix should be held personally liable for penalties and interest assessed against the succession because of late payment of the federal estate tax.

We affirm in part and reverse and render in part.

Eros Crosby Crain died on August 13, 1977. He was survived by his spouse, Sharon Haas Crain, the appellee, and two daughters by a prior marriage, Patricia Crain McDonald and Rebecca Crain Christ, the latter the appellant. Decedent's will confirmed the legal usufruct in favor of appellee and also named her as Testamentary Executrix. The two daughters were named as residuary legatees.

Appellee resigned from her position as Executrix and appellant was appointed as Provisional Administratrix. Appellee was later reinstated as Executrix. During the time that appellant was the administratrix, appellee filed a motion for payment of repairs to widow's home and for payment of widow's expenses in preserving property. Accountings prepared by appellant charged all expenses relating to the family home and the penalties and interest due to the late payment of taxes to appellee, individually. Appellee opposed the accountings.

The trial court rendered judgment in favor of appellee ordering the succession to bear one-half of the approved costs of repair work. The court also ordered the succession to reimburse appellee for one-half of the total mortgage payments, or $3149.73 and one-half of the expense for yard upkeep, the security system, homeowner's association, Terminex expenses, and plumbing expenses, or $866.97.

Appellant argues that all of the expenses related to the family home should be charged to appellee, individually; since appellee has enjoyed exclusively, and without disturbance, the usufruct over one-half of the family home, she should bear the costs associated with the usufruct. La. C.C. arts. 577, 578, 579, 588. Alternatively, appellant argues that appellee should pay rent to the succession.

As argument, appellee adopts a statement made by the trial judge in his "Reasons for Judgment":

> "Since this succession is under administration, the Testamentary Executrix is in possession of...(the) deceased's undivided one-half interest in this community home.... C.C.P. art. 3221... Therefore, one-half of any repair or maintenance which needs to be done to this community residence must be borne by the succession. C.C.P. art. 3221."

La. C.C.P. art. 3221 provides that "A succession representative shall preserve, repair, maintain, and protect the property of the succession."

La. C.C. arts. 1626 and 1628 provide that a testamentary executor who has seizin of the effects of the succession and who is at the same time a legatee, is not bound to demand the delivery of his legacy. He is deemed to be in possession. Succession of Villere, 411 So. 2d 484 (La. App. 4th Cir. 1982). Therefore, appellee is in possession of the property as a usufructuary, as well as an executrix. As a usufructuary, appellee is "answerable for all expenses that became necessary for the preservation and use of the property after the commencement of the usufruct." La. C.C. art. 581. Furthermore, "the usufructuary is responsible for ordinary maintenance and repairs for keeping the property subject to the usufruct in good order...."

Since appellee is a usufructuary and, as such, is entitled to the fruits of the property, she must assume those liabilities resulting from the usufruct. Therefore, we find appellee responsible for the costs of the "ordinary repair" items. We further classify the following items as "ordinary repairs."

Paint interior and exterior of house;
Repair leak spots;
Remove all glass mould in kitchen, den and bedroom and reseal water leaks;
Replace one frame of glass (solar equal film);
Erect iron post around electrical substation;
Remove small tree;
Repairs to air conditioning system.

The naked owner is generally only responsible for extraordinary repairs. La. C.C. art. 577. However, the usufructuary does not have the right to compel the naked owner to make the extraordinary repairs. His only remedy is reimbursement by the naked owner at the end of the usufruct. La. C.C. art. 579. We classify the following items as "extraordinary repairs":

Repairs to dock;
Repairs to boat slip;
Repairs to roof.

We find that La. C.C.P. art. 3221 does not apply when there is a usufructuary in possession. Therefore, appellee does not have authority to institute these repairs in her capacity as Testamentary Executrix. Furthermore, since the usufructuary cannot compel the naked owner to make the repairs, appellee's only remedy is to seek reimbursement at the end of the usufruct, if she chooses to make the repairs. C.C.P. art. 579.

For the same reasons stated above in reference to the repair costs, we find appellee responsible for the expenditures for maintenance of the family home, as outlined in the trial court's "Judgment on Rule Seeking Repair and Preservation Expense on Widow's Home."

Since we have found that appellee is in possession of the family home as a usufructuary, there is no need to discuss appellant's alternative argument that appellee owes rent to the succession.

The next issue raised by appellant is whether appellee should be held personally liable for penalties and interest assessed-against the succession because of late payment of the federal estate tax. The trial court held that appellee, as executrix, was not at fault in the handling of these taxes and therefore, the penalties and interest could not be taken from her share of the estate.

The trial court very meticulously reviewed the activities of Mrs. Crain in regard to the federal taxes and the penalties and interest thereon. We have carefully reviewed the record and agree with his conclusion that Mrs. Crain personally should not be assessed with the penalties and interest.

For these reasons, the judgment holding the succession liable for one-half of the cost of repair and maintenance of the family home is reversed and the appellee is declared responsible for these expenses. The judgment holding the succession responsible for the estate tax penalties and interest is affirmed. The costs of these appeals are to be shared equally.

NOTE

As *Walker v. Holt*, 888 So. 2d 255 (La. App. 3d Cir. 2004) revealed, the rule of CC art. 577 – that the usufructuary is responsible for "ordinary repairs" while the naked owner is responsible for "extraordinary repairs" – may have implications for third persons, that is, persons other than the usufructuary and the naked owner. Walker sustained person injuries when he stepped in a hole in the yard of a residential lot of which Holt and his siblings were the naked owners and of which Smith, father of the naked owners, was the legal usufructuary. Walker then sued the naked owners and the usufructuary to recover damages for those injuries. In response, the naked owners filed a motion for summary judgment, contending that, as mere naked owners of the lot, they could not possibly be responsible for damages caused by such conditions in the yard as "holes". The court of appeal, like the trial court before it, agreed. The court's rationale, in sum, was as follows. Liability to a third person for damages caused by a defect in a thing that is subject to a usufruct depends, at least in part, on who, as between the usufructuary and the naked owner, is responsible for remedying that particular defect. As to responsibility for repairs, that for "extraordinary repairs," defined as "those the reconstruction of the whole or a substantial part of the property," falls on the naked owner, whereas that for "ordinary repairs," defined as everything else, falls on the usufructuary. CC arts. 577 & 578. Here, because the "repair" in question – filing a hole in a yard – was an ordinary, not an extraordinary, repair, the usufructuary, not the naked owners, was responsible for making that repair. It follows that the usufructuary, to the exclusion of the naked owners, was solely liable for third-person damages caused by the defect that resulted from this default.

c. Payment of Debts:
Civil Code arts. 586-593

SUCCESSION OF DAVIS
536 So. 2d 495 (La. App. 1st Cir. 1988)

WATKINS, J. This is a succession proceeding wherein the forced heirs filed an opposition to the annual account and tableau of distribution filed by the surviving spouse, in her capacity as administratrix. The trial court ruled in favor of the forced heirs. The surviving spouse appeals devolutively.

Charles Edward Davis died intestate on August 9, 1984. He was survived by his widow, Irene Gregoire Davis (the administratrix), and his three children from a prior marriage, Darlene Davis Webb, Stanley Davis and David Davis (the forced heirs).

There are only two issues in this case. The first involves liability for mortgage payments, while the second involves the commingling of the deceased's separate funds with community funds.

Payment of Mortgage Debts

At the time of Charles Davis' death, the community owed two mortgage debts. One was a mortgage debt due Ford Motor Credit Corporation (Ford) in the amount of $2,133.67 secured by an automobile; the other was a mortgage debt due First Guaranty Home secured by a parcel of immovable property. The administratrix acquired a legal usufruct over the deceased's community interest in the automobile and immovable property, the naked ownership of the deceased's interest going to the forced heirs. During the administration of the estate, the administratrix paid off the Ford Motor Credit Corporation mortgage debt completely, and paid installments to First Guaranty totaling $6,899.10. Additional monthly installments on this debt continue to become due.

The administratrix takes the position that she and the forced heirs are proportionately responsible for the payment of these mortgage debts; whether it be by sharing the debt equally or, in the alternative, by her paying her half of the mortgage principal and interest as well as the mortgage interest attributable to the forced heirs half, with the forced heirs being liable only for their half of the principal. The forced heirs take the position that the administratrix, as usufructuary is alone responsible for the mortgage debts.

The trial court ruled in favor of the forced heirs, relying on Succession of Crain, 450 So.2d 1374 (La. App. 1st Cir. 1984).

Because our opinion in *Succession of Crain* did not go into detail regarding mortgage debt payments, we take this opportunity to do so.

C.C. art. 587 provides:

> When the usufruct is established mortis causa, the position of the usufructuary relative to the payment of the debts of the succession depends upon whether the usufruct is universal, under universal title, or under particular title. The usufruct of an entire succession is universal, of a fraction thereof is under universal title, and of individually determined things is under particular title.

The surviving spouse's legal usufruct over the deceased's share of the community property where the deceased also left separate property, is a usufruct under universal title. See Comments under C.C. arts. 587 and 591.

C.C. art. 589 provides:

Neither the universal usufructuary nor the usufructuary under universal title is liable for the debts of the succession. Nevertheless, the property subject to their usufruct may be seized and sold for the payment of succession debts.

C.C. art. 590 provides:

When it is necessary to satisfy a creditor of the succession, the succession representative with the authorization of the proper court or the universal successor may sell so much of the property subject to a universal usufruct or usufruct under universal title, as may be required to yield a sum for the discharge of the indebtedness. The usufructuary may prevent the sale by advancing the funds needed in accordance with the following provisions.

C.C. art. 591 provides:

The universal usufructuary must advance the funds needed for the discharge of all the debts of the succession.

The usufructuary under universal title must contribute to the payment of the debts of the succession in proportion to the value of the property subject to the usufruct.

C.C. art. 592 provides:

When the usufructuary advances funds needed for the discharge of the debts of the succession, he shall be reimbursed without interest at the end of the usufruct. When the usufructuary does not make such an advance, the universal successor may make the necessary advance, for which the usufructuary shall pay interest during the period of the usufruct, or sell a part of the property subject to the usufruct.

The usufructuary clearly has no legal obligation to pay the half of the mortgage debt attributable to the forced heirs' interest in the automobile and the property. However, assuming that either the usufructuary or the forced heirs elect to pay the succession debt in order to prevent seizure of the property, C.C. art. 592 then becomes applicable.

Article 592 must also be read in context with Article 591, which establishes the proportionate contribution of the usufructuary under universal title. If the usufructuary pays the succession debt, she or her estate is entitled to full reimbursement *when the usufruct terminates,* without interest on her proportionate contribution amount. Conversely, if the forced heirs pay the succession debt, they are entitled to interest payments from the usufructuary based on proportionate contribution amount.

We also note that the appellant confuses the interest referred to in article 592 with the interest amounts established by the mortgage contracts. The *succession debt* is comprised of the total mortgage obligation, both its principal and interest due. We construe Article 592 as referring to the rate of legal interest established by C.C. art. 2924(B)(l)(a). *Cf.* C.C. art. 2000. Accordingly, if the forced heirs choose to pay the mortgage installments as they come due, the usufructuary must pay legal interest to the forced heirs for her proportionate contribution amount of each installment until the usufruct terminates. The judgment of the trial court is modified in this respect.

5. TERMINATION OF USUFRUCT
Civil Code arts. 607-629

a. Causes of Termination

BARRY v. UNITED STATES FIDELITY & GUARANTY COMPANY
236 So. 2d 229 (La. App. 3d Cir. 1970)

CULPEPPER, J. This is a suit for damages arising out of an automobile accident. The plaintiffs are Miss Kathleen Barry, driver of one of the vehicles, and her mother, Mrs. A. E. Barry, who sues individually and on behalf of her minor son, Daniel Barry. Mrs. Barry and her son were passengers. The defendants are Mrs. Sadie F. Moon, driver of the other automobile, and her insurer, United States Fidelity & Guaranty Company. The district judge found the accident was caused solely by the negligence of Mrs. Moon.***

We find no manifest error in this conclusion. Accordingly, we affirm the holding of the district court that the accident was caused solely by the negligence of Mrs. Moon.

The next issue concerns the claim for damages to the Barry automobile. At the trial, it was stipulated that its value at the time of the accident was $1,125.00 and the salvage value is $200.00, which means that the total damage is $925.00. However, the vehicle was purchased during the marriage between Mrs. A.E. Barry and her deceased husband. As surviving spouse, Mrs. Barry owns an undivided one-half interest and has only a usufruct, under C.C. Art. 916 [Revised C.C. art. 890], of the remaining one-half which is owned by the 4 surviving children of the marriage. The district judge rejected Mrs. Barry's claim for damages to the automobile.

Defendants contend that under C.C. Art. 613 [Revised C.C. arts. 613, 614], "The usufruct expires before the death of the usufructuary, by the loss, extinction or destruction of the thing subject to the usufruct." Under this article, defendants argue that when the automobile was destroyed the usufruct terminated and hence tall naked owners are indispensable parties, C.C. Art. 641 [Revised C.C. art. 634], to this suit for damages to the vehicle. Here, only Mrs. Barry has sued for property damage. Defendants did not file an exception of non-joinder of a "necessary party," C.C. Art. 642 but if the heirs are "indispensable" parties, we may notice this deficiency, C.C. Art. 646, without an exception being filed.

Although the amount involved here is small, the question presented is res nova in our jurisprudence and this case may become an important precedent in the law of usufruct. The issue is whether all naked owners of property subject to the usufruct of a surviving spouse are indispensable parties to an action by the usufructuary for the total destruction of the property due to the wrongful act of a third person. Ultimately, we conclude that in this situation the usufruct of the surviving spouse does not terminate. Instead, it attaches to the claim for damages due by the wrongdoer. Hence, the naked owners of the interest subject to the surviving spouse's usufruct are not indispensable parties to the action.

It is true that Art. 613 [Revised C.C. arts. 613, 614], first paragraph, declares that "the usufruct expires before the death of the usufructuary, by the loss, extinction or destruction of the thing subject to the usufruct." Nevertheless, this provision contemplates a loss that is purely accidental, namely, a loss that is not attributed to the fault of any person. The second paragraph of Art. 613, by way of explanation, refers to "any other accident;" and Art. 615 [Revised C.C. arts. 614, 615] explains that "the thing subject to the usufruct is considered as lost, when it undergoes from accident,***" According to well settled French doctrine and jurisprudence, interpreting the corresponding provision in the Code Civil, if the loss is attributed to the fault of a person, the usufruct attaches to the claim for damages due by the wrongdoer. See 2 Aubry et Rau, Droit civil francais 694 (7th ed. Esmein 1961); Yiannopoulos, Personal Servitudes § 43, 87 (1968). The same solutions are followed in other civil law jurisdictions as in Germany and in Greece under the provisions of modern codes. See B.G.B. § 1045. 1046(1); Greek Civil Code Art. 1171.

Even if Art. 613, par. 1 were to be applied to all cases in which things are destroyed, whether by accident or as the result of the fault of a third person, still this article is inapplicable to the usufruct of the surviving spouse. According to well-settled Louisiana jurisprudence, the survivor's usufruct does not terminate "merely because the property to which the usufruct attached was changed in form." State Through Department of Highways v. Costello, 158 So. 2d 850 (La. App. 4th Cir. 1963), and cases cited. Indeed, termination of the usufruct would be inconsistent with the policy underlying the applicable legislation. In this respect, Louisiana courts apply the principle of real subrogation: the indemnity that the usufructuary has collected is substituted for the thing lost. See Yiannopoulos, Personal Servitudes § 43, text at note 107 (1968): "In cases involving usufruct of the surviving spouse, Louisiana courts may be expected to apply the principle of real subrogation, allowing the usufructuary not only to sue in his own name but also to recover and enjoy the payment for the period of the usufruct."

Quite apart from the policy considerations underlying the usufruct of the surviving spouse, Article 613 of the Civil Code [Revised C.C. arts. 613, 614] is inapplicable to usufructs under universal title, namely, usufructs of an assembly or a universality of things. It merely applies to usufruct under particular title, namely, to the usufruct of individual things. For the notions of usufruct under universal and under particular title, see Yiannopoulos, Personal Servitudes § 7 (1968). The usufruct of the surviving spouse is under universal title, as it comprises a variety of things, movables and immovables, corporeal and incorporeal. Ibid. Obviously, the usufruct of the whole does not terminate when only certain individual things are destroyed. And it would not be a good policy to allow partial termination of the usufruct whenever individual things are lost or destroyed, whether by accident or as a result of the fault of a third person. Of course, if things are destroyed as a result of the fault of the usufructuary, the question of the termination of the entire usufruct may well be raised.

From a pragmatic viewpoint, it is not logical to terminate the survivor's usufruct over an automobile that has been destroyed as a result of the fault of a third person. The survivor is entitled to have the use of the automobile until it is reduced to a state of junk. Why should he be deprived of this right without any fault on his part? It would seem that he ought to be entitled to the use of the proceeds collected from the wrongdoers by application of the principle of real subrogation. Application of this principle is not contrary to the interests of the naked owners. If the usufructuary had enjoyed the automobile to the end of its useful life, the naked owners would be entitled to take it as junk. If the automobile is destroyed, and the principle of real subrogation applied, the naked owners will have, at the end of the usufruct, a claim for the sum of money that the usufructuary has collected from the wrongdoer. See Yiannopoulos, Personal Servitudes, § 92, text at note 149 (1968).

Having concluded the usufruct of the surviving spouse has not terminated, it follows that the naked owners are not indispensable parties to the proceedings. Under the substantive law, the usufructuary has power of administration and is entitled to collect capital payments representing indemnities for injuries attributed both to the enjoyment and the ownership. In his capacity as administrator, the usufructuary effectively represents the interest of the owner. See Yiannopoulos, Personal Servitudes, §§ 36, 42 (1968). Barring collusion with the wrongdoer, which could be attacked collaterally by the naked owners, the usufructuary will normally seek maximum indemnity which will benefit the naked owners at the end of the usufruct. The usufructuary may, of course, implead the naked owners and the naked owners may intervene in the proceedings in order to safeguard their own interest; but there seems to be no compelling reason to classify the naked owners as indispensable parties in cases in which the usufruct has not terminated. On the contrary, due to the prevalence of the usufruct of the surviving spouse in Louisiana, it would be cumbersome to require the naked owners to become parties in all cases involving claims for the destruction of property subject to usufruct and to prove the value of their interest. In cases in which the usufruct does not terminate separate evaluation of the usufruct and of the naked ownership need not be made; the usufructuary will prove the value of the thing that has been destroyed and, if he recovers, he will enjoy an imperfect usufruct over the money collected. Rationally, the naked owners ought to be indispensable parties only in cases in which the usufruct terminates; in these cases the interests of the usufructuary and of the naked owners are distinguishable or even conflicting.

In Miller v. Colonial Pipeline Company, 173 So. 2d 840 (La. App. 2d Cir. 1965), a case in which there was no conflict of interests between the usufructuary and the naked owners, because recovery was sought for interference with the enjoyment only, we held that the naked owners were not indispensable parties. The rationale of that case may well be applied to the case under consideration, although, admittedly, the damage suffered here is attributed both to the enjoyment and the ownership.

The decision of the Louisiana Supreme Court in Tennessee Gas Transmission Company v. Derouen, 239 La. 467, 118 So. 2d 889 (1968), admittedly contains broad language which might lead to the conclusion that the naked owners are indispensable parties whenever their interests are affected by a judgment. "It is elementary," the court declared, "that every party who may be affected by a decree must be made a party to the suit, because no one should be condemned without a hearing." This case, however, is distinguished. In the first place, it was an expropriation, which involves special considerations. Secondly, it was the usufructuary who raised the exception of nonjoinder of indispensable parties. It ought to be the privilege of the usufructuary to implead the naked owners whenever he feels this is necessary for an adequate administration of justice. And thirdly, it would seem that the holding of the court is compatible with the idea that the naked owners are "necessary" rather than "indispensable" parties. The result would be the same under either classification.

It is our conclusion that the naked owners of the interest subject to the surviving spouse's usufruct are not indispensable parties. Furthermore, Mrs. Barry, as the naked owner of one-half and usufructuary of the remaining one-half, can recover all damages attributable to the total destruction of the vehicle.

For the reasons assigned, the judgment appealed is amended by increasing the award to Mrs. Barry by the sum of $925, her damages for destruction of the automobile. Otherwise than as herein amended, the judgment is affirmed.

BOND v. GREEN
401 So. 2d 639 (La. App. 3d Cir. 1981)

CUTRER, J. James and Ann Bond filed a rule to evict George and Mildred Green and J.B. and Freddie Powell from the following described property:

"LOTS 13, 14, 15, and 16 of Hedges Landing Lake Lots in Section 58 T5N,R7E, Concordia Parish, Louisiana, as per plat by James H. Tooke, Reg. Land Surveyor #3735 recorded in Plat Cabinet L, Envelope 150 B, Document Number 142064, of the Records of Concordia Parish, Louisiana."

The plaintiffs alleged that defendants were occupying the property without a lease and that the purpose of defendants' occupancy had ceased. In the alternative, the plaintiffs pleaded that, in the event it was determined that the defendants had a right to occupy the premises, the court should define the boundary of such occupied land. The defendants filed no pleading.

The trial court rendered judgment in favor of defendants, George and Mildred Green, recognizing that they had a usufruct over the following described property:

> "Lots 13, 14, 15 and 16 of Hedges Landing Lake Lots in Section 5, T5N, R7E, Concordia Parish, Louisiana, as per plat by James H. Tooke, Reg. Land Surveyor #3735 recorded in Plat Cabinet L, Envelope 150 B, Document Number 142064, of the Records of Concordia Parish, Louisiana and specifically as designated on plaintiff's exhibit number 6."

The court further ordered the Greens to reimburse the plaintiffs, James and Ann Bond, for taxes previously paid in the amount of $24.89. The court ordered the Greens to pay taxes for 1980 and future taxes. Plaintiffs appealed. We affirm.

The issues presented on appeal are:

(1) Whether, under the facts, the Greens' usufruct had terminated; and

(2) If such usufruct is still in effect, whether the trial court erred in its designation of the extent of property subject to the usufruct.

Whether the Usufruct Terminated

The facts are generally undisputed. In 1966, George and Mildred Green sold to Lloyd Love a tract of land containing approximately 55 acres of land. The instrument by which the property was sold contained the following reservations:

> "Vendors reserve unto themselves the usufruct of the house in which they now reside, the small house situated immediately on the west side of their residence and the yards surrounding the said residence."

Mrs. Green, 76 years of age, testified that following the sale to Lloyd Love in 1966, they continued to live in the larger of the two structures. She stated that at the time of the sale to Love, both structures were in bad shape or dilapidated. The Greens attempted to make repairs to the larger house where they resided. They changed the floor on the porch on two occasions. They installed bath fixtures and made other repairs, but the overall condition of the house could not be appreciably improved. The structural portions of the house had deteriorated to such an extent that the house could not be safely lived in.

The small house was not occupied and likewise was in a dilapidated condition when the sale was made to Love. The condition of this structure deteriorated to the point that it was falling down. Mrs. Green stated that in approximately 1976, she had her son-in-law remove the structures. This was done by pushing them down with a tractor. Mrs. Green explained the reason for removing the structures as follows:

"Q. What was the reason you tore the houses down?

"A. The reason? Well, the termites got in the seals [sic] and ate the seals [sic]. You know how termites will do. And the floors in the back of the house had fallen down about that far from the walls, and I didn't want the house falling down and injuring one of my grandchildren.

"Q. The termites had done great structural damage to the house?

"A. Yes. Both of them, as far as that's concerned."

After the removal of the structures, two mobile homes were moved onto the property and placed approximately in the location where the houses had been situated. The Greens occupied one mobile home and defendants, J.B. and Freddie Powell, daughter and son-in-law of the Greens, occupied the other.

Mrs. Green's daughter, Freddie Powell, testified that she and her husband moved a mobile home onto the property in order to assist her mother in caring for Mr. Green who was 76 years old. He had been sick for several years and was an invalid at the time of trial. The income of the Greens was limited to Social Security payments and food stamps ($439.00 per month). Mrs. Powell testified that the structures were old and literally had decayed and had become termite infested to the extent that they were falling down. She stated that at the time of the sale to Love, the structures were in very bad shape. She testified that her mother and father attempted to repair same but such repairs did not impede the continuing deterioration of the structures. She classified the larger house as not livable and a health hazard.

Lloyd Love testified that at the time he purchased the property both structures were in terrible shape. He stated that neither house was livable at that time. For this reason he attached no value to the structures when he purchased the property. Love stated that he wanted the Greens to have a place to live for the remainder of their lives, and had considered removing the structures and building a new house for the Greens to live in. Due to a financial problem, however, be could not carry out his intention. He stated that the Greens had his permission to remove the deteriorated structures.

Plaintiffs urge that, under the facts presented, the usufruct should be considered terminated on the ground that the property subject to the usufruct has been totally and permanently lost. Plaintiffs rely principally upon C.C. art. 613. This article reads as follows:

"The usufruct of nonconsumables terminates by the permanent and *total loss*, extinction, or destruction through accident or decay of the property subject to the usufruct." (Emphasis ours.)

Article 613 terminates the usufruct if the *total* usufruct is lost through decay. In the case at hand, the usufruct extended to *not only the two houses but the yards surrounding same.*

The facts are undisputed that the two houses were in unlivable, decayed condition with no value at the time the usufruct came into existence. The attempts of the Greens to repair the structures proved to be an exercise in futility. The removal of these structures did not effectuate a total loss of the usufruct. This was a partial loss of the usufruct. The usufruct remained on the land or yards surrounding the structures.

Paragraph (d) of the Comment to Article 613 explains this position as follows:

> "The usufruct terminates only if the loss is total. Thus, if the usufruct is established simply on a building, and this building is destroyed completely, the usufruct terminates.... If the loss is only partial, the usufruct continues and is exercised on whatever remains of the thing. C.C. art. 614 (1870). Thus, if the usufruct is established 'upon an estate of which the building is a part, the usufructuary shall enjoy both the soil and the materials.'...." (Emphasis ours.)

Since the loss of the structures was due to decay of only a part of the usufruct, and not a loss of the total usufruct, the trial court correctly held that the usufruct continued on the remaining land.

Plaintiffs further urge that the Greens committed waste or neglected to make ordinary repairs or abused their enjoyment of the usufruct, and under C.C. art. 623, the usufruct terminates.

This position of the plaintiffs is likewise without merit. The facts clearly reflect that these structures were old and decayed. A usufructuary is not bound to restore property that has been destroyed because of age. C.C. art.583 provides, in part, as follows:

> "Neither the usufructuary nor the naked owner is bound to restore property that has been totally destroyed through accident or because of age."

Finally, the plaintiffs contend that the defendants' failure to pay the property taxes on the land they occupied entitled the plaintiffs, as naked owners, to terminate the usufruct. C.C. art. 584 places the obligation to pay the property taxes on the usufructuary but does not provide for termination of the usufruct upon failure to meet this obligation. That article reads:

> "The usufructuary is bound to pay the annual charges imposed during his enjoyment on the property subject to the usufruct, such as property taxes."

This article clearly gives rise to an obligation on the part of the usufructuary to pay the taxes, but if the naked owner has paid the taxes he has only an action against the usufructuary for reimbursement, rather than a right to terminate the usufruct. We are buttressed in this opinion by the comments to that article. Comment (e) reads, in pertinent part, as follows:

> "The naked owner, in order to avoid a tax sale of his property, may pay the taxes due by the usufructuary and bring against him an action for reimbursement...."

Consequently, the trial judge was correct in ordering the Greens to reimburse the plaintiffs for back taxes. He also correctly concluded that the failure to pay the taxes was not a ground for termination of the usufruct.

Finally, we turn to the question regarding the extent of the property subject to the usufruct. Plaintiffs argue that the trial judge was erroneous in allowing the testimony of Lloyd Love as to the area covered by the Greens' usufruct. Plaintiffs argue that this testimony is parol evidence used to alter an authentic act. Again we disagree.

The general rule of law under our Civil Code art. 2276 [Revised C.C. art. 1848] is that parol evidence cannot be admitted to contradict or extend what is contained in a written instrument. However, where the instrument contains ambiguity, the court may resort to extrinsic evidence to clarify the ambiguity by showing the intention of the parties [citations omitted].

In the instant case the reservation of the usufruct over the "yards surrounding the residence," which is contained in the instrument conveying the property to Mr. Love, is ambiguous. The exact extent of the property included in the reservation of the usufruct is unclear. Mr. Love's testimony, however, revealed that at the time of the sale the parties to the agreement contemplated that the usufruct would cover the four lots in question. He delineated this area on the plat which has been introduced into evidence. The trial judge correctly considered this evidence and set forth the description of the area covered by the usufruct in his judgment as previously set forth herein.

For the reasons assigned, the judgment of the trial court is affirmed. Plaintiffs are to pay all costs of this appeal.

KIMBALL v. STANDARD FIRE INS. CO.
578 So. 2d 546 (La. App. 3d Cir. 1991)

LABORDE, Judge. On June 28, 1983, plaintiff, Bobbie Clark Kimball, filed suit against defendant, The Standard Fire Insurance Company of Hartford, Connecticut (Standard), seeking to collect fire insurance proceeds after a house purchased during her marriage to the late Guy W. Kimball was totally destroyed by fire. After the house burned, Michael H. Davis, who had been appointed provisional administrator of the Succession of Guy Kimball on June 24, 1980, gave notice to counsel for Standard that he intended to intervene in the suit on behalf of the succession. However, before a formal intervention was filed, Standard inadvertently sent a check directly to Mrs. Kimball's attorney and the check was cashed. Subsequently, on November 30, 1983, an intervention was filed by Mr. Davis and tried without a jury.

The trial court found that Mrs. Kimball was the only named insured under the fire insurance policy and that she did not intend to cover any interest other than her own insurable interest. Accordingly, the trial court determined that the Succession of Guy Kimball was not entitled to a share of the insurance proceeds and dismissed the intervenor's suit at intervenor's cost.

On appeal, intervenor argues that the trail court erred in failing to find that a portion of the insurance proceeds belonged to the Succession of Guy Kimball. After reviewing the trial record and appellate briefs, we find no error in law or manifest error in fact. Thus, we affirm the judgment of the trial court. Insofar as we are favored with its well-reasoned findings, we annex those reasons hereto. Costs of this appeal are to be paid by intervenor, the Succession of Guy W. Kimball.

Reasons For Judgment

The plaintiff in this suit and her three children were the owners in indvision of the family home located at 200 High Country Drive in Pineville. This included a substantial two story brick and frame home which was the property of the plaintiff and her husband before his death, and thereafter of the plaintiff and his heirs.

The plaintiff's husband was murdered in the home on March 8, 1980.[1] The plaintiff and two male friends were later charged in the murder of Guy Kimball. The plaintiff subsequently pled guilty to conspiracy to commit murder. She was being held in the Rapides Parish jail when the house was totally destroyed by fire on the afternoon of May 19, 1983.

Subsequent to the fire, a thorough investigation was done. The results tend to indicate that there is a very high probability that the fire was started and accelerated by means of arson. There were also strong indications that the home was unoccupied and had been unoccupied for a substantial period of time when destroyed. There are also reports that the home had been stripped of furnishings and fixtures prior to its burning.

Nonetheless, when the home burned on May 19, 1983, there was a policy of fire insurance in effect with The Standard Fire Insurance Company of Hartford, Connecticut covering the home and its contents. The policy covered the term June 3, 1982, to June 3, 1983. It was a renewal of a policy which had been in effect prior, but was renewed by Mrs. Kimball in her name alone. The premium was paid by her,

When the home burned, a claim was made on the policy. While the claim was being

---

[1] [Plaintiff's husband was actually murdered on March 8, 1979].

investigated, a sworn statement was taken from Mrs. Kimball in the parish jail, with her attorney, Eugene Cicardo, Sr., present. At that time Mrs. Kimball said that she alone had purchased the policy, but that the home was owned by herself and the late Mr. Kimball. The insurer was put clearly on notice of other potential ownership interests in the property, although the insurance was issued solely in Mrs. Kimball's name.

Subsequently, Mr. Michael Davis, who had been appointed the provisional administrator of the estate of Guy W. Kimball on June 24, 1980, gave notice to Mr. Edward Rundell, the attorney in Alexandria for Standard, that he intended to intervene in the insurance suit on behalf of the children who were owners in indivision with Mrs. Kimball in the house. A formal intervention was not at that time filed.

Standard, then at this juncture in the occurrence of events in the history of the suit, did a curious, unexplained and nonsensical thing. It mailed a check for $110,000.00 to Mrs. Kimball's attorney, Eugene Cicardo, Sr. No answer rationally explains why this payment was made or why it was made directly to the plaintiff, bypassing Standard's own attorney in Alexandria. The Court concludes that it was a mistake, suspicious, but not malicious. The insurer had nothing to lose through the intervention. It had nothing to lose in a concursus proceeding. It additionally had grounds for potentially avoiding payment on the policy; arson, vacancy. The payment appears not to have been incorporated in any settlement of the claim. Mrs. Kimball cashed the check, took the money and ran. She was not available for trial, and is apparently absent in violation of her probation terms.

The children of Bobbie Kimball and Guy Kimball have continued their intervention, bringing suit against Standard in an attempt to "raid" the proceeds of the claim payment to Mrs. Kimball. The theory of their right to do this is that they are owners in indivision with Mrs. Kimball as heirs of Guy Kimball. Since the whole of the destroyed property is insured, they claim that a proportion of the insurance policy reflective of their ownership interests is due to them.

In this suit this issue is greatly complicated by the unfortunate fact of the funds being gone. Mrs. Kimball has absconded with them, hence if monies are due to the intervenors under the insurance contract, the funds must come from Standard in excess of the policy payment previously made to Mrs. Kimball.

The Court determines that while the intervenors had an insurable interest in the insured property, that interest was not in fact insured. Mrs. Kimball by her actions showed an unequivocal intent not to insure the interests of the intervenors in the property, both before and after the loss. What is more, under the usufruct granted to Mrs. Kimball under La.C.C. Article 890 it would appear that the intervenors had very little interest in the property. Their interest being an undivided partial one, subject to usufruct for life or until the remarriage of Mrs. Kimball, a woman in her low thirties. The Court feels that Mrs. Kimball was entitled to insure the full value of the property.

Although neither party cited this authority, the crowning blow seems to come from Article 617 of the Louisiana Civil Code which reads:

When proceeds of insurance are due on account of loss, extinction, or destruction of property subject to usufruct, the usufruct attaches to the proceeds. If the usufructuary or the naked owner has separately insured his interest only, the proceeds belong to the insured party.

The usufruct of the house as community property subject to Article 890 would convert to a usufruct of insurance proceeds on insured property subject to usufruct. In a real sense, this intervention is a premature claim. Mrs. Kimball's Article 890 usufruct has metamorphosed into a usufruct of the insurance proceeds, a usufruct which does not terminate until her death or remarriage neither of which to the knowledge of the Court has occurred.

Additionally, the reasoning of the First Circuit enunciated in Hartford Insurance Company of Southwest v. Stablier, 476 So. 2d 464, leads to a conclusion that the intervention should not prevail, although emotions and equity might suggest otherwise.

Therefore, the Court is led to the abiding conclusion that the intervention should be dismissed with court costs assessed to the intervenors.

Alexandria, Louisiana, this 2nd day of May, 1989.

/s/LLOYD G. TEEKELL
LLOYD G. TEEKELL
District Judge
Division "D"
Filed May 2, 1989
/s/ Debra W. Boykin

NOTE
Introduction to *Watson*

The facts of the case that follows – *Watson* – are a little bit complicated, thanks to the number of parties involved in the litigation. A few words of introduction are therefore in order. First there's Margie, our usufructuary, who is Winston's surviving spouse. Then there are the four naked owners, who are Winston's four children. Winston had granted Margie a testamentary usufruct over all of Winston's property, which included the property at issue in this lawsuit. This property was apparently the couple's residence, but it was his separate property. Prior to his death, Winston mortgaged the property to Prudential. After his death, no one paid the mortgage, and Prudential foreclosed, causing the property to be sold at a judicial sale. From the proceeds generated by that sale Prudential was paid off in full, but there remained over $360,000, and some of the parties are fighting over this money. Land Bank is a judgment creditor of three of the four naked owners. As a judgment creditor, Land Bank has the right to seize property of its debtors (i.e., those naked owners) to satisfy its judgment. The issue in the case is the nature of those naked owners' interest in the money remaining after satisfaction of Prudential's claim.

WATSON v. FEDERAL LAND BANK OF JACKSON
606 So. 2d 920 (La. App. 3d Cir. 1992)

KALISTE J. SALOOM, Jr., Judge Pro Tem. This appeal questions the correctness of the trial court's granting of a motion for summary judgment in favor of defendant-appellee, Federal Land Bank of Jackson (hereinafter Land Bank). Plaintiff-appellant is Margie Nell Peloquin Estes (hereinafter Margie), wife of decedent C. Winston Estes.

FACTS

The facts of this case are not in dispute. On May 9, 1972, C. Winston Estes executed a mortgage on his separate property in favor of The Prudential Insurance Co. of America. His wife, Margie, joined in the mortgage solely to waive any homestead exemption rights she might have in the encumbered property. Subsequently, C. Winston Estes died and left to his wife, Margie, by testament dated September 26, 1973, the usufruct over all of his property, both community and separate, including the mortgaged property. He willed an undivided one-fourth interest in naked ownership of all of his property, to each of his four children. A judgment of possession, recognizing the usufruct and naked ownerships, was rendered in accordance with his will on January 27, 1977.

Thereafter, money judgments in favor of the Land Bank were rendered respectively against three of the four children, namely Charlotte Estes Luntsford on May 12, 1986, for $620,408.30; Walter Craig Estes on July 17, 1987, for $620,408.30; and Mahamala Estes Abshire on October 7, 1987, for $742,166.79. The fourth child, Irmaleta Estes Pousson, was not named in any judgment.

On October 27, 1987, Prudential filed suit for executory process on the property mortgaged by decedent in 1972 naming as defendants, the usufructuary, Margie, and the four children as naked owners. A judicial sale was conducted and after satisfying the Prudential mortgage debt and costs of the proceedings, there remained a balance of $360,620.12. This balance was paid over to the Land Bank in partial satisfaction of its money judgments against three of the Estes children.

Margie Estes and Irmaleta Estes Pousson, the fourth Estes child, and the only child not indebted to the Land Bank, filed suit to recover these funds. They then filed a joint motion for summary judgment, Margie seeking recognition of her usufruct over the entire balance of the proceeds, Ms. Pousson asking that the court recognize the wrongful conversion of her one-fourth interest. On September 27, 1990, the trial court denied the motion for summary judgment requested by the usufructuary, but recognized Ms. Pousson's right to her one-fourth share of the proceeds. Meanwhile, the Land Bank filed a separate motion for summary judgment against Margie, the usufructuary, seeking the rejection of her demands as a matter of law. The trial court subsequently granted summary judgment in favor of the Land Bank. This judgment is the subject of the present appeal. Neither Land Bank nor Margie appealed the trial court judgment insofar as it awarded Ms. Pousson one fourth of the excess proceeds.

LAW AND ARGUMENT

The sole issue to be considered in this appeal is whether a usufruct, which was subject to a prior superior mortgage, applies to any of the excess proceeds after the superior mortgage has been satisfied by a judicial sale. As recognized by the trial court, this is a case of first impression under Louisiana law. The trial court found that summary judgment in favor of Land Bank was required by application of C.C. art. 620 which provides as follows:

> Art. 620. Sale of the property or of the usufruct
>
> Usufruct terminates by the enforcement of a mortgage placed upon the property prior to the creation of the usufruct. The usufructuary may have an action against the grantor of the usufruct or against the naked owner under the third section of this chapter.
>
> The sale of the property by the naked owner after the usufruct has been created or the enforcement of a mortgage placed upon the property by the naked owner after the creation of the usufruct does not affect the right of the usufructuary.
>
> The judicial sale of the usufruct by creditors of the usufructuary deprives the usufructuary of his enjoyment of the property but does not terminate the usufruct.

According to the trial court, the enforcement of the superior Prudential mortgage terminated the usufruct in favor of the surviving spouse, thus vesting full ownership in the children, thereby allowing the Land Bank to receive the remaining proceeds from the judicial sale, as a judgment creditor.

Appellant relies on the second paragraph of C.C. art. 620 and C.C. art. 615 which provides:

> Art. 615. Change of the form of property
>
> When property subject to usufruct changes form without any act of the usufructuary, the usufruct does not terminate even though the property can no longer serve the use for which it was originally destined.
>
> When property subject to usufruct is converted into money or other property without an act of the usufructuary, as in a case of expropriation of an immovable or liquidation of a corporation, the usufruct does not terminate but attaches to the money or other property.

Appellant contends that the usufruct should terminate only insofar as necessary to satisfy the superior mortgage and that as there remained proceeds after the satisfaction, the usufruct should attach to those proceeds.

Land Bank, on the other hand, contended that this situation is not analogous to the situation contemplated by C.C. art. 615 in that although the usufructuary did not actively participate in the enforcement of the mortgage, she could have prevented it by advancing the funds necessary to discharge the Prudential debt. See C.C. art. 590 and 591. By failing to do so, Land Bank argues, she suffered the termination of her usufruct.

We recognize merit in each of these arguments, but believe that this decision must be resolved by reading the laws on usufruct in *pari materia*. By doing so, we believe that it is clear that C.C. art. 620 contemplates that the enforcement of a mortgage placed on property prior to the creation of a usufruct terminates the usufruct only to the extent necessary to satisfy the mortgage obligation. Should there be any proceeds remaining after the sale, the usufruct attaches to those proceeds.

We find that to interpret the law on usufruct as suggested by Land Bank would lead to an untenable result in that had there been no creditor of the naked owners of the property, upon enforcement of the mortgage, the naked owners would have become full owners of the proceeds. And although the appellant in this case, a universal usufructuary (See C.C. art. 587), is required to advance funds necessary to pay succession debts or suffer the seizure and sale of the property, she is not personally liable for these debts. C.C. arts. 589, 590, 591, and 592 and Succession of Weller, 107 La. 406, 31 So. 883 (1903).

Furthermore, the fact that there exists a creditor of the naked owner in this case causes the result to become even more absurd. Allowing the creditor to obtain the excess proceeds by interpreting the first paragraph of C.C. art. 620 as terminating the usufruct even as to the excess proceeds allows the enforcement of a judicial mortgage placed upon the property against the naked owners after the creation of the usufruct to the prejudice of the usufructuary in direct violation of the last paragraph of C.C. art. 620. We note that under C.C. art. 616, when the usufructuary and the naked owner agree to the sale of the property, the usufruct attaches to the proceeds. We see no reason to treat the enforcement of a mortgage any differently.

Therefore, we believe that paragraph one of art. 620 only contemplates complete termination when the enforcement of the superior mortgage exhausts the property and no proceeds remain. When proceeds remain, the most credible interpretation of C.C. art. 620 and the one that would lead to consistency in the law of usufruct is to read it in *pari materia* with arts. 615 and 616 as allowing the enforcement of a mortgage to terminate a usufruct only to the extent necessary to satisfy the mortgage obligation; the remaining proceeds are still subject to the usufruct.

This interpretation should cause no prejudice to the naked owner and *a fortiori* their creditors as they are protected by C.C. art. 618, by which they may require the usufructuary to invest safely the proceeds.

For the reasons hereinabove assigned, the granting of the summary judgment in favor of the Land Bank is hereby reversed and this case is remanded for further proceedings consistent with this decision. Costs of appeal are to be paid by appellees. Reversed and remanded

b. Consequences of Termination; Accounting:
Civil Code arts. 628, 629

SUCCESSION OF HAYES
33 La. Ann. 1143 (1881)

POCHE, J. At her death, on the 19th of October, 1862, Sarah E. Hayes, wife of Jesse B. Clark, who left no issue, but several legal heirs, left a will, under which she gave to her husband the usufruct of her share in the community property.

This litigation grows out of oppositions filed by the heirs to a final account and settlement of the community, filed by Clark in January, 1866, as dative testamentary executor. Although numerous items of the account were opposed, the issue on this appeal is confined to the correctness of the judgment of the lower court in dismissing oppositions to the following items:

1st. A credit of $1055.55 claimed by the executor for cotton belonging to the succession, sold by him for Confederate notes, which were converted into Confederate bonds, now valueless.

2d. A credit of $2000, claimed by him on account of his separate property and funds brought into the community, which, opponents contend, should be reduced by $254.

1st. The proper disposition of the opposition to the item of credit of $1055.55 requires an inquiry into the nature of Clark's possession of the succession cotton sold by him for Confederate money. If he held the cotton, as he contends, as testamentary executor, then under the great danger to which the cotton was exposed, either to confiscation or to destruction by fire, during the late civil war, during which the locality where the cotton was situated, was surrounded and overrun by contending forces, or by organized bands of robbers, the disposition which Clark made of the cotton is justifiable in Law, which exonerates him from responsibility in the premises.

If, on the other hand, he held the cotton as testamentary usufructuary, as opponents contend, his possession was under the imperfect usufruct, transferring to him the ownership of the cotton, with full power to dispose of it as he thought proper, entailing the obligation of returning the same, or the estimated value thereof, to the heirs, at the expiration of the usufruct. C.C. Art. 536-549 [Revised C.C. arts. 550-556].

Considering that, in his petition for the probate of his wife's will, Clark specially alleged that the usufruct of the wife's community property was bequeathed to him, and that the probating of the will was predicated upon and made with special reference to his petition; considering that, in his tableau of distribution, he claimed credit for two items charged in the inventory, on the ground that these items were for portions of crops, ungathered in October, 1862, when the usufruct began, and which he claimed as usufructuary, and that the accountant must be bound by his judicial admissions, we conclude that he took and held the twenty-two bales of cotton which he sold for Confederate money, in his right of usufructuary under the will, and that his responsibility must be tested under the provisions of our Code regulating the right of usufruct. This conclusion is further justified and absolutely confirmed by the fact, shown in the record, that the investment by Clark of the funds realized from his sale of the cotton, was not made in the name of the succession, but in his own name, and confusedly with other funds of his. We are clear that his administration, as executed, has been confined by law and by his own acts to the separate property of his wife, as shown by the inventory, and not subject to his usufruct. All these circumstances clearly differentiate this case from that of the succession of Frazier, 33 An. 593.

Had he kept, as some of his neighbors did, his cotton to the end of the war, and sold it at forty-five cents a pound, in legal currency, and realized from the transaction some five thousand dollars in such currency, he could not have been held accountable for more than the estimated value of the cotton, as shown by the inventory. In that case, he would have been entitled to the profits, in this, he must sustain the losses.

We are clear that the usufruct of cotton, the use of which would be of no value to the usufructuary, if he did not change the substance of it, by manufacturing or selling it, is of the imperfect kind, C.C. Art. 534 [Revised C.C. art. 545], and that Clark exercised his legal right in selling it, and has thus contracted the obligation of returning the same or the value thereof. Hence, in our opinion, the District Judge erred in refusing to amend the account in this particular.

2d. We are satisfied by the evidence that, among the property brought into the community by Clark, were some horses and cows, which he himself values at $254, for which animals he is not entitled to credit against the community. We. therefore, hold that the value of these animals must be deducted from the credit of $2000, allowed him by the District Judge, on account of his separate property and funds.

Appellants call our attention to the insufficiency in amount of the bond of the usufructuary, as fixed by the lower court. It must be increased from one thousand dollars to two thousand five hundred dollars.

It is, therefore, ordered, adjudged and decreed that the judgment of the lower court be amended by striking out the credit of $1055.55, allowed for the cotton sold by accountant for Confederate money, by reducing from $2000 to $1746 the credit allowed to accountant, on account of his separate property or funds, by increasing the usufructuary's bond from one thousand dollars to two thousand five hundred dollars; and that, as thus amended, said judgment be affirmed; costs of appeal to be paid by appellee.

SUCCESSION OF HECKERT
160 So. 2d 375 (La. App. 4th Cir. 1964)

McBRIDE, J. John Earl Heckert and Anna I. Buch were married in 1912 and two children were born of the marriage, viz. John E. Herkert, Jr. and Mrs. Isabelle L. Heckert Hardie. The two children were of the full age of majority when their mother died intestate on July 24, 1938; her succession was opened in the Civil District Court for the Parish of Orleans, Docket No. 227-393; as per judgment therein rendered and signed August 8, 1938, Heckert was recognized as decedent's surviving husband in community and as such was sent into possession as owner of an undivided one-half interest in 710 shares of the capital stock of S.H. Kress and Company belonging to the community as represented by eight certain certificates issued therefor standing in his name, said certificates being described by number in the judgment; the two children were recognized as the sole heirs of their mother and sent into possession of the other undivided one-half of said shares, subject to the usufruct of their father thereon. Notwithstanding the change of ownership decreed by the judgment of possession, the stock certificates remained as originally issued in Heckert's name and possession and he collected the dividends.

Besides the 710 shares inventoried in the wife's succession, there were 300 other shares of the Kress stock which belonged to the community represented by three certificates for 100 shares each standing in Heckert's name. These shares, for some unknown reason, were not mentioned in the succession proceedings. However, Heckert likewise had possession of the uninventoried certificates and collected the dividends. Of course, the two children acquired an undivided one-half naked ownership in said 300 shares immediately upon the death of their mother under the doctrine of *le mort saisit le vif.* C.C. arts. 940,941.

John Earl Heckert married his second wife, Eunice Knobloch, on August 4, 1939, in New York; it was then that his usufruct on the property derived by his children from the first wife's succession terminated by the operation of law. See C.C. art. 916 [Revised C.C. art. 890]. Heckert made no attempt to deliver to his children their portion of the 1010 shares of Kress stock on which his usufruct had existed, and the children made no demand on him therefor, but were content to permit him to retain possession of the certificates and to collect dividends.

Heckert departed this life on March 3, 1961, leaving a last will and testament which has been duly probated herein by which he bequeathed to his second wife, Mrs. Eunice Knobloch Heckert, the disposable portion of his estate and to his two children he left their legitime. Out of the 1010 shares of Kress stock of which Heckert had possession upon his first wife's death, only three certificates were found among his effects, these standing in his name as originally issued and being each for 100 shares. Two of said certificates

(7154 and 7155) were among those inventoried in the first wife's succession and one certificate (7158) was one of those which had been omitted therefrom.

The record discloses that Heckert had "donated" to his second wife at various times after their marriage 300 shares of the Kress stock which emanated from the first community, and that from time to time he had sold or otherwise disposed of 410 shares. In the bank box of decedent and his second wife were found six certificates representing 400 shares, all issued to Mrs. Eunice Knobloch Heckert. Said shares were the subject matter of gifts to her by Heckert.***

Decedent's children (more than 21 years after the termination of the usufruct) have brought a suit against Mrs. Eunice Knobloch Heckert, in her individual capacity and also as decedent's testamentary executrix, attacking the donations inter vivos and mortis causa insofar as their interests derived from their mother in the donated shares of stock are concerned; they also plead that no gratuitous transfer of any of the stock could be made to the prejudice of their rights as forced heirs of their deceased father; alternatively, they allege that if the donations be decreed to be valid, then the value thereof must be ascertained and brought back into the mass of his succession in order to determine their legitime. They pray that they be decreed to be the owners of and entitled to have delivered to them 605 shares of the capital stock of S.H. Kress and Company or the value thereof.* * *

Defendant, taking the position that what the two children by their suit are claiming is an accounting of the usufruct of their father on the property inherited from their mother, interposed the exception of ten years' liberative prescription provided by C.C. art. 3544 [Revised C.C. art. 3499] which reads as follows "In general, all personal actions, except those before enumerated, are prescribed by ten years."

Upon said exception being overruled, defendant filed a voluminous answer, the contents of which need not be recounted. After a trial on the merits, there was judgment (the nature of which will be hereafter set out) in favor of plaintiffs and against Mrs. Eunice Knobloch Heckert, individually, as well as testamentary executrix, and she has perfected this appeal.

Appellant in this court, as the sole ground for reversal of the judgment, relies on her exception of ten years' liberative prescription which she reurges.

We do not construe the suit to be one for an accounting. Plaintiffs are merely demanding their share of the capital stock of S.H. Kress and Company which they acquired as the sole heirs of their deceased mother and also for their legitime in their father's interest in the 300 shares remaining in her succession and also for a reduction of excessive donations inter vivos to the second wife so that their legitime may be reserved.

Upon deciding the case, the trial judge assigned comprehensive and well-considered reasons for judgment which encompass the factual situation and the applicable law, and since we are in accord therewith, we quote and adopt as part of our opinion herein the following portion of said reasons:

"***It is apparent to this Court that Mr. Heckert could have enjoyed the stocks to some extent without transferring or selling them, this by way of receiving the dividends.... Respondent insists that the legislation dealing with transfer of stock, R.S. 12:501, et seq. (Act 215 of 1912), has nullified the holding of the *Leury* case, *supra*. R.S. 12:501 provides:

"'***the person, firm or corporation, in whose name a certificate of stock stands, or to whom a certificate of stock is endorsed, whether in full or in blank and who has possession of said certificate shall be regarded as the legal owner thereof with full power to pledge, sell or otherwise dispose of said stock, and no person, corporation, firm nor transfer agent shall be responsible to any one claiming any interest in, or ownership of, said stock, or any part thereof, by virtue of any undisclosed or latent legal or conventional title or interest therein.'

"However, in the title of Act 215 of 1912 is found the following explanation of the purpose of the legislation:

"'To protect corporations, persons, firms and transfer agents, dealing in or transferring stocks where the transferor has the possession of the stock transferred, and where the stock stands in the name of the person, corporation or firm in full or in blank.'

"Thus, the Act was meant as a protective device for the benefit not of the transferor, but of the transferee. In other words, the transferee would be protected from actions on stocks where, on the face of the certificates or from the circumstances of the transaction, there is nothing to give the transferee notice of any latent defects in the transferor's title. Now, the answer to the question of whether this act broadens the powers or rights of the transferor, whatever might be his capacity or position, is answered by R.S. 12:525 (Act 180 of 1910, Sec. 2):

"'Nothing in this Act shall be construed as enlarging the powers of an infant or other person lacking full legal capacity, or of a trustee, executor or administrator, or other fiduciary, to make a valid endorsement, assignment or power of attorney.'

"Therefore, the holder of a perfect usufruct on common stocks in a corporation cannot, by the above mentioned acts, sell or transfer the interests or property rights of the naked owners. The above acts merely state that if the usufructuary does transfer the stocks without the permission of the naked owners, and the stocks stand in the name of the usufructuary, then the corporation is not liable to the naked owners for transferring the stocks. But, the usufructuary must still answer to the naked owners for the breach of fiduciary obligation. The holding of the Leury Case, *supra*, still stands as good law; Mr. Heckert's cancellations of the stocks representing the interests of the present petitioners was, therefore, a breach of his fiduciary obligation to the naked owners.***

"Respondent has sought to apply the ten year prescription of Civil Code Article 3544 [Revised C.C. art. 3499] to petitioners' rights. However, the cases cited by respondent on this point all relate to the seeking of an accounting under an imperfect usufruct. Cochran v.. Violet, 38 La. Ann. 525; In re Jones, 41 La. Ann. 620, 6 So. 180; Burdin v. Burdin, 171 La. 7, 129 So. 651. In fact, as relates to the property which was subject to a perfect usufruct in Burdin v. Burdin, *supra*, the court said:

> "'*** The only piece of real estate situated in Louisiana, in which the children of the deceased Mrs. Elizabeth Franz Burdin have an interest is a certain piece of swamp land in the Parish of Iberville, which apparently was not inventoried in Mrs. Burden's succession. Plaintiff does not allege that the defendant bas denied her proportionate interest in this particular land, which she is at liberty at any time to assert and liquidate by the proper proceeding.'"

"This 'quotation is cited to show that even though prescription may run on the right to an accounting under an imperfect usufruct, it cannot run as to rights of naked owners under a perfect usufruct. In an article by Leonard Oppenheim entitled The Usufruct of the Surviving Spouse, 18 Tulane Law Rev., the author states: "'The usufructuary being a precarious possessor cannot prescribe against the naked owner, no matter how long he holds the things subject to the usufruct.***' p. 217.

"This follows the code provision of Civil Code Article 3510 [Revised C.C. art. 3477]:

> "'Those who possess for others and not in their own name cannot prescribe, whatever may be the time of their possessior.. Thus, farmers, tenants, depositaries, usufructuaries, and all those generally who hold by a precarious tenure and in the name of the owner cannot prescribe on the thing thus held.'

"The law, as indicated by the above article, is that there can be no acquisitive prescription applied to a usufruct. As relates to the facts in the present case, were this Court to say that since the petitioners did not assert their rights to the stocks within ten years after the termination of the usufruct, their rights have prescribed; we would actually be saying that there can be acquisitive prescription under a usufruct. Such holding would be directly contrary to the clear and express provision of Civil Code Art. 3510 [Revised C.C. art. 3477].

Any contention that the usufructuary's transferring the stock and converting it to money transforms the usufruct to an imperfect one is met by the holding of the court in Wainer v. Wainer, 210 La. 324, 26 So.2d 829, where, in effect, the Court held that when stock has been converted to money by the usufructuary, the usufruct does not thereby become an imperfect usufruct.

"The stocks in the original succession were held in indivision after the termination of the usufruct of Mr. Heckert, Planiol, in Traité Élémentaire du Droit Civil, Vol. 1, part 2, No. 2497, says:

"'A thing belonging to several co-owners in indivision when the right of each owner bears upon the whole (and not upon a given part) of the thing held in common. The share of each, therefore, is not a tangible share but a portion expressed by a fraction: a third, a fourth, a tenth. It is the right of ownership that is divided among them. The thing is not. It is held in indivision. The right of each co-owner must be pictured as striking every molecule of the thing and as there encountering the right of the other co-owners for the portions belonging to them.'

"The application of this principle leads to the conclusion that petitioners did not merely own a certain number of shares in the stock of S.H. Kress and Co., but actually owned one-half of each of the certificates, each representing a certain number of shares. Thus, when Mr. Heckert sold or otherwise transferred a certificate, he was transferring a piece of property, half ownership of which was vested in petitioners.

"Based on this analysis the Court will determine petitioners' recovery as follows: From the original succession of Mrs. Anna Buch Heckert, petitioners received ownership of 505 shares of Kress stock, represented by the certificates in the inventory, and also the certificates numbered 7156, 7157 and 7158 which were inadvertently omitted from the inventory of that succession. In Mr. Heckert's succession there are only three certificates from that original succession still extant, these being numbered 7154, 7155 and 7158, representing in total 300 shares. Since petitioners are due 505 shares, the Court must award them full ownership of the three extant shares in Mr. Heckert's succession. This leaves petitioners 205 shares short. Certificate number H-9983,... Mrs. Heckert for 100 shares is dated December 17, 1942, the same date that certificate number 7153 was cancelled; therefore, the transaction would amount to an invalid donation of 50 shares belonging to petitioners, which shares must be returned to petitioners. Certificates numbered F-19232, F-19234, and F-10235 are dated July 17, 1944, the same date that certificates numbered 9178 and 9438 were cancelled; therefore, this transaction would amount to an invalid donation of 100 shares belonging to the petitioners, which shares must be returned to petitioners. Since the donations to respondent were valid as to Mr. Heckert's one-half interest at the time they were made, this Court will only require that the number of shares, or their value, as pertains to petitioners' one-half interest be returned to petitioners. This leaves the petitioners 55 shares short, for which the Court will award a judgment in favor of petitioners and against respondent in her capacity as testamentary executrix of the Succession of John E. Heckert in the sum of $1,100.00, being the value of 55 shares on the date of death of Mrs. Anna Buch Heckert, said sum to be chargeable as a debt of decedent's separate estate or chargeable to his one-half of the community..* * *

"There will be judgment accordingly."

Affirmed.

NOTE

It can be argued that neither the trial court nor the court of appeal successfully articulated the rationale behind the ruling in *Heckert*. There are several relevant articles: 481, 3448 and 3499. None of these articles expressly says that liberative prescription is inapplicable to the naked owner's claim for a nonconsumable. Article 481 says you cannot lose ownership by nonuse and that you can only lose ownership if another acquires that ownership through acquisitive prescription. Article 3448 says that real rights other than ownership can be lost through nonuse. And article 3499 says that personal actions prescribe after ten years.

One reason for the ruling can be drawn from articles 481 and 3448. These articles make it clear that the prescription of nonuse does not apply to ownership. Since prescription of nonuse produces more significant effects than mere liberative prescription (inasmuch as it extinguishes the right rather than merely barring the remedy), it follows *a fortiori* that liberative prescription ought not to apply to ownership.

Perhaps a more compelling reason for the ruling lies in article 3499. Personal actions prescribe in ten years. A personal action is one to enforce a personal right resulting from a personal obligation, as opposed to a real action, which is an action to enforce a real right. Ownership is a real right, not a personal right. Since article 3499 does not apply to real actions, but only personal actions, the article does not apply to the naked owner's claim for ownership of a nonconsumable. This is not the case with a consumable. Here the naked owner is bringing a personal action, to enforce the usufructuary's duty to pay the value the consumable had at commencement of the usufruct. The usufructuary owns the consumable–he holds all the elements of ownership, the entire real right. The naked owner has no real right to a consumable, but only a personal action at termination of the usufruct in which he seeks an accounting by the usufructuary.

6. LEGAL USUFRUCT

See A. N. YIANNOPOULOS, PERSONAL SERVITUDES
§§ 7:1 through 7:37 (5th ed. 2013)

NOTE
Kinds of Legal Usufruct

Article 544 of the Louisiana Civil Code declares that "Usufruct may be established by a juridical act either inter vivos or mortis causa, or by operation of law. The usufruct created by juridical act is call conventional; the usufruct created by operation of law is called legal."

There are several kinds of usufructs that are established by operation of law in Louisiana:

1.   Article 223: Parental usufruct over property of minor children during marriage.

2.   Article 890: Usufruct of surviving spouse.

3.   Article 891: Usufruct of parents over separate property inherited in naked ownership by siblings of the deceased child.

4.   Article 2434: Marital portion in usufruct over property inherited by descendants.

5.   Article 3252: Privilege of the surviving spouse in usufruct (the naked ownership devolving to the descendants of the deceased spouse).

a. The Law that Was: Legal Usufruct of the Surviving Spouse

A. N. YIANNOPOULOS, PERSONAL SERVITUDES
§ 7:8 (5th ed. 2013)
(footnotes omitted)

§ 7:8. Confirmation of the legal usufruct by will

***The Law that Was: Louisiana Civil Code of 1870.* A usufruct created by operation of law under Article 890 of the 1870 Code over the share of the deceased spouse in the community terminated upon the remarriage of the surviving spouse. The surviving spouse was not liable for the payment of Louisiana inheritance taxes; was relieved of the obligation to give security when the naked owners were children of the marriage; and there was no impingement on the legitime of forced heirs. When, however, a usufruct was created by testament, the incidents of the usufruct were quite different. In the absence of contrary testamentary disposition, the usufruct was for life; the usufructuary owed inheritance taxes; in the absence of testamentary dispensation, the usufructuary was bound to furnish security; and the usufruct could impinge on the legitime of forced heirs.

The distinction between legal usufruct and testamentary usufruct has been blurred in Louisiana by the doctrine of *confirmation* of the legal usufruct by will. According to the jurisprudence interpreting Article 916 of the Louisiana Civil Code of 1870, a testamentary disposition that was not adverse to the interests of the surviving spouse did not defeat the legal usufruct under that article. Such a disposition merely confirmed the legal usufruct.

The doctrine of confirmation of the legal usufruct by testament had no statutory foundation until the 1975 amendment to Article 916 of the Civil Code. Nevertheless, that doctrine became deeply imbedded in Louisiana law because it favored strongly the interests of the surviving spouse. Indeed, it allowed the surviving spouse in community to cumulate rights granted to him by law and those given by the will of the deceased spouse. In effect, the doctrine of confirmation of the legal usufruct by will was a part of the statutory scheme of the Louisiana Civil Code. A spouse could, confirm by testament "for life or for a shorter period" the legal usufruct in favor of the surviving spouse over the share of the community property inherited by descendants. A spouse could also grant a usufruct to the surviving spouse over separate property for life or for a shorter period, which was "to be treated as a legal usufruct." In all cases in which a spouse left by testament a usufruct to the surviving spouse, the question arose whether the usufruct of the surviving spouse was testamentary or legal.

The question of whether a testator intended to grant a testamentary usufruct or merely to confirm the legal usufruct of the surviving spouse could be answered in light of the intent of the testator as well as objective criteria. For example, a will granting a usufruct over separate property of the deceased or over property inherited by persons other than issues of the marriage was necessarily a testamentary usufruct. The question of confirmation of legal usufruct by will arise only as to community property inherited in naked ownership by descendants and in usufruct by the surviving spouse. In such a case, an interested party could claim that the usufruct was either a legal usufruct confirmed by will or a testamentary usufruct. Ordinarily, a surviving spouse would be expected to claim that the usufruct was legal. However, if the surviving spouse remarried, it would be to his advantage to claim that the usufruct was testamentary and, therefore, for life.

In *Succession of Chauvin*, the predeceased spouse left his entire succession to his son in naked ownership and to his wife in usufruct. The entire succession consisted of community property and thus all the terms for a legal usufruct under Article 916 of the Louisiana Civil Code of 1870 had been met. The Louisiana Supreme Court re-examined the doctrine of confirmation and established an objective test for the classification of a confirmed usufruct as testamentary or legal for all purposes. In the opinion of the court, a confirmed usufruct could be legal only when the disposition in favor of the surviving spouse was compatible with Article 916 of the Civil Code. Dicta indicated that when a testator varied the terms of Article 916, he did not confirm the legal usufruct but created a testamentary usufruct. This would be so in all cases in which the testator granted either greater or lesser rights than under Article 916. If a testator, for example, granted a usufruct *for life* prior to the 1975 amendment of Article 916, the usufruct would necessarily be testamentary. If the testator did not specify the duration of the usufruct over the share of the community property inherited by issues of the marriage, the usufruct would be a legal one confirmed by will. Thus, *Chauvin* did not only establish a clear distinction between legal and testamentary usufruct but also a clear test for the classification of a usufruct as legal or testamentary.

Subsequently, in *Succession of Waldron*, the Louisiana Supreme Court reaffirmed *Chauvin* to the extent that it had held that a legal usufruct could be confirmed by will and that a legal usufruct was defeated by an adverse disposition. However, the court repudiated dicta in Chauvin that confirmation required full compliance with the terms of Article 916 of the Civil Code. According to *Waldron*, a testator confirmed the legal usufruct when he gave to the surviving spouse *the same* or *greater* rights than those under Article 916. Thus, a usufruct granted for life prior to the 1975 amendment of Article 916 was held to be legal until the remarriage of the usufructuary. After remarriage, the same usufruct would be considered to be testamentary, that is, it would end at the death of the usufructuary.

b. The Law That Is: Legal Usufruct of the Surviving Spouse

LOUISIANA CIVIL CODE

Article 890 as revised by La.Acts 1996, 1st Ex. Sess., No. 77

Art. 890. Usufruct of surviving spouse

If the deceased spouse is survived by descendants, the surviving spouse shall have a usufruct over the decedent's share of the community property to the extent that the decedent has not disposed of it by testament. This usufruct terminates when the surviving spouse dies or remarries, whichever occurs first.

Revision Comments--1996

(a) This Article represents a policy decision to separate the multiple provisions of Article 890 of the Louisiana Civil Code, as it stood prior to the revision, and, in a more conceptually consistent approach, to use separate code articles to cover the different concepts. Like its predecessor (Civil Code Article 916 of the Code of 1870), Article 890 is located in the section of the Civil Code that deals with intestate succession. To the extent that the article provides a usufruct to a surviving spouse over community property inherited by descendants of the decedent, the article is appropriately placed. Over the years, however, amendments to the article (and its predecessor) have unduly complicated the article by expanding its application to matters of testate succession, such as authorizing a testator to grant a usufruct of separate property. Consequently, for reasons of stylistic purity and conceptual consistency, revised Article 890 deals only with a usufruct of the surviving spouse that arises by virtue of intestacy. A separate article covers issues of testacy, such as the ability of a testator to grant a usufruct over separate property, as well as other authorized impingements on the legitime. See Article 1499, infra.

(b) Since this usufruct arises by operation of law, it is a legal usufruct under C.C. Article 544. Although C.C. Article 573 provides that a legal usufructuary is not required to give security, C.C. Article 1514, infra, provides an exception to that rule.

NOTE
Attributes of Usufruct in Favor of the Surviving Spouse

The requirements for the creation of a legal usufruct under Article 890 of the Louisiana Civil Code are: (1) Existence of a community property regime between the spouses; (2) Devolution of the whole or of a part of the share of the deceased spouse in the community property by intestacy; and (3) Inheritance of the property of the deceased spouse by his descendants. Unless these requirements are met, there is no legal usufruct of the surviving spouse under Article 890 of the Civil Code. Thus, there is no legal usufruct if the spouses lived under a separation of property regime; there is no legal usufruct to the extent that the deceased spouse disposed by will of his share in the community; and there is no legal usufruct under Article 890 if the deceased spouse is survived by ascendants, collateral heirs, or strangers.

There is still an analytical distinction between the legal usufruct of the surviving spouse, governed by Article 890 of the Louisiana Civil Code, and testamentary usufruct in favor of the surviving spouse, governed by Article 1499 of the same Code.

1. *Impingement on the legitime.* Unlike prior Article 916 of the Louisiana Civil Code, Article 890 no longer decrees that the legal usufruct of the surviving spouse does not impinge on the legitime of forced heirs. The redactors apparently thought that the provisions of Article 1499 of the Louisiana Civil Code, governing testamentary dispositions in favor of the surviving spouse...also apply to the legal usufruct of the surviving spouse! Be this as it may, it would seem that the legal usufruct of the surviving spouse does not impinge on the legitime of forced heirs for the same reasons that the legal usufruct under Article 916 of the Louisiana Civil Code of 1870 did not impinge on the legitime of forced heirs. See Succession of Moore, 40 La. Ann. 531, 4 So. 460 (1888). See also Succession of Waldron, 323 So.2 d 434 (La. 1975).

2. *Louisiana Inheritance tax.* The usufruct of the surviving spouse, whether legal or testamentary, is free of the Louisiana inheritance tax. See La.R.S. 47:2402(1)(e).

3. *Dispensation of security prior to the 2004 amendments.* Unlike its predecessor (Article 890 of the Louisiana Civil Code, as revised by La.Acts 1990, No. 1075, *supra*), current Article 890, as revised by La.Acts 1996, 1st Ex. Sess., No. 77 does not mention the obligation of the usufructuary to provide security. It would seem therefore, that when the usufruct of the surviving spouse arose under the 1996 version of Article 890 of the Louisiana Civil Code, security was dispensed with even if the naked owners were forced heirs of the deceased spouse. However, Revision Comment

(d) under Article 890 states:

> (b) Since this usufruct arises by operation of law, it is a legal usufruct under C.C. Article 544. Although C.C. Article 573 provides that a legal usufructuary is not required to give security, C.C. Article 1514, infra, provides an exception to that rule.

It is highly questionable that Article 1514 provided an exception to the dispensation of security when the usufruct of the surviving spouse arose under Article 890 of the Louisiana Civil Code. Article 1514 declares:

> A forced heir may request security when a usufruct in favor of a surviving spouse affects his legitime and he is not a child of the surviving spouse. A forced heir may also request security to the extent that a surviving spouse's usufruct over the legitime affects separate property.

The second sentence of Article 1514 is only relevant when the usufruct is testamentary because there is no legal usufruct over separate property. Therefore, this sentence had no bearing on Article 890 and on the question of security under that article. In contrast, under the first sentence of Article 1514, a usufruct in favor of the surviving spouse may attach to both community and separate property of the deceased spouse and argument could be made that a forced heir, who was not a child of the surviving spouse, could request security even if the usufruct of the surviving spouse were a legal usufruct under Article 890 of the Louisiana Civil Code. However, Article 1514 does not mention legal usufruct and it is clear in context that this article applies to testamentary usufructs only.

Under the 1990 version of Article 890, *supra*, security was due only when a usufruct was testamentary and, by way of exception to Article 573 of the Civil Code, when the usufruct was a legal usufruct confirmed by testament over separate property or over property inherited by descendants other than issues of the marriage. See Louisiana Civil Code art. 890(4). The exception was found in the last paragraph of Article 890, which governed usufructs arising by operation of law as well as legal usufructs *confirmed* by testament. Under the 1996 revision, however, a legal usufruct established by operation of law under Article 890 is distinct and distinguishable from a testamentary usufruct authorized by Article 1499. Therefore, a surviving spouse who took a usufruct under Article 890 could well assert that the obligation to give security was dispensed with by Article 573 of the Civil Code. Further, under the 2003 amendment to Article 1499 of the Louisiana Civil Code, a surviving spouse having a testamentary usufruct is dispensed with security by operation of law unless the testator expressly provided otherwise or the usufruct attaches to the legitime of forced heirs, in which case Article 1514 of the Louisiana Civil Code still controls.

When the testator merely granted to the surviving spouse by testament the same rights that the surviving spouse would have enjoyed under Article 890 in the absence of the will, the usufructuary should be dispensed with security by operations of law, Article 1514 of the Louisiana Civil Code to the contrary not withstanding. It might be argued, of course, that naked owners, other than children of the marriage of the testator with the surviving spouse, could request security in accordance with Article 3154.1 of the Louisiana Code of Civil Procedure (repealed by La. Acts 2004, No. 158). However, despite broad language, that provision related to security due by the succession representative and only applied when the usufruct of the surviving spouse is testamentary.

4. *Dispensation of security by operation of law under the 2004 amendments.* Articles 571 and 573 of the Louisiana Civil Code governing the obligation of the usufructuary to provide security

were amended by La. Acts 2004, No. 518. For texts, see *infra*.

The second paragraph of the 2004 amendments to Article 573 effects a change in the law governing the usufruct of the surviving spouse under Article 890 of the Civil Code. After August 15, 2004, a surviving spouse having a usufruct under Article 890 of the Civil Code is dispensed with security by operation of law when the naked owner is a child of the usufructuary and not a forced heir of the deceased spouse. When the naked owner is not a child of the usufructuary, the surviving spouse may be compelled to provide security. When the naked owner is a child of the usufructuary and a forced heir of the deceased spouse, the surviving spouse may be compelled to provide security to the extent that the usufruct affects the legitime of the forced heir.

c. The Law that Is: Testamentary Usufruct of the Surviving Spouse

LOUISIANA CIVIL CODE

Art. 1499. Usufruct to surviving spouse

The decedent may grant a usufruct to the surviving spouse over all or part of his property, including the forced portion, and may grant the usufructuary the power to dispose of nonconsumables as provided in the law of usufruct. The usufruct shall be for life unless expressly designated for a shorter period, and shall not require security except as expressly declared by the decedent or as permitted when the legitime is affected.

A usufruct over the legitime in favor of the surviving spouse is a permissible burden that does not impinge upon the legitime, whether it affects community property or separate property, whether it is for life or a shorter period, whether or not the forced heir is a descendant of the surviving spouse, and whether or not the usufructuary has the power to dispose of nonconsumables. [Acts 1996, 1st Ex.Sess., No. 77, § 1. Amended by Acts 2003, No. 548, § 1].

Revision Comments—1996

(a) This Article is part of the effort to bifurcate the multiple provisions of former Civil Code Article 890, some of which dealt with testate succession and some of which dealt with intestate succession. See Revision Comments--1996 to Article 890, *supra*. The Article makes clear that a usufruct over separate property in favor of a surviving spouse does not constitute an impingement on the legitime. In Succession of Suggs, 612 So.2d 297 (La. App. 5th Cir. 1992) it was held that a usufruct to a second spouse over separate property comprising the forced portion was not permitted. The repeal of former Civil Code Article 1752 in 1995 effectively overruled Suggs by removing its only theoretical support. This Article leaves no doubt that under any circumstances, whether by clarification or by overruling, a usufruct in favor of a surviving spouse may be imposed over the legitime, whether the legitime is community property or separate property, and whether or not the spouse is a parent of the forced heir.

(b) This Article also clarifies an issue that has not yet been resolved in the courts, which is whether the testator may grant the usufructuary the power to dispose of nonconsumables as provided in the law regarding usufruct in Civil Code Article 568. There is disagreement among scholars as to whether the grant of such authority would constitute an impingement on the legitime. To remove any doubt and to establish that the grant of that right would not constitute an impingement, the Article expressly so provides.

(c) This Article does not supersede the provisions of the Louisiana Trust Code that protect a forced heir whose legitime has been placed in trust. See La. R.S. 9:1841 et seq.

(d) This Article legislatively overrules the case of Succession of B. J. Chauvin, 257 So.2d 422 (La. 1972) which held that when the will "merely confirmed" the legal usufruct to a surviving spouse over community property without specifying that it was for life, the usufruct was not a lifetime usufruct. See also Darby v. Rozas, 580 So. 2d 984 (La. App. 3d Cir. 1991), which involved a grant of a usufruct over separate property, but which was settled while an application for writs to the Louisiana Supreme Court was pending. There is a transitional provision that continues this rule for testaments executed prior to the effective date of this Act.

NOTE
Legal Usufruct and Testamentary Usufruct

The dichotomy between testamentary usufruct and legal usufruct has lost much of its significance as a result of legislative revision and it may be misleading to draw generalizations concerning "legal" and "testamentary" usufruct. It may be analytically preferable to discuss the law in terms of particular issues. For example:

Obligation to give security. This obligation is imposed, generally, on usufructuaries having a conventional usufruct, unless dispensed with by the grantor of the usufruct. However, when a spouse grants by testament a usufruct to the surviving spouse, the usufructuary is dispensed with security by operation of law. See La. Civil Code art. 1499. Nevertheless, *a forced heir* who is not a child of usufructuary may demand security when the usufruct in favor of the surviving spouse attaches to his legitime or when the surviving spouse's usufruct over the legitime affects *separate property*. See La. Civil Code art. 1514.

Article 1499, as amended by Acts 2003, No. 548, dispenses with security "except as expressly declared by the decedent or as permitted when the legitime is affected." The 2003 amendment, dispensing with security as matter of law, is pertinent for and should be inserted into Article 573 of the Louisiana Civil Code rather than Article 1499. Section 2 of Acts 2003, No. 548 declares that the provisions of this Act "are interpretative, procedural, and remedial and shall apply to testaments executed on or after June 18, 1996.

Obligation to pay Louisiana inheritance taxes. Any usufruct established in favor of the surviving spouse after December 31, 1991, whether by operation of law or by testament, escape Louisiana inheritance tax. See La.R.S. 47:2402(1)(e),

Impingement on the legitime. A usufruct established in favor of the surviving spouse under Article 890 or under Article 1499 does not impinge on the legitime of the descendants of the deceased spouse. It would seem that a usufruct established in favor of the surviving spouse under Articles 2434 and 3252 does not impinge on the legitime of the descendants of the deceased spouse for the same reason that a usufruct established under Article 890 is not an impingement on the legitime.

Termination of the usufruct. A usufruct established by testament is for life unless the testament specifies a shorter duration. A usufruct established by operation of law terminates as the law provides. Thus, a usufruct established under Article 223 terminates when the minor child attains majority, and a legal usufruct in favor of the surviving spouse established under Article 890 terminates upon the remarriage of the surviving spouse. It would seem that a usufruct established under Article 891, 2434, or 3252 is for life, and a legal usufruct that has been confirmed by will under Article 890 terminates upon the remarriage of the surviving spouse. However, argument may be made that, when confirmed by will, a legal usufruct, is to be treated as a testamentary usufruct that terminates at the death of the surviving spouse. See note Termination of Usufruct of Legal Usufruct Confirmed by Will, *infra*.

PROBLEM

A testator bequeathed to a legatee the naked ownership of property without making provision for the devolution of the usufruct. See Succession of Burguieres, 612 So. 2d 864 (La. App. 5th Cir. 1992). It should be clear that in such a case the usufruct devolves to the heirs of the testator under the laws governing intestate successions. It would be correct to state that this usufruct is established by operation of law. But is this usufruct a "legal" usufruct?

DARBY v. ROZAS
580 So. 2d 984 (La. App. 3d Cir. 1991)

LABORDE, Judge. Dr. Sidney J. Rozas died testate on April 6, 1986. In his last will and testament dated August 13, 1982, Dr. Rozas made the following bequests:* * *

> "I give and bequeath to my beloved wife, Dorothy Prejean Rozas, our home property located at 1115 Dietlein Boulevard, Opelousas, Louisiana, together with the vacant lot located to the south of such residence, including all funishing, furniture and contents. I also will and bequeath to my wife, Dorothy Prejean Rozas, the personal automobile which she may be using at the time of my death. Subject to the above, I will and bequeath to my wife, Dorothy Prejean Rozas, the usufruct of all properties owned by me, movable and immovable, separate and community, including the usufruct of all royalties and minerals. Subject to the above, I further will and bequeath to my wife Dorothy Prejean Rozas, such additional bonds, and stock and cash in order that she would receive, including the above bequest, one-half of the net value of my estate. Subject to the foregoing and to the payment of all debts and claims, including estate taxes, I bequeath all of the remainder of my

properties, movable and immovable, that I may own at my death to my two
daughters. Alice Augusta Rozas Bienvenue and Mary Ann Rozas Nicholson,
share and share alike, or per stirpes, to the descendants of any of them who
predecease me."* * *

Dr. Rozas' will was duly probated and the legatees were placed into possession of the
assets of the estate by Judgment of Possession rendered January 8, 1987, under Probate
No. P86-117-C of the 27th Judicial District Court, St. Landry Parish, Louisiana.

On June 8, 1988, defendant, Dorothy Prejean Rozas, the surviving spouse of Dr.
Rozas, contracted another marriage. Plaintiffs, Mary Ann Rozas Darby and Alice
Augusta Rozas Bienvenue, Dr. Rozas' children from a prior marriage, brought suit to
terminate defendant's usufruct. Plaintiffs also sought to recover all sums paid to
defendant as usufructuary since the date of her remarriage. The trial court ruled that the
usufruct did not terminate upon defendant's remarriage. Plaintiffs have now perfected
this appeal. We reverse and remand.

The sole issue raised by this appeal is whether the usufruct granted to defendant
terminates upon the remarriage or the death of the usufructuary. Resolving this issue
necessarily involves determining whether the usufruct granted to defendant is a legal or
testamentary usufruct.

Under Civil Code Article 544, a usufruct may be established by a juridical act either
inter vivos or mortis causa, or by operation of law. The usufruct created by a juridical act
is referred to as a conventional usufruct, and the usufruct created by operation of law is
referred to as a legal usufruct. Conventional usufructs are of two kinds: contractual
(created by an inter vivos juridical act) or testamentary (created by a mortis causa
juridical act). There are various kinds of legal usufructs in Louisiana; the one we are
concerned with is the legal usufruct of the surviving spouse over the deceased spouse's
share in the community that has been inherited by descendants.

For well over one hundred years, Louisiana has adopted some form of usufruct in favor
of the surviving spouse "to secure means of sustenance for the surviving spouse and to
prevent partition or liquidation of the community to the prejudice of that spouse."
Yiannopoulos, 3 Louisiana Civil Law Treatise: Personal Servitudes, at 381 (1989). In the
Civil Code of 1870, the usufruct of the surviving spouse was contained in Article 916. By
Act 919, which acquired the force of law on January 1, 1982, Civil Code Article 916 was
repealed and replaced by Article 890. Article 890 provides: "If the deceased spouse is
survived by descendants and shall not have disposed by testament of his share in the
community property, the surviving spouse shall have a legal usufruct over so much of
that share as may be inherited by the descendants. This usufruct terminates when the
surviving spouse contracts another marriage, unless confirmed by testament for life or for
a shorter period. The deceased may by testament grant a usufruct for life or for a shorter
period to the surviving spouse over all or part of his separate property. A usufruct
authorized by this Article is to be treated as a legal usufruct and is not an impingement
upon legitime. If the usufruct authorized by this Article affects the rights of heirs other

than children of the marriage between the deceased and the surviving spouse or affects separate property, security may be requested by the naked owner."

It is important to point out that a usufruct granted in favor of a surviving spouse can be legal or testamentary. When a usufruct is created by operation of law under Article 890, the following consequences attach: (1) the usufruct terminates upon remarriage; (2) the surviving spouse is not liable for the payment of Louisiana inheritance taxes; (3) the surviving spouse is relieved of giving security when the naked owners are children of the marriage; and (4) the usufruct does not impinge on the legitime. If the usufruct is testamentary: (1) in the absence of contrary testamentary disposition, the usufruct is for life; (2) the surviving spouse owes taxes; (3) in the absence of contrary testamentary disposition, the surviving spouse must provide security; and (4) the usufruct can potentially impinge on the legitime.

As Professor Yiannopoulos notes in his treatise, "[the distinction between legal usufruct and testamentary usufruct has been blurred in Louisiana by the doctrine of confirmation of the legal usufruct by will." Yiannopoulos, Personal Servitudes, at 392. Several early decisions interpreted Article 916 (the predecessor to Article 890) very narrowly, holding that any disposition by will defeated the legal usufruct in favor of the surviving spouse. See, e.g., Succession of Schiller, 33 La. Ann. 1 (1881); Forstall v. Forstall, 28 La. Ann. 197 (1876). However, later, a line of jurisprudence overruled these cases and determined that a testamentary disposition that was not adverse to the interest of the surviving spouse did not defeat the usufruct. See, e.g., Succession of Waldron, 323 So. 2d 434 (La. 1975); Succession of Chauvin, 260 La. 828, 257 So. 2d 422 (1972). In other words, the surviving spouse is entitled to the legal usufruct under Article 890 unless a testamentary disposition is adverse to the legal usufruct. The Louisiana Supreme Court in Succession of Waldron, *supra*, observed that such an adverse disposition may occur when the testator makes an excessive disposition to persons other than the surviving spouse of the portion of the estate which is subject to the legal usufruct, or, very simply, if the testator expressly states his intention that the legal usufruct does not apply.

Under Article 890, a testator may confirm by testament the legal usufruct of the surviving spouse over the share of the community inherited by descendants "for life or for a shorter period." A testator may also grant to the surviving spouse "for life or a shorter period" a usufruct over all or a portion of his separate property. Professor Yiannopoulos points out that whenever a testator grants the surviving spouse a usufruct, the question that naturally arises is whether that usufruct is testamentary or legal. He writes: "In all cases in which a predeceased spouse bequeaths to the surviving spouse a right of usufruct, the right may qualify as a legal usufruct, even if the usufruct is over separate property. However, it would be absurd to suggest that because the application of Article 890 ordinarily favors the interests of the surviving spouse a testator necessarily establishes a legal usufruct when he grants a usufruct to his surviving spouse. A testator enjoys testamentary freedom not to confirm the legal usufruct under Article 890, and he may by will enlarge or diminish the rights that the surviving spouse has under Article 890 in the absence of a will. As in the past, the question of the nature of the usufruct that the testator intended to create is a matter of testamentary interpretation. In the absence of express language qualifying the usufruct as legal or testamentary, the intent of the testator must be gathered from the provisions of the will. When a testator grants to the surviving spouse as usufructuary rights that are incompatible with the notion of legal usufruct, he intends to grant a testamentary usufruct." Yiannopoulos, Personal Servitudes, at 394. As examples of "rights that are incompatible with the notion of legal usufruct" Professor Yiannopoulos uses the hypothetical of a testator authorizing the usufructuary to grant a mineral lease without the consent of the naked owner, in contravention of Louisiana Mineral Code Article 190(B), and the hypothetical of the testator granting the usufructuary free reign to dispose of at his discretion corporeals and incorporeals, movables and immovables, contrary to Article 568 of the Civil Code.

In the case at bar, we can find nothing in Dr. Rozas' testament which would indicate that his intent was to create a testamentary and not a legal usufruct. Essentially, defendant received the disposable portion of the estate in full ownership and a usufruct over the community and separate property bequeathed to plaintiffs. We determine that such a bequest is not "incompatible with the notion of legal usufruct" and in no way constitutes an adverse disposition.

Defendant does argue, however, that the usufruct of all royalties and minerals is "incompatible with the notion of legal usufruct." We disagree. Under Louisiana Mineral Code Article 190(B).* * *

> "B. If a usufruct of land is that of a surviving spouse, whether legal or conventional, and there is no contrary provision in the instrument creating the usufruct, the usufructuary is entitled to the use and enjoyment of the landowner's rights in minerals, whether or not mines or quarries were actually worked at the time the usufruct was created. However, the rights to which the usufructuary is thus entitled shall not include the right to execute a mineral lease without the consent of the naked owner." We find nothing in the usufruct of royalties and minerals granted to the surviving spouse which would be "incompatible with the notion of legal usufruct."

Defendant also argues that the usufruct granted over separate property is an exclusive characteristic of testamentary usufruct. This is simply just not the case under Civil Code Article 890 and the jurisprudence construing it. Article 890 allows the testator to grant a usufruct over all or part of his separate property. Paragraph three of Article 890 states that "a usufruct authorized by this Article is to be treated as a legal usufruct and is not an impingement upon legitime." In Succession of Steen, 499 So. 2d 1338 (La. App. 3d Cir. 1986), rev'd on other grounds, 508 So. 2d 1377 (La. 1987), the decedent died possessing both community and separate property. By testament the deceased spouse gave his descendants the forced portion of his community and separate property and bequeathed to his spouse the disposable portion of his estate. The testament further confirmed the legal usufruct over all of his community property and granted his surviving spouse a usufruct over all of his separate property. This court observed in that case: "It is clear from the literal provisions of Article 890 of the Louisiana Civil Code that a decedent may by testament grant a usufruct for life to his surviving spouse over all or a part of his separate property.... Such a testamentary usufruct is a legal usufruct by operation of law." Succession of Steen, at 1342; see also Succession of Daly v. McNamara, 515 So. 2d 661 (La. App. 3d Cir. 1987), writ denied, 519 So. 2d 119 (La. 1988). The Supreme Court granted writs in that case and in its review stated, "by testament, a spouse may grant a usufruct over all or part of his separate property... any usufruct granted by a testator to a spouse is to be treated as a legal usufruct." Succession of Steen, 508 So. 2d 1377, 1379 (La. 1987). Additionally, Professor Yiannopoulos notes: "Normally, a usufruct created by a testament ought to be qualified as a testamentary usufruct; however, according to Article 890(2) and (3), the usufruct that a spouse establishes by a testament over his separate property in favor of the surviving spouse qualified as a legal usufruct." Yiannopoulos, Personal Servitudes, at 409. Accordingly, we find that the usufruct granted by Dr. Rozas over both his community and separate property qualifies as a legal usufruct.

In his testament, Dr. Rozas neglected to set out the duration of the usufruct over his community property and his separate property. It is clear that under Article 890 (paragraph one), if no period is designated for the confirmed legal usufruct over community property, it terminates on the surviving spouse's remarriage. See Succession of Chauvin, *supra*; Succession of Vallette, 538 So. 2d 707 (La. App. 4th Cir.), writ denied, 543 So. 2d 20 (La. 1989). Regarding the usufruct over separate property, Article 890 (second paragraph) states that the testator may grant it for life or shorter period, but nothing is stated concerning what happens when the testator neglects to set out the duration of the usufruct. Professor Yiannopoulos squarely addresses this point: "It is preferable ... to read Article 890(2) and (3) in the light of the first paragraph of the same article and to conclude that the usufruct should terminate upon the remarriage of the surviving spouse. The alternative would be to qualify the usufruct as testamentary, which, in certain cases at least, would be contrary to the intent of the testator." Yiannopoulos, Personal Servitudes, at 409. Professor Yiannopoulos' view makes good sense and we agree with it. Therefore, the usufruct granted over Dr. Rozas' community and separate property terminated on defendant's remarriage occurring June 8, 1988.

Plaintiffs would have this court remand this matter to the trial court for an accounting for all sums which may have been paid to defendant as usufructuary after her remarriage, as the trial court did not allow any evidence with regard to values. This court grants the remand for such purpose.

For the foregoing reasons, the judgment of the trial court is reversed. The case is remanded for further proceedings not inconsistent with this opinion. All costs are to be borne by defendant, Dorothy Prejean Rozas. Reversed and remanded.

FORET, J., dissents with reasons. I respectfully dissent from the majority opinion. I would affirm the result of the trial court judgment, although not necessarily the reasoning.

The uncertainty of the law in this area is exemplified by the fact that the majority, as I did as the original author, relied a great deal on Professor Yiannopoulos' treatise. In this dissent, as I did in my review, I will refer to the page numbers in 49 LLR 803 rather than the treatise as cited by the majority opinion. This is purely for my convenience and I apologize therefor. The articles are identical.

With all due respect to the majority opinion, and to Professor Yiannopoulos, I make mention of the fact that Professor Yiannopoulos' article and the majority reviewer vacillate a great deal in discussing the Louisiana jurisprudence and statutory law.

The fiction of the legal usufruct relied on by the majority is just that, a fiction. The "legal" usufruct evolved in this context as an inheritance tax avoidance device and to pronounce, in Article 890 (third paragraph), that such a usufruct "is not an impingement on the legitime."

A usufruct is either legal or testamentary. It is a legal usufruct where it comes into being by operation of law, ... period. If a usufruct does not come into effect by operation of law, then it is a conventional or testamentary usufruct. There is no other way. You can call it a flop-eared dog if you wish, but you are still dealing with a testamentary usufruct.

Testamentary usufructs terminate as specified by the testator, either specifically, or as gleaned from his intent. It appears to me that it is just as logical, if not more so, to hold that if a testator does not designate a term for the testamentary usufruct, that his intention can be presumed to be that it will terminate at the death of the usufructuary. To surmise, as does the majority, that the testator's intent was that it would terminate upon remarriage of the usufructuary, is rank speculation.

As for the majority's relying on Professor Yiannopoulos' observation that it is "preferable" that the usufruct terminate at remarriage, I would simply note here that some folks like their eggs scrambled; others hate broccoli.

One observation by Professor Yiannopoulos in an Epilogue to his article, that the majority fails to mention, is that in 1983 Senator Casey introduced Senate Bill 137. At 49 LLR, 803, page 839, Professor Yiannopoulos points out that, among other things, Senator Casey proposed to amend the third paragraph of C.C. art. 890 as follows: "A usufruct authorized by this article terminates when the surviving spouse contracts another marriage, unless confirmed by testament for life or for a shorter period. A usufruct authorized by this article is to be treated as a legal usufruct and is not an impingement on the legitime....Yiannopoulos goes on to say, at page 840, that: "The third paragraph of the proposed amendment would clarify the ambiguity of the present law concerning the termination of a usufruct granted to the surviving spouse over separate property without indication as to its duration. Under the proposed amendment, a usufruct over separate property would terminate, like a usufruct over community property, upon the remarriage of the surviving spouse, unless confirmed by testament for life or for a shorter period. "These modest amendments met resistance from professors and attorneys and were advisedly deferred." (emphasis provided.)

The "modest amendments" are still "deferred" by the Louisiana Legislature. The majority opinion, it seems to me, is indulging in judicial legislation by reading into the third paragraph of Article 890 an interpretation thereof that was declined by the Louisiana Legislature and advised against by professors and attorneys as being better left to triers of fact to determine the intent of the testator. To use the term "legal usufruct" as a tool to possibly thwart the intent of the testator and substitute the court's own sense of equity to dispose of the testator's will is injudicious. If the testator, a medical doctor, had intended the usufruct of his separate property to be for a shorter period, he would have said so. If he had intended the usufruct to terminate at the marriage of the usufructuary, he would have said so.

The term "legal" in the context of Article 890 is ambiguous when it is considered in the context of the other provisions of conventional, legal, and testamentary usufructs. As such, the legislative intent is determinative. The failure of the attempted amendment to Article 890 by Senator Casey loudly attests to the fact that the legislative intent is contrary to the majority opinion herein. I respectfully dissent.

NOTE
Termination of Usufruct of Legal Usufruct Confirmed by Will

Suppose that Mr. Taste Tator was married to Mrs. Alma Tator under the regime of community property. The couple had one child, Nick, an issue of the marriage. Mr. Tator died on October 13, 2004, in his domicile in New Orleans, Louisiana. He left a will and provided: *"I give to my beloved wife Alma the usufruct of my share in the community"* Is Alma's usufruct legal or testamentary? When should the usufruct in favor of Alma terminate?

Under the pre-1996 Revision law, Alma's usufruct was a legal usufruct that had been *confirmed by will.* See Succession of Chauvin 260 La. 828, 257 So 2d 422 (1972), In that case, the testator had left his entire estate to his son in naked ownership and to his wife in usufruct. The entire estate consisted of community property and, therefore, all the requirements for a legal usufruct under Article 916 of the Louisiana Civil Code of 1870 had been met. In the absence of a provision granting to the surviving spouse a usufruct *for life*, the court held that the testator had *confirmed* by his will the operation of Article 916 of the Civil Code and that the usufruct of the surviving spouse should terminate on remarriage.

Article 890 of the Louisiana Civil Code now declares that the surviving spouse "shall have a usufruct over the decedent's share of the community property to the extent that the decedent has not disposed of it by testament." The redactors apparently thought that this sentence suffices to suppress the pristine doctrine of *confirmation* of the legal usufruct by will. Comment (d) under Article 1499 asserts "This Article overrules the case of Succession of B.J. Chauvin." This assertion is highly questionable.

Take the above hypothet. Mr Taste Tator bequeathed to Alma Tator the usufruct of his share in the community. At first blush it would seem that because the testator disposed by testament of his share in the community, Article 890 of the Louisiana Civil Code does not apply and that under Article 1499 of the Louisiana Civil Code, (first paragraph, second sentence), the usufruct in favor of Alma Tator is a testamentary usufruct for life. In contrast, under *Chauvin*, the usufruct in favor of Alma would terminate on her remarriage and, to that extent, one may assert that *Chauvin* has been overruled legislatively.

One may seriously doubt, however, that the doctrine of confirmation of the legal usufruct by will, as established by Louisiana *jurisprudence constante,* commencing with the *Succession of Moore,* 40 La. Ann. 531, 4 So. 460 (1888), has been overruled legislatively *by a comment* which is neither law nor source of law. The pertinent language of Article 890, as revised in 1996, is the same as in prior Article 890, and it is reasonable to attribute to the new provision the meaning that was attributed to its predecessor. Courts may well continue to apply in appropriate cases the doctrine of confirmation of the legal usufruct by will that has been established by Louisiana *jurisprudence constante* despite the partial overruling of the *Chauvin* decision. Assume for example, that Mr. Taste Tator's will provided" *I give to my beloved wife Alma a usufruct as provided in Article 890 of the Louisiana Civil Code*". Mr. Taste Tator has merely confirmed by will the operation of Article 890 of the Civil Code and Alma's usufruct should terminate on remarriage under Article 890 rather than on her death under Article 1499. To that extent, *Chauvin* is alive and well.

Upon conclusion, the legal usufruct of the surviving spouse under Article 890 of the Civil Code terminates on remarriage whereas a testamentary usufruct in favor of the surviving under Article 1499 is for life. If a testator gave by will to the surviving spouse "a usufruct under Article 890," question would arise whether this usufruct is a legal usufruct or a testamentary usufruct According to the comments accompanying Article 1499, such a usufruct should be "for life" because the possibility of confirmation by will no longer exists. However, naked owners, and especially the descendants of the testator, may plausibly argue that the testator clearly intended to create a usufruct that should terminate on the remarriage of the usufructuary.

d. The Law that Is: Obligation to Give Security

LOUISIANA CIVIL CODE

Art. 571. Security

The usufructuary shall give security that he will use the property subject to the usufruct as a prudent administrator and that he will faithfully fulfill all the obligations imposed on him by law or by the act that established the usufruct unless security is dispensed with. If security is required, the court may order that it be provided in accordance with law [as amended by La. Acts 2004, No.158].

Art. 573. Dispensation of security by operation of law

Security may be dispensed with by the grantor of the usufruct or by operation of law when a person has a legal usufruct under Civil Code Article 223 or 3252.

Security is dispensed with by operation of law when a surviving spouse has a legal usufruct under Civil Code Article 890 unless the naked owner is not a child of the usufructuary or unless the naked owner, although a child of the usufructuary, is a forced heir of the decedent. In the latter case, the naked owner may obtain security only to the extent of his legitime.

Security is dispensed with by operation of law when a parent has a legal usufruct under Civil Code Article 891 unless the naked owner is not a child of the usufructuary.

Security is dispensed with by operation of law when a surviving spouse has a legal usufruct under Civil Code Article 2434 unless the naked owner is a child of the decedent but not a child of the usufructuary. Legal usufructuaries, and sellers or donors of property under reservation of usufruct are not required to give security [as amended by La.Acts 2004, No. 158].

NOTE

Article 573 of the Louisiana Civil Code, as revised in 1976, dispensed with security when a usufruct arose by operation of law under Articles 223, 890, 891, 2434 or 3252 of the Louisiana Civil Code. However, the provisions of that article were affected by the revision of the laws governing Successions and by the 2004 amendments (La. Acts 2004, No. 158, effective August 15, 2004. The 2004 amendments are not retroactive. Accordingly, a clear analysis of the prior law and of the changes effected by the 2004 legislation is desirable.

1. *The law in force before August 15, 2004.* Under the 1990 version of Article 890 of the Louisiana Civil Code, the surviving spouse in community could be compelled to give security when the legal usufruct attached to separate property of the deceased spouse or when the naked owners were persons other than children of the marriage. For discussion, see Yiannopoulos, 3 Louisiana Civil Law Treatise, Personal Servitudes § 121 (4th ed. 2000). However, after the 1996 revision of Article 890 security was dispensed with even if the naked owners were not issues of the marriage between the deceased and the surviving spouse. Further, after the 1996 revision of Article 890, the legal usufruct in favor of the surviving spouse attaches to community property only and a usufruct over separate property is necessarily testamentary. Therefore, when the usufruct of the surviving spouse attached to separate property of the deceased spouse, security was not dispensed with by Article 573 but it could be dispensed by Article 1499 that governs testamentary usufructs in favor of the surviving spouse.

2. *Security and forced heirs.* When the usufruct of the surviving spouse arose under the 1996 version of Article 890 of the Louisiana Civil Code, security was dispensed with even if the naked owners were forced heirs of the deceased spouse. When, however, the usufruct in favor of the surviving spouse was testamentary, forced heirs could in certain circumstances request security. See Louisiana Civil Code art. 1499, as amended by Acts 2003, No. 548; *id.* art. 1514.

Under the 1990 version of Article 890, security was due only when a usufruct was testamentary and, by way of exception to Article 573 of the Civil Code, when the usufruct was a legal usufruct confirmed by testament over separate property or over property inherited by descendants other than issues of the marriage. The exception was found in the last paragraph of Article 890, which governed usufructs arising by operation of law as well as legal usufructs *confirmed* by testament.

Under the 1996 revision, however, a legal usufruct established by operation of law under Article

890 is distinct and distinguishable from a testamentary usufruct authorized by Article 1499. Therefore, a surviving spouse who took a usufruct under Article 890 could well assert that the obligation to give security was dispensed with by Article 573 of the Civil Code. Further, under the 2003 amendment to Article 1499 of the Louisiana Civil Code, a surviving spouse having a testamentary usufruct is dispensed with security by operation of law unless the testator expressly provided otherwise or the usufruct attaches to the legitime of forced heirs, in which case Article 1514 of the Louisiana Civil Code still controls.

When the testator merely granted to the surviving spouse by testament the same rights that the surviving spouse would have enjoyed under Article 890 in the absence of the will, the usufructuary should be dispensed with security by operations of law, Article 1514 of the Louisiana Civil Code to the contrary not withstanding. It might be argued, of course, that naked owners, other than children of the marriage of the testator with the surviving spouse, could request security in accordance with Article 3154.1 of the Louisiana Code of Civil Procedure (repealed by La. Acts 2004, No. 158). However, despite broad language, that provision related to security due by the succession representative and only applied when the usufruct of the surviving spouse is testamentary.

4. *Dispensation of security by operation of law under the 2004 amendments.* The first paragraph of the 2004 amendments to Article 573 does not change the law. In accord with the prior law, security is dispensed with by operation of law when a usufruct arises under Article 223 or Article 3252 of the Louisiana Civil Code. New Article 573 declares that security may be dispensed with "by the grantor of the usufruct or by-ex (sic!) operation of law when a person has a legal usufruct under Civil Code Article 223 or 3252." The words "by the grantor of the usufruct" are superfluous and, in context, meaningless. Obviously, there is no "grantor of the usufruct" when the usufruct arises by operation of law as is the case under Articles 223 and 3252.

The second paragraph of the 2004 amendments to Article 573 effects a change in the law governing the usufruct of the surviving spouse under Article 890 of the Civil Code. After August 15, 2004, a surviving spouse having a usufruct under Article 890 of the Civil Code is dispensed with security by operation of law when the naked owner is a child of the usufructuary and not a forced heir of the deceased spouse. When the naked owner is not a child of the usufructuary, the surviving spouse may be compelled to provide security. When the naked owner is a child of the usufructuary and a forced heir of the deceased spouse, the surviving spouse may be compelled to provide security to the extent that the usufruct affects the legitime of the forced heir.

The third paragraph of the 2004 amendments to Article 573 clarifies that security is dispensed with by operation of law only when a parent has a legal usufruct under Article 891 of the Civil Code and the naked owner is a child of the usufructuary. A naked owner who is not the child of the usufructuary may, therefore, demand security. Security is also dispensed with by operation of law when the usufruct of a surviving spouse arises under Article 2434 of the Civil Code, if the naked owner is a child of the usufructuary. A naked owner who is the child of the deceased spouse and not a child of the usufructuary may compel the surviving spouse to provide security.

LOUISIANA CIVIL CODE

Art. 1514. Usufruct of surviving spouse affecting legitime; security

A forced heir may request security when a usufruct in favor of a surviving spouse affects his legitime and he is not a child of the surviving spouse. A forced heir may also request security to the extent that a surviving spouse's usufruct over the legitime affects separate property. The court may order the execution of notes, mortgages, or other documents as it deems necessary, or may impose a mortgage or lien on either community or separate property, movable or immovable, as security.

Revision Comment—1996

(a) The first sentence of this Article makes a limited exception to the rule that a legal usufructuary is not required to give security. See Civil Code Article 573.

(b) This Article allows the forced heir to request security in instances where the testator leaves the surviving spouse a usufruct that affects his legitime, and the forced heir is not a child of the surviving spouse. A forced heir may also request security to the extent the usufruct affects legitime composed of the decedent's separate property, and in that instance the security may be required even if the usufructuary is the parent of the forced heir.

(c) This Article essentially reenacts the provisions of the last paragraph of Civil Code Article 890, which was originally adopted in 1981 and was amended periodically thereafter. Article 890 expanded the law by which its predecessor Article 916 (1870) granted a usufruct to a surviving spouse that would terminate upon the death or remarriage of the surviving spouse, but only as to community property inherited by issue of the marriage. Civil Code Article 916 did not authorize a usufruct over community property that was inherited by children of a prior marriage or by illegitimate children, nor did it authorize a usufruct over separate property. When the law was expanded to permit a testator to grant such a usufruct to a surviving spouse, the last paragraph of Civil Code Article 890 was also added to authorize the naked owner in those instances to request security. In the absence of such an authorization, the usufruct of the surviving spouse would be a "legal" usufruct and security would not have been acquired. See Civil Code Article 573. The legislature made a policy decision that children of a prior marriage and illegitimate children are entitled to greater protection than are children of the marriage, or, in other words, to treat a surviving spouse who is the parent of the naked owner different from a surviving spouse who is not the parent of the naked owner. This Article continues that policy, but the language has been revised slightly and the provision itself has been appropriately moved to a different section of the Civil Code. Civil Code Article 1499 of this revision expressly authorizes a decedent to grant a surviving spouse a usufruct over all or part of his property, including the forced portion, and to grant the usufructuary the power to dispose of nonconsumables. This Article continues in place the rule that where the usufruct affects the legitime of a forced heir who is not a child of the usufructuary, then that child "may" request security. Where the usufruct applies to separate property, however, it matters whether the separate property forms part of the legitime but not whether the naked owner is a child of the surviving parent who is the usufructuary. This Article permits a naked owner, even one who is a child of the surviving spouse, to request security whenever the naked ownership comprising the legitime consists of separate property.

(d) There are no reported cases under the predecessor Article, Civil Code Article 890 (1981) interpreting the nature of the duty or obligation of the court to impose security when a naked owner requests it, or the extent of the security, or even the nature of the security. If one parses the sentence, it is apparent that the requirement of "security" is not automatic; the naked owner must first make a request for security to be required. And the very word "security" itself is susceptible of several different meanings. There are many forms of security, such as a surety bond, a legal or conventional mortgage, and perhaps, in a more colloquial sense, a designation of the nature of an investment. An example of that latter kind of provision is found in Civil Code Article 618, which applies when, for example, a usufruct of a nonconsumable is transformed into a usufruct of a consumable and the naked owner and the usufructuary are unable to agree on the investment of the proceeds within one year of the transformation of the property. In that case, Civil Code Article 618 authorizes the court to determine the nature of the investment. It is hoped that courts will not inflexibly apply the rule of this Article to require a usufructuary to post bond every time a naked owner requests security, but will consider all of the circumstances of the situation, such as the nature of the property that comprises the legitime, and whether the property is movable or immovable, consumable or nonconsumable, and what practical controls exist or may be used to protect the right of the naked owner without infringing on the rights of the usufructuary, or if so, by infringing in the least restrictive manner possible.

(e) It should be noted that since the testator can alienate the disposable portion in full ownership there is no reason to require a bond when he has donated something less than that, namely, a usufruct only.

NOTE
Power to Dispose of Nonconsumables

Article 1499 of the Louisiana Civil code declares that "[t]he decedent... may grant the usufructuary the power to dispose of nonconsumables *as provided in the law of usufruct*" (emphasis added). Article 568 of the Louisiana Civil Code declares:

The usufructuary does not have the right to dispose of nonconsumables unless the right has been *expressly* granted to him. Nevertheless, he may dispose of corporeal movables that are gradually and substantially impaired by use, wear, or decay, such as equipment appliances, and vehicles, provided that he acts as a prudent administrator... (emphasis added).

The wording of Article 1499 is either ambiguous or redundant. Apparently, this article refers to the requirement that the grant to the usufructuary of the right to dispose of nonconsumables be made *expressly*. It does not refer to the right of the usufructuary to dispose of nonconsumables that are gradually and substantially impaired by use, wear, or decay because the usufructuary has that right by operation of law.

EXERCISE ON LEGAL USUFRUCT

Antoine and Mary Boudoin were married in New Orleans, Louisiana, in 1968 under the regime of community property. It was the first marriage for both parties. There was a single issue of that marriage, Ernest.

Mary died on January 13, 1997, at her domicile in New Orleans. She was 78 years old, and was survived by Antoine, who is 82 years old, and her only child, Ernest, who is 50 years old. Mary's succession consists exclusively of her share in the community property and has an approximate value of $12,000,000.00. Mary has satisfied Ernest's legitime by a series of inter vivos donations. Mary's last will and testament executed on May 31, 1996, provides in pertinent part:

"I confirm Antoine's usufruct under Article 890 of the Louisiana Civil Code. Ernest's legitime has been amply satisfied by donations inter vivos.

Antoine shall be entitled to all mineral revenues, royalties and working interests. Antoine shall have the greatest possible freedom to act that can be given a usufructuary under the Louisiana Civil Code, and particularly but not exclusively the right to dispose of nonconsumables and to reinvest the proceeds in nonconsumables subject to the usufruct.

I name Antoine executor of my succession, and I relieve him of the obligation to furnish security."

Antoine and Ernest came to your office for a consultation. They wish to discuss with you the nature and effect of Antoine's usufruct. What is your advice?

Variation: Suppose that Mary's will was executed on July 31, 1996 and that Mary died on October 13, 2004. Would your answer be the same?

e. Reduction of Excessive Donations of Usufruct, Full Ownership, or Naked Ownership

LOUISIANA CIVIL CODE

Art. 1496. Permissible burdens on legitime

No charges, conditions, or burdens may be imposed on the legitime except those expressly authorized by law, such as a usufruct in favor of a surviving spouse or the placing of the legitime in trust.

Revision Comment 1996

This Article reproduces the substance of Article 1710 of the Louisiana Civil Code (1870). It retains the fundamental principle of prior law, that a forced heir is entitled to his legitime in full ownership. Despite that general principle, however, there are well-recognized impingements on the legitime that are permitted. The two most prominent exceptions to the general rule are the usufruct of a surviving spouse, in Civil Code Articles 890 and 1499, and the ability of the testator to place the legitime in trust, in La. R.S. 9:1841 et seq. and La. Constitution, Article XII, Section 5. Another example of a condition that may be imposed on the legitime is the short-term survivorship provision presently authorized by Civil Code Article 1521.

Art. 1503. Reduction of excessive donations

A donation, *inter vivos or mortis causa,* that impinges upon the legitime of a forced heir is not null but is merely reducible to the extent necessary to eliminate the impingement.

Revision Comments—1996

(a) This Article reproduces the substance of the first paragraph of Article 1502 of the Civil Code of 1870. It changes the law in part by eliminating the rule set forth in the second paragraph of Article 1502, to the effect that if each presumptive heir receives the same value of property during a calendar year the donation is not subject to reduction. There is no need for such a provision in light of the adoption of a three year cut off period as provided in La. R.S. 9:2372, as adopted by Act 402 of 1995, and Article 1505(A) of this revision. Under La.R.S. 9:2372 there is a three year cut off on including gifts in the calculation of the "active mass" to determine the forced portion as well as to be subject to the action to reduce. Section 2 of Act 402 may have been unnecessarily restrictive, in limiting the application of that act to donations made on and after January 1, 1996, and this revision contains a provision to make it more effective. Under Article 1505(A) of this revision whether gifts are of an equal value or not in the same year, if they were given three or more years before the decedent dies, they would not be included under any circumstances.

(b) Under this Article, if the husband's will leaves all to his wife and there is a forced heir who is entitled to one-fourth, the legacy to the wife is reduced to the disposable portion in full ownership and a usufruct for life, with the power to dispose of nonconsumables, over the forced portion, since that usufruct could have been left to her expressly under Article 1499. This is the maximum extent to which reduction is needed to eliminate the excess that impinges upon the legitime, since the decedent could legally have made such a bequest to his surviving spouse. No further reduction is necessary or appropriate.

NOTE
Dispositions in Favor of the Surviving Spouse

A disposition *in usufruct* in favor of the surviving spouse is never excessive. Article 1499 of the Louisiana Civil Code declares that a usufruct over the legitime in favor of the surviving spouse "is a permissible burden that does not impinge upon the legitime." However, a disposition in favor of the surviving spouse in full ownership or in naked ownership may be excessive. For example, when a testator leaves to the surviving spouse the naked ownership of his entire estate, the disposition impinges on the legitime of forced heirs because "the legitime may not be satisfied in whole or in part by a usufruct." (La. Civil Code art. 1502).

Under the prior law, the reduction of an excessive disposition *in naked ownership* in favor of the surviving spouse spawned divergent views concerning the method of reduction. Article 1503 now declares cryptically that such a disposition is "reducible to the extent necessary to eliminate the impingement" but it does not expressly provide guidelines as to the proper method of reduction of the excessive donation. It would seem that in such a case, the disposition in favor of the surviving spouse will be reduced to the naked ownership of the disposable portion and that the forced heirs will receive their legitime in full ownership. However, one might well argue that, since the disposition in favor of the surviving spouse is not necessarily an adverse disposition, the surviving spouse may claim, in addition to the naked ownership of the disposable portion, a legal usufruct under Article 890 of the Civil Code over the legitime of the forced heirs.

Questions also arise concerning the method of reduction when the excessive disposition in favor of the surviving spouse is *in full ownership.* It would seem that in such a case, the surviving spouse will receive the disposable portion in full ownership and, possibly, also a usufruct over the legitime of forced heirs. Under the prior law, this result was reached in *Winsberg v. Winsberg*, 253 La. 67, 96 So. 2d 44 (1857), and its progeny by application of the doctrine of confirmation of the legal usufruct by testament. However, if it were maintained that the doctrine of confirmation has been suppressed in the 1996 revision, the surviving spouse should merely receive the disposable portion in full ownership.

Comment (b) under Article 1503 states that "if the husband's will leaves all to his wife and there is a forced heir who is entitled to one-fourth, the legacy to the wife is reduced to the disposable portion in full ownership and a usufruct for life, with the power to dispose of nonconsumables, over the forced portion, *since the usufruct could have been left to her expressly under Article 1499.* This is the maximum extent to which reduction is needed to eliminate the excess that impinges upon the legitime since the decedent could legally have made such a bequest to the surviving spouse. No further reduction is necessary or appropriate" (emphasis added). The underscored phrase is a non sequitur.

The surviving spouse will be clearly entitled to the full ownership of the disposable portion, and, if the *Winsberg* decision has not been undermined by the revision, the surviving spouse will also receive a usufruct over the forced portion consisting of community property. There is absolutely no authority for the proposition that the surviving spouse will also receive a usufruct over the forced portion consisting of separate property of the deceased. A usufruct on separate property may be created by testament only. See La. Civil Code art. 1499. A usufruct by operation of law attaches to community property only. See La. Civil Code art. 890. Accordingly, in *Winsberg*, the surviving spouse received a usufruct over the share of the deceased in the community property. Further, there is absolutely no authority for the proposition that the surviving spouse will have power of disposition over non-consumables other than corporeal movables that are gradually and substantially impaired by use, wear, or decay. See La. Civil Code art. 568. The right to dispose of non-consumables generally may only be granted by *express* disposition. *Id.*

NOTE
Disposition in Usufruct in Favor of Persons other than
the Surviving Spouse

Testators adopt at times a plan of distribution whereby the usufruct of their estate is given to a chosen legatee and the naked ownership is left to forced heirs. According to Article 1496 of the Louisiana Civil Code a donation of usufruct to a stranger may not burden the legitime of forced heirs, and according to Article 1503 of the same Code such a donation is excessive and "reducible to the extent necessary to eliminate the impingement." The cryptic statements in Article 1503 and accompanying revision comments do not resolve the question of the mode of reduction of an excessive donation. The underlying assumption of the redactors seems to be that the usufruct will be removed from the legitime, and that the legatee of the usufruct will merely take the usufruct over the disposable portion. Correspondingly, the forced heirs will receive the legitime in full ownership as well as the naked ownership of the disposable portion. However, in the absence of a legislative text determining authoritatively the mode of reduction of excessive donations of usufruct, there is an invitation to uncertainty and conflicting opinions. Moreover, litigants and courts might be tempted to revisit Louisiana decisions involving the question of reduction of excessive donations of usufruct under the quite different regime of the Louisiana Civil Code of 1870.

Article 1499 of the Louisiana Civil Code 1870 provided for the mode of reduction of excessive donations of usufruct: if the testator had given to the legatee a usufruct of no more value than that of the disposable portion of his estate, the donation was valid. If however, the value of the usufruct exceeded the *value* of the disposable portion, the donation was excessive and should be reduced. In such a case, forced heirs had the option either to execute the disposition as made by the testator or claim the legitime in full ownership and abandon to the legatee the disposable portion of the estate in full ownership. According to the literal meaning of that provision, corresponding to Article 917 of the French Civil Code, forced heirs could not exercise the option unless the condition was met that the usufruct be of greater value than the disposable portion. Nonetheless, determination of the value of a usufruct was not an easy matter in the past, and difficulties connected with the valuation of usufruct gave rise to "most abstruse and unworkable theories in French law."

f. Intertemporal Conflicts of Laws

LOUISIANA REVISED STATUTES

R.S. 9:2441. Duration of usufruct in previously executed testament. A testament executed prior to the effective date of this Act leaves a usufruct to the surviving spouse without specifying its duration, the law in effect at the time the testament was executed shall govern the duration of the usufruct (La. Acts 1996, No. 77, eff. June 18, 1996).

LOUISIANA CIVIL CODE

Art. 870. Modes of acquiring ownership

The ownership of things or property is acquired by succession either testate or intestate, by the effect of obligations, and by the operation of law.

Testate and intestate succession rights, including the right to claim as a forced heir, are governed by the law in effect on the date of the decedent's death (as amended by La. Acts 2001, No.560, eff. June 22, 2001).

Art. 1611. Intent of the testator controls

The intent of the testator controls the interpretation of his testament. If the language of the testament is clear, its letter is not to be disregarded under the pretext of pursuing its spirit. The following rules for interpretation apply only when the testator's intent cannot be ascertained from the language of the testament. In applying these rules, the court may be aided by any competent evidence. When a testament uses a term the legal effect of which has been changed after the date of execution of the testament, the court may consider the law in effect at the time the testament was executed to ascertain the testator's intent in the interpretation of a legacy or other testamentary provision (as amended by La. Acts 2001, No.560, eff. June 22, 2001).

NOTE
Prescription of Claims

Article 3497 of the Louisiana Civil Code establishes a five year prescription for an action to annulment of a testament and for an action for the reduction of an excessive donation. This prescription is suspended in favor of minors during minority. Thus for successions opened five years ago, there is no annulment and no reduction, unless the prescription is suspended on account of the minority of heirs.

g. The marital portion in usufruct

See A.N. YIANNOPOULOS, PERSONAL SERVITUDES
§§ 214-218 (4th ed. 1999)

NORSWORTHY v. SUCCESSION OF NORSWORTHY
704 So. 2d 953 (La. App. 2d Cir. 1997)

MARVIN, Chief Judge. In this action by the widow, Rebecca Norsworthy, against the succession of her late husband, William Norsworthy, for the La. C.C. art. 2432 marital portion, the succession appeals a judgment awarding her the periodic allowance authorized by La. C.C. art. 2437. Appellant contends the trial court overvalued the net estate of decedent and miscalculated the marital portion to reach the monthly allowance of $2,500. We affirm the periodic allowance award.

DISCUSSION

Decedent died testate on May 27, 1995 after he had married plaintiff almost four years before. The Norsworthys agreed to a separate property regime, which did not and legally, could not, waive either spouses right to claim the marital portion if the other spouse died "rich" in comparison to the claiming spouse. La. C.C. arts. 2330, 2432.

Besides his widow, decedent was survived by two adult children, one of whom is the executrix of his estate. Decedent specially bequeathed to his widow their home, its furnishings, and a 1989 Jaguar automobile. The home secured a mortgage indebtedness of more than $36,000 and had a net value of $113,634. The household furnishings bequeathed to plaintiff were valued at $10,000, the Jaguar at $12,450. Decedent also named plaintiff as the beneficiary of a $250,000 insurance policy on his life. The executrix and plaintiff agreed that plaintiff was entitled to claim the marital portion (1/4 of the succession in usufruct in this instance, not to exceed $1 million) but did not agree on the amount or value of decedent's succession or estate.

After a hearing on the motion for periodic allowance, the trial court determined the periodic allowance by simply using the net value of the estate shown on the federal estate tax return, $3,716,727, which included $1,330,639 in life insurance proceeds payable to beneficiaries other than the estate and plaintiff.

The succession correctly argues that beyond exposure to federal estate tax liability, life insurance proceeds payable to a beneficiary other than decedent's estate are not considered as a part of a Louisiana decedent's estate. American Health & Life Ins. Co. v. Binford, 511 So. 2d 1250, 1253 (La. App. 2d Cir. 1987) (citing T.L. James and Company, Inc. v. Montgomery, 332 So. 2d 834 (La.1975)). See also Dupuy v. Dupuy, 52 La. Ann. 869, 27 So. 287, 289 (La. 1899). We agree that the Louisiana estate (decedent's succession for the purpose of determining the marital portion) should not include life insurance proceeds payable to beneficiaries other than the estate. We also agree that the life insurance proceeds payable to the spouse claiming the marital portion should be deducted from the marital portion.

We are here concerned only with the amount of the periodic allowance, whether the $2,500 monthly allowance is abusively high and potentially threatens to exceed the marital portion if it unduly continues for a lengthy period and to exhaust the estate. Otherwise, the Civil Code expressly allows for an adjustment upon the final fixing of the marital portion. La. C.C. art. 2437. Moreover, at this juncture, plaintiff, who is not in the position of a forced heir and who does not appeal or answer the executrix's appeal, cannot complain that the trial court included in its deductions from the marital portion its evaluation of the social security benefits to be paid to plaintiff during her lifetime, or urge that other properties should be included in decedent's estate, fictitiously or otherwise. La. C.C.P. art. 2133; Succession of Caraway, 25,879 (La. App. 2d Cir. 6/22/94), 639 So. 2d 415. See also A.N. Yiannopoulos, Personal Servitudes § 215, in 3 Civil Law Treatise (3d ed. 1989) (citing Francois v. Tufts, 955 So. 2d 813 (La. App. 4th Cir. 1990), writ denied, 575 So. 2d 368 (La. 1991)).

In any event, decedent's estate is solvent and liquid, able to pay the monthly allowance without unduly affecting the estate's solvency and liquidity. The appellant, decedent's daughter and executrix who complains of the amount of the monthly allowance, has the authority to promptly conclude the succession and effectively terminate the monthly allowance.

At this juncture the value of decedent's Louisiana succession and the marital portion has not been determined either by the trial court or this court. The trial court's calculations were made to serve only as a basis for determining the monthly allowance that is here complained of. We consider the trial court's calculations solely for the purpose of addressing the argument of each litigant. We do note relatively minor arithmetical mistakes in the trial court's calculations, which we have corrected in an unpublished appendix, not to be binding here or below on the litigants. For discussion purposes only, the net value of the federal estate appears to be at least $3,700,000. After the life insurance proceeds payable to beneficiaries other than the estate are excluded, the Louisiana estate appears to have a net value of about $2,400,000. The marital portion is 1/4 of the net value of the Louisiana estate. La. C.C. art. 2434.

Deductions from the marital portion mandated by La. C.C. art. 2435 include the assigned value of plaintiffs legacies, life insurance proceeds, social security death benefit [$255] and the value of social security benefits attributable to decedent's contributions to the social security system. We repeat that we need not pass on the trial court's deductions or calculations because the marital portion, after mandated deductions are made, will leave the net marital portion at more than $150,000. La. C.C. art. 2435. See unpublished appendix. The net marital portion will exceed most multiples of the $2,500 monthly allowance.

The succession also contends the trial court created a windfall for plaintiff by not discounting the marital portion (usufruct) to its present value of the usufruct. The succession reasons that because Mrs. Norsworthy received in full ownership legacies and other monetary benefits, her marital portion in usufruct should be discounted to its present value so that its true value relative to the legacies and benefits she received in full ownership can be ascertained. La. C.C. arts. 2434, 2435. In effect, the succession would have us find the value of one-fourth of the succession in usufruct by using the American Experience Table of Mortality in La. R.S. 47:2405, before making the mandated deductions, by first multiplying the marital portion by .7393 88, the present value of a life usufruct of $1 to a person Mrs. Norsworthy's age. Appellant then argues that after the mandated deductions that remaining figure is then to be secondly divided by .739388, which results in Mrs. Norsworthy being entitled to a marital portion of only $33,276. We cannot agree.

There being two surviving children of decedent, art. 2434 provides for a marital portion of one-fourth (1/4) of the succession in a lifetime usufruct. Art. 2434 does not provide that the marital portion is the present value of a lifetime usufruct over one-fourth of the succession. See A.N. Yiannopoulos, Personal Servitudes § 217, *supra*. The trial court correctly applied art. 2434, noting Comment (d) to this article, which states that:

> The surviving spouse is entitled to the usufruct of one-fourth or of a lesser fraction of the succession, depending on the number of children. He is not entitled to the value of such a fraction in usufruct or to a usufruct having a value equal to that of such a fraction of the succession. Succession of Henry, 287 So.2d 214 (La. App. 3d Cir.1973), is overruled to the extent that it is inconsistent with Article 2434.

We also note Comment (c) to the same article:

> The survivor receiving the marital portion in usufruct incurs, in principle, the rights and duties of usufructuaries under the general law. Taylor v. Taylor, 189 La. 1084, 1093, 181 So. 543, 546 (1938). *Cf.* Hartford Accident & Indemnity Co. v. Abdalla, 203 La. 999, 14 So. 2d 815 (1943). He is exempt, however, from the requirement of posting security. The usufruct attaches to the proceeds of a liquidated succession and is one of money. The principle of "le mort saisit le vif" does not apply to the marital portion. Since Article 2382 makes no provision for termination of the usufruct upon remarriage, this usufruct is for life and terminates in accordance with the general provisions governing usufruct. See C.C. Arts. 607- 629, as revised in 1976.

We used the correct method in Succession of Caraway, *supra*. Compare Succession of Mullin v. Mullin, 93-758 (La. App. 3d Cir. 2/2/94), 631 So. 2d 647, 650. We follow Caraway and not Mullin.

CONCLUSION

La. C.C. art. 2437 authorizes the periodic allowance. We emphasize its provisions:

When, during the administration of the succession, it appears that the surviving spouse will be entitled to the marital portion, he has the right to demand and receive a periodic allowance from the succession representative.

The amount of the allowance is fixed by the court in which the succession proceeding is pending. If the marital portion, as finally fixed, is less than the allowance, the surviving spouse is charged with the deficiency.

The record suggests that Mrs. Norsworthy's monthly expenses are about twice the amount of the periodic allowance awarded by the court. In this appeal by the succession, we review only the judgment awarding Mrs. Norsworthy the monthly allowance of $2,500 to determine whether it is abusively high. It is not. Considering that Mrs. Norsworthy's net marital portion in usufruct, when finally determined, will obviously be more than $150,000, we cannot say that the trial court abused its discretion in awarding the $2,500 monthly allowance during the administration of the succession as provided by art. 2437, *supra*.

DECREE

The judgment, at appellant's cost, is AFFIRMED.

From Federal Estate Tax Return:

Decedent's Estate Assets:
$2,293,000 Real Estate
1,330,639 Life Insurance with beneficiaries other than plaintiff 1,047,983 Stocks and Bonds
39,862 Annuities +11,404 Misc.
Total Assets 4,722,888

Less- 983,353 Debts [Undisputed]
Net Estate $3,739,535

We deduct -1,330,639 Life Ins, to beneficiaries other than plaintiff
Total Estate $2,408,896 x ¼ Marital Portion $602,224
Less 416,458 Art. 2435 Deductions
Marital Portion $185,766

Above figures and calculations, at this juncture, are not binding on litigants, on trial court or this court, but are offered solely for discussion purposes to resolve the respective arguments of appellant and appellee in this appeal.

CHAPTER XVIII. DEDICATION TO PUBLIC USE
La. Civil Code arts. 450, 455, 457-459

1. DEDICATION TO PUBLIC USE

A. N. YIANNOPOULOS, CIVIL LAW PROPERTY
§§ 91-95 (4th ed. 2001)
(footnotes omitted)

§ 91. Nature of Public Use

A member of the public has the right to use things that are subject to public use in accordance with their nature or destination. The exercise of this right may depend on compliance with laws and regulations designed to safeguard the public use in the interest of all. The power to regulate the public use is reserved to the state and its political subdivisions.

Things subject to public use are "out of commerce," that is, insusceptible of private relations incompatible with public use. They are inalienable, imprescriptible, and exempt from seizure as long as they are subject to, or needed for, public use. One encroaching on a thing subject to public use without right does not acquire the right to possess it; hence, he has no standing to bring a possessory action on the ground that his possession has been disturbed. Constructions encroaching on the public use may be removed at the instance of the state, its political subdivisions, or of a private person.

In Louisiana, public use has been likened to a servitude in favor of the general public or of the state and its political subdivisions. However, it would be preferable to distinguish between the right of a member of the general public to enjoy a thing subject to public use and a public servitude in favor of the state or its political subdivisions for the construction and maintenance of navigation facilities, roads, levees, and other public works. Thus, the right of a member of the general public to enjoy a thing subject to public use may properly be regarded as an incident of personality, whereas the right of the state or its political subdivisions to appropriate the banks of a navigable river for the construction of navigation facilities, roads, and levees may properly be classified as a limitation on the ownership of the banks in the nature of a legal servitude.

The conception that the right of the state or its political subdivisions over a private thing subject to public use is a legal servitude furnishes an acceptable basis for the resolution of several problems. The rights of the general public, of the state and its political subdivisions, and of the owner of a thing subject to public use may be defined, regulated, and protected by analogous application of the rules governing servitudes. In case of termination of the public use due to either natural or legal causes, the question of the ownership of the thing may find an easy solution. No longer burdened by a servitude of public use, the thing belongs to its owner, be he a private or a public person, in full unencumbered ownership.

§ 92. Public Use and Private Rights of Enjoyment

In Louisiana, a private person may have a real or a personal right for the enjoyment of a thing subject to public use. Such a right may be granted by the state or a political subdivision, or it may be reserved by the owner who dedicates a thing to public use. The state may grant a lease for oil and gas production from the beds of navigable water bodies, and a political subdivision may grant a franchise for the construction and operation of a tramway on a public street. In granting such a right, administrative authorities enjoy a wide measure of discretion. However, they may not grant a right that excludes public use or substantially interferes with it. Administrative acts are subject to judicial review and are annulled if they are found to be discriminatory, arbitrary, or capricious.

In civilian terminology, private rights on things subject to public use that are compatible with, and in most instances serve, the public interest are termed *concessions*. A concession is a unilateral act of the public authorities, even if it is based on a prior contract with the recipient of the right. The content, duration, and transferability of a right arising under a concession are matters depending on particular circumstances and the terms of the concession. Such a right is regarded as an administrative real right akin to a servitude. If a private thing is subject to public use, the consent of its owner is a prereq-uisite for a valid concession. Another prerequisite is that the private right granted should not exclude or obstruct the public use. A concession may be revoked only if the official act so provides. In the absence of such a provision, the concession may be taken away only under the law governing expropriation for public utility. This feature distinguishes a concession from a mere license that is freely revocable.

§ 93. Protection of Public Use

Public use gives rise to multiple legal interests. The state and its political subdivisions have a right of a public law nature in things that are common or public things and in private things that are subject to public use. This right is manifested in police power for the regulation of the public use. The owner of a private thing that is subject to public use has a private ownership under the Civil Code, but he may not exercise prerogatives that are incompatible with public use.

A member of the general public has a right to participate in the public use. This right is neither a personal nor a real right, but an incident of personality. In civil law systems, this right of a member of the general public is accorded a wide measure of protection. It may not be alienated, it cannot be lost by prescription, and it cannot be abandoned. Moreover, any unwarranted interference with that right gives rise to an action for damages or injunction

§ 94. Incidents and Effects of Public Use

An owner may convey to the public the ownership of a tract of land or a servitude to be used for designated purposes, such as a park, an open space, a cemetery, or a road. While public use continues, a thing dedicated to public use is "out of commerce," in the sense that it is not susceptible of private relations that are incompatible with public use. The owner of the thing, however, may still exercise prerogatives and derive advantages that do not interfere with the public use. Thus, he may be entitled to a treasure found in the land, to the proceeds of mineral operations, and to the civil or natural fruits of the property. Upon termination of the public use, ownership regains its full significance as it is freed of the burden of public use.

Things dedicated to public use may be put by the public authorities to uses other than those for which they are dedicated, provided that such uses are not contrary to the public interest. For example, a publicly owned park may be put to mineral production, provided that its use as a park is not materially impeded. A police jury may expand a courthouse in a public square owned by it, although the improvement may result in modification of the public use of the park as a place of rest, recreation, and entertainment. The public authorities enjoy a wide measure of discretion, but, in cases of palpable abuse, the state, its political subdivisions, or any citizen may bring an action for the preservation of the public use.

Courts and writers have experienced difficulties in distinguishing among the various modes of dedication and in determining the incidents and effects of each. Much confusion may be dispelled by abandoning efforts at generalization and by focusing attention on particular modes of dedication.

§ 95. Modes of Dedication to Public Use

The Louisiana Civil Code provides modes by which an owner may transfer to the public the ownership of lands or establish servitudes, but it does not deal with dedication to public use. As a matter of fact, Louisiana has never enacted comprehensive legislation dealing with dedication, and courts have had to struggle over the years to develop an impressive body of jurisprudence governing the requisites for, and the incidents and effects of, dedication to public use.

Under the Civil Code, an owner has always been able to dedicate land to public use in accordance with the provisions governing gratuitous dispositions. However, this faculty has not been frequently used. Since early in the nineteenth century, question arose whether dedication may be effected in a less formal way; and, in the course of almost two centuries, several forms of dedication have become established.

One mode of dedication is by virtue of a written act, whether in notarial form or under private signature. This mode of dedication is known as "formal dedication." A second mode of dedication is by virtue of the sale of lots with reference to a plan showing streets, squares, and other public places or by an informal offer to the public to use a road and acceptance by the public by actual use. This is known as "implied" dedication. A third mode of dedication is by compliance with the provisions of R.S. 33:5051, which impose on subdividers of land certain duties, including the filing of plats and the recordation of a formal dedication. This is known as "statutory" dedication. Finally, a fourth mode of dedication is by virtue of R.S. 48:491, that is, the maintenance of roads and streets by the public for three years. This is known as "tacit" dedication.

HAINES v. ST. JOSEPH BAPTIST CHURCH
96 So. 3d 1256 (La. App. 5th Cir. 2012)

EDWARDS, J. ...The matter arises as the result of a Suit to Quiet Title filed by Haines against St. Joseph. In the petition, Haines stated that he was the owner of immovable property in the Saddler Subdivision, Lots Nos. 19 and 20, at 5613 Fourth Street in Marrero, Louisiana. He urged that he had purchased the property from the Succession of Josephine Trupiano, wife of/and Frank Romano, in 1995. His predecessor in title had, in turn, purchased the lots in 1928 and 1929, and, in the early 1940's, had constructed their family home on the lots. It was admitted that the structure encroached on the adjoining lot, 210-A, owned by St. Joseph. Haines urged that he and his ancestors in title had maintained open, peaceful, and uninterrupted possession and that he should be recognized as owner of the encroachment by virtue of thirty years of acquisitive prescription. St. Joseph answered, urging that the encroachment constituted a trespass, and that lot 210-A is and has been used as a cemetery, is in the public domain, and is not subject to acquisition by possession.

Haines filed a Motion for Summary Judgment, following which St. Joseph also moved for summary judgment in its favor. The trial court conducted a hearing and subsequently granted Haines' motion while denying that of St. Joseph. St. Joseph has appealed.

Haines filed a copy of the 1928 Act of Sale of Lot 20 from Westminster Presbyterian Church of New Orleans to Mr. Romano as well as a copy of the 1929 Act of Sale of Lot 19 from Dominick Saladino to Mr. Romano. He also filed affidavits from Romano's granddaughter and grandson, attesting that the Romanos had owned Lots 19 and 20, and they had built the existing structure in the 1940's as their family home. A copy of the 1952 assessment roll for the Parish of Jefferson was filed, evidencing Mr. Romano as owner of the lots and improvements, as well as a copy of the 1995 act of sale to Haines. A copy of a 1995 survey indicates the improvements to the lots extend onto Lot 210-A, for a distance of eleven feet. Finally, Haines attached a copy of a Quitclaim deed dated January 30, 1996, in which Marrero Land and Improvement Association transferred Lot 210-A to St. Joseph.

In support of its motion, St. Joseph attached a copy of a survey done in 1996 evidencing Lot 210-A as a cemetery that contained at least one grave. Further, it attached an Affidavit of Ownership passed in March 1983, from the Rev. Talton W. Lewis, former Pastor of St. Joseph, establishing that the lot has been known as the St. Joseph Cemetery and that the church had participated in many burial rites there. The affidavit references a 1921 Plan of the "Robinson Avenue Subdivison," and describes the cemetery plot as the "last lot facing Fourth Street...next to Lot No. 210." According to the affidavit, the map indicates an official dedication of the cemetery plot, and the church has exercised control over it and been recognized as the owner. The affidavit stated it was to be recorded registering the plot in the name of St. Joseph.

The transcript reveals the trial court found that, prior to the present laws passed in 1974 (presumably *La. R.S. 8:1 et seq*), there was no specific delineation of "what constituted a cemetery, whether or not there was one indefinable [sic] headstone or not...." The trial court considered the date that the house was constructed and the "date of the dedication." The court then found there was no law detailing cemetery uses, that is, "what they must contain and what they must indicate," and granted summary judgment in favor of Haines while denying St. Joseph's motion. In so doing, the court determined that, although the building did encroach on the lot in question, it "did not really violate the law regarding...cemetery uses." The judge concluded that Haines was not in violation of the law, and his boundary should be "that line that an engineer might draw that would encompass just the house and the slab it's sitting on...allowing for any easements that may exist and be concomitant with any building structures."

Prior to codification of cemetery laws, our jurisprudence determined the law regarding cemeteries. According to the cases, a graveyard becomes dedicated for cemetery purposes by virtue of the long and exclusive usage of this property for these purposes. The Third Circuit summed up the law as follows:

> In *Locke v. Lester, 78 So.2d 14 (La.App.2nd Cir. 1955)*, plaintiffs sought to determine the boundary between a cemetery and the neighboring landowner. Landowner contended that the cemetery had never been properly dedicated, but the record showed that for over fifty years there had been no restrictions or conditions imposed upon the right of anyone to be buried in the cemetery, and it was informally dedicated to the public. The Court stated:

> "We are of the opinion the reservation of said tract of land for use by the public as a burial ground or cemetery, and its continuous use by the general public since it was set apart as a burial ground, [are] legally sufficient to dedicate said property for public use. In *Humphreys v. Bennett Oil Corporation, 1940, 195 La. 531, 197 So. 222, 227*, where under consideration was a plot of ground which had been transferred to a church for church and cemetery purposes, the court held that by making herself a party to the deed the vendor showed unmistakably an intention to set the lot apart for church and cemetery purposes to be devoted and consecrated to those purposes only. In the opinion Justice Odom said:

"It is our opinion, and we hold, that the dedication of this plot of ground for cemetery purposes was complete, and, since plaintiffs relied in good faith on the dedication made by the owners of the land and buried their relatives there under permits, it follows that they acquired rights therein which could not be divested by any subsequent disposition made of the property either by the fee owners or the churches, or both. 'The one-acre plot of ground having been set apart for a cemetery and its use for that purpose having been accepted by these plaintiffs and many others, neither the fee owners nor the churches could later use, or empower another to use, it for any purpose inconsistent with the use for which it was dedicated. * * *'

'Where the intent of the transferor has been to abandon certain property for public use and the property is used by the general public, the dedication thereof will be regarded as complete without necessity of formal acceptance by a public or quasi-public corporation. (Citations omitted)

'A parcel of land or property dedicated for use by the general public as a cemetery and which continues to serve that public purpose, is classified as a public thing under provisions of the LSA-Civil Code, and as such it is not susceptible of ownership, cannot be alienated and is not subject to prescription. *LSA-Civil Code Articles 453, 454, 458, 481, 482* and *483*. [Rev. La. Civ. Code of 1870; current numbers 450, 452, 453, 455], (other Citations omitted.) * * *' *78 So.2d 14, 15, 16.*[1]

Summary judgments are reviewed on appeal de novo. An appellate court thus asks the same questions as does the trial court in determining whether summary judgment is appropriate: whether there is any genuine issue of material fact, and whether the mover is entitled to judgment as a matter of law.

In the present matter, Haines contends that there is no evidence that the property in question was a cemetery until the Quitclaim deed was executed by Marrero Land Company in 1996. According to Haines, his ancestors in title had peaceable uninterrupted possession for thirty years prior to that act and, therefore, *La. C.C. art. 3486* applied to grant him title.

Our de novo review of the evidence of record discloses that St. Joseph has placed at least one material fact at issue, that is, how long has the subject property been a cemetery? The fact that it was transferred to St. Joseph by Quitclaim in 1996 does not put the question to rest. According to the affidavit of Rev. Lewis, the lot had been used for burial for many years prior to 1983, and there exists a survey evidencing its dedication as such at least as far back as 1921. If the dedication of the lot as a cemetery was complete

---

[1] Vidrine v. Vidrine, 225 So.2d 691, 696-97 (La. App. 3 Cir. 1969), writ refused, 254 La. 853, 227 So.2d 594 (1969). See also, In re St. James Methodist Church of Hahnville, 95-410 (La. App. 5 Cir. 12/27/95), 666 So.2d 1206, 1209, writ denied, 96-0278 (La. 3/15/96), 669 So.2d 421.

prior to the thirty years asserted by the plaintiff, then, under the existing law, Haines' ancestors in title could not assert acquisitive prescription. The jurisprudence quoted above appears to give St. Joseph standing to assert this action. Also see *Riverie v. Mills*, [481 So.2d 1050 (La. App. 1 Cir. 1985)], wherein the First Circuit found that plaintiffs who had relatives buried in the cemetery had a right to bring an action for declaratory judgment to require the defendant to remove a fence allegedly encroaching on cemetery property.

The existence of this material fact precludes summary judgment in favor of either party at this time. Haines was not entitled to judgment as a matter of law.

Therefore, we reverse the summary judgment in favor of Haines, affirm the denial of summary judgment in favor of St. Joseph, and remand the matter to the trial court for further proceedings. Because we set aside the summary judgment, the judgment denying a new trial is moot.

2. TYPES OF DEDICATION

a. Formal Dedication

A. N. YIANNOPOULOS, CIVIL LAW PROPERTY
§ 97 (4th ed. 2001) (footnotes omitted)

§ 97. Formal Dedication

In a strict sense, a formal dedication is a donation of a thing or of its use to the public for designated public purposes. As a donation, a formal dedication ought to conform with the requirements of substance and form governing gratuitous dispositions. For example, the act of dedication ought to be made in authentic form and it ought to be accepted by the public. Examples of this form of dedication are found in Louisiana jurisprudence.

However, strict compliance with the requirements governing donations would be cumbersome. It would discourage or even defeat dedication in many cases. For these reasons Louisiana courts have taken a much broader view of formal dedication that has no foundation in legislative texts. According to the jurisprudence, a formal dedication is a donation to the public that may be made by a written juridical act. Thus, neither authentic form nor acceptance of the donation by the public is required. There must be, however, a clear intent to dedicate.

A formal dedication must be proved. The production of an old city map showing streets and other public places does not establish a formal dedication, but it may establish an implied dedication. A formal dedication may not be revoked by the grantor. The public authorities, however, may revoke the dedication when the street is no longer needed for public use. In a formal dedication, the ownership of the property is transferred to the public, unless it is expressly or impliedly retained. For example, the act of dedication may expressly convey to the public a servitude only or it may convey the land to the public for designated uses with a reservation of ownership. In either case, the interest that the public acquires is a servitude of public use. A reversionary clause in an act of dedication is valid.

In Louisiana doctrine and jurisprudence, a dedication resulting from substantial compliance with R.S. 33:5051 is frequently called "formal" dedication. This usage is confusing. In this treatise, the words "formal dedication" are used to designate a dedication made by a written act whether executed in authentic form or under private signature. A dedication in compliance with the applicable statute is designated "statutory dedication."

CITY OF BATON ROUGE v. BIRD
21 La. Ann. 244 (1869)

LUDELING, C.J. In January, 1867, the plaintiff obtained an injunction to restrain the Sheriff from selling two squares of land situated in the city of Baton Rouge, designated in the pleadings as "Mexico Square" and "Government Landing." The petitioner alleges that the property belongs to the city of Baton Rouge, and that it has been in the possession of the city for more than twenty years without interruption. The petitioner then recites that the heirs of Elie Beauregard, having instituted proceedings for a partition of the property, obtained an order to sell these squares for that purpose. The plaintiff denies that said heirs have any right, title or claim to the property, and prays that the city of Baton Rouge may be declared the owner of the two squares of ground, and be quieted in its possession thereof.

The defendants deny all the allegations contained in the petition, and especially that the city of Baton Rouge has any title to the property in its own right; they aver that if the city has any title, it is for the benefit of and interest for them. They allege that they are the true and lawful owners of the property, the sale whereof has been enjoined, and they pray that judgment may be rendered quieting them in their title and possession, and dissolving the injunction with damages.

The nature of the titles under which the parties respectively claim is not stated in the pleadings. From the evidence and the brief in this case, it appears that the claim of the city of Baton Rouge to the property in question is founded on a dedication of these squares to public use by Elie Beauregard, the ancestor of the defendants, who now claim to be the owners of the two squares.

In the beginning of this century Elie Beauregard was in possession of a plantation adjoining the post of Baton Rouge, on which now stands the principal part of the city of Baton Rouge. He laid off a part of this tract into lots, streets and squares; he prepared a plan of the proposed city, and he published a notice of his intentions and plan.

This must have been done anterior to the acquisition of Louisiana by the United States, as the map contains sites (emplacements) for the location of "Government Palace," "Intendance," and "King's Store."

The map in evidence is admitted to be correct, and in exact accordance with the plan described in Beauregard's advertisement. This map, as well as the advertisement of the plan of the city, clearly shows that the squares in question were intended to be dedicated to public use.

On the map a space is designated as "Plaza de Mexico," and another space, fronting the river, is designated as "Plaza de Colomb." In his advertisement Elie Beauregard says:

> "J'ajouterai seulement quelques explications relatif au plan actuel."... "Il y a sept places publiques de differentes dimensions." ["I will add only some explanations related to the actual plan....There are seven public plazas of different dimensions." --trans. by ed.]

Of Plaza de Mexico and Plaza des Florides he says:

> "Ces deux places, que pourrai[e]nt être, par la suite, ornées d'une fontaine dans leur milieu, auront 230 pieds de large sur 340 de longeur, et communiqueront â la Grande Place par des rues de traverse." ["These two plazas, that could be, subsequently, ornamented with a fountain in the middle, will be 230 feet in width by 340 in length, and will communicate with the Grand Plaza by cross streets."--trans. by ed.]

Couisinard testified that he had known Mexico Square about thirty-eight or forty years — that it had never been held as private property, and was always considered as belonging to the city of Baton Rouge during that time. Government Landing, or Plaza de Colomb, is at the foot of Government street.

J. E. Elam testifies that he has known Mexico Square and Government Landing about twenty-five years; that neither of these places had ever been claimed or occupied as private property during that time. They were always considered and treated as public places. In 1865 Mexico Square was surveyed at the instance of the city; streets were laid off, and trees were planted on the square. What is known as Government Landing is designated as Plaza de Colomb on the plan of the city, and the tradition relating to it is that it was intended as a public landing.

Has there been a dedication of the two squares to public use?

"There is no particular form or ceremony necessary in the dedication of land to public use. All that is required is the assent of the owner of the land, and the fact of its being used for the public purposes intended by the appropriation." (Cincinnati v. White) 6 Peters, 110 (8 L. ed. 452); (New Orleans & C.R. Co. v. Town of Carrollton) 3 An. 282.

In this case an actual dedication has been proved. The consent of the owner is contained in the publication of his plan of the city, made at least as early as 1803, in which he says:

> "Il y a sept places publiques de differentes dimensions."***

> "Il y a aussi plusieurs autres emplacements destinés pour des etablissements publiques, tels que Palais du Gouvernement, Maison de Ville, Intendance," etc. ["There are also several other sites destined for public establishments, such as the Government Palace, City Hall, Supplies Office, etc." -- trans. by ed.]

The map of the city represents the two squares as public places; the spaces occupied by them are not divided into lots, and a name is given to each square—Plaza de Mexico and Plaza de Colomb.

The evidence in the record shows that the property in question has always been regarded as public places; that they have never been assessed as private property, and that they have been left unoccupied and open as commons for the use of the public from the date of the dedication till 1865, when trees were planted in the Plaza de Mexico.

Lots were bought and sold with reference to the plan of the founder of the city. After being thus set apart for public use and enjoyed as such for more than half a century, and private rights had been acquired with reference to it, the original owner or his heirs cannot be permitted to deny or revoke such dedication.

To do so would be a violation of good faith to the public, and to those who have acquired private property with a view to the enjoyment of the use thus publicly granted. We are authorized, therefore, in holding that there was a dedication to public use of the two squares in question, and that they are *"hors de commerce."[out of commerce*—trans. by ed.]***

The facts in this case are different from those in the cases in Livaudais v. Municipality No. 2, 5 Ann. 8; Livaudais v. Municipality No. 2, 6 La. 509; and David v. Municipality No. 2, 14 Ann. 872. In these cases there was "no evidence of dedication out of the plan (map) and none in the plan out of the word Coliseum," etc. The Court held that a Coliseum, market and church may be private property, and that merely writing these words across a square on a plan of a town was not proof of the intention of the owner to dedicate them to public uses. But in this case there cannot be room to doubt what Beauregard's intention was — his language, corroborated by the map in evidence, is unmistakable.

It is therefore ordered, adjudged and decreed that the judgment of the District Court be avoided and reversed, and that there be judgment in favor of the city of Baton Rouge, quieting it in its title and possession to Mexico Square and the Plaza de Colomb, and perpetuating the injunction issued in this case.

QUESTIONS

1. Given that there is "no particular form or ceremony necessary in the dedication of land to public use," what evidence does the court point to in support of its reversal of the trial court's injunction?

2. What policy with respect to the city's development does the court's rejection of private ownership in favor of dedication to public use foster?

b. Implied Dedication

A. N. YIANNOPOULOS, CIVIL LAW PROPERTY
§§ 98 (4th ed. 2001) (footnotes omitted)

§ 98. Implied Dedication

Since the early nineteenth century, question arose in Louisiana whether dedication may be accomplished without any written act at all. In Mayor v. Gravier, the earliest reported decision concerning dedication, a landowner had subdivided his plantation in accordance with a plan showing a public square and had sold lots surrounding the square with reference to the plan. When his heirs sought to erect buildings on the square, the court enjoined them on the ground that the square had been "destined to public use" by the former owner.

A few years later, in *DeArmas v. Mayor*, plaintiff brought a petitory action seeking recognition of his ownership of a tract of land adjacent to the Mississippi River in the city of New Orleans. The city defended the suit on the ground that the property in question was, according to the original city plan, a quay, a thing insusceptible of private ownership. The majority of the court held that the designation of an area as quay in the city plan did not operate as a conveyance of the property to the public. Judge Martin dissented. According to him a quay was a public thing that could not be claimed by an individual in a private action. The public could establish that it was a thing subject to public use by producing evidence showing "the plan of the city and the subsequent use."

In the following decades, after much litigation, it became settled that dedication to public use may be accomplished without any express or written act. This mode of dedication came to be known, in contradistinction with formal dedication, as "implied dedication."

The essential feature of implied dedication is the absence of requisite formalities. However, there must be, "a plain and positive intention to give and one equally plain to accept." Thus, the two indispensable elements of implied dedication are: proof of a positive intent to dedicate, frequently qualified as "offer," and proof of acceptance by the public. The offer may be implied from facts or acts of the owner that exclude any other rational hypothesis except an intent to dedicate and the acceptance may be inferred from actual use of the property by the public. The very idea of implied dedication was borrowed from common law jurisdictions; and, for this reason, implied dedication is also known as "common law" dedication. Louisiana courts have frequently relied upon common law authorities to support propositions concerning the incidents and effects of this mode of dedication. Cases are legion.

Courts have declared on several occasions that "it suffices that the owner permits the land to be used by the public with the intention of making the dedication." However, decisions establishing an implied dedication by the toleration of public use are extremely rare and may be explained on other grounds, such as estoppel vis-à-vis the public authorities. The jurisprudence is well settled that immemorial use by the public does not alone establish dedication. The two generally accepted examples of implied dedication are the sale of lots with reference to an original city plan or with reference to a sub-division plan showing streets, squares, and other public places. In contrast with a sale, the *donation* of lands with reference to a subdivision plat showing streets, squares, and/or public places does *not* result in dedication.

A dedication arising by application of R.S. 48:491, that is, the maintenance of a street by the public for a period of three years, is frequently qualified in Louisiana decisions as an implied dedication. This mode of dedication is more aptly designed as "tacit" dedication. In this treatise, the words "implied dedication" refer to a dedication arising from the sale of lots with reference to an original plan of the city or the plat of a subdivision.

The question of the nature of the interest acquired by the public as a result of an implied dedication was seldom raised in the nineteenth century. In most cases, the issue before the court was whether one could obstruct the public use of an allegedly dedicated street. If the court found that the street had been actually dedicated to public use, it would render a judgment enjoining obstruction of the public use without reaching the question whether the plaintiff or the defendant owned the bed of the street. If the court found that, despite sales of lots with plats annexed, there was no dedication either because the streets had not be opened or had not been used by the public, the question of the interest acquired by the public by virtue of an implied dedication was equally moot. The same is true of cases involving the public use of places other than streets. In certain cases, courts found an implied dedication to public use without ever considering the question of the ownership of such places. In other cases, however, courts refused to find dedication under the evidence before them. Dicta in these cases indicate that if there had been a dedication, it would have established merely a servitude in favor of the public.

When the issue of the interest acquired by the public as a result of an implied dedication was determinative, courts have held since early last century that an implied dedication establishes merely a servitude of public use. In an isolated instance, the Louisiana Supreme Court held that the sale of lots with reference to a subdivision plat vests ownership of the land under the streets in the public. Subsequent decisions, however, have cast doubt on the validity of this holding.

Late nineteenth century decisions have repeatedly held that the sale of lots with plats annexed establishes an "irrevocable" dedication. Such a dedication is what the word connotes: a dedication that may not be revoked. An irrevocable dedication, however, need not convey ownership to the public; it may convey merely a servitude. Thus, both a formal and an implied dedication may not be revoked; but one conveys ownership, whereas the other conveys a servitude.

CENAC v. PUBLIC ACCESS WATER RIGHTS ASS'N
851 So. 2d 1006 (La. 2003)

KIMBALL, J. In this case, we are asked to determine whether a privately owned boat launch and navigable canal have been impliedly dedicated to public use such that the property is now burdened with a servitude of use in favor of the public. After considering the evidence presented at trial, we conclude the evidence establishes only that the property has been used for a long period of time by the public with the permission of the owners. We find this evidence is insufficient to establish the requisite intent required for an implied dedication. For this reason, we affirm the judgment of the court of appeal.

FACTS AND PROCEDURAL HISTORY

On April 4, 2000, Arlen B. Cenac, Jr. ("Cenac") purchased from the Gheens Foundation ("the Foundation") a large tract of land known as Golden Ranch Plantation in Lafourche Parish. The tract included a portion of a canal, called Company Canal, and an adjacent boat launch and parking area. The canal connects Bayou Lafourche and Bayou Des Allemands and can be used to access Lake Salvador.

On October 19, 2000, Cenac filed a petition for injunction and damages against Public Access Water Rights Association ("PAWRA"), a local community association that seeks to preserve the fishing and water rights of the Gheens community, and [against] several individuals, alleging that on October 10, 11, and 17, 2000, he attempted to erect a security fence on his property and that PAWRA and the named individuals (hereinafter referred to collectively as "PAWRA") trespassed upon his property and prevented him from erecting the fence. Cenac requested a permanent injunction prohibiting PAWRA from engaging in acts that interfere with his use and enjoyment of the property.***

PAWRA filed an answer and reconventional demand to Cenac's original petition, denying most of Cenac's allegations and asserting the named individuals have for years had corporeal possession of real rights in the form of a servitude of right of way and use....PAWRA claimed they had peacefully used the boat launch and the canal for several years without objection and Cenac's attempt to erect the fence constituted a disturbance of their possession of the servitude....

PAWRA later added an alternative claim that the canal is a public canal, or has been formally dedicated for public use, or is a private canal subject to public use.

After a bench trial, the trial court entered judgment declaring Cenac the owner of the property in dispute. Furthermore, the trial court rendered judgment in favor of Cenac on the issue of the use of the boat launch and parking area and issued a permanent injunction [prohibiting the defendants] from launching, parking, or otherwise using the boat launch. Finally, on the issue of the use of the canal, the trial court rendered judgment in favor of ... PAWRA, declaring that Cenac's ownership of the canal is burdened by a servitude of use in favor of the public at large by virtue of implied dedication.

All parties appealed portions of the trial court's judgment to the court of appeal. The court of appeal affirmed the judgment of the trial court granting a permanent injunction as to the boat launch, but reversed the judgment of the trial court declaring that the canal was dedicated to the public use by implied dedication. Specifically, the court of appeal found that PAWRA and Cressionie failed to establish the plain and positive intent of the landowners to dedicate the canal and boat launch to public use. We granted certiorari to examine the issue of implied dedication.

DISCUSSION

The trial court's judgment declaring Cenac the owner of the boat launch[2] and canal has not been objected to and is not before us.... Thus, the sole issue presented for our review is whether the boat launch and/or the canal were impliedly dedicated to public use such that Cenac's property is burdened with a servitude of use in favor of the general public.

Our legislature has never enacted a comprehensive scheme governing dedication to public use.... In the absence of such a comprehensive scheme, our courts have recognized four modes of dedication to public use: (1) formal, (2) statutory, (3) implied, and (4) tacit. Only implied dedication is at issue in this case.

---

[2] For ease of reference, we will refer to the boat launch and its surrounding area, including the parking lot, as the "boat launch."

Implied dedication is a common law doctrine, but it has been recognized by Louisiana courts since the nineteenth century. No particular formalities are required to effectuate an implied dedication. 2 A.N. YIANNOPOULOS, LOUISIANA CIVIL LAW TREATISE, PROPERTY § 98, at 214 (4th ed. 2001). Traditionally, because implied dedication lacks the formalities and safeguards of the other modes of dedication, the two indispensable elements of implied dedication required by the courts are "a plain and positive intention to give and one equally plain to accept." [*St. Charles Parish Sch. Bd. v.*] *P & L Inv. Corp.*, 674 So. 2d 218, 222 (La. 1996); YIANNOPOULOS § 98, at 214. Thus, implied dedication requires an unequivocally manifested intent to dedicate on the part of the owner and an equally clear intent to accept on the part of the public.[3]

While traditionally the only requirements for implied dedication are the owner's plain intent to dedicate and the public's clear intent to accept, the additional requirement of maintenance by the municipality has sometimes erroneously been engrafted onto the concept of implied dedication. For example, in *B.F. Trappey's Sons, Inc. v. City of New Iberia*, 225 La. 466, 73 So. 2d 423 (1954), this court stated in part:

> The jurisprudence of this state appears to be well settled that where a street has been used and maintained by the city with the consent of the owner it creates an implied dedication of that street.
>
> .... Implied dedication operates by way of estoppel in pais by acceptance and use on the part of the public with the consent of the owner. The theory of all the decisions is that if there is no formal or statutory dedication there may be dedication by implication consisting of the assent of the owner, by his silence or otherwise, the use by the public and maintenance by the municipality. . . .

Id. at 469, 73 So. 2d at 424 (internal citations omitted).

This opinion appears to confuse tacit dedication, a dedication arising by operation of statute and involving public maintenance of a road or street for a specified period of time, with the concept of implied dedication at issue in the instant case. *See generally* YIANNOPOULOS § 98, at 216.... The jurisprudence suggesting that maintenance by the municipality is required before an implied dedication can be made is an aberration in our law. As explained above, all that has traditionally been required for an implied dedication is an unequivocally manifested intent to dedicate on the part of the owner and an equally clear intent to accept on the part of the public. While maintenance by the municipality might be a factor in determining whether an implied dedication has in fact been made, it is not required. Any language in our prior cases suggesting such a requirement is erroneous and hereby repudiated.

---

[3] An implied dedication has also been found when the owner of a tract of land subdivides the tract into lots, designates streets or roads on a map, and thereafter sells the property or any portion of it with reference to the map. *P & L Inv. Corp.*, 95-2571 at p. 5-6, 674 So. 2d at 222. This form of implied dedication is not involved in the instant case.

The weight of authority establishes that an implied dedication gives rise to a *rule* servitude of public use and does not transfer ownership.

The burden of proving the implied dedication falls upon the party asserting the dedication. The question of intent to dedicate to public use is one of fact. *Donaldson's Heirs v. City of New Orleans,* 166 La. 1059, 1063, 118 So. 134, 135 (1928).... The factual findings of a trial court should not be set aside by a court unless they are manifestly erroneous or clearly wrong.

In the instant case, Cenac argues PAWRA is prevented from acquiring a servitude of use over the boat launch and canal by the provisions of La. R.S. 9:1251, [under which a servitude of public use does not come into existence over land whose owner permits passage across it for the public's convenience in accessing either waters for boating or a recreational site]. PAWRA, on the other hand, contends the provisions of the statute do not apply to prohibit a landowner from creating a servitude of use by implied dedication....

We agree with the trial court that La. R.S. 9:1251 applies to the boat launch, but not to the canal. By its own terms, the statute applies to land used as a passage to reach waters for boating. It does not apply to prevent the acquisition of a servitude over the waters of the canal.... [I]f the owner has unequivocally manifested an intent to dedicate his land used to access waters for boating and the public has clearly accepted, then the provisions of La. R.S. 9:1251(A) do not apply to prevent the public from acquiring a servitude over the owner's land.

Like the boat launch, the canal is owned by Cenac. It is a private thing subject to dedication to public use, as are roads and streets. YIANNOPOULOS § 79. Although the canal is navigable, this fact alone does not render it public. In this case, the uncontroverted evidence reveals that when the canal was built, it did not divert any natural stream or water body. Thus, the privately owned canal is burdened with a servitude of public use only if [the defendants] prove the existence of an implied dedication.

....The sole question presented, then, is whether the boat launch and canal have been impliedly dedicated to public use such that the public has acquired a servitude of use over Cenac's property. *narrow issue statement*

The plain and positive intent to dedicate must be shown by language or acts so clear as to exclude every other hypothesis but that of dedication. The proof needed to establish an implied dedication has been accurately stated as follows:

> Ownership of land once had is not to be presumed to have been parted with, but the acts and declarations relied on to show a dedication should be unequivocal and decisive, manifesting a positive and unmistakable intention, on the part of the owner, to permanently abandon his property to the specific public use. If they are equivocal, or do not clearly and plainly

indicate his intention to permanently abandon the property to the public, they are not sufficient to establish a dedication. The intention to dedicate must clearly appear, though such intention may be shown by deed, by words, or [by] acts. If by words, the words must be unequivocal, and without ambiguity. If by acts, they must be such acts as are inconsistent with any construction, except the assent to such dedication.

Brusseau v. McBride, 245 N.W. 2d 488 (S.D. 1976) (quoting *Cole v. Minnesota Loan & Trust Co.*, 17 N.D. 409, 117 N.W. 354 (N.D. 1908)).

While recognizing that a plain and positive intent to dedicate must be proved, [the defendants] assert that the owner's mere toleration or acquiescence of continuous use on the part of the public is sufficient to establish an intent to dedicate. Louisiana jurisprudence does contain some language suggesting that long use by the public is sufficient to establish an implied dedication. *See, e.g., Emery v. Orleans Levee Bd.*, 207 La. 386, 21 So. 2d 418 (1945). These cases, however, have been criticized by the doctrinal writers and are contrary to the majority of decisions handed down by both Louisiana and common law courts. The majority of our cases establish the principle that continuous use by the public alone is insufficient to establish the requisite intent. Professor Yiannopoulos, a leading commentator, has explained: Decisions establishing an implied dedication by the toleration of public use are extremely rare and may be explained on other grounds, such as estoppel vis-à-vis the public authorities. The jurisprudence is well settled that immemorial use by the public does not alone establish dedication.

YIANNOPOULOS § 98, at 215 (footnotes omitted).

***We therefore conclude an owner's toleration of and acquiescence in long and continuous public use of his land, without more, is insufficient to establish a plain and positive intent to dedicate.

The evidence adduced at trial in the instant case showed that the public had been using both the boat launch and the canal for at least 60 years. During this time period, the prior owners of the canal, Mr. and Mrs. Gheens and, later, the Gheens Foundation, had knowledge of the public's use and never interfered when the public used the boat launch and the canal for passage into Lake Salvador. Melva Cressionie, one of the parties who lives across the highway from the boat launch, testified she never asked permission to use the boat launch and the canal because she thought they were public. She also testified that Mr. Taylor, a general manager of Golden Ranch Plantation, told her the boat launch was public. Other members of the public testified regarding their long use of the boat launch and canal and their understanding that the property was public. There was also testimony that the sheriff's office, the fire department, and an ambulance used the launch and canal in emergency situations.

PAWRA also presented evidence regarding maintenance of the boat launch and canal. Evidence was presented that some members of the community performed minor acts of maintenance around the boat launch such as placing shells in the holes made by vehicles using the launch, picking up trash, and installing steel cleats used to tie up boats. Additionally, evidence was presented that the Army Corps of Engineers sprayed the canal to keep it free of aquatic vegetation that would prohibit navigation. Ray Blouin, an inspector for the Army Corps of Engineers, testified the Corps was maintaining the canal when he began his job there in 1975. He also testified that the canal was generally sprayed from March or April through December of every year. A document was entered into evidence that showed the Corps sprayed the canal 27 times from August 1995 through May 1999. Mr. Blouin testified that he knew of no objection to the spraying by the owners. Finally, Mr. Blouin testified that while it is not the practice of the Corps to spray private canals, if the public used the canal, the Corps would spray it unless it was gated under lock and key. The parties stipulated that Mr. Russell Savoie, if called to testify, would state that he worked for the Parish of Lafourche and had done some spraying in the canal in the course of his employment.

Finally, testimony was presented that the parking area around the boat launch had been enlarged by the owners because they had liability concerns about the cars parking on the side of the highway when the parking area was full.

Cenac offered evidence and testimony purporting to show the owners' efforts to maintain the launch and canal as private. The record contains evidence that the previous owners placed signs at the boat launch and canal indicating that the property was "private" and "posted." Mr. Herman Robichaux, former general manager of Golden Ranch Plantation, testified he began working for the Gheens family in 1963 and posted and maintained private property signs at the boat launch and canal beginning around 1968. He testified the canal itself, including its points of entry and exit, were posted with private property signs. Mr. Robichaux stated he was always instructed by the owners to maintain the boat launch and canal as private. Mr. Robichaux testified his standing orders were that no public funds be spent on the property. He also testified that he ejected trespassers, commercial fisherman, and hunters from the canal. Criminal proceedings were sometimes instituted against people to keep them out of the canal. Mr. Robichaux testified the Foundation received a permit from the Army Corps of Engineers to conduct a marsh management project on the north side of the canal and spent about $ 120,000 completing the project. The Corps did not contribute any money to the project. Mr. Robichaux further testified that Foundation employees maintained the boat launch.

Additionally, Mr. Lanny Ledet, the property manager employed by Cenac, testified he recalled seeing signs asserting the private nature of the property around the boat launch and canal since his employment in 1987. Mr. Forrest Travirca, a security agent for Golden Ranch Plantation, also testified he saw the signs posted along the boat launch and canal. Because of the signs, he asked for and was granted permission to use the launch to reach his camp on Lake Salvador and, later, for use by his scout troop. He initially sought permission from the general manager, Mr. Taylor, but was told it was more appropriate to ask Mrs. Gheens directly for permission to use the property.

Mr. Donald Doyle, Vice-President of the Gheens Foundation and former attorney of Mr. and Mrs. Gheens, testified that both Mr. and Mrs. Gheens were very strict "relative to any use of the property that might in any way compromise their ownership or their right to exclusive use of the property." Mr. Doyle stated that the Gheens were against governmental work being done on the property without their permission and his instructions were that the parish should not be allowed to put shells at the launch. He testified that the public was given permission to use the boat launch and canal in an effort to be neighborly, but there was never any intention to grant the public any rights in the property. He also testified that when the Foundation sold the property to Cenac, it was the Foundation's intent to transfer the boat launch and canal to him free of any servitudes or right of public use.

Finally, evidence was presented to show that Mr. and Mrs. Gheens and the Foundation entered into various hunting leases with members of the public and allowed those persons to use the boat launch and canal in connection with the leases. Testimony at trial indicated that when large hunting groups were using the property, those groups were given a key to the "private boat launch" across the canal as the launch at issue was too crowded. Additionally, a letter purporting to show a draft of an agreement between Golden Ranch Plantation and the Gheens Jaycees was admitted into evidence. The letter indicated an agreement "for operation of the boat ramp," which provided that the Jaycees would keep the launch area clean, complete minor maintenance, and "monitor the use of the boat launch, prohibit use by the general public, insure availability of the facilities for the local community, and inform the Golden Ranch of any conflicts." The proposed agreement ended with the statement that Golden Ranch "reserves the right to prohibit anyone from using the facilities."

After considering the above evidence, the trial court found there was no evidence that anyone ever interfered with the public's use of the boat launch or canal. The trial court found the evidence showed the signs posting the property as private had been there for at least 30 years. The trial court determined that the Gheens family and the Foundation granted the community permission to use the launch and this permission has existed for at least 50 years.... With regard to maintenance, the trial court found the Corps had done some spraying, but had not spent overwhelming amounts of money maintaining the canal. The trial court stated, "The evidence of maintenance is sketchy and in this case, I don't think [it is] significant." The trial court concluded the Gheens family did not allow hunting from the canal or its banks and did not allow air boats in the canal. With regard to the navigable canal, the trial court found tolls were charged for its use in its early years of existence. The trial court found there were never any written acts dedicating the canal or the launch to the public. Finally, the trial court found that the possession of the public has always been with the permission of the owner, or precarious.

....[The trial court] considered the evidence to determine whether there was any intent to dedicate the [boat launch] to public use prior to 1958 and concluded the evidence was insufficient to show the owners had a clear intent to dedicate the launch to the public.

With regard to the canal, the trial court concluded the central question to be determined was the purpose for which the canal was built. Because it found the canal was built for navigation and has been used for navigation by the public for many years, it found the canal was impliedly dedicated to public use. The trial court did not, however, make any finding regarding the intent of the owners to dedicate the canal to public use. The trial court therefore legally erred in that it applied the wrong test to determine whether, in fact, an implied dedication of the canal had been established.

After reviewing the evidence presented in this case, we find the trial court was reasonable in concluding there is no evidence that any owner prior to Cenac interfered with the public's use of the boat launch and canal and that the canal was built for navigation and has been used by the public for many years. This evidence of mere toleration or acquiescence on the part of the owners, however, is not by itself sufficient to support a finding of implied dedication to public use. Because the trial court erroneously failed to consider whether the previous owners unequivocally manifested a plain and positive intent to dedicate the boat launch to public use... and whether the requisite intent was present with respect to the canal, we must review the record to determine whether such an intent was proved by ... PAWRA.

After a thorough review of the record and after considering the findings of fact made by the trial court, we find ... PAWRA failed to prove a plain and positive intent to dedicate by language or acts so clear as to exclude every other hypothesis but that of dedication. The evidence reveals that Mr. and Mrs. Gheens, and, later, the Foundation, took pains to ensure the property at issue remained private property not subject to any rights in favor of the public. While maintenance by the public is a factor in determining whether an implied dedication has been made, we agree with the trial court that the amount of maintenance provided by the public was somewhat "sketchy" considering the long period of time over which the property was used by the public. The record revealed that although the public provided minor maintenance, the owners did not turn over the maintenance of the property to the public, but continuously retained the responsibility to maintain the property. They gave instructions to their employees that no public funds were to be spent on their property. The minor maintenance provided by the public in this case is, by itself, insufficient to establish a plain and positive intent on the part of the owners to dedicate their property to public use.

The testimony of former employees of Mr. and Mrs. Gheens and the Foundation and that of the vice-president of the Foundation shows that the boat launch and canal were considered private by the owners and that they had no intention of dedicating any portion to the public. They posted signs at the launch and the canal, including its points of entry and exit, asserting the private nature of the property. They gave explicit permission to use the boat launch and canal to those who requested it. Although they gave the public permission to use the launch and canal, the evidence reveals they intended to retain the ability to revoke this permission and exercised this ability when people used the canal in an unapproved manner. The fact that the owners enlarged the parking area around the boat launch and repaired the launch itself is not inconsistent with their private ownership of the property and their decision to allow the public to use the property as long as their permission was given. Furthermore, the Foundation made no attempt to acknowledge any right of the public to the boat launch and canal when it sold the property to Cenac, although other servitudes were mentioned. Mr. Doyle testified that it was the Foundation's [intent] to transfer ownership of the property free of any servitudes of use in favor of the public.

In light of the above, we find [the defendants] have not presented evidence sufficient to show a plain and positive intent to dedicate by actions so clear as to exclude every other hypothesis but that of dedication. Instead, the evidence presented shows that the public was allowed to use the boat launch and canal for the purpose of traveling to other bodies of water for many years with the permission of the owners. This permissive use does not establish a plain intent on the part of the owners to permanently abandon the property to public use. Thus, like the court of appeal, we find neither the boat launch nor the canal is burdened with a servitude of public use established by implied dedication.
***

WEIMER, J. (concurring in part and dissenting in part). This matter involves a unique set of facts.

The small community of Gheens is located in an isolated area of a rural portion of Lafourche Parish. There is but one highway serving the community. One cannot drive through Gheens destined for anywhere else.

For decades and generations, the Company Canal provided the only navigable waterborne artery of ingress and egress to the area. The Company Canal was built by a joint public/private endeavor specifically for the purpose of navigation. Although the canal became private and tolls were charged at certain locations in the distant past, the record is clear that the portion of the Company Canal which connected the area where the community of Gheens is located was always utilized by the public as a waterborne thoroughfare.

In 1929 and 1930, C. E. Gheens purchased the Golden Ranch Plantation, which included the portion of the Company Canal at issue. Upon his death, his widow acquired title to the plantation. When she died in 1982, the Gheens Foundation became the owner of the plantation, including the canal and the land surrounding the canal. The evidence is clear the Gheenses always allowed the public to use the canal for travel. Prior to highways, waterways were virtually the only means of travel. The Gheenses apparently had a symbiotic, paternal relationship with the community that bore their name. So long as individuals used the canal as a means of transportation, that use was acceptable. Hunting, fishing, air boat use, and docking vessels in the canal were not tolerated; but navigation through the canal was not just permitted[;] it was encouraged. The encouragement did not come only in the form of allowing use of the canal. The Gheenses also built a boat launch, referred to as the "public boat launch," for the use of the public and later enlarged the boat launch, which further encouraged the use of the canal. In sharp contrast to this public boat launch is the so-called "private boat launch," located directly across the canal, that the Gheenses built for their own use.

At issue in this matter is whether there exists an implied dedication in favor of the public to use the canal and the boat launch. As explained by Professor Yiannopoulos, "After much litigation, it became settled that dedication to public use may be accomplished without any express or written act. This mode of dedication came to be known, in contradistinction with formal dedication, as 'implied dedication.' " 2 A.N. YIANNOPOULOS, LOUISIANA CIVIL LAW TREATISE: PROPERTY § 98 at 210 (1999).

Professor Yiannopoulos further states:

> The essential feature of implied dedication is the absence of requisite formalities. However, there must be, "a plain and positive intention to give and one equally plain to accept." Thus, the two indispensable elements of implied dedication are: proof of a positive intent to dedicate, frequently qualified as "offer", and proof of acceptance by the public. The offer may be implied from facts or acts of the owner that exclude any other rational hypothesis except an intent to dedicate and the acceptance may be inferred from actual use of the property by the public. The very idea of implied dedication was borrowed from common law jurisdictions; and, for this reason, implied dedication is also known as "common law" dedication. Louisiana courts have frequently relied upon common law authorities to support propositions concerning the incidents and effects of this mode of dedication. Cases are legion.

YIANNOPOULOS at 210-211.

While I am extremely reluctant to engraft a so-called common law concept such as implied dedication into our civil law system, it is clear that this concept has been fully adopted by the jurisprudence. See YIANNOPOULOS at 210 n.6. Sanctioned by the experience of ages, the common law doctrine of implied dedication rests on public convenience. 26 C.J.S. *Dedication* § 2, at 280 (2001), *citing Jack v. Fontenot*, 236 So. 2d 877 (La. App. 3d Cir. 1970). The doctrine is based on public policy and good faith, securing to the public only rights it has honestly enjoyed or depended upon, but taking nothing from the landowner that was not intended to be given. 26 C.J.S. *Dedication* § 2, at 280. The right conferred by common law dedication is a mere easement (or servitude), as contrasted with a statutory dedication that vests title in the public entity to which the dedication is made.

Further, despite its long history of being jurisprudentially recognized, the legislature has not abrogated the concept of implied dedication except in a limited situation. That situation involves a landowner allowing the use of his property to enable the public to get to a waterway. To encourage a landowner to allow such use, the legislature has expressed that such permissive use does not result in the establishment of a servitude. See LSA-R.S. 9:1251. I agree with the trial judge, the court of appeal, and the majority that LSA-R.S. 9:1251 acts to prevent a servitude from being established at the boat launch despite the public's use of the boat launch. For the public to acquire such a right of use, the landowner must specifically grant a servitude of passage or such must be purchased or acquired through expropriation. However, I believe a different result is compelled with respect to the canal.

From a civil law perspective, the concept of an implied dedication merely gives force and effect to the will of the parties based on the grantor's offer to donate and the grantee's acceptance of that offer. See LSA-C.C. art. 454. See also LSA-C.C. art. 455 and comments. The acts of the donor manifest an intent to dedicate. 26 C.J.S. *Dedication* § 58, at 358.

The comments indicate that although the provision is new, it does not change the law, thus implicitly recognizing legislatively the concept of implied dedication. The comments further state that in Louisiana decisions, private things subject to public use are frequently termed "public things", whether they belong to the state, its political subdivision, or to private persons. Private things of the state and its political subdivisions and things belonging to private persons may be subject to public use as a result of a legal provision or dedication.

Mr. Cenac and amicus on behalf of the Louisiana Landowners Association, Inc. express concern that the benevolence of a landowner, who tolerates use by the general public, should not be punished with the loss of ownership rights to his property. I agree. Mere tolerance of use by the general public is not enough to result in the loss of ownership rights. There must be an intent to give on the part of the benefactor. The law is not insensitive to the rights of property owners and recognizes that a servitude, being a restraint on the use of property, is generally not favored. However, in this case, there was enough evidence for the trial judge to find an intent to dedicate a right of use. This matter does not involve a taking of private property for public use. Rather, this matter involves voluntarily relinquishing rights. ...

The critical issue regarding the canal is whether there was adequate proof of a positive intent to dedicate. Mr. and Mrs. Gheens are no longer living, so their intent cannot be questioned directly. Rather, we must evaluate their acts to determine their intent. Particular acts of an owner which may be admitted in evidence as manifesting an intent to dedicate property to public use include making a canal through the property for general use and allowing maintenance at public expense. 26 C.J.S. *Dedication* § 58, at 358. However, as the court of appeal noted in the instant case, silence or acquiescence alone is generally insufficient to establish the unequivocal and positive intent necessary to find an offer to dedicate to public use.

Not one shred of evidence indicates that the Gheenses ever closed or intended to close the canal to waterborne traffic other than restricting the use of air boats. To the contrary, the evidence establishes they took steps to promote the use of the canal, even expanding the boat launch when it became overcrowded. I suggest the evidence indicates Mr. and Mrs. Gheens would not tolerate depriving their rural neighbors, who had used the Company Canal for generations as a means of travel to reach public waterways to fish, hunt, trap, and provide for their families, of the use of this canal.

Additionally, the canal was sprayed with herbicides at public expense to prevent the growth of water hyacinths. While maintenance by the public is not a requisite for implied dedication, it is a factor to be considered. See 26 C.J.S. *Dedication* § 58, at 358.... At trial, Ray Blouin, an Army Corps of Engineers inspector in the aquatic growth control unit, testified the Corps has sprayed the portion of the canal at issue in this case to keep it free from aquatic vegetation. Spraying was done from March or April through December of each year. He estimated that the canal had been sprayed by the Corps "in-house" for at least twenty years prior to 1995 when the Corps began contracting with private contractors to do the actual spraying. One such contract indicated the canal had been sprayed approximately 27 times from 1995-1999. The Corps maintains waterways that are used by the public to keep the waterways unclogged and navigable. Although the trial judge acknowledged the canal had been sprayed by the Corps, he indicated the expense to the public had not been monetarily significant. However, the evidence established that the maintenance was substantial and occurred over a long period of time. Without this spraying, which the evidence indicated had occurred numerous times, the canal would have long ago become clogged and non-navigable. The evidence established that the owners of the canal knew about the spraying.

Members of the Gheens community testified that for generations the canal was used by them and their ancestors. No one ever sought permission to use the canal; their use of the canal was never restricted. Understandably, they believed a right to use the canal had been established.

Two witnesses associated with the Gheenses testified no one was denied use of the canal so long as it was used as a thoroughfare. Herman J. Robichaux, Jr. testified he had worked for the Gheenses in one capacity or another since 1963. During questioning, he conceded it was trespassing on the property which caused him to intervene—not the use of the canal. He acknowledged the public had unrestricted access to the launch and canal to get to Lake Salvador during his employment.

Forrest Travirca was under contract to provide security for the Gheens Foundation since 1994. He was employed as a wildlife and fisheries enforcement agent from 1983 to April 1, 1999. He testified at trial regarding his actions in ejecting people from the property and the canal. He testified as follows:

> There was (sic) two individuals, while I was engaged in patrolling the properties, that I observed in the Company Canal engaged in hunting. The people were previously advised that that type of activity was not

allowed in the Company Canal. They could traverse the Company Canal going to and from[;] however, they could not hunt in the Company Canal.

When questioned as to whether there was ever any intent on behalf of Mr. Gheens to dedicate either the canal or the boat launch to public use, Donald Doyle, the attorney for Mr. and Mrs. Gheens and the Gheens Foundation, testified as follows:

> There was a feeling that within the community of Gheens, which was a small community at the time. There were people who did trapping on the property and there were some families that owned camps out on Lake Salvador. And that there was no reason why, as long as they obeyed the general rules about maintaining the property and not throwing trash, and debris, and garbage in it, that they could use it to go to their camps.

Doyle further testified it was his understanding the people using the boat launch and canal were using it with the permission of the owners. On cross examination, Doyle responded, "The type of use that we did not object to and thought that it was a perfectly neighborly thing for us to do was to accord to the community the right to use the canal." He also acknowledged on cross examination that there had been no objection to the spraying of the canal done by the Corps.

The learned trial judge heard the evidence and observed the witnesses. Although he did not make a specific finding regarding the intent to dedicate, his judgment was that the canal remain open to the public for navigation. The trial judge found "the canal is subject to an implied dedication to public use." In reasons for judgment, the trial judge stated:

> Certainly, the Gheens family and the foundation were interested in making certain that people who used the canal did not do so for illegal purposes. There were no efforts suggested by the evidence that the Gheens family at any time restricted or attempted to restrict the use of the canal by anyone or to any special group or category of persons. ***
>
> If there's one thing that the facts in this case show that cannot be contradicted or avoided, [it] is that the canal was built for navigation. And the difference between this case and all of these other cases cited on the issue of the canal is that it was built for navigation. There is no evidence that the state or any of the owners in this case have ever attempted to block the canal or interfere with its use. Even though over a period of time the canal has gone through periods where it may have been silted up in spots, where they didn't know who the owner was, where the owner was bankrupt, or the owner was a wealthy person, Mr. Barrow, who[m] nobody liked, none of that has anything to do with the use for which the canal was built or the use to which it has been put for the 100 plus years that it has been in existence. . . . If any case fits the implied dedication of public use for a canal, if the facts of any case fit it, it is this case, [b]ecause the facts in this case are overwhelming about why it was dug, why it was built, and the use

for which it was put. So my finding in this case is that there has been over a period of time, even if you take the period of years from the time that the Gheens family took ownership, that there has been an implied dedication to use of this canal by the owners that affects the title of Mr. Cenac. And as a result of that, there has been created a servitude of use in favor of the public to the Company Canal.

In civil cases, the appropriate standard for appellate review of factual determinations is the manifest error-clearly wrong standard which precludes the setting aside of a trial court's finding of fact unless those findings are clearly wrong in light of the record reviewed in its entirety. A reviewing court may not merely decide if it would have found the facts of the case differently; the reviewing court should affirm the trial court where the trial court judgment is not clearly wrong or manifestly erroneous.

As previously indicated, Mr. and Mrs. Gheens and then the Gheens Foundation allowed the use of the canal for transportation for generations. Testimony at trial indicates the Gheenses utilized significant efforts to prevent trespassers, but allowed and encouraged travelers. Despite occasional problems with trespassers and poachers on the property, the Gheens family never attempted to curtail the use of the canal for travel from one point to another. Members of the community testified they believed a right to use the canal had been established.

The trial judge did not find the right of passage exists merely because the canal was navigable. The trial judge found "an implied dedication to use of this canal by the owners. . . . There has been created a servitude of use in favor of the public to the Company Canal." There was no evidence to contradict the fact that the canal was always intended to be used for navigation[7]. The evidence clearly establishes that no one was ever prevented from using the canal so long as the canal was used as a highway for travel.

The evidence indicates the canal provided a link to other navigable waterways used for commercial as well as recreational purposes. The canal has a long history of being an artery of commerce. The Gheenses never intended the closure of the canal to the public which would have a detrimental effect on the lives of the residents of this small community of Gheens and the public at large.

As stated in the beginning, this matter involves a unique set of facts. Because of the unique facts of this case, I believe there is sufficient evidence to establish that the trial judge was correct in his assessment that a limited servitude of passage was established.

---

[7] "Navigable" as used above means able to support waterborne commerce, *i.e.*, width and depth of waterway sufficient for boat traffic. However, a waterway may be navigable, but there be no navigation because no boats travel on the waterway. "Navigation" as used in this context means boats actually used the waterway.

I do not agree that the trial court committed legal error in applying the wrong test to determine whether an implied dedication of the canal has been established or that the trial court was manifestly erroneous in its findings of fact. I would reverse the decision of the court of appeal and reinstate the judgment of the trial court.

QUESTIONS AND NOTE

1. The conclusion of the partially dissenting justice on the issue of the servitude of public use on the canal results from his different reading of the facts concerning that issue. Sometimes the same fact, such as the ejection of members of the public from the area by the Gheens's security company, is used to support both the majority and dissenting conclusions. What other examples of different interpretations of relevant facts exist? What style does each justice employ to present the facts in a way that supports her or his position?

2. What societal values underlying the law of implied dedication are expressed by the opinion of the majority and that of the partial dissent?

3. Is there a contradiction between the Court's adoption of the requirement of "an unequivocally manifested intent to dedicate on the part of the owner and an equally clear intent to accept on the part of the public," also termed "a plain and positive intention to give and one equally plain to accept" and the name "implied dedication"?

4. The majority opinion clarifies in dictum the confused jurisprudence on implied dedication that imported a requirement of municipal maintenance of the property to which the servitude attaches from the regime of tacit dedication: *a*): "While maintenance by the municipality might be a factor in determining whether an implied dedication has in fact been made, it is not required. Any language in our prior cases suggesting such a requirement is erroneous and hereby repudiated."

CITY OF HOUMA v. CUNNINGHAM
225 So. 2d 613 (La. App. 1st Cir. 1969)

MARCUS, J. On March 11, 1953 the Mayor and Board of Aldermen of the City of Houma, pursuant to the provisions of R.S. 33:3301-33:3316, adopted local Assessment Ordinance No. 1 of 1953, assessing property owners on a front foot basis for sidewalk construction in the City of Houma. Included in this ordinance was an assessment of property owners on the south side of Cherry Street, which is a narrow street one block in length running between Wilson Avenue and Gouaux Avenue. Among the assessments made was Assessment No. 76 against the property of the defendant Nolan J. Cunningham for 70.1 feet of sidewalk and curb at a cost of $193.38, 25 feet of special driveway at a cost of $73.25, *supra,* and 9 feet of drains at a cost of $5.86, making a total assessment of $277.49 against the property.

The sidewalk was constructed, but the defendant failed to pay any part of the assessment. Three years later, on July 2, 1956, the City of Houma filed this suit in the

Seventeenth Judicial District Court for the Parish of Terrebonne seeking $277.49 plus interest and attorney's fees.

In his answer the defendant alleged that the city had constructed the sidewalk entirely upon his property, and that under those circumstances the city could not assess the sidewalk lien against his property. In his answer the defendant included a reconventional demand for the damage caused by the allegedly unauthorized taking of his property.***

The piece of property in question is located at the corner of Cherry Street and Gouaux Avenue. Located on the premises are a number of apartment units owned by the defendant. The defendant's residence was located adjacent to the apartments on Gouaux Avenue. It is not disputed that the sidewalk was constructed on property which belonged to the defendant. He admitted that he had given his consent for the city to place the sidewalk upon his property, thus leaving room for the widening of Cherry Street, but con-tended that this permission had been upon the express condition that all the other property owners on the south side of Cherry Street do likewise.***

The record reveals that both Cherry Street and Gouaux Avenue were narrow streets, and that Mr. Cunningham did not have sufficient parking space for his apartments. It further shows that Cherry Street was in fact widened in front of the defendant's property, which widening encroached approximately one and one-half feet onto his property. The curb and sidewalk were located immediately adjacent to the street, and cover a total width of about three and one-half feet. This constitutes the five-foot encroachment claimed by defendant in his reconventional demand. The sidewalk was not constructed in a straight line from Gouaux Avenue to Wilson Avenue, but rather curves sharply upon leaving the defendant's premises and does not encroach upon any of the other lots on Cherry Street.

It is the contention of the City of Houma that the widening of Cherry Street in front of the defendant's property and the placing of the sidewalk upon his property was done at the request of, and solely for the benefit of, the defendant, who was himself a former councilman in the City of Houma. The city maintains that the defendant has impliedly dedicated this strip to public use, and is therefore estopped from denying his liability under the assessment ordinance and from claiming damages for the taking of his property.

The essential contention of the defendant is that he never consented to the placing of the sidewalk upon his property. He testified that when Mr. Cenac approached him about the signing of a right-of-way agreement he did not sign the paper.

Shortly after the sidewalk was constructed, Mr. Cunningham attended a meeting of the city council. He testified that at that time he again refused to sign the right-of-way agreement, but the testimony of the witnesses for the city was to the effect that he refused to sign because he did not feel that the work had been satisfactorily completed. Alphonse Badeaux, who was superintendent of streets and sanitation in the City of

Houma, testified that shortly after this meeting he had some men under his employ repair the defect complained of by connecting the driveway and walk on Mr. Cunningham's property to the city sidewalk.

Although Mr. Cunningham's residence was located adjacent to the property where the sidewalk was constructed, there is no evidence that he made any attempt to prevent the construction. On the contrary, Mr. Cenac testified that when the construction of the sidewalk began Mr. Cunningham asked to have the dirt thrown next to his house. Furthermore, a period of some three years passed from the time of the sidewalk construction until the filing of this suit. During this time there is no evidence that the defendant ever made any kind of protest. As far as the record reveals, his first protest was the filing of his reconventional demand in this lawsuit.

It is our finding that the defendant consented to the placing of the street and sidewalk upon his property, and that he intended to dedicate to the public use the strip of land on which they were constructed. The doctrine of implied dedication is well established in the jurisprudence of this state. Ford v. City of Shreveport, 204 La. 618, 16 So. 2d 127 (1943); Wyatt v. Hagler, 238 La. 234, 114 So. 2d 876 (1959); Best Oil Company v. Parish Council of East Baton Rouge, 176 So. 2d 630 (La. App. 1st Cir. 1965). "Implied dedication operates by way of estoppel in pais by acceptance and use on the part of the public with the tacit consent of the owner." Ford v. City of Shreveport, *supra*.

In this case we find that the defendant has impliedly dedicated a right-of-way across his property. Accordingly we affirm the judgment of the trial court in favor of the City of Houma as prayed for on the principal demand, dismissing the defendant's reconventional demand, with all costs to be paid by the defendant-appellant.

QUESTION

Would the result in *Houma v. Cunningham* remain the same if it had been decided after *Cenac v. Public Access Water Rights Ass'n*? Why or why not?

WHITE v. KINBERGER
611 So. 2d 810 (La. App. 3d Cir. 1992)

KNOLL, J. This appeal concerns a determination of whether a vacant 4,053-acre tract of undeveloped land in the Charles Park Addition Subdivision in Alexandria, Louisiana (the City) was dedicated to public use as a park. On defendants' motion for summary judgment, the trial court held that the City owned the property as a public thing by virtue of an implied dedication.

The plaintiffs (collectively referred to as "the Whites"), were attempting to develop the disputed property. They contend on appeal that the trial court erred in: (1) finding that the property was impliedly dedicated to the public by virtue of the filing of the plat of subdivision; [and] (2) finding that the property was a public thing owned by the City in its capacity as a public person by virtue of the implied dedication ....Finding the recording of a plat with a vacant tract marked "PARK", and the sale of lots according to the plat, constitutes an irrevocable dedication to the public use, we affirm.

FACTS

In January of 1977, Charles B. White, Inc. recorded a plat of the Charles Park Addition Subdivision. Although the plat showed many other lots, Charles Park Addition was identified as the lots numbered 316 through 326 on the plat. In addition to delineating lots, streets, and utility easements, the plat also referenced an undeveloped tract across Wycliff Way, the main Street through the subdivision, that was labeled "PARK." This undeveloped tract labeled "PARK" forms the basis of this dispute. The plat contained language dedicating the streets and utility easements to public use, but it failed to include a specific reference to the tract labeled "PARK." Lots in the subdivision were then sold which referenced the recorded plat.

In December of 1982, Charles N. White sold the disputed property with warranty to Paul D. White, Sr., who in turn sold the property in December of 1985 to the Whites, the plaintiffs herein.

In 1989, the Whites applied for permission from the Rapides Area Planning Commission to develop this property as a residential subdivision. Their request was denied after the neighboring landowners and the City claimed that the property was dedicated to public use as a park in 1977. The Whites then filed this possessory action against the eight adjoining landowners, the City, and the Levee District, all defendants herein, alleging that the actions of defendants and the recordation of certain documents amounted to a disturbance of their peaceable possession of the property.

The landowner defendants filed a motion for summary judgment, asking the trial court to declare that the disputed property was a "public thing" and was therefore insusceptible of possession by private persons. The Whites also moved for summary judgment, seeking a ruling that the property was not a "public thing." The Whites further asked the trial court to declare that the City and the landowners converted the suit into a petitory action when they pleaded the City's ownership of the property.... The trial court concluded that the City owned the property by virtue of an implied dedication.... The Whites bring this appeal.

DEDICATION OF PARK

The Whites contend that the trial court erred in its determination that there was a dedication of the park to public use in 1977.

A statutory dedication is effected when an owner of real estate files a subdivision plat that substantially complies with the requirements of R.S. 33:5051. The intent to dedicate is generally presumed from the act of filing the subdivision plan. Parish of Jefferson v. Doody, 247 La. 839, 174 So. 2d 798 (1965). A statutory dedication may exist even though there is no language in the plat formally dedicating lands to public use. Morris v. Parish of Jefferson, 487 So. 2d 647 (La. App. 5th Cir. 1986).

Nevertheless, the intention to dedicate must be clearly established. Banta v. Federal Land Bank of New Orleans, 200 So. 2d 107 (La. App. 1st Cir. 1967), writ denied, 251 La. 46, 202 So. 2d 657 (1967). If the fact of dedication is doubtful, the court must look to the surrounding circumstances to determine whether there was an intent to dedicate. Pioneer Production Corp. v. Segraves, 340 So. 2d 270 (La. 1976). When a rational construction of the record negates an intent of a landowner to dedicate a particular piece of land, the fact that reference to the land appears on a map does not effect a statutory dedication. Hailey v. Panno, 472 So. 2d 97 (La. App. 5th Cir. 1985).

An implied dedication results when there has been no substantial compliance with the statute but the property owner has nevertheless sold property by reference to a recorded plat. James v. Delery, 211 La. 306, 29 So. 2d 858 (1947).

In the present case, the Whites rely upon O'Quinn v. Burks, 231 So. 2d 660 (La. App. 2d Cir. 1970), to support their claim that the property was not dedicated to public use. In O'Quinn, the developer filed a subdivision plat in substantial compliance with R.S. 33:5051. The appellate court found that the developer did not intend to dedicate a tract designated as a "Proposed Park" on the plat where the plat contained language dedicating streets and utility easements, but not a park.

The landowner defendants assert that Town of Vinton v. Lyons, 131 La. 673, 60 So. 54 (1912), is dispositive of the issue before us. Vinton held that the word "Park" inscribed on a recorded plat manifested the developer's clear intent to dedicate the land to the public, and that an implied dedication became binding when the developer sold subdivision lots with reference to the plat. In Vinton, the plat did not contain any formal dedicatory language.

After carefully reviewing the record, we find that the Vinton case better addresses the issues before us. In O'Quinn, the developer only stated that the park was proposed, and his intent was not proven by a preponderance of the evidence. In Vinton, although there was no dedicatory language, the developer's intent was clear: the undeveloped land was designated, not simply proposed, as a park, and his intent to leave the land undeveloped was established.

In the present case, although the dedicatory language did not refer to the park, the undeveloped land was designated, just as in Vinton, as a park. Likewise, the developer's intent was established with his statement that "[the property was to remain] for the use and benefit of the owners of lots located in Charles Park." On this basis, we find that the Vinton case is more analogous to the present case.

Moreover, we are further convinced of the correctness of the trial court ruling when we consider the developer's recordation of the plat of survey, and its references to the plat in the sales to the lot owners. In Vinton, the Louisiana Supreme Court stated at page 678:

> "The word 'park' written on a block at the instance of the owner in a plat, subdividing a tract of land into lots and blocks for the purpose of founding a town, is as significant of the dedication of such block to the public for a park, as the word 'street' on such plat is of a dedication for a public street ... It would be contrary to equity and justice to hold that a real estate company could plat a town, make provisions for a park, sell lots from the plat after filing it for recordation and after the purchasers had built homes on their lots, and after the company no doubt received a better consideration for those lots, or many of them, because of the dedication, to then withdraw the dedication and make a sale of the property to a private individual."

We find that when a plat is filed of public record with an inscription, like "PARK", and lots are sold pursuant thereto, the subdivider should not profit at the expense of the purchasers who bought lots referenced to such a plat.

The O'Quinn case, relied upon by the Whites, was criticized by Professor A. N. Yiannopoulos in a case comment in The Work of the Appellate Courts for the 1969-1970 Term, 31 La. L. Rev. 202 (1971). The article questioned O'Quinn in light of recent cases which "tend to purport to protect the interests of persons buying property in a subdivision by finding a statutory dedication upon substantial compliance with the terms of the statute and by dispensing with the requirement of intention to dedicate." Id. citing Chevron Oil Company v Wilson, 226 So. 2d 774 (La. App. 2d Cir. 1969), cert. denied, 254 La. 849, 227 So. 2d 593 (1969). In Chevron Oil Company, the appellate court stated at page 777: "Where a plat is made and recorded and lots are sold with reference thereto, the requisite intention is generally indisputable.'" In like manner, we find it unjust in the case sub judice not to hold the original subdivider to the designations made on the plat, especially when he stated that it was his original intent to leave the disputed property undeveloped for use by the lot owners as a park.

The Yiannopoulos comment also questioned O'Quinn for its holding that "a dedication may be either statutory or implied but that it cannot be both." Addressing this conclusion, Professor Yiannopoulos pointed out, "There is no reason why the statutory dedication of streets and servitudes should exclude the possibility of this third dimension of dedication." Our holding further conflicts with O'Quinn in this regard. In the present case, the subdivision plat complies with the requirements necessary for a statutory dedication, and we have found that the inclusion of the word, "PARK", at least constitutes an implied dedication. Thus, it may be said that this case sanctions the inclusion of a statutory and implied dedication in the same recorded document. We cannot discern a reason for making these forms of dedication mutually exclusive.

Lastly, the Whites urge us to declare that the City and the landowner defendants have converted this suit into a petitory action because they pleaded ownership of the disputed property. In a possessory action, the claim that the subject property is a public thing is a defense and, if successful, defeats the action. Todd v. State, Dept. of Natural Resources, 474 So. 2d 430 (La. 1985). Accordingly, the Whites are not entitled to judgment declaring that this action was converted into a petitory action.***For the foregoing reasons, the judgment of the trial court is affirmed. Costs of this appeal are assessed to the Whites.

DOMENGEAUX, C.J. (dissenting). The developer in the instant case filed a plat of survey with language expressly dedicating the streets and utility easements shown on the plat to public use but with no mention of an undeveloped tract that was labeled "Park." These facts are almost identical to those presented in O'Quinn v. Burks, 231 So. 2d 660 (La. App. 2d Cir. 1970). Whether the tract was shown as a "Park" or a "Proposed Park" is unimportant. What is important is that in both cases the formal language of dedication did not include any reference to the undeveloped tract. Inclusio unius est exclusio alterius. A "park" or a "proposed park" is not a street or a utility easement.

The intent to dedicate must be established, whether the dedication is statutory or implied. If the fact of dedication is doubtful, the court must look to the surrounding circumstances to determine whether there was an intent to dedicate. Howard v. Louisiana Power and Light Co., 583 So. 2d 503 (La. App. 5th Cir. 1991). When a rational construction of the record negates an intent to dedicate a particular piece of land, the fact that a reference to the land appears on a map does not, of itself, effect a dedication to public use. Pioneer Production Corp. v. Segraves, 340 So. 2d 270 (La. 1976).

In an affidavit, the original developer stated that he intended the property to remain undeveloped "for the use and benefit of the owners of lots located in Charles Park."... This statement convinces me that the developer never intended to dedicate the disputed tract to public use. Lack of intent to dedicate is further found in the developer's subsequent sale of the property, with warranty, to the plaintiffs' ancestor in title.

The plat in Town of Vinton v. Lyons, 131 La. 673, 60 So. 54 (1912), contained the original layout of a proposed town. The tract involved was bisected by a railroad right of way, and there seemed to be no question that the area involved was meant to be a public park. In the instant case, a public park seems incongruous with the residential area depicted on the plat. Do the residents of Wyclyff Way really want a park open to all across the street from their homes? The disputed tract has never been used as a park, either public or private, and the City of Alexandria has required the plaintiffs (the record owners) to maintain the property.

If the plat in this case contained no formal words of dedication, then this case would be governed by Town of Vinton, supra. However, that language is present. The result reached by the majority requires us to either ignore the developer's express intent or to, in effect, say that a street "is a park." Other cases cited by the defendants, such as Parish of Jefferson v. Doody, 247 La. 839, 174 So. 2d 798(1965) and Garrett v. Pioneer Production Corp., 390 So. 2d 851 (La. 1980), hold only that the absence of a formal dedication clause will not defeat a statutory dedication of the streets and alleys shown on a recorded plat. The instant case is distinguishable in that (1) here, a formal dedication is present, and (2) the language of dedication does not include any reference to a valuable, undivided tract. I respectfully suggest that the majority opinion is based upon equitable considerations rather than an application of the law.

NOTES

1. *Inclusio unius est exclusio alterius* is a principle of interpretation that "the inclusion of one is the exclusion of the other." In this case, the dissenting judge thus explains his contention that the explicit dedication of streets and utility easements to public use excludes the dedication of the area marked "Park," since it was not named. The majority opinion implicitly rejected this argument, believing that the correspondences to the *Vinton* case called for a different result. What causes Judge Knoll to state that applying the dissenter's interpretive principle would be "unjust"?

2. The majority states that the trial court concluded that "the City owned the property by virtue of an implied dedication." But see the Yiannopoulos selection on "Implied Dedication," *supra*: "When the issue of the interest acquired by the public as a result of an implied dedication was determinative, courts have held since early last century that an implied dedication establishes merely a servitude of public use."

3. For the requirements of statutory dedication, see the recounting of the original legislation, Act 134 of 1896 in *Garrett v. Pioneer Production Corp.*, *infra*.

c. Statutory Dedication

A. N. YIANNOPOULOS, CIVIL LAW PROPERTY
§ 99 (4th ed. 2001)
(footnotes omitted)

§ 99. Statutory Dedication

In 1896, the Louisiana legislature enacted a statute that imposed on subdividers of lands certain duties, including the filing of plats and the recordation of a "formal dedication" of streets and other public places. The provisions of the statute remain in force as re-enacted in R.S. 33:5051.

Essential compliance with the provisions of the statute results in "statutory dedication." Noncompliance with the statute results in penal responsibility for the subdivider and either in another form of dedication or in no dedication at all.

The statute does not determine the effect of a dedication made in conformity with its provisions. For a few decades, Louisiana courts apparently assumed that the statute did not change the law and did not cite or discuss its provisions. Gradually, however, decisions began to indicate that substantial compliance with the statute vests ownership of the streets and other public places in the public. In 1938, the Louisiana Supreme Court faced the issue squarely and held that, when a subdivider sells lots with plats annexed in substantial compliance with the statute, the ownership of the land dedicated to public use is conveyed to the public. The court was influenced by common law authorities according to which a dedication by deed vests ownership in the public. Substantial compliance with the statute was considered to be the same as a dedication by deed.***

Courts have not developed a generally acceptable test as to what constitutes "substantial compliance" with the statute. They have merely held in certain cases that, under the facts involved, there was substantial compliance. In other cases, under different facts, courts have held that there was no compliance with the statute. In a leading decision, the recorded plat of a subdivision did not contain an express dedication of streets, had not been signed by the parish surveyor, and it did not show section, township, or range. Nevertheless, the Louisiana Supreme Court held that there was substantial compliance with the statute and that the streets of the subdivision had been dedicated to public use. There is no compliance with the statute, however, in the absence of recordation of the plat of a subdivision prior to the sale of lots, or when a plat is recorded by persons other than the subdivider or his representatives.

The dedication is ordinarily complete upon the recordation of a map or plat containing a description of the streets, alleyways, and other places dedicated to public use. There is no need for formal acceptance of the dedication by the public; nor is use by the public necessary. Proof of intent to dedicate is ordinarily dispensed with in a statutory dedication, the requisite intention being generally presumed. The Louisiana Supreme Court has declared that "implicit in the act of filing a plan of a subdivision in the map room of the parish, showing squares, lots, streets, alleys and walkways[,] is the intent on the part of the subdivider of dedicating the streets, walks, and alleys to public use." However, the same court held that "when a rational construction negates an intent on the part of the subdividing landowner to dedicate a particular piece of land, the fact that a reference to the land appears on a map does not, of itself, effect a dedication to public use." Thus, the mere designation of an area in the recorded plat of a subdivision as a "proposed park," as a "golf course," or as a space "reserved for schools," is insufficient to establish an intent to dedicate the property under the statute.

It has been held that the recordation of a survey showing a highway traversing the subdivision is a statutory dedication, although the road preexisted and was tacitly dedicated to public use. However, the statute does not "necessarily contemplate the dedication to public use of a bordering, existing right of way or highway"; the mere showing on the map of an exterior street which was subject to a previously recorded conventional servitude excludes the finding of an implied intent to dedicate.

The statute requires that a subdivider shall file, prior to any sale of lots, a map containing a "formal dedication," but it does not determine the meaning of these words. The requirement of a formal dedication is satisfied by a written recorded statement that the subdivider intends to dedicate the streets and other public places shown on the subdivision plat. A general statement of purpose ought to suffice; specific intent to dedicate each street, public square, or other public place appearing on the plat is unnecessary.

In the absence of a formal dedication there is no compliance with the statute, and, therefore, no statutory dedication. The jurisprudence is settled that noncompliance with the statute may result in another form of dedication or in no dedication at all. Thus, when a subdivider sells lots with reference to an unrecorded plat he dedicates the streets of the subdivision by virtue of an implied dedication. Further, despite noncompliance with the statute, the streets of a subdivision may be dedicated to public use by a written act that satisfies the requirements of formal nonstatutory dedication.

GARRETT v. PIONEER PRODUCTION CORP.
390 So. 2d 851 (La. 1980)

DIXON, C.J. This petitory action was brought to determine the various parties' ownership and mineral rights in property underlying certain streets in the City of Jennings, Louisiana. The plaintiffs include claimants to title and their lessees; the defendants are the City of Jennings and its lessees. Both groups claim to hold a valid interest in the mineral rights. Essentially, the controversy involves two disputes: whether the streets were dedicated to public use by the plaintiffs' ancestors in title so that full ownership is in the city and, if not, whether the leases held by the defendants-lessees should be dissolved. All parties applied for review of the decision of the Court of Appeal. Garrett v. Pioneer Production Corp., 378 So. 2d 945 (La. App. 3d Cir. 1979).

The plaintiffs' ancestors in title, Amanda and Austin Barber, acquired title to two tracts of land known as Barber's Addition and Barber's Subdivision in 1891 and 1901. Their titles can be traced to the sovereign. Beginning in 1901, the Barbers sold parcels of land in the addition and subdivision, regularly designating the lot and block number in the act of sale. In 1905, plats were recorded for both Barber's Addition and Barber's Subdivision. No signatures appear on these plats, and it is not known who filed them. Subsequent to the recordation, some lots were sold by the Barbers with reference to the plats, while other lots were sold without any such reference. In 1910, the Calcasieu Parish Courthouse was destroyed by fire; many of the records relevant to this case are taken from the files of a Lake Charles abstractor.

It is the defendants' contention that the filing of the plats, pursuant to Act 134 of 1896, effected a statutory dedication of the streets to public use, vesting full ownership in the city of all streets appearing on the plats. Alternatively, the defendants argue that a formal, non-statutory dedication occurred, again vesting full ownership in the city. The plaintiffs' position is that the filing of the plats was not proved to have been performed by the owners of the land, and that the plats themselves are not in substantial compliance with the statute. While plaintiffs concede that some form of dedication occurred, they argue that a non-statutory, implied dedication merely gives the public a servitude on the property, not ownership.

Act 134 of 1896 (basically the same as R.S. 33:5051) stated:

"Section 1. Be it enacted by the General Assembly of the State of Louisiana; That whenever the owner or owners of any real estate situated in this State shall desire to lay off the same into squares or lots with streets or alleys between such squares or lots and with the intention of selling or offering for sale any of said squares or lots it shall be the duty of such owner or owners of such real estate, before selling any square or lot or any portion of same, to cause to be made and filed in the office of the Keeper of Notarial Records of the parish wherein such property is situated and copied into the Conveyance Record book of such parish, a correct map of the real estate so divided, which said map shall contain the following:

1. The section township and range in which such real estate lies or subdivision thereof according to government survey.
2. The number of squares by numerals from 1 up, and the dimensions of each square in feet and inches.
3. The number of each lot or subdivision of a square, and its dimensions in feet and inches.
4. The name of each street and alley, its length and width in feet and inches.
5. The name or number of each square or plat dedicated to public use.
6. A certificate of the Parish Surveyor of the parish wherein the property is situated of the correctness of the map.
7. A formal dedication made by the owner or owners of the property or their duly authorized agent of all the streets, alleys and public squares or plats shown on the map to public use.

Sec. 2. Be it further enacted, etc., That any person or persons, agent or attorney in fact who shall violate any of the provisions of this act shall be deemed guilty of a misdemeanor and upon conviction before the District Court shall be fined not less than ten dollars nor more than five hundred for each offense.

Sec. 3. Be it further enacted, etc., That it shall be the duty of all clerks and ex officio recorders and notaries public in all the parishes of this

State, the parish of Orleans excepted, to refuse to place on record any deeds of sale of property coming under the provisions of this act, until the provisions of this act shall have been complied with; and to report to the District Attorney all violations of this act."

The statute only speaks of dedication "to public use." It does not explain or define the nature of the right acquired by the public through dedication. In fact, the legislature of this state has never enacted a comprehensive scheme of dedication to public use. For this reason, the subject of dedication has been a controversial one, and the task has fallen to the courts to decide the nature and effect of dedication.

Before Act 134 was enacted, the issues of dedication to public use and the nature of the public's interest in public property were frequently litigated. Consistent with provisions of the Civil Code, and relying upon Roman, French and Spanish Law, the earliest reported decisions squarely held that the soil underlying public roads was owned by the public. Morgan v. Livingston, 6 Mart. (O.S.) 19 (1819); Renthorp v. Bourg, 4 Mart. (O.S.) 97 (1816); Mayor, Etc., of New Orleans v. Metzinger, 3 Mart. (O.S.) 296 (1814). However, confusion arose as to what constituted a "public road." Hatch v. Arnault, 3 La. Ann. 482 (1848), discounted the applicability of ancient Roman law on the subject, observing that the roads in the "infant colony" of Louisiana were simply not comparable to Roman highways, "as permanent as the labor of man could make them." 3 La. Ann. At 485. This reasoning took into account the fact that roads in Louisiana were often washed away by inundation and the changing of river courses, and were sometimes abandoned along with the settlements they served. The court believed that the majority of roads in Louisiana could be classified according to the French system as "chemins publics," constructed on land subject to private ownership. The court conceded that a few "grands chemins," or highways, existed in Louisiana, and recognized that these roads were subject to public ownership. This decision obviously limited the principle set forth in earlier cases establishing public ownership of public roads. Note, "The Effect of Dedication to Public Use in Louisiana," 13 Tul. L. Rev. 606 (1939). By its own terms, however, the reasoning employed in the decision is now archaic. Were we to classify the ownership of roads in terms of their relative permanence, the large majority of roads in Louisiana, privately owned or otherwise, could be classified as "grands chemins." We do not believe that the matter of ownership can be determined by the relative stability of road beds; nor do we believe that the obscure distinction between "chemins publics" and "grands chemins" is of continuing vitality.

However, the Civil Code does appear to make some distinction between different types of roads. C.C. 454 and 458 (1870) [Revised C.C. arts. 450, 453] classify city streets as public property. C.C. 453 and 482 (1870) [Revised C.C. arts. 450, 452, 449, 455] refer to "roadsteads," "highways," and "high roads," apparently classifying them as public property as well. To the contrary, C.C. 658 (1870) [no corresponding article after Revision] deals with "public roads" that are built on the soil of privately owned estates, declaring that the public is limited to a servitude of use over such property. The indication given in this article that such "public roads" are largely rural is borne out by early jurisprudence. Landry v. Gulf States Utilities Co., 166 La. 1069, 118 So. 142 (1928); Hatch v. Arnault, *supra*. Different results were obtained in the case of urban areas such as city streets, public squares and quays. City of Shreveport v. Walpole, 22 La. Ann. 526 (1870); City of Baton Rouge v. Bird, 21 La. Ann. 244 (1869); Pickett v. Brown, 18 La. Ann. 560 (1866). In these cases the courts clearly found that the ownership of public places was in the public; the public interest was not limited to a servitude. Whatever ambiguities may exist in decisions prior to the passage of Act 134, there can be no doubt that the prevailing view was that ownership of municipal streets would ordinarily vest in the public body.

These early decisions are also informative as to the nature of the interest acquired by the public when property was dedicated to public use. In Pickett v. Brown, *supra* and City of Shreveport v. Walpole, *supra,* the area disputed by the parties was a tract of land between Commerce Street and the Red River, in the City of Shreveport. The original incorporators of the city had designated this particular property as "open space" on a map which was filed along with an act of partition. No use was ever made of this property except by the city. Both courts, considering all the circumstances, concluded that the original owners of the tract intended to dedicate the property to public use, and affirmed the city's title to the property. The same result was reached in City of Baton Rouge v. Bird, *supra*, where the ownership of public squares was in question. Once the intent to dedicate was inferred from the circumstances of the case, the court had no difficulty in deciding that title should vest in the public. In cases where no intent to dedicate was found, the courts uniformly held that the property in dispute was subject to private ownership. Leland University v. City of New Orleans, 47 La. Ann. 100, 16 So. 653 (1895); Mendez v. Dugart, 17 La. Ann. 171 (1865); Municipality No. 2 v. Orleans Cotton Press, 18 La. 122 (1841). Significantly, all of these decisions deal with property within municipalities, such as city streets and public squares.

From the foregoing we conclude that public ownership of property dedicated to public use is sanctioned by the Civil Code and was generally favored by law before the passage of Act 134 of the 1896, especially with regard to property within municipal limits. It is relevant to note that prior to the advent of the mineral industry in Louisiana, the subject of public ownership of dedicated property was important only insofar as it governed the use to which dedicated property could be put. By itself, ownership of the soil underlying public street was of no economic value. If dedicated property was exclusively subject to public use, there was no reason for the original owner to attempt to retain ownership while granting the public a servitude, since the economic value of the property was thought to consist entirely in its surface rather than in the minerals below. Property owners were simply not concerned with retaining ownership of the soil underlying a road except to the extent that they could reclaim the surface use of the property. This was especially true in the case of municipal streets and public squares, since there was little likelihood that such streets and squares would ever be abandoned by the public. When such streets were infrequently abandoned, the courts looked with disfavor upon claims of private ownership:

"***We think it may be safely asserted that much harm may result from the retention in remote dedications of the fee in narrow strips of land, valueless for many years, because of their public or quasi-public use which, on the abandonment of such use, become valuable for private purposes. Certainly such agreements are likely to be productive of disputes and litigation." Richard v. City of New Orleans, 195 La. 898, 928, 197 So. 594, 603-604 (1940).* * *"

In order to effect a statutory dedication, complete and detailed compliance with the statute is not required; substantial compliance will suffice. Parish of Jefferson v. Doody, *supra*; Metairie Park v. Currie, 168 La. 588, 122 So. 859 (1929). In the present case, the plats filed in 1905 fail to conform with the provisions of Act 134 in several respects. The plats were not recorded prior to the first sales, as required by § 1 of the act; all of the streets shown on the plats are not named, as required by § 1(4); and the plats contain neither a surveyor's certificate nor a formal dedication, as required by § 1(6) and (7). In all other respects, the plats satisfactorily meet the provisions of the act. In Parish of Jefferson v. Doody, *supra* the court concluded that the failure to include a surveyor's certificate and a dedicatory clause did not prevent the plat from being in substantial conformity with the law. The omission of a surveyor's certificate was ruled to be insignificant because it did not "render ineffective the plain intent of the subdivider to irrevocably dedicate the streets," 247 La. at 855, 174 So. 2d at 803. Similarly, the absence of a dedicatory clause was found to be insubstantial because the court believed that:

"***implicit in the act of filing of a plan of subdivision in the map book of the parish, showing squares, lots, streets, alleys and walkways, is the intent on the part of the subdivider of dedicating the streets, walks and alleys to the public use...." 247 La. at 854, 174 So. 2d at 803.

In 1929 this court considered the effect of the absence from the plat of a formal act of dedication of the streets in *Metairie Park v. Currie, supra.* The only penalty under the statute, said the court, was a fine on the owner, and the streets became dedicated as soon as a lot was sold in accordance with the plat:

"Defendant seems to contend that the owner of the subdivision is required by Act 134 of 1896 to imprint upon the map a formal act of dedication. If this be the case, the only penalty incurred under the statute for failure to comply with this requirement is a fine to be imposed on the owner or his agent. The title to the lot purchased is not affected by failure to observe this requirement of the statute, and, as the streets are shown and named in the Zander Plan, they become dedicated to public use as soon as a lot is sold in accordance with the plan. Jaenke v. Taylor, 160 La. 109, 106 So. 711." 168 La. at 595, 122 So. at 862.

In the present case, the trial court ruled that the subdividers achieved substantial compliance with the statute, despite the plats' insufficiencies. The Court of Appeal overturned this conclusion chiefly on the ground that there was "no proof that the

Barbers were responsible for the recordation." 378 So. 2d at 949.

If the fact of dedication is doubtful, "the conduct of the parties in interest ... may be considered as corroborative evidence." City of Alexandria v. Thigpen, 120 La. 233, 45 So. 253, 255 (1907). A search of the records reveals that in at least one instance prior to1905 the Barbers made a sale that referred to an unrecorded plat. In a sale executed on 10 December 1902, Austin and Amanda Barber sold to Robinson Coleman a parcel of land in Barber's Addition; the deed describes the tract and recites that it was "named in unrecorded plat as lot sixteen." The description and designation of this lot accurately follow the plat of Barber's Addition that was subsequently filed in 1905. This evidence is conclusive proof that the Barbers were aware that the plats existed: it is circumstantial proof that the Barbers were responsible for preparing the plats. The record also reveals that in sales made prior to 1905, the Barbers consistently designated the lot and block number of the property sold, in precise conformity with the plats later filed. This fact further substantiates the idea that the Barbers caused the plats to be prepared prior to making any sales.

Furthermore, after the recordation of the plats in 1905, many of the sales made by the Barbers were "according to plat," some of them designating the number of the page and book of conveyances where the plats could be found. Rather than disavow the plats, the Barbers expressly relied upon them in marketing their property, ratifying the filing and dedicating the streets.[1]

The 1905 plats have been official records for more than thirty years. They qualify as "ancient documents." R.S. 13:3729. According to R.S. 13:3730, it is "unnecessary to prove the *execution* of such a document, the mere fact of such instrument having been recorded for a period of thirty years, as herein provided, being sufficient to establish a prima facie presumption of the execution and of the genuineness of such instrument." The plaintiffs have presented no proof sufficient to overcome the presumption; in fact, the use which their ancestors made of the plats after they were filed is supportive of the presumption. See Carrollton Railroad Co. v. Municipality No. Two, 19 La. 62 (1841).

Because the Court of Appeal was in error in determining that there was no proof that the Barbers filed the plats in question or subsequently ratified the filing, there is no need to address the issue of nonstatutory dedication.[2] It is enough that the plats were

---

[1] Had the Barbers wished to retain ownership of the soil underlying the streets, they could have filed plats with an express stipulation to that effect. Wilkie v. Walmsley, *supra.*

[2] The defendants have alternatively argued that the sale of lots with reference to a recorded plat effects a "formal," nonstatutory dedication, vesting ownership in the public. See, e.g., Richard v. City of New Orleans, *supra*; Metairie Park v. Currie, *supra*; Jaenke v. Taylor, 160 La. 109, 106 So. 711 (1925).... See also A.N. Yiannopoulos, Property § 63, 2 La. Civ. Law Treatise (2d ed. 1980); Comment, "The Third Dimension of Dedication in Louisiana," 30 La. L. Rev. 583 (1970). However, in James v. Delery, 211 La. 306, 29 So. 2d 858 (1947), this court held that when property is sold with reference to a subdivision map, the owner creates a servitude of passage over the streets shown on the map. Earlier cases have been entirely

filed in substantial compliance with Act 134, and that the plaintiffs' ancestors in title, rather than objecting to or disavowing the plats, expressly relied upon them in their transactions involving the property. To conclude that the Barbers did not intend to statutorily dedicate the streets is to indulge in speculation that the record does not justify.

In holding that the City of Jennings has title to the disputed property underlying the streets shown on the plats, it follows that the city's mineral lessees are entitled to be maintained in their leases. However, there is some discrepancy in the record as to Carter Street, which does not appear on either plat, and another road described by the plaintiffs as "the former road running south from South Street." No statutory dedication has been proven as to these roads. In 1924, Amanda Barber sold a tract of land adjoining the latter road, designating the road as the eastern boundary line of the tract. Under R.S. 9:2971, a conveyance in these terms creates a conclusive presumption that the vendor is transferring all interest in the road, up to the center line, to the vendee. Despite the fact that the legislature intended this provision to have retroactive effect (see R.S. 9:2972), no such effect has been given it. State of Louisiana, through the Department of Highways v. Tucker, 247 La. 188, 170 So. 2d 371 (1965). We do not rule on the correctness of this decision; instead, we note that the statute cannot avail to the city's benefit in any case, since the city was not the vendee. Moreover, the language of the act of sale does not evidence an intent to convey ownership to the public body, nor does it fall within the category of a formal dedication. The City of Jennings, on the record before us, does not have a legitimate claim to the ownership of this property; nor can it claim anything other than a servitude over the property underlying Carter Street, which was never statutorily or formally dedicated to public use. Because the city has neither the ownership of the two properties nor an "executive interest" in the mineral rights, it cannot validly grant a mineral lease over the two streets. R.S. 31:15-16, 116. The city's lessee cannot be maintained as to these two strips of land.

The judgment of the Court of Appeal is reversed; it is ordered that the City of Jennings be recognized as the owner of the streets shown on the plats and described in the decision below. 378 So. 2d at 951-952. The city, however, is not to be recognized as the owner of Carter Street or the former road running south from South Street, which do not appear on any recorded plat. It is further ordered that the lessees and assignees of the City of Jennings be maintained in their mineral interests as to the property owned by the city; and that the plaintiffs' lessees-assignees are entitled to cancellation of that portion of the lease which the city granted over property that it does not own. The matter is remanded to the trial court for an accounting of all sums that maybe due to plaintiffs, consistent with this decision. The plaintiffs are cast for costs of these proceedings.

---

ambiguous as to the nature of the right acquired by the public when a subdivider sells with reference to a recorded plat. Iseringhausen v. Larcade, 147 La. 515, 85 So. 224 (1920); Flournoy v. Breard, 116 La. 224, 40 So. 684 (1906).

WEBB v. FRANKS INVESTMENT CO.
105 So. 3d 764 (La. App. 2d Cir. 2012),
cert. denied 110 So. 3d 579, 580, 581 (2013)

BROWN, C. J. These consolidated cases arise out of disputes over the mineral rights in two separate tracts of land in Caddo Parish, Louisiana. In both cases, in the early 1900s, a strip of land was dedicated for a public road. Both tracts were bisected by the roads. The ownership of the roadbeds is critical in determining who now owns the minerals underlying the roads and whether the mineral servitudes have prescribed through non-use. The district court consolidated the two cases and heard arguments on all motions for summary judgment pertaining to the ownership of the roadbeds. The trial court … found, as a matter of law, that Caddo Parish owned both roadbeds…. This appeal followed. We reverse, render and remand.

DISCUSSION

"It is relevant to note that prior to the advent of the mineral industry in Louisiana, the subject of public ownership of dedicated property was important only insofar as it governed the use to which dedicated property could be put." *Garrett v. Pioneer Production Corp., 390 So.2d 851, 855, (La. 1980)*. The dedications in these cases were made in 1913, 1914, 1924; and 1928. Today, these tracts are in the Haynesville Shale, and there are large bonuses and royalties at issue.

The Webb Tract and Flournoy-Lucas Road

The Webb case involves a strip of land across a 1,750-acre tract in south Caddo Parish. On September 11, 1913, J.W. Railsback executed a standard form dedication ("the 1913 dedication") with the preprinted language, "I … do hereby dedicate to the public use for a public road, the following described land," followed by a handwritten description of a 25- to 50-foot strip of land, "part of what is known as the Lucas-Forbing Road[,]" under which appears the preprinted statement, "The said property to be used for public road purposes only."

On June 14, 1914, F.F. Webb executed an identical standard form dedication ("the 1914 dedication") with a handwritten description of a 25-foot strip running diagonally across the lots described   in Sections 4 and 5, T 16 N, R 13 W.

On February 22, 1924, F.F. Webb executed yet another standard form dedication ("the 1924 dedication") with a typewritten description which "supercedes [sic] part of the previous deed[.]" The strip of land described in these dedications is now known as Flournoy-Lucas Road, which runs east-west across the middle of the tract.

In May 1979, Webb's successors partitioned the tract but retained the minerals; wells drilled north of Flournoy-Lucas Road have been maintained without any 10-year lapse. By cash deeds in 1985 and 1997, Franks Investment acquired mineral rights and surface rights in the tract, and leased them to Twin Cities Development, which subleased to

Chesapeake. These entities ("the Franks defendants") maintained that the 1913, 1914, and 1924 dedications conveyed to Caddo Parish full ownership of the roadbed of Flournoy-Lucas Road, thus splitting the mineral servitude pursuant to *La. R.S. 31:73*. They contended that operations conducted north of Flournoy-Lucas Road did not interrupt prescription as to the land south of the road; in essence, that the mineral servitude affecting the land south of the road prescribed for nonuse. Webb's successors countered that Caddo Parish had only a right of passage or servitude that did not divide the tract. Thus, operations north of the road maintained the mineral servitude to the south.

The Allen Tract and Blanchard-Furrh Road

The Allen case involves a strip of land across a 295-acre tract north of Shreveport. Jacobs Land Company is the common ancestor in title for all parties. On January 31, 1928, Jacobs Land Company executed the same standard form dedication as in the Webb case ("the 1928 dedication") with the same preprinted language, "I ... do hereby dedicate to the public use, for a public road, the following described land," followed by a typewritten description of a 100-foot wide strip traversing the tract, "known as the Blanchard-Furrh Road[,]" creating a northwest and southeast portion. Finally, the form provided, "The said property to be used for public road purposes only."

In 1991, Jacobs Land Co. sold the tract but retained the minerals; Allen and 42 others are the current surface owners. In 2003, Jacobs Land Co. sold the mineral rights to Huddleston Energy Reserves, which later (after the announcement of the Haynesville Shale) leased the minerals to Chesapeake. Allen and the other surface owners, however, maintained that the 1928 dedication conveyed to Caddo Parish full ownership of the roadbed of Blanchard-Furrh Road, thus splitting the mineral servitude.

Applicable Law

****The dedication of private property to a public use may be accomplished in a number of ways. Sometimes perfect ownership of the land passes to the public body; sometimes only a servitude is established in favor of the public. At issue in these consolidated cases is whether a servitude or fee title was given in the formal dedications of the roads. This will determine who owns the minerals underlying the roads and on each side of the roads. These dedications were all on a standard preprinted form used by the Caddo Parish Police Jury and were executed in 1913, 1914, 1924 and 1928. The parties are in agreement that these were formal dedications to the Caddo Parish Police Jury (now Caddo Parish Commission) for road purposes.

In each of the dedications, the preprinted form states: "I ... do hereby dedicate to the public use, for a public road, the following described land," followed by either a handwritten or typewritten description. Finally, the form provides, "The said property to be used for public road purposes only."

The plaintiffs in the Webb case and defendants in the Allen case point out that the granting of the dedications were voluntary, that no compensation was given, that they specifically limited the purpose for which the property could be used and contained no language conveying fee title to the Parish. On the other hand, the proponents of public fee ownership claim that the absence of any language in the instruments to the effect that the grantor retained ownership or that only a servitude was granted vest the Parish with full ownership of the property. In short, the grantors of the dedication would require a written clause in the deed that specifically conveys ownership to the Parish, while the other side would require the grantors to have a written reservation of ownership or specify that only a servitude was given. In this case, the instruments in question have no language either conveying or reserving title to the property.

In *Hatch v. Arnault, 3 La. Ann. 482 (1848)*, the supreme court was faced squarely with the issue and held that the public has merely a servitude on the soil on which the road is built. The court grounded its opinion on *Article 654 of the Louisiana Civil Code* of 1825, which is the same as *Article 658(2)* of the 1870 Code.

Article 658(2) (1870) provided that "the soil of public roads belongs to the owner of the land on which they are made though the public has the use of them." In 1978, *C.C. Article 457* was enacted.[*] The redactor's comments state that this article was based on *articles 704 through 706*, and *658(2)* of the Louisiana Civil Code of 1870 and "[I]t does not change the law."

The question is whether the dedicating instruments granted fee title to the Parish or just a servitude.
****

Those claiming that the dedications in the cases *sub judice* gave fee ownership to Caddo Parish argue that Louisiana's law of dedication to public use is summarized in *St. Charles Parish School Bd. v. P & L Inv. Corp., 95-2571 (La. 05/21/96), 674 So. 2d at 218, 221* as follows:

> Louisiana has never enacted a comprehensive scheme of dedication to public use. However, Louisiana courts have recognized four modes of dedication: formal, statutory, implied, and tacit. A landowner may make a formal dedication of a road by virtue of a written act, such as a deed of conveyance to the police jury of the parish. The written act may be in notarial form or under private signature. A.N. Yiannopoulos, Property § 95, at 204-205 [2 La. Civ. L. Treatise, 3 ed. 1991]. *A formal dedication transfers ownership of the property to the public unless it is expressly or impliedly retained*. Yiannopoulos, Property § 95, at 208-209. If the landowner retains ownership of the property, the public acquires a servitude of public use. (Emphasis added).

From Yiannopoulos's statement, as quoted by the Louisiana Supreme Court, the proponents of fee ownership in the Parish claim that "all formal dedications are, as a

---

[*] LCC art. 457 states, inter alia, "A public road is one that is subject to public use. The public may own the land on which the road is built or merely have the right to use it."— Ed.

matter of law, conveyances of full ownership unless some contrary expression of grantor's intent is provided." They would require a written retention of ownership by grantor or the inclusion of the word "servitude." We do not agree with such a restricting limitation.

The *St. Charles Parish School Board* case involved a tacit dedication; the school board constructed and maintained the road for more than three years. A tacit dedication arising by operation of statute involves public maintenance of a road or street for a specified period of time. *La.R.S. 48:491.* The public acquires by virtue of a tacit dedication a servitude of passage. *Gatson v. Bailey, 39,835 (La. App. 2d Cir. 06/29/05), 907 So. 2d 859.* The *St. Charles Parish School Board* case did not involve a formal dedication, as in the instant cases. See *Cenac v. Public Access Water Rights Ass'n, 02-2660 (La. 06/27/03), 851 So. 2d 1006,* which overturned *St. Charles Parish School Board* as to the requirements of a tacit dedication.

The quote from Yiannopoulos that "A formal dedication transfers ownership of the property to the public unless it is expressly or impliedly retained" must be read together with ... A.N. Yiannopoulos, 3 Predial Servitudes § 130, in 4 *Louisiana Civil Law Treatise* (4th ed. 2004).

An instrument granting a right of way may contemplate either the creation of a servitude of passage or the transfer of the ownership of a strip of land. Louisiana courts have repeatedly held that "whether the one or the other is meant in any particular instrument must be gathered from the instrument as a whole." The general rule is that "the conveyance of a right of way is generally meant to be merely a servitude, unless the deed itself evidences that the parties intended otherwise."...

Quite frequently, landowners granting servitudes employ language and forms generally used in sales of immovable property, coupled with qualifying clauses designating the creation of a servitude rather than transfer of ownership. In a typical case, an instrument declared that a described tract of land had been "sold and conveyed for railroad purposes only" and that the grant was "in perpetuity or so long as it is used by said Company, its successors and assigns, for railroad purposes, but if abandoned, for such use and purpose, then said land shall revert to the grantor herein or his heirs and assigns." The court, interpreting the instrument as a whole, reached the conclusion that the intention of the parties was to create a servitude only. [*Texas & P. R. Co. v. Ellerbe, 199 La. 489, 6 So. 2d 556, 557 (La.1942)*].

In the cases *sub judice*, the parties have historically treated the land underlying the roads as servitudes. In April 1930, the Parish Engineer wrote a letter ("the engineer letter") to an out-of-state landowner stating that a deed using the same standard form used in the 1913, 1914, 1924, and 1928 dedications "reads for public road purposes only and the Parish would have no right to exploit the mineral rights[.]"

In 1957, the Caddo Parish Police Jury received an inquiry from a landowner concerning a road created by a standard form deed like those in the present cases. In response, the police jury passed a resolution ("the 1957 resolution") stating that "in order to clear the title to the ownership of the mineral rights under a public road the Caddo Parish Police Jury hereby declares that it makes no claim to the ownership of the mineral rights by virtue of the deed[.]"

Finally, in 1983, the Police Jury passed another resolution ("the 1983 resolution") stating:

> [A]ll dedications of public road rights-of-way ... where the dedication instruments contained statements that the property was to be used for public road purposes only and where the instruments cited no financial consideration in favor of the grantors, shall be henceforth considered by Caddo Parish only to constitute grants of public servitudes and rights-of-way, ... and *Caddo Parish does hereby waive all present and future claims to fee title and to mineral rights relating to the property described in such instruments*. (Emphasis added).

This Resolution was immediately recorded in the Conveyance Records of Caddo Parish on April 25, 1983; and obviously, for the past thirty years has influenced title work in Caddo Parish.

The court in *Clement v. City of Lake Charles*, 10-703 (La. App. 3d Cir. 12/08/10), 52 *So. 3d 1054, 1058*, speaking to the difference between statutory and formal dedications stated:

> Statutory dedication and formal dedication are two different modes of dedication. See Yiannopoulos, Property § 97 (4th ed. [Pg 10] 2001). A landowner who ordinarily sells his land may never formally dedicate anything to the public use. On the other hand, a landowner who divides his property into lots with streets or alleys between them and then sells the lots must, in addition to performing other duties, dedicate to public use all the streets, alleys, and public squares or plats. *La. R.S. 33:5051*. Because in formal dedication the act of dedication is voluntary, there is a greater need to guard against a landowner's inadvertent mistakes. Thus, the landowner may impliedly retain ownership of the dedicated land without any specific reservation. *S. Amusement, 871 So.2d 630*; Yiannopoulos, Property § 97 (4th ed. 2001).

Unlike statutory dedication, formal dedications do not require fee ownership of the roadbed. The formal dedication is voluntary and there is no need for the public ownership of roadbeds. The public interest is in the use of the road. These roadbeds were given without compensation for a particular and limited purpose. The fact that the dedications did not include any language conveying fee title to the underlying roadbeds is indicative of an intent to retain ownership.

The dedications in the cases *sub judice*, clearly support the conclusion that only a servitude was given. There was no language dedicating fee title to Caddo Parish; there was no compensation given; there were specific limitations on the purpose for which the property could be used; and, the dedications have been historically treated as servitudes. The engineer's letter of 1930, the resolution of 1957, and the resolution of 1983 clearly expressed the Caddo Police Jury's (now Caddo Parish Commission's) understanding and intent that these instruments are "only to constitute grants of public servitudes . . ."

Focusing attention on the public policy (there was no need for the Parish to obtain fee ownership), the lack of consideration, stipulations pertaining to the use of the strips of land for road purposes only and the clearly expressed intent of the parties, we conclude that these stipulations are inconsistent with the idea that ownership was intended to be conveyed to the Parish; rather, they indicate strongly that a right of passage or servitude was intended to be given.

The intent of the dedications can be comfortably known from the deeds, but if ambiguous, the extrinsic evidence consisting primarily of the Resolutions and Parish Engineer's letter make clear the intent to give only a servitude. [The court concluded that, even if the dedication had been statutory and transferred ownership, Caddo Parish's 1983 resolution constituted a formal act of revocation "sufficient to relinquish the Parish's alleged and contested fee ownership and mineral rights to the strips of land in favor of a servitude." The resolution recognized "where the dedication instruments contained statements that the property was to be used for public road purposes only and where the instruments cited no financial consideration in favor of the grantors, shall be henceforth considered by Caddo Parish only to constitute grants of public servitudes and rights-of-way." It reversed the trial court's judgment and remanded.]****

MOORE, J., dissents. I respectfully dissent, remaining of the view that the district court properly interpreted the four dedications and subsequent documents in this case. The majority has adequately laid out the content of the dedications and correctly identified them as formal dedications. However, it has skirted the law in its zeal to avoid an unpalatable result. The supreme court, in its most recent ruling on the subject, *St. Charles Parish School Bd. v. P & L Inv. Corp.*, 95-2571, p. 5-6 (La. 5/21/96), 674 So. 2d 218, at 221, plainly stated:

> A formal dedication transfers ownership of the property to the public unless it is expressly or impliedly retained.

The majority attempts to circumvent this principle by saying that the dedication in *St. Charles* was not really formal but only tacit, and hence *St. Charles* does not govern this case. I do not join in this revisionism of *St. Charles*; the quoted language means what it says, a transfer of ownership. St. Charles is also consistent with this court's own jurisprudence in *Walker v. Coleman*, 540 So. 2d 983 (La. App. 2 Cir. 1989), which held that the effect of a dedication "to the public of the streets and alleyways" was to "divest the original owner of title and vest it in the political subdivision."

The four dedications in this case contain no retention or reservation of rights, either express or implied. By contrast, the dedications in *Jones Island Realty Co. v. Middendorf, 191 La. 456, 185 So. 881 (1939)*, and in *Texas & Pac. Ry. Co. v. Ellerbe, 199 La. 489, 6 So. 2d 556 (1942)*, prominently cited by the majority, plainly dedicated only a "portion of the right of way" and "the right of way now occupied," thus conferring only a servitude. *Jones Island* and *Ellerbe* do not govern this case. Likewise, the quotation from A.N. Yiannopoulos, 3 Predial Servitudes § 130 (4 ed. 2004), is limited to "instrument[s] granting a right of way" and "granting servitudes" and thus has no application here.

I also am unpersuaded that the provisions "to the public use, for a public road" and "to be used for public road purposes only" in the four dedications retain or reserve any interest to the donors. A statement of purpose merely makes the dedication an onerous donation. *Orleans Parish School Bd. v. Campbell, 241 La. 1029, 132 So. 2d 885 (1961)*. A purpose is crucial to the cause of the dedication. *Boutte Assembly of God Inc. v. Champagne, 00-340 (La. App. 5 Cir. 12/27/00), 777 So. 2d 619*. A statement of purpose does not defeat the tenor of the dedication.....

I certainly understand the majority's indignation at the prospect of declaring that these formally dedicated roadbeds belong to Caddo Parish rather than to the owners of the adjoining land. In light of the serious implications for public policy, it is perhaps time for the supreme court to revisit its pronouncement in *St. Charles* and affirm, clarify or reverse a ruling that seemed less controversial before the Haynesville Shale boom. Until it does so, I would follow the guidance of *St. Charles* and affirm the judgments of the district court.

d. Tacit Dedication

See A. N. YIANNOPOULOS, CIVIL LAW PROPERTY
§ 100 (4th ed. 2001)

LOUISIANA REVISED STATUTES

R.S. 48:491. Public roads. A. All roads or streets in this state that are opened, laid out, or appointed by virtue of any act of the legislature or by virtue of an order of any parish governing authority in any parish, or any municipal governing authority in any municipality, shall be public roads or streets, as the case may be.

B. (1) All roads and streets in this state which have been or hereafter are kept up, maintained, or worked for a period of three years by authority of a parish governing authority within its parish, or by authority of a municipal governing authority within its municipality, shall be public roads or streets, as the case may be, if there is actual or constructive knowledge of such work by adjoining landowners exercising reasonable concern over their property. Actual or constructive knowledge is presumed if prior to or during such work the public body notifies the last known adjoining landowners of same by written notice by certified or registered mail, return receipt requested. When such notice is given more than two years and ten months from commencement of such work, it shall suspend the foregoing prescription for sixty days. Actual or constructive knowledge is conclusively presumed within all parishes and municipalities except as otherwise provided by R.S. 48:491(B)(2) if the total period of such maintenance is four years or more, unless prior thereto and within sixty days of such actual or constructive knowledge, the prescription is interrupted or suspended in any manner provided by law.

(2) In the parish of Vermillion only, such maintenance operations are conducted by authority of a parish or municipal governing authority pursuant to a written contract with the landowner which specifies that a private road or street shall not be or become a public road or street.

C. All roads or streets made on the front of the respective tracts of lands by individuals when the lands have their front on any of the rivers or bayous within this state shall be public roads when located outside of municipalities and shall be public streets when located inside of municipalities.

JACKSON v. TOWN OF LOGANSPORT
322 So. 2d 281 (La. App. 2d Cir. 1975)

MARVIN, J. The Town appeals from a preliminary injunction granted plaintiffs which prohibits the Town from constructing a street across plaintiffs' property. The construction was ordered by the Town in October, 1974. The work began shortly thereafter, but stopped when plaintiffs barricaded their property after dirt was placed thereon in April, 1975, followed by plaintiffs bringing the action for an injunction. The Town contends that...it acquired a public servitude under the law; including, but not limited to L.R.S. 48:491.... We affirm.***

The riparian servitude provision is obviously inapplicable here. The Article 765 [Revised C.C. arts. 740, 742] servitude is also inapplicable because this article has been held not to apply within corporate limits of municipalities. See Bomar v. City of Baton Rouge, 162 La. 342, 110 So. 497 (1926). The record is also void of any declaration by the police jury. There is also no contention made of any formal dedication or disposition by the landowners to establish a public street. If the Town has the right to construct a street across plaintiffs' property, it must be founded upon the doctrine of informal dedication.

The jurisprudence divides informal dedication into two categories: implied dedication and tacit dedication. Implied dedication, non-statutory in nature, requires both the landowner's intent to create a public thoroughfare and the public's acceptance of the landowner's offer. Town of Eunice v. Childs, 205 So. 2d 897 (La. App. 3d Cir. 1968) writ refused 251 La. 937, 207 So. 2d 540 (1968). Such intention to dedicate may be manifested by the actions of the landowner; Wyatt v. Hagler, 238 La.

234, 114 So. 2d 876 (1959); while the acceptance by the public may be evidenced by public use. See 2 Yiannopoulos, Louisiana Civil Law Treatise, § 35, page 109.

Tacit dedication, on the other hand, is founded upon statute and its existence is determined by the application of L.R.S. 48:491, which reads in part as follows:

> "All roads...which have been or are hereafter kept up, maintained or worked for a period of three years by authority....of any municipal governing authority in its municipality shall be public roads or streets."

The "street" in question allegedly connected two existing thoroughfares about one block apart. The record is replete with circumstances indicating plaintiffs' desire not to create a public street on their lands. Approximately fifteen years ago, Prentis Jackson erected two fence posts to stop vehicles from entering or crossing his property. When plaintiffs became aware of the road construction in question, they complained to municipal authorities and erected barricades across their property. There was no implied dedication on the part of plaintiffs, Jackson and Guilliott.

The Town contends that a tacit dedication of a servitude by the Town's having "kept up, maintained or worked for a period of three years" the "street" in question. According to the Town's witnesses, prior to the enjoined road construction, the area in question was considered to be a "grass" street. Parts of the alleged street away from plaintiffs' property were mowed by town employees once a year, although no grass was ever cut on plaintiffs' property.

There is also testimony by a member of the town's maintenance crew that two or three loads of dirt had been dumped upon the alleged street during a thirteen year period before the litigation arose, but not necessarily on plaintiffs' property.

The jurisprudence construing R.S. 48:491 has consistently held that an occasional "brushing up" or token maintenance of private property does not establish a tacit dedication. Bordelon v. Heard, 33 So. 2d 88 (La. App. 1st Cir. 1947); Porter v. Huckabay, 50 So. 2d 684 (La. App. 2d Cir. 1951); Chargois v. St. Julien, 280 So. 2d 847 (La. App. 3d Cir. 1973).

The legislature, in enacting R.S. 48:491, and the cases interpreting the statute, contemplate more than an annual clipping of grass, accompanied every fourth year by the random deposit of a load of dirt, to establish a tacit dedication in favor of the public. Even if the Town's evidence is taken as true, this is at best token maintenance, under which no servitude is acquired.***

MEYERS v. DENTON
848 So. 2d 759 (La. App. 3d Cir. 2003)

EZELL, J. The primary issue in this case is whether Upper Little River Road located in Catahoula Parish is a public road. Bobby and Gladys Denton, who own the property on which the road is located, and E.C. and Rose Meyers, who use the road to access their property, all appeal the trial court's judgment.

FACTS

The Dentons own a 552-acre tract of land in Catahoula Parish next to Little River. They bought a 7/27 interest in the property at a federal court auction in April 1996 and bought the balance in February 1997. When the Dentons bought the property, there was an existing road, called Upper Little River Road, which runs parallel to Little River for some distance. Contending that the road was private, the Denton's erected gates on the property in 1998.

The Meyers own a 325-acre tract of land, which also fronts Little River, to the west of the Dentons. The Meyers use Upper Little River Road on the Denton property to access their property. The Meyers filed suit against the Dentons seeking removal of the gates, arguing that ...the road was a public road.

Lamar and June Poole, also owners of property to the west of the Denton land, intervened in the suit. As a result of a temporary restraining order filed by the Pooles, the Meyers and Pooles were provided with keys to the gates.

On March 24, 1998, the Meyers filed a motion for summary judgment. The trial court granted the motion, finding that the road in question was a public road and subject to a servitude in favor of the public pursuant to La.Civ.Code art. 665. The Dentons appealed the judgment to this court.

This court reversed the summary judgment, finding the existence of disputed material facts. The case was remanded to the trial court for a trial on the merits.

The trial court determined that the Catahoula Parish Police Jury formally adopted the Upper Little River Road as a public road on November 5, 1973, and for a period of more than three years performed maintenance work on the road. The trial court, therefore, found that pursuant to La.R.S. 48:491, Upper Little River Road is a public road. The trial court rejected the Dentons' claim for unjust enrichment in the amount of $9,592 for improvements made by them to the road. The court found that it did not need to address whether Upper Little River Road was a public river road pursuant to the legal riparian servitude found in Article 665. Both the Dentons and the Meyers appeal these findings.

PUBLIC ROAD

The Dentons argue that the trial court erred in finding that Upper Little River Road was a public road because the evidence indicates otherwise. They claim that the evidence supports a finding that the Catahoula Parish Police Jury did very little maintenance on this road which would support the dedication of this road as a public road pursuant to La.R.S. 48:491.

Whether a road is private or public is a factual determination.

Louisiana Revised Statute 48:491(B)(1)(a) provides:

> All roads and streets in this state which have been or hereafter are kept up, maintained, or worked for a period of three years by the authority of a parish governing authority within its parish, or by the authority of a municipal governing authority within its municipality, shall be public roads or streets, as the case may be, if there is actual or constructive knowledge of such work by adjoining landowners exercising reasonable concern over their property.

Furthermore, discussing the burden of establishing a tacit dedication pursuant to La.R.S. 48:491, this court in *Monfore*, 755 So. 2d at 910, stated:

> The legal existence of tacit dedication is determined solely by the application of the statutory criteria as enumerated in La.R.S. 48:491. Tacit dedication does not require intent by the landowner to dedicate the road way if there has been, in fact, sufficient maintenance without protest. However, token maintenance, or an occasional "brushing up" of a private road will not support a finding of tacit dedication.

See also St. Charles Parish School Bd. v. P & L Inv. Corp., 95-2571 (La. 5/21/96), 674 So. 2d 218.

The procedure of tacit dedication found in La.R.S. 48:491 was explained by *Winn Parish Police Jury v. Austin*, 216 So. 2d 166, 168 (La. App. 2d Cir. 1968), where the court stated:

> Within the purview of the statute, a road ceases to be a private passageway and becomes a public road only after it has been maintained for a period of three years. Hence the statute, in our opinion, presupposes, as it necessarily must, that for the period of time specified for the road to become public it remains a private road, at least, that it does not become a public road, a status assumed only after its maintenance for the requisite period of time. Therefore, for the initial statutory period of time while the road remains private, it can only be concluded that any action taken by the police jury as the governing authority, whether by

resolution or otherwise, is beyond the scope of its authority. The intention of the statute obviously extended no further and required nothing more than that the work and maintenance be done by appropriate authority, whether legally authorized or not, and accomplished with materials and labor provided from public funds.

Evidence indicated that road was constructed by Knickerbocker Construction for the Corps of Engineers in the early 1970's. The road was built to facilitate the construction of a low water structure or dam and was constructed and intended to replace an older road closer to the river.

On November 5, 1973, the Catahoula Parish Police Jury minutes reflect the following resolution:

SUBMITTED BY: Maizie Franklin, seconded by Grover Elliott.

WHEREAS, the Upper Little River Road and the portion of Old River Road in Catahoula Parish has been closed to the public traffic,

WHEREAS, said roads are vital to the Public's best interest as a Farm-to-market Road,

THEREFORE, The Catahoula Parish Police Jury hereby declares that the Upper Little River Road and the Old River Road in Catahoula Parish to the LaSalle Parish Line be and is hereby open to public traffic. . . .

Resolution unanimously adopted this 5th day of November, 1973.

According to *Winn Parish Police Jury*, this resolution did not dedicate the road as a public road. However, we do see it as evidence of an indication that the Catahoula Parish Police Jury intended to begin work to maintain the road for public road purposes. Further evidence also indicates that the maintenance of this road has continued to take place on the road located on the Denton property and was even requested by the landowners at times.

Ronald Renfrow, a police juror from 1984 to 1991, testified that all of Upper Little River Road was a public road which had been a school route at one time. He testified that he personally graded the road with his own grader.

Moses Poole testified that he worked off and on for the Police Jury since the 1960's. In addition to holding the job as motor patrol operator in the 1970's, Moses was also a road supervisor for two years. Moses testified that he graded the road a number of times to the end when it was an old dirt road with little gravel.

J.B. Morris also maintained roads for the Police Jury. He testified that he first worked for the Police Jury around 1974 for seven or eight years. He remembered the road being constructed before the dam and testified that a foot of gravel was placed on it. The Police Jury would call him every time the road needed grading. He testified that he went on the road and pulled ditches, filled the holes, and fixed the road. Morris graded the road all the way to the dam, which took about two days.

George Walton also worked for the Police Jury as grader operator. He testified that he graded Upper Little River Road four or five times in 1995 or 1996. He would grade the road past the railroad tracks, which are located on the Dentons' property, to a timber area. He testified that Morris had shown him where to grade.

The Dentons place a lot of emphasis on a road and bridge inventory that was prepared by Catahoula Parish in 1981 to comply with a legislative act that required a list of public roads for state expenditures. This roster shows Upper Little River Road as 4.3 miles and containing gravel. Upper Little River Road is 4.3 miles from New Deal Road to the east gates located at the beginning of the Denton land. They argue that this is the section of Upper Little River Road that is maintained by the Police Jury and a public road. Testimony revealed that the roster is not necessarily accurate. There was also testimony by Johnny McClendon, the road superintendent since May 1994, that he did not know if more than 4.3 miles was maintained. He simply relied on the information in the roster.

Tillman Gardner, the road superintendent from the early 1980's until 1989, and from 1990 until 1993, testified that a police juror told him to stop at the 4.3 mark until other information was obtained. He agreed that work may have continued past that point. He testified that the police juror could have been mistaken in telling him to stop there. Libby Ford, the police juror for Ward 6 when Denton acquired the property, testified that Bobby Denton requested that the Police Jury grade the road, which was done. It was only after Denton talked to another police juror who told him that 4.3 miles of the road was maintained that he decided to put the gates up.

Additionally, both E.C. Meyers and Lamar Poole, who have owned the property for forty-three and thirty-six years respectively, testified that they have seen the Police Jury grading the road. It was when the gates were placed on the road that the road was no longer accessible to the public.

Based on this evidence, we cannot say the trial court was clearly wrong in its assessment of the evidence. The evidence establishes that the Police Jury in the 1970's intended to maintain Upper Little River Road as a public road and that maintenance was actually performed on the road. We agree that the Meyers and Pooles established that Upper Little River Road located on the Dentons' property was maintained by the Police Jury for at least three years as contemplated by La.R.S. 48:491, making it a public road. With this finding we agree with the trial court's decision that there is no need to address the issue of whether Upper Little River Road is a public river road.

UNJUST ENRICHMENT

Since we agree with the trial court that Upper Little River Road is a public road, we will address the Dentons' disagreement with the trial court's rejection of their claim for reimbursement against the Police Jury for unjust enrichment. The Dentons claim they are entitled to $ 9,592 for improvements they personally made to Upper Little River Road.

In 1995, the principle of unjust enrichment was codified in La.Civ.Code art. 2298 and provides in pertinent part:

> A person who has been enriched without cause at the expense of another person is bound to compensate that person. The term "without cause" is used in this context to exclude cases in which the enrichment results from a valid juridical act or the law.

> The remedy declared here is subsidiary and shall not be available if the law provides another remedy for the impoverishment or declares a contrary rule.

Carriere v. Bank of Louisiana, 95-3058, p. 17 (La. 12/13/96), 702 So. 2d 648, 671, listed the five requirements for showing unjust enrichment:

> (1) there must be an enrichment; (2) there must be an impoverishment; (3) there must be a connection between the enrichment and the resulting impoverishment; (4) there must be an absence of "justification" or "cause" for the enrichment and impoverishment; and (5) there must be no other remedy at law available to plaintiff.

Bobby Denton testified that he made improvements to the road in the form of placing culverts, adding gravel, and maintaining the road since purchasing it. Denton relied on the information that one police juror member gave him that only 4.3 miles of Upper Little River Road was maintained by the Police Jury. He admitted that he saw other people using the road. Once Denton placed gates on the property in 1997, the Police Jury could no longer access the road to perform maintenance. Furthermore, in January 1998, when the Meyers instituted this action, Denton was aware that there was a dispute concerning the public or private nature of the road.

We find that the Police Jury was not enriched without cause. Denton knew there was controversy over the status of the road, yet he continued to perform acts of maintenance on the road. The Police Jury could not access the road to perform any necessary maintenance due to Denton's actions in placing gates on the road. Additionally, much of the maintenance he performed was beyond what was necessary for public road purposes in this case. We agree with the trial court that there was no unjust enrichment under the circumstances of this case. ***

For the reasons discussed in this opinion, the judgment of the trial court is affirmed. All costs of this appeal are assessed to the Dentons.

MARTIN v. CHERAMIE
264 So. 2d 285 (La. App. 4th Cir. 1972)

REGAN, J. Plaintiffs, Raoul Martin, the owner, and Martin's Marina, Inc., the lessee, filed this rule to compel the defendants to show cause why they should not be enjoined from blocking a section of land plaintiffs allege is a public roadway that leads into their property at Grand Isle, Louisiana, and why they should not be compelled to remove a series of barrels that form a blockade of the road.

Named defendants were Patterson Cheramie, Bertoul Cheramie, Jr., and Nelson Cheramie, who claim ownership of the strip of property across which the barrels were placed, and Clyde Pregeant. The latter defendant is Mayor of Grand Isle and the plaintiffs assert that he acted beyond the scope of his authority when he threatened to jail plaintiff Martin if the barrels were removed.

Defendants answered by virtue of a general denial. Pregeant additionally averred that any act he performed in connection with the disputed strip was an official act thus he was not individually liable.

From a judgment dismissing plaintiffs' request for injunctive relief, they have prosecuted this appeal.

The record discloses that Raoul Martin owns property fronting on Bayou Rigaud and leases it to a family-owned corporation designated as Martin's Marina, Inc. It is bounded on the east by the Cheramie tract. Louisiana Highway 1, the major traffic artery to this area of Bayou Rigaud, lies even further to the east. A 30 foot wide blacktop road, approximately 500 feet long, runs from the highway across the Cheramie tract to the eastern line of plaintiff Martin's property. Between the Cheramie property and the highway lies land owned by Michael Harris. Ownership of that portion of the blacktop road bounding the Harris property is not at issue. Plaintiff's land is bounded on the south by a 30 foot strip that surveys of the area show as a dedicated road. It junctures with the blacktop road near the eastern boundary of the Cheramie tract, and from there angles to the right.

We will refer to the dedicated road as the "Old 30" and the other as the Blacktop Road.

The incident that precipitated this litigation occurred on July 21, 1970. The Cheramies barricaded the Blacktop Road at the point where it junctures with the "Old 30" by placing seven metal drums across it; consequently the section of Blacktop Road crossing a portion of the Cheramie tract to the eastern boundary of plaintiffs' property was blockaded and plaintiffs and their customers could not use it. When the Martins removed the drums, the Mayor of Grand Isle supervised replacing the seven drums and added a few more. While plaintiffs were thereby prevented from using the road that ran in a straight line from the highway to the eastern boundary of their property, it was still possible to reach Martin's Marina by using the "Old 30" road.

Plaintiffs contend they are entitled to injunctive relief since the barrels obstruct their use of a public road. It is conceded the disputed strip was originally owned by the defendants; however, plaintiffs contend it was tacitly dedicated to public use in that it was maintained by the Louisiana Department of Highways for a period in excess of three years.***

The evidence adduced herein discloses that the disputed strip was tacitly dedicated as a public roadway since it was maintained by the Louisiana Department of Highways from 1953 through 1965. In 1953 the governing body of Jefferson Parish, then the Police Jury, contracted with the Louisiana Department of Highways to maintain certain roads in Grand Isle, one of which was the Blacktop Road. Between 1953 and 1958 or 1959, it was a shell road that was maintained approximately every three months by placing shells on it and grading it, according to Bruce Perdue, an assistant district engineer with the Department of Highways who was in charge of maintenance in the Grand Isle area. In 1958 or 1959 it was blacktopped by the state agency and required little maintenance thereafter.

When Hurricane Betsy struck the Louisiana coast in September 1965, a section of the Blacktop Road was washed away. Shortly thereafter, the Highway Department repaired the damaged roadway with sand and gravel. A short time later the Highway Department no longer worked or maintained the disputed section of the Blacktop Road because the Cheramies refused to permit the state employees to bring equipment upon the blockaded area. It was at this time that the state highway department built or rebuilt a shell roadway on the dedicated strip which we have referred to herein as the "Old 30."

The foregoing facts are attested to by several men employed by the Department of Highways during this period, and by Michael Harris, who was mayor of Grand Isle from 1959 to 1968 and by other witnesses. They all agreed that the Blacktop Road was used by the public as a means of ingress and egress to Martin's Marina until defendants erected the drum barricade.***

Although the lower court in written reasons offered in support of its judgment stated that it found as a fact that it was questionable whether the parish or the state performed sufficient maintenance to constitute a dedication, it appears that it based its decision primarily on the finding that a governmental agency had not maintained the disputed strip since 1965. It is conceded by all litigants that the Highway Department discontinued maintaining the section after 1965 because the Cheramies refused to permit highway employees to work on what they claimed was their property.

In our opinion, the fact that maintenance was discontinued after 1965 for whatever reason is of no moment and does not change the character of ownership. Under R.S. 48:491, once the disputed strip had been worked and maintained by the state Highway Department pursuant to an agreement with the Jefferson Parish Police Jury for a period of three years, the section became tacitly dedicated to public use. The more credible testimony establishes that the tract was shelled and maintained at public expense as a shell road for a period of at least five or six years and thereafter was blacktopped by the Highway Department. During this 12 or 13 year period, whatever maintenance was necessary was performed by governmental agencies. Thus, having been dedicated, it could revert to private ownership if the public discontinued using the tract as a public road for a period of ten years. Then the landowner would reacquire the tract by operation of C.C. art. 789 [Revised C.C. art. 753], which provides that a servitude (in this case in favor of the public) is extinguished by non-usage for a period of ten years. In this case, ten years has not elapsed since the public used the disputed area; therefore, it remains public.

Defendant argues that a tacit dedication did not occur because (1) the Cheramies did not impliedly consent to the dedication and (2) the maintenance performed was not sufficient to fall within the category of having been "kept up, maintained or worked for a period of three years" within the contemplation of R.S. 48:491.

The cases pointed out to us by the defendants to support the first argument are distinguishable. The most recent authority cited, Town of Eunice v. Childs, involved the effort to have a passageway adjudicated public by virtue of three years maintenance. It appears that what maintenance was done was insignificant and performed without the knowledge of the property owner for many years. When the landowner eventually observed shells being poured into a hole on her property, she protested immediately by registering a complaint with the city attorney. In this case the defendants consented to and invited public maintenance for a period of 13 years before they protested. When they finally resisted efforts by the state to maintain the road, it had already become public. One of the defendants testified that he evidenced his intention of retaining the privacy of the property by blocking the road once a year either with a piling or a truck.

Assuming arguendo that we accept the foregoing as a fact, a view which the defendants consider most favorable to their case, we do not see how this would convert the passageway into a private road because (1) more than three years maintenance had been performed when the annual blockading occurred and (2) during this same period the department of highways was still performing whatever maintenance was necessary.

Relative to the defendant's second contention, we agree that the jurisprudence establishes a mere "brushing up" or token maintenance is not sufficient to establish a tacit dedication to public use of property so maintained. But these are not the facts posed for our consideration. It appears that periodic shelling and grading during the 1950s and the blacktopping in 1958 or 1959 would constitute substantial maintenance. In fact, it appears that all the maintenance necessary was performed at public expense.

Finally the defendant argues that the disputed strip falls within the purview of R.S. 9:1251, which is an exception to R.S. 48:491. That section rationalizes that a passage made available to the public as ingress or egress to waters or a recreational area, even though maintained at public expense, does not become dedicated to the public after three years elapse. Clearly plaintiffs' land is used as a commercial marina and the public road giving ingress and egress is not subject to this exception.***

For the reasons assigned, the judgment appealed from is reversed in part and it is now ordered, adjudged and decreed that the defendants Patterson Cheramie, Bertoul Cheramie, Jr., and Nelson Cheramie must remove the drums blocking ingress and egress on the Blacktop Road to the eastern edge of the Martin property and defendants are further enjoined from interfering with the public use thereof or maintenance thereof in the future.

NOTE

La. R.S. 48:491B(1) states that "All roads and streets in this state which *have been* or hereafter are kept up, maintained, or worked for a period of three years by [public authorities] ...shall be public roads or streets [provided that any private owner had notice of the maintenance]." (Emphasis added). Concern that tacit dedication might result in takings in violation of the Louisiana and Federal Constitutions was addressed in *Town of Eunice v. Childs,* 205 So. 2d 897, 902 (La. App. 3d Cir. 1967):

> "The rationale behind the dedication of streets and roads for public use is that dedication is a type of *giving* and therefore is not a *taking* on part of the state governing agency. For this reason, no compensation is due the landowner; nor is there any violation of the due process clause of our State or federal constitutions. But were we to give retrospective effect to the statute in the instant case [in which much of the municipal maintenance took place before the statute was passed], we would in effect be *taking* the property of Mrs. Childs. Before 1954, Mrs. Childs could not have had any actual or constructive notice of the fact that she might lose or "give" her property to the City by the mere sufferance of it to work that alley periodically ... for a period of three continuous years. Thus, she knew of no way by which she could have protected her property interest before 1954."

e. Termination of Public Use

See A. N. YIANNOPOULOS, CIVIL LAW PROPERTY
§§ 104-105 (4th ed. 2001)

LOUISIANA REVISED STATUTES

R.S. 48:224. Abandonment of highway; sale by department; acquisition by parish

A. When the secretary determines that certain sections of the state highway system for any reason ceased to be used by the public to the extent that no public purpose is served, he may by appropriate certification, accompanied by a plat or sketch placed on record in the parish in which the section of highway is located, declare that section to be abandoned.

B. However, prior to certifying the abandonment of a highway or section thereof, the secretary shall notify the governing authorities of the parishes through which it passes of his intention. If the governing authority or authorities indicate by proper resolutions their willingness and desire to take over the section proposed to be abandoned and to maintain it, the declaration of abandonment shall so state and thereafter the abandoned highway shall form part of the parish road system of the particular parish.

C. If the governing authority or authorities are unwilling to take over the highways to be abandoned and to maintain them, or in the event of the abandonment of any property acquired in servitude for right of way purposes, the realignment of which has been changed so as to make the right of way no longer needed for that purpose, the secretary may at his discretion dispose of the property at either public or private sale, but the original vendor of the property to the department, or his successors in title, or the owner of adjoining property may purchase it upon payment of the original cost to the department or its present appraised market value, whichever is the greater.

D. However, nothing in this Section nor in Section 221 shall be construed as requiring the department to abandon or sell any property or property right, especially where local service or frontage roads, or the closing or portions of lanes in multilane highways are concerned. Further, where the secretary determines there is no market for any area owned by the department or over which it has a servitude, that portion may be abandoned in accordance with the general laws of the state.

R.S. 48:701. Revocation of dedication; reversion of property

The parish governing authorities and municipal corporations of the state, except the parish of Orleans, may revoke and set aside the dedication of all roads, streets, and alleyways laid out and dedicated to public use within their respective limits, when the roads, streets, and alleyways have been abandoned or are no longer needed for public purposes.

Upon such revocation, all of the soil covered by and embraced in the roads, streets, or alleyways up to the center line thereof, shall revert to the then present owner or owners of the land contiguous thereto.

Nothing in this Section shall be construed as repealing any of the provisions of special statutes or charters of incorporated municipalities granting the right to close or alter roads or streets.

R.S. 48:711. Authorization to sell or exchange immovable property

Upon a determination by the governing authority of any parish having a population in excess of three hundred twenty-five thousand persons, the parish of Orleans excepted, to the effect that any immovable property owned by the parish or title to which is in the public, including but without limitations, streets, roads and alleys, is no longer needed for public use, the same may be disposed of in the manner hereinafter set forth.

R.S. 48:712. Methods of disposition of property

The said property may be disposed of by one of the following four methods: (1) revocation of the dedication of the property if it consists of a street, road or alley dedicated to public use; (2) sale of any type of property at public auction; (3) sale of any type of property at private sale; or (4) exchange of any type of property for other property of approximately equal value.

R.S. 48:714. Streets, servitudes, roads and alleys

Where servitudes, streets, roads or alleys are involved, if the dedication of the same is revoked, upon the effective date of the revocation all of the soil covered by and embraced in such servitudes, street, road or alley up to the center line thereof shall revert to the present owner or owners of the land contiguous thereto.

R.S. 48:719. Applicability; alternative procedure

This part shall apply only to those parishes in the state of Louisiana having a population in excess of three hundred twenty-five thousand persons according to the official United States Census of 1970, the parish of Orleans excluded, and shall be construed as affording an alternative procedure to that set forth in R.S. 33:4711, 33:4712, 33:4717, 33:4718 and 33:4719, and shall supersede the provisions of R.S. 48:701 through R.S. 48:704 insofar as parishes having a population in excess of three hundred twenty-five thousand persons are concerned, excluding the parish of Orleans.

R.S. 33:4718. Revocation of dedication of parks, public squares or plots, reversion of property.

The parish governing authorities and municipal corporations of the state, except the parish of Orleans, may revoke and set aside the dedication of all parks, public squares or plots dedicated to public use within their respective limits, when such parks, public squares or plots have been abandoned or are no longer needed for public purposes.

Upon such revocation, the title to the land covered by and embraced in said parks, public squares or plots, shall revert to the person or persons who were the owners of such land at the time of the dedication, their heirs, successors or assigns.

COLISEUM SQUARE ASSOCIATION v. CITY OF NEW ORLEANS
544 So. 2d 351 (La. 1989)

ON REHEARING

MARVIN, J. We granted a rehearing to consider whether the New Orleans City Council (Council) has the legal authority to close the 2100 block of Chestnut Street and lease it to Trinity Episcopal Church (Trinity) and, if so, whether the decision of the Council, finding the property was no longer needed for public purposes, was arbitrary and capricious.

La. Const. art. VI, § 5(E) provides that a home rule charter "may include the exercise of any power and performance of any function necessary, requisite, or proper for the management of its affairs, not denied by general law or inconsistent with this constitution." There is no general law which prohibits a home rule entity from closing a public street and alienating it for a private purpose. Neither is there a constitutional prohibition. Neither the Civil Code nor the Constitution, therefore, prohibits the city from alienating a public street; in fact, specific authority to sell, lease, exchange or otherwise dispose of public property is authorized by both the home rule charter of New Orleans and the legislative statutes.

Under § 3-112(5)(d) of the home rule charter, the Council is empowered to adopt proposed ordinances alienating any immovable property and granting any servitude, franchise or privilege. Specifically, § 6-307(4) authorizes the leasing of public property.***

Moreover, La. R.S. 33:4712(A) grants authority to municipalities to sell or lease public property. It provides:

A municipality may sell, *lease for a term of up to ninety-nine years,* exchange, or otherwise dispose of, to or with other political corporations of this state, or *private persons,* at public or *private sale,* any property, or portions thereof, *including real property, which is, in the opinion of the governing authority, not needed for public purposes.* [Emphasis added.]

The authority of local governmental bodies to alienate public streets has been recognized by our courts. See Caz-Perk Realty, Inc. v. Police Jury of Parish of East

Baton Rouge, 207 La. 796, 22 So. 2d 121 (1945); Schernbeck v. City of New Orleans, 154 La. 676, 98 So. 84 (1923); .... In fact, the City of New Orleans has exercised that authority to lease and sell public things for many years in an effort to aid economic expansion and development in the city. Hence, we conclude that in the absence of a constitutional prohibition and in view of the express authority granted by the home rule charter and La.R.S. 33:4712(A), the Council possessed the legal authority to enter into a lease of the 2100 block of Chestnut Street with Trinity.

Having determined that the Council has the legal authority to lease the 2100 block of Chestnut Street to Trinity, we must next determine whether the exercise of that authority was proper in the instant case.

In reviewing the decisions of public bodies (the City Council in the instant case), the courts will not interfere with the functions of these bodies in the exercise of the discretion vested in them unless such bodies abuse this power by acting capriciously or arbitrarily. Caz-Perk Realty, Inc. v. Police Jury of East Baton Rouge, *supra*. In *Caz-Perk*, this court stated:

> It is our opinion, therefore, that when the Legislature delegated to the police juries and municipal corporations of this state full power and authority over the revocation of dedicated streets, roads, and alleyways that have been abandoned or are no longer needed for public purposes, it is necessarily within the scope of the police power thus delegated to these political bodies by the Legislature to look into and determine whether the street is an abandoned street or is no longer needed for public purposes and it is the well-settled jurisprudence that courts will not interfere with the functions of police juries or other public bodies in the exercise of the discretion vested in them unless such bodies abuse this power by acting capriciously or arbitrarily. 22 So.2d at 124. Generally, "capriciously" has been defined as a conclusion of a commission when the conclusion is announced with no substantial evidence to support it, or a conclusion contrary to substantiated competent evidence. The word "arbitrary" implies a disregard of evidence or of the proper weight thereof. Favrot v. Jefferson Parish Council, 470 So.2d 286 (La.App. 5th Cir. 1985); Torrance v. Caddo Parish Police Jury.

Plaintiffs contend that the Council's action in closing the street was arbitrary and capricious because the 2100 block of Chestnut Street is presently being used by pedestrian and vehicular traffic during weekdays (except when it is temporarily closed from 10:00 A.M. to 2:30 P.M.) and on weekends. Since the block is presently in use, they argue that the street is "needed"; hence, the decision to close the street "as no longer needed for public purposes" is arbitrary and capricious.

The mere fact that the street is being used by the public does not mean that it is "needed" for public purposes. "Use" and "need" are relative terms and it is the duty of the Council, after reviewing and weighing the evidence presented, to determine whether discontinuance of the present use and any inconvenience resulting therefrom would outweigh whatever benefit would flow from the closure of the street.

The 2100 block of Chestnut Street is presently a one-way street running in the uptown direction and is closed to public use from 10:00 A.M. to 2:30 P.M. five days a week. The traffic impact analysis performed by Urban Systems, Inc. analyzed the effect that the permanent closure of the 2100 block of Chestnut Street would have upon traffic volume and flow in the vicinity of the school. This report established that an average of 505 vehicles used the block each day and out of those vehicles, 220 or about 44% were directly school-related. (This does not include church-related or afterschool-activity-related traffic.) The report further determined that the vehicles that would be re-routed as a result of the closure could be accommodated on existing, adjacent streets without significantly negative impacts or reduction in service. The proposed circular driveway on Jackson Avenue for drop-off and pickup would remove Trinity-related traffic from the narrow one-way streets and also alleviate any potential traffic congestion on Jackson Avenue. The report recommended steps that could be taken to mitigate the impact, including reversing the one-way flow of traffic on Coliseum (the next street running parallel to Chestnut). This change would create a pair of one-way streets (Camp Street going downtown and Coliseum Street going uptown) that would work to the benefit of the neighborhood traffic flow. The relocation of the bike route from Chestnut Street as suggested by the study would simplify the route and improve safety. Implementation of the plan would result in a net increase of about eight parking spaces. Although plaintiffs contended that the closure would damage the historical character of the district by changing the "grid pattern" of the streets, it was the conclusion of the study that the reversal of Coliseum to flow in the uptown direction would preserve the internal grid pattern. The report was reviewed by both the City Planning Commission and the Council in reaching the determination to lease the street.

Trinity presently owns all of the property on both sides of the 2100 block of Chestnut Street. Many past and present Trinity students live in the neighborhood. The permanent closure of the block will not create a dead-end street, will not deprive any property owners of access to their property, and should not impede the access of emergency vehicles to the neighborhood residents.

Proponents contended that some of the benefits that would result from the permanent closure include increased security of the campus and safety of Trinity students as well as various other persons and groups who use the campus facilities on nights and weekends at all times of the year. Trinity has proposed a landscaping plan for the project that will increase the aesthetic quality of the neighborhood. The school's students have had a positive economic impact on the city and fulfillment of the school's long-term goals which include the use of the 2100 block of Chestnut will help the facility maintain its quality educational program. In fact, some residents of the neighborhood with no relationship to Trinity testified that the school's plans for the campus would enhance the value of the neighborhood in addition to increasing the quality of education at this inner city institution.

After weighing the substantial evidence presented to it, the Council determined that the present use made of the 2100 block of Chestnut Street could be served by alternative means and the benefits resulting from the permanent closure of the block outweighed whatever inconvenience the closure would have on the neighborhood in particular and the public in general. Based upon our review of the record, we are unable to say that the Council was arbitrary and capricious in its determination that the 2100 block of Chestnut Street is no longer needed for public purposes and it can be leased to Trinity under the terms and provisions agreed upon by the parties to the lease.

In sum, we find that the Council had the legal authority to close the 2100 block of Chestnut Street and lease it to Trinity and that the decision of the Council that the property was no longer needed for public purposes was neither arbitrary nor capricious. Accordingly, we should not substitute our judgment for that of the Council and will not. Hence, we reverse our judgment on original hearing and affirm the judgments of the courts below.

NOTES

1. Had it not been for the Home Rule Charter with its enhanced standard for challenging decisions of a municipality's governing authority, would the closure of the 2100 block of Chestnut Street and the lease to Trinity School have survived challenge by members of the public in *Coliseum Square*? The original opinion of the Louisiana Supreme Court, now withdrawn by the publisher, ignored the Home Rule provisions and examined whether the block was supporting public use. The Court judged that approximately 300 vehicles per day unconnected to the School constituted sufficient use to make abandonment improper. A strong dissent urged the Home Rule Charter standard of "arbitrary and capricious," which, as the rehearing indicates, requires great deference to the governing authority. Is this standard sufficient to protect the rights of the public?

2. Of what relevance to the issue of public use are the Court's observations that "fulfillment of the school's long-term goals which include the use of the 2100 block of Chestnut will help the facility maintain its quality educational program," that "some residents of the neighborhood with no relationship to Trinity testified that the school's plans for the campus would enhance the value of the neighborhood" and that the closure would "increas[e] the quality of education at this inner city institution"?

FORE v. VOLENTINE
385 So. 2d 860 (La. App. 2d Cir. 1980)

HALL, J. Defendants-appellants, Tollie Volentine and Mahlon Volentine, appeal from judgment of the district court declaring a road running through their property to be public, ordering them to restore such road to a passable condition and ordering them to desist from further interfering with its maintenance, use, and passage.

1

The road in dispute is a rural dirt road located in Caldwell Parish, running from Louisiana Highway No. 849 across the land of appellants and others not parties to the suit, and ending on land owned by appellee. The Caldwell Parish Police Jury originally built the road with parish funds approximately 40 years ago. The police jury also constructed a creosote piling bridge at a point where the road crosses a creek and installed an 18-inch culvert. The road was regularly maintained in the manner generally associated with this type of road in that area. Maintenance included grading, "pulling" the ditches and clearing the culvert of debris. It is undisputed that the maintenance occurred at least once a year, ceasing approximately eight years prior to the filing of this suit. Approximately five years prior to the filing of this action, the Volentines constructed a fence across the road. In 1977 and 1978 the road was plowed and soybeans were planted in the roadbed by the Volentines' lessee.

The trial court found that since this road was constructed by the police jury with public funds and maintained in excess of three years it was tacitly dedicated and became public by virtue of R.S. 48:491. The court further found that the road was used by the public until it was blocked by plaintiffs and had not lost its public character due to abandonment or 10-years nonusage.

Appellants argue that the road lost its character as a public road because there was a clear and well-established intent by the governing body to abandon the road. Appellants argue that this intent was evidenced by the fact that the police jury performed no maintenance on the road for approximately eight years, allowed the road to be fenced and planted, and did not include the road in their numbering system of public roads. Appellants cite Robinson v. Beauregard Parish Police Jury, 351 So. 2d 113 (La. 1977) and Starnes v. Police Jury of Rapides Parish, 27 So. 2d 134 (La. App. 3d Cir. 1946).

Robinson was a tort suit arising out of an accident which happened on a bridge and the issue was whether the allegedly defective bridge was owned by the police jury. Picking up on language from the Second Circuit *Starnes* case, the Supreme Court held:

> "Abandonment of a public road must be evidenced by (1) a formal act of revocation in accordance with R.S. 48:701, (2) relocation of the public road by the governing body, or (3) clear and well-established proof of intent by the governing body to abandon. *Starnes v. Police Jury of Rapides Parish, supra,* 27 So. 2d 134 (La. App. 2d Cir. 1946). Nonuse of a strip of land as a public road or street for a period in excess of ten years may also result in termination of the public use. C.C. 789; Yiannopoulos, 'Common, Public, and Private Things in Louisiana: Civilian Tra-dition and Modern Practice,' 21 La. L. Rev. 696, 736 (1961)."

Starnes was a suit by the plaintiff-landowner seeking to enjoin the police jury from using an allegedly abandoned roadway traversing his property. While the court held that the abandonment of public roads must be evidenced by clear and well-established proof of intent on the part of the governing body to abandon, the court found that the evidence in that case clearly failed to establish such intent. In the *Robinson* case the court likewise found the evidence did not establish an intent on the part of the governing body to abandon the bridge.

If these two cases stand for the proposition that the character of a road as a public road can be changed by an abandonment by the police jury without compliance with statutory requirements for abandonment, without formal action by the police jury, and without 10 years nonuse, they stand alone in Louisiana jurisprudence. Although the language of these cases supports the concept that a public road may be abandoned by a de facto abandonment of maintenance and upkeep of the road by the police jury, the context in which these holdings were made and the results in the two cases detract from the authority of the cases for that proposition.

In the instant case there was no formal action by the police jury to abandon the public road and there was certainly no formal revocation, or relocation in accordance with statutory provisions. There was no abandonment or nonuse for a period of 10 years. Accordingly, we hold that in the absence of compliance with statutory provisions, formal action by the police jury, or 10 years nonuse, the public road in question remains a public road and its use as such cannot be interfered with by the defendants whose property the road traverses. See R.S. 48:512.

The judgment of the district court is amended to refer to the highway mentioned therein as Louisiana Highway No. 849 instead of Louisiana Highway No. 128 and, as amended, is affirmed. All costs of these proceedings are assessed to appellants.

NOTE

Non-use by the public also does not cure a failed attempt at abandonment. In *Worthen v. DeLong*, 763 So. 2d 820 (La. App. 1st Cir. 2000), the Baton Rouge Metro Council had enacted in 1986 an ordinance pursuant to R.S. 408:701, conditionally revoking the dedication of a public right-of-way called "Princeton Avenue" in the College Town subdivision. The right-of-way had never been developed for public use because a majority of it had become submerged in College Lake owing to rising water levels. The condition imposed on the revocation was the execution by adjacent landowners of servitude agreements that would permit maintenance of a sewer system in the area. This condition was never met. Nevertheless, the city agency issued a permit to the defendants permitting them to construct a fence in the middle of the right-of-way. After they began construction, the plaintiffs sought to enjoin it on the ground that the dedication of the right-of-way had not been revoked because of the unfulfilled condition. The defendants argued that their fence did not obstruct public use because there was no evidence that the public used, or needed to use, the right-of-way. The First Circuit Court of Appeal remanded to the district court with instructions to issue the injunction, holding that because the right-of-way had not been revoked, the defendants had no right to obstruct the public's use of it.

ST. MARTIN PARISH POLICE JURY v. MICHEL
229 So. 2d 463 (La. App. 3d Cir. 1969)

SAVOY J. This suit was instituted by the governing authority of St. Martin Parish, Louisiana, against the defendants for an injunction enjoining said defendants from obstructing or blocking a public road in said parish. After issue was joined and a trial had, the district court granted the injunction. Defendants have appealed to this Court.

The facts are not in dispute. The only issue is a legal one.

A public road referred to as Richard Avenue located in Ward 6 of St. Martin Parish, Louisiana, was so created by being maintained for a period of three years by the Police Jury of St. Martin Parish, Louisiana, as provided for by R.S. 48:491 defining public roads. At the request of defendants or their representatives, the Police Jury, by Resolution dated and adopted July 11, 1967, abandoned Richard Avenue as a public road. Residents using the road and hearing of the action of the Jury appeared before the Jury and asked it to adopt a Resolution rescinding the July 11, 1967 Resolution. It did so at its next meeting held on August 1, 1967. The public continued to use the road until in the latter part of April, 1969, when defendants commenced blocking the road by the erection of chain link fences. Following this action by defendants this suit was filed.

In Washington Parish Police Jury v. Washington Parish Hospital Service District, 152 So. 2d 362 (La. App. 1 Cir. 1963) (certiorari refused 244 La. 669, 153 So. 2d 883), the rule of law applicable to the instant case is set forth in the second syllabus and states:

> "Police juries possess inherent as well as legislatively delegated power and authority to rescind their official actions provided such rescission does not abrogate or contravene other rules of law including, but not limited to, the legal prohibition against divesting of vested rights and the impairment of contracts lawfully made and entered into."

Using the *Washington* case, *supra*, as a guideline, we conclude that when the Police Jury adopted the July 11, 1967 Resolution abandoning Richard Avenue as a public road, the property then reverted back to the landowners of said road free and clear of any servitude and constituted a property right; and, that the Jury could not divest them of this property right by the passage of the August 1, 1967 Resolution rescinding the first resolution. To hold otherwise would allow the Police Jury to impair vested property rights in violation of Article 4, Section 15 of our State Constitution.***

For the reasons assigned the judgment of the district court granting plaintiff a permanent injunction is set aside and recalled, and plaintiff's suit is dismissed.

WALKER v. COLEMAN
540 So. 2d 93 (La. App. 2d Cir. 1989)

HALL, C.J. This suit involves ownership of a strip of land in Ouachita Parish which was statutorily dedicated as an alleyway by a subdivision plat filed in 1929 but was never opened or used, and which was sold in 1985 by the police jury to the plaintiff. The primary issue is whether the police jury may sell property dedicated as a street or alleyway, but never opened and no longer needed for public purposes, pursuant to R.S. 33:4711, which provides general authority to sell property not needed for public use, or whether the police jury's authority is limited to revoking the dedication in accordance with R.S. 48:701, in which case title to the street or alley reverts to the contiguous owner or owners. A second issue is whether R.S. 48:701 is unconstitutional as amounting to a donation of public property in violation of La. Const. Art. 7, § 14 (1974).

Finding that the property was not subject to alienation under R.S. 33:4711 and that plaintiff did not acquire ownership by purchase from the police jury, the district court dismissed plaintiff's suit against the defendant contiguous landowner on an exception of no right of action. The police jury, also named as a defendant, appealed. Plaintiff did not appeal and joins the defendant contiguous landowner in asking that the judgment be affirmed.

The police jury contends that the trial court erred when it found that property dedicated to public use in accordance with R.S. 33:5051, but never utilized as an alleyway or public road, was not subject to alienation under R.S. 33:4711. It also contends that if R.S. 48:701 is applied it will result in a donation to private landowners in violation of La. Const. Art. 7, § 14 (1974). For the following reasons, we affirm.

On April 13, 1929, Parker Realty Company dedicated to the public the streets and alleyways in DeSiard Terrace, a re-subdivision of Bon Air Home Place Subdivision in Ouachita Parish. The plat included a portion of Toulon Street, 50 feet in width and 295 feet in length, running east from Chatham Street and an alleyway, 200 feet north of Toulon Street, 25 feet in width and 245 feet in length, neither of which were ever improved or utilized by the public for access to the adjacent properties. A plat of the subdivision is attached to this opinion as Appendix A. In June of 1985, the police jury, upon the request of property owners adjoining the alleyway and street, adopted Ordinance No. 7962 which declared that the street and alleyway had not been improved or used by the public for access and that there exists no public use for said property. The ordinance authorized the sale of the property to the highest bidder under sealed bids. On June 21, 1985, plaintiff, Charles D. Walker, purchased the street and the alley for $6,100. The record is not clear, but apparently Walker is the owner of the property lying north of the alley and defendant James A. Coleman is the owner of the property lying south of the alley.

On June 4, 1987, Walker filed suit against Coleman demanding that he remove a metal building which encroached on the interior portion of the alleyway or pay damages. Coleman filed a peremptory exception of no right of action alleging that plaintiff did not have valid title to the property because the police jury could not sell property dedicated to public use. He alleged that the police jury could only revoke the dedication in accordance with R.S. 48:701 resulting in title reverting to the contiguous landowner. Walker subsequently amended his petition to add the police jury as a codefendant, and he demanded judgment against it for the return of the property's purchase price if the trial court determined that he did not acquire title to the alleyway. The trial court sustained the exception and dismissed plaintiff's suit against Coleman. The police jury appealed. Plaintiff did not appeal and joins with defendant Coleman in asking that the judgment dismissing his suit against Coleman be affirmed.

The police jury contends that since the street and alleyway were never improved or constructed on the property dedicated to the public, the property is a "private thing" subject to alienation by the police jury in accordance with R.S. 33:4711.

Walker and Coleman contend that streets and alleyways dedicated under R.S. 33:5051 are "public things" which are out of commerce and inalienable. They argue that police juries may not sell property dedicated to public use to private persons in parishes with a population of less than three hundred and twenty-five thousand persons. They further contend that R.S. 48:701 is applicable, and the police jury may only revoke the dedication in which case ownership of the street or alleyway reverts to the owner or owners of the land contiguous thereto.

R.S. 33:4711 provides:

> Police juries may sell or exchange with other political corporations of this state, and may sell or lease to the other political corporations or private persons, any property owned by the police jury or the parish, when such property is no longer needed for public purposes; and police juries may grant to municipalities within their respective parishes portions of roads, streets, alleys or other public ways which may lie along and parallel or approximately parallel to any boundary of any municipality in such manner as to be partly in the municipality and partly outside of the municipality; provided such transfer shall have no effect until accepted by the municipality to which it is made.

R.S. 48:701 provides:

> The parish governing authorities and municipal corporations of the state, except the parish of Orleans, may revoke and set aside the dedication of all roads, streets and alleyways laid out and dedicated to public use within the respective limits, when the roads, streets, and alleyways have been abandoned or are no longer needed for public purposes.

Upon such revocation, all of the soil covered by and embraced in the roads, streets, or alleyways up to the center line thereof, shall revert to the then present owner or owners of the land contiguous thereto.

Nothing in this Section shall be construed as repealing any of the provisions of special statutes or charters of incorporated municipalities granting the right to close or alter roads or streets.

When property is formally [statutorily] dedicated to the public, actual use by the public is unnecessary and the dedication becomes complete upon recordation of a map containing a description of the streets and alleyways dedicated. The effect of formal dedication is to divest the original owner of title and vest it in the political subdivision. The property so dedicated has the status of public property. City of Covington v. Glockner, 486 So. 2d 837 (La. App. 1st Cir. 1986), writ denied 488 So. 2d 693 (La.1986); Anderson v. Police Jury of Parish of East Feliciana, 452 So. 2d 730 (La. App. 1st Cir. 1984), writ denied 457 So. 2d 13 (La. 1984).

Public things cannot be alienated or appropriated to private use. The streets which belong to political subdivisions of the state are owned for the benefit of the public. A political subdivision owns a street subject to public use in its capacity as a public person. Such property, held as a public trust, is inalienable while it is being used by the public. C.C. Art. 450; Coliseum Square Association v. City of New Orleans, 538 So. 2d 222 (La. Sup. Ct. 1989).

Regardless of the use or improvement of dedicated streets and alleyways, they are public things until the political subdivision formally determines that they are no longer needed for public purposes. Although a dedicated street or alleyway may be unimproved, the police jury at anytime could decide to improve [it] for the benefit of the public. When the political subdivision formally determines that the thing dedicated to public use is no longer needed by the public, the thing ceases to be public and becomes a private thing of the political subdivision. After this determination, the private thing is alienable but only in accordance with applicable law. See Yiannopoulos, Louisiana Civil Law Treatise, Property, Vol. 2, § 71, p. 210 (1980).

Although R.S. 33:4711 provides the general authority for police juries to dispose of public property no longer needed by the public, R.S. 48:701 is a special law which specifically applies to streets and alleyways dedicated to public use in accordance with R.S. 33:5051. As a special law it takes precedence over R.S. 33:4711 which deals with alienation of parish or police jury property generally. Yiannopoulos, Louisiana Civil Law Treatise, supra. The authority of a police jury to revoke statutory dedications of streets or alleys is derived from R.S. 48:701 and necessarily is subject to the provisions of that statute. Caz-Perk Realty, Inc. v. Police Jury of Parish of East Baton Rouge, 213 La. 935, 35 So. 2d 860 (1948); Anderson v. Police Jury of Parish of East Feliciana, supra.

Therefore, in parishes with a population of less than three hundred twenty-five thousand persons, the police jury may determine that roads, streets, and alleyways dedicated to public use are no longer needed for public purposes but it may only revoke the dedication. Upon such revocation, all of the soil covered by and embraced in the roads, streets, or alleyways up to the center line thereof, shall revert to the then present owner or owners of the land contiguous thereto.

The police jury contends that R.S. 48:701 is unconstitutional since upon revocation of the dedication, the property, up to the center line, is transferred to the present contiguous landowners without consideration. It argues that such a transfer of ownership would be a donation in violation of La. Const. Art. 7, § 14 (1974).

The reversion of dedicated property by revocation of the dedication is not a donation as contemplated by Article 7, section 14. The statutory scheme of R.S. 33:5051 and R.S. 48:701, read together, is that subdividers are required to dedicate the streets and alleys shown on the subdivision plat to public use, but that upon revocation of such dedication ownership of the streets and alleys reverts to the contiguous owners. The legislature has authority to require the dedication and at the same time has the authority to regulate the effect of the dedication and a revocation thereof. Reversion of title under the statute does not amount to a donation under the constitutional article.

The judgment of the trial court is affirmed. Costs of the appeal are assessed to the police jury.

NOTES AND QUESTIONS

1. Why does the plaintiff ultimately join the defendant in requesting that the judgment under which the plaintiff's case was dismissed be affirmed?

2. Does the language of La. R.S. 48:701 and that of La. R.S. 33:4711 support the court's conclusion that the former is a specific statute that overrules the general principle of the latter?

3. Consider the difference in effect on ownership among the four types of dedication to public use (formal, implied, statutory, tacit). Under what circumstances does R.S. 48:701 apply to each of these upon revocation of dedication?

TABLE OF CASES
(Note cases in italics)

967

968

971

972